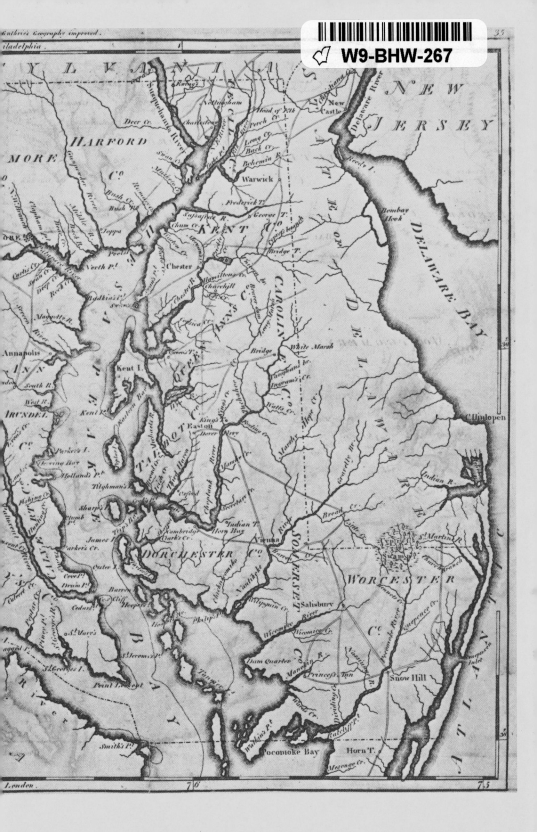

# MARYLAND: A HISTORY

## 1632 ، 1974

**Sir George Calvert, Founder of Maryland and the first Lord Baltimore.**
*Enoch Pratt Free Library.*

# MARYLAND

## *A History  1632·1974*

*Edited by*

RICHARD WALSH

*and*

WILLIAM LLOYD FOX

MARYLAND HISTORICAL SOCIETY

BALTIMORE, MARYLAND

1974

Press of Schneidereith & Sons, Baltimore, Md.

*For*

Harold Randall Manakee

*1908 ، 1974*

# PREFACE

This work fulfills a longstanding need for an up-to-date, balanced account of Maryland's rich and varied past. The stimulus for the book stemmed from Richard Walsh's experience as editor of the *Maryland Historical Magazine*, William Lloyd Fox's teaching Maryland history and the late Harold R. Manakee's many years of service as assistant director and, later, director of the Maryland Historical Society. Each from his vantage realized that a comprehensive history of Maryland, based on careful research, was overdue. Senator William S. James, president of the Maryland Senate, thought likewise and thus urged that the state support the publication of such a work, which the Maryland Historical Society would publish. The Board of Public Works (governor, comptroller, and treasurer) concurred; and so the project was launched in 1969 with two editors and ten contributors, each of whom, from his special competence, was to write a chapter.

Multiple authorship in a work of this kind inevitably makes for some differences in style as the reader can appreciate. It has, however, the advantage of providing special insights into and knowledge of various areas and developments of the past which one or two authors of a history of this nature and size would not necessarily have. More than a century ago David Hume noted in a letter that "the first quality of an historian is to be true and impartial; the next to be interesting." These two qualities the contributors and editors have set as their objectives. They have attempted to present the history of Maryland as an integral part of not only the political and economic but the social as well as cultural past of the United States from its colonial beginnings. In the unfolding of Maryland's nearly three hundred and fifty years of history, the authors recognize a development from a relatively simple, agrarian-oriented culture to an urbanized society which is a part of the eastern seaboard megalopolis. They also recognize the linkage of this development with Maryland's evolution from a southern colony to a mid-Atlantic border state which has embraced elements of both the North and the South in its economy, thought, and social development. Moreover, the authors readily acknowledge Maryland's long importance in the politics and the cultural life of the nation.

The editors are most grateful to the many people who helped and supported this publication. They wish especially to express their deep gratitude to the late Dr. Harold R. Manakee, Director Emeritus of the Maryland Historical Society, the Honorable William S. James, the Honorable Marvin Mandel, Governor of Maryland, the Honorable Louis L. Goldstein, Comptroller of the Treasury, the Honorable John Luetkemeyer, former Treasurer of Maryland, Mr. P. William Filby, Director of the Maryland Historical Society, and Professor Mary R. Dearing of Montgomery College. The editors are also appreciative of the secretarial services which Ms. Maria Stephens of Montgomery College provided; the professional assistance which the staff of the Maryland Room of the Enoch Pratt Free Library promptly gave, and the help which Mrs. M. Kathleen Thomsen of the Maryland Historical Society furnished in the selection of illustrations. The critique offered during the planning of the work by the Publications Committee of the Maryland Historical Society under the chairmanship of Dr. Rhoda M. Dorsey is gratefully acknowledged as is the assistance rendered to all of the contributors by the Hall of Records Commission under Dr. Morris L. Radoff.

To Betty J. Walsh and Lynn G. Fox, their editor-husbands say "thank you" for the help and understanding which they readily gave to the project.

For any errors of fact or interpretation the editors and contributors are alone responsible.

RICHARD WALSH
*Georgetown University*

WILLIAM LLOYD FOX
*Montgomery College*

# CONTENTS

# ILLUSTRATIONS

**From the Jefferson Fry Map of 1775**

# ABBREVIATIONS

H. R.                   Hall of Records Commission

*Arch. Md.*             *Archives of Maryland*

*M. H. M.*              *Maryland Historical Magazine*

M. H. S.                Maryland Historical Society

*M. G.*                 *Maryland Gazette*

J. H. Press             Johns Hopkins Press

*J. H. U. S.*           *Johns Hopkins University Studies in*
                        *Historical and Political Science*

L. C.                   Library of Congress

# I

## PROVINCIAL MARYLAND

BY

AUBREY C. LAND

UNIVERSITY OF GEORGIA

The history of provincial Maryland covers a span of almost a century and a half. Specifically, the chronicle begins on Annunciation Day of 1634 and ends on June 26, 1776, when the last provincial governor sailed away from a colony that had formally committed itself to independence. At first, to those English who knew the name at all, Maryland meant nothing more than an outpost perched somewhere on the rim of Christendom, a sign that the age of exploration and discovery was giving way to an era of settlement and exploitation. However dramatic and arresting this overseas expansion, the pressure of events at their very elbows distracted English eyes from remoter zones to sweeping changes at home—to gusts of the new capitalism that was transforming medieval into modern Europe, to tensions in church and state that were to cost two English kings their thrones and one of them his head. Amid such distractions some few still eyed the opportunities in overseas plantation, as the phrase went. Prominent among them was the Calvert family, inseparably associated with a century and a half of Maryland history.

### 1
### THE FOUNDATIONS

Ironically, George Calvert (c. 1580–1632), progenitor of the family, never laid eyes on Maryland soil, and he died before he even received a charter to this land he coveted. Yet he played a key role in the preliminaries of provincial history. Born into a Yorkshire County family, George Calvert had an Oxford education and the grand tour of the continent before entering the service of king and country. To the favor of King James I Calvert owed his rapid preferment: knighthood in 1617, the post of principal secretary of state in 1619, and a pension of £1000 a year in 1620.

Calvert's interest in overseas enterprise developed quite naturally from modest investments in joint stock companies concerned with trade: the East India Company and the Virginia Company. His first independent venture miscarried when he chose to plant a colony in 1620 on the bleak east coast of Newfoundland, which he euphorically named "Avalon." In 1625 Calvert's career altered sharply when he declared himself a Roman Catholic and resigned his office as secretary of state. Immediately thereafter the king raised him to the Irish peerage as Baron of Baltimore. Incapacitated for public office by his religion, George Calvert, now Lord Baltimore, devoted himself to cultivating his private estate. Now that he had sunk more than £25,000 in his colony of Avalon, he visited his property in person to discover that the climate with "ayre so intollerable cold" precluded successful colonization and wrote to the king requesting a "precinct of land" farther south, specifically in his majesty's dominion of Virginia.

Thereupon he sailed south to the Chesapeake Bay. According to the scanty evidence on his visit to Virginia, Lord Baltimore commanded respect as a person of "eminence and quality" but came under suspicion because he professed the "Romish religion." One aggressive planter threatened to knock him down. The more circumspect council rid themselves of their guest by tendering him the oath of allegiance and supremacy, which as a Roman Catholic Baltimore could not take. Before leaving, however, he had seen enough to convince him that his future lay in the Chesapeake. Back in England, Baltimore met discouragement from two sources. The king advised him "to desist from further prosecuting yo'r dessigns that way," observing with truth that new settlements "commonly have rugged and laborious beginnings." More pointedly, William Claiborne, secretary of Virginia, had come to England to take a hand in lobbying against the grant of any precinct within the colony. Undaunted, Baltimore carried his campaign and pushed his charter for Maryland—Terra Maria in the Latin of that document—through the first stage of authentication, the privy seal, a few days before his death on April 15, 1632.

As it happened, then, the charter of Maryland that finally issued under the great seal of the realm on June 20, 1632 named as grantee Cecil Calvert (c. 1608–1675), second Baron of Baltimore, son and heir of George, the first lord. The twenty-three articles of the charter conferred on Lord Baltimore a princely domain and the palatine powers of a lord proprietor. No one at the time could have told his lordship even the approximate size of his grant. The boundaries, apparently so clearly stated in Article III, traced an outline westward from the ocean along the fortieth parallel "unto the true meridian of the first fountain of the river Pattowmack," thence along the south bank of the river to a point "where it disembogues" into the Chesapeake, and then along the parallel that runs through Watkin's Point back to the ocean. Hidden in the future were the endless boundary disputes and lawsuits that cost his lordship thousands of acres before the final boundaries settled the extent of Maryland at 6,769,290 acres. His powers within his domain were staggering: "as ample rights, jurisdictions, privileges, prerogatives, royalties, liberties, immunities, and royal rights, and temporal franchises . . . as any bishop of Durham . . . within the county palatine of Durham." In return for these regal powers the Lord Baltimore was bound to yield the king two Indian arrows of those parts annually in Easter week as a rental.[1]

Cecil set about exploiting his grant without delay, though twenty months passed before his first expedition touched Maryland soil. Preparations took time: raising money and recruiting "adventurers." The initial cost came to an estimated £40,000 sterling. According to Lord Baltimore, he recruited some 300 laboring men, nearly twenty gentlemen "of good fashion," and his two younger brothers for the project. Probably his figure exaggerates the actual number. A London official boarded two vessels that Baltimore had chartered to transport the expedition and found only 128 persons, all of whom took the oath of allegiance. After departure from the Thames, the two vessels, *Ark* of 350 tons and *Dove* of about fifty tons, put in at the Isle of Wight,

---

1. A translation of the charter of Maryland appears in each edition of the *Maryland Manual*, cf. *Maryland Manual, 1967–68* (Annapolis: Hall of Records Commission, 1968), pp. 579-90.

where several Roman Catholic laymen and two Jesuit fathers came aboard to make up the total company. The mystery surrounding the composition and embarkation has strengthened the case of those who argue that Lord Baltimore founded his colony of Maryland primarily as a refuge for his persecuted coreligionists. Beyond doubt he wished to insure that Catholics in Maryland would be spared the discrimination they suffered in England. But the whole pattern of his conduct and that of his father before him resembles that of other colonial promoters of the day. Certainly his writings speak constantly of profit and loss and of the prospects for future gain. Doubtless his motives were mixed, but clearly he saw the main chance. He assuredly did not wish religious dissension to jeopardize the expedition and bade his brother Leonard, designated as governor, to "cause all Acts of Romane Catholique Religion to be done as privately as may be and . . . [to] instruct all the Roman Catholiques to be silent upon all occasions of discourse concerning matters of Religion."

The *Ark* and *Dove* departed England on November 22, 1633, in good time for an early spring arrival in the Chesapeake. The ships followed the usual route south and west to the West Indies, stopped at Barbados, then turned north to reach St. Clement's Island in the Potomac River on the Feast of the Annunciation, March 25, 1634. Here the company disembarked to erect a cross and celebrate mass. It is not difficult to understand why Governor Leonard Calvert and the Catholics recited litanies "with great emotion."[2]

For those adventurers who left accounts, the whole setting made for an emotional experience. Father Andrew White, one of the most literate, wrote with wonder of the Potomac: "The Thames seems a mere rivulet in comparison with it." He could not admire too much the trees: "You can drive a four-horse carriage, wherever you choose, through the midst of the trees." Here and there the native inhabitants had cleared fields for corn and vegetables and had built their huts or wigwams. The Indians proved friendly, and when they agreed peaceably to quit the area, leaving their fields and dwellings to the adventurers, Father White exclaimed, "The finger of God is in this."

Leonard Calvert proved a practical governor from the start. He

---

2. Charles M. Andrews, *The Colonial Period of American History*, 4 vols. (New Haven: Yale University Press, 1934–38), II, 285-88.

put the men to work piecing together a barge brought knocked-down from England and the women to washing clothing, while he explored some sixty miles up the Potomac. Within two days he had visited various Indian tribes on the Maryland side and had concluded an agreement with a petty chieftain of the Yaocomico for occupying the east bank of the St. Mary's River. Father White called the transaction a sale: "we bought from the King thirty miles of that land, delivering in exchange axes, hatchets, rakes, and several yards of cloth." Another eyewitness says only that the governor presented the chief and his advisers cloth and implements to make the entry peaceable and safe. Whatever the technicalities the colonists had housing and a little cleared land for planting, all within gunshot of the governor's seat in the community that came to be called St. Mary's City.

In two ways the beginnings were auspicious. Settlers solved the food problem by raising enough during the summer for their own use and a small surplus for export. Maryland avoided the annual famines that had plagued early Virginia. Beyond foodstuffs, they were able to begin planting tobacco, an export crop, after the manner of Virginians without a long period of experimentation. Then friendly relations with the Indians of the neighborhood spared Maryland colonists the horrors of such massacres as Virginia experienced in 1622 and again in 1644. Occasional alarms and almost continual petty disturbances grew out of thieving and murders perpetrated on each other by both Indians and whites. The single powerful tribe, the Susquehannahs on the upper Bay, was remote from the early settlements and partly neutralized by awesome enemies, the Iroquois, to their north. Other Maryland tribes gradually dwindled or moved away, leaving only place names as their memorials: Nanticoke, Wicomico, Port Tobacco, Patuxent, Piscataway.

The spectacular troublemakers were men of the same race as the colonists themselves. The deeds of William Claiborne, earliest and most notorious of them, fill many pages of the Maryland records. A bare recital of his doings would give him a disproportionate place in Maryland history at the expense of other and more enduring developments. Claiborne had opposed the Maryland charter in part because of his personal interest in Kent Island, where he had already established something like a colony of his own, a trading post with retainers who had laid out fields, orchards, and pastures. These properties clearly lay within the Maryland patent, but Claiborne stubbornly refused to acknowledge Lord Baltimore's jurisdiction. Governor Leonard Calvert, equally stubbornly, determined to assert the lord proprietor's rights to soil and government of the island. The impasse had complications touching Claiborne's superiors in England, the mercantile firm of William Cloberry and Company, and his unscrupulous rival in the fur trade, Captain Henry Fleet. Before an understanding could be negotiated, partisans of Claiborne and Calvert put the issue beyond amicable adjustment in an encounter described as the first naval battle in American history. On April 23, 1635, two proprietary vessels, *St. Helen* and *St. Margaret,* clashed with Claiborne's armed wherry, *Cockatrice,* at the mouth of the Pocomoke River on the Eastern Shore. After Claiborne's commanding officer and two of his men fell, the *Cockatrice* surrendered. Another encounter a fortnight later between Kent Islanders and Calvert's forces went in favor of Claiborne. Actual bloodshed ceased when Cloberry and Company replaced Claiborne with another factor, George Evelin, who promptly came to terms with Governor Calvert. For the moment Claiborne was stymied, but in neighboring Virginia he nursed his grudge and prepared to return in the day of trouble.[3]

And troubles did lie ahead in this first quarter century that forms the initial period of Maryland history. In England King Charles I, who had granted the province to Lord Baltimore, was having his differences with Parliament, soon to lead him into civil war and ultimately to the executioner's block. An infant colony, backed by dubious authority three thousand miles away, was fair prey to self-reliant adventurers nurtured on legends of Hawkins and Drake. As the struggle between king and Parliament moved into civil war, opportunities for interference in the American plantations increased. In 1644 one Richard Ingle, an adherent of Parliament, was seized for treason by the lord proprietor's officers while trading in Maryland waters. Ingle escaped to return the next summer with parliamentary letters of marque that permitted him to take ships trading to those places in sympathy with the king. Taking the broadest view of his authority, Ingle and his crew sailed their vessel, *Reformation,* into Maryland on a pirate bacchanal, taking ships and boats,

3. Matthew Page Andrews, *The Founding of Maryland* (New York: D. Appleton Century Co., 1933), pp. 94-112.

Cecil Calvert, First Proprietor of Maryland and the second Lord Baltimore. *M.H.S.*

7

looting plantations, and liberating indentured servants. Governor Calvert fled the terrorized country into Virginia. For some months Ingle had the province at his mercy.

Leonard Calvert's thirteen-year administration began and ended in struggle. He returned from Virginia in 1646 to restore proprietary authority with only a few months to live. In the end he had managed to hold the province for his brother against hostile forces. And over the years he had attended to the prosaic business of organizing the government with little help from the cryptic provisions of the charter. To serve the vital functions of lawmaking and law enforcement, Calvert instituted legislative and executive branches in embryonic form. A proper court system was yet to come, but the imprint of these earliest governmental arrangements remained indelibly stamped on the provincial constitution through all additions and refinements, until the Revolution finally ended the proprietary regime altogether.[4]

The executive branch proved easiest to adapt to the needs of a community that was destined to increase in numbers and complexity. Initial arrangements had been simple and functional to a colonizing expedition. Leonard Calvert had come as governor assisted by two "commissioners," Jerome Hawley and Captain Thomas Cornwalleys. Then in 1637 the lord proprietor dispatched a commission that erected the framework of a proper executive department. The commission created Calvert governor and chancellor, John Lewger provincial secretary, and the trio, Lewger, Hawley, and Cornwalleys, councillors. When Governor Calvert began appointing sheriffs shortly thereafter, the executive branch was substantially complete. Lord Baltimore left no doubt about his conception of government or the source of authority. To brother Leonard he wrote, "Certainly I have the power to revoke anie authority I have given you, either in whole or in part . . . for you are but meerly instrumental in those things to do what I direct."[5] As long as he remained obedient to his lordship's commands, the governor enjoyed the extensive powers of a viceroy: head of the military establishment as lieutenant general and admiral, keeper of the great seal and judge in equity as chancellor, and finally, the source of grants and writs.

4. *Ibid.*, pp. 113-20.

5. *The Calvert Papers*, No. I (Baltimore: M.H.S., 1889), p. 219.

Though subordinate, the secretary had even more duties: all the functions not assignable to the governor and chancellor. His post became the mother of offices, which were differentiated as separate posts as the province grew and the labors augmented over the years. Seven posts eventually came from the secretary's office in this process of subdivision: surveyor general (1642), agent and receiver-general (1651), attorney general (1657), commissary general (1673), naval officer (1676), rent roll keeper (1689), and judge of the land office (1738).[6]

The secretary, then, had initially among his many cares responsibility for the land system, a principal concern of proprietor and people. In his "conditions of plantation" Baltimore had promised 2,000 acres of land to every adventurer who transported five adult males as settlers and proportionately smaller acreage to those who brought fewer people. As a quitrent he asked ten pounds of good wheat for every fifty acres granted. During the next fifty years his lordship altered details of size and rentals without changing the method of granting land according to the number of immigrants—the headright system. But in 1683 he made money payment—"caution money"—the basis for acquiring title to land. At first he fixed the rate at two hundred pounds of tobacco (equivalent to sixteen shillings sterling) for every hundred acres. His successors increased this price from time to time until 1738, when it reached a peak of £ 5 sterling per hundred acres.

In order to distribute as much land as possible and hence realize maximum revenues, proprietary officials established a simple mechanism for the land office. Land-hungry settlers could perfect a grant in three steps. First, on establishing a headright, or in later years on paying caution money, a warrant was issued entitling the holder to have the surveyor lay out a stated number of acres on vacant land anywhere in the province. The certificate, returned by the surveyor with metes and bounds of the survey, authorized the holder to proceed to the third and final step: obtaining a patent under the seal of the province conveying title in fee simple subject to an annual quitrent.[7]

---

6. Donnell M. Owings, *His Lordship's Patronage: Offices of Profit in Colonial Maryland* (Baltimore: M.H.S., 1953), pp. 6-8.

7. Newton D. Mereness, *Maryland as a Proprietary Province* (New York, 1901), pp. 47-75.

Ironically, the successful land system undermined one of Lord Baltimore's designs for his province. He had clearly hoped to establish in Maryland the kind of landholding aristocracy familiar in the English countryside as a support for his own palatine overlordship. The idea of lords and retainers appeared in his first conditions of plantation and later had explicit expression in his offer to erect manors for his chief tenants with all the trappings of a medieval fief. A few manors were actually laid out and the records of two courts leet and baron have been preserved, relics of a feudalism that quickly withered in the new-world soil. Instead of manorial lords and faithful tenants, the single-family freehold prevailed. These family plantations of 250 acres or less that dotted the tidewater soon outnumbered the large grants manyfold and gave evidence of the aversion early settlers had for tenant status when they could acquire land in their own right, if not entirely free, then at least easily and relatively cheaply. Moreover, shortly after mid-century the proprietor gave less affluent provincials a political reason for preferring freehold to leasehold or copyhold of the manor. On his own motion Lord Baltimore in 1670 made possession of property a qualification for voting, specifically, a fifty-acre freehold or a visible estate of £ 40.[8]

This unilateral alteration of the franchise compounded the irony of Cecil, Lord Baltimore's proprietorship, which lasted until his death in 1675. His land system, designed to populate his province with numerous "heads" and to increase his revenues from quitrents by maximum patents to the soil, had worked at variance with his desire to introduce the manorial system into Maryland. Similarly, his authoritarian conception of government, illustrated in his arbitrary change in the franchise, involved him and his successor, Charles, the third lord, in struggles with the representative branch that lasted throughout their long lives.

From the first months of settlement the legislature gave both governor and proprietor trouble. When the first assembly convened on February 26, 1635, all questions of powers, structure, and franchise were unclear. On none of these did the charter give any real help. One phrase in Article VII spoke of "delegates or deputies . . . called together for the framing of LAWS." The first

---

8. Vertrees J. Wyckoff, "The Sizes of Plantations in Seventeenth Century Maryland," *M.H.M.* XXXII, (Dec. 1937), 338.

assembly did proceed to enact "wholesome laws" and sent them back for proprietary approval. Lord Baltimore vetoed the lot and announced that he had the sole right of initiative as provided in another phrase of Article VII, which gave him "free, full, and absolute power . . . to ordain, make, and enact LAWS . . . with the advice, assent, and approbation of the free men of the same PROVINCE." He would, he said, draft laws and send them over for the advice, assent, and approbation of the freemen. Some time before the assembly of 1638, Baltimore had yielded on the initiative and the freemen passed forty-one acts, which Governor Calvert duly signed.[9]

Settling the structure of the assembly took longer. These earliest assemblies were unicameral. Governor Calvert and his councillors sat together with the freemen at legislative sessions in a single chamber, an arrangement that some of the freemen found unsatisfactory. In 1642 Robert Vaughan "in the name of the rest desired that the house might be Separated & the Burgesses to be by themselves and to have a negative but it was not Granted by the Lieut General [Calvert]." Not until 1650 did the desired division into the now familiar upper and lower houses occur.[10] Over these same years the basis of representation was hammered out. As long as population hugged St. Mary's City, all freemen could attend sessions and participate personally in deliberations. The first assembly whose records are preserved, the session of 1638, was just such a body, though some of the freemen who could not actually attend gave their proxies to neighbors. As settlement pushed into outlying areas the primary assembly of all freemen became cumbersome, and subdivisions of the province, known as hundreds, took to choosing burgesses or delegates to represent the people of their vicinity. Not until after the assembly divided into two houses did the idea of a gathering of all freemen entirely give way to a representative system of elected delegates. By 1657 the records show a bicameral representative assembly that was to last throughout Maryland provincial history.

The central events of Maryland history during the two decades, 1640–1660, are curiously bound up with the fortunes of the king and Parliament back home, as many provincials put it.

---

9. *Arch. Md.* I, 20-24.
10. *Ibid.*, 130, 272–73.

In these turbulent years Lord Baltimore more than once saw his province threatened by outside forces or by troublemakers within. He had the misfortune to appoint as governors two men whose serious errors in judgment cost him heavily. In the summer of 1647 his brother, Governor Leonard Calvert, died after naming a senior councillor, Thomas Greene, his temporary successor. The following year the lord proprietor appointed as his regular governor a resident of Northampton County, Virginia, one William Stone, whose seven-year term was both eventful and full of unexpected turns.

Stone began his administration by inviting a number of Puritans in Virginia to settle along the Severn River. These dissenters from the Anglican Church followed Richard Bennett, one of their prominent laymen, in 1649 into the Severn area, which they called by the good Puritan name Providence and which later received the official name Anne Arundel. Sensing the risk from the new element just introduced into Maryland in the very year of crisis in the struggle between Anglicans and Puritans and between king and Parliament, Lord Baltimore urged passage of "An Act Concerning Religion," which provided that no person "be any waies troubled, molested, or discountenanced . . . in the free exercise" of his or her religion. Better known as the Toleration Act of 1649, this legislation was an astute move. It reflected, of course, the standing practice of the proprietary regime. But further it assured Protestants that they would not meet discrimination from a Catholic lord proprietor and at the same time protected Roman Catholics in the province from a rising tide of Protestant sentiment. Protestants already considerably outnumbered Catholics in Maryland by this date.

An accident brought crashing down the nice balance in Maryland only weeks after the Toleration Act became law. During a temporary absence from the province of Governor Stone, news of the execution of Charles I arrived. Forthwith the deputy governor, Thomas Greene, proclaimed Charles II as rightful monarch. Neither Stone's repudiation nor Lord Baltimore's disclaimer of this act could efface the implied disaffection to the parliamentary cause. Without delay an ancient foe of the Calverts, William Claiborne, and a coadjutor, Richard Bennett of the Puritan community, descended on Maryland with a commission to secure obedience to Parliament. Stone had no alternative but to submit. For several years the commissioners and their agents ran the province. The assembly of 1654, elected under their commission after Catholics were excluded from voting, set aside the Toleration Act and ignored proprietary authority.

At the nadir of his fortunes, Lord Baltimore struck back on two fronts. He ordered Governor Stone to reassert proprietary authority in Maryland and began his own campaign with Lord Protector Cromwell to recover his rights. Stone put together a makeshift government at St. Mary's, gathered a force of about 130 men loyal to Baltimore, and in March 1655 moved north against the Puritan stronghold at Providence, where the commissioners had established their government. The Battle of the Severn on the 25th day of the month ended in disaster for the proprietary forces. Stone, himself taken prisoner, barely escaped with his life. The Puritans maintained their control. At home Baltimore came off better with Oliver Cromwell, who had succeeded Parliament as the ultimate authority in England. After obtaining from Cromwell a decision in his favor, Baltimore first commissioned a new governor, Josias Fendall, who had fought among his troops at the Battle of the Severn. Then he negotiated a *quid pro quo* settlement with representatives of the Puritans. Baltimore regained his governmental rights in return for a promise to make no reprisals and to grant land without favor.

This pact of oblivion might have ended the trauma of the interregnum in reciprocal forgetfulness of the past had not Governor Fendall unexpectedly turned traitor to the proprietary cause. The transactions in this "pigmie rebellion" are obscure, but the outcome is clear: Fendall gave up his proprietary commission and accepted one from the delegates of the lower house, who adjudged themselves "a lawfull Assembly without dependence on any other Power." Fendall chose the least auspicious moment to stage his rebellion. Two months after the overt act "of mutiny and sedition," Charles II was restored to the throne. Baltimore, again in favor, commissioned his younger brother Philip Calvert as governor of his palatinate and quietly regained control.[11]

2

LIFE AND POLITICS IN SEVENTEENTH-CENTURY MARYLAND

Two restorations in 1660—Charles Stuart to the throne of his forefathers and Cecil Calvert to his palatinate—radically

11. Andrews, *Founding of Maryland*, pp. 221–49.

Diorama depicting the life and work of early Maryland settlers.
*Darnall Young People's Museum. M.H.S.*

14

changed previous uncertainties. Yet beneath the drama of change ran strong currents of continuity. After temporary interruptions, Cecil, Lord Baltimore, still had fifteen years ahead to complete the foundations of a successful colonizing enterprise. In the year following his "restoration" the lord proprietor sent his eldest son, Charles Calvert (1629–1715), then twenty-four years old, to administer a province that still hardly deserved the description, "flourishing." Pioneer conditions that had obtained since 1634 continued in all but the area of first settlement. Population stood at about 8,000 souls scattered over six counties, but two of these—Charles and Baltimore—were frontier wildernesses. Even the constitution still had flaws, and sharp conflicts over these lay ahead. To make matters worse, the tobacco trade, already the life blood of the economy, had fallen on evil days and continued in a depressed state for years to come. As the actual threat of loss by force faded, other ominous notes warned of troubles ahead. The interplay of economic and political themes surged like a fugue to a climax in 1689 to end this second period of Maryland history.

Among proprietary concerns population growth stood high, for on numbers of people and plantation units depended revenues from quitrents. From about 8,000 in 1660 the number of inhabitants increased by 1675 to nearly 15,000. In 1688 the figure stood at approximately 25,000 and by the end of the century over 32,000, a fourfold increase in four decades.[12] Local planters bred their own increase, but heavy immigration, encouraged by the lord proprietor, accounted for much of this steep rise. Among the promoters of immigration George Alsop has a unique place. With proprietary blessing, and quite probably assistance as well, Alsop produced a vivid pamphlet, *A Character of the Province of Maryland* (1666), which pictured an alluring future for the underprivileged in Maryland, especially for persons without funds and consequently obliged to sell themselves as indentured servants to pay their passage to the new world. Imported in numbers as laborers before Negro slaves became common, indentured servants doubtless found life somewhat rougher than Alsop's description. Field work was hard for these whites, who supplied "hands" for tobacco planters. Even so, as Alsop

12. Evarts B. Greene and Virginia D. Harrington, *American Population Before the Federal Census of 1790* (New York: Columbia University Press, 1932), pp. 123-24.

moralized, "The Son works as well as the servant, so that before they eat their bread, they are commonly taught how to earn it." At the end of their terms, four to six years' service, indentured servants did receive "freedom dues" of clothing and food and entered the estate of freemen—potential purchasers of plantations and payers of quitrents.

From freed servants and other immigrants with slender resources came the much misunderstood "planter" of early Maryland, who established his type in the tidewater during the second half of the seventeenth century. His plantation, literally a planted place, consisted of a few acres cleared from the ubiquitous forest that extended from the bayside back into a hinterland almost unpenetrated by whites. Here he built a rude dwelling, usually a single room, and planted his corn and his market crop, tobacco. From the beginning the Maryland planter practiced commercial agriculture and his wellbeing depended on a few hogsheads of tobacco he marketed each winter. With the proceeds he bought, first of all, necessary implements—axes and hilling hoes, guns, needles and the like, then whatever luxuries he could afford—sugar, and, occasionally, rum. For the rest he lived off his own cornfield, vegetable garden, and orchard, supplemented by hunting and fishing for sport and pot. Nearly every planting family kept chickens, cows, and pigs. Part of his living he made with his own hands: cups and bowls from dried gourds, plates and trenchers from slabs of wood, benches and bedsteads from hewn logs, even his mattress from corn shucks. These were the realities that appeared in the thousands of inventories of their modest estate preserved in the probate records. By actual count, more than two-thirds of all planters fell in this class, men with personal estates below £100 sterling. Nearly all were unlettered—few had a single book. Many were illiterate—they made their marks. None conformed to the stereotype of the moonlight-and-magnolia planter with gracious houses, elegant furniture, expansive fields, happy slaves, and the leisurely life. But if his sumptuary circumstances were bleak, the small planter had an ample country living and the opportunity to rise in the economic scale. He and his kind cleared the forest, built houses and wharves, made the roads, planted the orchards and made other "improvements" that in technical economics are termed capital formation. All this he did with his own hands, aided only by the simplest tools, and each tiny increment of capital formed in the process added to the common store of wealth. For one or another planter here and there, capital formation was the beginning of a different style of life.

Some few planters, about one in twenty or less, did rise to something like affluence by the standards of the time. Almost to a man they made their fortunes by combining their planting and capital formation with other profitable pursuits: merchandising, money lending, land speculation, petty manufacturing, and sometimes the law. Entrepreneurs in modern terminology, on the tongues of eighteenth-century men they were "traders" or—using the term in an older and unspecialized sense —"merchants." In a word, they were merchant-planters. Many of them operated stores on their plantations where they offered, at about a fifty per cent markup, English cloth, implements, and utensils for sale to the hordes of small planters, their neighbors about them. They also extended credit in the form of "book debts" to the small producer until his tobacco was ready for market. Then they received the hogsheads in settlement of the customer's account. The merchant-planters then, organized the commerce of the "Tobacco Coast." They sold essential imported goods, made loans in the form of credit, and assembled the cash crops for export. For their services they reaped rewards far beyond the common run of planters.

In every county a handful of merchant-planters forged to the front. William Worgan of Dorchester County followed such a path. At his death in 1676 Worgan's personal estate, excluding land and improvements, came to 202,616 pounds of tobacco, the Maryland money of account, or the equivalent of £844:4:8 sterling, a handsome fortune for his day and place. One-half his wealth was in the form of collectible debts on the books of his store, seventy-three in all. Dozens of Worgan's kind dotted Eastern and Western Shores: the Dashiells, Frisbys, Ringgolds, Galloways, Chews, Garretts, and—in the century ahead—the Lloyds, Taskers, Dulanys, Bordleys, Hammonds, and the Carrolls, both the Catholic and Protestant branches of the family. Not only did they accumulate fortunes, they also acquired social and political preeminence as vestrymen, justices of the peace, delegates to the assembly. A select few reached the apex, the governor's council. In brief, they became the provincial leadership. From their kind stems the planter of legend. They built larger houses and furnished them more amply. For heavier field

Interior of settler's log cabin, as faithfully reconstructed in the
*Darnall Young People's Museum. M.H.S.*

work they had indentured servants, or occasionally a slave or two. But they were few—perhaps five per cent of the planting families—and certainly not the typical or average of the whole planting society. They were a single thin stratum in a society that was achieving a permanent texture during the restoration decades just as the economy and political pattern were achieving designs that endured for a century.[13]

The state of the economy touched every soul in Maryland, small producer and wealthy merchant-planter alike. And in the middle decades of the seventeenth century a deadening malaise had descended as tobacco prices fell in many years to no more than one penny sterling per pound.[14] For all practical purposes prices responded to European supply and demand and consequently lay outside the control of both lord proprietor and provincials. Political doctors in the colony had, nevertheless, a kit of nostrums to prescribe for the sickly trade. The most popular remedy, a crude form of crop control, almost succeeded in 1666 and came up again periodically in one of its two forms: the jubilee, a total cessation of planting every seven years, or the "stint," a limitation on acreage or number of plants tended. Either required an act of assembly and to be successful needed cooperation of neighboring Virginians. Since the Virginia trade was also languishing, Sir William Berkeley, then governor, actively promoted an agreement and in 1666 made a hazardous midwinter trip to Maryland to tidy up final details. But the scheme met resistance and eventually categorical refusal from Lord Baltimore, who argued that the stint "would wholly ruin the poor, who are the generality of both Provinces." Instead, he recommended diversification of agriculture, particularly the raising of grain and cattle. In future years proprietors gave the same answer each time the question of crop controls came up in the assembly. Now and again frustrated planters took matters into their own hands in tobacco-cutting riots that broke out periodically.

Beside disastrous price fluctuations the tobacco monoculture created important side effects. Tobacco was not only the cash

---

13. Aubrey C. Land, "Economic Base and Social Structure: The Northern Chesapeake in the Eighteenth Century," *Journal of Economic History*, XXV, (Dec. 1965), 639-54.
14. Figures compiled by Russell Menard, St. Mary's City Project.

crop but the currency of the province as well, with all the limitations of commodity money. "The general way of traffick and commerce there is chiefly by Barter," commented one observer. Lord Baltimore toyed with a proprietary coinage bearing his own device and actually struck a few groats and shillings which became in after years fabulous collector's items. In the end this scheme for a specie currency with the Calvert arms came to nothing. Finally, in 1671 the assembly came into agreement on a method of stabilizing tobacco prices, at least for the purpose of quitrent payments. The assembly passed an act levying a duty of two shillings sterling on every hogshead of tobacco exported, one half to be used for the expenses of government, the rest to compensate the lord proprietor for receiving his quitrents in tobacco at the inflated rate of two pence per pound. This compensatory arrangement remained in force through the lifetimes of Cecil, Lord Baltimore, and his son and successor, Charles, the third lord. These export duties were in fact the principal revenues of the proprietors in many years when tobacco prices fell so low that quitrents hardly paid the costs of collection.[15]

Other measures to legislate prosperity failed. Acts establishing port towns to encourage trade were uniformly unsuccessful. Merchant-planters had already set the pattern of local commerce, which revolved about their country seats, and the urban communities simply did not materialize. Legislation designed to promote crop diversification recommended by the lord proprietor fared no better. The assembly offered subsidies and prizes for hemp and flax without getting more than an occasional experimental crop. Merchant-planters "understood" the tobacco business and planters had mastered the routines of tobacco husbandry. Like Virginia, Maryland was bound to the annual cycle of planting, tilling, and curing a single cash crop, with all the hardships that followed market gluts and attendant low prices.[16]

Economic discontent inevitably produced political overtones. Proprietor and people were even more at odds on political and constitutional questions in the restoration period. The principal bone of contention quickly came to be, who shall prevail in the

---

15. Beverly W. Bond, *The Quit-Rent System in the American Colonies* (New Haven: Yale University Press, 1919), pp. 178-81.

16. John W. Reps, *Tidewater Towns: City Planning in Colonial Virginia and Maryland* (Charlottesville: University of Virginia Press, 1972), Ch. V, 92-116.

common weal? On his side the lord proprietor had the wit to perceive the connection between his economic interest, which was paramount, and his continued political overlordship. "What Priviledges and Powers I have by my Charter are from the King, and that of Calling of Assemblies in any such manner and way as I shall think fitt being an undeniable one among the rest, I cannot Deem it Honorable Nor safe to Lodge it in the Freemen . . . being resolved never to part with Powers my Charter gives." Baltimore's conception, legally correct perhaps, represented a traditional outlook that had steadily lost ground in England during the century. On their side, his opponents among the freemen had long before recorded a countervailing assumption in words just as emphatic: "The lord Baltimore exercized an arbitrary and absolute government, undertook a princely jurisdiction, stiles himself absolute lord and proprietor, constituted a privy council, most of Papists, and the rest sworn thereto. This privy council must be the legislative power. . . . The people indeed are called to assemblies, but have neither legislative power nor judicature."[17] However partisan, this allegation contains an element of truth. Baltimore did claim palatine powers and he did use the royal "we" in referring to "our province" and "our faithful tenants" and sometimes to "our courts." Like benevolent despots elsewhere, he mistook his personal prejudices and aspirations for the best interests of Maryland. Many provincials had other and sharply different views of the common weal.

The party of resistance to the Lord Baltimore found in the lower house of assembly a forum for the long battle that reached crises in 1669, 1676, and 1681. In 1669 the Reverend Charles Nicholette, a Presbyterian divine, preached a sermon "to stir up the Lower House to do their Duty," namely, to assume "a Liberty equal to the people of England." The council fined Nicholette for his presumption and compelled him to apologize for his "seditious words," as they phrased it. But the damage had been done. The delegates proceeded to state "the real grievances of the province" in such high words that the upper house (the council) required them "to raze the mutinous and seditious votes . . . out of their journal." Over the two following decades delegates and their supporters aired many complaints against the proprietary regime. In the year after the Nicholette affair

---

17. Andrews, *Colonial Period*, II, 325.

Lord Baltimore by executive action limited the franchise, once enjoyed by all freemen, to those with a fifty-acre freehold or a visible estate of £ 40. The assembly protested this tampering with their representative system but failed to alter Baltimore's decision. Then in 1681 the proprietor added further to the constitutional dispute when he reduced the number of delegates representing each county from four to two. The assembly could with some color tax Baltimore with infringing on its parliamentary privilege of controlling its own membership.

Three other targets drew fire from the delegates. The proprietary veto over legislation evoked constant complaint. Frequently the lord proprietor exercised his undoubted right to a negative after laws had been in effect half a decade. As the delegates pointed out with justice, "our laws, whereby our Liberty and Property subsists, are subject to . . . Arbitrary Disposition." The land office, undoubtedly within the lord proprietor's prerogative, came in for similar criticism: frequent, arbitrary, and sometimes secret changes in rules and conditions of plantation. Finally, the patronage caused great bitterness. Baltimore's policy of preferment to office had been at best impolitic. The Calverts distributed posts with fattest fees and greatest powers lavishly to relatives and almost exclusively to Roman Catholics. Thus the gulf between a proprietary interest—largely Catholic—and an anti-proprietary element—predominantly Protestant—acquired a character at once dramatic and intense.[18]

It is a crowning irony that the lords proprietors, who had preached and practiced religious toleration for decades after the founding of Maryland, should move to policies that jeopardized the very principle of toleration itself. In western Christendom the age was hardly tolerant, as Europeans learned again in the 1680's when Louis XIV unleashed the dragonnades against French Protestants. Even in the haven of Maryland, Cecil, Lord Baltimore, had seen his policy of toleration set aside during seven years of Puritan control. At his death in 1675 the province devolved on his son, the resident governor, Charles Calvert, now third Lord Baltimore. Charles, as it happened, was the only proprietor who had first-hand acquaintance with his palatinate. After fifteen years as his father's lieutenant, he stayed on eight

18. Michael G. Kammen, "The Causes of the Maryland Revolution of 1689," *M.H.M.*, LV (Dec. 1960), 293-333.

more as lord and governor, beginning at the difficult time of Bacon's Rebellion in Virginia. Possibly the experience of carrying out his authoritarian father's wishes in a pioneer province beset with growth pangs and serious economic problems stultified his creative impulses. He certainly displayed little of the imaginative leadership called for in admittedly difficult circumstances. Faced with a contretemps, Charles, Lord Baltimore, responded with vetoes or ordinances, the stock in trade of authoritarian governments.

However valiantly the assembly championed popular causes in the constitutional forum, an active element centering in the southern counties—St. Mary's, Charles, and Calvert—advocated as the only solution direct and forceful measures. In 1676, the year of Bacon's Rebellion across the Potomac, trouble broke out in Charles County, where Josias Fendall of the "pigmie rebellion" and his restless accomplice, John Coode, provoked their neighbors into drafting a powerful indictment of the proprietor in a document headed "Complaint from Heaven with a Huy and Crye and a petition out of Virginia and Maryland." Written in a popular, rhetorical style, the paper aired the grievances against Baltimore: nepotism, tampering with the assembly, corrupting elected delegates with gifts, and royal pretensions. As a measure of relief, the authors asked the king to take over the government in order to prevent the proprietor from utterly ruining the people by oppression. On his side Baltimore dubbed Fendall and Coode "two rank Baconists" and stood pat. Both lines and issues had begun to harden thus early in the proprietorship of the third Lord Baltimore.[19]

Over the next decade the ranks of dissaffection swelled to include new leaders: Kenelm Cheseldine, Nehemiah Blakiston, Henry Jowles, and Ninian Beale, all of them substantial planters prominent among their neighbors in the southern counties. Consequently, when Charles, Lord Baltimore, sailed for England in 1684 to defend his charter against forfeiture to the crown and his boundaries against William Penn, he left behind opponents as well as widespread discontent. He had the further misfortune to leave behind a government that speedily compounded the dangers. He named as governor his nine-year-old son, Benedict

---

19. Francis E. Sparks, *Causes of the Maryland Revolution of 1689, J.H.U. Studies,* XIV (Baltimore: J.H. Press, 1896), 80-81.

Leonard, with the council members acting in his behalf. Soon after reaching England, Baltimore learned that his nephew, George Talbot, head of the council and *de facto* governor, had murdered the king's collector of revenue, Christopher Rousby, on board the royal ketch *Quaker,* near the Patuxent River.

Worse was yet to come. Baltimore's new council president, William Joseph, surpassed all records for tactless conduct. In the first year of his stewardship, Joseph informed the elected delegates to the assembly that the lord proprietor held the province by divine right, preached them a moral sermon, scolded them for misconduct, and commanded them to knuckle under to his lordship's government. When the delegates proceeded instead to draw up a bill of grievances, Joseph brought matters to a stalemate by proroguing the assembly. At this juncture news arrived in the province that King James II had fled to the continent before the armed forces of William of Orange, who had accepted the crown jointly with his English wife Mary. Amid "great uproar and tumult" in Maryland, the disaffected leaders formed "An Association in arms for the defense of the Protestant Religion, and for Asserting the Right of King William and Queen Mary to the Province of Maryland and all the English Dominions," with Nehemiah Blakiston at its head. Almost without resistance, troops of the newly formed Protestant Association, with Jowles, Cheseldine, and Blakiston leading them, took control of the province. They seized the records at St. Mary's and took into custody Governor Joseph and the councillors, who had fled to the country. Without delay Association leaders petitioned the new monarchs to assume dominion over the province.

3

THE ROYAL PERIOD

After years of discontent and wrangling, the revolution in Maryland came quickly and easily. Again the familiar element of Calvert mischance figured in the result. On the accession of William and Mary the Lord Baltimore had dispatched an emissary to proclaim the new monarchs in his palatinate. On the voyage the messenger died. Before a second could arrive, local tensions fed by wild rumors of popish plots and Catholic incitement of Indians had triggered direct action by the Protestant

Association, and Baltimore's palatine authority crumbled with the arrest of Joseph and the council. Without formally vacating the proprietary charter, the crown transformed the province into a royal colony by commissioning Lionel Copley governor, leaving Lord Baltimore substantially his rights to the soil only.

The quarter century of royal government in Maryland has attracted less attention than other and more colorful periods. Although lacking in high drama, this brief era left a permanent mark on ancient traditions and policies. Had the deposed proprietor visited his former palatinate in the last months of his long life, the final days of royal government in Maryland, he would have found many changes and very little merit in any of them.

Under the royal government the assembly took a firmer hand in provincial affairs.[20] Three strong royal governors, Francis Nicholson (1694–98), Nathaniel Blakiston (1698–1702), and John Seymour (1704–09), accorded the assembly more voice in policy-making and legislation than ever the Lord Baltimore had allowed. With some uncertainty at first, the lower house increasingly asserted its parliamentary character and in time made good its claims. The committee structure worked out by the delegates for the dispatch of business remained a permanent fixture: committees on privileges and elections, on laws, on grievances, and on accounts. Fed by the working committees, the assembly never lacked for fare. The legislative docket was uniformly large: altogether, eighty-five acts resulted from the first session of assembly under the royal government. Along with clearing up petty irritations and making minor adjustments, the assembly carried out more sweeping programs: establishing the Anglican Church, reforming the courts, and revising the legal code. In 1704 the two houses carried through a complete revision of the laws, much needed since the change from proprietary to royal government. The revision included deletion of obsolete acts and redrafting in proper form ambiguous or poorly drawn legislation. Probably the most substantial power acquired by representatives in the lower house was complete control over money bills, a power of vast import in the future.

A striking break with the past occurred in 1694 when Governor

---

20. The royal governors were: Lionel Copley (1691–93), Sir Edmund Andros (1693–94), Francis Nicholson (1694–98), Nathaniel Blakiston (1698–1702), Thomas Tench, president of the council (1702–04), John Seymour (1704–09), Edward Lloyd, president of the council (1709–1714), John Hart (1714–15).

Nicholson and the assembly moved the capital from the Catholic center of St. Mary's north to the heart of the old Puritan community on the Severn. Nicholson had a keen interest in town planning, and many of his personal touches in the layout of the new capital, Annapolis, still appear in State Circle and Church Circle on the high ground of the city.[21] Nicholson also brought his influence to bear in three different legislative acts for establishing the Anglican Church, all of them, as it happened, disallowed by the crown on technicalities. Nicholson was an ardent churchman, and he labored to put the Anglican communion on a footing of an established church. One of the charges laid at the door of Charles, Lord Baltimore, had been his neglect of the church. Whether he was responsible or not, the Anglicans were certainly not flourishing. All counties were in equally sad case. Anne Arundel County had four parishes but neither church buildings nor ministers. Calvert County had five parishes, three with churches but none with ministers. After several false starts over a decade, acts of establishment and endowment passed both assembly and crown in 1702 and 1704. This legislation provided parish organization—vestries elected by the communicants—and support for clergymen by a levy of forty pounds of tobacco on each taxable inhabitant. Beyond these obvious advantages, the Anglican communion, a minority element, received further benefits from a founder of the Society for the Propagation of the Gospel, Dr. Thomas Bray, who established parish libraries and recruited ministers for vacant pulpits.[22]

Other confessions faced a harder lot. None received financial support from official sources and some experienced severe penalties. The numerous Quakers lost their right to sit in the provincial assembly. Hardest hit of all, Roman Catholics were disbarred from holding any office and forbidden to celebrate mass except in privately owned chapels. Penalties against Roman Catholics reached a high point during the administration of Governor John Seymour. Notified of a public celebration of mass, Seymour hailed in the officiating priests and tongue-lashed them for their "gawdy shows and serpentine policy." His final warning was a token of the approaching death agony of

---

21. Reps, *Tidewater Towns*, pp. 117-40.
22. Nelson W. Rightmyer, *Maryland's Established Church* (Baltimore: Diocese of Md., 1956), pp. 14-54.

toleration: "In plain and few words Gentlemen if you intend to live here let me hear no more of these things for if I do and they are made good against you I'll chastize you, . . .Pray take notice that I am an English Protestant gentleman and can never equivocate."

The almost perpetual warfare of the royal period had its effect on religion and on the economy as well. King William's War (1689–97) and Queen Anne's War (1702–14) arrayed Protestant England against Catholic France. Though chiefly concerned with imperial and dynastic objectives, these wars insensibly swept religion into the toils with sorrowful consequences for the policy of toleration that had long prevailed in Maryland. More directly and demonstrably, the economy of the province suffered from the contraction of European markets for tobacco and the hazards to commerce. Tobacco prices remained uniformly low through the war years. Petitions of the times contain constant references to the "low state of the tobacco trade" and the consequent hardship on planters. Much of the economic legislation of the royal period must be viewed against the pinch of provincial poverty.

And yet the economy was not moribund. Planters still bought indentured servants as laborers at the rate of 500 to 950 annually at prices ranging from £12 to £20 per hand. Negro slaves, moreover, formerly rare in Maryland, arrived in growing numbers during these depression decades. In 1664 Governor Charles Calvert had tried to find a hundred planters who would promise to buy one slave each as a guarantee to the Royal African Company, an inducement to ship a cargo of blacks to the province. "I find wee are nott men of estates good enough to undertake such a business," he wrote his father, "but wish wee were for wee are naturally inclin'd to love neigros if our purses would endure it." After 1700 the picture changed. According to the census of 1704 the Negro population was 4,475. By 1712 it had almost doubled, and in 1720 had reached 25,000. Planters somehow found cash or credit to lay out sums as high as £25 to £30 sterling for prime hands. The social consequences of the influx of Negro slaves appeared in the decreased importation of indentured servants, drying up a source of future tenant farmers and freeholders. More affluent planters bought slaves, increasing their production and elevating their position in the social scale. Imperceptibly Maryland society was becoming more definitely stratified.

The bulk of planters, freeholders of modest personal estates without bond labor, still had the greater weight in numbers. The select few, men of considerable substance who held slaves and servants, formed a kind of squirearchy that furnished delegates to the assembly, justices of the county courts, vestrymen in the parishes, and officers of the militia. Some filled the offices of profit, the clerkships and collectorships that added tidy profits to their other sources of income.[23]

In a real sense the Maryland squires formed a power elite increasingly conscious of their position. More than once they gave royal officials a taste of their power. Governor Seymour grumbled when they set at naught one of his favorite schemes for reorganizing the judicial system. "The Country borne as they call themselves neither know their Duty to the Queens Matye nor the Respect they owe the Civill Magistrate." When delegates took their case to the electorate, Seymour called them a "restless and pernicious Crew" and described them as "busiest at Severall Elections in the Counties where they reside, to get Such ignorant & obstinate people return'd, who will pursue their destructive Notions and countenance their illegal proceedings."

Seymour's outburst of frustration bespoke the assembly's growing political maturity. The elected delegates were assuming the role of the "grand inquest of the province," the righters of wrongs, and they did not scruple to call in agents of the lord proprietor to account for those proprietary offices that were quasi-public in character. On one occasion the lower house placed under close arrest Baltimore's agent and receiver general, Henry Darnall, because he refused to produce the naval entry books for inspection. The delegates treated his successor, Charles Carroll the Settler, a man of massive talent and granite firmness, somewhat more circumspectly, without, however, hesitating to hold him to his responsibilities. Many a sheriff or other public official begged pardon of the house on his knees for some irregularity in the performance of his duties. Toward the end of the royal period the assembly had clearly acquired the habit of power that promised the Lords Baltimore a worthy champion when they recovered their governmental rights in 1715.

---

23. Margaret S. Morriss, *Colonial Trade of Maryland, 1689–1715, J. H. U. Studies,* XXXII (Baltimore: J. H. Press, 1914), 31-35.

4

## POLITICS AND PEOPLE

### IN EIGHTEENTH-CENTURY MARYLAND

Restoration of the proprietary government came with almost the suddenness of the revolution that had taken it away twenty-five years previously. Similarly, too, the restoration had occurred at a change in English monarchs, when at the death of Queen Anne in 1714 the Hanoverian line came to the throne in the person of George I. A year later on the death of old Lord Charles, last of the Catholic proprietors, a generous king returned full rights to Benedict Leonard, fourth Lord Baltimore (1675–1715), who had taken communion in the Anglican Church and now as a loyal Protestant could be entrusted with the government. Within a matter of weeks Benedict Leonard himself was dead, leaving the family province to his sixteen-year old son, Charles, the fifth Lord (1699–1751).

In Maryland the transition from royal back to proprietary government fell to John Hart (1714–1720), last of the royal governors, who continued in office five more years as proprietary chief magistrate in the province.[24] Hart brought to the task immense energy and modest talent. It was his misfortune to preside over provincial leaders far superior to him in native ability and to confront forces he could not grasp. In his final report to the Board of Trade in 1720 he wrote that since the restoration of "Lord Baltimore to his Government, [Maryland] is administered in the same manner, as when I formerly had the honour to be Governor by commission immediately from the Crown, save that in enacting of laws, holding of Courts, issueing of process, and granting of Commissions, the Lord Proprietor's name is solely made use of: as was done by his Lordsp's. noble ancestors."[25] Hart saw the form but missed the substance. In the uproar that marked his last gubernatorial years he imagined plots and evil designs when he was thwarted and saw plotters in the persons who thwarted him.

---

24. The proprietary governors after the restoration were: John Hart (1715–20), Charles Calvert (1720–27), Benedict Leonard Calvert (1727–31), Samuel Ogle (1731–32), Charles, Lord Baltimore (1732–33), Samuel Ogle (1733–42), Thomas Bladen (1742–47), Samuel Ogle (1747–52), Benjamin Tasker, president of the council (1752–53), Horatio Sharpe (1753–69), Robert Eden (1769–1776).

25. Cecil Headlam, ed., *Calendar of State Papers, Colonial: American and West Indies, 1720–21* (London: His Majesty's Stationery Office), XXXII, 129.

First of the provincials to cross the governor, Charles Carroll the Settler was also one of the ablest. Carroll could not qualify as "country borne" though he had become thoroughly seasoned since his arrival in 1688. As a Roman Catholic he had lost his post as proprietary attorney general in the overturn of 1689. Thereafter he had turned to private affairs and had become possibly the wealthiest man in Maryland, with many thousands of acres in plantations and personalty beyond the dreams of average planters. Toward the end of the royal period he had accepted from the proprietor the thankless post, agent and receiver general, or, in simpler terms, general manager of his Lordship's Maryland estate. At the restoration of the province Carroll had received his reward for faithful service to the proprietor in the years of adversity: no less than three major offices of trust and profit, including the important post, receiver general of the revenue. In his official capacity Carroll was now responsible to more than one master. He found himself bound to comply with provincial law and imperial regulations, both subjecting him to the oaths of abjuration and supremacy, to which he could not subscribe in good conscience. Feeling in the province against non juring office holders ran high for several months until the proprietary court in England relieved Carroll of those offices that required the oaths. But this was not before Hart had the satisfaction of seeing on the books new and stringent legislation disbarring Catholics from public office.

Even more drastic acts were to come in the frenetic days ahead as the Hart administration mired deeper in a morass of personalities and imaginary plots. Another provincial, Daniel Dulany (1685–1753), a coming young attorney of Prince George's County, incurred disfavor—in part at least—because of his association with prominent Catholics. Dulany had come to Maryland in 1703 as an indentured servant, served his term as clerk in the law office of George Plater, sometime attorney general, and had thereafter set up as an attorney in his own right. He had prospered in his profession and had married into a Calvert County family as old as the province itself. Now in his early thirties with a brilliant career ahead, Dulany brought official wrath upon his head. He had handled much of Charles Carroll's legal business, especially the debt collections, which were never popular. Furthermore, he had close ties amounting almost to a partnership with another lawyer, Thomas Macnemara, whose spectacular success in the courtroom was matched only by personal misconduct that brought on him such unbelievable charges as murder, sodomy, and rape in addition to the more ordinary offenses of drunkenness, brawling, and extortion. Reared as a Catholic, Macnemara had pretended to leave the church in order to qualify himself as an attorney by taking the oaths of abjuration and supremacy. Privately he made light of his perjury while he continued a highly remunerative practice. Dulany incurred guilt by association with such intimate connections as Carroll and Macnemara. He was, in Hart's words, "a noted favourer of the Papists." To head off the disaffected, Hart fanned into flame the embers of latent anti-Catholicism when he harangued the assembly on the machinations of priests and lay Catholics. Both houses thereupon rushed through an act that deprived Catholics of the franchise until they qualified themselves by oath. Thus in 1718 disappeared the last vestige of toleration that had been one of the glories of early Maryland.[26]

A brief season of tranquility descended on Maryland during the last fine days of summer in 1720. Within a space of weeks John Hart sailed for England, and his two chief villains, Macnemara and Carroll, died. The new governor, Charles Calvert (1720–27), cousin of the Lord Baltimore, had come with instructions from the proprietary court to pacify the wranglers and to still the tumult that had already begun to attract unfavorable comment in English political circles. Governor Calvert assured his first assembly that his lordship's aim was to live with "the good People of Maryland as a Bountiful Indulgent Father towards a dutiful Deserving son." His quotation of his lordship's own words about bringing "our Prerogative" and "your Privileges . . . into Ballance" revealed that Baltimore and his advisers had perceived more clearly than Hart the essential difference between proprietary and provincial interests. Plainly, too, Baltimore proposed to rest on his palatine authority, benevolently exercised to be sure, but nonetheless firmly.

Within two years the early peace of Governor Calvert's administration dissolved in strife sharper and more purposeful than the disorders of Hart's day. Provincials simply refused to conform to the lord proprietor's conception of government. When they spoke of "our happy constitution," they meant the

---

26. Aubrey C. Land, *The Dulanys of Maryland* (Baltimore: M. H. S., 1955), pp. 28-32, 40-41.

freedoms and powers won during twenty-five years of royal administration, and with these they were determined not to part. But the struggle as it shaped up was no more doctrinaire than constitutional conflicts of any date and country. Years of sharp economic distress goaded elected delegates to combat proprietary obstacles to any legislation designed for the well being of the province. And, as never before, the times and circumstances called for champions to lead the cause.

The beginnings of an era of struggle can be dated quite precisely from the first assembly after the elections of 1722, when many new faces appeared among the county delegations in the lower house. Early in the session the upper house clashed with the popularly elected body downstairs over a bill to prevent shipment of trash tobacco. Now in session time, the upper house comprised members of the council appointed by the proprietor and attentive to his wishes. After repeated failures to get agreement on legislation to improve the staple, the lower house thought fit to dramatize the conflict of interest in the dual function of the councillor-legislators upstairs who had blocked passage of the bill. The words of the lower-house polemic sound a note of eloquence:

> It is we that are the peoples Representatives for whom all Laws are made and Human Government Establisht. Your Honors Seem to be Assistants to Prerogative and Dependent on it, Rather than a State in which the people place a Confidence.

John Locke himself could hardly have improved this sturdy expression of the theory of responsible government.[27]

Certainly the House of Delegates had defined the constitutional issue: proprietary prerogative vs. popular aspiration. For ten years the battle raged, at times on great principles, at others on petty procedures. Once the delegates picked a fight over the trivial question of which house should have custody of the engrossed bills—those inscribed in a fair hand by a professional scrivenor—between the time they came from the copyist's hands and ceremonies at the end of the session, when the governor sealed them as laws. More serious, the lower house refused to include in the public accounts per diem allowances for members

27. *Arch. Md.*, XXXV, 356-57.

of the upper house on the ground that as councillors they were the proprietor's men and should be supported by him. Amid these briefer flurries the overarching question remained: who shall prevail, proprietary court or representatives of the country? And in due time the opposing elements came to be labelled "court party" and "country party."

Two leaders of the emerging country party first appeared in the lower house after the elections of 1722: Thomas Bordley and Daniel Dulany the Elder. Like Dulany, his rival at the bar, Bordley was an immigrant, a successful lawyer already wealthy and highly suspect in the governor's eyes. Before his early death in 1727, Bordley brought to Annapolis the printer, William Parks, who opened the pages of his *Maryland Gazette* to the propaganda of the country party. Meanwhile the collaborators had mounted a campaign that promised nothing short of a constitutional revolution. Specifically, they attacked the legislative veto, sparingly used during the royal period but more firmly and frequently exerted by the lord proprietor since his restoration. Their attack proceeded indirectly along two routes, one by introducing English statute law into the province and another by bringing the courts under assembly control. Dulany personally drafted an act binding judges to disregard personal directives and instructions from Lord Baltimore and "to do right and justice" according to the "laws, statutes, and reasonable customs of England and the acts of assembly and usages of the province of Maryland." The lord proprietor threw down the gauntlet by a peremptory veto.

After Bordley's death Dulany took the battle outside legislative halls. In 1728 he wrote for Parks's press a powerful pamphlet, *The Right of the Inhabitants to the Benefit of English Laws,* a piece instinct with the philosophy of natural law and English liberal thought. Dulany argued that the people of Maryland were justly entitled to the benefits of that great bulwark of English liberty, the common law. But, he continued, without the statutes that affirmed the common law, the rights conferred were wholly illusory. It followed then that the English statutes must necessarily be in force in Maryland. Dulany's performance had the strength of a lawyer's brief and the warmth of liberal sentiment he had absorbed from the great theorists in the western tradition of liberty. His pamphlet stated in concise form the position of the lower house and served Whiggish spokesmen for decades to come.[28]

Beneath the surface storms that all could see and hear churned powerful economic forces hidden from many eyes. Planters large and small labored to keep afloat in the grip of these currents by every means they and their representatives in the assembly could devise: limitation of tobacco production, destruction of inferior leaf, prohibitions on shipping trashy tobacco—anything to raise the price of the staple. Such measures represented their attempts to escape the simple economic truth spoken by a visiting ship captain: "The Largeness of the Quantity of Tobacco is the Grand Cause of the Lowness of the price . . . whilst it is so large, all . . . will be put palliating cures: for the weight of the Quantity, will break [your] strongest Resolution."[29] Production had indeed increased along with population since the end of the war in 1714, but the statistics of a decade and a half showed only two years when prices had been rewarding. As the year 1730 approached, an atmosphere of quiet desperation descended on the province. Here and there tobacco-cutting riots broke out. Profoundly depressed by the "unhappy Condition we are reduced to," Daniel Dulany wrote to a London merchant that he was in "despair of a cure [for provincial ills] without the Interposition of Providence."

A new governor, brother of the lord proprietor, Benedict Leonard Calvert (1727–1731), brought neither help nor consolation to Maryland. His term of office coincided with the bottom of the depression that had stricken the province, and his personal distaste for provincials and their ways did nothing to create a sense of rapport. Oxford bred and bookish by inclination, Calvert in a letter home spoke of Maryland as "this unpolished part of the universe," a description eloquent of his assumptions and of his social standards. By his measures Maryland stood low in the scale from all that he had seen. Not even the whole of the tidewater had yet come under cultivation, and, though population had moved up the Bay and out along the tidal rivers, large parts of Cecil and Baltimore Counties and the whole area west of Prince George's County were still wild country. One by one the assembly had erected new counties as settlers pushed away from

---

28. Land, *Dulanys*, pp. 76-85.
29. Letter of Captain Walter Hoxton, *M. G.*, April 1, 1729.

the original centers in the south, but fifty years of town legislation had not called into existence a single urban community
besides Annapolis. Oxford and Cambridge on the Eastern Shore
were no more than tiny bayside villages on the edge of an uniformly rural hinterland. Lacking urban centers that were natural
locations for schools, country families made shift to give their
children at least the rudiments of reading and writing. Wealthy
planters employed tutors, often indentured servants with a smat-
tering of letters, to keep a plantation school for their own children and those of nearest neighbors. A handful of these great
planters sent their sons to England or to Philadelphia to complete their education in an established preparatory school, to be
followed by college. Stephen Bordley, son of Thomas, was just
then in England for college and his final training in law at the
Inns of Court. Governor Nicholson had once entertained some
hopes for a local academy or college, King William's School, and
had opened a subscription with a handsome gift from his own
purse to launch it. But without the public support that kept
William and Mary College alive and healthy, King William's
School barely survived the decades just ahead and scarcely cut a
figure at all until many years later. By far the majority of planting
families instructed their own youth informally at home in letters
and simple arithmetic and in the practical lore of plantation
husbandry that one day would be their chief concern. And yet
the "Tobacco Coast" had its social dynamics even if not in towns
and schools familiar to Calvert. "Our Conversation," he wrote,
"runs on planting Tobacco and such other improvements of
trade, as neither the Muses inspire, nor Classic Authors treat of."
His most succinct summary, it misread the whole history and
culture of Maryland.

Calvert fully shared the traditional attitude of the proprietary
family toward provincials and their intransigent ways. "The
superiority, as I may term it, of the people over the government,
seems unnatural," he wrote his brother, "and is, I am sure,
repugnant to the very ends for which government was instituted,
*viz.*, an authoritative influence for the good order of society." But
Calvert had considerable powers of observation, and on the eve
of a new decade he sent his brother an acute analysis that within
two years brought about a showdown between proprietor and
province. First, Calvert predicted that the economy would continue to languish without a currency of some sort; he recom-

mended paper money as the tonic. Next he pointed out that proprietary officers, whose incomes depended on fees, could not collect without an authorizing act. "Every insolent fellow thinks himself free to refuse payment, and browbeat, as it were, the officers," he wrote. "And it is a continual bone of contention, and a specious handle to amuse the ignorant." The assembly had steadily refused to pass legislation without reducing the fees, which delegates considered exorbitant. Calvert recommended establishing the fees by prerogative action. Finally he questioned whether the proprietor was receiving the maximum revenues from his palatinate. During the lifetime of his grandfather, old Lord Charles, the revenues had come from an act granting the proprietor a duty of one shilling on every hogshead of tobacco exported as compensation for receiving his quitrents in tobacco at the rate of two pence per pound, a figure so inflated that in years of low prices on the London market the rent roll tobacco paid little more than the cost of collection. During the dominion of the current Lord Charles a new equivalent arrangement, worked out by the assembly, gave the proprietor an export duty of two shillings per hogshead in commutation of all quitrents whatsoever. But this temporary act ran only three years and came up periodically for renewal. Each renewal gave the lower house an opportunity to publicize the alleged bargain enjoyed by the proprietor and to demand concessions from him as a condition of continuing the act in force another three years. Governor Calvert frankly said that direct collection of quitrents by his own agents, however troublesome, would be more satisfactory.[30]

Calvert meant his advice for his brother's privy ear, but without doubt the proprietor had deep speech with his advisers about these matters. In the winter of 1732 Baltimore made a visit to his province, which had not seen a lord proprietor in person since Lord Charles, his grandfather, had sailed away half a century before. The visitation proved socially interesting, from the royal salutes and bonfires at his landing until his homeward-bound ship dropped down the Bay toward the high seas six months later. But for his lordship pleasure took second place to business, which he dispatched with relentless efficiency. Without demur he agreed to an act of assembly providing for the paper

---

30. *Arch. Md.*, XXV, 602-07.

currency—£90,000 in bills of small denominations—long desired as a stimulant to local trade. Then he turned to housekeeping. By proclamation he established a table of fees for proprietary officers and gave them the authority needed for collection. Rejecting further offers to renew the equivalent act, he instituted a rigorous system of quitrent collections and appointed Daniel Dulany as his agent at a handsome salary to set it in operation. Finally, he guaranteed his governor a salary independent of the assembly by reviving an act passed in 1704 "for settlement of an annual revenue on her majesty's governor." Many thought this highhanded reviver illegal and an abuse of authority. Constitutionally, Baltimore's actions represented a naked assertion of the prerogative.

The settlement of 1733 was to stand until the Revolution swept away proprietary property and governmental rights forever. However satisfactory administratively, the arrangement created a condition of permanent conflict between colony and proprietor, though at first relative quiet prevailed. The country party had lost its ablest and most articulate spokesman when Daniel Dulany elected to join the select company of wealth and talent that formed the establishment. The proprietor had in Samuel Ogle (1731–42), his governor, a political realist perfectly capable of systematically robbing the popular party by bestowing offices of profit on its leaders. "The Duke of New Castle is hard run in the political warehouse in Britain and in miniature I in Maryland," remarked a member of the proprietary court specially charged with appointments. In 1733 Ogle could count on such lieutenants as Dulany, Benjamin Tasker, and Edmund Jenings. Later and equally able recruits—George Plater, Stephen Bordley, Colonel Edward Lloyd of Wye House, Charles Goldsborough, and Daniel Dulany the Younger—gave the proprietor sturdy supporters of his regime and defenders of his rights. After a few years, when the leaderless country party regained its vigor, it retaliated on those who accepted offices of profit by disabling them to sit in the lower house.[31]

During the lull following Baltimore's visit, proprietary officials put the revenues in order. Dulany reorganized the quitrents, compiling rent rolls and appointing receivers. Naval

---

31. Charles A. Barker, *The Background of the Revolution in Maryland* (New Haven: Yale University Press, 1940), pp. 134 ff.

officers collected the new tonnage duties and the land office sold warrants and recorded patents in unprecedented numbers. The sheer value in money of these proprietary revenues was bound to evoke criticism. From all sources—quitrents, land sales, and tonnage duties—Lord Baltimore himself received an annual income that increased from £10,000 in the 1730's to more than £13,000 in the years immediately preceding the American Revolution. This sum, paid in scarce sterling exchange, went from the province to London and represented a direct tribute levied on the economy. Another £12,000 to £14,000 was paid by the planters to the select few who held places of profit—the collectorships and clerkships. Still another £8,000 went to support clergy of the established church, who received forty pounds of tobacco from taxables of every denomination, Catholic, Quaker, and Presbyterian as well as Anglican. Altogether, provincials paid out something more than £30,000 annually to Lord Baltimore and about 120 men in the civil and ecclesiastical administration who formed the nucleus of the court party.

It was well that a slowly turning cycle brought a long season of economic growth in the decades following 1733. The new paper money authorized during Baltimore's sojourn in Maryland had the tonic effect expected by its promoters on local trade. Already some of the Eastern Shore counties were turning from tobacco to grain, and when the western areas were settled, planters there grew no tobacco at all for paying tax and tithe. The currency proved a boon. But the principal stimulus to better times came from increased demand for Chesapeake tobacco abroad, particularly the rising port of Glasgow, where Scottish merchant houses did a volume business with France and northern Europe. Increased demand meant better prices for Maryland tobacco, never as high as planters wished, but tempting enough to encourage new slave purchases and greater consumption of store goods. Small planters profited by increased returns that afforded them ampler livings and—for some at least—an escape from debt. But the chief beneficiaries were the merchant-planters, who shipped the tobacco and sold the goods that small producers could not supply for themselves at home. The estates of Worgan and his like dwindle into insignificance beside the fortunes accumulated by the Chews, Galloways, and Bennetts during the golden age just dawning.

Like their prototypes half a century earlier, the new breed of merchant-planters organized the commerce of the province and in much the same manner—assembling cargoes of tobacco, extending credit, and selling goods. Their greater worldly success was in part the result of the sheer growth the province had experienced in population and in production. When Lord Baltimore visited Maryland in 1732, his faithful tenants numbered approximately 96,000 altogether, man, woman, and child. Thereafter increase proceeded at a rapid pace. By 1748 the population figure had risen to 130,000, by 1755 to 153,000, and to 164,000 in 1761, all well within a single generation. During the same years, decade by decade, the value of tobacco produced also expanded.

AVERAGE ANNUAL EXPORTS OF TOBACCO FROM MARYLAND

| Decade | Pounds of tobacco |
|--------|-------------------|
| 1721–30 | 13,033,000 |
| 1731–40 | 15,200,000 |
| 1741–50 | 20,200,000 |
| 1751–60 | 22,830,000 |
| 1761–70 | 25,000,000 |

Provincial shippers, the merchant-planters in correspondence with consignment houses of Britain, dealt in volume unknown in earlier days. Some of them, moreover, were taking profits in the slave trade as an adjunct to their tobacco business. Opportunity had new dimensions for the aggressive and prudent who could seize it.

In the 1730's a new type, the industrial entrepreneur, gained a foothold in the hitherto uniformly agrarian economy of Maryland. A syndicate of well-to-do planters in the Annapolis area formed the Baltimore Company to exploit the high-content iron ores lying on the surface in the Patapsco region. The five partners—Dulany, Tasker, and three Carrolls—each subscribed £750 sterling to a capital stock to get the iron works under way. By plowing back part of the profits into the enterprise, the partners soon enlarged the works to a respectable size and a level of output equal to individual iron smelters in England. The Baltimore works became something of a showpiece, commented on by nearly every traveler who came through the province. The annual profit to each partner ran higher than the entire estates of the majority of Maryland planters. Other smelters—the Snowden works, Stephen Onion's iron works on the Gunpowder

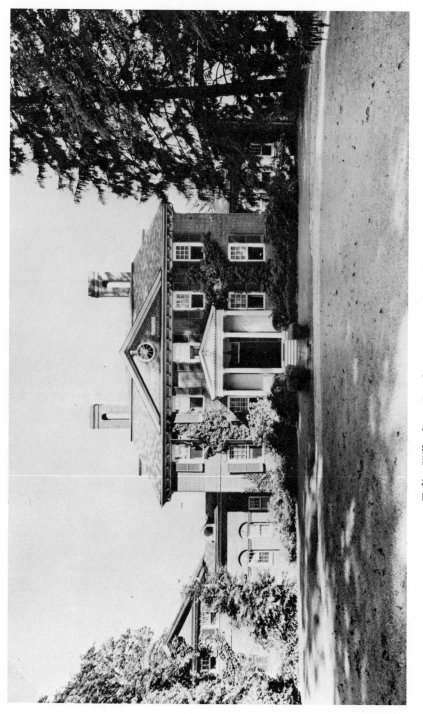

Tulip Hill plantation house, Anne Arundel County.
Typical of the finest of Georgian architecture. *M.H.S.*

River, the Nottingham and Principio companies at the head of the Bay—swelled iron production until by mid-century Maryland ironmasters were turning out annually an amount equal to about one-seventh of the output of England. Besides enriching the owners, the iron supplied provincial blacksmiths who otherwise paid scarce exchange for imported wrought iron. And the pig shipped to England by Maryland ironmasters put on the books of British merchant houses sterling balances for drawing bills of exchange.[32]

Still another highroad to fortune appeared as population moved out of the tidewater into the west. Tentatively at first, a few wealthy planters carved out tracts of wild land for future development. Daniel Dulany interested himself in this remote area in the 1730's to the extent of taking a mortgage on a 550 acre tract, Long Meadow, patented by his protegé Thomas Cresap, a colorful Indian trader in the great tradition of pioneers. Thereafter Cresap acted as a western agent for Dulany, now and again selling a farm to one of the migrating Germans following the route from Pennsylvania toward the Shenandoah in Virginia. Then, in the early autumn of 1744, Dulany went in person to the "western parts" on proprietary business. One look at the fat soils and the migrating Germans transformed him into a full-fledged land speculator. He went at his western enterprise with such ardor that his neighbors questioned his sanity. Already a large landholder, he patented an additional 20,000 acres of western land within half a decade, choice tracts selected and surveyed by his versatile agent, Cresap. Dulany went on to contact Dutch shippers and encourage them to bring Palatine Germans to the infant port of Baltimore, where his younger son, Walter, took them in hand. Then, to induce the immigrants to purchase from him, he sold farms on long term mortgages and laid out a market town, Frederick, as a commercial center for the west on a large tract he owned. Thus combining development with speculation, Dulany enlarged a respectable fortune into an immense one.

The middle years of the eighteenth century in Maryland have been called the golden age, probably with justice, as fortunes—made or enlarged—rose to new magnitudes and social life acquired a luster wholly unlike the dreary pioneering days.

---

32. Keach Johnson, "The Baltimore Company Seeks English Subsidies for the Colonial Iron Industry," *M. H. M.*, XLVI (Mar., 1951), 27-43.

An eighteenth-century plantation, a sign of prosperity, as depicted in one of the outstanding dioramas of the *Darnall Young People's Museum. M.H.S.*

42

Dulany's neighbor and business associate in iron works, Charles Carroll of Annapolis (1702–82), was building on the ample estate left by his father, Charles Carroll the Settler. Carroll also patented western land, lent money, operated several plantations, and shipped tobacco. In 1764 he appraised his net worth in personalty and real property at £88,380:9:7.[33] Almost every county could point to one or two families that had fattened their purses on the proprietary land system or other opportunities in trade and industry. In St. Mary's it was the Platers, in Calvert the Fitzhughs, in Charles the Hansons and Lees, in Anne Arundel the Garretts, Galloways, and Chews. Scattered over the Eastern Shore counties were the Lloyds, Tilghmans, Ringgolds, Goldsboroughs, and—at the pinnacle—Richard Bennett, a descendant of the troublesome Puritan of a century past. When Bennett died in 1749 the *Maryland Gazette* supposed him "the Richest Man on the Continent," and fulsomely described his many benefactions, among them the forgiving of a hundred fifty poor debtors in his will. These and their like built the mansions that are still showplaces of the tidewater and that ushered in the golden age of colonial culture.

Visitors expressed pleasant surprise at manners and fashions in Maryland, particularly in the miniature capital city. Annapolis had not developed either as an industrial center or port city, a future destined for the struggling village of Baltimore up the Bay near the iron works. But Annapolis streets were lined with stores and shops of artisans who purveyed imported luxuries and their own handiwork—wigs, furniture, silver—as fine as any to be had in London, if their advertisements in the *Maryland Gazette* are to be believed. These were the wares demanded by a residential community of wealthy inhabitants along with fine wines, imported cheeses, and books. Visitors also found the pleasures of their hosts "agreeable and varied." Horse racing became a gentleman's sport during the second administration of Governor Samuel Ogle (1746–52), who imported Arabian blood for his stable. Ogle's brother-in-law, Councillor Benjamin Tasker, Jr., had an abiding attachment to horseflesh and vied with the governor in bringing to the province some of the royal blood that still flows in the veins of descendants two centuries later. The Lloyds

33. Kate Mason Rowland, *The Life of Charles Carroll of Carrollton, 1737–1832, with his Correspondence and Public Papers,* 2 vols. (New York: G. P. Putnam's Sons, 1898), I, 60.

and Fitzhughs both bred turf champions that made the Annapolis races a social event of the Chesapeake tidewater.[34]

Other attractions usually coincided with the autumn races. Visiting theatrical companies found the gathering large, liberal, and appreciative. Dress balls were nightly occurrences. A visitor from Mount Vernon in Virginia faithfully kept his diary through eight days of the Annapolis races, noting dinners, balls, and theatricals without mentioning a single horse or race. Annapolis also boasted a succession of social clubs patterned after the lively Tuesday Club, founded in 1745 by Dr. Alexander Hamilton. While the secretary, "Sandy" Hamilton, kept mock heroic minutes of the doings of an assorted membership of lawyers and merchants, the new printer of the *Maryland Gazette,* Jonas Green, wit and *bon vivant,* amused the brethren with mystifying conundrums and atrocious puns. Among others, Walter Dulany frequented Tuesday Club meetings, where he earned the nickname "Slyboots Pleasant." A few touches of erudition scattered among Tuesday Club hijinx suggest another and more serious pursuit of the most ardent clubmen and horse fanciers. Many of them had excellently chosen libraries whose contents they knew from critical reading. Stephen Bordley carried on club antics with the best of them, but he also read widely and commented intelligently on his books. About one popular author Bordley said, "He seems to me to be an Empty & Modifying writer."

Maryland society included other strata than the highly visible set that frequented the capital or lived in the great country houses. Small planters elicited so little comment from either visitors or wealthy natives themselves that they have become the invisible people of the Chesapeake. Yet these petty producers who lived in one-room houses, raised tiny crops, and never read a book far outnumbered the merchant-planters at the top of the heap, even in the golden age. To be sure, they gathered to watch blooded horses run for purses of a hundred golden guineas, but their sports ran to wrestling, sometimes accompanied by eye-gouging, or to cudgelling, gander-pulling and foot racing. Cudgelling matches by rustics became major attractions at the annual fairs, among the first in America, that Daniel Dulany instituted at Frederick town. Such sports followed an ancient

---

34. William Eddis, *Letters from America,* ed. Aubrey C. Land (Cambridge: Harvard University Press, 1969), pp. 54-55.

English tradition of country frolics and attracted the gentlefolk as spectators, though never as participants. Nor did the lesser folk commonly intermarry with the gentry. Taskers married Dulanys and Galloways married Chews in a web of family alliances knit together by money and power. Nevertheless class barriers were neither rigid nor insurmountable. Even those at the bottom could ascend in the scale according to their talents, even from indentured servitude, as had Dulany and Macnemara or from an apprenticeship as Bordley. And no one, however rich or powerful, could ignore the force that sheer numbers gave the poor planters at the polls and in the economy. They were the strength of the country party whose leaders voiced their imperatives.

After a season of quiescence, the country party showed signs of reviving in the late 1730's as new leaders rose to direct strategy and write manifestoes. Foremost among them, Dr. Charles Carroll (1691–1755) and Philip Hammond rallied their colleagues to a new war of attrition on the entrenched proprietary interest. Dr. Carroll, a resident of Annapolis since 1715, was new to Maryland politics. Like other Roman Catholics ineligible for public office, he had for twenty years remained in a private station, first as a physician and surgeon but increasingly shifting his interests to shipping, land speculation, and iron manufacture as a partner in the Baltimore Company. After two decades in the province, rich and respected, Dr. Carroll was received into the Anglican communion and in 1738 was elected to the House of Delegates. The anti-proprietary movement dates from the assembly of 1739, when the new house drew up a formidable catalogue of grievances: the fee proclamation of 1733 violated the charter, the one-shilling duty of 1704 for support of the governor was illegal, the tonnage duties collected for his lordship's privy purse had lapsed, collection of alienation fines on land sales was contrary to terms of the land grants, the selling of clerkships tended to the ruin of the province, and the collection of naval officers' fees in gold and silver was a violation of the paper money law. As a token of their determination to right these grievances, the delegates voted to appeal their case to the king.[35]

From this position the lower house was never to recede. The issue was permanent: the relative authority of the representatives and the lord proprietor in ordering the affairs of Maryland.

---

35. Barker, *Background* pp. 223-30.

On his side the proprietor had a corps of officials carefully selected from the ablest minds of the province plus the advantage of an entrenched position won in the coup of 1733. To dislodge him, the lower house had its own cadre of talent backed by strong popular sentiment and the power of the purse. A whole generation lived through the politics of irreconcilabilities with occasional compromises that led to constructive legislation, such as the Tobacco Inspection Act of 1747.

Unexpectedly, the outbreak of imperial warfare after twenty-five years of peace gave the lower house political leverage. In 1739 the ancient enmity between Protestant England and the Catholic house of Bourbon broke out in King George's War (1739–48). Obedient to commands from England to put the colony in a posture of defense, Governor Ogle called on the lower house for a military supply bill, which the delegates passed for a period of one year only and with a provision appropriating minor proprietary revenues to the war effort. In dire need of funds, Ogle agreed to the measure, the first and last Maryland contribution to financing the war and a small temporary victory for the lower house over the proprietary prerogative. Thereafter annual supply bills failed when the delegates insisted on writing in provisions taking control of defense funds from the hands of the treasurers appointed by Baltimore and placing them in the hands of the speaker of the house. To this inroad Baltimore would not yield and specifically instructed his new governor, Thomas Bladen (1742–47), a native of Maryland, never to repeat Ogle's mistake of signing a bill that might abate proprietary revenues. The resulting impasse prevented further support of the war.

A single important piece of legislation, passed in the final months of King George's War, defined the narrow boundaries of constructive action in the prevalent atmosphere of irreconcilability. Samuel Ogle, who had just returned for his second term as governor (1747–52) was instructed by the proprietor to shepherd through the assembly a tobacco inspection law after the Virginia model that had given tobacco south of the Potomac a distinct edge in the trade. For once given some flexibility, Ogle carried out his seemingly impossible assignment. After twenty votes of record on details in the lower house, the Tobacco Inspection Act of 1747 became law. It had something for everyone. The inspection of tobacco by "viewers" promised to eliminate trash and "damnified leaves" from shipment and thus enhance both qual-

ity and price. Other provisions reduced tobacco due the clergymen of the establishment from forty to thirty pounds per taxable
head and trimmed officers' fees, also payable in tobacco, to rates
well below those of the proclamation of 1733. At last the fees
were established by law as the country party had always recommended, though the reductions promised no real loss because
they were made in the expectation of higher tobacco prices. A
few critics grumbled, but the majority thought an obstacle to
economic improvement was removed. The upper house invited
the delegates to the council chamber, where "all the Loyal
Healths, Success to the Tobacco Trade, &.&. were Drank." The
town battery boomed a ten-gun salute and "the Populace having
Punch and Wine distributed amongst them, made loud Acclama-
tions of Joy.' The majority judged more accurately than the critics. The first adequate tobacco legislation in twenty-five years,
the Inspection Act served its purpose for the next twenty-two.
But in passing it, neither country nor court had moved more than
a hair's breadth.[36]

During the brief pause following King George's War, major
changes occurred in high places within the Maryland system. In
1751 Charles, Lord Baltimore, died and was succeeded by his
son Frederick, sixth and last lord. A few months later Governor
Ogle was dead. Frederick, later to prove himself a degenerate
unworthy of his ancestry, appointed as his new governor Horatio
Sharpe (1753–69) and as principal secretary and his right hand
man a crafty uncle who always signed himself Cecilius Calvert.
The changes set the stage for the final two decades of Maryland's
provincial history, but they altered neither proprietary nor provincial attitudes in any significant way.

Almost as soon as he took office, Governor Sharpe had to face
the trials of the last and most savage stage of Anglo-French
rivalry in America, the French and Indian War. Again the sorry
play of partisan politics repeated itself. Time after time the lower
house tacked on appropriations bills one or another proviso
unacceptable to the proprietary court, usually in the form of a tax
on the lord proprietor's estate or his revenues. Though averse to
these tactics, the governor detested just as much a practice that
took a hold in Maryland politics during the war. From time to

---

36. Vertrees J. Wyckoff, *Tobacco Regulation in Maryland, J. H. U. Studies,*
New Series, XXII (Baltimore: J. H. Press, 1936), 164-84.

time county gatherings passed resolutions "instructing" representatives in the House of Delegates. Occasionally the *Maryland Gazette* gave province-wide circulation to a county resolve or instruction directing delegates to support one or another popular bill. And when these bills failed in the face of upper house or gubernatorial opposition, the *Gazette* printed the full text "for the perusal of the inhabitants." Such extramural political action, deeply distasteful to Sharpe, excited the people and sounded a note of popular government. Nor did Sharpe relish the outburst of anti-Catholicism engendered by the war and exacerbated by the out-of-doors politics in local instructions to delegates.[37] Possibly his hardest cross to bear was Cecilius Calvert, who meddled continually in provincial affairs behind his back. Somehow Sharpe preserved his equanimity through these tribulations, to be remembered, after the longest term of any proprietary governor, as also the ablest in Maryland provincial history.

The war in its active phase began with the ill-fated expedition of General Edward Braddock from western Maryland toward the forks of the Ohio. His stunning defeat exposed settlers in the west country to Indian reprisals and drove many from their frontier homes back eastward. Westerners understandably demanded protection against the savages and their French abettors. At the same time the crown was calling for troops and supplies to assist the imperial war effort.

The contributions of Maryland fell far below what was requested in supplies. It is also true that the lord proprietor was even stingier. Baltimore never willingly permitted his ample revenues to bear a part of the common burden. During the entire war only twice were supplies voted. First, in the earliest months of conflict, the lower house passed a war tax that appropriated among other items the proprietary income from tavern licenses. In his necessity Governor Sharpe signed the bill in violation of his instructions, though he protected himself by consulting his council. Baltimore grudgingly acquiesced in this tiny contribution of what he regarded as his revenue. The second and last appropriation, another violation of Sharpe's instructions, included two unpalatable taxes, one, a land tax that also fell on proprietary manors, and a second, a double tax on Roman

---

37. Barker, *Background*, pp. 254-55.

Catholics, a departure from the religious equality he was bound to uphold. Only the emergency following Braddock's defeat persuaded Sharpe to give his consent. Clearly, the delegates were using the war demands of the crown as a fulcrum to pry concessions from Lord Baltimore. In Sharpe's words, "His majesty's and the proprietary interest and instructions must be made to clash; and no money is to be raised unless his lordship's private claim be made to submit to demands and caprice of an infatuated assembly." But further he was not prepared to go. When the lower house proposed a five per cent tax on quitrents and incomes of officeholders, he would not agree, although the tax would have been no greater than that borne by other propertied men in the province. The country party rang the changes on the theme of proprietary greed during the remainder of the war in pamphlets and in the pages of the *Maryland Gazette.*

For the country party the war years proved an initiation into full maturity. Whiggish in outlook, its leaders found nothing amiss in the resolves, instructions, and petitions to delegates coming from the counties. Their forum, the *Gazette,* in turn informed the electorate of their legislative battles in behalf of "British rights," the heritage of the freemen of Maryland. The solidarity of leaders and led provoked Cecilius, always tampering with patronage, into a fantastic scheme of buying off country party leaders with minor offices at the proprietor's disposal. Sharpe had some difficulty persuading the infatuated old man that the planter delegates, several as wealthy as Dr. Carroll, would never be tempted. He recognized country party leaders as men of principle, even though he thought their Whiggish principles untenable.

At the war's end in 1763 proprietor and province remained at odds. In all the commotion the proprietor had neither yielded nor lost a particle of his prerogative nor, in any permanent way, his revenue. Outwardly, the anti-proprietary movement had gained nothing. But a subtle change—rather sensed than apparent—had effected a transformation in provincial attitudes that a perceptive mind might have recognized as an ill omen for the proprietary system. Cecilius Calvert, who never penetrated to essences, failed to grasp the toughness of American fiber. When Councillor Dulany died in late 1753 his son Daniel the Younger (1722–97) expected to inherit some of his father's offices and dignities. Schooled at Oxford and the Inns of Court, the younger Dulany had returned home to marry the daughter of Benjamin Tasker and to make his reputation as "an oracle of the law." As manager of proprietary patronage, Calvert appointed Dulany to office but could never bend the younger man to his will. Dulany's independent course as a member of the council occasionally collided with long-held proprietary positions, once so violently as to elicit the governor's comment: "That he is fond of being thought a Patriot Councillor & rather inclined to serve the People than the Proprietary is evident to everyone."[38]

If the war's end brought no significant impairment of proprietary rights, it brought no peace in Maryland politics either. Only the lack of openings for attacking the system diminished the hubbub of extramural politics. Yet there were those in the province who could seize and mould circumstances, among them young Daniel Dulany with the climax of a brilliant career ahead of him. Like his fellow provincials Dulany could hardly have known that a long chapter—the longest in Maryland history—was ending. But a new time was at hand, indeed had already begun by imperial reformers in Parliament.

---

38. Land, *Dulanys*, pp. 245-58.

BIBLIOGRAPHICAL ESSAY

CHAPTER I

The literature on provincial Maryland is huge, far too large for complete listing. Much of it is too specialized to interest the general reader. This bibliography aims at intelligent selection with brief annotation to guide the reader in the direction of his interest.

*General Works.* The oldest histories of Maryland, noteworthy for their time, are now almost curiosities: James McSherry, *History of Maryland; from its First Settlement in 1634 to the Year 1848* (Baltimore: J. Murphy & Co., 1849) and John V. L. MacMahon, *An Historical View of the Government of Maryland from its Colonization to the Present Day* (Baltimore: J. Lucas & E. K. Deaver, 1831). The massive work of John Thomas Scharf, *History of Maryland from Earliest Times to the Present Day*, 3 volumes (Baltimore: J. B. Piet, 1879), old-fashioned and leisurely but full and detailed, prints many scarce letters and documents in full.

Modern scholarship on Maryland begins with Newton D. Mereness, *Maryland as a Proprietary Province* (New York: The Macmillan Co., 1901), the standard institutional study. A more popularly written narrative account, Matthew Page Andrews, *The Founding of Maryland* (New York: D. Appleton Century Co., 1933) covers in detail the years up to 1689. His earlier *History of Maryland: Province and State* (Garden City:Doubleday, Doran & Co., 1929) deals extensively with both the seventeenth and eighteenth centuries. Clayton C. Hall, *The Lords Baltimore and their Maryland Palatinate* (Baltimore: J. Murphy & Co., 1904) treats briefly but attractively the relationships between proprietor and province.

Two superlative volumes cover the eighteenth century. Lawrence C. Wroth, *A History of Printing in Colonial Maryland, 1686–1776* (Baltimore: Typothetae of Baltimore, 1922) goes far beyond the scope implied by the title. Charles A. Barker, *The Background of the Revolution in Maryland* (New Haven: Yale University Press, 1940) is a masterly survey of the years from 1720 to independence.

*Special Studies.* Earliest years are covered in two detailed works by an elder scholar: Bernard C. Steiner, *Beginnings of Maryland, 1631–1639 (J. H. U. Studies*, XXI, Baltimore: J. H. Press, 1903) and *Maryland During the English Civil Wars*, 2 vols. (*J. H. U. Studies*, XXIV and XXV, Baltimore: J. H. Press, 1906–07). The older work of Francis E. Sparks, *Causes of the Maryland Revolution of 1689 (J. H. U.*

*Studies*, XIV Baltimore: J. H. Press, 1896) can be supplemented by Michael G. Kammen, "The Causes of the Maryland Revolution of 1689," *Maryland Historical Magazine*, XL, 293–333. Raphael Semmes, *Captains and Mariners of Early Maryland* (Baltimore: J. H. Press, 1937) contains much seventeenth-century local history charmingly written. On unfree labor two older works cover the whole colonial period: E. I. McCormac, *White Servitude in Maryland, 1634–1820* (*J. H. U. Studies*, XII, Baltimore: J. H. Press, 1904) and Jeffrey R. Brackett, *The Negro in Maryland: A Study in the Institution of Slavery* (*J. H. U. Studies*, Extra Volume X, Baltimore: J. H. Press, 1889). Abbott E. Smith, *Colonists in Bondage: White Servitude and Convict Labor in America, 1607–1776* (Chapel Hill: Univ. of North Carolina Press, 1947) has much new material to supplement the history of the unfree. On justice in early Maryland the fare is meagre: Conway W. Sams and Elihu S. Riley, *The Bench and Bar of Maryland*, 2 vols. (Chicago: Lewis Pub. Co., 1901) and Raphael Semmes, *Crime and Punishment in Early Maryland* (Baltimore: J. H. Press, 1938).

For a subject of such importance the literature on religion is surprisingly small: Nelson W. Rightmyer, *Maryland's Established Church* (Baltimore: Church Historical Society for the Diocese of Baltimore, 1956), H. S. Spalding, *Catholic Colonial Maryland* (Milwaukee: The Bruce Publishing Co., 1931), Theodore C. Gambrall, *Church Life in Colonial Maryland* (Baltimore: G. Lycett, 1885), and J. W. McIlvain, *Early Presbyterianism in Maryland* (*J. H. U. Studies*, VIII, Baltimore: J. H. Press, 1890).

Economic historians make a better showing, at least for the eighteenth century: Clarence P. Gould, *The Land System of Maryland, 1720–1765* (*J. H. U. Studies*, XXXI, Baltimore: J. H. Press, 1913), Vertrees J. Wyckoff, *Tobacco Regulation in Colonial Maryland* (*J. H. U. Studies*, New Series, No. 22, Baltimore: J. H. Press, 1936), Margaret S. Morriss, *Colonial Trade of Maryland, 1689–1715* (*J. H. U. Studies*, XXXII. Baltimore: J. H. Press, 1914), Clarence P. Gould, *Money and Transportation in Maryland, 1720–1765* (*J. H. U. Studies*, XXXIII: Baltimore: J. H. Press, 1915), Katheryn L. Behrens, *Paper Money in Maryland, 1727–1789* (*J. H. U. Studies*, XLI, Baltimore: J. H. Press, 1923), and Avery O. Craven, *Soil Exhaustion as a Factor in the Agricultural History of Virginia and Maryland, 1606–1860* (*University of Illinois Studies in the Social Sciences*, XIII Urbana: University of Illinois Press, 1926).

The architectural and urban history of colonial Maryland is recorded in several excellent books, among them the outstanding volumes by Morris L. Radoff, *Buildings of the State of Maryland at Annapolis* (Annapolis: Hall of Records Commission, 1954), *The County Courthouses and Records of Maryland. Part One: The Courthouses*

(Annapolis: Hall of Records Commission, 1960), and *The State House at Annapolis* (Annapolis: Hall of Records Commission, 1972). Walter B. Norris, *Annapolis, Its Colonial and Naval Story* (New York: Thomas Y. Crowell Company, 1925) and John W. Reps, *Tidewater Towns: City Planning in Colonial Virginia and Maryland* (Williamsburg: Institute of Early American History and Culture, 1972) cover these special subjects accurately and attractively.

Dieter Cunz, *The Maryland Germans, A History* (Princeton: Princeton University Press, 1948) deals with the most important ethnic group in early days.

To cover a hitherto neglected area J. A. Leo Lemay in *Men of Letters in Colonial Maryland* (Knoxville: University of Tennessee Press, 1972) has supplied a capital history of early Maryland literature, factually accurate in its fulsome detail but flawed by extravagant claims of the quality of colonial writing.

Of many possible biographical victims in a province rich in personalities only two have received adequate treatment, the Dulanys and Carrolls. See Aubrey C. Land, *The Dulanys of Maryland* (Baltimore: Maryland Historical Society, 1955, new edition, 1968). Charles Carroll of Carrollton awaits a proper biographer in the modern manner. Kate Mason Rowland, *The Life of Charles Carroll of Carrollton, 1737–1832, with his Correspondence and Public Papers,* 2 volumes (New York: G. P. Putnam's Sons, 1898), an old-fashioned life and times, still remains the most satisfactory. Three more recent accounts are flawed: Joseph Gurn, *Charles Carroll of Carrollton, 1737–1832* (New York: P. J. Kenedy & Sons, 1932), Ellen Hart Smith, *Charles Carroll of Carrollton* (Cambridge: Harvard University Press, 1942), Thomas O'Brien Hanley, *Charles Carroll of Carrollton, The Making of a Revolutionary Gentleman* (Washington: Catholic University of America Press, 1970). Among the many county histories two are outstanding: Oswald Tilghman, *History of Talbot County, 1661–1861,* 2 volumes (Baltimore: Williams & Wilkins, 1915) and George Johnston, *History of Cecil County, Maryland* (Elkton: The Author, 1887).

*Sources.* Four volumes of source materials on colonial Maryland are recommended to the general reader for their liveliness and flavor: Clayton C. Hall (ed.), *Narratives of Early Maryland, 1633–1684* (New York: Charles Scribner's Sons, 1910); Bernard C. Steiner (ed.), *Early Maryland Poetry; The Works of Ebenezer Cook, gent: laureat of Maryland* (Baltimore: J. Murphy & Co., 1900); Carl Bridenbaugh (ed.), *Gentleman's Progress: The Itinerarium of Dr. Alexander Hamilton, 1744* (Chapel Hill: University of North Carolina Press, 1948); William Eddis, *Letters from America* edited with an introduction by Aubrey C. Land (Cambridge: Harvard University Press, 1969).

Finally no bibliography would be complete without mention of two monumental series both published by the Maryland Historical Society: *The Archives of Maryland* (Baltimore, 1883—    ) which reprint in seventy-two volumes issued to date a large fraction of the source materials on provincial Maryland, and the *Maryland Historical Magazine* (Baltimore, 1905–    ), which in its sixty-nine volumes contains hundreds of articles, notes, letters, documents, and genealogies on all periods of Maryland history. For a special kind of literature readers should consult Dorothy M. Brown and Richard R. Duncan, "Master's Theses and Doctoral Dissertations on Maryland History," *Maryland Historical Magazine*, LXIII, 412–419; LXIV 65–73, 161–168. This useful checklist is available in an expanded form from the Maryland Historical Society under the same title.

During the past decade a surge of interest among younger scholars in the history of colonial Maryland has produced a spate of excellent articles in the scholarly journals, testifying to the wealth of fresh data and new interpretations that yet remain to be served up for readers. The volume by Lois Green Carr and David W. Jordan, *Maryland's Revolution of Government, 1689–1692* (Ithaca: Cornell University Press, 1973) shows the early fruits of this renaissance in Maryland studies. Others in preparation promise equally interesting results and threaten to put any bibliography speedily out of date.

# II

## THE ERA OF THE REVOLUTION

BY

RICHARD WALSH

GEORGETOWN UNIVERSITY

The French and Indian War ended in 1763, and England beheld a vast empire, but all of the problems of local political restlessness remained. Reports from the governors to the Crown, Horatio Sharpe's included, indicated the necessity for reform in general and defense of the frontier in particular. The cost of the war had been enormous, and the bills for governing the magnificent conquest continued to mount. English landowners who had shouldered the financial burden were in a rebellious mood. It was very clear to them that hereafter the empire should pay for itself.

Yet the Treaty of Paris had hardly been signed when a new war raged in the west. Influenced by the Pontiac conspiracy, the Indians of Maryland went on the warpath. The *Maryland Gazette* described the scene at Frederick:

> Every Day, for some time past has offered the melancholy Scene of poor distressed families drawing downwards through this Town, with their Effects, who have deserted their Plantations, for Fear of falling into the Cruel Hands of Savage Enemies, now daily seen in the Woods. And never was Panic more general or forcible than that of the Back Inhabitants, whose Terrors, at this Time exceed what followed on the Defeat of General Braddock, when the frontier lay open to the Incursions of both French and Indians.

Colonel Thomas Cresap of Old Town reported to Sharpe a list of the "desolate men and women and children who have fled to my house" which was enclosed by a stockade. The governor once again ordered out the militia to guard the frontier. The assembly generously resupplied Fort Frederick, and after July 1763 peace came to the frontier at last. But the general uprising only underscored the necessity for a new imperial policy.[1]

In 1763 a new ministry formed in England. Its titular head was George Grenville, and he with the rest of the ministers and an assortment of advisers undertook the reorganization of the imperial system. Piecemeal they attacked the American question with only a shred of knowledge about the colonies and of their political prejudices and prerogatives. It was this policy which reinvigorated the out-of-doors politics of Marylanders and refueled the smouldering fires of the anti-proprietary movement. When fused with the new British imperialism, the long and often frustrating struggle for local rights opened the way for the revolution in Maryland. That upheaval not only altered the governmental structure but changed men's minds and lives. The Revolution was a social as well as political one in Maryland. It affected the nature of government as well as religious, economic, and educational institutions. It installed new conceptions of individual rights which set Marylanders on a quest for equality which projects to the twentieth century.

1

THE POLITICS OF THE COMING REVOLUTION

Among the first measures the ministry took was the Proclamation of the King in Council, October 7, 1763. Designed to settle affairs in the west until a permanent policy could be secured, it forbade settlement across the mountains and made the newly acquired Ohio Valley an Indian preserve. While the proclamation was looked upon with shock, dismay, and anger in several of the colonies, it created hardly a ripple in Maryland.[2] Governor Sharpe reported that some hunters passed beyond the line, but there was little that could be done to prevent this, and besides, they caused no trouble. The governor stopped the granting of

1. Lady Edgar, [Matilda Ridout], *A Colonial Governor in Maryland: Horatio Sharpe and His Times* (New York: Longmans, Green and Co., 1912), pp. 200-01. *M.G.* July 19, 1763.

2. Gov. Sharpe to Earle of Shelbourne 23, December 1766, *Arch. Md., XIV,* 361–62. Barker, *Background of the Revolution,* pp. 290-91.

land west of the line. Evidently his orders were not enforced; in 1774 wealthy speculators of Annapolis applied for warrants for western lands, and these were granted. When they were challenged in court, the decision favored the speculators on the grounds that the line had for a long time been ignored in Maryland. Thus because of the laxity of enforcement those interested in western settlement, whether large speculator or the land-hungry poor, never became vocal over this matter.

Another measure of the Grenville administration addressed itself to the enormous amount of clandestine trade carried on in the colonies. The northern colonies were dependent upon smuggling for their commercial life. They had no money crop of stable value to compare with Maryland's tobacco. They needed the cheap sugar of the foreign West Indies to carry on the slave trade. The reaction to Grenville's new restrictions and increased number of customs officials was furious in the north. Secretary to the proprietor, Cecilius Calvert, at first believed Maryland would join the northern protestors who sought a general meeting of representatives of the colonies. Sharpe assured the secretary that no such move was afoot, and to Lord Halifax he reported "very few if any of the inhabitants of this Province have been concerned in Vessels employed in carrying on any illicit Commerce." Some unregistered vessels from other colonies occasionally entered the Chesapeake Bay and used the many rivers and inlets to unload contraband goods without detection by officials. Sharpe recommended an increased number of cutters in the area to stop what little smuggling existed.[3]

The governor described 1764 as among the most politically peaceful in years. But there was an uneasiness in the province over this new act of trade that Sharpe had overlooked. It erupted after the measure had been in operation for a year. The new procedures which the act demanded were time consuming, inconvenient, and expensive to shippers. The House of Delegates complained that the act subjected an "Infant Trade to new Delays, Ceremonials and Expenses" which "tends to discourage that Spirit of Traffic which an extensive View of the Interests of Great Britain" should "cherish."[4]

3. Paul Giddens, "Trade and Industry in Colonial Maryland, 1753–69", *Journal of Economic and Business History*, IV (May, 1932), 530-33. *Arch. Md., XIV*, 175-76; 181-82.
4. *Arch. Md., Acts and Proceedings of the General Assembly, LIX*, 208-09.

In its eagerness to raise a revenue and to tighten the screws on wrongdoers, Parliament prescribed in this Sugar Act that the arresting official or informer could elect trial of the accused in admiralty-courts, thereby avoiding the trial by jury. The recovery of losses incurred by a trial of an innocent person was made exceptionally difficult by virtue of the law's judicial recommendations. Marylanders remonstrated. It "seems to them as if Parliament esteemed it criminal to be an American." They warned, "How different is the Language of this Statute from that of Our Charter."[5]

Another important act of the Grenville administration was its attempt to curtail the supply of paper money issued by the colonies. Influenced by British mercantile interests, who feared that Americans would force payment of their debts in depreciated currency rather than sterling, the act forbade any further authorization for colonial money to be used as legal tender and demanded that money which had already been issued be called in and retired. For proprietary Maryland the tightening of currency came at a very bad time. It had been more than a generation since the last issue of paper money, and the province needed a viable medium of exchange to support expansion of agriculture and a growing population. Debts previously contracted would now become even more difficult to discharge. In commenting on the effect of the Grenville program in general and the monetary situation in particular, Benedict Calvert of Prince George's County and son of Charles, fifth Lord Baltimore, wrote to Secretary Calvert to paint a dark picture: "Our Trade is ruin'd; we are immensely in Debt, and not the least probability of getting clear. Our gaols are not half large enough to hold the Debtors. Upon every Road you ride you meet people going from different parts of the province to get out of the way of their Creditors."[6]

Colonial officials and men of political substance and wealth reacted strongly against the paper currency measure. Sharpe wrote to England that the commerce of the colony "must flag much from Want of paper currency." Proprietary Attorney General Daniel Dulany mentioned the necessity of a circulating medium of exchange and stated that if the colonies could not have one under public law then another means would be sought.

---

5. *Ibid.*, 209.
6. *The Calvert Papers*, No. 2, *Fund Publication* No. 34 (Baltimore: M.H.S., 1894), pp. 261-62.

Dulany questioned the competence of Parliament to pass such legislation and asserted that the "wisest Legislators are often mistaken, the Parliament of England are often, very often mistaken, even when the subject of their Deliberations is relative only to the internal Police of that Kingdom, which it may be presumed, they have understood, as well as the Affairs of America."[7]

In the fall of 1765 the last of the provincial paper money ran out. Angry residents of Frederick County protested the shortage of currency in a petition to the assembly, and Marylanders found that they had to rely on Pennsylvanian money as a medium of exchange. The House of Delegates sought a remedy. It passed an act to issue 173,733 dollars in paper money. The emission was to be backed by the stock that the province had invested in the Bank of England and by a collection of new purchases from surplus gold and silver accumulated in the loan and treasurers' offices. The new money was not to be used as legal tender but was made acceptable nevertheless in payment of public debts and by means of contracts between individuals who agreed to deal in the medium, thus circumventing the parliamentary prohibition. The council and the proprietor eventually approved the measure, but political embroilments both local and imperial prevented relief until December 1766. The delay unquestionably made these quarrels more bitter and intense.[8] Another emission was necessary to steady the economy by 1773.

Thus far the Grenville program caused disparate protests. Objections to its various restrictions came from different sections of the colonies and for that matter within colonies and even from different classes and occupations.

The last measure of the Grenville ministry, the climactic one, made common cause for all. It not only encouraged those who tended toward a radical view but also caused conservatives to join in the protest. It irritated every sore on the colonial body politic whether its origins were economic, social, political, or constitutional. It wrought colonial unity. The total effect of this,

7. Jack P. Greene and Richard M. Jellison, "The Currency Act of 1764 in Imperial-Colonial Relations," *William and Mary Quarterly*, 3rd Series, XVIII (Oct., 1961), 490-91.

8. William Lux to William Russell Aug. 4, 1766; to John Norton Aug. 20, 1766, William Lux Letterbook, New York Historical Society. Arch. Md., XIV, 174, 250-252; LIX, 193, 264-75, 319-21. Kathryn Laura Behrens, *Paper Money in Maryland, 1727-1789* (Baltimore: J.H. Press, 1923), pp. 52-53.

the Stamp Act, was a crisis in the empire that would never be forgotten by the colonists to the end.

All along the Grenville ministry had been confronting and trying to solve the postwar difficulties of the empire. Reorganization and some reform under a mercantilist view had been the watchwords of the program. England might reap the harvest of the ministry's actions, not the colonies.

Ironically, the Stamp Act was different in this respect. Its purpose was to protect the colonial frontiers. Surely, colonists would not mind paying for this worthwhile end. Stamps were to be placed on all legal and commercial documents and on all newspapers. Such stamps were commonplace in England. Colonial agents (Maryland had none, a sore point) were called in. They generally protested the act; Benjamin Franklin of Pennsylvania went so far as to support it, but the agents could present no alternative and all agreed the problem of the frontier wanted solution. The debate on the measure in Parliament was spiritless, and it passed with little opposition.

The colonies exploded, especially Maryland. What irritated Marylanders especially was the ministry's ignorance of the colonies. The high Anglican churchman, whose ambitions led him to entertain a bishop's crozier in America, the Reverend Jonathan Boucher, expressed annoyance at the measure to a friend. "Nobody of Consequence comes amongst us to get any personal Information of our affairs & Those Entrusted to communicate such intelligence are Themselves either too ignorant, or too knavish to give any to be depended upon." He continued: "In the Debates in the House, while the Bill for the Stamps in America was still in Debate, the Opulence of ye Americans was urg'd as an Argum't in its Fav'r; w'n there is not a more notorious Truth than it is, that they are immers'd over Head & Ears in Debt."[9]

Governor Sharpe chided his superiors in England that the proprietorship should have been less supine and more attentive to their interests while the act was taking shape. The proprietor ought to have reminded the administration that the original charter of Maryland forbade imperial taxation without proprietary consent. This was in Sharpe's view a "breaking of the charter." Sharpe perceived that such proprietary failures "will ren-

---

9. "Letters of Rev. Jonathan Boucher," *M.H.M.*, VII (Sept., 1912), 295-96.

Horatio Sharpe, governor of Maryland during the Stamp Act trouble. *M.H.S.*

der us more obnoxious than ever to the People & be a means of lessening our Authority over them."[10]

When Secretary Calvert finally presented this argument to the "Grand Financer," it availed nothing. The official observed that the clause in the charter could not be upheld against the sovereignty of Parliament. The province was under the jurisdiction of and allegiance to the king as others were. Since the time of Charles II acts of Parliament affected Maryland and "no Doubt he did suppose no doctrine could he advance under any colour to the contrary. . . ."[11]

Such constitutionally debatable opinions stirred Maryland's Attorney General Daniel Dulany to action. A man whose entire legal career had been spent in employing and dealing with questions of colonial rights, the British constitution and proprietary prerogative, Dulany wrote against the unconstitutionality of the Stamp Act.[12]

Ministerial claims to parliamentary prerogatives found in the pamphlets and books of Thomas Pownell and Thomas Whatley, the former an adviser, the latter secretary to George Grenville particularly irked the ordinarily conservative Dulany. Pownell's *The Administration of the Colonies* viewed the empire as a commercial whole which rightly should be centrally governed by Parliament. Whatley's *The Regulations Lately Made Concerning the Colonies and the Taxes Imposed upon Them* argued that the colonists were represented in Parliament as any Englishman, even though they had not directly voted for a member of the body. More concisely, a member represented all the empire, not merely the constituency which elected him. Thus there were no grounds whatever for the colonial claims of illegal "taxation without representation." Any and all members represented British subjects.[13]

In October, 1765, Dulany published his *Considerations on the Propriety of Imposing Taxes in the British Colonies, For the*

---

10. A. C. Land, ed. "Sharpe's Confidential Report on Maryland, 1765," *M.H.M.* *LXIV* (June 1949), 126-27; *Calvert Papers*, II, 259-63.

11. *Ibid.*

12. A. C. Land, *Dulanys*, pp. 260-73.

13. Helen M. and Edmund S. Morgan, *The Stamp Act Crisis: Prologue to Revolution* (Chapel Hill: Published for the Institute of Early American History by the University of North Carolina Press, 1953), pp. 71-87.

*Purpose of Raising a Revenue.* It answered the pamphleteers in England who had supported the measure. It addressed judicious men, rather than the rabble, which was by then aroused outside Dulany's very doors.

*Considerations* was not "easy" reading. Although it reached a polemical sharpness when the calculating attorney cannot hide his anger, its reasoning is mainly that of a constitutional lawyer. Dulany began by calling the Stamp Act a "rigorous and severe law." He loyally admitted that Parliament had a supreme power to rule. But Americans cannot submit to the notion that the body had an absolute power to tax. In English law, to take money without the consent of the people through their representatives was confiscatory. He contended that the notion of virtual representation was but a ploy to cover an unconstitutional act. Every inch of English soil had its representative, but where were the American representatives? They were certainly not in the British House of Commons. They were present in their own provincial assemblies. Only they were empowered to tax Americans internally. For more than a century they had acted in this capacity. England itself had recognized this right all during colonial history, as, for example, during the last war, when the ministry requested sums to be lawfully raised by the colonists in their assemblies for defense.

Americans also owed their allegiance to the Crown. But this could not admit, nor has it ever been the case, that the Crown can tax without consent of the people. That the executive has powers to act in an emergency—as it had during the war—Dulany conceded, but the Parliament never possessed this power. Nor for that matter did the Crown have the right to use it upon every fancied emergency.

The wisest policy and the constitutional one was to use the requisition system so that local assemblies could determine what sums were needed. These legislators were more familiar with American conditions than a distant ministry that was woefully ignorant of provincial affairs.

Dulany counseled remedies to his fellow colonists. They should dutifully protest an infringement upon the rights of Englishmen. But as good Englishmen they should submit to the law until the inherent justice of the British Constitution caused the repeal of such an unwarranted measure. Meanwhile a peaceful boycott of English goods should be effected as a reminder of the importance of the colonies in the empire. Americans should manufacture their own necessities and practice "frugality."[14]

The generally temperate and logical character of *Considerations* had a great impact. It gave conservative men not given to mobbing and violence a reasoned resistance. It was reprinted by American opponents of the Stamp Act for distribution in all the centers of resistance. It was widely hailed by moderate and radical alike. Even Governor Sharpe praised it and recommended its reading in England. There it was employed by political leaders who sided with the Americans. One of the most powerful of these, William Pitt, quoted from *Considerations* in his speeches for repeal of the act in the House of Commons.[15]

Despite Dulany's peaceful prescriptions, violence had already occurred in Maryland. One misguided merchant, Zachariah Hood of Annapolis, had the poor judgment to accept the position of stamp collector. On September 5 a mob of some 300 to 400 people went on a rampage in search of him. They pulled down a house which Hood had leased for storing goods. Hood fled for his life and finally wound up under the protection of royal troops stationed in New York under General Thomas Gage. Disorder, threats, and wild rumors became the rule thereafter, all of which were accompanied by inflammatory literature in the press.

The militia could not be depended upon to protect royal interests and keep order, for their sympathies were with the rioters. "Gentlemen of the town" were upset. It was thought that the attorney general was inciting the mob in the Hood affair, but this was untrue. He deplored what was happening. Yet not a great deal was done by public officials to prevent violence. A mob of men visited the sheriff in search of stamps. They demanded a bottle of wine and insisted he accompany them. He went with them to another house and there took a glass of wine, then broke away from them, went home and was abed during the whole affair at Hood's place.[16]

The governor entertained the idea of bringing troops in at Gage's suggestion. There were Royal Highlanders who could be moved from Pittsburgh. Sharpe wisely decided to wait, hoping

---

14. Daniel Dulany, "Considerations," *M.H.M. VI, VII.*

15. Land, *Dulanys*, pp. 265-67; *M.H.M., XLIV,* 127.

16. *Arch. Md.,* XIV, 222, 228-29, 233. "Resistance to the Stamp Act," *M.H.M., IV,* 134-39.

Daniel Dulany, the younger. Defender of American rights against Parliament in 1765-1766. *Courtesy of the White House.*

violence would subside. Had he acted precipitously and brought in troops, Maryland would have become a battleground, because the minds of the people were so inflamed.[17]

But the people made the right move to mitigate disorder. The electors from Anne Arundel County petitioned their delegates to seek an earlier-than-scheduled meeting of the assembly while at the same time instructing them to guard their rights under the charter. Maryland's lawyers petitioned the governor to convene an early meeting of the assembly so that delegates from Maryland could be sent to the congress on the Stamp Act which was to gather in New York. Maryland's council advised calling the assembly also. Its moderate and conservative members deeply resented the incursion by Parliament on proprietary privileges. Thus, as Sharpe put it, he called the assembly out of deference to the wishes of the members; otherwise it would have given "Occasion for general Discontent and Disturbance."[18]

Harmony reigned; the assembly drew up eight resolves ably summarizing all that had been said, even shouted, and written. It declared that Marylanders enjoyed the full rights of Englishmen, which embraced the Magna Carta, the Petition of Right, and the Bill of Rights protecting them against taxation without consent; that Marylanders especially were guaranteed these privileges in their Charter of 1632; that Maryland's assembly possessed the sole right to "levy taxes and impositions on the inhabitants of this province. . . ." For any other authority than the assembly to pass taxes or laws regulating the "internal" affairs of the province was unconstitutional.[19]

The assembly nominated Colonel Matthew Tilghman, William Murdock, and Thomas Ringgold, whom the council approved, as delegates to the Stamp Act Congress. They were instructed to join with representatives of the other colonies to present the resolutions and to secure repeal of the measure.

As soon as the assembly adjourned a new tactic was employed to undermine the act. No stamps were available, so public and private business closed down. In Frederick County the court determined, however, that its business should proceed without stamps. When the clerk of court refused to obey, the court jailed

---

17. *Arch. Md.*, XIV, 228-30.
18. *Ibid. M.H.M.*, XLIV, 128-29. *Maryland Gazette* Oct. 10, 1765.
19. *Arch. Md.*, XLIV, 30 *passim.*

him for contempt. Repenting his actions, he was freed and the court reopened. All of this was the occasion for a celebration of the court's independence and a demonstration for liberty in Frederick. An elaborate parade formed at the home of one Samuel Swearington.

In February 1766, an association styling itself the Sons of Liberty formed in Baltimore. Shortly thereafter another similar group was organized in Annapolis under Samuel Chase and William Paca. The object of the Sons of Liberty was to defy Parliament by forcing the courts to operate without stamps. In general they were successful, as the act went unheeded in Anne Arundel, Cecil, Queen Anne's, Somerset, and Worcester Counties and the law was violated. As one observer described these meetings of the Sons of Liberty: "The subscribers were men of little note; some expressions were very unguarded" and seemed to go beyond the object of mere repeal.[20]

Ten days after the victory over the courts, the province celebrated repeal of the Stamp Act. Most Marylanders paid scant attention to the Declaratory Act accompanying repeal. A hope to return to normal relations with the empire was uppermost in their minds, yet public and private affairs would never again be the same. William Lux, a merchant of Baltimore, wrote to a correspondent that Englishmen should be happy to see "the pure unpolluted British blood flowing through the veins of their children in this distant region warmed with the Sentiments which Freedom inspire, & be impatient with the Slavery they were threatened with." He hoped the dispute would be buried in oblivion and that the repeal "will make our Trade as Free as possible."[21]

In contrast, Henry Seymour Conway, Secretary to the Southern Department, wrote to Sharpe that this "open resistance" to the mother country should cease. It could "only have found place among the lower and more ignorant of the people. The better and wiser part of the colonies will know that decency and submission may prevail, not only to redress grievances, but to obtain grace and favor, while the outrage of a public violence can expect but severity and chastisement."[22]

20. Paul H. Giddens, "Maryland and the Stamp Act Controversy," *M.H.M.*, *XXVII* (June, 1932), 79-98.
21. Lux to William Molleson June 2, 15, 1766, Lux Letterbook.
22. *Arch. Md.*, XIV, 234.

Defiance of authority by the rabble did not cease in Maryland. New Maryland leadership found that the practice of "out of doors politics" was a potent weapon, especially when the lower classes were by no means in a submissive mood.

In the decade following repeal not only imperial efforts to command a revenue from the Marylanders but also substantially local issues heated the provincials. By 1775 most Marylanders became convinced that the proprietary government was as corrupt as the imperial system and that there was little hope of reforming either.

Two very different men, Samuel Chase and Charles Carroll of Carrollton, illustrate the Maryland mentality in these years. Charles Carroll was not impressed even by the repeal of the Stamp Act so long as the Parliament continued its claims of supremacy in the Declaratory Act. Suppose the Parliament should have the right, he asserted, "to restrain us from manufacturing woolens; this Restraint would be more oppressive than the Stamp Act itself—it would force thousands to go naked [or] to pay extravagant prices for the [advantage] of Britain. If I am to be fleeced, an American might say, if my money is to be taken from me without my consent, it is immaterial to me in what manner this is effected—whether by a tax upon paper, or by an exorbitant price for goods." Similarly, Samuel Chase focused his aim on those proprietary officials who were reluctant to join in the resistance and who had called him "a foul mouth'd common Disturber of the Public Tranquility" and "a ringleader of mobs." Chase accused some of them of esteeming the Stamp Act as beneficial. "Others, meanly grumbling in your corners," dared not to speak out for constitutional rights. Such officials were "unmanly," a condition natural to "Pimps and Tools of power" basking in the "proprietary Sunshine" of privilege at the expense of the people.[23]

One of the local political sores which the crisis of 1765–66 inflamed was the refusal of the proprietorship to permit a Maryland liaison with the Crown and Parliament through an agent. Frederick Calvert, the sixth Lord Baltimore, was held in low repute by local provincial leadership. It was generally felt that

23. Thomas Meagher Field, ed. *Unpublished Letters of Charles Carroll of Carrollton: . . . United States Catholic Historical Society Monograph Series II* (New York: U.S.C. Historical Society, 1902), p. 138. *M.G.* July 19, 1766. *To the Public,* July 18, 1766, in M.H.S.

His Lordship had been negligent in preventing passage of the act. In 1765 the House of Delegates sent its resolutions and letters of instruction to Charles Garth, agent for South Carolina and member of the House of Commons. In subsequent disputes over fees paid to proprietary officeholders by the people of Maryland, the council constantly turned back the house's demands for an agent to represent provincial as opposed to proprietary interests to the Crown. The upper house never denied the right of appeal of proprietary actions to the King in Council. It nevertheless refused appropriations for the support of an agent for the house.

Frustrated, the house members contributed personal funds, asked for donations, and raised a lottery for the support of such a representative. Advertisements of the lottery with accompanying anti-proprietary literature were published in the newspapers. It was called the "Liberty Lottery." These efforts failed, because the public declined to subscribe. In another respect, however, the propaganda value of the lottery was not lost on the public. On the tickets was the slogan "Life without Liberty is worse than Death."[24]

The real issue of which the public awareness was most evident was that of proprietary fees. Reduced to its simplest terms, His Lordship held an extensive power of appointment of officials throughout the colonial period. The fees of a number of offices were levied directly upon the people and were set by the proprietor, not the elected delegates. Over the years the number of offices had grown, and in the opinion of Marylanders the fees for services had become exorbitant, and salaries were excessively high for some of the inner circle who did little. In an atmosphere wherein taxation without the consent of the representatives brought angry responses against the empire, the proprietor inevitably brought down upon himself the same severe criticism and violent reaction.

By way of illustration: the proprietor's council and the peoples' House of Delegates had kept up a tedious dispute since 1756. The rub concerned the council's insistence that the salary of its clerk John Ross be paid by the House of Delegates. The house refused; it insisted he be paid from the special revenues of

---

24. *M.G.* Dec. 11, 1766; Mar. 11, 1767. *Unpublished Letters*, p. 141, Carroll to Jennings, Mar. 9, 1767.

the proprietor as any of his officials. In retaliation the council would not approve the journal of accounts in which Ross' as well as other public claims were listed.

When the house convened in November 1765 in that electric atmosphere, the old dispute over the journal of accounts took on new dimensions. The house broadened the entire issue to an investigation of all proprietary fees and salaries. Men such as Thomas Johnson, and Matthew Tilghman, already heady by the success of their anti-imperial activities, put new life in the old issue.[25]

By December the populace had stirred. Governor Sharpe accused the frontiersman, Indian-fighter and representative of Frederick, Thomas Cresap, of inciting the people to march on Annapolis and to settle the matter with tomahawk and musket if necessary. A not too sober group of men met at one Arthur Chaston's house on December 4 and resolved to muster a hundred armed men to march on the capital. Some restless spirits of Anne Arundel and Prince George's Counties, it was rumored, were also on the move. Clerk Ross was thoroughly frightened; he believed he would be accorded the same treatment as Zachariah Hood.

By the time the mob arrived, it had melted and sobered down to a small delegation. It petitioned the government, requesting that the journal of accounts be settled in accordance with the desires of the house and requested "they would Endeavour, like the Renowned antient true Roman Senate, to supress any further Attempt to deprive them of their Liberty." The petitioners whom Charles Carroll described as orderly and sensible men of property further asked that the journal be passed so that it would put badly needed money into circulation.

In spite of the excitement, the issue was not settled for two years, when the house passed the journal. But final passage was held up until an appeal on the whole matter of fees could be brought to the King in Council. That appeal was never made because of the unwillingness of the secretary of the proprietor, Hugh Hamersley, to make it.

As to proprietary collection of fees, His Lordship, championed by Attorney General Dulany, won the right to continue imposition of a tax on the amount of hogsheads of tobacco exported from

25. Donald MacClure Owings, *His Lordship's Patronage. Studies in Maryland History No. 1* (Baltimore: M.H.S., 1953), p. 104.

Maryland, but under Dulany's prodding the council recommended and the proprietor agreed to give up collecting money from the licensing of taverns.[26]

There supposedly followed a "dead time" in Maryland, according to Charles Carroll's observation. However, times were not quiet. As the journal fight and fee controversy ground to a temporary halt, the empire bestirred men again. Charles Townshend had risen to Chancellor of the Exchequer in England and, having been defeated on a proposal to increase the tax on landed estates in England, which should have moved him to resign, he made up the current deficit with new tax measures for America. But more than that, a month previously he had announced a plan of raising a revenue in America to support troops there and to increase the power of royal officials holding colonial offices by making their salaries independent of the legislatures. The most upsetting of these was the law which taxed paper, glass, tea, paint and certain other items imported to America. Townshend called the law an "external" rather than an "internal" tax by which he hoped to circumvent the constitutional objections raised against the Stamp Act. This tax was external, not internal as the Stamp Act, to control commerce. The deception fooled no one.

To a people already vexed with the high cost of proprietary government, the Townshend revenue measure only added to burdens; for among other things, it increased the number of customs collectors to prey on the purses of Marylanders and inhibit their commerce. It threatened to strengthen an already growing British patronage; whether it be proprietary or ministerial made not a whit of difference. Carroll, who had visited England (and there were many others similarly educated abroad) was aghast at the disintegration of political morals. "The numbers of great and lucrative posts in the distribution of the Crown should be lessened together with their profits," he commented. He decried the venality and avarice of men in the ministry. "These vices in all states have ever been distructive of liberty." The British system was being dismantled by the greed of men who had created "a corrupt aristocracy . . . the worst of all

26. *Arch. Md.*, XXXII, 110-13, 172-73, 174-75; XIV, 252-53; LIX, xlix-lvi, 220-21; *Unpublished Letters*, p. 105. Land, *Dulanys*, pp. 276-77. Daniel Dulaney, *The Right to the Tonnage* . . . (Annapolis: Jonas Green, 1766).

governments." The House of Commons had become the repository of special interests. Carroll's ugly picture of the seat of empire was widely held. The recently arrived Jesuit missionary Joseph Mosley, lamented that London "is a place of Business and Trade, but not of Virtue. . . ."[27]

While such wealthy Marylanders as Carroll lamented the breakdown of the system, the less mighty whose livelihoods were threatened joined with other colonists in resisting the ministry. In June 1769, new and younger merchants of Annapolis and especially Baltimore formed public assemblies and joined with their counterparts in the other colonies to set up a boycott of British importations to disrupt the commerce of the empire as far as possible.

Because these were men of business and property, the violent scenes of 1765 did not repeat themselves. Nonetheless, the threat of violence menaced those who disregarded the boycott. In 1770 the vessel *Good Intent* was held up at Annapolis, and finding that its owners James Dick and Anthony Stewart had broken the boycott, a committee of merchants sent it back to England unloaded. This kind of colonial fury, the death of Townshend, and the fear of "further mischief" brought an end to the Townshend Acts, excepting a tax on tea to keep up the principle. The traders of Baltimore ended non-importation because they feared its continuation would give advantage to rival Philadelphia merchants, who quit the association earlier. The more strident provincials, who desired to put political principle before economic interest, wished to continue contending against the parliamentary claims of taxation, but their arguments were unconvincing.[28]

Two local quarrels kept the fires of resistance stirring to the disadvantage of the proprietor, however. These were the Tobacco Inspection Act and the struggle to fix clerical salaries.

Nothing so greatly tarnished the authority and reputation of the proprietor than the type of cleric he appointed to Maryland's

---

27. J. G. D. Paul, ed., "A Lost Copy-Book of Charles Carroll of Carrollton," *M.H.M.* (Sept., 1937), 197-198. Joseph Mosley, S.J. to sister, June 5, 1772, Georgetown University Archives.

28. Robert Purviance, *A Narrative of Events Which Occurred in Baltimore Town During the Revolutionary War* . . . (Baltimore: Joseph Robinson, 1849), pp. 9-10. *Proceedings . . . of the Good Intent* (Annapolis: Anne Catherine Green, 1770), pp. xi, xii, 6 in Library of Congress. *M.H.M.*, III, 356.

established Church of England. Unquestionably there were some good men among the Anglican clergy, but there were very few who were not favor and place seekers, "dangling after Great Men," absentee pastors, who looked upon the provincials as boors.[29] One of the better of them, the ambitious Boucher, wrote to a friend: "There are many" parishes "nothing should tempt me to go to [;] the Mosquitoes of one Summer w'd kill me." Others were notoriously bad men. One ran a bawdy house in Philadelphia before taking orders and, after receiving an appointment to Maryland, he continued an inebriated and riotous existence. The clergy's salaries were high—as much as £500 sterling per year in some places. This was supported by a tax on everyone. One of the richest holdings was in Frederick "where" in the words of the worst miscreant of all the proprietary appointees, Bennet Allen, "three fourths of the inhabitants are foreigners, invincibly attached to their own Religion, Language and Manners, amongst whom no clergyman of the Church of England can hope for any more Respect than his Humanity entitles him to or his income commands."[30]

The dissenters, principally Lutherans, Quakers, and Catholics, despised the establishment they were forced to support. Anglicans, communicants themselves, wanted reform. The well-behaved clergy felt that a Maryland bishop would answer the need for discipline, as "the inhabitants look upon themselves to be in a state of the cruellest oppression with regard to ecclesiastical matters," victims of a patronage carried on "without any regard to the opinion of the parishioners."

Few among the laity accepted the proposition of a bishop. Instead, the establishment itself was attacked as unconstitutional and against "natural rights," by William Paca of Annapolis, one of the assertive politicos of the resistance against the empire and proprietor. The House of Delegates fundamentally accepted the necessity of reform and reorganized the Church of England

---

29. Francis Lister Hawks, . . . *Rise and Progress of the Protestant Episcopal Church in Maryland* (n.p., 1839), pp. 245-83. Rightmeyer, *Maryland's Established Church*, pp. 119 *passim*. Gerald E. Hartdagen, "Vestry and Clergy in Maryland," *Historical Magazine of the Protestant Episcopal Church, XXXVII* (Dec., 1968). A. C. Land, ed. William Eddis, *Letters from America* (Cambridge: Harvard University Press, 1969), pp. 26-29. William Stevens Perry, *Historical Collections Relating to the American Colonial Church* 4 vol. (New York: A.M.S. Press, (1878), 1969), IV *Maryland*, 333-44.

30. *Ibid. M.H.M.*, *XXXIX*, 49-60 *passim.*, *VIII*, 34-38, 238.

in Maryland by reducing the salaries of the clergy and setting up boards of discipline composed of local vestrymen and clergymen to review the activities of corrupt pastors. The proprietor kept appointments and hopefully would remove those whom the laity did not want. But as an insurance against the undesirables, some vestries negotiated contracts with appointees that guaranteed against abuses and proprietary supineness in not firing them.

Reduced income and lay control were far from the reform the clergy desired. Boucher called it a "Death Blow—and, without a total Revolution in American Politics," and he saw the whole establishment toppling. Bennet Allen, whose own street brawling and drinking had done much to end the old order, warned that it represented an erosion of proprietary power. The reformed Church satisfied Maryland Anglicans. But the Church remained a target of the dissenters who wanted it leveled.[31]

The arrival of a new governor in 1769, the gentle Robert Eden, and the death of Frederick, that "hipped Englishman," and the appointment of his illegitimate son, a minor, Henry Harford as proprietor, did nothing to allay the fears of corruption, cronyism, and distaste held by Maryland's anti-proprietary party for local government whose condition they equated with the cancerous body politic of England.[32]

The year 1770 saw the expiration of the Tobacco Inspection Act. The gentlemen planters, sitting in the house, wanted renewal, but not before seizing the opportunity to reduce the fees and influence of the great proprietary officials. This time the effort was more vigorous than ever before, and the arguments presented in the press were skillful and voluminous, reflecting a quest for power unmatched in provincial history.

The house members refused renewal of the old act and inaugurated a new investigation of fees. They arrested the clerk of the Land Office for executing the defunct act; the governor responded by proroguing the house to free the clerk, then, upon the advice of the council, issued a proclamation setting fees for the inspection of tobacco and other services. These were based on the old rate. The proclamation warned that fees should not be excessive for the service performed. This, the governor's defenders claimed, was for the public good, and the claim was

---

31. *Ibid.*
32. C.C.C. to Charles Carroll, Barrister, Dec. 3, 1771, *M.H.M., XXXII*, 209-10; *XLIV*, 125.

advanced that the setting of fees for proprietary appointees was a constitutional prerogative of the proprietor in Maryland.

Recalled Boucher, "There was a fierceness in opposition that was unusual." "Men's minds were restless and dissatisfied forever discontented and grumbling at the . . . state of things and forever projecting reformations."[33] The governor now legislated by decree, it was asserted, and attempts by some members of the House of Delegates at compromise with the executive failed. The failure produced Thomas Johnson's argument that Eden had acted unconstitutionally ". . . and shadowed . . . the practice of arbitrary Kings who, in their proclamations . . . generally covered their designs with the specious pretence of public good. . . . If the proclamation may rightfully regulate the fees, it has a right to fix any quantum. . . . If it has a right to tax us, then, whether our money shall continue in our own pockets depends no longer on us, but on the prerogative."[34]

The source of Eden's advice unquestionably was Daniel Dulany, the hero of 1765. To convince the public of the ultimate good that the proclamation served and of its constitutionality, Dulany went to press once more. In the *Maryland Gazette* he pretended a dialogue between two citizens. He ("Second Citizen") attacked opponents of the proclamation as disturbers who create distrust, suspicion, and confusion for selfish purposes. These were men who constantly canvassed votes at elections and interfered with the freedom of the electors. "First Citizen" was entirely convinced in the end by "Second Citizen" of the correctness of his argument.[35]

The learned lawyer was a formidable opponent. To pick up this verbal gauntlet was a challenge. Ironically, the challenger was one of the wealthy oppressed of the province. The Catholic, Charles Carroll of Carrollton, from his training at St. Omer's, was steeped in the political philosophy of Bellarmine, Locke, and Montesquieu and the republican ideal state, and its balances as taught by his Jesuit masters on the continent. In Carroll, resistance had been nurtured by his father. Letters sent to the younger while in England quaked with anger at the continued burden of triple taxation on Catholics by the proprietor, which he sus-

---

33. Jonathan Boucher, *Reminiscences of an American Loyalist* (Port Washington, N.Y.: Kennikat Press, reprinted 1967), pp. 68-9.

34. *Arch. Md., XXXII*, 493-501.

35. *M.G.*, June 7, 1773.

pected the Dulanys had advised, and disfranchisement, particularly of such a family as the Carrolls, who had been among the leaders of seventeenth-century Maryland.[36]

Carroll picked up the anti-proprietary cudgels in the newspapers, writing tauntingly under the pseudonym "First Citizen," who was now disabused of his earlier credulity. By doing so he not only affected the Catholics of Maryland, but also fellow communicants of other colonies. Maryland Catholics were sore under antipapist laws which were renewed during the last imperial war by the House of Delegates, held by Catholics in as low esteem as the delegates did the Proprietorship. Maryland under the provincial leadership of the house was more intolerant of Catholics than England itself.[37]

Carroll's "First Citizen" answers to Dulany moved Catholics out of the current of possible loyalism and identified them with the Revolution to come, making that event one of social as well as political change.

"First Citizen" drew wide acclaim for his verbal blows, his use of the natural rights philosophy, and for accusing Dulany of advocating the low principles of party politics at home, the same tactics that he had so effectively used to deprecate the empire in his *Considerations*. The fees were unjust and were tantamount to taxes without the consent of representatives of the people. Carroll evoked other voices against Dulany, those of Samuel Chase, Thomas Johnson and William Paca, who accused the attorney general of participating in the sale of proprietary offices and of advocating the dangerous stand that the prerogative of fixing salaries of appointed officials should be enjoyed not only by the proprietor but also the Crown.

Dulany answered "First Citizen" as "Antilon." But it was difficult to reply in legal terms. Legalisms did not make as easy reading as Carroll's rights of the people, which summarized their thoughts. At length, Dulany asked: Who is this "First Citizen?"

---

36. Charles H. Metzger, *Catholics and the American Revolution: A Study in Religious Climate* (Chicago: Loyola University Press, 1962), pp. 178-82; *M.H.M., X*, 343, *XII*, 277-78, 282, 285-87, Thomas O'Brien Hanley, "Young Mr. Carroll and Montesquieu," *ibid, LXII* (Dec., 1967); 394-18. Hanley, *Charles Carroll of Carrollton, The Making of a Revolutionary Gentleman* (Washington, D.C.: Catholic University of America Press, 1970), Ch. I, II, VIII; Land, *Dulanys*, 293-94.

37. Joseph Mosley to Mrs. Dunn, Jan. 5, 1772.

"He has no share in the legislature, as a member of any branch: he is incapable of being a member: he is disabled from giving a vote in the choice of representatives, by the laws and constitution of the country, *on account of his principles,* which are distrusted by those laws. He is disabled by an expressed resolve from interfering in the election of members, on the same account. He is not a protestant." This is the man, Dulany continued, who vehemently states, "the Proclamation *must not be endured.*" Our people are "instructed by the spirit of the laws, and constitution, by the disabilities you are laid under, not to place any trust in you, when your civil or religious rights may be concerned."[38] Dulany reminded his readers of the spectoral days of James II and "lawless prerogative."

Carroll replied warmly that he condemned James II and his bigotry. People have a right not to have "religion crammed down their throats." He bore malice toward no religious sect, but despised the knaves in any of them. From Alexander Pope he quoted:

> For modes of faith let zealous
> bigots fight,
> His can't be wrong, whose life
> is in the right.

He was aware of the disabilities against papists: Does this "preclude them from thinking and writing on matters merely of a political nature?" "Dulany has given some striking specimens of an arbitrary temper." "He will not allow me freedom of thought or speech."

Privately, Carroll wrote to William Graves that notwithstanding the legal disabilities as a Catholic, "I have done it," he explained, "as Eden or Dulany himself would acknowledge, could they forgive a man who had contributed to check their attacks on the constitution of his country."[39]

Dulany and Carroll held the provincials spellbound. As each

---

38. *M.G.* Jan. 7, Feb. 4, April 8, July 1, 1773. Published in Elihu Riley, *Correspondence between First Citizen and Antilon* (Baltimore: King Bros., state printers, 1902). Albert Silverman, "William Paca, Signer, Governor, Jurist," *M.H.M.,* XXXVII (March, 1942), 1-25. Edward S. Delaplaine, *The Life of Thomas Johnson* (New York: Grofton Press, 1927), p. 52. Bernard C. Steiner, *Sir Robert Eden, J.H.U.S. XVI,* (Baltimore: J.H. Press, 1898), Chs. IV, V. Land, *Dulanys,* Ch. XIX.

39. *M.H.M., XXXII,* 223.

piece came out, men relished their privacy to read them. When Dulany fired his personal attacks, the provincials sympathized with the papist. At an election and demonstration against the proclamation, Chase, Paca, and Johnson tendered the heartfelt thanks of Maryland to "First Citizen" for defending their liberties. The three anti-proprietary leaders projected that defense further. "Antilon" and "First Citizen" had contended that the British Constitution was the source of authority. In answering Hamersley, one of the counsellors who defended Dulany's position, Chase and Paca asserted that the people, not the Crown or constitution, was the source of all political authority.[40]

This appeal to popular power terminated in frustration for the anti-proprietary movement. It had produced long, sometimes learned debates over political and constitutional principles. But it had little effect for change. The house first tried an association for extra-legal inspection of tobacco. It did not work. The intransigence of the proprietary party in the council, with their many allies among the richer planters of the house, virtually achieved a victory. The poorer planters always despised the act; it prevented their getting some little money for their inferior tobacco.[41]

The house finally passed a tobacco inspection act, although without the list of fees. Thus the Proclamation of 1770 continued the old list, and the Proprietary held on to its patronage. That patronage was dearly purchased, however. The cost was the support of the people. Had the council and Eden given ground, the movement for independence from England might have been greatly retarded. Failure made radicals out of the moderate anti-proprietors.

In the radical view, there was a great resemblance between English politicians and the proprietor's favorites and friends. England passed the Tea Act in 1773, stubbornly insisting on the principle of its right to tax the colonists. In the face of the overt resistance to the act from New York and Boston and later from other centers of colonial resistance such as in Annapolis, where the tea ship, the *Peggy Stewart,* was burned before a howling, angry mob, the Parliament then passed the Intolerable Acts closing the Port of Boston, setting aside the Massachusetts Char-

---

40. *Ibid. XIV*, 368; *XXXVII*, 6 *et passim.*
41. Wyckoff, *Tobacco Regulation*, p. 196.

Charles Carroll of Carrollton, Signer of the Declaration of Independence. One of the principal figures in the revolutionary era, as well as political architects of the new nation. *M.H.S.*

ter and dissolving the assembly, and reorganizing the system of justice which discriminated in favor of Englishmen accused of crime in America.

Organization for colonial resistance had been present since 1765. It had grown more able and daring in the constant arguments with the empire and local proprietary officials. All of this had been within constitutional bounds. But not any longer. The veterans of anti-proprietary skirmishes now employed tight county organizations called associations. These associations were in constant contact with one another and with the people. When it became necessary, as the prospect of a peaceful securing of American rights dimmed, a Provincial Convention was elected. The statutes restricting the franchise were not attended to; at least the religious disabilities did not hold as Charles Carroll won a seat in the convention.

The Council of Safety, the executive arm of the convention, from its first meeting, began governing the province. By 1775 it had assumed all the operations of government. The Eden government held paper power. In the council three parties were identifiable: moderate to conservative—those who were opposed to independence but wanted the rights of Englishmen; the anti-proprietary forces, gaining a majority, wanted independence and reform of government. A new element now appeared which not only desired independence but also wanted radical changes along democratic lines in Maryland's social, political, and economic structure.[42]

2

ECONOMIC AND SOCIAL CONDITIONS ON THE

EVE OF REVOLUTION

The Revolution in Maryland was not merely fought over principles of the rights of Englishmen. The Revolution here as well as elsewhere was multidimensional. An examination of economic and social conditions is necessary to understand the Revolution in Maryland.

If one glances at statutes of trade in tobacco as the province's

42. John Heuser, "The Maryland Conventions: A Study in the Politics of Revolution," (M.A. thesis, History Department, Georgetown University, 1968), pp. 129-46.

main staple in the eighteenth century, one finds proof of a seeming rising production and expansion in the commodity. For the most part the eighteenth century witnessed a rise of wealth in the province and the creation of an aristocratic class of planters whose spokesmen dominated the House of Delegates and were powerful enough to contest the proprietory. Statistics of the value of exports to England in this commodity peak in 1763 and remain steady until 1767, when its export dramatically declined and would continue to remain low until 1770. Undoubtedly the political crises and embargoes of the decade before the Revolution had a depressing effect. Returns were low or negligible in these years, and give a bleak picture of economic distress.[43] The problem was not basically political, however. There was much endemically wrong with the cultivation of tobacco as a money maker, even during the best years when prices were good and credit easily attained with English or Scottish merchant houses. Marylanders, chiefly those of the southern counties, produced a tobacco—Orinoco—most of which was deemed unsaleable in the English market because of its harsh texture and strong flavor. It was reshipped to France (some to Holland) and there monopolized by a few houses that constantly kept down the price or manipulated it in their favor. The legal necessity of shipping to England before reshipment constantly drove up the price and narrowed markets, even in good years. Dulany, in his *Considerations*, was most critical of the English system. It hampered the plantation trade and lined the pockets of everyone involved except the producer. He observed that the commercial system gave English and Scottish merchants and shippers on an average £ 240,000 annually for freight, wharfage, and storage charges. Price agreements among factors also tended to lower prices, and yet such collusion raised the prices of imported goods. Carroll, his antagonist in 1773, was no less critical. The result was that only a handful of planters made any money from tobacco. They found that they were forced to supplement earnings with other enterprises—money lending, investment in tenant lands, production of other crops. Those who did not so engage themselves found they were growing more deeply indebted. They tightened their belts during the best times of the

43. U.S. *Historical Statistics of the United States* (Washington, D.C.: G.P.O., 1960), p. 757, 765, 767; *J.E.B.H.*, IV, 517-19. Samuel Galloway to Thomas Philpot, June 12, 1764, Galloway Papers, N.Y.P.L. *M.H.M.*, XXXVI, 341.

1760's and began importing less. Merchant houses in England tottered and fell by the 1770's because they were fearful of extending further credits to Americans who could not or would not pay them. Depression in the sot-weed was the effect.[44]

By the time of the Revolution, trade in the commodity was no longer very profitable. Cultivation of the crop was wasteful. It robbed the soil of its fertility. More land and greater labor were needed to produce a greater quantity, with the return per acre on the downgrade. That, coupled with the marked rise in population, made tobacco planting a very marginal pursuit at best. When this is considered with the burden of taxation, the restriction of currency on the colonists, and the threat of increased and expensive patronage from the Crown and proprietorship, revolution became pragmatic for Marylanders. Reform was nowhere in sight. To the British, reform of the imperial system meant further, not less, restrictions of the colonies' commerce and more centralization. In 1767 Carroll of Annapolis commented upon the stupidity of trade regulation and the necessity of free trade without the choking conditions and restraints of the mother country. He warned that radical changes might be necessary.

Carroll's complaints were significant. He was among the 2 per cent of rich planters in the colony. If such a man hurt, the majority of small producers hurt exceedingly.

These small people who were worth less than £ 500 were by far the greatest of the producers. At the same time, a study of their holdings indicates a style of life on a low scale. These men were not the importers. They owned few or no slaves to work their small lands and found it expensive to employ this kind of help. Their houses were rude and unspacious with little furniture, their clothing coarse, often homespun, their diet limited in the tastes, their liquor, far from the elegant delicate wines or brandies imported and advertised in the gazettes, was homebrew, better known as "busthead."[45]

---

44. Richard B. Sheridan, "The British Credit Crisis and the American Colonies," *J.E.H.*, XX (June, 1960), 178-179. Avery Odell Craven, *Soil Exhaustion as a Factor in the Agricultural History of Virginia and Maryland, 1606–1860* (Gloucester, Mass.: Peter Smith, 1965 [rep. of 1926]), pp. 67-71. Riley, *First Citizen*, pp. 210-11.

45. *J.E.H, XXV*, 639-54; A. C. Land, "Economic Behavior in a Planting Society: The Eighteenth Century Chesapeake, *J.S.H.*, XXXIII (Nov., 1967), 469-85. Joseph Mosley to Michael Mosley July 30, 1764.

They were frequently in debt, usually to the great planter and of the poorest class 70 per cent died insolvent; they more often bartered than bought, with corn, for there was little money in the province. They elected the upper bracket planter, and it behooved this man to keep taxes and fees at a low cost. Otherwise the fragile budgets of his constituents were broken. The noblesse obliged him, for political success meant economic power. Travellers remarked that roads and public buildings, bridges over streams, and other public works were astonishingly neglected. The House of Delegates had been tight with expenditures—but in the decade before the Revolution, both control of offices and their expenses were becoming more difficult.[46]

Since tobacco profits were falling for the upper income producer, they were negligible for the farmer. In order to enhance his income, the great planter entered into other entrepreneurial ventures; he began turning increasingly to wheat production. So also did the new arrival to Maryland, the tenant and the small producer, particularly in the western counties. By the eve of the Revolution the system of monoculture no longer existed. Southern Maryland remained, however, in the tobacco doldrums. The people there were conservative in their politics, too. By 1775 wheat production was nearly at par with the old staple.[47]

The wheat farmer brought changes to the economic structure. By 1775 Maryland was in a transitional stage economically with all of its attendant uncertainties of promise for some and altered conditions for others.

As a saleable commodity, wheat had its benefits and limitations. It was good for the small producer, since there was no restriction locally such as the tobacco inspection act. But it had been on the enumerated list of products which by law had to go to England. In England, the product faced the competition of the

46. *Ibid.* Tommy Thompson, "Marylanders, Personal Indebtedness and the American Revolution," (Ph.D. dissertation History Department, University of Maryland), 1972, p. 32 *et passim.* Of the two Chesapeake colonies, Maryland was the lesser in debt. Most of these debts were owed at home. The grandees were the heaviest debtors but able to pay them off. The lack of considerable debts to Britishers removes this as a cause of revolution.

47. David Skaggs and Richard MacMaster ed., "Letterbook of Alexander Hamilton" *M.H.M., LXII* (June, 1967), 145 *passim J.E.H., XX,* 184.

English farmer. Unlike tobacco, wheat did not enjoy a monopoly there. Wheat could be shipped to Portugal, *i.e.*, south of Cape Finisterre, where it competed with the French, Germans, Poles, and Russians for the continental market. It went to the West Indies but needed a broader market. It was a major money-maker in the coast-ways trade during times of revolutionary political crisis and embargo.[48]

Wheat suffered some disastrous years from British policy, however. An embargo placed by Parliament on the trade during the French and Indian War hurt. An open trade was enjoyed in later war years, particularly with Hispaniola, but in 1764, after the peace, such foreign places as this were closed, and the market suffered setbacks that were never forgotten by Marylanders.[49] With heavy competition from every quarter, wheat, although a very consumable and saleable commodity, was "not altogether profitable, because the market [was] precarious. When Russia, Poland and Germany [were] at Peace, Grain [was] purchased cheaper [in Europe] than in America. Consequently they [undersold] the Americans at the Spanish, Portugal, and Mediterranean markets."[50] Wheat producers and shippers often found themselves misinformed about a market situation and then, learning that it was glutted, they were forced to sell at a loss. Obsolete British policy forbade their going elsewhere, and the enforced system of indirect sale tended to raise prices and to take the Americans out of competition with other nationals unless there was a scarcity on the continent.

Statistics at Annapolis show a remarkable rise in exports in wheat between 1749 and 1774. In 1749, 82,684 bushels of grain left port; in 1774 it was recorded that 472,783 bushels were shipped out. Production of flour by the barrel shows a similarly phenomenal growth, and increased exportation of the commodity at Baltimore was even more dramatic. But the traffic, while

---

48. Malcolm Clark, "The Coastwise and Caribean Trade of the Chesapeake Bay, 1696–1776" (Ph.D. dissertation, Georgetown University, 1970), pp. 211 ff.

49. *Unpublished Letters*, p. 140. Clement Biddle to Samuel Galloway May 25, June 13, 1764; June 13, 1765. *J.E.B.H.*, IV, 524-25, 532. Vaughan W. Brown, *Shipping in the Port of Annapolis, 1748–1775, Sea Power Monograph No. 1* (Annapolis: United States Naval Institute, 1965), p. 26. Arthur H. Cole, *Wholesale Commodity Prices in the United States* (Cambridge: Harvard University Press, 1938), p. 138.

50. *Journal of Nicholas Cresswell 1774–77* (New York: Dial Press, 1924), p. 198.

always good, suffered during the postwar years and those of political crisis. Prices on the Philadelphia market exhibited declines in 1764 and 1765. Again, comparatively poor prices appeared in 1769 and 1770, with good returns during the five years, on the very eve of the Revolution.

Merchant and planter sources and statistics describing the conditions of the economy rarely present a picture of distress in this trade. Instead, they indicate one which promised expansion. Producers simply did not want the limited markets that the system of empire had caused with tobacco. Wheat-growing gave livings to far more folk than was the case with tobacco. Continued or increased restrictions clouded the future of the Maryland wheat grower and made him a proponent of independence. As the elder Charles Carroll asserted in a letter to a friend in England: ". . . Trade in its nature is free & open to all Mankind. . . ."[51]

Several supplementary industries round out the Maryland economic picture. Maryland was a growing capitalistic society; its people, particularly its leadership, were seeking profits in many ventures, with planting and land the base of investment. One gets the distinct impression of a people who were expansionistic and economically aggressive, who took their setbacks with the impatience of a young and vigorous society. They were in shipbuilding, for which Maryland ranked about sixth among the thirteen colonies—probably higher because of the numerous small craft designed to ply the unrecorded fishing and trade of the Bay.

Another important industry was in iron. Eight iron factories operated in Maryland by 1762 and many of the leading families either held stock in or worked them. After 1765 iron could be shipped in accordance with the law to England, to Ireland and south of Cape Finisterre. England and the proprietor encouraged the development of the pigiron industry. For example, iron laborers were exempted from taxes for four years. Encouragement possibly brought about increasing production, most of which went to England. Great increases were enjoyed together with good sales until 1766, when the political embroilments in the empire affected shipments. Bad years struck in 1772, but 1774 through 1775 witnessed recovery. The depression proba-

51. *M.H.M., XII*, 180.

bly reflected the generally gloomy conditions in England in the 1770's, and there was a fall-off in purchases.[52]

England, the best customer, was also the worst. Much depended upon purchases by the Navy Board and competition from English mongers. As early as 1763 Charles Carroll, Barrister of the Baltimore Iron Works, complained of the "inattention of the Merchants" in England "to our Interest." "No Person can have any Dependence on a Trade or Customers that seem actuated by Caprice or Whim only" or on "a Disposition" there "to Discredit and Depreciate Everything that we send from Hence. I do not see how we can subsist. I shall be glad to hear that Markets alter so that a Person may with any share of Prudence venture his Property to them."[53]

The Baltimore works never went so badly as the older Principio. Both because of the poor management and because iron from America became a "mere drug on the market," the Principio Company nearly folded on the eve of the Revolution. It received some new life during the war, and ownership was transferred to American citizens who made cannon and balls, but it never really recovered from its managerial mistakes and the poor years after the Townshend crisis.[54] Thus this important early industry suffered from the fragility of its infancy. Mismanagement at home or in the market place too easily brought economic death.

A merchant community developed slowly in Maryland until the mid-eighteenth century. The great planters whose lands were on or close to navigable waters handled the traffic chiefly in tobacco. They took care of the shipment of the small producer who reached the many plantation centers by means of rolling roads, i.e., roads down which hogsheads were rolled to wharfage. Attempts to centralize trade were constantly recommended by the proprietors, and, through legislation and, to some extent, convenience, such places as Port Tobacco and other areas became points of collection and shipping. Here planters increas-

52. *J.E.B.H.*, IV, 522-24; 535; *Historical Statistics*, 762-6. William Armstrong Fairburn, *Merchant Sail* (6 vol.; Center Lovell, Me.: Fairburn Marine Educational Foundation, 1945–55), I, 290. J. H. Clapham, "The Private Business of the Bank of England," *Economic History Review*, XI (1941), 79.

53. *M.H.M.*, XXXIII, 374-75.

54. Henry Whitely, "Principio Company," *Pennsylvania Magazine of History and Biography*, XI (1887), 288ff.

ingly made use of a local factor. Several Scottish houses from Glasgow developed their own system by employing such factors on commission. Thus, because of this kind of agent's ability to deal directly with houses in Scotland or England, a handful came to monopolize the tobacco trade in America.

By the middle of the eighteenth century, Annapolis had outstripped other places both because of its location on the Severn and easy access to the Bay and because of its position as center of government. A strong merchant community had therefore gathered there. Annapolis gave Maryland urban, social, and economic differentiation such as a politically vocal mechanics' community. Socially vibrant, it had theater, horse racing, plenty of gaming, an academy of learning, and evidences of luxury everywhere in the great houses erected by the grandees of government as well as commerce.[55] All of this reflected the rising commercial importance of the province. Signs of imperial expansion were evident. To corner trade as the Scots and English had done, the Annapolis partnership of Joshua Johnson, Charles Wallace and John Davidson, sent Joshua to London in 1774. In that city he was confronted with outright hostility by English merchants, who offered little or no help, and, as he reported, were downright resentful of this American ambitiousness. He nonetheless handled the "customs" of Charles Carroll, Barrister, Charles Carroll of Carrollton, and several business operations abroad of members of the anti-proprietary party. Johnson's firm was unusual, as it was the only one that coped with the colonial system by joining it.[56]

During the Revolutionary Era the progress of Annapolis paled when compared with the startling growth of Baltimore. In 1752 Baltimore was a struggling village of twenty-five houses. By 1788 it contained 2,000 houses, 14,000 people, and was vying for incorporation. Baltimore was, as a poet described it during the era, "A group of cabins to a city chang'd."[57]

---

55. David Ridgely, *Annals of Annapolis* (Baltimore: Cushing & Bro., 1841), Ch. *IV, V*. Land, *William Eddis*. Brown, *Shipping in Port Annapolis*, p. 15 *et passim*. Galloway, Maxcy, Marcoe Papers, L.C.

56. Joshua Johnson to Wallace and Davidson, Letterbook No. 1, July 3, 1771; to Davidson July 22, 1771. H.R. Annapolis.

57. *J.E.B.H.*, IV, 512-22. Clarence P. Gould, "Economic Causes of the Rise of Baltimore," *Essays in Colonial History Presented to Charles McLean Andrews* . . . (Freeport, N.Y.: Books for Libraries Press, repr. 1966 [1931]), pp. 250-51.

Baltimore in 1752. A sheltered settlement of about 25 houses—the nucleus of a great port city. *M.H.S.*

A number of things accelerated Baltimore's rapid rise. The construction of the Baltimore to Frederick road opened the wheat farming area to a ready, centralized, convenient market. Other roads from the community tapped the grain producing areas of Pennsylvania and gave its city, Philadelphia, a conscious rival for the trade. Thus a rapidly expanding mercantile community became the center for the grain trade to the West Indies and southern Europe. Also, the development of granaries first at nearby Elkton and then others in Baltimore itself commanded the flour-packing and bread industry.

The demand for labor was satisfied by a very heavy German immigration which moved into the western farming regions or remained in Baltimore. During the revolutionary period the town was nearly German speaking, and these Germans brought little love for English institutions or the tendency toward centralized authority in the empire. The town's growth and profitable prospects attracted colonists from Pennsylvania and from Maryland itself. Many of the leaders of the revolutionary movement were ambitious newcomers—restless under the restraints of Parliament. The city also received a constant influx of German redemptioners who were employed for their term and who then remained. Some 2,800 of this nationality arrived between 1747 and 1754.[58]

The flow of young entrepreneurs was a blessing in the long range, but it created problems on the eve of the Revolution. In 1767 when Baltimore flexed its political muscle against the Townshend program, William Lux, a merchant, claimed that there were about 350 houses in town with more being added every day. There were seventy or eighty "sail" loaded yearly. But he reported that "we have more merch'ts than employment." During these times he reflected the mercantile population's view. He dreamed that after the repeal of the Stamp Act the whole European continent would be "open'd to us" as well as all the West Indies. Thus they chafed under regulations that closed good markets to the law-abiding and benefited only a handful of smugglers.[59]

---

58. J. Thomas Scharf, *The Chronicles of Baltimore* (Baltimore: Turnbull Bros., 1874), 54 ff. Eugene Irving McCormac, *White Servitude in Maryland, J.H.U. Studies, XXII,* No. 3 (Baltimore: J.H. Press, 1904), p. 32.

59. William Lux to Mrs. F. Lux July 15, 1769: to Reese Meredith, Feb. 4, 1767 to William Molleson Sept. 15, 1766, N.Y.H.S.

Baltimore in 1796. During the Revolution, "a group of cabins to a city chang'd." by George Beck, oil on canvas. *M.H.S.*

90

Nor were they happy with the Scottish factors. Although Baltimoreans increasingly handled the commerce in wheat, they disliked the monopoly of the tobacco trade and felt that the Scots manipulated prices of goods to the Americans' disadvantage and that they held a stranglehold on the credit of the country. The letters of one of these factors, Alexander Hamilton, who acted for a Glasgow house, showed that the growing resentment of the natives was widespread. Hamilton blamed the attempted closure of the courts by debtors in 1765–66 on this feeling. He also related constant obstacles being thrown in the way of collecting debts and the general dislike of what amounted to a crop-lien system among Marylanders.[60]

Growth, together with the imperial regulation of the economy, brought social dislocations on the eve of the Revolution that were foreign to the provincial period. The population of Maryland between 1760 and 1780 increased by 83,207 souls and set population at 245,474. Of the increase, 31,511 were blacks, most of whom were destined to work the tobacco lands of the province. In addition, the arrival of servants after the Seven Years War was very heavy. For example, in 1774–1775, 1,124 servants left London for Maryland. Only 817 entered at Annapolis. A few went elsewhere, but 300 died en route or upon arrival, which attested to their hard lot. They were always held in port aboard ship because of quarantine, or until sold, which often meant months of waiting, bad food, disease, and misery. Descriptions of them affirm the meanness of their lives. They carried physical scars from small pox or the mark of an accident, a missing finger or a scarred face. Convicts augmented the labor supply. Their term of service was longer than the indentured servant which was about seven years. The convict served about fourteen years. Between 1766 and 1775 more than 12,606 servants and convicts came to Maryland.[61]

While under contract servant labor was productive, but after their term they often joined the unemployed, even though most of them were skilled craftsmen. The English Jesuit missionary

60. *M.H.M.*, *LXI*, 152. Henry Hull to S. Galloway Oct. 9, 1764: N.Y.P.L.

61. Abbot Emerson Smith, *Colonists in Bondage* (Chapel Hill: Published for the Institute of Early American History and Culture by the University of North Carolina Press, 1947), p. 325. Letterbook of Woolsey and Salmon, see Dec. 22, 1774, Jan. 3, 20, 28, Mar. 1, 1775 et passim; William D. Hoyt, "The White Servants of Northampton, 1771–74," *M.H.M.*, *XXXIII* (June, 1938), pp. 126-33.

Joseph Mosley vividly described conditions of indentured servitude on the Eastern Shore and in southern Maryland, where he resided for a time. In September 1770 he wrote to his sister: "I have seen white servants after their term of bondage is out ... strolling about the country without bread." Competition with black slavery was fierce. The price of good land was unattainable for them. Mosley did not recommend the country for a prospective redemptioner, and he continued describing his wide-sweeping mission in Talbot County: "I've often seen poor, miserable abandoned families, in poverty, want and misery. ... It has been a fine poor man's country, but now it is well peopled, the lands are all secured, and the harvest for such is now all over." Some unquestionably became tenant farmers if they could farm, though this was a long-term engagement whose prospects were meagre livings and growing indebtedness. There was a growing tenancy on the eve of the Revolution. In Prince George's County the number of land holders showed a very small increase between 1756 and 1771. In Talbot County there was actually a decline in land holding between 1756 and 1771.[62]

The problem of a rising poor was not an isolated one. Formerly, the poor were so few that the county housed them with private families. By the eve of the Revolution the cost of that system had grown prohibitive. In 1766 delegates from Worcester County pointed out that 40 per cent of their expenditures went for the purpose of caring for the poor. A tax list that they produced as proof of their statements seemed to indicate that about one-half were composed of women, children, the aged and infirm. The others appeared to be men without gainful occupation. Residents of Baltimore, Anne Arundel, and Prince George's Counties echoed Worcester's complaints. Attempts to alleviate the situation went for naught in 1765. The following year Samuel Chase brought in a bill on petition, but a general act was not passed until 1768.

Citing great burdens arising from the necessity, number, and continued increase of the poor, the law makers raised a general poor tax in and loaned money to the counties of need. These

---

62. Joseph Mosley to Mrs. Dunn June 5, 1772. David C. Skaggs, "Democracy in Colonial Maryland, 1753–66" (Ph.D. dissertation, Georgetown University, 1966), appendix I-III.

were Anne Arundel, Prince George's, Frederick, Charles; by 1773 Baltimore and Talbot were included. The act was no social milestone. It relieved the taxpayer more than the poor. The money raised was to provide a workhouse, part of which served as a jail. Wardens of the workhouses were to find work for the "able bodied vagabonds," their wages going for their support. The poor were to wear badges as though their condition did not already mark them. If not working, they were to be housed, fed and clothed on a meagre allowance.[63]

The poor laws were Elizabethan in tone and purpose. If this solution was old, the problem was new in the province. Optimists placed their faith in the natural rise of commerce and trade by which prosperous times would absorb the poor and unemployed, and, when the war broke out, productivity on farms and in shops increased. Many unemployed, and former servants joined the army as substitutes for the bounties in land and pay, promised inducements, however illusory they later proved to be to the poor man whose ilk composed a large element of the military forces. In the final analysis, Marylanders saw the break with England as a solution to economic and social problems.

3

THE WAR YEARS

The necessity for this change prescribed political action. It was not ideals which led to independence, however. Marylanders moved slowly, even tortuously, along that route. The convention that had been called to direct non-importation in 1774 was pushed by events. It was accused of "timidity" for continuing Governor Eden's presence. But news of Lexington and Concord made it necessary to arm, and fear of Governor Eden's collusion with Lord Dunmore, which threatened indentured servant and slave revolt, sent the moderates over to the independence

---

63. *Arch. Md., LXI*, xcv-xcvi, 5; *LXIV*, 380 ff. *Laws of Maryland*, 1740, Ch. *XI*; 1768, Ch. *XXIX*; 1744 Ch. *XIX*; 1770 Ch. *VII*; 1771 Ch. *XVIII*; 1773 Ch. *IX*, Ch. *XXX*. Clayton C. Hall, ed. *History of Baltimore* (New York: Lewis Historical Publishing Co., 1912), p. 23. For a study of the Maryland common soldier see Edward C. Papenfuse and Gregory A. Stiverson, "General Smallwood's Recruits: the Peacetime Career of the Revolutionary War Private," *William and Mary Quarterly*, XXX (Jan., 1973), 117-32.

group.[64] Eden was requested to leave.[65] Sensitive to the need for proprietary reforms, not fully ascertaining the need for independence, the convention called an election to get the sense of and instructions from the people in their counties on the issue. That call set forth a flurry of campaigning, as the delegates to the Continental Congress, particularly Samuel Chase and organizations in Annapolis and Baltimore such as the Whig Club, persuaded voters that we are now "engaged in war. It is now too late to look back or shirk; it is inglorious, effeminate and dastardly, unbecoming the Sons of Freedom." The colony that remained loyal would become the center of civil war. Moderation was a wise course six or eight months ago. It no longer was practical. One pamphleteer reminded his readers that "a house divided against itself can not stand." Independence was a necessity.

On June 28, 1776, the newly elected convention freed Maryland delegates to vote for independence. The elated Chase wrote to John Adams, with whom he had pressed members of the Continental Congress to arm, declare independence, and seek foreign alliances: "I am this moment from the House to procure an express to follow the Post with Unan[imous] Vote of our Convention for Independence. . . . see the glorious Effects of County Instructions. . . . our people have fire. . . . Now for a government."[66]

Legal government was an absolute necessity. The provisional government set August 2, 1776 for the election of a constitutional convention. The provisional group made changes in representation which immediately set the state on the long road of reform. Representation of the west was increased. Instead of the former two delegates from the oversized and heavily populated Frederick, that county was divided into three districts, each to elect four delegates. Recognizing the growth of Annapolis and Baltimore, the government ordered that each send two delegates. Any breach of the Continental resolves disqualified a voter. The

64. J. Archer Silver, *The Provisional Government of Maryland:* 1774–77 (Baltimore: J.H. Press, 1895), pp. 35-44; Herbert E. Klingelhofer, "The Cautious Revolution and Movement Toward Independence, 1774–76," *M.H.M., LX* (Sept. 1965), 261-313.

65. Woolsey and Salmon to John Pringle June 26, July 2, 1776.

66. *To the People of Maryland* by a Countryman, May 28, 1776 in L.C. and M.H.S.; Samuel Chase to John Adams 28 June, 1776, Ms., L.C.

provisional government made sure that the framers would hold pro-independence viewpoints. It was unwilling to liberalize the state further, but as Governor Robert Eden predicted: "Those who first encouraged the Opposition to Government, and set thereon this licentious Behaviour, will probably be the first to repent thereof." The prospect of recasting the framework of society had stirred minds. As the Methodist preacher Francis Asbury sighfully recorded in his journal after visiting the Jacob Giles home at Mount Pleasant outside of Baltimore: "... was confined to the company of men who were destitute of religion, and full of sin and politics."[67]

Independence fostered new political opinions. From Baltimore came the demand that no man be trusted with too much power. There should be rotation of office holders and a close watch over government which should govern little. "The right of examining the public conduct of their rulers is inherent in the people." Citing Montesquieu, the Baltimore writer thought that all governments should contain separation of powers. The vociferous Anne Arundel County militia observed that the basis of good government should be popular and free elections. The militiamen, most of whom could not vote, came to grips with basic issues. Plural office holding should be abolished. County officials should be elected. The poll tax should be ended along with other "oppressive fees." There should be a shift in the tax structure to those most capable of affording it—the wealthy and great landowners.

The provisional government drew critical fire for having retained the proprietary property qualifications for voting of a fifty-acre freehold or visible estate of £40 in the counties and in Baltimore. In Annapolis a voter had to have a visible estate of £20 sterling within the province or be a resident of the city for five years and a householder. The voting age was set at 21.

The question of the franchise became the hottest issue of the convention. On the day after its first meeting, August 15, a writer calling himself Watchman blasted the Convention as unrepresentative of the people. It was elected under a voting law "excluding near half the members of the state [from] the enjoyment of their inherent right of free suffrage. ... This inequality

67. Elmer E. Clark, *The Journals and Letters of Francis Asbury* (3 vol; Nashville: Abingdon Press, 1958), I, 355.

of representation cannot be justified on any principle. . . . It struck at the grandest right of freemen. It created strong sensations of disgust, and more than murmurs of resentment."[68]

The election had been the occasion for disturbances at the polling places in Queen Anne's, Prince George's, Worcester, and lower Frederick Counties where the qualifications for voting set by the convention were "broke." Evidently men under arms "in defense of their country" and those who simply paid taxes insisted upon voting and disregarded the legal qualifications. In Kent County voting proceeded peacefully, "til interrupted by a mob," and the electoral judges stopped the polling until a later date. Clearly the issue of franchise and the qualification of the members delayed the order of business. When the Convention met, it determined that new elections were necessary in the places where irregularities had taken place. Voice votes were taken, excepting on committees. Samuel Chase, no friend to this new democracy, had chaired a committee of five to examine the elections; sitting with him were also Brice Worthington and Carroll of Carrollton, equally anti-democratic. In accordance with the instructions to the delegates, the Convention proceedings were published. Secretiveness in government had been deplored by the radical element, and the functioning of their representatives was opened to the public where possible. Later, the debates in the Senate, on which the radical element kept a wary eye because of its conservative nature, occasionally were recorded in the newspapers.[69]

The Convention also responded to a demand of the people that they vote by delegate, not by county. The move tended to strengthen the more democratic forces in the Convention, but this augmentation of their strength was not enough to carry all their points, and their leadership did not enjoy the renown of the conservative anti-proprietary chiefs. Thus on August 17, those who had been heading the anti-proprietary party and had supported independence were elected to the committee to draw up a Bill of Rights and Form of Government. They were Samuel Chase, William Paca, Matthew Tilghman, George Plater,

---

68. *Maryland Journal and Baltimore Advertiser* July 3, 1776; *M.G.*, Aug. 15, 22, 1776; David Curtis Skaggs, "Maryland's Impulse toward Social Revolution," *Journal of American History*, LIV (Mar., 1968), 771-86.
69. *Proceedings of the Conventions of the Province of Maryland . . . in 1774, 1775 & 1776* (Baltimore: James Lucas & E. K. Deaver, 1836), pp. 210-15, 218.

Charles Carroll, Barrister, Charles Carroll of Carrollton, and Robert Goldsborough. Later Thomas Johnson was added to the committee.[70]

Charles Carroll, Barrister, and Samuel Chase resigned ten days later. Evidential of the conservative nature of the committee was their explanation that they felt bound by the instructions of their Anne Arundel constituency, which were "democratical in the extreme." The instructions, signed by 885 people, had, in the delegates' words, enjoined them to frame a system "destructive of a free government ... without a proper security for liberty or property." One of Chase's constituents had drawn up a plan of government, employed riders, and sent them through the county to enjoin the delegates to support this system "admirably calculated to promote the happiness of the poor people." In a new election Chase was returned but Carroll (Barrister) was not. Chase, who had a great deal to do with drawing up the new government, consistently voted against broadening the suffrage, the election of field officers by the militia and other democratic tendencies of the time. "I was averse that sheriffs and justices should be elected by the people at large," Chase recalled in 1777, "and that men without property should have votes for delegates. . . ."

Carroll of Carrollton blamed Rezin Hammond of Anne Arundel County for this assault on orderly government. He implored that the country be saved from "evil and designing men." "Should their schemes take place," he wrote, "and it is probable they will, unless vigorously counteracted by all honest men, anarchy will follow as a certain consequence; injustice, rapine and corruption in the seats of justice will prevail, and this province in a short time will be involved in all the horrors of an ungovernable and revengeful Democracy, and will be dyed with the blood of its best citizens."[71] Such disqualifications were repugnant to democrats. "That civil liberty is almost the only thing on earth in which every poor man is, to all intents and purposes, equally interested with every rich man; and

---

70. *Ibid.* p. 212 *et passim.*

71. *M.G.*, Aug. 22, 1776; Dec. 11, 1777; *M.G.B.A.*, Mar. 2, 1787. Peter Force, comp. *American Archives* 5th series (Washington: Congress of U.S., 1853), I, 1054-55; Philip A. Crowl, *Maryland during and after the Revolution, J.H.U. Studies LXI*, No. 1 (Baltimore: J.H. Press, 1943); C.C. of C. to Charles Carroll, Aug. 20, 23, Oct. 4, 18, 1776, IV, 361, 362, 366, M.H.S.

neither more nor less," wrote one who called himself Solon and he added, "to erect distinctions divides men in the cause."[72]

A few concessions were made to democracy. The property qualification for voting *was* reduced from a £40 sterling freehold to £30 currency. The revolutionary economy lowered such values more sharply than was intended. Maryland's revolutionary war paper money fell drastically from its original value. After the Convention there was not much public clamor against this qualification, whereas 1776–77 saw a great deal of criticism. Efforts to break down this barrier to participation in government by the common man were not again evident until 1792 when money achieved stability.

The Convention changed the sheriff's office from appointive to elective but set a high property qualification for the office. A bill of rights prevented governmental abuses. The Church of England was disestablished and religious freedom prescribed for Christians.[73]

On September 17 the Convention after ordering the Frame of Government and Bill of Rights published, adjourned until October 4 in order that the delegates might receive instructions from the people.

Upon the return of the members, the constitution was taken up by item, and voting rights became the principal argument. William Bayly and Turbutt Wright, who earlier had led a revolt of the Queen Anne's County militia against the officers appointed by the Convention, and threatened to throw them over the fence "if they took command," led the attack of the democrats in the Convention. Wright, moved that £5 currency be substituted for the £30 voting qualification. It was defeated, 34–20. Bayly then moved the question that payment of taxes for the support of government be a sufficient qualification for voting. He lost by a narrow margin of five votes, 24–29. On these important issues, Paca, Chase, Charles Carroll of Carrollton, leaders of the anti-proprietary party, invariably voted negatively. Urbanite delegates from Annapolis and Baltimore voted against, while their county neighbors voted affirmatively. Except for Queen Anne's, counties of the Eastern Shore, which witnessed violent Tory

---

72. *M.G.*, Feb. 13, 1777 Mar. 31, 1780.
73. John C. Rainbolt, "A Note on the Maryland Declaration of Rights and the Constitution of 1776," *M.H.M.*, *LXVI* (Winter, 1971), 420 ff.

Samuel Chase by the artist, Charles Willson Peale. *M.H.S.*

reaction against independence, opposed the measure, 9–4. The Western Shore was so badly divided that the democrats lost the cause there. Lower Frederick voted for the changes in suffrage, but the two western divisions voted against it.[74]

No issue divided the Convention more than that of the suffrage. The emergence of two factions was evident. Bayly moved to further liberalize the clause concerning religious freedom by permitting affirmation for the Quakers as an alternative to oaths taken in courts; nearly the same voting line-up for widening the suffrage took place. This issue the democrats also lost, 22–35, but they were rescued by the influential Thomas Johnson, who succeeded in exempting the Quakers and Mennonites from oaths and substituting "solemn affirmation" for all governmental purposes. Chase opened the door to plural office holding by winning the point that justices of the peace could be eligible as senator, delegate, or councillor. John Hall of Harford offered an amendment that salaries of such officials were to be controlled by the assembly. The democratic faction successfully opposed Chase, who tried to remove the power to nominate officials from the House of Delegates by placing it solely in the executive. Chase sought to change the office of sheriff from an elected to one appointed by the governor and council. Carroll concurred with him; but the democrats, who were bested on the high property qualification for that office, found allies and won handily, 9–45. But Bayly's democratic amendment that officers of the militia, justices of peace, and county clerks and surveyors be elected annually by county voters was slapped down, and then his final attempt to throw out the entire second article, providing the qualifications for electors, met failure.[75]

Conscious of the numbers and pressing problem of the poor, the authors of the original declaration of rights, in the thirteenth amendment, dropped taxation by the poll. It was a generally popular move and responded to several county instructions that taxes be equitable. In addition, they stated that no one should be taxed who did not possess at least a £30 freehold, thereby drawing a poverty line. However, the Convention later revised the declaration to read that paupers ought not to be "assessed for the support of government;" then in a following clause they obfus-

---

74. *Convention Journal*, pp. 329-30.
75. *Ibid.* pp. 308-10, 337.

cated that intention of excepting the poor from taxation by writing that "fines, duties, or taxes may properly and justly be imposed or laid with a political view for the good government and benefit of the community." William Fitzhugh, a surprising democrat, regularly voting with that faction despite having been seated on Eden's council, spotted the contradictory statement, and seeing that the ambiguity could devolve against the downtrodden, moved to delete it. Fitzhugh lost, and no vote was recorded.[76] Of Fitzhugh, Carroll of Carrollton wrote to his father that he "is ... most outragous, and acts a very weak and I think a very wicked part: he is uniting with Hammond, Cocky Dye" of Baltimore County "and such men, and seems desirous of impeding business and throwing everything into confusion."

Although some concessions were granted to the democrats, the constitution which finally emerged from the Convention was a limited aristocracy. The colonial aristocracy was in control. It contained Montesquieu-like balances. Still, it rested only on a portion of the people. It had been but little modified from the original plan. The guiding spirit behind its formulation had been expressed by Charles Carroll of Carrollton. In his thinking the governor and council must keep the democratic element in check. Regarding the members of the lower house he stated "Time may perhaps polish and soften their manners; wealth acquired by their own industry may satiate their avarice, and correct or at least moderate that eager longing after other men's property." He fulminated, quoting Horace on the commoner, "I hate the vile crowd, and keep them at a distance: *Odi profanum vulgus et arceo.*"

The democrats found some agreement with men of Carroll's belief that separation of powers diffused authority. They certainly shared the ideal of the Roman republic, which writers constantly cited as a model, that government should rest on virtue and that virtue was equated with patriotism. Anne Arundel had instructed Chase that a free vote was necessary by the associators—those who had pledged their loyalty to the revolutionary cause—regardless of property and who were above the age of twenty-one. But men like Chase and Carroll made property the standard of virtue, not loyalty or patriotism. Carroll lamented: "An infatuation seems to prevail over all America[,]

---

76. *Ibid.* pp. 301-02.

everywhere contending about forms of Govern[men]t and Liberty and likely by their inattention and divisions to lose the opportunity of securing either liberty or property." He thought that the internal political struggle had become so critical that only a reasonable peace with Great Britain could prevent chaos.[77]

As the constitution neared completion and acceptance, one of the many political poets of the era warned the framers with these lines that evil men raise a distinction between rich and poor and[78]

> Tho' man has often money made,
> And by it often been betray'd
> To think himself far excel
> Him that in humble station dwell.
>
> Another thing I find your darling
> You can't forget the name of sterling;
> But how you will exchange that coin,
> None but old Mammon can define.
>
> Then rouse, ye watchmen, on the tower,
> Before you have quite lost the power;
> Drive Mammon back from whence he come,
> And set up Virtue in his room.
>
> Let Virtue be the moving cause,
> Or summum bonum of your laws,
> Then may your state continue long.
>
> But if old Mammon bear the sway,
> He'll drive your virtuous sons away
> To other states, and you when scant,
> Will fall a venal mendicant.

Of the several potentially explosive issues that the Convention handled, the matter of the church was one. The state was religiously pluralistic, composed of Anglicans, who were the majority, and large minorities of Quakers, Roman Catholics,

---

77. *M.H.M.*, *LXII*, 394-418. C.C.C. to Charles Carroll, Sept. 16, 1760, Charles Carroll of Carrollton Papers, M.H.S., I, 57; May 16, I, 54; Aug. 17, 1766, *IV*, 360; Oct. 4, 1776, 366.
78. *M.G.* Feb. 15, 1777.

Presbyterians, Lutherans, Baptists, and Methodists. The Methodist preachers were making inroads at the expense of the Anglicans, "many of whom had abandoned their flock," both because they were disillusioned with their pre-independence treatment and the rebelliousness of their communicants against the mother country. By 1783 only thirty-eight ministers remained. A small Jewish community, gathered at Fells Point in Baltimore, was either ignored or blatantly discriminated against by the writers of the constitution, who would not allow their participation in government, though permitting them to practice their faith. In the early phases of the Revolution they had champions neither on the street nor in the legislature. In 1797, however, Solomon Etting of Baltimore petitioned the House for Jewish freedom and inaugurated the long struggle which did not end until 1826.[79]

Despite the Convention's blindness on the Jews, the aim in 1776 was nevertheless to avoid discrimination. Speaking as a Catholic, Carroll of Carrollton thought that religious tests were a device employed by the greedy to exclude men from the endowments of government.[80]

The members of the Convention were described by Asbury, who preached to them in the theater at Annapolis, as a very deistic audience. But deistic or not, the members felt that religion was necessary to society; to favor one church over another in the Revolution would ignite bitter internal strife which would surely lose the war. At the same time, caution in handling the wealthy Anglican Church was important. Its communicants despised its origins in the motherland, English clergy and the proprietors who profited from and supported it, but not its theological tenets.

In the Convention, Gustavus Scott sought to insure the continued support of the "Christian religion by permitting the legislature to pass a law for the collection of a "general and equal tax"

---

79. Ethan Allen, *The Clergy in Maryland of the Protestant Episcopal Church* (Baltimore: James S. Waters, 1860), pp. 86, 88. Joseph L. Blau and Saloman W. Baron, *The Jews of the United States: A Documentary History, 1790–1840* (3 vols.; New York: Columbia University Press for Jewish Publication Society of America, 1963), I, 33-35; *Votes and Proceedings*, Nov. Session 1797, pp. 26, 69, 71-72.

80. *M.H.M., XXXII*, 223; *X*, 251.

leaving the taxpayer to designate the sum to go to the religion of his choice or for the poor in general." Scott's resolution won, 41–18.[81]

In 1776 the Convention turned to the problem of the established church. Under the leadership of Samuel Chase, whose father, Thomas, was an Anglican minister, euphemistically called the "Pugnacious Parson," the convention rendered the church secure in its property and directed that repairs to certain edifices already contracted for should continue. Assessments were to be collected and the ministry paid until November 1, 1776. The Convention forbade any sale or devise of property for ecclesiastical purposes without the consent of the legislature.[82]

In the spring of 1779 the government enacted the Vestry Law by which the property of the church was conveyed to the parish vestrymen of known American loyalties.[83] "Vindex," the Presbyterian Dr. Patrick Allison of Frederick, spoke for the dissenters. He wrote that the property granted to the Anglican Church had been "plundered from their fellow Christians, by the operation of an irrational irreligious, anti-Christian establishment," during the colonial period when every man was taxed to support the church, regardless of his religion. He suggested that a restitution of such holdings should take place rather than a conveyance of them to a disloyal church.[84] Aside from other heated dissenter protests in the newspapers, the legislature did not engage in bitter partisan politics over the issue as in Virginia, even though by 1779 there were dissenter politicians in the House of Delegates. Attempts by vestrymen to raise the general tax for the support of religion were turned down in 1782 as unpropitious, and further meddling in the church by delegates who wanted the appointment of ordainers was prevented by the Reverend Samuel Keene, a minister in sympathy with the Revolution who eloquently led the cause of leaving church affairs to churchmen. Further reorganization was held in abeyance, therefore, until the war ended.

While legislators strained to preserve religion, revolutionary

---

81. *Convention Journal*, pp. 299, 307.
82. Hawks, *Narrative*, pp. 287-90.
83. Vindex [Patrick Allison], *Candid Animadversions* ... (Baltimore: Hayes & Hayes, 1783), p. 13 in L.C.
84. "Descriptive Sketch of Maryland" *M.H.M.* (June, 1924), XIX, 196-97.

Marylanders projected a secularism which one observer described poetically:[85]

> Religion here no gloomy garb assumes
> But sells her tears for patches and
> for plumes
> The blooming belle (some favorite
> swain to win)
> Talks not of angels but the world
> she's in
> Attach'd to earth, here born and to
> decay,
> She leaves to better worlds all
> finer clays.

Partly emanating from this secular spirit but chiefly as a result of the hatred for the Tories, and to insure the safety of the revolutionary movement, Maryland passed a law to license teachers and preachers.

This greatly discouraged the Anglican clergy and dampened the ardor of Methodist preaching whose leading light, Francis Asbury so much leaned toward England that he ceased work in the state during the war. On the other hand, an undaunted Methodist fellow with the *a propos* name of Freeborn Garrettson occupied as a lay preacher born near the mouth of the Susquehanna, defied mobs, and was upon several occasions, as he relates in his memoirs, chased by armed men. The government was in the dilemma of supporting freedom of speech and religion on the one hand and protecting the public safety on the other. As Boucher had put it earlier, there was more danger to liberty from licentious mobs than from the British constitution. Maryland's revolutionary government leaned to religious freedom. Although Garrettson refused the oath, he was permitted to continue his preaching.[86]

Father Joseph Mosley, an English-born Jesuit missionary who had ministered to a widespread flock for more than twenty years

85. Thomas O'Brien Hanley, "The Impact of Revolution on Religion in Maryland," (Ph.D. dissertation Hist. Dept., Georgetown University), 1961, 50-7; Nathan Bangs, *Life of Rev. Freeborn Garrettson* (New York: J. Emory and B. Waugh, 1829).
86. *A.C.H.S.*, *XVII*, 303-05.

on the Eastern Shore, continued his activity. But he would not take the oath. Despite his long ministry in Maryland, his letters indicate a warm attachment to his homeland. He awaited the decision of fellow priests on the oath-taking. When he learned that most had, he presented himself, yet he came under suspicion because the period prescribed by the law for compliance had expired. He petitioned the legislature and by special act he was licensed at the Talbot County court house. His letters indicated that his loyalty rested with the Faith, not a nation.

In 1785 he described the glowing condition of his religion. Religious freedom had brought prosperity to his believers, relieved of punitive taxation and now placed on an equal footing with others. A spirit of competition for converts prevailed among sects, with the Methodists abounding and in the thick of the contest for souls. The priest ordered books from England, with the *History of the Church* the most frequently read, worn-out, and reordered as a weapon in this happy fray. His chapel was now a place of public worship where once this had been forbidden, and the plantation which supported it was in a productive condition.[87]

Like the other dissenter sects, the Quakers were freed from the opprobrious taxation for Anglican support and granted the franchise and a role in government; yet the conscientious Quakers suffered.[88] As pacifists they were neutral and because they would not affirm loyalty tests, they were triple taxed. Their doctrines prohibited them from paying fines, taxes, or traffic in the revolutionary currency, because they considered that money as a war measure. Consequently, there were several arrests by rebel zealots, but perhaps worse, many disownments of members of the sect who considered their brothers' stand to be unreasonable. Several wealthy Friends, such as Joseph and Samuel Galloway, Samuel Chew and Gerard Hopkins, openly supported the Revolution, and some young men who could not suppress their enthusiasm bore arms in the rebel cause.[89]

87. Joseph Mosley to Mrs. Dunn, Oct. 3, 1784, Woolsey to Salmon, April 20, 1775. Thomas Haskins Journal, 1782, L.C.

88. John Thomas Guidas, "The Maryland Quakers in the Era of the American Revolution" (unpublished Masters thesis, History Georgetown University, 1969), pp. 82-8; 222-23.

89. J. McLure to Mordecai Gist, Aug. 2, 1776, Aug. 10, 1777, Gist to Thomas Johnson June 2, 1779, L.C.

The full brunt of the war never fell upon Maryland as it did upon its neighbors and other states such as South Carolina, New York, and New Jersey. General Robert Howe moved as far as Elkton after his invasion of Pennsylvania; this caused a flurry of military activity, but the British soon returned to quarters in Philadelphia and the good life of urban encampment. The British navy captured several vessels in the Chesapeake Bay and disrupted commerce briefly at the beginning of the war. The state's response of a naval force under Commodore James Nicholson and privateering generally cleared the Bay during most of the war. Still, the people were constantly apprehensive as fighting raged all around them. Finances were very strained by the expense of fortifications such as Fort Whetstone (McHenry), planned by Colonel Mordecai Gist,[90] and of maintaining a large militia.

The militia, as well as the Maryland Continental troops, were a restive, impatient soldiery. They were restive because of the generally poor conditions under which they served. They were drafted for a long period, while richer men were enabled to buy their way out of service if they could find a substitute and pay him a bounty. It is doubtful that (regarding their political desires) the soldiers were entirely pleased with the political compromises and outright conservatism as they saw it, of the Convention of 1776. Some of the militia units were outspoken on the matter.

Maryland's people were succumbing to the egalitarian spirit of the times, though its conservative party dominating the legislature, moved cautiously. Many took the earlier writings on equality of Paca, Chase, Carroll, and other spokesmen of the Revolution at face value. Such spirit was reflected in the army. Apparently so many incidents occurred between rich and poor soldiers that the legislature reorganized the battalions. It was done along class lines. A law of 1780 ordered that the counties be surveyed and that classification by property holding be made of those men subject to military service. Anyone who would not serve was fined in accordance with the value of his holdings or until he could find a substitute of his class. The legislature also recommended that those of great and small property be mixed in the battalions. The object was to obliterate class distinctions in

90. *M.H.M.*, VI, 256-61, *XLII*, 184-87, 192. *M.G.*, Mar. 10, 1780.

service and force all classes to serve. Those who volunteered for three years received $200 and a fifty-acre bounty of land and were relieved of paying taxes during their time in uniform and for four years after their discharge.[91]

Whether this seeming democratization of the army, in so far as that was possible, had good effect is difficult to determine. A few rich men served, but others continued to find and enlist substitutes for their class, though the new law made the financial burden greater. The Maryland Line nevertheless was one of the most dependable fighting units of the Revolutionary War, particularly in the black days after 1780 and the near collapse of the South. Valiant feats by such officers as Otho Holland Williams, Mordecai Gist, and John Eager Howard are legendary, but the deeds of the nameless men who obeyed their orders put these figures in the military history books.

Soldiers in general continued to dislike their constitutional disabilities. Officers could not serve in the executive or legislative branch, even if otherwise qualified, without resigning their position. Much ink was used to criticize this prohibition, asking the question, "Why should strong patriots be so discriminated against?" An amendment to the constitution permitting soldiers to hold office passed one legislature, but that change did not survive the following session, as required by the constitution.[92] Maryland's revolutionary rulers resisted too military-minded a government in a period when every uniformed man was thought to be a guardian of the cause of liberty and men of high military rank could easily have attained office and endangered civilian control of policy.[93]

By 1780 the need to supply men for the continental army became critical. As a result, the state took apprentices and servants in the last year and a half of their indenture, into the ranks but only with the permission of the master, who was to be paid a bounty. Apparently this proved unworkable and the law was repealed. A year later each county was ordered to take up ablebodied unemployed vagrants for military service; if accepted, they received a small bounty, but if they chose to enlist for three years they were given the usual bounty plus a bonus. The law

---

91. *Laws of Maryland*, 1780 Ch. XLIII.

92. *M.G.*, June 28, 1781. C.C. of C. to Charles Carroll June 23, 1780, VII, 597.

93. *Laws of Maryland* Ch. XV, III, X, 1781. Gist to Capt. J. H. Lowe June 23, 1777, L.C.

allowed them to be used as substitutes for draftees, who brought them to the recruiting officer. If they did not want to serve at all, they could appeal to the field commander. Poor persons with a wife and two or more children totally dependent upon their earnings were, however, excused from the draft.[94]

In 1780 and 1781 Maryland permitted slaves to enlist with the consent of the master and slave. Free black men were subjected to the drafts. It was hoped that 750 Negroes could be supplied, but it is doubtful that so many served, as the return of the 2nd Maryland Brigade of the continental army showed that only sixty blacks were enrolled. The reason was clear, as one free black, David Randall, complained in a letter to Governor Thomas Lee. Randall had consented to serve as a substitute, and then both the man whose place he was to take and the recruiting officer cheated him out of all his bounty money. Not many slaves consented to enlist, for the law was vague and promised them nothing—neither freedom nor the bounty. It appears that a slave could only be freed if he was enlisted by a white who falsely claimed ownership of him. But the true master was to receive double the slave's value from the false one, which discouraged the practice.[95]

Enlistment in the Maryland forces appealed to the poor and young. The allure of land and money and relief from taxation temporarily alleviated the conditions of unemployment which were pressing on the eve of the Revolution. Prosecution of the revolution required a program combining enticing self-interest and patriotic principles.

The Revolution produced a new breed of fighting man—the citizen soldier. Once his interests were reasonably secured, at least, in his mind, he could become a formidable partisan of a cause, and he could suffer the worst privations of campaigning.

The Marylanders, like the other states' citizen-soldiers, were very vocal about their rights. They performed badly under leadership for which they held a low esteem. Such was the case in the Battle of Brandywine under the soldier politician, Major General John Sullivan. The Maryland Line ran in the face of the

---

94. *Ibid.* 1780 Ch. *XLIII. Md. Arch., XLVII*, 196, 249-50; Jeffrey R. Brackett, *The Negro in Maryland . . . J.H.U. Studies*, VI (Baltimore: J.H. Press, 1889), pp. 196-97. C.C. of C. to Charles Carroll June 4, 1781, VII, 666.

95. Harold T. Pinkett, "Maryland as a Source of Food Supplies during the American Revolution," *M.H.M., XLVI* (Sept., 1951), 157-72.

enemy—self-preservation was a high priority to the citizen soldier—because of Sullivan's confusion. Just the year before, however, under their own General William Smallwood the same First Maryland Regiment had earned an outstanding reputation for fighting a rear-guard action in the Gowanus Swamp in Brooklyn and before Fort Washington which enabled Washington to make good his escape to New Jersey.

It was after the dark days of 1780 that Maryland troops gained their reputation as among the most dependable of the war. With Savannah and Charles Town having fallen to the British, the Maryland regiments were transferred to the Southern Department. At the Battle of Camden, South Carolina, August 16, 1780, the First Maryland Regiment fought so savagely that the troops threatened to turn a British rout into an American victory; and had not the commander, General Horatio Gates, miscalculated at the outset his need for cavalry and had he not already been in hasty and full retreat himself, a triumph might have been the outcome. In addition, the embattled troopers were sick from a meal Gates had ordered the previous night composed of some meat and cornmeal and instead of the usual rum they were issued a gill of molasses. Colonel Otho Holland Williams reported that "the men were breaking the ranks all night and were certainly much debilitated before the action commenced in the morning." "Instead of enlivening our spirits" as would have the rum, the molasses "purged us as well as if we had taken jallep," commented Sergeant Major Seymour of Delaware.

Following that debacle, Nathanael Greene replaced Gates and proceeded to carry out the cautious campaigning which would end in the British evacuation of Charles Town on December 14, 1781. The Maryland Line participated in all of those major battles, taking and suffering decimating casualties. They were responsible for the "very complete victory" at Cowpens, South Carolina. Colonel Daniel Morgan set them against the best troops of Lieutenant Colonel Banastre Tarleton and the First Regiment sent the British regulars running before their bayonets. Meanwhile, while Lord Charles Cornwallis chased Greene into North Carolina, Marylanders under Colonel Williams constantly harassed his advance. Finally at Guilford Court House in North Carolina, Greene offered battle. Unfortunately the Fifth Maryland Regiment composed of raw troops broke and ran; yet the First Regiment fought so fiercely that it shattered a

British brigade and menaced the whole action. Cornwallis was forced to pour grape shot into the death-locked combatants, killing friend and foe alike.

At Hobkirk's Hill, South Carolina, Lieutenant Colonel Francis Rawdon (Cornwallis had proceeded into Virginia to his defeat at Yorktown) surprised Greene and to the consternation of their officers, the wearied First Regiment could not be solaced because of the death of Captain William Beatty Jr, one of their favorite officers, and so they ran, to be rallied by Lieutenant Colonel John Eager Howard, but too late.

The siege of Ninety-Six saw slaughter of a Maryland contingent under Lieutenant Isaac Duval, but at Eutaw Springs they had revenge. Here the Maryland Line with the Virginians forced the action and effected a breakthrough causing the enemy to panic and run. The British managed to rally and avert a thorough drubbing. Their casualties, numbering a thousand, were too great to sustain any further major campaign. Greene was soon enabled to lock them up in Charles Town.

In the beginning, the wartime economy glittered with promise for Marylanders. The state was not a theater of war and was not as greatly disrupted by embattled armies as other states.

Wheat replaced tobacco as the staple crop along with other foodstuffs for feeding the American forces, and Baltimore became the major trading market.[96] After 1776, English and Scottish tobacco factors left the country and Maryland merchants, centering chiefly in Baltimore, took over.

As soon as the risk of ship capture by the British was minimized, merchants reopened trade with the West Indies and European ports. An Annapolis merchant spoke of profits on a safe voyage rising to as high as 500 per cent of the investment.[97] After the French alliance was signed, shippers sent cargoes to Bordeaux, Lorient, Nantes, and Dutch ports.[98] Merchants were using everything that floated "rotten or sound" in the newly-freed trade. One enterprising merchant partnership arranged to deal with a company in Bordeaux, where a variety of manufac-

---

96. M.G., May 12, 1777. Woolsey to Salmon June 18, 1776; to John Pringle Sept. 1, 1776.

97. Woolsey and Salmon Letterbook, 1774–84: Sept. 28, 1779, April 14, 1780, May 24, April 27, June 20, Aug. 15, 23, 1780 *et passim*.

98. Rhoda M. Dorsey, "The Pattern of Baltimore Commerce during the Confederation Period," *M.H.M., LXII* (June, 1967), 119-34.

tured goods was exchanged for foodstuffs, and the cargo they somehow insured by the British through the resourcefulness of a French correspondent. Tobacco was the major cargo carried to the French. Shipping statistics during the war were not kept exactly, sometimes not at all; but one historian found that in 1780 Baltimore cleared 236 ships, 105 of which went to foreign ports, 21 to the continent, 84 to the West Indies, the others, 131, to United States destinations.[99]

Trading abroad and with the other states caused great scarcities of provisions at home and endangered the supply to the military forces, so that the government was obliged to impose short term embargoes on overseas shipping and to send its commissioners into the countryside to commandeer foodstuffs. But that did not close off profits. Merchants, particularly those of Baltimore, invested in privateering. Between 1776 and 1781 some 224 letters of marque and reprisal were issued by the Continental Congress to Marylanders. Some lost heavily, as for example, John and Robert Purviance, who invested about £ 35,000 in a venture to clear British vessels from the Capes. Because privateering was a gamble with heavy stakes, other merchants chose to invest in land, particularly those of Baltimore who speculated in town lots; for the war by no means impeded the growth of the city. Rather it gave impetus to the city's development and by the end of the era Baltimore was the largest city in the state and the third largest in the United States. During the war growth came with such rapidity that roads went unpaved and housing was inadequate. The Continental congressmen who met there briefly because of the British occupation of Philadelphia, crabbed at the inconveniences and appearance of the place. To William Hooper the place was a "dirty boggy hole" which "beggars all description." For Oliver Wolcott it was "infinitely the most dirty place I ever was in. No one can walk except in Boots." John Adams, however, enjoyed it and saw a glowing future for this war-time boom town.[100]

The newspapers of Annapolis and Baltimore were filled with commentary on the economic conditions of the state. Writers

---

99. Bernard C. Steiner, "Maryland Privateers in the American Revolution," *M.H.M.*, III (June, 1908), 99-103; John Sterett to M. Gist, Nov. 26, 1777; Samuel Smith to Otho Holland Williams, Feb. 16, 1779, Williams Papers, M.H.S.

100. Edith Rossiter Bevan, "The Continental Congress in Baltimore Dec. 20,1776–Feb. 27, 1777" *M.H.M.*, *XLII* (Mar., 1947), 22-26.

frequently blamed nameless disloyal persons who attempted to corner the market on grains and provisions, who caused the depreciation of money by not accepting anything but specie, or who, supposedly in collusion with the British, were responsible for the scattered raids on Maryland's commerce.[101]

Those persons who did not take the oath of allegiance prescribed in 1777 were especially the targets of attacks. Mounting intolerance of them saw the organizing of Whig Clubs, whose members ran suspects out of town. While the clubs claimed to be democratic and supporters of the constitution, the Bill of Rights and its freedoms, they were nonetheless ill-directed and often attacked the innocent.[102] In this the Whig Legion of Baltimore made itself notorious. For printing what the Legion misconstrued to be a pro-British piece in the *Maryland Journal*, William Goddard, the founder of the paper, was roughly used by the club and ordered banished. Subsequent investigation of the incident by the legislature revealed that Samuel Chase had requested the printing of the essay in question and that he had also placed a contrasting and biting commentary along with it. The legislature condemned the action of the Legion and insisted that such vigilantism cease.[103] The intrepid Goddard pamphleteered that the members of the Legion, particularly the mechanics, should stick to their work with awls and needles and patch shoes, not the state. Those who fancied themselves a Solon or Lycurgus and usurped the power of the executive could not but meet with contempt. From Jonathan Swift he hurled the lines:[104]

> Brutes find out where their talents lie: . . .
> But man we find the only creature,
> Who led by folly combats nature
> Who when she loudly cries, forbear
> With obstinancy fixes there;
> And where his genius least inclines,
> Absurdly binds his whole designs.

---

101. *M.G.*, Dec. 19, 1776; Dec. 1, 1780.

102. *Arch. Md., XII*, 517-18; 526-27. *M.G.* April 17, 1777. C.C. of C. to Charles Carroll of Annapolis, Mar. 9, 1776, IV, 376.

103. Ward L. Miner, *William Goddard Newspaperman* (Durham: Duke University Press, 1962), pp. 150-62. William Goddard, *The Prowess of the Whig Club* . . . (Baltimore: author, 1777), pp. 7, 16, in L.C.

104. "Sentry" in *M.G.*, Mar. 3, 1780; Mar. 10, 1780. Mar. 17, 15, 24 *passim*. "Censor" is identified as Chase: Aug. 23, 1781.

In this atmosphere of suspicion, invective, and anti-Tory violence, the legislature considered the confiscation of British property. By 1779 the war in the South had gone badly; Savannah had fallen to the British. Charles Town was threatened, and by the spring of 1780 the British occupied it. With the major military defeats, continental money plummeted disastrously. The value of Maryland money declined, too. People hated to accept paper money in trade, even though a law of 1777 declared it legal tender. Creditors bitterly complained and avoided payments of debts in the currency; consequently in 1780 the legal tender act was repealed, but only after a divisive fight in which the issue of seizing British property was involved.

The state faced financial disaster. Efforts to reevaluate money above its worth and to reduce the amount in circulation proved fruitless. The government taxed heavily, but not so heavily as the times and economic conditions necessitated. Such a policy was politically inexpedient; in this era it might well have had fearful consequences.

Thus the house turned to an earlier suggestion of congress that Tory property be seized to sink continental issues. The Senate had refused the first attempt and became adamant over the new one. Heated debates ensued between the two bodies, but at no time was the position advanced that the measure was one to democratize the state through a redistribution of property as historians later argued. Confiscation was an expedient to relieve the state of its awesome wartime financial obligations.

The acrimony between the two houses and between the democratic and conservative parties spilled into the newspapers of Baltimore and Annapolis. Samuel Chase, Charles Ridgely of Baltimore, and many others, some writing under unidentifiable pseudonyms but probably members of the house, supported confiscation. All of the essayists insisted that the British had caused the war, and they spared no adjectives describing the maliciousness of the Tories and the enemy's responsibilities for the damages and expenses of the war. The need to finance the war and spare the people from taxation were also main themes of the pro-confiscation authors, but even they were couched in war-time emotion. One who called himself "A Sentry" exclaimed: "Good-God! What is this state come to, to be subjects of Great Britain? and we can not take the property of our enemies to pay our taxes, when if it was in their power, they would take our lives. ... I have borne a firelock and I can say that the writings ... and proceedings of the Senate is damned Toryism."

Another, from Montgomery County, addressed the Senate: "Let the assembly give it to us, and all the devils in hell shall not take it from us."[105]

Not nearly so numerous as their antagonists, several writers explained the Senate's aversion to confiscation. Two authors bore the weight of the verbal battle, Thomas Sim of Prince George's County ("Plebian") and Charles Carroll of Carrollton ("Senator"), both members of the Senate. Mainly they argued that other means must be found to pay the cost of the war. To confiscate property was contrary to the Bill of Rights. A sweeping bill such as the house proposed condemned men without trial. The disorganized state of society made it impossible to ascertain who was a British subject. The fate of enemy aliens, if they were aliens, must await the results of the war, and confiscation would greatly complicate, if not entirely prevent, negotiations for peace and independence.[106]

As to the state's profiting from the sale of British lands, Carroll saw another, far different, goal. Confiscation would increase speculation and profiteering among the people in general, especially among a small clique in particular that had been hungry to purchase confiscated property in cheap money.[107] He attacked Chase for his attempt while a member of Congress to monopolize the flour trade with the French army for his own company. Alexander Hamilton had exposed the maneuver, warning that "There are seasons in every country, when noise and impudence pass current for worth: and in popular commotions especially the clamours of interested and factious men are often mistaken for patriotism." The Maryland legislature, acting with dispatch, had passed a law prohibiting members of Congress to engage in trade, and Chase lost his seat. Carroll asserted that Chase's leadership of the pro-confiscation and the pro-tender factions had analogous self-serving motives. Chase and his cohorts answered

105. *M.G.*, Mar. 10, Feb. 11, 18, 25, 1780, Debate in Senate in April 14, 1780.
106. *Ibid.*, Aug. 23, 1781.
107. *Papers of Alexander Hamilton*, Harold Syrett and Jacob E. Cooke (New York: Columbia University Press, 1968), I, 562-63. *Laws of Maryland*, Ch. II, Mar. 1779. C.C. of Annapolis to S. Chase, June 6, 1776, June 5, 9, 1777 S. Chase to C.C. of Annapolis June 6, 1776: V 401a, 402, 404 *et passim; M.G.* Sept. 27, 1781.

in kind: The Senate was pro-Tory, aristocratic, and was a cumbersome body which from its anti-Whig predilections could not act in the interest of the people, and Carroll was trying to protect his holdings in England from retaliatory measures.[108]

After a year of resistance, the Senate finally assented to confiscation. That body's position became virtually untenable when it was learned that the Bank of England would not honor Maryland's bills of exchange backed by stock purchased before the war, that British forces had sequestered rebel estates in South Carolina, and that sister states had already confiscated British property.[109]

The Confiscation Act of 1780 weakly met some of the Senate's objections. The law tried to define British citizenship as those persons living in Great Britain who had abandoned the state, even if on business, and those who left the state since the 30th of April, 1775, and those who had not taken the oath of allegiance or had in any way aided England. It gave persons who had left Maryland until March 31, 1782, to return and take the oath. Another act appointed commissioners to "discover" and declare British estates and to keep an account of them. British property was placed at auction by the commissioners, and payment for purchases was to be made in hard money or the equivalent in three installments over a period of nine months. Later laws permitted buying on credit from the state with payment of interest on the debt.[110] In the beginning avid purchasing took place. Valuable properties were sold in large lots and were

---

108. *M.G.* Aug. 30, 1781. Charles Carroll of Carrollton to Joshua Johnson, 21 Nov. 1779, Arents Collection N.Y.P.L.; C.C. of C. to Charles Carroll of Annapolis, May 11, 1780, VII, 584 *et passim*.

109. *Laws of Md.*, 1780 Ch. XLV. *M.H.M.*, VIII, 369-70. John Kilty, *The Landholder's Assistant* (Baltimore: G. Dobbin and Murphy, 1808), pp. 332-37.

110. Sale Books: Confiscated Lands, H.R. *Landholders Assistant*, 538, 343-47; Smallwood's Report on Bounty Land, H.R. (1788); Brown Books, II Aug. 7, 14, 1781 Smallwood to Gov. T. S. Lee. *M.G.* Feb. 14, 21, Jan. 3, 1782; Report on Confiscated Estates, Nov. 9, 1784. Md. Miscellany, L.C. Doris Maslin Cohn, "The Haynie Letters," *M.H.M.*, XXXVIII (Dec. 1943), 347-48. Bounty Land: Soldiers Entitled to Land Westward of Fort Cumberland, H.R.; Richard Arthur Overfield, "The Loyalists of Maryland during the American Revolution" (Ph.D. dissertation History Department, University of Maryland, 1968), pp. 46-7, 339-40; 348-354; 361-79. Crowl, *Revolution*, 50-51, 57-60 *et passim*. I was also aided in the research for these conclusions by Mr. Ivan Kauffman, Ph.D. candidate, Georgetown University. John Hosmer Stone to Daniel St. Thomas Jenifer, Annapolis, Mar. 9, 1782, Revolutionary War Collection M.H.S.

bought by the great merchants and large landholders, many of them the proponents of confiscation in the house—men of wealth, extensive credit, and political influence. Proprietary land was set aside for purchase by former tenants. A few managed to buy the land they worked, but most of these people had no money. Confiscated land in the west at Cumberland was set aside for soldiers. A few took up their acreage. Many others, however, sold it at low prices, particularly in the postwar depression years.

After 1782 the sale of British property went very slowly. The threat of possible litigation, disputes between parties claiming property, bad surveys of land, and the fear of fraud were among the reasons. By the middle 1780's there was little money with which to buy anything, and many who had bought confiscated property were unable to pay for it. Rather than easing the financial burdens of the war, confiscation added to them.[111]

4

## THE IDEALS OF A NEW SOCIETY

The Revolution in Maryland stimulated minds to weigh and reexamine the old institutions. The measuring rod was republicanism. Definitions of republicanism varied. To some it meant total freedom of expression for all classes where formerly only the aristocrats had license to think, bespeak themselves, and act on public matters. To others, only those of education, wealth and social position were capable of constructive thought and leadership.

In Maryland's revolutionary society a clash of ideas on the meaning of the Revolution and how it affected institutions was inevitable. Almost every piece of writing in the newspapers, the broadsides, the pamphlets, the letters, no matter what the subject, indicated a willingness to experiment.

Thoughts on the new society were given free rein. For example, most men agreed that a simplicity of dress and manner of living best symbolized this republicanism, in contrast to the monarchical courts of Europe; contrarily one genteel writer, possibly A. C. Hanson, found the inauguration of Governor Thomas Johnson vulgar because of its plainness. Pomp and cir-

---

111. *M.G.* Nov. 26, 1776; Nov. 24, 1780.

cumstance were necessary, he thought, because they reflected the dignity of the state and the power of the people on which it rested. Charles Willson Peale, the Maryland and Pennsylvania master painter, who captured the epic scenes and heroes of the Revolution forever in oils and drawings, was fond of upsetting the masculine ego by proclaiming his fervent belief in the intellectual equality of the female with the male.[112] One who called himself "Republican Philosopher" wrote a series of articles in the *Maryland Gazette* advocating freedom from imprisonment for debtors. He also wrote of the need for reform in criminal justice along the lines of Cesare Beccaria's *Des delitte e delle pene.* "Republican Philosopher" found slavery inconsonant with his ideals, and though he saw no practicable way of abolishing the system, he called for more humane treatment of the slaves in the Maryland codes. Perhaps this was the same man who managed, in the earliest draft of the Constitution of 1776, to get a statement against slavery, only to have it deleted by the conservative element before the document reached final form. Maryland liberalized naturalization, gave public notice for eight weeks before passing any private acts, and let the door of legislative debate be opened to the people.[113]

A continuing revolution seemed targeted on the issues of religion, education, slavery, the expansion of the economy, the perfection of the union, and the fuller participation in government through the broadening of the suffrage.

The Church of England occupied considerable attention. In 1783 Governor Paca called for an adequate support of the Christian religion. Under the leadership of Dr. William Smith, the church asked for incorporation and the right to determine and alter its own liturgy and to speak on purely spiritual matters. Dissenter critics saw this move as a new threat of collusion between the state and church, intending a governmental reestablishment. But such was not the case. The charter which the legislature granted declared the church's independence of the

---

112. *M.G.*, April 28, 1780. *M.H.M.*, LXVI, 435; Charles Coleman Sellers, *Charles Willson Peale* 2 vol. (Philadelphia: American Philosophical Society, 1947), I, 80.

113. Debtors were freed of prison. However, this would be only upon appeal to the assembly and after having given their creditors all of their assets except necessities. 1779 Ch. VII; *M.G.* Sept. 17, 1779. Bond, *State Government in Maryland*, p. 78. See also: *M.G.* Nov. 26, 1776; Nov. 26, 1779; June 25, Jan. 17, May 17, 1781; June 14, 1781; Dec. 12, 1782.

state and its separation from the Church of England, while recognizing the parenthood of that church. The Episcopal Church of Maryland thereafter structured its government along lines dictated by the events of the Revolution, that is, a full participation in all church affairs by the laity. In 1784, the laity and the clergy both defined the spiritual duties of the ministry and both arms of the church met annually in convention. In 1788 a standing committee for each shore composed of five clergy and five laymen executed the orders of the convention.

The parish vestry was charged with overseeing each parish and with lodging complaints against bad ministers to the convention who were tried by that body.

Support of the church was made to rest solely with member-parishioners, a fact of life whose hardships brought sighs for the old days. Thomas Gates, parson for Talbot County's Saint Peter's and a member of the Standing Committee for the Western Shore, wrote a relative: "I often cry out *quando* to *revisam*. The truth is I am weary of being a *Subscription Parson*." "As a clergyman, I can have no agreeable prospect before me; the church is as democratic as the state. . . ."[114]

Few churches were as disorganized as the Methodists. The end of the war found them with only one ordained minister remaining in America, Francis Asbury, with a large group of preachers and converts and its spiritual guide and founder, John Wesley, very critical of the revolutionary movement. The Methodists at the same time were not separated from the Anglican church.

Recognizing the American Methodists' difficulties, John Wesley sent the Reverends Thomas Coke and Richard Whatcoat to meet with Asbury and to convene representatives of the church in America in 1784. The conference took place in Baltimore at Lovely Lane Chapel beginning December 24th. Approximately sixty of the eighty-one American preachers attended. They were a youthful, vigorous, enthusiastic lot. Asbury and Coke dominated the assembly. The preachers resolved to sever ties with England and set up a separate church styled the Methodist Episcopal Church in America. Asbury was ordained superintendent, but the ministry assembled in conference controlled his

114. Allen, *Episcopal Church*, p. 14; Hawks, *op cit.*, pp. 296-300; Thomas Gates to Horatio Gates May 4, 1785, June 30, 1787; Gates Papers, N.Y.P.L.

powers and could dismiss him from office for abuses. Coke, apparently carried away with the revolutionary fervor, then sermonized the assemblage on the corruption of the Anglican church, "filled with the parasites and bottle companions of the rich and great." He spoke of the "anti-Christian union of church and state" which the Revolution had broken asunder. All doubts of the Methodists' loyalties to the American cause which had plagued them during the war were now removed.[115]

Like most of the dissenter sects, Catholics were in a euphoric state because of their newly-won freedom. Yet the church was faced with new problems of status. Directed by the vicar-general at London, that tie was now broken. Most of the clergy were Jesuits, and they were demoralized because of the Papal dissolution of the order on the eve of the Revolution. There were about 15,000 Catholics in Maryland, with few priests, many of whom had grown old in their service to attend them, yet Maryland Catholics were better ministered to than those in the rest of the country.

At first a meeting of the clergy of Maryland indicated that they did not want a bishop. American Catholics would not accept one, they argued, and their compatriots would not understand the office. Such a posture put the American church gravely in danger of intrigues. For example, Benjamin Franklin, United States minister to France, was promoting a Frenchman's appointment to please that nation and further cement the alliance.

An attack on the church seemed to galvanize matters. This came from Reverend Charles Wharton, an apostate Jesuit. He not only criticized the essential teachings of the church as false but also accused the church of suppressing freedom of thought. It was a hackneyed attack, but it required an answer in this revolutionary age when freedom of thought and expression were watchwords. Father John Carroll was chosen to reply to Wharton. This ardent patriot, who had returned to Maryland in 1774 from training and work in Europe and who with Charles Carroll of Carrollton and Samuel Chase had been sent on a fruitless mission to Canada by the Continental Congress of 1776 to enlist the aid of Quebec, wrote a 116-page pamphlet. It was respected

---

115. Diary of Thomas Haskins Dec. 21, 1784–Jan. 1, 1785, L.C. N. C. Hughes, Jr. "The Methodist Christmas Conference: Baltimore Dec. 24, 1787–Jan. 2, 1784," *M.H.M.* LIV (Sept., 1959), 272-92.

generally, especially for the sentiments on religion in America. John Carroll felt anguished at Wharton's "natural tendency to embitter against us the minds of our fellow citizens." He did not want to "disturb the harmony now subsisting amongst all Christians in this country, so blessed with civil and religious liberty; which if we have the wisdom and temper to preserve, America may come to exhibit a proof to the world, that general and equal toleration, by giving free circulation to fair arguments, is the most effectual method to bring all denominations of Christians to an unity of faith."

By 1784–85 Carroll was appointed vicar-apostolic by Pius VI. By 1788 the priests who had stated sentiments against a bishop changed their minds. The difficulties encountered by Carroll in unifying the far-flung church (particularly in New York where two warring factions tore that church asunder) and the continued intrigues for foreign control moved the clergy to convene at Whitemarsh, Maryland, where they nominated Carroll for Bishop, 24–1. The Pontiff met the solution with enthusiasm, and Carroll, whose nationalistic nature caused him to prefer the vernacular in church services, though this was far off, set about the herculean task of forging an American Catholic church, free of foreign influence.[116]

Both religion and the Revolution gave thrust to the improvement of education. When the Methodists met in Baltimore and organized their church, one of the principal projects on their minds was the founding of a college. Methodists generously contributed funds for a college. In December 1786 enough money was collected to establish Cokesbury College at Abingdon in Harford County. The intention of the founders was not only to educate in a religious atmosphere but to implement this goal with the ideals of Locke and Rousseau. The school took in both poor and tuition students.

Cokesbury struggled for a few years with Asbury, often going from house to house in Baltimore "through the snow and cold, begging money for the support of the poor orphans at Cokesbury." Misfortunes were too great to overcome. A fire in 1795

---

116. John Tracy Ellis, *Catholics in Colonial America* (Baltimore: Helicon Press, 1963), pp. 416-17 *et passim;* Peter K. Guilday, *The Life and Times of John Carroll* (New York: Encyclopedia Press, 1922), p. 126, Ch. XIII. John G. Shea, *The Life and Times of . . . John Carroll* (New York: John G. Shea, 1888), Ch. V.

St. John's College, Annapolis. An early nineteenth-century view. *M.H.S.*

caused the school's removal to Baltimore next to the Light Street Church. Another fire there ended the effort.[117]

Like the Methodist bishops, John Carroll gave high priority to the founding of a college. At the convocation of Whitemarsh plans were laid for a college to be erected at George Town. "Agreeable to the liberal Principle of our Constitution, the Seminary will be open to students of Every Religious Profession. ..." The college was inaugurated in 1789 and received its first student in November 1791. It was to supply vocations for an American clergy as well as to train youth generally. The college had a peculiarly nationalistic cast about it. Carroll feared the potential damage of a foreign clergy who might well be comprised of the troublesome castoffs of Europe—adventuresome clerics who had left Europe under a cloud.[118]

The conviction that higher education was a necessary foundation for the republic and that training in European institutions served to corrupt the young were among the principal motives for public support of a state university. Marylanders believed that "lasting provisions must be made, by Good Education for training up a succession of Patriots, Lawgivers, Sages, and Divines; for Liberty will not ... dwell, but where her fair companion Knowledge flourishes by her side."[119]

This kind of thinking spawned the first university in Maryland. Establishment wanted only energetic leadership, and this it found in the Reverend William Smith who captured Benjamin Franklin's attention with his philosophy of education as stated in his book *College of Mariana*. He became Provost of the College of Philadelphia, but the Revolution and his loyalism ended in dismissal from the college and exile. In 1780 he took a position as pastor in Chestertown, Maryland, and began teaching at Kent Academy. During Smith's brief presence the academy bulged with students. In 1782 it was incorporated as Washington College. Two years later Smith induced the legislature to establish a tax supported university, transforming King William's Academy

---

117. Bernard C. Steiner, *History of University Education in Maryland, J.H.U. Studies,* IX, (Baltimore: J.H. Press, 1891), pp. 27-29, 171-73.

118. John M. Daley, *Georgetown University: Origin and Early Years* (Wash.; Georgetown University Press, 1957), pp. 47-51 *passim.*

119. William Smith, *A General Idea of the College of Mirania* (New York: J. Parker & W. Weyman, 1753). George H. Callcott, *A History of the University of Maryland* (Balt.: M.H.S., 1965), pp. 8, 15, 12-14.

Washington College in Chestertown which combined with St. John's to form the first university in Maryland.
*Enoch Pratt Free Library.*

in Annapolis into St. John's College and combining it with Washington to form the University of Maryland.[120]

Smith outlined two distinct and innovative curriculums for the period. The first was classical, one designed for the aristocracy, who ordinarily sent their youngsters abroad for schooling. Even this introduced practical subject matter for the use of modern republican society. These subjects were English, history, modern languages, chemistry and botany. The other curriculum appealed even more to the pragmatic strain in revolutionary Marylanders. It was designed to help men earn a livelihood rather than delve into philosophical questions.

Classics and philosophy were virtually eliminated. Modern languages, history, and science formed the core of study, together with English composition. Accounting, economics, geography, surveying, navigation, architecture, and agriculture were also offered as additional courses. This was the much hailed "Republican curriculum."[121]

Whether the second curriculum ever fully went into effect is doubtful. By 1789 the two colleges were flourishing, but the university was not. Public support for collegiate education was victimized by factionalism. The democratic small-farmer based politicians were highly critical of tax support for the university, as they viewed it, aristocratic education "only for the rich and extravagant."[122]

When Smith resigned to pursue the office of Episcopal bishop, the "university" lost its best public-relations man, and before the

---

120. Smith, *Account of Washington College in the State of Maryland* (Phil.: N.P. 1784), pp. 3, 14-20, 42-43. Callcott, *op cit.* Steiner, *Hist. of Univ. Ed. Md.*, 105. Tench Francis Tilghman "The Founding of St. John's College, 1784–89" *M.H.M.*, *XLIV* (June 1949), pp. 75-92.

121. Callcott, *op. cit.*, p. 14.

122. *M.G.*, April 21, Dec. 22, 1785; Nov. 20, 1794; Mar. 12, 1795, Mar. 10, 1803. James McHenry, a high Federalist, voted as a democrat on the school issue: see Bernard C. Steiner, *The Life and Correspondence of James McHenry* (Cleveland: Burrows Bros., 1907), 18 Dec. 1794, pp. 154-55. *Votes and Proceedings House Nov. Session*, 1798, pp. 49, 67-68. Feelings were so feverish over the issue that schoolmasters fell to fighting. Conservative divine John Bowie and Republican Jacob Gibson engaged in a war of words. Bowie, insulted by minister Gibson's remarks, hunted for him and, finding him at the courthouse in Easton, laid down his clerical coat: "Lie there Divinity while I *thrash* rascality." One of the best brawls ever in Talbot county ensued, but ended in a draw. The legislature gave their respective schools some money. God was on both sides: Lucy Leigh Bowie, "The Rev. John Bowie, Tory," *M.H.M.*, XXXVIII (June, 1943, 156-57.

era ended, it suffered reduced support. Eventually the two schools became private in character.

Education unfortunately was a continuing issue between democrats and their conservative rivals. The democrats resented higher education for the sons of the gentry at public expense, and its exclusiveness. The democrats wanted support for the three R's on the county level. The conservatives argued that provision had always been made for poor scholars. A well-educated leadership was the foundation of the republic.

The struggle continued until 1798, when the master of Frederick Academy, Samuel Knox, addressed the legislature. Winner of a prize essay on education awarded by the American Philosophical Society, he commanded attention. He stressed the necessity of diffusing knowledge to all corners of the state instead of wasting funds on the institutions at Annapolis and Chestertown. "In all ages," he told them, "it has been the policy of those governments that existed by the slavish ignorance of the people to establish one or two sumptuously endowed schools for the sons of fortune and affluence—the expecting brood of despotical succession, leaving the canaille, the ignorant herd, to live and die, the profanum vulgus, the despised, enslaved and stupid multitude." He advocated the founding of primary schools and academies as the "nurseries" of the colleges with a national university at the pinnacle. The legislature should establish a board of education and maintain a uniform system of training. By the early nineteenth century the legislature merely committed itself to subsidizing the county schools that were already established and supporting new ones upon application by the people of the locality.[123]

The Revolution not only gave impetus to organized education but also stimulated learning generally. The revolutionary mind reasoned that if man would rule himself, ignorance became the enemy of that new order of things. The newspaper was the most popular instrument of information and education. At the beginning of the Revolution there was only the *Maryland Gazette* of Annapolis. In 1776 Goddard produced a Baltimore paper, and by 1787 the *Palladium of Freedom*, a daily, was undertaken there.

---

123. Samuel Knox, *An Essay on the Best System of Liberal Education Adopted to the Genius of the Government of The United States* . . . (Balt.: n.p., 1799); Leo Joseph McCormick, *Church State Relationships in Maryland* (Wash.: Catholic University of America Press, 1942), p. 78.

Weekly or biweekly newspapers were published at Easton, Georgetown, and Frederick, where Matthias Bartgis' weekly became a fiery organ reflecting German and small farmer viewpoints.[124]

The growth of newspapers indicated increased interest in book publishing in the urban areas of the state, but especially in Baltimore, which became one of the important printing centers in the country. Printers frequently augmented income by book selling, and merchants also listed books for sale, so that Marylanders had a ready availability of reading matter in politics and philosophy, religion, soldiery, history, and business methods, as well as in the always popular ancient writers. Before the Revolution there was one circulating library—this in Annapolis, whose owner, William Aikman, boasted holdings of 12,000 titles. Upon visiting Annapolis in 1800, however, Mason Locke Weems stated that there was no library in the city, though a little earlier (1784) Father John Carroll found the Annapolis library "adequate" in preparing his answer to Wharton. In 1787 a circulating library was opened in Baltimore. By 1790 there were three of them.[125]

Despite the numerous and severe problems which Maryland revolutionaries dealt with, they were not a somber lot. The theatre at Annapolis continued to stage plays. In Annapolis an advertisement of the playhouse had a tragedy—*The Grecian Daughter* and a comedy, *The Lying Valet* on the same bill. In 1782 a theatre was founded in Baltimore. Horse racing at Annapolis and Baltimore was not suspended by the rebels, nor were dancing and popular lectures on literature and science— these usually held in the taverns.

Men of the period were not only absorbed in the maxims of self-government, but in the universal laws of nature. Science greatly absorbed Marylanders. For example, the work in mathematics and astronomy of Benjamin Banneker received acclaim on both sides of the Atlantic. The influence of the Medical College of nearby Philadelphia caused a strong contingent of medical practitioners to come to Baltimore and incorporate their own medical society. A lively debate over the practice of

124. Joseph Towne Wheeler, *The Maryland Press,* 1777–90 (Balt.: M.H.S., 1938), pp. 57-9, 71-75.
125. *Ibid.,* pp. vii-viii Joseph Towne Wheeler, "Booksellers and Circulating Libraries" *M.H.M. XXXIV* (June 1939), 111-37. *M.G.*, June 5, 1777.

medicine by unqualified persons occupied the pages of the newspaper and was just as hot as the issues over the Senate, paper money, or the new federal union. Dissection of human cadavers brought stormy protests in 1793, but earlier a Maryland poet wrote:[126]

> Our Life's a storm and let the
> science be,
> To turn its rigors to felicity.

Revolutionary Marylanders were optimists. Feeling that man could unlock the secrets of the universe, they were not deterred by seemingly insurmountable social problems. Slavery was one of these. A strong strain of abolitionism ran through Maryland revolutionary thought. Religious conviction was responsible for the movement, and this, mated to the high ideals of freedom then current, stirred Maryland consciences. The movement against the keeping of slaves had grown among Quakers since the visit of the abolitionist Quaker John Woolman to the Eastern Shore in 1766. Meetings of the Friends resolved to discourage slavery by forbidding candidates for the eldership to hold slaves, by visiting and persuading brothers to free their slaves, and finally by the disowning of a Quaker slave-holder who proved stubborn.[127]

The Methodists also opposed the institution. Before the war, John Wesley adamantly opposed slavery, and American leaders such as Asbury, Coke, Garrettson, and Thomas Haskins constantly preached against slavery as a sinful practice and on their circuits joyfully witnessed manumission by members of the church. Typical of the combined religious and political sentiments of the era was that of the Methodist Wingott family: "slavery is contrary to the Golden Law of God on which hang all the law and prophets and to the Glorious Revolution that has lately taken place in America."

At the Baltimore Christmas Conference of 1784, the abolition of slavery was accepted as a rule of membership. But among the general Methodist membership the resolution proved so unpopular that it was suspended in six months. Yet abolitionism

---

126. *M.G.* Sept. 10, 1779; Jan. 28, 1780; Mar. 27, 1783. Silvio A. Bedini, *The Life of Benjamin Banneker* (New York: Charles Scribner's Sons, 1972). Scharf, *Chronicles of Baltimore*, p. 255.

127. Kenneth Carroll, "Religious Influences on the Manumission of Slaves," *M.H.M.*, LVI (June, 1961), 176-97.

was not forgotten; in 1796 it revived. The conference ruled that every official of the church must emancipate his slaves. Slaveholders who sought membership must be admonished by the ministers about slavery, and members could not buy slaves unless provision be made for the freedom of their offspring. Slave-traders were excommunicated. Traveling preachers must free their slaves where state law permitted it.[128]

Abolition was not exclusive to churches. Though quickly deleted, the earliest draft of the Declaration of Rights contained a clause to end the importation of slaves. In 1789 Charles Carroll, Nicholas Hammond, and John Hull stunned the legislature by introducing a law for gradual abolition of slavery. All female slave children were to be bought by the state. They were to be educated and bound out to the age of 28 when they were to be freed. Slaves under forty-five were also to be freed under certain conditions. The bill also intended to prevent the "rigorous exportation of Negroes and mulattoes." A move to commit the bill to a joint committee of both houses was defeated, 39–15. Members from the large slaveholding counties voted against it, while lesser slaveholding counties were divided. This was a culmination of frequently unsuccessful petitions to the house from 1785 on the the subject of abolition.[129]

In 1789 citizens of Baltimore formed the Maryland "Society for Promoting the Abolition of Slavery and the Relief of Poor Negroes unlawfully held in Bondage." Among its officers were several of the leading men of the period: Samuel Chase, Luther Martin, Gerard Hopkins. It soon boasted a membership of between two and three hundred and procured a suitable building in the city for its activities. In 1791, at a public meeting of the society, George Buchanan, a physician of the Medical Society who was daring enough to give lectures on obstetrics in that age, addressed the public on the inconsistency of slavery and liberty.[130]

---

128. N. C. Hughes, Jr., "The Methodist Christmas Conference: Baltimore, Dec. 24, 1784–Jan. 2, 1785," *M.H.M.*, LIV (Sept., 1959), 288. Haskins Journal, L.C.: Dec. 3, 1782; April 2, 1785.

129. Jeffrey R. Brackett, *The Negro in Maryland . . . J.H.U. Studies*, Extra vol. VI (Baltimore: J.H. Press, 1889), pp. 52-54. *V.&P.* House 1789 pp. 10-14; 64-65. Senate, 1789, 5-34. Petitions relative to abolition came from Queen Anne's, Kent, Caroline, Dorchester, Worcester, Talbot in 1785 and were read and rejected 32–22; *V.&P.* House 1785, pp. 36-9.

130. Scharf, *Chronicles*, pp. 255-56. William Frederick Poole, *Anti-Slavery*

What a distressing scene is here before us. America, I start at your situation. The idea of these direful effects of slavery demand your most serious attention. What! Shall a people, who flew to arms with the valour of Roman Citizens, when incroachments were made upon their liberties by the invasion of foreign powers, now basely descend to cherish the seed and propagate the growth of evil, which they bodily sought to eradicate? To the eternal infamy of our country, this will be handed down to posterity, written in the blood of African innocence.

Buchanan reminded his hearers (and readers, for the address was published) not to become "apostates" to their revolutionary principles of equality and "life, liberty, and the pursuit of happiness."

The society, which backed the gradual abolitionist move in the legislature, was very active. It assisted runaway slaves or those who were enslaved but claimed to be freemen. So blatant were their operations that the society became the target for numerous complaints in petitions to the legislature. A committee to investigate its activities reported that the society had acted in an "indecent and unjustifiable manner" in a case in which it had refused to turn over two runaway blacks to their owners. The legislature condemned the society, but refused, by three votes, to resolve that it operated in repugnance to the laws of the state. The populace became so militantly opposed to the society that it was forced to discontinue as an antislavery organization, although it supported a school for teaching Negro children. Other societies, however, persisted on the Eastern Shore, and Maryland abolitionists sent delegates to attend the first convention of antislavery societies in Philadelphia in 1794.[131]

The antislavery movement was not a popular one despite the fact that it was spawned by the Revolution. The situation was as Ezekiel Haynie warned his brother Luther, a professor at Washington College, to stop disputing with slaveholders ", . . . people who would not be likely to hear reason, or even the pathetic voice of *Human Misery* when it tended to diminish their *Idol* Property."[132] Yet the small number of avid supporters were

*Opinions before the Year 1800* (Cinn.: Robert Clark Co., 1873), reprints Buchanan's speech, p. 82 ff. p. 12.

131. *Maryland Society for the Promoting the Abolition of Slavery at a Meeting . . .* 4 February 1792 (Balt.: Goddard and Angel, [1792]), in M.H.S. Poole, *Anti-Slavery Opinions;* Brackett, *Negro in Maryland.*

132. *M.H.M., XXXVI,* 212.

among the revolutionary leadership and were influential. In 1796, under the direction of William Pinkney, the legislature approved the right of a master, even in his last illness, to manumit slaves.[133] There was a marked increase in manumissions during the era and thereafter so that on the eve of the Civil War Maryland held the largest free-Negro population of any of the old southern states.

The Revolution not only caused men to tackle insurmountable social problems; they also dreamed of commercial empire, one of national unity into whose orbit the vast western territories would be tightly drawn. In 1784 General Washington journeyed to his lands in the west to reassert his prewar claims in Ohio. More than ever impressed with the potential wealth of the northwest, he realized that its natural flow of commerce would move southward into Spanish territory and that the eastern seaboard states would be divested of economic and consequently strong political ties with those who eventually settled the region.

Washington therefore proposed to Virginia and Maryland that the navigation of the Potomac be improved by canal building and other projects in order to open an eastward flow of commerce. Commissioners appointed by both states agreed, and the Potomac Company was thus formed. Each state promised the purchase of fifty shares of stock, and a public sale of stock was subscribed to enthusiastically. The Potomac Company was the first of the great projects for the internal improvements of the state. Only the Baltimore business interests were critical of it, as they were of any state-supported commercial route that threatened their supremacy of trade. Another canal, proposed from Philadelphia, mainly threatened Baltimore commercial hegemony over a wide area about the Susquehanna. This canal, which would join the Elk and Delaware rivers, was vigorously opposed. As a Baltimore writer suggested, Maryland's best pol-

---

133. *American Museum,* VI (July, 1789), 74-77 contains Pinkney's speech against slavery in the House, also *ibid* (1798), pp. 79-89. Mary Stoughton Locke, *Anti-Slavery in America . . . 1619–1808* (Boston: Ginn & Co., 1901), pp. 120-21. For Maryland Negro opinion on slavery and the revolution, *Journal of Negro History,* I (Jan., 1916), 49-54. One who signed himself "Othello" addressed his contemporaries from Baltimore and wrote of the principles of the revolution and adds: "Blush ye revolted colonies, for having apostasized from your own principles," May 10, 1788 p. 49. See also Benjamin Brawley, *Early American Negro Writers. Essay Index Reprint Series* (Freeport, N.Y.: Books for Libraries, 1968: reprinted from the original by Univ. of N.C. Press, 1935), pp. 79-83.

icy was to "adopt some wholesome provisions to retain the exportation of these important articles [wheat and flour] from her own seaports, [rather] than assist in forming a highway for their safe passage into Delaware."

The people were still mercantilist-minded internally but not internationally, as the state licensed, gave franchises or bounties to stages, ferries, road builders and inventors as encouragements leading to a strong economy.[134]

The work on the Potomac Canal proceeded with characteristic optimism. There were immediate problems of management. Labor proved to be scarce so that James Rumsey, the manager of the enterprise who was working also on the perfection of a steam-propelled craft, was forced to hire slaves and purchase servants. Clashes among those workmen proved an obstacle as did also conflicts between the workmen and the people who had settled their homes along the river. In their opinion the workmen behaved riotously and drank too much after hours. Runaway servants plagued management. The elements—heavy rains particularly—caused many a slowdown and loss to the operation. Deepening the river proved an insurmountable feat for the engineering of the period. Yet by 1789 by-passing canals were completed at Shenandoah, Seneca, and Great Falls so that a few vessels arrived from Fort Cumberland to within nine miles of Georgetown.[135]

It was neither the combat with nature nor human problems that almost killed this and other important dreams of internal improvements, but the downturn in the economy generally. For example, the Potomac Canal Company discovered that it had underestimated the cost of the project and very quickly it was in need of more money. The problem was then compounded by the inability of subscribers to the stock to pay for their holdings. The original subscribers were substantially wealthy men, but by

---

134. Ralph D. Gray, *The National Waterway: A History of the Chesapeake and Delaware Canal, 1769–1965* (Urbana: University of Illinois Press, 1967), p. 11. James Weston Livingood, *The Philadelphia-Baltimore Trade Rivalry, 1780–1860* (Harrisburg: Pennsylvania Historical and Museum Commission, 1947), pp. 14-16, 83-86. Mary Jane Dowd, "The State in the Maryland Economy, 1776–1807." *M.H.M.*, LVII (June–Sept. 1962), 90-132; 229-258.

135. Mrs. Cora Bacon-Foster, "Early Chapters in the Development of the Potomac Route to the West," *Records of the Columbia Historical Society* (Wash.: C.H.S., 1912), pp. 125, 128-132, 264 *et passim*.

1785–86 many of them were nearly penniless.[136] This was typical; the entire population of the state was in dire financial straits by then.

The enormity of the wartime economy plagued Maryland within a few years of the peace of 1783. Money, apparently hard money, was exceedingly scarce since the war, and that situation worsened.[137] A paper issue of 1781 was not sufficient to meet needs. Many business men would not traffic in any kind of paper currency. The inflation of the war years destroyed their faith in this kind of currency. The state began a policy of retiring the paper so that by the middle of the decade even it was scarce.

The state was bankrupt from the great debts incurred during the war. It was not meeting its obligations to pay its soldiers, let alone the new promises made for internal improvements and education. It found its citizens frequently petitioning for relief from payment of taxes. When the state sought to enforce laws to confiscate for non-payment of taxes, officials were resisted, sometimes violently, by the people. If a debtor's property was put up for sheriff's sale, the neighborhood prevented such disposal. The receipts from the confiscation of British property, which it was hoped would pay debts and be sufficient to stabilize the paper issue of 1781, proved negligible. Much of the property was purchased on credit, and credit extensions became the rule rather than the exception. Finally, the state allowed holders to keep their property if the interest on the debt was at least paid; even this was not often met.

The number of bankruptcies and cases of private indebtedness in the courts mounted annually, and by 1789 it was staggering. Not only the poor and middling were dunned to death but many

---

136. *Ibid.* H. Gates to William Hartshorne Mar. 31, 1787; John Hopkins to H. Gates Dec. 18, 1786.
137. Capt. Charles Ridgely letters between 1784–88 are composed of dunning notices. Ridgely Family Papers, M.H.S. Woolsey & Salmon Letterbook, 1783–84 evidences growing mercantile distresses. Louis Maganzin, "Economic Depression in Maryland and Virginia, 1783–87" (Ph.D. dissertation, History Department Georgetown University), 1967, pp. 100-101, 103, 106, 112-18, 121-24, 143-44, *passim* Galloway Papers, 1784–87, L.C. Paul Bentalou to Mordecai Gist, Oct. 11, 1787, L.C. on trouble with French ports; Peter Changeur to M. Gist, July 30, 1787. O. H. Williams writes to Merchants Elliot & Williams, June 18, 1788: "... appearances are dark now—save yourselves if you can," O. H. Williams Papers, *M.H.S.* item *Calendar*, 409. Delaplaine, *Life of Johnson*, pp. 431-32 *M.H.M.*, *XXI*, 192-97, LV, 237-38. Stuart Weems Bruchey, *Robert Oliver, J.H.U. Studies, LXXIV*, No. 1 (Balt.: J.H. Press, 1956), p. 61.

great planters and merchants, as creditors unable to receive payments, themselves fell victim to the depression.

Marylanders, not unlike other Americans, thought the commercial millennium had arrived with peace. Trade in their staples so expensively encumbered by the old imperial restrictions was unfettered after 1783. Trade should now flower and flourish in the new freedom. Such was not soon to be the case; almost a decade would pass before expectations would be satisfied. Meanwhile, Marylanders found that British mercantilism adversely affected them. British ports were closed and British houses which had long extended credit were not only adamant about collecting old debts but were indeed unwilling to extend further credits. Allowed by law to sue for prewar debts in the Maryland courts, British creditors met with extra-legal resistance. In Charles County a riot ensued when a representative of a British firm tried to recover prewar debts. The bitterness infected healthy commercial relations with the old empire, and they remained at a low point.

The trade with the continent which freedom opened up proved illusory during the decade. The mid-1780's witnessed bumper crops of grains for sale on the European market, so that Maryland's flour and wheat had to be sold at disastrously low prices. Furthermore, the French, Dutch, and Spanish traders drove hard bargains with American shippers, and they were unwilling to offer the long terms of credit that Americans were accustomed to receiving from the English. Nor did these nations produce the needed and cheap manufactures, particularly in tools and cloth.

Added to these economic complexities of the new freedom, Marylanders were angered by international banditry. In 1783 vessels had penetrated the Mediterranean market. The following year, Algerian pirates seized two ships and thereafter virtually closed traffic in the region, so that another commercial vista was beclouded while the nation was unable to do anything about it.

As the depression deepened, it seemed that even nature was against the Marylanders. The winter of 1784–85 was so severe that the Baltimore port was iced-in well into March. Shipping could not move. The spring thaw brought freshets which wiped out farms and stock.

In their distress the people turned to government. Petitioning the governor, one group lamented:[138]

> We were unhappily involved in debt before the late war, some of us to the British and others to domestic creditors ... and taxes are unusual and very burthensome. The scarcity of specie [is] great. We are not able to pay the present taxes, and satisfy our creditors. We are really in a most deplorable situation. The most wealthy, (a very few excepted) can not command cash to answer the present demands of their creditors. The very great number of suits for debt in the general courts and the county courts prove the melancholy truth. Our tobacco and lumber bear a very low price, and the value of our wheat has fallen. Our property is at the mercy of sheriffs and collectors and [when] sold will not bring one-third of its real value. If our government [will not offer] relief, many of us, with our families, must be inevitably ruined.

The more responsive House of Delegates considered various forms of debtor relief, while the Senate tried to abridge the right of appeal in cases of indebtedness that were used by debtors to stave off final payment. The act "to prevent mischievous suits" was sarcastically vetoed by the house, 43–9: reflecting upon the present situation of this country ". . . our citizens largely involved in debt . . . we cannot agree to a bill tending . . . to deprive distressed debtors . . . of that time within which they may be enabled to extricate their persons and property out of the power of cruel or oppressive creditors."

Meanwhile, the house decided that a reissue of bills of credit was necessary and that measure passed, 38–22. It was unanimously rejected by the Senate. This inaugurated a political fight between the two houses, until finally, at the insistence of the delegates, the issue was referred to the people for instruction. This was to include, however, commentary from the people as to whether the upper house was open to instruction by the electorate, and this last was regarded as a blow at the independence of the Senate.

Senators bestirred themselves, therefore, and campaigned in the press and otherwise on the constitutional issue. The returning opinions were favorable to the Senate, and the paper money politicians of the house moved with greater caution. The result

---

138. *To His Excellency the Governor and Council*, 1784, Broadside, L.C.

was that no paper money was issued by Maryland, nor for that matter was much done in the way of debtor relief; for other attempts to lighten the burden of debt were victims of the battle between the two houses.[139]

Unquestionably, the leaders of the house were mistaken in confusing a constitutional question with an economic one.[140] Perhaps the people did not think that a paper issue was the answer; fears of that remedy still remained to haunt them. Besides that, the anti-paper money advocates readily let it be known that the leadership of that faction, Chase, Paca, Ridgely, and others, were not disinterested parties. Most were deeply indebted to the state for purchases of confiscated property, and they had a special interest in that panacea for economic ills. Nor was the voter ready at this point to reform the upper house.

5

POLITICAL GOALS

The fight over paper money and the Senate still raged when Congress issued a call for delegates to revise the Articles of Confederation, and thus such leaders on both sides as Chase and Carroll were fearful of leaving the state. Elected instead were Luther Martin, James McHenry, Daniel Carroll, Daniel of St. Thomas Jenifer and John Francis Mercer. Of these, Martin and McHenry were the most active in the convention, even though McHenry was absent for a long period owing to the illness of his brother.

Several developments greatly motivated Maryland in the formation of the new union. The people were nationalists. During the war the state's troops had fought not for the home state, but in New York, New Jersey, Pennsylvania, Virginia, the Carolinas, and Georgia. The campaigning on the continent had inculcated notions of national unity in officer and enlistee alike. Maryland was instrumental in founding the first union under the confederation by insisting that western lands be granted to the union as a national domain and for the support of that government. Maryland's reasoning was not entirely altruistic, for the

---

139. Crowl, *Maryland during and after the Revolution*, pp. 90-2, Ch. IV.

140. Jackson Turner Main, *The Upper House in Revolutionary America* (Madison: University of Wisconsin Press, 1967), pp. 212-14.

state had no claims to the west and Maryland feared domination by those states that did. There were other important signposts of nationalism through the period. Since 1776, citizens of the state always wrote favorably toward a strong union. The revolutionary organization of the church was along nationalistic lines and Marylanders even envisioned their local schools culminating in a national university. At one point the legislature and the City Council of Annapolis offered the city as the national and permanent capital.[141] Maryland's accommodation with Virginia concerning the improvement of the navigation of the Potomac was one of the prime examples of inter-state cooperation rather than of the too frequent rivalry and divisiveness of states, and thus the Annapolis convention was called, from which the seeds of stronger national unity germinated. Fear of further weakening the confederation government prevented the attendance of a Maryland delegation. But generally the perfection of national union was inextricably an object of the Revolution in Maryland, not a reaction against it.

At the moment, the strongest motive behind a new unification was economic. The state government obviously was ineffective in halting economic decline. Paper money had failed. Indebtedness continued and threatened general disorder. The state alone could neither effectively threaten nor bargain with a piqued Great Britain, with stagnation of commerce as a result; nor could a local government implement and protect the new avenues of commerce. Every farmer, large or small, whether wheat or tobacco producer, was an exporter and needed the overseas market and the kind of government that could assure it.

A petition to the new government from the politically active and vocal mechanics, tradesmen, and manufacturers of Baltimore underscored economic problems which it was hoped would be solved by the "General Government." It spoke of the failures of the state government to enact a viable economic program. It addressed itself to the "gloomy future this country exhibits" and described "the number ... of poor increasing for want of employment; foreign debts accumulating, houses and lands depreciating in value; trade and manufactures languishing and expiring." The list was impressive. There were 726 signatures, very few of them prominent men, except Daniel Carroll

---

141. Md. Misc. May 12, 1783, L.C. *V.&P.* April 1783, p. 18.

and William Goddard. Most were mechanics and laboring men, though not all; some were merchants and planters such as Robert Purviance. Two were evidently illiterate, giving marks instead of signatures.[142]

Martin and McHenry reflected the general desire of the new government to handle the economic difficulties. In the convention, Martin supported the state power to emit bills of credit, which he thought necessary from time to time. But in this he found himself alone, not just in the Maryland delegation but in the convention as a whole. In the committees, in the after-hour convention socializing, and in the Maryland caucuses, McHenry was a proponent of increasing the commercial powers of the central government, allowing it to levy taxes on imports, so long as these were fair and equal and would not serve the interests of one state against another.[143]

Luther Martin played the largest role of the Maryland delegation. This was as a political dissenter to the new system. He spent nearly a month in silence, he recalled, to listen and observe the unfolding of the new plan. He generally lined up with the small states with their inherent fears of domination by the larger states. Whether Martin grasped the Maryland situation is questionable. Geographically, Maryland was small in area, but her population of 319,728 persons was the third largest of the southern states and larger than seven of the thirteen comprising the union. The amount of her commerce and productivity ranked Maryland with the largest states. Nevertheless, Martin opposed the system of representation based upon population. He considered the counting of slaves for purposes of representation and taxation an anomaly in a republican system. He argued that to legalize the system of slavery in this manner was wrong and "inconsistent with the principles of the Revolution, and dishonorable to the

---

142. *American State Papers: Documents Legislative and Executive* (Wash.: Gales & Seaton, 1832), V, 5-8.

143. *M.H.M., XXVII*, 280-93; Jonathan Elliott, *The Debates in the State Conventions on the Adoption of the Federal Constitution* . . . (Phil.: J. B. Lippincott Company, 1836), I, 369-70 *passim:* Martin's, *Genuine Information . . . Relative to the Proceedings of the General Convention* (Hereafter *Elliott's Debates*); Max Farrand, ed. *The Records of the Federal Convention of 1787* (4 vol.; New Haven: Yale University Press, 1937), III, 144-47 *passim;* McHenry, *Life and Correspondence,* 97-110.

American character, to have such a feature in the constitution."[144] McHenry may have agreed with this position. He was a gradual emancipationist. Here was probably reflected that minority of Maryland's revolutionaries who did not like slavery. Martin wanted the election of justices controlled by the states. He feared the potential for judicial review by the Supreme Court. He desired a weak executive rather than a strong one, and he suspected the potential for an overriding power in according the executive the veto over legislation, and he agreed with the executive's power to nominate administrators. All of these things built a monarchical system which the Revolution had wiped out. He wrote critically that the convention was"eternally troubled with arguments and precedents of the British government." However negative Martin's work seemed, his abilities at law and his effective oratory probably prevented the erection of a stronger central government. His most persuasive device was to remind fellow convention members that the new plan would need approval by the people. Although he won several battles—equality of representation of the states in the Senate the major one—he nevertheless returned to Maryland lividly opposed to the erection of the new government. Of the system, Martin remarked to Jenifer: "I'll be hanged if ever the people of Maryland agree to it." "I advise you" said Jenifer, "to stay in Philadelphia lest you should be hanged."[145]

The delegation returned home. Besides Martin, only John Francis Mercer opposed the results of the convention. McHenry had opposed many parts of it, but the patriotism and abilities of several of the gentlemen at Philadelphia persuaded him to sign the document before leaving.

During the summer of 1787, while the convention met, the Baltimore papers carried a few items on the convention; most of these were complimentary and looked toward improvement of the system, though one writer fretted about the secrecy of the proceedings. After the adjournment of the convention, the Baltimore papers in particular reported the early state ratifications. The articles in the newspapers were generally federalist in sen-

---

144. *Life and Correspondence,* pp. 124-25; *Records,* III, 151-59. *M.H.M.,* *XXVII,* 286.
145. *Records,* III, 85.

timent. As early as possible the text of the constitution was printed.[146]

A new House of Delegates was due for election. The federalists began a campaign to elect men favorable to the new system, for opponents could stop ratification by not voting for a state convention. In general, that campaign went smoothly. The powerful Samuel Chase spoke on the Court House steps in Baltimore. He asserted that he favored a strong union and "increase of powers in Congress"; yet he said the constitution would overthrow the Maryland constitution, and that the new government must be approved by two successive sessions of the legislature. He also said "I think the federal government must be greatly altered. I have not formed my opinion, whether the plan proposed ought to be accepted, as it stands, without any amendment or alteration. The subject is very momentous and involves the greatest consequences. If elected, I will vote for and use my endeavors to procure a recommendation by the legislature to call a convention, as soon as it can conveniently be done, unless otherwise directed by this town."[147] The town must have instructed him to clear up the contradictions in his address, for the next day he sent a note to the journal and advocated a call for a convention as early in the spring as possible.

Chase, who seemed to have been regarded as a proponent of the new plan, polled three-fourths of the votes cast. Once elected, he clarified his position. In his letter of October 12 to the inhabitants of Baltimore town he warned the people against a petition circulated through the town requesting an immediate call for a convention and approval for the constitution without alteration or amendment. He cautioned against surprise and stated that the new government should have the maturest and most careful deliberation. Chase now showed his hand as an antifederalist.[148] The main tactic of the antifederalists was to cause delay, since these moves were already successful in New Hampshire and Virginia. Delay could cause defeat of the new government. Given time, it could be shot through with sugges-

146. Bernard C. Steiner, "Maryland's Adoption of the Federal Constitution," *American Historical Review*, V (Oct. 1899; Jan. 1900), 22-44; 207-24.

147. Paul Leicester Ford, *Essays on the Constitution of the United States* (Brooklyn: Historical Printing Club, 1892), pp. 325-26.

148. *Ibid.*, pp. 327 ff.

tions for changes and amendments so that it would be inoperable.

Why was there antifederalist opposition in Maryland? The antifederalists were the proponents of paper money. They had been beaten at home and the new system also contained prohibitions against it. More legitimately, the Philadelphia convention had committed a grievous error; it had omitted a bill of rights. When the question arose in Philadelphia, the answer was that the state constitutions included such rights.

McHenry reported to the legislature briefly. He praised the new government and generally described its evolution from the Virginia plan. Luther Martin's report took three meetings to present and received a wider audience by its publication in the *Baltimore Advertiser*. He continued to be vehemently critical of the work of the convention and implied a conspiracy between Washington and Franklin to increase the national power of Massachusetts, Pennsylvania, and Virginia. He emphasized those things which might strike home to Marylanders. For example, he expressed fear of the appointing power and of the enormous increase in the number of such offices created by the new government. He stated that the greatest part of the work of the convention was done in the last few days after many of its members had departed, especially those who had opposed the new government. In this period the executive was strengthened and allowance was made for his reelection whereas earlier this had been prohibited. That no state should impair the obligations of contracts was a product of the committee on style rather than the full convention. One of the delegates, probably McHenry, interrupted Martin's long indictment of the secrecy of the proceedings: Martin's assertion was untrue that the reason for the departure of New York's Robert Yates and John Lansing was their disgust with the proceedings.[149]

Martin's partisan speech did not prevent the legislature's call for a convention. The Senate resolved to have the convention meet March 1, 1788. But the house postponed the meeting by a close vote, 24–23 until April 21; this, although regarded as a defeat for the Constitution, was accepted by the Senate. By a

---

149. "Genuine Information," *Elliott's Debates*, I 344-89. Farrand, *Records*, III, 147-50; Paul Clarkson and Samuel R. Jett, *Luther Martin of Maryland* (Baltimore: J.H. Press, 1970), pp. 136-39.

narrow margin, 28–21, the antifederalist forces lost a stratagem when the House allowed a majority vote of the convention for approving the Constitution, rather than unanimous consent of the delegation, which possibly would have defeated ratification.[150]

It was obvious that the federalist advantage in the house was uncomfortably small, only about nine votes. The federalists set about to strengthen their position and undo the powerful influence of Chase and Martin.

The public was bombarded with pro and con arguments on the Constitution. Martin elaborated his attacks further, many of which were published outside the state. The anti's employed scare tactics: the Constitution would undermine basic liberties; the militia could be sent outside the state by this new and all powerful government; the Constitution was the result of a French plot forwarded by Robert Morris.[151] Of all the many federalist writers, the most effective was Judge Alexander Contee Hanson who wrote under the pen name of Aristides. Assuaging fears of power, he played particularly on the theme of necessity for order. He spoke of the need for unity and its economic benefits, especially in trade with Europe where new respect would be gained for the republic. A grand policy whose aims were the "Restoration of Public and Private Faith" in credit, he stated, was one of the principal benefits to be derived from the new union.[152] He described the dangers inherent in antifederalist calls for amendments or a new national convention. Such would result in confusion and a more deteriorated situation among the states than had obtained before. Lastly, the Constitution had to be approved without alterations.[153]

The campaigning was vigorous. In Montgomery County, John Mason of Virginia made several antifederalist speeches to counteract the federalism of the lawyer, John Dorsey. Dorsey won, and three federalists to one antifederalist were elected. In Anne Arundel County, despite the efforts of the Carrolls, the county

---

150. *A.H.R.*, V, 30-31.

151. Daniel Carroll to James Madison May 28, 1788, *Documentary History of the Constitution* . . . Part 1 (Wash.: Dept. of State, 1905), IV, 636-37.

152. Paul Leicester Ford, *Pamphlets on the Constitution* (Brooklyn: De Capo Press, repr. 1968 [1888]), pp. 234-35.

153. *Ibid; Remarks on the Proposed Plan of a Federal Government* . . ., pp. 221-34, 242-48, 250-56.

went to the anti's. Mercer's and Jeremiah T. Chase's efforts apparently changed the political picture there in the last days before the polling. Harford and Baltimore Counties elected antifederalist delegates. In Baltimore many irregularities took place at the polls. Such persons ineligible to vote as servants, slaves, apprentice boys, and unnaturalized citizens helped turn the tide for the federalists.[154]

The final results were disappointing for the anti's. Only twelve antifederalists were chosen; even frontier Washington County favored the federalists unanimously. With only the exceptions mentioned, every other county was federalist, and these delegates came armed with instructions from their constituents to ratify the Constitution without delay or amendment.

The convention met in Annapolis on Monday, April 21. It consisted of seventy-six members, two of whom were unable to attend because of illness. Some may have dodged their creditors. One, long-suffering creditor R. Furguson, attended the "clambake to dun delegates, one of whom he referred to as 'Robinhood'."[155]

The small antifederalist minority was led by Samuel and Jeremiah T. Chase, William Paca the former governor, and like Chase a Signer of the Declaration of Independence, and Francis Mercer. Martin's sore throat prevented his speaking, and, as the federalist William Smith put it ". . . . saved a great deal of time and money to the state." But Martin was busy in the evenings in the tavern, where he asserted that the federalists plotted for a king, and that he had the names of these conspirators. He was very ineffective.[156]

On April 22 the convention organized, elected George Plater as the president, and accepted some simple rules of procedure. The convention determined that the Constitution should be considered as a whole, not debated in parts. Delegates feared delay; time was crucial. As matters stood with the rest of the states, Maryland's ratification was a turning point in favor of the new government. The delegates insisted that they should

154. *A.H.R.*, V, 38, 39–44.

155. R. Furguson to Alexander Hamilton May 14, 1788, Georgetown University Archives.

156. William Smith to O. H. Williams April 28, 1788, item 401; Daniel Carroll to James Madison, May 28, 1788, *Documentary History*, IV, 638.

The State House at Annapolis, scene of ratification of the Federal Constitution and other important acts of the Revolution. *M.H.S.*

144

strictly adhere to the instructions from constituents, plainly stating that they should ratify without changes.[157]

On Thursday Samuel Chase arrived and the opponents of the Constitution stirred. Chase spoke for two and one-half hours. The Constitution was defective: "The powers to be vested in the new government are deadly to the cause of liberty and should be amended before adoption." His speech was received with a "profound silence." That afternoon Paca stated that he had a variety of objections to the Constitution and that he had several amendments in mind that he thought should not be a condition of ratification but should be given the members in Congress as instructions. He asked for time to present these, which Johnson amiably recommended be allowed. On Friday morning he began to offer his amendments. He was repeatedly interrupted, however, by members from Frederick, Talbot, Kent, Somerset, Prince George's, Worcester, Queen Anne's, Dorchester, Calvert, and Caroline Counties, as well as others from Annapolis and Baltimore cities. All cited instructions to ratify without amendments. Paca was thus unable to read them, and the vote for ratification was taken. It was, 63–11.

On Saturday afternoon Paca said that he had voted for the Constitution. But that in order that he and his people would support the government, he felt that amendments must be peaceably proposed; otherwise his constituents might oppose the government firmly, "he believed even with arms." Many delegates now persuaded themselves that they could consider amendments and suggested them in their private capacities as citizens. A distinctly novel idea, commented staunch federalist Hanson, who believed that the convention was entangling itself and falling into an antifederalist trap to delay the whole process. A committee to report amendments was voted favorably, nevertheless, 66–7.

A committee of nine federalists and four anti's was formed. Paca presented his amendments. These contained provisions for trial by jury in criminal cases—that Congress hold none but the delegated powers of the Constitution, a guarantee of rights under search and seizure, that there be freedom of the press, that there be no quartering of soldiers on the people in time of peace. These were agreeable to the committee. But the federalist mem-

---

157. The truncated Journal of the Convention is in *ibid.*, IV, 97-122.

bers would not assent to such amendments as those to limit
Congressional power to use the militia beyond the state; to alter
the time and place of elections, and to impose taxes. Nor would
they agree to a prohibition against standing armies in time of
peace or to a limitation on the president as commander of the
armed forces or a declaration concerning freedom of religion.
Thus the committee was unable to report, and the federalist
majority decided against bringing in even those amendments
which had been approved.

As chairman, Paca explained to the convention what had occurred in the committee and read all the proposed amendments.
An attempt to consider the amendments was refused. A motion
was then carried to adjourn, 47–27.[158]

Ratification had won. Federalists in Virginia rejoiced, as it
threw more weight in their favor.[159] When the Maryland result
was known in South Carolina, at least one delegate there
changed his mind and cast his vote in favor of ratification. But the
struggle for amendments was not ended. The hasty action of the
federalists was "exposed" in the newspapers, and the proposals
for amendments were published. Antifederalists continued to
complain that the Constitution could not be approved by the
state unless two successive General Assemblies passed it.
Otherwise, it altered the state's constitution. It was alleged that
insufficient time had been given before the election for the
convention, and that of 25,000 qualified voters only 6,000 had
voted.

The election for the House of Delegates of 1788 saw another
hard-fought contest. The issue was that the house should petition the new federal Congress for amendments. On that issue
Samuel Chase lost his Baltimore town seat along with David
McMechen; McHenry and John Coulter, federalists, replaced
them. Disorders and violence again marked the election and
were the subject of investigation by the house. One antifederalist was threatened by a mob that was determined to pull
down his home.[160] The house did not reflect such violence; it

---

158. Elliott's *Debates* II, "Fragment of Facts," 547-56; *Documentary History*,
IV, Hanson's "Narrative," 645-64.

159. *Ibid.*, IV, 615.

160. Delaplaine, *Johnson*, pp. 452-53. McHenry, *Life and Correspondence*,
pp. 114-15; *Maryland Journal and Baltimore Advertiser* Sept. 23, 1788; O. H.
Williams, *Calendar*, items. 429, 431. *M.H.M.*, XVIII, 311-12.

William Paca, Signer of the Declaration of Independence and proponent of amendments to the Federal Constitution to include basic rights. by Charles Willson Peale. *Peabody Institute—on deposit in M.H.S.*

accepted an oath to support the Constitution, and established electoral districts for representation in the federal Congress. Lastly, it brought peace to the political atmosphere by voting in favor of sending a petition to the Congress for amendments to the Constitution. The efforts of the antifederalists had at least been recognized as a contribution to the new government instead of an obstruction.[161]

Political parties did not directly organize from the debate over the Constitution. New parties really arose after 1776. As Chase observed in 1781: "There is no government in which parties do not sometimes arise, and party as naturally creates factions, as summer produces heat, as winter cold." By that time the revolution ended the court or antiproprietary party and the country or popular party dominated. After 1776 its major leaders, such as Chase and Charles Carroll of Carrollton, were conservative, but they were so often divided that it prevented that party from effectively maintaining the old system.

A new and interesting political phenomenon took place. Since the constitutional convention of 1776, a democratic party had formed. This is discernable from its voting pattern in the years after independence. Its members showed a consistency of voting together. They tried to reduce taxes and governmental expenses; they were anti-religious establishment; they opposed a strong executive; they wanted, since 1776, elective rather than appointive offices and fewer of them. Once they voted against the entire civil list. As we have seen, they were not opposed to education, but distrusted the founding and fought the support of the university. They were careful guardians of the Bill of Rights. Anti-Tory in the extreme, they supported confiscation to lift the burden of taxes. They wanted paper money and debtor relief. They had been advocates of broadening the franchise in 1776 and continued to be. Their leadership was county-oriented—not known nationally or even statewide.

The conservative party had strongholds in the urban areas and generally in the older settled regions of large slaveholders and plantations, namely southern Maryland and the Eastern Shore. Their voting indicates opposite stands. They were proponents of the strong executive, of higher education, and opponents of

---

161. McHenry, *Life and Correspondence*, p. 115, 124-25.

debtor relief measures, on which issue Chase left the fold but otherwise was a consistent voter with the conservative group.[162]

The new national issues after 1789 tended to galvanize both groups. For a time there was some unanimity through compromise in the early years of the new federal Republic. That was broken with the Jay Treaty and the Whiskey Rebellion.

The stronghold of the whiskey rebels was west of Frederick. They were angered at the national law taxing every gallon of whiskey distilled from their surplus corn and wheat for cheaper transport and sale eastward. Resistance to the law smouldered because of the Indian war. When that danger was removed, men of the West then turned on the government. Agitation by Pennsylvania whiskey rebels in Maryland left little to the imagination. They told stories of the federal government not only taxing whiskey, but also taxing parents for their children—15 shillings for a boy; 10 shillings for a girl.

As the rebellion heated up in Pennsylvania, the Maryland government drafted militia from Washington County. This set off riots; a band of rebels whose headquarters were at South Mountain moved to Frederick to take the magazine. They set up a liberty pole and, when someone cut it down, were further enraged. The mob made demands, written in German and English, to reerect the thing.

The governor found that he had to call the militia from other counties. General Samuel Smith was placed in command, and the whole matter proved embarrassing. Smith, while no supporter of disorder, was no friend of federalist policies. The army moved slowly. It found itself without shoes or proper clothing and equipment. Finally, some advanced forces made arrests and brought order. The culprits were treated leniently. The rebels discovered that much of the state opposed their disorder. When matters became reasonably quieted, President Washington made a tour of the west and stayed a night at Hagerstown. The presence of the hero of the Revolution brought assurance and peace.[163]

---

162. Jackson Turner Main, "Political Parties in Revolutionary Maryland" *M.H.M.*, LXII (Mar., 1967), 1-27; Ronald Hoffman, "Economics, Politics and the Revolution in Maryland" (Ph.D. dissertation, History Dept. University of Wisconsin, 1969), Ch. X-XII.

163. Thomas J. C. Williams, *A History of Washington County, Maryland . . .* (Hagerstown: Mail Publishing Co., 1906), pp. 111-14. Thomas Sprigg to Gov.

The Whiskey Rebellion, however, strengthened democratic politics in Maryland. After 1780 the voting patterns of delegates show the western counties democratic, and in the decade after the constitution the tendency is increased. After the presidential election of 1796 the democrats took the name Republican. In the meantime, disappointment over the Jay Treaty caused democratic inroads to be made elsewhere. Some two dozen Democratic Republican Societies were formed after 1794. Composed of friends of the French Revolution, unregenerate antifederalists, and people who thrived on trade with the French, they pledged "incessant watchfullness" to safeguard freedom. Of those in Baltimore City, the weakening conservative bastion, McHenry commented that the criticism of the treaty came from the democratic clubs. "These will, I am convinced, go on. They assume a ground so plausible in a free country that they will still flourish and occasionally produce convulsions, or rather prepare the mind for them."[164]

One of the great issues of 1776 had been the question of broadening the suffrage. It had never died. There were frequent murmurings in the newspapers about the illiberality of the constitution. Many hot or closely-contested elections brought complaints that the unqualified had been permitted to vote—this usually coming from the loser. The electoral system was grudgingly obeyed as a rule. Yet on one occasion a party of Baltimore mechanics was narrowly prevented from hurtling Samuel Chase into a chair "and ... carry him to the Dock & there leave him to find his way out the best ... he could" because he had "acted in the most arbitrary & outrageous manner" as judge of an election.[165]

In 1792 a bill to end property qualifications for voting was introduced in the house. It suffered defeat. In 1794 the bill to incorporate Baltimore met aroused angry cries because it in-

---

Thomas Sim Lee Sept. 11, 1794, *Calendar of Maryland State Papers*, Brown Books, #4, H. R. Dorothy M. Brown, "The Maryland Federalists" (revised Ph.D. dissertation "Party Battles in Maryland, 1786–1812," Hist. Dept. Georgetown University, 1962), pp. 104-109; revision in possession of the author.

164. *Ibid.*, pp. 109-10; McHenry, *Life and Correspondence*, p. 155.

165. J. R. Pole, "Constitutional Reform and Election Statistics in Maryland", *M.H.M.*, LV (Dec., 1960), 275-92; *J.S.H. XIV*, 218-28. William Smith to O. H. Williams Oct. 8, 1792, *Calendar*, item 747.

cluded property tests for voting in the city and required a voice vote by which the mighty could overcome the poor and minimize popular control of the city government. One writer in the *Baltimore Intelligencer* went further than the local issue to accuse the framers of 1776 of establishing a government for the rich. Men in "Rags" had no hand in drawing up the Constitution. True republican doctrine should have recognized that the poor had an interest in society. The writer foretold that such inequities would in time destroy liberty.

In 1797 Michael Taney of Calvert County (and father of Chief Justice Roger Brooke Taney) introduced a bill to establish universal manhood suffrage. Taney was a Federalist, at least on national issues, and the bill found no distinct political pattern at this juncture. Conservatives and Democrats could be found on both sides of the issue. The house voted in favor of the bill, 30–21. The Senate rejected it, and considerable criticism was now heaped upon both the Senate and those who had opposed it in the house. "Some lost favor" with the voters. When the Senate attempted to tighten the franchise by even stricter property controls, criticism against that body rose to a crescendo. Warned a writer in the *Baltimore American and Daily Advertiser* "It was the maintenance of this right, that the hero of '76 bled in the field, and the patriotic statesman deliberated in council." Another stated his general dissatisfaction with the system. Only the man of wealth has freedom of election. "By comparison, the man of rags, when he has assurance enough to attempt to choose an elector, or a member of the second branch is under pressure to vote the wishes of the thousand dollar men." The poor one "must make his election viva voce ... in order to let the man of *wealth* know, whether the man of *rags* has merited further employment, or another loan or further indulgence in time of paying *his* debt, or whether upon occasion he can be intrusted with any other post than a whipping post."[166] The theme of the revolution was reiterated by Bartgis' *Frederick Town Hornet* "Who stood in the ranks as soldiers and fought the battles of the revolutionary war? ... Is not the poor man now bound to do military duty? And do not the farmers and mechanics now fill the ranks of the militia companies? The soldier is as much entitled to vote as the Captain of the company or the Colonel of the regiment."

166. *Baltimore American & Daily Advertiser*, Sept. 28, 1799; *Baltimore Daily Intelligencer* Feb. 8, 1794.

The conservatives of old such as Chase and Carroll still found the propertyless voter inconsonant with responsible government. Chase called the pro-suffragates the "degenerate sons" of the founding fathers. When the house revised the bill, ironically, to exclude the free black from voting which, as it was explained, removed "Republican" prejudices against the measure, it became more difficult for the Senate to stand in the way. That body finally approved it, though it was too late to rescue the Senate and the Federalists who dominated that branch from public opprobrium. The election of 1801, when the conservatives suffered mortal defeat, saw the *Baltimore American and Daily Advertiser* rejoice that the names of "a Carroll, a Ridgely . . . or a McMechen" were "banished" from "our Councils." "They have uniformly opposed and defeated the privilege of universal and equal suffrage." Property was not the measure of liberty. Universal white manhood suffrage became constitutional in 1802.[167] One of the great political principles of the Revolutionary Era in Maryland was won.

---

167. Chilton Williamson, *American Suffrage From Property to Democracy* (Princeton: Princeton University Press, 1960), pp. 146-47, *passim; Baltimore American*, Aug. 21, 1801; Brown, "Federalists," 173, 177, 353-56, appendix; *A Plain History of the Federal Party on the Subject of General Suffrage . . .* 1797–1816, in Enoch Pratt Free Library, Baltimore.

BIBLIOGRAPHICAL ESSAY

CHAPTER II

Many useful works on the Colonial Period extend into the first phase of the revolution. But there is a dearth of good monographs on the Revolution in Maryland. Through the years, the *Maryland Historical Magazine* has partially filled this void. Some of the articles are outstanding, not only for what they offer in the way of information on the period, but also for the questions they raise. These are Paul H. Gliddens, "Maryland and the Stamp Act Controversy", XXVI (June, 1932); an analysis of the convention of 1776 is contained in John C. Rainbolt, "A Note on the Declaration of Rights and the Constitution of 1776", LXVI (Winter, 1971); and the Confederation period is studied by two scholars, the political side, Jackson T. Main, "Political Parties in Revolutionary Maryland, 1780–1787", LXII (March, 1967) and the economic, Rhoda Dorsey, "The Pattern of Baltimore Commerce during the Confederation Period", LXII (June, 1967). Bernard C. Steiner, "Maryland's Adoption of the Federal Constitution", *American Historical Review*, V (Oct., 1899, Jan., 1900) and J. R. Pole, "Suffrage and Representation in Maryland," *Journal of Southern History*, XIV (May, 1958) touch the important political aspects of the Federalist era.

Of books on the Revolution in Maryland, sound and readable works in general are Barker's *Background*, Philip A. Crowl, *Maryland During and After the Revolution* (Baltimore: Johns Hopkins Press, 1943) and David Curtis Skaggs, *Roots of Maryland Democracy* (Westport, Conn.: Greenwood Press, 1973). Ronald Hoffman's excellent study, *A Spirit of Dissension Economics, Politics, and the Revolution of Maryland. Maryland Bicentenial Studies* (Baltimore: Johns Hopkins Press, 1974) should be read in tandem with Crowl's and Skagg's works.

Secondary works for economic and social history make slim picking. A seminal article is Aubrey C. Land, "Economic Base and Social Structure: The Northern Chesapeake in the Eighteenth Century,"*Journal of Economic History*, XXV (December, 1965); also Land's "Economic Behavior in a Planting Society: the Eighteenth Century Chesapeake," *Journal of Southern History*, XXXIII (November, 1967). Baltimore's economic rise in this period is traced in C. P. Gould, "The Economic Causes of the Rise of Baltimore," *Essays in Colonial History Presented to Charles McLean Andrews* (New Haven: Yale University Press, 1931). Still important is Avery Odelle Craven's, *Soil Exhaustion as a Factor in the Agricultural History of Virginia and Maryland* (Glouster,

Mass., Peter Smith, 1965 reprint of 1926 edition). For the maritime trade see Arthur Pierce Middleton, *Tobacco Coast: a Maritime History of Chesapeake Bay in the Colonial Era* (Newport News, Virginia: the Mariners Museum, 1953). The volume also describes plantation methods and some description of the wheat trade.

A thorough and scholarly study of the Annapolis merchant is to be found in Edward C. Papenfuse's *In Pursuit of Profit: the Annapolis Merchant in the Era of the Revolution, 1763–1805* (Baltimore: Johns Hopkins University Press, 1975). This work is important because the author uses the new historical approaches and speaks not only of the merchants' politics but the social mobility of that class.

There are a few ethnic studies for the period. These are in addition to Dieter Cunz's *The Maryland Germans,* Eugene Irving McCormac, *White Servitude in Maryland, 1634–1820* (Baltimore: Johns Hopkins Press, 1904) and the dated but useful Jeffrey R. Brackett, *The Negro in Maryland* (Baltimore: Johns Hopkins Press, 1889).

Works on religious and educational history are wanting. Somewhat filling the need are Rightmeyer's, *Maryland's Established Church* and the poorly done Bernard C. Steiner's, *History of Education in Maryland* (Washington: Government Printing Office, 1894).

Of the primary sources for Maryland there are many unexploited manuscript materials both in the Hall of Records and the Maryland Historical Society, making it advisable to consult the *Guide to Manuscripts in the Maryland Historical Society* (Baltimore: M.H.S., 1965) and the *Calendar of Maryland State Papers, No. 3, 4, Parts 1–3, 5* (Annapolis: Hall of Records Commission, 1948–58).

Good biographies are few because the personal materials on Maryland's leading figures are scarce and scattered. Charles Carroll of Carrollton has had several biographers; a good biography of Johnson is Edward S. Delaplaine, *The Life of Thomas Johnson* (New York: Grafton Press, 1927), also Matilda Ridout, *A Colonial Governor in Maryland: Horatio Sharpe and His Times* (Longman's, Green and Co., 1912), Aubrey C. Land, *The Dulanys of Maryland* (Baltimore: Johns Hopkins Press, 1970). For other important men see the *Dictionary of American Biography.* Useful articles on William Paca and Samuel Chase are contained in the *Maryland Historical Magazine* volumes XXXVI "William Paca..." by Albert Silverman (March, 1942) and LVII (June, 1962) "Sam Chase Disturber" by Frances F. Beirne and Neil Strawser, "Samuel Chase and the Annapolis Paper War" (September, 1962). There is no worthy military history of Maryland's revolutionary soldiers. James McSherry, *History of Maryland* (Baltimore: Baltimore Book Co., 1904) contains fair summaries of the action. More accurately done and with perspective is Christopher Ward's *War of the Revolution,* 2 volumes, (New York: Macmillan Co., 1952). Hopefully a history will be written of the Maryland Line and will follow the direction of Edward C. Papenfuse and Gregory A. Stiverson "General Smallwood's Recruits: the Peacetime Career of the Revolutionary War Private," *William and Mary Quarterly, 3rd Series, XXX* (Jan., 1973).

Printed primary sources which are readily available are the *Archives of Maryland* embracing Governor Sharpe's *Correspondence, the Proceedings of the Assembly* and the *Records of the Committee of Safety.* The *Maryland Gazette* so useful for all phases of this period is complete and accessible on microfilm and the *House and Senate Journals* (*Votes and Proceedings*) published each year after 1776 are available on microcard.

# III

## ECONOMIC DEVELOPMENT, SOCIAL AND CULTURAL CHANGES: 1800–1850

BY

JAMES S. VAN NESS

ST. LAWRENCE UNIVERSITY

From Revolution to a new government to a new century: the birth of the year 1800 should merit great celebrations. Marylanders planned a variety of events, formal and informal, religious and secular, to welcome the new year and the new century. Many halted their plans short of execution. Others quickly shifted the focus of activities from celebration to commemoration as news spread, late in December 1799, that the nation's leading citizen would not witness the transition of centuries. The *Maryland Gazette* reported that on January 1, the theater in Annapolis "was 'full to overflowing,' " and the audience "displayed a scene calculated to impress the mind with the utmost solemnity and sorrow."[1] George Washington was dead.

Some might have viewed Washington's death as signifying the passing of the revolutionary generation and, indeed, of the revolutionary idealism. Such individuals soon were to find themselves and their complacent attitudes rudely shaken. Both on the national scene and in Maryland, evidence that aspects of the revolutionary ideology were alive and well in 1800 soon presented itself. Although this continued vitality appears most prominently in the political realm, the implications of this evidence for societal values more broadly considered is important.

On the national scene, two members of the original committee appointed by the Continental Congress to prepare a Decla-

---

1. *M.G.*, January 2, 1800.

ration of Independence in 1776, John Adams and Thomas Jefferson, contested for the presidency in 1800. Jefferson's political lieutenant and master tactician, James Madison, not only could claim extensive service during the Revolution, but had served brilliantly in the Philadelphia Constitutional Convention and almost singlehandedly had pushed the Bill of Rights through the Congress. George Washington's death, then, signified neither the passing of the revolutionary generation nor of that generation's idealism.

1

PROMISE, DIVERSITY AND DISAPPOINTMENT: 1800–1815

Two concerns presented to the Maryland legislature in the 1790's which continued to generate discussion after the turn of the century stemmed from the ideas surrounding both the Declaration of Independence and the Bill of Rights. The first of these typified the kind of conflict that often arises between ideas and behavior, and represented for Marylanders the most obvious example of man's failure to carry out in fact what he has pledged in words. In 1789 Charles Carroll of Carrollton had introduced into the Maryland Senate a bill aimed at the gradual abolition of slavery in the state. Although an owner of many slaves, Carroll, a signer of the Declaration of Independence, and a man of great intellectual depth, understood the hypocrisy of his situation. He sought the support of fellow political leaders in eliminating the most telling contradiction of the phrase he had endorsed in 1776: that all men had the right to "life, liberty and the pursuit of happiness." The second measure had aimed at eliminating a property qualification on the franchise and on officeholding. It, too, arose in the state legislature in 1797.

In contrast to the underlying motivation of Carroll's proposal, the effort to expand the franchise and broaden opportunities for elective officeholding had aimed at securing the ascendancy of one of several competing ideologies. Property qualifications for voting and officeholding represented two widely held ideas of the revolutionary generation: that only those with a genuine stake in society (as seen in property holding) should participate in the governmental process and that unbridled political democracy held as strong a potential danger to society as did a dictatorship. Many saw the institutionalization of these concepts in state constitutions as being equally as essential to the security of individual freedom as was their effort at ensuring a representative form of government.

By the end of the century, growing faith in the rationality of one's fellow man (including the landless laborer) and growing pride in the accomplishments of the American nation had prompted members of the House of Delegates to look with favor on increasing the rights of the white male half of the state's free population.

Most Maryland legislators turned a deaf ear to Charles Carroll and to the normally influential and respected men who led the Maryland Society for Promoting the Abolition of Slavery. The contradiction between the words of 1776 and the actions of men continued for another half century and more. On the other hand, before the new century passed through its third year, the legislature did eliminate property holding as a restriction on the franchise. Ironically, in doing so, the elected leaders of the state reaffirmed one of the corollaries of slavery: racial prejudice. Free black men lost the franchise. The idea of elitisms, as represented in the substantial property qualifications required of legislators and officers of the state executive department, held fast for another eight years.[2]

The human animal often is seen as being composed of a bundle of contradictions. Just as the state legislature's actions regarding slavery and the franchise and officeholding exhibited an inconsistent pattern of behavior, so a general view of Maryland society early in the nineteenth century brought forward curious inconsistencies. Many individuals were greatly concerned with securing the greatest financial advantage possible to them, perhaps typified by the Elkton innkeeper who assured an English traveler he had ample accommodations, with "no less than eleven beds in one room alone." On the other hand, individuals and groups in distress could count on the private and public generosity of Marylanders.[3]

---

2. Constitutional Convention Commission, *Constitutional Revision Study Documents of the Constitutional Convention Commission of Maryland* (Baltimore, King Bros., Inc., 1968), pp. 393, 396. See above, Ch. II, Section 4; and below, Ch. IV, Section 1.

3. Henry Adams, *The United States in 1800*, ed. by Dexter Perkins (Ithaca,

Perhaps the Elkton innkeeper's financial groveling resulted from his harsh experiences during times of war and depression. Occasionally others found less demanding avenues to economic security. On a trip down to Maryland from Philadelphia to look at a piece of property, John Pershouse met an Englishman who acquired a tavern by marrying "an old woman with some cash." The traveler also noted that the immigrant tavernowner "had also purchased his couple of Negroes observing that he did not come into this country to work." Still, the bulk of Maryland's free residents worked hard and expected others to do likewise; maintained a skeptical attitude toward the beneficence of government while participating actively in the charitable activities of the churches in the state; held fast to established lines of business and economic activity; and gave scant attention to those seeking to foster educational and cultural endeavors. Despite this generally conservative outlook, though, aspects of what today might be called an "open society" existed.[4]

The most obvious test of openness in an American society in the early years of the new century was its treatment of nonwhite members of the population. In Maryland, of course, this could be equated with treatment of blacks. The government, and therefore the society, accepted slavery as an institution. This put an obvious taint on the free Negro. Such individuals suffered much more than the social stigma accompanying the knowledge that they were brothers to those in bondage. Maryland law declared blacks to be inferior to whites: Negroes could not testify against whites in court. Other dehumanizing restrictions also infringed on the freedom of the free blacks. In truth, though, the Maryland pattern of restraint on this beleaguered population was no worse than other state codes throughout the nation in the early nineteenth century.[5]

Rapid growth of the free black population in Maryland in the early 1800's indicated a degree of openness not reflected in the

N.Y.: Cornell University Press, 1964), p. 32; Walter C. Hartridge, "The Refugees from the Island of St. Domingo in Maryland," *M.H.M.*, XXXVIII (June, 1943), 103-106, 108-110; Douglas G. Carroll, Jr., & Blanche D. Coll, "The Baltimore Almshouse An Early History," *M.H.M.*, LXVI (Summer, 1971), 135-152.

4. John Pershouse to James Pershouse, July 5, 1811 in John Pershouse Papers, American Philosophical Society Library.

5. Winthrop D. Jordan, *White Over Black* (Chapel Hill: University of North Carolina Press, 1968), Ch. XI.

statutes. In 1790, Maryland had almost thirteen times the number of slaves as of free blacks; by 1810, the growth of the free black population changed the ratio to just over three to one.[6]

Reflecting upon their injustices, individuals in at least some areas of the state felt sufficiently secure to speak out against limitations imposed upon them. In Baltimore County following the state's removal of property qualifications for voting and simultaneous disfranchisement of all blacks, a man accustomed to voting learned that he was now denied the vote because of his race. He spoke to those at the polling place "in a strain of true and passionate eloquence."[7]

That same county had been the home of one of the most accomplished black men of the post-revolutionary era: Benjamin Banneker. The son of a mulatto woman and a freed slave (who took the name of his wife: Banneker), Benjamin enjoyed the exceptional opportunity of attending school. After being tutored by his grandmother, the youngster enrolled in a local school run by Quakers. Then, while earning his livelihood through farming, he pursued mathematical studies on his own and developed a rather wide correspondence with accomplished scientists and mathematicians. He achieved a degree of fame with the publication of an annual almanac, first printed in Philadelphia about 1792 and later in Richmond. Locally, he generated sufficient respect for his mathematical ability that he earned an appointment to a commission to survey the boundary of the new District of Columbia. Despite these successes, Banneker seldom traveled far from his home near Ellicott City. He died in relative obscurity about 1804.[8]

---

6. By 1850, the ratio was less than two to one, and by the time of the Civil War it had virtually reached one to one. See: Bureau of the Census, *A Century of Population Growth*, (Washington: Government Printing Office, 1909), p. 82; U.S. Census Bureau, *Aggregate Amount of Persons Within the United States in the Year 1810* (Washington: n.p., 1811), p. 11.

7. As quoted by Brackett, *The Negro in Maryland, J.H.U. Studies*, Extra Volume VI (Baltimore: J. H. Press, 1889), 187.

8. Details about Banneker's life and work are sketchy. His papers and possessions were destroyed when his home burned shortly after his death. See: "A Sketch of the Life of Benjamin Banneker," paper read by J. Saurin Norris before the Maryland Historical Society, October 1854; Paul Wilstach, *Tidewater Maryland* (New York: Tudor Pub. Co., 1945), p. 264. Banneker received some international acclaim through Jefferson's correspondence with the Frenchman Marquis de Condorcet. Paul Leicester Ford (ed.), *The*

Nearby, in the city of Baltimore free blacks developed both social and religious organizations, worked with interested whites in promoting Negro education, and secured increasing amounts of real estate. One member of this free black community, Joshua Johnston, became locally prominent as a portrait painter. Employing techniques similar in important respects to the then more widely acclaimed Baltimorean, Charles Peale Polk, Johnston painted at least twenty-one canvases. His subjects included the families of successful Baltimore merchants, a southern Maryland ship captain, and a prominent Calvert County plantation owner. The willingness of such prominent Maryland families as the Kennedy Longs, Hugh McCurdys, John Moales, Samuel Smiths and Bennett Sellers to commission works by Johnston speaks for his high professional standing. He pursued his artistic profession for at least thirty-five years including the first quarter of the nineteenth century.[9]

The relative conditions of free blacks when compared to whites in the early 1800's was generally better than that of their kinsmen in the deep South. It was to deteriorate somewhat in later decades, but always remained significantly higher than was the case in states where slavery impacted on most of the economic activities. These factors contributed to Maryland's steady, though gradual, movement toward an eastern, and away from a southern, orientation.[10]

Population movement within the state indicated a degree of openness. In the first decade of the nineteenth century individuals were leaving the old, worn-out farms of the Eastern Shore and southern Maryland to take up land in Frederick and Harford Counties and, to a lesser extent, in Allegany County. Baltimore City enjoyed continued growth at a high rate, contributing to a notable decline in the population of Baltimore County. Baltimore, Calvert, Kent, Prince George's, St. Mary's and Somerset Counties all declined in population between 1800 and 1810. Baltimore City increased some 76 per cent in the same decade; Harford County grew 21 per cent and Frederick County over 9 per cent. For the most part, the mobile

*Writings of Thomas Jefferson* (New York: G. P. Putnam's Sons, 1904), V, 379. Also Bedini, *Life of Benjamin Banneker*, pp. 9 *et passim*.

9. J. Hall Pleasants, "Joshua Johnston, the First American Negro Portrait Painter," *M.H.M.*, XXXVII (June, 1942), 121-149.

10. See below, section IV of this chapter.

population represented younger offspring of established families who had few reasons to remain at home or to try to persevere on low-yield land, or they represented the small farmer who no longer could face the trial of competing with his slave-owning neighbor. This last group had the least degree of mobility because of its heavy investment in human property. Some of these planter aristocrats did choose to leave the state and take their slaves with them to Kentucky or Tennessee, or to newly opened land in the southern Mississippi Valley following the purchase of Louisiana in 1803. Except for Baltimore County, which had a relatively small percentage of slaves in its population, all the counties losing population in the decade registered declines in both white and slave inhabitants. Curiously, the free black population in those counties generally did not decline.[11]

Most of the moves Marylanders made are represented simply by statistics, with little concrete evidence of individual actions. One exception to this affords a modest degree of insight into the openness that existed within the state as the new century dawned. As is usually the case, this example comes from a family of means: the Michael Taneys of Calvert County. An established man of some importance in that county before the Revolution, Taney could afford to secure a satisfactory professional education for his son after the war. Young Roger B. Taney chose to study law and, after completing his formal education, returned to Calvert County to begin legal practice and try his hand in politics. He found the demands for legal counsel in the area slim and, following his defeat for reelection to the House of Delegates after serving one term, he wrote that "there was no object to be gained by continuing there any longer."

Taney senior thought his son should move to Baltimore, but the young man demurred and proposed the alternative of Frederick City, arguing that "next to Annapolis and Baltimore, it was, with a view to profit, the best point of practice in the State." Indeed, the reasoning was sound. With the two senior attorneys in Frederick verging on retirement, the town had need of able, energetic lawyers.

In 1801, when Roger Taney moved to Frederick, the town

11. Arthur E. Karinen, "Numerical and Distributional Aspects of Maryland Population, 1631–1840" (Ph.D. dissertation, University of Maryland, 1958), pp. 111-137; 208.

had a population of some 3,000, was a developing commercial and industrial center, and served as a way station for individuals traveling from Cumberland to Baltimore and return. Further, this route soon was to be developed into the Baltimore-Cumberland Pike, a toll road that became the eastern leg of the National Pike. In Frederick and the surrounding communities were iron and glass works; tanneries; textile, hat, shoe and wagon manufacturers; a cooperage; powder mills; breweries and distilleries; and pottery works. Among these the forty-seven tanneries produced goods valued at approximately $140,-000 annually; the furnaces and forges around $80,000 and breweries and distilleries some $75,000. In addition, Frederick City housed banks, printers, and the usual assortment of commercial establishments. These businesses frequently had call for the services of an attorney, as did the emigrés who sought to secure clear titles for the land they wished to purchase. Taney received a warm welcome when he reached Frederick and one of the most respected barristers in the region introduced him to the county court. His business prospered and within five years he had secured sufficient income to be able to marry the daughter of a locally prominent man of means: Anne Key, sister of Francis Scott Key. Taney also joined the temporarily demoralized Federalist party and, with several other young men, infused new energy, new ideas, and generated electoral majorities at the polls. Business, marital and political success resulted from the decision by one young man to leave the old, established area of the state and enter a developing community. Ability more than pedigree proved the key to success as far as Frederick residents were concerned.[12]

Just as Charles and Frederick Counties might be cited as representing two contrasting areas, with one holding to tradition and the other welcoming youthful energy, so one could look at the homes recently completed or under way within the state as representing holdovers from eighteenth century architecture or as showing youthful signs of innovation. In both cases—the atti-

---

12. Samuel Tyler, comp., *Memoir of Roger Brooke Taney, LL.D.* (Baltimore: John Murphy & Co., 1872), pp. 94, 95, 96-100. See also: Bernard C. Steiner, *Life of Roger Brooke Taney, Chief Justice of the United States Supreme Court* (Baltimore: William & Wilkins Co., 1922), Ch. I-III; Tench Coxe, Compiler, *A Statement of the Arts and Manufactures of the United States of America for the Year 1810* (Philadelphia: n.p., 1814) pp. 79-87.

tudes of the population and the architectural developments—
the story is far more complex than would appear from the re-
citing of simple contrasts, yet a stress on the contrasts points
out the range of values and perspectives at play.

Georgian style persisted as a favorite among home builders
through the mid-eighteenth and well into the nineteenth century and even retained some acceptance to mid-century. This
style had adherents throughout much of the settled area of the
state. For example, Pleasant Prospect, a home built by a Quaker
family in Baltimore County in the 1820's, with its single room
depth, two story elevation and highly symmetrical pattern, is a
classical example of mid-eighteenth century Georgian architecture. Other examples could be found in both southern Maryland and Baltimore City. For the latter, one need only look at
the famous Flag House built in 1793 on East Pratt Street as
clear proof that the American Revolution did not completely
sever cultural ties with Britain. The conservative attachment to
Georgian architecture might best be dramatized by viewing
the home Richard Turner ordered built for his family in Kent
County. Named Ellwood, this frame house was completed
about 1851. Members of the county's revolutionary Committee
of Safety would have found the exterior—if not the interior—
charmingly typical of Shore homes in 1775.[13]

At the other end of the spectrum one can find occasional attempts at a "new" style for the new century: Gothic Revival.
The first notable structure employing this form in America was
not a house but rather a church, and the architect was a French
emigré, J. Maximilian M. Godefroy. He designed and supervised the construction of the Chapel of St. Mary's Seminary
between 1806 and 1808. Several important details of the original plans never were completed, in fact, and a number of careless errors in design detracted from the overall impressiveness
of the chapel. The architect also willingly diluted the purity of

---

13. For this and succeeding paragraphs on architecture in early 19th century
Maryland see: H. Chandler Forman, *Maryland Architecture, A Short History
from 1634 Through the Civil War* (Cambridge, Md.: Tidewater Pub. Co.,
1968), Ch. III; Joseph Jackson, *Development of American Architecture 1783–
1830* (Philadelphia: David McKay Co., 1926) Ch. I, III, IV, VII, XI; Richard
M. Ketchum, "Maryland," *The American Heritage Book of Great Historic
Places* (New York: American Heritage Pub. Co., 1957), pp. 132-134; Beverly
Da Costa, ed., *Historic Houses of America* (New York: American Heritage
Pub. Co., 1971), pp. 103-109.

design by some interior ornaments. Still, this first effort produced a gradual groundswell of support for what later became known as "Gothic," and became visible in churches, country mansions, town houses, and even outbuildings.

The style most generally representative of the post-revolutionary era was, of course, Classical (or Greek) Revival. Actually, the roots of this Federal style, as it is also known, predate the Revolution in Maryland, as seen in White Hall, built for Governor Horatio Sharpe in Anne Arundel County at the close of the French and Indian War. By the early 1800's architects and craftsmen proliferated Baltimore City with homes based on Classical Revival and, to a lesser extent, the counties. In the countryside, the broad porches, Doric porticoes and temple shapes could be designed and effected by local artisans; the straight lines, vertical panels and Doric porches of Baltimore town houses generally came from the hands of professional architects. Ironically, though, this style supposedly symbolized at once America's independence from Europe and her heritage from classical democratic Greece; yet the designers of outstanding homes and buildings of the Federalist style arrived in the new nation from Europe after the Revolution!

A fundamental problem for anyone desiring to sponsor a notable, architecturally sophisticated building—house, church, or public structure—was the absence of trained, professional architects in the young land. For Maryland this difficulty eased appreciably in the early nineteenth century when two young but accomplished architects began taking commissions for works within the state, particularly in Baltimore. One of these, already mentioned, was Godefroy who fled to the United States following the upheavals of revolution. Although remaining in Maryland less than two decades, he had a profound effect on the development of both the Federal and Gothic styles. In addition, he contributed mightily to Baltimore's title, the Monumental City, by designing a remarkable memorial to those who fell in the Battle of Baltimore during the War of 1812. This Battle Monument, constructed on Court House Square, began to rise at the same time as the more famous Washington Monument, designed by the Philadelphia architect, Robert Mills. Where Mills chose to stress mass and simplicity in his column, Godefroy presented a unique—though not necessarily attractive—combination of an Egyptian base and a Roman column. Perhaps he chose a Romanesque style for the tower since the statuary for the monument came from the hands of an Italian sculptor, Antonio Capellano.[14]

Far more important for the developing styles in Maryland were the habitable structures Godefroy designed. His versatility in relating design to purpose is perhaps most clearly symbolized by comparing the Gothic design of St. Mary's Seminary Chapel with the classical Unitarian Church in Baltimore which stresses plainness on the outside and simplicity and grace on the interior, with heavy reliance on straight lines, squares and circles. The simplicity was in keeping with the Unitarian ideology. The importance of this building in the eyes of those espousing this newly emerging faith in the United States may be seen in one of its early historic events. William Ellery Channing, principal ideologue of Unitarianism, traveled from Boston to preach the ordination sermon of Jared Sparks when the latter assumed the ministry of the recently completed home of Baltimore Unitarians. In that 1819 sermon Channing laid down in clear terms the tenets of Unitarianism. The published version of this sermon quickly became a fundamental tract for Unitarian laymen and clergy across the North.[15]

Important as he was to architectural developments in Maryland, Godefroy must be considered second to the Englishman who came to America following several years of formal study, apprenticeship, and practice in and around London: Benjamin Henry Latrobe. Fortunately for Latrobe, and for Marylanders, he had studied and apprenticed under architects and engineers who had stressed "plain style," and who had associated with those of an English Whig political orientation. With a mother who traced her heritage to Pennsylvania Mennonites, political and professional associates who had criticized Britain's vigorous prosecution of the American Revolution and who looked with favor on the French Revolution, and with significant training and experience in designing and overseeing the construction of buildings during London's remarkable post-war growth,

---

14. Two other Italian sculptors also contributed to Baltimore's architectural development, both as sculptors and teachers. See Richard R. Borneman, "Franzoni and Andrei: Italian Sculptors in Baltimore, 1808," *William and Mary Quarterly*, 3rd. Series, X (January, 1953), 108-111.

15. William Warren Sweet, *Religion in the Development of American Culture 1765–1840* (Gloucester, Mass.: Peter Smith, 1963), p. 195.

Latrobe enjoyed virtually all the assets needed by an immigrant to make good. In every respect except financial, the transplanted Englishman built upon his assets and left behind him a series of remarkable accomplishments in Maryland, Pennsylvania, and the nation's capital.[16]

Latrobe was an artist as well as an architect; a romanticist as well as an engineer. His remarkable combination of talents and attitudes comes through with the story of his role in the design and construction of the first cathedral to be erected in the new nation.

Following the official organization of the Roman Catholic Church in the United States and the appointment of Father John Carroll as Bishop, the next step was the construction of a cathedral. Someone had already developed a design for such an edifice and, aware of Latrobe's talents as overseer of construction of the Chesapeake and Delaware Canal and also as the appointed Surveyor of the Public Buildings of the United States (he had so impressed President Thomas Jefferson) that an assistant of Bishop Carroll's sought the architect's advice. Latrobe responded by offering to design the cathedral without charging a fee. A building committee accepted and Latrobe began at once to outline his proposals. Here he combined his romanticism and professionalism, producing two detailed sketches; one of a Gothic design; the other Romanesque. Openly admitting his personal preference for the former, he acknowledged certain practical advantages of the Romanesque style. His descriptions of the two plans reveal a dedication to objectivity; his willingness to submit alternative proposals and to acknowledge the authority of the building committee to make a binding decision displayed a singular lack of authoritarianism on his part. This generosity did not prevent Latrobe from demanding—to the point of withdrawing his plans—that once the committee accepted his designs, his instructions be followed faithfully by the builder.

The story of the cathedral's construction is a protracted one, due partly to Latrobe's insistence on the faithful execution of his design specifications, and partly to the War of 1812 and the depression in the city at that time. Finally the cathedral was

16. See the excellent, sympathetic biography of Latrobe: Thomas Hamlin, *Benjamin Henry Latrobe* (New York: Oxford University Press, 1955), Ch. I–III, XII, XV, XX, XXII–XXIII.

Benjamin Henry Latrobe by Charles Willson Peale. The great architect and
painter set styles in both fields for Maryland and the nation.
*Courtesy of the White House.*

completed and dedicated in 1821, seventeen years after Latrobe first associated himself with the project. And so, appro-
priately enough, the colony that created a haven for Catholics
provided the setting for their faith's first cathedral in the
United States. Unfortunately, Bishop Carroll did not live to see
the dedication. All the while, Latrobe used his talents both to
design this magnificent church and at the same time to teach
the intricacies of style and structure to several young Americans who aspired to a career in architecture and who worked
for modest fees on the plans. Notable among these was Robert
Mills whom one author credits with being "the first architect of
note to be born in the United States." Indeed, throughout his
career, Latrobe gave generously of his talents both in his architectural work and in his supervision of those who sought to follow in his footsteps.[17]

Latrobe and Robert Goodloe Harper were close friends. This
friendship netted for Latrobe not only the assignment of designing a town house and a second dwelling for Harper but, in addition, a commission of sizable proportions: design and supervision of the construction of the Baltimore Exchange. Harper, a
member of the inner circle of Baltimoreans planning this project, helped Latrobe win the appointment as architect. Hardly
an artistic masterpiece, the building became known for its size,
massiveness, and utility. Its construction, starting before and
completed in the midst of the depression of 1819–21, illustrated
the forcefulness and underlying stability of the Baltimore business and merchant community then. Its simple, classical exterior contrasted with the imaginative interior that included
representations of the commercial activities conducted on a
daily basis in the various rooms and halls of the Exchange. This
contrast between exterior and interior also symbolized the sto-
lidity on the one hand and derring-do on the other of Baltimore's men of commerce and business.

The Exchange was the secular temple of Baltimore as the
Cathedral was the sacred. Where the Cathedral served as the
home of a rapidly expanding and still-emerging American Catholicism, the Exchange served as the home of men who had
already approached their peak of inventiveness and creativity.
Baltimore grew rapidly following the American Revolution and

---

17. See *ibid.*, Ch. XII; Forman, *Maryland Architecture*, p. 73.

The Roman Catholic Cathedral—the first in the United States. A water color painting by the architect, Benjamin Henry Latrobe. *Papers of Benjamin Henry Latrobe, M.H.S.*

was to continue to grow in the decades ahead. Early expansion owed much to the natural attributes of the region and to the ability and audacity of merchants and businessmen. The continued energy of these men kept Maryland clearly in the northeastern sphere of influence; their limited creativity held Baltimore in the second layer of the nation's most powerful mercantile and industrial centers.

Even before the Revolution, Marylanders were changing their economic base. No longer did they rely primarily on tobacco for income. Instead, influenced by the low tobacco yield on the Eastern Shore, the decline in the European market, and the natural agricultural heritage of German immigrants in the west, grain began replacing tobacco as the staple. With the development of iron works near Baltimore and discovery of the excellent power generated by racing streams and little falls near the emerging town of Baltimore, the Revolution served as the death knell of business leadership for Annapolis and the clear emergence of Baltimore as the new state's commercial center. Agriculture, geography, and business enterprise combined to make Baltimore the fastest growing city in the new nation and secure for Annapolis the twin distinctions of being both a state capital and a sleepy, stately town. The national government recognized the situation in 1790 when it erected a customs house in Baltimore.[18]

Blessed with natural sources of power and a terrain that allowed for easy land connections with western Maryland and southern Pennsylvania, Baltimore had only to contend with a harbor that filled steadily from the runoff generated by Jones Falls and Herring Run. Most large ships had to anchor off Fells Point, a mile from the Pratt Street piers where only ships drawing less than six feet of water could dock safely. Naturally, enterprising merchants and the port wardens tried a variety of devices and methods to dredge a deep-water channel to the piers. Despite the ingenuity of the Ellicott brothers, who developed a mud machine for dredging, and the labor of horse and man engaged in clearing a channel, the situation by the mid-

18. Charles Carroll of Carrollton noted that by the mid-1770's he could make a greater profit selling his tobacco locally than by shipping it to England. See letter to Wallace and Co., Sept. 18, 1775, in Charles Carroll of Carrollton Letterbook 1771, Arents Collection, N.Y. Public Library. See also: Craven, *Soil Exhaustion,* pp. 68-70; Clement Eaton, *The Growth of Southern Civilization* (New York: Harper & Row, 1961), pp. 4-5.

1820's was worse than in the 1790's. The advent and use of a steam-powered dredge, though, caused the deep water channel to draw closer to Baltimore. However, by that time the city had lost ground rapidly to the port of New York.[19]

Whether they had a particularly easy time docking or not, ships came to and left Baltimore at a great rate in the early years of the century. The advent of the Baltimore clipper, a sleek, fast, shallow-draft vessel, designed to outmaneuver the blockading British warships and to serve as privateers, gave local merchants reason to expect that the city would continue to thrive despite the docking difficulties. These ships proved especially useful in carrying grain to the West Indies and, somewhat later, to various South American ports.

The home vessels, though, did not have exclusive control over Baltimore commerce by any means. Many ships from the northeastern states and from various foreign nations customarily made Baltimore one of their stops because of the availability of manufactured products and access to the foodstuffs produced in the interior of Virginia, Pennsylvania, and Maryland. For this, Baltimore and much of Maryland could be thankful for the roads that extended across western Maryland into Virginia and those tying Baltimore to central Pennsylvania along with the Susquehanna River that often served as a one-way route for goods coming down from Lancaster and York. Although serious limitations hampered the usefulness of all these transportation routes, in the early 1800's the only superior form of transportation for those in the Susquehanna Valley or in western Maryland seemed to be canals. Construction of one canal up the Susquehanna soon was to be tested and others were to follow. Transportation of goods from the Eastern Shore and southern Maryland was appreciably easier: overland to a local port and then transshipment of the goods on Bay craft up to Baltimore. Despite these realities, local groups understood the need for improvements and sought interesting, though generally ineffective, ways of achieving their goals.[20]

19. R. J. Robinson, "How Baltimore Became a Port," *Baltimore*, XLVIII (July and August 1955).

20. See generally: Howard I. Chapelle, *The Baltimore Clipper, Its Origin and Development* (Hatboro, Pa.: Tradition Press, 1965); George Rogers Taylor, *The Transportation Revolution 1815–1860*, IV of *Economic History of the United States*, ed. by Henry David, *et. al.* (New York: Harper & Row, 1968),

Four problems confronted leaders of such internal improvement projects in the early nineteenth century: capital, technology, the lack of interstate cooperation, and intrastate jealousies. Many of the early turnpike, navigational, and canal projects were undercapitalized, causing the company directors first to approve the use of shortcuts in construction which in the long run generally proved very costly, and second to allow completed works to deteriorate until they were virtually unusable and sometimes unrepairable. In addition, much of the capital came from state legislatures in the form of stock purchases. When a company proved incapable of continuing, the legislature hesitated to allow bankruptcy proceedings to clear the slate since the state owned much of the outstanding stock. This then prevented new projects from being developed in the same region. In Maryland this happened with both the Potomac Company and the Susquehanna Canal Company. Technological limitations and the dearth of qualified engineers plagued the early river channelization companies such as the Potomac Company as well as the canal companies. Between its founding in 1784 and the first of the new century, the Potomac Company "ran through" almost a chief engineer a year.

The Susquehanna Canal, running from Port Deposit to the Pennsylvania border alongside the Susquehanna River, demonstrated the two problems of technological limitations and lack of interstate cooperation. The locks on this canal proved to be too narrow for the large size canal boats that were most efficient in carrying down grain and other bulky products. The canal could not be built up to any of the Pennsylvania trading centers on the river because it had only a Maryland charter (the first such charter granted to a canal company in the United States: 1793). Philadelphia merchants successfully blocked the passage of a charter for the company to operate in Pennsylvania, hoping to preserve that city's commercial ties with the interior of the state. As a result of these two liabilities, the Susquehanna Canal Company never was a financial success and the canal itself was unusable before the end of the War of 1812.

---

Ch. I; Jeremiah Young, *Political and Constitutional Study of the Cumberland Road* (Chicago: University of Chicago Press, 1904); and William Hollins, *Intercourse of Baltimore with the Western Country* (Baltimore: n.p., 1818).

The fourth problem, intrastate jealousies, alternately hampered the financial support a single major project could secure from the state legislature and generated impractical local projects that had little value except in winning some state funds for construction work. These difficulties became most apparent in Maryland in the decade of the 1830's, though intrastate jealousies clearly could be discerned in the vote patterns of the House of Delegates on such questions as support for the Potomac Company and the Susquehanna Canal Company.[21]

Prior to the War of 1812, roadways were the only practical way to tie Baltimore to the West. Consideration of canal construction along the Potomac River Valley was out of the question because of the monopoly enjoyed by the Potomac Company. This beleaguered concern limited its activities to clearing a channel in the river and constructing some locks around the falls just above the town of Georgetown. Even when the river was in condition to handle barges, only downstream commerce was possible. Obviously, too, the use of this route provided effective commerce only with Georgetown, Washington, southern Maryland and northern Virginia. Such activity did nothing to improve conditions for the millers in Baltimore County or the merchants of the city. These individuals turned to the construction of toll roads that would provide good overland transportation between the port city and both western Maryland and the Ohio River Valley.

By persuading the legislature to require new banking concerns to enter into the turnpike business as a prerequisite to securing a state corporation charter, a kind of turnpike authority was formed and the "Frederick Pike" began to emerge. Actually, this turnpike connected Cumberland with Baltimore and later was tied into the National Pike that ran into the Ohio River Valley. Alas, by the time the pike neared completion, some portions of the road needed major repairs; then came the first effective river steamboats and many producers in the Ohio Valley discovered they could ship their goods more easily and less expensively down the Ohio and Mississippi Rivers to New Orleans than by wagons over the toll road to Baltimore. A new

21. See Charles Fisher, "Internal Improvement Issues in Maryland, 1816 to 1826," (M.A. thesis, University of Maryland, 1972), Ch. I, II; James W. Livingood, *The Philadelphia-Baltimore Trade Rivalry 1780–1860* (Harrisburg, Pa.: The Penn. Historical & Museum Commission, 1947), Ch. I, III.

technological problem came into view: obsolescence. In some cases the steamboat would make toll roads unprofitable and therefore unmanageable. The problem was not to end with the competition between toll roads and steamboats. While Baltimore businessmen lamented the limited success of the turnpikes to the west, they had to wait until a decade after the termination of the second war with Britain to see the possibility of an alternative system that could tap the resources of the Ohio Valley.[22]

Western Maryland's attention to grain agriculture and the considerable difficulties farmers had in transporting bulky loads of grain overland to Baltimore or down river to Georgetown actually prompted the development of local businesses. These concerns processed the grain in one of two forms so that the product was more manageable as an item of shipment. They ground the grain into flour or they distilled it into whisky. Numerous visitors to Baltimore in the early years of the century commented about the excellent flour mills in the vicinity of the city, and with reason. By 1810, over fifty mills ground out flour worth almost $50,000 annually. What these visiting businessmen failed to realize was that to the west there existed about three times as many mills. Frederick County housed some 100 mills and Washington County more than fifty. Further, these mills operated at a swifter rate than did the Baltimore establishments. The annual value of their product amounted to more than one and a half million dollars. In the business of turning grain and fruit into alcohol, the two western counties also surpassed Baltimore City and County. The latter pair distilled about 140,000 gallons in a year, while the two western counties distilled almost 350,000 gallons. Most of the western concerns produced relatively small quantities of flour or liquor and many quickly disappeared after economical rail transportation became available, but they contributed substantially to the economy of the region for some years, both by providing reasonable markets for local farmers and by bringing eastern capital into the area since the processed product could be shipped down to Georgetown or over to Baltimore.[23]

Baltimore and agricultural Maryland faced some severe eco-

---

22. See Fisher, "Internal Improvement Issues in Maryland," Ch. II.
23. Coxe, *Arts & Manufactures of the U.S.A. for the Year 1810*, pp. 83, 87.

nomic trials in the early nineteenth century. These problems related to the international aspects of the state's economy. The first of these stemmed from the economic warfare conducted by the British and French as an adjunct of the Napoleonic wars and the subsequent foreign policy decision of President Jefferson: he placed an embargo on American exports headed for international markets in an effort to secure recognition of American neutrality by the warring powers in Europe. The impact of this policy is clearly illustrated by the story of Maryland exports and Baltimore flour inspection. Going into effect just before Christmas in 1807, the embargo hit Maryland heavily in 1808 but had substantially less effect in 1809 (the year it terminated). The total value of Maryland exports dropped from fourteen million dollars in 1807 to two million in 1808. It rose to six million the following year and remained at about that level until the United States declared war on Britain. Flour inspection shows a somewhat different pattern, probably because some of this commodity went to southern states rather than out into the international market. Inspectors cleared just under 500,000 barrels in 1807, with only about 250,000 being inspected the following year. After that point the number of barrels increased to a point in excess of the 1807 figure by 1811.[24]

Jefferson's embargo proved highly unpopular at home and came to an end with his retirement from the presidency. Although the Madison administration attempted to employ economic trade sanctions as a pressure tactic against the warring French and British in the hope that those nations would treat American merchantmen with respect, the information reaching Washington was less than encouraging. Harassment of American vessels and confiscation of American products continued to anger long-suffering producers and embarrass the Administration. Though American shipowners took grave risks when they sent their vessels into waters patrolled by British or French

---

24. Livingood, *The Philadelphia-Baltimore Trade Rivalry*, pp. 24, 26. For the impact of the European wars and the American foreign policy decisions on one Baltimore firm, see: Stuart W. Bruchey, *Robert Oliver, Merchant of Baltimore, 1783–1819, J.H.U. Studies*, LXXIV (Baltimore: J.H. Press, 1956), 336-345. John Pendleton Kennedy's father attributed his bankruptcy in 1809 to the embargo and subsequent trade problems. The elder Kennedy apparently had not been able to market the copper from his mines. Charles H. Bohner, *John Pendleton Kennedy* (Baltimore: J.H. Press, 1961), pp. 11-12, 16.

vessels, and sailors sometimes found themselves forced off a merchant vessel and onto a British warship, the loudest cries came from the American producers whose goods were confiscated and who paid dearly in loss of income. This group of businessmen—largely farmers, millers and small manufacturers—had suffered through the embargo and now were seeing their goods stolen from them by marauding British warships. Their representatives in Congress, tired of Jefferson's and Madison's unsuccessful efforts to secure recognition of American sovereignty, demanded and then declared war on Britain. The Maryland congressional delegation voted seven to four in favor of the declaration.[25]

Farmers, merchants, congressmen might be exasperated with the crass treatment by the British and might assume that Britain would come to terms quickly with the United States because of her involvement in the massive war on the European continent, but Britain failed to see either of these points. The War of 1812 lasted longer, and was more severe, than most Americans expected. Britain brought to bear her vastly superior naval strength and taught Marylanders, among others, that war involved more than naval clashes and armed combat. With a powerful fleet of ships, the British began blockading the Chesapeake Bay in 1813 and extended their control in 1814 until Bay trade came to a virtual standstill. The impact is clearly illustrated by the precipitous drop in Maryland exports. While Maryland exports in 1812 were valued at five million dollars, the following year the figure fell by forty per cent to three million dollars, and in 1814 only some $200,000 worth of goods were exported. The only substantial profits stimulated by the war went to a few fortunate owners and captains of privateers. Sleek, swift Baltimore clippers sailed from the Maryland port in record numbers to harass British shipping and, if they escaped capture, won valuable prizes. Only New York sent into the fray

---

25. See "The Report of the Committee on Foreign Relations of the United States House of Representatives, November 29, 1811," *Annals of Congress of the United States*, 12th Congress, 1st Session, Pt. I (Washington: Gales & Seaton, 1853), columns 374–77. President Madison called for a declaration of war on June 1, 1812, and the Congress obliged. James D. Richardson, ed., *Messages and Papers of the Presidents 1789–1907* (Washington: Bureau of National Literature & Art, 1908), I, 499-505; Scharf, *History of Maryland*, II, 635.

a number of privateers comparable to Baltimore's contribution of some fifty-five vessels.[26]

Despite the economic success of privateers, the hiatus in international trade caused by both the embargo and war actually halted the rapid growth of Baltimore. Never again in the years before the Civil War did Baltimore's economic or population rise approach the boom years of 1775–1805. Indeed, in subsequent years Baltimore's growth merely reflected general national expansion.[27]

The war affected Maryland in ways other than military and economic affairs. It brought out the violent temper of some of her citizens, revealing that, despite the first amendment to the United States Constitution and the provisions of the Maryland Declaration of Rights, freedom of speech and of press had its limits, as exemplified in the mobbing of Alexander Contee Hanson and his associates.[28]

In the first decade and a half of the nineteenth century Maryland's society continued developing along the lines staked out earlier, with modest expansion in the attitudes toward openness, with growing acceptance of cultural change, but with continued examples of intolerance toward those expressing generally unpopular views. Economically and demographically the state witnessed a growing shift away from the Eastern Shore and southern Maryland counties toward northern and western Maryland and, of course, Baltimore City. While the growth in the hinterland continued at a generally strong rate, Baltimore City's population growth slowed dramatically and her early economic growth was reversed as a result of adverse international conditions and the War of 1812. When the war ended,

---

26. *Ibid.*, III, 32-136; Smelser, *The Democratic Republic 1801–1815* (New York: Harper & Row, 1968), pp. 274-275; Livingood, *The Philadelphia-Baltimore Trade Rivalry*, p. 24.

27. David T. Gilchrist, ed., *The Growth of the Seaport Cities* (Charlottesville, Virginia: University of Virginia Press, 1967), pp. 39, 31, 56, 62-67, 203-204.

28. See Ch. IV. A number of the documents relating to the attacks on the editors and friends of the *Federal Republican,* as well as on other residents of the city are found in Scharf, III, 4-25. See also *Niles Weekly Register,* August 8, 1812. The city almost experienced a similar destructive attack on the homes of private citizens when the gruff but brilliant Maryland lawyer Luther Martin took as a client in 1810, Aaron Burr who was charged with treason. Smelser, *Democratic Republic,* pp. 122-23.

Baltimore did not enjoy a return to economic expansion but rather lost out to the enterprising merchants and financiers of New York.

## 2

### CALAMITIES, CONFLICTS AND CHANGES: 1815–1839

All Maryland celebrated the dramatic military victory over the British in the Battle of Baltimore. The celebration was institutionalized architecturally in the construction of the Battle Monument and literarily in *The Star-Spangled Banner*. Baltimore's theatre attempted to immortalize the victory by producing *The Bombardment of Baltimore in a New Patriotic, Military and Naval Entertainment*. This endeavor generated modest attendance, however. Indeed, the martial spirit and general enthusiasm generated by the successful defense of Baltimore and the Treaty of Ghent ending the war proved rather short lived. Marylanders quickly found themselves occupied with other thoughts and more pressing concerns.

Perhaps the reality of the war to Marylanders, with the frequent British raids among Bay plantations and towns as well as the assaults on Bladensburg and the commercial center of Baltimore, generated increased awareness by many residents that life is transient. Whether from this or other causes, intellectual and religious activities, along with theological conflicts, rose in prominence. Organization of the Delphian Club in 1816, which sponsored *The Portico*, a magazine of rather nationalistic tone but stressing essays dealing with serious rather than trivial topics, stimulated the development of those competing organizations of an intellectual bent. Choral societies dedicated to the serious study of music also gained in popularity after the war. The Newtonian Society focused, understandably, on natural sciences. Rembrandt Peale's Museum of Natural History and Art Gallery attracted many visitors and the serious student could choose from among 14,000 volumes at the Baltimore City Library. Interestingly, one of the practically-oriented groups that one would assume to have a large following—the Agricultural Society—could barely keep functioning either in Baltimore or any of the agricultural counties, because of very low membership. Such developments indicated at once a growing urbaneness in Maryland society and a developing division of labor that allowed time for humanistic pursuits.[29]

Organized religion added adherents, modified longstanding policies, and underwent some painful schisms in the two decades following the War of 1812. Two major church organizations looked to Maryland as their home, and both enjoyed remarkable growth nationally as well as locally. Both also suffered from internal controversies in Maryland. In this respect they were joined by several other church groups.

With the appointment of John Carroll as the first Bishop of the Catholic Church in the United States, Baltimore naturally became the headquarters for American Catholicism. A very astute judge of character and a tactful administrator, Bishop Carroll effectively promoted the church in Maryland and elsewhere, stressing the cultural and religious diversity of the American people to the European clergy who came to serve in the new nation, and stressing the nondenominationalism of the American government to the Catholic hierarchy in the Old World. Not only did the church prosper under Carroll's leadership, but the political and military controversies in Europe, as well as post-war famines, prompted increased migration of French, German and Irish Catholics to America. Many of these settled in Baltimore and northern Maryland. Nationally, the growth of the Catholic Church is reflected in its increasing representation in the population. In 1790 Catholics comprised just over one per cent of the white population. Thirty years later, with an increase of more than five fold, some two and one half per cent of the white population in the United States was Catholic. This very rapid expansion provided both opportunities and problems for Bishop Carroll and his successors. In Maryland, Carroll had a very strong nucleus for the church. The original American haven for persecuted Catholics, communicants continued to immigrate to Maryland even after the colony revoked its policy of toleration in 1689, and with the Revolution Maryland Catholics regained civil and religious freedom.

By the time peace returned to the American continent in 1815, Catholic churches existed in Baltimore, Frederick, Ha-

---

29. Bohner, *John Pendleton Kennedy*, pp. 28-31; Lubov Keefer, *Baltimore's Music: The Haven of the American Composer* (Baltimore, n.p., 1962), pp. 64-69; Raphael Semmes, *Baltimore as Seen by Visitors* (Baltimore: M.H.S., 1953), pp. 65-66; Craven, *Soil Exhaustion*, p. 104.

gerstown, Emmitsburg, and Bohemia. In addition, priests served several other congregations. Furthermore, as with the Puritans almost two centuries earlier, Bishop Carroll recognized the need to establish indigenous educational institutions to prepare both men and women to serve the particular needs of American Catholics. Although having lost Georgetown College to the District of Columbia, St. Mary's remained to develop in Baltimore and Mount St. Mary's at Emmitsburg. Separate institutions to prepare women for work in the church and the community were being organized in Emmitsburg and by a convent at Port Tobacco.[30]

With the development of churches came a problem unknown to the Catholic Church in Europe: legal ownership of land, buildings, and furnishings. Generally speaking, the most convenient arrangement was to follow the established Protestant arrangement of creating a board of lay trustees to hold legal title and to administer the secular aspects of real and personal property. Such an arrangement facilitated the development of Catholic churches in the United States without doing violence to church doctrine. The complicating factor was the rather natural extension of this trustee arrangement by the laymen involved. Taking their cue from longstanding American Protestant practice, some groups of laymen saw their role as extending to the selection of the parish priest and even to the government of the church.

In his waning years, Bishop Carroll found his authority to appoint priests challenged on several fronts, including Baltimore, by trustees who were determined to secure control over local affairs. These actions came in the face of an announcement made in 1810 by Bishop Carroll and the four bishops serving under his leadership in the United States that lay bodies were not to permit individuals claiming to be priests to exercise any religious function in their churches before the priests "exhibited authentic proofs of their having obtained the Bishop's permission" to serve in the local church. Although the Baltimore challenge proved short-lived, such controversies continued in nearby congregations for more than a decade following Bishop Carroll's death in 1815. Not until the First Pro-

---

30. Thomas T. McAvoy, *A History of the Catholic Church of the United States* (Notre Dame, Indiana: University of Notre Dame Press, 1969), pp. 75, 80, 87, 88, 112.

vincial Council, held in Baltimore in 1829, formally authorized bishops to punish severely clergy who participated in lay challenges to church authority and to place rebellious churches under an interdict did the independent-minded lay groups bow to authority.[31]

The ease with which the Bishop put down the lay challenge to his authority in Maryland, if not elsewhere, may have stemmed from an earlier case that centered on a priest's challenge of Bishop Carroll's judgment. That dispute was resolved both by church authorities and by civil courts in favor of the Bishop. The controversy related to a problem confronting not only Catholic leaders but the leaders of several Protestant denominations as well: maintaining European nationalistic identity within given congregations. Father Caesarius Reuter, a German priest, arrived in Baltimore with the self-appointed task of ministering to the German Catholic inhabitants of the city. Although Father Reuter's activities generated no overt opposition from Bishop Carroll, the ambitious priest overstepped his authority when he announced plans to form a separate German congregation. Basically opposed to the creation of such ethnically oriented congregations, Bishop Carroll blocked this move on the rational grounds that the small German Catholic community in the city could not support a separate church. After an unsuccessful visit to Rome where the German nationalist found the church authorities unsympathetic to his charges against Carroll, Father Reuter returned to Baltimore still determined to pursue his goal. While he was trying to set up a schismatic congregation, Father Reuter found himself in the center of a court challenge to his authority. As had the church authority in Rome, the court ruled that Bishop Carroll had jurisdiction over German priests as well as those of other nationalities serving within the prescribed geographical authority of Bishop Carroll. The rebellious priest was forced to yield and abandon his hopes of creating a German Catholic church in Baltimore.[32]

---

31. *Ibid.*, Ch. V; Sweet, *Religion in the Development of American Culture* (Nashville: Abingdon Press, 1954), p. 131. Ray Allen Billington, *The Protestant Crusade, 1800–1840* (Gloucester, Mass.: Peter Smith, 1963), p. 38; Peter Guilday, *A History of the Councils of Baltimore (1791–1884)* (New York: Macmillan Co., 1932), pp. 73-74, 90-92.

32. Sweet, *Religion in the Development of American Culture*, p. 122.

Some Maryland Lutherans faced a problem of national identity in their congregations. The difficulty did not involve an assimilation of various European nationalities into one body, rather a disagreement developed over retaining Germanic ways in religious activities. In the two decades following the War of 1812, the congregations centered in both Frederick and Hagerstown engaged in extended internal controversies over the use of English in church meetings. Slowly, German yielded to English, first in occasional sermons, then in services held at other times than on Sunday morning, next in the official records of the congregation, and finally in the offering of separate German and English language communion services.

Careful records maintained in the Hagerstown congregation show the growing support for English services: in 1820, fewer than fifty persons attended the English language communion service while over 200 attended the German language service. In the succeeding four years the growth of the church was entirely in favor of those preferring English: the number of communicants at the German language service changed only slightly and remained just over 200, while those attending the English language service rose to almost 120. By 1828 attendance at the two services was almost identical, each drawing over 180. By 1840 the picture of 1820 was almost reversed: ninety at the German language communion service and over 200 at the English. In anger and frustration, some of the congregation who wished to maintain a pure German Lutheran community broke from the Hagerstown church to form a new congregation. They soon found this to be a futile effort and returned to the parent church. In fact, despite a number of controversies, some generating considerable heat among members or between clergy and congregation, the Maryland Lutherans retained greater unity than any other Protestant church in the state except the Episcopalians.[33]

Maryland Methodists and Quakers proved the most volatile of Protestant groups in the state. Their actions, however, did not place Maryland in a unique position. Rather, for the Methodists, some Maryland groups led a split in the Church that

---

33. Dieter Cunz, *The Maryland Germans* (Princeton: N.J., Princeton University Press, 1948), pp. 204-220; Abdel R. Wentz, *History of the Evangelical Lutheran Synod of Maryland of the United Lutheran Church in America, 1820–1920*, (Harrisburg, Pa.: Evangelical Press, 1920), pp. 147-157, 161-163.

lasted a century, while Quaker dissidents in Maryland joined with others from Pennsylvania, New York, and elsewhere to effect a breach in the ranks of that faith. In both cases the splits emerged in public during the second decade after the War of 1812, just as was the case with the Americanization of German Lutheran congregations in western Maryland.

The divisions that occurred among congregations of the Society of Friends (Quakers) generated little public discussion and were effected much faster than the internal division in the Methodist churches. The central issue in the Quaker dispute was theological, yet the immediate cause of the split proved to be a conflict over leadership. In fact, discussions as to the fundamental tenets of Quakerism generated considerable disagreement for much of the first quarter of the nineteenth century. Leader of the forces to modify Quaker teaching and practice was a New Yorker, Elias Hicks. His call to devote greater attention to one's inner self and less to determine the literal meaning of Bible passages reached out from Long Island into the heart of American Quakerism: Pennsylvania, Maryland, and the frontier. It went even across the ocean to Britain. Not until Hicks' liberal teachings reached the home of Quaker orthodoxy in England did a division of congregations loom large. Representatives of the London Yearly Meeting traveled to Pennsylvania in 1827, and their challenges to the liberal forces in the Philadelphia Yearly Meeting generated a split that spread all the way to Ohio. The following year at the Baltimore Yearly Meeting, a visiting Friend from England precipitated a formal decision by members as to their support for liberal or orthodox doctrines. As happened in several New England Congregational churches when a dispute split congregations between orthodox and developing Unitarian doctrines, the new Quaker doctrines generated such strong support that conservative elements had to depart their old home and relocate, leaving it to the insurgents. So in Maryland, the orthodox Quakers found themselves decidedly in the minority. By the time the reorganization of individual meetings within the Baltimore district was complete, Hicksites outnumbered the orthodox four to one. Interestingly, the rural Quaker congregations in western Maryland and on the Eastern Shore remained almost completely unified but supported the liberals; only in Baltimore did a substantial split within a local society occur. The supporters of

English orthodoxy developed a new organization which, while continuously in agreement on theological questions, became divided on peripheral issues and suffered an additional rift in 1854.[34]

Unlike the Quakers, Methodists split over organizational disputes centering primarily on representation in policymaking bodies. Such a dispute actually was rather slow in coming. Methodism emerged from a reform movement within the Church of England and developed as a separate denomination in America. Organized at the Christmas Conference held in Baltimore in 1784, this dynamic new institution built into itself an almost irreconcilable conflict. By accepting key Episcopal organizational concepts on the one hand and on the other a doctrine that contained strong democratic implications of the Revolution and relying heavily on both local preachers and active lay participation, the Church placed administrative theory and religious doctrine at odds. Demands for a concept of authority flowing up from the congregation and the active ministry rather than down from the bishops and superintendents grew gradually. That the dispute emerged in the host city for the first Methodist conference is not surprising; that the conflict took more than forty years to develop is less easy to understand.[35]

A New Jersey layman began what proved to be an abortive effort to reform the Methodist administrative organization in 1821. Though generating substantial support among laymen and some preachers, this movement collapsed when the General Conference of 1824 rejected petitions for reform. At that point the focus of agitation shifted to Baltimore and came under the direction of Nicholas Snethen, a former traveling companion of Francis Asbury who was the first leader of organized Methodism in America, and Alexander McCaine who became one of the dominant theoreticians of the reformers. Among

---

34. The original Baltimore Yearly Meeting included the Western Shore of Maryland, two counties of southern Pennsylvania and part of northern Virginia. See Anna B. Thomas, *The Story of Baltimore Yearly Meeting from 1672 to 1938* (Baltimore: Weant Press, Inc., 1938). Summaries of the yearly meetings as well as an index of extant documents are in: Phebe R. Jacobsen, *Quaker Records in Maryland, Publication No. 14, Maryland Hall of Records Commission.*

35. William W. Sweet, *Methodism in American History* (New York: Methodist Book Concern, 1933), Ch. VI.

other arguments advanced by the reformers was the charge that while American citizens were democratizing their state governments and individuals were speaking out freely on issues of great moment, the Methodist hierarchy not only refused to broaden its representation but also stifled free speech by closing official church publications to reform authors. What made the situation all the worse for those defending the establishment was the essential validity of the reformers' charges. To publicize their protests, the Baltimore reformers began a periodical commonly called *Mutual Rights*. They soon organized local Union Societies to further their cause. Before long, groups as far away as Ohio sought advice from the Maryland dissidents on how to establish Union Societies. The mutation from reform to rebellion occurred in 1827–28 when a committee of the Baltimore Conference heard charges against a traveling preacher in the Harford circuit, Dennis B. Dorsey, that he had circulated with approval an "improper" publication. Dorsey lost the right to preach for a year. Soon after this another thirty-odd preachers and laymen were tried in Baltimore and either suspended or expelled. Appeals made to the 1828 Baltimore Annual Conference, meeting in Carlisle, Pennsylvania, proved fruitless. Between these two fateful decisions, almost fifty female supporters of the convicted preachers and laymen formally withdrew from the Church in protest. Similar disputes and expulsions developed in areas to the west, north and south of Maryland.

From these actions a new Methodist Church emerged, again in Baltimore. Ministers and members of congregations consisting of expelled and resigned members of the Methodist Episcopal Church met as delegates to a general conference of the "Associated Methodist Churches" in Baltimore in November 1830. Stressing the representative nature of the newly emerging organization, these delegates banded together as the Methodist Protestant Church, formally severing any remaining ties with the parent organization. The new church emphasized representation of clergy and laymen in its hierarchy, along with a decentralized system of government. Primary responsibility rested with each regional conference. Curiously, the subsequent organization of the Baltimore Conference, housing some of the most forceful Maryland advocates of democratic reform, gave its chief executive—an elected official—sole authority to appoint ministers and committees. The reformers felt no need to place institutional checks on the authority of this person.

Unlike the division within the Quaker congregations, the schism in Methodism did not leave the conservative forces severely weakened. Numerous able and energetic preachers did associate with the new Methodist Protestant Church, both in Maryland and elsewhere, but the Methodist Episcopal Church continued to dominate Methodism.

A far more severe trial was to confront the conservatives when sectional conflicts focusing on the question of slavery entered the debates of annual conferences in the 1840's. Slavery and the Civil War again split the church but on sectional grounds. A general reunification of the three major branches of Methodism was not possible until a century later, in 1940.[36]

While doctrinal and organizational disputes troubled Catholics, Quakers and Methodists, the steadily-growing Jewish community in Maryland received long-deserved recognition from the state. Individuals within the Baltimore Jewish community had served and contributed to city, state, and nation for years. President Thomas Jefferson appointed Ruben Etting to the post of United States Marshal in Maryland, yet the Maryland constitution prohibited any Jew from serving in an official capacity with the state government. This stigma had a debilitating effect on local congregations and proved especially glaring in the years following the War of 1812 which Maryland Jews had supported in liberal fashion. A decade following the termination of the war, and more than half a decade after Thomas Kennedy of Washington County began what amounted to a one-man crusade in the House of Delegates, all legal restrictions on Jews were removed from Maryland law and constitution. The closeness of the votes on the legislation indicates that prejudice continued to exist within the state, but the flow of democratic thought into Maryland and growing egalitarian attitudes could be perceived in this action. The beneficiaries of this were not just Maryland Jews, of course, but all those striving to secure freedom of thought and expression. Naturally,

36. *Ibid.*, 178-183; Gordon P. Baker, ed., *Those Incredible Methodists, A History of the Baltimore Conference of the United Methodist Church* (Baltimore: The Baltimore Conference, 1972), Ch. VI. Documents relating to the Methodist controversy of 1827 and picturing the reformers' point of view are found in: *The Mutual Rights of the Ministers and Members of the Methodist Episcopal Church*, III (1827), IV (1828).

too, this fundamental change in policy allowed the Maryland government to move able Jews into official positions.[37]

Although Protestant denominations in Maryland enjoyed considerable expansion in the second and third decades of the nineteenth century, and some new denominations developed, one national religious trend that emerged in the years following the War of 1812 bypassed Maryland with barely a ripple. This was the development of interdenominational moral and religious societies such as the American Bible Society, the American Sunday School Union, and the American Home Missionary Society. To a great extent, Marylanders chose to operate within their own denominational organizations rather than diffusing their efforts among these groups. The American Home Missionary Society, for example, enlisted over 1,000 missionaries nationally. Two lived in Maryland.[38]

Changes and mutations in Maryland religious institutions stemmed variously from theological conflicts, disagreements over organizational theory and practice, and changing attitudes about preserving aspects of a group's cultural heritage. The counter trends that created conflicts belied an underlying popular commitment to church support and religious activity. As such, these confusing cross currents represented similar conflicts and consistencies in popular attitudes and values in a number of economic and social concerns.

In the post-war years, many Marylanders tended to react to changing economic conditions while a few daring souls took the initiative in creating new markets or in employing technological advances that had proven successful elsewhere. As had been true since the beginning of Maryland, most residents relied on agriculture for their livelihood. Despite this fact, agriculture continued its relative economic decline after the War of 1812 as had been true before the war. There were several causes for this. One was the continued depletion of natural

---

37. Joseph L. Blau, "The Maryland Jew Bill: A Footnote to Thomas Jefferson's Work for Freedom of Religion," *Review of Religion,* VIII (1944), 227-239; See E. Milton Alfred, *The Jew's Struggle for Religious and Civil Liberty in Maryland* (New York: DaCapo Press, 1970). For more information on the Jewish community see Moses Aberbach, "The Early German Jews of Baltimore," *A Journal of German-American History,* 1972, ed. by Klaus Wust (Baltimore: The Society for the History of the Germans in Maryland, 1972), pp. 27-36.

38. Sweet, *Religion in the Development of American Culture,* pp. 162-165.

nutrients in the soils, especially in the tidewater regions. Various individuals experimented with natural and artificial means of restoring the soil, but they were very definitely the exception to the general rule of avoiding innovation. The aggressive, optimistic individual tried various fertilizers, most commonly gypsum. Successes with such endeavors did not generate widespread adoption of fertilizers. The introduction of the iron plow allowed deep plowing which a few saw as a major factor in restoring or preserving soil productivity. As with the use of various fertilizers, most farmers held back from using the new plow. In one Frederick County locality a distributor for the deep furrowing plow waited almost a year after receiving his first shipment to make a sale. A single example of an experiment with fertilizers or plows which failed seemed to receive greater attention than the several examples of conspicuous success. Such negativism on the part of farmers certainly was not limited to Marylanders. Farmers to the south of the Potomac and north of the Mason-Dixon Line generally reacted in a similar vein.[39]

By 1815 most farmers outside of Prince George's County had given up growing tobacco as their basic money crop. Not only had repeated growing of that crop greatly depleted the soil, but the conflicts in Europe made the market precarious. Many had turned to wheat as the basic money crop only to suffer a new setback: attacks by the Hessian fly. Annually thousands of bushels of wheat were lost to this little pest. Indeed, the fly's destructive activities became so extensive that several West Indian ports, normally major importers of Maryland wheat, temporarily closed their docks to the Maryland product. The basic concern there was that the small West Indian wheat crop would be infested since the Hessian fly laid its eggs in the grain to hatch the following year. There was no sure method to detect or kill the eggs without ruining the wheat.

In desperation, a number of farmers returned temporarily to tobacco, only to find themselves in even worse economic straits. From these problems, a system of diversified agriculture emerged in those instances where farmers had the initiative and the resources to change. Many owners of depleted land on the Eastern Shore simply allowed scrub pine to grow up, hop-

---

39. Paul W. Gates, *The Farmer's Age: Agriculture 1815–1860*, (New York: Holt, Rinehart and Winston, 1960), pp. 1-5, 107-10; Craven, *Soil Exhaustion*, Ch. III.

ing nature would regenerate the soil. To the west, in the foot-hills and valleys farmers fought the fly as best they could and turned their crops into either liquor or flour. They also grew clover, legumes and began dairy and beef herds. Though often classified as "stolid," the German farmers in the piedmont of Maryland tended to be more receptive to experimentation and change than did their Anglo-Saxon counterparts to the south and east. By almost any economic standard, though, the condition of Maryland agriculture, extending well into the 1820's, may be classified as stagnant if not regressive. Expansion of cultivated acreage in the piedmont and improvements in farming methods that produced greater yields there were more than counterbalanced by the abandonment of farm lands and declining production in the tidewater areas.

Another difficulty in promoting the practical growth of agriculture to the west was the problem of markets. With haphazardly maintained roadways, farmers in Frederick, Washington and Allegany Counties faced substantial expense in marketing their crops. The small farmer, therefore, had little chance to grow prosperous until someone provided him with an economical means for transporting his produce.

The problem facing the small farmer who desired to expand and lacked capital, plagued most Marylanders. Few could follow the lead, or even hope to secure sufficient partners to enter into a venture one-quarter the size of the Warren Manufacturing Company that raised $200,000 in 1815 to open a large textile mill in Baltimore County at Gunpowder Falls.

Symptomatic of the dearth of capital was the large number of lotteries working in Maryland following the war. Jacob Cohen and his brothers found the lottery business so profitable that they opened Cohen's Lottery and Exchange Office in Baltimore and later branched to five other cities. Of course, the lottery business succeeded largely because individuals willingly took risks with only small amounts of money, but the momentum stemmed from the desire of groups in need of capital to finance the development of such public institutions as the Maryland Medical College and the Baltimore Cathedral. Later, the state established its own lotteries. The success of such fundraising projects may have stimulated businessmen in the 1820's to organize corporations and sell stock to the public in projected business ventures. Certainly the astute capitalists would not lose sight of the fact that even during the depths of the depression of 1820–21, when Baltimore commerce almost stood still, individuals bought lottery tickets.[40]

Marylanders certainly must have had a difficult time keeping an optimistic outlook toward the economy through the first two decades of the nineteenth century. Although the first few years seemed bright, there followed a series of problems and calamities that would have taxed the most enthusiastic advocate of the power of positive thinking: embargo, war and invasion, natural disasters, and topped off in the years 1819–22 with the deepest depression Maryland or the nation had yet known. Baltimore, which had long suffered from insufficient capital and limited banking facilities, felt the depression more than any other major commercial center in the United States. The City Bank failed; many individual businesses and partnerships closed; and the Warren Manufacturing Company in the nearby county, capitalized at $200,000 only four years earlier, declared bankruptcy and sold its assets for a mere $36,000 with the original investors recovering not a cent. The British consul in Baltimore reported that: "The trade of this city was never more depressed, pecuniary embarrassment beyond anything ever before known, many failures, more expected and no one knows who to trust." Ten thousand laborers walked the streets looking for work. Hardly the way to end the decade![41]

Once the debilitating effects of the depression began to diminish, commercial farmers, small merchants, and businessmen throughout the Western Shore began looking for means of improving their condition. Sentiment developed rapidly for massive investments in new transportation systems. Little, if

---

40. W. Ray Luce, "The Cohen Brothers of Baltimore: from Lotteries to Banking," *M.H.M.*, LXVIII (Fall, 1973), 288-308; Richard W. Griffin, "An Origin of the Industrial Revolution in Maryland: The Textile Industry, 1789–1826," *M.H.M.*, LXI (March, 1966), 32-33; Hugh S. Hanna, *A Financial History of Maryland (1789–1848)*, *J.H.U. Studies*, XXV (Baltimore: J.H. Press, 1907), 52-53, 57-60.

41. Quoted in Livingood, *Philadelphia-Baltimore Trade Rivalry*, p. 18. Samuel Smith, the "Defender of Baltimore" in 1814 found himself hounded so much by his creditors that he almost committed suicide. Frank A. Cassell, *Merchant Congressman in the Young Republic, Samuel Smith of Maryland, 1752–1839* (Madison: University of Wisconsin Press, 1971), pp. 223-24; Gilchrist, *Growth of the Seaport Cities*, pp. 122, 123, 131, 132-133; Joseph G. Rayback, *A History of American Labor* (New York: Macmillan Co., 1959), p. 57.

anything, could be done to overcome the miserable navigational conditions of the Bay. Early faith in the efficacy of turnpikes had been forgotten. Stories of rapid progress in the construction of the Erie Canal gave credibility to proposals for
canals through the interior of Maryland as well as up the Potomac Valley and on into the Ohio Valley. A fundamental problem still existed, though: regional loyalties and interregional
antagonisms. Advocates of a Potomac Valley canal could generate little or no enthusiasm for their plan from residents of Baltimore and northern Maryland; calls for a new Susquehanna
canal fell on the deaf ears of western Marylanders; no canal
proposal generated the slightest interest in an Eastern Shoreman. A tremendous amount of political activity, including the
organization of paper companies, pledges for support of projects
that were patently impractical, and basic logrolling, produced
state support for the one project that appeared feasible: the
Chesapeake and Ohio Canal. This support followed an interstate Chesapeake and Ohio Canal Convention held in 1823, for
generation of federal support and incorporation of the company
by Virginia. The Maryland legislature's 1824 decision to incorporate the Chesapeake and Ohio Canal Company proved to
be that political body's first step down a road that took the
state perilously close to financial ruin. It did create a monster
that drained the capital and dashed hopes of many small investors. However, buoyed by the stories of rapid progress and
relatively reasonable financial costs of the Erie Canal, a project
begun in 1817 and within a year of completion in 1824, the enthusiastic supporters of the C & O Canal forecast quick completion of the project tying Georgetown to Wheeling, (West)
Virginia and the Ohio River. With that, they said, would come
a dramatic increase in commerce and provide ready markets for
farm products from the Maryland interior.[42]

Although counties abutting the Potomac River above Washington—Montgomery, Frederick, Washington, and Allegany—
supported the canal project, and though some Eastern Shore
support was bought with the promise of state funds to improve
navigation along Shore rivers and to drain low-lying areas, Baltimore economic leaders could see no benefit from the canal. To
be sure, a pledge existed to build a connecting canal between

42. Fisher, "Internal Improvement Issues in Maryland," Ch. III; Scharf,
*History of Maryland*, III, 154-165.

Georgetown and Baltimore, but virtually no one really expected to see the project leave the drawing boards. Too many practical obstacles existed. No—if the harbor was to be tied to the vast market of the Ohio Valley, some alternative plan, not involving turnpikes or canals, had to emerge.

Promising reports on British experiments with rail transportation were read carefully by leading businessmen of the state. There emerged a plan for the incorporation of a company that would construct a railroad line from Baltimore to the Ohio River: the Baltimore and Ohio Railroad Company. Petitioners to the state legislature in support of the company's incorporation included the venerable Charles Carroll of Carrollton, respected Jewish merchant Solomon Etting, and prominent mill owner Thomas Ellicott. After securing legislative endorsement early in 1827, the company quickly sold its authorized stock and determined the basic route the track was to follow. On the same day the first spade of earth was dug for construction of the C & O Canal, Charles Carroll of Carrollton laid the railroad's cornerstone: July 4th, 1828. Although his nine-plus decades of life led Carroll to view events in which he partook with a cautiously conservative perspective, he expressed the opinion that his symbolic inauguration of the B & O ranked second only to his signing the Declaration of Independence.

Neither Carroll's lofty support of the railroad nor President John Quincy Adams' efforts in turning the first spade of dirt to build the C & O Canal assured success for these ambitious transportation projects. To complete them the two companies involved needed to secure a combination of astute engineers; business leaders possessing tact, wisdom, and personal dynamism; and massive funding. While both companies enjoyed enthusiastic support in their initial public stock offerings, both also vigorously pursued financial support from local, state, and national governments with considerable success.[43]

---

43. *Ibid.*, 167-169; Hanna, *Financial History of Maryland*, pp. 80-81; Alfred R. James, "Sidelights on the Founding of the Baltimore and Ohio Railroad," *M.H.M.*, XLVIII (December, 1953), 288-89, 293; Louis B. Schmidt, "Internal Commerce and the Development of National Economy Before 1860," *Journal of Political Economy*, XLVII (December, 1939), 811-14. The basic studies of the two projects are: Walter S. Sanderlin, *A History of the Chesapeake and Ohio Canal*, *J.H.U. Studies*, LXIV (Baltimore: J.H. Press, 1946); and Edward Hungerford, *The Story of the Baltimore and Ohio Railroad, 1827–1927*, 2 vol. (New York: G. P. Putnam's Sons, 1928).

Charles Carroll of Carrollton turns the earth at the laying of the 'first stone'
for the construction of the Baltimore and Ohio Railroad in 1828.

*Courtesy of B & O Transportation Museum*

194

Ironically, the two sleeping giants secured state financial support by employing almost opposite appeals. Time after time, the C & O Company pleaded an insufficiency of capital to keep construction going, noting that until at least Georgetown and Cumberland could be connected, no revenues worth mentioning would accrue. In contrast, less than two years after construction began on the railroad, trains were running between the city and Ellicott Mills, generating a modest income. By the spring of 1832, the railroad had reached the Potomac River at Point of Rocks. Systematic expansion of the line promised continually increasing financial returns and more importantly, vigorous economic activity in the vicinity of the roadbed. Both arguments struck responsive chords in Annapolis. Once the legislature invested funds in the C & O Canal Company it was loath to see the project abandoned with the consequent loss of state investments. With promising results by the B & O Railroad Company, possibly increased state support would reap hoped-for rewards more quickly if additional funds went to that institution.

Between 1826 and 1840, the state borrowed over ten million dollars to support the two projects. In addition, it borrowed another four and one half million dollars to support the Baltimore and Washington Branch Railroad (later taken over by the B & O), Baltimore and Susquehanna Railroad, Tidewater Canal, Annapolis and Elkridge Railroad and Eastern Shore Railroad. At the time this borrowing spree began in 1826, the state's operating budget was averaging less than $300,000, and it had a funded debt of just under $58,000. In sum, the state went almost fifteen million dollars in debt to promote a variety of sectionally oriented transportation projects, sometimes fully aware that the grants were really made merely to supply the legislative votes needed to secure backing for other projects. Further, though seemingly aware of the deepening financial morass into which they were wading, legislators refused to consider the long-range implications of their actions, always rationalizing the situation with hopeful statements that the transportation projects would all be successful and yield handsome returns to the state treasury. Indeed, for a time the combination of dividends from the few successful transportation projects and modest interest charges on outstanding loans allowed the state to meet its obligations without undue difficulty. In fact, between 1833 and

PETER COOPER'S "TOM THUMB" 1829~30 BALTIMORE & OHIO R. R.

**Replica of the first railroad engine of the Baltimore and Ohio.**
*Courtesy of B&O Transportation Museum*

1839, the average annual interest payments above returns amounted to just over $50,000.

Then came the reckoning. In 1840, dividends and payments to the state from internal improvements companies dropped precipitously and at the same time interest payment from recent substantial loans made by the state government came due. Where the state had to make payments of slightly less than $98,000 in 1839 to meet the difference between receipts from the internal improvements companies and interest on loans, the sum required in 1840 amounted to nearly five times that figure: almost $500,000. By various combinations that included temporary suspension of interest payments, transfers of federal payments, manipulation of bank stock and drastic revisions of the state's tax structure (including adoption of a very unpopular stamp tax), the legislature finally met its obligation. Full payments on the loans resumed in 1848.[44]

The Chesapeake and Ohio Canal finally was completed to Cumberland and served intermittently throughout the second half of the nineteenth century and first quarter of the twentieth as a means of shipping coal from the western Maryland mines to the Washington area. Of course, foodstuffs and other supplies also were shipped along the canal as well, but coal proved to be the most frequently seen item on canal boats. Considering that federal, state, and local government investments in the canal ran to some eleven million dollars, as compared to seven million dollars for the Erie Canal, and that long before the C & O had been completed to Cumberland the railroad was serving that area and nearing a link with the Ohio Valley at Wheeling, only by the most warped logic can one call the project even a limited success.[45]

In addition to its dismal financial story the building of the canal also involved violent conflicts among construction workers and management. Six years after construction began on the canal, violence among workers broke out and disturbances ranging from simple riot to armed conflict and killings continued intermittently for five years. Both the first and last of these disturbances were bloody, including murders and ultimate suppression by armed troops. The latter conflict, in 1839, differed substantially from the outbreaks of 1834 that witnessed Irish laborers battling among themselves with such ferocity that five men died and at least five others sustained serious injury. In response to state appeals at that time, President Andrew Jackson sent federal troops into the area to restore peace. Following the riots work continued, of course, but company engineers continued to face a problem that had plagued them from the start: labor shortages. Never able to stimulate much enthusiasm for employment opportunities among laborers in the Potomac region, company officials first relied on indentured

---

44. Hanna, *Financial History of Maryland*, pp. 79-125, 130-131.

45. Douglass C. North, *Growth and Welfare in the American Past* (Englewood Cliffs, N.J.: Prentice-Hall, Inc., 1966), p. 102; Charles S. Sydnor, *The Development of Southern Sectionalism*, V in *A History of the South*, ed. by Wendell H. Stephenson and E. Merton Coulter (Baton Rouge: Louisiana State University Press, 1948), pp. 271-72.

servants and, after that source of manpower disappeared, hired immigrants, chiefly Irishmen and Germans. As more of these workers joined the canal operations, some Irish organizers saw a chance to force management to provide improved salaries. Although initially successful in securing higher wages, the leaders ran afoul of changing conditions. For one, the C & O Canal Company became desperately short of working capital. For another, the labor market opened up as a result of the major national depression that hit the country in 1837 following President Jackson's unrealistic economic measures with its overexpansion of state banking and improvement programs. Subcontractors on the C & O Canal began arbitrarily slashing salary payments, some by as much as seventy-five per cent, and also began hiring German and American laborers. Infuriated by these tactics, the Irish workers first sabotaged work on the canal and then, on August 11, 1839, some 100 of them attacked German labor camps near Hancock. Although inflicting relatively limited bodily injury, the Irish stole nearly all the valuables held by the Germans and destroyed many of the shanties in which the Germans lived. After considerable indecision, Maryland militia moved into the area, destroyed much private property themselves, including some taverns where the Irish supposedly had met to conspire, arrested over two dozen suspects, and thoroughly struck fear into the workers. Ultimately, fourteen Irish laborers were convicted of major offenses and received jail sentences ranging from four to seventeen years. Several individuals who lost homes or businesses to militia axes successfully sued for recovery of damages.[46]

The combination of depression and military suppression of the Irish workers ended organized Irish labor activities on the C & O project and also enabled management to drop wages from $1.25 to under ninety cents per day. This significant set-

---

46. The stories of the two major labor disputes are told, with substantially different interpretations, in: Richard B. Morris, "Andrew Jackson, Strike Breaker," *American Historical Review*, LV (October, 1949), 54-68; and W. David Baird, "Violence Along the Chesapeake and Ohio Canal: 1839," *M.H.M.*, LXVI (Summer, 1971), 121-34. Labor violence on a Baltimore and Ohio Railroad construction project in 1829 caused one death and considerable property damage before a militia unit arrived to quell the disturbance. John R. Commons, *et al.*, *History of Labour in the United States* (New York: Augustus M. Kelly, 1966) I, 416-17.

back to organized labor was no isolated case, as labor groups throughout the industrialized East lost out to the combined economic pressures of the depression, vigorous resistance of businessmen, and the application of British common law concepts by state courts that recognized strikes by organized labor as conspiracies.[47]

Baltimore was a hotbed of labor organization in the early 1830's, reaching a level of activity that surpassed similar endeavors in any other city south of Philadelphia. The flurry of organizational activity and strikes that lasted from 1833 to the depression of 1837, began when journeyman hatters struck in protest against a wage reduction. In June 1833, master hatters notified their employees of a forthcoming 25 per cent reduction in wages. Protesting the action as completely unwarranted, the Journeyman Hatters' Society, which had been in existence in Baltimore for almost two decades, appealed both to other unions and to the public for aid. A remarkable degree of support came from other trade unions in the city, and newspapers printed the public appeals of the society. Lasting about a month, the defensive action of the hatters, aimed simply at blocking a wage reduction, proved successful. The master hatters agreed to continue paying the old wage rate.[48]

One success led to other efforts. The rash of threats and strikes following the Journeyman Hatters' Society's modest victory differed from the hatters' endeavor in one very important particular. Baltimore mechanics, feeling the pulse of Jacksonian democracy in their veins, wanted both respect for their respective callings and leisure to participate in community affairs. They wanted a ten-hour work day between April and September (the months of long daylight) at existing wage rates. Rational arguments coupled with threats of strikes persuaded some masters to agree. Others settled for ten-hour work days during summer months only after a short strike. A few trades,

---

47. Organized Baltimore shoemakers had to defend themselves in two criminal conspiracy suits because of their labor activities in 1809. The shoemakers won one case; the outcome of the other is unknown. *Ibid.*, I, 138.

48. Richard B. Morris, "Labor Controls in Maryland in the Nineteenth Century," *Journal of Southern History*, XIV (August, 1948), 386. See the July 1833 issues of: *The American and Commercial Advertiser, Baltimore* (County) *Commercial Chronicle and Daily Marylander*, and *Baltimore Republican and Commercial Advertiser.*

however, continued with working hours unchanged until 1835.[49]

Female employees of the clothing trades cared more for securing a living wage than shortening their working hours. They received payment by the piece rather than the hour. In general, these hard-pressed women averaged a scant one-quarter of the weekly wage received by male laborers. Organizational activities and strikes in the fall of 1833 apparently led to a new piecework scale for the ladies and stimulated the organization of the Female Union Society, United Seamstresses Society and, ultimately, the integrated United Men and Women's Trading Society.[50]

The flurry of labor activities in the summer and fall of 1833 eventually led groups of skilled laborers to form a Baltimore Trades' Union and, somewhat later, to factions within the labor movement branching into political endeavors, all of which enjoyed a degree of short-term success. As the 1837 depression engulfed the American economy, these activities collapsed and every man and woman laborer was forced to pursue an independent course as all laborers, skilled or otherwise, desperately struggled to keep roofs over their heads.[51]

A sad tale of irresponsible financial manipulation, duplicity, and unethical behavior by several leading Marylanders led to a temporary panic in the midst of the Baltimore labor activities. The tragedy of this situation is that the banking institution that collapsed, the Bank of Maryland, held the deposits of hundreds of Baltimore middle class and lower class inhabitants. What made the bank's demise particularly galling to many depositors was the combination of a very slow audit of the books, taking more than two years from the March 1834 closing, and the public airing of disputes among the directors of the bank as to the

49. *The American and Commercial Advertiser*, August 9, 13, 15, 24, 26; *The Baltimore Gazette and Daily Advertiser*, August 12, 21, 26; *The Baltimore Republican and Commercial Advertiser*, July 30, August 13, 19, 21, 24, 26, 1833.

50. *The American and Commercial Advertiser*, October 19, 1833; J. B. Andrews and W. D. Bliss, "History of Women in Trade Unions," *Report on Condition of Women and Child Wage Earners in the United States*, X, U.S. Senate Document No. 645, 61st Congress, pp. 38-39.

51. Rayback, *History of American Labor*, p. 76; Commons, *History of Labour in U.S.*, I, 358-62, 373, 378-83.

culprits responsible for the failure. Included in the machinations and the public conflict were Evan Poultney, president of
the bank, Reverdy Johnson and John Glenn, two directors of the
bank, and Roger B. Taney, at that time secretary of the treasury
in President Jackson's cabinet. Had the depositors realized how
self-serving Johnson and Glenn had been, no doubt they would
not have been as patient as they were. Had Marylanders in
general understood that Taney cavalierly threw hundreds of
thousands of government dollars away by secretly trying to bail
out the Bank of Maryland with United States Treasury receipts,
they would have treated him with much less respect in subsequent years.

As it was, the auditors' delay in filing a report and the extended newspaper war between involved financiers stimulated a riot in Baltimore that resulted in the destruction of
Johnson's home and serious damage to several other residences. Although bodily injury did not reach the extent of the
riot of 1812, the city did experience almost a week of mob rule.
Ironically, while the little depositors in the Bank of Maryland
generally had to sell their credits at substantial losses even before the auditors completed their examination, in order to sustain themselves, Reverdy Johnson and others who had suffered
property damage from the mob action, thanks in part to the political intervention of Taney, secured compensation from the
state for their losses, with Johnson receiving almost $41,000.[52]

Although the legislature easily succumbed to the lobbying of
Taney, Johnson, and their cohorts and granted exorbitant compensation for the loss of private property from mob violence,
and though legislators continued pouring state money into internal improvement projects of dubious merit, these same
elected officials consistently rejected or obfuscated plans to develop a free school system for the state.

Delegates to the colonial Maryland legislature had attempted
to establish a loose system of free education, and their successors following the revolution also had devised plans for a public
education system; but these endeavors led only to the operation
of a few schools. Even the promising plan of uniting the private

---

52. Scharf, *History of Maryland*, III, 176-82; paper read by Professor David
Grimsted to University of Maryland History Department Faculty Seminar,
April 1972; Peter L. Payne and Lance E. Davis, *The Savings Bank of Balti-
more, 1818–1886, J.H.U. Studies,* LXXII (Baltimore: J.H. Press, 1956), 82-83.

schools of Washington on the Eastern Shore and St. John's on the Western Shore into a state university had come to naught.

Several governors of Maryland actively encouraged legislative involvement in creating a system of elementary schools in the state. In 1816, the General Assembly did authorize appointment of county school boards and allocation of taxes from banking and turnpike companies for use by the schools. This sum of money proved so paltry that many counties directed the treasurer to leave the money in their accounts until sufficient funds had accrued to be of some use. Further, the principle of county federalism, that is equality among the counties regardless of size, wealth, or population, was applied so that the least populous county received the same percentage of funds as the most populous. Nine years later Governor Samuel Stevens in his last year in office successfully goaded the legislature into authorizing a survey of state educational needs.

The following year, 1826, the General Assembly reluctantly responded to the survey report by creating an administrative hierarchy to effect a state system of primary education. The new governor, Joseph Kent, appointed Littleton D. Teackle, who had conducted the survey, as the head of this paper system. Still, federalism survived, with each county having to conduct a referendum for involving itself in a state primary education system before coming under the crude arrangements. Not surprisingly, some of the counties most in need of a free system to provide education for the children of poor laborers or impoverished small farmers rejected offers of state aid. These included Allegany, Caroline, Dorchester, Somerset, Washington and Worcester Counties. Even the counties voting in favor of involvement with the state received little worthwhile support for their positive outlook and often local school boards became so politically oriented that existing schools suffered severe reverses. Primary education in the counties, then, depended almost entirely on the vagaries of local officials. Egalitarian and reform concepts stemming from Jacksonian Democracy did not appreciably affect Maryland attitudes toward education.

So divided were state and county political leaders on the question of public education that the "reform" constitutional convention of 1850 debated the question at great length and then voted to say nothing regarding education in the constitution. In 1856 Governor Thomas W. Ligon lamented that outside

Baltimore City public education lay in "utter and hopeless prostration." Not until the Constitutional Convention of 1864 did a mandate for an effective state system of education emerge and the Constitutional Convention of 1867, by slashing from the constitution most of the 1864 section on education, demonstrated that the moral commitment to free public education for children in the state was not deeply and widely held.[53]

Unlike the laggardly, temporizing attitudes of the state legislators and the selfish attitudes of county officials, Baltimore leaders recognized the importance of public education to the industrial and commercial future of the city. As a result, the city received concessions from the state to develop and fund its own school system. This led to the formation of a Board of Commissioners of Public Schools and a taxing system sufficient to foster an expanding public school system. With the first public elementary school opening in 1829, the commissioners oversaw an ever-growing system that could be considered well-functioning by the time of the depression of 1837. That economic disaster did not affect public education as it did labor unions. Although enrollments dropped by almost one-quarter, the schools weathered the depression and soon both a night school and high schools were open for students. Interestingly, though most public schools in the nation at the time tended to cater to boys, and though the Baltimore system segregated students by sex, female enrollments accounted for a substantial minority of the school population. While only thirty-four girls enrolled in the first female school founded in 1829 compared with 235 boys in the two male schools opening that year, a decade later, in 1839, with the worst effects of the depression over, the city had five male schools and four female, with just over 700 male students and just under 425 female. By 1850,

53. State financial support of all educational institutions in Maryland clearly indicates the priority legislators gave to education. Between 1819 and 1848, the annual expenditure ranged from a low of $10,600 in 1825 to a high of $24,100 in 1836. Between the peak in 1836 and the year 1848, the annual expenditure in education averaged $19,600. These funds were to support the University of Maryland, private academies and public primary schools. Cooperating counties would have received only some $1,000 each for their primary schools. Hanna, *Financial History of Maryland*, p. 480. Governor Ligon quoted in *ibid.*, 69. See: Steiner, *History of Education in Maryland*, pp. 53-63; William H. Shannon, "Public Education in Maryland (1825–1868) With Special Emphasis Upon the 1860's," (Ph.D. dissertation, University of Maryland, 1964), pp. 2-33.

there were almost twice the number of female schools as male, and girls accounted for forty-nine and one-half per cent of the school enrollment. By the time of the Civil War, girls represented a majority of students and both male and female high schools were functioning.

There is no reason to believe that students in these schools received particularly good teaching by twentieth century standards. Indeed, various protests over the teaching methods and instructional philosophy occasionally generated press reaction. However, despite serious instructional limitations, both male and female students received instruction in the Three R's and training in various skilled trades.[54]

From the end of the War of 1812 through the Jacksonian depression of 1837–39, Maryland experienced a shifting population, with substantial growth in Baltimore City, modest increases in the piedmont of northern and western Maryland, and stable or declining populations in the slave areas of southern Maryland and the Eastern Shore. Economically, the state suffered substantial setbacks in the post-war era, enjoyed comfortable, though not vigorous, growth in the middle twenties and early thirties, only to see itself weakened by the depression and the oncoming state obligations to European bankers holding internal improvement bonds. The one truly bright aspect was the continued expansion of the Baltimore and Ohio Railroad that was serving much of western Maryland by 1839. Socially, Marylanders displayed considerable independence— some would say stubbornness—in their religious controversies. They also displayed considerable lack of foresight in refusing to give wholehearted support to public basic education. While this failure is frequently attributed to the selfishness of slaveholding aristocrats, it must be remembered that two counties voting not to join the proposed state system, Allegany and Washington, were the westernmost counties of the state and

---

54. Because of its relatively advanced educational system by 1850, Baltimore City politicians did not support plans for a state system of education based on general taxation, reasoning that city residents would be paying for the creation of county programs rather than contributing to the advancement of their own educational institutions. L. E. Blach, "Education and the Maryland Constitutional Convention, 1850–1851," M.H.M., XXV (June,1930), 182-83; Shannon, "Public Education in Maryland," Ch. II; Vernon S. Vavrina, The History of Public Education in the City of Baltimore, 1829–1856 (Washington: Catholic University of America Press, 1958).

had populations that were overwhelmingly free and white. Though during this period important changes occurred in the state's political system, and while stirrings from the rising tide of Jacksonian Democracy moved into social institutions nationally, Marylanders generally turned away from social activism. Some Jacksonians stressed the value of honest labor and helped stimulate a labor movement in Maryland as elsewhere, but the ignorance of the Jacksonians in the area of economics accelerated and deepened the depression of 1837, bringing the labor movement down with it.

3

ANTE-BELLUM STATUS QUO: MARYLAND IN THE 1840'S

In 1844, when the Rev. Isaac Van Bibber toured southern and central Maryland on a one-man fundraising drive for the Episcopal Church of Westminster he visited the state capital and found the sleepy little town of Annapolis full of "many fine old houses," which he romanticized as having "an English and aristocratic air about them, such as is seldom seen in our more modern structures." In stark contrast, Van Bibber found the land in Anne Arundel County, formerly used for tobacco culture, "one of the dreariest and most poverty-stricken countries I ever saw." Annapolis and Anne Arundel County changed little in physical appearance over the first half of the nineteenth century.[55]

The continually depressed state of the agricultural economy in southern Maryland, outside of Prince George's County and in most of the Eastern Shore, prompted many area children to look for greener pastures when they reached their majority. Some, as Roger Taney, moved to western Maryland or to Baltimore City. Many left for good, heading into the Appalachian region of Tennessee or on into the Ohio Valley. Others, especially the plantation owners who realized they soon would be unable to maintain farm, family, and slaves, moved into the new south of Mississippi, Louisiana and Alabama, or over into Tennessee or Missouri. In all, by the end of the 1840's, more than 125,000 Marylanders had resettled out of the state.[56]

55. J. Alexis Shriver, ed., "A Maryland Tour in 1844; Diary of Isaac Van Bibber," *M.H.M.*, XXIX (September, 1944), 246, 247, 249.

56. Craven, *Soil Exhaustion*, p. 123.

As with the farmers, others looked for fertile fields outside of Maryland. One of these was a rising young poet and author who had spent several years in Baltimore living with his aunt following a disastrous experience at the United States Military Academy at West Point. He then went on to literary greatness in Richmond, Philadelphia, and New York, returning to Baltimore only long enough to suffer his final illness in 1850. This was Edgar Allan Poe. Poe published a number of short poems and three collections of poems before coming to live with his aunt in 1831, but his first notable achievement stemmed from his Baltimore years when in 1833 he won first prize in a literary contest sponsored by the *Baltimore Visitor* with his story of a weird adventure: "MS. Found in a Bottle."

Two years later he left for Richmond to assume the position of literary editor for the *Southern Literary Messenger*. Although Poe, as did his farmer friends, left Maryland for greener pastures, the comparison ends there. Certainly the literary and cultural fields of Baltimore were nowhere as barren as the agricultural wastelands to the south and east of the city. Indeed, in each of the years Poe resided in Baltimore, at least two new literary journals emerged. Of course, several of these entered the publishing field for only a brief stay, disappearing from circulation in a few months, but others continued to provide authors with outlets for their creative talents. In addition, the city claimed as home several authors and artists of note who visited widely among the culturally inclined. Poe knew a few of these individuals and, after winning the *Visitor* prize, apparently met the most illustrious of Baltimore's men of letters: John Pendleton Kennedy. In any case, Kennedy, who had been a judge in the contest, later recommended Poe for a position on the *Messenger*. Certainly Poe and Kennedy rank at the top of all Baltimore authors for the first half of the nineteenth century. In national repute, the youthful, eccentric, sometimes fitful Poe has far outshone Kennedy. A master practitioner of the fantastic tale and creator of a distinctive literary esthetic, Poe's greatest achievement may have been the impact made by his fiction and critical concepts on two of the founders of modern poetry,—the Frenchmen, Baudelaire and Mallarmé. Most of his work was translated into French by the latter. If Poe is habitually (and rightfully) praised as being the father of the detective story, far more important is his position as one of those who laid the grounds for the particular kind of poetry most characteristic of the present age.[57]

While John P. Kennedy's generous recommendation helped boost Poe's literary career, Kennedy's own career was at its peak. A man who never really knew whether to be a dashing hero, man of business, literary giant, or what he often coveted but only occasionally achieved—a politician. Critics of Kennedy might have charged him with the familiar sobriquet: jack of all trades, master of none. Actually Kennedy came perhaps as close as one might reasonably expect to mastering them all. A delegate to the Maryland legislature, representative to the United States Congress, and secretary of the navy in President Millard Fillmore's administration, as a youth Kennedy also had a brief and honorable combat with the British while serving with the militia during the War of 1812, both in the unsuccessful defense of Washington and the far more glorious defense of Baltimore. He then settled down to the mundane but rewarding program of winning admission to the Maryland bar. From then on it was politics, literature, society, and business. For a brief period in the middle 1850's he even served as president of a small but prosperous railroad, the Northern Central Railroad Company.

Kennedy's literary career included the usual mixture of works for a man of his temperament: fiction, biography, and nonfiction. He developed his fictional style with the aim of blending historical fact and fiction, not simply developing fictitious characters in a historical setting, but rather rounding off the rough edges of what he might have considered objectionable aspects of historical fact. Thus while his *Horse Shoe Robinson* sought to employ minor characters to keep the focus away from unnecessary violence, in *Rob of the Bowl* he mixed characters and settings (the latter being St. Mary's City in the seventeenth century) from various times and localities in order to downplay the harshness and uncertainties of frontier life. At the same time,

---

57. Edwin Markham, ed., *The Works of Edgar Allan Poe* (New York: Funk & Wagnalls, 1904), I, v-xii; John C. French, "Poe's Literary Baltimore," *M.H.M.*, XXXII (June, 1937), 101-108; Joseph M. Garrison, Jr., "The Function of Terror in the Work of Edgar Allan Poe," *American Quarterly*, XVIII (Summer, 1966), 136-38, 144-47. A defense of Poe's genius as an American writer despite his frequent use of European settings is found in: Charles L. Sanford, "Edgar Allan Poe: A Blight Upon the Landscape," *American Quarterly*, XX (Spring, 1968), 54-66.

though, he did challenge the standard romantic format by tainting his heroes and even letting a pirate escape death.

Probably the most interesting major fictional work of Kennedy was the political satire *Quodlibet,* a biting criticism of Jacksonian Democracy. Though some saw this work in narrow political terms, it was broad in scope and of exceptionally high quality for satire. Indeed, several critics who associated themselves closely with the Democratic party of Jackson and Van Buren wrote reviews praising it as a masterpiece of humor. Yet with this, his fourth novel in a decade, Kennedy hit the "dry" 1840's. Early in that decade he wrote a little work in defense of the Whig party and, near the end of the decade, completed a laborious and uncritical biography of the noted Maryland lawyer, United States Attorney General and author William Wirt.

Despite its ponderous style and other defects, and in spite of the sectional animosity of reviewers, the *Life of Wirt* proved very popular, second only to *Horse Shoe Robinson* in the sale of Kennedy publications. Yet Kennedy realized that his literary endeavors in the 1840's had not lived up to his potential. Complaining in 1852 to his friend, the very prominent southern writer, William Gilmore Simms, that while Simms produced works of great merit Kennedy only planned them. The Baltimore author said in exasperation: "My time is absorbed, *wasted,* with the little villainous shuffles of the business of the day—letters—an occasional railroad report—an *infernal* lecture, now and then, and driblets of occupation which leaves me no time to write *what I have in hand.*" Indeed, while his political and business activities proved personally rewarding, the 1840's were as barren for Kennedy literarily as for the southern Maryland farmer economically.[58]

With the youthful Poe dead and Kennedy out of steam, Baltimoreans also lost another important artist in the 1840's when Henry Dielman, who had come to the city from Germany in

---

58. Kennedy quoted in Lloyd W. Griffin, "The John Pendleton Kennedy Manuscripts," *M.H.M.,* XLVIII (December, 1953), 335-36; Kennedy's accounting of his literary successes is in Charles H. Bohner, *John Pendleton Kennedy* (Baltimore: J.H. Press, 1961), p. 185. See also Bohner's article: "J. P. Kennedy's *Quodlibet:* Whig Counterattack," *American Quarterly,* XIII (Spring, 1961), 84-92; and William S. Osborne, "John Pendleton Kennedy's *Horse Shoe Robinson:* A Novel with 'The Utmost Historical Accuracy,'" *M.H.M.,* LIX (September, 1964), 286-96.

1828 at age fifteen and had demonstrated remarkable musical talent as performer, composer and musical director, departed to take the music chair at the little Catholic college of Mount St. Mary's in Emmitsburg. In a few short years that school had already secured a wide regional reputation in music. This, coupled with the less demanding schedule of performances there, lured the maturing Dielman away from his admiring audiences. Yet the musical stage was not dark in the Monumental City during the 1840's. A wide range of visiting European performers played to the delight of the city's growing ethnic minorities, culminating with a visit by the popular rage of the day, Jenny Lind.[59]

Not all Maryland cultural institutions found the 1840's to be a barren time. On the one hand, the Library Company of Baltimore, that aristocratic and exclusive organization for the city elite, limited to those who could afford to purchase a share at fifty dollars and pay an annual fee, was at death's door. Founded in 1797, it suffered from chronic, if modest, indebtedness in the 1840's. Though enjoying a temporary spurt of prosperity at the end of the period, the company passed from the scene in 1854, leaving only the more egalitarian Mercantile Library Association (initiation fee two dollars, annual dues three dollars) functioning in the city. By contrast, it was in 1844 that the Maryland Historical Society emerged, and by 1848 exhibits under its auspices were opened to the public. The Maryland Institute of Art, too, was expanding and by the end of the decade was preparing to move to quarters it was to enjoy for over half a century. Before that time, though, its night school classes had stimulated William H. Rinehart to begin a lifetime of artistic achievement as a sculptor, an inspiration he later repaid by establishing a handsome trust fund which formed the base for the Rinehart School of Sculpture at the Institute.[60]

Seen in isolation, the cultural life of Baltimore and vicinity may appear to have been both extensive and of considerable

---

59. Locally, German male choruses made popular the minstrel show. Keefer, *Baltimore's Music*, pp. 104-105. See also pp. 70, 84, 104, 114, 119-35.

60. Stuart C. Sherman, "The Library Company of Baltimore," *M.H.M.*, XXXIX (March, 1944), 21-24; Latrobe Weston, "Art and Artists in Baltimore," *M.H.M.*, XXXIII (September, 1938), 213-19; Samuel K. Dennis, "A Brief Summary of the Maryland Historical Society's Hundred Years," *M.H.M.*, XXXIX (March, 1944), 1-5.

quality. Yet before the trials of Civil War engulfed the state, sculptor Rinehart fled to keep from starving and, ironically, made his fortune in Italy as a sculptor, sending back to his native Maryland the funds to encourage young artists. The 1850 census of professions recorded the combined total of artists, dancing teachers, musicians and music teachers in the entire state as 170. By comparison, there were 194 barkeepers. More immediately, when Ralph Waldo Emerson came to Baltimore to give two lectures to the Mercantile Library Association, only one newspaper saw fit to report his talk, indicating, perhaps, a general lack of interest in cultural events. Emerson, himself, after searching in vain for suitable intellectual companionship, wrote: "Charles Carroll the Signer is dead, and Archbishop Carroll is dead, and there is no vision in the land." Indeed, when compared with Boston, New York, Philadelphia, even Charleston, Baltimore's cultural life perhaps needed as much care and cultivation as Maryland's farmland.[61]

Part of the trouble in Baltimore, as in much of the state of Maryland, stemmed from its uncertainty as to regional and national allegiance. The latter 1840's, of course, were filled with controversy over the Mexican War, extension of slavery, and the rising tide of abolitionism that continually pressed hard moral questions on unwilling listeners. These abolitionist arguments generated very few political debates in the state. They were heard and debated, rather, in the councils of the various church organizations. Even there, the arguments over slavery surfaced most frequently in national and regional conferences. They seldom got down to the basic level of the Sunday sermon in Maryland.

Still, if churchmen within a given denomination found themselves irreconcilably split over such an issue, was that disagreement symptomatic of developing conflicts in the popular mind? Disputes within denominational hierarchy led to sectional splits in most Protestant churches and might have even caused a division within the Catholic Church had not that institution's leadership accepted a temporizing attitude toward the question. These divisions, as they occurred, caused many sleepless

61. Emerson quoted in George E. Bell, "Emerson and Baltimore: A Biographical Study," *M.H.M.*, LXV (Winter, 1970), 343. J. D. B. DeBow, comp., *The Seventh Census of the United States: 1850* (Washington: Government Printing Office, 1853), pp. 225, 226.

nights for Maryland clergy and lay leaders. Most churchmen opposed the establishment of official denominational policies regarding slavery, realizing that such a move would force a split in the national organization. Still, when splits occurred, as with the Baptists in 1845, and the Methodists a year later, Maryland leaders tended to support the southern contingent. At home in their own Maryland communities, even the Quakers, who were the strongest opponents to slavery of any church organization, came under pressure to oppose the institution more vigorously. Maryland Friends, however, preferred to preach their abolitionist doctrine "in the meek and peaceful spirit of the lamb" rather than in the more fiery language of some of their more northerly brethren.[62]

Among the Maryland population, the 1840's were indeed the preparatory time of the 1850's. Both in terms of population mobility and growth and social activism, the last decade in the first half of the nineteenth century proved to be evolutionary, with significant action coming in the closing years of the 1840's.

As with the preceding decades, growth in population centered around Baltimore. Outside the city, the population growth in northern Maryland had stimulated the splitting of Baltimore and Frederick Counties in 1836 and the creation of Carroll County. Still, the growth rates were not particularly high. Sev-

---

62. The fateful meaning of the church divisions is stated clearly by a noted historian of the growth of sectionalism: "The division of the churches was something more than an ecclesiastical event. The churches were among the great cohesive forces in America, serving along with the Whig and Democratic parties, business organizations, and other institutions to reinforce the Federal government in the maintenance of the American Union. The snapping of any one of these bonds under the stress of sectional tension inevitably increased the strain upon the others. The churches were the first to break; and when they did, tension upon other national organizations was brought nearer to the danger point," Sydnor, *Development of Southern Sectionalism*, pp. 299-300. See also: Robert G. Torbet, *A History of the Baptists* (Philadelphia: Judson Press, 1950), pp. 305-10; H. Shelton Smith, R. T. Handy and L. A. Loetscher, *American Christianity* (New York: Scribner, 1963), II, 168-79. A leading authority on American Catholicism explained how that church avoided taking a stand against slavery in the face of a statement by Pope Gregory XVI in 1839 condemning slave trade: "So long as Catholics regarded the question of the liberation of slaves not as a moral question but as a political question under the guise of abolitionism, Catholics did not divide over it." He also noted that the basic stance of Maryland Catholic leaders was to condemn the abolitionist movement on the grounds the abolitionists' actions only assured the stability of slavery in the nation. McAvoy, *History of the Catholic Church*, p. 161.

eral counties on the Eastern Shore began showing growth rates reflecting a virtual ending of the white outward migration of earlier years, most notably Somerset, Talbot, and Queen Anne. Caroline, with an overall twenty-four per cent increase in the decade, led the shore in population growth. Significantly, where Caroline's small slave population had declined by forty per cent between 1830 and 1840, it actually increased by seven per cent in the 1840's. The numbers are not significant, a slave population of 752 in 1840 and 808 in 1850, comprising only some ten per cent of the population in 1840 and eight per cent a decade later. The county grew no tobacco for sale during the decade. It modified its agricultural base only slightly, greatly increasing its production of wheat and Indian corn and, logically, its herds of cattle. County farmers devoted less land and effort to growing rye and oats and to raising sheep.[63]

For the state as a whole, the decade was transitional in the relative decline of individuals leaving the state and the beginning of what was to prove a massive influx of foreign immigrants as the unsuccessful German revolution and the Irish famine stimulated hundreds of thousands to flee to the New World. Averaging the annual birth and death rates for whites and free blacks to derive an annual growth rate, and excluding emigration from Maryland as a factor, the state's population should have shown a natural increase of approximately 52,000 during the decade. The 1850 census recorded some 51,200 foreign born in Maryland. Assuming that all of these persons arrived during the decade, the growth of population of the state actually exceeded these two combined elements. At least 9,000 other individuals migrated to the state from within the nation during the 1840's. All of these figures do not place Maryland in the forefront of the nation, but they do indicate the state was growing at a rate at variance with the states to the south. A very significant statistic is that regarding the foreign born within Maryland. Standing at over 50,000 in 1850, Maryland's foreign born population was larger than the foreign born populations of Virginia, North Carolina, South Carolina, and Georgia combined.

In terms of national and regional percentages of foreign born

---

63. *Seventh U.S. Census, 1850*, pp. 218-228; Thomas Drake, *Quakers and Slavery in America* (New Haven: Yale University Press, 1950) p. 117.

in the overall population, Maryland had 114 foreign born residents per 1,000. The average for the nation was 115; the average for the southern states, including Maryland, was thirty-two.
The importance of Baltimore City and its environs in this
demographic analysis must be stressed. Almost seventy per
cent of the foreign born registered in the 1850 census for Maryland lived in the city. The arrival of large numbers of Germans
in the late 1840's prompted the Baltimore German population
to reinvigorate the work of the German Society of Maryland
(1783) to protect the new arrivals from pernicious laws and unsavory people and profiteers. In contrast, Talbot County, a
county showing fourteen per cent growth in the 1840's following a decline of six per cent in the 1830's, had only seventy-
three foreign born out of a population of just over 13,800 in
1850. Similarly, its residents born outside the state accounted
for less than two per cent of its population. Ten per cent of
Baltimore's population had been born in the United States but
outside of Maryland. On the Western Shore, Frederick long had
been a home for migrating Germans. Yet in 1850, only three
per cent of its population was foreign born (approximately
1,400) and five per cent had come into the county from another
state or territory in the nation (2,200).[64]

While Maryland public schools could hardly be called collectively a state system, they were more extensive than farther
south. Local social and political leaders gave considerable attention to academies, mostly privately run, as did their southern
brethren. Every county except Caroline and Queen Anne had at
least one such academy. Carroll County had the amazing number of thirty academies (though only forty-seven teachers)

---

64. For a detailed social analysis of key areas in Maryland during the 1830's
see: Whitman H. Ridgway, "A Social Analysis of Maryland Community
Elites, 1827–1836: A Study of the Distribution of Power in Baltimore City,
Frederick County, and Talbot County" (Ph.D. dissertation: University of
Pennsylvania, 1973). Philip Taylor, *The Distant Magnet* (New York: Harper
& Row, 1971), p. 125; data for 1840 is in: *Sixth United States Census, 1840,
Compendium of Enumeration* (Washington: Thomas Allen, 1841); data for
1850 is in: DeBow, *Seventh U.S. Census, 1850*. See also: M. Ray Della, Jr.,
"An Analysis of Baltimore's Population in the 1850's," *M.H.M.*, LXVIII
(Spring, 1973), 20-35; Bureau of the Census, *A Century of Population Growth*
(Washington: Government Printing Office, 1909), p. 129; Karinen, "Numeri-
cal and Distributional Aspects of Maryland Population." Louis P. Hennig-
hausen, *History of the German Society of Maryland* (Baltimore: W. E. C.
Harrison & Sons, 1909), pp. 5 *et passim*, 171.

teaching just under 1,000 students. By contrast, that county had no public schools, and only three per cent of the academies' funds came from public monies. Frederick had seventeen academies with an average of four teachers and forty-three students each.

The arrangements for education left the state with a much larger population of illiterate whites than was true to the north, but the illiteracy rate was only half as poor as in southern states. Unfortunately, the very limited attention given to educating Maryland's large free black population left that group of people with an illiteracy rate among adults of almost sixty per cent, or approximately six times that of whites. The actual attendance figures for children in county schools and academies when compared with school age population (ages five through fourteen) gave a strange picture of school enrollments. If the figures are to be believed, St. Mary's County, with the highest illiteracy rate among white adults in the state, had the highest percentage of white children in school: ninety-eight per cent. Across the state as a whole, sixty-one per cent of the male white children and fifty-five per cent of the female white children of school age were enrolled. Of all the counties, Prince George's stands out as having had a higher percentage of girls than boys in school. Somerset County, with twenty-six per cent of the white school-age population in school, and Allegany with thirty per cent, represented the most educationally backward counties. The illiteracy rate among white adults in those counties reflected the average rate for the state.[65]

Higher education in Maryland developed along religious, private, and public lines in the first half of the century. The public aspects centered around various professional schools of the University of Maryland in Baltimore, particularly the medical and dental schools. Liberal arts aspects of this institution barely managed to survive the bombast and avarice of Horace Morison who supposedly administered and taught in the liberal arts "college," and by the early 1850's doubt existed whether the college would survive him. Several church-related colleges, founded at the beginning of the century, disappeared or went up in smoke as their buildings blazed to the ground; but such

65. Eaton, *Growth of Southern Civilization*, pp. 117-18, 160; DeBow, *Seventh U.S. Census, 1850*, pp. 120, 123-25.

private institutions as St. John's College and Washington College, along with the growing Catholic school, Mount St. Mary's College, provided solid academic programs for youth of the state and region. Mount St. Mary's, in particular, won wide acclaim for its curricula and professors—attracting outstanding students from many parts of the nation.[66]

Economically, Marylanders had overcome the extended problems of the early years and of the depression of 1837–39. Additionally, the state was repaying the massive debt it had incurred for promoting internal improvements and was on a sound financial footing. Legislative development of conservative financial standards kept banks solvent through the financial vagaries following the demise of the Bank of the United States.

Enterprising Baltimore merchants and shipowners were losing out to New York in several ways. One important factor was the failure of local ship builders to adjust to changing styles and to new technological developments. While the Baltimore clippers proved very valuable in both the privateering activities during the War of 1812 and the Hispanic American wars for independence, as well as in the South American coffee trade and in the illegal slave trade, they lacked sufficiently large holds to prove competitive in the Atlantic as well as the rapidly developing China trade. New clippers coming out of northern shipyards were much larger and also of a different design than the small, slender Baltimore clipper. Yet Maryland shipyards built few of the new vessels.

Similarly, the development of steamboats brought new opportunities both for construction and for trade. Indeed, successful navigation of the lower Susquehanna River by a steamboat greatly lessened interest in an expanded canal along that waterway. Still, Baltimore money generally did not go into the local construction of these craft. This does not mean that city businessmen were inactive. Flour merchants shipped an average of a quarter million barrels annually to the West Indies and South America in the 1840's. The point is that Baltimore's growth was not remarkable when compared with New York, and this was due in considerable part to the failure of businessmen to pursue actively and vigorously new, developing markets or to push

---

66. Bell, "Emerson in Baltimore," p. 346; Callcott, *History of the University of Maryland,* pp. 96-97. See generally, Steiner, *History of Education in Maryland.*

Sleek, swift Baltimore clippers which led the British navy many merry chases during their reign of the open seas. Watercolor by M. J. Huggins. *Maritime Museum. M.H.S.*

new products aggressively. The growth that city and state experienced in the decade could be ascribed primarily to natural increase rather than to unusual industriousness or to the exercise of creative talents.[67]

Agriculturally, Maryland farmers began to recognize the value of investing time, energy, and money into their business. Agricultural societies grew, study of technical reports increased, and large quantities of money went into the purchase of fertilizer, both natural and chemical. The latter development spurred a few enterprising manufacturers into developing some of the largest chemical fertilizer plants in the nation. The most popular fertilizer, though, proved to be Peruvian guano which came into the state by multi-ton shipments. With first large-scale importation in 1843, it quickly became very popular. Montgomery County farmers spread more than seventy tons of the manure on their farms in 1847. This investment paid off in both increased crop production and higher land values. The steady growth of Baltimore and Washington caused some farmers in the vicinity of those two centers to begin what today would be called truck farming, and by the middle forties some good dairy herds were being developed. The Baltimore-Washington branch of the B & O Railroad with its convenient and rapid service contributed substantially to this growing industry.[68]

Successful completion of the rail line between Washington and Baltimore served to do more than promote truck farming. One of the great technical feats of the mid-century was demonstrated along the right of way of this railroad when Samuel F. B. Morse chose that route to establish his first telegraph. Because the train operated so conveniently between the two cities,

67. Craven, *Soil Exhaustion*, p. 131; Charles C. Griffin, "Privateering From Baltimore During the Spanish American Wars of Independence," *M.H.M.*, XXXV (March, 1940), 1-25; Howard I. Chapelle, *The Baltimore Clipper* (Hatboro, Pa.: Tradition Press, 1965), pp. 110-11, 140-45; George R. Taylor, "American Economic Growth Before 1840," *Journal of Economic History*, XXIV (December, 1964), 430-32; Marion V. Brewington, "Chesapeake Sailmaking," *M.H.M.*, LXV (Summer, 1970), 144.

68. The trip between Baltimore and Washington took two hours and ten minutes. Donald J. McCauley, "The Limits of Change in the Tobacco South: an Economic and Social Analysis of Prince George's County, Maryland, 1840–1860," (M.A. thesis, University of Maryland, 1973), Ch. II; Craven, *Soil Exhaustion*, pp. 146-47; Vivian Wiser, "Improving Maryland's Agriculture: 1840–1860," *M.H.M.*, LXII (Summer, 1962), 105-32.

Morse could secure free transportation between the terminals of his line as it was being constructed. Although the official test of the experiment came May 24, 1844, with the transmission of the message: "What hath God wrought!" some three weeks earlier, with the line almost to Baltimore, news of Henry Clay's nomination as the Whig party's candidate for President, reached the nation's capital from Whig convention headquarters in Baltimore over the telegraph almost two hours before newsmen in Baltimore could file their stories in Washington via the train.[69]

A second impact the rail line had on the Maryland countryside was to turn the Laurel area into a little industrial center. The combination of easy access to markets, both for raw materials and finished products, and modest land prices, made Laurel quite attractive to several Prince George's County businessmen. The Patuxent Manufacturing Company began operating there in 1835, and in the 1840's was prospering as a cotton mill. With up to 500 employees, 100 looms and possibly as many as 7,000 spindles, it became the largest such plant in the Southeast. To complement this manufacturing concern, smaller concerns went into operation in the area, including a machine shop, a woolen mill, and a second small cotton sheeting mill. By 1850, over one-half million dollars had been invested in capital improvements for manufacturing concerns in the Laurel area. The firms produced goods valued at just under $360,000 in that year and made a combined profit of almost $50,000.[70]

Completion of the main B & O line to Cumberland furthered the expansion of the coal mines in western Maryland and also provided encouragement for expansion in Pennsylvania and northwestern Virginia. Conversely, this improved transportation system spelled doom for many small home manufacturing concerns such as farmers' grist mills and whisky stills. The more efficient businesses in the hills around Baltimore gained much of that business.

By 1850, Maryland's economic, social, and cultural institutions clearly were superior to those of the more southern states, though generally behind similar institutions in Pennsylvania, New York and Massachusetts. With a diverse economic base, a

69. Oliver W. Larkin, *Samuel F. B. Morse and American Democratic Art* (Boston: Little, Brown & Co., 1954), pp. 150-51; James A. Robertson, contributor, "A Letter from Samuel Morse," *M.H.M.*, XXXIV (March, 1939), 40.

70. McCauley, "Limits of Change," Ch. II.

population that included substantial, though localized, mixtures of recent immigrants, and educational facilities that represented a greater balance between basic learning and advanced scholarly and professional training than any state to the south or west, Maryland clearly did not fit into the classical image of a southern state. Only one element tied Maryland to the South: the American aberration, slavery.

4

## WAS MARYLAND A SOUTHERN STATE?

Marylanders began holding blacks in bondage within twenty years of the founding of the "Old Line State." Still, slavery developed more gradually in the colony than in Virginia, partly because many white indentured servants came to Maryland who could be purchased with much less capital. Whether white prejudice against blacks developed as gradually as the institution of slavery or was already imbued in the transplanted Englishman before he even arrived is debatable. However, it developed, certainly even before the nineteenth century began that whites in Maryland tended to look with a jaundiced eye upon fellow inhabitants who were black, whether those persons were living in bondage or as free men. By the antebellum era, then, the existence of slavery within Maryland for well over a century had made an impact on its society, economy, and government. One consequence of this impact was the tendency on the part of many whites to picture themselves and their state as part of the South. Others failed to see a clear relationship with the southern states; for them, Maryland owed as much to other regions and could derive as much benefit by maintaining ties with northern and western communities as with southern. Included in this latter group, by 1850, were businessmen, recent immigrants, and a free black population of some seventy-five thousand individuals.[71]

Slavery as an institution was found in all geographical areas of Maryland, but well before the nineteenth century its area of concentration had been set: southern Maryland and the Eastern Shore. Of course, the primary positive reason for this was the

---

71. A clear picture of the early development of slavery in Maryland is drawn in: Ross M. Kimmel, "The Negro before the Law in Seventeenth Century Maryland" (M.A. thesis, University of Maryland, 1971.)

early reliance on tobacco culture in those two regions. Still, the institution remained strong even when the agricultural activities changed. As tobacco and poor farming methods drained the soil of its productivity, planters began growing other crops or undertaking other endeavors. But they did not shift their ownership of human flesh as rapidly as they did their means of livelihood. Changes occurred, of course, and the number of slaves in the tidewater area declined through most of the first half of the nineteenth century, although the institution remained focused there. Yet even after the agricultural economy began to improve in the 1840's, the institution of slavery did not expand again. Only in three southern Maryland counties, Calvert, Charles' and St. Mary's, did the relative number of slaves to total population maintain itself. Even Prince George's County, fast becoming one of the two largest producers of tobacco in the nation, failed to maintain a constant relationship between the number of whites and slaves in the 1840's. While more slaveholders increased, there was an augmentation also in the percentage of heads of households in the county holding no slaves. The editor of the county *Planters' Advocate* could argue that slavery was more profitable in Prince George's County than in the best cotton regions of the deep South, but apparently a decreasing percentage of the residents agreed with him. This may have been due to the growing economic diversification within the county during the 1840's.[72]

If slavery was on the wane for much of the era, what happened to the slaves? Generalizing from the birth and death statistics of bondsmen given in the 1850 census, had all Maryland slaves remained within the state and under bondage, the slave population in 1850 should have been almost seventy-five per cent higher than it was. A recent analysis of available records indicates that the remarkable decline of the number of slaves in the state cannot be attributed to escapes. The only hard evidence on the frequency of slave runaways is in the 1850 census which listed 279 in 1849. Even if one were to assume that to be a typical number, the total escapes for the first half of the century would account for about a decade's natural increase in the slave population within the state. A second rea-

72. Eugene D. Genovese, *The Political Economy of Slavery* (New York: Random House, 1967), pp. 142, 143; McCauley, "The Limits of Change in the Tobacco South," Ch. IV.

son for the decline of the slave population could be manumissions. Some individuals did, indeed, free their slaves, frequently by the will of a dying master. Geographically, most manumissions occurred in northern and western Maryland. Despite occasional legislative enactments aimed at discouraging such actions, numbers of slaves became free annually. Yet overall, somewhat fewer lost their chains through the voluntary action of masters than would represent the hypothetical number of escapees. This includes those who were released from bondage to journey to the Maryland colony in Liberia.

A third explanation for the decline of slavery could be wholesale sale of slaves to the "New South" of Louisiana, Alabama and Mississippi. Certainly slave traders traveled through Maryland soliciting business, and no doubt many bondsmen found themselves transported from Maryland to the Gulf Coast states. However, serious doubt has been thrown on the old belief that Maryland became a principal trading and "slave breeding state" when productive agricultural work declined. The most pressing explanation for large scale departure of slaves is that masters took them when they started a new life outside of Maryland. The decline of white population in areas of the state where slavery was concentrated during the 1820's and 1830's would indicate by correlation that slaveowners did not rid themselves of their human property and remain themselves in a depressed community. They left and took their slaves with them.[73]

Many factors affected the conditions of slaves who lived in the state in the nineteenth century. Most masters held slaves for agricultural field work. Those few whites who had large farms singled out some slaves to work as artisans, especially for smithing, wagon and barrel making, and harness work. In addition, a select few slaves became house servants and livery men. Some artisans and craftsmen secured slaves to work as helpers; a few shipbuilders, warehousemen and manufacturers either owned or hired slaves to work in their establishments. Of course,

---

73. Elwood L. Brinder, Jr., "The Fugitive Slaves of Maryland," *M.H.M.*, LXVI (Spring, 1971), 33-50; Brackett, *The Negro in Maryland*, Ch. IV; *Seventh U.S. Census, 1850*, p. 222; William Calderhead, "How Extensive was the Border State Slave Trade? A New Look," *Civil War History*, XVIII (March, 1972), 42-55; Craven, *Soil Exhaustion*, pp. 122-23; McCauley, "Limits of Change in the Tobacco South," pp. 20-23.

wealthy merchants, lawyers, doctors, and politicians sometimes owned slaves as house servants. But without a doubt, the vast majority of Maryland slaves toiled in the fields.

During times of relative prosperity, slaves of "good masters" could expect to receive equitable treatment, given their condition. Their master passed out occasional supplements to their basic food ration of corn meal, pork, flour, and vegetables. In addition, the slaves were permitted to maintain small gardens near their quarters. They also received warm, if rough, clothing for the winter and were given several extra holidays during that season. They were allowed to participate in celebrations off the plantation. Even during the good times, though, they received no form of education. Field hands had virtually no opportunity to develop their intellectual talents or even learn about the "outside world" except through word of mouth from fellow slaves. Masters saw no benefit for either themselves or the slave from education; indeed, they recognized that the reverse could be the case. A person fit for field work, hard and boring as that work was, would be no better at such menial tasks if he were literate; rather, he would be likely to realize with greater perception that his condition as chattel was both inhuman and intolerable. That realization naturally would lead to conflict between master and slave, with the slave often losing. Such a condition would be detrimental to the master in the form of decreased productivity from the slave. Indeed, by the 1830's, farmers in the piedmont began realizing that a slave, who had nothing to gain by working hard, was less productive than a hired free person.[74]

During periods of depression slaves greatly suffered. The material items usually provided decreased in quantity and quality, and the demands placed upon them to work increased. Some farmers who chose to ride out bad times imagining an eventual economic reversal, tried to hire out their slaves. Others, recognizing that fellow agriculturalists were facing similar trials, either sold their slaves or moved to a newly developing territory outside the state. Only the owners of farms adjacent to an urban area or near a canal or railroad construction project

---

74. One observer suggested in the mid 1830's that there was "a rapidly growing conviction among the landholders of the state that hired labour is cheaper for all their agricultural purposes, excepting the culture of tobacco, than slave labour." Quoted in *ibid.*, p. 30.

**Overseer doing his duty, during the slavery days.** Print by Benjamin Henry Latrobe. *Papers of Benjamin Henry Latrobe, M.H.S.*

could hope to hire out some of their field hands as laborers. Even in bad times, though, masters disliked hiring out their slaves to work on construction gangs because of the dangerous work involved and the consequent chance that their property would suffer permanent injury.

Very few slaves being literate, autobiographical evidence, with others, concerning their daily lives and treatment as field hands is limited. Their statements at best provide only an impressionistic picture of the conditions under which they lived and worked.

Normally, slaves who were part of a family lived in a two-room house. One former slave described the living conditions in this manner: "I lived with my mother, father, and sister in a log cabin built of log and mud, having two rooms; one with a dirt floor and the other above, each room having two windows, but no glass . . . I slept on a home-made bed or bunk, while my mother and sister slept in a bed made by father . . . while dad slept on a bench beside the bed and that he used in the day as a work bench. . . ." The work varied, of course, according to the season and to the crops being raised on the farm. Naturally the distribution of work also depended upon the number of slaves owned by the farmer. There is a tendency to perceive the slave-owning farmer as a planter-aristocrat. In fact, many farmers had only a few slaves; the large plantation with twenty or more slaves was not common in Maryland, either at the beginning or the middle of the century.[75]

Another slave recalling his youth on Kent Island commented that his master's family, "being poor, not having a large place or a number of slaves to increase their wealth, made them little above the free colored people and with no knowledge, they could not teach me or anyone else to read." A slave from western Maryland, noted: "The farm was like all other farms in Frederick County, raising grain, such as corn, wheat and fruit and on which work was seasonable, depending upon the weather, some seasons producing more and some less. When the season was good for the crop and crops plentiful, we had a little money as the plantation owner gave us some to spend." He reminisced, however, that "My father used to tell me how

75. George P. Rawick, ed., *The American Slave: A Composite Autobiography* (Westport, Conn.: Greenwood Pub. Co., 1972), XVI, No. 8, 51-52.

Frederick Douglass (Frederick Augustus Washington Bailey) the Maryland-born abolitionist who denounced slavery in speeches and writings throughout the world. *Photo in M.H.S.*

he would hide in the hay stacks at night, because he was whipped and treated badly by his master who was rough and hard-boiled on his slaves."

Large farm or small, good season or bad, the treatment slaves received depended on the temperament of the master or mistress. Several slaves commented on their fear of the "nine ninety-nine," meaning a severe whipping which lasted until the slave collapsed. Others told of good masters but harsh mistresses. Slaves who could congregate after work, attend services at their own church on Sunday, enjoy the same holidays whites celebrated, hunt and fish, and not feel afraid of being sold to a dealer considered their masters as good persons. This might best be illustrated by the recollection of Charles Coles, "I do not know who my parents were nor my relatives. I was reared on a large farm owned by a man by the name of Silas Dorsey, a fine Christian gentleman and a member of the Catholic Church." He added: "Mr. Dorsey was a man of excellent reputation and character, was loved by all who knew him, black and white, especially his slaves." Coles said he believed no slave ever ran away from the Dorsey farm. The man's ignorance of his family apparently did not disturb him as much as was the case with Maryland's most famous slave, Frederick Douglass. In his memoirs, Douglass attributed his lack of contact with his mother to his master's desire to dehumanize his slaves.[76]

Although Maryland was a border state close to free territory where a runaway slave might secure his liberty, the frequency of successful escapes from the area was not high. Of course, over the years hundreds of slaves escaped to freedom, but the rate even in the counties bordering free land was surprisingly low. One evidence that this was the case was the general absence of slave patrols. Periodically, slave owners met to complain about the number of runaways and to discuss means of preventing further escapes. As a result slave patrols were formed, but only rarely did they function longer than a few weeks. Even the sensation of Nat Turner's uprising in Virginia stimulated very little activity.

With the proximity of Maryland to the Pennsylvania and Dis-

---

76. *Ibid.*, pp. 49, 44, 61, 4-5; Frederick Douglass, *Life and Times of Frederick Douglass Written by Himself* (New York: Collier Books, 1962), p. 2.

Harriet Tubman, the intrepid Maryland free black woman who led hundreds of slaves to freedom through the underground railway. *Photo in M.H.S.*

trict of Columbia borders, and with very limited patrols to stop runaways, why did so few slaves escape? Certainly the answer is not that Maryland blacks held in bondage were happy and content with their lives, nor that they lacked a vision of freedom. Rather, the basic reason was that they were ignorant of the logistics of escape. Who could tell the person planning to flee how to reach safety or to know when he had arrived in free territory? Several poor souls, for example, following either directions or crude maps, thought they were safe when they crossed the lower Susquehanna River, only to emerge from hiding and find themselves in the hands of the Harford County sheriff. Others never attempted escape because of lurid stories their masters told them. As one black related it: "At every gate through which we were to pass, we saw a watchman—at every ferry a guard—on every bridge a sentinel—and in every wood a patrol. We were hemmed in upon every side . . . when we permitted ourselves to survey the road [to freedom] we were frequently appalled. Upon either side we saw grim death, assuming the most horrid shapes. Now it was starvation, causing us to eat our own flesh;—now we were contending with the waves, and were drowned;—now we were overtaken, and torn to pieces by the fangs of the terrible bloodhound. . . ." This latter point received confirmation in southern Maryland, where one plantation owner bred large numbers of bloodhounds to sell to slave owners and sheriffs for hunting runaways![77]

The lure of freedom sometimes overcame fear and despite the risks, slaves managed to escape. They received support from free blacks and whites. Although authenticated reports of such activities by white Marylanders are few in number, there are some examples of such daring actions. But the most famous and successful person who helped slaves escape was a former Maryland slave: Harriet Tubman, who reentered the South fifteen times to lead over two hundred to freedom. The stories

---

77. *Ibid.*, p. 85. Douglass noted that on the Lloyd plantation where he lived much of his early life, only "three classes, slaveholders, slaves, and overseers" came within the gates. "Not even commerce," he said, "was permitted within its secluded precincts." How could slaves in such isolation learn that they were near a free border? *Ibid.*, p. 38. The Stafford Farm in Charles County was known as "Blood Hound Manor" because blood hounds were raised there and trained to track runaway slaves. Rawick, *The American Slave*, XVI, No. 8, 22.

of her successful missions could rival the most dramatic spy stories of the twentieth century.[78]

Slavery itself did not make Maryland a southern state. The attitude of whites and free blacks would be a stronger determinant of that classification. Some Marylanders held attitudes quite in keeping with the generalized southern attitude. Whether conscious or not, many slave owners classified their bondsmen as cattle. One Marylander bequeathed his daughter: "three negroes . . . also one gray mare and one cow." The law, too, distinguished between slave and free white in a manner comparable to southern states generally. This is evidenced both in the statutes and in court cases. In the latter area, for example, a woman slave of Lewis Hann was found dead, presumably from "being whipt & abused." Nobody was accused of committing the crime because of a lack of testimony. Thus, a conspiracy of silence protected the culprit, buttressed by the fact that slaves could not testify against whites.[79]

Private attitudes, too sometimes reflected a Southern orientation. The former governor, Charles Goldsborough, for example, felt the economic pinch in the mid-1830's. Seeking a way to ease his financial problems, he realized that he simply had too many blacks to feed and clothe. Acknowledging that "if I keep them at all I must keep them well," Goldsborough could not bring himself to sell a portion of his human property because "it is inevitably to a certain degree inhuman and offensive to one's own feelings." He concluded that the best solution was to retain ownership but to resettle all or most of his slaves in a more southern location, because: "To them the removing is just the same as the migration of any poor white family seeking their future in the Southern or Western country." In so do-

---

78. Caroline Hammond told of escaping from a farm in Anne Arundel County with her parents, being shielded by "a white family on Ross Street"—now Druid Hill Ave., "where we were sheltered by the occupants, who were ardent supporters of the Underground Railroad." The family then was given transportation in a covered wagon to Hanover, but on the trip "we never alighted on the ground in any community or close to any settlement, fearful of being apprehended by people who were always looking for rewards." *Ibid.*, pp. 20-21; Gerald Sorin, *Abolitionism, A New Perspective* (New York: Praeger, 1972), p. 101.

79. Quoted in Kenneth M. Stampp, *The Peculiar Institution* (New York: Vintage Books, 1956), p. 204; manuscript #234, Maryland Room, McKeldin Library, University of Maryland. Counter examples are given in Brackett, *The Negro in Maryland*, pp. 138-43.

ing he hoped "to send out as my own property a sufficient number to stock a good large cotton plantation." Although Goldsborough never accomplished the plan, his attitudes reflected the views of the more enlightened slaveowners of southern Maryland. It was an ambiguous situation, with the master at once viewing the slaves as property and as humans. John Pendleton Kennedy, author and politician, displayed a somewhat similar ambivalence. After freeing his inherited slave, and expressing the view that a slave was "the persecuted child of misfortune," Kennedy continued in the same vein, noting that "I cannot reconcile myself to the opinion that one man can ever obtain a lawful title to the possession and ownership of another." Yet when he heard arguments from abolitionists he remarked: "Manifestly emancipation would be a greater evil than the continuance of slavery." Thus, his primary concern was ultimately to protect his own class even at the perpetuation of a system he said he abhorred. Even here, though, while this attitude might be classified as southern, similar expressions came from many northerners and westerners. In fact, prejudice against slaves and against blacks in general permeated the American scene. This prejudice took the form both of words and deeds.[80]

Organization of the Maryland Colonization Society is pictured by some as the institutionalization of southern prejudice against both slaves and black people generally. After all, the whites who organized the society sought the removal of blacks from Maryland on the grounds that the prospective emigrés could not live a wholesome life among the dominant white population in the United States. After Nat Turner's rebellion in 1831 support grew for emigration on the grounds that free blacks in Maryland were stirring up trouble among slaves and also serving to aid runaways. White spokesmen feared another Turner-like uprising. Thereafter with some exceptions the great thrust of the society was to persuade free blacks to migrate to Cape Palmas rather than as formerly to induce masters to liberate their slaves and send them to Africa.

In the 1830's abolitionists began raising the cry of discrimi-

---

80. No author, "Governor Charles Goldsborough's Views on Slavery," *M.H.M.*, XXXIX (Dec., 1944), 333; Bohner, *John Pendleton Kennedy*, pp. 46, 170; Herbert Aptheker, ed., *A Documentary History of the Negro People in the United States* (New York: The Citadel Press, 1951), pp. 147, 176, 188.

nation against supporters of both the American Colonization Society and the Maryland Society on the grounds that the organizations were perpetuating a negative view of blacks. William Lloyd Garrison, the most outspoken and dynamic abolitionist, condemned Maryland colonization plans in his famous newspaper, *The Liberator*. Lest his statements be pictured as representing only the extreme wing of abolitionist thought, and that the attacks focused just on Southerners, one need only read an address drafted at a mass meeting in New York City by blacks of that locale, attacking plans for formation of a New York branch of the American Colonization Society. Contending that "This is our home, and this is our country," members of the meeting asked "in what respects are we inferior?" The attitudes of those supporting and opposing colonization, then, cannot be labled neatly northern or southern. Marylanders shared the range of attitudes found elsewhere.[81]

Clearly, rapid expansion of the free black population in Maryland during the first half of the nineteenth century set Maryland apart from southern states. In that half century, the state's white population increased by 93 per cent; its slave population rose briefly, but gradually declined by 14 per cent from 1800. In dramatic contrast to both variations, the free black population of Maryland increased by 282 per cent between 1800 and 1850. No South Atlantic state witnessed such startling changes in the ante-bellum years.[82]

How can the dramatic growth of the free black population be explained? The answer does not lie in an official state policy of benevolence. While Maryland statutes did not place as harsh

---

81. The standard work on the Maryland Colonization Society and its beleaguered little (900 colonists) colony is Penelope Campbell, *Maryland in Africa, The Maryland State Colonization Society, 1831–1857* (Urbana: University of Illinois Press, 1971). Baltimore free blacks actively counseled prospective emigrés not to leave for the colony. They had significant success when talking with individuals who had been living in the rural areas of the state. The agent for the society complained that Baltimore City and County blacks "left no means unturned to put obstacles in the way of our expedition." Quoted in: Aaron Stopak, "The Maryland State Colonization Society: Independent State Action in the Colonization Movement," *M.H.M.*, LXIII (Sept., 1968), 278; Sorin, *Abolitionism*, pp. 48-49; Apthecker, *Documentary History of the Negro People*. A courageous but temperate Quaker abolitionist, Benjamin Lundy, sought to publicize the range of sentiments and ideas regarding the abolition of slavery through his newspaper published in Baltimore, *The Genius of Universal Emancipation*.

82. *Seventh U.S. Census, 1850*, p. 222.

and extreme limitations on free blacks as did some states to the south, there certainly was no encouragement for their immigration into the state. Rather, the laws affecting free blacks in Maryland were comparable to those in northern states. Maryland blacks could marry, own property, execute wills, engage in commercial activities, and institute suits in courts. Ample evidence exists that they exercised these rights with success. On the other hand, they were subjected to a variety of harassments, including threats to their freedom. For example, free blacks could expect to be challenged by anyone seeking to locate a runaway slave. When this happened, the free person of color had to show proof of his status or face at least temporary incarceration. In such situations, he was presumed guilty until proven innocent, hardly in keeping with the Bill of Rights of either the United States or Maryland. Still, despite oppressive statutes and imminence of being returned to slavery, the free black population in Maryland rose dramatically. No definite explanation can be offered for this growth.[83]

A somewhat complex hypothesis may suggest reasons why Maryland served as a magnet to attract thousands of free blacks. First, geographically, and especially climatically, Maryland was reasonably comparable to more southern states. An individual moving to the tidewater area of Maryland from any South Atlantic state north of Florida would have had minimal difficulties in adjusting. If he had gone just one state farther north—to Pennsylvania—this generalization would not have held true. Second, in the Ante-Bellum period, even after Nat Turner's uprising, Maryland's black code was far less severe in practice than in theory. Furthermore, while restrictions increased over the decades, many efforts to place legal threats over the heads of "free persons of color" were rejected. This was in contrast to states in the deep South which increased their efforts to force

---

83. Eaton, *Growth of Southern Civilization*, p. 92; Sydnor, *Development of Southern Sectionalism*, p. 31; James M. Wright, *The Free Negro in Maryland, 1634–1860* (New York: Octagon Books, 1971) pp. 191-196. Richard Wade showed that many blacks in Baltimore were detained for not having proof of their free status. Some of these were fugitives; others were not. Richard C. Wade, *Slavery in the Cities* (New York: Oxford University Press, 1964), p. 219. A black minister recalled being stopped by a group of whites who decided he was a runaway, and "dey wuz gwine to give me a coat of tar and feathers when de boss rode up and ordered my release." Rawick, *The American Slave*, XVI, No. 8, 75.

out the free black population, fearing recurrences of Turner's rebellion. A third point is the decline of slavery in the key area where jobs might be obtained: Baltimore. In contrast to such cities as Richmond, Norfolk, Charleston, Mobile, Savannah, and even Washington, D.C., where the number of slaves increased over the decades, the number of slaves in Baltimore declined by over thirty per cent between 1820 and 1850. This decline was not due to a high incidence of escapes, for proportionately fewer slaves ran away successfully from Baltimore than from rural areas in Maryland. Instead, it seems to have come from the recognition that hired was cheaper than slave labor in terms of productivity.[84]

The three points suggested here are all somewhat negative: moving to Maryland from the lower South required no major adjustments in one's style of living; life in Maryland, while restricted, was considerably less oppressive than southward; the decline of slavery in a large labor market, Baltimore, reduced competition for jobs. On a positive note: free blacks in Maryland exercised their freedom to promote themselves socially, culturally, and economically.

Although Maryland had no efficient educational system in the first half of the nineteenth century, at least many free schools for white children existed and enjoyed a minimal public support. Little in this way was given to free black children. Yet many private endeavors, often successful, provided some educational opportunities for young blacks. While a number of these programs were financed and promoted by whites, especially in the early years by white churches, a large number of educational activities stemmed from the initiative of "concerned" blacks. When black Methodists revolted against the white domination of that institution and established the separate African Methodist Episcopal Church, a number of Sunday schools appeared, providing basic education for those in attendance. Some such projects, whether founded privately or

---

84. Although the 1850 census only showed two per cent of the free blacks in Maryland having been born outside the state, the figures do not compare closely to the birth and death rates of free blacks. Probably many fugitives who were included in the census reported Maryland as their birthplace in order to prevent their recapture. Wade indicates that many fugitives lived in Baltimore. *Seventh U.S. Census, 1850*, pp. 219-22; Wade, *Slavery in the Cities*, p. 219; McCauley, "Limits of Change in the Tobacco South," p. 30; Wright, *The Free Negro in Maryland*, p. 173.

by churches, failed because of harassment by bigots; but in most cases perseverance was rewarded.[85]

Social organizations which also served as agents of benevolence abounded among Maryland's free black population. These included branches of such prominent international fraternal orders as the Masons and the Odd Fellows. In addition, a substantial number of secret social clubs created specifically by blacks sprang up and drew membership from young persons. Although farther south these would have provoked very strong reactions among whites, most institutions of this kind in Maryland grew into important supporters of the wayward or unfortunate black.[86]

Black churches provided the strongest organizational bond of all. Except in a few rural areas, free blacks were able to create and maintain their own religious institutions. Some of these affiliated directly with national sectarian denominations; others, as the Methodists, formed as separate administrative units; still more were completely independent and operated strictly in one locale. In addition to the usual religious and social activities and aggressive work in education, black churches also strove to alleviate the needs of the impoverished. Their efforts in this area were aided substantially by specially created benevolent societies dedicated to the same purpose. Individuals coming into Maryland, then, could turn for succor to a variety of institutions dedicated to the protection and promotion of the free black society within the state. Perhaps in no other state did this group of people create as extensive and diverse a series of institutions as could be found in Maryland.[87]

Many other circumstances may have contributed to the unique condition of Maryland's free black population. Unquestionably the combination of fewer restraints and more supportive institutions than elsewhere goes far in explaining the unusual population development throughout the first half of

---

85. 45 per cent of the adults were able to read and write in 1850, but only 8 per cent of the children between ages five and fifteen were regularly enrolled in school. This does not include the many children who received instruction in Sunday schools, *Seventh U.S. Census, 1850*, pp. 219, 224, 225; Wright, *The Free Negro in Maryland*, pp. 202-208.

86. John Hope Franklin, *From Slavery to Freedom* (New York: Knopf, 1967) p. 226.

87. Wright, *The Free Negro in Maryland*, pp. 209-38, 250-52. This was in contrast to the Southern states. Eaton, *Growth of Southern Civilization*, p. 93.

the nineteenth century. However the statistics are explained, the presence of this large free black population both in the rural and urban areas of the state adds very strong support to the argument that except in an emotional sense nurtured in a minority of the white population, Maryland was not a southern state. Economically, the diverse agriculture, the presence of manufacturing and trades, the aggressive, extensive development of railroads, and the wide "mix" in commerce placed Maryland out of the southern sphere. The existence of a two-party system, if not for all localities, tied Maryland closely to the national political scene. Socially, the changing population patterns, the internal mobility, and the development of a numerous foreign-born population certainly set Maryland apart from such states as Alabama, Georgia, or even Virginia.

During the first half of the nineteenth century, Maryland's social institutions developed along diverse lines so that individuals had a variety of options to consider in determining how they would relate to others. While Marylanders did not promote comparable diversity in the arts, artistic endeavors showed a wide range of interests as witnessed by the variety of architectural achievements completed during the period. Economically, Maryland developed a variegated system which grew at a very halting pace but expanded in such a manner that no one aspect of it dominated all others. Maryland's economic strength was in its diversity compared to the colossal sameness of "King Cotton." Socially, culturally, and economically, Maryland identified better with American nationalism than sectionalism between the death of Washington and the Compromise of 1850.

BIBLIOGRAPHICAL ESSAY

CHAPTER III

Because scholars have given primary attention to political issues in
Maryland between 1800 and 1850, the opportunities to investigate
and report social, cultural and economic developments during that
era are almost unlimited. Unfortunately, this places the general reader
at a decided disadvantage, for no single source may be utilized to
learn about Maryland's socio-economic history. Rather, a multitude of
regional or national studies as well as specialized articles must be
pieced together to secure a comprehensive understanding of any aspect of the period.

Perhaps the best single secondary source is biographies such as the
previously cited: in economics, Stuart W. Bruchey, *Robert Oliver,
Merchant of Baltimore, 1783–1819, Johns Hopkins University Studies*
LXXIV (Baltimore: J.H. Press, 1956); in architecture, Thomas Hamlin, *Benjamin Henry Latrobe* (New York: Oxford University Press,
1955); and in literature (along with a liberal sprinkling of politics), Charles H. Bohner, *John Pendleton Kennedy* (Baltimore: J.H.
Press, 1961). For those who lived in slavery, the early autobiographical chapters of Maryland's most famous slave must be consulted:
Frederick Douglass, *Life and Times of Frederick Douglass Written
by Himself* (New York: Collier Books, 1962). Supporting most of the
biographies are primary sources from the collections of family papers.
These are becoming available through editorial projects recently completed or under way. Most notable at the moment is the editorial
and compilation project of the Benjamin Henry Latrobe papers, sponsored by the Maryland Historical Society and financed primarily by a
grant by the National Endowment for the Humanities. Editorial direction is by Dr. Edward C. Carter, II.

The strongest area of secondary information in social history centers
around religious studies. Although some state studies have been completed, the best approach is through general and denominational
works. The numerous volumes authored by William Warren Sweet
provide an abundance of information, though one must sort out the
data relating to Maryland from his extensive accounts of events
within congregations, conferences and denominations. Within Maryland proper, the very important projects at the Hall of Records in
Annapolis will continue to produce guides to church records in the
near future. Under the careful scrutiny of Mrs. Phebe R. Jacobsen,

the Hall of Records is compiling and microfilming available documents. The first completed study is: Phebe R. Jacobsen, *Quaker Records in Maryland*, Publication No. 14, Maryland Hall of Records Commission (Annapolis: Hall of Records Commission, 1966).

Culturally, the literary leaders of Maryland have provided the greatest inspiration to historians and critics, with reviews of Kennedy and Poe leading the list. In addition, a number of general studies of architectural developments that encompass Maryland have provided interesting insights into changing patterns of artistic values. An early and still valuable example of this is: Joseph Jackson, *Development of American Architecture 1783–1830* (Philadelphia: David McKay Co., 1926). The primary difficulty with works that focus exclusively on Maryland is their limited view which restricts efforts to understand trends within the nation, or within architectural styles generally. As a result, local studies tend to offer little more than a description of structures that cannot be related to changes within society; see for example H. Chandler Forman, *Maryland Architecture . . . 1634 Through the Civil War* (Cambridge, Md: Tidewater Pub. Co., 1968).

Economically, studies of agriculture, transportation, and Baltimore's businesses provide many interesting insights into the pluralism of the state. Fundamental to the understanding of agricultural problems and developments is: Craven's, *Soil Exhaustion as a Factor in the Agricultural History of Virginia and Maryland, 1606–1860.* For transportation, consult: Walter S. Sanderlin, *A History of the Chesapeake and Ohio Canal, J.H.U. Studies*, LXIV (Baltimore: J.H. Press, 1946); and Edward Hungerford, *The Story of the Baltimore and Ohio Railroad, 1827–1927* (New York: G. P. Putnam's Sons, 1928). For Baltimore, the interesting comparison of Baltimore and Philadelphia, James W. Livingood, *The Philadelphia-Baltimore Trade Rivalry 1780–1860* (Harrisburg, Pa.: The Pennsylvania Historical & Museum Commission, 1947), should be compared with the more general study: David T. Gilchrist, ed., *The Growth of the Seaport Cities* (Charlottesville, Virginia: University of Virginia Press, 1967); it places Baltimore's growth and problems in context with the contemporary situations of Philadelphia, New York and Boston.

In surveying the growth of ethnic minorities in Maryland, Dieter Cunz, *The Maryland Germans* (Princeton, N.J.: Princeton University Press, 1948) must be consulted. Additional works, especially focusing on the Irish, are badly needed. Studies of Maryland's black populations, slave and free, are sadly lacking. Two old but excellent studies are Brackett's, *The Negro in Maryland, A Study of the Institution of Slavery, Johns Hopkins University Studies*, Extra Volume IV (Baltimore: J.H. Press, 1889); and James M. Wright's recently republished *The Free Negro in Maryland, 1634–1860* (New York: Octagon Books, 1971). An important study of racial control in ante-bellum Maryland is nearing completion under the direction of Dr. Dan T. Carter, Professor of History, Department of History, University of Maryland. Other demographic and social studies are needed to provide more comprehensive understanding of the slave and the vastly important free black populations in Maryland during the first half of the nineteenth century.

Generalized studies that integrate social and economic data similar to the pioneering work, Whitman H. Ridgway, "A Social Analysis of Maryland Community Elites, 1827–1836," (Ph.D. dissertation, University of Pennsylvania, 1973), are much needed.

With primary materials including a range of city and county newspapers available on microfilm, general editorial and compilation projects completed and under way that include the papers of the Maryland Colonization Society and the papers of Benjamin Henry Latrobe; with the easily available public documents at the Hall of Records in Annapolis, with most of the Maryland Historical Society's collections outlined in Avril J. M. Pedley, *The Manuscript Collections of the Maryland Historical Society*, and the expanding catalogued collection of private papers in the Maryland Room of McKeldin Library at the University of Maryland, College Park, plus the published census data, scholars do not need to fear for the availability of sources. Neither do teachers who would like to see their students delve into Maryland history.

# IV

## POLITICS AND DEMOCRACY
## IN MARYLAND, 1800–1854

BY

W. Wayne Smith

INDIANA UNIVERSITY OF PENNSYLVANIA

The elections of 1800 and 1801 provided stunning changes in the political character of Maryland. After several years of energetic organizing and campaigning, the Jeffersonian Democratic-Republicans swept the Federalists from power. The Republicans delivered five of Maryland's ten electoral votes to Thomas Jefferson in 1800, elected a majority of congressmen, gained the dominant position in the General Assembly in 1800 and 1801, and chose John Francis Mercer as governor. Republicanism was the ascendant force in Maryland and congratulations seemed in order for the state's Republican leaders. Accordingly John Randolph of Virginia wrote his friend and political cohort, Joseph Nicholson of Maryland: "I heartily wish you joy of the regeneration of Maryland. Under the auspices of her present political opinions I doubt not, that like other converted reprobates, she will prove a zealous disciple of the orthodox faith."[1]

### 1

### THE JEFFERSONIAN PERIOD

Several factors accounted for the success of the Republicans. Towards the end of the Federalist decade they identified with

1. John Randolph to Joseph Nicholson, October 1, 1801, Joseph Nicholson Papers, L.C., quoted in Brown, "Party Battles and Beginnings in Maryland, 1786–1812," p. 237.

the rising liberal mood by attacking the constitutional requirements of property ownership for the right to vote. The Republicans advocated a free suffrage for all white adult males and were
instrumental in the passage of the Reform Bill of 1802. The
Federalist party, in contrast, offered a deaf ear to the demands for
the liberalization of politics. The Federalists, additionally, were
identified with unpopular measures such as the Alien and Sedition Acts and the proposals in 1800 that the legislature rather
than the voters choose the presidential electors. Elitism and
conservativism ran counter to the mood of Maryland and the
country.[2]

Besides their more popular stance on the issues of the day, the
Republicans were better organized than their opponents. Their
position as the political "outs" in the 1790's had compelled them
to be more active and systematic in their campaigning. Consequently they had devised a better disciplined and coordinated
political organization than the Federalists. Though they lacked a
statewide structure, the Republicans had district and county
committees that effectively directed and coordinated party activity. One of the strongest cogs in the Republican machinery was
the Smith faction in Baltimore. General Samuel Smith, forty-
eight years old in 1800, was the tall, handsome, and popular
gentleman-merchant and congressman who led the faction. As a
prominent merchant and Revolutionary War hero, it seemed
natural that he became one of Maryland's leaders in the early
days of the republic. He originally had entered politics as a
Federalist and built a powerful organization in Baltimore that
included his extensive family and commercial associates,
tradesmen, and the local militia. Elected to Congress in 1792, he
had become disenchanted with Federalist policies and switched
his allegiance to the Jeffersonian Republicans. He became an
influential politician, and his organization became a strong
foundation for Republicanism in Maryland. Elsewhere the Republicans had created elaborate party machinery in Allegany,
Washington, Frederick, Prince George's, and Anne Arundel
Counties.[3]

2. *M.H.M.*, LV, 278-81; J. R. Heller III, "Democracy in Maryland 1790–1810"
(Senior thesis, Princeton University, 1959), pp. 37-40; Edward G. Roddy,
"Maryland and the Presidential Election of 1800," *M.H.M.*, LVI (Sept., 1961),
252-55.
3. Noble Cunningham, *The Jeffersonian Republicans* (Chapel Hill: The Uni-

Republicanism was strongest in the areas of Maryland that were experiencing dynamic demographic, social, and economic changes. These areas included Baltimore City, the northern Chesapeake counties, and western Maryland. The commercial growth of Baltimore generated a boom that expanded throughout these areas and provided increased economic opportunities. As the paths to success were opened, men on the make became less respectful of the established elites. Competition for economic and social power encouraged an egalitarian spirit that spilled into politics. The ambitious newcomers gravitated to Republicanism, while the older leaders remained loyal to Federalism. The areas of the Eastern Shore and the southern tobacco counties, which were more homogeneous and static, were the bastions of the Federalists. Here the planter class provided social and political leadership and identified with the more conservative Federalist party.[4]

For several years the Republican ascendancy in Maryland was nearly unchallenged. As Table 1 below reveals, the Republican power in the House of Delegates increased. It included eighty members with each county electing four delegates, and Baltimore and Annapolis each electing two. Since the house was elected annually in October, the returns served as a remarkable gauge of public opinion and political organization.

Republican control over the state government was made more secure by their victories in the 1801, 1806, and 1811 elections for the state senate. That house was chosen every five years by an elected senatorial electoral college. Whichever party elected the majority of the electoral college could choose all fifteen members of the senate and thus control the upper house for five years.

By holding the upper hand in the General Assembly the Republicans were able to wrest the executive department from the

---

versity of North Carolina Press, 1957), pp. 158-59, and *The Jeffersonian Republicans in Power* (Chapel Hill: The University of North Carolina Press, 1963), pp. 176-177; Frank A. Cassell's *Merchant Congressman in the Young Republic: Samuel Smith of Maryland, 1752–1839* (Madison: University of Wisconsin Press, 1971), pp. 3-102.

4. Paul Goodman, "The First American Party System," in *The American Party Systems,* eds. William Nisbet Chambers and Walter Dean Burnham (New York: Oxford University Press, 1967), pp. 65-69; David Hackett Fischer, *The Revolution of American Conservatism* (New York: Harper & Row, 1965), pp. 211-19.

TABLE 1
Composition of House of Delegates, 1800–1822

| Year | Republican | Majority | Federalist |
|------|------------|----------|------------|
| 1800 | 48 | R | 32 |
| 1801 | 54 | R | 26 |
| 1802 | 47 | R | 33 |
| 1803 | 57 | R | 23 |
| 1804 | 53 | R | 27 |
| 1805 | — | R | — |
| 1806 | — | R | — |
| 1807 | — | R | — |
| 1808 | 40 | — | 40 |
| 1809 | 44 | R | 36 |
| 1810 | 58 | R | 22 |
| 1811 | 44 | R | 36 |
| 1812 | 26 | F | 54 |
| 1813 | 31 | F | 49 |
| 1814 | 21 | F | 59 |
| 1815 | 32 | F | 48 |
| 1816 | 24 | F | 56 |
| 1817 | 35 | F | 45 |
| 1818 | 45 | R | 35 |
| 1819 | 50 | R | 30 |
| 1820 | 49 | R | 31 |
| 1821 | 61 | R | 19 |
| 1822 | 67 | R | 13 |

SOURCE: This chart is compiled from the official election returns reported in various newspapers. Incomplete reporting prevented the collection of total and accurate data for 1805, 1806 and 1807. In those years, however, the Republicans maintained their majority.

Federalists. Since the legislature selected the governor and the governor's council, the Republicans were able to choose the executive department from 1801 to 1812.

The Republican successes in the early 1800's compelled the Federalists to make dramatic adjustments or face political extinction. Some Federalists, whom David Hackett Fischer has dubbed the "Young Federalists," recognized the political realities and tried to emulate the Republicans in soliciting popular support. Among these was Robert Goodloe Harper, who had moved to Maryland from South Carolina and married the daughter of Charles Carroll of Carrollton. A self-made man from South Carolina's hill country, Harper had entered Congress in 1795 when he was only thirty years old. Supercilious but ambitious, Harper was sensitive to the changing forms of politics. He acknowledged that "the public is the judge, the two parties are the combatants, and that party which possessed power must employ it properly . . . in order to ensure public approbation, and retain their power."[5] Assisting Harper in the organization of a Maryland Federalist party was Alexander Contee Hanson. Twenty-two years old in 1808 when he founded the newspaper *Federal Republican,* Hanson quickly earned a reputation as one of the more caustic critics of Republicanism. Typical of his acidic charges was the accusation "There is scarcely an act of tyranny and oppression complained of against George the Third which has not been committed by Jefferson and his political pimp . . . whiffling Jemmy, [Madison]!"[6] A third Young Federalist leader could be found in the shadows of the Catoctin Mountain range at Frederick. This was Roger Brooke Taney, thirty-one years old in 1808, scion of the prominent family in Calvert County. Young Taney moved to Frederick to practice law and followed in his father's footsteps by joining the Federalist party. By 1808 he was influential enough to be presidential elector on the Federalist ticket.[7]

Organization was not achieved overnight by the Maryland Federalists. Harper proposed a state convention meeting in Baltimore in 1808, but apparently his call fell on deaf ears. Two years later Harper and Hanson created a party directory called the Washington Society with Harper as the president. Hanson, obviously distraught about the anti-organizational attitude of the Federalists, argued that the party "has long been under the exclusive direction . . . of spiritless and temporizing men who have neither the ability to be our leaders nor the firmness to face the opposition." Proposing that Harper assume the presidency of the society, Hanson declared that "the times require

5. Fischer, *ibid.,* pp. 36-38.

6. Joseph Herman Schauinger, "Alexander Contee Hanson, Federalist Partisan," *M.H.M.,* XXXV (Dec., 1940), 354-55.

7. Carl Brent Swisher, *Roger B. Taney* (New York: The Macmillan Company, 1936), pp. 54-55. See also for a recent and readable biography of Taney, Walker Lewis, *Without Fear or Favor* . . . (Boston: Houghton Mifflin Co., 1965).

us to set aside such men and to choose a leader whom no motive will restrain from serving his country."[8]

But the Young Federalists encountered stiff resistance from the more conservative and older members of the party. Samuel Chase and John Eager Howard broke entirely with the party. Michael Taney, father of Roger Brooke Taney, another prominent Federalist who disdained organizational activity, remained associated with the revamped party only in deference to the pleas of the younger Taney.[9] Not surprisingly, then, it was 1811 before the Federalists had a party that was comparable to the Republican organization in Maryland.

Indicative of the Young Federalists' acceptance of more democratic politics was their support of a bill to remove property qualifications for officeholding. These requirements, ranging from £500 for delegates to £5,000 in property and £1,000 in currency for governor, had restricted officeholding to the wealthier class. By 1809 the qualifications were incongruous with the growing egalitarian attitudes. The impetus for reform came accidentally in 1809 when the legislature was called into a special session to elect a governor to replace Robert Wright, who had resigned. The legislature decided that if a governor died or resigned, the president of the council should become the successor. Then it was noted that the property requirements for the council's president would not qualify. This small episode contributed to the demand that property requirements be abolished. In the next session of the General Assembly John Hanson Thomas, one of the Young Federalists, introduced a bill to remove the property qualifications for holding office. Through the cooperation of the Republicans and the Young Federalists this bill was passed along with other reforms, including the extension of manhood suffrage to presidential elections and the opening of jury duty to non-Christians.[10]

As both political parties attained greater maturity, iden-

---

8. Victor Sapio, "Maryland's Federalist Revival, 1808–1812," *M.H.M.*, LXIV (Spring, 1969), 2-3.

9. Fischer, *The Revolution of American Conservatism*, pp. 162, 360, 363.

10. Governor Wright resigned in May 1809 in anticipation of gaining an appointment as a justice to the Court of Appeals of Queen Anne's County. See Frank F. White, Jr., *The Governors of Maryland, 1777–1970* (Annapolis: The Hall of Records Commission, 1970), pp. 56-57; Heller, "Democracy in Maryland," pp. 98-100.

tification with the national leaders was inevitable. Consequently the successes and failures of the Jefferson administrations had repercussions in the grass-roots. Jefferson's thorniest problem was to find a peaceful way to protect American commerce from English and French depradations. War had erupted again in 1803 between the European powers, and they imposed a blockade on each other's coast. Neutral ships trading with either belligerent were subject to seizure or having their crews impressed. American merchant vessels and crews fell prey to the belligerent powers. Jefferson, preferring peace to war, took no action beyond protests against the seizure of American ships and crews as violations of American neutral rights. Then in June, 1807, an incident occurred that inflamed the American temper. A British vessel, H. M. S. *Leopard*, attacked an American naval frigate, U.S.S. *Chesapeake*, off the Virginia coast. The British impressed four sailors from the American ship, and the *Chesapeake* limped back into port damaged and with twenty-one injured crewmen.

News of the *Chesapeake-Leopard* affair spread like oil thrown on a fire. Americans, already incensed about the disregard for their neutral rights, prepared to go to war to vindicate their honor. War fever swept up and down the coast as Americans demanded retribution. In Maryland partisan rivalry was temporarily put aside as Republicans and Federalists pledged in public meetings to avenge the *Chesapeake*. Maryland's General Assembly adopted a bellicose resolution pledging the state "to brave all the calamities of war rather than tamely submit to the tyranny and indolence of any nation."[11]

President Jefferson retained a cooler head than most Americans. He proposed a boycott on trade with England and France in the hope that their economies would suffer enough to compel them to recognize American neutral rights. Republicans in Congress agreed with the President that a boycott, or embargo, offered a more desirable course than a declaration of war. Samuel Smith, spokesman for the merchant interests in Baltimore, who had been exasperated about the seeming pusillanimous efforts of the Federalist administration, now gladly welcomed Jefferson's sterner attitude and sponsored the bill in the Senate to prohibit

---

11. Maryland. *Resolutions of the Senate, 1804*, p. 24.

American trade with the belligerents. The embargo won passage by Congress in December 1807.[12]

The embargo bore heaviest upon seaports like Boston, New York, Philadelphia, and Baltimore since it reduced their outgoing trade. But Americans accepted the sacrifice, expecting the embargo's duration to be brief. In Baltimore newspapers applauded the administration's new policy, and at Annapolis the Maryland legislature passed a resolution endorsing the Embargo Act. Expressing the view of the commercial interests in Baltimore was John Hollins, who wrote that "all ranks and degrees at this time are satisfied that it was a measure both proper and well-timed, and which saved the mercantile men from total ruin."[13]

Americans soon learned that their trade was not as vital to Europe as they had supposed. England and France did not budge, and Americans became the unexpected sufferers. Baltimore merchants and seamen quickly saw that their sacrifice was greater than they had anticipated. Baltimore's exports declined more than eighty per cent, which must have caused considerable anxiety among the merchants and vast unemployment among the sailors. The economic distress spread into the hinterland as farmers lost markets for their wheat but saw the prices of imported manufactured goods rise. Hanson, through his *Federal Republican*, bemoaned that "the Farmer is nearly ruined by Mr. Jefferson's experiments, who cannot sell his crop for half price, and whose grain is rotting upon his hands. . . ."[14]

Economics and politics are intricately bound together and nothing illustrates this tie better than the Embargo Act and the revival of Federalism in Maryland. The economic distress occurred as the Young Federalists were gaining control of their party, and they acted swiftly to exploit the disillusionment with the embargo. The *Federal Republican* asserted that "the only way for the people to save themselves from ruin is to run such unworthy servants out of office and elect men who they know will vote against the embargo and all such measures as are in-

---

12. John S. Pancake, "Baltimore and the Embargo, 1807–1809," *M.H.M.*, XLVII (Sept., 1952), 175.

13. *Ibid.*, p. 177.

14. *Ibid.*, p. 178.

tended to destroy commerce and injure agriculture which is her hand-maid."[15]

Inspired by the opportunity handed to them by the discontent with the Embargo Act, the Maryland Federalists eagerly prepared for the 1808 campaign. Labeling their slate the Anti-Embargo Ticket, they directed their appeal to the agrarian interests. They charged that Baltimore merchants gained some relief from the embargo's restrictions through widespread evasions, while the farmer had no such recourse available to him. Only by voting for the Federalist candidates, the campaign oratory claimed, could the farmers hope for relief.[16]

The Federalist tactics succeeded in uniting the wheat belt of western Maryland with the traditional Federalist strongholds in the tobacco counties and the Eastern Shore to give the party control of the House of Delegates for the first time in eight years. Evidence of the intense interest in the election in the hard-pressed wheat counties of western Maryland is best seen in the voter turnout. In Frederick County 84 per cent of the electorate voted in the congressional election, an increase of 24 per cent over the 1806 turnout; in Washington County, 75 per cent, an increase of 16 per cent; in Allegany County, 72 per cent, an increase of 31 per cent. But the following month the Federalists failed to maintain their momentum in the presidential election. Voter participation declined dramatically, and they lost the western district by 130 votes. They captured only two electoral votes from the southern Maryland and Eastern Shore districts, while the remaining nine electoral votes went to James Madison.[17]

Despite Madison's victory in Maryland and the nation it was obvious to the Republicans that the Jeffersonian experiment with the embargo had proved politically disastrous. It failed in its original purpose of winning concessions from England and France and had incurred an economic depression at home. Moreover, it had provided the Federalists with an issue and enabled them to win in areas traditionally regarded as Republi-

---

15. *Ibid.*, pp. 178-79.

16. Dorothy M. Brown, "Embargo Politics in Maryland," *M.H.M.*, LVIII (Sept., 1963), 205-06.

17. Pole, "Constitutional Reform and Election Statistics," pp. 289-90; *M.H.M.*, LVIII, 208-9.

can preserves. The only way the Republicans could salvage the party and bring economic relief was to admit the failure of the Embargo Act and repeal it. Consequently, the Republican Congress in 1809 voted for repeal of the detested embargo.[18]

Foreign policy continued to influence state politics in the next few years as President Madison struggled with the maritime problem inherited from Jefferson. England and France still refused to recognize American neutral rights, and Madison's diplomatic efforts were ignored. The President had to contend, too, with pressure from within his party as a group of young congressmen, the "war hawks," clamored for retribution for American losses. Indian problems on the frontier that resulted in the Battle of Tippecanoe were attributed to English agents crossing the Canadian border and further incensed Americans. Then Napoleon in 1810 coyly announced that he would lift French restrictions on American shipping, but the English remained quiet. As the nation's patience with England wore thin it appeared that war was the only recourse. Accordingly, President Madison asked for and received from Congress a declaration of war against England on June 19, 1812.[19]

The Federalists, who were traditionally sympathetic to England, regarded the war as a plot by Francophiles to ally the United States with Napoleon. They opposed the war and became trenchant critics of Madison's war policy for the next several years. Alexander Contee Hanson on Saturday, June 20, 1812, used the columns of his *Federal Republican* to attack the war policy. In an editorial entitled "Thou Hast Done a Deed Whereat Valour Will Weep" he announced that the Federalists intended to show that the war was "unnecessary, inexpedient, and entered into from . . . motives bearing on their front marks of undisguised foreign influence. . . . We mean to use every constitutional argument and every legal means to render as odious and suspicious to the American people . . . the patrons and contrivers of this highly impolitic and destructive war. . . ." Federalist editors quickly followed Hanson's lead in criticizing the decision for war and predicted that horrifying consequences would ensue, including the loss of "thirty thousand lives," bur-

---

18. Pancake, "Baltimore and the Embargo," p. 185.

19. Marshall Smelser, *The Democratic Republic, 1801–1815* (New York: Harper & Row, Publishers, 1968), pp. 151-218, offers a most recent summary of the war's background.

densome taxes, "the capture of our vessels, the blockading of our ports, the bombardment of our cities" and the increase of the national debt by millions of dollars.[20]

Intemperate partisanship such as this only served to heighten the tensions in a nation already aroused by the patriotic appeal. The result was an equally intemperate response in the form of mob violence against the Maryland Federalists. On Monday, June 22, two days after Hanson's initial editorial blast against the war, a crowd of nearly three hundred stormed the office of the *Federal Republican* and destroyed the presses. This attack set off a summer of violence in Baltimore as mobs roamed the streets assaulting Federalists and destroying their property. In July Hanson defiantly opened a new office at 45 South Charles Street, only to be besieged again by a mob. Prominent Baltimore Federalists, determined to defend their press from destruction a second time, quickly gathered in Hanson's office. Tempers flared, stones were flung, guns were fired, and Charles Street became a battlefield. Perhaps only the intervention of the militia saved the stout defenders of Hanson's office from being lynched. Fearing for their lives, the Federalists took refuge in a jail. But the next night a mob gathered at the jail, stormed it and pulled the Federalists into the streets and mercilessly clubbed them. General James Lingan, a Revolutionary War veteran and aged Federalist, was killed, and others were beaten and left for dead.[21]

Public indignation over the Baltimore riots swept over the state. It appeared that the Republicans were emulating the French Jacobins by repressing political opposition and the press. The stout defenders of the *Federal Republican* became political martyrs.[22] Reacting against the Republican tactics, the voters gave the Federalists a 54–26 margin in the House of Delegates, which enabled that party to elect the governor's council and Levin Winder as the governor. The Republicans were able to retain a majority of the congressional delegation,

---

20. *M.H.M.*, LXIV, 11-12.

21. Brown, "Party Battles and Beginnings in Maryland," pp. 335-38; Libero Marx Renzulli, Jr., "Maryland Federalism, 1787–1819" (Ph.D. dissertation, University of Virginia, 1961), pp. 359-70.

22. Brown, "Party Battles and Beginnings in Maryland," p. 338; Renzulli, "Maryland Federalism," p. 378.

An artist's conception of the bombardment of Fort McHenry during the defense of Baltimore, September 1814. Aquatint by J. Bowers. *M.H.S.*

though Alexander Contee Hanson was one of the Federalists elected.

While the Maryland Federalists exuberantly tallied the votes in the state elections, they had few expectations of defeating President Madison in the presidential contest. Much of the nation applauded the President's call for war and was in no mood to replace him. Even the Federalists divided on the war issue, with the Adams wing of the party supporting the President. Moreover the Federalists lacked a strong personality to challenge Madison. Federalists in Maryland and other states even countenanced the thought of supporting DeWitt Clinton, an anti-war Republican, for the presidency. Robert Goodloe Harper believed that such a course was the only feasible one open to the Federalists. He advised John Hanson Thomas to discuss the plan with the Federalists of western Maryland because it was "thoroughly approved by the great body of Federalists in this state."[23] A subsequent meeting of leading Federalists took place in New York at which nominations of John Marshall, Rufus King, and Clinton were discussed. But the party caucus came to no firm decision and left the party's strategy in 1812 completely muddled. Lacking unity, it was doomed to failure.

The returns in the presidential election, however, revealed that Maryland's electorate remained divided over the war policy. The Republicans continued to win in Baltimore and the upper Chesapeake counties, giving Madison six of the state's electoral votes. The western and southern counties and the Eastern Shore gave the other five electoral votes to the Federalist ticket.[24]

As the war progressed the threat of England's military power muted some of the vestiges of partisanship. Some Federalists gradually abandoned their rigid anti-war stance and shifted to support the defense against England. In Maryland a faction of the Federalist party gave its support to the war effort. That faction's most notable member was Roger B. Taney. Other Federalists, Harper and Hanson particularly, continued to criticize the war.

In the spring of 1813 the appearance of a British fleet in the Chesapeake Bay heightened the need for cooperation in defending the homeland against the enemy. The British fleet sailed into

23. *M.H.M.*, LXIV, 14.
24. Brown, "Party Battles and Beginnings in Maryland," pp. 351-52.

Marshalling of the troops for defense of Baltimore, September 12–13, 1814. Oil painting by Thomas C. Ruckle. *M.H.S.*

252

the Chesapeake region simply to harass traffic and smaller ports. Only Havre de Grace, Frenchtown, and a few Eastern Shore communities suffered any damage before the English fleet withdrew in autumn. A feint at Baltimore, however, alerted the citizenry there of the need to strengthen their defenses.

Baltimore was protected somewhat by Fort McHenry, located on the entry to the main harbor at Whetstone Point. Since less than fifty regular troops manned the fort, it was obvious that the principal defense of the city depended upon the local citizenry and the militia under General Samuel Smith's command. General Smith, combining both his military experience from the Revolution and political influence in Baltimore, proved to be one of the nation's principal defenders against the English threat. He solicited funds for military equipment from the federal and state governments, drilled the militia, and coordinated the plans to make Baltimore secure. Smith's leadership succeeded in shoring up the weak defenses of Baltimore and in encouraging the citizens that they could withstand a British attack.

In September 1814 the British tested the mettle of Baltimore's defenders. A major British invasion force, combining fifty ships and seven thousand troops, reentered the Chesapeake in August and proceeded to the Patuxent River where they landed. Marching north through the Maryland tobacco country, the British force headed for the nation's capital. At Bladensburg the British encountered the first American resistance in the form of militiamen and volunteers under General William Henry Winder. The disciplined and experienced British force quickly scattered the American defenders and continued their march on the exposed District of Columbia. On August 24 the British force occupied the seat of the American government. They lingered in Washington twenty-four hours, taking time only to burn some public buildings, before they returned to their ships at the Patuxent River.

Encouraged by their conquest of Washington, the British found the temptation of attacking Baltimore too strong to resist. They headed up the Bay. By Sunday morning, September 11, the sails of fifty British ships lined the horizon at the entrance of the Patapsco River. The British planned to attack Baltimore with a combined land and sea operation. The land force, comprising four thousand troops, debarked on September 12 at North Point and moved up the narrow peninsula between the Patapsco and Back rivers. A successful march here would bring them to the environs of Baltimore from the east. Simultaneously, frigates and bomb vessels sailed up the Patapsco, expecting to enter the Northwest Branch beneath Fort McHenry and assault Baltimore from its inner harbor.

The British strategy was obvious to General Samuel Smith, and he prepared to meet it. He assigned 3,200 troops to Brigadier General John Stricker to meet the British advance upon the peninsula from North Point. Smith then ordered that the mouth of the Northwest Branch, between Fort McHenry and the Lazaretto, be blocked with barges. He reinforced the troops and cannon at Fort McHenry and the garrison across the river at the Lazaretto.

On September 12 and 13, 1814, the two forces moved to carry out the strategy planned for them. General Stricker's militia met the seasoned British regulars, but unlike the battle at Bladensburg, the American militia held their ground. After two costly engagements and the death of their commander, Major General Robert Ross, the British retired to their vessels at North Point.

While the land forces were in combat, the British ships blasted away at Fort McHenry. Beginning early on the morning of September 13, a terrific hammering of cannon continued throughout the day and into the night. At dawn on the morning of September 14 aboard a flag-of-truce ship down the Patapsco, Francis Scott Key peered through spyglasses and to his joy and amazement saw the American flag still flying over Fort McHenry. Key had made contact with the British to seek the release of a captured Dr. William Beanes and had witnessed the bombardment aboard ship. As he gratefully discerned the flag in the foggy dawn, his emotions stirred his poetic nature, and he quickly jotted down phrases on the back of a letter he carried. Released and ashore, he published the verses written in celebration of the victory. Thus "The Star-Spangled Banner" came into being. The light of day also brought relief and joy to the defenders of Fort McHenry. They had withstood the British assault and for a few days tensely girded for another. But the disheartened British sailed away. Though Washington had been sacked Baltimore stood un-

General Samuel Smith, Revolutionary War hero, congressman, merchant, and defender of Baltimore in 1814. *Peale Museum.*

touched, and by this defense the nation's honor was partially restored.[25]

National honor was a central issue in the war with England. With the end of fighting, Americans rejoiced that their republic's integrity was intact. Consequently, those who had defended the nation earned praise; those Federalists, called the "Blue Lights," who had condemned the war effort were disgraced. General Samuel Smith, for example, emerged a hero of the war, and Baltimore's citizens appreciatively elected him to the House of Representatives. For the Federalists, on the other hand, their anti-war posture brought them into disfavor. At that point Federalism in the United States was moribund, and the party's leaders thereafter lived under a cloud of opprobrium.

While the Federalist party withered away elsewhere, for a time it retained some vitality in Maryland. The Federalists won control of the state Senate and House of Delegates in 1816, though they could deliver only three of Maryland's electoral votes to the Federalist presidential ticket. In the postwar years the complexion of the party changed as Taney's faction, called the "Coodies" assumed the reins and purged the "Blue Lights." In the 1816 election, for example, the Montgomery County "Coodies" cooperated with the Republicans to defeat Alexander Contee Hanson's bid for a seat in the House of Delegates. Expectedly, Hanson fumed, "I was disposed to curse the hour when first I attached myself to so base a party."[26] Robert Goodloe Harper, the U.S. Senator, was still a power with which the "Coodies" had to contend. Harper resigned from the Senate in 1817 and picked Hanson as his successor. Taney's faction supported General William H. Winder, but the General Assembly elected Hanson. Within two years ill health incapacitated Hanson, and in April, 1819, death silenced the youthful Federalist volcano.[27]

Although the Federalists controlled the upper house until 1821, their sagging popularity could be seen in their constant

---

25. Reginald Horsman, *The War of 1812* (New York: Alfred A. Knopf, 1969), pp. 75-79; Walter Lord, *The Dawn's Early Light* (New York: W. W. Norton Inc., 1972), pp. 19-300; Cassell, *Merchant Congressmen in the Young Republic*, pp. 128-212.

26. Quoted in Renzulli, "Maryland Federalism," p. 412 ff.

27. Swisher, *Roger B. Taney*, p. 75; Schauinger, "Alexander Contee Hanson," p. 364.

loss of power in the lower house. From a commanding 56–24 majority in the House of Delegates in 1816, the Federalists lost seat after seat in the ensuing annual elections, until by 1820 they had only thirty-one. Moreover, they had no national party with which to affiliate, as the Federalists conceded defeat and nominated no candidate to oppose President Monroe in 1820. The following year's campaign marked the last gasp of Federalism in Maryland. They lost the battle for the state Senate and elected only nineteen candidates to the House of Delegates. The Federalist party was dead, and an era of political partisanship ended in Maryland.

Politics in Maryland then entered an amorphous state. Political organization became atomized and public interest in politics dramatically declined. In 1822 and 1823 the once partisan press nearly ignored the annual state elections. The papers listed only the candidates and the winners with no regard to votes polled. The candidates were nominated in caucuses and ran without party designations. In some of the counties former Federalists continued to run for office as independents, but the campaigns more often were intra-party battles between Republicans.

The end of partisanship in Maryland had an interesting effect on the vitality of democracy. Without an organized competition, the politicians deemed active electioneering unnecessary. The electorate on the other hand saw little need to vote, because candidates ran unopposed. Apathy set in, and popular participation in the electoral processes declined. The best example of the complacency is the voter turnout in the 1820 presidential election, in which President Monroe's opponent received only one electoral vote. In Baltimore, whose voting population was estimated at seven or eight thousand people, only 568 votes were cast in the presidential election.[28] Within a year newspapers whose columns had once bulged with campaign news and propaganda were silent on political matters.

Though the intensity of partisan politics mellowed in this "era of good feelings," an additional step toward democratic reform was taken. Maryland's constitution stipulated that only Christians could hold public offices or commissions; as a result, the

---

28. *Niles' Weekly Register* explained that "there was no excitement because there was no opposition." XIX (December 9, 1820), 240; Charles S. Syndor, "The One-Party Period of American History," *American Historical Review*, LI (April, 1946), 439-51.

state's small Jewish population was denied fundamental political privileges. Attention had been directed to this discrimination as early as 1797, when Solomon Etting, a Jewish merchant in Baltimore, petitioned the General Assembly to grant Jews all the rights of citizenship. But Etting's and subsequent petitions met with no success in the state legislature.

Notwithstanding the denial of these political rights, Jews moved to Baltimore in the early 1800's as the city became a major commercial center. By 1820 the Jewish population in Maryland exceeded 150 citizens. As they assumed prominent positions within Baltimore's mercantile and banking community, the political restrictions on Jews attracted more attention. Jacob Cohen, a prominent merchant, for example, could not accept a captaincy in the local militia; and Solomon Etting's son could not gain admission to the Maryland bar.

The restrictions on the Jews seemed glaringly incongruous with the interests of the state, and several Marylanders sought to have the discriminations removed. Hezekiah Niles, editor of the influential *Niles' Weekly Register*, argued that "the number of persons professing the Jewish religion in the State of Maryland is very small but if there were ONE such, the constitution ought to be altered in his favor." Within the state legislature Thomas Kennedy, a Washington County delegate, assumed the crusader's role to have all religious restrictions for officeholders removed. He originally introduced a bill in 1818 to grant full equality for all religious groups, but not until 1822 did the legislature approve such a measure. Since Kennedy's bill was in the form of a constitutional amendment, the subsequent session of the General Assembly had to approve the measure before it became a law.

But the measure aroused considerable opposition throughout the state. Opponents argued that Kennedy's proposal would permit even atheists to hold public office. While Marylanders might have been willing to grant Jews equal rights, they found Kennedy's bill too liberal. Thus the measure became a political issue in the 1823 campaign and caused Kennedy and other supporters of the bill to lose their bids for re-election. Consequently, the 1823 General Assembly rejected the Kennedy bill.

Kennedy won re-election in 1824 and again proposed a bill to liberalize the religious requirements for officeholders. This time, however, his bill specifically called for the removal of restrictions on Jewish citizens. The legislature was willing to accept this milder bill and on the last day of the session approved the so-called "Jew Bill." It went into effect in 1826 and in that year Solomon Etting and Jacob Cohen celebrated their newly acquired political rights by winning seats on the Baltimore city council.[29]

2

REVIVAL OF PARTISANSHIP, 1824–1836

Beneath the placid surface and unknown to the public some politicians were stirring in anticipation of the forthcoming 1824 presidential election. Many eyes turned toward that election, for it would end the reign of the Virginia Dynasty of Jefferson, Madison, and Monroe with no apparent successor. The situation was rendered more uncertain by the absence of any national organization to offer candidates for the contest. There was even no acceptable mechanism to nominate candidates, and, in retrospect, the significance of the 1824 campaign was that another step toward democracy was taken in the debate over the nomination of the candidates.

Among the politicians quietly plotting for the 1824 campaign was Virgil Maxcy, gentleman farmer of the Tulip Hill estate in Anne Arundel County. Strongly handsome with dark wavy hair and deep sideburns, Maxcy had moved from New England to Baltimore to practice law. He soon married the daughter of the deceased Joseph Galloway and moved to Tulip Hill to assume the managerial responsibilities of the estate. Maxcy became active in politics as a Federalist and was appointed the postmaster at West River in 1814.[30] With his party defunct in 1821, Maxcy became John C. Calhoun's chief promoter in Maryland. His rationale was that "the great object to be desired is that the principles of Federal policy should predominate," and this could be accomplished by Federalists allying with the Calhoun

29. Edward Eitches, "Maryland's Jew Bill," *American Jewish Historical Quarterly*, LX (March, 1971), 258-79; Issac M. Fein, "Niles' Weekly Register on the Jews," in Abraham J. Karp, ed., *The Jewish Experience in America* (Waltham, Mass.: American Jewish Historical Society, 1969), II, 97-101.

30. J. Reaney Kelly, " 'Tulip Hill,' Its History and Its People," *M.H.M.*, LX (Dec., 1965), 387-91.

wing of the Republican party.[31] Throughout 1821 and 1822 Maxcy corresponded with Calhoun about strategy, contacted influential editors, and sought disciples in Maryland. By early 1822 Robert Goodloe Harper, the former Federalist leader, and Republicans Peter Little and Joseph Kent enlisted in the Calhoun ranks. Maxcy's quiet campaign gained such headway in Maryland that some urged that a Calhoun ticket for the state offices in the 1822 elections be announced. Such an expression of support for Calhoun, it was believed, would enhance the candidate's chances within the state and in larger states like New York and Pennsylvania. The suggestion came too late to prepare for the state elections, but it was acknowledged that "things must be better managed next fall . . ." in order to boost the South Carolinian's chances.[32]

Political activity was by no means restricted to the Calhounites. William H. Crawford, the Secretary of Treasury and acknowledged front-runner among the presidential candidates, was being boosted by the old Jeffersonian, Samuel Smith. Now in his seventies and hard-pressed because of financial losses in the recent depression of 1819, Smith worked tirelessly for Crawford. He no longer commanded the political leverage of his earlier years and conceded that Crawford was not popular in the Old Line State. Edward Lloyd, U.S. Senator and noted planter of the extensive Wye Plantation on the Eastern Shore, and Luke Tiernan, a prominent Irish-Catholic Baltimore merchant, assisted Smith in quietly promoting Crawford.

The political calm in Maryland was disturbed in May 1823, when the *Baltimore American* opened its columns to the public discussion of the candidates.[33] Immediately letters deluged the *American*'s office advertising or attacking the various candidates. Many of the letters were little more than scurrilous attacks; some sensibly examined the candidates' qualifications, and a few attempted to raise serious issues. The letters revealed, in all, that no single candidate possessed a strong enough appeal, program, or following to sweep Maryland.

An astounding number of the letters advocated the candidacy

---

31. Virgil Maxcy to William Sullivan, March 25, August 18, 1821, Galloway-Maxcy-Markoe Papers, L.C.

32. George Peter to Virgil Maxcy, September, n.d., November 5, 1822, *Ibid.*

33. May 23, 1824.

of John Quincy Adams. Nothing had been said about him before in Maryland's press, but it was evident that many people had been thinking about him. Other letters indicated that the boom for Andrew Jackson sweeping through other states was spilling into Maryland. At this early date few Maryland politicians took Old Hickory's candidacy seriously and one emphatically predicted in private correspondence that "Jackson's pretensions have risen like a rocket & like a rocket will expire."[34]

Anxious to exploit every opportunity to advance his own campaign, John C. Calhoun urged Virgil Maxcy to use the *American*'s columns for some free publicity. Calhoun suggested, too, that young John Pendleton Kennedy, a rising star in Maryland's literary and political circles, be enlisted to use his facile pen in Calhoun's behalf.[35] Kennedy subsequently agreed to write for Calhoun, and within weeks the South Carolinian had a regular correspondent "Republican" promoting him in the *American*.[36]

Samuel Smith joined the newspaper fray under the pseudonym "A Democrat" with a series of letters championing Crawford. As Crawford's defender Smith found sufficient work, for the *American*'s columns bulged with attacks on Crawford. Undaunted by the criticisms of his candidate, Smith faithfully provided letter after letter defending Crawford and sucessfully extended the campaign to the Eastern Shore by persuading Edward Lloyd to publish his essays in the Easton newspapers.[37]

Crawford's campaign in Maryland hit many snags. A steady stream of critical letters against him appeared in the press, and one Crawford supporter bemoaned, "Were the friends of Mr. Crawford here arraigned before the public for arson or murder not a press would do them justice."[38] Crawford's emergence as the whipping boy of the campaign occurred in part because he

---

34. J. S. Skinner to Edward Lloyd, n.d. [early 1824], Lloyd Papers, M.H.S., No. 2001.

35. John C. Calhoun to Virgil Maxcy, June 11, 1823, Galloway-Maxcy-Markoe MSS, L.C.

36. Several letters appeared in the *American* espousing Calhoun's candidacy under this pseudonym, e.g., July 31, September 1, and November 4, 1823. Whether the writer was Kennedy, Maxcy or several persons has not been determined.

37. Samuel Smith to Edward Lloyd, June 5, 1823, Lloyd Papers, M.H.S., No. 2001.

38. J. S. Skinner to Edward Lloyd, n.d. [early 1824], *ibid.*

was running counter to the democratic currents in Maryland and the nation. His strategy called for his nomination by a caucus of congressional leaders, the customary means of nominating candidates in the Republican-Federalist years. Because the caucus placed the nominating power in the hands of a few politicians, this method was inconsistent with demands for greater participation of the people in the electoral processes. Critics across the country repudiated it as "King Caucus" and insisted that it be abandoned.[39]

"King Caucus" quickly became the hottest political issue in Maryland. Meetings throughout the state repudiated caucuses and the *American* published letters railing against caucus nominations. In Anne Arundel County caucus and anti-caucus tickets appeared in the race for the House of Delegates. When the anti-caucus ticket won, the *Maryland Gazette* exclaimed that "caucusing has received its death blow in this county."[40] The anti-caucus sentiment was so intense that it pervaded the General Assembly in the 1823–24 session. A set of anti-caucus resolutions arrived from the Tennessee legislature, giving the Maryland anti-caucus and anti-Crawford politicians an opportunity to register their disapprobation of the practice and the candidate who intended to use it. Robert Bowie, state senator from Prince George's County, led the attack on "King Caucus" by introducing resolutions that Maryland's congressional delegation were to discourage any caucus nomination for the presidency. Both houses approved the resolution and placed Maryland in the midst of this democratic assault on "King Caucus."[41]

The General Assembly's resolutions by no means settled the issue among Marylanders. Despite the impairment of Crawford's popularity because of the caucus issue his Maryland supporters still believed that only a congressional nomination could ensure his election.[42] Within the Maryland congressional delegation were Crawford's strongest supporters, Senators

39. William G. Morgan, "The Decline of the Congressional Nominating Caucus," *Tennessee Historical Quarterly*, XXIV (Fall, 1965), 249-51.
40. *M.G.*, October 9, 1824. Anti-caucus meetings were reported by this newspaper on August 21 and September 4, and by the *Baltimore American*, August 6, September 9, 1823.
41. The Senate vote was 9–2; House of Delegates, 51–23, *American*, December 12, 19, 1823; *M.G.*, December 25, 1823.
42. J. S. Skinner to Edward Lloyd, October 7, 1823, Lloyd Papers, M.H.S., No. 2001.

Smith and Lloyd. Both endorsed the caucus strategy and felt no obligation to abide by the instructions from the General Assembly. Lloyd fired a retort to Annapolis and then with Smith and Congressman William Hayward joined the congressional caucus on February 14, 1824, that nominated Crawford.[43]

The issue was now before the public. Crawford, though ill from a paralytic stroke suffered in the previous summer, was the "King Caucus" candidate. If he had had any chances of winning the presidency before, they were now dissipated. Association with "King Caucus" proved to be the political kiss of death. Caucus nominations were discredited as aristocratic anachronisms subject to political intrigue. Hereafter the process of nomination had to encompass a broader selection of the country than through representatives sitting in Washington. In 1824 and 1828 nominations were made by various state legislatures, but that procedure gave way to national conventions in 1832.

The political kaleidoscope in Maryland transformed dramatically through 1822 and 1823 and still showed no signs in 1824 of stabilizing in a definite pattern. Calhoun's boom had failed to materialize, and he accepted the wise counsel to bid for the vice-presidency. He made known his preference for Jackson, which prompted his Maryland supporters, including Maxcy, Harper, and Kennedy, to declare for Old Hickory.[44] Henry Clay, who was running well in other states, aroused only scant attention in Maryland, and there was no organized group working for him. Crawford, though weakened by the caucus issue and his health, remained a formidable contender in Maryland. Crawford rallies took place in Kent, Montgomery, and Charles Counties, and a full slate of electors announced for him in mid-summer.[45] Adams and Jackson were acknowledged as the strongest candidates in Maryland, with Old Hickory especially popular in Baltimore City and Adams's strength dispersed throughout the state.

The campaign of 1824 reflected the amorphous state of politics in Maryland. Parties were absent, activity was sporadic, and the discussion was often vacuous. However, 53.7 per cent of the

---

43. *M.G.*, February 19, 1824.
44. Shaw Livermore, Jr., *The Twilight of Federalism* (Princeton, N.J.: Princeton University Press, 1962), p. 159; Robert Goodloe Harper to Virgil Maxcy, March 1, 1824, Galloway-Maxcy-Markoe MSS, LC.
45. *M.G.*, June 26, September 16, 19, 1824; *American*, July 15, 1824.

eligible voters went to the polls, a healthy increase since President Monroe's election four years before. Maryland voted according to a district system which enabled Jackson to win seven electoral votes, Adams three, and Crawford one. It was a closer race than the electoral vote indicated, as Jackson polled 14,573 to Adams's 14,442. Old Hickory ran slightly ahead of Adams in Baltimore City and county, western Maryland, and the upper Chesapeake. Adams won the tobacco counties and the Eastern Shore except for Lloyd's Talbot-Caroline district, which went to Crawford.[46]

Nationally Jackson led the other candidates in the popular and electoral votes but lacked the necessary majority of the electoral votes to win. For the second time in twenty-five years the election was thrown into the House of Representatives. The story of that decision needs no retelling here except to note that the Maryland delegation was divided with five congressmen favoring Adams, three for Jackson, and one for Crawford. Maryland's vote therefore went to Adams. Considerable bargaining occurred in Washington, and it was generally believed that Clay influenced congressmen to vote for Adams. When Adams won and quickly appointed Clay as secretary of state most politicians gave credence to the rumors that a bargain had been reached. The rhetoric of the "corrupt bargain" haunted both men for many years thereafter.[47]

The 1824 presidential contest ended with two healthy political embryos, the Jackson and Adams factions. Eventually they became the dominant parties. But maturation of these factions to full-fledged parties was slow even in Maryland, where a strong political system had existed less than a decade before. The 1825 elections for the House of Delegates revealed that the political system in Maryland was still fragmented and diffused. Virgil Maxcy reported that in visits to the Eastern Shore and Baltimore prior to the elections he discerned no interest in the revival of parties.[48]

Circumstances in 1826 offered an opportunity for the renewal

---

46. *Niles' Weekly Register*, XXVII (November 13, 1824), 161-62, with corrected totals.

47. Livermore, *The Twilight of Federalism*, pp. 172-82, covers the story as well as the pressure on the Maryland delegation.

48. Virgil Maxcy to n.n., November 15, 1825, Galloway-Maxcy-Markoe MSS, LC.

of party organizations in Maryland. Elections for the House of Delegates, state Senate, House of Representatives, and U.S. Senate were on the agenda. With so many elections at hand and with party organizations appearing in other states, a propitious time for party development seemed at hand in Maryland. Yet the opportunity was ignored, for politics remained confused and haphazard. Only a few candidates announced as either Jackson or Adams supporters. In counties where Jackson was popular some candidates announced as his supporters, while the opponents ran as independents. In counties favorable to Adams the reverse was true. The House of Delegates and the Senate retained a nonpartisan character, though within a year several of the state legislators became active Jackson or Adams leaders. After the election the congressional delegation comprised four Jackson men, three Adams men, and three independents. The elections for the U.S. Senate seats revealed an equally non-partisan attitude. Edward Lloyd had resigned, and Ezekiel F. Chambers, an avowed Adams supporter from Chestertown, was elected by the General Assembly to the Senate. Samuel Smith's term had expired and he was returned, though he was correctly suspected of having shifted to Jackson.[49]

Though the politicians had not used the 1826 campaign to construct viable parties, it was clearly evident in early 1827 that organized parties would appear once again on the Maryland scene. The *American* in March accurately expressed the mood in Maryland and the nation:[50]

> A new era has arrived in the politics of our country. The old party names are laid aside. The old party distinctions seem to have been extinguished; or, at all events are forgotten in the deep interest which pervades the Union on the subject of the next presidential election. Who is to be our next President—Jackson or Adams? This is the great question which now agitates the country. . . .

Perhaps the *American* was alluding to the activity of the Jacksonians in Maryland. In early March Virgil Maxcy, Roger B. Taney, and other Jackson supporters met privately in Baltimore to plan a statewide convention, and meetings were taking place

---

49. Mark H. Haller, "The Rise of the Jackson Party in Maryland, 1820–1829," *The Journal of Southern History*, XXVIII (Aug., 1962), 315-17.
50. March 21, 1827.

in the counties.[51] On May 21, 1827, the Jacksonians gathered in Baltimore for their first state convention. Thomas Forman, elderly Eastern Shore veteran of the American Revolution, presided; but younger, if less prominent, Marylanders guided the proceedings. Maxcy delivered the main address and used the rhetoric of the "corrupt bargain" to denounce Adams and Clay and champion Jackson as the people's choice in 1824. He also refuted charges that Jacksonians were unfriendly regarding government subsidies for internal improvements. The convention then created a state central committee, with Roger B. Taney as the chairman, to direct and coordinate party activity during the campaigns.[52]

The leadership of the Jackson party illustrated that a complete political realignment had indeed taken place in Maryland. The old party lines had been snapped, and Republicans and Federalists now collaborated to promote Jackson. The new party drew heavily from the former Federalist party with Taney, Virgil Maxcy, Benjamin C. Howard, and George Winchester. Another dimension of the party was the Crawford element, including Samuel Smith, Edward Lloyd, and William Hayward. The Jackson organization included a talented corps of young politicians who would play a role in Maryland's politics in the next several decades. Among these were John Pendleton Kennedy, Reverdy Johnson, John Van Lear McMahon, Francis Thomas, Beale Randall, and Dabney Carr.[53]

The clarion calls of the Jacksonians had the effect of arousing their opposition as well as their own people. An Adams committee met on May 5, 1827, in Baltimore to plan a summer convention. The committee confessed its reluctance to organize so early but acknowledged that a response to the Jacksonians was imperative.[54] Obviously, if the Jacksonians monopolized the news and organized, the public might be swayed to Old Hickory's camp while Adams supporters were sitting on their haunches. Thus the Adams forces responded with a statewide convention in Baltimore on July 23. The Adams party, or Na-

---

51. Virgil Maxcy to John C. Calhoun, March 2, 1827, in *John C. Calhoun, Correspondence*, J. Franklin Jameson, ed., in American Historical Association, *Annual Report*, 1899, II, 793.

52. *Journal Southern Hist.*, XXVIII, 317-18.

53. *Ibid.*, pp. 318-19.

54. *American*, May 7, 1827.

tional Republicans as they were officially called, issued an address to the voters calling attention to what they believed were Adams's superior qualifications. Except for Jackson's victory at New Orleans, the National Republicans boasted, "he never would have been thought of as one of those from whom a selection is to be made to fill the presidential chair."[55] The National Republicans, like their opponents, included a conglomeration of Republicans and Federalists who years before had feuded with each other. But now they were united in their opposition to Jackson. They included Thomas Emory, Robert H. Goldsborough, Thomas W. Veazey, and John Leeds Kerr of the Eastern Shore; Daniel Jenifer, John G. Chapman, Richard Thomas, and Robert Bowie of the tobacco counties; John Archer, William Price, and Henry Warfield of western Maryland; and such Baltimoreans as Luke Tiernan, Nathaniel F. Williams, Solomon Etting, Charles S. Walsh, and Isaac Munroe, editor of the *Baltimore Patriot*.[56] Two influential persons who played a role in party organization but who were not on the published convention roster were Hezekiah Niles and Governor Joseph Kent. Niles became an active participant among the National Republicans, though he scrupulously maintained a neutral position in the columns of his *Weekly Register*. Governor Joseph Kent, formerly a supporter of Calhoun, joined the Adams ranks in 1824 and became one of the state leaders.

While the parties presented an array of candidates in 1827, voters had not totally committed themselves to one party or the other. At least ten of the nineteen counties elected delegations that were divided between the two parties, and some confusion existed about which party had won the election. A test of party strength occurred in the elections for the speaker of the House of Delegates and the governor in which the Adams delegates beat back the Jacksonian challenge. Kent reported that the Jacksonians misjudged his popularity and had to abandon their attempted coup.[57]

Both parties had organized for bigger stakes, and early in 1828 preparations were underway for the autumn presidential

---

55. *Ibid.*, July 27, 1827.
56. *Ibid.*
57. *Journal Southern Hist.*, XXVIII, 320-21; Joseph Kent to Henry Clay, January 21, 1828, Henry Clay Papers, L.C.

election. While personal qualities of the candidates dominated the campaign rhetoric, both parties groped for issues which might convert voters to their side. The Jacksonians reiterated the "corrupt bargain" argument, which contended that political intrigue in 1824 had cost the people their choice for the presidency. Vindication, the Jacksonians argued, would come with Old Hickory's election in 1828. The National Republicans countered with appeals to the growing interests in internal improvements. They contended that the southern interests behind Jackson's candidacy would prevent federal money from being used for roads and canals.[58] Yet the National Republicans faced a formidable candidate in Andrew Jackson. His popularity was sweeping the country, and criticism of him had to be delicately stated. As one National Republican explained,[59]

> In advocating the cause of Mr. Adams great skill & prudence are necessary to prevent injury. You must not detract too much from Genl Jackson . . . but to admire him for some qualities & wish you could think him qualified. But prudence & reason forbid . . . admit him to be brave & chivalric but we do not choose to make a Priest of a muscleman or a soldier of a Brain as well might you attempt to convert a cook into a sailor or make a soldier of a goose as to make a statesman of a man without coolness & prudence. . . .

The October elections for the House of Delegates suggested the balance in the state. The Adams slate won forty-eight seats, the Jacksonians thirty-one with a tie for one position in Cecil County. As expected, the presidential election a month later was close. Adams won 25,527 voters and six electors to Jackson's 24,565 and five electors. Southern Maryland and the Eastern Shore went for Adams, while Baltimore and the northern and western counties voted for Jackson.

Old Hickory won more decisively in other states and was elected president. His election momentarily boosted the Jacksonians in Maryland. Appointments now in Jackson's hands strengthened the sinews of the party as Marylanders entered positions in the federal government. Virgil Maxcy, after suffering a ruinous fire at Tulip Hill, secured a minor post in the

---

58. *Journal Southern Hist.*, XXVIII, 321.
59. MS Diary, April, 1828, John G. Chapman Papers, owned by William Chapman, La Plata, Maryland.

Treasury Department. Several offices in the diplomatic corps went to Marylanders, including a post for Christopher Hughes, son-in-law to Samuel Smith. Other positions in the Baltimore customs house and various post offices went to Jacksonians. In 1831, with the reorganization of the President's cabinet, Roger B. Taney became attorney-general. The various appointments, coupled with Jackson's popularity, enhanced the Maryland Jacksonians while demoralizing the National Republicans. In the 1829 elections the Jacksonians won six of the nine congressional seats, thirty-nine of the seats in the House of Delegates, which with their supporters in the state Senate, enabled them to elect the governor, Thomas K. Carroll.[60] All signs pointed to a potent Jackson party which might dominate the state's politics for years.

The game of politics, however, is inexact and unpredictable, as the Maryland Jacksonians quickly learned. Within a year the situation turned topsy-turvy, and the Maryland Jacksonians plunged into the depths of near political ruin. The turnabout came prior to the elections of 1830 as President Jackson vetoed a bill that appropriated funds for the construction of the Maysville Road in Kentucky and a turnpike that ran from Washington, D.C. to Frederick, Maryland. These presidential vetoes reinforced the National Republican charge that the Jackson party opposed federal assistance to internal improvements. Enthusiasm for internal improvements was particularly intense in Maryland, as it was believed that canals and railroads could link Maryland with the lucrative traffic of the West. Two years before, on July 4, 1828, work had begun on two major projects, the Chesapeake and Ohio Canal, the successor to the Potomac Company of the revolutionary era, and the Baltimore and Ohio Railroad, with substantial funds from the Maryland treasury. Marylanders had hoped that federal funds could be tapped to underwrite these and other projects. With President Jackson's vetoes in 1830, hopes for federal assistance faded.

The Maryland Jacksonians immediately recognized that the vetoes could have disastrous political repercussions at home. On the Eastern Shore, where enthusiasm for internal improvements was slight, a Jacksonian leader, William Grason, expressed dismay over the vetoes. "I should have been pleased," he wrote

60. *Journal Southern Hist.*, XXVIII, 321.

Senator Smith, "if some thing could have been got for the railroad because the interest of our state is now essentially connected with its completion."[61] As the Jacksonians feared, the public's disapprobation of the vetoes affected the elections for the lower house. The ascendant Jacksonians' balloon was punctured; they won only sixteen seats, the National Republicans sixty-four. The following year disaster continued to plague the Jacksonians as they lost again in the house and senate elections.

Additional woe came to the Jackson party with the defection of many of its young and talented members. Among these was John Pendleton Kennedy, who confided in his diary,[62]

> Jackson's Maysville message . . . is the most absurd state paper I ever read, and will consign him to oblivion. My objection to the veto message being known, an overture was made to me from the Clay party here to bring me out for the Legislature, and afterwards for Congress upon condition that I would vote for Clay. . . .

In time Reverdy Johnson and John Van Lear McMahon would also leave the ranks of Jacksonianism as that party subscribed to doctrines obnoxious to them.

The introduction of the internal improvements issue marked a significant change in Maryland's political climate. The revival of a two-party system in the mid-1820's had stemmed primarily from a power struggle between various factions that had associated themselves with Adams or Jackson. But with the growing interest in internal improvements and Jackson's vetoes, substantive issues divided the parties. Each party was developing an ideological base. This caused men like John Pendleton Kennedy to have second thoughts about the attractiveness of Old Hickory, and some like him looked for a new political home.

A second economic issue, bank reform, further stimulated a readjustment of political views in Maryland. Jackson's administration was soon identified with critics of the Bank of the United States. The bank reformers included an assortment of state bankers envious of the national bank's power, hard money advocates who essentially disliked all banks, and persons who simply believed greater federal supervision over the Bank of the United States was necessary. Roger B. Taney, who went into the cabinet

---

61. William Grason to Samuel Smith, July 7, 1830, M.H.S., Vertical File.

62. Journal, September 28, 1830, John Pendleton Kennedy Papers, Peabody Institute.

in 1831, was among the advisers who encouraged the President to restructure the banking system. Taney's opposition to the Bank of the United States stemmed in part from his belief that it exercised too much authority over the nation's financial system. Without being too uncharitable to Taney, it should be noted that his bias resulted, too, from his association as investor and counsel with the Union Bank in Baltimore. Its president, Thomas Ellicott, was one of the state bankers who was envious of the power of the Bank of the United States.[63]

Nicholas Biddle, the president of the bank, detected the Jacksonian prejudice against his bank and acted in 1832 to thwart any attempt to bring it under federal control. Though the bank's charter was not to expire until 1836, he applied for a renewal in 1832 from Congress. By this premature application for renewal Biddle expected that congressional approval would force the President to accept the Bank of the United States. Biddle believed that he had the public's support and that the President would not risk a veto of the charter in an election year. Old Hickory was not one to cower before a challenge, however, and after Congress renewed the bank's charter the President forcefully vetoed it. This was the opening salvo in the bank war and the battleground became the 1832 campaign. Jackson ran against the bank and its staunch defender, Henry Clay, the National Republican candidate.

Maryland in 1832 offered little hope for the Jacksonians. The National Republicans controlled the state government, and following Clay's nomination by a national convention which met in Baltimore in December, 1831, the General Assembly in early 1832 endorsed him. Moreover, Taney's views on the bank did not typify Maryland's sentiment. It had many friends in Maryland, including the Jacksonian Senator Samuel Smith, Reverdy Johnson, one of the original Jacksonians, and the influential family of Charles Carroll. Excepting for Thomas Ellicott, the state bankers in Maryland generally were sympathetic to the Bank of the United States.[64] Jackson's position on internal im-

63. Swisher, *Roger B. Taney*, p. 166 *et seq.*; Frank Otto Gatell, "Secretary Taney and the Baltimore Pets: A Study in Banking and Politics," *The Business History Review*, XXXIX (Summer, 1965), 207-26.
64. Jean Alexander Wilburn, *Biddle's Bank: The Crucial Years* (New York: Columbia University Press, 1967), pp. 87-89. In September 1831 the Anti-

provements and banking consequently strengthened the popularity of his opponent, Clay, in Maryland.

Yet the fall elections were disappointing to the National Republicans. Their majority in the lower house was trimmed to four seats, and Clay carried Maryland by only fifty-two votes. Clay's slim margin may have resulted from the relatively low turnout of Maryland voters. In all counties except Talbot County and Baltimore City the vote declined, as only 53.9 per cent of the eligible voters went to the polls. Maryland barely stayed in the National Republican's electoral column, but Old Hickory won nationally in a landslide victory.

Jackson regarded his resounding victory as a popular mandate against the bank and determined he would kill it. He decided to remove government funds from the Bank of the United States, a course which Taney had constantly urged him to do.[65] Taney was now appointed Secretary of the Treasury and directed the final attacks on the bank. In October, 1833, he began the removal of government funds and expectedly deposited the revenue in state banks partial to the Jackson party. One of these "pet" banks was the Union Bank in Baltimore under the directorship of Taney's friend Thomas Ellicott.[66]

As the Jacksonian attack on the Bank of the United States persisted, its president Nicholas Biddle tried to defend his institution by a severe constriction of its operations. This policy quickly upset the nation's economy and a recession in the winter of 1833–34 resulted. In Baltimore banks failed, money became scarce, and hundreds lost their jobs. "Distress—Distress—is the only cry," one Marylander reported. "The experiment [removal of the deposits] works badly. Mr. Taney does not keep the wheels well greased."[67]

Discontent in Baltimore quickly took the form of a public protest. On February 6, 1834, such a gathering appointed a delegation to visit President Jackson and insist upon the restoration

Masonic party also met in Baltimore and nominated the Maryland author and former U.S. Attorney General, William Wirt. A Clay man, Wirt hoped to swing the Anti's to Clay: John Pendleton Kennedy, *Memoirs of William Wirt* (2 vol. Phil.: Lea and Blanchard, 1850) II, 299-315.

65. Swisher, *Roger B. Taney*, p. 228.

66. Frank Otto Gatell, "Spoils of the Bank War: Political Bias in the Selection of Pet Banks," *The American Historical Review*, LXX (Oct., 1964), 37-39.

67. James Tongue to Virgil Maxcy, April 12, 1834, Galloway-Maxcy-Markoe MSS, L.C.

of the public funds in the Bank of the United States.[68] Whether
the National Republicans in Baltimore planned the meeting for
political purposes is uncertain. Obviously, large public meetings
did not occur spontaneously, and prominent National Republicans were among the officers of the meeting and the delegation
which went to Washington. Nevertheless, this meeting initiated
a chain of events that led to the formation of the Whig party in
Maryland. The announcement of the gathering to organize the
new party came from Isaac Munroe's *Patriot,* the organ for the
National Republicans. On April 12 Munroe announced that a
meeting would be held and for the first time used the term
"Whig" in reference to Maryland anti-Jacksonians. "So sure as
the Whigs of the Revolution opposed arbitrary power," Munroe
wrote, "so sure will the Whigs of this day and this community
oppose it now."[69] On April 23 the Whig party was organized in
Baltimore, and Reverdy Johnson, formerly a Jacksonian, was
appointed chairman.[70]

The elections for the House of Delegates in 1834 was the first
test of strength for the newly-organized Whig party in Maryland.
As expected, they hammered away at the Jacksonians on the
economic issues and on President Jackson's assertive role as
President. They claimed he had usurped the power of the government and caused the depression. The Whig strategy struck
responsive chords. Taney visited Maryland and found the Jacksonians enveloped in gloom.[71] Their anticipatory pessimism was
borne out by a Whig landslide. After the elections the Whigs had
sixty seats in the lower house, the Democrats a paltry eighteen.
In 1835 the Whigs maintained a satisfying majority of thirty seats
in the House of Delegates and captured four of the eight congressional seats.[72]

Economic issues provided the framework for party battles in
Maryland from 1830 to 1835, but in 1836 political reform became
the central issue. In recent years the more populous areas around
Baltimore and in western Maryland had become exasperated

---

68. *Baltimore Patriot,* February 6, 1834.

69. *Ibid.,* April 12, 1834.

70. *Ibid.,* April 24, 1834.

71. Roger B. Taney to Martin Van Buren, September 17, 1834, Martin Van
Buren Papers, L.C.

72. W. Wayne Smith, "The Whig Party in Maryland, 1826–1856," (Ph.D. dissertation, University of Maryland, 1967), pp. 112-13.

about their apportioned power in the state legislature. Though these areas were growing in population, their representation in the House of Delegates only equaled that of the smaller counties. In 1830, for example, Baltimore County with a population of 40,250 or Frederick County with 45,789 residents elected the same number of delegates as Calvert with 8,900 people and Caroline with 9,070. The city of Baltimore with 80,620 residents enjoyed only half the representation as that of the smaller counties.[73]

Considerable attention was given also to the undemocratic methods of electing state senators as well as the governor and his council. Voters exercised little choice in the election of the upper house, because the state constitution provided for an election first of a senatorial electoral college, which then chose the senators. The method of selecting the governor and his council further raised the animus of the reformers. A joint ballot of the legislature annually elected members of the executive branch, and the party which controlled the senate enjoyed an advantage of fifteen votes in the balloting. Moreover the equal status of the counties in the legislature gave the rural areas, notably the less populous eastern and southern counties, an edge in the choice of the state's leadership.

The publication of the 1830 census called attention once again to the gross inequities in the representation and stirred interest in reforming the state government. Reform meetings and petitions urged that the General Assembly consider modifications of the state constitution. Delegates from the more populous counties from time to time introduced bills proposing reform. Among them was Stephen Boyd, a Whig delegate from Harford County, who in the 1835–36 session suggested the popular election of the governor and state Senate, abolition of the governor's council, and a more equitable representation for the counties.[74]

The House of Delegates between 1833 and 1836 considered six definite reform proposals that either called for a constitutional convention or specific reforms. An analysis of the voting on these proposals reveals the division within the state on the issue. In the voting twelve Whigs and nineteen Democrats voted for

---

73. *Ibid.*, p. 118.

74. Maryland, *Journal of the Proceedings of the House of Delegates, 1835*, pp. 90-91.

reform, while four Whigs and one Democrat assumed a moderate position by voting for some of the proposals. Forty Whigs and seven Democrats opposed all the proposals. The question divided the parties and actually pivoted on sectional differences, with the smaller among the southern counties and the Eastern Shore opposing the reform and the western and northern counties advocating change.[75]

As the 1836 campaign opened the Maryland Democrats decided to exploit the reform issue to their advantage. Three contests were on the agenda that year: first, the election for the senatorial electoral college, followed by the annual lower house elections, and then the presidential election. Since the Democrats were strong in the more populous counties, the reform issue was a natural tool for them. The genius behind this strategy appears to have been the Democratic boss in Frederick County, Francis Thomas. A tall and slender man with small eyes peering over a long pointed nose, Thomas gave the impression of a crafty fox. His political instinct and cunning further accentuated this image. He had organized the Jackson party in Frederick County, served in congress, and in 1841 would be elected governor. In 1836 his energies were directed to winning Maryland for Martin Van Buren. He and Samuel Harker, the volatile editor of the *Baltimore Republican*, orchestrated Democratic maneuvers during the campaign.

The first election that fall was for the senate electors. The Democrats polled 53.4 per cent of the vote and won a majority of 4,000 votes, but the senate electoral college was chosen on a county basis, which favored the Whiggish rural areas. Consequently the Whigs had twenty-one electors, the Democrats, nineteen. Undoubtedly this portended the election of a Whig senate that would sit until 1841, and give the Whigs an advantage over the choice of the executive branch for five more years.

Frustrated by the outcome, the Democrats altered their tactics to salvage some gains. They noted that the constitution specified the necessity for a quorum of twenty-four electors before the college could conduct its business. The Whigs needed three Democrats in attendance in order to elect a senate. On September 9 Samuel Harker's blistering editorial "Reform or Revolution" hinted that the Democrats would not join the electoral

75. Smith, "The Whig Party in Maryland," p. 121.

college.[76] The following day a reform meeting in Frederick County adopted resolutions submitted by Francis Thomas which instructed the Frederick electors, all Democrats, not to join the college until the Whigs agreed to choose eight reform Democrat senators. Democratic meetings quickly followed in Elkton, Bel Air, Hagerstown, and Baltimore endorsing similar resolutions.[77]

The Democratic electors presented these demands to the Whigs at Annapolis on September 19, the day on which the electoral college was scheduled to sit. The Whigs naturally rejected the demands, and for a week each side played a waiting game. Sprigg Harwood, one of the Democratic electors, later recalled that the atmosphere in Annapolis remained calm. He remembered that "there was no personal animosity among the participants. I used to associate with the Whig electors outside and they would ask me to go up to the Senate, but I would say—'No, you will lock me in.' "[78]

A week passed with neither side budging. The Whigs then appealed to public opinion with a manifesto arguing that they were abiding by their constitutional obligation. Raising the specter of anarchy, they argued that the Democrats had caused a constitutional crisis and threatened to ruin the government. But "we are determined" the manifesto read, "that, if confusion, anarchy and ruin are to come upon us . . . we will have the consolation of reflecting, in the midst of our afflictions, that we have faithfully performed our duty."[79]

Both sides obviously appealed to public opinion to support their respective positions. The Whigs staged rallies to counter the Democrats, echoing the refrain that reform must come peacefully, not by revolution. In Cumberland one meeting nearly resulted in fisticuffs between reform Democrats and Whigs. The reformers extinguished the lights in an attempt to end the meeting, but the Whigs restored illumination and adopted resolutions condemning the Van Buren electors.[80] Whig newspapers eagerly

---

76. *Baltimore Republican*, September 9, 1836.
77. Bernard C. Steiner, "The Electoral College for the Senate of Maryland and the Nineteen Van Buren Electors," *American Historical Association Annual Report for 1895* (Washington: Government Printing Office, 1896), pp. 150-51.
78. Riley, *A History of the General Assembly of Maryland*, pp. 340-41.
79. *Niles' Weekly Register*, 51 (September 24, 1836), 69-70.
80. A. Clarke Hagensick, "Revolution or Reform in 1836: Maryland's Preface

published letters accusing the Democratic electors of subverting the constitutional government of the state. "Like Satan, they would rather 'reign in Hell, than serve in Heaven,' " one letter ran, "They would rather see anarchy and confusion supersede law and good rule."[81]

Some Democrats found themselves in a dilemma. While wishing to maintain party loyalty, they could not with a free conscience endorse the tactics of Francis Thomas and his followers, the "Glorious Nineteen" as they were called. Isaac McKim, former congressman and a staunch Jacksonian in Baltimore, feigned illness rather than participate in a Democratic rally. He confessed to his party's presidential candidate, Martin Van Buren, that "although being as much in favor of Reform as any one in the State, yet I wished it to be effected according to Law and not by the 19 Electors refusing to join to go into the Election of State Senators."[82] Rumors also circulated that Taney disapproved of the tactics, and despite pleas that he spike the rumors with a statement, none was forthcoming.[83]

The controversy over the "Glorious Nineteen" occurred while the campaign for the House of Delegates was being conducted. That contest assumed a newer and more significant complexion as politicians looked to its results for some sign of the public attitude toward the electoral college imbroglio. The house election demonstrated that the Democrats' strategy had backfired. The Whigs polled 53.9 per cent of the vote in the house elections, gaining five more seats in the house and appreciably reducing the Democratic vote in the northern and western counties.[84]

This vote threatened to fragment Democratic unity, and Francis Thomas scurried to Baltimore for a hasty caucus. After the meeting Dr. Washington Duvall, the elector from Montgomery County, issued a statement in which he said he would continue to absent himself from the college. Thomas and the other Democrats undoubtedly hoped this statement would

to the Dorr Rebellion," *M.H.M.*, LVII (Dec., 1962), 362; Steiner, *AHA Annual Report 1895*, pp. 146-48.

81. *Easton Gazette*, September 24, 1836.

82. Isaac McKim to Martin Van Buren, September 23, 1836, Van Buren MSS, L.C.

83. F. P. Blair to Roger B. Taney, September 24, 1836, Roger B. Taney Papers, M.H.S., No. 800.

84. Steiner, *AHA Annual Report*, pp. 149-150; Smith, "The Whig Party in Maryland," p. 128.

bolster the sagging unity of the Democratic electors. By this time Thomas could see that the party's strategy jeopardized Van Buren's chances in Maryland the following month.[85] Thomas's doubts were confirmed in November as the Whig candidate Harrison swept Maryland by more than 3,500 votes and carried every county except Baltimore, Cecil, and Baltimore City. The Democratic gamble had brought them nothing but defeat.

Governor Thomas W. Veazey, a Whig who had remained quiet throughout the controversy for fear that any precipitate action of his party might unite the Democrats, now instructed the Senate chosen in 1831 to continue to serve. Four Democratic senate electors, sensing public obloquy, then conceded defeat and returned to the electoral college. The constitutional crisis was over, continuity in goverment was preserved, and the Whigs' domination of Maryland remained secure.

A political revolution in Maryland had been avoided, but the victorious Whigs recognized that the reform clamor could no longer be ignored. They had committed themselves during the campaign to constitutional reform, and accordingly the Whiggish 1836–37 General Assembly devoted most of its time to modifying the constitution. The legislature passed the Reform Bill of 1837, which thoroughly overhauled the state government.

First, the Reform Act of 1837 revamped and reapportioned the legislature. It called for the popular election of a new Senate in 1838 and arranged for one-third of the Senate to be elected thereafter biennially. The legislators still adhered to the principle of federalism by providing that each county and Baltimore City have equal representation. In the lower house federalism gave way to the more democratic principle, representation according to population. The reform session reapportioned the house on a temporary basis until the end of the decade. Then, with the 1840 census statistics and every second census thereafter, representation in the House of Delegates would be determined more accurately. In the new formula Baltimore City was entitled to representation equal to the largest county.

The reform session wielded the scalpel deftly with the executive branch, too. It abolished the governor's council and called for the popular election in 1838 of a new governor. A governor's

<hr>

85. Francis Thomas to James K. Polk, October 14, 1836, James K. Polk Papers, L.C.; Smith, "The Whig Party in Maryland," pp. 129-30.

term was limited to three years, and no governor could succeed himself. To prevent any section from dominating the executive branch, the reform bill stipulated that a new governor must be elected alternately from either the eastern, southern, or north-western gubernatorial districts.

The enactment of the 1837 reform bill represented a major step in the democratization of Maryland's political structure. Counties were represented according to their population in the lower house, and the people now had a voice in the selection of the Senate and the governor. With two minor alterations, the abolition of the Eastern Shore's separate staff of officials and the change to a biennial legislative session, Maryland's constitutional framework remained fixed until the 1850 constitutional convention.[86]

### 3

### POLITICAL EQUILIBRIUM AND DEMOCRACY

The constitutional restructuring of Maryland's government in the 1836–37 reform session equalled the 1802 suffrage bill in its significance. While legislative reapportionment failed to satisfy all reformers, at least Baltimore and the western counties gained more power in the General Assembly. For the first time, too, the people had a voice in choosing the governor. These constitutional reforms had attendant effects on the operations of the political parties. Since the district or county organizations had to meld together for gubernatorial elections, the renovated constitutional structure, in effect, created an entirely new political cosmos.

Among the reforms was the creation of gubernatorial districts which corresponded with the three geographical sections of the state and alternated in the nomination of candidates. The gubernatorial election of 1838 was the first election to occur in the new cosmos, and the Eastern Shore had the privilege of nominating the parties' candidates. The Whigs nominated John Nevitt Steele, a forty-two-year-old Dorchester County lawyer-planter who had served in the state house and the Congress. William Grason, the Jacksonian leader of the Eastern Shore, was the Democrats' candidate. In a very close election Grason

---

86. W. Wayne Smith, "Jacksonian Democracy on the Chesapeake: The Political Institutions," *M.H.M.*, LXII (Dec., 1967), 383-84.

won by 313 votes in 55,131 cast. His victory, combined with the reduction of the Whig majority in the lower house to five seats and in the newly elected Senate to three seats, portended the end of a Whig hegemony in Maryland's legislature. The reform measures had boosted the Democrats who were popular in the western counties and thereafter neither party could monopolize power in the state legislature. In a sense, then, the election of 1838 marked the point at which Maryland attained a modern political system.[87]

For the next ten years the parties waged intense but fairly even contests. No party was assured of victory, as the gubernatorial results indicate. Francis Thomas won in 1841 by only 379 votes, Thomas G. Pratt in 1844 by 545 votes and Philip F. Thomas in 1847 by 638 votes. The composition of the state legislature also reflected the political balance of the 1840's:

TABLE 2

Composition of the General Assembly, 1838–1853

| Election Year | State Senate | | | House of Delegates | | | |
|---|---|---|---|---|---|---|---|
| | Whigs | Major-ity | Demo-crats | Whigs | Major-ity | Demo-crats | |
| 1838 | 12 | W | 9 | 42 | W | 37 | |
| 1839 | | | | 32 | D | 47 | |
| 1840 | 16 | W | 9 | 60 | W | 19 | |
| 1841 | | | | 35 | D | 43 | |
| 1842 | 13 | W | 8 | 35 | D | 47 | |
| 1843 | | | | 47 | W | 35 | |
| 1844 | 15 | W | 6 | 61 | W | 21 | |
| 1845 | | | | 43 | W | 39 | |
| 1846 | 13 | W | 8 | 53 | W | **29 | |
| 1847 | | | | 54 | W | 28 | |
| 1848 | 14 | W | 7 | | | | |
| 1849 | | | | 46 | W | 36 | |
| *1851 | 10 | D | 11 | 30 | D | 43 | |
| 1853 | 14 | W | 8 | 34 | W | 30 | 10 |

SOURCE: Smith, "The Whig Party in Maryland." *Election result Wash. Ct. unknown. **Temperance Party Delegates.

In presidential elections the Whiggish nature of Maryland was more apparent. Maryland's electoral votes consistently went to the Whig candidates from 1828 to 1848; not until 1852 did a Democratic presidential candidate carry Maryland.

---

87. Smith, "The Whig Party in Maryland," pp. 147-148.

Victory depended upon a fortuitous combination of several ephemeral factors. Voter turnout, energetic party organizers, party loyalty, appealing candidates, the weather on election day, and even fraudulent voting determined the outcome of elections. To some degree decisive issues affected the campaigns, but party ideology played a lesser role in Maryland's politics than has heretofore been suggested. More significant factors influencing the state's politics were the jealousy of the rural counties for Baltimore's looming preeminence, the sectional differences between the tidewater tobacco counties and the piedmont areas, and the rivalry between the eastern and western shores.

Traditional historical explanations for party differences held that the Whigs represented the silk-stocking, broadcloth gentry of the cities and plantations while the Democrats were drawn from the homespun-garbed farmers or urban laborers. Recent analyses in Maryland and other states have proved that such an explanation of party battles is too simplistic and distorts the political realities. Different examinations of the parties' rank and file in Maryland has shown that the Whigs and Democrats were strikingly similar in their socio-economic composition.[88]

The parties' leadership came from the planter-merchant-lawyer class, while the lesser party workers came from the sprawling middle class. In property ownership, slaveholding, or religion no real differences between the two parties were discernible. The social factor that appeared to have most affected Maryland's politics was ethnicity. Voting statistics and contemporary observations suggest that recently naturalized citizens in Baltimore voted consistently Democratic.

Since the early colonial period certain families had dominated Maryland's politics. The sweep of democracy in the early nineteenth century had eroded the power of these families, but in some counties they continued to exercise considerable influence. Perhaps the best example of the family party in the 1830's and 1840's is the Bowie family of Prince George's County. Robert William Bowie, Whig and scion of the Jeffersonian Republican governor, Robert Bowie, was the key figure in the family network. His sons-in-law, brother-in-law,

---

88. W. Wayne Smith, "Jacksonian Democracy on the Chesapeake: Class, Kinship and Politics," *M.H.M.*, LXII (Mar., 1968), 55-67.

and several nephews comprised both the Bowie clan and the Prince George's County Whig party. They shared in the officeholding and patronage of the county, and through other family ties extended their influence into Montgomery, Anne Arundel, and Worcester Counties and Baltimore City. Other families who exerted an inordinate political influence were the Goldsboroughs, Kerrs, and Bozmans of the Eastern Shore, and the Keys and Thomases of southern Maryland. The sons of John Eager Howard offer a most interesting case of family involvement in politics. Benjamin Chew Howard became the silk-stocking leader of the Jacksonian Democrats in Baltimore, while brother George was a prominent Whig in Anne Arundel County and briefly served as governor.

Family networks and politicians from the gentry, however, met with new challenges in the 1830's and 1840's. A new breed, the professional, was emerging and supplanting the older gentry leader who depended upon his social standing to retain his political power. John Leeds Kerr, a conservative Eastern Shore Whig, perceived the "silent revolution" as politics became more professionalized and lamented that "politics is now become a complete trade and what is worse every fellow follows it fool or knave & aspires to the best jobs. This subject once the study of patriots & statesmen, is now conveyed to such as to make it disgusting."[89]

A recent study details more precisely the "silent revolution" about which Kerr wrote. This study examined Maryland's leadership from 1789 to 1860 and found that the prototype politician after 1830 contrasted sharply with the leaders of the state in the earlier decades. Maryland's leaders from 1789 to 1830 were drawn primarily from rural areas, with two-thirds from the Eastern Shore or southern Maryland. In every respect gentry politicians, they were planters with extensive estates and numerous slaves, well-educated, and having considerable political experience and blood-ties with the social elite throughout the state. After 1835 their influence diminished steadily, until by 1843 only one per cent of the political leaders came from the planter class. The new leaders who ousted the planters were predominantly lawyers who became the professionals. From 1841 to 1860 over sixty per cent of the elected state officials

---

89. John Leeds Kerr to n.n., n.d., John Leeds Bozman Papers, L.C.

were lawyers. The new breed tended to be younger (the median age dropping from forty-six years to forty-two) and to reside in Baltimore or county seats. The new breed owned less property than the planters and lacked the family ties that distinguished the older leaders. While this change in leadership was not a social revolution in the classic sense whereby a lower class came to power, political leadership was no longer the special province of the social and economic elite.

As power shifted to the professional politician its locus became more favorable to Baltimore and western counties. In the 1790's, for example, only twenty-four per cent of the congressmen came from the western counties, while in the 1850's that area accounted for forty-four per cent of the congressmen. With the constitutional reforms establishing gubernatorial districts and appropriating more power to the northwest, more state leaders came from that area.[90]

The emergence of this new breed of politician between 1835 and 1845 contributed to and was symptomatic of a more democratic political style. The central features of the new politics were the professional politician, the party machine, and the active solicitation for votes. Atop the structure of both parties in Maryland was the state central committee, which became the administrative arm of the party. It issued the call for state conventions and the opening of the campaigns, formulated party policy, disseminated party propaganda, collected and appropriated money, and aided in the distribution of patronage. Beneath the state committee, the county central committees directed the party at the county level. Frequently these county leaders served as ex-officio members on the state committee. The local district or ward organization provided the broad base for the pyramidal party structure. These organizations conducted the campaigns on the local level and enjoyed immediate contact with the voters. At the outset of every election the various organizations met in a county convention to nominate candidates for the local and state offices. Or, in the case of a gubernatorial campaign, the county conventions appointed delegates to attend the state convention where the party leaders nominated the candidate.

90. Robert E. Leipheimer, "Maryland Political Leadership, 1787–1860," (Master's thesis, University of Maryland, 1969). While I have relied upon the entire thesis, the conclusion provides an excellent summary, pp. 101-10.

Electioneering required money, and the parties had to devise ways to raise the necessary funds. Private donation, then as now, was the major source for money. Persons holding federal or state offices necessarily donated a portion of their salaries to retain their party in power. On some occasions the party extracted large chunks from the officeholder's salary, "some giving as much as one half their whole earnings."[91] The parties judiciously distributed their money to aid campaigners where victory might be most rewarding. Whenever a state election seemed decisive for the national party, the local politicians received financial aid from Washington. John Pendleton Kennedy informed a fellow Whig that the Democratic national administration had contributed $1,000 to carry the congressional election in Baltimore.[92] Recognizing that many residents were oblivious of the generalized rhetoric of the campaigns, the party workers solicited the votes with jobs, gifts, and money. In 1830 Hezekiah Niles reported to his friend Henry Clay that "whiskey flows like water, & money abounds very much for real bribery in the presentation of coats, hats, boots, etc. in nearly balanced counties."[93] Rather than donating gifts or money the party bosses frequently found jobs for unemployed laborers. The Whigs attributed their loss in 1837 in Baltimore City to such practices in the first and second wards. William Frick, a Democratic boss who held a position of customs collector, instructed a building contractor to hire more men who would vote for the Democrats and release those who were Whigs.[94]

A necessary adjunct to every political party in the nineteenth century was a partisan press. The newspapers reported the party's activities and policy, and filled their columns with vitriolic attacks on the opposition. The Baltimore daily newspapers were the principal party organs. The *American, Patriot,* and *Chronicle* were the Whig papers, while the *Republican* and *Sun* identified with the Democrats. Principal weekly papers that served smaller communities were the Whiggish *Frederick*

91. Hezekiah Niles to Henry Clay, September 17, 1830, Clay MSS, L.C.
92. John Pendleton Kennedy to Thomas Duckett, December 26, 1847, Kennedy Papers, Peabody Institute.
93. Hezekiah Niles to Henry Clay, September 17, 1830, Clay MSS, L.C.
94. William Brown to William H. Watson, February 26, 1841; William H. Watson to William D. Merrick, February 28, 1841, Sub-Officers Applications, Treasury Department, Record Group 56, National Archives.

Herald, Cambridge Chronicle, Easton Gazette, The Cecil Whig (Elkton), The Maryland Republican (Annapolis), and The Civilian (Cumberland), and the Democratic Dorchester Aurora (Cambridge), Easton Star, The Republican Citizen (Frederick), and The Torch Light (Hagerstown).

The meetings, rallies, parades, and speeches combined to make the campaign a central feature of Maryland's political life. The campaigns assumed a carnival-like atmosphere with touring candidates addressing citizens at innumerable barbecues and fishfries. During the frequent campaigns which featured that period the parties assumed they were fighting duels to the death. Politicians castigated opponents as jackals who intended to undermine the American way of life. This, however, was largely for effect, for frequently their opponents were relatives or close friends. Ebenezer L. Finley, a Baltimore politician, confessed that his opponent was one of his best friends. During the canvass, Finley related, "we travelled in the same carriage, ate at the same table, lodged at the same inn, and then appeared as opponents on the same platforms."[95]

In the nineteenth century the political rally was the prime medium by which the politicians communicated with the voters. Replete with banners, bunting, and placards, the party workers opened the rallies by parading through the community to enlist an audience for the party orators. Then the crowd marched to a nearby open field, church, or other hall where the party workers had decorated a temporary platform with American flags and the party's paraphernalia. John Pendleton Kennedy, one of the most popular Whig orators in Maryland, described an 1848 rally in Hagerstown at which he spoke:[96]

> The country people are assembling in town. Drums are beating. A large wagon filled with a military band of music came in with a banner, and on the wagon printed, the Clear Spring band. They belong to a delegation from Clear Spring which arrives with them. At half past eleven we go to a grove about a mile from town on the Williamsport road, where we find a stage erected—seats prepared for auditors, and tables set out covered with bread, mutten, [sic] beef, pork & etc. eats for one or two thousand per-

---

95. Quoted in George Wilson Pierson, *Tocqueville and Beaumont in America* (New York: Oxford University Press, 1938), p. 502.

96. MS Journal, September 26–27, 1848, Kennedy Papers, Peabody Institute.

sons. In the course of half an hour the procession arrives from town. The meeting is organized.

During the campaign, politics attracted a good deal of public attention and served as a regular form of recreation. If he lived in Baltimore City, the voter might attend a political rally at a nearby tavern, where politicians gathered for their ward meetings. The tavern, in fact, provided a most effective political channel to reach the voter. For the poorer class, an evening spent at the neighborhood tap provided the primary entertainment. In the informal atmosphere of the tavern, where men of all ranks quenched their thirst together, political and social discussion could be intertwined easily, and converts won. And politics also invaded the churches. After drinking with his companions at a political rally during the evenings, the voter frequently heard a partisan preacher on the following Sunday morning. Hezekiah Niles, for example, reported that his wife enjoyed a "Clay" sermon at her church, while a friend heard an "American System" sermon at another church. Moreover, the local civic or social clubs offered the politicians an additional vehicle. The fire companies, for example, in Baltimore, as in most cities, operated as a political organization on the grass roots level.[97]

Naturally, political activity intensified with the approach of election day. Weekly meetings of local organizations became common, and the party workers received specific assignments for election day. The ward leaders appointed committees to distribute circulars, to challenge suspected illegal voters, to hire hacks to transport voters to the polls, and to provide lodging and board for those "unfortunate men who may be found without homes between now and the day of election provided they were *bona fide* voters."[98]

One of the unsavory aspects of the elections in a democracy is that politicians utilize people who are not *bona fide* voters. The use of bribed voters is a common experience which is probably as old as elections, and many commentators have described the practice during the Jackson period. In Maryland, as in other states, the "bought voter" was a common feature of political

97. Hezekiah Niles to Henry Clay, July 4, 1832, Clay MSS, L.C.
98. MS Proceedings of the 6th Ward Democratic Association, October 1, 5, 1847, William A. Stewart Papers, M.H.S., No. 1432.

practice. One account vividly described the use of the so-called "floating vote" in the 1844 election in Maryland:[99]

> The amount of money expended by the Locos during the battle is best known to themselves but it must have been tremendous—"The floating vote," which comprises the loafers, rounders and rowdies, cost them no small sum—In this state there is always a class, an indefinite number of chaps who lean against lamp posts during the day and knock store-boxes around at night, and who care a fig for neither party, having no knowledge or interest in the principles which divide the more reflecting portion of the people of the country—The Locos have supported these fellows like lords for the last three months —They have fawned upon them, and coaxed them; they have cajoled; and carressed them; and swilled them in whiskey, until they look as slick as any other cattle well cared for. . . .

The election campaign was somewhat akin to a religious crusade, and, like a crusade, the political canvass engendered excitement that nearly obliterated rational thought. Instead, emotion held sway. In the early nineteenth century the passions aroused by the intense rivalry of the parties frequently led to violence. Because of the riotous behavior that regularly occurred at election times and during wars, Baltimore acquired the sobriquet of "mob town." The first gubernatorial campaign in Maryland, for example, sparked a rash of riots at the polls in Baltimore. Fear spread throughout the city as the rioting continued late into the night after the polls had closed. *The Whig*, a campaign journal, reported that Democrats "stationed themselves at the corners of streets to waylay and attack with clubs, pistols, and stones, every prominent Whig that passed along." Several persons were injured—at least two were shot—in the violent aftermath of the election. Two years later, when the Whigs massed for a monstrous rally and parade, the Democrats attacked with rocks and bricks. During the fray one Whig fell dead and later another person was found in the street after having been mauled. Tempers continued to flare up during the presidential campaign of 1840, and Sheppard C. Leakin, the Whig mayor of Baltimore, received pleas for protection from Duff Green, who had begun that year the publication of a new Whig paper, *The Pilot*. After the election Leakin attempted to

99. Mason Parsons to Jesse Parsons, October 25, 1844, Mason Parsons Papers, Duke University.

quell a riot and was injured. Disorder at the polls became as regular as election day, and gun battles were not infrequent.[100]

Though the ballot box had replaced *viva voce*, the resident did not enjoy the luxury of a secret ballot. Each party printed its ballots and assigned party workers to distribute the tickets to voters at the polls. When the voter received his ballot, he was undoubtedly under the scrutiny of watchful eyes. Often, a party counterfeited the opposition's ballots by placing the wrong candidates on the ticket. To guard against such fraudulent tactics, parties stationed vigilance committees at the polls, but with infrequent success. The local organizations also kept a careful record of the political habits of the residents in their districts. A list of the residents in Baltimore's sixth ward, which was kept by the Democrats, indicates some voters as independents, but they were rare. The parties used these collations to round up their voters, to notice laggards, and distribute the patronage.[101]

The excitement engendered by the campaigns was certainly reflected in Maryland's voter turnout. Maryland's voter participation in the early nineteenth century was extraordinarily high. In 1840 Maryland's voter response was approximately 84.6 per cent of the eligible males and in 1844, 80.3 per cent.[102] In all, the changing political forms and intense public interest indicated a healthy state of democracy in Maryland.

4

FINANCIAL PROBLEMS AND CONSTITUTIONAL REFORM,

1840–1851

Though the maturation of the political system associated national issues and leaders with the state organizations, state and

---

100. J. Thomas Scharf, *History of Maryland*, III, 196; *The Whig* (Baltimore), October 4, 1838; Allan Nevins (ed.), *The Diary of Philip Hone* (New York: Dodd, Mead and Company, 1927), I, 478; Duff Green to Sheppard C. Leakin, October 17, 1840; transcript of a clipping from the *Pilot* (Baltimore), n.d., Leakin-Sioussat Papers, M.H.S., No. 1497.

101. W. W. Levy to Richard C. Holliday, March 19, 1848, Executive Papers, 1848, H.R.; MS Proceedings of the 6th Ward Democratic Association, Stewart Papers, M.H.S., No. 1432.

102. Richard P. McCormick, "New Perspectives on Jacksonian Politics," *The American Historical Review*, LXV (Jan., 1960), 292.

local problems exerted a prevailing influence in the 1840's. The most immediate political concern was the huge state debt that accrued from Maryland's heavy investment in the internal improvement projects of the previous decades. Anxious to make Maryland a principal market for the growing western commerce, the General Assembly in the 1820's and 1830's handsomely subscribed to railroad and canal companies.

The era of internal improvements revived in 1827 when the state underwrote the Baltimore and Ohio Railroad and the Chesapeake and Ohio Canal with subscriptions of $500,000 each. Work on both projects began on July 4, 1828, with the venerable Charles Carroll, last surviving signer of the Declaration of Independence, attending the railway festivities at its construction site at Mount Clare. Not to be outdone, the C&O Canal invited President John Quincy Adams to turn over the first shovelful of dirt in a ceremony north of Georgetown. The dedication ceremonies portended the next decade's competition between the two companies for land rights along the Potomac Valley and funds from private and public investors. The B&O leaped ahead in the race, and in 1834 traffic between Baltimore and Harper's Ferry opened. The iron horse was winning the race while construction of the canal inched along. The canal company was constantly beset with financial, engineering, and labor problems. As construction of the railway sped along enthusiasm for the canal venture waned, and investors channeled their money into the B&O. With construction costs rocketing upward and sources for money becoming scarce, the C&O pleaded with the General Assembly for additional funds. In 1833 the state loaned an additional $125,000 to the C&O and then again in 1835 granted a substantial loan of $2,000,000. Still the C&O Canal teetered on the brink of collapse as debts and costs mounted. In an effort to salvage the canal project and boost other internal improvements, the Maryland legislature in May 1836 appropriated $8 million to several companies. The C&O Canal received $3 million, the B&O Railroad, $3 million, the Eastern Shore Railroad Company, $1 million, the Annapolis and Potomac Canal Company, $500,000, and the Maryland Canal Company, $500,000. The state's generosity continued until 1840, with smaller subscriptions going to smaller companies. The state raised the money for these projects through the sale of bonds, principally in Europe, thus accruing a debt of nearly $15 million, with the yearly interest amounting to $585,819 by 1840.[103] Since the state government operated on a relatively small budget, no provisions for the massive accumulation of funds had existed in Maryland. Consequently, the state was trapped in 1840 with insufficient funds to meet the interest payments. State leaders knew that only taxes could raise the money to meet the state's financial obligations, but they also recognized that taxation was politically an explosive issue. Neither party wanted to accept the responsibility for levying taxes. In 1839 the Democratic Governor Grason recommended a state property tax, but the Democratic legislature failed to enact one. Then in 1841, with the recognition that the state could not meet the interest payments due the following year, a special session of the legislature levied a property tax of twenty cents per $100 of property.[104]

While the enactment of the state tax exemplified fiscal responsibility on the part of the legislature, it proved to be an unwise political move. The tax was enacted prior to a gubernatorial election campaign, and the new taxes became the principal issue. Since the Whigs had dominated the legislature that levied the taxes, William Cost Johnson, the thirty-five-year-old Whig candidate from Frederick County, had to bear the onus of the criticism. His opponent, wily Francis Thomas, the genius behind the revolt of the "Glorious Nineteen" in 1836, hammered at the issue of taxation throughout the campaign. "The Whig party having had control of the state since 1830," Thomas charged, "were responsible for the reckless policy which had squandered the public money, bankrupted the treasury, and imposed an onerous Direct Tax. . . ."[105] Despite the discontent with the taxes, Thomas barely edged Johnson by 479 votes to win the governorship. The house elections, perhaps, revealed better the dissatisfaction with the Whigs, as the Democrats gained control of the lower house by a 43–35 margin.[106]

No sooner had Thomas entered office than he had to confront the state's money problem. The assessments on property levied

103. Walter S. Sanderlin, *The Great National Project* (Baltimore: J.H. Press, 1946), pp. 83-84; Hugh Sisson Hanna, *A Financial History of Maryland, 1789–1848* (Baltimore: J.H.Press, 1907), pp. 79-95.

104. Hanna, *A Financial History of Maryland*, p. 105.

105. *The Easton Star*, September 9, 1841.

106. Smith, "The Whig Party in Maryland," pp. 177-78.

according to the 1841 law showed that the actual taxable property base in Maryland was too small for the needed revenue.
Additionally, the counties were negligent in the levying and
collecting of the taxes. They resisted the new taxes by failing
to levy taxes or appointing collection officials. With insufficient
funds forthcoming, the Thomas administration was compelled
to suspend payment of the interest due on Maryland's debt in
January 1842.[107]

The state was now faced with bankruptcy, and Marylanders
anxiously sought ways to pay off the debt. Some proposed that
Maryland seek assistance from the federal government, while
others suggested new taxes. Finally, in 1843, the legislature
decided to divorce Maryland from the transportation projects
entirely by offering to sell its stock in various companies. It was
believed that $11,700,000 could be raised, and Maryland ad-
vertised its desire to sell its stock in American and European
newspapers. But financiers were reluctant to invest in Maryland's transportation companies. The state treasurer received
only a single bid for the Tide Water Canal stocks; it was below
the acceptable minimum price and therefore was rejected.[108]

The financial pressure led others to recommend retrenchment in government operations. This resulted in the reduction
of the salaries of the governor and other officers, the abolition of
several minor posts (including a separate staff of officials for the
Eastern Shore), and the decision of the legislature to meet
biennially rather than annually.[109] Retrenchment, while perhaps removing some extravagances, offered no real cure to the
state's financial woes.

Increasingly, Marylanders talked about repudiating the debts.
This offered a simplistic approach for the fancied wishes of
citizens who wished to avoid taxation. Advocates of repudiation
could be found in all counties, but the Harford and Carroll
County Democrats seemed most interested in that approach.
They intended to make repudiation the Democratic party's solution to the state's financial difficulties. But not all Democrats,
and in particular the Baltimore Democrats, would accept re-

107. Hanna, *A Financial History of Maryland*, pp. 116-19. Scharf, *History of
Maryland*, III, p. 211.
108. Hanna, *A Financial History of Maryland*, pp. 121-22; Scharf, *History of
Maryland*, III, 211.
109. Hanna, *A Financial History of Maryland*, p. 122.

pudiation, and the issue threatened to divide the party in the 1843 elections. Harford County fell to the Whigs in 1843, but reconciled factions in Carroll County kept that delegation safe for the Democrats. Nonetheless, the issue of repudiation was introduced into the political rhetoric as a Democratic approach, while the Whigs were looked upon as protectors of the state's integrity, though their solution might be taxation.[110]

The images of the parties' positions on the debt intensified when Governor Thomas G. Pratt's administration grappled with the problem. Pratt, a Whig elected in 1844, exhorted the legislature to enforce the existing tax laws and to find new sources of revenue. The legislature responded to Pratt's leadership by expanding the tax program with a new stamp tax. The new tax law required that a specially stamped paper be used in drafting of bonds, bills of exchange, and promissory notes. The new tax policy, combined with a general improvement in the nation's economy, made the Maryland government's financial situation look healthier than it had for more than a decade. By mid-1846 the revenues of the treasury, in fact, exceeded the state's expenditures.[111]

As Maryland's financial picture brightened, state leaders hoped to resume payment of its debt. As with taxation, it was the Whigs who provided the leadership in the resumption policy. Aided by campaign funds from Baring Brothers, the London banking house which had purchased most of the Maryland bonds, the Whigs gained control of the House of Delegates in a relatively quiet state election in 1846. This gave the Whigs a majority of twenty-eight seats and enabled them to elect John Pendleton Kennedy speaker of the house. Kennedy assisted the resumption plans by appointing as chairmen of the committees those who favored the policy. Yet even with Kennedy's expert management and the influence of Governor Pratt, the resumption plans encountered stiff resistance in both houses. Yet the advocates of resumption won the passage of a bill directing the state treasurer to begin paying interest on all state bonds.[112] For Kennedy and other Whigs Maryland appeared to be back on the proper course.

---

110. Smith, "The Whig Party in Maryland," p. 212.

111. Hanna, *A Financial History of Maryland,* pp. 114, 118-19, 123.

112. Smith, "The Whig Party in Maryland," pp. 214-17; Hanna, *A Financial History of Maryland,* pp. 124-25.

The identification of the Whigs with resumption and taxation continued to haunt them in the subsequent party battles in Maryland. The Democrats, on the other hand, became associated with more popular programs, retrenchment in state expenditures, and reform of the malapportioned legislature. The Democrats argued that the inequitable representation by which the eastern and southern counties still ruled Maryland prevented advocates of retrenchment from gaining control. Consequently, the Democrats rationalized that reform of the state government was necessary in order to reduce expenditures and taxes. This rhetoric, reform and retrenchment, admirably exploited the growing reform and anti-tax sentiment and shaped the political contests for the next several years.

With the enactment of the stamp tax in 1845 the reform spirit converged with the opposition to taxes. Several reform meetings were held in the summer of 1845 and culminated in a state reform convention in August in Baltimore. There the reformers pledged themselves to vote only for candidates who favored the calling of a state constitutional convention and reduction of the state budget. The reformers flooded the General Assembly with petitions calling for a state constitutional convention, but the legislature failed to respond. Thus, the reform spirit and anti-tax sentiment were ripe for exploitation as the Whigs and Democrats prepared for the 1847 gubernatorial campaign.[113]

It was the Eastern Shore's turn to nominate the gubernatorial candidates, and the Whigs drew their candidate from the Goldsborough clan, William T. Goldsborough, the gentleman farmer of Horn's Point. The Democrats nominated Philip Francis Thomas, a prominent lawyer in Talbot County who had served in Congress and the House of Delegates. "Reform and Retrenchment" became the rallying call of Thomas and the Democrats in the campaign. They accused the Whigs of incurring the huge state debt with "Utopian schemes of Canals and Railroads" and urged the calling of a constitutional convention to reform the malapportioned state legislature.[114] While Thomas stumped the state throughout the summer, Goldsborough failed to emerge from Horn's Point until late September. It was evident that Goldsborough's failure to campaign jeopardized his

113. Smith, "The Whig Party in Maryland," pp. 217-19.
114. *Baltimore Republican,* August 27, 28, 1847.

chances. Even the Eastern Shore, traditionally Whig in its political temper, appeared to be leaning toward Thomas. However, it
was a close election again, as Thomas won by only 638 votes.[115]
Whether Thomas' victory came because of Goldsborough's failure to tour the state or because of the Democrats' association
with retrenchment and reform is undeterminable. Still the reformers interpreted the outcome as a victory, and they generated
a campaign toward the calling of a state constitutional convention.

   Despite Governor Thomas' recommendation in his inaugural
address that a constitutional convention be called, the General
Assembly refused to budge. The opponents of reform in the
1840's, as earlier, represented the smaller counties of the Eastern Shore and southern Maryland who feared that a new constitution would result in their loss of representation and power.
In 1849 the reformers opened an active campaign to generate
more interest in a constitutional convention and in a definite
reform party. They held rallies in several towns where delegates
to the state reform convention were selected. In Worcester and
Somerset Counties the reformers attracted some support from
the tax resisters, who called a reform meeting in Snow Hill.
Delegates from several counties assembled in Baltimore on July
25, 1849, for a two-day session to discuss reform proposals and
plans to persuade the state legislature to call a convention.
Though delegates from Worcester and Somerset Counties were
present, the convention was comprised mainly of Baltimore and
western Maryland representatives. The meeting, too, had a
strong bipartisan flavor, with John Pickell, a prominent Baltimore Whig, acting as presiding officer and Beale Richardson, a
Baltimore Democrat, serving as secretary. The delegates
petitioned the General Assembly to convene a state constitutional convention and pledged themselves to vote only for candidates who were committed to reform. In a relatively quiet
election campaign in 1849 some tickets for the lower house were
bipartisan "reform" slates. In Baltimore, for example, both parties came out for a state constitutional convention. In the election

---

115. Thomas Hicks to Theodore Buchanan, September 2, 1847, Theodore
Buchanan Papers, Duke University; Smith, "The Whig Party in Maryland,"
pp. 219-24.

the Whig's majority was cut by ten seats and most politicians attributed this to the growing reform sentiment.[116]

The General Assembly could no longer ignore the demands for constitutional reform, and, after considerable haggling in its 1849–50 session, passed a reform bill. The bill first provided for a vote to determine whether the people of Maryland favored a constitutional convention; if so, it called for its election; and finally, its revisions had to be submitted to the people. On May 8, 1850, the Maryland voters were polled, and the turnout was quite poor; but the reformers won by 23,423 votes to 4,935. Only Charles, Dorchester, Prince George's and St. Mary's Counties were recorded against the constitutional convention.[117]

Since the election for delegates to the constitutional convention coincided with a gubernatorial campaign, the parties agreed to delay the latter campaign until the election for the constitutional convention had taken place in September. Partisanship nonetheless crept into the election for the convention, and in many counties both parties nominated slates. William T. Goldsborough, the former Whig candidate for the governorship, revealed a strong competitive spirit when he reported that in his area "our people are at last beginning to be roused up. I have had quite an active time of it, and seen more of the county than I have ever done before. . . ."[118] The results gave the Whig delegates a fifty-five to forty-eight majority, though in the actual proceedings of the convention party lines broke apart. John W. Crisfield, an Eastern Shore delegate, wrote to his wife that "parties as such act without consent of its members and hence on all questions the voting is wild and unaccountable."[119]

In the gubernatorial campaign which opened subsequent to the election for the constitutional convention, reform remained the topic of debate. Enoch Louis Lowe, the thirty-year-old

---

116. James Warner Harry, *The Maryland Constitution of 1851* (Baltimore: J.H. Press, 1902), pp. 406-07.
117. In Somerset County the reformers won by 356–350! No vote was recorded in Calvert County, *ibid.*, p. 463.
118. William T. Goldsborough to Edward Lloyd, August 27, 1850, Lloyd Papers, M.H.S., No. 2001.
119. John W. Crisfield to Mary H. Crisfield, January 13, 1851, Crisfield Papers, M.H.S., No. 1248.

Democratic candidate, accused the Whigs of opposing reform and warned that a Whig governor would subvert the constitutional convention. William B. Clarke, the Whig candidate from Washington County, debated with Lowe on a tour of the state, but was unable to convince the voters that the Whigs advocated reform, too. The results showed that the Whigs could not escape their image as a party of taxation and anti-reform. Lowe was elected by a majority of 1,482 votes, the largest margin for a gubernatorial candidate since the 1838 election.[120]

As that campaign closed the delegates to the constitutional convention assembled on November 4, 1850, in Annapolis. The most controversial subject which concerned the convention was the question of representation of the counties and Baltimore City under a new constitution. The more populous areas naturally wanted to establish population as the basis, but the smaller counties insisted that representation be apportioned as in the past. The Eastern Shore and southern Maryland delegates naturally feared that their interests would be subverted if Baltimore gained control of the legislature. Thomas Hicks, the Dorchester County delegate, expressed the fears of the Eastern Shore when he asked, "Were people of the Eastern Shore to be retained as men serfs, hewers of wood and drawers of water for the city of Baltimore? . . . If they could be allowed to go [secede] from the Western Shore, they would gladly do it."[121] Like Hicks, other Eastern Shore delegates spoke of secession. Sectional antagonisms were raised, too, by the proposal that gubernatorial and senatorial districts be abolished; again the Eastern Shore and southern Maryland delegates fought to retain their districts for fear that the removal of districts would mean that Baltimore and its populous environs would always elect the state leaders.

The convention probably lasted longer than anticipated and became a tedious affair. Absenteeism was high, tempers flared, and men of patience undoubtedly moaned in despair. Still the delegates thoroughly examined all facets of Maryland's government and laws. Questions of representation, gubernatorial powers, budgetary questions, elective judges, restrictions of

---

120. Smith, "The Whig Party in Maryland," pp. 247-50.
121. Maryland. *Debates of the Constitutional Convention of 1851*, II, 282.

freedmen and slaves—all came under the scrutiny of the convention. Given the scope of their task, the sectional tempers and the clash between progressives and conservatives, it is not surprising that the finished document was regarded as a patchwork of compromises. Disappointment with the new constitution was deep, and most delegates accepted it only because they believed it was the best document they could obtain.

The new constitution effected the most sweeping and democratic changes ever attempted in Maryland's government. Imitating the federal government's pattern, the state's organic law assigned each county and the city of Baltimore one seat in the Senate but based representation in the House of Delegates on population, though Baltimore could have no more than four delegates than the largest county. The new formula effectively shifted the power in the General Assembly to Baltimore and the western counties. In the lower house the representation of southern Maryland and the Eastern Shore was reduced from forty to twenty-nine seats, while the remainder of the state (including Anne Arundel and Cecil Counties) gained four additional seats. State senators served four years, and one-half of the Senate was elected biennially. Delegates served only two years. The governor's term was increased from three to four years, and the gubernatorial districts were retained. The governor's appointive power was severely limited, since all state officials from constable to governor were now elected. Even the judges were elected for terms of ten years. Reflecting the exasperation of the state with the debt problems in the previous decade, the new constitution imposed tight restrictions on the debt levels that might be incurred. The state could not incur a debt beyond $100,000, and it had to be paid off within fifteen years. No state appropriations for private internal improvement projects were permitted.

The new constitution was submitted to the voters on June 4, 1851, and was ratified by a majority of 10,418 votes. It went into effect in 1851 and lasted until 1864.[122] The ratification of the 1851 constitution marked the end of an era of increasing democratic changes in Maryland.

---

122. Harry, *The Maryland Constitution of 1851*, pp. 446-62; Scharf, *History of Maryland*, III, 241-43.

5

SECTIONALISM, NATIVISM, AND UNIONISM, 1850–1854

Marylanders, of course, had not been oblivious to the growing slavery and sectional controversy that plagued the nation.
The slaveholders and slave population had steadily declined in
Maryland, but the state's cultural attitudes aligned her with the
South. Yet rare was the Marylander in the early stages of the
sectional controversy who advocated secession in order to protect slavery. Attachment to the Union was as powerful a force in
Maryland as was the attachment to slavery. Marylanders
wanted slavery protected and maintained, but they also wanted
to preserve the Union.

An aggravation that Marylanders knew must be removed if
slavery and the Union were to be preserved was the fugitive
slave problem. While precise data on the number of runaways is
impossible to obtain, Maryland certainly suffered as much as
any other state from the fugitive slave problem. The 1850 census reported that 271 slaves escaped from Maryland in 1849,
and, according to the 1860 census, 115 ran away in 1859. These
and other statistics suggest that the number of slaves escaping
was as low as one per cent of the slave population.[123]

Marylanders, of course, lacked this minimal data and based
their estimates of the number of fugitive slaves on erroneous
reports and dramatic events. They read newspaper reports of
abolitionist plots to aid slaves and saw advertisements periodically describing Negroes who had escaped. Undoubtedly the
bold attempt of thirty-eight slaves who escaped on July 8, 1845,
from southern Maryland gave credence to the suspicions about
the severity of the problem. This band marched together just
outside Washington and Rockville before they were apprehended on the Frederick Pike as they made their way toward the Mason-Dixon Line.[124] Reading about these events
made the rumors of plots and escapes believable. Marylanders
naturally joined with other southerners in demanding federal
assistance and tougher laws for capturing slaves and punishing
abolitionists who abetted the fugitives.

123. Elwood L. Bridner, Jr., "The Fugitive Slaves of Maryland." *M.H.M.*,
LXVI (Spring, 1971), 33-36.
124. *Niles' Weekly Register*, 68 (July 12, 1845), 293.

The fugitive slave problem became a core issue in the 1849–50 session of Congress. Southerners demanded a stronger fugitive slave law and insisted that slavery be permitted in the southwestern territory recently acquired from Mexico. Following the lead of John C. Calhoun, southern congressmen coupled their demands with threats of secession if Congress failed to act favorably toward them. In the deep South state leaders planned a convention at Nashville to consider secession and apply additional pressure on Congress to enact favorable legislation.

In Maryland the extremist views of the South found little acceptance. Instead, Unionism prevailed, and, as Congress groped for compromises, Marylanders reflected a strong sense of political unity. In the House of Representatives Maryland's congressmen, Whig and Democrat, voted alike. Like the two senators, their vote reflected a desire for compromise with protection for slavery. The Whiggish state legislature, moreover, passed resolutions calling for compromise but with the recognition that slaveholders might take their property into the territories. While calling for protection of southern rights, the legislature avoided any flirtations with extremism by ignoring the invitation to send delegates to the Nashville Convention. As might be expected, the prevailing temper among Maryland's citizens was one of moderation. Typical was the attitude reflected by one speaker when he urged Congress: "In the name of God, take the compromise, and don't let us hear any thing more about this matter."[125] When Congress passed the Compromise of 1850, including a new fugitive slave law, Marylanders breathed a sigh of relief, thankful that a crisis had been averted and hopeful that the sectional issues had been resolved.

But sectionalism persisted and became a factor in the 1852 presidential election. With little difficulty the Democrats united behind Franklin Pierce. Sectionalism, however, plagued the Whigs as they prepared for their national nominating convention in Baltimore. The northern Whigs touted Winfield Scott and Daniel Webster, while the southern Whigs, including Marylanders, staunchly supported the incumbent President, Millard Fillmore. Maryland Whigs preferred Fillmore because he was a moderate who had endorsed the fugitive slave law.

---

125. *The Sun*, January 24, 1850.

View of Baltimore from Federal Hill in 1857. *M.H.S.*

John G. Chapman, Maryland's congressman from Charles County, was chosen the presiding officer of the national convention, and he expressed Maryland's view in his opening remarks: "We differ as to men, but we do not differ as to principles. . . . If we have any sectional feelings, let us bury them, and like patriots look to the interests of the entire country."[126] Sectional tensions could not be easily extinguished, and the convention went through fifty-three ballots before settling on Scott. But Whigs in Maryland and throughout the South refused to accept Scott, and as the campaign unfolded Whigs defected to the Democrats. Pierce carried the nation, and for the first time since the reappearance of the two-party structure in the 1820's, Maryland fell to the Democrats. Two years later the debate over the Kansas-Nebraska bill completely divided the Whigs along sectional lines, and for all practical purposes the Whig party was dead.

As the two-party structure deteriorated nationally, reverberations ran through the state organization. In Maryland, Whigs became thoroughly demoralized, and the Democrats nearly gained an unchallengeable preeminence. The Democrats won with Enoch Louis Lowe in the gubernatorial election of 1850, capitalized on the reapportioned legislative structure to win decisive control over the General Assembly in 1851, carried the state in 1852 for Pierce, and won the governorship in 1853 with T. Watkins Ligon.

Sectionalism was not the only force affecting political conditions in Maryland. The public, increasingly disgusted with politics, held the political leadership in low esteem. The electorate had grown weary of the fraud and violence in the campaigns and the apparent disregard of significant problems by the politicians as they vied for the spoils of office. A political malaise gripped the state, and the people were turning away from the established parties.[127] Indicative of the public's revulsion were editorial blasts like the one in the *Baltimore Clipper* denouncing the parties for manipulating votes of the masses and forcing "upon them by means of party discipline men to-

---

126. *The American*, May 21, 1852.

127. Douglas Bowers, "Ideology and Political Parties in Maryland, 1851–1856," *M.H.M.*, LXIV (Fall, 1969), 198; William J. Evitts, "A Matter of Allegiances: Maryland from 1850 to 1861, (Ph.D. dissertation, Johns Hopkins University, 1971), pp. 62-63.

The city of Frederick about 1850. *Unsigned print in M.H.S.*

302

tally unqualified."[128] John Pendleton Kennedy, veteran of so many campaigns, withdrew from public life in disgust and confided to his diary: "Nothing can be more contemptible than the state politics and management of Maryland. We have not a man in public office above mediocrity, and the whole machinery of our politics is moved by the smallest, narrowest, most ignorant and corrupt men in the State."[129]

As men like Kennedy withdrew from politics and party organization sagged, a political vacuum resulted. Independent, nonpartisan, or "fusion," candidates ran for office, each arguing that the electorate should be more concerned about the quality of candidates than political affiliation. To the electorate the parties had become simply political machines, contesting for power without regard to the real problems of the state. Perhaps the *Baltimore American* best expressed the mood of the public when it observed after the 1853 elections that the "results of the elections shows [*sic*] with great significance the abatement of party feeling, and the difficulty of an organization under party banners. . . . The superior interest which the people have taken in questions of moral reform or of local interest . . . prove . . . the power of the party is certainly losing its influence."[130]

With the Whigs enervated by sectionalism and failure on the state level, the Democrats divided by interparty squabbling, and the electorate generally disgusted with conventional politics, the ground was fertile for a new political party. It came in the form of the Temperance party. In Maryland the temperance enthusiasts attracted Whigs who were looking for a new party and nativists who believed the social disorder stemmed from alcohol-prone immigrants. Encouraged by the success of a Temperance party in Maine that enacted prohibition there in 1851, Maryland temperance leaders turned to politics in 1853. While the enthusiasm for temperance percolated in all counties, its adherents preferred to encourage the regular parties to adopt a temperance posture. In Baltimore, however, the feebleness of the party structure was more apparent, and the temperance leaders decided to nominate candidates for the House of Delegates. The Democrats nominated outspoken anti-

---

128. Baltimore *The Clipper*, September 17, 1851.
129. MS Journal, April 20, 1850, Kennedy Papers, Peabody Institute.
130. *The American*, November 4, 1853; *M.H.M.*, LXIV, 198; Smith, "The Whig Party in Maryland," pp. 268-69.

temperance candidates, and the issue was joined in Baltimore. The Temperance party easily elected the entire slate of Baltimore's ten delegates to the House of Delegates. When the General Assembly met in December for its annual session, the Temperance delegates immediately prepared to bring prohibition to Maryland. They introduced a bill which would outlaw alcoholic beverages save for medicinal purposes and steered its passage through the house by a 42–23 vote. The rigidity of their bill raised objections among more moderate reformers in Maryland, and the press came alive with criticisms of the bill. The state Senate, sensing the public objections, rejected the house bill and proposed instead a system requiring stricter liquor licenses. The temperance movement in Annapolis was stalemated, and no compromise could be reached between the two houses. The session ended with nothing gained by the temperance delegates. Temperance enthusiasm then dissipated as a more potent force, nativism, emerged in Maryland's politics.[131]

Nativism, the hatred of immigrants, had been a latent force in Maryland for over two decades. It had contributed to the violence in Baltimore in the late 1830's and appeared as a political force in Baltimore in 1845. It surfaced again in 1852 when the Catholics attempted to obtain state funds for parochial schools. A bill sponsored by Martin J. Kerney, Catholic editor of the *Metropolitan* and chairman of the House Committee on Education, called for the appropriation of funds to religious schools. When his bill came under attack in the Baltimore press, he withdrew it only to try again in the 1853 session with a milder bill. His second effort stirred the Protestant clergy, the Baltimore City Council, and various newspapers to denounce and lobby against the bill. The house referred his bill to a special committee, where it died.[132] The Kerney bill along with other events in Maryland aroused the latent nativism. It was a force ready to be harnessed and channelled into politics.

By the spring and summer of 1854 reports of a new and secret political organization, the American party, circulated throughout Maryland. Known members of the secret organization, when queried about their party, replied, "I know nothing," and thus gained the sobriquet "Know-Nothings." The Americans, or

---

131. *M.H.M.*, LXIV, 208-09; Evitts, "A Matter of Allegiances," pp. 87-89.
132. *M.H.M.*, LXIV, 203-05.

Know-Nothings, expressed the ultraconservative sentiments of a nation caught up in the sectional problems and social changes of the ante-bellum period. While they despaired of the influx of foreigners, their greater concern was for the preservation of the union as founded by the revolutionary generation. They believed that the social breakdown and political malaise stemmed from the nation's abandonment of the principles of the Founding Fathers. Hence the Americans called for the return of the simpler politics and purer precepts of a bygone day. "Heed the warnings of Washington, Jefferson, Madison, Jackson," intoned the Hagerstown *Herald and Torch*, "and . . . inscribe the soul-stirring motto upon the Star-Spangled Banner—'Americans shall Rule America.' " They hoped to cleanse politics of its demagoguery and corruption by extending the period of naturalization and electing qualified, statesmanlike candidates to office.[133]

The conservative feature  of Know-Nothingism is reflected, too, in the types of people playing a role in the party. The leaders of the party in Maryland were usually scions of distinguished families. Well-educated and socially prominent, these "sons of blue-bloods" had achieved success as lawyers, bankers, merchants, and railroad executives. Through the Know-Nothing movement they were entering public life for the first time. These Know-Nothing leaders presented a sharp contrast to the Democratic leadership. The Know-Nothings tended to be younger men (average age, thirty-four years; for Democrats, forty-three years) drawn from the business class, while the Democrats were the professional-politician-lawyers. The Know-Nothings were outspokenly in favor of such business legislation as a high tarriff and were less defensive of slavery and the South than the Democrats.

The electorate attracted to the Know-Nothing column had distinctive features, too. The Know-Nothing tickets polled well in urban areas or small towns among the middle class proprietors and clerks. The party fared poorly in slaveholding areas and among the wealthy and poorer wards in Baltimore City. Moreover, contrary to conventional beliefs, in Baltimore it was the Democrats, not the Whigs, who enlisted most in the American party ranks. Additionally, it is believed that a remarkable

---

133. Evitts, "A Matter of Allegiances," pp. 114-18.

portion of Know-Nothing votes came from persons who were voting for the first time.[134]

In the 1850's the Know-Nothing movement accorded perfectly with Maryland's political sentiments. The party offered fresh candidates who were untainted by the corrupt politics of the day and who promised statesmanlike leadership. The Know-Nothings evoked a pride in the Union, while the other parties seemed under the sway of sectional interests. Finally, of course, the Know-Nothings capitalized on the latent nativism. Without question, the American party seemed the most promising new star in the political constellation.

6

CONCLUSION

By mid-century Maryland's political structure was substantially different from what it had been in 1800. The trend toward a more democratic society had wrought fundamental changes to the political scene. Since the passage of the 1802 suffrage law nearly half a century before, the aristocratic features of Maryland's government and politics had disappeared. Gentry rule had given way to the professional politician and the party machine. Deference politics had disappeared with the widely-expanded suffrage and the politics of participation. The people had a voice in the selection of nearly every state leader, with the notable exception of United States Senators who were still chosen by the General Assembly. The locus of power had shifted to correspond with the democratic changes as the more populous areas now exercised more influence in the state government. At mid-nineteenth century it could be said that the advent of democracy had been witnessed on the shores of the Chesapeake. The question next facing Maryland and the nation was in what direction would the forces of sectionalism and nativism take them.

---

134. Jean H. Baker, "Dark Lantern Crusade—An Analysis of the Know Nothing Party in Maryland," (Master's thesis, Johns Hopkins University, 1965), pp. 13-28, 32-51; see Bibliographical Essay Ch. V.

BIBLIOGRAPHICAL ESSAY

CHAPTER IV

Maryland's political history from 1800 to 1850 has been a neglected chapter in the state's history. A single volume that synthesizes the politics of that period still awaits some historian. Meanwhile we can find ample primary sources and monographs that serve as building blocks for an overview.

Among the most significant manuscript collections available for Maryland's political history is the collection of John Pendleton Kennedy Papers located at the Peabody Institute. Other notable collections include the papers of Benjamin Howard, Roger B. Taney, and the Lloyd Family at the Maryland Historical Society; the Thomas Family papers at the Hall of Records; and the papers of John Leeds Bozman and the Galloway-Maxcy-Markoe families at the Library of Congress.

A bountiful supply of newspapers, including Baltimore dailies and county seat weeklies, exists within the vaults of the Maryland Historical Society.

Monographs, biographies and scholarly articles offer considerable insight into Maryland's politics. For the Republican-Federalist years valuable volumes include David Hackett Fischer, *The Revolution of American Conservatism* (New York: Harper and Row, 1965), and Frank A. Cassell, *Merchant Congressman in the Young Republic: Samuel Smith of Maryland* (Madison: University of Wisconsin Press, 1971). Useful articles are Dorothy Brown, "Embargo Politics in Maryland," *Maryland Historical Magazine* LIII (1963), pp. 193–210; John S. Pancake, "Baltimore and the Embargo, 1807–1809," *Maryland Historical Magazine*, XLVII (1952), pp. 173–187; and Victor Sapio, "Maryland's Federalist Revival, 1808–1812," *Maryland Historical Magazine*, LXIV (1969), pp. 1–17.

Carl Brent Swisher, *Roger B. Taney* (New York: Macmillan Company, 1936) is the definitive biography of a figure that bridges both the Jefferson and Jackson eras.

For the Jackson party battles no monograph yet exists. One must rely on doctoral dissertations such as W. Wayne Smith, "The Whig Party in Maryland, 1826–1856," University of Maryland, 1967, and William Evitts, "A Matter of Allegiances: Maryland from 1850–1861," Johns Hopkins University, 1971. Indispensable articles for this period include Douglas Bowers, "Ideology and Political Parties in Maryland,

1851–1856," *Maryland Historical Magazine*, LXIV (1969), pp. 197–217; Frank Otto Gatell, "Secretary Taney and the Baltimore Pets: A Study in Banking and Politics," *Business History Review* XXXIX (1965), pp. 207–226; A. Clark Hagensick, "Revolution or Reform in 1836: Maryland's Preface to the Dorr Rebellion," *Maryland Historical Magazine*, LVII (1962) pp. 346–366; Mark H. Haller, "The Rise of the Jackson Party in Maryland, 1820–1829," *Journal of Southern History*, XXIII (1962) pp. 307–326; and W. Wayne Smith, "Jacksonian Democracy on the Chesapeake . . . ," *Maryland Historical Magazine*, LXII (1967), pp. 381–393; LXIII (1968), pp. 55–67.

Frank White, Jr., *The Governors of Maryland* (Annapolis: The Hall of Records Commission, 1970), is a valuable reference.

# V

# THE ERA OF THE CIVIL WAR

BY

RICHARD R. DUNCAN

GEORGETOWN UNIVERSITY

The period between 1854 and 1868 was a tumultuous era in
the history of Maryland and the nation. The growth of sectionalism in the decade of the 1850's shattered the old political
alignment, while the ominous sectional confrontation over slavery ultimately ended in a test of arms over the issue. A reluctant
Maryland, conservative by instinct, was swept into the vortex of
the Civil War and in the upheaval underwent a social revolution
in race relations. Maryland was to remain loyal to the Union, but
Marylanders experienced serious trauma in their decision. The
questions of loyalty and emancipation became serious divisive
issues during the war years. Ultimately the triumph of the Unconditional Unionists in 1864 ridded Maryland of her "peculiar
institution," while Southern sympathizers were to suffer penalties for their wartime position. Radical ascendancy, however,
was short lived and rapidly collapsed with peace. In the following political realignment, conservatives and moderates, now in
control of the Democratic party, once again regained their dominance over the state by 1868.

1

THE RISE AND COLLAPSE OF KNOW-NOTHINGISM

Politically the decade of the 1850's was one of upheaval, violence, and realignment in Maryland. The 1851 Constitution
marked the end of a period of stability and Whig domination. The
struggle between the more reform-minded Democrats and con-

servative Whigs had ended in a victory for reform. Now lacking issues, the two major parties were threatened with increasing dissatisfaction with the party system. Emerging independent movements were soon challenging old allegiances. Nationally, the sectional confrontation over slavery also had its ramifications for Maryland. In 1854 the uneasy peace established by the Compromise of 1850 was suddenly exploded by the Kansas-Nebraska Act. The bill shattered the Whig party and even Democrats were badly shaken by the repercussions. The collapse of the Whigs nationally and the political vacuum it created offered an excellent opportunity for the emergence of a nativist movement and, as events unfolded, the American party to fill the need for a second major party in the state.

Nativism as a political movement had briefly emerged in Baltimore as early as 1844 but had quickly collapsed in the following year after its failure in the municipal election. Yet nativism was kept alive by the activities of secret societies and by a few Protestant ministers. Fuel was added to the nativist impulse when in the late 1840's and in the following decade immigration to the United States rapidly increased. Most of the immigrants were Germans and Irish, and many native Marylanders reacted sharply to the Roman Catholicism and clannishness of both groups and to the presumed radicalism of the Germans.

The controversy over the Kerney School bill, which would have provided public funds for parochial schools, and the visit of the Papal legate Bedini to the United States and Baltimore in the early 1850's also helped to accentuate the sensitive religious issue. With the increase in agitation over religion, nativist societies became active and a more potent force in the state. Strong additional impetus was given to the movement in Maryland from Know-Nothing activity in New York. By August the movement had gained sufficient momentum for its leaders to hold a mass meeting in Monument Square in Baltimore, where the estimated 5,000 in attendance heard speakers advocate the principle, "Americans should rule America." The crowd was told that the public schools should continue to be run as they were, and that there should be additional restrictions on immigration. They were also called upon to resist any attempts to curtail freedom of speech; to adhere to the principle of separation of church and state; and, paradoxically, to oppose the formation of secret societies by a religious denomination for political purposes.[1]

The early nativist societies had eschewed politics, but by 1852 many of them were merging and coordinating their activities with the growing Know-Nothing movement or temporarily cooperating with the Maine Law Temperance movement. In the autumn 1853 election, Baltimore nativists, after receiving favorable responses to a circular containing questions on the church-school issue, endorsed temperance candidates for local offices. Nativist support quickly demonstrated its potential power. While the Democratic candidate for governor, T. Watkins Ligon, carried Baltimore by over 3,000 votes, the local slate was defeated by less than a thousand.

But it was in the following year that the nativist movement began to come into its own. The appearance of the Papal legate Bedini in Baltimore helped to intensify the religious issue and brought about a violent outbreak of anti-Catholic sentiment in the city. By 1854 nativism had taken hold in western Maryland as well. The April municipal election in Hagerstown caused a sensation. The anti-Maine Law and Know-Nothing candidates were swept into office. A month later Cumberland Know-Nothings selected a ticket drawn from both the Democratic and Whig parties and succeeded in electing it.

By fall the movement had gained considerable strength and momentum. Democrats, apprehensive about the fall election, denounced the Americans or, as they were better known, Know-Nothings, as being a party "contrary to the principles of the Constitution." They boasted that they would carry the election "in spite of the combination of Whigs, Know-Nothings and Temperance men."[2] However, their cry soon had a hollow ring.

Two weeks prior to the Baltimore municipal election the American party, still shrouded in secrecy and mystery, publicly announced their candidate for mayor. On September 27 the *Baltimore Clipper* reported that Samuel Hinks had been selected in a secret meeting the night before to oppose the Democratic nominee, William G. Thomas. The campaign was

---

1. Benjamin Tuska, *Know Nothingism in Baltimore* (New York: n.p. 1925), p. 9.
2. Quoted in Laurence Frederick Schmeckebier, *History of the Know Nothing Party in Maryland* (Baltimore: J.H. Press, 1899), p. 18.

short, lively, and a surprise. And it was also one in which the Know-Nothings demonstrated their political sagacity. Unknown to the Democrats, the Americans had printed their ballots with the same blue stripes on the back as had the Democrats. The trick came too late to counteract and was a disaster for the party in traditionally Democratic Baltimore. Hinks won by a margin of 2,744 votes. The American party also elected fourteen members to the first branch and eight to the second branch, gaining control over the city council.[3]

In the following year Americans added to their successes in Baltimore, Hagerstown, and Cumberland by expanding their political base to include victories in Annapolis and Williamsport. In the wake of the Whig party's collapse and with these nativist successes in Maryland and other victories in such states as Massachusetts and Delaware, the Americans threatened to become the second major national party. When the party's national council met in Philadelphia, it threw off the mantle of secrecy which had surrounded its activities and drew up a public platform of principles which stressed unionism and nationalism. The platform called for changes in immigration and naturalization laws, resistance to the aggressive policies of the Catholic church, the use of the Bible in the public schools, and other governmental reforms. On the sticky question of slavery, the Americans endorsed a resolution condemning the agitation that the issue had produced and denied congressional authority to interfere with the institution. The party's attempt to avoid the divisive issue was unsatisfactory and unacceptable to many northern Know-Nothings who were infected with anti-slavery stirrings. Ultimately American inability to resolve the dilemma led to schism within the party.[4]

However, jubilant Baltimore Know-Nothings, meeting en masse in Monument Square in June, endorsed the actions and principles which had been adopted at the national council's meeting. Other meetings throughout the state adopted a similar stand, and when in the following month the state convention met to nominate candidates, they too ratified the platform. Yet there was concern in Maryland over Article 8 which called for resistance to the "aggressive policies and the corrupting ten-

---

3. Scharf, *History of Maryland* III, 246.
4. Schmeckebier, *Know Nothings*, pp. 19-22.

dencies of the Roman Catholic Church." A number of Know-Nothing local lodges had given up the religious test for admission. They wished to confine the test to political allegiance to the party as the only membership requirement and thus avoid the religious issue. Maryland nativists, shifting the issue from intolerance to a question of loyalty and patriotism, attempted to distinguish between native and foreign-born Catholics.[5]

By 1855 the emerging Know-Nothing movement had great appeal to the Protestant middle class in Maryland, and for its leadership it began to draw heavily on the upper-middle class business community. Prior to 1854 most of the leadership had come from the clerical and proprietary classes, but after that date there was an influx from business and professional groups. Interestingly, lawyers constituted only 38 per cent of the American leadership as compared to 72 per cent of the Democrats. Know-Nothing leaders were more likely to be Protestant businessmen, especially Episcopalians, and live in an urban area. Jean Baker, in an interesting study of forty Know-Nothing and thirty-five Democratic leaders, found that the average age for the Americans was 34 as compared to 43 for the Democrats. Most of the older and prominent Whig leaders had refused to join the Know-Nothings, which in part accounts for some of this, but it is also obvious that the movement had an appeal to the younger and newer politicians. Professor Baker feels that a key in understanding the attraction of the leaders to the party was that "Young men who were Masons, businessmen, and pro-Union were attracted to the party which promised a return to 'America for the Americans' and to 'The Spirit of '76.' "[6] No less appeal, probably, was the political opportunity allowed by the new coalition for young aspiring politicians.

The Democrats, on the other hand, were vociferous in their denunciations of the movement, and its principles were declared as "unconstitutional, anti-republican, dangerous to free institutions, and destitute of sound morals and true religion."[7]

5. *Ibid.*, pp. 21-23; William Joseph Evitts, "A Matter of Allegiances: Maryland From 1850 to 1861" (Ph.D. dissertation, Johns Hopkins University, 1971), p. 108.

6. Jean Hogarth Harvey Baker, "Dark Lantern Crusade: An Analysis of the Know Nothing Party in Maryland" (M.A. thesis, Johns Hopkins University, 1965), Ch. II, III (an excellent Master's thesis and analysis of the Maryland Know-Nothing movement).

7. Quoted in Schmeckebier, *Know Nothings*, pp. 24-25.

Know-Nothings were also accused of being merely Whigs in disguise. But the newly emerging political coalition not only drew from the ranks of the former Whigs but also cut into Democratic strength in the middle class as well. To meet the new challenge Democrats not only nominated their own candidates but also joined with Whigs in some counties in fusion tickets. Yet, in southern Maryland, where the plantation economy was the strongest and where the population ratio of blacks to whites was higher, the move eventually was towards strengthening the Democratic party. In an area which was originally settled by Catholics many reacted negatively to the anti-Catholic principles of the American party, and more positively many responded to the growing attraction of the Democratic party's Southern wing. The accusation that the Know-Nothings were abolitionists hurt the Americans.[8]

The resulting election campaign of 1855 was active and vociferous on both sides. A majority of the old Whig newspapers, despite a distaste for the secrecy and the rhetoric of the Know-Nothing movement, supported American candidates.[9] In an open address to Maryland voters, American candidates attacked the misrepresentations of their party and maintained that their only purpose was "to rescue the Republic from the control of factions, combinations, sectional, sectarian and political." They further maintained that they had "no secret pledges, no hidden purposes, no object not declared." In listing their purposes they maintained that they wished "to protect the country from illegitimate foreign influences" by making sure that candidates for public office were imbued with a knowledge of the American language, laws, and spirit. They denied that they had any intention of proposing laws which would revoke any "right now conferred on naturalized citizens," but they did oppose allowing unnaturalized persons the right to vote. They also maintained that they did not oppose immigration, but that they favored laws to prevent "the outpourings of the poorhouses and jails— the criminals and fugitives from justice— the halt and blind and insane of Europe and China." Finally they

---

8. Evitts, "Matter of Allegiances," pp. 122-30.

9. Douglas Bowers, "Ideology and Political Parties in Maryland, 1851–1856," *M.H.M.*, LXIII (Fall, 1969), 215.

pledged themselves to resist any violation "of American law, which forbids religious sects to meddle in politics."[10]

Unfortunately for the Democrats the tide of victory was still rising for the Know-Nothings. The party carried Baltimore City and thirteen out of the twenty-one counties. The party had also cut into the Democratic strongholds of Baltimore, Carroll, Harford, and Howard Counties. Their chief opposition came from southern Maryland.[11] When the new legislature met on January 2, 1856, the Americans controlled the House of Delegates, and with cooperation from a few of the Whig holdovers, they had sufficient strength to organize the Senate as well.

With the political campaign over, party warfare now shifted to a new battle ground. In his annual message to the legislature, Democratic Governor T. Watkins Ligon, who had been elected in 1853, called specific attention to the Know-Nothings and charged that the "new element" had already been "productive of more baneful consequences" by its secrecy in dividing Marylanders. In a free society, he charged, secret societies were not justified and tended "to the subversion of the well established and most dearly cherished principles of our Government . . . plainly prohibited both by the letter and spirit of each and all of them." He decried the attempt to divide citizens into classes against one another, and he believed that

> it may require already a most vigorous exercise of public virtue to turn back the tide of evil flowing upon us, from an improvident introduction of religious issues into the field of political agitation and to restrain that proclivity to intolerance and proscription, which has recently been developed in different sections of the country.[12]

The governor's attack was quickly answered by Anthony Kennedy of Baltimore, who had that part of the message attacking the Know-Nothings referred to a select committee of five to investigate the charges. Needless to say, with American control over the legislature and therefore a majority on the committee, the resulting report became more of a vehicle for a counterattack than an impartial investigation. The majority sarcastically

---

10. *Address of the Candidates of the American Party, to the People of Baltimore* (Baltimore: n.p., 1855).
11. Bowers, "Ideology and Political Parties," p. 215.
12. Maryland, *House Documents, 1856*, Doc. A., pp. 28-29.

made fun of the governor's fears and then in turn used the report to defend the principles of the American party. The report charged that his fears stemmed from the proceedings of the national council of the American party and asserted that it "appears that the secrets which have contributed to the Executive's disquiet are the political doctrines avowed in a paper called the Platform of that Party." Therefore, since its principles had been amply published by the press, they found little necessity in investigating the party.[13]

The minority disagreed. After setting forth the many difficulties and frustrations that they had encountered in attempting to make an investigation, the minority, ignoring past history, denied that there had ever been any religious agitation before the appearance of the Know-Nothings and accused them of having introduced the issue. Yet, despite their attack on the Americans, they did not recommend any legislative action against the societies.[14]

With control over the assembly in the hands of the Americans, there was the logical expectation that the anti-Catholic and anti-immigrant rhetoric of the campaign would be enacted into law. But such was not to be the case. None of the Know-Nothing program was enacted into law during the session. Petitions praying for protection for individuals held in convents against their will were received by the House of Delegates and were duly turned over to a select committee of five to investigate the charges. Much to the surprise of many, the committee's report was unanimous. Confining its attention to the single purpose, that of determining whether persons were being held illegally in convents and if so whether there were existing legal remedies for such persons, the committee felt that mere complaints without sufficient evidence were not justification for legislative interference, since "no allegation has been substantiated, nor has proof been exhibited that any person is now unlawfully confined in any religious house or Convent." But the committee went on to say that even if there were such cases, "the writ of Habeas Corpus, throws ample protection around even the humblest citizens of our Commonwealth." Therefore they concluded "that no further legislation is necessary."[15]

13. *Ibid.*, *Report of the Majority of the Committee on Secret Societies.*
14. *Ibid.*, *Report of the Minority of the Committee on Secret Societies.*
15. *Ibid.*

Meanwhile in the senate such petitions were merely laid on the table. Calls for changes in the naturalization laws met a similar fate and were buried in committee. An attempt was made to secure the passage of a joint resolution calling upon Maryland's congressmen to use their influence in securing a modification of the naturalization laws, but even this died without legislative action.

Once in office, the Americans demonstrated their practical political nature rather than their ideological rhetoric. Typically, the Know-Nothings became pragmatic politicians. The distribution of spoils and offices became a more pressing concern than the enactment of their party's program. Paradoxically, the General Assembly's major accomplishment under the Know-Nothings was a party matter: the election of Anthony Kennedy to succeed Senator Thomas Pratt in the United States Senate.

For fear that Governor Ligon would appoint an interim Democrat to fill Pratt's expiring term, which would end after the legislature adjourned, the Americans pushed for the election of their candidate. Democrats, meanwhile, hoping that the next session would see their return to power, attempted to block the vote. In selecting a suitable candidate, the question of party loyalty was a crucial and determining factor. John P. Kennedy, a Know-Nothing supporter but not a society member, had hoped to be the candidate, but his brother, Anthony, who was a member, was chosen instead. To John Kennedy the reason was obvious, a ". . . disposal to be loyal in its appointments to those who have gone through the forms of initiation."[16]

With a series of brilliant successes behind the party in 1855, Maryland Know-Nothings looked optimistically towards the 1856 election. For despite some defeats and setbacks in Virginia and Ohio, the Americans nationally had been fairly successful. Yet the ominous issue of slavery continued to threaten the unity of the Americans as it had the Whigs. The party, meeting in Philadelphia symbolically on Washington's birthday, prepared for the forthcoming campaign and easily nominated former President Millard Fillmore and Andrew Jackson Donelson of Tennessee as their candidates. But again party unity in drawing up a platform was threatened by the slavery issue. Controversy over the issue had already caused some anti-

---

16. Quoted in Baker, "Dark Lantern Crusade," p. 74.

slavery delegates to walk out of the meeting of the national council in the previous year. Therefore, prior to the opening sessions of the convention, the national council had again tried to straddle the issue, but the inability to frame a plank acceptable to the anti-slavery men ultimately led to a bolt of many northern delegates from the convention. Eventually they were absorbed by the Republican party. Meanwhile the remaining delegates proceeded to criticize the Pierce administration for re-introducing the slavery issue but then with little regard for consistency adopted a plank endorsing the principle of popular sovereignty as its solution.

Later on September 17 remnants of the Old Line Whigs from twenty-one states met in Baltimore to hold their last convention. They too endorsed Fillmore's candidacy, but they refused to approve of the American party's platform. Instead they drew up their own. But with their acceptance of Fillmore they were quickly absorbed by the Know-Nothings.

For Baltimoreans 1856 was a municipal election year as well, and since the local election preceded the presidential one by a month, Marylanders were most interested in witnessing the first test of party strength. Baltimore Americans chose for their mayoralty candidate Thomas Swann, a former president of the Baltimore and Ohio Railroad, to oppose the Democratic nominee, Robert Clinton, another former railroad president. Excitement ran high in Baltimore and as early as August political violence had erupted when Democratic clubs, on their way to a party meeting, were ambushed by members of Know-Nothing clubs. Again in September there was fighting between the various opposing clubs. Mayor Hinks, seemingly taking into account the growing apprehension over the violence, ordered General George H. Steuart to ready the city militia for possible use on election day. But suddenly, after the orders were made public, the mayor decided to suspend the military preparations.

Unfortunately in what followed, the fears of many were fully justified. Disorders were far worse than in previous elections. At least two serious riots between warring clubs occurred, and in one case the Rip Raps, after defeating the New Market Fire Company in Lexington Market, sacked the company's fire house. Out of the disorder, intimidation, and confusion the American party maintained its hold on the city by electing Swann with a majority of 1,567 votes. The Americans also continued to control the city council by electing thirteen members out of twenty to the first branch, while in the second branch the parties were evenly divided.[17]

Governor Ligon, in reacting to the spectacle of the municipal election as well as a concern for the Democratic vote in the city, now went to Baltimore in an attempt to secure the cooperation of city officials in helping to prevent a recurrence of the violence in the forthcoming presidential election. Municipal authorities, however, were not receptive and rejected his overtures "with cold civility." Frustrated in his efforts, the governor had no time to make other arrangements. Another attempt had also been made to force the mayor to undertake necessary precautions when a committee of citizens asked him to convene the city council into extra session in the hope that it would take action to prevent a recurrence of the October disorders. But the mayor was unreceptive. He told them that he did not fear a repeat of the violence and assured them that he had already made appropriate arrangements to secure a peaceful day. And seemingly the mayor was formulating contingency plans. He ordered the militia to report to their armories to stand in readiness if their services were needed. But later the order was suddenly countermanded, and the men were merely placed on stand-by duty.[18]

Again, fears for an orderly election proved to be justified. Without an adequate police force violence flared up. In the ensuing disorders even a small cannon was utilized, and at least ten were killed and over 150 injured in the fighting. And again the Know-Nothings, with the muscle power of their clubs, not only swept to victory in the election but increased their margin to over 7,000. Every ward was carried for Fillmore, giving him 16,900 votes to Buchanan's and Fremont's 9,871 and 214 respectively.[19] The remainder of the state also added to Fillmore's margin. But for Marylanders it was a singular victory. Fillmore's only electoral votes came from the Old Line State.

The 1856 election exposed the weakness of the American party on the national level. Schism over slavery and defections within the party's ranks over the issue fatally sapped the

17. Tuska, *Know Nothings*, p. 15; Bernard C. Steiner, *Citizenship and Suffrage in Maryland* (Baltimore: Ginn, 1895), p. 39.

18. Maryland, *House Documents, 1858*, Doc. A., pp. 21-22.

19. Tuska, *Know Nothings*, p. 16.

movement's strength. Following the national election the party's demise quickly came in the meeting of its national council at Louisville, Kentucky in June 1857. There the council recommended that each state should adopt a platform best suited to its needs.[20] For Maryland Know-Nothings, despite their ability to deliver the state's electoral vote, the national party's collapse was a disaster. Isolated and no longer a part of a viable national party and cut off from future federal patronage, continuation would be difficult. Yet, in the immediate sense, the party's structure and political achievements, resting on local rather than the state and national councils, allowed it to survive the initial shock.[21]

The interacting issues of slavery and growing sectionalism which had destroyed the national party, however, could not indefinitely be ignored and sidetracked by Marylanders using anti-Catholic and anti-immigrant rhetoric. Nor could they be avoided by their increasing stress on unionism and Americanism. As a border and slave-holding state, the slavery issue was a very sensitive one, especially in areas where there were heavy concentrations of slaves in southern Maryland and on the Eastern Shore. It was in these areas where the Know-Nothings first lost their support, primarily to the Southern rights wing of the Democratic party.[22]

Yet despite this, the American party temporarily remained a viable political coalition in Maryland and was to achieve an even more meaningful triumph in 1857. Success in the previous year had made the gubernatorial nomination extremely attractive. Consequently, a number of candidates were eager to be the party's choice. After a bitter fight in the convention Thomas Hicks emerged as the nominee, while the other contenders were selected for the lesser offices. William Purnell was nominated for Comptroller, D. H. McPhail for Lottery Commissioner, and L. W. Seabrook for Land Commissioner. Later Hicks' chief opponent, James B. Ricaud, was nominated for Congress.

Meanwhile the Democratic party was reeling from its political setbacks, and Democratic newspapers such as the *Cecil Democrat* lamented that original strongholds of the party were

---

20. Schmeckebier, *Know Nothings*, p. 45.
21. Baker, "Dark Lantern Crusade," pp. 65-66.
22. *Ibid.*, pp. 11-12.

Cartoon depicting political campaign violence during the "Know-Nothing" period.
M.H.S.

now "hot beds of Know Nothing profligacy." A number of papers such as the *Cecil Democrat, Democratic Alleganian* and the *Planter's Advocate* called upon the "opponents of bigotry and intolerance" to unite in defeating the Americans by supporting conservative candidates.[23] Later, in April, the Democratic State Central Committee, in issuing the call for the party's convention on July 30, extended an invitation to "all voters who have acted or disposed to act with us upon existing political issues" to send delegates to the meeting.[24]

When the party did meet it was dispirited and divided by internal factionalism. Ultimately the Democrats made no formal nominations but only recommended candidates. Baltimore Democrats, also torn by internal fighting, selected candidates only for the city council. However, a number of disgruntled Americans united with Democrats to put forth candidates for the House of Delegates.

Baltimore politically expected the worst. And again the October municipal elections erupted into violence and produced the usual victory for the Know-Nothings. Despite increasing concern that disturbances would take place in the city, Governor Ligon made no effort to intervene. Swann had attempted to take precautions by adding additional men to the police force, and the governor had hoped that this would be sufficient. But election day saw the usual fights and brawls everywhere and a riot in the Irish-Democratic eighth ward, where a police sergeant was killed. Devices such as tubs of bloody water, designed to intimidate immigrants by threatening to plunge them into it, were used near the polls. Intimidation again proved to be a powerful weapon. A number of candidates withdrew before the voting ended, while some election judges feared to serve. Democratic leaders were greatly angered by the virtual disenfranchisement of their voters.[25]

Governor Ligon became quickly convinced that the municipal authorities were either unable to cope with the situation or were unwilling to incur the displeasure of their allies, the Know-Nothing clubs. The governor now decided to go to Baltimore and to use his own authority in preserving order. From Barnum's

23. Cumberland, *Democratic Alleganian*, Feb. 28 & April 4, 1857.
24. *Ibid.*, May 2, 1857.
25. Maryland, *House & Senate Documents, 1858.* Doc. A.; Tuska, *Know Nothings*.

Hotel he sent Mayor Swann a message asking for his cooperation in the forthcoming election. In the letter Ligon indicated that he had received complaints from a large number of respectable citizens over the conditions surrounding elections and that therefore a sense of constitutional duty impelled him to consult with the mayor "as to what provision should be made by you to guarantee personal security, and the free exercise of suffrage by the legal voters." Ligon charged that many people had been prevented from voting in the previous presidential election by the violence and intimidation. He now asked the mayor's cooperation in maintaining order.[26]

Swann did not agree. He maintained that Ligon's proposal infringed upon his jurisdiction, and the mayor charged that the governor did not have a constitutional right to interfere in the internal affairs of the city. In replying to Ligon, Swann expressed surprise at his apparent "summary judgment upon the inefficiency of the city government." In defending himself and his administration, the Mayor pointed out that he had had "no official connection" with the events of 1856. He also reminded the governor that it was the duty and prerogative of the city authorities to determine the best manner in securing peace and order. He did agree with the governor on the necessity of maintaining order. But he pointed out that some violence was a natural product of excited elections. Finally, after indicating that he had made proper arrangements to keep order, he declined the governor's offer on the grounds that he could "recognize 'subordination' to no other power within the sphere of my duty."[27]

Rebuffed, Ligon began to initiate his own measures. Major General George H. Steuart was ordered to hold the First Light Division of the militia in readiness, while Major General John Spear Smith was authorized to enroll six regiments of militia for possible use. The governor then in a proclamation publicly expressed his concern and apprehension over the failure of the municipal authorities to cooperate with him. In keeping with his constitutional duty to uphold the laws, he called upon the moral support of the people and warned all those who might engage in illegal activities to refrain from such acts. He also announced the

---

26. Maryland, *House & Senate Documents, 1858*, Doc. A., Appendix; see also Scharf, *History of Maryland*, III, 253-62 and Schmeckebier, *Know Nothings*, pp. 74-86 for exchange between governor and mayor.

27. *Ibid.*, Appendix, pp. 35-36.

possibility of using military force to preserve order if necessary.[28]

The governor's proclamation made the confrontation between himself and the mayor public. In the ensuing hassle, both sides sought legal counsel. After consulting an imposing array of prominent and legal authorities, Ligon sent Swann another letter in which he set forth the case and the necessity for intervention to "see that the laws are 'faithfully executed,' by every constitutional power." He again called upon the mayor to cooperate with him in "uniting in a harmonious effort to assert the supremacy of the law."[29]

The mayor too had consulted his legal advisers; but after doing so, he decided not to discuss the legalities of the question. In a curt reply to Ligon he maintained that since the governor had decided to place the city under military supervision, "The responsibility is with your excellency." In a closing barb, he wrote: "In the exercise of my functions, I shall be governed by the authority of law, and, I trust by the support of the entire community."[30]

Much to the chagrin and frustration of the governor, his efforts to enlist additional militia failed. But in the meantime a number of prominent citizens attempted to find a solution to the impasse. Finally, the entering wedge occurred on November 1; Mayor Swann made public his plans for preserving order in a proclamation which laid down the rules and procedures for conduct on election day. He also announced the appointment of a special police force to aid the regulars in their supervision of the city and to aid the election judges at the polls.

The governor was now urged to accept the sincerity of the mayor's arrangement as sufficient and "to abandon your purpose of resorting to the military on that day." The governor, in a weak political position without an effective militia, acquiesced, and in a letter to the mayor he expressed his gratification over the announced plans and indicated that he no longer contemplated the use of the militia in the city. Yet in acquiescing, Ligon chose his words with care; he refused to withdraw the proclamation. He felt that to do so would mean a surrender of his constitutional

28. *Ibid.*, pp. 36-38.
29. *Ibid.*, pp. 38-43.
30. *Ibid.*, pp. 43-44.

authority. Second, he also felt that it would not be wise to fore-close the possibility of such action in case of necessity.[31]

The mounting tension was quickly relaxed when that evening an excited crowd at Barnum's Hotel was told of the governor's decision. On the following day Ligon's decision appeared publicly and put an end to the crisis. The election itself was probably less violent than previous ones. Yet the decrease in overt violence did not mean that it was free from fraud and intimidation. In many instances, the police, despite good intentions on the part of some, proved to be ineffective, while in other cases, they continued to be unconcerned about protecting voters. The special police, without much support from the regular force, found themselves powerless, and many resigned before the day was over.

Again with the use of specially-marked ballots and with favorable locations of the polling places the Know-Nothing clubs were not only able to continue their domination of Baltimore but to increase their margin of victory as well. For the Hicks' candidacy American control over the city was crucial. Hicks carried the city by 17,850 to his opponent, John C. Groome's 8,211. In the remainder of the state the results were different. There Groome won by a majority of 1,179.

In the election American candidates still had generally done well. They carried the other state offices, elected four congressmen out of six and continued their control of the state legislature. Yet the 1857 election marked the first obvious defections from the party. Whereas in the 1855 election the Know-Nothings had sent fifty-four members to the House of Delegates, this figure now dropped to forty-three. In western Maryland the American candidate, Henry W. Hoffman, who had won handily with a 749 majority in 1855, now was defeated by Col. Jacob Kunkel by 168 votes. Later, in February, in a special election for delegate to the House of Delegates in the same district, a Democrat again defeated the Know-Nothing candidate.[32] As a result of a strong Democratic revival, Hicks carried only one county in southern Maryland, while on the Eastern Shore he lost in a majority of the

---

31. Maryland, *House & Senate Documents, 1858*, Doc. A., pp. 24-25 and Appendix, pp. 44-48.
32. Thomas J. C. Williams, *History of Washington County* (Hagerstown: John M. Runk & L. R. Titsworth, 1906), pp. 274-75.

counties. These trends, coupled with a collapsed national organization, were ominous signs for the Americans in Maryland.

When the new legislature assembled in January, Governor Ligon in his last annual message delivered one final blast at the Know-Nothings. He charged that it was his "deliberate opinion that the election [in Baltimore] was fraudulently conducted . . . and that the whole of the returns from the city are vicious, without a decent claim to official recognition anywhere. . . ."[33] The Americans were furious with the content of the message and the governor's added insult of allowing the press to make use of the message before it was sent to the legislature. In retaliation for his partisan slur, by a party vote of forty-one to twenty-eight in the House of Delegates, Ligon's message was laid on the table. Eventually it was read, but only one hundred copies were initially authorized to be printed. Later approval was given for the printing of an additional 5,000.

Ligon was severely denounced in the assembly and, after an acrimonious debate ending in disorder, the House censured the governor by a strict party vote. Ligon was condemned for libeling the people of Baltimore and for meddling in the affairs of the city "under circumstances, ill-advised, reckless, unnecessary and dangerous to the peace of the city."[34] Later, even Governor Hicks could not pass up the opportunity in his inaugural address to attack Ligon's attempted use of the militia in Baltimore as unconstitutional.[35]

In his message to the legislature Hicks reflected much of the rhetoric of the Know-Nothing movement. He called attention to the problems involving immigration and maintained that the people of Maryland were determined to find a remedy. Hicks also reaffirmed his party's adherence to the principle of the separation of church and state and his firm opposition to past attempts to use public money to support sectarian schools. Continuing his religious attack, the governor denounced all those who would "acknowledge an allegiance superior to the laws and the Constitution of the State."[36]

Yet, as in the case of the previous session of the legislature, Americans made little effort to translate rhetoric into law. There

33. Maryland, *House & Senate Documents, 1858*, Doc. A., pp. 25-26.
34. *Ibid.*, "Joint Preamble and Resolutions," pp. 49-52.
35. *Ibid.*, Doc. E., pp. 9-11.
36. *Ibid.*, pp. 4-6.

was little pressure to enact measures against convents or for stricter naturalization laws. Only one petition calling for the suppression of convents was received and that was quickly buried. Instead, the Know-Nothings were much more concerned with the problems of retaining power and holding on to public office. Political concern produced probably the session's only interesting proposal: the call for a new constitutional convention. Since this had not been an issue in the election and would not normally come up for consideration until after the 1860 census, the Know-Nothings were charged with playing politics and attempting to concentrate the power of appointment in the hands of the governor for political purposes. Democrats also viewed with suspicion the proposal to change the basis of representation in the legislature to one based on population. Such a plan would allow Baltimore to control one-third of the assembly. The specter of Know-Nothing control of the city made Democrats less than enthusiastic.

Despite the opposition, the Americans secured the measure's passage by a strict party vote. The question was then submitted to the people in a special election. The issue created little excitement except among the Know-Nothing clubs in Baltimore. Enthusiasm there produced the expected majority in its favor, but in the counties the question was overwhelmingly defeated.

By the fall of 1858 it had become obvious that the Americans were slipping in the counties and that Baltimore was increasingly becoming their last bastion of power. Continuing success in the city, therefore was essential to the party. And in 1858 the municipal election, involving not only council positions but also the mayoralty, would be the key to continued control there. Swann expressed the desire not to run again, but with the party in need of a winner, the Americans, despite his reluctance, renominated their most popular and available candidate.[37]

City Democrats were in a demoralized state and made no effort to select a candidate to oppose the mayor. Yet there were those who were unwilling to allow the election to go to Swann by default. An emerging independent movement was determined to field an opposition candidate. A few disgruntled Americans

---

37. Diary of Richard H. Townsend (Transcribed by the Works Progress Administration of Maryland at the Enoch Pratt Free Library, Enoch Pratt Free Library, Baltimore, 1937), 1858, Ninth Month, p. 788.

united with interested Democrats to nominate Colonel A. P. Shutt.

The Independents made a determined, but not a successful effort to challenge the power of the Know-Nothings. On election day, despite an attack on the newspaper office of the *Deutsche Correspondent*, outbreaks of violence were less frequent than previously. And again the Americans used election gimmicks such as marked ballots. But Shutt, fearing for the safety of his supporters and charging that the mayor countenanced a partnership of the police and the lawless in controlling the ballot box, withdrew his name at noon. Swann was overwhelmingly reelected. Shutt's only strength had come from the eighth ward, which had never been controlled by the Americans.[38] However, many respectable and prominent citizens were coming to lament that the "so frequent occurrence [of elections] was becoming a sorrow to every well disposed person."[39]

Unfortunately for Swann, the violence and rowdyism displayed in the municipal and state elections obscured the more positive aspects of his tenure in office. As mayor, Swann did much to strengthen the role and power of the office. He tightened up the administration of the city by making the various city departments accountable to him. The fire department and the police department were reorganized and were made directly responsible to the mayor. Among his other achievements were the change in the city's operation of the almshouse, the construction of a new jail, the drawing up of a map showing the sewer system, the development of the City Passenger Railway, and an interest in parks and public health.[40]

The 1857 municipal election produced two important byproducts: the reorganization of the police department and the formation of the City Reform Association. The growing national reputation of Baltimore for violence and disorder frightened many in the business and professional community. There was increasing fear that such an image would ultimately hurt the city economically. On August 26, in response to this growing concern, the *Baltimore American* called for a town meeting to dis-

---

38. Schmeckebier, *Know-Nothings*, p. 97; Tuska, *Know Nothings*, pp. 24-25; and Scharf, *History*, III, p. 264.
39. Townsend Diary, p. 792.
40. See Joanna H. Spiro, "Thomas Swann and Baltimore: The Mayor and the Municipality, 1856–1860" (M.A. thesis, Loyola College, 1964).

cuss the affairs of the city. A committee was quickly appointed to set up the machinery of such an organization and a call for a mass meeting, to be held on September 5, was soon issued.

Bad weather forced its postponement until three days later. But when the reformers did meet, they denounced the political conditions of the city and declared that the situation was both socially and economically destructive of the interests of Baltimore. Their purpose, they maintained, was to work for good government on a nonpartisan basis. A central committee was created to select nominees for the municipal election. The committee was then directed to call upon the mayor to appoint honest and impartial election judges and to ask him to commission two hundred special deputies, or those necessary in each ward, to cooperate with the regular police force in preserving order. The mayor was also asked to close all drinking houses on election day and to reply to their suggestions in writing so that his statement could be published in the newspapers.

Swann, in countering the committee's demands, indicated his willingness to appoint a special force if it could be composed of conservative men and free from party bias. Yet the mayor's reply showed a reluctance to cooperate in what he deemed an "attempt to share with him the powers and responsibilities of his office." In a second letter to the mayor, the committee complained that many of the previous election judges had already been reappointed, and they charged that a number of them had received and recorded illegal votes in the past. Swann countered by demanding legal proof to support the charges, which the committee was unable to provide. Frustrated in their efforts to gain cooperation from Swann, they next turned to the sheriff of Baltimore, but he too demurred. He maintained that he was satisfied with the arrangements made by the mayor.[41]

On the day of the election, much to the despair of the reform group, the disorders continued. The reform candidate in the ninth ward withdrew, while in the case of the twentieth ward the Plug Uglies destroyed the ballot box.[42] Yet the reformers did enjoy some success in electing six members to the city council, as opposed to thirteen for the Americans.

The results merely heightened the excitement and interest in

---

41. Scharf, *History*, III, pp. 271-74.
42. Tuska, *Know-Nothings*, pp. 27-28.

the following statewide election in November. The returns of October also stirred Know-Nothings to greater activity. Intimidation became flagrant. As a symbol of power in Baltimore, the Know-Nothings displayed the awl in transparencies and on floats as a menace to the opposition, while American leaders, such as Henry Winter Davis and Anthony Kennedy, engaged in fiery political rhetoric. Older methods, such as the use of coops, were also employed to deliver the necessary majority for Know-Nothing candidates. Benjamin Tuska maintains that the election was the "most lawless and riotous that Baltimore had ever experienced."[43] However, the majority that the Know-Nothings produced in the city was not sufficient to offset their collapse of power in the counties. The election produced a new legislature in which the majority now shifted to the Democrats. In the Senate the Democrats controlled twelve seats to the Americans' ten, while in the house the margin was even greater, forty-five Democrats to twenty-nine for the Americans. The results were disastrous for the Know-Nothings. Now, even their power in Baltimore was in jeopardy.

The state results were very encouraging to Baltimore reformers. And on November 17 another meeting was held to appoint a new central committee to give the movement a greater thrust. Another committee was created to present evidence to the legislature of the frauds in the municipal election, while still another one was selected to draw up measures which might curb the abuses.[44]

Consequently Baltimore affairs were a major concern when the legislature, now under Democratic control, met in January 1860. Numerous memorials, praying relief from the corruption and violence in the city, poured into the assembly. Democrats, feeling their renewed vitality and utilizing the heightened negrophobia following John Brown's raid on Harper's Ferry in 1859 to strengthen their unity, were quick to strike a mortal blow at the last bastion of Know-Nothing power. An indication of the changed political situation came quickly with the passage of a resolution declaring the office of the clerk of the circuit court in Baltimore vacant. The house charged that his election was "in contempt of law and in violation of the freedom of election" by

---

43. *Ibid.*, p. 28.
44. Scharf, *History of Maryland*, III, pp. 275-76.

virtue of the "tumult, disorder, riot, intimidation and injustice in the election." But far more important, the subject of a proper police force for Baltimore was immediately put forth for consideration. The resultant legislation took control over the police from the mayor and placed it in the hands of a board elected by the assembly. The mayor was reduced to ex-officio membership on the board. The measure further undermined Know-Nothing power by dividing the city into election precincts.[45]

An additional blow was struck at Baltimore lawlessness with the impeachment of Judge Henry Stump of the criminal court. Stump was regarded as a major impediment to law and order in the city because of his conduct on the bench. The legislature, responding to citizens' petitions, asked the governor for his removal. As a final insult to the Americans, the assembly in its closing days declared that the election of the delegates from Baltimore was void.[46]

The American party, with its power base already gone in the remainder of the state, collapsed with the actions of the assembly. In a last desperate effort, the Swann administration challenged the constitutionality of the police bill in court, but with the failure of this move the essential elements for Know-Nothing control over the city were gone. In looking to the 1860 election, the question for the Americans was now whether they should make a mayoralty nomination or to fuse with the newly emerging Constitutional Union party. After first attempting to nominate Charles M. Keyser, they turned to Samuel Hindes in opposing the Reform Committee's candidate, George William Brown, for their last political contest.

In the election the new reforms made the difference. The day remained peaceful, and the Know-Nothings, without the ability to utilize the muscle of their clubs, suffered a stunning and deadly defeat. Brown, along with the entire Reform ticket, swept to victory by a landslide of 17,771 to 9,575. Not only was the mayor's office secured by the Reformers but both branches of the city council as well.

But far more important to Marylanders was the rising concern over the presidential election. National politics were very much in disarray. The Democratic party had split in two. The schism

45. *Laws of Maryland* (Annapolis, 1860), Ch. VII and Resolution no. 7.
46. *Ibid.*, Resolution no. 7.

that had erupted in Charleston in April was reinforced when the party reassembled in Baltimore in June. The regular Democrats, after a bolt by Southerners, nominated Stephen A. Douglas, while the Southern wing chose John C. Breckinridge as their candidate. In the meantime the Republican party meeting in Chicago nominated their most available candidate, Abraham Lincoln. Meanwhile, conservatives in the upper South viewed the evolving political events of 1860 with increasing alarm. Fearing the consequences of sectionalism, they had met earlier in Baltimore on May 9 and formed the Constitutional Union party. Their platform and political solution was simple: support for the Constitution and the Union.

Of the four candidates, Marylanders were concerned primarily with only two, Breckinridge and Bell. Both campaigns stressed conservatism and unionism. Bell supporters, drawing heavily upon the old Whig element, called upon "men of property —conservative men—you who earn bread by the sweat of your brow—merchants, manufacturers, mechanics and men of every pursuit of life—look to the impending crisis, realize its manyfold enormities and apply the remedy."[47] They underlined the party's unionism and conservatism and maintained that Bell would stand "like a wall of fire, backed by the conservative masses of enlightened freemen" against political sectionalism.[48] Bell newspapers stressed several themes. They pointed to the secessionist background of the Breckinridge movement and then underscored the theme that the issue in the election was union or disunion. They reasoned that if Lincoln won, the Breckinridge people would have to bear that responsibility, since the only national candidates were those of the Constitutional Union party.

In Maryland even the Breckinridge campaign emphasized unionism. A strong effort was made to disassociate him from Southern ultraism. Breckinridge Democrats maintained that a vote for him would unite Maryland with the South and rebuke fanaticism, while they declared that one for Bell would separate the state from the South. Democrats charged that the Bell party was tainted with "Black Republicanism." A speech by Henry Winter Davis, a leading American, had raised suspicions that

---

47. *Baltimore Clipper*, Sept. 6, 1860.
48. *The American Union*, Sept. 25, 1860.

the charge might indeed be true, and in Baltimore the Breckin-ridge ticket profited from the connection between the Constitu-tional Union party and Know-Nothing elements. Breckinridge also enjoyed the support of the regular Democratic organization in Maryland, while Douglas had the support of only a small minority. The Republicans were at an even greater disadvan-tage. Republicanism was equated with abolitionism and fanati-cism, and for many it was the embodiment of all the "isms" of the era.

By a small margin the Breckinridge party carried the state over Bell. Breckinridge won 42,482; Bell, 41,760; yet it was a hollow victory and, unfortunately, an ominous achievement. Lincoln and the Republicans swept to victory nationally by carrying eighteen free states with 180 electoral votes to Breckinridge's seventy-two. Much to the despair of Maryland-ers, the results had elected a President that neither the people of Maryland nor the South wanted and had rejected.[49]

2

THE CRISIS OF LOYALTY

The political crisis of 1860 had severe economic and political ramifications for Marylanders. Maryland, as a border state, had strong commercial ties with both the North and the South. Tra-ditionally, much of Baltimore's trade was tied to the South, but by 1860 the city's coastwise trade had shifted to where 60 per cent of this was with Northern ports.[50] Baltimore's rail connec-tions had also forged important bonds with the North and Northwest in the 1850's. And in the crisis, Marylanders were deeply concerned over the threat to their commerce with both sections. Initially, uncertainty and fear had a sharp depressing effect in the state. Banks suspended making specie payments and stocks dropped in value. Business stagnated, and unem-ployment rose rapidly. Economically, Maryland was not to re-cover until 1862. But in the crisis the strong commercial links

49. See Ollinger Crenshaw, *The Slave States in the Presidential Election of 1860* (Baltimore: J.H. Press, 1945), pp. 112-21 and Evitts, "Matter of Al-legiances," Ch. VI.
50. William Bruce Catton, "The Baltimore Business Community and the Secession Crisis, 1860–1861" (M.A. thesis, University of Maryland, 1952), pp. 22-26.

with the North, despite Southern appeals that Baltimore would become the New York of the Confederacy, were important in sustaining and creating support for the Union.

Politically as well as economically, Marylanders traditionally looked south. Sharing a common heritage, forged by the "peculiar institution" of slavery, Marylanders had strong sympathies for the South. Yet they were strongly attached to the Union as well. Preferring compromise, Marylanders remained indecisive in the sectional crisis, and it was not until the fall of 1861 that Maryland's adherence to the Union was firmly settled beyond doubt. By then the initial Southern stirrings to join the Confederacy were offset by a strong Unionist movement. Unionists were further strengthened by the increasing presence of the federal government in the state. Maryland's geographical position, in surrounding the capital and in controlling the rail line to Washington, made the state's continued loyalty essential. Federal presence and intervention into state affairs ended all real ability of Marylanders to make any other decision.

Response initially to the crisis varied from strong support of the Union to secessionist in expression.[51] However, Marylanders were basically more cautious, moderate, and Unionist in sentiment than they were secessionist. Aware of their geographical position and their social and economic ties with both sections, compromise was preferred as a solution to the crisis. Kentucky Senator J. J. Crittenden's proposals of providing guarantees for the South, for many, were the appropriate position for Maryland to adopt in defense of Southern grievances against Northern anti-slavery agitation, personal liberty laws, and the non-execution of the fugitive slave law. Marylanders, at the most, saw secession only as a last resort.

In the western counties strong expression of Unionist sentiment was exhibited in newspapers and mass meetings. The Cumberland *Democratic Alleganian,* while deploring Lincoln's election, denied that this was sufficient cause for the dissolution of the Union.[52] Another Cumberland paper, the *Civilian Telegraph,* denounced both secession and coercion; yet it maintained that the government had the right to collect

---

51. Carl M. Frasure, "Union Sentiment in Maryland, 1859–1861," *M.H.M.,* XXIV (Sept., 1929), pp. 210-24.
52. *Democratic Alleganian,* Nov. 10, 1860.

revenues at ports of entry and to repel any attack against its property and forts. Other journals, such as the Hagerstown *Herald and Torch*, believed that since Lincoln had been constitutionally elected, he should be allowed to take office. If he then violated the Constitution, the newspaper felt that sufficient remedies were available to the South.[53] Even in Baltimore the Breckinridge paper, the *Baltimore Exchange*, while expressing its sympathy for the South, denied that there was sufficient cause for secession.[54] The Baltimore *Sun* felt that there was really no disunion or secessionist spirit in Maryland. The *Sun*'s editor wrote:

> We are for the Union—for the restoration of the Union. . . . It should be our duty to aid the South, not by secession, but by such firm measures as will be protective in themselves, conciliatory in the end, and reconstructive of the federal Union.[55]

In southern Maryland and the Eastern Shore, the plantation regions, the slavery issue was a very sensitive one; and the accent there was placed more on Northern wrongs and Southern grievances. Unionist expression in these areas was more qualified and predisposed towards a Southern position. A January meeting in Easton expressed the feelings of many at that time:

> That Maryland is essentially a Southern State in association, in feeling, in interest and in her domestic relations; that her destiny is interwoven with that of her sister Southern States; and that her action will be firm and unyielding in the maintenance and vindication of her Constitutional rights.[56]

Stronger pro-Southern sentiment was exhibited in a meeting at Port Tobacco in the same month. There the delegates did express their attachment to the Constitution and Union and recommended the adoption of the Crittenden proposals "for the purpose of preserving or reconstructing the Union." But they also went on to state that Maryland's interests were "indissolubly connected with Virginia, Kentucky and the border States of the South" and that if a reunification of the Union was impossi-

---

53. Hagerstown, *Herald and Torch,* Nov. 14, 1860.
54. *Baltimore Exchange,* Nov. 9, 1860.
55. Baltimore, *Sun,* Jan. 10, 1861.
56. *Easton Gazette,* Jan. 5, 1861.

ble, "then Maryland will share the fate and future of her Southern sisters, let that fate and fortune be what it may."[57]

A more pronounced rise in pro-Southern sympathy came with the actual secession of the lower South in December and January. Yet those who pushed for the adoption of an extreme Southern position found strong resistance. In a meeting of prominent Baltimore Democrats at the Custom House, William H. Norris, an extreme Southern man, was told by those present that they were all for the Union and only for the South if the Union could not be saved.[58] But pressure mounted rapidly for Governor Hicks to call the legislature into special session so that it might deal with the exigencies of the crisis. There was also pressure for the governor to adopt a more pro-Southern position. Some hoped that the legislature would provide for the calling of a state convention to give expression to Maryland's feelings. But Hicks, fearing and distrusting the Democratic-controlled assembly, refused to do so, and as early as November he had set forth his reasons against calling a special session.[59]

Hicks also refused to receive officially the southern commissioners. In a public reply to Alexander H. Handy, special commissioner from Mississippi, he expressed Maryland's identification with the South in feeling and institutions, but he told Handy that Maryland was conservative and "devoted to the Union." He further indicated that "not until every honorable and constitutional and legal effort is exhausted" would Maryland "consent to any effort for its dissolution."[60] Later in January Hicks took an even stronger stand in a letter to J. L. M. Curry, commissioner from Alabama. He wrote:

> The people of Maryland, in my opinion, regard any such measures of co-operation among any State of this Union, especially with any view to secession therefore, as a violation of the very terms of that Constitution under which this Union was formed and is preserved.[61]

Pressure on Hicks continued to mount as the crisis deepened.

57. *Charles County Convention*, Jan. 25, 1861, Broadside collections, M.H.S.
58. John Glenn Diary, Jan. 1861, Glenn Papers, M.H.S.
59. *Annapolis Gazette*, Nov. 29, 1860.
60. Charles Branch Clark, "Politics in Maryland during the Civil War" (Ph.D. dissertation, North Carolina, 1941), p. 88; *Annapolis Gazette*, Dec. 27, 1860.
61. *Annapolis Gazette*, Jan. 24, 1861.

A large meeting in Baltimore on December 22 at the Universalist Church, where arguments for and against secession were presented, appointed a committee to urge the governor to call the legislature into session.[62] Later a group of state senators met and eleven of them sent a signed petition to Hicks urging such a call. Five others merely sent accompanying letters of approval.[63] Governor Hicks remained adamant, and, on January 3, after replying to the legislators, he issued a "Proclamation to the People of Maryland." It constituted a formal statement of his views. Again he stated the case against convening the assembly. And again he denounced Northern evasions of the fugitive slave law and expressed a desire to always live in a slave state. However, Hicks maintained that he did not feel that secession was wise and that it was an act only of the last resort. In closing his address he ended "with a touching appeal" that he hoped to spend the remainder of his days in the Union.[64]

Several days later a group of prominent Baltimore citizens met to discuss the state of affairs. After considerable debate and a short recess, they adopted a series of resolutions affirming Maryland's loyalty to the Union, favoring the Crittenden compromise, and appointing a committee to urge the governor to allow the people, by a referendum, to decide on the question of calling a convention.[65]

Another Baltimore meeting in February was more decidedly Southern in its orientation. The members expressed their continued adherence to the Union, but along strict constructionist lines, and a desire for a policy of conciliation rather than one of coercion. The majority in the meeting preferred to accept secession rather than a Union maintained by force, but they expressed a hope of an eventual reconciliation. In the meantime they wanted to have the matter discussed in a state convention.[66]

Later in the month the Southern Rights Convention met in Baltimore to apply pressure to Hicks as well. Denying that they were a secessionist group, although it was obvious where their

---

62. *Sun*, Dec. 24, 1860.

63. George L. Radcliffe, *Governor Thomas H. Hicks of Maryland and the Civil War* (Baltimore: J.H. Press, 1901), pp. 29-30.

64. *Annapolis Gazette*, Jan. 10, 1861; Radcliffe, *Governor Hicks*, pp. 30-31.

65. Radcliffe, *Governor Hicks*, pp. 31-32.

66. Clark, "Politics in Maryland," pp. 103-04.

sympathies lay, delegates urged the governor to convene a convention and also warned him that if Virginia seceded and if he did not call one, the Southern Rights Convention would reassemble to recommend to the people of Maryland "the election of delegates to such a Sovereign Convention." They blamed secession on Northern aggression "in violation of the Constitution of the United States" and that "the moral and the geographical position of the State" demanded that they cooperate with Virginia in maintaining the Union. If this failed, Maryland's destiny was "to associate with her in Confederation with our sister States of the South." Finally, the delegates resolved to resist any effort to make Maryland "a highway for federal troops, sent to make war upon our sister States of the South," and that any attempt on the part of the federal government to coerce the South would result in "civil war and the destruction of the government itself."[67]

Southern Righters then adjourned with the understanding that if the governor had not called a convention by March 14, they would reassemble. And with no call forthcoming from Hicks, they again reassembled in Baltimore. But after much discussion as to their course of action, they finally decided merely to send a delegation to a proposed border-state convention.

In the crisis Governor Hicks wavered and vacillated considerably in his public and private addresses and correspondence, but despite this, Hicks' position remained basically within a conservative-Unionist framework. He refused to take any action which might have precipitated a secessionist movement, and his leadership, such as it was, helped to preserve Maryland for the Union. His policy of "masterly inactivity" had wide support. Bishop William R. Whittingham of the Episcopal Church wrote to Hicks endorsing his policy and allowed the governor to make the letter public.[68] Numerous county conventions and newspaper editorials also approved of the governor's position. A Unionist meeting in the Maryland Institute on January 10, featuring an imposing array of prominent Unionists, also endorsed the governor's stand.[69]

---

67. *Address and Resolutions Adopted at the Meeting of the Southern Rights Convention of Maryland* (Baltimore, 1861).

68. *Baltimore American and Commercial Advertiser*, Jan. 18, 1861. Hereafter cited as *American*.

69. Clark, "Politics in Maryland," pp. 98-101.

In the meantime Governor Hicks had been active in helping to promote the Virginia Peace Convention which convened in Washington on February 4, 1861. Maryland delegates in the conference denounced both the doctrine of secession and the idea of coercion. The convention, in attempting to solve the crisis, proposed a constitutional amendment which was substantially the same as the Crittenden proposal. But the conference, lacking the full participation of all the states, was doomed to failure. And when the suggested amendment was submitted to Congress, it was defeated in the Senate by a vote of twenty-eight to seven. With its failure the last serious attempt at compromise came to an end.

Finally, in April a cluster of inter-reacting events precipitated an immediate and serious crisis for Maryland and Baltimore in particular. The firing upon Fort Sumter on April 12 sent shock waves throughout the upper south and the nation. Lincoln now called for 75,000 volunteers to suppress the insurrection. Virginia, reacting to that call for troops, joined her sister states in secession. In Maryland, Lincoln's call for troops created a wave of excitement. Governor Hicks, in an effort to allay the mounting tension, left Annapolis for Baltimore. From there he then proceeded to Washington to consult with Secretary of War Simon Cameron. Hicks told Cameron that Maryland strongly opposed coercion and was in turn assured by the secretary that state military units would be used only to protect Washington and public property within Maryland.[70]

Later Cameron, on April 18, warned Hicks that there were "unlawful combinations of misguided citizens" in the state who were determined to prevent the transit of soldiers through Maryland. The governor, who was now in Baltimore, responded to the warning by issuing a proclamation counseling Marylanders to practice restraint and to refrain from heated debates which might provoke violence. He further reiterated that Maryland military units, except in the defense of Washington, would not be sent out of the state. Hicks also asked Mayor George Brown to issue a similar statement to help allay fears. Brown concurred and went on to state his personal determination to preserve peace and order.[71]

---

70. Maryland, *House & Senate Documents, Extra Session, 1861*, Doc. A., pp. 9-10.

71. *Ibid.*, pp. 10-11; George William Brown, *Baltimore and the Nineteenth of*

The Massachusetts Sixth Regiment of Volunteers fires into the mob of citizens as it passes through Baltimore on April 19, 1861. *M.H.S.*

Northern troops passed through Baltimore on the 18th, but resistance to their continued passage had also considerably heightened. The *Baltimore Exchange* expressed its opposition to their transit, while in a meeting of southern men on the morning of the 18th one speaker, Wilson C. N. Carr, had asked "whether the 75,000 minions of Lincoln should pass over the soil of Maryland to subjugate our sisters of the South." The response was a "deafening shouts of No, Never!" However, the only action that was taken by the meeting was the appointment of a committee to consult with the presidents of the various railroads leading into Baltimore to urge them not to transport the soldiers.[72]

Hope by state and municipal authorities to maintain calm and order was quickly shattered on April 19. Suddenly five months of political and economic frustration erupted into a storm of protest against the federal government. With the unexpected arrival of Massachusetts troops in Baltimore, rioting and fighting broke out between citizens and the Sixth Massachusetts Regiment, while city officials attempted in vain to protect the soldiers.[73] By evening authority in the city had collapsed, and Baltimore was engulfed by hysteria. The governor, mayor, and the president of the police commissioners attempted to exert control over the deteriorating situation by immediately ordering the assembling of the city's militia and the convening of a large public meeting at 4:00 P.M. in Monument Square.

A large crowd assembled to hear an assorted group of speakers. Several severely denounced the policy of coercion and demanded that Northern troops which would be used against the South should not be allowed to pass through the state. Mayor Brown reflected much of this sentiment, but at the same time he denied that a state had the right to secede. Governor Hicks concurred with Brown's statement, but he also expressed a de-

*April* (Baltimore: J.H. Press, 1887), p. 40; Frank Moore, ed., *The Rebellion Record: A Diary of American Events* (New York: G. P. Putnam's), I, pp. 76-77; John Glenn Diary, April 13 and 17, 1861; U.S. War Dept., *The War of the Rebellion: A Compilation of the Official Records of the Union and Confederate Armies* (Washington: Government Printing Office, 1880–1901), series 1, II, p. 577. Hereafter cited as *OR*.

72. *Republican-Extra*, April 18, 1861; John Glenn Diary, April 18, 1861.

73. For contemporary reports see *OR*, series 1, II, pp. 7-20; Brown, *Baltimore and Nineteenth*; J. Morrison Harris, *A Reminiscence of the Troublous Times of April, 1861* (Baltimore: M.H.S., 1891).

sire to see the Union preserved. Hicks' comments brought about an angry response from the gathering, and a badly shaken Hicks was forced into compromising his statement by asserting that "I bow in submission to the people. I am a Marylander: I love my state and I love the Union, but I will suffer my right arm to be torn from my body before I will raise it to strike a sister state."[74]

In the meantime Governor Hicks and Mayor Brown sent off reports of the rioting to Washington and requested the federal government not to send any additional troops to the city. They claimed that city and state military units, which had been called into service, would be sufficient to restore order. On receiving the reports, federal authorities misinterpreted the message to signify that no additional troops were needed merely to restore order, but a clarification of its meaning was soon forthcoming in a telegram to John W. Garrett, president of the Baltimore and Ohio Railroad, from Governor Hicks, Mayor Brown, and Charles Howard, president of the police board. The dispatch advised Garrett to return all Northern troops to the state line. Garrett, in acknowledging the telegram, indicated his approval of the move and stated that he would act accordingly. Subsequently, the Baltimore and Ohio informed the presidents of the Northern Central and the Philadelphia, Wilmington, and Baltimore railroads that the Baltimore and Ohio would not forward any additional troops to Washington. Both railroads agreed that temporarily they would comply and not pass troops over their lines to Baltimore.[75]

In conjunction with these moves, Mayor Brown sent H. Lennox Bond, George W. Dobbin, and John C. Brune to Washington by express train to inform Lincoln that further passage of federal soldiers through the city was not feasible. In support of this contention, the three expressed concern over the maintenance of order if additional troops were sent through Baltimore. They indicated that the local authorities would not be responsible for the consequences if it were done.

No immediate reply was forthcoming from Washington. In the meantime, rumors of approaching troops continued to circu-

---

74. Radcliffe, *Governor Hicks*, pp. 54-55; Charles B. Clark, "Baltimore and the Attack on the Sixth Massachusetts Regiment, April 19, 1861," *M.H.M.*, LVI (March, 1961), 53-54; Brown, *Baltimore and Nineteenth*, pp. 56-57; John Glenn Diary, April 19, 1861.

75. *Sun*, April 20, 1861.

late in the city. Having received no reply by the evening, Mayor Brown, Marshal George Kane, and the police board met with Governor Hicks. The group was informed by S. M. Felton, president of the Philadelphia, Wilmington, and Baltimore Railroad, that additional troops were indeed heading for Baltimore. In response to this information it was generally agreed that for the maintenance of safety and peace no further troops should be permitted to pass through the city. A proposal was also put forth to implement the decision by burning the bridges leading into the city. This was generally agreed upon. Later Hicks denied giving any consent, but historians feel that "there can be little doubt but that Hicks gave that night some form of authorization for the burning of the bridges."[76] A number of groups, one being personally led by Marshal Kane, put the plan into effect and a number of bridges were destroyed.[77]

In the confusion and near chaos, city authorities began to move in three directions; the protection of Baltimore from outside attack, the restoration of order within the city itself, and continued communication with the federal government at Washington. For defensive purposes the mayor called upon all citizens to deposit their guns with the board of police for the city's use, while the city council appropriated $500,000 for defense. The board also put into effect a series of regulations which restricted the exportation of provisions, breadstuffs, and coal in preparation for a possible siege.[78]

The Bond-Dobbin-Brune delegation, which was already in Washington, conferred with Lincoln. In addition, at the request of Mayor Brown, Representative J. Morrison Harris and Senator Anthony Kennedy also met with Lincoln. Later Lincoln wired that he wished to consult with both Hicks and Brown in Washington. The governor was unable to go, but the mayor and three others did confer with the President, cabinet, and General Winfield Scott. A general understanding was reached in which the administration promised that no more troops bound for Washington would be sent through Baltimore if they could be taken

---

76. Radcliffe, *Governor Hicks*, p. 57; John Glenn Diary, April 19, 1861; Brown, *Baltimore and Nineteenth*, pp. 58-59.

77. Brown, *Baltimore and Nineteenth*, pp. 57-59.

78. "Baltimore and the Crisis of 1861" (Isaac Trimble Papers), *M.H.M.*, XLI (Dec., 1946), 259-63.

successfully around the city. In return municipal authorities promised to use "all lawful means to prevent their citizens from leaving Baltimore to attack the troops in passing at a distance."[79]

The most serious problem facing the local authorities was in bringing under control the boisterousness and lawlessness in the city. The arrival of militia from the surrounding counties and from communities as far away as Frederick merely added to the turmoil, confusion, and difficulty in maintaining order. The police board, in an attempt to channel the energies of the mob and the militia into a controlled and manageable form, announced that it would accept volunteers to aid in the defense of the city under the command of Colonel Isaac R. Trimble. The board then quickly ordered those men under Trimble's command to refrain from using martial music, in the streets. This was to prevent crowds from collecting and thereby curb the circulation of rumors. All unnecessary parading was also prohibited. Amusement places and saloons were ordered closed and the display of all flags, except those on federal buildings, was prohibited.[80]

By April 27 the board of police felt that the general excitement had sufficiently subsided to relax the restrictions and regulations in Baltimore. Most of the military units under Colonel Trimble were dismissed and by the last of April the city had returned to normal. There were also signs of the revival of Unionist sentiment, which had been suppressed by the rioting and its aftermath. A number of Union meetings were soon being held in Baltimore, and Union supporters began to circulate a petition expressing their support for the right of federal troops to pass through the city unobstructed.[81] In the middle of May a large Union meeting quickly passed a series of resolutions denouncing the right of a state to secede, affirming Maryland's loyalty to the Union, and expressing the federal government's right to transport troops through the state.[82]

---

79. Brown, *Baltimore and Nineteenth*, pp. 71-73; Harris, *Troublous Times; OR*, series 1, II, pp. 581-82 and series 2, I, pp. 564-65; Roy P. Basler, ed., *The Collected Works of Abraham Lincoln* (New Brunswick, N.J.: Rutgers University Press, 1953), IV, 340-41.
80. *M.H.M.*, XLI, 260-263; *Republican-Extra*, April 20, 1861; Alexander Randall Diary, April 21, 1861, MS. 652, M.H.S.
81. *New York Times*, May 2, 1861.
82. *Sun*, May 15, 1861.

Yet, during the tumultuous days of April, movements were in motion which were rapidly to bring Baltimore and the remainder of the state under close federal supervision. Another detachment of Massachusetts soldiers under General Benjamin F. Butler had been forced to stop at Perryville by the rioting. In his effort to get to Washington, Butler took his troops to Annapolis by steamer. His arrival in the state capital caused great consternation. Both Governor Hicks and Mayor John R. Magruder opposed his landing. But Butler insisted and quickly set up his base at the Naval Academy. When the general found that the tracks of the Annapolis and Elk Ridge Railroad were being torn up, he seized the railroad over the protests of Governor Hicks. Butler then secured the route to Annapolis Junction where the railroad joined the Washington branch of the Baltimore and Ohio Railroad which led to Washington.[83]

The federal government quickly extended its control over both the Annapolis and Elk Ridge and the Baltimore and Ohio railroads and temporarily seized control of the rolling stock of those roads between Annapolis and Washington.[84] General Winfield Scott promptly ordered the stationing of troops along the rail line to protect it against sabotage.[85] But a more significant and important act came from Lincoln. He ordered the commanding General of the Army to suspend the writ of habeas corpus at any point or in any vicinity which offered resistance to the federal government on the line of communication between Philadelphia and Washington.[86] With increasing control over the railroads in the state, military authorities began to supervise rail traffic going west and south as well. Military officers began to check and search passengers and baggage for contraband items that might be headed for Virginia.[87]

83. Maryland, *House & Senate Documents, Extra Session, 1861*, Doc. A., pp. 17-22; *OR*, series 1, II, pp. 586-87; 589-90.

84. *OR*, series 1, II, pp. 603-04; *Sun*, April 25, 1861; Thomas Weber, *The Northern Railroads in the Civil War: 1861–1865* (New York: King's Crown Press, 1952), pp. 35-36.

85. James Ames Marshall, ed., *Private and Official Correspondence of Gen. Benjamin F. Butler* (Norwood, Mass.: Privately issued, 1917), I, 42.

86. *OR*, series 2, I, p. 567, and series 1, LI, pt. 1, p. 337; Basler, *Works of Lincoln*, IV, 347.

87. *OR*, series 1, II, pp. 629-30, 633; General George Cadwalader to Col. Edward Jones, May 22 and 29, 1861, Col. Edward Jones Papers, MS. 1331, M.H.S.

Meanwhile Butler, without notice to the administration or warning to city officials, in the midst of a thunderstorm, occupied Baltimore on the evening of May 14. When the inhabitants of the city awoke the next morning, Butler was militarily well situated on Federal Hill. To the surprised Baltimoreans, he announced his presence and intention of enforcing respect and obedience to federal law and, if the civil authorities wished, to state law as well. At the same time the general was careful to point out that he had no desire to interfere with the normal functions and activities of the municipal authorities and of loyal citizens. However, Butler did order that all weapons which were designed to be used against the government were to be seized and that all assemblages of armed men, except the police, were prohibited. All displays of Southern flags or banners were equally forbidden within the city.[88] General Scott, angered over Butler's actions which he thought jeopardized the government in Baltimore, wired Butler that "It is a godsend that it is without conflict or arms" and on the following day he ordered Butler to stop issuing proclamations. Nevertheless, Butler was quickly promoted by Lincoln to major-general on May 15.[89]

The increasing presence of troops in Maryland allowed the federal government to supervise state affairs and suppress activities and sentiments which were deemed subversive to federal authority. Butler had been authorized to arrest individuals who committed hostile acts against the government. His successor, General George Cadwalader, was also given similar authority and, under certain circumstances, was authorized to detain prisoners in spite of a presentation of a writ of habeas corpus.[90] And within a month the constitutional issue of suspending and refusing to honor the writ was quickly raised with the arrest of John Merryman.

John Merryman, a secessionist who lived near Cockeysville, was arrested for acts of treason stemming out of the burning of the bridges and for holding a commission as a lieutenant in a company of men with hostile intentions toward the government. In a previous Baltimore case involving the writ, military au-

88. Marshall, *Correspondence of Butler*, I, 83-85; *OR*, series 1, II, pp. 29-32; *Sun*, May 15, 1861.
89. *OR*, series 1, II, p. 28; Benjamin F. Butler, *Butler's Book* (Boston: A. M. Thayer & Co. 1892), p. 235.
90. *OR*, series 2, I, pp. 571-572 and series 1, II, p. 639.

thorities had already refused to honor it. Therefore in this instance application was made directly to the Supreme Court of the United States. Taking note of the seriousness of the issue, Chief Justice Roger B. Taney went to Baltimore to hear the petition.[91] Subsequently, General Cadwalader was served with a writ for him to appear in the Baltimore federal circuit court on May 27 with John Merryman and there to make known the reasons for the latter's arrest. Cadwalader refused. The general informed the chief justice that Merryman was charged with acts of treason and that his arrest had been made by virtue of the authority of the President of the United States to suspend the writ of habeas corpus in the interest of public safety. In his reply Cadwalader requested the postponement of any further action until he could receive additional instructions from higher authorities. In the forthcoming instructions, the general's power to arrest such persons was confirmed, and he was directed to continue holding "in secure confinement all persons implicated in treasonable practices." Cadwalader was further instructed to reply that he would comply with the writ at the conclusion of "the present unhappy difficulties."[92]

Taney, in reviewing the case, questioned the constitutionality of the military's position. The chief justice saw the case hinging upon the issue of arrests being made on vague and indefinite charges and then having persons incarcerated without recourse to the writ in order to investigate the legality of the charge. Taney declared that the President "cannot suspend the privilege of the writ of habeas corpus, nor authorize a military officer to do it."[93] He argued that the executive branch did not possess this authority and that only Congress had that right. Taney further maintained that persons, who were not subject to the articles of war and who were arrested by the military, had to be delivered over to civil authorities for judicial proceedings. But, the chief justice in his written decision declared that the court had "exercised all the power which the Constitution and law confer on me, but that power has been resisted by a force too strong for me to overcome." Taney then filed his opinion with the federal circuit court

91. Matthew Page Andrews, *Tercentenary History of Maryland* (Chicago: S. J. Clarke Publishing Co. 1925), I, 841.

92. *OR*, series 2, I, pp. 574-77.

93. Samuel Tyler, *Memoirs of Roger Brooke Taney, L.L.D.* (Baltimore: J. Murphy & Co., 1872), Appendix, p. 645.

in Baltimore and sent a copy under seal to Lincoln indicating that it was now up to the President to fulfill his constitutional obligations and to decide "what measures he will take to cause the civil process of the United States to be respected and enforced."[94] Later Lincoln, in his message to the special session of Congress on July 4, defended his authority to suspend the writ.[95] But the issue of the military holding persons without civil trial or procedure was not to be settled until after the war.

Military authorities, especially after General Nathaniel P. Banks assumed command on June 11, continued to tighten their hold on Maryland and Baltimore in particular. The city's police commissioners had long been suspected of being Southern sympathizers, and on June 24 General Scott, seeking to strike a damaging blow at secessionist sentiment in Baltimore, decided to have them arrested.[96] He ordered General Banks to carry out such a command on the 27th. But Banks arrested only Marshal George P. Kane. At the same time, in order to allay public fears of increasing military intervention, Banks assured the public that he did not wish to interfere in the legitimate functions of civil government. But he emphasized that the federal government could not permit any unlawful combination of persons that had designs of resisting the laws to enjoy the very protection and privileges of the government. In Kane's place Banks appointed Colonel John R. Kenly of the Maryland Volunteers to serve as provost marshal and authorized him to organize a police force of four hundred men.[97]

Banks, in informing Mayor Brown of Kenly's appointment, also told him that he was suspending the functions of the police board as well. The board, however, refused to accept the legality of the general's action. Yet they indicated that they would do nothing to excite the public or to obstruct the order, though they

---

94. OR, series 2, I, pp. 577-585; see also Tyler, Memoirs of Taney, Appendix, pp. 640-59.

95. Basler, Works of Lincoln, IV, 430-31. See also J. G. Randall, Constitutional Problems Under Lincoln (Baltimore: J.H. Press, 1945) and Carl Brent Swisher, Roger B. Taney (New York: Macmillan Company, 1936), Ch. XXVI. See in particular, for a most recent treatment, Jean Baker, The Politics of Continuity: Maryland Political Parties from 1858 to 1870 (Baltimore: J.H. Press, 1973), pp. 58-61.

96. OR, series 1, II, pp. 138-39.

97. Ibid., series 1, II, pp. 138-45 and series 2, I, pp. 623-25; Sun-Extra, June 27, 1861, Broadside Collection, M.H.S.

did declare that his act had suspended the operation of police law in Baltimore and placed the police on off duty status.[98]

The ensuing confrontation between civil and military authorities created a tense situation in Baltimore. The absence of police on the streets and the growth of boisterousness quickly moved the army to organize a new force. Banks also placed the city in military readiness in case of any outbursts of violence.[99] Later, on July 1, Banks, in the interest of public safety but not for serious reasons of treason, finally announced the arrest of the remaining commissioners on the grounds that the board had continued to meet in secret session after its suspension. He further charged that in suspending police law they had made an "unwarrantable construction" of his proclamation and that they also held under their control a large group of men whose existence and intentions were deemed inconsistent with the authority of the government. Banks took the precaution of stationing troops throughout Baltimore to prevent any outbreaks of rioting over the arrests.[100]

Federal officials were not totally insensitive to the mounting opposition from the increasing number of arrests. Secretary of War Simon Cameron, in taking note of the growing volume of complaints, ordered officers in Maryland to use greater care in making arrests and then only for good cause. He suggested that the officers themselves should be Marylanders in order to make them more acceptable to the public.[101] In attempting to improve public relations, Banks consulted with Unionists in the city and then removed Colonel Kenly as provost marshal and appointed Colonel George R. Dodge of Baltimore to the position. He also announced that the military units which had been sent into the city to preserve order at the time of the arrests had been withdrawn to their former positions in the suburbs.[102]

The growing volume of arrests also caused federal officials to become increasingly aware of their limited facilities to handle prisoners. To cope with some of the problem, Banks suggested that prisoners should be divided into two categories: those de-

---

98. *Sun*, June 28, 1861.
99. *Sun*, June 28, 1861; Dr. Samuel A. Harrison Journal, June 27–28, 1861, MS 432.1, M.H.S.
100. *OR*, series 1, II, p. 141 & 139 and series 2, I, pp. 625, 586-87.
101. *Ibid.*, series 2, I, pp. 586-87.
102. *Sun*, July 10, 1861.

tained temporarily for the public safety and those charged with high crimes and misdemeanors.[103] When General John A. Dix assumed command, he became increasingly suspicious of charges of disloyalty. He refused to accept such accusations unless they had support from a reliable source.[104] Dix was determined that greater care should be exercised in interfering in civilian affairs. He ordered that the police should be used to search private homes rather than the military. The general also relaxed the prohibition against hunters leaving the city with their firearms, although suspicious vehicles were still to be searched for goods and arms intended for the South.[105]

Newspapers also quickly came under the scrutiny of federal officials who were concerned with their editorials, and at times their contents. Before February 1862, newspapers were suppressed only on specific orders from the War Department, but on February 18 General Dix was given wide discretionary power to take such action himself.[106] Generally, three methods were used to suppress those regarded as "disloyal": the physical closing of an office, the arrest of the editor, or the denial of the use of the federal mails. A number of editors were arrested and imprisoned during the course of the war, and in the latter part of the war it was not uncommon for an offending editor to be banished beyond federal lines as a form of punishment. The denial of mail facilities had disastrous consequences for smaller papers. Quite early the Baltimore *Daily Exchange*, the Marlboro *Planter's Advocate*, and the Frederick *Herald* were placed on the proscribed list. As a result, both the *Advocate* and *Herald* were forced to suspend their publishing activities.[107] Some newspapers, like the Baltimore *Sun*, ceased carrying an editorial for fear of suppression. During the war at least nine Baltimore papers were either temporarily or permanently suppressed.

Meanwhile, following the rioting on April 19, Governor Hicks finally called the legislature into special session. But Hicks

---

103. *OR*, series 2, I, pp. 586-87.
104. *Ibid.*, series 2, I, p. 599.
105. *Ibid.*, series 2, I, p. 597.
106. *Ibid.*, series 2, II, p. 789.
107. *Sun*, June 26 & Oct. 26, 1861; Bel Air *The Southern Aegis*, Sept. 14, 1861; Jacob Englebrecht Diary, Sept. 24, 1861 (microfilm), M.H.S. For a good article on the suppression of the press see Sidney T. Matthews, "Control of the Baltimore Press during the Civil War," *M.H.M.*, XXXVI (June, 1941), 150-70.

chose Frederick, not Annapolis, as the meeting place. Hicks in this unusual move chose the western city for two reasons: General Butler's presence in Annapolis and, probably more important, Frederick's Unionist reputation.[108] Federal authorities were highly suspicious of the convening of the legislature. But Lincoln decided against trying to prevent the Maryland assembly from meeting, although he did take precautionary steps in case an attempt was made to adopt an ordinance of secession. In case such a move was made, the President directed General Scott "to adopt the most prompt, and efficient means to counteract, even, if necessary, to the bombardment of their cities —and in the extremest necessity, the suspension of the writ of habeas corpus."[109]

However, at the very outset the Maryland Senate in an "Address to the People of Maryland" denied that it had any power to pass such an ordinance, and the House of Delegates also adopted a similar measure. Much to the surprise of many, the legislature also opposed the calling of a state convention. Yet the assembly through various acts and expressions showed its antagonism to federal policies. Strong protests over treating Maryland as a "conquered province" were heard, and in the early sessions the house adopted a report calling the war unconstitutional. The delegates, "while recognizing the obligations of their State, as a member of the Union," expressed their sympathy with the South and maintained that Maryland was for peace and reconciliation. In the resolutions they not only denounced the war but also called for the recognition of the Confederacy. But while they protested the military occupation of Maryland, they declared that it was inexpedient to call a state convention.[110]

After a short adjournment in May, the legislators reassembled in an even uglier mood. In the interim a number of irritations, including arrests and the clash between Taney and Cadwalader over John Merryman had occurred, and by this time Governor Hicks was also beginning to take a more decidedly Unionist stand in support of the federal administration. Now the House

---

108. *OR*, series 1, II, pp. 592-593; Maryland, *House & Senate Documents, Extra Session, 1861*, Doc. A.
109. Basler, *Works of Lincoln*, IV, 344; *OR*, series 1, II, pp. 601-02.
110. *Journal of Proceedings of the House of Delegates* (Baltimore, 1861), pp. 106-109.

of Delegates lashed out at both the governor and the federal government. In response to a message from Jefferson Davis, the assembly adopted a series of resolutions, even more radical in tone, in which they strongly protested the suspension of the writ of habeas corpus. But again the legislature temporarily adjourned without taking any action. By the time the legislature reconvened, another series of sensational arrests had been made. Marshal Kane and the police commissioners had now joined the list. Reacting to federal "tyranny" the legislators sent a memorial to Congress protesting the arrest of the city officials. Finally, however, the legislature adjourned until September, but it did so in a bitter and hostile mood. The federal administration, however, was greatly relieved.[111]

Yet federal authorities remained suspicious of the intentions of the legislators. When in September the assembly was to meet again, federal officials, in the wake of the disaster of Bull Run, finally decided to arrest all those members who were regarded as southern sympathizers as a matter of public safety. Preparations for the arrests were planned well in advance, and when the legislators began to gather in Frederick, martial law was proclaimed and the town was sealed off by federal troops. No one was permitted to leave the city without a pass although free entrance was still permitted.[112] Simultaneously, arrests were also made in Baltimore. A few legislators who were still there, as well as Mayor Brown and the editors of the Baltimore *Exchange* and *South*, were rounded up by marshals. Except for those released under oath, the prisoners were sent to Annapolis and then taken to Fort Monroe for confinement.[113]

Legislators and city officials were not the only ones to feel the sometime heavy hand of the military. Judges, too, found that they were not immune to federal scrutiny. Richard Carmichael, judge of the circuit court for Talbot, Queen Anne's, and Kent Counties, was considered to be one of the principal leaders of disloyalty on the Eastern Shore. Quite early, Carmichael had

---

111. *OR*, series 2, I, pp. 587-588; Radcliffe, *Governor Hicks*, Chap. XI. For composition of Legislature see Ralph A. Wooster, "The Membership of the Maryland Legislature of 1861," *M.H.M.*, LVI (March, 1961), pp. 94-102.

112. J. Thomas Scharf, *History of Western Maryland* (Philadelphia: L. H. Everts, 1882), II, 205-206; Englebrecht Diary, Sept. 18, 1861; *OR*, series 1, V, p. 193.

113. Scharf, *Western Maryland*, II, 205-206; *Herald & Torch*, Oct. 2, 1861.

expressed his opposition to the war, and during the November 1861 session of court the judge had openly attacked the government in his instructions to the Grand Jury of Talbot County for its use of arbitrary arrests.[114] As early as October, Secretary of State William Seward had suggested that Carmichael should be arrested even if it had to be done in his courtroom.[115] Finally, in May 1862, General Dix decided to send a detachment to Easton to arrest the judge. Unfortunately the officers, without taking into account public opinion, actually did make the arrest within the confines of the courtroom. Carmichael refused to recognize their authority and had to be forcefully dragged from the room. The government's poor handling of the case created a strong reaction against federal authorities on the Eastern Shore, and even many Unionists felt that the situation had been badly handled.[116]

Politically, even without federal intervention, events in early 1861 had moved decidedly against those in sympathy with the South. By spring both the Know-Nothing and Constitutional Union parties had collapsed, while the Democrats, on the other hand, were internally divided between Unionists and Southern men. Yet out of the turmoil a new political coalition had emerged by May. Meeting in convention in Baltimore on May 23, Unionists set about organizing the Union party on a statewide basis. A state central committee was appointed; and Brantz Mayer, chairman of the committee, issued an address to the people of Maryland setting forth the principles of the party. In the platform the Unionists denounced secession, endorsed the federal government's right to preserve the Union by force, and supported Lincoln's war policies.[117] The Unionist party, suppressing potential internal difficulties over specific issues, wrapped itself in the patriotic garb of defending the Constitution and Union against treason.

---

114. Richard B. Carmichael to James A. Pearce, July 23, 1861, James A. Pearce Papers, MS 1384, MHS; *Judge Carmichael's Charge to the Grand Jury of Talbot County, On Arbitrary Arrests, November Term, 1861,* Broadside collection, *M.H.S.*; *Easton Gazette,* Nov. 23 & 30, 1861.

115. *OR,* series 2, II, p. 85.

116. *Easton Gazette,* May 31, June 3 & 7, 1862; Harrison Journal, May 27–30, 1862; Charles B. Clark, "Suppression and Control of Maryland, 1861–1865," *M.H.M.,* LIV (Sept. 1959), pp. 254-56.

117. Brantz Mayer, *Address of the Union State Central Committee, of Maryland* (Baltimore).

Unionist candidates in the special June congressional election for representatives were opposed by various factions known as the "peace party" or "State Righters" or those who stood for "Constitution and Equality." The first test of strength between the two parties came in Annapolis and Hagerstown in April and then again in the June election. Unionist candidates did extremely well in June and carried every congressional district.[118] Yet the main test for the Unionist cause came in November when the governorship and control of the legislature were at stake.

Unionists were soon looking for a suitable successor to Governor Hicks. The name that was most frequently mentioned was that of Augustus W. Bradford, a conservative Unionist. When the Union convention met in Baltimore in August, the delegates unanimously nominated him as their candidate.[119] His nomination was greeted, in large measure, with enthusiasm. Many felt that he was their strongest and most available candidate.

Initially, the opposition lacked a candidate. However, the Baltimore *Daily Exchange* soon took the offensive and charged Bradford with being an "extreme coercionist" and an "unconditional" supporter of the government. Bradford was also linked with the Republican party and Lincoln in order to capitalize on what this symbolized to many Marylanders. The States Righters at first merely attacked Bradford, but finally in October they generally agreed to put forth Benjamin C. Howard to oppose him. The States Rights party, in the remaining campaign, made a strong appeal to the prejudices of labor by maintaining that a vote for Bradford was a vote for the war, the Republican administration, additional taxes, and especially abolitionism.[120]

Fear of the appeal that the States Rights party was making caused considerable concern in the Unionist party and forced them to make stronger efforts. Unionists were anxious to achieve, as Governor Hicks told General Banks, "a Killing majority." Consequently, Unionists were soon appealing to federal authorities for help and were in consultation with Generals Banks and Dix. A responsive War Department directed Banks

---

118. *Annapolis Gazette*, June 20 & 22, 1861; Middletown *Register*, April 5 & 12, 1861; Charles B. Clark, "Politics in Maryland during the Civil War," *M.H.M.*, XXXVII (Dec., 1942), p. 379.

119. For sketch of Augustus W. Bradford see *ibid.*, pp. 381-82.

120. *Ibid.*, 384-88.

and General George B. McClellan to give furloughs to soldiers of the Maryland Volunteers so that they might return home and add their weight at the polls. General Banks was also directed to send detachments of men to various points to protect Union voters from intimidation by "disunionists" and to arrest any such persons who had just returned from Virginia. If necessary, he was authorized to suspend the writ of habeas corpus. General Dix was also asked by Bradford to authorize the use of oaths "to all persons of doubtful loyalty." Dix, however, maintained that he did not have this power, but he did issue an order "to arrest any persons who have been in arms in Virginia if they appear at the polls . . . and to take into custody all who aid and abet them in their treasonable designs."[121] The States Righters strongly protested the threat of intervention, but there was little that they could do.

In general, the election was peaceful. Military interference, even though a few arrests were made, was on the whole restrained. Yet, the presence of the military was an obvious intimidating factor to many voters. For some, like Ramsay McHenry of Harford County, the credit for the Unionist victory on the Eastern Shore went to General Dix's proclamation.[122] The election returns swept Bradford to victory with 57,502 votes to Howard's 26,070. Howard carried only four counties: St. Mary's, Charles, Calvert, and Talbot. The results were similar for the House of Delegates where the Unionists now controlled the house with sixty-eight members to six for the States Righters. In the Senate the margin was thirteen to eight in favor of the Unionists. Not only were Unionists in Maryland relieved and jubilant over the results, but Lincoln and the administration had similar feelings.[123] The results also virtually ended any hope for pro-Southern elements to gain control in the state. Union strength, in its own right but fortified by the presence of the military, was too much to overcome.

Governor Hicks now called the new legislature into special

---

121. Major General John A. Dix to Augustus W. Bradford, Nov. 1, 1861, Augustus W. Bradford Papers, MS. 1215, M.H.S.: *Secret Correspondence Illustrating the Condition of Affairs in Maryland* (Baltimore, 1863), pp. 30-39; *OR*, series 1, V, pp. 628-29, 641.
122. Ramsay McHenry to Col. George Gale, Dec. 9, 1861, George Gale Papers, MS 1282, M.H.S.; *Herald & Torch*, Nov. 13, 1861; *OR*, series 1, V, pp. 645-47; *Secret Correspondence*, p. 37.
123. Basler, *Works of Lincoln*, V, 24.

session. Southern men were quite concerned that the assembly, now under the control of the Unionists, would undertake reprisals and pass laws requiring the taking of loyalty oaths.[124] When the legislators did meet in December, they quickly undid the work of the previous legislature. Resolutions of loyalty to the government and support for the prosecution of the war replaced the earlier protests. Yet the legislators did qualify their support by emphasizing that the war's purpose was to defend the Union, not to subjugate, conquer, or interfere with the institution of slavery. And when the legislature met for its regular session in January, it quickly ratified a proposed constitutional amendment which would have forbidden Congress the right to interfere with slavery in any state.

Maryland's loyalty was a serious matter to the Unionist legislators; and when Jefferson Davis in his inaugural address on February 22 referred to Maryland as "already united to us by hallowed memories and material interests, will, I believe, when able to speak with unstifled voice, connect her destiny with the South,"[125] members of the house denounced the assertion as unfounded and a "gross calumny upon the people of the State." The delegates reiterated their continued devotion and adherence "to the Union devised for us by our fathers, and absolutely necessary to our social and political happiness, and the preservation of the very liberty which they fought and bled to achieve for us."[126] For many, both in and out of Maryland, the real test of this loyalty came with Lee's invasion of the state late in the summer of 1862.

By the summer of 1862 the military situation had changed considerably. The Peninsula Campaign under General George B. McClellan had collapsed by July. Lee, taking advantage of McClellan's withdrawal from the Peninsula, had then struck at General John Pope's army at Manassas in Northern Virginia. Stunned, Pope withdrew his army into the defenses of Washington. The Confederate victory now in turn posed the question for Lee as to what to do with the Army of Northern Virginia. An invasion of Maryland had definite advantages for the

---

124. Harrison Journal, Nov. 23, 1861.
125. James D. Richardson, ed., *The Messages and Papers of Jefferson Davis and the Confederacy Including Diplomatic Correspondence: 1861–1865* (New York: Chelsea House-Robert Hector Publishers, 1966), I, 186.
126. *M.H.M.*, XXXVIII, 237.

South. An army threatening Washington, Baltimore, or Philadelphia would relieve pressure on Richmond and would also
allow farmers in Virginia to gather their crops without interference. Another important consideration was the liberation of
Maryland from Union control. Most Southerners believed that
federal forces were denying Marylanders the right to choose
their destiny freely; and therefore, it followed that the presence
of a Confederate army in the state would allow them that opportunity to express themselves and, very likely, declare for
the Confederacy. But one of the most important factors was that
Maryland, a rich area thus far untouched by the war, was a potential source of urgently needed supplies and additional recruits for Lee's army.[127]

By September 3 Lee had decided to risk crossing the Potomac
River, and within two days the Confederate army was moving
into Union territory at White's Ford. With shouting, cheering,
and a brass band playing "Maryland, My Maryland," the Southerners assumed the spirit of a liberating army as they marched
into the state. Despite their enthusiasm, their reception was not
what they had anticipated. The huzzahs for the Confederacy
failed to materialize. Unionists received them coolly; and many
who sympathized with the Southern cause held aloof, not wishing to be identified with the Confederates.

Both Generals Lee and Thomas "Stonewall" Jackson, before
entering Maryland, had been advised by Bradley Johnson, a native of Frederick, that the western portion of the state was Unionist in sentiment and that Southern sympathizers would look
for some assurance of a continued occupation before they would
materially aid the Confederate army. Lee was therefore not surprised by the reception. In a dispatch to Jefferson Davis on September 7, Lee wrote: "Notwithstanding individual expressions
of kindness that have been given, and the general sympathy in
the success of the Confederate States, situated as Maryland is,
I do not anticipate any general rising of the people in our behalf."[128]

---

127. *OR*, series 1, XIX, pt. 2, pp. 590-92; Clifford Dowdey and Louis H.
Manarin, eds., *The Wartime Papers of R. E. Lee* (Boston: Little Brown and
Company, 1961), pp. 292-295, 312-14, 287; Douglas Southall Freeman, *R. E.
Lee: A Biography* (New York: Charles Scribner's Sons, 1934–1935), II, 351-52.
128. *OR*, series 1, XIX, pt. 2, pp. 596-597, 601-602; Freeman, *Lee*, II, 356-357;
*American*, Sept. 12, 1862; Lenoir Chambers, *Stonewall Jackson* (New York:
William Morrow & Co., 1959), II, 181.

"Burnside's Bridge" at the Battle of Antietam—one of the bloodiest engagements of the Civil War September 17, 1862.
*M.H.S.*

358

In crossing the Potomac River Lee had done so to the east of the Blue Ridge Mountains in an effort to draw Union forces out of Northern Virginia. He had then moved quickly to Frederick, where he hoped to be joined by ex-Governor Enoch L. Lowe, who had joined the Southern cause. When Lowe did not appear, Lee issued a proclamation to the people of Maryland explaining why his army had come to the state. Lee expressed the South's sympathy over the "wrongs and outrages" inflicted upon a sister state, which he maintained had been reduced to a conquered province. Therefore the army had come to Maryland to restore her "independence and sovereignty." He promised that no constraint would be placed on the freedom of Marylanders "to decide your destiny freely."[129]

From Frederick the main Confederate army moved towards its rendezvous point in the Hagerstown area, while Jackson was sent to reduce the federal garrison at Harper's Ferry. In the meantime McClellan was again placed in command and was soon moving his army into western Maryland in pursuit of Lee. Surprisingly, the usually cautious McClellan was moving more rapidly than Lee had expected. He had guessed Lee's intentions and then had them confirmed with the discovery of Lee's Special Orders No. 191 which showed the disposition of the Southern army. Initial contact between the advanced and rear units of the two armies came at the passes of South Mountain. The Confederates, fighting a delaying action, suffered defeat, but the Battle of South Mountain gave Lee valuable time. Jackson was able to reduce the garrison at Harper's Ferry and then to rejoin the main army at Sharpsburg. Lee, with the news of Jackson's victory, now decided to stand and meet the Union army on September 17.[130]

Militarily, Antietam ended in a draw after the war's bloodiest single day's encounter, though on the following day Lee retreated into Virginia. But diplomatically the battle was a serious reverse in the South's attempt to secure British and French recognition and possible intervention. The repulse of Lee's army from Union soil also gave Lincoln his awaited opportunity to issue his Preliminary Emancipation Proclamation on September 20.

129. *OR*, series 1, XIX, pt. 2, 601-02; Freeman, *Lee*, II, 356-57.

130. Warren W. Hassler, Jr., "The Battle of South Mountain," *M.H.M.*, LII (March, 1957), 39-64.

But also, with the retreat of the Confederate army, the belief that Marylanders, if given an opportunity, would rise up in support of the Confederacy was shattered. Maryland's response to Lee's invitation to join the Southern cause was negative. Coolness and indifference were far more pronounced than enthusiasm. Many Southern sympathizers, lacking confidence and assurance that Confederate forces could maintain their control over the state, were cautious in their reception of Lee's army. Although pro-Southern manifestations continued to persist, the invasion affirmed Maryland's adherence to the Union, atoned for her early indecision and the April 19 rioting, and dispelled many of the North's suspicions concerning the state's loyalty.

3

SLAVERY AND EMANCIPATION

Slavery had long been a sensitive issue in Maryland, and the growing sectional confrontation had increasingly accentuated the concern of Marylanders over it. Concern, motivated by the fear that the institution was becoming primarily the "peculiar institution" of southern Maryland and the Eastern Shore, had brought about a demand as early as the late 1840's for its protection in the state. In the Constitutional Convention of 1850 delegates from these areas managed to have inserted in the constitution a clause which stated: "The Legislature shall not pass any law abolishing the relation of master or slave, as it now exists in this State."[131] Later when the American party in 1857 succeeded in passing a bill calling for a new constitutional convention, an amendment was added to the measure which would have limited the convention's power to change the provision on slavery.[132]

Nationally, agitation over slavery had brought about the collapse of the Whig party in the 1850's, while the emerging American party had attempted to straddle the thorny issue. Maryland Know-Nothings were more than eager to demonstrate their orthodoxy on slavery, but their opposition was soon making telling charges in associating them with "Abolitionism" and

---

131. Constitution of Maryland, 1851, Art. III, sec. 43.
132. Schmeckebier, *Know Nothings*, p. 95.

"Black Republicanism." And for the Americans their first defections came in those areas dominated by slave interests.[133]

John Brown's raid in 1859, instead of freeing any slaves, sent shock waves of fear throughout the upper South, and in Maryland the legislature reacted by passing additional restrictive laws to secure the institution. Republicanism and abolitionism by 1860 were so repugnant to many Marylanders that in the bill creating the Baltimore police commission, legislators inserted a clause "that no Black Republicans or endorser" of Hinton R. Helper's *Impending Crisis*, which criticized slavery "should be appointed to any office under said Board."[134]

On the eve of the war sensitivity to the slavery issue was at the boiling point. Maryland Methodists, for instance, were in a turmoil of outrage at their national body. Northern Methodists had brought about a change in the Discipline on slavery in the 1860 General Conference at Buffalo. The action was sharply denounced by the Baltimore, East Baltimore, and Philadelphia conferences in March 1861. The Baltimore Conference, meeting in Staunton, Virginia, severed its ties to the national body, while Eastern Shore circuits in the Philadelphia Conference called for similar action.[135]

With the eruption of the sectional crisis of 1860, many Marylanders feared that secession and war would ultimately destroy slavery in the border states. When actual hostilities began, Marylanders feared the possibility of federal interference with the institution.[136] In Congress Maryland representatives showed their concern by fully supporting the Crittenden resolution on the purpose of the war, and in May members of the Union meeting at the Maryland Institute, which organized the Union party, also indicated that the war was not to be for abolition. Union delegates warned against the possibility of mixing the slavery issue with the defense of the Union. When the Maryland State Union Convention met in August, delegates endorsed a plan similar to the Crittenden resolution. And in Governor Bradford's inaugural address to the new legislature in

---

133. Jean Baker, "Dark Lantern Crusade," pp. 11-12.
134. Schmeckebier, *Know Nothings*, pp. 105-06.
135. Richard R. Duncan, "Maryland Methodists and the Civil War," *M.H.M.*, LIX (Dec., 1964), 350-59.
136. *Easton Gazette*, July 13, 1861.

January 1862 his support of the war contained the semblance of a veiled threat. He told the legislators that Maryland would continue to remain loyal to the Union as long as the federal government remained faithful to the constitution. This expression obviously referred to slavery and was given as a warning to the federal administration not to interfere with the institution. The assembly concurred in Bradford's sentiments and ratified a proposed constitutional amendment which would have prohibited federal "interference in the domestic institutions of any state."[137]

Initially the federal government was very cautious in its handling of the sensitive issue. When General Butler landed his troops at Annapolis in April 1861 and heard a rumor of an impending slave insurrection in the area, he offered his services to Governor Hicks in suppressing such an uprising.[138] In late July army officers in the Department of Washington were warned against allowing fugitive slaves to be harbored within army camps or to accompany troops on the march.[139] Later, in October, General Dix, appreciating the sensitivity of the issue, ordered that no slaves, except laborers and servants who had the consent of their masters, could enter military camps. He also ordered that if any did without the knowledge of the officer in charge, the slave was to be immediately surrendered on the owner's demand. Again in November Dix reiterated his position in directing his subordinates to use special care not to interfere with slavery or to commit any actions which might be misconstrued or misrepresented.[140]

Troops were also cautioned against inciting slaves to insubordination or insurrection. As early as September 1861, orders were given against any conduct which might provoke such; but there were also indications that the orders had been violated on several occasions. This finally provoked General Charles Stone to recommend that all such violators read the thirty-third article of war. He promised that offenders would be punished for any infraction of the article and furthermore, on the request of the

---

137. Charles Lewis Wagandt, *The Mighty Revolution: Negro Emancipation in Maryland, 1862–1864* (Baltimore: J.H. Press, 1964), p. 36.
138. Marshall, *Correspondence of Butler*, I, 26-27.
139. *Annapolis Gazette*, July 25, 1861.
140. *OR*, series 2, I, pp. 772-75.

civil authorities, the culprits would be turned over to them for additional proceedings.[141]

The problem of slaves escaping from their masters quickly became a serious one for slave owners in Maryland. Concerned over the matter, the legislature appointed a special committee to express their complaints to General McClellan over the admission of slaves within army lines. The general, however, was ill, and the committee saw Lincoln instead. At a later visit they spoke with McClellan. They expressed their fear of the disastrous economic consequences that the massive loss of slave labor would have on agricultural interests. John Bayne, in writing to Lincoln, protested that "The fugitives find employment in various capacities as wagoners, servants, wood choppers, etc. And if the legitimate owners pursue them, they are treated with great indignities; ejected from the camps and in some cases they are threatened with the loss of life."[142]

A citizens' committee from Prince George's, Anne Arundel, and Calvert Counties complained bitterly to Governor Bradford about the numerous slaves escaping from their counties to Washington. They accused federal officials in Washington of refusing to aid in helping to return them to their proper owners, and they asked the governor to establish an armed force in those counties to prevent the flight of slaves. Bradford refused to create such a force, but he did attempt to see Lincoln. Unable to see the President, Bradford saw Representative John W. Crisfield about the matter. Crisfield assured him that the fugitive slave law was being enforced.[143]

Yet the concern that Washington had become a haven for fugitives alarmed slave owners in the surrounding counties. A delegation of 300 to 400 planters went to Washington to protest directly to Lincoln. A subcommittee, consisting of planters and Maryland members of Congress, saw the President and complained of their difficulties with military officials who refused to relinquish slaves despite executive orders. Lincoln assured them that he would give the matter his immediate attention.[144]

---

141. *Ibid.*, series 1, V, p. 641; *Times*, Feb. 12, 1862; Moore, *Rebellion Record*, IV, p. 11.

142. John H. Bayne to Lincoln, March 17, 1862 (copy), John H. Bayne Papers, MS 1200, M.H.S.

143. Bradford to Wm. D. Bowie, May 19, 1862 (copy), Bradford Papers.

144. *American*, May 21, 1862.

Complaints still continued to persist. Meanwhile, Lincoln did attempt to secure compliance with the law by his subordinates, who regarded blacks entering the district as having been freed by the Confiscation Act of 1861, and to reconcile a conflict of jurisdiction in Washington between the civil and military authorities. Efforts to enforce the law quickly sent blacks scurrying across the Potomac River to military areas there. Similar complaints were soon heard concerning the provost marshal in Alexandria, who refused to give up slaves fleeing from Maryland.[145]

Meanwhile, in 1862, the beginnings of a shift of policy on slavery was evident in Lincoln's administration. In a March message to Congress Lincoln urged the passage of a resolution indicating that the federal government would cooperate and give "pecuniary aid" to any state that provided for compensated emancipation. He pleaded that such a step in the border states would end the hope of the South that the border states would join them. As a spur to its acceptance, Lincoln warned that "it is impossible to foresee all the incidents, which may attend all the ruin which may follow it [war]."[146]

Lincoln's plan for compensated emancipation was soon put into a practical form in the following month with the passage of the act abolishing slavery through compensation in the District of Columbia. Marylanders, however, opposed the bill. Former Governor Hicks wrote Lincoln urging him to veto it. Hicks appealed to the President on the grounds, "one thing at a time, let us first down the Rebellion then I care nothing for Slavery." He was very concerned that the measure would give the Democrats an issue.[147] Other Unionists had similar feelings, and Unionist papers such as the *Baltimore American* expressed hope that Lincoln would veto the bill.[148]

The next administration move against slavery came in the aftermath of Antietam. Lee's retreat into Virginia gave Lincoln the appropriate moment that he had been waiting for to issue his Preliminary Emancipation Proclamation. In terms of the

145. Bayne to Lincoln, July 3, 1862 (copy), Bayne Papers; Ward Hill Lamon, *Recollections of Abraham Lincoln: 1847–1865* (Chicago: A. C. McClurg and Company, 1895), pp. 249-55.
146. Basler, *Works of Lincoln*, V, 144-46.
147. Thomas H. Hicks to Lincoln, May 26, 1862, Thomas Holliday Hicks Papers, MS 1313, M.H.S.
148. *American*, April 14, 1862.

border states, the proclamation was not a radical shift, for in the document Lincoln still supported compensated emancipation and "the effort to colonize persons of African descent, with their consent, upon this continent, or elsewhere."[149]

Maryland response to the proclamation varied from ignoring it to outright bitterness. Montgomery Blair, fearing an adverse reaction to the proclamation in the fall election, had earlier advised Lincoln in July against such a move. Again in the cabinet meeting at which Lincoln announced his intention to issue the proclamation, Blair opposed the measure on the same grounds.[150] Frederic Bernal, British Consul for Maryland, in writing to Lord Russell described its impact on Baltimore: "The President's Emancipation Proclamation has fallen like a thunderbolt on the Union men here. . . ."[151] In the House of Representatives both John W. Crisfield and Charles B. Calvert openly attacked it, while Cornelius L. Leary and Francis Thomas joined with them in voting for a resolution of opposition to Lincoln's action. Bradford, attending a governors' conference gathered at Altoona, refused to sign an endorsement of the proclamation.[152]

Following Republican reverses in the November election, Lincoln tried to take some of the sting out of the issue by proposing in his annual message to Congress a constitutional amendment which would compensate states which freed their slaves before 1900 with interest bearing bonds. And again he left open the door to colonization schemes. Journals such as the *Baltimore American* warmly greeted the message, and as a result it pacified the anger of some towards Lincoln.[153]

However, fugitives remained a serious problem for Marylanders. The Hagerstown *Herald and Torch* in western Maryland referred to the fleeing slaves as a process known as emancipation without compensation.[154] In western Maryland frequent military operations in September 1862 and again in the

---

149. Basler, *Works of Lincoln*, V, 433-36.

150. Wagandt, *Mighty Revolution*, pp. 73-75.

151. Charles L. Wagandt, ed., "The Opinion of Maryland on the Emancipation Proclamation: Bernal to Russell, Sept. 23, 1862," *M.H.M.*, LVII (Sept., 1963), 250-51.

152. Wagandt, *Mighty Revolution*, pp. 76-78; William B. Hesseltine, *Lincoln and the War Governors* (New York: Alfred A. Knoff, 1955), pp. 258-59.

153. Basler, *Works of Lincoln*, V, 527-37; *American*, Dec. 11, 1862.

154. *Herald & Torch*, Sept. 30, 1863.

summer of 1863 also helped to shake the institution's stability. In 1863 another factor emerged which accelerated the institution's collapse. In early July the War Department ordered the recruitment of free blacks into the army and informed General Robert E. Schenck that a regiment was to be organized in his department by Colonel William Birney.[155] The zeal and vigor with which Colonel Birney and his men performed their task brought forth a storm of protests in Maryland.

Non-slaveholders were as concerned with the issue as slaveholders as they feared its effect on the labor market. They believed that such recruitment would deprive certain areas of needed labor and that the resulting scarcity, along with the reluctance of free labor to come into the state so long as slavery continued, would double the value of the institution by increasing slave prices. Therefore, they reasoned that the recruitment of freedmen would in effect be giving indirect aid to the very element which was hostile to the government. They, in turn, proposed that both freedmen and slaves should be recruited for the army.[156] State leaders such as Judge Hugh Lennox Bond and Henry Winter Davis agreed and began to urge the recruitment of slaves, with or without compensation, to a receptive Secretary of War, Edwin M. Stanton.[157]

Slaveholders firmly resisted any move on the part of the government to enlist slaves, but soon there were cries that agents were recruiting slaves. Colonel John P. Creager's activities in western Maryland caused a wave of excitement and outrage among slaveholders in August. Colonel Creager, in response to an attempt of slave owners to reclaim their slaves, refused to give them up. He told them that they would have to appeal to a higher authority "and even threatened to arrest some of the masters." Finally one slaveholder swore out a warrant for the colonel's arrest for "enticing slaves away from their owners" against state law.[158]

A similar situation existed on the Eastern Shore. The arrival of a government steamer brought huge crowds of blacks to the

155. OR, series 3, III, pp. 470-71.
156. The American Annual Cyclopaedia (New York: D. Appleton & Company, 1866), III, 614; American, Sept. 7, 1863.
157. John W. Blassingame, "The Recruitment of Negro Troops in Maryland," M.H.M., LVIII (March, 1963), 21.
158. American, Aug. 13, 17, & 20, 1863.

docks. At Eastern Neck Island slaves and blacks appeared in such numbers that many were left behind by necessity. It was estimated that between 150 and 200 were carried off in the steamer.[159] Critics quickly accused Colonel Birney and his agents of interfering with slavery on the Eastern Shore. Such criticism prompted the government to order Birney on September 2 to revoke any authority that he had given to civilians to act as his agents. The order also stated that only commissioned officers were to be employed in such a capacity.[160]

By September ex-Governor Hicks was warning Lincoln about the confusion and excitement which were being created by recruiting agents in the Cambridge area. He feared the results of their indiscriminate enlisting of slaves of both loyal and disloyal persons during the harvest season when labor was at a premium. Hicks also warned that the situation was creating an adverse public reaction toward the government just before the approaching election. Hicks, in indicating to the President that he did not object to the use of blacks in the army, did express the fear that the news that Colonel Birney, accompanied by black troops, was intending to enlist slaves as well as freemen on the Eastern Shore had caused considerable public anxiety. He informed Lincoln that he had been visited by a deputation of Union men from Talbot County who were most concerned about its effect on their area. Finally Hicks told the President that even though he believed that enlistments should be continued, he strongly warned the administration against using blacks in this work.[161]

Governor Bradford was even more upset about administration policies and the excitement that they were creating in Maryland. He complained to Montgomery Blair that he had gone to Washington in late August and had been assured by Lincoln and Stanton that "the enlistment of slaves has not been determined on, and no one was authorized to enlist them, the practice not only continues, but seems from what I hear and see to be every day increasing." He complained that Union men in Talbot County had not even been allowed on board a steamer to determine whether any of their slaves had enlisted so that they

159. Washington, D.C. *National Intelligencer*, Sept. 30, 1863.
160. *OR*, series 3, III, pp. 760-61.
161. *Ibid.*, series 3, III, pp. 767-68.

could later present proof for compensation. Bradford was especially concerned that these complaints were coming from
Union men and about the possible repercussions in the forthcoming election. Bradford predicted to Blair that ". . . I tell you
and mark my prediction—if such practices are not speedily arrested, we are given over in spite of all we can do, once more to
Democratic rule."[162]

Bradford continued to complain. On September 28 he wrote a
long letter to Reverdy Johnson and Hicks charging that slaves of
loyal masters were being indiscriminately recruited in Maryland. Johnson and Hicks, in turn, took the letter to Lincoln who
then wired Bradford to come to Washington to discuss the matter with him.[163] In the meantime, to keep Lincoln abreast of the
controversy, Stanton sent the President a report on his previous
interview with the governor. He told the President that he
thought a basic understanding had been reached between Bradford and the War Department on three propositions:

> First, that free persons of color in Maryland should be enlisted;
> second, that slaves should be enlisted by consent of their own-
> ers; third, that if it were necessary for the purpose of the Gov-
> ernment that slaves should be enlisted without regard to the
> consent of their owners, there would be no objection to a general
> regulation by which loyal owners of slaves could receive just
> compensation for the labor or service of such slaves upon filing
> in this department deeds of manumission—disloyal owners not
> being entitled to any such compensation.

Stanton regarded the enlistment of slaves in Maryland as a
military necessity which would allow the release of white soldiers for other duties. Also, the secretary of war, in answering
the charge that irregular practices were being used, maintained
that recruiting officers had given receipts to owners claiming
slaves, and if there had been departures from this, it had been
without the department's approval and redress would be made.
In a memorandum to Stanton, Lincoln essentially agreed with
the basic general policy. But at the same time he also made his
disapproval of any offensive recruiting and of any practice of
taking away slaves who were unfit for service in the army.[164]

---

162. Bradford to Montgomery Blair, Sept. 11, 1863 (copy), Bradford Papers;
*OR*, series 3, III, pp. 787-89.
163. Basler, *Works of Lincoln*, VI, 491.
164. *OR*, series 3, III, pp. 855-56.

Three days later the War Department issued the confidential order, General Orders No. 329, which covered the general policy of black enlistments. It authorized the establishment of recruiting stations by the Bureau for Organizing Colored Troops and established regulations governing recruiting activities. It directed that all able-bodied men were subject to being drafted and would be credited to the state's quota. Everyone serving in the army was to receive his freedom, and slaves of loyal persons, except in cases of necessity, were required to have their master's written permission. Their owners were to be granted compensation not to exceed $300, if within ten days, they filed a claim of manumission and an oath of allegiance to the government. The order established a board of three persons appointed by the President whose duties were to make rolls and information available to the general public and to investigate claims and issue certificates for payment by the chief of the bureau. Those persons who were regarded as disloyal were, however, to be denied any form of compensation.[165]

The enlistment policy which had been worked out seemed to give general satisfaction and was instrumental in relieving some of the burden of conscription on the white populace. It also provided a step in the direction of emancipation and compensated slave owners at the same time.[166] Even though the misunderstanding between Governor Bradford and the War Department had been cleared up, Bradford did ask Stanton to postpone temporarily the implementation of the order in Maryland. He asked for delay in order to inform and educate the public as to the government's actions. Probably more important, he believed that postponement during the harvest season would be advisable in view of the general shortage of labor in certain areas of the state.[167]

Yet complaints and irregularities still remained. Reverdy Johnson, speaking in the United States Senate, maintained that federal officers were visiting farms and enlisting slaves without the owner's consent by merely telling them that they must enlist.[168] In May Governor Bradford, in a letter to Colonel James

---

165. *Ibid.*, series 3, III, pp. 860-61.
166. Charles B. Clark, "Politics in Maryland during the Civil War," *M.H.M.*, XLI (June, 1946), 144.
167. *OR*, series 3, III, pp. 862-63.
168. *American*, Jan. 5, 1864.

B. Fry, Provost-Marshal-General, complained that Maryland had not received proper credit for blacks recruited in the state. He also blamed irregularities in enlisting those unfit for military service as a factor in the drain on the state's labor supply.[169]

Finally, in December 1863, the board of claims, in session in Baltimore, began to award compensation to loyal claimants. Claims for compensation, along with a deed of manumission, an affidavit of ownership, and an oath of allegiance, certified by two witnesses, were required to be presented to the board before March 1. By October the board had acted on some 244 cases and had rejected only nine.[170]

By 1864 slave values in Maryland had virtually collapsed. In 1860 the value of slaves in the state had been estimated at $35,331,111.[171] By March 1864 Samuel Harrison could confide to his diary that "Slavery has become valueless and can be made to pay . . . only by attaining compensation for the slaves at a stated valuation either from the general or state government. Negroes have no market value."[172] As early as April 1862 prices were in sharp decline, and at a slave auction in Frederick a set of slaves, which would have brought $2,500 two years before, sold for only $400.[173] The *Easton Gazette* in August 1863 estimated that slaves were bringing only one-third of what they had five years before.[174] Appraisers in Hagerstown in 1864, in evaluating seventeen slaves ranging in ages between four to over forty-five set their price at $5.00 each.[175] Finally, with the adoption of the new constitution, the value of the institution was totally destroyed by article twenty-four in the Declaration of Rights and article I, section 36, in the constitution, which prevented the General Assembly from ever compensating former slave owners for their loss.[176]

Politically the issue of slavery and emancipation created se-

---

169. *OR*, series 3, IV, pp. 279-80.
170. *Ibid.*, series 3, IV, p. 790; *American*, Jan. 5, 1864; *Easton Gazette*, Jan. 2, 9, 1864; *M.H.M.*, XLI, 146-47.
171. Scharf, *History of Maryland*, III, 583.
172. Harrison Journal, March 1, 1864.
173. *American*, April 3, 1862.
174. *Easton Gazette*, Aug. 29, 1863.
175. *Sun*, March 10, 1864.
176. Frances Newton Thorpe, ed., *The Federal and State Constitutions* (Washington: Government Printing Office, 1909), III, 1743-57.

vere strains within the Union coalition, and ultimately it brought about an open schism within the party. An internal struggle had developed in the spring of 1862 when the Union state central committee resisted the calling of the full committee into session for fear of possible controversy over the issue. But the Unconditional Union men of Baltimore decided to apply force, and on May 21 they met and adopted a resolution affirming their support of Lincoln's offer of compensated emancipation. The action of the Unconditional Unionists created a stir within the party and opened the way for the coming intraparty struggle in the spring.

By the spring of 1863 the party, differing on approach and strategy rather than principle, was ready for an open split. The Unconditional men began their assault on slavery at a meeting of the Union League in Baltimore on April 20 where they declared "that Slavery should cease to be recognized by the law of Maryland, and that the aid of the United States as recommended by the President ought to be asked and accepted. . . ."[177] During the next month, at the annual City Union Convention, they not only endorsed the resolutions of the Union League but also issued the call for a constitutional convention.[178]

Estranged over the black issue, both groups, Unconditional men and conservatives, decided to meet separately. The Radicals meeting on June 16 declared that "unconditional Union men of Maryland ought to vote for no candidate for Congress who does not avow himself in favor of giving a hearty support to the whole policy of the Administration. . . ," and that they should vote "for no candidate for the General Assembly who does not pledge himself to call a constitutional convention," and that "the policy of emancipation ought to be inaugurated in Maryland."[179] The Radicals had ultimately hoped to get the more conservative Unionists to agree and to cooperate with them. In order to facilitate this, they appointed a committee to confer with the Conservatives when they met on June 22.

The Radicals had hoped that the Conservatives, or now the State Central Committee Convention, would create a similar

---

177. *American*, April 21, 1863; quoted in Wagandt, *Mighty Revolution*, pp. 98-99.
178. Wagandt, *Mighty Revolution*, pp. 99-100.
179. *American Annual Cyclopaedia*, III, p. 616.

committee for discussions so that a third, but joint convention, could be held to nominate candidates for state offices for the forthcoming election. Instead, the Conservatives refused. The state central committee affirmed its loyalty to the Union and Constitution, but declared that "this convention ignores all issues, local or national, but those of war, until treason shall succumb before an offended people." The Conservatives, preferring to continue their focus on support of the Constitution and Union, were politically opposed to submitting the highly charged black question with its various ramifications to the electorate. They did, however, pass a resolution indicating that the new legislature should submit the question of calling a constitutional convention to the people.[180]

Between May 15 and November 14 the two Unionist factions vigorously battled one another. By September the lines were tightly drawn. The Conservatives accused the Unconditional men of "demanding pre-emptory emancipation, without regard to constitutional rights. . . ." They further charged them with making emancipation the paramount issue in the election and in doing so risking the harmony of the Union party. Conservatives believed that the subject should be left for consideration in a constitutional convention and that "it is advisable in order to secure all shades of opinion in a common effort to restore the Union, to ignore all side issues."[181]

In answer to the Conservative charges Unconditional Unionists issued an address on September 16 in which they disavowed "all measures for the violent abrogation of slavery in our midst." Yet they did assert that slavery should be abolished "legally and constitutionally . . . at the earliest period compatible with the best interests of the State. . . ." They believed, "That men who seek to legislate in this crisis need first to emancipate themselves from the influence of the great disturbing interest. . . ." An appeal was made for Unionists to rid themselves and their interests from the domination of the slaveholders. The Unconditional men believed that with the elimination of slavery the major cause of the war would thereby be removed.[182]

---

180. *Ibid.*, p. 616.

181. *Ibid.*, pp. 616-17.

182. *Ibid.*, pp. 617-18; Wagandt, *Mighty Revolution*, pp. 142-44; Charles B. Clark, "Politics in Maryland during the Civil War," *M.H.M.*, XXXVIII (Sept., 1943), p. 242.

With division obvious within the ranks of Unionists, Democrats in certain areas now tried to make a comeback and in the fifth district ran Benjamin C. Harris for Congress. In other areas they ran as Peace men. Democrats opposed the introduction of the emancipation issue into the campaign and adopted a conservative constitutional stand. They further denounced the Lincoln administration for violating the Constitution and maintained "That our devotion for the Union increases with its perils . . . we yield it our heartfelt allegiance, and will ever support it by legal and constitutional means."[183]

Both Conservatives and Democrats feared that in the election the power of the military would be used in support of the Unconditional Unionists. Prominent Conservative leaders expressed their concern over possible federal interference. Thomas Swann, chairman of the state central committee, wrote directly to the President and told him of suspicions that the government was intending to interfere in the election. Therefore in order to clarify the matter, he wanted Lincoln's views to be known to loyal voters of Maryland. Lincoln quickly responded that there were no grounds for such suspicions and that he was "somewhat mortified that there could be any doubt of my views upon the point. . . ." He went on to indicate that he wished "all loyal qualified voters in Maryland & elsewhere, to have the undisturbed privilege of voting at elections."[184]

Several days later Governor Bradford also wrote to Lincoln to express his concern over rumors that troops were going to be dispatched to certain counties to be at the polls on election day and that their presence in turn would exert pressure on its outcome. He had heard, Bradford wrote, that military orders were to be soon issued restricting the right of suffrage. Bradford asked the President to prevent this. Lincoln again was prompt in his reply. He had just conferred with General Schenck, he stated, and the general had told him that provost guards would be needed at a number of polls to protect loyal voters and to maintain order. He also reminded Bradford of the support that the government had given to him in the 1861 election. As to the second point, a test of loyalty for voting, Lincoln defended the need of such a measure. He wrote: "Nor do I think that to keep

---

183. *M.H.M.*, XXXVIII, 242.
184. *American*, Nov. 2, 1863; Basler, *Works of Lincoln*, VI, pp. 542-43.

the peace at the polls, and to prevent the persistently disloyal from voting, constitutes just cause of offence to Maryland."[185]

Meanwhile, just prior to Bradford's letter to Lincoln, General Schenck issued his General Orders No. 53, which called for the arrest of all disloyal persons who were found "hanging about or approaching any poll or place of election." Provost marshals were ordered to assist the election judges in requiring an oath of any voters whose loyalty was challenged. The general further charged his officers to report any election judge who refused to carry out the order.[186]

Lincoln told Bradford that he had reviewed the order and revoked part of it, not because it was wrong in principle, but it "is too liable to abuse." Instead the President substituted: "That all Provost Marshals, and other Military Officers, do prevent all disturbances and violence at or about the polls, whether offered by such persons as above described, or by any other person or persons whomever." Bradford, despite the order's modification, still remained suspicious.[187]

In the meantime the governor and General Schenck were moving towards an open confrontation. Bradford began to prepare his own proclamation and instructions to election judges. He told them to use their own judgment, regardless of the general's orders, in determining the right of any voter to participate in the election and that state authority would protect them. He maintained that Maryland was loyal and protested any military interference. After receiving Lincoln's reply to his letter, Bradford added a supplement to the proclamation in which he cited the change, but he still felt that it did not alter the "general principle of the order."[188]

Schenck ordered the *Baltimore American* not to publish the governor's proclamation until he gave permission. In a similar action he ordered the American Telegraph Company not to transmit it over their wires.[189] Schenck now issued a second proclamation in which he indicated that he did not believe that the governor was intentionally inviting a collision between the

---

185. *Ibid.*, Nov. 3, 1863; *ibid.*, VI, pp. 556-57.
186. *Ibid.*, Nov. 3, 1863; *OR*, series 1, XXIX, pt. 2, pp. 394-95.
187. Basler, *Works of Lincoln*, VI, 555-558; *OR*, series 3, III, p. 981.
188. *American*, Nov. 4, 1863; *M.H.M.*, XXXVIII, 250-51.
189. *OR*, series 3, III, p. 983.

military and civilian authorities but that "its obvious tendency is to invite and suggest such disturbance." Resentful of having his motives questioned, the general defended himself and denied that his orders were directed at any candidates or meant to interfere with the voting rights of loyal voters. His only interest, Schenck maintained, was in preventing persons who "are hostile to the Government of which Maryland is a part" from voting. He also indicated that there was a large disloyal element in some counties of the state and that numerous letters had asked him to employ a test oath. Schenck also admitted that he had restricted the publication of Bradford's proclamation until a copy of Lincoln's letter to the governor could accompany it.[190] Now he permitted its publication.

The military presence in the election, especially on the Eastern Shore, was obvious. There interference was often direct. In some areas ballots for Crisfield were prohibited, while some military officers, reflecting their own political interest, endorsed candidates and a number of arrests were made. Yet military interference was undoubtedly magnified by Democrats and Conservatives, and many historians have probably been guilty of literally accepting these protests as fact.[191] In a light voter turnout the results were an overwhelming victory for the emancipationists and those pledged to the calling of a convention. In the newly elected legislature the emancipationists controlled twelve out of the twenty-one seats in the Senate, while in the house the margin was even greater, fifty-two out of seventy-four seats. The most striking victory was that of the Unconditional Unionist candidate Henry M. Goldsborough, for comptroller by a two to one margin. In the congressional districts they won four seats out of five districts. Benjamin Harris was the lone Democrat to win election to Congress.

A number of Unionists, recognizing the results of the election and the need of political expediency, were ready to join the move for emancipation. Governor Bradford called for "immediate measures" to end slavery. Even the Union State Central Committee recommended that institution's destruction but

---

190.  Thomas H. Hicks to Major General Robert Schenck, Oct. 26, 1863, Bradford Papers; *American,* Nov. 4, 1863.
191.  *M.H.M.,* XXXVIII, 254-57; Harrison Journal, Nov. 4, 1863. For a challenge to the interpretation that the outcome of the election was determined "by sword," see Baker, *Politics of Continuity,* pp. 88-91.

asked for federal compensation and the adoption of an apprenticeship system in helping to make the transition. When the
General Assembly met in January 1864, the Unconditional Unionists, despite some anxious moments, were in command and
secured the necessary majority to pass a convention bill. The
measure provided for the holding of a referendum on the issue,
but in order to expedite the matter, delegates to the proposed
convention were also to be elected at the same time. But also
included in the measure was a provision requiring voters to
take an iron-clad loyalty oath.

In this election, unlike the one in the previous fall, there was
no conflict between military and civil authorities. Yet the military and the federal administration were very interested in its
outcome.[192] General Lew Wallace, who had just assumed command in Maryland, was also far more politic in his dealing with
the governor. This allowed for more room for cooperation between the two.[193] Governor Bradford now authorized the use of
an oath far more sweeping than that which had been used in the
previous election. In many areas the military notified election
judges that they were at their disposal to maintain order and to
render any assistance to them. On election day the army used
restraint and won praises from many conservative Unionists.
Voters overwhelmingly gave the convention issue a wide margin of victory, 31,593 in favor to 19,514 opposed. Only southern
Maryland and the slave counties of Kent, Queen Anne's, Dorchester, and Somerset resisted the move towards emancipation.

Delegates to the constitutional convention quickly assembled in Annapolis on April 27. The membership represented a
radical shift in Maryland thinking. Whereas a discussion by
politicians of abolishing slavery would have virtually been unthinkable before the war, now however, one of the main objectives of the delegates was to do just that. Finally, on June 7,
delegates took up the matter in their debate on the Declaration
of Rights. After a heated debate, the "peculiar institution" was
struck down by a strict party vote of 53 to 27. The constitution,
which was soon to be ratified in October, now read "there shall
be neither slavery nor involuntary servitude, except in punish-

---

192. Lew Wallace to Mrs. Wallace, April 1 & 3, 1864, Lew Wallace Papers, Ind.
Hist. Soc.; Basler, *Works of Lincoln*, VII, 276-77.
193. Wagandt, *Mighty Revolution*, pp. 208-11.

ment of crime, whereof the party shall have been duly convicted; and all persons held to service or labor, as slaves, are
hereby declared free."[194]

4

## DISENFRANCHISEMENT, RECONSTRUCTION, AND

## REALIGNMENT

The Constitution of 1864 represented a triumph for the Radical faction of the Union party. Not only did the Unconditional
Unionists rid Maryland of her "peculiar institution," but they
also laid the basis for their continued control over the state
through the disenfranchisement of Southern sympathizers. Yet
their triumph was shortlived. With the collapse of the Confederacy, political forces moved to establish a more natural
realignment, and a conservative reaction was not long in coming. Peace undermined the Union coalition, while Democrats
began to make efforts to revitalize their party. Ultimately the
conservative upsurge culminated in a new constitution and
Democratic control of Maryland politics.

The question of loyalty was brought into sharp focus during
the summer of 1864. In July Confederate units under General
Jubal Early once again poured into western Maryland. The invasion was closely tied to Union military movements in eastern
and western Virginia in the spring. The successful penetration
of a federal army under the command of General David Hunter
into western Virginia complicated Lee's already hard-pressed
defense of Richmond against General Ulysses S. Grant. The
necessity of defending the west and Lynchburg against Hunter
forced Lee to detach Early's corps to challenge the Northern

194. See William Starr Myers, *The Maryland Constitution of 1864* (Baltimore:
J.H. Press, 1901). For further works on blacks following emancipation see: W.
A. Low, "The Freedmen's Bureau and Education in Maryland," *M.H.M.*,
XLVII (March, 1952), 29-39; W. A. Low, "The Freedmen's Bureau and
Civil Rights in Maryland," *Journal of Negro History*, XXXVII (July, 1952),
221-47; and Richard Paul Fuke, "The Baltimore Association for the Moral
and Educational Improvement of the Colored People 1864–1870," *M.H.M.*,
LXVI (Winter, 1971), 369-404; and Charles L. Wagandt, "Redemption or
Reaction?—Maryland in the Post-Civil War Years," in Richard O. Curry, ed.,
*Radicalism, Racism, and Party Realignment: The Border States during
Reconstruction* (Baltimore: J.H. Press, 1969).

advance. It was also decided, if it proved feasible, to send Early's army down the Shenandoah Valley to threaten either Washington or Baltimore. Lee hoped that such a move would force Grant either to attack his army or to send troops to defend the capital. If the latter decision were made, then a weakened Grant would be more vulnerable to attack.

There were also a number of other considerations important in Lee's thinking. An invasion of Maryland would force Hunter away from the Kanawha Valley and would thereby remove the Union threat to southwestern Virginia. Also, if the Shenandoah Valley were again successfully brought under Southern control, there would be little advantage in having Early remain inactive, while an expedition into Union territory would help to replenish needed military supplies and stores. In addition, he hoped that a successful movement into Maryland could be coupled with a plan for the liberation of Confederate prisoners held at Point Lookout.[195]

During the 1862 campaign Southerners had stressed the idea that Maryland was a sister state, but after three long years of warfare, Confederates regarded the area as Union territory. The army of liberation now became a predatory one. In overrunning western Maryland municipal authorities in Hagerstown, Middletown, and Frederick were forced to pay ransoms in order to prevent their towns from being burned.

In the Southern army's move through western Maryland towards Washington, General Lew Wallace attempted to slow its advance at Monocacy Junction. Located on the Monocacy River, Wallace secured a strong defensive position. With few fords and with the commanding heights of the river on the eastern bank, the number of points to defend allowed the general's smaller army more effectiveness. Wallace's decision to fight was motivated by several factors. He hoped to determine whether Washington or Baltimore was the intended Southern objective. A battle would also help to determine the size of the Confederate force as well as to delay its advance. General Grant would then be allowed additional time to reinforce Washington.[196]

---

195. OR, series 1, XXXVII, pt. 1, pp. 346, 766-770; Dowdey & Manarin, Papers of Lee, pp. 806-08, 811, and 822-823; Jubal A. Early, War Memoirs (Bloomington, Ind.: Indiana University Press, 1960), p. 371.

196. OR, series 1, XXXVII, pt. 1, pp. 191-200; Lew Wallace, Lew Wallace: An Autobiography (New York: Harper and Brothers, 1906), pp. 753-54.

Unfortunately Early defeated Wallace and the Confederates plundered the Western Shore now at their mercy. Before Early's army returned to Virginia, the homes of Governor Bradford and Postmaster General Montgomery Blair were included in the destruction committed by the Southerners in retaliation for Northern depredations in Virginia.

Early's raid intensified the bitterness of Unionists towards Southern sympathizers. The Union press called for strong retaliatory measures. A number of newspapers accused Southern men of having prepared for the invasion and of guiding Confederate forces through the state.[197] Papers such as the Baltimore *American, Baltimore Clipper*, the *Baltimore County Advocate*, the Cumberland *Civilian and Telegraph*, and the Frederick *Examiner* vehemently denounced them. Some demanded that Southern sympathizers should be punished by assessing them to pay for the damage done to Unionists.[198]

Delegates in the constitutional convention, then meeting in Annapolis, reacted sharply on July 9 to the news of the invasion. A majority of the delegates quickly adopted a denunciatory resolution condemning the action as being ". . . by bands of robbers and murderers under the authority of the so-called Confederate states . . ." and reaffirming the state's unwavering loyalty to the Union at all costs. As for Southern sympathizers, they were described ". . . as unworthy citizens of Maryland, as recreant to the faith of their fathers, forsaken of God, and instigated by the devil."[199]

Confederate presence in the Baltimore-Annapolis area forced a temporary adjournment of the convention until July 18. When the delegates reassembled, they quickly passed resolutions calling upon the President and the commanders of the military departments in Maryland to assess known sympathizers for damages sustained by loyal citizens during the raid.[200] Later an even more scathing set of resolutions, introduced by Archibald

----

197. *Baltimore Daily Gazette,* July 9, 1864; *American,* July 13, 1864.

198. *American,* July 13 & 15, 1864; *Baltimore Clipper,* July 9, 1864; *Baltimore County Advocate,* July 23, 1864; *Frederick Examiner,* July 23, 1864.

199. *The Debates of the Constitutional Convention of the State of Maryland, Assembled at the City of Annapolis, Wednesday, April 27, 1864* (Annapolis: Richard P. Bayley, 1864), II, 787.

200. *Ibid.,* II, pp. 800-801; *Proceedings of the State Convention of Maryland to Frame a New Constitution* (Annapolis, 1864), pp. 257-58.

Stirling, was adopted by the delegates. The Stirling resolutions demanded that the government either banish or imprison all citizens who refused to sign a loyalty oath, who persisted in open sympathy with the South, or who had expressed sympathy with or aided the Confederates during the raid.[201]

Despite the storm of Unionist indignation and demands for action, actual retaliation remained limited in scope. Federal authorities checked over-zealous military commanders, while the people themselves were reluctant to take extreme measures. However, Unionists inserted a provision within the constitution disenfranchising all those who had sympathized with the South by requiring voters to take an ironclad oath of past and future loyalty.

Disenfranchisement had its practical political uses. The Unconditional Unionists could easily use it as a political device to maintain their control over the state by disqualifying many Democrats who could not take the oath. Shrewdly the radicals also made the suffrage provision a condition for voting on the constitution. But there was yet another important change in the document. The basis of representation in the House of Delegates was changed to give Baltimore and the western and northern counties a greater voice. This lessened the power of the old slaveholding areas in the assembly.

Opposition to the constitution and in particular to the provisions calling for registration and disenfranchisement quickly emerged. Democratic convention delegates, denouncing it, issued a public protest in September. They characterized it as "wholesale robbery and destruction perpetrated by those whose cardinal duty was to provide for the security of the persons, the protection of the property and the preservation of the inalienable rights of all citizens of the state."[202] When Democrats met in their state convention in Baltimore, they rallied in opposition to its adoption. Even Conservative Unionists, especially those who had been opposed to emancipation, were also unhappy over disenfranchisement. Conservative Unionists such as Reverdy Johnson openly attacked the use of the test oath "as the condition and qualification of the right to vote upon the new Constitution." Johnson declared that "the exaction of

---

201. *Ibid.*, II, pp. 830-31 and 849-51; *ibid.*, 265-66 and 273-77.
202. Myers, *Maryland Constitution*, pp. 92-93.

the oath was beyond the authority of the Convention, and as law is therefore void."[203]

But the Unconditional Unionists had wisely taken that precaution against defeat by applying the oath in the October election. Provision had also been made to allow soldiers to vote. The Radicals had planned well, for even with the disenfranchisement of many Marylanders, the constitution would have suffered defeat if it had not been for the soldiers. Without them it would have lost by a margin of 1,995. The soldiers voted 2,633 to 263 for the constitution and carried it to victory by a 375 majority.[204]

The strains in the Unionist coalition over the black issue were quick to emerge again in the controversy over disenfranchisement. Conservatives such as Montgomery Blair, Thomas Swann, and William Henry Purnell were soon challenging the Radical leadership of the party. One of the earliest battles between the forces of Blair and Henry Winter Davis came in February 1864 over the selection of delegates to the National Union Convention. On this occasion the Davisites easily carried the day and elected their slate.[205] Later, despite their defeat and misgivings, Conservative leaders did support the fight for the new constitution. But with the rising reaction to the Radicals, the Conservatives by fall had secured the selection of William H. Purnell as chairman of the State Central Committee and Thomas Swann as the party's gubernatorial candidate to oppose the Democratic nominee, Ezekiel F. Chambers.

Disenfranchisement under the new constitution proved to be a powerful tool for the Unionists in retaining control in the November election. In areas such as Baltimore, election judges adopted strict guidelines in applying the test oath.[206] The military, on the other hand, took special care "to avoid the slightest demonstration looking to military interference."[207] Voter turn-

203. Reverdy Johnson, *Opinion of the Hon. Reverdy Johnson* (1864).

204. Myers, *Maryland Constitution*, pp. 95 and appendix.

205. Reinhard H. Luthin, "A Discordant Chapter in Lincoln's Administration: The Davis-Blair Controversy," *M.H.M.*, XXXIX (March, 1944), 34.

206. *Biographical Sketch of Hon. A. Leo Knott with a Relation of Some Political Transactions in Maryland, 1861–1867*, from *History of Baltimore* (Baltimore, n.d.), pp. 27-28.

207. General Wallace to Lt. Col. S. B. Lawrence, Oct. 4, 1964 (copy), Wallace Papers.

out reflected the change in the suffrage and dropped more than 20 per cent from the 1860 presidential total.[208] Swann easily defeated Chambers for governor, while Lincoln carried the state by a majority of 7,432 over his Democratic opponent, General George B. McClellan.

The election results, however, left the Unconditional Unionists in disarray. Swann represented the upsurge of conservative Unionism. Henry Winter Davis, who had not run for re-election to Congress, was succeeded by a Conservative. The Democratic party, utilizing its county organizations, also gave evidence of its revival. The party had been reorganized in February 1864 with the immediate objective of defeating the call for the constitutional convention. Democrats, sensitive to charges of disloyalty, had also begun to project an image of being the defenders of civil liberties which were threatened by the Radicals. They decided, if the new constitution provided for disenfranchisement, to begin a campaign against such a provision.[209] In the election Democrats actually did fairly well. Two congressional candidates, Benjamin G. Harris of southern Maryland and Hiram McCullough on the Eastern Shore, won seats to the United States House of Representatives. But a more serious threat for the Unconditional men came with the collapse of the Confederacy in April 1865. Support for the war, as a cohesive core for the Union party, was now gone and could no longer be used to submerge divisive issues in the coalition. The movement was little improved by the April 14 assassination of President Lincoln at the hand of John Wilkes Booth, a native of Harford County. Vice president Andrew Johnson succeeded Lincoln as the nation's chief executive. Soon after, more normal political forces were moving towards a new political realignment in Maryland.

Yet despite the emergence of a powerful conservative force, the legislature was still controlled by the Unconditional Unionists. When the assembly met in January 1865, Governor Bradford charged the lawmakers to implement the newly adopted constitution. Bradford also submitted the thirteenth amendment to a responsive assembly for ratification.[210] They then destroyed

---

208. Wagandt, "Redemption or Reaction?", p. 152.

209. *A. Leo Knott*, pp. 11-13.

210. *Laws of Maryland, Jan. 1865–March 1865 Session* (Annapolis, 1865), pp. 406-07.

much of the old ante-bellum slave code as well. But their most controversial measure was the Registry Bill. This act to list voters by registrars became one of the most divisive issues in Maryland politics until its repeal. By it the Unionist registrar could disqualify Democrats particularly those returning from Confederate service. The Baltimore *Sun*, reflecting the thought of many Conservatives, called for repeal by maintaining that the conditions and motives which were present at the time of adoption of the constitution "may now be presumed no longer to possess the same force." But for the Radicals the Registration Act was the key for maintaining power, and they were not likely to allow its repeal without a fight.[211]

Following the regular session, Swann called the legislators back into session to deal with the finances of the state. Yet he spent his opening address mostly on political matters. Swann pointed to the need of revising the state's laws towards blacks. "In proclaiming freedom to the colored race," Swann declared, "the State of Maryland designed to confer upon the negro something more than a mere nominal benefit: she intended freedom in all that relates to personal property." He expressed the hope "that steps may be taken, at an early day, to confer upon the freedmen the privilege of testifying in our Courts."

In reply to the complaints and threats of resistance to the Registration Act, the governor, to the relief of the Radicals, stood opposed to its repeal and maintained that such action would "not materially benefit any class of voters who have been heretofore disenfranchised under its provisions." In moving into a discussion of Reconstruction, Swann cordially approved of President Andrew Johnson's efforts at reuniting the country and opposed "the threats held out by some, that no State should resume her former status in the Union, without a transfer of the political power which she had always exercised, to the control of the negro race." The governor, while favoring the right of testimony, stood opposed to black suffrage.[212]

Swann's approval of Johnson's Reconstruction policy was endorsed by the House of Delegates by a vote of forty-seven to twenty-four.[213] Yet there was growing division within the Union

---

211. Richard Paul Fuke, "The Break-Up of the Maryland Union Party, 1866" (M.A. thesis, University of Maryland, 1965), pp. 26-28.
212. Maryland, *House & Senate Documents, Extra Session, 1866*, Doc. A.
213. *Laws of Maryland, Extra Session, Jan.–Feb., 1866* (Annapolis, 1866), pp. 316-17.

party over Johnson's policy. The Unconditional men were fearful of the effects of the President's policy on their program in Maryland, and when the confrontation came between Johnson and Congress over the Freedmen's Bureau and the Civil Rights Act, they sided with congressional Radicals. The Conservatives, on the other hand, continued their support of the President.

By early 1866 Democrats, noting their support in traditionally Democratic areas, were busy attempting to build on their limited success in 1864. At an informal meeting in January, they issued a call for an "anti-Registry Law" convention to be held in Baltimore on the 24th. The response was enthusiastic. Even many Conservative Unionists joined in support of the convention. When the meeting assembled, Montgomery Blair was chosen its president. Blair, a strong supporter of the President and opponent of the Davisites, hoped to become a symbol pointing the way for cooperation between Democrats and Conservatives. Blair, maneuvering to bring about a party realignment, accused the Unconditional Unionists of attempting to use the Registry Bill as a device to keep themselves in power. He also introduced a new element in the rising political debate: Negro suffrage. Even though the Radicals had not endorsed the idea, Blair, and soon others as well, began unfairly to use the issue as a powerful weapon for partisan purposes against the Unconditional Unionists.[214]

Swann was not slow in joining the attack and in using the suffrage issue as well. Rapidly the governor moved towards a conservative position. When the Baltimore City Unconditional Unionist convention endorsed Senator John A. J. Creswell's vote in favor of the Freedmen's Bureau bill, Swann publicly objected. By May the governor had become even more pronounced in denouncing Negro suffrage. And by mid-month he had finally broken with the Radical faction of the party.

With the rising attacks on the Registration Act and black suffrage, the Unionist coalition began to crumble. Schism finally came in the May meeting of the party's executive committee. The Conservatives, with William H. Purnell as chairman, attempted to gain control over the party by securing the passage of resolutions approving Johnsonian Reconstruction

---

214. *American*, Jan. 18 and 25–26, 1866; Fuke, "Break-Up of Union Party," pp. 35-40; William Starr Myers, *The Self-Reconstruction of Maryland, 1864–1867* (Baltimore: J.H. Press, 1909), pp. 43-45.

and demanding a change in the Registration Act. Unconditional Unionists balked and refused to accept the majority decision. Both factions now called for separate conventions. Governor Swann's endorsement of the Conservative actions made his break with the Unconditional Union men official. Undoubtedly personal ambition—the desire to become a United States Senator—played an important role in Swann's motivation as well as his more natural conservative proclivities.[215]

The Unconditional Unionists met first on June 6, while Conservatives followed on July 25. In the campaign Conservatives struck at the Radicals through the suffrage issue and especially at their support of the Registry Law. But the central issue was the Registration Act with the two groups dividing on it. The Conservatives reiterated their charge that the Radicals were using it to maintain their control over the state.

But the key figure who was to shape the course and the outcome of the fall election was Governor Swann. The Registration Act authorized the governor to appoint the registrars who were responsible for drawing up the voter registration lists. Therefore much depended upon his choice of registrars. Swann in a mass meeting in Baltimore gave little doubt as to his course in the matter. In addressing the crowd he promised: "I shall take care that the Registration Act is not made the instrument of degradation of our people in the hands of vindictive and radical agents." He promised that the law would be "fairly and justly administered."[216]

Actually, Swann had already moved in the direction of seeking conservatives, who supported Johnson's policy and who would interpret the law liberally, to appoint as registrars. When the appointments were announced, much to the despair and anger of the Unconditional Unionists, their conservative nature was obvious. Included within the appointees were a number of Democrats who could also aid in forging some of the necessary links in a new coalition of Conservatives and Democrats.

In the meantime, Democrats on the day following the Conservative meeting in July issued a call for the holding of a convention on August 8 to select delegates to the Philadelphia Union Convention. Democrats urged all those who believed in

215. Myers, *Self-Reconstruction*, pp. 56-57.
216. Quoted in Fuke, "Break-Up of Union Party," pp. 49-50; *American*, June 22, 1866.

the convention to join with them in August. The invitation was repeated in subsequent meetings, and when the Democratic State Convention met in Baltimore, they too indicated their willingness to cooperate with the Conservatives.

A number of interacting factors were present in the summer of 1866 which were to promote a political realignment. Principally the Registration Act provided a common cause to unite both Conservatives and Democrats in opposition to the Unconditional Unionists. And Governor Swann's appointment of sympathetic registrars made it possible for many who would otherwise have been barred to vote and produce a Conservative-Democratic majority. This majority in turn would owe its existence to Swann. A second factor was that both Conservatives and Democrats could agree on their support for President Johnson's Reconstruction policy and in their opposition to the ratification of the Fourteenth Amendment. Finally, both were opposed to black suffrage.[217]

Yet despite the stimulus of the Philadelphia Union Convention of encouraging a united front, there were difficulties on the local level. In areas where Democrats were traditionally strong, little interest was shown in cooperation, while in weaker areas they were much more receptive. Also, Democrats refused to give up their party identity and to meet in a joint convention with the Conservatives. But the key to the election remained in how broad the electoral base would be in the fall election. In this the Swann-appointed registrars had certainly done their part well. Voter registration soared. In many areas the number of voters doubled and in some cases even tripled.[218] Yet Baltimore remained a threat to a Conservative-Democratic victory.

There Conservatives and Unconditional Unionists had clashed over the Registration Act and its applicability to the October municipal election. Radicals, having the support of Attorney General Alexander Randall's decision that the 1865 registration list should apply, won the first battle. With suffrage still limited, the Unconditional Unionists easily re-elected John Lee Chapman as mayor and continued their control over the city council. Democratic leaders, such as A. Leo Knott, charged

217. Ibid., pp. 66-69.
218. Wagandt, "Redemption or Reaction?" p. 166.

that the conduct of the election judges caused "the disenfran-chisement of a great majority of the registered Democratic vot-ers of the city."[219]

For the Conservatives the October results were ominous un-less the political situation was somehow changed. Baltimore's eighteen seats in the House of Delegates were crucial in the control of the assembly. To prevent a recurrence of the Oc-tober debacle, Swann was now asked to rectify the situation by removing the police commissioners, Samuel Hindes and Nicholas L. Wood, who appointed the election officials, on grounds of "official misconduct." Baltimore Conservatives, meeting in Rechabite Hall, also joined in asking for their re-moval and the appointment of impartial election judges.

Swann happily responded to the cry for action and im-mediately ordered the commissioners to stand trial before him to answer charges of misconduct. Radicals met the challenge with stiffening opposition. At first armed resistance by Radical organizations, such as the "Boys in Blue" and the Union Leagues, seemed imminent. Swann countered by issuing a warning against "military and other combinations" forming "for the purpose of obstructing and resisting the execution of the laws of this State." In the meantime the governor consulted with federal military and government officials. General Edward Canby was sent to Baltimore to report on the situation. General Grant after conferring with Canby indicated to Johnson that the situation did not warrant military interference "in advance of even the cause (the removal of said commissioners) which is to induce riot." But he did indicate that "If insurrection does come, the law provides the method of calling out forces to sup-press it."[220]

The trial of the commissioners had the expected results. Swann found them guilty, and on the following day, November 2, he appointed James Young and William Thomas Valiant to the vacant offices. Hindes and Wood, however, refused to va-cate their offices. Judge Hugh Lennox Bond now issued warrants for the arrest of Young and Valiant on charges of conspiracy.

---

219. *A. Leo Knott*, p. 66.
220. Maryland, *House & Senate Documents, 1867*, Doc. A., pp. 9-11; *A. Leo Knott*, pp. 70-71; Myers, *Self-Reconstruction*, pp. 69-70.

Jailed, Young and Valiant then secured writs of habeas corpus, but arguments on the writs were delayed until two days after the election.[221]

Swann remained determined not to allow the Radicals to block his efforts and to continue their control over Baltimore. He was soon in contact with federal authorities after the jailing of his two appointees. Swann hurried to Washington to see President Johnson and was given assurances of military aid if necessary in order to maintain order. General Grant, returning with the governor to Baltimore, was sent to the city to investigate conditions there. In the meantime, there was an attempt at negotiations between Conservatives and Unconditional Unionists in an effort to reach a compromise. It was understood that "one judge and one clerk of Conservative proclivities" would be appointed in each precinct.[222] But the compromise failed, and none were appointed. Grant also attempted to mediate between the two groups, but since the election judges had already been selected by Hindes and Wood, little could be done on the matter. But yet, it was agreed that the judges would be reasonable in the election.

When election day arrived in November, despite the efforts of the Unconditional Unionists to maintain power, Conservative-Democratic efforts secured an overwhelming victory. With the inability of the election judges to refuse all the newly registered voters and the presence of the military to support Swann if necessary, all eighteen delegate seats were lost by the Radicals. In the remainder of the state the coalition did almost as well. In the House of Delegates Unconditional Unionists held onto only twenty-one seats out of eighty. It was an especially victorious election for the Democrats. Most of the Conservative and Democratic gains came from traditionally Democratic areas, and with the national collapse of the Union party movement, Conservatives had little place to go except into the Democratic party. Blair's attempt to create a new party had failed. The Unconditional Unionists, on the other hand, now ultimately became Republicans.[223]

When the newly elected legislature met in January 1867,

---

221. Myers, *Self-Reconstruction*, pp. 71-72.
222. A. *Leo Knott*, pp. 81-82.
223. Fuke, "Break-Up of Union Party," pp. 100-02, and 105.

Democrats and Conservatives dominated the assembly and were determined to make a number of changes. In his message to the legislature Swann called for a new municipal election in Baltimore, opposed ratification of the Fourteenth Amendment, and endorsed Johnsonian Reconstruction. The governor also sounded the call for a new constitutional convention.[224]

Legislators were only too eager to undo some of the work of the previous assembly. Approval was expressed over Swann's support of the President's Reconstruction efforts and "in the just and liberal execution by him of the existing Registry Law . . . and a proper recognition of their [the people's] inalienable right to participate in its government by the exercise of the elective franchise."[225] The legislators then virtually repealed, in effect, section 4 of Article I of the 1864 Constitution. The legislators obviated the necessity of taking an iron-clad oath by substituting a simple oath of allegiance. Under a new registration act voters had a choice of taking either to fulfill the qualifications for the suffrage.

Consideration was also given to the ratification of the Fourteenth Amendment to the federal Constitution. A joint committee of both houses was appointed to consider the amendment. Again the matter of disenfranchisement, along with states' rights arguments and objections to the section prohibiting future federal compensation for emancipation, arose in the debate over ratification. The committee's majority recommended rejection, and the assembly agreed.[226]

But, the most important piece of legislation was the call for a new constitutional convention. Some difficulty was encountered in the House of Delegates in securing the bill's passage, but in the Senate the measure met serious resistance. A majority of the Senate's judiciary committee adopted an unfavorable report. When the bill was considered by the Senate, even though it passed by a vote of fifteen to seven, Lieutenant-Governor Cox declared that the measure, lacking a necessary two-thirds, had failed. His ruling was quickly appealed and eventually a new vote secured the needed support.[227]

224. Maryland, *House & Senate Documents, 1867*, Doc. A.
225. *Laws of Maryland*, 1867, p. 869.
226. Maryland, *House & Senate Documents, 1867*, "Joint Resolutions," pp. 882-911.
227. Myers, *Self-Reconstruction*, pp. 95-99.

Appreciative Democrats and Conservatives were also anxious to pay their political debt to Governor Swann. The reward was to be his election to the United States Senate. To accomplish this, a series of inter-related measures were passed in the assembly. The requirement of rotating senators between the Western and Eastern Shore was set aside, a change in representative apportionment in the assembly, and the constitutional convention bill paved the way for his election. Swann was eager but soon became cautious. Fearing the consequences of Cox becoming governor and the threat that he would be blocked from taking his seat in the Senate, Swann, at the last moment, refused the offer. He rationalized his decision as being in response to "appeals from the representative men of the State . . . asking my continuance in the Gubernatorial chair. . . ." A disappointed Swann declared that it was his "duty to the people of the State of Maryland, to decline the Appointment. . . ."[228]

The Unconditional Unionists saw the work of the assembly, especially the call for a new constitution, as a threat and denouement of their power. In a desperate attempt to thwart disaster, the Radicals appealed to Congress for federal intervention. They maintained that the legislators in the assembly had been ". . . elected in great part by the deliberate violation of the election law of the State, by the votes of men who were in active accord with the rebellion. . . ." They also asserted that the call for a new convention had been made illegally. In another effort, Radicals attempted to secure an injunction in the Superior Court of Baltimore to prevent holding the election. However, all such efforts failed. The election was held on the appointed day, April 10, 1867, and the question carried with an overwhelming 10,350 majority.[229]

The new constitution reflected the newly-changed political situation. Since the Unconditional Unionists, who had adopted the Republican Union party label, had made no nominations for delegates, the convention was virtually a Democratic conclave. As was expected, the old constitution was shorn of its Radical taint. Only a simple oath of allegiance was now required for

---

228. A. *Leo Knott*, pp. 95-115; Myers, *Self-Reconstruction*, pp. 87-92; Wagandt, "Redemption or Reaction?" pp. 170-71.
229. Myers, *Self-Reconstruction*, pp. 103-11.

office holders. However, the expanded franchise was restricted to white males of legal age. Blacks were denied this right. They would have to wait until the Fifteenth Amendment to the federal constitution. But blacks were, after considerable debate, allowed to testify in court. Also the delegates did retain the section prohibiting compensation for emancipation, but as a gesture, hope was held out for future federal compensation.

The constitution also temporarily brought about a new shift in power. Provision was made for new elections in Baltimore. But far more important was the fact that now both blacks and whites were counted in determining representation in the assembly. Since whites were only eligible for the franchise, a voter in southern Maryland and on the Eastern Shore was overrepresented in comparison with the remainder of the state. In addition a new county, Wicomico, was created on the Eastern Shore and thereby further increased the strength of the former slave-holding areas in the Senate. The northern and western portions of the state were shorn of their political dominance. Even though much of the work of the Radicals was undone, the Unconditional Unionists had left an important legacy: emancipation.

The finished document finally went to the voters on September 18, and despite Republican opposition, it was approved by a two to one vote. And on October 5 the new constitution became the basic law of the state. The municipal and state elections bore further witness to the renewal of Democratic ascendency. Democrats carried the mayoralty election in Baltimore, while in the gubernatorial race the party's candidate, Oden Bowie, trounced Republican Judge Hugh Lennox Bond by 63,694 to 22,050. For the first time since Governor Ligon the Democrats were again in control and were to remain there for an extended tenure.

With Bowie's victory a decade of social and political turmoil essentially drew to a close. By 1867 Maryland's period of "Self-Reconstruction" had come to an end and a more stable party alignment had emerged. The remaining capstone to party realignment came with the extension of the franchise to blacks. The successful ratification in 1870 of the Fifteenth Amendment to the United States Constitution and the protection of black voters by the passage of the enforcement acts by Congress added a new dimension to Maryland politics.

Out of the political flux of the previous decade, Democrats —now augmented by Conservative Unionists, new voters, and returning veterans—emerged as the dominant party in Maryland and would remain so for years to come. Yet a new party had also appeared to act as a serious check on Democratic dominance. The Republican party, drawing heavily on the Unconditional Unionist faction, at first was forced to rely on federal patronage to support its organization. But yet, Republicans, aware of their weakness, pragmatically took hope in the move for black enfranchisement. As early as 1867 Unconditional Unionists had openly called for universal manhood suffrage and had begun to integrate their party. Success in their strategy was finally realized with the Fifteenth Amendment and the enforcement acts. And with the increase of the potential electorate by approximately 30 per cent, the Republican party in Maryland was given the necessary infusion of strength to become a viable opposition party in the decades to follow.[230]

---

230. See Margaret Law Callcott, *The Negro in Maryland Politics 1870–1912* (Baltimore: J.H. Press, 1969).

BIBLIOGRAPHICAL ESSAY

CHAPTER V

A sizeable bibliography of literature exists for the Civil War era. Yet, most of the work has been concentrated on the war period, while the decade of the 1850's and the reconstruction era have comparably suffered more neglect until recently. Within the past decade much of this has been rectified by a number of fine scholarly monographs, articles, and theses.

For the decade of the 1850's the dated, but still useful, standard work is Laurence Schmeckebier's *History of the Know-Nothing Party in Maryland* (Baltimore: Johns Hopkins Press, 1899) and Benjamin Tuska's *Know-Nothingism in Baltimore 1854–1860* (New York: n.p., 1930?). Newer and more balanced studies can be found in Jean Baker's excellent master's thesis, "Dark Lantern Crusade: An Analysis of the Know-Nothing Party in Maryland" (M.A., Johns Hopkins University, 1965); William Evitts' doctoral dissertation, "A Matter of Allegiances, Maryland from 1850 to 1861" (Ph.D., Johns Hopkins University, 1971); and in an article by Douglas Bowers, "Ideology and Political Parties in Maryland, 1851–1856," *M.H.M.*, LXIV (Fall, 1969).

The war period has always attracted scholarly attention. The older and more narrative work, but still significant, on Civil War politics is Charles Branch Clark's "Politics in Maryland during the Civil War" (Ph.D., University of North Carolina, 1941) which was largely reprinted in serial form in the *Maryland Historical Magazine* and later published in book form. A newer study which minimizes military and federal interference is the excellent analysis and synthesis by Jean Baker in *The Politics of Continuity: Maryland Political Parties from 1858 to 1870* (Baltimore: Johns Hopkins Press, 1973). Other works of note are: George L. Radcliffe, *Governor Thomas H. Hicks of Maryland and the Civil War* (Baltimore: Johns Hopkins Press, 1901); William Starr Myers, *The Maryland Constitution of 1864* (Baltimore: Johns Hopkins Press, 1964); and Harold Manakee, *Maryland in the Civil War* (Baltimore: Maryland Historical Society, 1960). Articles of interest are: Carl M. Frasure, "Union Sentiment in Maryland, 1859–1861," *M.H.M.*, XXIV (Sept., 1929); William A. Russ, "Disfranchisement in Maryland (1861–67)," *M.H.M.*, XXVIII (Dec., 1933); and Sidney T. Matthews, "Control of the Baltimore Press during the Civil War," *M.H.M.*, XXXVI (June, 1941); Herman Belz, "Henry

Winter Davis and the Origins of Congressional Reconstruction,"
*M.H.M.*, LXVII (Summer, 1972); and Gerald S. Henig, "Henry Winter
Davis and the Speakership Contest of 1859–1860," *M.H.M.*, LXVIII
(Spring, 1973). Two recent doctoral dissertations, "Henry Winter
Davis: A Biography" (Ph.D., City University of New York, 1971) by
Gerald S. Henig and "Henry Winter Davis" (Ph.D., Louisiana State
University, 1972) by Milton L. Henry, fill the need for an updated
work on Maryland's controversial congressman.

The economic impact of the war is treated in such studies as Walter
S. Sanderlin's *The Great National Project* (Baltimore: Johns Hopkins
Press, 1946) and in his articles, "A House Divided—The Conflict of
Loyalties on the Chesapeake and Ohio Canal" in *M.H.M.*, XLII (Sept.,
1947) and "The Vicissitudes of the Chesapeake and Ohio Canal during the Civil War" in the *Journal of Southern History*, XI (Feb., 1945);
Festus P. Summers' *The Baltimore and Ohio in the Civil War* (New
York: G. P. Putnam's Sons, 1939) and in his article, "The Baltimore
and Ohio—First in War," *Civil War History*, VII (Sept., 1961); William Bruce Catton's "The Baltimore Business Community and the
Secession Crisis, 1860–1861," (M.A. thesis, University of Maryland,
1952) and in his doctoral dissertation, "John W. Garrett of the Baltimore and Ohio: A Study in Seaport and Railroad Competition, 1820–
1874" (Ph.D., Northwestern University, 1959); and Katherine A.
Harvey's article, "The Civil War and the Maryland Coal Trade,"
*M.H.M.*, LXII (Dec., 1967).

Various aspects of the impact of the war on churches, education, and
social life can be seen in articles by Dieter Cunz, "The Maryland
Germans in the Civil War," *M.H.M.*, XXXVII (Dec., 1941); Isaac M.
Fein, "Baltimore Jews during the Civil War," *American Jewish His-
torical Quarterly*, LI (Dec., 1961); and Richard R. Duncan, "Maryland
Methodists and the Civil War," *M.H.M.*, LIX (Dec., 1964), "Bishop
Whittingham, The Maryland Diocese, and the Civil War," *M.H.M.*,
LXI (Dec., 1966), and "Impact of the Civil War on Education in Mary-
land," *M.H.M.*, LXI (March, 1964).

Recently considerable attention has been given to the black community. For the decade of the 1850's two articles by M. Ray Della, Jr.,
"The Problems of Negro Labor in the 1850's," *M.H.M.*, LXVI (Spring,
1971) and "An Analysis of Baltimore's Population in the 1850's,"
*M.H.M.*, LXVIII (Spring, 1974), Elwood L. Brinder, Jr.'s "The Fugitive Slaves of Maryland," *M.H.M.*, LXVI (Spring, 1971), and William
Calderhead's "How Extensive Was the Border State Slave Trade? A
New Look," *Civil War History*, XVIII (March, 1972) are of note. For
the War and Reconstruction periods older studies would include W.
A. Low's articles, "The Freedmen's Bureau and Education in Maryland," *M.H.M.*, XLVII (March, 1952) and "The Freedmen's Bureau

and Civil Rights in Maryland," *Journal of Negro History*, XXXVII (July, 1952). Newer works are by Charles L. Wagandt, *The Mighty Revolution*, previously cited, and his article, "The Army versus Maryland Slavery, 1862–1864," *Civil War History*, X (June, 1964); John W. Blassingame, "The Recruitment of Negro Troops in Maryland," *M.H.M.*, LVIII (March, 1963); and of special note Richard Paul Fuke's article, "The Baltimore Association for the Moral and Educational Improvement of the Colored People 1864–1870," *M.H.M.*, LXVI (Winter, 1971) and his doctoral dissertation, "Black Marylanders, 1864–1868" (Ph.D., University of Chicago, 1973).

Material on the military campaigns in Maryland is voluminous. However, a few of those principally concerned with the state are: James V. Murfin, *The Gleam of Bayonets* (New York: Thomas Yoseloff, 1965); Frank Vandiver, *Jubal's Raid* (New York: McGraw-Hill Book Company, Inc., 1960), and articles by Warren Hassler, Jr., "The Battle of South Mountain," *M.H.M.*, LII (March, 1957) and Richard R. Duncan, "Marylanders and the Invasion of 1862," *Civil War History*, XI (Dec., 1965), and "Maryland's Reaction to Early's Raid in 1864: A Summer of Bitterness," *M.H.M.*, LXIV (Fall, 1969).

The Era of Reconstruction has recently come in for additional research and evaluation by Maryland scholars. The older standard work is by William Starr Myers, *The Self-Reconstruction of Maryland, 1864–1867* (Baltimore: Johns Hopkins Press, 1909). Newer works of note include Charles L. Wagandt's "Redemption or Reaction?— Maryland in the Post-Civil War Years" in *Radicalism, Racism, and Party Realignment: The Border States During Reconstruction* (Baltimore: Johns Hopkins Press, 1969), edited by Richard O. Curry; Jean Baker's excellent analysis in her previously cited *Politics of Continuity;* Richard Paul Fuke's fine master's thesis, "The Break-up of the Maryland Union Party" (M.A., University of Maryland, 1965); and Reinhard H. Luthin's article, "A Discordant Chapter in Lincoln's Administration: The Davis-Blair Controversy." *M.H.M.*, XXXIX (March, 1944).

# VI

## THE INDUSTRIALIZATION OF MARYLAND
## 1860–1914

### BY

### ELEANOR BRUCHEY

### NEW YORK CITY

THE TABLES referred to in this chapter will be found
at the end of the chapter.

Maryland emerged from the Civil War to pick up old
economic threads and to forge ahead in new directions. The war
had badly disrupted economic ties with the South, but soon
Baltimore had reestablished the old patterns of domestic commerce with that region and Baltimore's financial institutions
were investing heavily in southern economic development.
After the war Baltimore likewise resumed its position as an
important and competitive port in foreign trade. But agriculture, also much disrupted by the war, now entered a period of
decline, especially in relation to the increasing strength of the
industrial sector of the economy. Maryland, particularly Baltimore and environs, took new strides in industrialization. Some
older industries expanded while new ones flourished. The increasing size of companies, many with headquarters out-of-
town, encouraged the development of impersonal administrative bureaucracies in corporate management.

Dramatic population shifts supplied the labor force necessary
for this industrial growth. In Maryland most important was the
great exodus from the farm to the city and towns. It was only in
this period for the first time that more people were engaged in
industry than agriculture[1] and, necessarily, more lived in urban
than in rural areas. Foreign immigration was of only secondary

1. See Table 1; U.S., Department of Commerce, Bureau of the Census, *Census of Manufactures: 1914*, I, 553.

importance in Maryland in building the labor supply. Often caught in the hard discipline of increasingly mechanized factory routines, many workers tried to better their condition but with only sporadic and incomplete success.

To what extent Maryland was transformed into an urbanized, industrial state and with what attendant problems will be explored in detail in the following pages.

# 1

## AGRICULTURE

Until nearly the end of the period agriculture was still the leading economic activity of the state, but, as in the United States, it underwent marked changes. First, Maryland as a slave state suffered some deep and permanent agricultural and social upheavals due to the Civil War. Southern Maryland and the Eastern Shore, particularly, suffered critical shortages of farm labor during and after the war. Slaves ran away, encouraged by the recruitment policy of the federal army, which was constantly in need of manpower. The emancipation of the slaves further exacerbated farm-labor problems as even more Negroes left the plantations. The magnitude of losses to capital and labor can be grasped from the estimate that slave-property in Maryland in 1860 was worth $50 million, and about 100,000 slaves were farm laborers.[2] A serious scarcity of farm labor resulted, which signaled the decline of the large estate as an agricultural unit and brought an immediate decline in the production of some staples and rising wages for farm labor. In addition, many farmers heavily mortgaged their holdings, especially during the long agricultural depression which blighted the 1870's.[3]

Another major factor necessitating adjustment on the part of Maryland agriculture was the westward movement of the center of agriculture so that Maryland was no longer an important bread basket as it had been in the eighteenth century. Although the state's chief crops continued to be corn and wheat, they could not compete with the scale of production of corn in Illi-

---

2. Richard R. Duncan, "The Social and Economic Impact of the Civil War on Maryland" (Ph.D. dissertation, Ohio State University, 1963), Chap. V.

3. Maryland, Board of World's Fair Managers, *Maryland, Its Resources, Industries and Institutions* (Baltimore: Sun Printing Office, 1893) p. 154.

nois and Iowa and wheat in Kansas. Acreage in these staple crops in Maryland had to be reduced in the face of western competition and only the most productive land used, causing a shift in the traditional patterns of farming in the state.[4] More precisely, agriculture in Maryland in this period lost significance in relation to the nation.

Moreover, within the state itself, agriculture declined in importance as manufacturing grew in scale and attracted an increasing labor force. Specifically, by 1900 for the first time the proportion of those engaged in agriculture was less than those in manufacturing. Table 1 (at the end of the chapter) shows the declining proportion in agriculture as against the rising one in manufacturing. By 1910 the percentages had reversed themselves from 1870. Indeed, this drop in farm population characterized the whole country. The chief cause was the greatly increased use of farm machinery, replacing men, women, and children. A major result was a faster tempo of internal migration. A swelling tide of population moved from farm to town and city. By 1910 the trend had gone so far that for the first time the federal census showed 51 per cent of the people located in cities, with 49 per cent on the farm.[5]

The average size of a farm in Maryland fell steadily from 212 acres in 1850 to 103 in 1910. The decline which, started even before the Civil War, showed that the impact of the war was not the only factor causing the movement toward smaller farms. By 1910, 44 per cent of the farms were between 50 and 174 acres and 18 per cent were over 174 acres.[6]

Some aspects of agriculture, on the other hand, remained largely unaltered over the period. The federal census indicates that the pattern of farm tenure changed very little from 1880 to 1910, amounting roughly to 70 per cent operated by farmers who were owners and 30 per cent by tenants. These were the only years when such figures were available. Nor did the proportion of share-croppers versus cash tenants vary much be-

---

4. *Ibid.*, pp. 156-57.

5. U.S., *Census of Manufactures: 1914*, I, 553.

6. U.S., *Thirteenth Census: 1910* as cited in Maryland, Bureau of Statistics and Information, *Annual Report: 1911*, (Baltimore: 1912) pp. 212, 216. (hereafter cited as Maryland, BSI).

tween 1880 and 1910. Approximately 23 per cent were share-croppers and 8 per cent cash tenants.[7]

Nor were there any major changes in the racial and ethnic characteristics of all those engaged in farming, including plant-ers, stock raisers and herders, tenants, and laborers as well as farmers. The federal census collected such data beginning only in 1880, and that year it was concerned only with the place of birth. It found that 95.8 per cent were born in the United States, including blacks as well as whites, compared with 95.4 per cent in 1890, 95.9 per cent in 1900, and 97.2 per cent in 1910. Thus no real change occurred. Table 2 shows no significant changes in racial and nativity patterns: 66 to 68 per cent were native whites, 29 to 30 per cent Negro and a very small percentage were immigrants, the largest proportion of whom were German.

Immigrants never figured importantly in terms of numbers in modern Maryland farming. Nevertheless there was an effort throughout the period to divert to the Maryland countryside some of the newcomers pouring into the country to repopulate land abandoned because of the Civil War and the migration of Negro and white farm labor to the city, as well as land left un-cultivated for other reasons. An official immigration commis-sion was established in the 1860's and later a State Bureau of Immigration. Officials traveled to Europe to advertise the state. Pamphlets were written cataloging and extolling its opportuni-ties and resources.

To get much data on the wages for farm labor is difficult, but some idea can be gleaned from the 1901 report of the Bureau of Industrial Statistics of Maryland. Wages remained unchanged at 50 to 75 cents a day from 1890 through 1901.[8] This compares unfavorably with wages for unskilled labor in Baltimore at the time, yet there was constant reference in the immigration drum-mer literature to the scarcity of farm labor making for very high wages and thus adding to the farmers' problems.[9]

The two most important regions for agriculture in the state were the tidewater area, which includes the entire Eastern Shore and part of the Western, and the Blue Ridge division,

---

7. *Ibid.*, p. 213.
8. Maryland, Bureau of Industrial Statistics, *Annual Report: 1901* (Baltimore, 1902), p. 6. (hereafter cited as Maryland, BIS).
9. Maryland, BIS, *Annual Report: 1894*, p. 12 ff.

Tobacco in bloom. A. Aubrey Bodine, *My Maryland.*

which is the Piedmont plateau just behind the tidewater region and extends to the foot of the Catoctin mountains.[10] Agriculture was less profitable in the western part of the state and in the mountains impractical. Tidewater Maryland was traditionally associated with tobacco since colonial times. Tobacco remained an important crop in the southern counties, but truck farming, resuming after the Civil War, grew rapidly, especially on the Eastern Shore. With the growth of railroads in the region a great variety of fruits and vegetables were supplied early in the season to the adjacent and northern cities such as Baltimore, Philadelphia, New York, and even Boston, as well as Washington and Georgetown. By 1909 many thousands of acres on the Eastern Shore were devoted to this type of farming.

The Blue Ridge division includes Montgomery, Howard, Carroll, Frederick, Washington, and the greater part of Baltimore and Harford Counties. With the development of good railroad transportation, truck farming developed here also, supplying northern cities and, in Harford and Baltimore Counties especially, the local canneries. Excellent grasslands enabled dairy farming to be very profitable as well. While corn was grown throughout the state by four out of five farmers in 1910,[11] the highest yields were in this division, particularly in Carroll, Frederick and Washington Counties. These were also the main wheat-growing areas. Germans had settled these counties in considerable numbers since colonial times and engaged successfully in agriculture. Frederick County in particular was renowned for the careful farming and emphasis on agricultural improvement associated with German settlers.

By 1910 the leading crops for the entire state, in the order of their value, were corn, wheat, hay and forage, potatoes and tobacco, the latter two being far behind the others.[12]

2

INDUSTRY

As we have seen, the post-Civil War period was characterized by dramatic industrial development. The contours of

---

10. The description of Maryland agriculture is based largely on James Higgins, *A Succinct Exposition of the Industrial Resources and Agricultural Advantages of the State of Maryland* (Annapolis: Henry Lucas, 1867), *passim*.
11. Maryland, BSI, *Annual Report: 1911*, p. 225.
12. *Ibid.*, p. 224.

Maryland's industrial progress can be quickly established by the following figures. In 1860 the federal census reported a total of over three thousand manufacturing establishments with a capital of a little over $23 million, a labor force of almost twenty-nine thousand and an annual value of product of almost $42 million. By 1890 the number of establishments was 7,485, the aggregate capital $120 million, the average number of workers ninety-eight thousand, and the value of products was $172 million. By 1914 the number of establishments had shrunk to not quite four thousand, the work-force had grown to almost 112 thousand, capital to $293 million, and the value of products to $378 million.[13]

Measured in decades and current dollars, the value of products increased 84 per cent between 1860 and 1870, 39 per cent between 1870 and 1880, 61 per cent the next decade, 41 per cent between 1890 and 1900, almost 50 per cent between 1899 and 1909, and 20 per cent between 1909 and 1914.[14] The average was 55 per cent each decade between 1860 and 1910. Although this is far from a reliable index, in part because of the rise and fall of prices over the period, it at least serves to indicate that economic development did take place. Another indication of this, for which there are only partial figures in the United States census, is the rising proportion of industrial wage earners in the total population of the state: 4 per cent in 1860, 8 per cent in 1880, 9 per cent in 1900 and 8 per cent in 1910.[15]

Maryland was not an industrial giant. Comparing the value of products per capita in Maryland with that of the United States as a whole, Maryland's rate of growth is not so far behind the average of the country. Maryland's per capita value of products more than quadrupled between 1849 and 1909, while that of the United States nearly quintupled between 1850 and 1905. But compared with leading industrial states, Maryland did not fare as well. In 1860 it ranked twelfth in value of products among the states; by 1870 it had dropped to fourteenth; in 1880 it rose

13. U.S., *Eighth Census: 1860, Manufactures*, p. 230; U.S., *Eleventh Census 1890*, II, *Manufacturing*, pt. 1, 55-56; U.S., *Census of Manufactures: 1914*, I, 578-79.

14. U.S., *Census: 1900*, VIII, *Manufactures*, pt. 2, p. 329; U.S., *Census: 1910*, IX, *Manufactures*, pt. 1, 61; U.S., *Census of Manufactures: 1914*, I, 553.

15. U.S., *Census: 1900*, VIII, *Manufactures*, pt. 2, p. 329; U.S., *Census: 1910*, IX, *Manufactures*, pt. 1, 57.

to thirteenth; in 1890, 1900, and 1904 it was fourteenth; in 1909 it was fifteenth and in 1914 it rose again to fourteenth. Thus after 1870 the ranking neither improved nor deteriorated very much. Maryland's proportion of the total value of manufactures for the entire country fell from 3 per cent in 1849 to 1.6 per cent in 1914. Even though Maryland ranked first in the value of products and in the value added by manufactures in 1910 in the South Atlantic United States, which included Delaware, Maryland, Virginia, West Virginia, North Carolina, South Carolina, Georgia and Florida, the region itself was not a leader in manufacturing.[16]

Nor was there one predominant industry within the state throughout the period. Table 3 shows the major industries as gauged by a number of different criteria. For the most part, the same ones appeared under the different categories. Taking the value of products as the most important index, men's clothing emerges as the single most significant industry throughout the entire period, holding first place indeed, from 1880. By 1914 it stood well ahead of the other important manufactures, even when it did not include men's shirts, and thus might be said, by this date, to be the predominant industry of the state. Some form of the iron and steel industry, including foundry products and machinery, also was almost consistently important. Presumably the figures in Table 3 do not include the output of the huge steel plant at Sparrows Point, which the Bureau of Statistics and Information of Maryland in 1912 declared to be "easily the largest and most interesting of Maryland's manufacturing industries."[17] Figures for the iron and steel industry were not given by the federal census in 1909 and 1914 because it would have been tantamount to publishing the particulars of the operations of the Sparrows Point plant since it so dominated the steel industry in Maryland. A third consistently important industry in the state was the canning of fruits and vegetables, which was prominent on the list from 1880 on.

By 1880 three items from the original list of 1860 had been removed: leather, sugar refining, and boots and shoes. Replac-

16. U.S., *Census: 1900*, VIII, *Manufactures*, pt. 2, 329; U.S., *Census: 1890*, II, *Manufacturing*, pt. 1, 6.; U.S., *Census: 1910*, IX, *Manufactures*, 461; U.S., *Census of Manufactures*, I, 553; U.S., *Census: 1910, Manufactures*, pt. 1, 57.
17. Maryland, BSI, *Twenty-first Annual Report: 1912*, p. 123.

ing them were the canning, fertilizer, and iron and steel industries. By 1890 cotton goods were no longer of prime importance and were replaced by copper, tin and sheet-iron works. Finally, after 1900 flouring and grist mill products disappeared from the list and slaughtering and meat packing came into the picture. A comparison of the main industries in 1860 with those in 1914 shows that while most of the individual ones had changed, it was still light industry that remained predominant throughout the period, except after 1910 when the steel industry became the largest in the state.

In comparison with other states, Maryland ranked sixth in the value of product of men's clothing in 1860, and fourth in 1900, 1909, and 1914.[18] Figures are scarce for the canning of fruits and vegetables, but the importance of the state in this area can be appreciated from the fact that in 1900 and 1905 it ranked second in the nation in value of the product. Indeed, Maryland had been an important producer from the early history of the industry around 1850. In 1904, when canning was a major industry in the nation, it ranked third in value of product of all three types of canning combined: fruits and vegetables, fish and oysters, pickles, sauces and preserves. In the canning of oysters Maryland was preeminent, ranking first in 1900. Unfortunately, this branch of the industry did not have so large a value of product as that of fruits and vegetables.[19] The fertilizer industry dated from 1832. By 1879 Maryland was the national leader for this manufacture and remained so until 1904, when it slipped to second place.[20]

Other locally important products achieved only undistinguished national rank. In 1900 Maryland ranked eleventh in iron and steel, fifteenth in slaughtering and meat packing (which rose to ninth in 1914), thirty-second in lumber and timber products, thirteenth in cotton goods, and eighteenth in flour and grist mill products.[21]

The federal census omitted two very important industries in its tabulations, petroleum refining and copper smelting and refining, because figures would disclose the operations of individ-

18. U.S., *Census of Manufactures: 1914*, I, 555.

19. U.S., *Census: 1910*, IX, *Manufactures*, 463; U.S., *Census: 1900*, VIII, *Manufactures*, pt. 1, clxxxiv.

20. U.S., *Census: 1910*, IX, *Manufactures*, 463-64.

21. U.S., *Census: 1900*, VIII, *Manufactures*, pt. 1, clxxxiv.

ual firms. For example, there were only three petroleum refineries in 1880 and 1890, which then consolidated into one.
There were fewer than three establishments in the refining of
copper in 1905.[22] Thus there is no way of knowing where these
two industries fitted in relation to the top six industries of the
state as determined by census data.

Another industry omitted from the above discussion is mining. It hardly rises above the level of local interest and color
in this period. Bituminous coal was by far the most important
mineral mined in the state. Coal mining in western Maryland
developed rapidly in the 1840's to 1860, suffered a setback in
the early years of the Civil War due to the disruption of the
transportation systems by the Confederate forces, then revived
and grew from 1863 for a decade. With the general industrial
activity of the 1880's coal mining expanded and prospered.
However, in value of product it was not among the top six industries of the state. In 1860 the value of product was only $464
thousand. Even though the industry ranked fourth in the nation
in 1870 and 1880, its worth in 1870 was only somewhat over $2
million, and in 1880 and 1890 it was under $3 million. In 1902
the census evaluated it under $6 million, and in 1909 under $5
million.[23]

The Cumberland coal field supplied all the coal mined in
the state and had been operated since the early nineteenth century. The area was about twenty-five miles long and five miles
wide, but only about one-half of the field was actually
worked, with most attention centered on the "Big Vein," a
fourteen-foot seam. Most of the mining was in Allegany County,
just west of Cumberland, in what is called the Frostburg basin
or George's Creek basin. The latter was named for the river that
drains the region. A string of mining towns lies in the area, the
most important of which are Frostburg, Lonaconing, and West-
ernport.

The nearest bituminous field to the North Atlantic seaboard,
this area supplied a high grade of coal used to produce steam.
The operators shipped coal down the Chesapeake and Ohio
Canal or on the Baltimore and Ohio Railroad to be marketed

22. U.S., *Census: 1890*, II, *Manufacturing*, pt. 3, 360; U.S., *Census of Manufactures: 1905*, pt. 1, p. ccxxxvii.
23. U.S., Bureau of the Census, *Special Report on Mines and Quarries: 1902*,
pp. 229-30; U.S., *Census: 1910*, XI, *Mines and Quarries*, 95.

primarily in northern coastal cities. The executives and main offices of the mining companies were mostly located in Baltimore. The largest and best known company was the Consolidation Coal Company, which was organized in 1860 and capitalized at well over a million dollars in 1880. By 1870 it controlled half the coal lands and all of the local railroad facilities in the area. By 1909, through further mergers, it became the largest coal mining concern in the country.[24]

Iron ore had been mined in Maryland since colonial days, but by the second half of the nineteenth century was of only marginal importance. As measured by tons produced, Maryland ranked seventh in the nation in 1860, fifth in 1870, ninth in 1880 and then plummeted to eighteenth in 1889. In 1880 the value of product was merely $422 thousand. By 1909 this had slipped drastically to $44 thousand.[25] Nor was the quarrying of granite and limestone of sufficient importance to be considered among the leading industries of the state.

Two major influences on the course of Maryland's economic development remain outside the direct scope of the federal census: the impact of the Civil War and business cycles. The Civil War had a dual effect on Maryland's industrial economy: an initial recession which started just before the outbreak of the war and remained in certain lines of economic activity, and a gradual readjustment of the economy to wartime demands and opportunities, beginning about 1862.[26] Being a border state with many economic ties to the South, uneasiness about the political instability and the possibility of a coming conflict caused a tightening of credit and a retraction of trade in Baltimore and most of Maryland. The recession deepened in April 1861 with a sharp depression of trade affecting especially traffic in dry goods, hardware, provisions, guano, and whiskey with the South and Southwest. Manufacturing slumped and unemployment soared in Baltimore and western Maryland particu-

24. Katherine A. Harvey, *The Best Dressed Miners, Life and Labor in the Maryland Coal Region, 1835–1910* (Ithaca: Cornell University Press, 1969), pp. 166, 360.
25. U.S., *Census: 1890, Report on Mineral Industries in the United States,* p. 14; U.S., Bureau of the Census, *Special Report on Mines and Quarries: 1902,* p. 229; U.S., *Census: 1910,* XI, *Mines and Quarries,* 95.
26. This discussion is based on Richard R. Duncan, "The Social and Economic Impact of the Civil War on Maryland," Chapters I-IV.

larly. Severe shortages of cotton and South Carolina rice struck Baltimore. The Baltimore and Ohio Railroad was very vulnerable to damage by Confederate raids and the invasion of southern armies, since much track lay on the border between Maryland and West Virginia. In the early months of the war the railroad was maintained with great difficulty. The Chesapeake and Ohio Canal suffered many of the same problems of interruptions in service with the result that the supply of Cumberland coal in Baltimore was seriously curtailed. Sharp restrictions on Baltimore trade irritated local businessmen, who felt that the military authorities went beyond the dictates of military necessity to discriminate against the city in favor of northern cities. Federal authorities commandeered vessels for troops and supplies, virtually ending Baltimore's coastal trade with the North, and a strict surveillance of ships and railroads prevented trade with the South.

By 1862 the economic picture began to improve. Government contracts played an increasingly important role, so that by 1863 Baltimore enjoyed prosperity and economic stability. The federal government spent liberally for supplies, produce, and transportation, and by 1863 its influence was pervasive, directly or indirectly, in many sectors of the state's economy. The flour trade revived and flourished, supplying both the federal army and South American markets. The iron, copper, and shipbuilding industries boomed. Both the Baltimore and Ohio and the Northern Central railroads profited from servicing the government. The petroleum industry began to prosper in Baltimore with a growing number of refineries, and the coal trade revived with the improvement of transportation services. The foreign commerce of Baltimore picked up after reaching an initial plateau and decline. Thus despite the loss of southern markets and persistent problems of inflation and disruptions of rail and canal traffic, Maryland's economy adjusted to the war and in certain sectors even prospered.

The other aspect of economic development which is only incidentally treated in the census is business cycles. Recording the economy every ten years does not reveal adequately its instabilities. Most dramatic, of course, in terms of human suffering are the depressions. Long and severe ones occurred following 1873 and 1893, and shorter ones following 1865, 1882, 1904, and 1907.

3

INDUSTRIAL GROWTH OF BALTIMORE

Throughout the period, Baltimore was the leader and center for manufactures in Maryland. The primacy of commerce in Baltimore, like that of agriculture in the state, began to give way in this period to industry. In 1890 the federal census reported for the first time a gross value of products of manufactures for the city that surpassed the overall value of her foreign trade. It is unlikely that manufacturing outranked in value the entire commercial sector, including the domestic trade, both coastal and interior, but it is incontestible that manufacturing rose to greater prominence in Baltimore than ever before and helped to change the character of the city.

Baltimore's industrial preeminence in the state is clear from the census figures on the ratio of the aggregate value of product for the city to that of the whole state. In 1860 Baltimore accounted for 50.5 per cent of Maryland's total value of products, in 1880 73.4 per cent, in 1890 82.5 per cent, in 1900 66.5 per cent, in 1910 59 per cent and in 1914 57 per cent. Figures are not available for 1870. The growth from 1860 to 1890 is what one would expect. Several circumstances explain the subsequent decline. First, the largest drop came in the 1890's. Of this decade the census noted that a number of industries experienced a decline, namely, brick and stone masonry, brass castings and finishing, planing mill lumber products, and glass. Boots and shoes and musical instruments fell off too, but by smaller amounts. Secondly, a change in the method of classification by the census served to reduce the value of canning and preserving fruits and vegetables. In this industry there was also a certain amount of migration out of the city to be nearer the source of supply. Baltimore's proportion of the industry declined from 75 per cent in 1900 to 48 per cent in 1905. The canning of oysters, however, remained largely in the city.[27]

Finally, some of the decline can be attributed to the movement of industry to the suburbs, which was a characteristic of urban development of this period. Improved transportation and electric power enabled industry to move out of the central city

27. U.S., *Census: 1900*, VIII, *Manufactures*, pt. 2, cclxxxiii-cclxxxiv, U.S., *Census of Manufactures: 1905*, pt. 2, p. 398.

Urban Transportation West Baltimore Street, Baltimore, during the late 1880's.
*M.H.S.*

to take advantage of lower rents and taxes and the greater availability of space. In the early twentieth century decentralization of industry was a general pattern among industrial cities and towns and was clearly indicated in manufacturing statistics. Furthermore, a study by the federal census for the period 1899–1904 shows a greater growth of the labor force in the suburbs than in the central city in twelve of the thirteen largest industrial districts.[28] Of course, industry moved even beyond the suburbs as the Maryland Bureau of Industrial Statistics and Information noted in its 1890 report.

> Many of the manufacturers of Maryland have during the past years, sought more advantageous locations in the rural districts for the conduct of their business, notably, in the towns of Laurel, Frederick, Hagerstown and Cumberland in the west, and Havre de Grace, Cambridge, Easton and Salisbury in the east. In many of these towns new factories have been erected and many hands have been given employment to the great advantage of the rural population.[29]

Interestingly enough, the census noted in 1900 that Maryland was one of the few exceptions to the rule that the average manufacturing establishment in urban districts was much larger than in the rural.[30]

Table 4 presents the percentage of growth in value of product for all Baltimore industries combined for each census year from 1880 to 1914. According to this index of aggregate growth, the decade of the 1880's appears the most vigorous and indeed outstripped the state's rate of growth (61 per cent).[31] The smallest progress is shown for the 1890's which, of course, reflects the prolonged depression in that decade, and also, very likely, the accelerated movement of industry out of the city as mentioned above. The rate of growth for the state was 41 per cent, far greater than that of the city. On the other hand, the percentage of growth for the decade 1899–1909 was 35.6, which indicates a strong comeback in a period marred by the great fire as well as a short recession in 1904, and a sharp plunge in 1907.

28. Charles N. Glaab and A. Theodore Brown, A History of Urban America (New York, Macmillan Co., 1967), pp. 275, 277.
29. Maryland, Bureau of Industrial Statistics and Information, Fourth Biennial Report; 1890–91 (Baltimore: 1892), p. 6 (hereafter cited as BISI.).
30. U.S., Census: 1900, VIII, Manufactures, pt. 1, ccxxiv.
31. Ibid., p. cclxxxiii.

Table 5 at the end of the chapter presents the major industries in Baltimore by value of product. There are no figures available for 1870; hence those for Baltimore County are used for that year. They give a rough idea of Baltimore's industrial activity. Despite the constant qualifying and regrouping of the categories used by the censuses, it is clear that the most consistently important industries were: men's clothing, canning (first of oysters and then of fruits and vegetables), foundry and machine shop products, slaughtering and meat packing, tin, copper and sheet ironware, and tobacco. Sugar refining and boots and shoes disappeared and printing and publishing, and car construction and repair of the rolling stock of steam railroads (which in the tables is abbreviated to cars) joined the list.

Changing the criterion of measurement of industrial importance, Table 6 (at the end of the chapter) presents three possible alternatives: the amount of capital, the average number of wage earners, and the net value of production (or value added by manufacture). No figures for the latter are available for 1860 and 1870, and again in 1870 figures for Baltimore County had to be used. The amount of capital is admittedly a very uncertain standard to apply. The authorities responsible for the census itself from 1880 through 1914 were agreed on the special partiality to error of the statistics collected under this rubric, since few establishments had an accounting system capable of calculating accurately the return from capital. Despite their inadequacies the figures for capital do not turn up any surprises. In fact, the conclusion is clear that no matter which of the four criteria of measurement is used, very much the same industries emerged as the leaders with simply small changes of position over the period. However, the importance of the fertilizer, printing and publishing, and malt liquor industries is revealed more clearly by the figures on capital, labor force, and net value of production.

Implicit in all the above discussion and tabulations based on census reports is the reservation that the figures cited are by no means necessarily or probably complete. Not only can individual firms be omitted from an industrial count but also whole fields of industry can be lumped together at the end of each itemization of manufactures in the census as "all other industries" to avoid disclosing the operations of any individual firm. In the 1914 census of manufactures, for example, it was noted that twenty-one industries were omitted, of which fourteen reported values of product as exceeding $1 million.

Likewise buried beneath all the foregoing discussion is another reservation: all that has been said concerns only manufacturing inside the boundaries of the incorporated city of Baltimore. Gradually the census became aware of the importance of suburbs to complete the industrial picture. Statistics began to be collected to this end in 1899 for the "metropolitan district." Briefly stated, the metropolitan district of Baltimore experienced the following growth within the period 1899–1914. The population grew from 577,670 to 693,253, an increase of 17.9 per cent. The number of manufacturing establishments rose from 2,352 to 2,698, or 14 per cent. The average number of wage earners increased from 71,688 to 84,937, or 16.2 per cent. The value of products rose 66 per cent from almost $177 million to almost $314 million, while the value added by manufactures increased by 57.6 per cent from about $68 million to $113 million. In this last category Baltimore's metropolitan district ranked ninth in 1914 among others in the nation. Naturally Baltimore proper always dominated the metropolitan district throughout the period measured and in 1914 accounted for 83 per cent of the district's population, 68 per cent of the value of products, 92.7 per cent of the manufacturing establishments and 86.9 per cent of the wage earners.[32]

Taking into account the wider area of Baltimore business activity does not, therefore, fundamentally alter the industrial profile given above which was for the incorporated section of the city. The major industry of the metropolitan district was clothing, which was located entirely within the bounds of the city proper. The industries which operated to an important extent in the part of the district which was not inside the city limits also in 1914 figure heavily within the city limits, namely, copper, tin and sheet-ironware products, malt liquors, and slaughtering and meat packing.

The same limitations, of course, plague the census figures for the metropolitan district as for the city. Particularly distressing is the necessity for the census to leave totally out of considera-

32. U.S., *Census of Manufactures: 1914*, I, 563; U.S., *Census: 1910*, X, *Manufactures, 1909*, 963-64; U.S., *Census of Manufactures: 1914*, I, 563-64.

tion such industries as petroleum and copper refining, both of which operated extensively in Canton, on a national scale of importance.

The steel industry at Sparrows Point, which likewise was of immense significance, had to be skipped because, as in the other two cases above, one firm so dominated the field that any figures would in effect reveal its operations. Thus it is necessary to supplement the evidence from even the metropolitan census to gain an accurate picture of the major industries of Baltimore in this period.

The overlap between the major industries of Maryland and Baltimore, and hence the industrial importance of Baltimore to the state, is strikingly evident from a comparison of the figures for value of product in Tables 3 and 5. They repeatedly show the high proportion of Maryland's value of product accounted for by Baltimore. Indeed, the only major industries on the list located largely outside the city were flour milling and cotton goods. This comparison, of course, is confined to the top six industries in both state and city and merely presents a telescoped view of the city's industrial leadership within the state. Presumably a more expansive list would show its predominance more completely.

Of considerable interest are the operations, sources of raw materials, markets and some problems of the major industries in Baltimore. The manufacturing of ready-to-wear clothing in Baltimore had begun before the Civil War, as early as 1838, reaching sizeable proportions by 1859, when it emerged a national leader in the field. The Civil War brought disruption with the loss of the southern and western markets.[33] After the war, however, these were regained and the growth of the industry resumed, particularly rapidly after 1870. By 1880 local firms were constantly competing with New York for supplying the West and the South. The South at this time was purchasing over one third of Baltimore's output and the Middle West about one fourth. Surprisingly, an amount equivalent to about one-third of the value sent to the South was consumed in New York and New England. By 1895 Baltimore practically dominated the

---

33. Maryland, State Planning Commission, "Report on Men's Clothing Industry," by A. A. Imberman (mimeographed, 1936), p. 15.

southern market for boys' and men's clothing, and this remained the case for the rest of the period.[34] Because of the emphasis on the southern trade, summer clothes were a local specialty. The market was not confined exclusively to the South, however, but rather by 1914 had become definitely a national one in response to the national advertising of several local companies. Indeed, clothing was one of the few Baltimore manufactures that was well advertised by this latter date. As of 1883, the materials came mainly from New York and New England. As of 1914, production was concentrated on the medium and high-priced grades.[35]

The related industry of shirts, overalls, and underwear was also a most active one throughout this period, competing vigorously with Troy, New York, the acknowledged center of men's furnishings. By 1883 Baltimore had built up a large business in overalls, which went mainly to the South and the West. Ladies underwear too became something of a specialty, supplying both northern and western markets as well as New York, which drew heavily on Baltimore output in this field. Shirts were made mainly from northern cotton textiles and marketed in the South and West, following the routes of the general dry goods jobbing trade. By 1914 the picture had shifted somewhat. The overalls were being made from the cheap southern textiles and marketed all over the country. Even dress shirt manufacturers were using southern textiles increasingly and by this time were having difficulty meeting the competition from Troy. Certain types of men's underwear and pajamas were, however, of growing importance and made Baltimore a leader in this area. The materials were from both New England and southern mills, and the market was national but with a southern emphasis.[36] Looking beyond Baltimore's activity in this field for a moment one finds that the manufacture of ready-to-wear clothing was a major industry in the nation and a kind of index to industrialism as it gave

---

34. Charles Hirschfeld, *Baltimore, 1870–1900: Studies in Social History* (Baltimore: J.H. Press, 1941), p. 41; John R. Bland, *A Review of the Commerce of the City of Baltimore* (Baltimore, n.d.), p. 86.
35. *Industrial Survey of Baltimore: Report of Industries Located Within the Baltimore Metropolitan District* (Baltimore: 1914), p. 34. (Hereafter cited as *Industrial Survey*); Bland, *Review of Commerce*, p. 86.
36. Bland, p. 102; *Industrial Survey*, pp. 35-37.

a clear view of the increasing reliance on standardized factory products, which were eventually sold all over the country.

Sugar refining dated back at least to the early nineteenth century in Baltimore and by the early 1870's there were four refineries and two establishments preparing sugar from molasses and supplying a western as well as a local market. By the early 1880's, however, the business was extinct. Baltimore producers apparently floundered somewhere on the shoals of import duties, drawbacks, and price wars in a business that was becoming highly centralized in the hands of a few big firms in New York, Philadelphia and Boston.[37]

The boot and shoe industry expanded rapidly in Baltimore during the 1860's in response to the introduction of power machinery and the growth of the leather-tanning business in Maryland. By 1870 twenty-six wholesale manufacturers flourished in the city, supplying not only the local needs but also the South and West. By the early 1880's at least, production was geared mainly to the out-of-state markets.[38]

Baltimore had been a center of the canning industry since the 1840's, and indeed was called "the cradle of the canning industry."[39] Initially, oysters were the main product, the packing season lasting from September through April. In the summer the canneries turned their attention to fruits and vegetables, although on a much smaller scale. In 1870 over a hundred packing houses were thriving in Baltimore, supplying a national market as well as Europe and even the Far East. By the mid 1880's fruits and vegetables became the more important branch of the industry locally, outstripping the packing of oysters in value of product. Until the turn of the century, however, Baltimore remained the leading center for oyster packing. By 1914 fruits and vegetables constituted 97 per cent of the value of product for the entire canning industry. This branch of the industry supplied a national, and to some extent, a foreign market. However, by the turn of the century, Maryland was slip-

---

37. Victor S. Clark, *History of Manufactures in the United States* (1929 ed.; New York: Peter Smith, 1949), I, 304 and II, 511; George W. Howard, *The Monumental City, its Past History and Present Resources* (Baltimore: Ehlers & Co., 1873), p. 115; Hirschfeld, p. 44.
38. Clark, II, 131; Howard, p. 161; Bland, p. 84-85.
39. U.S., *Census: 1900*, IX, *Manufactures*, pt. 3, 480.

Oyster dredging on the Choptank. A. Aubrey Bodine, *My Maryland.*

416

ping from its national number-one position.[40] This was not due to lack of enterprise, the Maryland Bureau of Industrial Statistics believed, but rather to a relative lack of produce at hand compared with the amount grown in larger agricultural states. Vegetables were always more important in Maryland canning than fruits. In 1910 the state packed 46 per cent of the entire tomato pack of the country, 9 per cent of the corn, and 5 per cent of the peas. By 1914 tomatoes were the single most important item packed, making up about two-fifths of all of the tomatoes canned commercially in the country. Oysters came next in importance. The city had, however, dropped radically in its national standing in the canning of peas, from first to sixth place. Further loss had come when pineapple canning, which had been centered in Baltimore, moved to the islands of supply around 1904. Nevertheless, from 1910 on the industry as a whole showed very strong growth.[41]

The fertilizer industry had been first established in the United States in Baltimore about 1850. Initially it relied heavily on the importation of guano from the West Indies, Peru, and Chile. Later this was replaced by crude phosphate rock after the discovery of extensive deposits in South Carolina. By the early 1880's, phosphate rock formed the main ingredient in the local manufacture. But with this change in raw material the industry by the 1890's began to move south, closer not only to the source of supply but also to the main market, the cotton fields. At this time the South used more fertilizer than any other section of the country. Baltimore's early predominance began to wane. By 1914, however, the local industry was reported to be in excellent shape, with Baltimore described as the largest fertilizer manufacturing center in the world and growing every year. The market had been expanding at the rate of about 10 per cent per year for the previous few years largely due to the intensive educational efforts of the Department of Agriculture and various state agricultural colleges. The South constituted an increasing proportion of the market (about 60 per cent in 1914) not only because of its cotton but also because of its expanding acreage in truck and intensive farming. The demand

40. U.S., *Census of Manufactures: 1914*, I, 555; Howard, pp. 101-102.
41. Maryland, BIS, *Tenth Annual Report: 1901*, p. 74; *Industrial Survey*, p. 13; Maryland, BSI, *Annual Report: 1910*, p. 193.

Girls canning oysters. Interior view of Gibbs Preserving Oyster Company, Baltimore, ca. 1910. *M.H.S.*

418

from the West was of next importance and constantly increasing.[42]

Foundries and machine shops embraced a variety of specialties. The manufacture of machinery, although very hard hit by the depression in the 1890's, supplied a national and a foreign market. In the 1880's it had supplied the South as well, but by 1896, at least, this area was no longer an important market for Baltimore machinery. Freight rates were blamed by the producers for this loss. By 1914, Baltimore was the leader in the number and the value of machines made for the canning industry. The market for these, incidentally, was not local but largely out of town, where the new canning establishments were rising and giving the local canning industry increasing competition. Baltimore was also important in the field of machinery to make tin cans, a close corollary of the canning industry. A great variety of other types of machines was made here, such as turbine water wheels, boilers, engines, and machinery for breweries as well as for preparing fertilizer and tobacco.[43]

Architectural iron work, iron bridges, stoves, furnaces, and steam-heating apparatus were marketed widely throughout the country in this period with no one section attaining specific preponderance. In the larger firms, quite often, iron foundries formed part of the same company as machine shops, but in most instances they were separate by at least 1914. They supplied mainly the local market, in many cases machine shops. About 40 per cent of their output was shipped to a geographically limited market of nearby points in the state, the District of Columbia and Pennsylvania. The weight of the products, mainly iron castings, combined with the slim margin of profits to make it imperative to minimize freight charges and thus to limit the extent of the market. The general complexion of these three related branches of activity was one of health throughout the period, except, of course, for the serious setback in the 1890's. In general, this was an area of steady importance rather than spectacular growth.[44]

Slaughtering and meat packing was a notably growing and healthy industry in Baltimore throughout this period. It is an ex-

---

42. Clark, III, 289; Bland, p. 91; *Industrial Survey,* pp. 7–8.
43. Maryland, BIS, *Fifth Annual Report,* p. 14; *Industrial Survey,* p. 17.
44. Bland, p. 98; *Industrial Survey,* pp. 18–19.

cellent illustration both of an industry which was growing to fill
the demands of the increasing and increasingly urban market,
and also of local resistance to the western meat packers' attempt
to build up a national market. In 1914 the local situation was so
strong that it was reported that slaughtering was "fast becoming
the leading industry of Baltimore."[45] Although aggressive competition from the western packers as well as local restrictions
on the location of the plants were considered serious threats to
continued growth, vigorous effort on the part of the local industry was, for the time being, it seemed, retarding the inroads of
outside suppliers. The energies of the local packers were
mainly directed towards "educating" the local butchers and
banding together to sell the offal.[46] This was in partial imitation
of some of the big western packers who had realized the commercial value of this by-product and had gone into the fertilizer business on the side.

Tin, copper, and sheet-iron ware manufactures really lump
together several quite separate and independently important
industries. Tin itself was manufactured in Baltimore for a variety of purposes, especially for roofing and household cooking
articles. The market for these was increasing in this period with
the growth of the city. The local canning industry promoted a
large manufacture of tinware in the making of tin cans and consumed in 1883 an estimated eighty to a hundred million cans.
The market for all the types of tin goods discussed above extended beyond the local scene to include the rest of the state,
Pennsylvania and the South. The tin plate necessary in all these
manufactures was imported, presumably from Britain, as that
was the prevalent practice before the McKinley tariff (1890)
boosted the domestic manufacture of the plate. The replacement of handmade by machine-made cans began in 1880 and
was nearly complete by 1896, when the great majority of can-
making factories used the fully mechanized process whereby a
can was made by machine from a piece of sheet tin. As a result,
output was increased and the price of cans reduced. By 1914
Baltimore was making more tin cans than any other city in the
United States and was supplying a national market. Local demand accounted for only 15 per cent of the output, even though

---

45. Industrial Survey, p. 13.
46. *Ibid.*, pp. 13-14.

the local canners bought all their cans from Baltimore producers. About 50 per cent was sold within two hundred miles of Baltimore and the rest distributed over the country. There was also some export trade, which was on the increase. By 1914 the sheet tin for this product was supplied almost entirely by Pittsburgh.[47]

The processing of copper in Baltimore dates back to the first half of the nineteenth century, when the city was a center of copper refining along with New York and Boston. The industry was located in these shipbuilding ports because the materials were imported and much of the product was used in shipbuilding. After some difficulties immediately following the Civil War, the industry resumed its local importance. The business, as was previously mentioned, was located in Canton. In 1883 the smelting of copper was reported to have been of large proportions, producing up to 20 million pounds annually. The ores, which had always been imported from Cuba and Chile, after 1869 came mainly from Arizona and Montana. Despite the increasing tendency for the refining industry to move west to be closer to the enormous domestic sources which were being increasingly exploited, much of the Montana ore was still being shipped to Baltimore in 1892. In response to the tendency to smelt the ore at the mine, however, Baltimore's role shifted somewhat. Increasingly copper came to Baltimore in the form of pig to be refined and rolled into sheet. The electrolytic refining plant which was built at Canton in 1891 was the largest in the country. In 1907 the American Smelting and Refining Company gained control of the Baltimore Copper Smelting and Rolling Company, which had an annual output of 144 million pounds. By 1914 Baltimore ranked first in the nation for the amount of copper smelted and rolled. The value of the smelting and refining works, together with the coppersmithing business, was estimated at $20 million in 1912. Baltimore supplied a world market, but particularly Europe and the United States.[48] The strong demand for this semimanufacture was excellent evidence of the tide of urbanization and the dimensions of the

47. Bland, p. 104; Clark, II, 373; Hirschfeld, p. 34; *Industrial Survey*, p. 44.
48. Bland, p. 104; Clark, II, 97, & 368-369; E. Emmet Reid, "Commerce and Manufactures of Baltimore," *Baltimore, Its History and Its People*, ed. Hall, I, 525; Maryland, BISI, *Twenty-first Annual Report*, p. 184; *Industrial Survey*, p. 50; *The Sun*, Dec. 24, 1910, p. 16; Clark, I, 525.

urban market, since copper was a mainstay of electrical equipment in lighting city streets and buildings.

In the tobacco industry Baltimore had the advantage of being near some of the sources of supply; hence some form of the manufactured product was important throughout almost the entire period, especially if one looks beneath the top six industries. In 1883 the tobacco came from four areas: 53 per cent from Virginia and North Carolina, 20 per cent from Maryland, Ohio and Kentucky, 15 per cent from Pennsylvania, Connecticut, and Wisconsin, and 10 per cent from Cuba and other foreign sources. In the early 1880's Baltimore's tobacco products were distributed to a national market with 53 per cent to the West, 20 per cent to the South, and 27 per cent to Pennsylvania, New York and New England. Cigars were manufactured extensively in the 1860's and 1870's; but as in the national tobacco industry, cigarettes showed the most striking growth in this period. This again reflected the growth of the urban market since cigarettes were sold mainly in cities. Unfortunately only sparse information is available on the snuff and smoking tobacco branch of the industry, which was well established in Baltimore with several large factories. Their brands were well known in Europe as well as in this country.[49] In 1891 they were bought out by the American Tobacco Company, and thereafter no figures are available in the census as they would reveal the operations of a single firm, a practice which the census authorities were careful to avoid.

Cotton textiles were a major part of the economy of Baltimore, for although all but two of the mills were located outside the city, they were owned by Baltimore men, had their central offices in the city, were run by Baltimore capital, and their products were marketed through Baltimore. An estimate of the value of product in 1883 of over $6 million and of the value added by manufacture of almost $2 million established the industry as one of the leaders in the city. It was ignored, however, by the census, which canvassed only the part of Baltimore that was incorporated. Then, of course, several of the mills were outside even the metropolitan district. Most, however, were clustered at Woodberry, which, until it was annexed in 1888, was a small manufacturing town in Baltimore County. In 1883 there were

---

49. Bland, p. 105; Clark, II, 513; Maryland, BIS, *Sixth Annual Report*, p. 60.

altogether twenty-one mills with a total of 128,514 spindles, 2,469 looms, and a labor force of about 4,795. A great variety of goods was produced, such as shirtings, sheetings, drills, yarns, netting, and twine. A very heavy grade of cotton duck was the main product, for which the Baltimore area was the manufacturing center for the entire country. Duck had been made in this area well before the Civil War and had then received a great impetus from the war demand. After the war the manufacturers had expanded their facilities further. By 1883 it was estimated that this area had more than double the number of duck looms in the rest of the country and produced about four-fifths of all this fabric in the United States. At this time the duck and heavy goods had a world market, while the lighter goods were distributed on the national market.[50] By 1889 the number of mills had increased to twenty-five with a total of 175,642 spindles and 3,536 looms. In 1894 a rough estimate of the value of cotton manufactures was $16 million. By 1914 the emphasis was still on heavy goods and Baltimore still led in the production of cotton duck. Although formerly most of the duck had been used for sails, this demand, of course, had fallen off dramatically and now only about 1 per cent of the output was used for that purpose. By this time it was used principally for awnings, grain conveyors, deck and life boat coverings, and tents,[51] which very probably meant a lessening of the importance of the local industry, although there are no readily available figures to prove this.

Baltimore had always been the leading iron center in Maryland, and it established a reputation for high-quality charcoal pig. In the late nineteenth century with the introduction of new technological methods, the importation of iron ores expanded into importance about 1880 to meet the needs of eastern steelmakers for high grade Bessemer pig. Baltimore was a point of importation of these ores from northern Spain and Algiers. In the late 1880's ore from Cuba was also coming into Baltimore. Despite the tradition of Peter Cooper, who had owned and operated iron forges here that eventually became the well-known Abbott Iron Works, maker of iron plate and armor for ships

50. *Manufacturers' Record*, Sept. 29, 1883, p. 196. (Hereafter cited as *M.R.*); Bland, p. 88.
51. *M.R.*, Aug. 10, 1889; George W. Engelhardt, *Baltimore City, Maryland* ([Baltimore]: 1895), p. 133; *Industrial Survey*, pp. 33-34.

in the Civil War, iron and steel production at Baltimore was not impressive in the 1880's.[52] This was the transitional period, not only in metallurgical methods in the industry, but also in transportation. Furnaces in uneconomic locations in terms of the new technology were being dismantled in favor of increased output in better-located plants. In Baltimore the shift was made away from the small-furnace production of charcoal iron to large-scale production in 1889, when the first of four giant furnaces at the new steel plant at Sparrows Point went into blast. The tract of land at Sparrows Point had been bought in 1887 by the Pennsylvania Steel Company. The plant, although built by that company, was nominally owned by the Maryland Steel Company, which was closely tied in with the parent company just noted. By 1891 three blast furnaces were in operation, and Bessemer steel was beginning to be produced. The next year an annual capacity of 400,000 tons of steel had been reached, and the shipbuilding division began operation. The location was convenient to the raw materials, the Cuban and Mediterranean ores, the Pennsylvania coke and the Baltimore County limestone. The site had been selected also with distribution in mind. Much of the output was in the form of rails, about one-half of which went to foreign customers. Bleak times came, however, when 1893 brought a prolonged, though not permanent, setback. The industry was extremely hard hit by the depression; production had to be cut back and parts of the plant idled. The company itself went into receivership and had to be reorganized administratively as well as financially. After 1896 the picture brightened, production rose impressively, and the turn of the century proved to be a period of rapid expansion. The census for 1909, necessarily vague to avoid revealing a firm's operations, stated that the combined value of product of the steel works, blast furnaces, steel shipbuilding yards and coke ovens reached into the millions. The census of 1914 simply asserted that the steel works at Sparrows Point were among the most important in the country.[53]

In two moves, one in 1875 and the other in 1877, the Standard Oil Company successfully took over the oil refining indus-

---

52. Reid, p. 525; Clark, II, 198, 204; *M.R.*, Sept. 4, 1886, p. 115; Reid, p. 526.
53. Clark, II, 199-200, 204, 232; Reid, p. 527; Clark, III, 38; Maryland, BIS, *Fifth Annual Report*, p. 18; U.S., *Census: 1910*, IX, *Manufactures, 1909*, p. 963; U.S., *Census of Manufactures: 1914*, I, 564.

try in Baltimore. Later, the city's oil industry was placed under the jurisdiction of Jersey Standard. Although few figures are available, the indications are that the refining business was expanding locally in this period. In 1883 the estimated capacity for refining crude oil was about 800,000 barrels per year. Most of the crude oil came directly by pipe line from Pennsylvania, and, to a less extent, West Virginia, with only a relatively small amount handled by rail. The refined product was distributed domestically throughout the state and to Virgina, the Carolinas, and Georgia. The export trade amounted roughly to three-quarters of the amount of the domestic consumption. The combined value of the two in 1883 was not quite $2½ million. The plant was enlarged in 1895, and between 1893 and 1897 its consumption of crude oil increased by 67 per cent. By 1906 the refinery at Baltimore had a daily capacity of 6,046 barrels, a total that by 1911 had risen slightly to 6,654 barrels. Despite its progress it was the smallest of the three refining plants operated directly by the parent company.[54]

Finally, there are two manufactures traditionally associated with Baltimore which were more famous than quantitatively important: rye whiskey and straw hats. Before the Civil War Maryland distilleries had achieved an excellent reputation for the quality of their whiskey. In 1880 the industry was very active, producing over 1,500,000 gallons. Approximately 50 per cent was consumed in the North, 25 per cent in the South and Southwest and the rest locally. By 1913 output had risen to about 4,750,000 gallons, of which 85 per cent was distilled in the unincorporated part of the metropolitan district.

The manufacture of straw hats was very insignificant in Baltimore in 1870, but by 1883 the value of product was about $852,-000, and the business was reported as steadily growing. From the beginning the quality was very high.[55] By 1914 it was observed that "for more than a generation Baltimore had led the country in both the amount and factory value of product in this industry."[56] Whereas formerly the market had been largely in

54. Ralph W. Hidy and Muriel E. Hidy, *Pioneering in Big Business, 1882–1911* (New York: Harper, 1955), pp. 18-20, 290; Bland, pp. 74-75; Hidy and Hidy, pp. 289, 291, 414, 420-21.
55. Bland, p. 90 and 67; *Industrial Survey*, p. 4; Hirschfeld, p. 45.
56. *Industrial Survey*, p. 49.

the South, by 1914 it was nationwide and included Canada as well.

Finally, it is important to consider Baltimore's industrial position in the nation. The city ranked among the leading industrial cities in this period, but with increasing difficulty. Unfortunately, figures are lacking for the years prior to 1880. Baltimore slipped from eighth place in 1880 to eleventh by 1914 as measured by the gross value of product (see Table 7). On the basis of this scale the cities which ranked ahead of Baltimore by 1914 were: (1) New York (decidedly first), (2) Chicago, (3) Philadelphia, (4) Detroit, (5) St. Louis, (6) Cleveland, (7) Boston, (8) Buffalo, (9) Pittsburgh, and (10) Milwaukee.[57] Baltimore's loss of pace with other leaders was slow until 1909. It clung to eighth place until 1905, when it dipped to ninth. In 1909 it plummeted sharply to thirteenth, and then partially recovered by 1914 to achieve eleventh place.

Other indicators point to the same general conclusion that Baltimore's position as a manufacturing center was respectable, if lacklustre, and that it was gradually being outstripped by more energetic cities. Table 7 shows the irregular decline in terms of the net value of product, or as it was later called, the value added by manufacture. Starting in ninth place in 1880, rising to eighth in 1890, it dipped back to ninth in 1900. There was a plunge in 1909 to thirteenth place and in 1914 a mild recovery, this time only to eleventh place. This indicator is perhaps the most valuable, as it singles out the essence of the contribution of manufacturing.

Another scale of comparative measurement is the number of wage earners. In this category, as is seen in Table 7, the decline was gentle, with Baltimore hovering between fifth and fourth place from 1880 through 1905 and then after a pronounced drop to seventh place in 1909, slipping further to eighth in 1914. The ranking and number of wage earners given for 1890 are incompatible with those of the other years as they include officers, firm members, and clerks. For that reason they have been omitted in the above discussion.

As one would anticipate from the gradual loss of place previously detailed, Baltimore's manufactures figured more prominently in 1880 than in 1914. (See Table 8.) In 1880 Baltimore

---

57. U.S., *Abstract of the Census of Manufactures: 1914*, p. 280.

Baltimore retorts and fire brick works, George C. Hicks & Company. *M.H.S.*

ranked among the top six cities in nine types of industry. Its copper and sheet ironware industry was first in the nation. This proved to be the only first ranking for the entire period. In fourth place came the manufacture of brick and tile, in fifth, carpentry, and in sixth place the city offered not one but six industries: bread and other bakery goods, men's clothing, marble and stonework, saddlery and harness, shipbuilding, and, finally, tobacco (cigars and cigarettes). In 1890 the list had shrunk to three industries: brick and stone masonry taking third place, and both bread and other bakery goods and men's clothing reappearing in sixth place. In 1900 one can see the rise in importance of men's clothing, which now ranked fourth nationally. Tobacco manufactures had risen to fifth place. This ranking for these two industries was repeated in 1905. In 1909 the men's clothing industry had risen to third place in the nation. Heavy industry climbed into national view again after having been missing from the chart since 1880, with the manufacture of cars and general shop construction and repairs by steam railroads emerging in fifth place in 1904 and fourth place in 1909.

The censuses of 1904 and 1909 give a few fragmentary figures which supplement Table 8. In 1904 men's clothing, including shirts, ranking third in the nation, accounted for 6.2 per cent of the national value of product in that field. Five years later Baltimore accounted for 6.4 per cent of the nation's men's clothing, including shirts. In the manufacture of cars, general shop construction and repairs by steam railroads, Baltimore in 1904 contributed a mere 1.4 per cent of the national value of product in the industry and in 1909 a slightly larger contribution of 1.8 per cent.

Baltimore throughout this period was constantly reminded of its industrial potential and encouraged to make the most of it or else be hopelessly outranked by faster-growing cities. Spearheading a veritable campaign to change Baltimore from a predominantly commercial to a leading industrial center was the Merchants' and Manufacturers' Association, founded in 1880 to galvanize business opinion and efforts. The Association created a host of committees to report on various aspects of the city's economic situation. In a pamphlet published in 1882, it asserted that "Baltimore is primarily and above all things else, not a commercial city,"[58] nor a distributive center but a manu-

---

58. Edward Spencer, *A Sketch of the History of Manufactures in Maryland* (Baltimore, 1882), p. 51, quoted in Hirschfeld, p. 36.

facturing center, even though it may be in a state of arrested development. The *Manufacturers' Record* picked up the cry. Established in 1882, it was ever ready to itemize Baltimore's manufacturing advantages and to predict with fulsome cheer the rosiest industrial development just around the corner. Joining the chorus were the Board of Trade, *The Sun,* the special supplements of the *Baltimore American* and a number of small incidental publications such as guides to the city. On the other hand, genuine concern for the continued economic progress of Baltimore was expressed by many local leaders after the fire of 1904. There were fearful references to the crushed spirit and sapped vigor of Baltimore's citizens emerging from the Civil War, and there was worry that this catastrophe would have like results.[59]

For all the optimism, in the cold light of fact, Baltimore's industrial growth in this period was disappointing. Such was the verdict of the committee supervising a local industrial survey, the results of which were published in 1915. J. E. Aldred, the president of the Consolidated Gas, Electric Light and Power Company, sparked the investigation, and an advisory committee carried it out. The committee consisted of Jacob Hollander, professor of Political Economy at The Johns Hopkins University, John R. Bland, president of the United States Fidelity and Guaranty, who, as erstwhile secretary of the Merchants' and Manufacturers' Association, had conducted a rather similar examination of 1883, and Frederick W. Wood, president of the Maryland Steel Company. The committee felt that the survey was "a deliberate and sober inquest designed to acquaint our citizen-body with facts as they are."[60] It proceeded to sum up the conclusions of the report:

> The one clear and emphatic impression left upon our minds by the data hereinafter presented is that the industrial growth of Baltimore has been less pronounced than it should have been, having in mind the general economic progress of the country and the forward strides of other cities no more favorably circumstanced.
>
> The population of Baltimore has increased less rapidly than

---

59. Hirschfeld, pp. 36-37; James B. Crooks, "Politics and Progress: The Rise of Urban Progressivism in Baltimore, 1895 to 1911" (Ph.D. dissertation, Johns Hopkins University, 1964), p. 185.
60. *Industrial Survey,* p. v.

that of certain competing communities and it has fallen back in relative rank among the great cities of the United States. Real estate values, a reasonable index of industrial activity, have been, with some notable exceptions, relatively immobile and there have been considerable areas of absolute decline marked by vacant properties and reduced rentals. The number of newly established industries is less considerable than it seems reasonable to expect and there are certain discouraging instances of the decay of one-time flourishing establishments. There is no evidence of any considerable influx of industrial workers, such as inevitably occurs in a growing manufacturing center.

We deem it mistaken policy in anywise to suppress or gloss over the fact that the industrial progress of Baltimore has been thus sluggish.[61]

The committee attributed this retardation to "an economic transition the ill effects of which have been too long tolerated."[62] The transition was from the commercially-oriented ante-bellum economy of the city which was smashed by the Civil War. Thus disrupted, the economy of Baltimore tried to change over to manufactures and in this new area to make up for the losses caused by the war. It was not an easy transition and was made even worse, according to the committee, by the fact that Baltimore did not fully realize the situation. "In a word, the industrial retardation of Baltimore is largely traceable to the absence of organized effort to make easy an abrupt change in our business life."[63] As an illustration of this the committee pointed to the lack of any material progress in the years just before the survey was taken. Recent expansion in industries such as copper smelting and refining, the manufacture of tin cans, canning of fruits and vegetables, and slaughtering and meat packing, the committee elaborated, was counter-balanced by the gradual curtailment, sometimes even the elimination, of other industries such as sugar refining, the manufacture of iron bars, railroad cars, chrome, crockery and pottery, boots and shoes, wall paper, and soap. It was the committee's opinion that, basically, what was lacking was not individual initiative or talent but rather "a collective consciousness and a communal effort which should take account of existing difficulties growing

61. *Ibid.*
62. *Ibid.*
63. *Ibid.*, p. vi.

out of the historical change of Baltimore from a commercial to a manufacturing city, and which should encourage and facilitate the endeavors of individual enterprise to adapt itself to this necessity."[64]

The future need not look bleak, according to the committee. Baltimore probably had not only about equal advantages in geographic location, manufacturing sites, taxation exemption, climatic conditions, and municipal spirit as any other place. It could offer three other essential advantages as well: a labor supply with lower wages, a coal supply, and favorable freight rates.[65] The conclusion was, in effect, that if given the proper hardheaded encouragement, the industrial development of Baltimore could markedly improve. Thus at the end of the period, the cry was for greater effort so that Baltimore would rise to the eminence of front-running American manufacturing cities.

4

INDUSTRIAL GROWTH OF THE LESSER CITIES

No other city in Maryland came close to Baltimore in industrial significance. A glance at Table 9 shows the smallness of the value of product for the three next largest cities: Hagerstown, Cumberland, and Frederick. Unfortunately, figures are not available before 1899. In 1914 collectively they accounted for 4 per cent of the total value of product of manufactures of the state. By that date Hagerstown emerged as the second manufacturing city in Maryland in terms of value of product, edging out Cumberland, which heretofore had held that position. In population Hagerstown grew from 6,627 in 1880 to 16,507 in 1910. It supported a variety of industries, the most important being machine shops, steam railroad repair shops, flour and grist mills, furniture, knit goods, and organs.

A population in 1914 of just over 25,000 made Cumberland the second largest city in the state throughout the period. Well situated within easy access to local iron ore and bituminous coal, it developed an iron and steel industry, machine shops, and repair works for steam railroads. Local timber enabled the development of a lumber industry. Besides these there were

64. *Ibid.*       ·
65. *Ibid.*, p. vii.

glass, cement, and brick works, flour mills, breweries, and leather works.

Frederick, located in the center of an important agricultural district, supported flour mills as its chief industry along with a vigorous canning business as well. Foundry and machine shops, knitting mills, and leather works about completed the roster of manufactures. By 1910 its population was only a little over 10,000, and it was decidedly the least aggressive of the three secondary cities.

Beneath these three were a host of towns, with populations under 10,000 by 1914, which, together with rural districts, accounted for 38 per cent of the value of product of the manufactures of the state in 1914. Salisbury, for example, had a large lumber industry as well as flour and textile mills. Elkton in the 1890's bestirred itself to establish pulp mills, machine shops, fertilizer plants, and canneries. Cambridge in the 1890's was the third largest oyster packing center in the state and had a variety of other manufactures as well. Crisfield's main industry was oyster packing as was that of many tiny towns dotting both sides of the Chesapeake Bay. Similarly, many inland towns in agricultural areas had canneries or flour mills such as Ellicott City, historically famous for its flour mills. Ship yards, iron foundries, and lumber mills were also scattered throughout the state.[66]

One final aspect of industrial development in Maryland remains to be considered: organizational changes. The need for ever larger amounts of capital caused the growth of the corporation. Not until 1905, unfortunately, was the census able to make accurate calculations on the subject, and from then on it recorded steady growth. By 1914, 21 per cent of the establishments in Maryland were under corporate ownership, accounting for 70 per cent of the total value of products and 61 per cent of the wage earners. However, these figures, as usual, are not complete, since several important industries had to be omitted by the census. By 1909 firms with corporate management produced the largest proportion of the total value of product for such major industries in the state as canning, steam railroad cars and general shop construction repairs, copper, tin and sheet

66. The whole discussion of other cities relies largely on: U.S., Census of Manufactures: 1914, I, 553, 563, 565-67; Maryland, Board of World's Fair Managers, Maryland, Its Resources, pp. 352-53, 355-58.

iron products, foundry and machine shop products, lumber, printing and publishing, and slaughtering and meat packing. The men's clothing industry and flour and grist mills were conspicuous exceptions. As most of these industries were located largely in Baltimore, this reflected the city's industrial structure as well.

In Baltimore, by 1914, 21 per cent of the establishments had corporate ownership, accounting for 61 per cent of the total value of products and 57 per cent of the wage earners. The city fell somewhat below the national proportion of incorporation of all industrial firms, 23.6 per cent in 1905, but the trend toward corporate organization is clear.

The tendency for business to concentrate in larger establishments was evident in the state as well as in Baltimore. By 1914, 11 per cent of the total number of establishments in the state had a value of product of $100,000 and over, accounted for 83 per cent of the total value of products, and hired 73 per cent of the wage earners. In Baltimore, in 1914, 14 per cent of the firms had a product value of $100,000 and up, accounted for 83 per cent of the total value of products and hired 79 per cent of the workers. Yet to keep in mind an accurate picture of manufacturing as late as 1914, it must be remembered that while a small proportion of the firms controlled most of the output and labor, the great majority of firms, as in 1860, were still operating on quite a small scale.[67]

Nor did Baltimore develop into a center for huge corporations aggressively acquiring plants and other properties across the nation. Rather, Baltimore firms were in many instances themselves bought out by giant corporations and made part of out-of-state complexes. Mergers with national companies, as well as those merely between local firms, occurred quite frequently at the turn of the century. Mention has already been made that the Standard Oil Company and the American Tobacco Company bought out local firms. Other excellent examples are the American Agricultural Chemical Company, which in 1898 purchased eight local fertilizer plants, and the American Can Company, which in 1900 acquired all of the city's major can manufacturing plants.[68]

---

67. U.S., *Census of Manufactures: 1914*, I, 565-67. The author's calculations are based on data from the above, p. 568.
68. Hirschfeld, p. 80.

5

LABOR

Turning to an examination of industrial labor in Maryland, let us first consider its size and composition. Table 10 at the end of the chapter gives the number of wage earners engaged in manufacturing and mechanical industries in both Maryland and Baltimore throughout the period. For the state, in absolute terms, the figures rose steadily from decade to decade except for 1910. Clearly, however, the percentage of increase was larger in the earlier than later years, specifically before 1890. Looking over the proportion of the state's population engaged in manufacturing, growth is even more strikingly pinpointed in the early years. In 1860, 4 per cent of Maryland's population was engaged as wage earners in manufacturing,[69] while by 1880 this had doubled to 8 per cent. Thereafter it leveled off. In 1900 it was 9 per cent, in 1910, 8 per cent and in 1914, 8 per cent.

Throughout the period, of course, men predominated, ranging between 62 and 76 per cent of the work force. (See Table 11 at the end of the chapter.) The figures for 1860 are particularly unsatisfactory since they merely divide the labor force by sex and not by age as well, mixing child labor with adult. There is, therefore, little point in calculating the proportion of men and women for that year. In 1870 women made up 18 per cent and children 6 per cent of the group. In 1880 adult men constituted 62 per cent of the group, adult women 29 per cent, and children and youth 9 per cent. In 1890 women accounted for 25 per cent and children 4 per cent, in 1910 women were 27 per cent and children 6 per cent, and in 1914 women were 28 per cent and children 3 per cent. After 1880 there is amazingly little change in the proportion of women in the work force.

As Table 11 indicates, most of the women and children worked in Baltimore. With the increase in the city's industrialization the number of male wage earners in industry increased, but only by 87 per cent between 1870 and 1900, while that of women rose 363 per cent.[70] This was caused by the introduction

69. Percentage is the author's calculation.
70. Hirschfeld, p. 62. Percentages for 1860 & 1870 are author's calculations. U.S., *Census: 1880*, Manufactures, p. xxxv; U.S., *Census of Manufactures: 1914*, I, 557.

of machinery, enabling women and children often to replace skilled men. Also there took place an increasing division of labor. Unskilled and poorly paid women and children replaced the skilled male when the employer divided his job into a number of simple operations. This latter process is well illustrated by the garment industry: here the introduction of the "Boston system" substituted the factory for the sweatshop. In the sweatshop, under the "task system" a team of five men, headed by a skilled tailor and assisted by a girl or two to sew buttons, produced the garment. Men predominated as workers under that system. Under the factory system the making of the garment was divided into many more simple operations performed quickly by a large number of women under the direction of a few skilled tailors. "Factories exist where more than 100 persons are engaged in the making of one coat, a procedure whereby it is possible to introduce a large number of unskilled workers to work with a few skilled ones,"[71] observed the census in 1900. By 1910 more women were employed in men's clothing than in any other industry in the city.

Other industries with a high proportion of women workers were the canning industry in which in 1910 they constituted 52 per cent of the adult wage earners. These two industries together accounted for 50 per cent of the adult female employees in manufacturing in Maryland in 1910. Women also predominated in the manufacture of shirts, cigars and cigarettes, boots and shoes, chemicals and drugs, and tinware.[72]

Most of the child labor in Baltimore was in the clothing and canning industries: young girls sewing buttons, pulling stitches, and preparing fruits and vegetables for canning. In this latter industry whole families worked together, a mother bringing her entire brood to the factory. In 1909 Baltimore ranked third in the nation in the size of its child labor force, which constituted 6 per cent of the city's work force. In the state, by 1910, 34 per cent of the children working in manufacturing were in either men's clothing or canning. Large numbers were also to be found in the glass, brick, shoe, tobacco, and tinware industries. By 1914 five industries in the state accounted for most of the child labor: clothing, department and other large

---

71. U.S., *Census: 1900*, IX, *Manufactures*, pt. 3, 297.
72. U.S., *Census: 1910*, IX, *Manufactures*, 465; Hirschfeld, pp. 60-62.

retail stores, copper, tin and sheet iron products, telegraph and telephone service, and printing and publishing. By this date the number of children engaged in manufacturing was substantially less than previously, owing to the progressive tightening of the child labor laws. This period as a whole also witnessed the disintegration of the apprenticeship system due to the increased use of machinery and the increased division of labor.[73]

An examination of Tables 3 and 6 will show the industries in Maryland and Baltimore which used the largest number of workers. In both the state and the city men's clothing and canning were the two largest employers during most of the period.

The sources of supply for Baltimore's labor force were threefold: natural increase within the city itself, internal migration, and foreign immigration. Part of Baltimore's native labor supply, white as well as black, came from another part of the state and was newly arrived in the city. It has been estimated that 48 per cent of the city's total increase in population between 1870 and 1900 consisted of native Americans born outside of Baltimore. Of these, two thirds were white. Only a small percentage came from other states and a very large majority (70 per cent) from Maryland itself. The Negro population increase in Baltimore was even more dramatic. It accounted for almost 90 per cent of the growth of that population in the city between 1870 and 1900. As with the whites, most Negro migrants to Baltimore came from within the state.[74] The influence of this horizontal mobility in shaping the labor force, black and white, cannot be detailed here statistically as the necessary research has not yet been done. Its importance, however, is confirmed by the Maryland Bureau of Industrial Statistics and Information in its 1886–7 report which referred to the "young, native Americans, crowding in from the farms of Maryland and Virginia."[75]

While Baltimore was an important port of entry for immigrants in this period, most went on to settle in the West. It is estimated that between 1870 and 1900 only about 5 per cent of the city's total increase in population was due to foreign immigration. (Table 12 classifies the manufacturing labor force of

---

73. U.S., *Census: 1910, Manufactures,* pt. 1, 275, IX, 465; Hirschfeld, p. 63; Maryland, BS & I, *Annual Report: 1914,* p. 68.
74. Hirschfeld, pp. 20-21.
75. Maryland, BISI, *Second Biennial Report, 1886–1887,* p. 13.

Maryland by race and nativity for the years when the data are available from the census.)

In 1880, 80 per cent of the manufacturing work force in Maryland consisted of native-born Americans, both black and white. In the light of the figures for 1890 and 1900, one might deduce that the black proportion would be around 5 per cent and the native white about 75 per cent. The striking stability of the labor force in Maryland is clear from Table 12, as well, of course, as the dominance of native white Americans. The fact that foreign white immigrants made up such an unchanging proportion at a time when immigrants were pouring into the country suggests a stable, conservative society in Maryland. The only significant change was the growth of the percentage of blacks in the manufacturing labor force between 1900 and 1910.

A systematic survey of wages and wage rates in this period is impossible with the fragmentary, haphazard information available. It is a task which is often little more than tantalizing, if not frustrating. Before the establishment of the Maryland Bureau of Industrial Statistics and Information in 1884 the data are even more scarce. The founding of the Bureau brought at least somewhat systematic research to the subject coupled with great interest and concern for the workers' welfare. The Bureau conducted a number of studies of wages in this period, but even so, there is the discouraging problem of the incomparability of much of the data which over time were collected in different ways. Furthermore, it can be very difficult to determine, without detailed knowledge of an industry, whether a job is skilled or unskilled. Finally, some mining and textile companies provided houses and fuel at very low cost to their workers, the value of which were not often included in wage rates.

All that can be done here is to trace a trend in the wage rates of certain types of workers. This gives some impression of the period and is a first step toward determining the condition of the workers.

Taking a few examples from skilled labor, one learns that money wages for a cutter in the boot and shoe industry rose from $1.50 per day in 1860 to $3.33 by 1884 and dropped to $2.50 in 1890. An overseer in the carding, spinning, or weaving rooms of a cotton textile mill fluctuated from $2.71 in 1870 to $2.17 in 1880, to $2.25 in 1884 to $3.50 in 1890. In 1905 the average wage rate for men was $7.86 a week and in 1913, $9.76. At six days a week, the weekly wages in 1870 would be $16.26, markedly higher than in 1905. But the comparability of the data is far from certain, since the figures for 1870 and 1880 are from a shirting and drilling mill, whereas those from 1905 and 1913 are a composite, presumably of several companies and several branches of the cotton textile industry. Moreover, the cotton duck manufacture faced a steady decline as the demand for canvas sails dropped off, and this would reduce wages for some part of the industry. In foundries and machine shops a machinist or boilermaker received $2.50 per day in 1884 and in 1890, averaged about $2.30 to $2.50 a day in 1900 and 1902, in 1905 got $12.62 a week and in 1913, $15.31 a week. This represents $2.10 a day in 1905 and $2.55 a day in 1913.[76] Thus in general the rates remained about the same in this line of work.

Wage rates, however difficult to determine in this period, of course do not give the full picture in themselves of the welfare of the worker. "Real wages" or wages in relation to price levels, are much more relevant to the problem of a workingman's welfare. Modern economists estimate that, for the nation as a whole, while money wages rose on the average about 10 per cent between 1870 and 1890, real wages rose between 10 and 20 per cent in the 1870's, and by more than 25 per cent in the 1880's. Further estimates find a $50 increase per year in real wages in the 1890's, a $100 increase in the period 1900–1910, and a $50 rise in the decade 1910 to 1920. Still another overall calculation asserts that taking into account the complex interactions between the rise in productivity (which is considered the basis for the rise in real wages), the tides of immigration, and the business cycle, there was a fairly steady rise in real wages of about $7 a year from 1880–1920.[77] These are the broadest statements of the worker's condition, and pertain, once again, to the nation as a whole. They, of course, obscure the individual's

---

76. These figures were drawn from the U.S. *Census: 1860, 1870, & 1880*, Maryland, BISI *Biennial Report* 1884, BSI *Annual Report*, 1902, 1905, 1909, 1913, U.S. *Census of Manufactures: 1905*, pt. 4, 780.

77. John A. Garraty, *The New Commonwealth, 1877–1890, The New American Nation Series*, ed. Henry S. Commager and Richard B. Morris (New York: Harper & Row, 1968), p. 128; Stanley Lebergott, *Manpower in Economic Growth: the American Record Since 1800, Economics Handbook Series*, ed. Seymour E. Harris (New York: McGraw-Hill Book Co., 1964), pp. 154-55, 163.

experience of variations between regions, industries, occupations, and companies, as well as the sudden jolts of unemployment due to panics, depressions or company mismanagement.

Maryland's Bureau of Industrial Statistics and Information put the subject of wages and living costs into quite human terms. Its first report covered a depression year, 1884–5, and naturally, times were difficult. The Bureau stated flatly, "the bulk of our working people find it more difficult to live than they did a few years ago."[78] In 1901 the Bureau still argued that, despite the rise in wages for some skilled workers, generally the situation for labor had not improved because of the rise in the cost of living. The unskilled laborer's situation lagged the most since he got, on the average, $1.25 a day, a rate unchanged since 1890, despite the rise in prices.

In 1903 the Bureau studied what it considered to be twenty typical Baltimore workingmen's families and discovered that only two were able to save anything from their income, while eight were in debt at the end of the year.[79] Another sampling of "forty industrious, sober and economical"[80] workingmen, including both skilled and unskilled, in Baltimore, showed that fourteen managed to save a little at the end of the year and nine ran into debt. Of those who saved something, some had taken in boarders. The Bureau declared that wages had not kept pace with the cost of living in Baltimore, even in the building trades, which had experienced substantial gains in hours and wages from 1890 to 1902.[81]

The complaints of the Bureau continued each year until 1908, along with increasingly detailed tabulations of retail food prices in Baltimore. Between 1892 and 1906 the retail cost of some basic foods advanced 52 per cent. Prices were always rising faster than wages and, in fact, the Bureau stressed, only the wages of skilled, organized workers had risen substantially over the period 1894–1904. Even these did not catch up with prices. The Bureau painstakingly indicated that its researches were based on the fairly remunerative occupations under conditions of steady employment, and not on shiftless, casual labor. In

78. Maryland, BISI, *First Biennial Report, 1884–1885*, p. 31.
79. Maryland, BIS, *Annual Report, 1901*, p. 6; BSI, *Annual Report, 1902*, p. 7.
80. Maryland, BSI, *Eleventh Annual Report, 1902*, pp. 10-11.
81. *Ibid.*, pp. 7-11.

1906 it estimated that a family of six could live in Baltimore on $742 a year with all necessities covered but no luxuries. At such a rate, in fifteen out of thirty-one occupations studied by the Bureau, the male head of the family made less than that amount. Among these were porters making $375, laborers making $421, cigarmakers making $571, and planing mill hands making $675. Among those earning more than the minimum amount established by the Bureau were machinists averaging $786 and clothing cutters averaging $751. Even though Baltimore was a cheaper place to live than New York or Chicago, it was much more difficult to make ends meet in 1906 than in 1892, although the Bureau asserted that the cost of production was much lower due to combinations and the increased use of machinery. Clearly, wages failed to keep pace with advancing productivity.[82]

From 1907 until 1911 the bureau noted that food prices were decreasing or at least steady, and some wages increased a little. The frantic race with the cost of living seemed to have relaxed after 1911, and the bureau no longer addressed itself to the problem.

It is well known that women and children received lower wages than men. The federal census for 1905 gives a succinct picture of the distribution of wages in Maryland. Men constituted 70 per cent of the work force in manufactures and received 84 per cent of the earnings. Women made up 25 per cent of the force and received 15 per cent of the earnings, and children made up 5 per cent and received 2 per cent.[83] Unfortunately, comparable data are not available for the entire period. It is painfully clear, however, that men's wages were inadequate for a family budget requiring in many cases the supplementary mite from a wife and children.

In aggregate terms, it has been estimated that per capita real earnings in all manufactures in Maryland combined, fell from $493 in 1899 to $484 in 1904, rose to $536 in 1909 and dipped back to $499 in 1914. These fluctuations, through 1909 at least, mirror the distressing conclusions of the Bureau. In short, the change in purchasing power of the incomes of all manufactur-

---

82. Maryland, BSI, *Annual Report, 1906*, pp. 148-50, 164.
83. U.S., *Census of Manufactures: 1905*, pt. 4, 679.

ing labor in Maryland for the period 1899–1914 amounted to 1 per cent.[84]

Two factors tending to lower wages were the increasing use of machinery—given the failure of unions or minimum wage laws to equate wage rates with advances in the value of labor's marginal product—and the influx of large numbers of immigrants into the labor force. Immigration had in general a twofold effect on the economy. In the long run it was a source of productivity, but in the short term it tended to depress wages by increasing the labor force, especially since many European workers were accustomed to lower standards of living. However, the stability of the ratio of immigrants to the rest of the work force (as seen in Table 12) suggests, at least, that for the period 1890–1910 in Maryland, immigration was not an important factor tending to lower wage rates.

The decrease in wages in Maryland due to the introduction of machinery, while impossible to pinpoint, can still be illustrated in a general way. The increased use of machinery meant the replacement of the skilled craftsman by an unskilled worker who simply tended the machine. Furthermore, mechanization could out-produce more than one craftsman. More was produced by fewer workers at lower wages. Women and children could now do the work once done by skilled men. Skilled workers objected vociferously and tried to prevent the introduction of machinery. A dramatic example is that of the canning industry, where both the canmakers and the workers who filled the cans fought mechanization, but to no avail. The cans had been handmade and the fruits and vegetables processed by hand. The 1880's saw machinery perform both tasks. By 1890 one-half to three-quarters of the men had been replaced by women and children. A single automatic machine made a can from a sheet of tin. Other machines labelled and boxed the filled cans. Thus not only were wages reduced, but the size of the work force in 1900 was much diminished while production increased impressively.[85]

It should also be noted that the reduction of wages and jobs

84. U.S. Bureau of the Census. *Earnings of Factory Workers, 1899–1927*, by Paul F. Brissindon. *Census Monographs*, X (Washington, D.C.: Government Printing Office, 1929), pp. 81, 150.

85. U.S., *Census: 1900, Manufactures*, pt. 1, p. cxxiii; Hirschfeld, pp. 48-51.

in one industry, however deplorable, was relieved to some extent by improvement in working conditions, increased jobs in other industries (especially in the machine tool industry) and lower prices for consumers.

Hours are closely related to wages. In this period the trend in the length of the working day edged downward. The prevailing hours of work in 1860 were ten a day and this remained true for most of the period until very near the end, constituting a sixty-hour week. There was still a great deal of variation between industries and occupations, however. Bakers worked long hours, while potters had an eight-hour day and a five-day week in 1884. A coal mine required a ten-hour day in the 1860's, raised it to eleven hours in the 1870's, and in the 1880's dropped it to nine. By 1884, as a rule, coal miners in Maryland worked ten hours in winter and eleven in summer. In the canning industry the general practice in the 1880's was a twelve-hour day for the season which, for fruits and vegetables, lasted about a hundred days beginning in May. Because of the seasonal nature of the employment, the laborer worked at other jobs the rest of the year. The blacks often became domestic servants, white girls went into the clothing industry and still others into oyster shucking and canning.

The clothing industry itself was an important exception to the ten-hour day as much work was done at home by underpaid and overworked women. Often, whole families were stuffed into cramped living quarters, all working at the needle trades. It was not uncommon for women to sew eighteen hours a day at home and earn $3 to $5 a week. Twelve hours a day was about the rule, but fourteen to eighteen was not exceptional, reported the Maryland Bureau of Industrial Statistics and Information in 1884.[86]

By the late 1890's a nine-hour day was noticeably edging into the picture, for example, in the building trades, iron works, and with clothing cutters. By 1902–5 even the eight-hour day appeared in the building trades as well as among cigarmakers and structural iron workers. Laborers, excepting those in the building trades, still worked ten hours. However, even by 1910 nearly three-fourths of the total number of workers in the manu-

---

86. U.S., *Census: 1880, Statistics on Wages*, p. 44; Maryland, BISI *Biennial Report, 1884–1885*, pp. 80, 62, 87.

facturing industries worked a nine- to ten-hour day, six days a week. More than one-half of these worked ten hours. Eighteen per cent of all manufacturing workers worked fewer than fifty-four hours a week and 8 per cent worked over sixty hours. The sixty-hour week prevailed in the canning industry, brick and tile, copper, tin and sheet iron products, fertilizer, lumber, slaughtering, and cotton goods. By 1910 the largest number of workers was in the men's clothing industry, with about one-third working between forty-eight and fifty-four hours, one-third between fifty-four and sixty, and one-third sixty hours.

The trend toward shorter hours continued, and by 1914 only about one-third of the total average number of wage earners in all industries combined toiled a sixty-hour week or more, while 66 per cent labored under sixty hours. There was also a decided increase in the proportion working under fifty-four hours.[87]

Some workingmen turned to unions to gain higher wages, shorter hours, and better working conditions and to battle the introduction of machinery. Unfortunately unions were at best ephemeral organizations throughout the period, constantly disintegrating in times of depression. And depressions pockmarked the era with distressing frequency. Because of the paucity of historical sources, estimates of union membership in the state are all but impossible, and thus we are unable to give an accurate indication of the proportion of union men to the total working force. Not only did the unions themselves keep very scanty and unreliable records of membership, but as the eminent labor historian Leo Wolman warns in discussing unions in the country as a whole from 1880 to 1895:

> Statistics of membership during such a period must naturally be severely discounted. Diverse cross-currents in the labor movement were simultaneously in operation, workingmen at the same time held membership in more than one of the competing unions, and joining a union was often only a temporary incident in the conduct of a strike.[88]

Furthermore, some industries were difficult to organize. New

---

87. Maryland, BSI, *Annual Report, 1902*, pp. 6-9; *Annual Report, 1905*, p. 263; U.S., Census: 1910, IX, *Manufactures*, 466; U.S., *Census of Manufactures: 1914*, I, 560.

88. Leo Wolman, *The Growth of American Trade Unions, 1880–1923* (New York, 1924), p. 31.

unions replaced old ones with no more permanent success. A notable example was the coal industry. Despite the efforts and temporary successes of the Knights of Labor and, after 1891, the United Mine Workers of America, the Cumberland coal field remained unorganized and unionism inactive after 1909 due to the power and determination of the coal companies to prevent unionization. The union gained recognition only during the New Deal. The Maryland experience in mining unionization during this period fits the national pattern of violent and frequent fluctuations in union membership in that industry.[89]

Nevertheless, with all the evanescence of unions and the attendant difficulties in gauging membership, it was generally true that skilled workers were the ones to organize. But they were a minority in the labor force. Thus it should be emphasized that we are dealing with only a small and fluctuating fraction of the labor force.

In general, most of the available information concerns unions in Baltimore and the mining region of western Maryland. The rest of the state remains largely a mystery. It is reasonable to assume, however, that union activity was most important precisely in these two areas. Most of the record is from the Maryland Bureau of Industrial Statistics and Information. It became interested in compiling a complete list of labor organizations in the state, their membership, address, secretary, wages and hours of the members, and the condition of the trade. Beginning in 1884 the bureau published occasional lists of unions with these data, but they were far from complete, as the bureau itself constantly lamented. The unions not only failed to keep systematic records of membership but also often did not even cooperate with the bureau's requests for information.

Trade unions existed in Baltimore before the Civil War. Indeed Baltimore was the birthplace of the National Labor Union in 1866, which embraced on a national scale all unions, workingmen's associations, eight-hour leagues and national organizations. But union membership everywhere declined during the depression of the late 1860's, and Baltimore was no exception. It was not until the prosperity of the late 1870's that unions in the city began to build in a more substantial way.

One of the most important was the Knights of Labor, which

---

89. Harvey, p. 361 & *passim*; Wolman, p. 35.

organized a local district assembly in Baltimore in 1878. The Knights had been formed in Philadelphia in 1869 as an ecumenical brotherhood of labor, cutting across narrow self-interested union lines to include all trades, sexes, and sometimes Negroes as well as whites. Its membership was secret, and it leaned heavily toward ritualism. In Baltimore and in the coal fields of western Maryland its membership grew steadily. By January 1886 the Knights in Maryland exclusive of the mining region totalled 4,000, with about 16,000 in the state as a whole, including the mining region. The year 1886 witnessed an astonishing growth of all types of labor organizations and of the Knights in particular.[90]

The bureau in its first report in 1884 observed the change in the course of labor organization from primary emphasis on trade unions to the great popularity of the Knights of Labor. The bureau enthusiastically reported:

> The year 1886 will be marked in the social history of the American people for the extraordinary impetus which has been given to labor organizations. Simultaneously, all over the states, following no given track, bounded by no minor geographical limits, confined to no particular industries, the impetus to organize seems to have possessed the wage-workers of the country, and since writing the body of this report, within three months, the trade unions have multiplied and increased with a rapidity which amazes the observer. . . .
>
> For some years, with varying success, the trade unions of Maryland have slowly increased their membership, but during these few months it is no exaggeration to say they have more than quadrupled their numbers. . . .
>
> Neither is this an organization of separate trades. The groups are not coming together as blacksmiths, or bakers, or leather workers, but the tendency is to consolidate, to recognize the dependence of one branch of industry upon another, and (in the expressive language of the West) "to pool their issues."[91]

During the year it was estimated that the ranks swelled to about 25,000 in Baltimore alone. Then the Haymarket Affair in Chicago and subsequent employer opposition, a disastrous miners' strike, and the depression of 1893 rained heavy blows. A rapid

---

90. Hirschfeld, p. 67 ff.; Maryland, BISI, *Biennial Report, 1884–1885*, p. 13 n.

91. Maryland, BISI, *First Biennial Report, 1884–1885*, p. 12 n.

and permanent decline set in. By 1890 only about 489 members remained in the state, exclusive of the mining region. The Knights never recovered.

Along more conventional trade lines, some old unions of skilled workers reorganized and new ones were born. The bureau counted ninety-six unions in Baltimore in early 1886, noting that some joined the Knights while others joined one of the other two city-wide organizations: The Baltimore Federation of Labor, which was formed in 1883 and included the local District Assembly of the Knights, or the German Central Labor Union, formed in 1885. For the entire state the bureau estimated there were 27,000 organized workers in early 1886. Just as with the Knights, membership shrank in the late 1880's, and by 1903 only ten of the unions formed in the 1880's survived. In the early 1890's unionization resurged, only to meet a setback in the long depression beginning in 1893.

With the return of prosperity in the late 1890's unions again grew and multiplied. By 1901 the bureau made an educated guess that there were about a hundred trade unions in the state, but no membership figures were available. By 1902 the bureau estimated a total membership of over 21,000 for the seventy-two organizations in Baltimore that responded to its questionnaire. This figure is probably an overstatement, for it includes the members of the Metal Trades Association, who seem also to be counted in the list under separate unions. Thus a more accurate estimate for union membership in Baltimore would be closer to 15,000. Of the seventy-two organizations, forty-two were formed after 1896, and of these, fifteen were organized in 1902. Indeed, that year witnessed the greatest rush in membership since the peak year of 1886. Growth seems to have continued in 1903 with a total of 117 organizations reporting to the bureau from the entire state, thirty-one from the counties, mostly in western Maryland and eighty-six from Baltimore. Together the total membership was slightly over 22,000.

By 1904 the unions of the building trades in Baltimore were the most active in gaining members because the great fire of 1904 gave a spur to construction in the city. Other unions experienced some small losses. That same year 112 organizations responded to the bureau's annual union counting effort, thirty-seven in the counties (mainly Allegany County), and seventy-five in Baltimore. Membership was reported at 14,000, but since the figure was evidently incomplete, the bureau felt fully 20,000 to be a more accurate estimate for the unions reporting that year.[92] Thereafter there was a steady decline in the number of unions reporting and in membership given. By 1909 the bureau no longer gave membership estimates. Thus the ebb and flow in membership and in the life span of the unions themselves were blurred by the inability of the bureau to get systematic cooperation from the unions.

The Baltimore Federation of Labor, which was founded in 1883 with thirty-two affiliated unions, grew rapidly in membership and prestige, so that by 1900 most of the local unions were affiliated with it. By 1906 the bureau declared it to be "the most potent factor in labor circles in Baltimore, or in the state."[93] It had no direct membership of its own, but consisted of representatives of local labor organizations that had a charter from the American Federation of Labor. Its function was purely advisory, without the power either to call or to end a strike except with the consent of the locals involved. Although loosely organized, its power lay in its ability to solidify the unions and bring the pressure of a unified opinion to bear on specific issues. It had been affiliated with the AFL since 1889.[94]

The AFL, founded in 1886 with Samuel Gompers its first president, was the "rallying point for the unions of skilled workers, the trade unions."[95] During the 1880's, although there was much overlapping membership, basically there was competition with the Knights of Labor for leadership of the labor movement. The Knights peaked in 1886; their membership and strength thereafter declined. The strength of the AFL rose, so that by 1890 the latter was clearly at the helm. It represented a victory for the idea of the trade-autonomous labor organization over that of industrial unionization.

Collective bargaining and strikes were the two chief weapons used in dealing with employers. In a survey conducted by the bureau in 1901 all but one organization out of the twenty that replied to the question stated that they favored conciliation and arbitration. The photoengravers replied "no"; and the boiler-

92. *Ibid.*, p. 13 n.; Maryland, BIS, *Annual Report, 1901*, p. 30; BSI, *Annual Report, 1902*, pp. 52-53; BSI, *Annual Report, 1904*, p. 42.
93. Maryland, BSI, *Fifteenth Annual Report, 1906*, p. 153.
94. Hirschfeld, p. 69; Maryland, BSI, *Annual Report, 1906*, p. 153.
95. Wolman, p. 30.

makers, iron ship builders, milk dealers, and plumbers and gas-fitters avoided the answer. By 1900 one-fourth of the unions in Baltimore had trade agreements with their employers; these established the working conditions for a prescribed time and prevented strikes. Generally only well organized workers could manage to get trade agreements.[96]

Much more dramatic than the business of negotiation—and frequently engendering our sympathy—was the strike. But strikes were a double-edged sword. They might precipitate lockouts or severely damage a union if they proved unsuccessful, or arouse hostile public opinion. Most of the strikes in the period stemmed from a desire either to raise wages, prevent a reduction in them, or to reduce working hours.

The most dramatic strike was against the Baltimore and Ohio Railroad in 1877. Cutting across state lines, it involved not only Maryland but also West Virginia, and because of its violence was in the center of national attention. It began just outside of Baltimore on July 16 over the 10 per cent cut in wages by the company. The cut came on top of such other belt-tightening measures so that men worked only two or three days a week for about one dollar a day. The national economy was in a downswing, and 1877 was the fourth bad year in succession. The strike began spontaneously, without planning or union direction. It spread to Martinsburg, West Virginia, where the state militia proved unable to handle the strikers, and from there to Cumberland, where coal miners and canalmen were sympathetic. The Maryland governor appealed for federal intervention when the state militia was stoned in Baltimore by a mob that had joined with the strikers. Actually, order was restored before federal troops arrived. More importantly, the calling of the federal and state troops in both states reflected the high-handedness of the B & O officials rather than the scope and seriousness of the provocation.

Riots in Baltimore continued for a day, with considerable damage to railroad property before the local situation came completely under control. In three weeks the strike was entirely quashed, and the strikers had gained nothing except the loss of their jobs and a blacklisting. Interestingly enough, none of the leaders of the riots in Baltimore were strikers. Indeed

---

96. Maryland, BIS, *Annual Report, 1901*, p. 30: Hirschfeld, p. 69.

most of the B & O railroadmen remained loyal to the company. The two national rail unions, the Brotherhood of Locomotive Engineers and the Locomotive Firemen's union, denounced the strike. The complete tie-up of the lines was effected only because the strikers held strategic jobs. Starting as a local incident near Baltimore, the expression of discontent spread to fourteen states and ten major railroads, resulting in millions of dollars of damage, about a hundred people killed, and countless injured. The violence and bloodshed alarmed much of the public over a "labor problem" and stirred up fear for the safety of property.[97]

The second large interstate industrial conflict was the 1894 coal mining disturbances. The strike over a reduction in wages was organized by the United Mine Workers as part of a national strike, but was joined only reluctantly by Maryland miners. The latter had vivid memories of the disastrous strike in 1882, which had wrecked the Knights of Labor in the coal fields and set back unionism for over a decade. In 1894 soft coal miners all over the country were on strike in response to the United Mine Workers, but the Maryland miners had only begun to be organized by the UMW that year. The strike was in vain. The companies again emerged victorious, using the courts, the militia and foreign laborers to replace strikers. Unionism all but ceased among the miners until another effort was made by the UMW in 1899.[98]

At the local level, but noteworthy because of the importance of the industry and the deplorable working conditions, were the strikes by the clothing workers. Their first strike was in 1892, when over a thousand workers stopped work to demand of the employers written agreements with the union establishing a ten-hour day, weekly payment of wages, and an end to the task system. The strike was fairly successful, but sweated conditions still prevailed. In 1896 over 4,000 clothing workers struck for an end to the blacklist, higher wages, a written trade agreement between employers and the unions, and the closed shop. This time the union suffered defeat and a serious setback.[99]

97. This discussion of the B. & O. strike relies heavily on Clifton K. Yearley, Jr., "The Baltimore and Ohio Railroad Strike of 1877," *M.H.M.*, LI (Sept., 1956), 188-211.
98. Harvey, pp. 296 ff.
99. Hirschfeld, p. 72.

Besides coping with employers directly, many labor organizations endeavored to get laws enacted by the state legislature setting standards for working conditions. In part, they sought to arouse public support for such measures. Most labor organizations campaigned for some proposal designed specifically for the needs of their trade. The bakers, for example, pushed for a sanitary bakeshop inspection law, which passed in 1894. On the other hand, the printers, whose union was the oldest surviving one in the state, were an interesting exception. They had little or no interest in legislation.

Besides laws tailored to one industry, there were four larger goals affecting labor as a whole which were endorsed by many labor organizations in the 1880's: the eight-hour day, abolition of child labor, compulsory education, and workmen's compensation. Only partial success, slowly achieved, attended all these efforts. Still, enough was accomplished to be considered progress. Necessarily, only the most important laws can be discussed here.

In Maryland it was not until the late 1870's that labor groups began to emulate efforts being made elsewhere in the nation to obtain remedial legislation. Although trade unions had existed in the state for almost half a century, they had been concerned solely with conditions in their own trade. It was the Knights of Labor who first worked for labor legislation, especially in the 1880's, their peak years. Because they lacked definitiveness of purpose, they were not effective in securing legislation, although several measures were introduced in the General Assembly. The Federation of Labor was more successful. Its initial demands, made in 1883, included an eight-hour day for municipal employees, (effected in 1898), a bureau of labor statistics, (established in 1884 with much help from the Knights, however) and an end to applying conspiracy laws to trade unions. This was achieved in 1884, when trade unions were declared to be not indictable as conspiracies if their actions did not constitute an offense when committed by an individual.[100]

In this period legislation shortened the working hours for some employees but never established a generally applicable

100. *Ibid.*, pp. 74-75; H. Wirt Steele, "The Influence of Labor Unions Upon Legislation in Maryland," *The Johns Hopkins University Circular*, New Series, 1911, No. 4. Whole No. 234, pp. 42, 38-39.

work day for men. Rather it imposed restraints for certain classes of workers and certain industries. As mentioned above, first nine hours, and then, in 1910, eight hours became the legal day for municipal employees and employees of contractors engaged in, public work. Overtime was permissible for the protection of life and property, but this could easily be stretched to include ordinary overtime. For public safety, street car workers' hours were cut back from eighteen to twelve after a vigorous campaign by organized labor and a concerned public. Train dispatchers on railroads using the block system were limited to an eight-hour day. In 1884 the working day for cotton and woolen mill operatives was established as ten hours, and of coal miners in Allegany and Garrett Counties as ten hours, beginning at seven A.M. But both laws provided that male workers over twenty-one years of age could contract to work longer.

In 1912, after a bitter fight, a law was passed limiting the working day for women to ten hours and the week to sixty hours, with two industries excepted: the canning of fruits and vegetables and retail mercantile establishments outside of Baltimore. Night work was limited to eight hours, but without a uniform starting time this was next to impossible to enforce.[101]

Restrictions on child labor were not very stringent until 1916. Trade unions had pressed for legislation in this area, and finally in 1894 the legislature passed a law prohibiting the employment of children under twelve years of age in any mill or factory in the state, exempting the canning industry and sixteen counties. In 1902 the law was amended to raise the age level to fourteen years, but again the canning industry was excepted, as were all children who were the support of a widowed mother, invalid father or themselves. Furthermore, nineteen out of the twenty-three counties were excepted, so that it was applicable only to Baltimore City, Allegany, Anne Arundel, Charles, and Dorchester Counties. Even so, it was practically a dead letter, as no provision had been made for its enforcement. When in 1906 the law was repealed and reenacted with amendments, the Maryland Bureau of Statistics and Information was given the power of enforcement, with six additional inspectors

101. Malcolm H. Lauchheimer, *The Labor Law of Maryland* (Baltimore: J.H. Press, 1919), pp. 102-03; Hirschfeld, p. 75; H. Wirt Steele, "Labor Laws in Maryland," *The Johns Hopkins University Circular*, New Series, 1908, No. 5, whole No. 206, p. 48.

specifically for this purpose. No child under twelve could be employed in any gainful occupation. No child between twelve and sixteen could work without a permit from the bureau, which first had to ascertain the child's age. Farm labor was excepted, as were all counties during the summer months. In 1912 children under eighteen were prevented from working in dangerous occupations, which were specifically enumerated. Finally, in 1916 a tighter law was passed, prohibiting children under sixteen from working in almost all occupations, except canning and domestic labor, for more than eight hours a day, six days a week.[102] Enforcement was considerably strengthened by the provision that the mere "presence of such a child in any establishment shall be prima facie evidence of its employment."[103]

Laws making public education compulsory for children, long desired by labor organizations, were first enacted in 1902 for the benefit of those between the ages of eight and twelve years. In 1912 another more complicated law further spelled out school attendance.[104]

Maryland had no minimum wage law in this period. Brief mention, however, should be made of legislation in two related areas. Maryland passed a law forbidding railroads doing business within the state to withhold any part of the wages of their employees for the benefit of any relief association or the members thereof. This was to prevent fraud on the part of an employer acting as trustee of the workers' unpaid wages. Another series of laws dating back to 1868 dealt with the evils of the truck system or the company store, specifically in the coal-mining counties. Company stores could be an obvious convenience in out-of-the-way communities where miners often lived, but the possibilities for employer control over the worker were all but unavoidable. Wages, even if paid in legal tender rather than in credits at the store, were not much above subsistence, and soon the miner was in debt to the company through the store. Also, a worker might very well feel a compulsion to do some buying at the company store even if others were available, just in the hope of making his job a bit more secure. In the dual posi-

---

102. Steele, "Labor Laws," 51; Lauchheimer, pp. 101-105.
103. Lauchheimer, p. 102.
104. Hirschfeld, p. 76; Lauchheimer, p. 118.

tion of monopolist supplier of goods and credits the company could raise prices substantially and enjoy double profits. After 1900 it became the law in Allegany County, at least, that wages be paid only in legal tender and by 1911 the whole truck system was dying out.[105]

Gradually a body of legislation was accumulated whereby the state tested the qualifications of certain types of workmen and issued a license to work. Certification was required of plumbers, barbers, horseshoers, moving picture operators, stationary engineers, electricians, and chauffeurs. Unions favored this type of legislation as a stimulus toward organizing.[106]

In the area of factory safety and sanitation laws, Maryland was by 1914 still very deficient. Provisions against fire applied only to Baltimore and even there were inadequate. State protection laws regarding the use of dangerous machinery were even less satisfactory. Legislation setting sanitation standards dated back to 1884 and was impossible to enforce because of the generality of its provisions. The Maryland Bureau of Industrial Statistics and Information was empowered to enforce it, but in vain. In 1914 more effective legislation was passed, but there were still no uniform standards applicable to the whole state.[107]

The strikes of the clothing workers in 1892, 1894, and 1896 highlighted the conditions in the sweatshops and brought about legislation in 1894, 1896, and 1898 that sought to eliminate health hazards of communicable diseases and to set minimum requirements for cleanliness, lighting, ventilation, and the size of workrooms. Little improvement occurred. In 1902, however, legislation passed that was much more effective. The bureau was vested with broad powers of inspection and licensing. Two deputies of the chief of the bureau were to be factory inspectors and a permit was necessary before any building, or part of one, could be used in the manufacture of clothing, furs, or accessories. After a place of manufacture had been inspected, the chief of the bureau issued a permit specifying the number of persons that could work in the rooms. The law was tightened in 1914 and, although not exceptional, was considered adequate.

---

105. Lauchheimer, pp. 105-12.
106. Steele, "Labor Laws," 49; Lauchheimer, p. 113.
107. Lauchheimer, pp. 81-87.

While the inspection and licensing powers of the bureau were strengthened, a great loophole existed—the laxity of the officials of the local health department with which the bureau had to work in ascertaining the health conditions of the work premises.[108]

The conditions in the clothing industry leading to the enactment of these laws were notorious. In his recommendation of a factory inspection system, the chief of the bureau commented in 1890 on the terrible exploitation of labor, especially women and children "on inadequate premises and without any restriction of law."[109] After a tour of inspection in 1895 of some 200 places where clothing was manufactured, the chief summarized conditions as follows:

> The bulk of the places that fall within the category of sweatshops are to be found in the territory bounded by Lexington street, Eastern avenue, Caroline street and Jones' Falls, though there are a number of others in various sections of the city. The Hebrews are the most numerous of those engaged in the business, although Lithuanians and Bohemians form no inconsiderable part of the number. The shops are usually in dwelling houses, in some of which special apartments have been prepared, notably by the coat tailors, and in these an effort has been made to admit as much light and air as possible and to avoid many of the discomforts of the business. In a majority of the places visited, however, a large number of persons of both sexes were found crowded into a second story and attic rooms, surrounded on all sides by piles of clippings from the garments upon which they are engaged. . . . In addition to the clippings lying about, which is true of all shops, in many of them are found all sorts of dirt and filth either in the room where the work is being carried on, or in the adjoining ones, and the halls and stairways are swarming with half-clothed children, the imprints of whose unclean hands are found everywhere. The only entrance to some of the shops is through a malodorous side alley filled with stagnant water and other filth; thence up a crooked stairway and dingy hall strewn with pots, pans and other cooking utensils. . . .[110]

While lacking the color of detailed individual cases, the above

---

108. Hirschfeld, p. 75; Steele, "Labor Laws," 49; Lauchheimer, pp. 90-93.
109. Maryland, BISI, *Biennial Report, 1890–1891*, p. 7.
110. Maryland, BIS, *Annual Report, 1895*, pp. 80-81.

description has the virtue of being based on a fairly large number of cases.

Other important legislation in the area of safety and health was a series of laws on the ventilation and inspection of mines passed in 1876 and 1898 and amended in 1900. It applied to the mines in Allegany and Garrett Counties and provided for a mine inspector, specifying his duties and the conditions under which a mine should be operated. A penalty was attached for violations in a 1904 amendment.[111]

One other field of labor law which should be mentioned briefly is that of workmen's compensation. It began in 1902 for certain small categories of workers, covered about 10,000 workers, and was in effect for only two years. Its chief value was as an opening wedge for further legislative efforts, which came in 1910 to the mining industry and in 1912 to industry in general. Since the latter, however, was elective rather than compulsory, it was a dead letter. In 1914 the three earlier laws were repealed and a new and better law passed. It provided for a compulsory system of compensation insurance covering certain enumerated, extremely hazardous occupations. All other employments might elect such insurance, although this was not likely. Yet because of the resistance on the part of the employers to the increased costs in the form of insurance, the legislature did not enact an adequate law.[112]

Finally, the legislature provided that the Bureau of Statistics and Information could organize a court of arbitration in any important labor dispute. This came as the result of a massive strike of the coal miners in the George's Creek region in western Maryland in 1899, after which the chief of the bureau suggested establishing a court of arbitration to intervene in serious strikes at the request of either party involved. About three-quarters of the labor organizations in the state supported this proposal, but it was not enacted into law until 1904.[113]

In all, Maryland labor law in the period 1860–1914 was characterized as rather backward and almost totally unsystematic. Modelled fairly closely on the legislation of New York and more progressive than those of the southern states, its labor laws

---

111. Harvey, pp. 209, 325; Steele, "Labor Laws," 49-50.
112. Hirschfeld, p. 76; Lauchheimer, pp. 47-54.
113. Steele, "Influence," 42.

were far from pioneering or experimental. In this and in the lack of system, Maryland was unexceptional among the states. There was a welter of legislation in the field. Antiquated and useless legislation was left on the books, new legislation was enacted without repealing conflicting laws, criminal laws were enacted without penalties as sops to reform movements,[114] and "high sounding laws with fatal exceptions [were] in endless abundance."[115]

The trade unions, while always fragile and beset with difficulties, can be credited with three achievements, however incompletely realized in this period. The first was a definite improvement in wages and hours. As the bureau reported in 1902:

> . . . in whatever trade or calling you find a strong, compact union, there you find higher wages, a shorter work-day and average intelligence greater. . . . We have yet to hear of any considerable increase of the wages of the unskilled, or common laborer, or farm hand.[116]

Secondly, their own gains influenced the working conditions of other, unorganized workers in general, uplifting the standard of living. As the bureau noted in its 1905 report:

> the work they have really done in reducing the hours of labor, increasing wages, and bettering the condition generally of the working classes, because the high standard of living and the continual effort for a less number of hours of labor has, after all, been the basis for every advancement of the standard of living in this country. . . .
> It should be understood that the union rate of wages, in all mechanical industries especially, creates a standard wage rate in the community, and often unorganized workers secure considerable benefit from the efforts of the organization.[117]

Thirdly, their efforts gradually achieved an increasing amount of protective state legislation.

---

114. Lauchheimer, pp. 16, 96.
115. *Ibid.*, p. 96.
116. Maryland, BSI, *Annual Report, 1902*, p. 1.
117. Maryland, BSI, *Annual Report, 1905*, pp. 237-38.

## 6

### TRADE AND COMMERCE

Trade had been a natural, indeed vital, aspect of Maryland's economy since earliest days. The Chesapeake Bay abounds in protected harbors, on both the Eastern and Western Shore, giving easy outlet for exchange to local agricultural products, natural resources and manufactures. Crisfield, on the lower end of the Eastern Shore, was a port of entry in the customs district and prominent in the shipping of locally-packed oysters. Salisbury enjoyed a large trade in grain, fruit, lumber, and the products of its textile and flour mills. Cambridge shipped fish, oysters and lumber, and Easton traded in grain and fruit. On the Western Shore, Annapolis was a port of entry in the customs district; Havre de Grace traded in lumber and fish; and Port Deposit in lumber and quarried stone.[118] Nor does this exhaust the list of small ports.

The "Queen of the Chesapeake," the center of foreign and domestic trade, was, of course, Baltimore. Its long history of commercial vigor dated from the Revolutionary Era. Later on local shipbuilders produced the "Baltimore clipper," the fastest sailing vessel before the Civil War. Besides an excellent coastal location, Baltimore enjoyed the natural advantage of comparative closeness to the West, making transportation costs there cheaper and thus helping Baltimore as a distributive as well as an export center. During the ante-bellum period Baltimore was a commercial rather than a manufacturing city, with its economy focused on the import of sugar and coffee and the export of flour and grain. Its domestic traffic was in large part with the South, especially its extensive wholesale and jobbing trade. The Civil War disrupted the city's trade dramatically. Baltimore was occupied by federal troops and an embargo erected. Commerce with the South ended abruptly.[119]

After the war new patterns of foreign trade emerged for the nation, reflecting largely the growth of industrialization after

---

118. James Higgins, *A Succinct Exposition of the Industrial Resources and Agricultural Advantages of the State of Maryland* (Annapolis: 1867), *passim*; Maryland, Board of World's Fair Managers, *Maryland, Its Resources, Industries and Institutions* (Baltimore: 1893), pp. 352 ff.
119. Reid, pp. 501-12.

Commission Merchant: L. W. Gunther, tobacco and cotton,
at No. 9 South Gay Street, Baltimore. *M.H.S.*

1880. Nationally the export of crude foodstuffs rose initially from 1860 to 1880, mainly because the railroads were able to reach the western grain supply, and then declined thereafter to 1915. The proportion of foodstuffs in national exports fell steadily from 55.8 per cent in 1880 to 21.6 per cent in 1910. Manufactured foodstuffs rose until 1880, remained on a plateau until 1905, and then dropped until 1914. The export of raw materials declined over the period 1860–1914 while that of manufactures and semi-manufactures increased steadily. In 1880 manufactures formed 14.8 per cent of the exports of the nation. The proportion rose steadily until by 1910 they constituted 44.9 per cent of exports. The national import picture likewise reflected to a large degree the impact of industrialization. The proportion of raw materials and semi-manufactures escalated, while that of finished manufactures declined. The import of crude foodstuffs remained about the same.[120]

Baltimore's foreign trade pattern paralleled national trends in part, reflecting to some extent her own as well as the nation's industrialization. The proportion of the value of each category to the total value of Baltimore's export or import trade was calculated and presented in Table 14. As a gauge of the flow of Baltimore's exports and imports, the eight major articles imported and exported each decade are itemized in Table 13 at the end of the chapter. Then they are grouped into the five larger categories of commodities used in summarizing national trade patterns. Since for eleven out of the fourteen years examined, the eight items in Table 13 constitute well over one-half the total value of merchandise, this synoptic gauge is adequate as a very rough estimate. Admittedly, it is more accurate for exports than imports, and it is of uncertain value for imports in the year 1914. In both Tables 13 and 14, the year 1871 had to be used instead of 1870 because that volume of the Treasury Department's *Report on the Commerce and Navigation of the United States* was unavailable. Likewise, in both tables the data for 1914 is for Maryland rather than Baltimore alone, but this would not much affect the comparability of the 1914 information, since Baltimore was by all odds the most important port

---

120. Ross Robertson, *History of the American Economy* (2d ed.; New York: 1964), pp. 369–71; U.S., Department of Commerce and Labor, Bureau of Statistics, *The Foreign Commerce and Navigation of the United States: 1910*, p. 19.

in the state. In both tables exports are domestic and do not include re-imports; imports, of course, are exclusively foreign. Despite these reservations, the data are sufficiently representative to indicate the major trends in foreign trade.

In exports crude foodstuffs mainly paralleled the national trend, except for an insignificant growth in the 1860's. In the 1870's, however, there was phenomenal growth, reaching a peak in 1880 and declining thereafter. Grain was the major crude foodstuff exported from Baltimore. (See Table 13.) A glance at the grain trade in absolute terms—then a comparison of ten-year annual averages of the volume of corn and wheat combined—shows almost a doubling in the 1890's over the 1880's average, and in the decade 1901–1910 a drop in the average almost to the figure for the 1880's. While always second to New York as a grain market on the Atlantic coast throughout this period, Baltimore's relation to the leader improved rather than declined. Whereas in 1875 Baltimore exported not quite one quarter the amount of grain that New York did, by 1901 its proportion had risen to three-quarters. Before the 1870's local grain from Maryland, Virginia, North Carolina, Delaware, and Pennsylvania was exported from the city; but thereafter most of the grain came from the West, hauled by two trunk lines, the Baltimore and Ohio Railroad and the Pennsylvania Railroad. The relative closeness of the city to the Middle West as compared with the other northern Atlantic ports gave Baltimore a natural advantage in the competition for grain exports. By 1883 both lines had a total of seven large grain elevators, with a total capacity of over five million bushels, in the harbor right on deep water's edge. Corn and wheat were the most important grains, but occasionally rye, oats, and others figured significantly. Europe was the chief market, and by 1910, at least, Great Britain was Baltimore's best customer for corn. Germany also consumed a lot of both corn and wheat. Holland, Denmark and Belgium were the other large customers. Sensitive to poor western harvests, Baltimore was also vulnerable to the demands of the market. Poor European harvests caused the spectacular soaring of the city's grain exports from 1897 to 1899. All previous records were broken, and local hopes rose that Baltimore was capturing first place. Indeed, in 1897 the port achieved first rank in corn and second in wheat. But there were downs as well as ups. The European grain market contracted sharply between 1909 and 1910, and Baltimore's exports dropped suddenly.[121]

Cattle, while not nearly of the importance of grain, figured prominently in 1890 and 1900. The export of cattle began in 1878 and grew with the expansion of the railroads. The cattle came from Virginia, West Virginia, North Carolina, Tennessee, Kentucky, Pennsylvania and the Middle West. England was the chief consumer.[122]

Exports of manufactured foodstuffs showed a partial parallel with the national trend. The proportion of Baltimore's exports to its total exports fell from 1860 to 1880, rose in 1890 and fell thereafter, as Table 14 indicates. As can be seen in Table 13, lard and flour remained important throughout the period, while pork, bacon, hams, and corn meal figured occasionally. Baltimore remained an important flour market supplying the West Indies and South America, using mainly local grain grown in Virginia and Maryland and milled locally. By the 1870's western grain was hauled by rail to be processed in Baltimore, and by the 1880's western flour from Illinois, Indiana, and Minnesota superseded the importance of the local product, although flour continued to be produced locally. Exports went chiefly to Great Britain, the West Indies and Brazil, which in the 1880's was consuming over one half the amount exported by Baltimore. By 1910 the market was more diverse and was affected by two major developments: the drop in European demand for American foodstuffs and the gradual atrophying of Baltimore's coffee trade with Brazil. Coffee had formed the basis of the city's trade with that country. Lard by the 1870's came from the West and went to the West Indies, South America, and at least half to Britain and Germany.[123]

In general, Baltimore's exports of crude materials conformed to the national pattern. The proportion fell over the period, as can be seen in Table 14, but unlike the national trend, there is some suggestion of a possible rise from 1900 to 1914, although

121. Author's calculations based on figures cited in Reid, pp. 515-16. These figures apply only to corn and wheat shipments, and exclude all other varieties; Reid, pp. 516, 530; Bland, pp. 63, 66; Maryland, BIS, *Annual Report: 1899*, pp. 73, 119.

122. Maryland, Board of World's Fair Managers, *Maryland, Its Resources*, p. 328; Maryland, BISI, *Annual Report: 1911*, p. 323; Reid, pp. 520, 530.

123. Howard, pp. 133, 106-109; Maryland, Board of World's Fair Managers, *Maryland, Its Resources*, p. 326; Bland, p. 59; Reid, pp. 530, 517, 520.

not a very spectacular one. Leaf tobacco and raw cotton were the most important items throughout the period. Tobacco had always been a staple of trade, and after the Civil War almost the entire crop of Maryland and Ohio as well as some from Kentucky, North Carolina and Virginia was shipped from the port. France, England and Germany were the best customers. Quite early a system of state inspection was established by the legislature, and by the early 1870's there were six state warehouses in Baltimore.

Raw cotton, coming largely by steamer from Norfolk and Savannah, became an important consideration in Baltimore trade after the Civil War with the establishment of a cotton exchange and a state-chartered system of warehouse storage. The city shipped cotton mainly to Liverpool and Bremen.[124]

Semi-manufactures did not form a significant proportion of the city's exports until after 1900, when they rose steadily. Copper, in the form of pigs, ingots, bars, plates, and sheets, was the major item in this category. It became important in 1894, and in 1900 was the second most important article in terms of value, constituting 14 per cent of total exports. In 1910 and 1914 it was the leading item of export, accounting for 28 per cent and 39 per cent, respectively, of total exports. It went mainly to England, the Netherlands, and Germany.[125] The rising importance of semi-manufactures in Baltimore's exports after 1900 conforms to the national pattern, but for the United States as a whole the rise took place over the entire period, from 1860 on.

Unlike the national trend, Baltimore's exports of finished manufactures remained insignificant over the whole period, with fluctuations indicating no particular trend. Nor was there any single item of sustained importance. Cotton manufactures, illuminating oil, railroad rails, and agricultural implements all figured occasionally.

On the import side of the picture, crude foodstuffs rose in importance from 1860 to 1880 and then declined steadily, indeed precipitously. Basically, the nation had no such definite pattern, remaining relatively unchanged over the period. Coffee was by far the most important item, and its decline and disappearance constituted the dominant local trend in the flow of

---

124. Howard, pp. 184-85, 176-77; Bland, pp. 54, 79; Reid, pp. 530, 519-20.
125. Reid, p. 529.

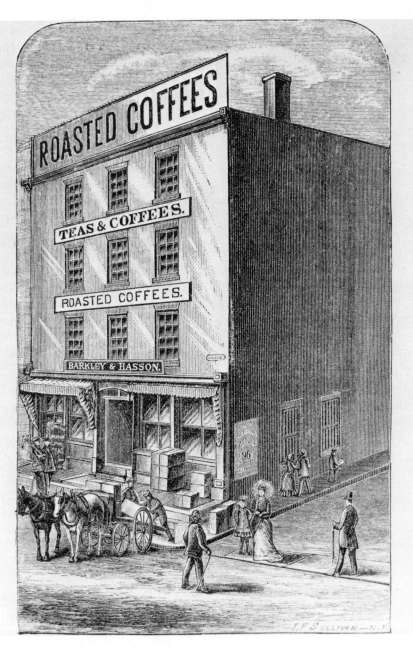

Coffee and Tea Importers—Barkley & Hasson's of Baltimore.
Engraving by J. F. Sullivan. *M.H.S.*

incoming foodstuffs in the period. Indeed, the decline of Baltimore's coffee trade went counter to the national increase in the importation of coffee. Baltimore's prominence in the importation and distribution of coffee dated from the late eighteenth century. As mentioned before, it came principally from Brazil and much of it was shipped west. While in 1871 Baltimore was second to New York and that year imported twice the amount of Boston, Philadelphia and New Orleans combined, it floundered in the sharp race with New York. One of the main reasons was that New York used steamers extensively in this trade, while Baltimore still depended on sailing vessels. Also New York, as a superior distributive center, could bring a mixed cargo from Brazil. Baltimore could import only coffee. In one month during 1883 New York nearly surpassed Baltimore's intake for that entire year.[126] By 1910 coffee had disappeared from the ranks of Baltimore's leading imports.

As in the nation, the importation of tropical fruit was of increasing importance. Bananas, in particular, came to Baltimore for both local consumption and general distribution. Nevertheless, in this period they did not begin to reach the level of importance that coffee had maintained.

While on the national scene there appeared no firm trend, manufactured foodstuffs imported into Baltimore rose proportionately between 1860 and 1871, dropped precipitously, and then disappeared. Sugar, molasses, and syrup from sugar cane were the items involved. They supplied at least six local refineries,[127] but by 1890 they had vanished from among the leading imports, and the refineries had ceased operation.

From 1860 through 1880 Baltimore went counter to the national trend in that the import of crude materials declined. Then from 1890 through 1910, it followed the national trend in the steady rise of this type of goods to meet the needs of a rapidly industrializing economy. Table 13 shows the great variety of articles in this category, such as copper, iron and manganese ores, guano, sulphur, muriate of potash, and nitrate of soda and tropical fibers. The guano, potash, and soda were for the local fertilizer industry.

---

126. Maryland, Board of World's Fair Managers, *Maryland, Its Resources*, p. 330; Howard, p. 116; Frank R. Rutter, *South American Trade of Baltimore* (Baltimore: J.H. Press, 1897), pp. 74, 85; Bland, p. 125.
127. Howard, p. 114.

The import of semi-manufactures into the city does not seem to have conformed to the national pattern. They rose proportionately from 1871 through 1900 and then declined, while those of the country at large continued to rise. Tin plate for the local canning industry, pig copper and pig iron were the chief items, as seen in Table 13.

Finally, finished manufactures arriving in Baltimore did not follow the national pattern. They dipped in proportionate importance in 1871 and rose from 1890 through 1914, as Table 14 indicates. Throughout, however, they remained insignificant. On the national scene they declined.

Throughout the period Baltimore remained an important port. Ranking fifth in the nation for imports in 1860, it rose to third in 1871, hovered between fifth and sixth from 1880 through 1910 and then fell to ninth in 1914. In exports it ranked seventh in 1860 and 1871, jumped to third in 1880 and 1890, reached second in 1900 and glided down to fourth in 1910 and fifth in 1914. Thus initially Baltimore was more important as an import center, and then beginning in 1880 and for the rest of the period it figured more importantly as an export center. Between 1880 and 1900 imports averaged only about $15 million per year, which increased, at least, to $27 million per year from 1901 through 1910. On the other hand, exports averaged $50 million per year from 1881 to 1890, $89 million for 1891–1900, and somewhat over $88 million for 1901–1910. From 1880 Baltimore illustrated in miniature the favorable balance of trade which characterized foreign commerce during this period.[128]

Baltimore was also the center of an extensive domestic trade, supplied by both ship and rail. Systematic figures on the tonnage, value and content are simply not available for the period, but a few scattered ones are at least helpful in sketching the impressive dimensions of the trade. In his annual report for 1890 the Chief of Engineers of the United States Army calculated that, making allowances for the unreported tonnage as well as ballast, the total tonnage for the coastal trade would be

128. U.S. Bureau of Statistics, *The Foreign Commerce and Navigation of the United States: 1880*, p. xxiii; *Foreign Commerce and Navigation: 1900*, I, 50-51; *Foreign Commerce and Navigation: 1910*, pp. 38-40, 54-55. All figures are in current dollars and have been rounded to the nearest million; Maryland, BSI, *Annual Report: 1913*, p. 171.

about 3,379,460 tons as compared with 1,956,226 tons for foreign commerce. From colonial times the coastal trade had been vital in Maryland's economy. By now it covered not only the Atlantic seaboard, but also the Gulf of Mexico and around to the Pacific coast to San Francisco.[129] Coal, ore, ice, lumber, and resin were among the chief articles, as well as "products of farm, mine and mill."[130] In 1896 coastwise tonnage exceeded export tonnage by 60 per cent. However, it should be kept in mind that in describing the coastal traffic in 1895 the Board of Trade of Baltimore commented that it was larger in tonnage than the foreign trade but somewhat less in value. In 1902, however, it was valued at $175 million as compared with $99 million for total foreign trade, and in the calendar year 1914 coastal trade was worth $240 million as compared with $144 for foreign trade. These scant and haphazard estimates suggest the possibility that at some point around the turn of the century coastal trade superseded foreign trade in importance. Without more complete figures, however, the picture remains unclear. In 1913 and 1914 the most important items in the trade were general merchandise, boots and shoes, tobacco, coal, fertilizer, cotton manufactures, whiskey, lumber, canned goods, and raw cotton. To transport these and other goods, Baltimore commanded the second largest bay and coastal fleet on the Atlantic by 1896.[131]

The coastal trade was oriented toward the South as indeed was most of the domestic trade of Baltimore in this period.[132] In the southern jobbing trade, which had begun before the Civil War and had very much revived and grown after the war, dry goods, clothing, hats, provisions, boots and shoes, hardware,

---

129. U.S. Dept. of Commerce, Bureau of Foreign and Domestic Commerce, "Ports of the United States," by Grosvenor M. Jones, Miscellaneous Series, No. 33 (Washington, D.C.: Government Printing Office, 1916), p. 144; U.S. War Department, *Annual Report of the Chief of Engineers, U.S. Army: 1890*, pt. 1, pp. 991-92.
130. *Ibid.*, p. 992.
131. Hirschfeld, pp. 32-33, 33 n., Engelhardt, p. 66; Reid, p. 529; *M.R.*, Sept. 3, 1914, pt 2, p. 50; U.S. Dept. of Commerce, "Ports of the U.S.," by Grosvenor Jones, p. 143.
132. For a somewhat different view see William B. Catton, "The Baltimore Business Community and the Secession Crisis, 1860–61," (M.A. thesis, University of Maryland, 1952), pp. 22-26. He estimates that in 1860 60 percent of Baltimore's coastal trade was with the North.

canned goods, notions, and drugs predominated.[133] Table 15
gives the estimated value of the chief items of domestic trade
in 1883. These figures are available through the publication by
the Baltimore Association of Merchants and Manufacturers of a
long and careful report on the nature and condition of the city's
economy as of the early 1880's.

Grain, bread, and breadstuffs made up the largest part of
Baltimore's trade, as can be seen in Table 15, and were mostly
exported. Dry goods, notions, and toys likewise represented a
substantial portion of the domestic trade. Southern and New
England textiles, as well as some from the middle states and
California, were distributed to the Middle West, Southwest,
Denver, San Francisco, New York, and Philadelphia. New England supplied 37 per cent of the goods, while Maryland supplied 18 per cent, especially heavy textiles. It held a virtual
monopoly of the supply of overalls to the West. The middle
states, including New York and Philadelphia, supplied 34 per
cent, mainly clothing accessories. Notions and toys came both
from abroad and from home. Trade in livestock consisted
mostly of cattle from the Virginias, Maryland and Pennsylvania,
and, to a lesser extent, Ohio and Illinois. As of 1883 the cattle
were mostly for home consumption. A small proportion was
shipped south and northeast, and an even smaller number was
exported. It was a growing business, having doubled in size
since 1873.

Baltimore had long been a center for the distribution of gro-
ceries, including tea, spices, and roasted coffee. About half of
the items were supplied domestically, namely canned goods,
flour, sugar, molasses, prepared spices, soap, candles, and soda.
Maryland, Delaware, Virginia, and West Virginia constituted
half of the market, the South 35 per cent, and Ohio 15 per cent.
Raw cotton came to Baltimore mainly from Norfolk, Charleston,
and Savannah by steamer, and from Cincinnati and St. Louis by
rail. Baltimore manufacturers used only a small portion; most of
it was exported. Provisions, consisting of meat and meat products, came largely from the Middle West, especially Illinois
and Indiana, and were exported as well as distributed to Maryland, Virginia, West Virginia and the Carolinas. The wood for
the wholesaling and jobbing of lumber came from Maryland,

---

133. Howard, p. 142; Bland, p. 34; Engelhardt, p. 6.

Virginia, the Carolinas, Georgia, Pennsylvania, and the Middle West and Northwest. Most of the coal distributed from Baltimore in 1883 was bituminous and went to New York, New England, Southern ports, and San Francisco. A small amount was consumed locally and an even lesser amount exported. The jobbing of coffee was done partly in Baltimore and partly in New York with coffee purchased there by Baltimore jobbers. Various types of hardware were supplied mainly from Maryland, Pennsylvania, New York, Connecticut, Massachusetts and Ohio. The articles were distributed about 25 per cent locally, 35 per cent to the South, 25 per cent to West Virginia and the Middle West, and 15 per cent to the middle states. Hides for the wholesaling of leather were imported from abroad as well as from the South and the Middle West, while leather came from the South, Ohio, Pennsylvania, and New York. Almost a million dollars worth of sole leather was consumed locally, and large quantities went to New York, Philadelphia, upper New York state, the Middle West, and the South. The jobbing of boots and shoes was a very vigorous part of domestic trade. It had grown substantially in the 1870's, so that Baltimore was an acknowledged center by 1883. Most of the shoes, about 65 per cent, came from New England, and about 25 per cent came from Maryland. Sales were mainly to the South, Maryland and Pennsylvania.[134] The trade in domestic liquors grew substantially after the Civil War. Maryland whiskey supplied about one quarter of the business, much of which went to the South and neighboring states such as Pennsylvania and New York.

To sum up, there were three geographic areas where Baltimore was paramount in the distributive or jobbing trade. The first, of course, was the state of Maryland itself and contiguous areas, such as the District of Columbia, part of Delaware, Pennsylvania, and Virginia. Because of the short distance involved, Baltimore had the advantage of lower freight charges over Philadelphia and New York and outstripped their competition. Trade in this section was on the increase in the early 1880's.

The second area comprised the South, from the Atlantic states to the Mississippi, Texas and Arkansas, Tennessee and Kentucky. Baltimore had a larger percentage of trade than such competitors as Boston, New York, and Philadelphia, but faced

---

134. The entire discussion is based on Bland, pp. 48-82.

some competition from southern cities and especially such western and southwestern cities as St. Louis, Chicago, Cincinnati and Louisville. A very rough estimate of the importance of the southern and southwestern trade to Baltimore business is given by an 1883 description of the warehouse district in the city which was devoted to a trade "70 per cent of which lies in . . . Virginia, North Carolina, South Carolina, Georgia, Tennessee, Alabama and Mississippi."[135]

The third area consisted of parts of Ohio, Indiana, West Virginia, and western Pennsylvania. Competition here was stiffest and came both from such eastern cities as Boston, New York, and Philadelphia, and such western ones, as St. Louis, Chicago, and Cincinnati.

Some goods distributed from Baltimore were marketed all over the country. These included such local products as straw goods, leather, millinery, paper, coal, and naval stores and such imports as coffee, sugar, molasses, foreign fruits, chemicals, iron and steel.[136]

Although there are no systematic figures for the value of Baltimore's domestic commerce, there are a few scattered estimates. In 1883 it was valued as $381 million and in 1910 at about $400 million.

Finally, two interior cities, Cumberland and Hagerstown, were centers of substantial internal commerce. Cumberland shipped mainly coal to the seaboard, and Hagerstown traded primarily in flour and farm products.[137]

7

TRANSPORTATION

A necessary underpinning to the industrial development of Maryland was a growing system of transportation. The site of the first railroad in the country, Maryland soon became jabbed and then laced with small lines and two major national lines, the Baltimore and Ohio and the Pennsylvania systems. Beginning in 1860 with approximately 373 miles, the total railroad mileage in the state by 1914 was 1,430 miles.

---

135. Bland, p. 34.
136. *Ibid.*, pp. 82-84.
137. Maryland, Board of World's Fair Managers, *Maryland, Its Resources*, pp. 332-36.

Locust Point terminus for the Baltimore and Ohio Railroad, Baltimore, 1870's. *M.H.S.*

470

Sustaining the vigor of Baltimore's commerce and manufacturing was a network of railroads. By 1861 Baltimore was an important railroad center. The Baltimore and Ohio, the Northern Central, the Philadelphia, Wilmington and Baltimore, and the Western Maryland railroads tied the city directly to West Virginia, the Susquehanna Valley of Pennsylvania, Washington, D.C., Wilmington, and Philadelphia; indirectly to points beyond, via connections with other railroads. By the early 1880's Baltimore was served by five railroads directly, including the two trunk lines to the West, the Baltimore & Ohio, and the Pennsylvania Railroad. The latter had absorbed two local lines: the Northern Central Railway in 1874 and the Philadelphia, Wilmington and Baltimore Railroad in 1881. Three local lines supplemented the two major lines: the Baltimore and Potomac Railroad, the Western Maryland Railroad, and the Maryland Central Railroad. Despite Baltimore's importance as a distributive center for the South, there was no direct railroad to that area. Three southern lines made use of steamship connections on the Chesapeake Bay to service the city: the Richmond and Danville, the Atlantic Coast Line, and the Seaboard Air Line.

The two trunk lines were instrumental in hauling grain from the West for the export sector of Baltimore's economy, as has been previously mentioned. Although Baltimore actually was closer to the western grain than either of her sharp eastern competitors, New York and Philadelphia, it was only after intense squabbling between the various trunk lines linking Chicago with the eastern seaboard that a differential was established in 1877 of one cent per hundredweight over Philadelphia and three cents over New York. This enabled Baltimore to be competitive with the other export ports.[138]

By 1914 the railroad picture was little changed in contour. The two major lines had grown larger, and the Baltimore & Ohio had the largest terminal on the Atlantic coast at Locust Point. It covered a mile of waterfront and handled thousands of immigrants and millions of tons of freight each year. Two very large grain elevators for the export trade and large coal piers completed its facilities. The Pennsylvania Railroad had

138. Bland, pp. 38-41; J. Wallace Bryan, "Transportation System and Facilities," *Baltimore, Its History and Its People*, ed. Hall, I, p. 492; Reid, pp. 512-13.

absorbed the Baltimore and Potomac Railroad. Its steamship terminal with two huge grain elevators was at Canton. The Western Maryland Railroad had been reorganized, modernized and considerably expanded since it had been taken over in 1901 by New York interests, headed by George J. Gould. It had been bought into a little later by John D. Rockefeller as well. Its importance to Baltimore was much increased by its connection with the New York Central System. Its waterfront terminal was at Port Covington, which had storage capacity for 2,000 freight cars. Last and decidedly least was the Maryland and Pennsylvania Railroad, an independent line formed in 1901 of seventy-eight ambling miles from Baltimore to York, Pennsylvania, with but slim *raison d'etre*. The route southward by rail was still considered unsatisfactory by those who wished a direct line to the deep South without recourse to rail connections in Washington or steamboat connections on the Bay to Virginia.[139]

Two canals were in operation in the state throughout the period. The Chesapeake and Ohio Canal, which paralleled the Potomac River, went from Cumberland to Georgetown, D.C., a distance of about 200 miles. It carried mainly coal. Outmoded by the building of the Baltimore and Ohio Railroad, it was plagued with financial difficulties and declining traffic. The Chesapeake and Delaware Canal provided a second and northern exit from the Chesapeake Bay to the ocean via the Delaware River and Bay. It was fifteen miles long. Most Chesapeake Bay traffic went south, but in 1916 the canal still carried almost as much as it had in 1880, mostly lumber.

The Chesapeake Bay itself, some 200 miles long and with numerous small harbors, provided Maryland with the basis of a natural system of water transportation. Baltimore, of course, was the major harbor; its natural advantages were improved a number of times throughout the period by the Army Corps of Engineers, who dredged and deepened the channel. By 1896 the nineteen miles of dredged ship channel was 600 feet wide and twenty-seven feet deep. This was the depth maintained off the Canton piers, Fells Point and Locust Point. By 1910 the

---

139. *M.R.*, Sept. 3, 1914, pt. 2, pp. 38, 42-44; George W. Hilton, *The Ma and Pa, A History of the Maryland and Pennsylvania Railroad* (Berkeley, Calif.: Howell-North, 1963), *passim*; Bryan, p. 498.

depth of the channel had been improved still further to thirty-five feet.[140]

Steamboats and sailing vessels plied the Bay between the smaller ports and, more importantly, connecting Baltimore with Norfolk and the Eastern Shore. Regular steamship lines also tied Baltimore directly to Boston, Providence, New York, Charleston, Savannah, and Jacksonville throughout the period. Ocean liners connected Baltimore on a regular basis with a number of ports in Great Britain as well as Copenhagen, Hamburg, Bremen, Antwerp, Rotterdam and Le Havre. While in the early 1880's thirteen lines had engaged in coastal traffic and six went to foreign ports, by 1914 a total of thirty-four lines in domestic and foreign trade were in operation. Of the regular lines running to Europe, the North German Lloyd, which had started service in Baltimore in 1868, was the oldest. Fruit steamers plied regularly to Cuba, the West Indies, and Central America, and at all times there were tramp steamers visiting the harbor.[141]

## 8

### FINANCE

Turning briefly to the field of finance, we note that by 1897 Baltimore had a total of thirty commercial banks, twenty-one of which were national banks. The aggregate capital amounted to almost $14 million.

In the 1890's Baltimore, along with the rest of the country, experienced a marked acceleration in the formation of trust companies. Thirteen such companies sprang up between 1895 and 1900 with an aggregate capital and surplus of $40 million. By contrast, in the early 1880's there had been but one.[142]

The South was a prime area for Baltimore investment, and many journalistic claims were made that the city was the financial center of that region. Soon after the Civil War, Baltimore had been quick to realize the attractiveness of investments in that area, and capital flow to the South had been a trend ever

---

140. Bryan, p. 500.

141. *Ibid.*, pp. 498-99; Bland, p. 24; *M.R.*, Sept. 3, 1914, pt. 2, p. 41.

142. Maryland, BIS, *Annual Report: 1897*, p. 76; Hirschfeld, p. 34; *M.R.*, Sept. 3, 1914, pt. 2, p. 33.

since. The *Manufacturers' Record* stated unequivocally in 1914
that Baltimore had been the financial center of the South for
fifty years. It estimated that by 1900 the amount of Baltimore
capital in that area was about $100 million, spread in a wide
variety of enterprises such as railroads, street railways, utilities,
cotton mills, coal, iron and phosphate mines, and lumber tracts.
The paper's conservative figure for the 1914 situation had
climbed to $400 million. However, the bias of the *Manufac-
turers' Record* is unmistakable. It constantly boomed both Baltimore and the South, presenting as encouraging a picture as
possible to induce further investment. As it reported no figures
for any other city's (especially New York's) relation with the
South, it cannot be stated with certainty whether or not Baltimore was indeed the financial keystone of the region. Baltimore's interests in the area, however, were heavy and of long
standing. The most dramatic examples were the Atlantic Coast
Line and the Seaboard Air Line, both of which had been initiated, promoted and knit together by Baltimoreans during the
Reconstruction period. The securities of a third railroad, the
Southern Railway Systems, were held extensively in Baltimore.
Individuals aside, trust companies, bonding companies, and
savings banks all invested substantially in southern securities.[143]

## 9

### SUMMARY

In retrospect, the period 1860–1914 was a pivotal one
wherein the economic life style of the state was permanently
altered. The balance between agriculture and commerce on the
one hand, and industry on the other, shifted in favor of industry. The relative importance of agriculture receded. Spurred by
the end of slavery, competition with western agriculture, and
improvements in railroad transportation, Maryland farms were
trimmed of their sprawling acreage and increasingly turned into
truck farms, supplying urban markets on the Atlantic seaboard.
Urbanization forged ahead until by 1910 more people lived in
towns and cities than in rural areas of the state. Most striking,
of course, was the growth of metropolitan Baltimore. Manufacturing grew, so that by 1900 it engaged more people in the state

---

143. Hirschfeld, p. 34; *M.R.*, Sept. 3, 1914, pt. 2, pp. 33-34.

Alex. Brown & Sons, Baltimore's oldest investment banking firm,
135 E. Baltimore Street, Baltimore. *M.H.S.*

than did agriculture. In its development, a mixture of light and heavy industry evolved as Maryland became a center for the manufacture of men's clothing, iron and steel, canned goods, and the refining of copper and petroleum. Baltimore remained a very important port, especially for the export of western grain and semi-finished copper. Its domestic trade supplied the South and Southwest and rivalled the export sector in importance.

The economic character of the city changed as industry became increasingly important. Essentially, Baltimore in this period maintained and improved its high rank as a commercial center, while at the same time developing into a moderately important industrial center. In the area of industrial organization the trend towards large corporations was unmistakable, if not yet dominant.

An industrial labor force developed, self conscious enough to attempt to organize unions and to press for collective bargaining and protective state legislation. Although not systematically successful, the efforts were sustained throughout the period. In all, Maryland prepared for the economic challenges of the twentieth century.

BIBLIOGRAPHICAL ESSAY

CHAPTER VI

This chapter is based almost entirely on primary sources. Most important are the United States census reports, the foreign trade reports of the U.S. Treasury and the reports of the Maryland Bureau of Industrial Statistics and Information. Systematic use was made of the federal census volumes on population, agriculture, manufacturing, and mining for the years 1860–1914 and of the United States Treasury reports on foreign trade for the same period. They provide not only the most detailed and reliable data but in addition often show the position of Maryland relative to the nation in these areas. The most helpful volumes printed by the Government Printing Office were: U.S. Census Office, *Eighth Census of the United States: 1860, Manufactures, Population* (1864); *Ninth Census: 1870,* III, *Statistics of the Wealth and Industry of the United States* (1872); *Tenth Census: 1880,* I, *Population,* II, *Manufactures, Report on the Productions of Agriculture* (1883); *Eleventh Census: 1890,* I & II, *Population, Report on Manufacturing Industries,* Parts I, II & III, *Report on the Mineral Industries* (1892); *Twelfth Census: 1900,* VI, *Agriculture,* Parts I & II, VIII, *Manufactures,* Parts I–IV, *Special Reports, Occupations* (1902). U.S. Bureau of the Census, *Special Reports, Mines and Quarries, 1902* (1905); *Manufactures, 1905,* Parts I–IV (1907); *Thirteenth Census: 1910,* II & IV, *Population,* VI, *Agriculture,* VIII, IX, *Manufactures,* XI, *Mines and Quarries* (1913); *Census of Manufactures: 1914,* I & II (1918); Census Monographs, X; Paul F. Brissindon, *Earnings of Factory Workers, 1899–1927* (1929); U.S. Treasury Department, *Report on Commerce and Navigation of the United States: 1860–1914* (1860–1914). Useful for estimates of the volume, cargoes, and number of ships engaged in domestic trade, particularly in the latter part of the period, are United States War Department, *Annual Report of the Chief of Engineers, U.S. Army: 1871, 1881, 1890, 1900, 1915* (1871–1915).

Important information for economic history of the era is found in Maryland Bureau of Industrial Statistics and Information, *Biennial Report* (Baltimore, 1884–1891); *Annual Report: 1893–1901* (1894–1902); *Annual Report: 1902–1914* (1902–1915). Unfortunately, the volumes do not cover the period of the Civil War to 1884. They are, however, the best source of labor statistics (such as they are) and contain a serious and sympathetic discussion of workmen problems and trends.

Valuable and detailed contemporary descriptions of the economic resources and development of Maryland are provided by James Higgins, *A Succinct Exposition of the Industrial Resources and Agricultural Advantages of the State of Maryland* (Annapolis: Henry Lucas, 1867). Note that it was a drummer booklet, published to encourage immigrants to settle in Maryland. John R. Bland, *A Review of the Commerce of the City of Baltimore* (Baltimore: N.P., 1886), compiled by the secretary of the Baltimore Merchants and Manufacturers Association at the request of the Bureau of Statistics of the U.S. Treasury Department, is a concrete and systematic treatment of the Baltimore economy in 1880. It indicates Baltimore's strengths and weaknesses and has some statistics. *The Industrial Survey of Baltimore: Report of Industries Located Within the Baltimore Metropolitan District* (Baltimore, 1914) is an examination of Baltimore's industrial growth to 1914 that supplies a thorough view of local manufactures.

*The Sun* (1860–1914), was the major newspaper used in writing this chapter. *The Manufacturers' Record, A Weekly Southern Industrial Railroad and Financial Newspaper* (Baltimore: 1882–1909) began in 1882 to encourage southern industrial development and is enlightening. Two special supplements give highly favorable descriptions of the Baltimore economy: *Blue Book of Southern Progress* (Baltimore: 1909, 1911), and *Baltimore: As It Was, As It Is, and As It Will Be* (Baltimore: 1914).

Two useful books that are a combination of primary and secondary sources and that include historical assessments and contemporary data are: George W. Howard, *The Monumental City, Its Past History and Present Resources* (Baltimore: J.D. Ehlers & Co., 1873), whose facts are abundant but undocumented, and Board of World's Fair Managers, *Maryland, Its Resources, Industries and Institutions* (Baltimore: Sun Printing Office, 1893). The latter consists of a series of essays written mainly by The Johns Hopkins University professors, who presented popular but responsible coverage of many aspects of Baltimore in 1893.

## Secondary Sources

To date no first-rate economic history of Baltimore or Maryland exists; little in the way of solid scholarly monographs in the area of economic history has been published. Of the older works the best is Clayton C. Hall, ed., *Baltimore, Its History and Its People.* The first volume consists of essays by different contributors, and although none venture very far from the approach of a chronicle, one in particular,

E. Emmet Reid's contribution, "Commerce and Manufactures of Baltimore," is thorough and well informed. Among few valuable monographs, Charles Hirschfeld, *Baltimore, 1870–1900: Studies in Social History* (Baltimore: J.H. Press, 1941) remains outstanding. Hirschfeld carefully analyzed the changes in the population, economy, public education, and charity. In the field of labor Malcolm H. Lauchheimer, *The Labor Law of Maryland, The Johns Hopkins University Studies in Historical and Political Science,* Series XXXVII, No. 2, (Baltimore: J.H. Press, 1919) is very clear and fairly detailed. Also helpful but so brief as to be sketchy are: Wirt H. Steele, "Labor Laws in Maryland," The Johns Hopkins University Circular, New Series, 1908, No. 5, Whole No. 206, and, by the same author, "The Influence of Labor Unions Upon Legislation in Maryland," New Series, 1911, No. 4. Whole No. 234. Katherine A. Harvey, *The Best Dressed Miners, Life and Labor in the Maryland Coal Region, 1835–1910* (Ithaca: Cornell University Press, 1969) contains much useful information written in an excellent style. Two works in the field of foreign trade are: Frank R. Rutter, *South American Trade of Baltimore, The Johns Hopkins University Studies in Historical and Political Science,* Series XV, IX, (Baltimore: J.H. Press, 1897) and Grosvenor M. Jones, "Ports of the United States," Dept. of Commerce, Bureau of Foreign and Domestic Commerce, *Miscellaneous Series,* No. 33 (Washington, D.C.: Government Printing Office, 1916). Clifton K. Yearley, Jr., "The Baltimore and Ohio Railroad Strike of 1877." *M.H.M.* LI (Sept. 1956), 188–211, is excellent. Less penetrating but a clear narrative of events is Doris Olszewski's "Strike on the Baltimore and Ohio, 1877," (M.A. thesis, George Washington University, 1952). Three good, unpublished studies on important subjects are: William B. Catton, "The Baltimore Business Community and the Secession Crisis, 1860–1861," (M.A. thesis, University of Maryland, 1952), his "John W. Garrett of the Baltimore and Ohio: A Study in Seaport and Railroad Competition, 1820–1874," (Ph.D. dissertation, Northwestern University, 1959), and Richard R. Duncan, "The Social and Economic Impact of the Civil War on Maryland," (Ph.D. dissertation, Ohio State University, 1963).

Finally, three broader studies helped provide perspective: John A. Garraty, *The New Commonwealth, 1877–1890, The New American Nation Series,* edited by Henry S. Commager and Richard B. Morris (New York: Harper and Row, 1968), Stanley Lebergott, *Manpower in Economic Growth: The American Record Since 1800, Economics Handbook Series,* edited by Seymour E. Harris (New York: McGraw-Hill Book Co., 1964) and Leo Wolman, *The Growth of American Trade Unions, 1880–1923,* (New York: National Bureau of Economic Research, Inc., 1924).

# TABLES

# APPLYING TO

# CHAPTER VI

*Much of the research in the United States census was done with the diligent help of Helen Camp.*

TABLE 1

TOTAL NUMBER OF PERSONS ENGAGED IN AGRICULTURE AND
IN THE MANUFACTURING AND MECHANICAL INDUSTRIES
IN MARYLAND, 1860–1910

| | Agriculture[a] | | Manufacturing and Mechanical Industries[b] | |
|---|---|---|---|---|
| | Number | Percentage of State Population | Number | Percentage of State Population |
| 1860[c] | 41,286 | 6.0 | 78,824 | 11.4 |
| 1870[d] | 79,602 | 10.1 | 58,540 | 7.4 |
| 1880[e] | 89,098 | 9.5 | 77,769 | 8.3 |
| 1890[f] | 88,195 | 8.4 | 83,260 | 7.9 |
| 1900[g] | 93,318 | 7.8 | 118,169 | 9.9 |
| 1910[h] | 101,166 | 7.8 | 137,687 | 10.6 |

[a]Includes farmers and planters. Percentages are author's calculation.
[b]Includes businessmen and labor, but excludes miners, fishermen, oystermen, and lumbermen.
[c]U.S., *Eighth Census: 1860, Population*, pp. 216–17. These figures are inexplicable and therefore are not discussed in the text.
[d]U.S., *Ninth Census: 1870, Statistics*, III, 812–23.
[e]U.S., *Tenth Census: 1880, Population*, I, 827.
[f]U.S., *Eleventh Census: 1890, Population*, pt. 1, 566.
[g]U.S., *Twelfth Census: 1900, Special Reports, Occupations 1900*, pp. 294–301.
[h]U.S., *Thirteenth Census: 1910, Population*, IV *Occupation Statistics*, 468–70.

TABLE 2

PERCENTAGE[a] OF PERSONS ENGAGED IN AGRICULTURE IN
MARYLAND BY NATIVITY AND RACE, 1890–1910

| | 1890[b] | | 1900[c] | | 1910[d] | |
|---|---|---|---|---|---|---|
| Total Native White | | 65.7 | | 67.1 | | 68.2 |
| Native Parents | 61.1 | | 62.1 | | 64.0 | |
| Foreign Parents | 4.5 | | 4.9 | | 4.1 | |
| Total Foreign White | | 4.5 | | 4.0 | | 2.7 |
| Total Negro | | 29.7 | | 28.8 | | 29.0 |
| Total | | 100 | | 100 | | 100 |

[a]Percentages are author's calculation based on census data.
[b]U.S., *Eleventh Census: 1890, Population*, pt. 1, 566.
[c]U.S., *Twelfth Census: 1900, Special Reports, Occupations 1900*, pp. 294–301.
[d]U.S., *Thirteenth Census: 1910, Population*, IV, *Occupation Statistics*, 468–70.

TABLE 3

THE LEADING INDUSTRIES IN MARYLAND, 1860–1914, AS
DETERMINED BY CAPITAL, SIZE OF LABOR FORCE, VALUE OF
PRODUCT, AND VALUE ADDED BY MANUFACTURE

*(In Current Dollars, Rounded to Nearest Thousand)*

## 1860[a]

| CAPITAL | | WAGE EARNERS | | VALUE OF PRODUCT | |
|---|---|---|---|---|---|
| Industry | Amount | Industry | Average No. | Industry | Amount |
| Flour and meal | $2,547 | Clothing, men's | 6,053 | Flour and meal | $8,231 |
| Cotton goods | 2,235 | Cotton goods | 2,649 | Clothing, men's | 3,271 |
| Machinery, steam | | Boots and shoes | 1,954 | Cotton goods | 2,941 |
| engines (etc.) | 1,384 | Oysters, canned | 1,698 | Sugar, refined | 2,300 |
| Clothing, men's | 1,270 | Machinery, steam | | Leather | 1,880 |
| Gas | 1,196 | engines (etc.) | 1,665 | Machinery, steam | |
| Leather | 1,088 | Brick | 1,250 | engines (etc.) | 1,611 |

## 1870[b]

| | | | | | |
|---|---|---|---|---|---|
| Flouring and grist | | Clothing, men's | 7,316 | Sugar, refined | $7,008 |
| mill products | $2,791 | Boots and shoes | 3,228 | Flouring and grist | |
| Cotton goods | 2,734 | Cotton goods | 2,860 | mill products | 6,786 |
| Clothing, men's | 2,238 | Brick | 2,051 | Clothing, men's | 5,832 |
| Iron, pig | 2,005 | Fruit and vege- | | Cotton goods | 4,853 |
| Gas | 1,820 | tables, canned | 1,985 | Iron, forged and | |
| Paper, printing | 1,122 | Oysters and fish, | | rolled | 3,573 |
| | | canned | 1,531 | Boots and shoes | 3,111 |

## 1880[c]

| | | | | | |
|---|---|---|---|---|---|
| Iron and steel | $4,962 | Fruits and vege- | | Clothing, men's | $9,579 |
| Cotton goods | 4,606 | tables, canned | | Flouring and grist | |
| Fertilizers | 4,272 | and preserved | 14,998 | mill products | 7,954 |
| Clothing, men's | 3,895 | Clothing, men's | 11,294 | Fruits and vege- | |
| Flouring and grist | | Cotton goods | 4,055 | tables, canned | |
| mill products | 3,146 | Foundry and | | and preserved | 6,245 |
| Foundry and | | machine shop | | Fertilizers | 5,770 |
| machine shop | | products | 3,150 | Cotton goods | 4,689 |
| products | 2,684 | Boots and shoes | | Iron and steel | 4,470 |
| | | including custom | | | |
| | | work and repair | 2,943 | | |
| | | Iron and steel | 2,763 | | |

TABLE 3—Continued

**1890[d]**

| CAPITAL | | WAGE EARNERS | | VALUE OF PRODUCT | |
|---|---|---|---|---|---|
| Industry | Amount | Industry | Average No. | Industry | Amount |
| Clothing, men's | | Fruits and vege- | | Clothing, men's | |
| factory product | $9,783 | tables, canning | | factory product | $15,033 |
| Cotton goods | 7,297 | and preserving | 13,048 | Masonry, brick | |
| Fertilizers | 6,936 | Clothing, men's | | and stone | 10,282 |
| Liquors, malt | 5,825 | factory product | 12,700 | Fruits and vege- | |
| Foundry and | | Masonry, brick | | tables, canning | |
| machine shop | | and stone | 4,467 | and preserving | 7,196 |
| products | 4,670 | Cotton goods | 4,256 | Flouring and grist | |
| Iron and steel | 4,068 | Foundry and | | mill products | 6,905 |
| | | machine shop | | Fertilizers | 6,208 |
| | | products | 3,352 | Tinsmithing, | |
| | | Tinsmithing, | | coppersmithing, | |
| | | coppersmithing, | | sheet-iron | |
| | | and sheet-iron | | working | 5,538 |
| | | working | 3,280 | | |

**1900[e]**

| | | | | | |
|---|---|---|---|---|---|
| Gas, illuminating | | Clothing, men's | | Clothing, men's, | |
| and heating | $18,554 | factory product | 9,725 | factory | |
| Liquors, malt | 13,857 | Fruits and vege- | | product | $17,328 |
| Clothing, men's, | | tables, canning | | Fruits and vege- | |
| factory product | 8,458 | and preserving | 7,505 | tables, canning | |
| Cotton goods | 7,709 | Cotton goods | 4,727 | and preserving | 11,996 |
| Fertilizers | 7,003 | Foundry and | | Iron and steel | 8,739 |
| Foundry and | | machine shop | | Foundry and | |
| machine shop | | products | 4,695 | machine shop | |
| products | 6,382 | Shirts | 3,998 | products | 8,444 |
| | | Cars and general | | Flouring and grist | |
| | | shop construc- | | mill products | 8,035 |
| | | tion | 3,620 | Tobacco, chewing, | |
| | | | | smoking, snuff | 7,054 |

TABLE 3—Continued

### 1909ᶠ

| CAPITAL | | WAGE EARNERS | |
|---|---|---|---|
| Industry | Amount | Industry | Average No. |
| Gas, illuminating and heating | $26,954 | Clothing, men's including shirts | 19,784 |
| Copper, tin, and sheet-iron products | 24,719 | Canning and preserving | 8,613 |
| Clothing, men's including shirts | 19,578 | Lumber and timber products | 7,003 |
| Foundry and machine shop products | 10,324 | Cars and general shop construction | 5,549 |
| Lumber and timber products | 9,182 | Copper, tin, and sheet-iron products | 5,275 |
| Fertilizers | 9,098 | Foundry and machine shop products | 4,798 |

| VALUE OF PRODUCT | | VALUE ADDED BY MANUFACTURE | |
|---|---|---|---|
| Industry | Amount | Industry | Amount |
| Clothing, men's including shirts | $36,921 | Clothing, men's including shirts | $15,955 |
| Copper, tin, and sheet-iron products | 16,909 | Copper, tin, and sheet-iron products | 6,101 |
| Canning and preserving | 13,709 | Foundry and machine shop products | 6,021 |
| Slaughtering and meat packing | 13,683 | Printing and publishing | 5,895 |
| Lumber and timber products | 12,134 | Lumber and timber products | 5,627 |
| Foundry and machine shop products | 11,978 | Tobacco manufactures | 4,893 |

TABLE 3—Continued

1914<sup>g</sup>

CAPITAL

| Industry | Amount |
|---|---|
| Gas, illuminating and heating | $20,663 |
| Clothing, men's | 17,364 |
| Fertilizers | 16,325 |
| Stamped and enameled ware | 11,483 |
| Tinware | 10,755 |
| Canning and preserving, fruits and vegetables | 10,370 |

WAGE EARNERS

| Industry | Average No. |
|---|---|
| Clothing, men's | 12,909 |
| Canning and preserving, fruits and vegetables | 8,354 |
| Cars and general shop construction | 5,969 |
| Shirts | 5,153 |
| Stamped and enameled ware | 4,155 |
| Cotton goods | 3,424 |

VALUE OF PRODUCT

| Industry | Amount |
|---|---|
| Clothing, men's | $29,000 |
| Canning and preserving, fruits and vegetables | 17,500 |
| Slaughtering and meat packing | 16,607 |
| Fertilizers | 13,987 |
| Cars and general shop construction | 13,229 |
| Stamped and enameled ware | 12,615 |

VALUE ADDED BY MANUFACTURES

| Industry | Amount |
|---|---|
| Clothing, men's | $13,983 |
| Liquors, distilled | 5,715 |
| Stamped and enameled ware | 5,243 |
| Liquors, malt | 5,086 |
| Canning and preserving, fruits and vegetables | 4,896 |
| Shirts | 4,467 |

<sup>a</sup>U.S., *Eighth Census: 1860, Manufactures*, pp. 228–30.

<sup>b</sup>U.S., *Ninth Census: 1870*, III, *Statistics of Wealth and Industry*, 526–28, 762.

<sup>c</sup>U.S., *Tenth Census: 1880*, II, *Manufactures*, 128–30.

<sup>d</sup>U.S., *Eleventh Census: 1890, Manufacturing*, II, pt. 1, 444–45.

<sup>e</sup>U.S., *Twelfth Census: 1900*, VIII, *Manufactures*, pt. 2, 336–41.

<sup>f</sup>U.S., *Thirteenth Census: 1910*, VIII, *Manufactures, 1909*, pt. 1, *General Report and Analysis*, 482–85.

<sup>g</sup>U.S., *Census of Manufactures: 1914*, I, 578–83.

TABLE 4

BALTIMORE CITY'S AGGREGATE INDUSTRIAL GROWTH:
PERCENTILE INCREASE IN THE VALUE OF PRODUCTS

*(In Current Dollars, 1880–1914)*

| Years | Per Cent |
|---|---|
| 1880–1890[a] | 80.7 |
| 1890–1900[a] | 13.8 |
| 1899–1904[b] | 11.1 |
| 1904–1909[b] | 24.5 |
| 1909–1914[c] | 15.1 |

[a]U.S., *Twelfth Census: 1900, Manufactures*, pt. 2, 334.
[b]U.S., *Thirteenth Census: 1910*, VIII, *Manufactures*, pt. 1,
   *General Report and Analysis*, 99.
[c]U.S., *Census of Manufactures: 1914*, I, 563.


TABLE 5

THE MAJOR INDUSTRIES IN BALTIMORE, 1860–1914,
BY GROSS VALUE OF PRODUCT

*(In Current Dollars, Rounded to Nearest Thousand)*

| 1860[a] | | 1870[b] | | 1880[c] | |
|---|---|---|---|---|---|
| Industry | Value of Product | Industry | Value of Product | Industry | Value of Product |
| Clothing, men's | $3,124 | Molasses and sugar | | Clothing, men's | $9,447 |
| Sugar, refined | 2,300 | refined | $7,008 | Fruits and vege- | |
| Copper, smelting | 1,300 | Clothing, men's | 5,574 | tables canning | |
| Oysters, packed | 1,026 | Iron, forged and | | and preserving | 5,201 |
| Boots and shoes | 872 | rolled | 2,873 | Fertilizer | 4,287 |
| Cigars | 673 | Boots and shoes | 1,937 | Foundry and | |
| | | Iron, pig | 1,499 | machine shop | |
| | | Fruits and vege- | | products | 3,910 |
| | | tables canned | 1,402 | Boots and shoes | 3,412 |
| | | | | Tin, copper and | |
| | | | | sheet ironware | 3,371 |

TABLE 5—Continued

| 1890[d] | | 1900[e] | | 1909[f] | |
|---|---|---|---|---|---|
| Industry | Value of Product | Industry | Value of Product | Industry | Value of Product |
| Clothing, men's | $15,033 | Clothing, men's | $17,291 | Clothing, men's | $36,269 |
| Masonry, brick and stone | 10,190 | Fruits and vegetables canning and preserving | 8,477 | Copper, tin and sheet iron products | 12,833 |
| Fruits and vegetables canning and preserving | 5,723 | Tobacco, chewing, smoking and snuff | 7,054 | Tobacco manufactures | 10,270 |
| Tin and coppersmithing and sheet iron work | 5,218 | Foundry and machine shop products | 6,120 | Slaughtering and meat packing | 10,082 |
| Foundry and machine shop products | 4,718 | Tin and coppersmithing and sheet iron work | 5,421 | Foundry and machine shop products | 9,074 |
| Slaughtering and meat packing wholesale | 4,311 | Slaughtering and and meat packing, wholesale | 5,308 | Printing and publishing | 7,553 |

| 1914[g] | |
|---|---|
| Industry | Value of Product |
| Clothing | $44,482 |
| Copper, tin and sheet-iron products | 18,842 |
| Printing and publishing | 10,284 |
| Cars | 10,039 |
| Slaughtering and meat packing | 9,504 |
| Canning and preserving | 7,789 |

[a]U.S., *Eighth Census: 1860, Manufactures*, pp. 220–22.
[b]U.S., *Ninth Census: 1870*, III, *Statistics of Wealth and Industry*, 672–73.
[c]U.S., *Tenth Census: 1880*, II, *Manufactures*, 383–84.
[d]U.S., *Eleventh Census: 1890*, II, *Manufacturing*, pt. 2, 46–57.
[e]U.S., *Twelfth Census: 1900*, VIII, *Manufactures*, pt. 2, 340–45.
[f]U.S., *Thirteenth Census: 1910*, IX, *Manufactures. Statistics for Maryland*, 648–49.
[g]U.S., *Census of Manufactures: 1914*, I, 584–87.

TABLE 6

THE LEADING INDUSTRIES IN BALTIMORE CITY, 1860–1914,
AS DETERMINED BY CAPITAL, SIZE OF LABOR FORCE,
AND VALUE ADDED BY MANUFACTURE[a]

*(In Current Dollars, Rounded to Nearest Thousand)*

### 1860

| CAPITAL | | WAGE EARNERS | |
|---|---|---|---|
| Industry | Amount | Industry | Average No. |
| Clothing, men's | $1,219 | Clothing, men's | 5,811 |
| Gas | 1,100 | Oysters, packed | 1,698 |
| Oysters, packed | 652 | Boots and shoes | 1,340 |
| Copper, smelting | 600 | Brick | 865 |
| Leather | 335 | Cigars | 505 |
| Iron, castings | 328 | Ship and | |
| | | boatbuilding | 442 |

### 1870

| | | | |
|---|---|---|---|
| Clothing, men's | $2,157 | Clothing, men's | 7,033 |
| Gas | 1,658 | Brick | 1,712 |
| Molasses and | | Boots and shoes | 1,563 |
| sugar refined | 958 | Oysters and fish, | |
| Brick | 927 | canned | 1,286 |
| Copper, milled | | Fruits and vege- | |
| and smelted | 800 | tables canned | 1,282 |
| Printing and | | Iron, forged and | |
| publishing | 782 | rolled | 1,192 |

### 1880

| CAPITAL | | VALUE OF PRODUCT | | WAGE EARNERS | |
|---|---|---|---|---|---|
| Industry | Amount | Industry | Amount | Industry | Average No. |
| Clothing, men's | $3,849 | Clothing, men's | $3,433 | Clothing, men's | 11,157 |
| Fertilizers | 3,241 | Foundry and | | Fruits and vege- | |
| Foundry and | | machine shop | 2,053 | tables canned | 10,923 |
| machine shop | 2,240 | Boots and shoes | 1,779 | Boots and shoes | 2,694 |
| Printing and | | Fertilizers | 1,598 | Foundry and | |
| publishing | 1,954 | Fruits and vege- | | machine shop | 2,676 |
| Iron and steel | 1,632 | tables, canned | 1,346 | Shirts | 1,696 |
| Shipbuilding | 1,493 | Tin, copper and | | Brick and tile | 1,529 |
| | | sheet-iron | 1,120 | | |

### 1890

| | | | | | |
|---|---|---|---|---|---|
| Clothing, men's | | Clothing, men's | | Clothing, men's | |
| factory product | $9,783 | factory product | $6,910 | factory product | 12,700 |
| Foundry and | | Masonry, brick | | Fruits and vege- | |
| machine shop | 4,523 | and stone | 4,913 | tables, canned | 5,195 |
| Liquors, malt | 4,456 | Foundry and | | Masonry, brick | |
| Fertilizers | 3,979 | machine shop | 2,924 | and stone | 4,376 |
| Masonry, brick | | Liquors, malt | 2,209 | Foundry and | |
| and stone | 3,011 | Fruits and vege- | | machine shop | 3,222 |
| Tin, sheet-iron and | | tables, canned | 2,209 | Tin, sheet-iron and | |
| coppersmithing | 2,335 | Tin, sheet-iron and | | coppersmithing | 3,061 |
| | | coppersmithing | 2,200 | Oysters, canned | 2,666 |

TABLE 6—Continued

## 1900

| CAPITAL | | VALUE OF PRODUCT | | WAGE EARNERS | |
|---|---|---|---|---|---|
| Industry | Amount | Industry | Amount | Industry | Average No. |
| Liquors, malt | $9,689 | Clothing, men's, factory product | $7,067 | Clothing, men's factory product | 9,690 |
| Clothing, men's factory product | 8,435 | Tobacco (chewing) | 4,558 | Fruits and vegetables, canned | 4,360 |
| Foundry and machine shop | 4,971 | Foundry and machine shop | 3,972 | Foundry and machine shop | 3,375 |
| Fertilizers | 4,450 | Carpentering | 2,623 | Shirts | 2,475 |
| Fruits and vegetables, canned | 2,862 | Liquors, malt | 2,312 | Cars | 2,438 |
| Cars | 2,236 | Fruits and vegetables, canned | 2,045 | Tin and coppersmithing and sheet-iron | 2,227 |

## 1909

| | | | | | |
|---|---|---|---|---|---|
| Copper, tin and sheet-iron | $20,655 | Clothing, men's and shirts | $15,597 | Clothing, men's including shirts | 18,596 |
| Clothing, men's factory product | 19,283 | Printing and publishing | 5,326 | Copper, tin and sheet-iron | 4,172 |
| Foundry and machine shop | 7,863 | Foundry and machine shop | 4,870 | Cars | 4,163 |
| Tobacco manufactures | 6,442 | Tobacco manufactures | 4,740 | Foundry and machine shop | 3,719 |
| Printing and publishing | 5,625 | Copper, tin and sheet-iron | 4,661 | Tobacco manufactures | 3,294 |
| Liquors, malt | 5,350 | Patent medicines, compounds and druggists' preparations | 3,335 | Canning and preserving | 3,166 |

## 1914

| CAPITAL | | VALUE ADDED BY MANUFACTURES | | WAGE EARNERS | |
|---|---|---|---|---|---|
| Industry | Amount | Industry | Amount | Industry | Average No. |
| Clothing | $19,749 | Clothing | $16,627 | Clothing | 15,770 |
| Fertilizers | 7,544 | Copper, tin and sheet-iron | 6,660 | Copper, tin and sheet-iron | 6,289 |
| Liquors, malt | 6,767 | Shirts | 4,223 | Shirts | 4,449 |
| Foundry and machine shop | 6,560 | Printing and publishing | 3,418 | Cars | 3,490 |
| Shirts | 5,099 | Liquors, malt | 3,306 | Fruits and vegetables, canned | 3,290 |
| Printing and publishing | 4,244 | Bread and other bakery products | 2,855 | Foundry and machine shop | 3,071 |

[a]U.S., *Eighth Census: 1860, Manufactures*, pp. 220–22.
[b]U.S., *Ninth Census: 1870*, III, *Statistics of Wealth and Industry*, 672–73.
[c]U.S., *Tenth Census: 1880*, II, *Manufactures*, 383–84.
[d]U.S., *Eleventh Census: 1890*, II, *Manufacturing*, pt. 2, 46–57.
[e]U.S., *Twelfth Census: 1900*, VIII, *Manufactures*, pt. 2, 340–45.
[f]U.S., *Thirteenth Census: 1910*, IX, *Manufactures. Statistics for Maryland*, 648–49.
[g]U.S., *Census of Manufactures: 1914*, I, 584–87.

TABLE 7

BALTIMORE AS COMPARED WITH 99 OTHER
INDUSTRIAL CITIES IN THE U.S.: 1880–1914

*(Current Dollars)*

| | GROSS PRODUCT | | NET PRODUCT | | WAGE EARNERS | | TOTAL WAGES | |
| Year | Rank | Value | Rank | Value | Rank | Number | Rank | Amount |
|---|---|---|---|---|---|---|---|---|
| 1880[a] | 8 | $78,417,304 | 9 | $30,443,007 | 5 | 56,338 | 9 | $15,117,489 |
| 1890[b] | 8 | 141,723,599 | 8 | 67,953,598 | 8 | 83,745 | 8 | 35,914,854 |
| 1900[c] | 8 | 135,107,626 | — | — | 4 | 66,571 | 8 | 23,493,427 |
| 1905[d] | 9 | 151,546,580 | — | — | 5 | 65,224 | 9 | 25,633,550 |
| 1909[e] | 13 | 186,977,710 | 13 | 79,953,827 | 7 | 71,444 | — | — |
| 1914[f] | 11 | 215,171,530 | 12 | 94,638,311 | 8 | 73,769 | — | — |

[a]U.S., *Tenth Census, 1880, Manufactures,* II, p. xxiv.
[b]U.S., *Eleventh Census: 1890,* II, *Manufacturing,* pt. 2, p. xxxii.
[c]U.S., Bureau of the Census, *Special Report on Manufactures, 1905,* p. cclxxxii.
[d]*Ibid.*
[e]U.S., *Thirteenth Census: 1910,* X, *Manufactures,* 84.
[f]U.S., Bureau of the Census, *Abstract of the Census of Manufactures: 1914,* p. 282.

TABLE 8

BALTIMORE AS COMPARED WITH OTHER LEADING
INDUSTRIAL CITIES IN THE UNITED STATES AS
MEASURED BY THE VALUE OF PRODUCT IN
LEADING INDUSTRIES: 1880–1909

| Rank | 1880[a] | 1890[b] | 1900[c] | 1905[d] | 1909[e] |
|---|---|---|---|---|---|
| 1st | tinware, copperware and sheet-ironware | | | | |
| 2nd | | | | | |
| 3rd | | masonry (brick and stone) | | | clothing, men's including shirts |
| 4th | brick and tile | | clothing | clothing | cars and general shop construction and repair by steam R. R. Co's. |
| 5th | carpentry | | tobacco manufactures | tobacco manufactures | |
| 6th | bread and other bakery goods men's clothing marble and stonework saddlery and harness shipbuilding tobacco (cigars and cigarettes) | clothing, men's factory product bread and other bakery goods | | | |

[a]U.S., *Tenth Census: 1880, Manufactures*, II, p. xxvi.
[b]U.S., *Eleventh Census: 1890*, II, *Manufacturing*, pt. 2, p. xxxv.
[c]U.S., Bureau of the Census, *Special Report on Manufactures, 1905*, p. cclxxx.
[d]*Ibid.*
[e]U.S., *Thirteenth Census: 1910*, X, *Manufactures*, 91.

TABLE 9

AGGREGATE MANUFACTURES OF HAGERSTOWN, CUMBERLAND,
AND FREDERICK, 1899–1914,
AS MEASURED BY CAPITAL, LABOR FORCE, VALUE OF
PRODUCT, AND NUMBER OF ESTABLISHMENTS

*(In Current Dollars, Rounded to Nearest Thousand)*

| | HAGERSTOWN | | | |
| | ESTABLISHMENTS | CAPITAL | AVERAGE NO. WAGE EARNERS | VALUE OF PRODUCT |
|---|---|---|---|---|
| 1899[a] | 80 | $1,121 | 1,515 | $1,820 |
| 1904[a] | 67 | 2,194 | 2,210 | 3,027 |
| 1909[a] | 76 | 2,970 | 1,718 | 3,197 |
| 1914[b] | 113 | 6,713 | 3,574 | 7,412 |

| | CUMBERLAND | | | |
|---|---|---|---|---|
| 1899[a] | 56 | $2,352 | 1,643 | $2,900 |
| 1904[a] | 72 | 4,139 | 2,276 | 4,595 |
| 1909[a] | 71 | 4,095 | 1,936 | 4,534 |
| 1914[b] | 74 | 5,135 | 2,817 | 7,113 |

| | FREDERICK | | | |
|---|---|---|---|---|
| 1899[a] | 54 | $1,033 | 939 | $1,438 |
| 1904[a] | 56 | 1,421 | 1,032 | 1,938 |
| 1909[a] | 55 | 2,370 | 1,026 | 2,911 |
| 1914[b] | 57 | 2,788 | 1,146 | 3,167 |

[a]U.S., *Thirteenth Census: 1910,* IX, *Manufactures. Statistics for Maryland,* 643–44.
[b]U.S., *Census of Manufactures: 1914,* I, 577, 586.

TABLE 10

TOTAL NUMBER OF WAGE EARNERS, MALE, FEMALE, AND
CHILDREN IN MANUFACTURING, MECHANICAL AND
MINING INDUSTRIES AND THE PERCENTAGE OF
GROWTH, IN MARYLAND AND BALTIMORE,
1860–1914

| | MARYLAND | | | BALTIMORE |
|---|---|---|---|---|
| | TOTAL | MANUFACTURING AND MECHANICAL | PERCENTAGE GROWTH[h] | TOTAL |
| 1860[a] | 28,703 | 27,422 | — | 17,054 |
| 1870[b] | 48,661 | 44,860 | 66 | — |
| 1880[c] | 78,564 | 74,945 | 66 | 56,338 |
| 1890[d] | 101,901 | 97,808 | 30 | 76,489 |
| 1900[e] | 113,546 | 108,325 | 10 | 78,738 |
| 1910[f] | 114,880 | 107,921 | — | 71,444 |
| 1914[g] | — | 111,585 | 3 | 73,769 |

[a]U.S., *Eighth Census: 1860, Manufactures*, pp. 222, 230; *Population*, pp. 216–17.
[b]U.S., *Ninth Census: 1870*, III, *Statistics of Wealth*, 526, 762.
[c]U.S., *Tenth Census: 1880, Manufactures*, II, 128; *Population*, I, 827;
    U.S., *Twelfth Census: 1900, Manufactures*, VIII, pt. 2, 334.
[d]U.S., *Eleventh Census: 1890, Manufacturing*, II, pt. 1, 444–45, *Population*, pt. 1,
    566; U.S., *Twelfth Census: 1900, Manufactures*, VIII, pt. 2, 334.
[e]U.S., *Twelfth Census: 1900*, VIII, *Manufactures*, pt. 2, 329, 334;
    U.S., Bureau of the Census, *Special Reports, Occupations, 1904*, p. 298.
[f]U.S., *Thirteenth Census: 1910*, IX, *Manufactures*, 482, 486; *Population*, IV, 468.
[g]U.S., *Census of Manufactures: 1914*, I, 566, 584.
[h]Author's calculations.

TABLE 11

TOTAL NUMBER OF WAGE EARNERS IN THE MANUFACTURING
AND MECHANICAL INDUSTRIES IN MARYLAND AND IN
BALTIMORE BY SEX AND AGE DISTRIBUTION
1860–1914

|  | MARYLAND | | | BALTIMORE | | |
|  | Men | Women | Children | Men | Women | Children |
|---|---|---|---|---|---|---|
| 1860[a] | 21,930 | 6,773 | — | 12,388 | 4,666 | — |
| 1870[b] | 34,061 | 8,278 | 2,521 | — | — | — |
| 1880[c] | 46,698 | 21,700 | 6,547 | 34,086 | 18,137 | 4,115 |
| 1890[d] | 67,261 | 26,432 | 4,115 | 53,626 | 21,030 | 1,833 |
| 1900[e] | 72,824 | 29,617 | 5,884 | 50,954 | 23,710 | 4,074 |
| 1910[f] | 72,416 | 28,957 | 6,548 | 44,258 | 22,875 | 4,311 |
| 1914[g] | 76,262 | 31,649 | 3,674 | 47,613 | 26,926 | 2,650 |

[a]U.S., *Eighth Census: 1860, Manufactures,* pp. 222, 228.
[b]U.S., *Ninth Census: 1870,* III, *Statistics of Wealth,* 526.
[c]U.S., *Tenth Census: 1880, Manufactures,* II, 128;
   *Report on Social Statistics of Cities,* pt. 2, 24.
[d]U.S., *Eleventh Census: 1890,* II, *Manufacturing,* pt. 1, 445, pt. 2, 47–49.
[e]U.S., *Twelfth Census: 1900,* VIII, *Manufactures,* pt. 2, 337, 992–93.
[f]U.S., *Thirteenth Census: 1910,* IX, *Manufactures, Statistics for Maryland,* 648;
   U.S., *Census of Manufactures: 1914,* I, 556.
[g]U.S., *Census of Manufactures: 1914,* I, 556, 584.

TABLE 12

TOTAL LABOR FORCE IN MANUFACTURING IN MARYLAND
BY RACE AND NATIVITY
1890–1910[a]

|  | Percentage Native White | Percentage Black | Percentage Foreign White Immigrants |
|---|---|---|---|
| 1890[b] | 76 | 5 | 19 |
| 1900[c] | 78 | 5 | 17 |
| 1910[d] | 71 | 12 | 17 |

[a]Percentages are the author's calculation based on census data.
[b]U.S., *Eleventh Census: 1890, Population,* pt. 1, 566.
[c]U.S., *Twelfth Census: 1900, Special Reports, Occupations 1900,* pp. 294–301.
[d]U.S., *Thirteenth Census: 1910, Population,* IV, *Occupation Statistics,* 468–70.

TABLE 13

THE MAJOR ARTICLES OF THE FOREIGN TRADE OF BALTIMORE,
1860–1914[a]

*(In Current Dollars)*

IMPORTS

| 1860 | | 1871 | | 1880 | |
|---|---|---|---|---|---|
| Coffee | $3,271,110 | Sugar, brown | $9,504,261 | Coffee | $8,473,698 |
| Sugar, brown | 2,116,172 | Coffee | 8,759,397 | Iron, pig | 1,691,210 |
| Copper, ore | 469,200 | Guano | 1,067,221 | Iron, scrap | |
| Tobacco, cigars | 262,443 | Tin, plates | 786,233 | and old | 1,449,514 |
| Molasses | 258,607 | Iron, railroad | | Tin, plates | 1,447,767 |
| Iron, railroad | 253,375 | bars or rails | 765,083 | Sugar, brown | 616,761 |
| Guano | 233,672 | Molasses | 671,352 | Molasses | 486,825 |
| Hides and skins, | | Fruits, all kinds | 317,524 | Copper, pig | |
| raw | 207,174 | Melado and syrup | | bars, ingots | 334,100 |
| | | of sugar cane | 233,119 | Sulphur or | |
| | | | | brimstone, | |
| Percentage major articles | | | | crude | 313, 342 |
| are of total imports | | | | | |
| | 72 | | 89 | | 72 |

| 1890 | | 1900 | | 1910 | |
|---|---|---|---|---|---|
| Coffee | $3,248,072 | Copper, pig, | | Iron, ore | $3,068,246 |
| Tin, plates and | | bar ingots | $4,310,740 | Iron, pig | 2,797,098 |
| terne plate | 2,857,037 | Coffee | 1,849,940 | Copper, pig | |
| Iron, ore | 774,724 | Manganese, ore | | ingot, bar | |
| Soda, | | and oxide | 1,515,322 | plate | 2,632,619 |
| carbonate | 665,958 | Sisal grass | 1,335,498 | Soda, nitrate | 1,771,190 |
| Iron, pig | 613,230 | Earthen, stone, | | Earthen, | |
| Sulphur | 322,018 | chinaware | 853,518 | stone, china- | |
| Bananas | 210,336 | Bananas | 681,375 | ware | 1,400,354 |
| Earthen, stone | | Iron, pig | 677,149 | Bananas | 1,266,015 |
| and chinaware | 176,067 | Cement | 500,096 | Toys | 1,117,306 |
| | | | | Potash, | |
| Percentage major articles | | | | muriate | 1,040,460 |
| are of total imports | | | | | |
| | 65 | | 61 | | 50 |

| 1914 | |
|---|---|
| Iron, ore | $2,471,677 |
| Iron, pig | 2,322,001 |
| Cork, manu- | |
| factures | 2,037,068 |
| Potash, | |
| muriate | 1,904,911 |
| Soda, nitrate | 1,655,044 |
| Wood, pulp | 1,424,165 |
| Bananas | 1,404,590 |
| Toys | 1,177,904 |
| | |
| Percentage major articles | |
| are of total imports | |
| | 42 |

TABLE 13—Continued

EXPORTS

| 1860 | | 1871 | | 1880 | |
|---|---|---|---|---|---|
| Tobacco, leaf | $3,124,993 | Tobacco, leaf | $4,092,368 | Wheat | $43,573,729 |
| Flour, wheat | 2,183,487 | Flour, wheat | 3,484,157 | Corn | 9,664,802 |
| Cotton, manu- | | Cotton, raw | 2,376,501 | Cotton, raw | 6,386,960 |
| factures | 429,078 | Corn | 840,687 | Tobacco, leaf | 4,107,405 |
| Lard | 349,522 | Oil-cake | 613,350 | Flour, wheat | 2,833,360 |
| Pork | 201,216 | Wood, shooks | | Lard | 2,411,267 |
| Corn meal | 196,393 | staves | 588,620 | Bacon and | |
| Corn | 180,882 | Wheat | 396,460 | hams | 1,583,387 |
| Lumber | 138,746 | Lard | 302,567 | Oil, illu- | |
| | | | | minating | 1,399,975 |
| Percentage major articles | | | | | |
| are of total imports | | | | | |
| | 77 | | 84 | | 94 |

| 1890 | | 1900 | | 1910 | |
|---|---|---|---|---|---|
| Flour, wheat | $15,562,609 | Corn | $18,189,623 | Copper, pig | |
| Corn | 9,581,081 | Copper, bars | | etc. | $21,813,742 |
| Cattle | 7,139,050 | ingots etc. | 16,655,872 | Tobacco, leaf | 8,734,926 |
| Cotton, raw | 6,090,305 | Flour, wheat | 11,388,582 | Corn | 5,517,261 |
| Wheat | 5,394,465 | Cotton, raw | 8,001,051 | Flour, wheat | 4,395,928 |
| Lard | 4,624,118 | Lard | 7,914,492 | Cotton, raw | 4,178,526 |
| Copper, ore | 4,382,786 | Tobacco, leaf | 6,547,573 | Lard | 4,164,850 |
| Tobacco, leaf | 3,927,378 | Wheat | 5,452,079 | Wheat | 3,304,023 |
| | | Cattle | 4,838,850 | Steel rails | 3,049,062 |
| Percentage major articles | | | | | |
| are of total imports | | | | | |
| | 77 | | 68 | | 71 |

| 1914 | |
|---|---|
| Copper, pigs | |
| etc. | $36,091,900 |
| Cotton, raw | 12,534,654 |
| Wheat | 12,419,723 |
| Tobacco, leaf | 11,334,699 |
| Copper, plates | |
| and sheets | 6,900,144 |
| Mowers and | |
| reapers | 3,801,621 |
| Flour, wheat | 3,721,332 |
| Lard | 2,900,710 |

Percentage major articles
are of total imports
82

aCommodities are listed in sections on imports and exports in U.S., Treasury Department, *Annual Statements of the Chief of the Bureau of Statistics on the Commerce and Navigation of the United States,* for the years designated. Percentages are author's calculation.

## TABLE 14

FOREIGN TRADE OF BALTIMORE, 1860–1914:
MAIN COMMODITY GROUPS AS PERCENTAGE
OF TOTAL IMPORTS AND EXPORTS[a]

### IMPORTS

|  | Crude Foodstuff | Manufactured Foodstuff | Crude Materials | Semi-Manufactures | Finished Manufactures |
|---|---|---|---|---|---|
| 1860 | 33 | 24 | 9 | — | 5 |
| 1871 | 37 | 42 | 4 | 3 | 3 |
| 1880 | 42 | 6 | 2 | 25 | — |
| 1890 | 26 | — | 13 | 26 | 1 |
| 1900 | 13 | — | 15 | 29 | 4 |
| 1910 | 4 | — | 20 | 18 | 8 |
| 1914 | 4 | — | 17 | 11 | 9 |

### EXPORTS

| 1860 | 2 | 33 | 35 | 2 | 5 |
|---|---|---|---|---|---|
| 1871 | 8 | 25 | 43 | 8 | — |
| 1880 | 70 | 9 | 14 | — | 2 |
| 1890 | 30 | 27 | 19 | — | — |
| 1900 | 25 | 17 | 13 | 14 | — |
| 1910 | 11 | 11 | 17 | 28 | 4 |
| 1914 | 11 | 6 | 22 | 39 | 3 |

[a]Author's calculations based on data in Table 13.

## TABLE 15

MAJOR ARTICLES IN THE DOMESTIC TRADE OF BALTIMORE
IN 1883[a]

*(In Current Dollars, Rounded to the Nearest Million)*

| COMMODITY | VALUE |
|---|---|
| Grain, bread and breadstuffs | $37 |
| Dry goods, notions and toys | 31 |
| Livestock | 23 |
| Groceries | 23 |
| Raw cotton | 18 |
| Provisions | 14 |
| Lumber | 11 |
| Tobacco | 11 |
| Coal | 9 |
| Coffee | 8 |
| Hardware | 8 |
| Leather | 7 |
| Liquor, domestic | 7 |
| Boots and shoes | 7 |
| Flour | 5 |

[a]Bland, pp. 81–82.

# VII

## SOCIAL-CULTURAL DEVELOPMENTS FROM THE CIVIL WAR TO 1920

BY

WILLIAM LLOYD FOX

MONTGOMERY COLLEGE

The half century following the Civil War was a time of impressive development in the social-cultural history of Maryland. During this period the state's population rose above one million, European immigration having helped to swell the number; public education was expanded and improved; several public and private institutions of higher learning were established, as were also a library and a museum of art in Baltimore, both of which shortly gained national distinction; the American penchant for social organizations was reflected in this period by the founding and fostering of more than a few clubs and fraternal bodies in Maryland; and interest in other forms of recreation was shown in the establishment of parks and in such sports as baseball, bicycling, lacrosse, football, and rowing. Maryland, more particularly Baltimore, became in these years one of the most important medical centers in the United States. Moreover, there was among Maryland artists and writers a creative and intellectual vibrancy as reflected in the quality and extent of their works.

Like all periods of history, the half century following Lee's surrender at Appomattox Courthouse had in Maryland its unfortunate and at times tragic results. The ugly shadow of Jim Crowism fell across the state, not only on public education but on public transportation as well, accompanied by unsuccessful attempts to deny the Negro the ballot.[1] In 1868 a flood struck Baltimore, doing more damage than the one of thirty-one years before; and in 1873 and again in 1904 the city experienced severe fires, the latter ranking as one of the worst in damage and extent in American history.

While in many ways Maryland's historical development in the five and a half decades following the Civil War was parallel to that of the country in general, it also revealed some differences from the national pattern. "It is difficult to see," wrote Sir John Bland-Sutton (1855–1936), "the past in true perspective: the years seem almost on one plane like images in a kaleidoscope."[2] The truth of this observation is to be found in the social-cultural history of Maryland between 1865 and 1920. Its fascinating richness is a worthy challenge to try to see it "in true perspective."

1

POPULATION

As both a small and a border state, Maryland between 1870 when the *Ninth Census* was taken and in 1920 when the *Fourteenth Census* was made reflected a steady increase in population though below the national rate of growth.[3] This was also true of the other south Atlantic states. Not until the 1930's did Maryland's rate of growth in population exceed the national.

In 1870 the population of Maryland amounted to 780,894, Baltimore City's population constituting almost one-third of that figure. Only nine of the then twenty-two counties—Garrett County, the twenty-third and last, was created in 1872—had populations in excess of 20,000 each. Other than Baltimore City, no city in Maryland had a population of more than 9,000, e.g. Annapolis (5,744), Cumberland (8,056), Frederick (8,526),

---

1. See Chapter VIII. On July 1, 1904, a "Jim Crow" law in Maryland requiring railroads and steamships to provide separate accommodations for Negroes went into effect.

2. John Bland-Sutton, *The Story of a Surgeon* (London: Methuen & Co., 1930), p. 1.

3. Donald J. Bogue, *The Population of the United States* (Glenco: The Free Press of Glenco, Ill., 1959), p. 65.

Frostburg (6,131), Havre de Grace (2,281), Leonardtown (2,957), and Rockville (5,437).[4]

During the 1870's every county with the exception of Allegany, from which Garrett County was carved, grew in population; three counties were added to the list of those having populations of 20,000 or more.

By 1890, when the *Eleventh Census* was taken, Maryland's population had risen slightly above one million (1,042,390). The number of counties having 20,000 or more people remained unchanged from the previous census. Baltimore County's population fell by 10,000, inasmuch as a part of the county was annexed to Baltimore City in 1888 as the result of a plebiscite. The Census of 1890 also showed that Maryland's birth rate 51.20 (per 1,000 women 15 to 50 years of age) was below the national rate of 54.68 and that 9.05 per cent of its population was foreign born compared with 14.77 per cent of the national population.[5] Moreover, the *Eleventh Census* of 1890 reported the interesting fact that "besides the District of Columbia there are four states in 1890 where the Negro population represents from 25 to 50 per cent of the white population, the same as in 1880, namely, Arkansas, Tennessee, Texas and Maryland."[6]

While the Negro population of Maryland increased in the 1890's by 9 per cent, it continued to decline in proportion to the white population of the state. By 1900 the Negro population of Maryland equalled 19.8 per cent of the total population and was to continue its relative decline during the early decades of the twentieth century.

When the *Twelfth Census* was taken in 1900, the United States had a population of nearly seventy-six million, indicating an increase of 20.7 per cent since 1890. The country had become a world power with a colonial empire which had recently been acquired. Its international status was based on its industrial supremacy, the American production of iron and steel

---

4. *Ninth Census*, I, Table III, 163-65.

5. *Report on Vital and Social Statistics in the United States at the Eleventh Census: 1890*, Part I (Analysis and Rate Tables) p. 482; *Report of the Population of the United States at the Eleventh Census: 1890*, Part I, lxxxv.

6. *Report of the Population of the United States at the Eleventh Census: 1890*, Part I, xcix.

having surpassed that of its nearest rivals, Germany and Great Britain.

In 1900 American industrialization was reflected in Baltimore City's population of over a half million, which represented a rise of 17.2 per cent during the past decade. Maryland's population rose 14 per cent in this period, which indicated the greatest gain in any decade from 1880 to 1930.[7] Furthermore, the *Twelfth Census* revealed that Maryland was one of five states (Pennsylvania, Delaware, Illinois, and California) which had between 40 and 50 per cent of its total population in places of 8,000 or more.[8] Nearly 47 per cent of Maryland's population lived in urban areas (8,000 or more as defined by the Census Bureau). Only eight of the twenty-three counties had populations of less than 20,000. Allegany County's population by 1900 had shot upward during the past ten years by 29.2 per cent as reflected in the growth of Cumberland, and Baltimore County's residents had increased by nearly 25 per cent.

Although Baltimore City's population had increased significantly as reported in the *Twelfth Census*, the foreign born constituted only 13.5 per cent of the city's inhabitants, compared with 35.1 per cent for Boston, 37.0 per cent for New York, 22.8 per cent for Philadelphia, 34.6 per cent for Chicago, and 32.6 per cent for Cleveland.[9] The increase in Baltimore's population, however, must be viewed as a part of the total demographic picture of the city during the past thirty years as is shown by Charles Hirschfeld:

> If natural increase played a comparatively small part in the growth of the population of Baltimore, a major portion of the total increase of the population between 1870 and 1900 must have been the result of the migration to the city of both native Americans and foreigners. If only about 75,000 people were added to the population of the city as a result of natural increase, and some 39,000 by the annexation of two suburban wards in 1888, then about 126,000 must have come into the city from elsewhere in

7. Ara A. Asadorian, "Population Trends in Maryland from 1880 to 1930" (M.A. thesis, University of Maryland, 1938), p. 76.
8. *Twelfth Census of the United States Taken in the Year 1900*, Population, V, Part I, lxxxii-lxxxiii.
9. *Ibid.*, cix.

order to make the total population increase by 240,000 in the course of thirty years.[10]

Of this increase the native Americans who migrated to Baltimore contributed an impressive number, amounting to about 114,000 or 47.5 per cent. "The state of Maryland furnished the majority of native white migrants to the city." Nearly 57,000, or 70 per cent of the total number of such migrants, came to the city from other parts of the state."[11] (Negro migration to Baltimore also increased during this period, nearly 65 per cent of the black migrants having come from elsewhere in Maryland.) Obviously, the rural counties of the state were the source of much of the increase in Baltimore's population. Several of these counties consequently suffered a net loss of inhabitants by the turn of the century.

Ten years later Baltimore's population had increased even less than it had between 1890 and 1900, having grown by a little less than 10 per cent. Prior to 1890 the city's rate of growth in population "was considerably larger than that of the state . . ."; however, between 1890 and 1910 the growth rates for the city and the state approached one another.[12] By 1910, when the *Thirteenth Census* was taken, 43.1 per cent of Maryland's population lived in Baltimore City, which then ranked as the seventh largest city in population, having exchanged the sixth and seventh positions with Cleveland since 1900.

Of the nine cities in Maryland in 1910, Cumberland showed the highest percentage of increase in inhabitants (27.5 per cent) during the past decade and Annapolis, the lowest (1 per cent). Cumberland's population had risen to 21,838. Hagerstown's population of 16,507, which had increased by 3,000 in the corresponding period, made it the third largest city in the state, followed by Frederick, whose population numbered 10,411.

When the census of 1910 was completed, it was found that Maryland was twenty-seventh among the then forty-six states in size of population but ranked seventh in density. Whereas the

10. Charles Hirschfeld, *Baltimore, 1870–1900: Studies in Social History*, *J.H.U. Studies*, Series LIX, No. 2 (Baltimore: J. H. Press, 1941), p. 19. Reprinted by permission of The Johns Hopkins Press.

11. *Ibid.*, p. 21.

12. *Thirteenth Census of the United States Taken in theYear 1910*, I, "Statistics for Maryland," p. 569.

Immigrants arriving at Locust Point, Baltimore, ca. 1880. *M.H.S.*

United States had experienced a growth in population of 21.0 per cent, Maryland had only a 9.0 per cent increase, the smallest gain for any decade between 1880 and 1930.[13]

The *Thirteenth Census* also included an interesting comparison between Maryland's population and that of the original thirteen states from 1790, the year of the first decennial census, and 1910. Whereas the total population of the first thirteen states had increased tenfold in the 120-year period, that of Maryland had only multiplied fourfold.

The four years following the census of 1910 were a period of international tension and diplomatic crises in Europe, ultimately leading to an ignition of war in the summer of 1914. The Great War, or World War as the conflict came to be called, was to last four years, the last eighteen months of which found the United States involved as a belligerent on the side of the Allies. One of the many consequences of this war was a reduction in the number of European immigrants coming to the United States.[14] While the *Fourteenth Census*, taken in 1920, showed that the American population had increased 14.9 per cent since 1910, there had nevertheless been a decrease in the rate of growth from that of the first decade of the century, due in large part to the drop in the numbers of immigrants. In contrast, Maryland's population actually increased by 11.9 per cent in the decade ending in 1920, reflecting an increase of nearly 3 per cent more than the increase as noted in the Census of 1910.

Four of Maryland's five largest cities reported very significant percentages of increase in population in 1920. The population of Annapolis advanced 30.3 per cent, of Baltimore 31.4 per cent, of Cumberland 36.6 per cent, while that of Hagerstown skyrocketed 70.0 per cent.[15] Stimulated by the war, the urban migration continued, as the number of farms, which had increased from 1880 to 1910, began in the latter year to diminish.[16]

---

13. *Ibid.*, I, p. 50. Asadorian, p. 76.

14. The decade ending in 1910 saw the largest number of immigrants enter the United States for any decade in the history of the Federal Census: 8,795,386. For the years 1911 to 1920 inclusive 5,735,811 immigrants came to the United States. *The 1972 World Almanac and Book of Facts*, p. 289.

15. *Fourteenth Census, State Compendium Maryland: Statistics of Population, Occupations, Agriculture, Manufactures, and Mines and Quarries for the State, Counties, and Cities*, p. 8.

16. Asadorian, p. 78.

In keeping with the urban trend, thirteen of Maryland's twenty-three counties showed in 1920 a decline in population, varying from three tenths of 1 per cent in Frederick County to 11.4 per cent in Kent County. "The large decrease in Baltimore County [from 122,349 in 1910 to 74,817 in 1920] was due to the annexation of part of its territory to Baltimore City in 1919."[17] Although Anne Arundel County also ceded a portion of its territory to Baltimore City in 1919, it actually gained some 3,800 in population by 1920.

Reflecting the urban trend in Maryland, the population of the Eastern Shore, which had steadily increased from 157,254 in 1870 to 200,171 in 1910, began in the latter year a gradual decline which did not level off until about 1930. For the decade ending in 1920 the area showed a decrease of 2.7 per cent.[18] During the half century culminating in 1920 the percentage of native whites of native parentage on the Eastern Shore rose, so that 67.7 per cent of the people living there were by 1920 of that demographic grouping. "As late as 1910 ninety-two per cent of the 200,000 whites on the Eastern Shore were native born, of native parents, and in most cases of old English stock."[19]

An examination of the nativity of Maryland's total population in 1900 provides an interesting comparison with that of the Eastern Shore. The native born constituted 92.1 per cent of the state's population, whereas the foreign born included only 7.9 per cent. In the *Twelfth Census* (1900) the foreign born inhabitants of Maryland and Baltimore City were reported as coming from the following countries:[20]

| Maryland | | Baltimore City | |
|---|---|---|---|
| | (Country of Birth) | | |
| Germany | 44,990 | Germany | 33,208 |
| Ireland | 13,874 | Russia | 10,493 |
| Russia | 11,301 | Ireland | 9,690 |
| England | 5,299 | England | 2,841 |
| Bohemia | 2,813 | Bohemia | 2,321 |
| Italy | 2,449 | Italy | 2,042 |
| Poland (Russian) | 2,227 | Poland (Russian) | 1,694 |
| Scotland | 2,128 | Austria | 1,356 |
| Austria | 1,756 | | |
| Canada (English) | 1,143 | | |

17. *Fourteenth Census, State Compendium Maryland*, p. 7.
18. Frank Goodwin, *A Study of Personal and Social Organizations: An Ex-*

Ten years later the *Thirteenth Census* revealed that for both Maryland and Baltimore City the foreign born population was drawn in order of numbers from these countries: Germany, Russia, Ireland, Austria, Italy, England, and Hungary. From 1850 to 1910 the Germans had clearly composed the largest percentage of foreign born in Maryland: 50 per cent (1850), 56 per cent (1860), 56 per cent (1870), 55 per cent (1880), 55 per cent (1890), 48 per cent (1900), and 35 per cent (1910). (The percentages are approximate.)[21] As the number of foreign born increased after 1880, the percentage of those born in Germany declined from 55 per cent to 35 per cent, as noted above. In his fine study, *The Maryland Germans: A History*, Dieter Cunz observed:

> During the last decades of the nineteenth century about 85 per cent of all those residents of Maryland who had been born in Germany lived in Baltimore City and Baltimore County. In 1900 more than half of all the foreign-born residents in Baltimore were German immigrants; in Allegany County, where the city of Cumberland is located, a quarter of all the foreigners were German. (1,270 German-born in Allegany County.) On the other hand, the two old German counties, Frederick and Washington, which had received the main stream of German immigrants in the middle of the eighteenth century showed no more than 516 German-born in 1900, a little more than one per cent of the total of Maryland Germans. We can see how the weight shifted from the western counties to Baltimore.[22]

One of the significant aspects of the history of the Maryland Germans is that in Baltimore between the Civil War and World War I "... there emerged a type which never appeared in Hagerstown and Frederick: the German-American."[23] In the earlier period the Germans who settled in Western Maryland "... remained German until their deaths. However, their

---

*plorative Survey of the Eastern Shore of Maryland* (Philadelphia; by the author, 1944), p. 32.

19. Charles B. Clark, "Politics in Maryland During the Civil War," *M.H.M.*, XXXVI (September, 1941), 243.

20. *Twelfth Census*, I, 732-35 and 758-59.

21. Dieter Cunz, *The Maryland Germans: A History*, p. 392.

22. *Ibid.*, pp. 392-93. Reprinted by permission of the Princeton University Press.

23. *Ibid.*, p. 320.

grandchildren were completely Americanized."[24] In contrast, the German-Americans were able to maintain a strong ethnic and cultural identity, at first due to attacks on them by the Know-Nothings, American nativists who became fearful of the influx of foreigners coming to the United States before the Civil War. The German-American reaction was to close ranks. "They cut themselves off, founded their own societies, churches, schools, newspapers and built a wall around their German-American individualism that was to hinder the acclimatization of even the next generation."[25] And of course the constant flow of immigration from Germany to Baltimore and its environs to the turn of the century did much to maintain this Germanic identification, which was of such force that the Maryland General Assembly enacted a law in 1868 requiring that "every public general law . . . shall immediately after its passage be published, at the expense of the state, daily for one week in two daily newspapers of the city of Baltimore, one of which shall be printed in the German language. . . ."[26] This law was in effect until it was repealed during World War II.

When the census was taken in 1920, it was found that among the foreign-born population of Maryland and Baltimore City the Germans had fallen to second place as a national group; the Russian immigrants outnumbered them. Of the foreign-born the Germans comprised 21.6 per cent in the state and 20.8 per cent in the city of Baltimore compared with the Russians, including Jews, who accounted for 24.3 per cent and 27.7 per cent respectively. Clearly, in 1920 the census showed that in Maryland as well as in the other states which comprise the northeastern quadrant of the United States the "new" immigration from southern and eastern Europe was outdistancing the "old" immigration from the northern and western parts of the continent. The Poles and the Italians ranked third and fourth respectively among the foreign-born in both the state and Baltimore City.[27]

The end of World War I in 1918 was a watershed in the history of immigration to the United States. Disillusionment

24. *Ibid.*
25. *Ibid.*, p. 320.
26. *Ibid.*, p. 321.
27. *Fourteenth Census, State Compendium Maryland*, p. 21.

with Europe and its perennial problems, fear of Bolshevism, chauvinism (coupled frequently with blatant racism), and an inclination toward retreating into hemispheric isolation appeared in American thought and behavior within a few years after the war. In 1921 and again in 1924 quota laws were enacted greatly restricting immigration, especially from southern and eastern Europe. "The era of the hyphen was past" for the German-Americans as well as for other ethnic groups.[28] A new day in the history of Maryland's population profile had consequently been reached.

## 2

### EDUCATION

Before 1850 there had been discussion from time to time about the desirability of a state school system. Baltimore City and some counties had obtained special legislation by which public schools were established in their jurisdictions and were supported in turn by state aid and local taxes.[29] As no provision was made in the Maryland Constitution of 1851 for a state school system, the counties were free to do what they liked. "... By 1864 each had made some provision for public education. Among the counties there was no uniformity at all."[30]

A significant landmark in the state's history, therefore, was the adoption of the Constitution of 1864 which "was the first legal enactment for a uniform system of public schools in Maryland, excepting the rather abortive law for primary schools in 1826."[31] Meeting in Annapolis from April 27 to September 5, 1864, the constitutional convention included among its standing committees a "committee on education and the encouragement of literature" which, after two months of study, presented a unanimous recommendation. The report called for an article on education consisting of seven sections to be put in the new constitution, each section providing in turn: a state superintendent of public instruction, an assistant superintendent of public

28. Cunz, p. 402.
29. L. E. Blauch, "Education and the Maryland Constitutional Convention, 1850–51," *M.H.M.*, XXV (June, 1930), 174-75.
30. *Ibid.*, 226-27.
31. L. E. Blauch, "The First Uniform School System of Maryland, 1865–1868," *M.H.M.*, XXVI (September, 1931), 205.

instruction for each county, a state board of education, five school commissioners for each county, a uniform system of free public education, an annual state tax for free public education, and a permanent state school fund.

> The report proposed a thoroughing State system in which all the officials were to be appointed by the State and the schools were to be supported by the State. Public education in Maryland was to turn a complete somersault.[32]

The governor, according to the constitution, was to appoint a state superintendent who was to present to the General Assembly in 1865 "a plan for a uniform system of free public schools." The General Assembly had the obligation to provide such a system; if it did not, then the state superintendent's report would go into effect. There was, however, no provision in the system for the education of Negro children.

> Few emancipationists fought for Negro children. A handful believed in it and supported the idea, but they were too few to force their position. Most Unionist delegates to the constitutional convention feared that a proposal to educate Negroes would touch off such strong reaction that the constitution would meet with defeat at the polls. People were simply not ready for Negro schools.[33]

Efforts were made in the constitutional convention to provide for white education only, but they were voted down as it would mean that the lower counties would receive less public funds than they otherwise would on the basis of total population.[34]

Much of the credit for the establishment of Maryland's public school system belonged to the Reverend Libertus Van Bokkelen, a native of New York who had come in 1845 to Catonsville, Maryland, as the rector of St. Timothy's Church and had in turn established St. Timothy's Hall, a fine private school. Later, declining the presidency of St. John's College and the Maryland

---

32. L. E. Blauch, "Education and the Maryland Constitutional Convention, 1864," *M.H.M.*, XXV (September, 1930), 233. Richard R. Duncan, "The Impact of the Civil War on Education in Maryland, *ibid.*, LXI (March, 1966), 37-52, *passim*.

33. Richard Paul Fuke, "The Baltimore Association for the Moral and Educational Improvement of the Colored People 1864–1870," *M.H.M.*, LXVI (Winter, 1971), 369-70.

34. *M.H.M.*, XXV, 245-47.

Agricultural College, Van Bokkelen strove to bring about the establishment of a complete state educational system. At the constitutional convention in 1864 he ". . . attended as a lobbyist to capitalize on the prevailing democratic sentiment and to crusade for his long cherished public school system."[35] His crusading effort, as noted above, was obviously quite successful.

On November 12, 1864, Governor Augustus Bradford appointed Van Bokkelen as State Superintendent of Public Instruction. Immediately the new superintendent drew up

> a complete system of Public Instruction, beginning with the Primary School, progressing through the Grammar School to the County High School, in which young men (were) to be prepared for the State Colleges, whence they (should) pass to the Schools of Medicine or Law, or the practical duties of active business.[36]

Van Bokkelen's plan also included provisions for "an asylum for the blind, an asylum for the deaf and dumb, a school for idiotic and feebleminded youth, and other benevolent and remedial institutions" such as industrial homes and houses of refuge. Before the Civil War Maryland had begun to give attention to these areas through special funds but not by the establishment of such institutions.

In 1867 the Maryland General Assembly provided for the establishment of a school for deaf and dumb children at Frederick. The state also made provision for the education of the indigent blind and for financial assistance in the building of the Maryland Institution for the Instruction of the Blind, a private school. Moreover, the House of Refuge as well as a number of other private benevolent institutions received some state aid. The State Board of Education, however, had no supervising authority over these institutions.[37]

An interesting facet of the educational developments which Van Bokkelen wrought was the reaction of Baltimore City. For nearly forty years the city had enjoyed "a well organized system

---

35. George H. Callcott, *A History of the University of Maryland*, p. 168.
36. Blauch, "The First Uniform School System of Maryland, 1865–1868," *M.H.M.*, XXVI (September, 1931), 206-207. *Report of the State Superintendent of Public Instruction to the General Assembly of Maryland* (Annapolis, 1865), 7.
37. *M.H.M.*, XXVI (September, 1931), 221-22.

of schools under special legislation."[38] The Civil War, the Baltimore school commissioners believed, by

> ... inducing many of the wealthier families to send their children to public schools rather than to private ones, ... had broadened the base of support for public education in Baltimore. In support of this, they cited the continued patronage of the system by many of this group.[39]

The school law of 1865, which was based on Van Bokkelen's plan, applied not only to the counties but to Baltimore City as well. After this legislation was enacted, strong though unsuccessful efforts were made in the General Assembly to exempt the city from the application of the law. Ignoring this statute, the school officials of Baltimore City did not use the uniform series of textbooks required by the law until they were ordered to do so by the Court of Appeals. Apparently, no satisfactory resolution of the educational "problem between the State and City officials appears to have been made."[40]

The school year 1866–67 found 71,000 children in 1,279 schools and taught by teachers who had been pedagogically examined. To his challenging task Van Bokkelen brought vision coupled with administrative ability. Inevitably there arose some opposition to the state school system. Objections were made about the organization and supervision of the system. Criticism was also leveled at what was considered the inordinate expense of public education. ". . . The Constitution of 1867 was in educational matters happily brief in laying down fundamental principles without creating cumbersome machinery."[41] In addition, during that school year the selection and administration of the series of uniform textbooks were denounced.

Despite these attacks on the new public school system, there were 105,435 children (97,761 white; 7,674 black) attending school in 1870, five years after the Public Instruction Act became law. Among the classes of schools in Maryland in 1870 there were: three high schools, forty-nine grammar schools, 159

---

38. *Ibid.*, 218.
39. *M.H.M.*, LXI, 46-47.
40. *M.H.M.*, XXVI, 218-19.
41. Andrews, *A History of Maryland: Province and State*, p. 638.

graded common schools, 1,266 ungraded common schools, and seventy-two classical, technical and professional schools.[42]

Although the public kindergarten was first introduced in this country in St. Louis in 1873—private kindergartens had been operating since Elizabeth Peabody opened the first one in Boston in 1860—none was established in Maryland by 1890. Baltimore City was therefore not among the cities then maintaining public school kindergartens (St. Louis, Milwaukee, Philadelphia, and Boston), nor among those cities which provided free kindergartens supported by benevolent associations (San Francisco, Denver, Louisville, Chicago, Indianapolis, and Cincinnati).[43] Not until the first decade of this century was the public kindergarten introduced in Maryland.

While public education for the Negro was not delayed as long as the introduction of the public kindergarten in Maryland; nevertheless it was not before the early 1870's that any legislative action was taken. Although Superintendent Van Bokkelen's plan included provision for Negro children in separate schools, the General Assembly balked. "The Public Instruction Act of 1865 simply suggested a procedure and made funds available for counties that wished to use it for educating black children."[43] For Negro education there was nothing compulsory about this legislation. Meanwhile, in 1867 the Baltimore City Council did take over the Negro schools in the city, as described below.

Even though there was an

> ... absence of either state or popular support, the years 1864 to 1870 witnessed in Maryland the inauguration of a widespread, centralized system of Negro schools. In the combined efforts of a handful of Baltimore citizens, northern relief societies, and the Freedmen's Bureau, the state underwent a revolution in black education.[44]

The most important group in this effort was a new organization, the Baltimore Association for the Moral and Educational Improvement of the Colored People, or, as it was more com-

---

42. *Eleventh Census, Report on Population of the United States at the Eleventh Census,* 1890, II, 34-35.
43. Fuke, 371.
44. *Ibid.,* 372.

monly called, the Baltimore Association. Organized in November 1864 by a group of business and professional men who "brought in outside financial aid and encouraged teachers to work in Maryland,"[45] this association opened twenty-five schools enrolling more than 3,000 Negro children during the ensuing year. Seventeen of these schools were located in the tidewater counties, seven in Baltimore City, and one in Cumberland.

While the Freedmen's Bureau provided the school houses, the Baltimore Association recruited the teachers and paid their salaries. "The combined operation was basically straightforward and most of the time it ran quite smoothly. Between them, the two groups built up a Negro school system which rivalled that of any other state."[46]

Having established 130 schools in three years, the Baltimore Association's fortunes declined from the summer of 1867 until it closed its doors in June 1870. The Association's persistent efforts led the Baltimore City Council on July 10, 1867, to request the city's school commissioners to establish immediately separate schools for Negro children.[47] This action was a harbinger of the state's resolve five years later to establish "at least one school for colored children in each election district provided the average attendance was fifteen."[48]

Five years after the close of the Civil War, the Baltimore Association terminated its operation, having done much during its nearly six-year history ". . . to dispel white Marylanders' doubts and fears over educating black children."[49] Many whites came to realize that a black neighborhood school made for economic as well as social improvement of the Negro and that it also tended to keep black farm hands in the community where they were needed. The Baltimore Association, together with the Freedmen's Bureau, had provided a valuable bridge by which the city of Baltimore and the state could cross in their

---

45. *Ibid.*, 373.
46. *Ibid.*, 396-97.
47. *Ibid.*, 399. Vernon Sebastian Vavrina, "The History of Public Education in the City of Baltimore, 1829–1956," I (Ph.D. dissertation, Catholic University of America, 1958), 224.
48. Adelyn B. Venezky, "Negro Education in the State of Maryland since the Civil War" (M.A. thesis, University of Maryland, 1929), p. 3.
49. Fuke, 404.

assumption of the responsibility for the education of Negro children. "By 1900 the attitude of the state toward public education for the Negro had become crystallized."[50] Nevertheless, as late as 1916 there were no high schools for Negroes in the counties, "Baltimore City having the only high school for colored in the state."[51] Not until after 1919 were there any public high schools for Negroes on the Eastern Shore; this was not surprising, as "the general status of education on the Eastern Shore . . . has always been lower than that provided elsewhere in the state."[52] Other instances of discrimination in public education were reflected in the length of the school year for Negroes and for that of whites and in the minimum salaries paid respectively to white and black teachers. "White schools in Frederick County closed on May 28 in 1909 whereas the colored school closed on April 8."[53] In 1918 the minimum salary in Maryland for a white teacher was $300.00 per year and for a black teacher, $280.00. These discriminatory differences were of course to be found in other states of the upper and deep South.

By the time a state public education system was established in Maryland, the city of Baltimore's school system was nearly forty years old. It is interesting to note that

> In contrast with the rapid growth and development of the Baltimore Public Schools during the formative period, the period from 1866 to the reorganization of the schools in 1900 was an era devoted more to maintaining the status quo than to expanding the services of the schools. In this period of arrested development, the educational system experienced few significant developments. The beginnings of the colored schools, the English-German schools, and the manual training schools represent exceptions and were innovations which marked progress in public instruction.[54]

Unfortunately the public schools had not kept pace with the city's growth. From 1866 to 1900 the overcrowding of students

---

50. Helen Marie Plater, "A History of Public Education of the Negro in Maryland, 1865–1940" (M.A. thesis, Howard University, 1942), p. 92.
51. Venezky, p. 12.
52. Emily Wanda Wilson, "The Public Education of Negroes on the Eastern Shore of Maryland" (M.A. thesis, Howard University, 1948), p. 2.
53. Plater, p. 141.
54. Vavrina, I, 381.

in "unhealthy quarters" was the rule rather than the exception. Furthermore, "the schools were caught in the maze of municipal politics and the professional educators and those commissioners who were not pawns of political bosses were faced with endless frustrations. . . ."[55] Baltimore teachers, moreover, were confronted with an inadequate salary schedule and the lack of a pension plan.

As already indicated, significant innovations appeared in the instructional program of the Baltimore City schools. In 1874 the first English-German school was established with six teachers and 260 pupils. By 1900 there were eight such schools enrolling 6,977 pupils taught by 170 teachers. These schools, which were obviously popular, provided instruction in both German and English.

In October 1883 the school commissioners of Baltimore City established a manual training school which opened its doors the following March as the Baltimore Manual Training School and which was renamed in 1893 the Baltimore Polytechnic Institute. This was "the first free public school to give practical training," and it was "the only absolutely free public school of the kind in the world."[56] Eight and one half years later the Colored Manual Training School opened. In 1897, like its white counterpart, it underwent a change of name to the Colored Polytechnic Institute.

With the notable exceptions previously mentioned, the period from 1866 to 1900 was for Baltimore City public education one of "arrested development." However, the first two decades of the twentieth century "provided the transition between the traditional school system of the nineteenth century and the modernization of the schools in postwar years."[57] Moreover, by 1925 the school commissioners had secured enough independence from city hall to allow them to develop in time a fine educational system.

Meanwhile, there was a compelling need to examine the state's entire system of public education. This was met in 1914 by the creation of the Maryland Educational Survey Commis-

55. *Ibid.*, p. 3.
56. *Sixtieth Annual Report of the Board of Commissioners of Public Schools,* (Baltimore, 1888), p. 151.
57. Vavrina, II, 554.

sion (Chapter 844, Acts of 1914), which was to present "a comprehensive study" of the educational system from the elementary grades through the level of higher education.[58] In the preface to the professional report made at the request of the commission, whose members included B. Howell Griswold, Jr., Chairman, J. McPherson Scott, and Albert W. Sisk, the commissioners noted:

> The Federal Census of 1910 ranks Maryland among the states of the Union as thirty-first in point of illiteracy. If full allowance is made for the 18 per cent Negro population of the state, the results are still very discouraging.[59]

Abraham Flexner and Frank P. Bachman, who prepared the Report to the Commission, found that public education in the state was "on the whole soundly organized" but that it produced "extremely unsatisfactory results."[60] They found that while a few counties had good schools as well as ones in which there was steady improvement and that there was a scattering of good schools in the other counties,

> . . . the large majority of the schools are poor; teachers are, for the most part, poorly trained; instruction is ineffective and obsolete; children attend school with disastrous irregularity; school buildings are far too often in unsatisfactory condition, school grounds frequently neglected and untidy.[61]

Among the reasons cited for this depressing situation in Maryland's public education system were the lack of sufficient staff in both the State Department of Education and in the county superintendents' offices, the distribution of money "almost unconditionally" from the state's rather large educational fund regardless of the ineffectiveness of some county programs, and the pervasive and inhibiting influence of politics in the operations of the State Board, the selection of county superintendents and "even . . . of the one-room rural teacher."[62] Moreover, public education suffered from a lack of a sound

58. Abraham Flexner and Frank P. Bachman, *Public Education in Maryland: A Report to the Maryland Educational Survey Commission*, 4th ed. (New York: The General Education Board, 1919), p. vii.

59. *Ibid.*, p. xi.

60. *Ibid.*, pp. xv and xvi.

61. *Ibid.*, p. xvi.

62. *Ibid.*, pp. xvii-xviii.

attendance law. "In consequence, her public schools are now reaching less than three-fourths of the white children of school age (6-18)," noted Flexner and Bachman in their interesting report, "while probably half of her white children are taking up the duties of parenthood and of citizenship with a fifth-grade education or less."[63] Contributing also to the depressing picture of the state's public education system, as reflected in the Flexner and Bachman report, was the inferior quality of the Negro schools, a condition which was considerably rectified in the 1920's.

The General Education Board Report of Flexner and Bachman indicated improvements here and there in Maryland's public schools such as the establishment in each of sixteen counties of at least one central industrial school for Negroes where older girls were taught cooking and sewing and older boys woodwork, and the increase in the number of high schools from twenty-eight in 1905 to sixty-five in 1914 (with an additional year added in the meantime and with more exacting standards). The general tenor of the report was, however, an indictment of public education. As will be shown later, this report was a necessary stimulus to improving the state's public school system during the next decade, as was the Strayer Report (1920) to strengthening the public education program of Baltimore City.

The development of the Maryland State Teachers' Association paralleled in several ways the development of public education in the state. At a meeting on December 2, 1865, the Public School Teachers' Association of Baltimore, an organization that had been founded sixteen years before, invited the teachers of Baltimore County and any others present to participate in the activities of the session. One important item of business at this assembly was the adoption of a motion to have a committee of five plan a meeting during the Christmas holidays for the purpose of establishing a state teachers' organization. Again the Baltimore County teachers were invited to establish a committee to cooperate in the realization of this proposal. The meeting took place on December 27, 1865, at Western Female High School under the leadership of Thomas D. Baird, Principal of Baltimore City College, with the primary concern of for-

---

63. *Ibid.*, p. 101.

mulating plans for a state teachers' association. Several committees were appointed, and arrangements were made for a meeting the following summer (July 10, 11 and 12, 1866) again at Western Female High School. "In agreement with the new state educational program and pledging support to the state superintendent, the organization was to aid in the implementation of the new educational order for Maryland."[64] At this first regular meeting about sixty members attended although the membership was officially listed at eighty-three. With the establishment of the Maryland State Teachers' Association, Maryland became the twenty-seventh state to form a teachers' association, which was to come nine years after the founding of the National Teachers' Association, the original name of the National Education Association.

The first three decades of MSTA's history revealed within the association "a reluctance to make any major change in the status quo."[65] In 1890 the General Assembly incorporated the association, and in 1900 and 1910 reorganizations occurred "at which time the constitution was changed to make the body more effective."[66] The first reorganization called for additional standing committees, and the second created a departmental organization. To make MSTA more democratic, a representative assembly was instituted in 1921 because the organization had grown from 71 members in 1900 to 2,580 in 1919. "New horizons were beginning to come into view, and the Association had helped to bring them about."[67]

During its first half century of operation MSTA had shown for the most part a disinclination to push for educational reforms. For example, from 1865 to 1916 several agencies had the authority to grant teaching certificates, a situation which led to the issuance of no less than five different kinds of elementary certificates until 1916, when this authority was given to the State Superintendent of Education. Moreover, till 1886 there were no requirements for the preparation of teachers in teach-

---

64. Benjamin Paul Ebersole, "A History of the Maryland State Teachers' Association" (Ed.D. dissertation, University of Maryland, 1964; copyright, 1965), p. 21.
65. *Ibid.*, p. 289.
66. Gardner Shugart, "A History of the Maryland State Teachers' Association" (M.A. thesis, University of Maryland, 1933), p. 50.
67. Ebersole, p. 127.

ing methods.[68] Although a state salary schedule for teachers had been established in 1904, it was not until 1920 that "the greatest increase in this salary schedule took place. ..."[69] Two years before the establishment of the state salary schedule, the General Assembly had passed a pension law that provided for $200 per year, later advanced to $400, for a retired teacher; but it was not until 1927 that the Maryland Teachers Retirement System was inaugurated.

These deficiencies of educational administration and delays in reform were not due to indifference of the Maryland State Teachers' Association, whose membership was quite small until after 1900 but rather to the lack of public concern. After 1920 significant improvements were made in the operation of Maryland's public school system, due in large part to the Association.

No review of Maryland's social history from 1865 to 1920 would be complete without noting briefly some of the developments in private and parochial education. The *Eleventh Census* of 1890 reported a total enrollment of 19,426 in the denominational, including parochial, schools of Maryland compared with an aggregate of 184,251 enrolled in the public common schools of the state. The division of enrollment of the church-related schools was as follows:[70]

|                      |        |
|----------------------|--------|
| Catholic             | 16,210 |
| Lutheran             | 983    |
| Methodist            | 738    |
| Presbyterian         | 247    |
| Protestant Episcopal | 800    |
| All others           | 448    |

As one can readily see, the largest denominational school enrollment was in the Catholic schools, most of which were at the elementary level. Catholic secondary education began in 1791 with the establishment of Georgetown Academy, which later was moved to Garrett Park, Maryland. "During the first

---

68. Rexford B. Hartle, "The Teacher in Maryland Since 1865" (M.A. thesis, University of Maryland, 1931), p. 51.
69. *Ibid.*, p. 53.
70. *Eleventh Census*, II, 113-17.

half of the nineteenth century five secondary schools were established. . . ."[71]

The development of Catholic secondary education in the second half of the nineteenth century was very slow. This was due
no doubt to the social and financial upheaval caused by the Civil
War. Yet, five high schools were founded during this period.[72]

An interesting facet of Catholic education in Maryland in the
years following the Civil War was the establishment of St.
Mary's Industrial School for Boys. Archbishop Martin John
Spalding wished to establish a school for Catholic boys who
either had no home or who had been committed by the court for
some offense. Spalding invited the Xaverian Brothers to establish such a school, which opened on October 3, 1866, with two
registrants on a tract of land on the south side of the Frederick
Turnpike Road and the Washington Turnpike Road, near the
village of Carrollton in what was then Baltimore County. Mrs.
Emily MacTavish, a granddaughter of Charles Carroll of Carrollton, leased forty-eight and a half acres to the Archbishop and
provided in her will that that land as well as an adjacent property, totaling one hundred acres, should go to him upon her
death.

Years later, in the Forty-Sixth Annual Report of the Superintendent of St. Mary's, there was a reference to the departure of
one of the boys, George Herman "Babe" Ruth, who was committed to the school on June 13, 1902, at the age of eight. " 'It is
not unusual,' " noted the superintendent, " 'for some of these
players of the school to adopt baseball as a profession. One boy
created a sensation this year by his excellent work.' "[73] This
was apparently in reference to Ruth, who had left the school
late in February, 1914, to become in time one of the "immor-
tals" of professional baseball.

Five years later, St. Mary's experienced a fire that destroyed
practically all of the plant. The school was subsequently rebuilt, but in 1950 it closed its doors; it had run into serious

---

71. Francis W. McConville, "The History of Catholic Secondary Education in
the Counties of the Western Shore of Maryland" (M.A. thesis, Catholic University of America, 1944), p. 128.

72. *Ibid.*, p. 129.

73. Jordan Buckley, C.F.X., "The History of St. Mary's Industrial School for
Boys" (M.A. thesis, Loyola College, Baltimore, 1951), p. 27.

financial trouble, even though for the last eleven years of its operation the State of Maryland had increased its financial aid.

In 1867, the year following the opening of St. Mary's, the Sisters of Mercy established in Mount Washington, Mount Saint Agnes, a boarding school for girls, to which was later added on the same campus Mount Saint Agnes College (1890) and in 1899 Mount Washington Seminary, a school for boys from six to thirteen years of age. The name of the boys' school was later changed to Mount Washington Country School for Boys.

During the more than five decades following the Civil War, several nonsectarian college preparatory schools for boys and girls were established in Maryland, especially in and around Baltimore.[74] One of the first of these private institutions was Oldfields School for girls that Mrs. John Sears McCulloch began in 1867 on a small farm at Glencoe, Maryland, twenty miles north of Baltimore. Six years later the McDonogh School was established in Green Spring Valley, northwest of Baltimore City. John McDonogh had left a sizable estate, which was to be used for charitable and educational ends in his home city of Baltimore and in New Orleans, where he had made his fortune. The money McDonogh bequeathed to Baltimore was to be used "in establishing a farm school for worthy boys."[75] At Catonsville, just outside of Baltimore, St. Timothy's School for girls was founded in 1882; it remained at that location until 1951, when it moved to Stevenson, Maryland. The next private school to be opened was the Bryn Mawr School for Girls of Baltimore, which "was founded in 1885 by a group of women determined to establish . . . a school that should offer to Baltimore girls a secondary education equal in every respect to the best offered for boys."[76] Two years later Samuel Ready opened a school "for girls who had lost one or both parents." Since 1949, however, the school has taken paying students in both the day and the boarding departments.[77] About 1894 Baltimore saw the opening

---

74. *Schools In and Around Baltimore*. Compiled by The Baltimore District, Maryland Federation of Women's Clubs (Baltimore: Consolidated Engineering Co. Inc., 1955), *passim*.
75. *Ibid.*, p. 74.
76. *Ibid.*, p. 27.
77. *The Handbook of Private Schools: An Annual Descriptive Survey of Independent Schools*, 50th ed. (Boston: Porter Sargent, 1969), p. 446.

of yet another school for girls that six years later would be provided with larger quarters by the Roland Park Company, then engaged in developing a suburb of that name. Until 1908 the company served as the school's sponsor; then the school became an incorporated non-profit institution known as Roland Park Country School.

"It was in October, 1897, that a small school, later to be called Calvert, opened its doors to about fifteen day pupils. This was above a drug store at the northeast corner of Madison Street and Park Avenue."[78] In time this school became renowned for its home instruction courses, which began with kindergarten and extended through the ninth grade. "By May of 1915, Calvert School was educating more than 1,000 children yearly by mail," both in the United States as well as abroad.[79] Not only did bedridden and handicapped children thus receive instruction; so also did those whose parents were stationed overseas.

At the time of the Calvert School's opening, the Gilman Country School was established. "In a vigorous maternal fashion, Baltimore gave birth in the fall of 1897 to the Country School for Boys of Baltimore City."[80] This school owed its start to Mrs. Francis King Carey, who believed that what her son and other boys equally blessed needed was a "day school in the country" as the city's schools offered little to college-bound youth. Among those consulted about the proposal for a country day school was Dr. Daniel Coit Gilman, president of The Johns Hopkins University, in whose honor the school was renamed in 1910. "Dr. Gilman had been immensely interested and helpful in the founding of the school and had actually drawn up its initial prospectus."[81]

For the first thirteen years of its operation, the Gilman Country School was located at "Homewood," the lovely old home of Charles Carroll, Jr. on North Charles Street and the future site of the new campus of The Johns Hopkins University. In the fall of 1909, the school's board of trustees bought a tract of sixty-eight acres at the southeast corner of Roland and Belvedere

---

78. *Schools In and Around Baltimore*, p. 29.
79. *Ibid.*, p. 30.
80. Bradford McE. Jacobs, *Gilman Walls Will Echo: The Story of the Gilman Country School 1897–1947* (Baltimore, 1947), p. 1.
81. *Ibid.*, p. 50.

Avenues in the northwest part of Baltimore City. This became the permanent campus of Gilman, a pioneer in its field as Frank S. Hackett, the headmaster of Riverdale Country School, New York, wrote in the *New York Evening Post* for September 2, 1911:

> There has recently sprung up in America a new type of school which aims to afford country life to the boy who remains at his own home in the city. . . . The oldest and most successful school of this type in America is "The Country School for Boys of Baltimore City," founded as recently as 1897. This has been followed in New York, Boston, Philadelphia, Buffalo, Kansas City and Richmond with suburban schools which have met with so hearty a response from parents that there is no question of the spread of the movement. The benefit to the city boys has been proven so great that a study is being made by public school authorities in a number of large cities. . . .[82]

Three years after the Gilman Country School opened at Homewood, The Tome School for Boys, located at Port Deposit, Maryland, on the palisades of the Susquehanna River near its union with Chesapeake Bay, opened to boarders and received its first students in 1894. It was part of a system of schools beginning with kindergarten and extending through high school, collectively known as The Jacob Tome Institute and named for its affluent founder. The Tome School, which today is coeducational, was established as a nonsectarian college preparatory school for boys.

In the decade ending in 1920 four more college preparatory schools were established in Maryland. Mary Moncrieff Livingston opened a school in the fall of 1910 in a house in Garrison, a small community in the Green Spring Valley, twelve miles northwest of Baltimore. Fifty small boys and girls were the first pupils of the Garrison Forest School. A year later Mr. and Mrs. Samuel R. Middleton founded the Gunston School as "a family school for girls" in Centreville on the Eastern Shore,[83] and in 1912, as a result of parental dissatisfaction with the public schools, the Park School opened in Baltimore with an enroll-

---

82. *Ibid.*, p. 51.
83. *The Handbook of Private Schools: An Annual Descriptive Survey of Independent Schools*, 50th ed. (Boston: Porter Sargent, 1969), p. 451.

ment of ninety-eight in a rented mansion near Druid Hill Park. The campus of the Park School is now located on Old Court Road in Baltimore County. In 1914 Rolland M. Teel founded the Severn School at Severna Park in order to prepare boys for admission to the United States Naval Academy; however, from 1920 the objectives of the school were broadened in order to prepare boys for such institutions as The Johns Hopkins and the University of Virginia.

The limitations of space in this chapter do not permit a review of the developments in the years following the Civil War, of those Maryland preparatory schools that were founded before 1865. Schools such as Friends School (established 1784) in Baltimore; Charlotte Hall School (established 1774) in southern Maryland, in continuous operation since 1796; and West Nottingham Academy (established 1744) at Colora in northeastern Maryland, an affiliate of the Synod of the Chesapeake of the United Presbyterian Church in the United States of America, continued their academic programs throughout the period reviewed here as well as in the years after 1920.

The private or college preparatory schools founded in Maryland during the half century following the Civil War reflected as elsewhere in America the dissatisfaction of the middle and upper income families with public education and their desires to provide their sons and daughters with a schooling that would prepare them well for college.

Not only were many preparatory schools established throughout the United States in the decades after the Civil War; so also were scores of public as well as private colleges and universities. By 1907 there were nearly a dozen and a half collegiate institutions in Maryland, most of which had been founded after 1865.

A part of State Superintendent Van Bokkelen's plan for public education in Maryland involved higher education. He wanted to unite the colleges in the state in order to make each an integral unit of the University of Maryland; however, the General Assembly accepted the plan only in part. St. John's College, Washington College, Maryland Agricultural College, the Faculty of Arts and Sciences and the Law School (University of Maryland in Baltimore) were organized as the University of Maryland; "but no provision was made for its management, and the University was therefore not organized under the proposed scheme."[84] As George H. Callcott has noted in his history of the university:

> The general assembly was not fundamentally opposed to the ambitious university system, but with many advocates of higher education disfranchised, it hesitated. In principle it approved the plan, declaring the four colleges united as the University of Maryland. Thus for the third time—in 1784, in 1826, and in 1865—the legislature created a state university. Actually, however, it put off its zealous superintendent by delaying an appropriation to acquire the colleges from their owners.[85]

Van Bokkelen was not easily balked. Early in 1866 he urged the General Assembly to purchase the then bankrupt Maryland Agricultural College. "As his favorite of the four colleges, it would, he thought, serve to launch the rest of the university system. His maneuvers were masterful."[86] The state superintendent pointed out to the legislators that public support meant that the state would have control of the land grant college. In turn he told the institution's stockholders that the only way that the college could be reopened would be through state aid. Van Bokkelen skillfully brought the legislature and the stockholders together in a compromise providing that the state pay $45,000 for half-ownership in the Maryland Agricultural College and for the retention by the stockholders of seven of the eleven seats on the institution's board of trustees.

Meanwhile, the state continued its annual contributions to Washington College and St. John's College as well as to the Maryland Agricultural College, and increased the amount it gave to the Baltimore Female College. Although annual appropriations were also provided for the Faculty of Arts and Sciences and the Law School of the University of Maryland, these divisions of the university failed to meet the conditions of the appropriations and so did not receive state aid.

After visting normal schools at New Britain, Connecticut, and Albany, New York, Van Bokkelen recommended in his report of 1865 to the General Assembly the establishment of a state normal school. The legislature accepted this proposal for the train-

84. Blauch, "The First Uniform School System of Maryland, 1865–1868," *M.H.M.*, XXVI (September, 1931), 220.
85. G. H. Callcott, pp. 169-70. Reprinted by permission of the Maryland Historical Society.
86. *Ibid.*, p. 170.

ing of teachers with virtually no change. According to the law the State Board of Education was to establish the school in Baltimore City, and the new institution was to be put under the supervision of the state superintendent, who *ex officio* was the principal. After much difficulty, Van Bokkelen finally found space in Red Man's Hall, 24 North Paca Street, the rental of which the state board approved at $1,000 per year. Before the school opened on January 15, 1866, with an enrollment of eleven students, Mr. M. Alexander Newell was made principal. By the time the first session closed, forty women and eight men had enrolled, one-third of them from the counties. The following June sixteen graduated: four of the graduates were teachers of the grammar grades and twelve, of the primary grades.[87]

For the fall term, 1866, the Maryland State Normal School began with forty-eight students and ended with ninety-three. By 1869 there were 144 enrolled. Five years later the General Assembly appropriated $100,000 for land and construction of a new building at Carrollton and Lafayette Avenues. Until 1915 this site was the home of the Normal School, which in that year moved to its present campus in Towson, north of Baltimore City.

When the school year ended in 1921, the Normal School at Towson, with an enrollment of 234, closed the academic department and the fourth-year high school class which until that time had been "the lone survival of the gradual elimination of the under classes."[88] The State Board of Education adopted a policy of accepting only four-year high school graduates for the following year. "This elimination made possible the raising of the standards of the normal school to that of the college level."[89]

Within three or four years following the opening of the Normal School in 1866, several colleges were founded in Maryland. Reference has already been made to the establishment of Mount St. Agnes Academy in 1867 and to its incorporation as a college in 1890.

> During the early history of Westminster [Maryland] a number of private academies operated from time to time, but not until

---

87. Blauch, *M.H.M.*, XXVI (September, 1931), 219. Elmer Kirk Chandlee, "A History of the Maryland State Normal School for White Students" (M.A. thesis, University of Maryland, 1935), pp. 20 and 22.
88. Chandlee, p. 66.
89. *Ibid.*

1865, when Professor Fayette R. Buel came from New York state to Westminster and opened an Academy, was the idea of a college conceived.[90]

Professor Buel presented in March 1866, the idea of a college to the Maryland Conference of the Methodist Protestant Church, a denomination which had split off from the Methodist Episcopal Church more than thirty years before. The cornerstone for the new college at Westminster was laid on August 29, 1866; but it was not until 1868, when it appeared that the college, organized in 1867, might not survive, that the Maryland Conference appointed thirty-three men to be incorporated by the state legislature as a board of trustees for Western Maryland College. On August 12, 1868, the college received its charter.[91] "Under the inspiring leadership of Dr. J. T. Ward [the first president] and due greatly to the unselfishness of Mr. John Smith, Mr. Isaac Baile and the lovers of education in the Methodist Protestant Church, the college finally became a reality."[92]

During the 1870's the academic program of Western Maryland College was divided into six departments: collegiate (three years for women; four years for men), preparatory and classics, theology, music, lecture, and extras, the last of which included instruction in vocal music, drawing, oil, Grecian and water-color painting, wax fruit and flowers. By the end of its first twenty-five years of operation the Westminster college had a student body of 258 and a faculty of eighteen.

In 1867, when Western Maryland College opened, Centenary Bible Institute was founded in Baltimore as a school for Negroes under the patronage of the Baltimore, Washington, Wilmington and Delaware Conferences of the Methodist Episcopal Church. Renamed Morgan College in 1890 in honor of Dr. Lyttleton Morgan, who had given the school a substantial sum of money so that it could have a college-level program, the institution remained under the jurisdiction of the church until 1939 when the state purchased it.

---

90. Western Maryland College, *College Bulletin*, III, No. 9 (July, 1890), p. 1.
91. Joe Corby Newcomer, "The Origin and Early History of Western Maryland College" (M.A. thesis, University of Maryland 1941), pp. 28-29.
92. *Ibid.*, p. 30.

Meanwhile, in 1886, the Methodist Episcopal Church established the Delaware Conference Academy for Negroes at Princess Anne on the Eastern Shore. Gradually Morgan College assumed control of this two-year school, which was later called Princess Anne Academy and which received through Maryland Agricultural College federal funds as provided by the Second Morrill Act (1890), ". . . probably the first national legislation in American history providing education 'without distinction of race or color.' "[93] The Academy's program gave special emphasis to agricultural training, blacksmithing, plumbing, printing, and home economics and postponed until 1927 the offering of college courses. In 1935 the General Assembly "acquired from Morgan College full title to Princess Anne and made it a part of the University [of Maryland] which had long been supplying most of the smaller school's inadequate budget."[94]

Like Western Maryland and Morgan State Colleges, Bowie State College was founded in 1867 as the Baltimore Normal School, a private institution. The state purchased the school for Negroes in 1908 and moved it to its present site under the name of the State Teachers College at Bowie. In 1963 the institution was renamed Bowie State College.

In addition to the founding of the colleges mentioned in 1867, the General Assembly enacted early in March of that year a charter "for the purpose of establishing a house of studies for young men intended for the ministry of the Roman Catholic Church. . . ."[95] Meanwhile, in January of the previous year the Society of Jesus had purchased a 139-acre farm at Woodstock, twenty-five miles from Baltimore in Baltimore County, on the Baltimore and Ohio Railroad and the Patapsco River. A few months later the order added 110 acres to this purchase. By September, 1869, the Jesuit college was ready to begin operation.

The Philosophy and Theology taught there acted as background for the instruction and ideals offered by Jesuit administrators and teachers in Jesuit educational institutions throughout

93. G. H. Callcott, p. 191.

94. *Ibid.*, p. 352.

95. Rev. Edmund Granville Ryan, S.J., "An Academic History of Woodstock College in Maryland (1868–1944): The First Jesuit Seminary in North America" (Ph.D. dissertation, The Catholic University of America, 1964), p. 24.

the entire United States and Canada during the last quarter of the nineteenth century and, since 1900, of Jesuit schools on the Eastern seaboard.[96]

Besides its academic program, Woodstock College operated the Woodstock Press, established in 1869, and sponsored, beginning in 1872, the *Woodstock Letters*, "a private-circulation quarterly magazine devoted to contemporary or former Jesuit activity in the home and foreign apostolate."[97]

Within a few years after the opening of Woodstock College, another Catholic institution was established in Maryland. Founded in Baltimore as a school for girls by the School Sisters of Notre Dame, the Academic and Collegiate Institute received its charter in 1873. A little more than twenty years later this school, having been authorized to grant college degrees, became the College of Notre Dame of Maryland, the first Roman Catholic college for women in the United States. It continued to operate, however, its preparatory program until 1961, when the Notre Dame Preparatory School was established at Towson as an institution independent of the college.

Speaking at St. John's College, Annapolis, in 1869, two years after Johns Hopkins was incorporated and seven years before it opened, former Mayor George William Brown, a regent and faculty member of the University of Maryland, where he taught constitutional law, observed:

> A great university hereafter to be established in Baltimore, has been planned by the wealthiest of her citizens, a native of this county [Anne Arundel], and at some future day we may confidently expect that it will be so liberally endowed out of his large fortune as to enable it to take rank among the first and most useful universities in the land.[98]

Brown's observation was prophetic indeed. On the day before Christmas, 1873, Johns Hopkins, at the age of seventy-eight, died quietly in his sleep. A Baltimore bachelor and Quaker who had made a fortune in finance, he had provided in his will that the twelve trustees who were to establish the university bearing his name were to use half of his seven-million

---

96. *Ibid.*, p. 2.
97. *Ibid.*, p. 243.
98. Hugh D. Hawkins, "George William Brown and His Influence on The Johns Hopkins University," *M.H.M.*, LII (September, 1957), 183.

Johns Hopkins (1795-1873), Baltimore philanthropist
who gave his name and fortune
to two world-renowned institutions. *M.H.S.*

dollar estate for that purpose and that Clifton, his country home, was also to be a gift to the university.[99] The other half of the Hopkins estate was to be used for the establishment of a hospital which, though independent of the university, would be used for clinical teaching by a projected medical department or school.

Three years after the incorporation of the university, the trustees met and elected a president and a secretary of the board. Not until after Mr. Hopkins' death did the trustees again meet. In seeking answers about the nature of the institution which they were to create, the trustees sought the advice of such leading university presidents as Charles William Eliot of Harvard, James Burrill Angell of Michigan, and Andrew Dickson White of Cornell. "Eliot and Angell, but not White, stressed the ideal that Hopkins should establish professional schools, which, they implied, would make it a true university."[100] All three agreed, as did President Noah Porter of Yale, that Daniel Coit Gilman, who was then president of the University of California, was ideally suited to be the first president of The Johns Hopkins. Eliot had been the first of the group to suggest his name and White had known Gilman and his "organizing faculty" while a fellow student at Yale twenty-five years before. In December, 1874, the Hopkins board of trustees elected Gilman president, a position he was to hold until his resignation in 1901.

> Soon after Gilman accepted the presidency of Hopkins, a friend wrote him, "You will have your pick of professors all the world over, and I presume the colleges are shaking in their shoes and waiting to see what will happen to them." But it was not so easy as that.[101]

Many established scholars and scientists were unwilling to "pioneer" in bringing to life a new university. Except for such proven scholars as the English mathematician James Joseph Sylvester and Basil L. Gildersleeve, a professor of Greek at the

---

99. Hugh Hawkins, *Pioneer: A History of the Johns Hopkins University, 1874–1889* (Ithaca: Cornell University Press, 1960), p. 3. (Hereafter cited as *Pioneer*). Helen Hopkins Thom, *Johns Hopkins: A Silhouette* (Baltimore: J. H. Press, 1929), *passim*.

100. Hawkins, *Pioneer*, p. 13.

101. Hawkins, *Pioneer*, p. 38. The internal quotation was from a letter of Frederick J. Kingsbury to Gilman, Feb. 23, 1875.

University of Virginia and the first professor to be appointed to the Hopkins faculty, Gilman, in his recruitment of faculty, had to be largely content with men of promise.

For the first quarter of a century of its history, Johns Hopkins University was situated in the heart of Baltimore within sight of the Washington Monument and by 1900 was housed in nine distinct buildings. There were no dormitories; so students lived in private boarding houses or at home, for of the 4,089 students who had enrolled at the University during this period, 1,298 were residents of Baltimore (1,617 were from Maryland).[102]

By the time of President Gilman's retirement in 1901 there were 143 members of the faculty and 651 students; 473 had already graduated from a college or some other university. "At commencement in June, 1901, the degree of Bachelor of Arts was conferred upon forty-one candidates, the degree of Doctor of Medicine upon fifty-three, and thirty were promoted to the degree of Doctor of Philosophy."[103]

Four months before that commencement William Wyman, R. Brent Keyser, Francis M. Jencks, Samuel Keyser, J. LeRoy White, and William H. Buckler gave to the university a 176-acre tract on "Charles-street avenue" on the condition that $1,000,000 should be raised for the erection of buildings. Shortly afterward the condition for raising that sum was withdrawn, when the city of Baltimore offered to buy from the University Clifton, the suburban estate of Mr. Johns Hopkins. This made possible the removal of the university to "Homewood," its present campus, which took its name from the lovely colonial mansion that Charles Carroll built and that served for several years as the president's home. Wyman Park, which is adjacent to the Homewood campus, is named to honor the first donor of a part of the land.

In 1912 the state of Maryland contributed to the Homewood campus when the General Assembly appropriated $600,000 for the purpose of building and equipping a school of advanced technology as an integral part of the university. The legislature, moreover, provided $50,000 for its annual support. In turn, Johns Hopkins was to establish 129 free technical scholarships

---

102. Ira Remsen, "The Johns Hopkins University," *Baltimore, The Trade Queen of the South* (Baltimore: John Murphy Co. Publishers, 1902), p. 160.
103. *Ibid.*

for Maryland boys who could meet the requirements. The university was to have, the state agreed, administrative control of the new school.[104]

After carefully reviewing the early development of Johns Hopkins under Gilman's leadership, Hugh Hawkins makes the interesting observation:

> That Gilman was not as single-eyed in his interest in graduate education and research as tradition pictures him, that he bent with the wind of public opinion, that he placed the effect of higher studies on the student over their contribution to the advancement of knowledge, should not lessen his stature. Much of his importance and most of his success came because his aims were plural, his method pragmatic, and his values centered in the living individual.[105]

Upon his retirement from the presidency of Hopkins, Gilman became president of the newly-established Carnegie Institution of Washington, where he remained for two years. His successor at Hopkins was Dr. Ira Remsen, a distinguished organic chemist, known especially for his work on saccharin, and as the university's first professor of chemistry. After serving as president for twelve years, Remsen retired in 1913.

Eight years after Johns Hopkins opened its doors, the Baltimore Conference of the Methodist Episcopal Church, at its one hundredth session held in Washington, D.C., in March, 1884, made plans for the establishment of the Women's College of Baltimore (later renamed Goucher College). The college was incorporated in Maryland early in 1885; and three years later, under the leadership of its first president, the Reverend Dr. John F. Goucher, classes began at this college for women. In the 1940's, it began moving out of Baltimore City to Towson, a transfer that was completed in 1953.

In 1893 the Potomac Synod of the Reformed Church in the United States founded the Women's College of Frederick, Maryland. Henry Joseph Apple having been selected as president, the college commenced operation with a student body of eighty and a faculty of eight on the site of the Frederick Female Seminary, dating from 1839, on East Church Street. The college was incorporated four years after it was established, and in 1913

104. *The Baltimore Sun Almanac*, 1913, p. 89.
105. Hawkins, *Pioneer*, p. 66.

its name was changed to Hood College as a result of Mrs. Margaret E. S. Hood's benefactions. Two years later the school moved to its present campus in Frederick. Apple, who was of Pennsylvania-German descent, was president of Hood from its beginnings to 1934 and was considered "one of the leading educators in the state."[106]

A year after Hood College was established, Mr. and Mrs. John Irvin Cassedy, formerly of Norfolk, Virginia, founded at Forest Glen, Maryland, the National Park Seminary, an institution for young women. At first it was called "The Glen School" and continued to be colloquially referred to by that name in later years. In 1903 the school was chartered as the National Park Seminary, a name derived from the institution's proximity to the National Rock Creek Park. Nine years later it was organized as a junior college; and in 1916, after Mr. Cassedy had sold his interest in the school that meanwhile had become fashionable, Dr. James Ament became the president. During World War II the federal government purchased the wooded campus, with its intriguing buildings of varied occidental as well as oriental architecture, as an extension of the Walter Reed Army Hospital. As a consequence the nearly fifty-year-old junior college and preparatory school for young women came to a close.

In 1898, four years after the establishment of the National Park Seminary, the Maryland General Assembly appropriated funds for the building and support of a normal school at Frostburg, located ten miles west of Cumberland on a plateau 2,200 feet above sea level. The new normal school, the second in the state, opened with fifty-seven students on September 15, 1902, in a three-story brick and stone building that housed all of its activities. By the end of the first year the enrollment had risen to ninety-four, of whom seventy-one were women and twenty-three were men. In 1914–15, the school's enrollment reached 200, but took a decided drop within the next five years as a consequence of World War I. Meanwhile, for the first eight years of the normal school's operation Edmund Dandridge Murdough served as principal. In 1912 the General Assembly authorized a second unit for the school, which included a gymnasium and space for a model school which a year later was opened for use.

---

106. Cunz, p. 341.

In the meantime the Board of School Commissioners of Baltimore City established at the turn of the century the Colored Training School to prepare Negroes for teaching positions. This school, more than two decades later, was renamed the Fannie J. Coppin Normal School in memory of Fannie Jackson Coppin, a former slave who bought her freedom and became the first American Negro woman to earn a college degree.[107] The state assumed control of the normal school in 1951, and twelve years later its name was changed to Coppin State College.[108]

By 1907, it is interesting to note, there were seventeen colleges and universities in Maryland. Several of the private institutions subsequently closed, among them Rock Hill College (Roman Catholic, Ellicott City), New Windsor College (Presbyterian, New Windsor), Maryland College for Women (Lutheran, Lutherville), and Kee Mar College (nonsectarian, Hagerstown). But while some colleges were closing in Maryland as the twentieth century wore on, new ones were being established.

One year after the armistice ending World War I was signed, the Baltimore Hebrew College opened for the purpose of giving instruction in Hebrew and cognate languages to both men and women, training teachers for Jewish religious schools, and providing pre-theological instruction for people planning to enter the rabbinate.

It was not until some time after the turn of the century that a serious effort was made to transform the University of Maryland into a genuine state university. There were several reasons for the delay, including the nature of the university's charter, which had been drafted in 1807 without provision for adequate government for a state university and which apparently could not be modified except by the unanimous consent of the faculty.[109]

> One could point to geographical and religious divisions within the state as explanations of the delay, or to the traditionally economy-minded state government or to the lack of educational leaders. A more formidable obstacle lay, not in the failure, but in

---

107. *Maryland Manual 1971–1972*, p. 961. Vavrina, II, 728.

108. As Salisbury Normal School (now Salisbury State College) did not open until 1925, its establishment and early history do not fall within the scope of this chapter. It did for the Eastern Shore what Towson and Frostburg had done for the western part of the state.

109. G. H. Callcott, pp. 276-77.

the very success of the private institutions which had risen to take the place of a state university. The Johns Hopkins served the scholars, proprietary schools served the professions, the Maryland Agricultural College served the farmers, state normal schools provided teachers and such private institutions as Washington, St. John's, Loyola, Western Maryland, St. Mary's, Morgan and Goucher served for regular collegiate training. The general assembly had fallen into the peculiar custom of providing regular appropriations to almost all of these institutions. By 1912 Johns Hopkins alone received over $600,000 from the state, and by 1920 the legislature was doling out, in pork-barrel fashion, almost $1,000,000 annually to unregulated private, denominational and proprietary institutions. Each institution had a vested interest in the system. Each institution feared that a state university which might include it meant loss of independence, and that a state system which might exclude it meant the loss of its state subsidy. Generally the established colleges considered the idea of a state university unnecessary and socialistic.[110]

In 1907 Dr. Eugene F. Cordell, a member of the medical faculty of the University of Maryland, recommended to Governor Edwin Warfield a merger of St. John's College with the university. Warfield, in turn, arranged a meeting with officers of the two institutions as well as with the Maryland Agricultural College in College Park. The latter, however, decided to stay aloof from any proposed merger. Eventually a temporary agreement was hammered out between the University of Maryland and St. John's for the establishment of "an advisory super-government," as Callcott called it, composed of the governor as chancellor, provosts of the respective institutions, and an eight-man faculty council. As a result of this arrangement, St. John's referred to itself as the university's Department of Arts and Sciences. In 1912, when Dr. Bernard Carter, the president of the University of Maryland, died, Dr. Thomas Fell, president of St. John's, was asked to become provost of the University of Maryland. Fell strove for legislation granting legal recognition to the merger; this appeared imminent in 1914, but failed when Dr. Fell declined the presidency of the university, as did a few others in turn.

A further attempt to provide an undergraduate college for the

---

110. *Ibid.*, p. 276. Reprinted by permission of Maryland Historical Society.

university came after World War I when the medical faculty of the University of Maryland, reflecting the goal of the American Medical Association to close down the proprietary schools (see the section in this chapter on Medicine and Public Health) and needing an undergraduate program, tried again to negotiate a merger with St. John's College. The effort failed, as did also an attempt to make Western Maryland College the liberal arts division of the university. Finally, arrangements were made with the Maryland State College of Agriculture, which the state had taken over and renamed in 1916, for a consolidation of the University of Maryland in Baltimore with the College Park agricultural institution under the name of the University of Maryland. The enabling legislation, which was introduced by Millard Tydings, speaker of the House of Delegates, provided that the trustees of the Maryland State College were to become the Board of Regents of the University of Maryland and were thus to have complete responsibility for the university, including the ownership of its property. On April 9, 1920, Governor Albert Ritchie signed the Tydings bill, which had been passed unanimously in both the House of Delegates and the Senate. For the future of higher education in Maryland this was an occasion of historic importance.

3

MEDICINE AND PUBLIC HEALTH

The history of medicine in Maryland after 1800 is intimately associated with the Medical and Chirurgical Faculty of the State of Maryland, the official name of the state medical society. Through the efforts of Dr. John Archer of Harford County, one of the first physicians to receive a medical diploma in this country (M.B., College of Philadelphia, 1768), and Dr. Upton Scott of Annapolis, the faculty's first president, legislation to establish and incorporate the Medical and Chirurgical Faculty was enacted on January 20,1799. This act provided for a medical board of twelve examiners drawn from the faculty, seven from the Western and five from the Eastern Shore. Their responsibility was directed to the issuance of licenses upon examination or identification by diploma "from some respectable college" that the physician was qualified.[111] In 1838 the Medical and Chirurgical Faculty lost the authority to license practitioners but regained it by the Medical Act of 1892, which established the Board of Medical Examiners. This was in keeping with a trend after 1875 in which state medical societies "encouraged by the better [medical school] faculties, reasserted themselves and helped to reform the schools through the revival of state boards."[112]

No applicants for license applied to the Maryland Board of Medical Examiners in 1892 but fifty did so the following year, nine of whom were not admitted. "A number of those applying were debarred by reason of not having studied medicine three years and not having attended three courses of lectures."[113]

Two years after the enactment of the Medical Act of 1892 an amendment to it was passed "so as to provide for a general official registration of all physicians practicing in the state on or before the first day of June, 1892. This registration was directed to be made in the Circuit Courts of the counties or of Baltimore City."[114] Until the adoption of this amendment there was no way of knowing how many physicians had settled in Maryland since the spring of 1892, nor therefore how many had been practicing illegally.

Meanwhile, in 1882, two important developments occurred in the history of the Medical and Chirurgical Faculty: the admission of the first Negro physician to the faculty and the establishment of a nurses' directory "modeled after the one founded in Boston in 1879, 'which is already a pronounced success.' "[115] Dr. Whitfield Winsey, a graduate of Harvard, became the first Negro to be admitted to the faculty, after having been unanimously elected. By 1890 three Negroes were members of the state medical society. "Nevertheless, the University of Mary-

111. *The Act of Incorporation and Supplementary Acts, with the By-laws of the Medical and Chirurgical Faculty of Maryland to which is added A List of the Officers and Members of the Faculty* (Baltimore: Richard J. Matchett, 1848), pp. 3 and 5.

112. Richard Harrison Shryock, *Medical Licensing in America, 1650–1965* (Baltimore: J. H. Press, 1967), pp. 111–12.

113. Eugene Fauntleroy Cordell, *The Medical Annals of Maryland 1799–1899* (Baltimore: Williams and Wilkins Co., 1903), p. 241.

114. *Ibid.*, pp. 241–42.

115. *Ibid.*, p. 177.

land medical college and all others in the state had refused to open its [sic] doors to the colored people."[116]

For almost the first sixty years of its history the Medical and Chirurgical Faculty of Maryland had no home of its own. In 1858 it secured a house on Calvert Street in Baltimore, which it sold nine years later, using the proceeds from the sale to buy a house at 60 Courtland Street. As a consequence the faculty took on renewed life, with an attendant increase in the membership.[117] The headquarters of the faculty remained at the Courtland Street house for only five years, after which they were moved to Fayette Street at the northwest corner of Park Avenue, where they stayed for four years. In 1878 the state medical society moved to a hall across Fayette Street, which served as its home for the next eighteen years. It then moved in 1896 to 847 Eutaw Street, and finally in 1909 to a building at 1211 Cathedral Street, which was specifically designed to house the faculty.

While located at the Eutaw Street address the Medical and Chirurgical Faculty celebrated its centennial anniversary with a four-day, elaborate program, beginning on April 25, 1899. The program opened with the presidential address of Dr. Samuel C. Chew on the appropriate subject "Medicine in the Nineteenth Century." Chew reviewed the great discoveries of that century which was drawing to a close, noting that "no period can be compared as to the number and importance of its achievements."[118]

Toward the end of the century the Medical and Chirurgical Faculty sought in several ways to raise the quality of medicine and public health in the state. In 1886 the Lunacy Commission of Maryland was established, and in the following year an institution for feeble-minded children was founded. Eight years following the creation of the Lunacy Commission a second state mental hospital (Sykesville) became a reality. Moreover, the faculty also urged the establishment of a municipal bacteriological laboratory in Baltimore to supervise the city's water supply, analyze suspected foods, and provide early detection of communicable diseases. In 1892 the state medical society

---

116. Plater, p. 88.
117. Cordell, pp. 147-49.
118. *Ibid.*, p. 271.

urged the Baltimore City Council to establish a hospital for infectious diseases and a disinfecting plant. At the national level the Medical and Chirurgical Faculty successfully fought, as did other organizations, the efforts of the antivivisectionists, who in 1896 had introduced a bill in Congress to prevent cruelty to animals. If passed, this bill would have closed governmental biological laboratories such as those of the Marine Hospital Service, Surgeon General, and Bureau of Animal Husbandry, and in addition would have prevented medical schools in the District of Columbia from experimenting with live animals. The state medical society, largely through the efforts of Dr. (later Sir) William Osler, the president of the Medical and Chirurgical Faculty in 1896–97 and professor of medicine at The Johns Hopkins University School of Medicine until his departure for Oxford in 1905, was instrumental in the establishment of the Maryland Public Health Association (1897). This new organization was founded ". . . for the purpose of calling attention to sanitary measures throughout the state and thereby forcing reforms upon a timid and reluctant legislature."[119]

Five years before Osler assumed the presidency of the faculty, his friend and colleague, Dr. William H. Welch, professor of pathology and the dean of The Johns Hopkins University School of Medicine when it opened in 1893, became president of the state medical society. Both Welch and Osler did much to advance the work and status of the faculty during the last decade of the nineteenth century.[120] And when the building on Cathedral Street in Baltimore which now houses the faculty was dedicated on May 13, 1909, "Osler's fifteen years in Baltimore had had much to do—indeed nearly everything to do—with making it possible."[121] It was, therefore, not surprising that a room in the new quarters—Osler Hall—was dedicated to him, as he had given his time, talent, and interest to the development of the faculty and as a devoted bibliophile, to its library.

119. Harvey Cushing, *The Life of Sir William Osler* (Oxford: Oxford University Press, 1926), I, 446.
120. *Ibid.*, I and II, *passim*. Simon Flexner and James Thomas Flexner, *William Henry Welch and the Heroic Age of American Medicine* (New York: Viking Press, 1941), p. 156.
121. Cushing, II, 175.

In the decades following the Civil War one of the most serious problems which continued to plague American medicine in
general and Maryland medicine in particular was the inferior
quality of medical education.

As early as 1876 progressive faculties had founded the Association of American Medical Colleges in order to promote reform
from within. Although twenty-two colleges were represented at
the first meeting, this effort was premature and was abandoned in
1883.[122]

The medical colleges in Baltimore and the staff of the newly-
opened Johns Hopkins Hospital requested seven years later a
meeting in Nashville to revive the association at which
sixty-five medical schools were represented. "The association
immediately called for a three-year curriculum, and grew during ensuing decades into a representative and influential
body."[123]

It was not until the publication of Bulletin Number Four in
1910 by The Carnegie Foundation for the Advancement of
Teaching that the need for considerable improvement in
American medical education was dramatically underscored.
This report, entitled *Medical Education in the United States
and Canada*, was prepared by Abraham Flexner and was a general indictment of the deficiencies of medical education, including the training of physicians in Maryland:

There are seven medical schools in Maryland, a state whose
population increases slowly and in which there are between two
and three times as many physicians as it now requires. Of these
seven schools, two belong to the worst type of American medical
school, *viz.*, the Atlantic Medical College and the Maryland
Medical College. That such unconscionable concerns should at
this day continue to flourish is a blot upon the state of Maryland
and the city of Baltimore.[124]

The seven medical schools included the University of Mary-

122. Richard Harrison Shryock, *Medical Licensing in America, 1650–1965*
(Baltimore: J. H. Press, 1967), p. 55. Reprinted by permission of The Johns
Hopkins Press.
123. *Ibid.*
124. Abraham Flexner, *Medical Education in the United States and Canada:
A Report to The Carnegie Foundation for the Advancement of Teaching*,
Bulletin Number Four (New York, 1910, Reprinted 1960), p. 238.

The four doctors. Johns Hopkins University's famous "Big Four" of the medical faculty (left to right Dr. William H. Welch, Dr. William Stewart Halsted, Sir William Osler, and Dr. Howard A. Kelly). Artist: John S. Sargent, R.A. *M.H.S.*

land School of Medicine, organized in 1807; the College of Physicians and Surgeons, established in 1872; Baltimore Medical College, founded in 1881; Women's Medical College of Baltimore, organized in 1882; Atlantic Medical College, established in 1891 "as an independent homeopathic institution"; The Johns Hopkins Medical School, established in 1893; and Maryland Medical College, instituted in 1898. Flexner was scathing in his evaluation of six of the seven medical schools.

> The Johns Hopkins Medical School, for which neither the state of Maryland nor the city of Baltimore has ever done anything, is thus the only medical school in Maryland that either ought to or can live, and to its development greatly increased means should be freely devoted.[125]

In 1893, seventeen years before the famous report on *Medical Education in the United States and Canada* was published, The Johns Hopkins University School of Medicine opened through the efforts and gifts of Miss Mary Garrett, who had inherited a large fortune from her father John W. Garrett, a former president of the Baltimore and Ohio Railroad, and of The Women's Fund for the Higher Medical Education of Women. The latter was a national undertaking which Miss Garrett and several of her young women friends including Miss M. Carey Thomas, a daughter of a university trustee and the dean of the newly established Bryn Mawr College, had organized. Miss Garrett initially gave $10,000 in 1890 and two years later added $306,977 to the amount collected by the Women's Fund, thus providing the university with the $500,000 necessary for the establishment of the medical school. "It was a condition of her gift that women should be admitted on equal terms with men and that all students should, preliminary to admission, have the degree of Bachelor of Arts or of Science, have had training in physics, chemistry and biology, and possess a reading knowledge of French and German."[126]

Writing thirty years later to Dr. Harvey Cushing, the renowned neurosurgeon and biographer of Sir William Osler, Dr.

---

125. *Ibid.*, p. 239.

126. Lewellys F. Barker, "The Early Days of The Johns Hopkins Hospital," *M.H.M.*, XXXVIII, (March, 1943), 11.

William H. Welch, the first dean of The Johns Hopkins Medical School, noted:

> The terms of admission to the medical school were not the invention of Miss Garrett or Miss Thomas, but years before I had set them down in a document which Mr. Gilman and the Trustees asked me to prepare soon after I came to Baltimore. Miss Garrett got this document through her lawyer, Mr. [Charles J. M.] Gwinn, who was an influential trustee of the university. She naturally supposed that this was exactly what we wanted. It is one thing to build an educational castle in the air at your library table, and another to face its actual appearance under the existing circumstances.[127]

The high admission requirements exacted by Miss Garrett as a condition for her substantial gift to the medical school were finally accepted by the university's trustees upon the recommendation of Dr. Welch, even though he had entertained reservations about starting with such imposing prerequisites. Osler no doubt expressed a general feeling when he remarked: "Welch, we are lucky to get in as professors, for I am sure that neither you nor I could ever get in as students."[128] These requirements for admission as well as the quality of instruction offered in The Johns Hopkins Medical School set an example in American medical education which was long overdue. Within a decade the school of medicine achieved an international eminence.

Moreover, it had an advantage of a teaching hospital nearby, as The Johns Hopkins Hospital had opened in 1889 on a site in East Baltimore that Mr. Hopkins had selected before he died. The new hospital included fourteen distinct though connected buildings; and in conjunction with it a school for nurses was established, one that soon earned, like the medical school, an excellent reputation. Much of the credit for the planning of the hospital was due to Dr. John Shaw Billings, the distinguished librarian of the Surgeon General's Library in Washington (now the National Library of Medicine in Bethesda, Maryland) and the principal adviser to the hospital's board of trustees.

---

127. S. and J. T. Flexner, p. 220. Copyright 1941 by Simon and James Thomas Flexner. Reprinted by permission of The Viking Press, Inc.
128. *Ibid.*

The Johns Hopkins Hospital as it appeared on opening day, May 7, 1889. *M.H.S.*

Maryland, in addition to the establishment of The Johns Hopkins School of Medicine and some inferior medical schools in the decades after the Civil War, witnessed the continued development of dental education. It will be recalled that in 1840 the Baltimore College of Dentistry was established through the efforts of Horace H. Hayden and Chapin A. Harris, thus becoming the first school of dentistry in the world. Between 1840 and 1865 only seven dental schools were chartered throughout the United States. "After 1865, however, there was a renascence of enthusiasm for dental training; and a continually increasing number of schools were chartered and put in operation in many of the larger cities throughout the United States."[129] In 1873 the Maryland Dental College was founded in Baltimore as one such school. Operating only for six years, this dental school conferred degrees on about seventy students. In its last class was Dr. Richard Grady who became known as the "Father of the Oral Hygiene Movement."

Three years after the Maryland Dental College closed a dental department of the university opened with a clinic of twenty-five chairs, each having a window in front of it. Dental students, it was felt, should receive instruction in a medical atmosphere, as the leading medical associations had come to recognize "the art and science of dental surgery."[130] Generally the students studied anatomy, chemistry, *materia medica*, physiology, and surgery in the same classes with the medical students.

"There is no explanation of why, in 1895, a charter was issued for the establishment of still another dental school in Maryland, to be known as the Dental Department of the Baltimore Medical College. . . ."[131] During its eighteen years of operation this department enjoyed a fine reputation. When the Baltimore Medical College merged with the University of Maryland School of Medicine in 1913, its dental department likewise came to an end.

Unfortunately cutthroat competition between the Baltimore dental schools in the early 1880's had led to a decline in their standards. "With the danger apparent to everyone the dental

129. Harry Bryan McCarthy, "A History of Dental Education in Maryland" (M.A. thesis, University of Maryland, 1948), p. 31.
130. *Ibid.*, p. 42.
131. *Ibid.*, p. 48.

colleges tried desperately to halt the slide. In 1883 they formed the Maryland State Dental Association, and the following year obtained state legislation requiring all dental college graduates to take a licensing examination."[132] Within the next three years the Baltimore colleges of dentistry had restored their two-year requirement and in turn instituted ". . . a graded curriculum with different courses for the junior and senior years."[133]

By 1909 there was a need for the establishment of the Dental Education Council of America. In cooperation with the National Association of Dental Examiners, it worked for higher admission requirements and the increase in the length of dental courses. In 1918, when the Dental Education Council made its first classification of dental schools, both the Baltimore College of Dental Surgery and the Dental Department of the University of Maryland were rated as Class B. Both had been proprietary operations, the latter being so from its inception in 1882 to 1920, when the University of Maryland was reorganized. The poor ratings (loss of accreditation) resulted in declining enrollments for the two schools. However, the state aid that the university's dental department commenced to receive following the reorganization meant virtually the end of the senior dental college. After considerable negotiation the faculty of the Baltimore College of Dentistry agreed to sell its interest to the University of Maryland for $12,000, a reduction from the original request of $30,000. The merger became effective in June 1923.

Like the status of medical education, public health conditions in Maryland were generally deplorable in the decades following the Civil War. The efforts to improve public health in the state during the first two decades of the twentieth century will be discussed in the chapter on "Maryland Progressivism."

Among the diseases which had high mortality rates in Maryland from the Civil War to the turn of the century were consumption (tuberculosis), cholera infantum, diarrhea, dysentery, diphtheria, pneumonia, enteric, scarlet, and typhoid fevers. Cancer and the cardiovascular diseases, of course, also produced high death rates. The census of 1890 reported that

---

132. G. H. Callcott, p. 219.
133. *Ibid.*

whereas the national death rate (per 1,000) was 13.98, that of Maryland was noticeably higher, 17.27.[134]

In 1900 the *Twelfth Census* revealed that in the coastal counties of Maryland, which were included by the census as part of the middle Atlantic coastal region, the proportion of deaths from consumption, pneumonia, diarrheal diseases, Bright's disease, apoplexy, bronchitis, diphtheria, and hydrocephalus were above the average proportions for these diseases in the United States. On the other hand, the proportions of deaths in these counties from such diseases as typhoid fever, cancer, meningitis, influenza, malarial fever, croup, and diabetes were less than the national averages.

The census of 1900 designated Frederick, Maryland, as one of the registration cities in the Central Appalachian Region. Here the death rates for apoplexy, paralysis (poliomyelitis?), diphtheria, convulsions, scarlet fever, kidney diseases and peritonitis were higher than the national averages, whereas the proportions for such diseases as consumption, typhoid, influenza, malarial fever, measles, appendicitis, and hydrocephalus fell below the averages for the country at large.[135]

The lamentable state of public health in Baltimore was carefully noted in the *Tenth Census' Report on the Social Statistics of Cities* (1880).[136] The condition of the city's drainage was observed: ". . . Baltimore is mainly still in the condition of a small country town with paved streets." And Dr. McShane, the city's assistant commissioner of health and general superintendent of streets, stated in his annual report (1880): "Baltimore has no regular system of sewers, the present sewers of the city being constructed for the removal of storm-water."[137] Practically all excrement went into the 80,000 cesspools and privy-vaults, then estimated to be in use. Moreover, laundry and kitchen wastes and all foul liquids except urine were sent across or under the sidewalks into the gutters. The city did provide from May to November for the daily removal of garbage

---

134. *Eleventh Census, Report on Vital and Social Statistics in the United States*, Part I, pp. 548-49.
135. *Twelfth Census*, III, Part 1, c-cii.
136. *Tenth Census, Report on the Social Statistics of Cities*, XIX, Part II, 17-21.
137. *Ibid.*, p. 19.

and ashes and during the remainder of the year for their removal three times a week.

> In 1892 the role of modern hygiene was brought dramatically
> to the attention of the American people; a severe epidemic of
> cholera broke out in Hamburg and seven ships brought almost a
> hundred cases to New York. The foremost bacteriologists of the
> country sprang into action; Biggs, Prudden, and Welch [of Johns
> Hopkins] conferred; and the first municipal bacteriological
> laboratory in this country was hastily fitted up by the New York
> City Board of Health. Dr. Edward K. Dunham, working under
> Biggs' direction, obtained cultures of cholera bacilli which were
> confirmed by Prudden, Welch, and Ernst, as well as by the Im-
> perial Board of Health in Berlin. The disease was arrested in the
> port of New York.[138]

Welch, with his colleagues at the The Johns Hopkins Medical
School, took full advantage of the cholera scare to urge specific
reforms in public health in Baltimore and the state. "There was
much to be done," as the Flexners observed in their biography
of Welch.

> Although two generations of citizens' committees and public
> health officials had urged cleansing the soil and providing a safe
> water supply for Baltimore, sewage contamination in Lake Ro-
> land, the source of drinking water for a large part of the city, was
> known to exist, and in other public health matters Baltimore was
> equally backward.[139]

It was Welch who provided, according to Harry S. Sherwood
of the Baltimore *Sun*, "the first impulse" for building a modern
filtration plant for the city. Welch's concern was not confined,
however, to Baltimore City. In 1898 he was appointed to the
Maryland State Board of Health and two years later became its
president, a position which he held until its abolishment in
1922. During his years as president of the Board of Health,
Welch was able to replace the old politically-oriented county
health officers, who gave only a small portion of their time to
their responsibilities, with men who were scientific in their
work and who devoted their full time and attention to their
public health duties.

---

138. S. and J. T. Flexner, p. 343. Reprinted by permission of The Viking
Press, Inc.

139. *Ibid.*, p. 346. Reprinted by permission of The Viking Press, Inc.

Another facet of public health in Maryland to which Welch as president of the State Board of Health and his Johns Hopkins colleague Dr. William Osler gave attention was the prevention and treatment of tuberculosis. Through Governor John Walter Smith the state board recommended to the General Assembly the establishment of a tuberculosis commission, which became a reality in 1902. Two years later the Maryland Association for the Prevention and Relief of Tuberculosis was founded. "By 1904, 23 state and local associations had been formed. Finally, after a preliminary meeting in Baltimore in January 1904, the idea of a nationwide organization was adopted and the National Association for the Study and Prevention of Tuberculosis was formed at Atlantic City in June of that year."[140] In 1918 the name was shortened to the National Tuberculosis Association. Both Osler and Welch were among the medical founders of the association; and in 1911 Welch became its president, working "for the better control of 'the disease of the people' which was responsible for one-third of the deaths suffered during the prime of life."[141] In 1908 Welch prophetically stated: "At least one-half of the existing sickness and mortality from tuberculosis could be prevented within the next two decades by the application of rational and entirely practicable measures" such as providing proper diet, fresh air, well-ventilated homes and places of employment, and shorter working hours. By 1933, twenty-five years later, "the mortality from tuberculosis had dropped 62.5 per cent."[142] Both in Maryland and in the country at large the efforts of Welch and Osler in combating the "white plague" were truly impressive.

## 4

### RELIGIOUS AND CULTURAL LIFE

Although religious life and thought, due to the impact of science and technology, underwent some changes in Maryland and elsewhere in the United States during the half century following the Civil War, religion continued to play an important

---

140. George Rosen, *A History of Public Health* (New York: MD Publications, Inc., 1958), p. 389. Reprinted by permission of MD Publications, Inc.
141. S. and J. T. Flexner, p. 348.
142. *Ibid.*

part in the lives of the people in the Old Line State. The census of 1890 indicated that Maryland stood twelfth from the top among the states (including the District of Columbia) in proportion of church members to aggregate population.[143] (It must be remembered that church membership statistics as a rule are subject to inflation and so discretion should be exercised in their employment.)

Of the 2,328 Maryland religious bodies (parishes and congregations) in 1890 indicated in the *Report on Statistics of Churches in the United States at the Eleventh Census*, more than 1900 were listed as Methodist (1,340—all bodies), Roman Catholic (180), Protestant Episcopal (170), Lutheran (131—all bodies), and Baptist (104 including 38 Regular (Negro) Baptists). The remainder were divided among such denominations as: Church of God (21), Disciples of Christ (14), Dunkers (36), Religious Society of Friends (23), Jewish Congregations (12), Presbyterian (93), Reformed (67), United Brethren (57), Unitarian (2), and Universalist (1).

The two largest churches in Maryland between 1865 and 1920 were the Methodist Episcopal and the Roman Catholic, both of whose historical beginnings in America were intimately associated with Maryland. Robert Strawbridge, a follower of John Wesley, the founder of Methodism, began in 1763 to preach not far from New Windsor, Maryland. As a separate American denomination freed of its English connection (Wesley), the Methodist Church was established at the "Christmas Conference" of December 24, 1784, in Baltimore, at which time the name "Methodist Episcopal" was adopted at the suggestion of John Dickins.

It will be further recalled that George Calvert, the first Lord Baltimore, and his eldest son Cecil, who inherited the title and the proprietorship of Maryland and in turn founded the colony, were Catholic. Although the Catholics never constituted a majority in Maryland before or after the Revolution, they were important in its affairs by reason of their numbers and historical association. Shortly after the War of Independence John Carroll, a Jesuit priest and a member of an old and distinguished Roman Catholic family of Maryland, became Prefect Apostolic

---

143. *Report on Statistics of Churches in the United States at the Eleventh Census: 1890*, Book 3, pp. xx-xxi. Hereafter referred to as *Eleventh Census Report*.

with episcopal powers in the United States and in 1790 was consecrated Bishop of Baltimore, thus becoming the first American Catholic bishop. "Upon the recommendation of Bishop Carroll, Pope Pius VII, in 1808, raised Baltimore to metropolitan status, with Carroll as archbishop. . . ."[144] Thus the roots of Roman Catholicism and Methodism in Maryland extended well back into the colonial and early national periods.

In 1890, when the *Eleventh Census* was taken, there were only two counties of Maryland in which there were less than one thousand Methodists: St. Mary's and Charles. In all the others as well as Baltimore City the Methodists numbered more than one thousand respectively; the city of Baltimore boasted more than 20,000. The concentration of Methodists continued to be strong in the Eastern Shore counties.[145] It is interesting to note that while some Maryland Methodists at about the time of the Civil War joined the Methodist Episcopal Church, South, established in 1845, most of them remained loyal to the older church. In the coal regions of western Maryland, as Katherine A. Harvey notes,

> Methodism had spread rapidly among English miners during the nineteenth century, and to it they owed much: free education for their children, improved living and working conditions, and training in leadership. Consequently, the Maryland mining towns supported many Methodist and Methodist Episcopal churches.[146]

At the beginning of the 1890's, the Roman Catholics numbered more than one thousand respectively in thirteen of Maryland's twenty-three counties as well as in the city of Baltimore. They were most numerous in Baltimore City (77,047), St. Mary's County (11,884), Allegany County (9,315), Baltimore County (7,821), Charles County (5,950), and Prince George's County (5,305). In turn their numbers were smallest in Garrett, Calvert, and the Eastern Shore counties, Somerset recording nineteen and Wicomico only eight in the Census of 1890.[147]

---

144. Clifton E. Olmstead, *History of Religion in the United States* (Englewood Cliffs, N.J.: Prentice-Hall, Inc., 1960), p. 236.
145. *Eleventh Census Report*, p. 511.
146. Harvey, *The Best-Dressed Miners*, p. 116. Reprinted by permission of the Cornell University Press.
147. *Eleventh Census Report*, p. 240.

During the quarter of a century following the Civil War the city of Baltimore continued to be a center of national Catholic activity. In 1866 and again in 1884 American Plenary Councils were held there, as also in 1852. The centennial celebration of the establishment of the Catholic hierarchy in the United States and the appointment of Bishop John Carroll to the See of Baltimore also occurred in Baltimore on November 10, 11 and 12, 1889. It was immediately following this occasion—on November 13—that The Catholic University of America opened in Washington, D.C., largely through the efforts of James Cardinal Gibbons, whose see and place of birth were Baltimore. Pope Leo XIII appointed him as the first chancellor of the new institution, the only American pontifical university. Cardinal Gibbons, who was the second American to be appointed to the cardinalate, held that office until his death in 1921.[148]

Compared with the numbers of Roman Catholic and Methodist churches and communicants in Maryland, the Protestant Episcopal, Lutheran, Presbyterian and Baptist denominations were smaller. Only in Anne Arundel, Baltimore, and Prince George's Counties and in Baltimore City were there respectively more than one thousand Episcopalians.

In five of the northern counties—Allegany, Baltimore, Carroll, Frederick, and Washington—the Lutherans (General Synod) numbered more than one thousand, with the heaviest concentrations in Baltimore and Frederick.[149] ". . . Maryland may claim to be the birthplace of organized Lutheranism," for the Lutheran General Synod was established in Hagerstown in 1820, and a year later its second meeting was held in Frederick. Despite this relationship, many German-speaking Lutheran churches in Baltimore City preferred to be members of the Synodical Conference of the Missouri Lutherans.[150]

The Presbyterian Church was not numerically strong in Maryland during the decades following the Civil War, nor was it concentrated in any particular region as was true of some of

---

148.  John J. Pritzl, "James Cardinal Gibbons: Champion of Christian Education" (M.A. thesis, The Catholic University of America, 1935), pp. 1-8.

149.  *Eleventh Census Report*, pp. 440 and 713.

150.  Bernard C. Steiner, "Maryland's Religious History," *M.H.M.*, XXI (March, 1926), pp. 16-17. The Reverend Dr. John G. Morris, a distinguished Lutheran clergyman in Maryland, became the first Librarian of the Peabody Institute and was president of the Maryland Historical Society in 1895 when he died at the age of ninety-three.

the other churches. "During the division in the Presbyterian Church from 1837 to 1869, the Maryland Churches adhered to the 'Old School' and only a very few of them joined the Southern Presbyterian Church at the close of the Civil War."[151]

As was true in the ante-bellum period, the strength of the Baptist Church in Maryland in the half century following the Civil War was confined largely to the Negroes, as the white Baptists (Southern Baptist Convention) were never strong in the state.

Among the oldest religious denominations in Maryland was the Religious Society of Friends; the first Quakers arrived there in the 1650's. By the end of the eighteenth century their meetings were found on both the Eastern and Western Shores. During the early years of the twentieth century the Quakers witnessed a significant change in their condition on the Eastern Shore, where they had once enjoyed some degree of strength: "A steady decline in membership year by year, resulting from few convincements, the departure of younger members to the city, and a low birth rate, can be seen."[152]

Another Christian denomination having historical ties with Maryland was that of the Winebrennarians, whose founder, John Winebrenner, a German Reformed minister, was born in Woodsborough, Frederick County, in 1797. Ordained at Hagerstown in 1820, Winebrenner was excluded eight years later from his pastorate in Harrisburg, Pennsylvania, as a result of his evangelistic practices. He created a new denomination called the General Eldership of the Church of God, to which was later added "in North America." "The only requirement for membership in the church was regeneration. There was no creed but the Bible."[153] By the early 1920's the Winebrennarians had twenty-five churches in Maryland and were confined largely to Pennsylvania as well as Maryland. Their churches are now located in other states as well.

In the years after the Civil War, the number and size of Negro churches in the United States increased.

Unlike the Negroes of South Africa who divided into hundreds of separate denominations, American Negroes developed no

---

151. *Ibid.*, p. 8.
152. Kenneth Carroll, *Quakerism on the Eastern Shore* (Baltimore: M.H.S., 1970), p. 193.
153. Olmstead, p. 303.

new denominational types of major significance. They preferred to follow those basic structures with which they had become familiar during their period of slavery, leaning heavily on Baptist and Methodist doctrine and polity.[154]

This was indeed true of the Negro churches of Maryland in general and of Baltimore in particular. "By 1895, the city [of Baltimore] with a population of 79,739 Negroes, had nineteen outstanding African Methodist Episcopal Churches. . . ." Perhaps "the most phenomenal gains made by the Baltimore Negro had been along religious lines."[155]

In the last two decades of the nineteenth century, as the result of a new wave of anti-Semitism sweeping Europe, Jewish immigration to the United States rose precipitously. "Between 1881 and 1898 a half million Jews entered the United States; between 1899 and 1907, 700,000 came, while 600,000 had entered the country between 1908 and 1914, and by the latter year the total number of Jews in the United States had risen to 3,000,000."[156] Most of the Jews in Maryland during the colonial and early national periods were the Sephardim (Spanish or Portuguese). Their numbers in Maryland and elsewhere were comparatively small. After the collapse of the Revolution of 1848, many German Jews or Ashkenazim made their way to the United States and to such cities as Baltimore. About 1890, as a consequence of European anti-Semitism, large numbers of Polish and Russian Jews began to settle in Baltimore and other large eastern cities. A committee composed of several prominent Baltimore clergymen prepared resolutions protesting the attacks on these people and formulated a plan of action to help them. In a letter of December 15, 1890, to B. H. Hartogensis, James Cardinal Gibbons declared: "Every friend of humanity must deplore the systematic persecution of the Jews in Russia."[157] By the outbreak of World War I a substantial

---

154. *Ibid.*, p. 409. Reprinted by permission of Prentice-Hall, Inc., Englewood Cliffs, New Jersey.

155. Grace Hill Jacobs, "The Negro in Baltimore, 1860–1900" (M.A. thesis, Howard University, 1945), p. 153.

156. William Warren Sweet, *The Story of Religion in America* (New York, Evanston, and London: Harper & Row, Publishers, 1950), p. 369.

157. B. H. Hartogensis, "Christian Prelates of Baltimore on Russo-Jewish Persecution," *M.H.M.*, XXVIII (March, 1933), p. 4.

number of Jews were living in the city of Baltimore, where either they or their parents had migrated from central and eastern Europe.

In addition to organized religion, the family, and government, the newspaper was an important social force in the lives of most Marylanders from the close of the Civil War to the years immediately following World War I. When the American War of Independence began there were only two newspapers in Maryland. When the *Tenth Census* was taken in 1880, over one hundred years later, there were in the state 143 daily, weekly, Sunday, and monthly newspapers, including fifteen daily papers, nine of which were published in Baltimore.[158]

One of the significant developments associated with newspaper publishing that occurred in Baltimore during this period was the invention of linotype by Ottmar Mergenthaler. Born in Germany in 1854 and trained as a watchmaker, Mergenthaler migrated to the United States in 1872. His first four years in America were spent in Washington, D.C., where he checked and repaired clocks in government buildings. Moving subsequently to Baltimore, he developed the linotype, which he patented in 1884. This machine was to revolutionize the process of typesetting.

Four years later, Arunah S. Abell, who had founded the Baltimore *Sun* a little over fifty years before, died at his home in Baltimore after having made that newspaper one of the most outstanding in the country. *The Sun*, which was one of the first to use the telegraph for gathering news, reduced its price per copy in the spring of 1902 from two cents to one cent; the Sunday edition, however, remained at two cents.

In addition to publishing morning and afternoon daily editions as well as the Sunday edition, *The Sun* annually issued from 1874 to 1916 *The Sun Almanac*, which contained election statistics and vignettes as well as facts and figures about Maryland and the city of Baltimore. The successor to *The Sun Almanac* was the *Maryland Almanac*.

Intimately associated with *The Sunpapers* from 1906 to the late 1940's, H. L. Mencken became a journalist, critic, and linguistic scholar of international reputation. Born September 12, 1880, into a middle-class Baltimore family, Mencken lived from

---

158. *Tenth Census, The Newspaper and Periodical Press*, VIII, 27, 68, 194.

1883 in the same row house at 1524 Hollins Street for the rest of his life, except for the five years of his marriage, which ended in the death of his wife Sara in 1935. In 1900 he began his newspaper career as a reporter for the *Baltimore Herald*. Within a short time he became in turn the dramatic critic, city editor, managing editor, and, finally, as an attempt by the owners to head off disaster, editor-in-chief. As city editor "he got the paper running with a sprightliness it had never shown before. . . . Then came the Great Fire of Baltimore, which literally and figuratively incinerated the *Herald*."[159] In June 1906, the *Herald* folded, sixteen months after the Great Fire. Mencken went to the Baltimore *Evening News*, stayed with it but a few weeks, and then joined the staff of the Baltimore *Sun*, where he remained but for two interruptions for the rest of his journalistic career. Serving first as editor of the *Sunday Sun*, he became in 1910 the associate editor of the *Evening Sun* when that edition began publication; a year later he was made editor. Soon Mencken "began his 'Free Lance' column which gained him lasting fame in Baltimore."[160] As one of his biographers notes:

> It gave the effect of a brightly colored mosaic. There were quotable sentences from outraged or enthusiastic readers; there were comments in "American" as heard, for instance, on the streetcars; there were assorted jibes and catcalls from Mencken; there were pungent pen portraits; there were items of curiosa; there were his alkaline observations on the politics and politicians of Baltimore.[161]

From May 8, 1911, to October 23, 1915, "The Free Lance Column" was published daily on the *Evening Sun*'s editorial page. Almost any topic was fair game to Mencken, an avowed agnostic, who on one occasion wrote prayerfully that he be saved

> . . . from all persons who lift their eyebrows when one mentions sauerkraut, and from fat women who loll grotesquely in automobiles, . . . from barbers with pale, freckled hands, and from

159. Carl Bode, *Mencken* (Carbondale and Edwardsville, Ill.: Southern Illinois University Press, 1969), p. 39.
160. Herbert M. Simpson, "Mencken and Nathan" (Ph.D. dissertation, University of Maryland, 1965), p. 17.
161. Bode, p. 44. Reprinted by permission of Southern Illinois University Press.

neighbors who do not drug their children at night, and from German waiters wearing detachable shirt fronts, . . . from young pests selling tickets for church fairs, and from bassos with prominent Adam's apples, . . . from argumentative Christian Scientists, . . . from street car conductors who are new to the line and don't know the names of streets, . . . from adult males who wear diamonds, and from all boosters of tinpot fraternal orders, . . . and from persons who believe that "alright" is an English word.[162]

Not only was Mencken able to edit a newspaper and to write a daily column during those years, but to prepare monthly book reviews for *Smart Set*, an uninhibited, though sophisticated literary magazine for which, as the literary critic, he had begun to write in 1908. Six years later Mencken and George Jean Nathan, who had meanwhile become the magazine's drama critic, were made co-editors, positions which they held until 1923, when they left to establish *The American Mercury*. Three years before Mencken joined the staff of *Smart Set* and while he was still with the *Baltimore Herald*, he published the first American study of George Bernard Shaw, entitled *George Bernard Shaw: His Plays*, which possibly resulted from Mencken's "interest in drama, but more probably grew out of his appreciation of the iconoclasm of Shaw."[163] This work and his occasional journalistic reviews of books and plays had more than likely been instrumental in the *Smart Set*'s invitation to him to become its literary critic.

It was while he was co-editor of *Smart Set* that Mencken defended in 1916 Theodore Dreiser's *The Genius* against criticism and censorship and did the same in 1920 for James Branch Cabell's *Jurgen*.

> In 1920 Mencken sanctioned revolt from the village as a theme in fiction by praising Zona Gale's *Miss Lulu Bett* and Sinclair Lewis's *Main Street*. Mencken's suggestion that some enterprising novelist should portray life in a medium-sized American city encouraged Lewis to persevere in his plan to use such a setting for his next novel, *Babbitt*.[164]

---

162. *Ibid.* Reprinted by permission of Southern Illinois University Press.
163. Simpson, p. 11.
164. Douglas C. Stenerson, *H. L. Mencken: Iconoclast from Baltimore* (Chicago and London: University of Chicago Press, 1971), p. 214. Reprinted by permission of the University of Chicago Press.

As early as 1910 Mencken had written articles about the American language "as opposed to English as it was spoken in England." During World War I, when because of his pro-Germanic feelings he had to avoid comment on public issues, Mencken began work on an extended study of the American language. In 1919 he published *The American Language: A Preliminary Inquiry into the Development of English in the United States*, a significant study as it was "an early prefiguration of the study of linguistics in America."[165] This study and its subsequent editions gives Mencken, probably more than anything else he ever did, an enduring claim to fame. "Mencken derided Americans in a dozen different ways but never about the language that they and their forefathers had created."[166]

A writer who could at once produce hypertensive outrage and sardonic laughter by his invective ("An archbishop is a Christian ecclesiastic of a rank superior to that obtained by Christ"), a critic who fearlessly scrutinized American life and literature, Mencken, after several years of poor health, died at his home in Baltimore on January 29, 1956. Some years before, he had written that moving, now famous, eulogy: "If, after I depart this vale, you ever remember me and have thought to please my ghost, forgive some sinner and wink your eye at some homely girl."[167]

Another Maryland literary figure whose career as a composer, editor, and poet centered mostly before the Civil War was John Hill Hewitt (1801–1890). To ante-bellum Americans he was "Father of the American Ballad," because much of his fame stemmed from "The Minstrel's Return from the War." In the 1870's he published *Shadows on the Wall*, a book of reminiscences of famous Americans he had known.[168]

Worthy of mention among Maryland writers of the late nineteenth and early twentieth centuries are Hester Dorsey Richardson and Lizette Woodworth Reese. From 1887 to 1891 Hester Richardson wrote under the pseudonym "Selene" for

165. Simpson, p. 27.
166. Bode, p. 121.
167. *Ibid.*, p. 376.
168. Marianne Ellis Alexander, "John Hill Hewitt—A Shadow on the Wall: A Study of the Reflections and Contributions of a Nineteenth Century Composer, Editor, and Poet" (M.A. thesis, University of Maryland, 1964), p. 1.

the *Baltimore American*, a paper which encouraged women to enter the professions," while at the same time she served as a special correspondent for the *Philadelphia Press* and the *New York Herald*.[169]

Spending most of her life teaching English in Baltimore's Western High School, Lizette Reese published her first book of poetry, *A Branch of Spring*, in 1887. Louis Untermeyer, the well-known American poet and anthologist, has considered the poems in this work as "an entire generation ahead of the times."[170] Twelve years after the appearance of *A Branch of Spring*, Reese published in *Scribner's* a sonnet entitled "Tears," which was widely acclaimed.

In the decades following the Civil War several notable Maryland painters and sculptors were engaged in professional endeavors. "There was, in fact, in Baltimore between 1870 and 1890, an activity and general interest in art and artists that has never since obtained. Men of wealth of that period, traveling in Europe, took pride in purchasing and bringing home with them valuable paintings to adorn their residences."[171] Among the nearly dozen Maryland artists of this period was Alfred J. Miller, who was born in Baltimore in 1810 and died there sixty-four years later. His paintings of the American Indian are considered his finest work. "The dress and customs of tribes that, so far as their former manner of life is concerned, have now passed utterly away, are graphically depicted in these sketches."[172] Having at one time studied with Thomas Sully, Miller in turn taught such younger artists as A. J. H. Way and Frank B. Mayer.

Except when he was a student in Paris, A. J. H. Way (1826–1888) spent his whole life in Baltimore, where, in addition to his own work, he kept a record of the art life of the city. He developed a reputation as an excellent still-life artist.

His contemporary, Frank B. Mayer (1827–1899), was an Annapolis painter who was known for his paintings of life in the state capital, especially that of "My Lady's Visit," which is in

---

169. Mildred K. Sheff, "The Position of Women of Maryland in the Nineteenth Century" (M.A. thesis, University of Maryland, 1946), p. 84.

170. *Ibid.*, p. 85. Louis Untermeyer, ed., *Modern American Poetry* (New York: Harcourt, Brace and Co., 1931), pp. 115–16.

171. Latrobe Weston, "Art and Artists in Baltimore," *M.H.M.*, XXXIII (September, 1938), 225.

172. *Ibid.*, 215.

the possession of the Maryland Historical Society. He also did "The Burning of the Peggy Stewart" and "The Founding of Maryland." For his painting "Michael the Fiddler" Mayer received at the Philadelphia Centennial Exposition in 1876 the gold medal awarded for figure painting.

During a ten-year period in the 1870's and 1880's, John Dabour, who was born in Smyrna, Asia Minor (Turkey), in 1837, did portraiture in Baltimore. Among his portraits were those of Enoch Pratt, Thomas Shryock, Grand Master of Maryland Masons, and Jerome Bonaparte, the second son of Betsy Patterson, and her husband Jerome.

Another painter who contributed to the art life of Baltimore in this period was Charles Yardley Turner, who was born there in 1850 of a large family of Quaker origin. He did the murals depicting Calvert's treaty with the Indians and the burning of the Peggy Stewart, both of which are in the Baltimore court house. Moreover, he was the principal assistant to Francis D. Millett in the decoration of the buildings of the Columbian Exposition in Chicago in 1893.

Born two years after Turner, Louis Dietrich migrated to the United States from Germany when he was a child. He later became in Baltimore a portrait painter of distinction whose studio, at Charles and Mulberry Streets, after his death in 1924, was continued by his son Waldemar.

Before his marriage, Harper Pennington also did portraiture in Baltimore. Born into a prominent family of the city in 1854, Pennington became while in England an admirer of James Abbott McNeill Whistler.

Richard Curzon Poultney's career was somewhat the opposite of Pennington's. Born in 1861, Poultney spent his early years as an artist in Baltimore, after which he departed for England, where, painting miniatures of socialites, he enjoyed during the rest of his life the patronage of Lord Frederick Hamilton.

Although most of William Henry Rinehart's life and career as a distinguished sculptor occurred before 1865, he did complete one of his best known works a little less than two years before he died: the seated figure of Chief Justice Roger B. Taney before the State House in Annapolis. A sculptor in the classical tradition, Rinehart was born in 1825 on a farm near Union Bridge, Maryland. Employed in the stone-cutting trade in Bal-

timore as a young man, he did beautiful work in many fashionable homes of the city, including that of William T. Walters, a
wealthy merchant, who in turn became Rinehart's friend and
major patron. During his early Baltimore days he studied at
night at the Maryland Institute of the Mechanic Arts but apparently never mastered drawing. Upon his return from Florence,
where he had gone in 1855, Rinehart opened a studio in Baltimore at Baltimore and Calvert Streets. He did not stay there
long; he left for Rome in 1858, where he remained (except for a
few trips to America) until his death in 1874.[173]

Besides the modelling and casting of the United States House
of Representatives' bronze doors, Rinehart did, among his several works, *Hero*, (Pennsylvania Academy of Fine Arts), *Latona
and Her Children* (Metropolitan Museum of Art), and *Clytie*
(Peabody Institute), the last of which may be considered his
masterpiece. (Some forty-two casts of Rinehart's sculpture, as
well as three of his marble originals, are in the collection of the
Peabody Institute, Baltimore.)

When on December 10, 1872, the Taney statue on the State
House lawn was unveiled, Rinehart was present for the cere-
mony. The General Assembly, five years before, had voted
$5,000 for the monument to the distinguished Marylander, the
fifth Chief Justice of the United States; and in 1870 it had provided the additional $10,000 that was necessary for the comple-
tion of the statue as the original amount was not enough to cover
the cost of the material.[174]

When the Taney sculpture was completed in 1872, Ephraim
Keyser, a native of Baltimore, was twenty years old. A sculptor
of less renown than Rinehart, Keyser nevertheless, created
some fine sculpture, including *The Rose* (Maryland Institute), a
bronze bust of Sidney Lanier (The Johns Hopkins University),
and the bronze guardian angel at the tomb of President Chester
Arthur (Albany Rural Cemetery).[175]

While these Maryland artists were active during the half century following the Civil War, William T. Walters and his son
Henry were becoming collectors and patrons of the arts in Baltimore. Born in 1820 in Pottsville, Pennsylvania, of Scotch-Irish

173. William Sener Rusk, "Notes on the Life of William Henry Rinehart,
Sculptor," *M.H.M.*, XIX (December, 1924), 309-338.
174. *Ibid.*, 325.
175. Weston, 217-18.

stock, William Thompson Walters arrived in Baltimore in 1841. He subsequently became involved in the commission-merchant business, later took an interest in the Baltimore and Susquehanna Railroad, and, in turn, as his business interests extended southward, bought several small bankrupt railroads which after the Civil War led to the establishment of the Atlantic Coast Line. In 1850 Walters began the collection that in time was to include a large number of modern European paintings, especially those of such French artists as Corot, Daumier, Delacroix, Millet, and Théodore Rousseau. In later years Walters opened his home on Mount Vernon Place in Baltimore to the public on certain days, a practice which his son Henry continued.[176] "Like other self-made men of this period in the United States or in Europe, he began by supporting local talent. In 1854, for instance, he provided financial aid which permitted the Maryland sculptor W. H. Rinehart to study in Florence and Rome."[177]

A decade and a half after the elder Walters' death in 1894, his son, for whom art collecting had become "a serious study and a ruling passion," opened the present gallery.[178] (Although the Walters Gallery was private, it was opened to the public on certain days of the year.) As Denys Sutton notes: "It says much for Henry Walters' strength of character that as the son of such a determined man, he did not rebel against art, especially as his father made him write essays on artistic themes when a youth!"[179] When Henry died in 1931, he left to the city of Baltimore and the state his art gallery and its contents, together with one-fourth of his estate as an endowment.

Two other wealthy benefactors who contributed to the cultural life of Baltimore and the state in the half century following the Civil War were George Peabody and Enoch Pratt, both of whom were born and reared in Massachusetts.[180] Peabody, re-

---

176. Denys Sutton, *The Walters Art Gallery*, originally published in *Apollo Magazine*, LXXXIV (December, 1966), 2 and 4. *Report to Honorable J. Millard Tawes by Maryland Committee to Review the Desirability of State Assistance for The Walters Art Gallery*, appendix, pp. i-ii.

177. Sutton, p. 2.

178. Broadus Mitchell, "Henry Walters," *Dictionary of American Biography*, 1936, XIX, 399.

179. Sutton, p. 7.

180. Franklin Parker, *George Peabody: A Biography* (Nashville: Vanderbilt

**Henry Walters (1848-1931). Artist: Thomas C. Corner, 1938.**
*The Walters Art Gallery.*

turning in 1866 from England, where he had lived for many years as a merchant and investment banker, dedicated the Peabody Institute in Baltimore, which "provided for a library, a course of lectures, an academy of music, a gallery of art, and prizes to encourage private and public school pupils."[181] Construction was begun in April 1875, on the Peabody Library, which was located on Mount Vernon Place. The building, with a capacity of 300,000 volumes, was completed and opened to the public in 1878.

By the late 1870's Enoch Pratt believed that "the greatest present need of the city of Baltimore" was "a free circulating public library, open to all citizens regardless of property or color."[182] The success of the Workingmen's Institute, which included a library of several thousand books, was probably an encouragment to Pratt to establish a much larger library. Building began late in 1881, without the formality of laying a cornerstone, on a lot owned by Pratt on Mulberry Street. In a letter of January 21, 1882, to the mayor and city, he wrote about his plan to erect a central library with a capacity of 200,000 volumes and with branches in the four quarters of Baltimore. Costing about $225,000, the central library building was deeded by Pratt to the city. He noted in his correspondence with the city's officials:

> The title to all the books and property is to be vested in the City, and I will pay to your Honorable Body, upon its completion, the additional sum of $833,333.33 making $1,058,333.33 provided the City will grant and create an annuity of $50,000 per annum forever, payable quarterly to the Board of Trustees, for the support and maintenance of the Library and its branches.[183]

On January 5, 1886, the central library opened with approximately 28,000 books. By the middle of March four branches were in operation, each with a collection of over 4,000; and the fifth branch opened early in November 1888. "In his first annual report Dr. [Lewis Henry] Steiner [the librarian] claimed,

University Press, 1971) *passim*. Richard H. Hart, *Enoch Pratt: Story of a Plain Man, Fiftieth Anniversary Publication* (Baltimore: Enoch Pratt Free Library, 1935), *passim*.
181. Parker, p. 90.
182. Hart, pp. 48-49.
183. *Ibid.*, pp. 52-53.

George Peabody (1795-1869). Photograph (1867). *M.H.S.*

with justice, that the Enoch Pratt was the largest free circulation library, founded by private liberality, in the United States."[184] On February 3, 1933, the present central building of the Enoch Pratt, at Cathedral and Franklin Streets, opened. With regard to his own interest in library endowment, Andrew Carnegie once observed that Pratt was his "pioneer."

In 1902, sixteen years after the central library of the Enoch Pratt opened, the Maryland General Assembly enacted legislation calling for "the establishment and efficiency of free public libraries and public school libraries in the State."[185] The governor was required to appoint biennially four people (at least two of whom had to be women) who, with the state librarian, superintendent of public instruction, and the librarian of the Enoch Pratt Free Library, formed the State Library Commission.

Not only was there a growing interest in the establishment of public and quasi-public libraries in this period in Maryland as well as elsewhere, but as historian Wendell H. Stephenson observed: "A renaissance in state histories as well as in historical societies developed in the post-war years."[186] Founded in 1844, the Maryland Historical Society expanded its collection during the half century following the Civil War, and among the valuable additions were the Calvert Papers, which the society acquired in 1888 through contributions of a few wealthy members. These manuscripts included over one thousand documents on paper and parchment that were purchased from Colonel F. H. Harford, a retired British army officer and a descendant of the Calverts.

An important and necessary step in the development of the Maryland Historical Society came at its annual meeting on February 12, 1906, whn it was announced that a quarterly, the *Maryland Historical Magazine*, would be published. Under the editorship of Dr. William Hand Browne, a professor of English literature at The Johns Hopkins University since 1879, the first number of the *Maryland Historical Magazine* appeared in

---

184. *Ibid.*, p. 61. On February 3, 1933, the present central building of the Enoch Pratt, at Cathedral and Franklin Streets, opened.

185. *Baltimore Sun Almanac*, 1903, p. 55.

186. Wendell H. Stephenson, "Herbert B. Adams and Southern Historical Scholarship at The Johns Hopkins University," *M.H.M.*, XLII (March, 1947), 2.

Enoch Pratt (1808-1896). Photography by Bachrach. *Enoch Pratt Free Library.*

March 1906. Serving as the editor for four years, Browne was succeeded by Louis H. Dielman, who edited the *Magazine* from 1910 through 1937, the longest period of service of any of the publication's eight editors. Since its inception, the *Maryland Historical Magazine* has been regarded as one of the best publications among those of state historical societies.

Another notable development in the annals of the Maryland Historical Society came with the expansion of its facilities through a gift of Mrs. Mary Washington Keyser shortly after World War I. Wishing to provide a memorial to her late husband H. Irvine Keyser in the form of a permanent home for the historical society, Mrs. Keyser made it possible for the society to move into the former residence of Enoch Pratt, a four-story house on the southwest corner of Monument Street and Park Avenue in the heart of Baltimore. Moreover, for the library and picture gallery she provided funds for the construction of a fire-proof building with an entrance on Park Avenue, which was only briefly used after the building opened.

The expansion of the Maryland Historical Society's plant and collection, the establishment of the Enoch Pratt Free Library, the Peabody Institute, and the Walters Art Gallery, together with the artistic, literary, and religious activity in Maryland, especially in Baltimore City, revealed indeed a vibrant religious and cultural life which compared favorably with that found in other states.

5

SOCIAL OUTLETS: ORGANIZATIONS AND RECREATION

A long-standing observation about the American people has been that they are a nation of joiners—of this or that association, club, lodge, or society. Whether they really are greater joiners than people of other nations is debatable, but joiners they have been; and the Marylanders have been truly American in this regard. Recent evidence suggests that the South River Club, located eight miles south of Annapolis, is one of the oldest social organizations in the United States. Founded some time before 1739, the club was established for the purpose of "fellowship and fullsome discussion." The extant minutes of the club date back to the first meeting in the present club house on February 11, 1742. Noted, among other things, for its South

First home of the Enoch Pratt Free Library, Baltimore.
Engraving by H. McDowell. *M.H.S.*

River Club punch, the organization remained active through the period covered in this chapter and continues so today.[187]

Although a much younger organization than the South River Club, the Maryland Club, composed of twenty-nine men, was formed in 1857 at Guy's in Baltimore. In the spring of 1858, the club, whose first president was Jerome N. Bonaparte, the son of Baltimore's celebrated Betsy Patterson Bonaparte, moved into a house on the northeast corner of Cathedral and Franklin Streets. Temporarily closed for a time during the Civil War, the Maryland Club moved in 1891 to its present quarters, designed by the prominent architects E. Francis Baldwin and Josias Pennington. By the end of the century the Maryland Club had become famous for its cuisine and its bar.[188]

Another club that had its beginnings shortly after the establishment of the Maryland Club was the Wednesday Club, an organization formed from social gatherings held in Otto Sutro's bachelor quarters in Baltimore from 1858 to 1869. After his marriage, Sutro decided to give up these convivial evenings; but his friend William Prescott Smith suggested that the gatherings be converted into a Wednesday evening club meeting. During the nearly two decades of its activity, the Wednesday Club "was an amateur music and dramatic club which played an integral part in the cultural life of Baltimore and helped to raise it to a high artistic level. Its members were among the socially elite. . . ."[189] In time, difficulties arose over obtaining professional talent to supplement the club's amateurs and the attempt to limit the membership. Its clubhouse, completed in 1879, subsequently became Albaugh's Lyceum Theater. Yet "for twelve years succeeding 1875, six plays and six concerts were given annually."[190] When the Wednesday Club closed, its activities, observed Ottilie Sutro, were "at the peak of achievement."[191]

---

187. Arthur A. Ageton, "The Old South River Club: Vestige of A More Gracious Way of Life," *The Washington Post*, Nov. 23, 1969, *Potomac*, pp. 21-31.

188. Betty Ann Howard, "Of Terrapin and Oysters: A History of the Maryland Club," ms in Maryland Club, 1969, 70 pp. William Stump, "Maryland Club: A Civilized Centennarian," *The Baltimore Sunday Sun Magazine*, May 19, 1957, pp. 15-18.

189. Ottilie Sutro, "The Wednesday Club: A Brief Sketch from Authentic Sources," *M.H.M.*, XXXVIII (March, 1943), 60.

190. Weston, 223.

191. Sutro, p. 67.

Meanwhile, in 1878, the Baltimore Club, another men's club, was established. Located first in a room on Franklin Street, then in turn at one or two other addresses, it finally settled in the Abell Mansion on Mount Vernon Place. In 1932, because of financial difficulties, the Baltimore Club closed. Many of its members were invited to join the Maryland or the University clubs.

Not only did men's clubs in Maryland develop in the years after the Civil War; so did clubs for women, the oldest of which, the Mutual Improvement Association of Sandy Spring, was founded in May 1857. It is thereby one of the oldest women's clubs in the United States. Of its fifteen charter members, all were Quakers except one, and all were married women between the ages of thirty and fifty. Meetings, which were held once a month in members' homes, were devoted to readings in prose and poetry and discussions of such topics in home economics as canning and soap making.

For the most part, the women's club movement in Maryland was restricted to the city of Baltimore and its environs. "It was preceded, as in other parts of the country, by church and charitable societies, which in those days had few social and no intellectual features."[192] In Mount Washington, a northern suburb of Baltimore, there was begun in 1872 the Lend-a-Hand Club, whose purpose was initially philanthropic, but was broadened in 1888 to include the study of literature and music.

In January 1889, the Sorosis Club of New York City, at the suggestion of Mrs. Jenny June Croly, proposed that, as a way of celebrating its twenty-first anniversary or reaching its majority, a call be made for a national convention of women's clubs. Meeting at the Madison Square Theater on March 20, 1889, delegates from various women's clubs appointed a committee to draw up a constitution and a plan of organization which were ratified a year later in the first convention of the General Federation of Women's Clubs.

Ten years after the establishment of the General Federation and largely as a result of the work of Mrs. John T. Graham of the Lend-a-Hand Club of Mount Washington, the Maryland Federation of Women's Clubs was formed. Among the nineteen charter clubs, besides the Lend-a-Hand Club, were: the Friday

192. *History of the Maryland Federation of Women's Clubs 1899–1941*, I (Federalsburg, Md.: J. W. Stowell, 1941), 29.

Club, Twalif Club, Sorosis Club, Women's Club of Roland Park, Eastern Female High School Alumnae Association, Mothers' and Teachers' Educational Union, Council of Jewish Women, Baltimore Chapter of Women's College Alumnae, Hytheham Club of Port Deposit, and Frederick Art Club. By 1911 sixty-eight clubs with a combined membership of 6,000 women belonged to the Maryland Federation. In April 1900, six months after the formation of the Maryland Federation, the General Federation admitted it into membership.

The early work of the Maryland Federation centered on education, traveling libraries, "purity of the press," need for a women's club section in the newspapers, cooperation with the international movement for holding meetings to commemorate the Peace Conference at The Hague, assisting sufferers from the Baltimore Fire of 1904, and medical inspection in the public schools. Thus much of the federation's attention was devoted to civic matters.

In addition the Maryland clubs for men and women already mentioned, there emerged in the 1890's the country club:

> ... horsiness, whether mere hacking in the park, polo or fox hunting, was guarded by the dollar sign from the mass popularity that successively overcame baseball, bicycling, golf and tennis. Hence it was fitting that the new institution of the country club, where the Quality could indulge in outdoor sports without the lower orders breathing down their necks, was associated with the importation of polo from England and the Anglophile revival of fox hunting in the Northeast in the 1880's.[193]

Two country clubs were established in Maryland before the turn of the century: The Chevy Chase Club and the Baltimore Country Club. The Dumblane Club, devoted to fox hunting and a forerunner of the Chevy Chase Club, was organized in 1885 by S. S. Howland, a well-known horseman. Seven years later, after Howland had resigned as the Dumblane Club's Master of the Hunt, the Chevy Chase Club was established in Montgomery County, just north of the Maryland-District of Columbia line. Mr. Francis G. Newlands, the organizer of the Chevy Chase Land Company, wanted the new club in Chevy Chase

---

193. J. C. Furnas, *The Americans: A Social History of the United States 1587–1914* (New York: G. P. Putnam's Sons, 1969), p. 815. Reprinted by permission of G. P. Putnam's Sons.

and at a price that would be attractive.[194] As it developed, the club concerned itself not only with fox hunting but with those increasingly popular sports, golf and tennis.

Organized four years after the Chevy Chase Club in 1896, the Roland Park Golf Club, located in the northwest part of Baltimore City, was the foundation on which the Baltimore Country Club was established with an initial membership in 1899 of six hundred.[195] That same year the Columbia Country Club formed the previous year was incorporated in the District of Columbia. Located first on the east side of Brightwood Avenue (later Georgia Avenue) and later at two other sites in the District of Columbia, the Columbia Country Club moved to its present location in Chevy Chase, Maryland, in 1911. Not only the outdoor recreation but the dinners, dances, card parties, and general conviviality of these country clubs appealed to women as well as men among the affluent people.

No review of social organizations in Maryland from 1865 to 1920 would be complete without consideration of fraternal orders, some of which antedated the Civil War. Attracted by the opportunity to socialize, to enjoy the esoteric mysteries of the orders' rituals, symbols, and badges, many men joined such bodies as the Masonic Order, the Odd Fellows, or the Knights of Columbus. The oldest of these organizations in Maryland was the Masonic Fraternity, which dated back to the eighteenth century. Following the American Revolution, the Grand Lodge of Ancient Free and Accepted Masons of Maryland was established on April 17, 1787, at Talbot Court House, now Easton, on the Eastern Shore. Individual Maryland lodges had already existed since before the war. By 1887 there were seventy-five lodges under the Grand Lodge of Maryland, and by 1921 the figure had risen to 117. More than 2,000,000 Americans were Masons in 1920, nearly 26,000 of whom belonged to Maryland lodges.[196] Moreover, in Maryland

 . . . many Germans were members of the various Free Mason

194. John M. Lynham, *The Chevy Chase Club: A History 1885–1957* (Chevy Chase, Md., 1958), p. 6.

195. *Thirty-Sixth National Amateur Golf Championship: Early History of the Baltimore Country Club* (Baltimore Country Club, n.d.).

196. Carl N. Everstine, *History of the Grand Lodge of Ancient Free and Accepted Masons of Maryland 1888–1950*, 2 vols. (Baltimore: King Brothers, Inc., 1951), p. 1011.

lodges. Even in this field the strong tendency of the Germans of that time [post Civil War] to create separate German-American groups may be seen; in 1872 and in 1886 two exclusively German lodges—Germania Lodge and Sincerity Lodge—were founded within the Masonic Order.[197]

It was on February 2, 1825, that the first lodge of Negro Masons in Maryland was warranted by the First Independent African Grand Lodge of North America, No. 1, of the State of Pennsylvania, under the name of Friendship Lodge No. 6 of Baltimore. Twenty years later three subordinate lodges created the first Negro Grand Lodge in Maryland, followed two years afterward by another Grand Lodge. As a result of a meeting of these two Grand Lodges in 1876, the First Union Colored Grand Lodge of the State of Maryland was established. Subsequently the name of this body was changed to the Most Worshipful United Grand Lodge of the State of Maryland.[198] Many years later, as a result of a conference of Grand Masters, it was decided that all Grand Lodges of Negro Masons were to be incorporated under the name of The Most Worshipful Prince Hall Grand Lodge, Free and Accepted Masons; and the Grand Lodge of Maryland incorporated under this name in 1946.[199] Prince Hall, it should be noted, was a leader in American Negro Masonry in the late eighteenth century.

Another fraternal order that, like Freemasonry, had British roots was the Independent Order of Odd Fellows, whose first American lodge originated on April 26, 1819, when Thomas Wildey and four others founded Washington Lodge, No. 1, at the Seven Stars Tavern in Baltimore. In time, Baltimore became the seat of the Sovereign Grand Lodge of I.O.O.F. in the United States. By 1917 there were 166 Odd Fellows lodges in Maryland with a total membership of 16,124.[200]

When the International Order of B'nai B'rith was established in New York City on October 13, 1843, "for the expressed pur-

---

197. Cunz, p. 323. Reprinted by permission of Princeton University Press.
198. William H. Grimshaw, *Official History of Freemasonry Among the Colored People in North America* (New York: Negro Universities Press, 1903).
199. *Prince Hall Masonic Yearbook* (N.P.: The Fraternal Press, 1955), pp. 99-100.
200. *Odd Fellows Art Business Souvenir* (Ellicott City, Md. Edition, May, 1902) p. 10. *Report of Special Sessions and Committee Reports: Odd Fellows, Independent Order of Maryland Grand Lodge*, [1927], pp. 41-43.

pose of ending, or at least reducing, the chaos and anarchy in Jewish life—or, as one of the founders put it, of 'uniting and elevating the Sons of Abraham,' " several of the twelve founders were Odd Fellows and Masons.[201] In 1844 the Jeshurun Lodge was organized in Baltimore, the third lodge of this Jewish fraternal order to be established in the United States. "By 1875 there were six well-functioning B'nai B'rith lodges in the city. Although it was a purely fraternal order, the lodges were involved in some charity work."[202] During the decade between 1910 and 1920, B'nai B'rith's American membership increased by almost one hundred per cent to a total membership of some 23,000. Maryland lodges enjoyed a corresponding increase in new members.

Among American fraternal organizations, two were founded in Baltimore, one before the Civil War and the other shortly afterward. The Improved Order of Red Men, which, according to the organization's publication, is "the oldest patriotic and fraternal organization of American origin," had its inception in 1834.[203] The Maryland General Assembly, three years later, granted a charter to the Order's Great Council of Maryland, which was followed a decade later by the establishment of the Great Council of the United Sates. Like the other organizations mentioned, the Improved Order of Red Men appeared to thrive in the post Civil War years in Maryland, although its membership was smaller than that of the Masons or Odd Fellows.

The other fraternal body whose origins were in Baltimore was the Order of the Knights of Pythias, founded on November 27, 1867, on the precepts of friendship, charity, and benevolence, with friendship, as reflected in the story of Damon and Pythias, regarded as the cornerstone. By 1912 the Knights of Pythias in Maryland included approximately a hundred lodges and a membership of 11,000, about one-half of whom were residents of Baltimore City and its suburbs.[204]

---

201. Edward E. Grusd, *B'nai B'rith: The Story of A Covenant* (New York: Appleton-Century-Crofts, 1966), pp. 12, 14.

202. Fein, *The Making of An American Jewish Community: The History of Baltimore Jewry from 1773 to 1920*, p. 131.

203. *The Maryland Indian Magazine*, I (October, 1947).

204. *The Baltimore American Almanac 1885*, p. 74. *Catalogue: Exhibition Sale of Paintings and Sculpture by Maryland Artists, Great Pythian Fair and Bazaar and States Exposition*, Baltimore, October 1–12, 1912.

Although the Knights of Columbus, a Catholic fraternal order, was chartered in Connecticut on March 29, 1882, it was not until 1896 that a national organizer for the Supreme Council, Thomas Harrison Cummings, came to Baltimore, sought out some of the distinguished Catholic laymen, and convinced them that the K. of C. was worthy of support. The order, he explained, was created "for the purpose of developing a practical Catholicity among its members, and to promote Catholic education and charity and furnish temporary financial aid to families of deceased members."[205] James Cardinal Gibbons gave his approval and blessing; so on February 21, 1897, Baltimore Council No. 205, with fifty-four charter members, became the first Knights of Columbus council in Maryland. From this beginning other councils were to be established in the state.

> Religious prejudice was particularly strong in the outlying sections of Maryland and [K. of C.] State Deputy [Edgar N.] Ganster (1915–1918) and the State Officers were active in these sections in order to bring Catholic men together so that in unity they may [sic] combat this anti-Catholic feeling.[206]

Thus in December 1916, Brute Council No. 1860 was established at Emmitsburg.

In addition to these fraternal organizations there were many others in Maryland from 1865 to 1920, only a few of which can be mentioned here by name: Loyal Order of Moose, Fraternal Order of Eagles, Ancient Order of Hibernians, Fraternal Order of Orioles, Knights of the Golden Eagle, and Improved Order of Heptasophs.

Besides the clubs and fraternal organizations in which Marylanders were active during the half century after 1865, there was a variety of organized as well as informal recreational activity to attract their interest. In the western part of the state

> . . . some forms of entertainment were linked to national backgrounds. The Irish had great celebrations on St. Patrick's day; the Scots annually observed the anniversary of Burns' birth; and the Welsh had their Eisteddfods. Ties with the old country were strong, and trips to Scotland and England were mentioned as

---

205. John P. Bauernschub, *Columbianism in Maryland 1897–1965* (Maryland State Council: Knights of Columbus, 1965), pp. 25-26.
206. *Ibid.*, p. 60.

George Herman (Babe) Ruth as a member of the Baltimore Orioles.
(Standing, left to right, Manager Jack Dunn and Lefty Caporal.
Seated, left to right, Jack Dunn, Jr., and Babe Ruth). *M.H.S.*

casually in the newspapers as a journey to Baltimore or Philadelphia.[207]

Among the miners of Allegany and Garrett Counties not only were baseball, foot-racing, and curling on the C & O Canal popular; so also were boxing, cock-fighting, and pigeon-shooting. "In fact, a United Mine Workers' delegate, disgusted with Maryland's aloofness toward unionism, said on one occasion that only two things would bring the George's Creek miners together—'prize fighting and chicken-sparring.' "[208]

Less savage sports that Marylanders enjoyed, besides baseball, included bicycling, football, lacrosse, horse racing, fox hunting, rowing, and sailing. The Civil War, in considerable measure, popularized baseball, which emerged from several bat-and-ball games as town ball and one old cat. "Every large enough piece of flat ground near an encampment saw a baseball game with improvised equipment."[209] Yet even before the war broke out, the Baltimore Excelsiors had played the Brooklyn Excelsiors in what was apparently the first intercity baseball game known to have been played in Baltimore. The Brooklyn team won by a crushing score of 51–6. The Baltimore Excelsiors soon declined and merged with another Baltimore team, the Waverlys, under the name Pastime. This newly consolidated club put up Baltimore's first grandstand and charged a small admission to its games. The Pastimes' greatest opponent was the Marylands, who by the summer of 1867 had upset the Pastimes, remaining on top through 1870, the last year before organized league baseball. Later the Maryland Baseball Club, which was semi-professional, was enticed to become fully professional by some businessmen in Fort Wayne, Indiana, the club's new home. Shortly thereafter Baltimore had a new team with a new name, the Lord Baltimores, and with a new park (Newington Park). By this time the club had joined the National League of Professional Baseball Ball Clubs, the oldest professional baseball league. However, from the beginning of 1875 through 1881 Baltimore was represented in no league. Then in 1882, in opposition to the National League, the American Association, comprising teams from six cities (including one from

207. Harvey, p. 119. Reprinted by permission of Cornell University Press.
208. *Ibid.*, p. 122.
209. Furnas, p. 656.

Baltimore) was formed. A year later the Brooklyn Athletics became the Baltimore Orioles, the first time that this name was used. Operating for nine years, the American Association was forced to merge with the National League in 1891 to form a league of twelve clubs. Under the masterful leadership of Edward Hanlon, the Orioles won three consecutive championships—in 1894, 1895, and 1896—and placed second in 1897 and 1898. Among the best known players of this famous team was John Mcgraw, the star third baseman, who managed the Orioles in 1899, helped to organize the American League in 1900 after the team was dropped from the National League, and served as the colorful manager of the New York Giants from 1902 to 1932.[210]

The first college football game having been played between Princeton and Rutgers in 1869, intercollegiate football by the turn of the century was well-established in Maryland. The Johns Hopkins University, for example, played seven games in 1892, winning all but one. Its opponents included the Baltimore Athletic Club, Maryland Agricultural College, Delaware Field Club, Columbia Athletic Club, Kendall College and St. John's College, which was played twice for the Maryland championship.[211] In the fall of 1897 an intercollegiate football association composed of Maryland and District of Columbia institutions was established. Among the members were Gallaudet College (which won the association's championship that year) St. John's College, The Johns Hopkins University, Western Maryland College, and Maryland Agricultural College.

In addition to baseball and football, lacrosse, which "has one of the longest and most colorful genealogies in American history,"[212] became popular in Maryland, especially in Baltimore, by 1920. "However lacrosse first got to North America, it was played by the Indians from one end of the continent to the other."[213] Played at first by clubs in the North, East and Mid-

210. James H. Bready, *The Home Team: A Full Century of Baseball in Baltimore 1859–1959,* (n.p. 1958), 62 pp. Ralph J. Robinson, "The Glamorous Days of The Old Orioles," *Baltimore Chamber of Commerce* (October, 1953).
211. *The Baltimore Sun Almanac for 1893,* p. 96.
212. N. A., "The Great Game," *The Johns Hopkins Magazine* (April, 1956), 8.
213. *Ibid.*

Johns Hopkins University's lacrosse team, spring, 1898. *M.H.S.*

west, by the late 1870's the National Amateur Lacrosse Association was established in the United Sates. In the meantime,

> . . . a track and field team composed of the scions of Baltimore's leading families went, in August 1878, to compete in a three-day sports carnival at the Westchester Polo Club in Newport, Rhode Island. While there they got their first look at lacrosse and liked it so well that they bought sticks and had them sent to Baltimore.[214]

Soon the members of the Baltimore Athletic Club held an intra-club practice game. In May 1879, the Ravenswood Lacrosse Club of New York defeated the Baltimore Athletic Club three to one in the first inter-club game to be played in Baltimore. Two more lacrosse clubs were established in Baltimore by the spring of 1880. As many of the players on these teams were high school students, they carried lacrosse with them to college: Johns Hopkins, Harvard, Yale, Lehigh, Princeton, and Stevens Institute. The game was first played at Hopkins in 1885 but then apparently disappeared until 1888, when it was permanently incorporated into the athletic program of the university, which a year later enjoyed its first unbeaten season. In 1890 Hopkins joined with Lehigh, Princeton, and Stevens to form the Intercollegiate Lacrosse Association. Since that time Hopkins has been prominently associated with the game and has won several national championships.

Marylanders also enjoyed racing of various kinds in the half century following the restoration of the Union. Established in 1864, the Ariel Rowing Club of Baltimore competed with other clubs in Maryland, among them the Arundels and the Naval Academy in such events as the single scull, double scull, four- and eight-oared shells, and six-oared barge. Horse racing, long a favorite sport in the state, continued to be popular, as was evidenced by the opening of Pimlico, Maryland's "premier" track, in the city of Baltimore in 1870 under the auspices of the revived Maryland Jockey Club. "Pimlico, or 'Old Hilltop,' as it is affectionately known, is the only race course to which the United States Congress ever adjourned to attend in a body. The National legislators came over from Washington in a special train one October day in '77 to see Pierre Lorillard's Parole win the Great Sweepstakes."[215] At Pimlico the Preakness became

---

214. *Ibid.*, pp. 9 and 20.
215. D. Sterett Gittings, *Maryland and the Thoroughbred*, Sponsored by the

Holliday Street Theater, Baltimore. Attributed to John H. B. Latrobe. *M.H.S.*

the outstanding race, the winner of which from 1917 received the Woodlawn vase, a gift to the Maryland Jockey Club from Thomas Clyde, who had obtained possession of this famous trophy through the victories of his horse, Short Hose. Reflecting on a need for the supervision of horse racing, the Maryland General Assembly enacted and Governor Albert Ritchie signed a bill (March 31, 1920) to regulate, control, and license the sport within the state and to establish a racing commission which, among other responsibilities, could set the license fee.[216]

Providing another form of racing which Marylanders enjoyed, "the bicycle had first enjoyed extended American notice at the Philadelphia Centennial. But it was then solid-tired and grotesquely composed of one five-foot wheel and one tiny one. . . ."[217] This was the "ordinary," to be supplanted by the "safety" or low model which attracted women as well as men. By the tenth annual meet of the League of American Wheelmen, held at Hagerstown on July 2, 3, and 4, 1889, bicycle riding and racing had become increasingly popular in Maryland and elsewhere in the United Sates.

Although organized yachting in America began with the founding of the New York Yacht Club in 1844 and continued with the establishment of such clubs as the Boston Yacht Club (1865), Chicago Yacht Club (1875), and Larchmont Yacht Club (1880), it was not until 1885 that the Chesapeake Bay Yacht Club on the Eastern Shore, the oldest club for yachtsmen in Maryland, was organized aboard the schooner yacht *Gaetina* off Oxford on the Choptank River. The *Gaetina's* owner, William O'Sullivan Dimpfel, became the first commodore of the club, whose declared objectives were "the purchase of real estate, navigation, and . . . scientific and social purposes."[218] In time, other yacht clubs were established on the Bay and its estuaries.

By 1880 still other means of recreation were afforded the people of Maryland, especially those of Baltimore City. Four major public parks—Druid Hill, Patterson, Riverside, and Federal Hill—and smaller areas known as squares—were sup-

Maryland Horse Breeders Association (Baltimore: Hoffman Bros., 1932), p. 121.

216. *Ibid.*, p. 125.
217. Furnas, p. 810.
218. *Chesapeake Bay Yacht Club* (Easton, Md., 1935), p. 8. Gray Johnson, "Yachting on the Chesapeake Bay," *The Maryland Spectator*, I, No. 4, 10.

ported by a 12 per cent tax on the gross earnings of the city railway, from which the interest was deducted on bonds issued for the purchase of Druid Hill and Patterson Parks.[219] Other parks in Baltimore were subsequently opened, among them Mount Royal Terrace, Carroll, and Clifton,thus providing the city's population with a superior park system by 1900.

In addition to the parks, Baltimoreans and those Marylanders who could travel to the city by train or horse and buggy enjoyed as of 1880 performances of plays, operas, and vaudeville put on by road companies at such theaters as the Academy of Music, Holliday Street Theater, Front Street Theater, Concordia Opera House, Central Theater, and Ford's Grand Opera House, which John Thompson Ford, a native Baltimorean, opened in October 1871 with a performance of Shakespeare's *As You Like It*. "The early years at Ford's were dominated by the plays of Shakespeare, but the audiences were exposed to a complete range of entertainment."[220] Joseph Jefferson performed in his famous role in *Rip Van Winkle* at Ford's, where in the 1890's Otis Skinner, Alexander Salvini, Ethel Barrymore, and James O'Neill "were among those who made their initial appearance. . . ."[221]

With numerous clubs and fraternal orders, special occasions such as church socials and steamboat excursions on the Bay, holidays, a variety of sports, parks, and theaters, there was indeed a wide array of social outlets for the people of Maryland to enjoy in the years from 1865 to 1920, years which in demographic, educational and cultural activity were among the most interesting and exciting in the long history of the state.

219. *Tenth Census, Report on the Social Statistics of Cities*, 1880, XIX, Part II, 18.

220. Clyde Victor Kuemmerle, Jr., "A History of Ford's Grand Opera House, Baltimore: From its Origins in 1871 to its Demise in 1964" (M.A. thesis, University of Maryland, 1965), p. 130.

221. *Ibid.*, p. 132.

BIBLIOGRAPHICAL ESSAY

CHAPTER VII

Comprehensive studies of Maryland's social-cultural history from the Civil War to 1920 do not exist. Official reports as well as published and unpublished monographs of this aspect of the state's history are located in such repositories as the Enoch Pratt Free Library and the Maryland Historical Society in Baltimore, the McKeldin Library of the University of Maryland, College Park, the libraries of Howard University and The Catholic University of America, Washington, D.C., and the Maryland Room of the Prince George's County Public Library, Hyattsville.

In examining population patterns and trends the six official Census Reports beginning with 1870 are of course important. Ara A. Asadorian's "Population Trends in Maryland from 1880 to 1930" (M.A. thesis: University of Maryland, 1938) is helpful, as is Charles Hirschfeld's *Baltimore, 1870–1900: Studies in Social History* for the demographic study of Baltimore during the last three decades of the 19th century. An important study of the German migrations, settlement, and culture in Maryland is Dieter Cunz's *The Maryland Germans: A History*.

Invaluable to the study of public education in the half century following the Civil War are three articles by L. E. Blauch, "Education and the Maryland Constitutional Convention, 1850–51," *M.H.M.*, XXV (June, 1930); "Education and the Maryland Constitutional Convention, 1864," XXV (September, 1930); and "The First Uniform School System of Maryland, 1865–1868," XXVI (September, 1931). The significant survey which Abraham Flexner and Frank P. Bachman prepared, *Public Education in Maryland: A Report to the Maryland Education Survey Commission*, 4th ed. (New York: The General Education Board, 1919), provides a clear insight into the condition of the public schools sixty years ago. Benjamin Paul Ebersole's "A History of the Maryland State Teachers' Association" (Ed.D. dissertation, University of Maryland, 1964; copyright, 1965) carefully examines the origins and development of the state teachers' organization.

As the Gilman School was a pioneer in the field of country-day school education, Bradford McE. Jacobs' study, *Gilman Walls Will Echo: The Story of the Gilman Country School 1897–1947* (Baltimore: n.p., 1947) is of interest in the realm of the independent school in Maryland.

For a study of higher education in the state the following are of considerable value: Hugh Hawkins, *Pioneer: History of the Johns Hopkins University, 1874–1889* (Ithaca: Cornell University Press, 1960); Rev. Edmund Granville Ryan, S.J., "An Academic History of Woodstock College in Maryland (1869–1944): The First Jesuit Seminary in North America" (Ph.D. dissertation, The Catholic University of America, 1964); and George H. Callcott, *A History of the University of Maryland*.

A careful inquiry into the history of Maryland medicine and public health must include Eugene Fauntleroy Cordell's *The Medical Annals of Maryland 1799–1899* (Baltimore: Williams and Wilkins Co., 1903); Harvey Cushing's *The Life of Sir William Osler*, 2 vols. (Oxford: Oxford University Press, 1926); Simon and James Thomas Flexner's *William Henry Welch and the Heroic Age of American Medicine* (New York: Viking Press, 1941); Abraham Flexner's famous report, *Medical Education in the United States and Canada; A Report to The Carnegie Foundation for the Advancement of Teaching*, Bulletin Number Four (New York, 1910); Alan M. Chesney's *The Johns Hopkins Hospital and the Johns Hopkins University School of Medicine*, 3 vols. (Baltimore: J. H. Press, 1943–1963); and Harry Bryan McCarthy's "A History of Dental Education in Maryland" (M.A. thesis, University of Maryland, 1948).

The further study of the religious and cultural life of Maryland during the half century following the Civil War should include Bernard C. Steiner's "Maryland's Religious History," *M.H.M.*, XXI (March, 1926); Kenneth Carroll's recent study, *Quakerism on the Eastern Shore* (Baltimore: Maryland Historical Society, 1970); Katherine A. Harvey's fine monograph, *The Best-Dressed Miners: Life and Labor in The Maryland Coal Region, 1835–1910*; Carl Bode's engaging biography, *Mencken* (Carbondale and Edwardsville, Ill.: Southern Illinois University Press, 1969); Douglas C. Stenerson's *H. L. Mencken: Iconoclast from Baltimore* (Chicago and London: University of Chicago Press, 1971); Latrobe Weston's interesting article, "Art and Artists in Baltimore," *M.H.M.*, XXXIII (September, 1938); Richard H. Hart's *Enoch Pratt: The Story of a Plain Man* (Baltimore: Enoch Pratt Free Library, 1935); and Franklin Parker's recent biography, *George Peabody: A Biography* (Nashville: Vanderbilt University Press, 1971).

Among the books and articles which deal with Maryland clubs and fraternal organizations, either directly or indirectly, the following are of importance: *History of the Maryland Federation of Women's Clubs 1899–1941*, I (Federalsburg, Md.: J. W. Stowell, 1941); John M. Lynham's *The Chevy Chase Club: A History 1885–1957* (Chevy Chase, Md., 1958); Carl N. Everstine's *History of the Grand Lodge of*

*Ancient Free and Accepted Masons of Maryland 1888–1950*, 2 vols. (Baltimore: King Brothers, Inc., 1951); William H. Grimshaw's *Official History of Freemasonry Among the Colored People in North America* (New York: Negro Universities Press, 1903); Edward E. Grusd' *B'nai B'rith: The Story of A Covenant* (New York: Appleton-Century-Crofts, 1966); Isaac M. Fein's *The Making of An American Jewish Community: The History of Baltimore Jewry from 1773 to 1920*; and John P. Bauernschub's *Columbianism in Maryland 1897–1965* (Maryland State Council: Knights of Columbus, 1965).

Of particular interest in the field of recreation are James H. Bready's *The Home Team: A Full Century of Baseball in Baltimore 1859–1959* (n.p. 1958); an excellent article on lacrosse, N.A., "The Great Game," *The Johns Hopkins Magazine* (April, 1956); D. Sterett Gittings' *Maryland and the Thoroughbred.* Sponsored by the Maryland Horse Breeders Association (Baltimore: Hoffman Bros., 1932); Gray Johnson's article, "Yachting on the Chesapeake," *The Maryland Spectator*, I, No. 4; and Clyde Victor Kuemmerle, Jr.'s well-written, unpublished monograph, "A History of Ford's Grand Opera House, Baltimore: From Its Origin in 1871 to Its Demise in 1964" (M.A. thesis, University of Maryland, 1965).

# VIII

## MARYLAND PROGRESSIVISM

BY

JAMES B. CROOKS

UNIVERSITY OF NORTH FLORIDA

The years between the end of Reconstruction and World War I were most strikingly characterized by the urbanization and industrialization of America. Maryland, despite the predominantly rural character of the Eastern Shore, southern counties and the mountainous coal-mining region to the west, underwent similar changes, particularly around Baltimore.

### 1

### POLITICS IN THE GILDED AGE

From 1870 to 1920, the state's population grew from 780,894 to 1,449,661 for a gain of 85 per cent. Meanwhile Baltimore's population jumped from 267,354 to 733,826, a gain of 170 per cent. Clearly most of the state's population increase centered around Baltimore, and if one subtracts Baltimore's gains, the rest of the state's population increase was only 25 per cent over a fifty-year period. As a result, where the state was almost 60 per cent rural in 1880, it became 50.8 per cent urban in 1910, and 60 per cent urban in 1920. With slightly over half the population in Baltimore, the urbanization of Maryland was well under way.[1]

---

1. U.S. Department of Commerce, *Fifteenth Census of the United States, 1930, Population,* I: Number and Distribution of Inhabitants, 485–87. Maryland's other cities were considerably smaller, though generally they also enjoyed substantial growth during this time. Annapolis grew from 5,774 in 1870 to 11,214 in 1920. Cumberland more than tripled in size from 8,056 to 29,837. Frederick remained relatively static increasing from 8,526 to 11,066 over the fifty years. Hagerstown, almost quintupled in size from 5,779 to 28,064, while the Eastern Shore's major city, Salisbury, grew from 2,064 to 7,553. The largest of these cities, Cumberland, was in 1920 less than one-twentieth the size of Baltimore.

590

As the city grew in size and importance relative to the small towns and rural areas of Maryland, so too did manufacturing grow relative to agriculture and commerce. Major industrialization took place in the 1880's, particularly again in the metropolitan area in and around Baltimore. Most striking was the construction of the steel works at Sparrows Point, but in addition shipbuilding, oil refining, copper smelting, clothing manufacturing, canning, and meatpacking were among a range of enterprises that either began or expanded during the period. In addition, commerce flourished through the busy port of Baltimore, as well as along the Chesapeake and Ohio Canal, the Baltimore and Ohio Railroad, and Pennsylvania Railroad. Contemporaries worried about a comparatively slow industrial growth rate within the city limits of Baltimore, but industrial expansion in the metropolitan area moved at a substantial pace, providing jobs, income and profits for increasing numbers of Marylanders migrating to the city.[2]

Inevitably, industrialization and urbanization brought many changes to the lives of Marylanders. Industrialization meant more factories and more jobs, but it also meant more sweatshops, industrial accidents, unemployment during slack seasons, and child labor. It meant more people—immigrants, blacks and rural white migrants—crowded into tenements, alley houses, and row-house slums. Housing in Baltimore neighborhoods like Canton, Old Town, Locust Point, Hampden or Woodberry, lacked adequate light, ventilation, fresh water, or sewage facilities. Medical care was minimal; mortality rates were excessive, and too frequently eight and ten-year-old children went to work full time rather than to school. Increased poverty, however, was only one aspect of increasing urbanization. The growing city also required paved roads, sewers, schools, hospitals, and leadership that too often was not forthcoming.

Both city and state governments in Maryland, as in other states, were slow to respond to the changes brought by the urbanization and industrialization. The reasons were numerous. Social change accelerated in the late nineteenth century. Simply keeping pace with building schools or roads was costly. The application of medical science to public health problems

2. See Chapter VI. Eleanor S. Bruchey, "The Development of Baltimore Business, 1880–1914," LXIV, *M.H.M.* (Spring and Summer, 1969), *passim.*

was only just beginning. Few people understood the impact of factory life and urban living upon the city dwellers. In addition, many city, state, business, and professional leaders seemingly did not care about the inhuman effects of industrialization or urbanization. Either they were oblivious to the rapid social and economic changes, or they believed such conditions as poverty to be the responsibility of the poor themselves. It was the era of Social Darwinism, when community elites saw their successes and others' failures as the result of natural evolution.

Another factor contributing to the slow response to social change was the urban-rural split in the state's population, accentuated by the over-representation of the counties in the Maryland General Assembly. Baltimore, with one half the state's population, sent only eighteen of the ninety-six delegates to the House of Delegates, and three of twenty-six senators to the state Senate. Rural legislators were hardly concerned about the social effects of industrialization and saw little reason to spend state tax money for urban problems. Though the state had subsidized railroad and canal building before the Civil War, the current tradition stressed a frugal government, one which maintained order, limited its expenditures, and performed mainly ceremonial functions. Finally, boss rule characterized the structure of post-bellum party politics in Maryland, as in other states. In Maryland the Democratic party was dominant under the leadership of Arthur Pue Gorman of Howard County, and it showed little concern for responding to urban industrial change.

Gorman controlled Maryland politics from 1875 until his death in 1906. A personally devout, modest, and generous man, he was one of the most astute politicians in an age of rough and tumble partisan politics. Beginning with his election to the House of Delegates in 1869, under the sponsorship of William T. Hamilton of Hagerstown, Gorman maneuvered quietly and effectively in the political arena. He supported first one faction, then another, until he put forward his own candidate for governor in 1875, electing John Lee Carroll of Howard County. In due course Gorman became speaker of the House of Delegates, president of the Chesapeake and Ohio Canal (which offered financial security plus a political base and control over substantial patronage), state senator, chairman of the state central committee, and finally, in 1880, United States Senator. In the process Gorman worked closely with Democratic leaders of the Eastern Shore, in Harford, Carroll, Montgomery, and Anne Arundel Counties. Most important, perhaps, was Gorman's cooperation with Isaac Freeman Rasin, the political boss of Baltimore City.[3]

Like bosses in other American cities in the late nineteenth century, Rasin was a self-made, sometimes ruthless man who had entrepreneurial talents for power and profits comparable to the business barons of the age. Unlike other big city bosses, however, Rasin was not of recent immigrant stock, but came instead from an old Eastern Shore family that had migrated to Baltimore before the Civil War. As a young man Rasin became active in the political club of his ward. Later he was elected to the Democratic party's executive committee, where he allied himself with William Pinkney Whyte. Whyte subsequently became mayor, governor, and United States Senator. In 1871 Rasin backed Whyte in his successful bid for governor and became head of the city organization. Factional leaders challenged him, but during the succeeding decade Rasin replaced them with loyal ward lieutenants such as John J. "Sonny" Mahon, and by the mid-1880's, Rasin controlled the party that won the elections in predominantly Democratic Baltimore. Rasin met Gorman at Annapolis in 1870, and they quickly recognized one another's political talents. Rasin probably helped to engineer Gorman's election as speaker of the House that year, and the city-county alliance was born.[4]

Their control over Maryland politics was never complete. Governors such as Whyte (1871–75), Hamilton (1879–83), and Frank Brown (1891–95) had power bases or popular support independent of the Gorman-Rasin machine, but while governors came and went the organization's influence over the General Assembly remained dominant. Except for Republican control over the black belt southern counties and the counties to the west, state legislators in both houses generally followed the political leadership of Gorman and Rasin.

Their leadership, however, was not geared to solving the

---

3. John R. Lambert, Jr., *Arthur Pue Gorman* (Baton Rouge, La; Louisiana State University Press, 1953), pp. 16–48, *passim*.

4. Sister Mary Anne Dunn, OSF, "The Life of Isaac Freeman Rasin, Democratic Leader of Baltimore from 1870–1907" (M.A. thesis, Catholic University of America, 1949), pp. 1-8.

problems of urbanization and industrialization. Rather, they looked first to maintaining and expanding their own power and influence. Next, they sought to satisfy their constituency, which ranged from farmers to business and professional people, and by the 1880's included organized labor. Thirdly, they sought to promote the general welfare and prestige of the state.

In the process the goals at times conflicted. The needs of city Democrats conflicted with those of county Democrats; the interests of labor Democrats conflicted with those of business Democrats. Following the formation of a Workingmen's party in the 1876 Baltimore mayoral campaign, Rasin responded first by co-opting their leaders into the Democratic party with patronage, and then by obtaining legislation in the 1884 General Assembly to guarantee their rights to organize by exempting labor unions from the state's conspiracy laws. But labor's gains were limited. While responding to their demands, the Democrats could not ignore the conflicting concerns of businessmen and farmers. Too often the result was a factory safety code with sizable loopholes and minimal enforcement, or the rejection of child labor laws that would prohibit youngsters under the age of ten from working. The Democratic organization was reluctant to enact social or economic legislation for fear of antagonizing parts of its supporting coalition, and they continued in this posture until public pressures forced them to act differently.[5]

Consequently, the organization worked to secure its hold on government, cultivated friendly if superficial relations with its constituencies, and promoted the state of Maryland for industrialization—and urbanization—without taking into account the disruptive effects of their actions.

2

## ORIGINS OF REFORM

Except for the brief appearance of a Workingmen's party in Baltimore in 1876, opposition to the Gorman-Rasin machine did not focus upon the Democrats' failure to respond to the urban-industrial changes of the day, but rather on the organization's power and how it was used. Gorman's successful maneuvering

---

5. Margaret Law Callcott, *The Negro in Maryland Politics, 1870–1912* p. 47; Hall, ed., *Baltimore, Its History and Its People,* I, pp. 249 and 251.

Charles Joseph Bonaparte (1851-1921), Baltimore lawyer and reform leader
and, later, secretary of the navy and attorney general in turn during
President Theodore Roosevelt's administration. *M.H.S.*

of John Lee Carroll's gubernatorial nomination in 1875 provoked anti-organization Democrats and Republicans to form a
fusion ticket in the hope of defeating the machine. The effort
failed in a turbulent and disorderly election marked by violence, repeat-voting and stuffed ballot boxes. Though the
Democratic victory assured Gorman's dominance in the Democratic party, it also created an independent or reform Democratic group committed to opposing the Gorman-Rasin machine
and its corrupt manipulation of the electoral processes.[6]

These reformers were essentially purists in politics, a small
group of elite business and professional men—mostly in Baltimore, but also spotted across the state—who viewed government as a public trust. They attacked the spoils system of the
Gorman-Rasin machine, which used patronage to strengthen
the party in power. Charles J. Bonaparte, though a Republican,
spoke for his fellow reformers when he wrote that he could
accept and even welcome differences of opinion on most issues,
but the spoils system used public office for private, partisan
gains and was unequivocally, immorally wrong. Bonaparte,
patrician lawyer and descendant from the famous marriage between Jerome Bonaparte and Baltimore's Betsy Patterson,
joined with reform Democrats in 1881 to form a Civil Service
Reform Association of Maryland as a state chapter in the National Civil Service Reform League. Following the particularly
tumultuous mayoral election of 1885, Bonaparte and his reform
friends organized the Baltimore Reform League to "secure fair
elections, more honest and efficient government, and to expose
and bring to punishment official misconduct."[7]

Supporting the reforms in their opposition to the Gorman-
Rasin machine was John K. Cowen, general counsel of the Baltimore and Ohio Railroad. At one time the Baltimore and Ohio
worked hand in glove with the Democratic party in Maryland.
Both the city and state had invested in the railroad's construction before the Civil War. Under John Work Garrett, during and
after the war, the railroad had expanded rapidly, becoming the
dominant business in the state as well as exerting influence on

6. Frank Richardson Kent, *The Story of Maryland Politics* (Baltimore:
Thomas and Evans Printing Co., 1911), pp. 42-52.
7. James B. Crooks, *Politics and Progress: The Rise of Urban Progressivism
in Baltimore, 1895–1911* (Baton Rouge, La.: Louisiana State University Press,
1968), pp. 13-15; and Baltimore *Evening Sun*, March 26, 1937.

the General Assembly. After the war, however, the Democrats sought to limit the railroad's political power, first by authorizing the right-of-way to Washington for the Pennsylvania Railroad, and then by upgrading the similarly state-sponsored Chesapeake and Ohio Canal under Gorman's leadership in order to provide greater competition in the coal traffic from the west. The result was increased power for the party organization at the expense of the railroad. At the same time the General Assembly levied increased taxes on the Baltimore and Ohio's earnings, while the Pennsylvania received special exemptions. The Baltimore and Ohio was not accustomed to loss of special privileges and tax exemptions. In addition, the railroad was locked in a rate war with the Pennsylvania. Not surprisingly, after Garrett's death in 1884 an open rupture occurred between the railroad and the Democratic organization, with Cowen attacking the iniquities of the Gorman-Rasin machine.[8]

Also opposed to the Gorman-Rasin dominated Democratic party were the Republicans, but in Baltimore, as across the state (except for western Maryland and three southern black belt counties) they lacked substantial support. Historically, the Republicans were unpopular for their suppression of civil liberties in Maryland during the war as well as for their Reconstruction policies and their support by black voters since ratification of the Fifteenth Amendment. Many, if not most, white Marylanders outside the western counties had been sympathetic to the Confederate cause. They supported the Democratic party's election platforms endorsing white supremacy as well as its commitment to state's rights and frugal government. In addition, in the port city of Baltimore, merchants frequently voted Democratic in support of lower tariffs for increased foreign trade. Where the Democrats appealed to Marylanders with southern sympathies, particularly among the farmers, trade unionists, and merchants, Republican support was limited to the smaller number of Union sympathizers, blacks, and a small but growing number of industrialists such as textile manufacturer James Gary, who became President McKinley's postmas-

---

8. Paul Winchester, *The Baltimore and Ohio Railroad* I (Baltimore: The Maryland County Press Syndicate, 1927), pp. 50-78, *passim*; Matthew Page Andrews, *History of Maryland: Province and State*, pp. 576-78, 587-88; and Lambert, *Gorman*, pp. 21-22, 124-25, 135-36.

ter general. Not surprisingly, the Democrats won every state-wide election from the end of Reconstruction until 1895.

Despite the coalition of reformers with the Republicans, backed by the B&O, their cause was not a popular one. Most voters in the 1870's and the 1880's were intensely partisan; Maryland Democrats saw no point in voting Republican and little value in supporting the highly moralistic elitist policies of the civil service reformers. To the victor belonged the spoils of office, and good government was an ideal that seemed to have little relevance to their lives in the changing urban-industrial world.

Still, the Civil Service Reform Association and the Reform League continued a running attack upon the Democratic organization. In a series of technical reports issued in the late 1880's, the Reform League analyzed voter registration lists, the appointment of election officials, and election returns. Their studies pointed to fraud, to the apparent collusion between officeholders, and excessive laxity in the state government's administration of the election machinery. Attempts to prosecute election officials were undermined by a lack of governmental cooperation, while efforts to enact election law reforms in the 1886, 1888, and 1890 General Assemblies resulted in delays, amendments and finally passage of statutes with substantial loopholes. Though the Australian secret ballot was finally accepted in 1890, partisan election registrars, judges, and supervisors controlled by the Democratic organization still remained.[9]

The reformers' reports were largely ignored by the press of the state. The Baltimore *Sun* briefly championed a reform movement in 1882 to prevent the Rasin machine from extending its control over the city's judiciary, but then lapsed back into a quiescent mood, advocating, in the words of the newspaper's biographer, "happiness in a guarded way." For lack of newspaper support to help educate public opinion, the reform movement lagged in Maryland until the arrival of Charles H. Grasty from Kansas City. Grasty moved to Baltimore in 1891. With the backing of four wealthy, reform-minded Baltimoreans the following year, he bought the nondescript Baltimore *Even-*

---

9. Crooks, *Politics and Progress*, pp. 15-17. See also issues of the *Civil Service Reformer* on deposit at the Enoch Pratt Free Library and the M.H.S.

Charles Henry Grasty (1863-1924),
reform editor of the
Baltimore *Evening News*. M.H.S.

*ing News*. One colleague subsequently described Grasty as "a warm, charming, friendly fellow, a grand companion, who loved to talk, liked to drink, and understood not only the newspaper game, but the game of politics." Grasty's newspaper philosophy derived from watching William Rockhill Nelson run the Kansas City *Star*. Nelson and the *Star* were the regional exponents of the "new journalism" developed by Joseph Pulitzer of the New York *World* before the onset of yellow journalism. The new journalism emphasized thorough news coverage, editorial writing of high character, a crusading spirit, and a touch of sensationalism. Grasty had watched Nelson direct the *Star* in a wide range of crusades against municipal corruption in Kansas City, and in Baltimore he took up the cause.[10]

In an early editorial the *News* proclaimed its attitude toward Baltimore city government. Baltimore probably was as well governed as most American cities, but it could stand substantial improvements. Improvement, however, would come only when the people demanded it. "We do not believe," said the *News*, "that public sentiment is ever lightly treated by the politicians or corporations, nor that the unanimous demands of the people will ever be ignored. . . . The responsibility for all shortcomings in the conduct of public affairs rests directly upon the people. Our City, State and Federal governments are just as good or as bad, as the people choose to make them."[11]

On the basis of this belief, the *News* began to enlighten Baltimoreans on the inadequacies of their city government. It began with an attack on the Consolidated Gas Company, condemning its high prices, uneven gas pressures and watered stocks. Next, it exposed the telephone monopoly with its free rights-of-way, its federal tax to prevent competition, and its exorbitant rates. In March 1892 the *News* turned on the streetcar companies and advocated a state public utilities commission to regulate all utilities. In May the paper began a series exposing the letting of street paving contracts. The following September the *News* ran a series on the slum conditions in Baltimore. In the immigrant section of Old Town, Russian Jews worked in crowded, filthy, malodorous, dilapidated sweatshops. Spavined children in rags played nearby. The walls, ceiling, and stairway

10. *Ibid.*, pp. 17-18. For the description of Grasty, see Gerald Johnson, et. al., *The Sunpapers of Baltimore* (New York: Knopf, 1937), p. 172.
11. Baltimore *News*, January 9, 1892.

of one building "were blackened with grease and smoke, the floor was littered with dirt. . . . From cellar to roof of these houses," wrote one reporter, "there is an unbearable stench of sewer gas and . . . other odors; plastering has fallen from the walls that are damp and black with dirt." Another newsman described an alley nearby, "piled high with a villainous composition of mud, dead cats and rats, old shoes and offal from [nearby] cow stables." Reporters interviewed slum residents and discovered that many were illiterate and incapable of coping with their squalid environment. They could not afford doctors or medicines, and did not know about charity services. Reporters looked in vain for city health inspectors. Street cleaners were non-existent. They interviewed the city health commissioner, who claimed his hands were tied. For years he had asked the city council for the power and funds to pave and clean the streets, inspect food, and remove garbage. Clearly, the boss-ridden city government had neglected poverty in the slums.[12]

Along with its efforts to awaken public opinion to the iniquities of the political machine, the *News* also supported the lagging efforts of Baltimore reformers. When the first National Conference for Good City Government met in Philadelphia in 1894, the *News* urged the Reform League to send a delegation. Municipal reform was the great issue of the day, wrote one editorial writer, and "Baltimore must be abreast of the times."[13]

The times were exciting ones in municipal politics across the country. Though reform campaigns had taken place in New York, Philadelphia, and elsewhere before the 1890's, the long steady pull to respond to urban change had just begun in Detroit, Boston, Chicago, and San Francisco. Reform associations from a dozen cities sent delegates to Philadelphia to attend the first conference on good city government, laying the ground work for the formation of the National Municipal League. Bonaparte attended as a delegate from the Reform League and in a speech described the evils of Maryland machine politics.[14]

Back in Baltimore after the meetings, the Reform League's executive committee met and established watchdog groups to

12. *Ibid.*, January 23, 29, February 11, 12, March 3, 4, 6, September 9, 17, 20, and 21, 1892.
13. *Ibid.*, December 31, 1893.
14. Crooks, *Politics and Progress*, pp. 23-27.

check the operations of the city's departments of street cleaning, paving, schools, taxes and assessments, municipal finance,
and public health. Meanwhile a handful of Baltimore churchmen, responding to the social gospel movement in American
Protestantism, began to participate in the reform agitation,
preaching the role of Christianity in all areas of man's life, including politics. Finally, the Republicans, long dormant in local
elections, began to show signs of renewed vitality. In the city
elections of 1894 they nominated a judicial candidate who was a
member of the Reform League, and in a vigorous campaign
elected him and a Republican majority to the first branch of the
city council, defeating the Democratic machine.[15]

Victory in the 1894 election, however, was only the preliminary round in the renewed struggle against the Gorman-Rasin
machine. The mayoral and gubernatorial elections of 1895 became the main event. The reformers recruited new additions to
the Reform League. They began further investigations into
governmental maladministration and election violations; they
organized good government clubs in predominantly middle and
upper middle class wards; they brought together a citywide
group of normally Democratic business and professional men to
oppose the machine. Meanwhile the new majority of Republicans in the city council's first branch began their own investigations into city government, exposing the incompetent and
wasteful administration of the street paving department. No
large-scale corruption was revealed, such as the Tweed scandals in New York, but one authority questioned whether the
long-term seepage of funds in Baltimore's generally mismanaged government was not more costly than a single outright
looting.[16]

At the state Democratic Convention in July, Gorman once
again forced the nomination of his candidate for governor, a
respectable Baltimore dry goods merchant named John E.
Hurst. The action was a mistake. Where party loyalists had accepted the boss's dictates in the past, this time they revolted.
The venerable William Pinkney Whyte announced his opposition to the Democratic candidate, and the Federation of Labor
resolved against the party nominee. Of even greater importance

15. *Ibid.*, pp. 24-25.
16. *Ibid.*, pp. 27-32.

were the determined protests of the Baltimore *Sun*. Since 1890, the *Sun* had been gradually shifting its position, endorsing the secret ballot, utility regulation, civil service reform, clean streets, and efficient non-partisan government. Unlike the *News*, however, the *Sun* did little to expose social injustice or misgovernment. Though at times critical of Gorman, especially for his senatorial role in sabotaging tariff reform in the Wilson-Gorman act, it never sought to overturn him or the organization. Instead, it urged the bosses to reform the party from within and consider public opinion in their choices of candidates. Gorman's dictatorial nomination, however, finally provoked a break. Editorially, the *Sun* joined the crusade to turn the bosses out.[17]

Meanwhile, the Republicans gathered at Cambridge in mid-August to choose their slate. Much depended upon the caliber of their selections. A good ticket could win the vote of most anti-Gorman Democrats. Reform elements within the party persuaded the Republicans to nominate Lloyd Lowndes, a banker from Cumberland. They then drafted a platform endorsing civil service reform and the Reform League's election bill, and voiced strong opposition to boss rule by any party.[18]

The Baltimore mayoral nominations that followed in October attracted less attention than the state conventions. The Democratic organization again dictated its candidates, while the Republicans endured a three-cornered fight which resulted in the selection of Alcaeus Hooper, a textile manufacturer who had led the city council investigation the previous spring. Hooper immediately promised to divorce partisan politics from governmental administration, promote higher standards of public education, and conduct government on business principles of efficiency and economy.[19]

The selection of the candidates and the drafting of party platforms set the stage for a campaign fight in which the rhetoric focused on good government versus machine politics. The weeks that followed reinforced this view in the minds of not

---

17. *Ibid.*, pp. 32-34, and Baltimore *Sun*, August 6, 10, 1895.
18. Crooks, *Politics and Progress*, p. 34.
19. Baltimore *Sun*, September 1, 26 and October 4, 1895; Baltimore *News*, October 4, 1895; and Baltimore *Morning Herald*, October 10, 1895.

only the reformers, but a large number of Marylanders. The machine's emphasis on party loyalty, Democratic party principles, and white supremacy built on fear of Republican victory with blacks taking office for once had little effect.

The reformers, supported by the press (and the county newspapers generally reprinted much of the political news from the *Sun* or *News*), kept a close watch on the campaign. When registrars, ballot clerks, and election judges were appointed by the State Board of Supervisors of Elections, Reform League investigators charged that officials were being reappointed who had fraudulently registered voters in the last election. In addition, the minority members of the three-member election teams were supposed to be Republicans and too often were not. Many were Democrats accepted by the predominantly Democratic board as Republicans. Distrustful of the appointed election officials, Republicans sent unofficial watchers to supervise voter registration in Baltimore. Some were barred, others evicted, and four even jailed. When the Republicans protested, the board of supervisors claimed that they already had minority representation, and that the watchers were disrupting the registration procedures. It took a court order to open voter registration to public observation.[20]

The Reform League petitioned Governor Frank Brown for the removal of the uncooperative, excessively partisan Board of Elections Supervisors. Public hearings were held in which it became apparent that the Republican supervisor was old and infirm, and that one man, a Rasin lieutenant, ran the show. When challenged for rejecting the Republican recommendations for minority party election officials, he claimed that his appointments to Republican positions were better than those recommended by the party organization. Clearly, the Board of Election Supervisors was run in the interest of the Democratic organization, and the press broadcast the fact across the state.[21]

Next, the reformers spot-checked for fraudulent voter registration. In Baltimore's ninth ward, supervised by "Sonny" Mahon, Rasin's top lieutenant, they found 186 persons registered from three houses. In 1894 only eleven had been registered from these same houses. At another place in the same

20. Baltimore *News*, August 24, 30, September 3, 16, 17, 18, 21, 23, 1895.
21. *Ibid.*, September 23, 26, October 2, 4, 5, 10, 11, 1895.

ward, seventy-two persons were registered from a cheap lodging house located upstairs over a saloon. Reform League counsel John C. Rose checked voter lists by mailing 1,152 registered letters to presumably registered voters. Only 190 could be delivered. The rest were presumably fraudulent. Reports circulated that black voters in good standing who presumably would vote Republican were being disqualified.[22]

Election day approached amidst the hoopla of parades and rallies, of which the most important was the visit of New York City's Police Commissioner Theodore Roosevelt to Baltimore to endorse the crusade for good government. Reform League officials issued a call for election watchers to observe the polls on election day, report any misconduct on the part of police or election officials, challenge suspected repeaters, and generally help where possible to prevent election frauds. Almost fifteen hundred Baltimoreans responded to the call, including reformers, college students, Republicans, and clergy. One elderly Presbyterian minister offered his services, adding: "I think my years should exempt me, but I helped in the dark days of the Republic in [18]60 to 65 to protect my country, and now under the pending danger to the Ballot Box, I am prepared to take my part as a nonpartisan republican."[23]

Meanwhile, the press kept up its clamor. On the Sunday preceding the election, moreover, at least ten Protestant clergymen urged their congregations to vote against boss rule and for good government. Across the state, voters made up their minds. The result on election day was an overwhelming Republican victory. Almost 125,000 voters chose Lowndes for governor against 106,000 Marylanders who voted for Hurst. It was a 53 per cent majority and the first Republican gubernatorial victory in Maryland since the Civil War. Nineteen of twenty-three counties plus Baltimore City voted Republican. Further, the voter turnout was heavy: 86 per cent of the state's electorate voted compared to 85 per cent in the presidential campaign of 1892 and 79 per cent in the gubernatorial race of 1891. Even in the state legislature, the reform-Republican coalition beat the machine. The Senate retained a fourteen-to-twelve Democratic edge only

22. *Ibid.*, October 11, 15, 17, 22, 24, 25, 29, and November 29, 1895.
23. Crooks, *Politics and Progress*, p. 39; and Rev. George Morrison to Charles J. Bonaparte, October 18, 1895, Bonaparte Papers, L.C.

because half the senators were not up for reelection. Of the thirteen who were, nine Republicans were returned and only four Democrats, while in the new House of Delegates, seventy of ninety-one new legislators were Republican. Even the Senate Democratic majority was precarious, because the one holdover from Baltimore City was reform leader William Cabell Bruce, who along with a Harford County reform Democrat could be counted on to vote on the issues rather than simply from loyalty to party organization. In Baltimore the reformers also elected Republican Alcaeus Hooper for mayor.[24]

Election postmortems raised the obvious question of how and why the Republicans so resoundingly beat the Gorman-Rasin machine. In Baltimore, it was clear the substantial vote shifts occurred among the upper, middle, and working class white voters. The immigrant wards shifted along with silk-stocking wards. The least shift came in the areas that were already Republican, such as in the southern and western counties and the black wards of Baltimore. Also, Democratic strongholds such as Mahon's ninth ward and Queen Anne's, Wicomico, and Worcester Counties on the Eastern Shore maintained their loyalties to the Democratic candidate.[25]

The reasons for these voter shifts are less clear. Voter awareness resulting from the adverse publicity in the *Sun* and *News* about the Gorman-Rasin machine was great. Voter organization through good government clubs and among anti-Gorman Democratic businessmen was substantial. The depression in progress also may have had some impact. On neither the city nor state level had the Democrats responded with aid to the unemployed. For the more well-to-do, misgovernment was costly in times of tight money. In addition, underlying the issues, the appeal of the American ideal of honesty and fair play may have had its effect. Perhaps Marylanders were beginning to see through some of the political hypocrisies of the Gilded Age. If their awareness of the urban-industrial changes doubtless remained slight, they did subscribe to an ideal of democratic government responsive to the people. Clearly the Gorman-Rasin machine had not been responsive; in fact, it had tried to undermine the entire election process in order to win.

---

24. Baltimore *News*, November 6, 1895; Crooks, *Politics and Progress*, p. 42; and *Sun Almanac* (Baltimore, 1896), pp. 64-65.
25. Crooks, *Politics and Progress*, pp. 42-47.

3

## REPUBLICAN REFORM AND REACTION

The machine's defeat provided the Republicans with a chance to respond to urban, industrial change, but partisan politics intervened. Reform Leaguers pushed through election law reforms which substantially eliminated fraud and violence at the polls, but efforts to obtain civil service reform failed. Similarly, an attempt to pass a corrupt practices act to publicize and control the use of money in election campaigns was defeated. Party professionals sustained over the years by federal patronage fought reform attempts to control and purify the Republican party. The result was intraparty conflict similar to that within the Democratic party, a conflict that detracted from efforts to cope with social change.[26]

The best example of this partisan strife can be seen in the reform administration of Baltimore's Mayor Alcaeus Hooper. Hooper had pledged a good government administration upon taking office in November 1895. One of his first actions as mayor was to begin a ward-by-ward inspection of the city, checking the condition of streets, schools, and sewers. Hooper was even seen in the downtown district after midnight checking the work of street cleaners. Finding the work inadequately done, Hooper hired replacements, employing the first gang of Negro sweepers in the city. When word of water pollution reached him, Hooper drove out to the country to inspect the rivers and lakes that fed the city. Such executive activity was unprecedented in Baltimore. In his annual message to the city council in February, 1896, Hooper urged administrative and financial reforms for greater efficiency. In addition, he called for a juvenile detention home, along with a quarantine hospital for infectious diseases.[27]

Initially, the mayor's administrative reforms provoked little overt opposition, but his nonpartisan appointments soon drew grumbling criticism from Republican city councilmen. The councilmen grudgingly accepted Hooper's choices to nonpaying boards, including the first appointment of women to gov-

26. *Ibid.*, pp. 49-51, 89-92.
27. *Ibid.*, pp. 86-87.

ernmental posts, but they resisted the renomination of capable Democratic officeholders to salaried positions such as health commissioner. Hooper remained adamant, and on February 27 Republican spoilsmen forced through the city council ordinances that withdrew the mayor's power to appoint any salaried officer of the city government. Reformers called a mass meeting to protest the action. Theodore Roosevelt came down from New York to castigate the spoilsmen; President Woodrow Wilson of Princeton University, in town for a lecture at The Johns Hopkins University, challenged the audience to stay active in politics and fight for good government; Bonaparte, in a brilliantly sarcastic speech, awarded the Republican councilmen a "political booby prize" for exhibiting their "conspicuous unfitness for their respective tasks."[28]

The protest accomplished little. Efforts at compromising the differences between the mayor and council failed, with both sides obstinately refusing to give ground. When Hooper vetoed the bill taking away his appointive power, the council passed it over his veto. When the council chose a new city collector, the mayor refused to administer the oath of office. The conflict went to the courts. Eventually the Maryland Court of Appeals decided for Hooper, but the effect was to leave the mayor and council stalemated for the remainder of Hooper's term.

In the 1897 mayoral election good government Republicans put forward Theodore Marburg, one of their number, for nomination, but the party organization refused to accept him. With little choice, Marburg withdrew and William T. Malster, a popular and successful local shipbuilder, was chosen. Reformers, both Republican and Democrat, reluctantly supported Malster in preference to the candidate of the Democratic organization. The primary object still remained to break the Gorman-Rasin machine.

Malster won the election, and almost immediately the mayor's office was besieged by spoilsmen. Incumbent Democrats were replaced by partisan Republicans, and efficiency in city departments declined. In 1898 Malster's supporters and the city council began a campaign for a series of public works projects. Grasty and other reformers saw it as a first step in a raid by

28. *Ibid.*, pp. 87-88.

spoilsmen on the city treasury. Clearly, the Republicans appeared to be no improvement over the Democrats.[29]

Still, the Malster administration did make one substantial contribution to political reform. This was the provision for a new city charter, a major structural change in response to urban needs. Fortunately, both Republicans and Democrats approached charter reform in a nonpartisan spirit. Malster appointed a charter commission consisting of prominent Democrats such as William Pinkney Whyte, former United States Senator and seven-times mayor of Baltimore, Ferdinand C. Latrobe, good government Republicans such as Reform Leaguers Lewis Putzel and George Gaither, and nonpartisan community leaders such as President Daniel C. Gilman of The Johns Hopkins University. Once the commission had completed the charter draft, both the city council and the faction-split General Assembly accepted it. As the twentieth century began, Baltimore had a modernized, more efficient governing instrument with which to respond to urban and industrial change.

By the end of 1898, however, despite the charter achievement, the reformers had had enough of Republican rule in both city and state. That December William Keyser, reform leader, retired B&O Railroad executive, iron manufacturer, and copper magnate, called together business and professional leaders to organize the New Charter Union, a group whose purpose was to put pressure on both parties to nominate good candidates. Though the Union was small in numbers, its members were leading Baltimoreans of independent persuasion, and both the *News* and *Sun* endorsed its efforts. The Republican party professionals, however, were satisfied with Malster's performance as mayor and ignored the reformers' pressures. The Democrats, on the other hand, having lost the 1895 election, the McKinley-Bryan contest, and the legislative campaign of 1897, were less settled. The machine was not functioning well. Rasin temporarily withdrew from active leadership in favor of former Governor Frank Brown. Brown, popular and ambitious for power, saw the possibility of reuniting Democrats by choosing candidates acceptable to both partisans and independents. His proposal of Thomas G. Hayes received support from the re-

29. *Ibid.*, pp. 92-93.

formers, and the Democrats won the mayoral election. Back in office, the Democrats would not be dislodged in Baltimore for another twenty years, but the party organization paid a price. For the rest of the progressive era, Democratic mayoral candidates would be competent men, independent of boss control, responsive for the most part to enlightened public opinion and willing to work to promote the welfare of the city.[30]

At the state level, on the other hand, the fight for independent progressive government responding to social change was less successful. Lowndes was renominated by the Republicans in 1899, while the Democrats chose John Walter Smith, a Gorman lieutenant from the Eastern Shore. Like Baltimore's mayoral candidate that same year, Smith also promised good government. Grasty of the *News* was unconvinced, but most Marylanders, including the *Sun's* policy-makers accepted Smith's promises at face value and elected him. Reformers feared the worst, but Smith stood by his platform promises during the legislative session of 1900.

The break came in 1901. Under the direction of Gorman, Governor Smith called a special session of the General Assembly. Ostensibly the session was planned to take steps to correct frauds in the federal census of 1900, authorize a sewage system for Baltimore, and make minor revisions to tighten the election laws. The purpose of the election law revision, said Gorman, was to reduce to a minimum the purchase of votes. The reality, however, was a Democratic strike for a return to unchallengable power, The party had suffered election defeats for three consecutive years from 1895, and a Republican General Assembly had replaced Gorman in the United States Senate. Though the outlook brightened with the victory of 1899, McKinley carried Maryland in 1900, and a coalition of Republicans and Democrats acting independently continued to threaten organization rule. In 1902 the legislature was due to elect another United States senator. In order to return to Washington, Gorman needed a Democratic victory in the 1901 election. To insure that victory Gorman planned to disfranchise the state's 25,000 illiterate adult male Negroes, who presumably voted Republican, by an

---

30. *Ibid.*, pp. 97-99. H. L. Mencken remembered Hayes as "a very shrewd lawyer, an unreconstructed Confederate veteran, a pious Methodist, and a somewhat bawdy bachelor" (H. L. Mencken, *Newspaper Days, 1899–1906* [New York: A. A. Knopf, 1941], p. 41).

election law reform that prohibited aid to illiterate voters in marking their ballots. By removing the Negro vote, Gorman also would destroy the effectiveness of the reform-Republican coalition.[31]

Bonaparte, Grasty, and the reformers recognized Gorman's strategy at once. The Reform League lobbied against the election bill and held mass meetings, but without effect. The bill passed the General Assembly essentially as planned. Gorman's strategy, however, did not work as well as anticipated in the legislative elections of 1901. In the counties he managed to increase his majority in the legislature sufficiently to return him to the Senate, but in Baltimore the election law revisions boomeranged. Voters in the city replaced eighteen Democratic delegates with fifteen Republicans and only three Democrats.

Dissatisfied with the result of the election law revision, Gorman sought next to have adopted a constitutional amendment which would disfranchise Maryland's Negro voters. Gorman's biographer, John R. Lambert, claims that this decision was based completely on political considerations; personally Gorman had no aversion to Negroes. But Marylanders did, and Democratic politicians used this prejudice to unite the party just as mid-western Republicans waved the "Bloody Shirt" to unite theirs.[32]

In 1899 Democratic leaders called on party members to back their nominee, because Republican success was dependent upon black support. In 1903 Democrats were told that good government could be achieved only by their party and that "the political destinies of Maryland should be shaped and controlled by the white people of the State." Two years later, during the first disfranchisement campaign, the platform called the black vote "a perpetual menace to the prosperity and peace of Maryland . . . for it is ignorant, corrupt, the blind instrument of unscrupulous and selfish leaders." That the statements were false bothered few Democratic politicians. In Maryland, Negroes accounted for only 18 per cent of the population. With their vote, Maryland had a two-party system. Without them, the Democrats would rule unchallenged as in their sister states to the South.[33]

---

31. Crooks, *Politics and Progress*, pp. 54-55.
32. Lambert, *Gorman*, pp. 315.
33. *Sun Almanac for 1900*, p. 53; *for 1904*, p. 38; and *for 1906*, p. 51.

The opportunity to disfranchise Maryland's Negroes came following the Democratic election victory in November 1903. The popular Edwin Warfield, a Howard County gentleman farmer, weekly newspaper editor, and Baltimore banker, had been elected governor along with a General Assembly in which there was a three-fifths Democratic majority, sufficient to pass a constitutional amendment. In December, Gorman asked John Prentiss Poe, dean of the University of Maryland Law School, to draft an amendment which came to bear Poe's name.

There were many precedents for Negro disfranchisement. Ten southern states had already eliminated blacks by "grandfather clauses," poll taxes, property qualifications, and requirements that prospective voters interpret passages from the constitution in a "reasonable" way. Gorman chose to disfranchise by two methods. The first, the grandfather clause, stated that any person or his lineal male descendant who was entitled to vote on January 1, 1869, was eligible to vote. Prior to that date when the Fifteenth Amendment to the Constitution became effective, Negroes in Maryland as in many other states, were disfranchised. The second clause enabled a person to vote who could read and give a "reasonable" interpretation of any section of the state constitution to a voter registrar. If unable to read, the prospective voter must be able to understand and give a reasonable explanation of any section read to him. The "reasonableness" of the explanation was left up to the discretion of the partisan voter registrar.[34]

The Poe amendment was introduced in the Senate in February, 1904, read three times over the next two weeks, and passed without delay in early March. Republicans fought a rear-guard action, but the measure passed without change by a party vote. The House of Delegates followed suit, despite protests from the Religious Society of Friends in Maryland and the Congregationalist ministers of Baltimore. Submission of the amendment to the voters of Maryland took place at the next general election in November 1905.

During the summer preceding the election, opponents of the Poe amendment began to organize. Their coalition was reminiscent of the 1895 campaign. In addition to the Republicans,

---

34. *Laws of Maryland* 1904, Ch. 96.

who made the Poe amendment the only issue of the campaign, reform Democrats created the Democratic Anti-Poe Amendment Association, consisting of some five hundred business and professional men opposed to the organization's method of disfranchising Negroes. The association's platform, however, was no call to racial equality. They supported white supremacy and an honest disfranchisement amendment, but they strongly opposed the understanding clause. Election judges were not qualified to apply the interpretive tests, and the chances for unscrupulous partisan activity were too great. Association president Leigh Bonsal stated the group's position succinctly when he said, "For my part, I fear much more the old Democratic ring . . . than I do the bugaboo of Negro domination."[35]

A more detailed indictment of the Poe amendment was prepared by Bonaparte in a special report to the Reform League. In addition to criticizing the understanding clause, Bonaparte argued that the amendments were subversive of republican and democratic principles of government, endangering the very fabric of self-government in Maryland. The amendment was unconstitutional because it would take away the rights of certain voters retroactively. Also, by its grandfather clause, it would create hereditary honors. Finally, Bonaparte claimed that the amendment could disfranchise all white foreign-born voters and their descendants who could not qualify under the grandfather clause. If the amendment were honestly administered, foreign-born voters as well as Negroes would have to face the "understanding" clause.[36]

The last claim burst like a bomb upon the large foreign-born community in Baltimore. The Maryland League of Foreign-Born Voters, representing nine nationalities, was formed to oppose the amendment. The German-American Independent Citizens Union, representing the largest foreign-born group, denounced the measure. In the tenement-ridden third ward of East Baltimore, William J. Garland asked five hundred Russian Jews to support him in his efforts to oppose the amendment and

35. Baltimore *News*, June 1, 20, 1905.
36. *Special Report of the Executive Committee to the Baltimore Reform League on the Poe Amendment, presented at the Annual Meeting, April 19, 1905*, Edwin Warfield Papers on deposit at the M.H.S.

guarantee their vote. Garland was the organization's ward leader there, but his loyalty to his "foreign friends" came first.[37]

Meanwhile, the black community mobilized its resources. A Maryland Suffrage League was formed to organize and educate Negro voters to the threat. *The Afro-American Ledger* of Baltimore urged its readers to vote against the amendment. Black churchmen were asked to get their congregations prepared by registering potential voters and getting out the vote.

Editorials criticized voter apathy, and praised the fine work of black leaders who, without white Republican help, had raised money, held meetings, and organized and aroused the people to oppose the amendment.[38]

The Democrats, meanwhile, were having their troubles. Rumors circulated in Baltimore that Rasin was trying to keep his legislative candidates independent of the amendment in order to insure their victory. Already four ward leaders, including Garland, had broken with the organization over the issue. On election day every Baltimore ward but "Sonny" Mahon's returned a majority against the amendment, while statewide, except for the Eastern Shore, only Gorman's Howard County voted for disfranchisement. The amendment lost by a wide margin of 104,286 to 70,228. A coalition of Republicans, reform Democrats, and foreign-born voters defeated the Poe amendment, believing it to be a political attempt to insure permanent Democratic rule under the Gorman-Rasin machine.[39]

Despite the defeat, the Gorman-Rasin machine at the state level continued intact until the deaths of the two leaders in 1906 and 1907, respectively. Subsequently, the strength of the partisan appeal ebbed in both parties, easing the way for progressive reform. As long as Gorman lived, however, the reformers could only block the excesses of the machine. After 1906, though partisan politics continued, the combination of a viable two-party system supported by nonpartisan citizens' lobbies, special interest groups, and a reform-minded press provided a milieu for change that began to respond to urban industrial conditions. This was particularly true in Baltimore,

---

37. Baltimore *News*, August 11, September 16, 1905; and Baltimore *Sun*, October 15, 1905.
38. *Afro-American Ledger*, September 23, October 7, 21, November 4, 1905.
39. Crooks, *Politics and Progress*, pp. 63-64.

where victory in the 1899 mayoral campaign began an era of responsible and innovative municipal government.

## 4

### URBAN REFORM IN BALTIMORE

In Maryland the wide-ranging political, economic and social reforms that characterize the progressive era in American history began largely in Baltimore City, where the greatest urban-industrial changes were taking place. Yet most Baltimoreans were not involved. Of Baltimore's approximately half million population during the era, only men over the age of twenty-one, or about 114,000, were registered voters. Of these, 82 per cent voted in the much ballyhooed election of 1895 with 53,183 people, or only 10 per cent of the total population, supporting the reform candidacy of Alcaeus Hooper. Even acknowledging the male dominated character of early twentieth century America, only 44.7 per cent of the eligible male voters chose Hooper. In 1899, again only 44 per cent of the possible voters chose Thomas G. Hayes, though he received 53 per cent of the votes cast, while in 1907 only 33.8 per cent of the voting population elected J. Barry Mahool as mayor. On referenda for public improvement, the voter returns were even less. In 1905 less than 20 per cent of Baltimore's eligible voters authorized the package of proposed public improvements to be built. Clearly, the urban reform movement was undertaken by a minority of the population.[40]

The leadership of this minority were bright young men, frequently under forty, of established American stock, college-educated, Protestant, Democratic, and often prominent professional men or business executives. A disproportionate number were listed in the Baltimore social register; urban reform had an elitist tone. Yet if most reformers were clearly from the establishment, an important minority were immigrants, Jews, Catholics, Republicans, from the working class, or lesser business and professional men who did not represent Baltimore's elite. There was also a significant group of women working for social change.[41]

---

40. *Ibid.*, p. 220.
41. *Ibid.*, pp. 195-200.

Baltimore's urban progressivism essentially broke down into two categories. On the one hand was a concern to modernize city government and make it respond more effectively to urban change. In the process professional expertise was introduced in the areas of planning, public health reforms, and modern management practices. Autonomy from state interference as well as fair representation in the General Assembly were important means. At its best these structural or administrative reforms were more than simply good government for greater efficiency, honesty, or economy. Reformers sought to modernize city government in order to use and develop more effectively both the city's physical and human resources.

The second classification of urban reform sought social, political, and economic change for the reduction of poverty, sickness, discomfort, and stunted growth, partly for the relatively recent casualties of industrialism, but also for the city dwellers whose infirmities had preceded the industrial revolution. In a broader sense, historians and contemporaries have called these humanitarian reforms the movement for social justice.[42]

Many of the reforms overlapped these two categories in their effects. A park development program combined city planning with recreational benefits for slum dwellers. The sewage system was a public works project essential to any large, twentieth century city; yet its effect was also to improve the public health conditions for all city dwellers. Thus the practical decision-making to modernize urban structures was often intertwined with a concern for the working child, the tenement dweller, or sweatshop employee. They were signs of an enlightened self-interest on the part of progressive Baltimoreans, whether a reduction in the rate of tuberculosis was seen as a humanitarian ideal or simply a lessening of the chances that one's gardener, maid, or governess might spread the dread disease to members of one's own family.

---

42. Otis Graham, Jr., *The Great Campaigns: Reform and War in America, 1900–1928* (Englewood Cliffs, N.J.: Prentice Hall, 1971), pp. 129-59, discussed with considerable insight three classifications of reform: (1) attempts to impose order and modern procedures upon an archaic nineteenth-century society; (2) attempts to come to the aid of the casualties of industrialism—the ghetto dweller, the female factory laborer, the working child; and (3) attempts to impose nineteenth-century moral codes on a twentieth-century world (p. 129). The last named was weakest in the cities with perhaps stronger impact at the state level, particularly on issues like prohibition.

Administrative reforms began with Mayor Hooper's two-year term, but the first major breakthrough was undoubtedly the city charter of 1898. The old one, dating from the city's incorporation in 1796, was antiquated. Governmental departments were inefficiently organized; the ward system of representation favored local as opposed to a citywide outlook in municipal affairs; and finally, the entire administration of city government was crippled by periodic ravages of partisan politics and the spoils system. The worst example of these deficiencies was the school system. The Board of School Commissioners consisted of twenty-two men, one from each ward, appointed with the advice and consent of the ward's councilman. Each appointment was by patronage. The school commissioners frequently chose the teachers as well as the librarians, clerks, and janitors on the same basis. There were no standards for teacher qualifications, and the caliber of teaching was low. One exposé showed that the commissioners bought obsolete texts at prices higher than those paid for up-to-date books in other cities. Schools were old and overcrowded, and attendance was not compulsory. One national authority in a series of articles on the nation's schools described the Baltimore system as being in a "deplorable condition of affairs."

Other city departments varied in quality. Some, like the water department, were generally well run. Most of them combined inefficiency with politics and got mediocre results. There was little coordination between departments, and the superstructure of authority was clumsy and inefficient.

Mayor Malster's nonpartisan charter commission worked quickly and harmoniously to modernize the administrative structure. To reform the schools, Daniel Gilman proposed the appointment of a nine-member school board chosen by the mayor on a citywide basis. The board would establish policy and select a professional superintendent. The superintendent would then hire teachers on a merit basis, plan curriculum, and supervise all phases of administration. In other areas of city government, the commission followed the model of the new charter of greater New York. Executive powers were strengthened at the expense of the city council. A new five-member Board of Estimates, composed of three elected and two appointed officials, became the dominant power in the city government. The three elected officials were the mayor, the comptroller, and the president of the second branch of the bicameral city council. The two appointees were the city solicitor and the city engineer. The board proposed the city's annual budget, granted franchises, and set limits to municipal expenditures. All of these functions were formerly undertaken by the city council. Meanwhile, a Board of Awards, similar in makeup to the Board of Estimates, took over the council's function of granting contracts on an honest and competitive basis.

In theory and in practice, both boards represented the best in contemporary municipal institutions. New York, Boston, Cleveland, and Toledo had them. Other charter innovations were equally reform-minded. One provision, limiting public utility franchise grants to twenty-five years, was similar in scope to the recommendations of the National Municipal League. Another shifted city elections from November to May in an attempt to separate local issues from politics on the state and national level. Finally, administrative departments were reorganized to promote greater efficiency in municipal government.

There were also limitations to the new charter. It failed to provide for home rule or sufficient autonomy from state legislative interference in local affairs. It failed to include civil service reform; the inefficient and ofttimes irresponsible bicameral city council was retained; and the mayor's appointive powers were limited by the council's right to advise.

These limitations reflected an awareness of the realities of political life in Baltimore in 1898. Both party organizations had to accept a new charter on both city and state levels in order for it to pass. In Baltimore the organization's strength lay in the city council, which prevented the pruning of one of its legislative branches then and later in another proposed charter revision effort in 1909. The organizations also prevented civil service reform from replacing the more popular spoils system in both 1898 and 1909. Yet the charter commissioners did make progress in restricting the council's powers; this resulted in the "half a loaf" that political reformers were frequently obliged to accept. In comparison with other American cities, Baltimore's new charter was not in the forefront of municipal reform, but it was a substantial step to enable city government to function more effectively in coping with urban-industrial change.[43]

---

43. Crooks, *Politics and Progress*, pp. 93-96.

The second major advance in the modernization of Baltimore came with the gradual introduction of city planning after the adoption of the new charter in 1898. The impetus came from William Keyser, by then the president of the Reform League, Theodore Marburg, vice president of the Reform League, and Charles Grasty of the Baltimore *News*. In January 1899 Marburg organized the Municipal Art Society of Baltimore, a group of more than 500 predominantly upper and upper-middle class Baltimoreans who were initially concerned about making their city a more attractive place to live. Within a year the society appointed committees to plan for suburban development and to implement the recent recommendations of the Baltimore Sewerage Commission. The commission was the third of its kind appointed by Baltimore mayors over the previous forty years to propose remedies for the city's unsanitary conditions.

In 1900 Baltimore was the only major city in the United States without a sewage system. In the city's early history cesspools or outdoor privies had been adequate for sewage disposal, but the introduction of indoor plumbing, including the toilet, the new habit of more frequent bathing, and increased population magnified the problem of sewage disposal. Except for wealthy home owners and business establishments with private sewage systems, all bathroom wastes drained into cesspools, causing the ground to become increasingly saturated. Home owners in the densely packed rows of brick houses contracted for their cesspools to be cleaned periodically, but the ground saturation was not relieved. In the older, most crowded sections of the city, dirt-packed basement floors became softened as saturated ground below failed to drain liquid wastes. Public health authorities could only recommend that such cellars be paved.

By 1900 agreement had been reached to build an expensive filtration system to avoid any possibility of polluting the Chesapeake Bay. Grasty in the *News* urged the construction of the system as Baltimore's "paramount need." Keyser, who was also a director of the Municipal Art Society and one of the city's largest property taxpayers, urged Mayor Hayes to support the project, and the Municipal Art Society endorsed Keyser's stand.

At the special session in 1901, the General Assembly authorized construction, but the city council refused to go along for partisan reasons. The council passed an authorization bill the following year, but the General Assembly tabled it. Finally, in 1903, both political parties in their platforms pledged to build a sewage system on a nonpartisan basis, and authorization was secured by both city and state governments in 1904.[44]

Meanwhile, the Municipal Art Society undertook its second major project in January 1902, when Marburg announced the decision to engage a landscape architect to draw up a plan for park and suburban development in Baltimore. The firm of Olmsted Brothers, noted for its work at the Chicago World's Fair as well as for cooperating on the implementation of L'Enfant's plan for Washington, D.C., agreed to undertake the Baltimore plans. The contract called for planning suburban and park development, but no topographical survey had been done for the

---

44. *Ibid.*, pp 129-136.

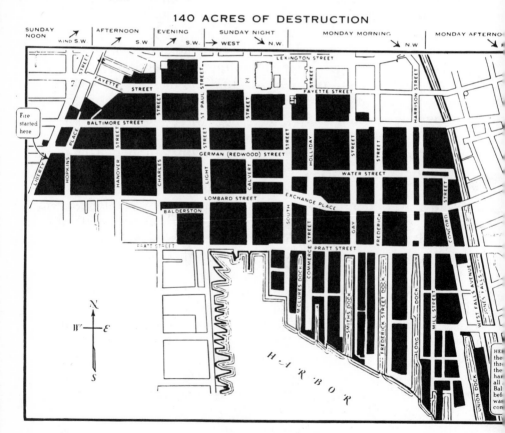

PROGRESS OF THE FIRE

suburbs, and the firm was limited to developing a system of parks. The park plan completed in November 1903, however, was a masterpiece that served as a basis for park development for two generations. It recommended the acquisition of thirty-six small parks in the densely populated areas of Baltimore, additions to the five major existing parks—Wyman, Druid Hill, Clifton, Montebello, and Patterson—and the acquisition of outlying areas along Back River, Loch Raven, the Patapsco River Gorge, Curtis Creek, and in the Green Spring Valley, in anticipation of future metropolitan growth. In all, the plan recommended the acquisition of 2,600 acres of park land, including parkways along Gwynns Falls, Jones Falls, Stoney Run, and Herring Run. It also provided for widened commercial highways that fanned out from downtown Baltimore in all directions.[45]

Following the report, Grasty again issued a call for a public works campaign. City officials responded by putting together an authorization package that included parks, sewers, paved roads, new schools, and firehouses. Baltimore's delegation to the General Assembly announced its readiness to support the bills on February 6, 1904. This action came just in time; further delay might have buried the program in the ashes of the Baltimore fire.

The great Baltimore fire of February 7, 1904, began on a quiet winter Sunday. A spark from a discarded cigar or match burst into flame in the basement of a downtown dry goods firm, igniting the blankets and cotton goods that were stored there. The fire spread rapidly, and within minutes was blazing out of control. The flames leaped from building to building and overcame efforts of more than 1,200 firemen to extinguish them. The fire raged for thirty hours. It threatened residential East Baltimore, but the wind shifted and drove it into the harbor. Seventy blocks, from Liberty Street to Jones Falls, and Fayette Street to the harbor were burned out, including 1,526 buildings and more than 2,500 business enterprises. Twenty banks, eight hotels, nine newspaper plants, and nine transportation offices, including the home office of the Baltimore and Ohio Railroad,

---

45. Olmsted Brothers, *Report on the Development of Public Grounds for Greater Baltimore* (Baltimore: The Lord Baltimore Press, 1904), pp. 11-50 *passim*.

Devastated area of the heart of Baltimore after the fire of February 1904.
Photograph by J. W. Schaefer. *M.H.S.*

were gutted. Fortunately, no one was killed and few homes were destroyed.[46]

On the Friday following the fire, Mayor Robert McLane appointed a Citizens Emergency Committee under the leadership of William Keyser to plan the rebuilding of the burnt district. Proposals ranged from widening and smooth-paving the city's streets to construction of municipally owned docks and a recreation pier. The General Assembly authorized a bond referendum, but the city council dragged its feet on widening Baltimore Street. Subsequently the parks were also eliminated, but harbor renewal continued, along with sewer construction, street paving, and a height limitation on new building construction. Private interests rebuilt rapidly and within two years few scars remained from the fire. Unfortunately, no plan coordinated the private reconstruction in terms of form or function. City planning in Baltimore and across the nation had not yet reached that stage of development. The result was a renewed business district in Baltimore, but a lost opportunity to rebuild the city's center with creativity and coordination.

While Baltimoreans coped with the fire's devastation, the General Assembly authorized the sewage, park, and other

46. Harold A. Williams, *Baltimore Afire* (Baltimore: Schneidereith and Sons, 1954).

improvements. In preparation for the referendum to follow, reform leaders called a General Public Improvements Conference to organize public support. The idea caught the imagination of Baltimoreans. Delegates from center city and suburbs, business associations and trade unions, immigrant and charitable groups, neighborhood improvement associations and the Municipal Art Society, joined to campaign for the referendum. Only Baltimore's Negroes were not represented. The loans passed by substantial majorities in May 1905, and over the next six years Baltimoreans endorsed eleven of twelve bond referenda for planned public improvements.[47]

Meanwhile the Municipal Art Society continued to work toward a city plan. Over the next decade it sponsored a series of proposals to pave over Jones Falls, to build a civic center of governmental buildings east of City Hall (rather than have them scattered throughout the city), and to coordinate development of South Baltimore, including a plan to eliminate railroad grade-crossings, build Key Highway, construct sewers, smooth pave other streets, and replace an obsolete market with a community center.[48]

---

47. Crooks, *Politics and Progress*, pp. 141-149.
48. *Ibid.*, pp. 149-154, and Municipal Art Society, *Partial Report on City Plan* (Baltimore: n.p., 1910).

By 1911 city planning was being established as an important tool in urban development. Compared with other American cities, Baltimore was keeping pace. By contrast to European cities, however, all American cities were backward. By 1900, planners in Europe were preparing and executing programs of slum razing, low cost housing, and residential and commercial zoning. In Baltimore, as in most American cities, social reformers might recognize slum conditions but they lacked authority to do anything about them. Zoning did not become municipal policy in Baltimore until 1927, and government-sponsored housing waited for the New Deal. But a beginning had been made, both with the new charter, piecemeal city plans coordinating public construction and improvements, and the creation in 1906 of a Department of Legislative Reference, which served as a technical resource for city and state lawmakers.

All of these gains reflected a progressive concern to modernize the way city government responded to urban growth, using outside expertise, greater efficiency, and technology for the welfare of all its inhabitants. At the same time, it was clearly limited progress, initiated by the business and professional elite, in their own self-interest as doctors, lawyers, merchants, and manufacturers living and working in Baltimore.

The second category of urban reforms more directly benefited the urban poor. Social reform began in the 1880's with the formation of the Charity Organization Society under the sponsorship of Daniel Gilman of The Johns Hopkins University. The management, again, was largely composed of leading Baltimoreans. The Charity Organization Society sought to replace traditional almsgiving, which offered gifts of food, clothing, and coal (mixed with religious homilies) to the poor, with volunteer "friendly visitors" who worked on a one-to-one basis with needy families. These visitors assisted them with food or, if necessary, medical care, and also with jobs that worked toward individual self-sufficiency.[49]

Along with the volunteers from the Charity Organization Society, Baltimore's clergy also became concerned with social

---

49. Crooks, *Politics and Progress*, pp. 158-59. See also the *Annual Report of the Charity Organization Society* (Baltimore 1885–1906); Charles Hirschfeld, *Baltimore, 1870–1900* (Baltimore: J. H. Press, 1941), pp. 138-48; and Mary E. Richmond, *The Long View* (New York: Russell Sage Foundation, 1930), *passim*.

conditions among Baltimore's poor. Most outstanding was James Cardinal Gibbons, Archbishop of Baltimore, defender of organized labor, Negroes, consumers, and immigrants working in unhealthy sweatshops. Perhaps the leading Protestant clergyman supporting social reform was Edward H. Lawrence, a Congregationalist minister who preached the social gospel to Johns Hopkins students. In 1893 he and a Hopkins graduate student moved into a tenement in southwest Baltimore to live and work with the poor. Lawrence died prematurely of a ruptured appendix the following year, but friends, including Robert Garrett, the Baltimore banker and philanthropist, and Bernard Steiner, librarian at the Enoch Pratt Free Library, formed the Lawrence Memorial Association to begin the first settlement house in Baltimore. Other settlements followed, begun by Episcopalians, Unitarians, and Jews, working primarily among immigrants to provide nurseries and kindergartens for children, sewing and cooking classes for girls and women, handicrafts and athletics for boys and men, as well as adult education to promote literacy. None of the Baltimore settlements had the cultural scope and diversity of Chicago's Hull House, but few anywhere did. Yet frequently the settlement house became the neighborhood center. Unfortunately there were too few of them. Baltimore's half dozen privately-financed settlements met only a tiny fraction of the need; most immigrants and Negroes probably never saw one.[50]

A third group to become concerned with the poor before 1895 was a nucleus of medical men who advocated social reform in the name of public health. Their leaders were Doctors William H. Welch and William Osler of The Johns Hopkins Hospital and Medical School. Welch's speech on "Sanitation in Relation to the Poor," delivered to the Charity Organization Society in 1892, probably marked the beginning of efforts to improve environmental health conditions in Baltimore. In it he noted that the death rate among the poor was two to three times greater than among the "better situated" people of America. He estimated that better sanitation in the cities could save 100,000

---

50. Crooks, *Politics and Progress*, pp. 160-64; John Tracy Ellis, *The Life of James Cardinal Gibbons* (Milwaukee: Bruce Publishing Co., 1952) I, 486-546; Margaret Woods Lawrence, *Reminiscences of the Life and Work of Edward A. Lawrence, Jr.*, pp. 431-99, *passim*; and *Charities Record*, October, December 1895; February, May 1896; February 1897; October 1900; and May, 1905.

lives each year, besides improving the physical, mental, and moral conditions of the poor, who daily were condemned to breathe impure air, eat contaminated food, and live in filthy, overcrowded surroundings. Cities like Baltimore, he said, must provide pure water, food inspection, clean streets, hospitals, and a sanitary sewage system as well as adequate housing conditions to remedy environmental deficiencies and insure the health and welfare of all of their citizens. It was clear to Welch that in Baltimore the machine-dominated political leaders had failed to provide for the public's health.[51]

A fourth group concerned about poverty and the workingman was organized labor, first the Knights of Labor in the 1880's and later the Baltimore Federation of Labor. The latter group, under the leadership of Edward Hirsch, supported child labor, sweatshop and tenement legislation, as well as higher wages and the eight-hour day.

The early efforts of these groups and their coalition into the Union for Public Good, under the leadership of Bonaparte, was a good start. Real accomplishment, however, had to await the removal of the Gorman-Rasin machine. The reformers obtained passage of a factory inspection act in 1894, but, typically, the General Assembly crippled it at the last minute by providing for only one enforcement inspector.

Combined with such actions as that of the General Assembly to sabotage reform efforts was the machine's failure on both the city and state level to aid victims of the depression that began in 1893. It was the worst depression to that time in American history. Unemployment statistics are incomplete, but the Maryland Bureau of Industrial Statistics estimated that in the first year 11 per cent of the labor force was unemployed. Subsequent estimates of unemployment ranged from one-third to one-half the labor force of Baltimore. The Charity Organization Society took the lead among the numerous voluntary organizations in Baltimore to provide work or assistance for heads of household, but they were able to help only about one-third of the unemployed. Thoughtful observers like Mary Richmond of the Charity Organization Society began to realize that self-help and private initiative were no longer sufficient tools to relieve

---

51. Crooks, *Politics and Progress*, pp. 164-66; and William Henry Welch, "Sanitation in Relation to the Poor," *Paper and Address* (Baltimore: J. H. Press, 1920), I, 588-96.

poverty. Increasingly, she saw that the physical and social environment, as well as individual ignorance and indolence, caused poverty and sickness. Private initiative must continue, but only government could clean up slums and make healthy the urban environment.[52]

Following the defeat of the Gorman-Rasin machine in 1895, fresh forces joined the fight for social reform. Particularly important were the women's clubs and a new generation of well-educated young business and professional men who were concerned about urban conditions and who joined with the clergy, organized labor, the medical men, and the older, establishment reformers to support social change.

Their concerns focused mainly in the two areas of child welfare and public health. Where reforms in both areas might help upper and middle class Baltimoreans, they primarily aided the poor. The poor were those who were most susceptible to the diseases associated with garbage-strewn alleys, contaminated foods, and overcrowded housing. Moreover, once incapacitated by sickness, they also lacked the resources to obtain medical care. Miss Richmond estimated that one quarter of all urban poverty could be traced to sickness and disease. In addition, it was the poor child who lived in a tenement, worked in a factory, missed school, and was forced to play in the busy streets.

The four main areas of child welfare legislation were education, correction, employment, and recreation. The women of the Arundell Good Government Club, first organized in the election of 1895, provided the initiative on behalf of a compulsory school attendance law. The principle was long established in the North, but heretofore neglected in the southern states. In 1902 the law was passed by the General Assembly as local legislation. It was also supported by the Charity Organization Society and organized labor.[53]

Tied with the plan for compulsory education were the educational reforms in progress after 1898 under the new charter and

52. Maryland Bureau of Industrial Statistics, "The Unemployed of Baltimore," *Bulletin* No. 6 (March 1, 1894); Hirschfeld, *Baltimore*, pp. 54-55; and Richmond, *The Long View*, pp. 129.

53. Crooks, *Politics and Progress*, pp. 169-74; *Annals of the Arundell Club, 1894–1925* (Baltimore: A.C., 1926); and Minutes of the Meetings of the Arundell Good Government Club, Arundell Club of Baltimore, 1896–1952, on deposit at the M.H.S. Local legislation referred to laws applicable only to one's own constituency and permitted by legislative courtesy.

school board. In 1900 the board hired James H. Van Sickle from Denver as the new superintendent, and Van Sickle proceeded to modernize the school system, raising academic standards, enlarging the curriculum with vocational education, special education, and kindergartens, and putting teachers under a modified merit system where promotions were based on classroom performance and civil service examinations. The last innovation provoked increasing opposition from public school teachers, particularly on the elementary level, resulting in public conflicts and the eventual ouster of Van Sickle in 1911. Nevertheless, major educational reforms were introduced in Baltimore during this era, and standards were raised.[54]

In the second area of child welfare reform, the Charity Organization Society took the initiative in establishing a juvenile court. They were supported by the Arundell Good Government Club and the Consumers League of Maryland. This bill, too, was passed by the 1902 General Assembly as local legislation, the Baltimore delegation at that session being composed largely of young reformers who had helped to defeat the Gorman-Rasin machine in the city at the previous November's election.[55]

The third bill of the session outlawed child labor for youngsters under fourteen years of age in manufacturing establishments. Mercantile businesses were exempt. Again the women, organized labor, and the Charity Organization Society cooperated. Subsequently, the Maryland Bureau of Industrial Statistics, in cooperation with the Consumers League, studied the law's enforcement and found it negligible. The League organized a Maryland Child Labor Committee composed of representatives from the Charity Organization Society, the Arundell Club, organized labor, and the churches to push for a more effective law. The Merchants and Manufacturers Association, local affiliate of the National Association of Manufacturers, opposed the bill by arguing that children and their mothers needed their wages, and besides, child labor was a healthy discipline. Jane Addams, of Hull House fame, responded in an address to the child labor committee with evidence that in Il-

54. George D. Strayer, "The Baltimore School Situation," *Educational Review* (November, 1911), XLII, 325-45; and Harlean James, "A Twelve Years' Fight for School Reform: the Situation in Baltimore," *New England Magazine*, XLIX (May, 1913), 118-24.

55. Crooks, *Politics and Progress*, p. 175.

linois the extra money earned through child labor frequently went to improve the parents' standard of living at the expense of the child. After considerable lobbying, press agitation, and a ground swell of public opinion, the General Assembly of 1906 passed a child labor law with enforcement provisions again on a local basis. Children under twelve were absolutely prohibited from working; children from twelve to sixteen needed work permits certifying minimum health standards and literacy; six inspectors were authorized to enforce the act; and employers hiring youngsters without permits could be fined.

The law was enforced. In the first year, 23,000 children between the ages of twelve and sixteen obtained work permits. Another 3,000 were turned down for reasons of health, age, or illiteracy. Forty arrests were made for law violations, while Federated Charities (successor to the Charity Organization Society) established twenty-five "school scholarships," an early form of aid to dependent children, to enable youngsters in poor families to stay in school and still support their parents. Further refinements of the Child Labor legislation followed in the 1912 General Assembly, raising the minimum age to fourteen, and a standard of law enforcement was set in perhaps the most important child wefare issue of the era.[56].

The fourth area of child welfare reform was the program to provide recreational facilities for city children. The playground movement, along with kindergartens, had begun in Germany as an outgrowth of urbanization. As building construction filled vacant lots and the countryside receded beyond the reach of city children, municipal authorities recognized the need for setting aside park land as playgrounds. In the United States, Boston and Rochester pioneered the movement. In Baltimore, Miss Eliza Ridgely organized support for the first city playgrounds in cooperation with a local woman's club, and by 1899 had started the Children's Playground Association, which supervised five playgrounds. The number increased to eighteen by 1902, and twenty-four by 1906, but the operation was run on a shoestring. Lack of funds limited the program to small children and girls attending morning sessions for only one month each summer. Financial support finally came from the city as a result of Coun-

---

56. *Ibid.*, pp. 175-78; *Annual Reports of the Bureau of Statistics and Information of Maryland* (Baltimore: B.S.I.M., 1906 and 1907).

cilman (later mayor, 1907–1911) J. Barry Mahool, who achieved appropriations for it.

Meanwhile, Baltimore banker Robert Garrett, a participant in the 1896 Olympic games in Athens, had become interested in establishing recreational facilities for young boys in the city. In 1908 he organized the Public Athletic League to provide a complete recreational program for adolescents and young men. That year in Baltimore recreational personnel supervised twenty-eight park and school-yard playgrounds, twenty-two of which were located in the inner city, five of them open to Negroes. The playgrounds were open for six hours daily throughout the summer, with special services, including library facilities, children's gardens, a baby's milk station, and track meets. When school resumed in September, the programs continued indoors in twenty schools, churches, and settlement houses.[57]

Closely allied with the playground and other child welfare programs were the public health reforms of the era. They stressed decent housing, pure food, hygienic working conditions, and programs of disease prevention for all city dwellers, but especially for the poor.

While the medical profession began the public health campaigns, social reformers soon joined with them in organizing the Maryland Public Health Association in 1897. The membership of over 300 came from all parts of the state. For the first years of the progressive era, the association provided the leadership for public health reforms, though other groups like the Charity Organization Society often supported them. In 1897 the association provided a forum for discussing the proposed sanitary sewage system. In subsequent years it focused attention on the need for public baths, a municipal hospital for infectious diseases, and the crusade against tuberculosis.[58]

Most important was the campaign against tuberculosis, which got under way in 1902. Of the 10,000 consumptives in Baltimore, 1,000 died each year from the disease. In Baltimore, as

---

57. Crooks, *Politics and Progress*, pp. 179-82; *Children's Playground Association, Biennial Report for 1907–1908 and 1908–1909* (Baltimore, 1909), pp. 7-9; Children's Playground Association, *Proceedings of Annual Meeting, April 4, 1910 and Annual Report for Year Ending March 31, 1910* (Baltimore, 1910), p. 6; and Public Athletic League, Inc., *Second Annual Report and Proceedings of the Second Annual Meeting* (Baltimore: P.A.L., 1910), p. 59.
58. Crooks, *Politics and Progress*, pp. 182-84.

across the nation, tuberculosis was the most widespread and fatal of all known diseases. The death rates were highest in the most densely populated areas, where standards of living were lowest. In Baltimore, these areas were the Negro ghetto and the new immigrant sections of East Baltimore. Compared with other major American cities, Baltimore's death rate from tuberculosis was not excessive, but other cities, particularly Philadelphia, New York, and Boston, were acting to combat the disease. Baltimoreans, as yet, were doing nothing.

In January 1902, the Maryland Public Health Association, together with the State Board of Health and a small private tuberculosis society connected with The Johns Hopkins Medical School, sponsored a public meeting to support the establishment of a state tuberculosis commission. In a blistering speech to his "long-suffering, patient, inert fellow-citizens," Dr. William Osler lambasted the community for its failure to do "one solitary thing that a modern civilized community should do" to combat tuberculosis. Through The Johns Hopkins Medical School, Osler had undertaken a survey of tuberculosis cases in Baltimore and discovered that few patients had any idea of the proper treatment for the disease or the prevention of its spread. The city government did not even recognize that the disease existed. There were no registration of cases, no dispensaries for outpatient care, and no sanitarium for either curable, incipient or incurable advanced cases. Osler excoriated the politicians for their lack of concern about the city's health needs and challenged his listeners to do something to correct the situation.[59]

Governor Smith responded by requesting the General Assembly to create a tuberculosis commission, which it did. In its report of 1904, the commission recommended strongly the passage of laws in Baltimore to require registration of all tubercular cases, prohibition of spitting in public places, a program of education, the building of sanitaria, and a practice of disinfecting all houses vacated by tuberculars. On the state level, it urged the building of a state sanitarium.

---

59. *Ibid.*, pp. 184-85; see also *Report of the Tuberculosis Commission of the State of Maryland, 1902–1904* (n.p., n.d.), 8; *Report of the Maryland Association for the Prevention and Relief of Tuberculosis for 1909–1910* (Baltimore: M.A.P.R.T., 1910); Harvey Cushing, *The Life of Sir William Osler* (New York, Oxford University Press, 1925) I, 570-71.

To publicize the report, the State Board of Health and the Maryland Public Health Association cosponsored with the commission a week-long tuberculosis exhibit at The Johns Hopkins University. The exhibition dramatized the history and nature of the disease, presented statistics on its prevalence and rate of mortality, displayed models of proposed dispensaries and sanitaria, and sponsored daily lectures on the subject. Among the displays was a series of photographs of Baltimore tenements and sweatshops showing overcrowding, inadequate ventilation, and poor sanitation, all of which were conducive to the spread of the disease. Speakers urged employers to limit working hours for children and provide sanitary workshops; philanthropists to build model tenements, sanitaria, and public baths; and cities to build sanitaria and public housing as was done in Glasgow, Scotland. An estimated fifty thousand people saw the exhibit.[60]

Subsequently, public health reformers organized the Maryland Association for the Prevention and Relief of Tuberculosis, which promptly called for a national convention at Atlantic City that summer, leading to the formation of the National Association for the Study and Prevention of Tuberculosis.

In Baltimore the Maryland association's primary purpose was educational: to alert people to the threat of tuberculosis and to show them how to prevent and relieve it. It also supported legislation to require the registration of all tuberculars, prohibit spitting in public places, and provide the construction of sanitaria. In addition to activity directed toward the immediate causes of the disease, the association supported all legislation "bearing upon social and economic conditions which make for or against the spread of tuberculosis." It cooperated with Federated Charities in its efforts to improve housing conditions, supported the child labor laws, and endorsed pure food legislation. Again and again speakers reiterated the association's belief that the state was responsible for safeguarding "the lives of its working people by defining proper standards of employment, proper factory conditions . . . prohibiting the labor of immature children, and limiting the hours of work for women." Advocates stressed the interrelationship between overcrowded

<hr>

60. *Report of the Tuberculosis Commission*, pp. 1-22, *passim*; and *Report of the Maryland Association for the Prevention and Relief of Tuberculosis, 1907–1908*, p. 21.

housing, the lack of playgrounds, contaminated food, and tuberculosis, seeking to awaken public opinion to change conditions.[61]

The association's achievements may be measured in three ways. First, it persuaded the General Assembly to appropriate funds to subsidize one private sanitarium north of Baltimore and to authorize construction of the first public sanitarium in western Maryland. The legislature also passed registration laws that became the model for laws subsequently enacted in New York, Wisconsin, California, and Washington, D.C. In Baltimore, reformers supported the city health department's opening of a tuberculosis hospital in 1904 and persuaded the Mahool administration to create a tuberculosis commission in 1910 to administer a complete medical care program for all tuberculars in Baltimore. The association's second standard of achievement was its growing company of supporters. Initially, some three hundred people contributed to the cause, and by 1910 the number of contributors had increased tenfold. Finally, the third standard of progress was the declining mortality rate attributable to tuberculosis after 1910.[62]

Despite the progress, however, tuberculosis treatment facilities remained inadequate. The state's public and private sanitaria had beds for approximately five hundred patients in 1910; registered cases numbered at least eight times that. Dispensaries in Baltimore only partially relieved the load. The association advocated progressive policies in both tubercular care and social reform, but city and particularly state officials moved slowly to meet the needs. The association's greatest failure was its inability to do more for Maryland's Negroes, whose death rate from tuberculosis was more than twice that of whites. The association, along with the Municipal Tuberculosis Commission, urged treatment for them, but by 1910 the city and state's Democratically controlled governments had yet to provide facilities. Progress was for whites only.[63]

61. *Ibid.*, pp. 35-37; and *Report of the Maryland Association for the Prevention . . . of Tuberculosis for 1909–1910*, p. 10.
62. *Ibid.*, Crooks, *Politics and Progress*, pp. 187-188; and William T. Howard, *Public Health Administration and the Natural History of Disease in Baltimore, Maryland, 1797–1920* (Washington: The Carnegie Institution of Washington, 1924), p. 382.
63. *Ibid.*, p. 411; and *Report of the Maryland Association for the Prevention . . . of Tuberculosis for 1909–1910*.

The Maryland Association for the Prevention and Relief of Tuberculosis was the most successful of the special interest groups formed during this decade in Baltimore. Other groups, however, were also active in support of specifically directed reforms. The Anti-Saloon League established a chapter in Maryland in 1898, and in Baltimore eight years later. It campaigned for temperance on a local option basis, but made little headway in Baltimore. Many Protestant clergymen and most county residents probably favored local option, but in Baltimore Cardinal Gibbons and the Roman Catholic Church opposed it, as did the Hebrew congregations, the Federation of Labor, the strong German-American Independent Citizens Union, and the vast majority of the city's politicians and reformers. Local option prohibition was one environmental reform that most of Baltimore's reform leaders did not want. Other special interest groups organized with varying successes in the causes of sex education, state care of the mentally retarded and the insane, and prison reform.[64]

Meanwhile, the older reform groups were also active in the other fields of public health besides tuberculosis. Organized labor, in particular, had since 1880 been trying to improve factory conditions in the garment industry. Following his appointment to the Bureau of Industrial Statistics in 1899, Jacob Schonfarber, formerly of the Knights of Labor, took the lead in an effort to obtain legislation for inspecting Baltimore's sweatshops.

Baltimore's sweatshops, like others across the United States, originated in the early nineteenth century, when farmers' wives and family craftsmen plied the needle trades at home. The Civil War and its aftermath stimulated the public's demand for ready-made clothing. New manufacturers entered the trade, enlarging the industry but without changing the home-craft system. As demand for ready-made clothes increased, the new immigrant from eastern and southern Europe became the main source of labor. Where the newcomers were unskilled, established craftsmen became middle men between the manufacturer and the newcomer, "sweating" the latter for a portion of his meager earnings. Where the newcomers were craftsmen—as

---

64. On early Anti-Saloon League activity, see Baltimore *News* November 19, December 11, 1907, January 27, February 5, 18, 25, 27, and March 11, 1908.

many of the Italians and Russian Jews were—their ignorance of the language provided employment for middle men who contracted for the work and "sweated" the workers. In either case, the work continued at home in the dirty, overcrowded, unhealthy tenements of the city.

Schonfarber estimated that there were three hundred sweatshops, mostly in East Baltimore, employing an average of ten workers per shop. Compared to New York's forty thousand sweatshops, this number was small, but conditions were as bad. Schonfarber, in cooperation with Jacob Moses, a young Democratic state senator from Baltimore, drafted a factory inspection act in 1902. Baltimore's delegation supported the bill, and it passed as local legislation.

The law provided two inspectors to enforce its provisions; Schonfarber considered this adequate. During the next decade, encouraged by the support of Cardinal Gibbons, these inspectors worked to eliminate Baltimore's sweatshops. Their success was substantial. By 1910 only 5 per cent of Baltimore's garment workers labored in their homes. The rest worked in factories established by the clothing manufacturers. More important, through the implementation of factory inspection, Baltimore may have avoided such horrors as the 1910 Triangle Fire in New York, were 146 garment workers died in the flames. With the foresight lacking in many cities, Baltimore's reformers enforced the factory inspection act and eliminated the sweatshop evil from their city.[65]

Another public health hazard that required correction was the condition of housing in Baltimore. Because the city lacked the ugly tenements of New York, most Baltimoreans ignored the division and subdivision of the old brick row houses into tenements in East Baltimore. A United States Bureau of Labor report on the slums of Baltimore, Chicago, New York, and Philadelphia in 1894 noted their existence, but it produced little reaction under the old political machine.

Baltimoreans continued to ignore housing problems until 1906, when the Federated Charities sponsored a study of slum conditions. The report showed that East Baltimore tenements,

---

65. Crooks, *Politics and Progress*, pp. 189-90; see also annual *Reports* of the Bureau of Industrial Statistics of Maryland, later renamed the Bureau of Statistics and Information.

occupied primarily by new immigrants from eastern Europe, were subdivided row houses with inadequate space, ventilation, light, and sanitary facilities. Indoor plumbing, especially toilets, was lacking, while the foul outdoor privies were shared by three or four families. Overcrowding was less pervasive in the Negro alley homes of northwest Baltimore, but the houses were frequently in ramshackle condition, with rotted floors and leaky roofs. They also lacked the simplest utilities such as piped running water.

The report of the housing investigator prompted a campaign to rewrite Baltimore's housing code. The Federation of Labor, the Maryland Association for the Prevention and Relief of Tuberculosis, and the women's groups joined with Federated Charities to obtain passage of a new code in 1908. The ordinance enlarged the scope of housing surveillance and increased the number of inspectors with some immediate results, but the code did not establish standards for one and two family homes, so that the deplorable conditions of the Negro alley homes remained unremedied.[66]

The final health reforms of this era concerned legislation for pure food and pure milk. An Osler-inspired pure milk bill, despite its failure to provide adequate enforcement provisions, began the doctor's efforts in 1894. Following the election of 1895, reform Mayor Hooper appointed experts to administer the health department. These health officials and their successors achieved a considerable reduction in the contamination of the reservoir, adulteration of milk, and unsanitary conditions of local slaughterhouses. Still more needed to be done to regulate the content and distribution of milk. In 1906 the State Board of Health sponsored a milk exhibit at The Johns Hopkins University, similar to the tuberculosis exhibit of two years earlier, to show the need for "stable to table" regulation. An infant cholera scare in the summer of 1907 stimulated additional public support for more rigid milk inspection which the health department introduced that fall. During the winter months, health officials drafted a comprehensive ordinance to regulate all dairies and farms doing business in Baltimore. The proposal

---

66. U.S. Bureau of Labor, *The Slums of Baltimore, Chicago, New York and Philadelphia* (Washington: G.P.O., 1894); Janet E. Kemp, *Housing Conditions in Baltimore* (Baltimore, 1907); Crooks, *Politics and Progress*, pp. 191-92.

provoked opposition from city councilmen representing small dairymen who feared being driven from business due to the added cost of meeting higher standards. Health officials claimed the standards were necessary and enlisted the support of the Federated Charities, the Arundell Club, and the Federation of Labor. Finally, even Democratic boss John J. "Sonny" Mahon endorsed the bill, and it became law. Despite its added restrictions, the new law still omitted provision for bacteriological inspection. This step, leading to the eventual pasteurization of all milk, finally came in 1912.[67]

The progressives' achievements in promoting public health and child welfare reforms were substantial, but incomplete. Yet they did stimulate a growing awareness that people in Baltimore were victimized by the physical and social environment in which they lived. The social Darwinian attitude of survival of the fittest and laissez-faire began to decline. As time went on, it became increasingly clear to Baltimore progressives that government had a responsibility for the health and welfare of the people.

The climax to the urban progressive reform in Baltimore came with the organization of the City-Wide Congress in March 1911, to discuss ways of furthering efficient government, city planning, and social reforms. Of the 132 groups that supported the congress, there were forty businessmen's associations, thirty-five neighborhood improvement associations, twenty-two welfare and reform groups, fourteen professional associations, a dozen or so fraternal organizations, plus governmental commissions and the Federation of Labor. Every white business group, improvement association and civic organization in Baltimore was represented.

The character of sponsoring agencies exemplified the evolving nature of Baltimore's urban progressive movement. Where earlier civic groups like the Reform League and Municipal Art Society were predominantly upper-class in membership, the sponsors of the congress more nearly represented a cross section of Baltimore. Old-line Baltimoreans continued to serve, but they shared direction with leaders from the middle class, organized labor, old and new immigrant groups. No vocational interest dominated. Businessmen composed almost half the or-

---

67. *Ibid.*, pp. 192-93.

ganizers, but they represented such diverse categories as bankers, large and small manufacturers, publishers, wholesalers, and retailers. Every white neighborhood from working class East Baltimore to the town houses on Bolton Hill and the new suburbs to the north was represented. Partisan politics were absent, as Democrats and Republicans, including the bosses, cooperated for the city's welfare. With the exception of Baltimore's Negroes, and a big exception it was, Baltimore progressivism by 1911 represented all segments of the community.

The three-day congress brought national standards of urban progressivism into comparison with reform achievements in Baltimore. There was very little sense of self-congratulation, but rather a look at from whence the progressives had come, and where they were going. Recent progress in public health, city planning, governmental reforms and social justice in its various forms were recognized as responses to the rapid growth, urbanization and industrialization of Baltimore. Much, however, remained to be done in all areas. Dr. J. Hall Pleasants, president of the Board of Supervisors of Baltimore City Charities, summed up one progressive viewpoint when he said: "We hear a great deal of emphasis laid upon a mere increase in a city's population, but most of us forget that these increases are really detrimental unless at the same time the condition of the individual in his relation to his surroundings is considered, and there is at least a corresponding increase in the health and happiness of the individual." Pleasants, who was from an old Maryland family and who taught at The Johns Hopkins Medical School, stressed society's responsibility for the physical environment. The city should provide for improved housing, better schools and more playgrounds, he said, as well as take care of the dependent classes. Above all, "the conditions giving rise to dependency must be wiped out of existence."

The congress produced a series of resolutions in behalf of complete city planning, home rule, civil service reform, street paving, more playgrounds and hospitals, water filtration, milk pasteurization, and tax reform, most of which were achieved in the following years.[68]

---

68. *Ibid.*, pp. 209-20; see also *Addresses, Delivered at the First Citywide Congress of Baltimore* (Baltimore, 1911) for the various speeches and comments.

The subsequent though not precipitant decline of the reform impulse following the city-wide congress was due in part to a resurgence of partisan politics. Partisan politics had been relatively subdued since the election of Mayor Hayes in 1899. Four years later, when Hayes sought to build an organization to perpetuate himself in office, reformers proposed and the Democratic organization accepted the candidacy of Robert C. McLane. When he died suddenly in the spring of 1904, his Republican successor, E. Clay Timanus, worked closely with and even brought additional reformers into the city administration. Hayes, McLane, and Timanus were what one historian calls "structural reformers," seeking the modernization of city government and responding particularly with new approaches to more effective government such as city planning or systematic, efficient administration. In contrast, Barry Mahool, the mayor elected in 1907, was also a social reformer. His selection by the organization, some of the reformers, and the establishment reflected partly the shifting attitudes towards reform and also opposition to George Stewart Brown, a more radical reformer concerned about municipal ownership and higher taxation of public utilities. Mahool's election led to legislation establishing a public utilities commission, charter revision, plans for a civic center and South Baltimore renewal, increased funds for recreation, the building of a quarantine hospital, new tenement regulation, more rigid food inspection, an eight-hour day at a two-dollar minimum wage for municipal employees, and a city tuberculosis commission. Progressives urged his reelection in 1911.[69]

The Democratic organization in Baltimore, meanwhile, was undergoing change. From the distant autocratic rule of boss Rasin, who died in 1907, power shifted to John J. "Sonny" Mahon, an affable and generous son of Irish immigrants. Mahon was a shrewd politician who responded to the shifting tides of public opinion. In 1911 he backed James H. Preston for mayor. Preston was a popular, long-time member of the organization who was also progressive in supporting a new charter, city planning, and public health reform. Mahon's move split the

---

69. Crooks, *Politics and Progress*, pp. 102-94, *passim*. The structural reform-social reform dichotomy is explained in Melvin G. Holli; *Reform in Detroit; Hazen S. Pingree and Urban Politics* (New York: Oxford University Press, 1969), pp. 157-81.

reformers down the middle. Veteran critics of the organization such as Grasty and Bonaparte, who remembered Preston's mediocre record before 1900 as a member of the House of Delegates and of the police board, vehemently opposed his nomination. Yet Democrats seeking reform from within the party backed him, as did the united party organization in all but the silk-stocking wards. Preston beat Mahool in the primary by a three to two majority. In the mayoral election Preston faced former Mayor Clay Timanus. Again reformers split, and Preston edged his Republican opponent by 699 votes out of 96,330 ballots counted.[70]

In office, Preston showed the extent to which the Democratic machine had changed. Mahon still controlled patronage in appointments, but the Democrats he selected were qualified for their jobs. Preston was a party man, but he was also determined to provide efficient, honest government. Mahon agreed, and for eight years the two men ran city government and politics in tandem.

Preston's major accomplishments were administrative. He was a doer. During his tenure, he completed smooth paving of the previously predominantly cobblestone city streets; he completed the sewage system, a water filtration plant at Montebello, Loch Raven Reservoir, Jones Fallsway, Key Highway, Preston Gardens along downtown St. Paul Street, nine new schools (including the Polytechnic Institute), and harbor renewal. World War I postponed the completion of the civic center east of city hall, but land was acquired. Preston's administration secured the expansion of the city limits by annexing sixty-two square miles of Baltimore and Anne Arundel Counties. Preston obtained charter amendments to provide for the civil service reform and unicameral council that his predecessors could not get. He also began the first city symphony in the United States and adopted a city flag. Progress was made toward home rule in city government, but the General Assembly blocked complete autonomy, as it blocked representation proportionate to the city's population in the legislature.[71]

70. Crooks, *Politics and Progress*, 212n; and *Sun Almanac for 1912*, pp. 36, 45. For a slightly cynical view, see H. L. Mencken, *Heathen Days* (New York: A. A. Knopf, 1955), pp. 107-18, *passim*.

71. See the "Mayor's Message" in the Annual *Reports* of Baltimore for 1911, 1912, 1913, 1914, 1915, 1918; and *The Municipal Journal* (Baltimore, 1913–1919).

In all of these reforms, Preston was largely a structural reformer seeking to modernize the city with good roads, modern harbors and sufficient schools to meet population needs. Annexation was an attempt to expand the city's control over the suburbanites in the metropolitan area in order to prevent the balkanization of the region into many small, noncooperating, autonomous units, as would occur in the years following World War I. Preston supported planned metropolitan development as the citywide congress recommended in 1913. He also believed in adequate representation in the General Assembly in order to govern more effectively.

Preston's accomplishments in his first term virtually guaranteed his reelection in 1915. Skeptical reformers came around to his support, and former opponents like Barry Mahool, Dr. Welch, and former Governor Warfield endorsed his candidacy. He was not challenged in the primary and beat his Republican opponent easily in the mayoral election.

On the debit side of his record, Preston endorsed the West ordinance, passed in 1911, which wrote racial housing segregation into law. Democrats saw it as a progressive measure "for preserving peace, preventing conflict . . . and promoting the general welfare of the city." Critics saw it as not only restricting the growing black population to their already overcrowded ghetto, but also as a deprivation of property rights without due process. It was on the latter grounds that the Maryland Court of Appeals—and subsequently the Supreme Court—declared it unconstitutional.[72]

Preston also politicized the Baltimore school system after a decade of nonpartisan progress. He responded in part to the complaints of the Public School Teachers Association, which opposed the reforms of Superintendent Van Sickle. The superintendent had fired teachers he considered to be unfit and had begun supervision of instruction. Merit rating was particularly unpopular, as was enforced retirement at age sixty-five; but Van Sickle argued that his goal was professionalism for quality education. He had introduced special education, manual training, home economics, school building, and health inspections. He argued for tailoring instruction to the individual child, and recommended reading groups in the elementary grades. Parents complained about academic frills, as did business men about

---

72. Baltimore *Sun*, April 28, 1911; *The Municipal Journal*, October 24, 1913.

new styles of penmanship. By the time of Preston's primary fight in 1911, the conflict had spread beyond the bounds of the school system to the city council, where the politicians backed the teachers and the older progressives supported Van Sickle.[73]

When Preston won the mayoralty, he quickly arranged for Van Sickle's dismissal, justifying his actions in terms of restoring harmony to the system. For most Baltimoreans, it was a popular move, but educational standards were undoubtedly weakened and future progress delayed. The reconciliation of quality education with democratic rule remained to be solved.

As a strong mayor, Preston tended also to be a bulldozer. He got things done, but frequently ran roughshod over people in the process. This happened in the Van Sickle dismissal, when Preston refused to wait for a report on the schools by the United States Office of Education, which was then in progress. It happened when he ignored the law in seeking to transfer park funds to the school system, and when during his second term he continued building Preston Gardens and renovating the Washington Monument area despite a plea to conserve funds and resources for the war effort.

Preston ran for a third term in 1919 at the urging of Mahon. His opponent was George Weems Williams, former head of the park board. Williams criticized the mayor's handling of park funds, his domineering approach to administration, and his politicization of the school system. Most progressives backed Williams, as did East Baltimore boss, Frank Kelley, who was challenging Mahon's authority in the Democratic organization. Williams won the primary, but lost the mayoral election to Republican William Broening, a popular politician who may have had Mahon's support as well as that of his own party. The postwar return to normalcy doubtless hurt the Democratic candidate, too.[74]

For Baltimoreans, the election of a Republican in 1919 appeared to end an era. Democrats had been elected to office continually since 1899, and generally had been reform-minded. Upon closer scrutiny, however, the picture becomes more complicated. In terms of modernizing the city in response to urban

---

73. Strayer, "The Baltimore School Situation," pp. 325-45; and James, "A Twelve Year Fight for School Reform," pp. 118-24.

74. Clippings from the George Weems Williams scrapbooks on deposit at the M.H.S.

change, the process continued into the 1920's. The annexation of the suburbs required urban services of water, roads, sewers, police, and fire protection. The first civic center was built and zoning eventually passed. Civil service reform and the unicameral council went into effect. Responding to urban change was a continuing process of city government which the progressive era began but did not end. Eventually, suburbs like Towson blocked further annexation, and state legislatures blocked adequate tax powers and representation disrupting the process. The gap between urbanization and governmental response widened more rapidly with regard to social reform than to structural ones. Urban progressivism in terms of social reform lost its impetus at city hall when Preston split the progressives and beat Mahool in the 1911 primaries. Yet, though Mahool was more advanced in his views than Preston, he was less effective with the voters, city council, and state legislators. Social reform groups continued to agitate issues into the second decade of the twentieth century, recommending housing, health, educational, and child welfare advances. Some were implemented; others were not; and the schools apparently regressed.

In addition, the war distracted people's attention from reform issues, while the migration of factory workers to Baltimore aggravated problems of overcrowded housing among the working class. Throughout, black Baltimoreans received short shrift from the city government and the reformers. Baltimore's urban progressivism, like progressivism elsewhere, was racist and primarily for whites. Yet given these substantial limitations, the era saw impressive gains structurally as well as limitations upon child labor, the abolition of sweatshops, provision for recreational facilities, improved juvenile justice, raised health standards for food and water, and a decreased rate of tuberculosis. Further innovations were clearly needed in terms of social security, health care, housing, and working conditions; but compared to the decades preceding, urban change from 1890 to 1920 was substantially progressive.

## 5

## STATE PROGRESSIVISM, 1907–1919

State progressivism, in contrast to urban progressivism, was less dynamic in Maryland, partly because so many of the social problems were urban in character, and partly because state government was either powerless or reluctant to challenge the politico-economic power structure that opposed increased taxation and close corporate regulation. In addition, boss rule undermined representative government in the Democratic party until Gorman's death. The party's ofttimes conflicting, rural-urban coalition of support from farmers, business men, and workers also slowed necessary progress. Perhaps most important, Marylanders from the counties who were involved in the political process tended to be conservative in outlook —supporting limited, frugal government, minimal tampering with the free enterprise system, white supremacy, and maintenance of the status quo. Their horizons were limited and their trust in their party leaders occasionally naive.

Still, progressivism came to Maryland, slowly at first, but substantially over the long haul, not only in the area of modernizing state government, but also in terms of economic, social, and political reform.

Following the defeat of the Gorman-Rasin machine in 1895, the Lowndes administration secured a number of laws modernizing state and local government. As already noted, the General Assembly passed an election reform bill and a new charter for Baltimore City. In addition, the legislature in 1896 established a Geological and Economic Survey to investigate more fully the potential for development of the state's natural resources. It enlarged the Supreme Bench in Baltimore City by adding a judge to relieve overcrowded court dockets, and it created an immigration commission to recruit new settlers to the state. On the advice of Dr. Welch, Governor Lowndes appointed Dr. John S. Fulton to be executive secretary of the State Board of Health. He, in turn, organized the Maryland Public Health Association in 1897.[75]

Following the election of John Walter Smith as governor in 1899, the reform impetus subsided. The General Assembly in 1900 did authorize a token increase in Baltimore City's legislative representation from three to four senators (out of twenty-seven), and from eighteen to twenty-four delegates (out of 101). It also reorganized the police board by shifting the appointive power from the legislature to the governor, although, given

75. Hall, ed., *Baltimore*, I, 297.

Smith's loyalty to the Gorman machine, this may not have been a step forward.

The 1901 special session was a backward step, with its so-called election law reform to disfranchise illiterate voters. The election that fall was a reaction against the special session and resulted in the selection of a reform-minded Republican majority in the House of Delegates, along with a reform nucleus in the Senate.

As a result, the 1902 session of the General Assembly saw the first substantial progressive legislation. The House of Delegates under the leadership of reform Democrat Isaac Lobe Straus, in cooperation with Republicans, passed the compulsory education, juvenile court, and child labor laws on a local basis, as already mentioned. They also secured a direct primary law for Baltimore City and supported the creation of a statewide tuberculosis commission.

Working closely with the house reformers was the Baltimore delegation in the Senate led by Jacob Moses, which secured passage of the factory inspection act to regulate Baltimore sweatshops as well as a law to permit women lawyers to practice in Maryland. In addition, there was the remarkable little state senator from Allegany County by the name of David J. Lewis, a lawyer who had been born into poverty. He began to work in the coal mines at the age of nine, never attending school. He was taught to read at home by his mother until she died when he was twelve. Despite these handicaps, Lewis was able by age seventeen to begin reading law and subsequently pass the state bar examination. He later was both corporation counsel for the B&O Railroad in Cumberland and attorney for the United Mine Workers.[76]

Elected to the state Senate in 1901, Lewis made sure that the compulsory education, direct primary, and child labor laws secured by the Baltimore delegation were applied also to Allegany County as local legislation. In addition, he secured a mine inspection act for Allegany County as well as the nation's first workmen's compensation law to replace the hodgepodge of common law interpretations concerning employer liability for

---

76. Thomas D. Masterson, S. J., "The Formation of a Progressive; the Early Career of David J. Lewis of Maryland" (M.A. thesis, Georgetown University, 1969).

industrial accidents that the courts too frequently decided against the worker.

The law, though subsequently struck down by the courts on a technicality, was desperately needed. An estimated 500,000 workers were killed or injured each year in the United States, and liability was difficult to prove. Lewis' bill, based on English and German precedents, covered mine, streetcar, railroad, and construction workers. It created a systematic program of compensation under state administration without regard to negligence. Later it was passed again in the 1910 General Assembly on a voluntary basis and made compulsory in 1914. Meanwhile, Lewis went on to the House of Representatives, by which time he was a leading proponent of the Federal Workmen's Compensation Law that was passed in 1912.

The accomplishments of the 1902 General Assembly were substantial, but the pace slowed again with the return of a three-fifths Democratic majority following the election of 1903. The new governor, Edwin Warfield, had good intentions, particularly about insuring that Baltimore's program of planned public improvements would not get further enmeshed in partisan politics. But generally, governors in this era did not yet provide legislative leadership. Instead, the General Assembly looked to its own leadership under the still potent domination of the Gorman-Rasin machine. The result was the Poe Amendment to disfranchise black voters. Also passed as local legislation was authorization for Baltimore's public works program and a limited reorganization of the state Department of Education.

Following the defeat of the Poe Amendment in 1905, the General Assembly the succeeding year authorized construction of the state's first tuberculosis sanitarium in western Maryland and passed registration laws for tuberculars that became models for similar laws enacted in other states. The legislation also tightened the child labor law providing sufficient personnel for its enforcement and passed the first in a series of major oyster conservation bills to regulate development of the major natural resource in the Chesapeake Bay.

A significant breakthrough for progressive reform came after the death of Gorman in 1906 and of Rasin the following year. Prior to that time, Democratic party control had been centralized largely in the bosses' hands, and reforms came as a result of dissident Democrats working with Republicans. Following the bosses' deaths, no one man could take their place. The result was a factionalism which worked to the advantage of Democratic progressives pushing reforms from within their party. Their help in electing Governor Austin L. Crothers in 1907, and their efforts in the General Assembly afterwards, produced the second major round of reform activity that lasted until the eve of World War I. It also helped to implement an informal direct election of a United States senator in 1907, which the General Assembly subsequently ratified, six years before a constitutional amendment formally shifted the power from the State House to the people.[77]

The 1908 term of the General Assembly started slowly with what the Democrats considered to be two political reforms: the Corrupt Practices Act to limit and publicize campaign spending, and the Straus amendment to disfranchise black voters again. This time, however, there was little concern about the party organization seeking monopolistic control. Instead, it was clearly a white racist amendment seeking to "purify" the electorate. Requirements included the perennial grandfather clause, special provision for naturalized immigrants, an educational requirement and a $500 property requirement. Frank Kent of the Baltimore *Sun* called it "as fair a proposition of the kind as has ever been presented," but opposition once again organized to defeat it.[78]

Reform Leaguers repeated their argument that the grandfather clause was unconstitutional and in addition that the educational clause was unreasonable. One had to write the full name of the President of the United States, one justice of the Supreme Court, the governor of Maryland, one judge of the Maryland Court of Appeals, and one's mayor or chairman of the local board of county supervisors. Who could remember the middle name of Governor Austin L. Crothers?

Cardinal Gibbons declared his opposition to the amendment: "I do not believe the Negro should be disfranchised solely on the ground of color." Property and educational qualifications were permissible, he added, provided they were applied to blacks and whites alike. Subsequently, numerous priests at-

77. Crooks, *Politics and Progress*, p. 52.
78. *Ibid.*, pp. 64-70; also Kent, *Maryland Politics*, p. 42.

tacked the amendment from the pulpit as contrary to brotherly love, and so did a number of Protestant clergymen.[79]

The amendment attempted to provide for the foreign-born voter, but Reform League counsel John Rose concluded that immigrants not yet naturalized and future immigrants would have to pass either the educational or property test. Karl Scholtz of the German-American Independent Citizens Union argued that to vote for the amendment would mean for the foreign-born "giving up an assured right for an uncertainty." The American League of Foreign-Born Citizens, claiming 8,600 members in Baltimore from twelve different nationalities, resolved against the amendment, as did smaller groups of Jews, Italians, Poles and Lithuanians.[80]

The Colored Men's Suffrage League, having protested passage of the amendment in the General Assembly, registered black voters and passed out sample ballots in Baltimore. The *Afro-American Ledger* bitterly attacked advocates of the amendment. Despite racial discrimination, prejudice, humiliation and abuse, wrote one editorial writer, the Maryland Negro in forty years had eradicated 65 per cent of his illiteracy and accumulated property amounting to between five and six million dollars. "What would have been his condition had he had an open field with no discrimination . . .? " The *Afro* did not oppose educational or property qualifications provided they applied to whites and blacks alike.[81]

The election referendum in 1909 resulted in the second defeat of the disfranchising amendment. Again the foreign-born, especially the new Russian and Italian immigrants, voted with the Republicans, both blacks and whites, and with reform Democrats. The margin was less than the one against the Poe amendment, but still sufficient to maintain the two-party system and the Negro franchise in Maryland.[82]

Following the defeat of the Straus amendment in 1909, the General Assembly the next year passed the greatest amount of

---

79. Baltimore *Sun*, January 28, 1909.

80. Baltimore *American*, September 28, 1909; Baltimore *Star*, September 17, 1909; and Baltimore *American*, September 23, October 5, November, 1909.

81. *Afro-American Ledger*, December 12, 1908, September 11, October 23, 30, 1909.

82. *Sun Almanac* (Baltimore, 1910), pp. 117-160; and Crooks, *Politics and Progress*, p. 70.

progressive legislation since 1902. For the first time, the intiative came from the governor, who, working at his office full time, spoke out forcefully in behalf of a public service commission to regulate public utilities, supported workmen's compensation, and demanded that party regulars vote for a statewide direct primary or be read out of the party.[83]

The creation of the public service commission, like workmen's compensation, was a major challenge to the unlimited powers of a few major corporations. Maryland progressives had been agitating the issue on and off since the early 1890's. Grasty was one of the first to speak out. His views were largely pragmatic and probably typical of the later progressive position. He criticized the overcapitalization, exorbitant rates, and uneven gas pressures provided by the Consolidated Gas Company. Although competition was the usual relief from high prices or poor service, Grasty saw it as an impossible solution with public utilities. Competition in the distribution of gas meant that rival companies would be tearing up city streets to lay mains. Temporary rate wars were followed by consolidations and then high rates to recoup profits lost during the competitive phase. If competition was impossible, so was unregulated monopoly, which was responsible for the existing unsatisfactory situation. Grasty looked with misgivings to the European successes in municipal ownership. Americans were too familiar with municipal graft and inefficiency in New York, Philadelphia, and elsewhere to accept municipal ownership as a panacea. In Baltimore, the water department worked efficiently under municipal ownership, but the municipal street cleaning operation and the city's markets were ineptly managed. There was no guarantee that municipal ownership of utilities might not be similarly mismanaged. Municipal ownership, concluded Grasty, was dependent upon good government.[84]

The same kind of reasoning was applied to proposals for state regulation of the utilities. Theoretically, the state always held the power of regulation, but too frequently in the past politicians had used this power to propose confiscatory rate legislation in order to extort money from the corporations for them-

---

83. *Ibid.*, pp. 74-75.
84. *Ibid.*, pp. 110-21, *passim.*

selves or their party. Also, the utilities, by various means of persuasion, used the city and state legislatures for their own ends to reduce taxes, increase rates, or extend franchises. Again, in the minds of reformers, good government had to precede either municipal ownership or regulation.

On the basis of this reasoning, reformers initially concentrated on achieving good government as a prerequisite to owning or regulating the public utilities. After the defeat of the Gorman-Rasin machine in 1895, reformers over the next ten years introduced a series of bills to regulate or authorize ownership of utilities. None passed on a statewide basis, though a small municipal lighting plant for park use was built in Baltimore, which resulted subsequently in a 50 per cent reduction in electricity rates there. Public opinion was quiet on the issue, and reform efforts, confronted by utility lobbyists in Annapolis, made little headway.

A change in attitudes occurred in the summer of 1908 after a grand jury examined complaints from users of electric power. That September, it charged that the Consolidated Gas Company, which had combined gas and electricity distribution into an unregulated monopoly in 1906, was extorting increased electricity rates from Baltimore consumers. In its report, the grand jury recommended a commission to regulate all public utilities.

At Annapolis, Governor Crothers began to study the problem. Prior to the state political conventions the following August, Crothers announced his support for utility regulation and proposed it as a plank in the party's platform. The Democrats adopted the proposal, and, not to be outdone, the Republicans did likewise. After the election, Attorney General Straus drafted a bill based on the Wisconsin law creating a public service commission with powers to set rates, investigate conditions, and subpoena witnesses, books and papers. Public opinion mobilized in behalf of the bill, including even the Merchants and Manufacturers Association. Consolidated Gas fought the measure, even to the point of hiring the son-in-law of Senator John Walter Smith, Gorman's successor as the head of the state organization, to fight the bill. But the combined pressure of public opinion and Governor Crothers proved sufficient, and on the last day of the session, the General Assembly passed the bill creating the commission.[85]

---

85. *Ibid.*, see also Baltimore *Sun*, February 15-27, 1910, *passim*.

Maryland was not in the forefront of this movement nationwide as it had been with workmen's compensation and the fight
against tuberculosis; but it was not a laggard either. The New
Jersey legislature enacted utility regulation the same year as
Maryland, but its law was introduced by the utility corporations
to forestall effective legislation, which came during the administration of Governor Woodrow Wilson in 1911.

In addition to his triumph for utility regulation, Governor
Crothers also secured passage of a $6 million appropriation for
good roads, a first step toward paving, widening, and extending
Maryland highways to accommodate the increasing use of au-
tomobiles. The General Assembly also passed legislation authorizing construction of Baltimore's civic center, a comprehensive pure food law, provision for state care of the insane, and a
strengthening of the powers of the State Board of Health.

Progress, however, was limited. The statewide direct primary
was flawed by the unit rule in convention, and workmen's compensation was limited to miners. Despite the hostility of county
legislators, a delegation from Baltimore's Just Representation
League did achieve a constitutional amendment increasing
Baltimore's legislative delegation, adding two senators and six
delegates, only to see it soundly defeated in a 1911 referendum
by county voters. Charter revision for Baltimore also was defeated on partisan grounds, as were bills for woman's suffrage
and statewide local option. Overall, though, the accomplishments of the Crothers administration brought Maryland into the
mainstream of American progressivism on the state level.[86]

In the 1911 gubernatorial race, Crothers was not a candidate
for reelection, perhaps because of his accomplishments. He had
made too many party organization and corporate enemies in the
process of achieving progressive legislation. In his stead, State
Senator Blair Lee of Montgomery County represented the reformers and contested with the organization's candidate, Arthur
Pue Gorman, Jr., of Howard County. The conflict was similar to
the Baltimore City primary of the same year. The organization
candidate took progressive positions on statewide issues and
moderates stayed with the organization, resulting in Gorman's
victory. But the Gorman name was still anathema to many voters, and combined with a minor election scandal in Baltimore,
served to persuade sufficient reformers once again to switch

---

86. Andrews, *History of Maryland*, pp. 610-12.

parties and elect Phillips Lee Goldsborough of Cambridge to be the first Republican governor since Lloyd Lowndes. Again the strength of the two-party system and the Negro vote maintained a healthy balance in Maryland politics, a balance lacking in states to the south.

Goldsborough's administration continued the progressive legislation of its precedessor, but continued some of its limitations as well. The General Assembly in 1912 enacted legislation for presidential primaries, made the child labor law statewide in coverage, passed a statewide compulsory education law, limited the workday to ten hours for women, continued road building, provided funds for the care of the indigent insane, and expanded programs of oyster conservation. At the same time it also emasculated Baltimore City's charter revisions which Governor Goldsborough subsequently vetoed, and limited expansion of workmen's compensation by making coverage voluntary rather than compulsory for Maryland employers.[87]

In the biennial session of 1914, the General Assembly continued its progressive ways, passing a home rule amendment for Baltimore and the counties, providing that 10,000 or 20 per cent of the voters initiated it by petition. It was subsequently defeated, however, in an election referendum. The General Assembly also authorized a survey of Maryland's schools to determine what measures were necessary to improve the caliber of statewide education; it instituted penal reforms by creating advisory boards of parole and prison administration in order to run the state's prisons on a more humane and scientific basis; it authorized the referendum procedure for voters to ratify state legislation (as well as constitutional amendments); it directed the State Board of Health to push forward in the areas of sanitation and health conservation; it created a state tax commission to rationalize the tax system in the interests of equity and uniformity; and it finally passed a compulsory statewide workmen's compensation bill approved by the state Federation of Labor, the fulfillment of David J. Lewis' efforts of a dozen years before. The moderately progressive Baltimore *Sun* praised the General Assembly for its nonpartisan and capable work.[88]

---

87. Baltimore *Sun*, April 2, 3, 1912.
88. *Ibid.*, April 5, 6, 1914.

In addition to these legislative accomplishments, Governor Goldsborough appointed the Goodnow Commission, under the direction of President Frank J. Goodnow of The Johns Hopkins University, to examine governmental operations and recommend changes that would increase administrative efficiency and economy. He also appointed a County Life Commission to investigate rural conditions and make recommendations.

The Republican administration of Governor Goldsborough was probably the climax of progressivism in Maryland. His successor, Emerson C. Harrington, a Democrat from the Eastern Shore who was elected in 1915 by a narrow margin in a straight party contest, provided relatively weak executive leadership in an administration that came to be dominated by its attorney-general, Albert C. Ritchie of Baltimore.[89]

Ritchie was a striking figure, a handsome bachelor, scion of an old Virginia-Maryland family, and a graduate from Johns Hopkins and the University of Maryland Law School. After practicing briefly with a prestigious Baltimore firm, he entered public service, first in the city solicitor's office and then as a counsel for the Public Service Commission. In both offices he got on well with both reform and organization Democrats. In 1912 Ritchie was appointed People's Counsel on the Public Service Commission. Two years later he successfully sued the Consolidated Gas Company to reduce rates from 90 cents to 80 cents per 1000 cubic feet. Ritchie also received credit for pressing a private suit against the company that same year to improve the quality of its product.[90]

In the spring of 1915, Ritchie announced his candidacy for attorney general. Although he supported a variety of reforms, his main concern was for administration. "It should be the task of our next administration," he announced, "not so much to enact laws as to direct the intelligent administration of the laws we have."[91] In the primaries, Ritchie beat his opponent handily, while Harrington barely nosed out Blair Lee for the gubernatorial nomination. In November, Ritchie ran ahead of his ticket as the Democrats won. As attorney general, he revamped the state's legal services and supported the legislature's efforts

89. *Ibid.*, April 4, 1916.

90. *Ibid.*, March 24, 1915; *Labor Leader*, August 7, 1915; see also extensive scrapbook clippings in the Albert C. Ritchie Papers on deposit in the M.H.S.

91. Baltimore *Sun*, March 24, 1915.

in 1916 to establish a budget system, implement governmental reorganization on the basis of the Goodnow Commission's report, and carry out the results of the educational survey to bring county schools up to professional standards. Clearly in contrast to the governor, who equivocated on annexation for Baltimore City and who criticized the Goodnow Commission on partisan grounds for having too many Republicans on it, Ritchie appeared to be both progressive and forceful. He was also popular with many Marylanders for his forthright stand opposing prohibition and woman's suffrage.

The popularity of Ritchie's prohibition stand was perhaps a surprising one in a state in which most of the counties were already dry and in which a formidable alliance of Woman's Christian Temperance Unioners, Anti-Saloon Leaguers, and Protestant churchmen had been pressing the issue for a generation. Their goal was local option, a reasonably democratic approach whereby voters in each county could determine whether to make their area wet or dry. In 1910 they had almost succeeded in persuading the General Assembly. In 1916 the legislature passed a local option bill subject to a referendum the following year. The campaign was a lively one, with temperance folk holding rallies in Frederick and Hagerstown as well as a major rain-soaked parade in Baltimore the Saturday preceding the election. Even the Baltimore *Sun* conceded much of the justice of their cause when they quoted statistics showing the correlation of alcoholism with homelessness and poverty. The *Sun*'s self-interested editorial solution, however, was to keep Baltimore wet and vote the counties dry. The election returns gave an almost three-to-one majority for the wets in Baltimore while Allegany, Baltimore, sections of Anne Arundel including Annapolis and Prince George's Counties also voted for "demon rum." Frederick, Washington and Carroll Counties joined the already dry Eastern Shore and southern Maryland counties. A year later, the county-dominated General Assembly ratified the Eighteenth Amendment that imposed prohibition on the entire state.[92]

Unlike prohibition, woman's suffrage was never taken seriously by most Marylanders. Beginning in 1910, suffragists lobbied for the ballot at each legislative session and were blocked

---

92. Baltimore *News*, October 20, 28, November 5, 10, 1916; Baltimore *Sun*, October 9, 1916; and Baltimore *Evening Sun*, October 13, 1916.

every time. They cornered candidates for office and most (Barry Mahool was an exception) rejected their support. Opposition to woman's suffrage was put on both racist and sexist grounds. Governor Harrington opposed it for fear that the black woman's vote could not be controlled by the Democrats. Others thought that politics was the work of men and a woman's place was in the home. When the Nineteenth Amendment was submitted to the 1918 General Assembly, the legislators rejected it. Ritchie had substantial support for his stand against women voting.[93]

The declaration of war in April 1917 prompted Governor Harrington to call a special session of the General Assembly to establish a Maryland Council of Defense, authorize the construction of Camp Meade in Anne Arundel County, and enact a compulsory work law. Apparently state officials overlooked the draconian implications of the last bill in their zeal to ensure total mobilization in the war effort.

At the 1918 legislative session, Ritchie recommended absentee ballots for soldiers and sailors, annexation for Baltimore City, a state legislative reference bureau, and further prison reforms, including the abolition of contract labor, a major progressive concern in most southern states.

In June, Ritchie took a leave of absence from the attorney general's office to become chief counsel for the War Industries Board in Washington, but was back in Annapolis by December, after the Armistice. His campaign for governor in 1919 was virtually a foregone conclusion. He had become the leading Democrat on the Maryland scene, and his record as attorney general was acceptable to both progressives and conservatives. His nomination was uncontested, and his election victory over Harry Nice by 165 votes out of 106,000 cast was a personal triumph in a year of strikes, inflation, and a general shift to normalcy and Republican rule.[94]

Nationwide, the progressive era was clearly over. Yet Ritchie's campaign showed that a moderate supporting civil service reform, road building, financial aid to oystermen, increased salaries for teachers and police, scientific aid to agriculture, further governmental reorganization, and support of Wilson and the League of Nations could still win on the state level

93. *Ibid.*, July 25, 1916.
94. Baltimore *Sun*, June 3, 24, December 24, 1918, May 19, July 24, and November 6, 1919.

and provide a basis for continuing structural reforms that might modernize state government through the 1920's.

But progress was limited, particularly in the areas of social and economic justice. Ritchie still opposed woman's suffrage and prohibition, and never would enforce the latter. There was little inclination to redistribute income in the interests of the poor, despite a small inheritance tax passed in 1916. Appropriations for education, public health, and welfare remained far below need. Yet the reaction to the accumulated reforms of the progressive era that year was much less in Maryland than on the national scene. Perhaps there was less of a backlash because of the conservatism of Maryland progressivism. Its response to urban industrial change was determined by a predominantly rural legislature only partially affected by the changes. This rural character was fundamental to these limitations. Its achievements were due largely to the maintenance of the two-party system in which reform Democrats could join with black and white Republican voters periodically to choose legislators who would respond to change. Given the rural, racist, and conservative domination of the Democratic party organization, reforms were limited and often dependent upon Republican victories. In Maryland, the Republicans became generally the party of progress, aided by a minority of reform Democrats. Their achievements enabled state government, first of all, to modernize its administration, to a lesser extent provide Baltimore with authorization to meet its most immediate needs, and, finally, to begin to reshape the notion of state government as responsible for the political, economic, and social welfare of its peoples. Recent criticism of American progressivism rightly shows the substantial limitations to its reforms, but ignores the distance travelled from what went before. In the continuity of history, Maryland progressives brought substantial though not sufficient change to the government's role in state affairs.

6

SIGNIFICANCE OF MARYLAND PROGRESSIVISM

Compared with other states, Maryland was in the mainstream but not the forefront of progressive change. Perhaps if the impetus of the 1902 legislature had not been undercut by the resurgence of the Democratic organization in 1903, Maryland would have been a national leader of reform. Certainly the workmen's compensation law and urban reforms concerned with juvenile courts, factory inspection, and direct primaries ranked with the early innovations in Wisconsin and the South. But as politics developed in the Free State, the bulk of progressive reform from 1910 through 1914 paralleled legislative action in California, Colorado, Ohio, and New Jersey.

The origins of reform were pluralistic. A major factor in Maryland was the influence of The Johns Hopkins University and the Medical School, an influence comparable to that of another great university upon the progressive reforms achieved by Robert M. LaFollette in Wisconsin. The Maryland connection, however, was on a more informal basis. Not only were President Gilman and Doctors Welch and Osler early leaders of the movement, but in the decades of the 1880's and 1890's, the university had a significant educational impact upon a generation of graduates, many of whom became progressives. The influence of Richard Ely teaching economics, Herbert Baxter Adams in history, and Woodrow Wilson lecturing on the possibilities of municipal government is impossible to measure. Yet a substantial number of graduates like Theodore Marburg, Jacob Moses, Isaac Lobe Straus, Albert Ritchie, Jeffrey Brackett, George Stewart Brown, Eli Frank, Jacob Hollander, William Maltbie, and J. Hall Pleasants had a significant influence upon progressive reform.[95]

The press, particularly Grasty's Baltimore *News*, played an important role in both exposing urban and state problems, as well as in educating public opinion. Its influence was comparable to Pulitzer's New York *World* and Nelson's Kansas City *Star*, as Grasty hoped it would be. Similarly the churches and synagogues contributed to the reform-mindedness of the progressive era, expanding the social gospel beyond the traditional Protestant character seen elsewhere.

Equally important, such events and experiences of the era as the depression, the rigors of the coal country in the west, the muck-raking and reform politics on the national scene, and the growing realization of urban conditions deepened the realization that both city and state must respond in terms of enlightened social, political, and economic self-interest.

---

95. Crooks, *Politics and Progress*, p. 203.

Progressivism's accomplishments were substantial though limited. In enacting political reforms ranging from the direct primary and direct election of United States senators to the initiative, referendum, and Corrupt Practices Act, it still fell short on woman's suffrage. To Maryland's credit, blacks were not disfranchised as in the states to the south, but it was tried. On economic grounds, public utility corporations were regulated by the Public Service Commission. Banks and insurance companies, however, were not. The railroads also continued without consistent control, though the Interstate Commerce Commission operated nationally, and periodically the General Assembly imposed controls and closed tax loopholes. Economic reform was doubtless the least consequential because of the substantial influence of big business as well as the conservative temper of the reformers. Social reforms, however, were significant. Included were standards set for food, schools, factories, prisons, child labor, and hours for women. Outside of Baltimore, however, there were no wage and hour laws. In addition, tentative steps were taken toward taxing inheritances, providing aid to mothers with dependent children, conserving natural resources, and combatting the dread disease of tuberculosis. Perhaps most far-reaching in terms of changes brought about were the administrative reforms which not only made government more efficient, but also brought to the state the responsibility to act on behalf of the welfare of its citizenry. Remnants of governmental frugality remained, but Ritchie in 1920 was a substantial improvement over his post-Reconstruction predecessors in conceiving of the role of government as one that stressed responsibility for roads, schools, public health, and conservation. In comparison with what needed to be done for Maryland to become truly a just society, the gap continued to remain immense. In comparison with what went before, Maryland progressives could take some satisfaction in things accomplished.

Maryland's role on the national scene during this era was not an important one. Gorman was the state's most prominent national political figure because of his long tenure in the Senate, his successful management of Grover Cleveland's presidential victory in 1884, and his undercutting of the free trade principles in the Wilson-Gorman tariff of 1894. The other United States senators were a relatively insignificant group either in ability or

because their tenures of office were too short. Textile manufacturer James A. Gary was briefly Postmaster General in President McKinley's administration; he contributed little of lasting
importance. The two most important progressives on the national scene were the patrician, Charles Bonaparte, and the
mineworker, David Lewis. Bonaparte, as secretary of the navy
and attorney general in Roosevelt's cabinet, played a part in the
President's limited trust-busting program. He also helped to
organize the Civil Service Reform League in 1881 as well as the
Progressive party in 1912. Lewis in the House of Representatives sponsored the Parcel Post Act that was passed during
Taft's administration and supported a range of progressive bills
during the Wilson administration. Theodore Marburg was a
member of the National Civic Federation and worked actively
in the National Society for Judicial Settlement of International
Disputes before World War I. President Taft appointed him
minister to Belgium in 1913. During the war, the Wilson administration appointed Maryland progressives to national posts,
Ritchie the most prominent among them. Maryland's political
leaders did not make a big splash on the national scene.[96]

The record of Maryland's voters in national elections was
generally a conservative one; in each presidential election from
the end of Reconstruction to 1896 a majority of them voted
Democratic. In the latter year substantial numbers of Gold
Democrats crossed party lines (the precedent had been set in
the gubernatorial election of 1895) to vote for McKinley over
Bryan. The pattern held four years later. In 1904 and 1908, the
vote was extremely close. Alton B. Parker, the Democratic
nominee, won in 1904 seven of eight electoral votes, but the top
individual vote getter was Roosevelt's number one elector,
Bonaparte. In 1908 Bryan won six of eight electoral votes, but
again, if one tabulated the ballots of the highest elector on each
ticket, Taft would have won. Thus from 1896 to 1912, the overall pattern of political behavior in Maryland shifted away from
party loyalties toward conservatism when the two did not
coincide.[97]

---

96. For pertinent biographies, see Lambert, *Gorman*; Masterson, "Lewis";
Eric F. Goldman, *Charles J. Bonaparte, Patrician Reformer, His Early
Career*, J.H.U. Studies (Baltimore: J.H. Press, 1943); and Henry A. Atkinson,
*Theodore Marburg, The Man and His Work* (New York: Harper & Row, 1951).
97. For the presidential returns through 1912, see the *Sun Almanac* for the

In 1912, the picture was more complex. In the presidential primaries authorized that year, Roosevelt defeated Taft in Maryland and Champ Clark beat Wilson. When the Chicago convention nominated Taft anyway, Bonaparte led a faction into forming a Maryland Progressive Party to support Roosevelt. Though sketchily organized, their charismatic candidate outdrew Taft in the fall. The party continued in existence for another two years, but merely in skeletal form.

Meanwhile, a group of Baltimore businessmen had persuaded the Democratic National Committee to hold their convention at the new National Guard Armory in Baltimore. There, in the blistering heat of August, without air conditioning, the perspiring delegates nominated Wilson after prolonged debate and partisan maneuvers.[98] Maryland's Democracy accepted the former Johns Hopkins graduate student and guest lecturer enthusiastically, and gave him a substantial plurality but not a majority in the fall, 112,674 votes to Taft's 54,956 and Roosevelt's 57,579. Wilson repeated with a victory over Hughes in 1916, but in the landslide return to normalcy in 1920, most Marylanders, including the women who cast their first ballots, chose Harding.[99]

In the heyday of the Gorman machine, the Democrats won virtually all of the statewide elections. Beginning in 1895 in state politics and the following year in national politics, Marylanders became a less predictable state, tending toward conservatism regardless of party affiliation. Yet both Roosevelt and Wilson were popular figures to Marylanders and received substantial voter support. Still the top vote-getter from 1870 to 1920, with the blessing of the newly enfranchised women, was the handsome, debonair Warren G. Harding.

Historians in recent years have been examining progressivism and its relations with various minority groups, partly to evaluate the reformers' sincerity and commitments to assist the underdogs of American society. Generally, the resulting picture

---

respective years. After 1912, returns may be found in the *Maryland Manual* for the appropriate year.

98. For a colorful description of the Democratic National Convention, see Walter Lord, *The Good Years: From 1900 to the First World War* (New York: Harpers, 1960), pp. 289-319, *passim*.

99. *Maryland Manual, 1912–1913*, pp. 249-54; and *Maryland Manual, 1916–1917*, pp. 262-63.

has not been favorable to the progressives; and Marylanders, with some exceptions, proved no different. Progressive Marylanders wanted to disfranchise black voters and deny the ballot to women. Their links with immigrants and organized labor were tenuous. At the same time minority group people generally supported progressive reform.

Margaret Callcott in her book on *The Negro in Maryland Politics, 1870–1912*, clearly shows black Marylanders supporting reform from within the Republican party while receiving few benefits in return. They participated in the work of the Charity Organization Society, with more than fifty doctors, ministers, teachers, and housewives manning supervisory boards or becoming friendly visitors in the black ghetto. They formed the Colored Law and Order League to fight crime, vice, and immorality,but were thwarted by a generally unsympathetic city government. They organized the Maryland Suffrage League and the Colored Men's Suffrage League to get out the vote against disfranchisement. In cooperation with the Woman's Civic League, they also organized the Woman's Cooperative Civic League in 1912 to work for better education, clean streets, and pure milk.[100]

A small number of white progressives—men like Gilman, John Rose, Bonaparte, and Garrett—cooperated with the black groups, but they were the exceptions. Similarly, the setting up of playgrounds, public baths, and a black teachers' college were exceptions to the general discrimination of an era that saw the passage of Jim Crow laws to segregate railroads and steamboats in 1904, the West ordinance to enforce neighborhood segregation in 1911, the omission of black housing from the enforcement of tenement standards, the failure to provide facilities for black tuberculars, and the exclusion of blacks from the city planning conferences, and the citywide congress. The failure of disfranchisement was a victory for the two-party system, not for racial justice.

Women in Maryland also suffered substantial discrimination during the progressive era. Although women had organized the Arundell Good Government Club under Bonaparte's sponsorship in 1895 to fight the machine and later used the vehicle to support compulsory education laws, child labor reform, and the

---

100. In addition to Callcott, see Crooks, *Politics and Progress*, p. 211n.

creation of a juvenile court, Maryland politicians generally regarded their involvement as a nuisance. After 1900 the Maryland Federation of Women's Clubs and later the Woman's Civic
League became active in support of public health and child
welfare reforms.

The Maryland Woman's Suffrage Association was first formed
in the 1890's with branches in Baltimore City and Montgomery
County. By 1904, however, it still had fewer than 200 members.
Large scale suffrage activity came after the annual convention
of the National American Woman's Suffrage Association in Baltimore in 1906, and with the formation of the Equal Suffrage
League as an offshoot of the socially elite Arundell Club.
Within two years it had a membership of 800, but its goals were
limited. These women wanted the municipal franchise in order
to have a voice in the school, public health, and welfare issues
of Baltimore City. The Maryland Woman's Suffrage Association,
on the other hand, wanted complete suffrage as a fundamental
right of citizenship. The two groups split, and each presented
its suffrage bill to the General Assembly in 1910. The municipal
suffrage proposal had support from Mayor Mahool, "Sonny"
Mahon, the Federation of Labor, and a men's Just Government
League, but the General Assembly tabled both bills.[101]

In 1912 some 800 suffragists descended upon Annapolis to
lobby for a constitutional amendment granting women the right
to vote. The Republican state chairman endorsed the bill, but
again it was overwhelmingly rejected, this time by a seventy-
four to eighteen vote in the House of Delegates. The pattern
continued. Suffragists and their male allies held street rallies,
parlor meetings, distributed pamphlets, and in 1912 paraded
past the Democratic National Convention at the National Guard
Armory. The Socialist, Prohibition, and Progressive parties endorsed women's suffrage that year, but the major parties held
back. By 1915 the Just Government League, endorsing
woman's suffrage, claimed 17,000 members, but the following
year the General Assembly again turned down an amendment
by a two-to-one majority. Even when the national political parties endorsed it in 1916, Maryland's political leaders remained
aloof. In 1919, following congressional passage of the
Nineteenth Amendment, Attorney General A. Mitchell Palmer

101. *Ibid.*, pp. 78-82; and Mal Hee Son, "The Woman Suffrage Movement in
Maryland from 1870 to 1920" (M.A. thesis, University of Maryland, 1962).

and suffragists asked Governor Harrington to call a special session of the General Assembly to ratify the amendment, but he refused. Maryland's legislators never did ratify the Nineteenth Amendment, as they never ratified the Fifteenth Amendment granting Negro suffrage until 1973. Other states did, however, and Maryland women voted for the first time in the presidential election of 1920.[102]

Organized labor fared better than either blacks or women during the progressive era, but ironically, they were normally associated with the less progressive of the two parties. This was due partly to the class consciousness of the era. The Republican party more clearly represented big business, especially manufacturing interests. Partly too, Boss Rasin in Baltimore had responded to labor's concerns in the 1880's, and had invited labor into the Democratic coalition. As a result, the Federation of Labor in Baltimore generally supported the Democratic machine, though 1895 was an exception. It also lobbied in behalf of child labor, sweatshop, workmen's compensation, public health, and compulsory educational reforms. Although its participation was limited, it supported city planning conferences and the citywide congress. Clearly, organized labor was at times part of the progressive coalition as well as part of the Democratic coalition in Maryland, a harbinger of the New Deal.

Yet there were also substantial differences between labor and many Maryland progressives. Labor was stronger in support of social reform and less concerned with structural reform, just the reverse of progressives generally. The Federation of Labor took no position on the bill to create a public service commission, believing it offered no benefits for the workingman. In return, some progressives dragged their feet on workmen's compensation and on an eight-hour day for women. In Baltimore, where organized labor was strongest, it obtained the eight-hour day and a two-dollar minimum wage in municipal employment. Yet support for the measure came from the Democratic machine, not from most progressives. The relationship between progressivism and organized labor was a pragmatic, sometimes tenuous one, and this was especially true on the state level, where an anti-labor, county vote was strong.[103]

---

102. *Ibid.*, pp. 64-101, *passim*.
103. Crooks, *Politics and Progress*, *passim*; see also *Labor Leader*, the Federation's weekly newspaper on deposit in the Enoch Pratt Free Library.

Like labor, the immigrants generally voted Democratic unless they were threatened, as in the election of 1895, or by the disfranchisement referenda of 1905 and 1909. Among the older waves of first and second-generation immigrants, the Germans and Irish were relatively well established in politics, business, the professions, and civic groups. Cardinal Gibbons, "Sonny" Mahon, Theodore Marburg, and Jacob Moses belonged in this category. A number of German-Americans, particularly, were progressive, and their largest civic group, the Independent Citizens Union, supported both structural and social reforms. Among the newer Russian, Polish, and Italian immigrants, there were fewer leaders; yet they did work effectively for sweatshop, housing, and public health reforms.

Again, however, the relationship of the immigrants with the progressives and the community at large was tenuous. Concerns of the former were also primarily for social reforms, not structural ones. Doubtless progressives held less prejudice toward them than white Marylanders had against blacks, or management against organized labor, yet German Jews looked down upon Russian Jews, and socially elite Episcopalians undoubtedly looked down upon both. Still, newcomers did support city planning, the citywide congress and public health reforms. A nucleus of first and second generation Americans was a part of the Maryland progressive movement.[104]

The progressive relationship with businessmen in Maryland was ambivalent. Clearly, the leading businessmen in Baltimore supported most of the structural reforms, from city planning to public improvements and to charter revision, and more efficiency and expertise in government. Both the Merchants and Manufacturers Association and the Board of Trade were strong endorsers of the citywide congress in 1911. The former also supported the National Municipal League and the creation of a public service commission. At the same time, however, the Merchants and Manufacturers Association opposed the regulation of child labor, the eight-hour day, mothers' pensions, a minimum wage and the inheritance tax. In its claim to be progressive, the association fit the patterns of revisionist historians who see big business dominating the reforms of the era in order to control and limit them. It was enlightened self-interest and

---

104. Crooks, *Politics and Progress*; and Cunz, *The Maryland Germans*.

economical good sense to try to rationalize utility rates, urban growth, governmental administration, and public health programs to eradicate tuberculosis and provide pure foods. The association had little to do directly with assisting the underdog or redistributing economic power and wealth to the poor. In the same pattern, these reforms were also opposed frequently by those small businessmen who could not afford to raise health standards in their dairies, bakeries, and slaughterhouses, or who were penalized by the withdrawal of a special privilege because of competitive bidding on contracts.[105]

In addition to these structural reforms, largely supported by the established business interests and frequently opposed by the marginal businessmen, were the social reforms which were concerned with helping the poor and underprivileged. Here businessmen split. Contrasted with the opposition of the Merchants and Manufacturers Association was the support for many of these reforms that came from the publishers of the Baltimore *News*, individual bankers like Robert Garrett and B. Howell Griswold, merchants David Hutzler and Jacob Epstein, corporation executives William Keyser and Waldo Newcomer, plus pharmacists, photographers, printers, and salesmen. Their commitments were comparable to those of the reform-minded lawyers, social workers, academics, and clergy. Yet business support for social reform was clearly mixed, and where achievements were substantial, as in child labor, sweatshop, and tenement reforms, it was frequently over the opposition of business interests.

Generally, World War I had a disruptive effect upon progressivism, as it had upon the nation at large, though the reform impetus was probably on the downswing before the war began. Prejudice against foreigners increased; the German-language newspapers had to switch to English or suspend publication. The vitality of the Independent Citizens Union waned. German Street in downtown Baltimore was renamed Redwood Street, after the first Maryland officer to die in combat, and the use of German in the public schools and churches declined. Generally, German-Americans, particularly in Baltimore, lived under suspicion for the duration of the war.[106]

---

105. *Baltimore* (1910–    ), the periodical of the Merchants and Manufacturers Association, presents the major business perspective.
106. Cunz, *Maryland Germans*, pp. 401-02.

In Baltimore, too, a serious manpower shortage developed, especially at city hall, when 2,000 employees, including 600 in the street cleaning department alone, quit their jobs to either enlist or take better paying positions in war industries. The city's public works program, particularly the paving operations and the construction of the civic center, were delayed or postponed for the duration. The vast migration of men and women to work in factories in the metropolitan area put a severe strain on housing accommodations and temporarily worsened public health conditions, particularly during the influenza epidemic. Welfare problems increased as heads of families joined the armed services, leaving behind wives and children without adequate means of support. Fuel was scarce, to the extent that during the particularly cold winter of 1917–18, people were burning furniture, factories were shut down, and some children even froze to death. Power shortages came suddenly, with electricity simply cut off for extended periods of time. There were food shortages, with sugarless Mondays, meatless Tuesdays, wheatless Wednesdays, porkless Fridays, and only two meals on Saturday. After skyrocketing, prices were fixed, and crafty Marylanders tried to hoard their food.[107]

To produce more food, the progressive-minded Woman's Civic League urged Marylanders to grow vegetables at home in "liberty gardens." In addition, they sponsored thirty-one community gardens in vacant lots, five playgrounds, and eleven school yards that raised, they claimed, $500,000 worth of crops. To combat inflation, the women kept a weekly check on food prices, and held home canning demonstrations. They distributed food during the influenza epidemic and also folded bandages for the Red Cross.

Other progressives became involved in a variety of programs supporting the war. Some enlisted in the armed forces; others went off to Washington or served on the Maryland Council of Defense. In Baltimore, the Alliance of Charitable and Social Agencies established the Baltimore Fund to raise initially $300,000, later $1.5 million, and to provide and coordinate relief resulting from the dislocations of war. The Red Cross, families of servicemen, the sick, and the impoverished benefited. A committee of fifty, including many progressives,

---

107. Various newspaper clippings in the Vertical File entitled "World War I" in the Maryland Room of the Enoch Pratt Free Library.

contacted 32,000 potential donors through home meetings and mailings, and then worked through business firms and fraternal orders to canvass for gifts and pledges using such slogans as "Fight, Farm or Fork-up!" It was the predecessor of the United Fund or Community Chest campaign, and it worked.[108]

The war contributed to the decline of progressivism by shifting priorities and expending energies on the war effort rather than on reform. Yet both candidates for governor in 1919, as well as both mayoral nominees in Baltimore that year, were moderates, supporting quality schools, public health reforms, good roads, and efficient, honest government. At the same time, however, there was little inclination to initiate reforms in new areas, particularly in those of social reform. Rather, the tendency was to consolidate past gains and to consider competent administration of the new governmental responsibilities to be the primary aims. The limited postwar reaction in Maryland —and there was less of the Red Scare, labor, radical or anarchist hysteria in Maryland than elsewhere—was due partly to the same conservative qualities that limited reform at its peak.

The waning of progressivism stemmed also from a variety of ideological, personal and institutional factors. Ideologically, reform had achieved about as much as the mainstream of progressivism would accept. More thorough city planning or governmental controls seemed to lead to socialism. More welfare provisions, such as unemployment compensation or social security, ran contrary to the American work ethic or challenged the property rights of businessmen. They also cost money, which meant either new or increased taxes. Thus the goals of the reform era were limited. A David Lewis or a George Stewart Brown might push for more, but they were on the fringe of reform; the mainstream was more cautious in its views.

In addition, progressivism declined for a variety of personal reasons. Old age took pioneers like Bonaparte and Gilman from the ranks. Grasty moved on to the *New York Times* as a war correspondent. Jeffrey Brackett moved to Boston to direct the school of social work at Simmons College. George Stewart Brown became a federal customs judge in Brooklyn. Lewis went to Congress. Marburg went to Brussels. Osler went to

---

108. Walter A. Parcelle, "Baltimore Underwriting a Blanket War Insurance Policy," *The American City*, XVI (June, 1917), 573-78.

Oxford. New leaders succeeded the earlier ones, but then the war came.

Institutions changed. Both major political parties adapted to a measure of reform. Blatant boss rule was gone. Reform Democrats could vote easily for Harrington in 1915 after the defeat of Lee in the primaries and support Ritchie in 1919 with few qualms. The parties absorbed moderate progressivism, leaving the more advanced reformers the choice of heading to oblivion with a third party or seeking further change within the major parties. Most progressives made the latter choice after 1912. Similarly, business institutions, especially the public utilities, but also the clothing manufacturers and others, seemed less rapacious by 1914 or 1915. The era of welfare capitalism was beginning.

Then too, the progressives themselves were rarely a cohesive group. Some were Democrats with varying attachments to their party organization and some were Republicans. Some were trade unionists and others were merchants and manufacturers. Most were primarily structural reformers on political, economic or social issues, but a minority were equally concerned with social reform. Progressives differed over Negro suffrage, woman's suffrage, municipal ownership versus regulation of public utilities, priorities in city planning, and the extent of social welfare and public health programs. No wonder they could not coalesce for long except on specific issues like boss rule or child labor reform. Such coalitions rarely endured, once the specific issue passed.

There were also opponents of change: the old organization, many rural legislators, tradition-minded businessmen and farmers, and—perhaps greatest of all—the uninformed and apathetic voter and non-voter. From the beginning of the era, reformers like Grasty and Bonaparte had urged Marylanders to be concerned about politics in their communities. Throughout the era, the theme continued to be sounded. Many responded, but despite the range of programs and the concerns of municipal and state leaders, in the elections after 1900 the percentage of voter participation declined.

Thus the progressives were a pluralistic, often fragmented minority group of people, who for a generation helped to change the direction of American politics. Their goals resulted largely from enlightened self-interest. Their methods were pragmatically political. They saw the changing urban industrial world around them and the failure of boss rule to respond adequately to the change. So they became involved, in the words of David Lewis, "to adapt both state and national governments to the change of conditions which two generations of material development have brought upon us." That was the dominant, rational motive.[109]

There were others. Robert Garrett spoke for the social reformers in one of his reports to the Public Athletic League when he rejected traditional *laissez-faire* government on the grounds that it contributed to the causes of poverty, sickness, and crime. Instead, he added, governments must act to reform the environment, which will produce "not merely happier people, but a people possessing intellectual and moral power unknown to us today in the mass."[110]

Maryland progressives pieced together a point of view that eventually led to the welfare state. Their attempts to secure individual freedom in a just society were often timid by modern standards, frequently were blocked by a majority who were either apathetic or opposed to progressive change, and were not carried further sufficiently by their successors. In seeking to respond to the twin forces of urbanization and industrialization, Maryland progressives operated in a conservative political, economic and social milieu. Perhaps the striking phenomenon is not that they failed to do more, but that they accomplished as much as they did. In Maryland, as across the nation, progressivism meant conservative reform.

---

109. Masterson, "Lewis," p. 20.
110. Public Athletic League, *Second Annual Report*, p. 18.

## BIBLIOGRAPHICAL ESSAY

### Chapter VIII

The most valuable sources for the study of Maryland history from the 1870's to 1920 are the newspapers and periodicals from Baltimore City and the counties. Their biases, however, must be taken into account. For example, the state's most important newspaper, The Baltimore *Sun*, was a strongly partisan Democratic paper until the opening of the twentieth century when it shifted toward moderation and standards approaching dispassionate journalism. The best progressive paper was the Baltimore *News* under Charles Grasty's editorship from 1893 to 1907. Other helpful newspapers included *The Afro-American Ledger*, *Labor Leader*, and the Baltimore *Municipal Journal*. The numerous scrapbooks of statewide newspapers in the Edwin Warfield and Albert C. Ritchie collections on deposit in the Maryland Historical Society added a broader perspective for the state as a whole. Useful periodicals included *The Civil Service Reformer*, *Charities Record* and *Baltimore*.

Supplementing and at times correcting the press are a range of other primary sources including the extensive Charles J. Bonaparte Papers, on deposit at The Library of Congress; the Arthur P. Gorman Papers, on deposit at the Maryland Historical Society; the Mayors' Papers at City Hall, Baltimore; and the Governors' Papers in the Hall of Records at Annapolis.

Also significant were the various reports of the Maryland Bureau of Industrial Statistics, Tuberculosis Commission, Charity Organization Society, Maryland Association for the Prevention and Relief of Tuberculosis, Municipal Art Society, Baltimore Reform League, Sewerage Commissions, and Public Athletic League referred to in footnotes in the text.

Among secondary sources, James B. Crooks, *Politics and Progress: The Rise of Urban Progressivism in Baltimore, 1895–1911* (Baton Rouge: Louisiana State University Press, 1966) focuses on the history of Maryland's largest city. Margaret Law Callcott, *The Negro in Maryland Politics, 1870–1912*, traces the political role of the state's largest minority group. Cunz, *The Maryland Germans: A History*, presents an overview of the state's largest immigrant group. Gerald Johnson, et. al., *The Sunpapers of Baltimore* (New York: Knopf, 1937), provides a popular history of the state's most influential newspaper. Frank R. Kent, *The Story of Maryland Politics* (Baltimore: King Brothers, Inc.,

1911), is a gossipy, contemporary's view of the state political scene. Mal Hee Son, "The Woman Suffrage Movement in Maryland from 1870 to 1920" (M.A. thesis, University of Maryland, 1962), traces the efforts of Maryland women to obtain the vote.

Among biographies, John R. Lambert, *Arthur Pue Gorman* (Baton Rouge: Lousiana State University Press, 1953), is the most important in its examination of the state's dominant political figure. Other useful biographies include John Tracy Ellis, *The Life of James Cardinal Gibbons*, 2 vols. (Milwaukee: Bruce Publishing Co., 1952); Simon Flexner and James Thomas Flexner, *William Henry Welch and the Heroic Age of American Medicine*; Harvey Cushing, *The Life of Sir William Osler*, 2 vols.; Thomas J. Masterson, S. J., "The Formation of a Progressive: The Early Career of David J. Lewis of Maryland" (M.A. thesis, Georgetown University, 1969); and Sister Mary Anne Dunn, OSF, "The Life of Isaac Freeman Rasin, Democratic Leader of Baltimore from 1870–1907," (M.S. thesis, Catholic University of America, 1949).

Morris L. Radoff, ed., *The Old Line State, A History of Maryland* has a somewhat dated essay on this era in Maryland history. An older statewide study of some value is Matthew Page Andrews, *History of Maryland: Province and State*, but unfortunately it has little on the progressive era.

# IX

## MARYLAND BETWEEN THE WARS

BY

DOROTHY M. BROWN

GEORGETOWN UNIVERSITY

Muted by the world war and its aftermath in the big red scare, progressive voices and issues persisted but did not dominate in the decades between the wars. Battles for social justice and political and economic morality captured national headlines only intermittently. So changed was the national climate that in February, 1926, *Survey* magazine questioned, "Where Are the Pre-war Radicals?" Progressive William Allen White explained that there was an inability to dramatize injustices. The average man "puts his hand to his mouth, yawns and walks off. . . . New issues will produce new causes."

1

RITCHIE

Maryland faced these issues and the deep and pervasive changes in the decades between the wars under the leadership of her most remarkable governor, Albert C. Ritchie. His four administrations spanned the euphoria of the Coolidge twenties, the chilling reality of the depression, and the early relief and reforms of the New Deal. His philosophy of state sovereignty —in the face of increasing federal expansion—his efforts to achieve governmental economy and efficiency, and to safeguard the liberties of the citizen not only dominated the Old Line State but won him serious consideration for the presidential nomination. In Maryland and the nation, the end of the Age of Ritchie in 1934 and the emergence of the Age of Roosevelt would be symbolic of more than a simple changing of the guard.

672

Descended from a Virginia family that boasted a governor and rector of the University of Virginia on his mother's side, Ritchie was the only child of Elizabeth Cabell and Judge Albert Ritchie of the Supreme Bench of Baltimore. He was educated in private schools, graduating in 1896 from The Johns Hopkins University with the yearbook prophecy that he would be elected President by one vote and reelected for life. Departing for a grand European tour, the traditional climax to the education of a gentleman, the handsome Ritchie was described as "almost a manifestation of the Gibson man." Back in Baltimore, he earned his law degree at the University of Maryland, joined its faculty, and entered private practice. Ritchie's public service began with his appointment as assistant city solicitor in 1910. Two years later he served as assistant general counsel to the Public Service Commission and led a successful fight for cheaper gas and electric rates, saving Baltimore consumers an estimated $500,000 annually. Approaching the Democratic political leaders Senator John Walter Smith and Baltimore businessman Frank Furst, the popular young attorney sought a position on the party ticket. Told to "prove himself," Ritchie's diligent work won him the attorney general's nomination on Smith's slate in 1915. In a bitter primary battle and general election, Ritchie ran well ahead of the ticket. Accepting an invitation during World War I to serve the War Industries Board, Ritchie became one of Bernard Baruch's protégés and was known as "the intelligent and highly geared young attorney for the group." On his return to Maryland politics, Attorney General Ritchie announced his candidacy for governor in 1919. Still no favorite of the bosses, Ritchie was a proven vote-getter with a good war record. Chastened by the disastrous party bloodletting of 1915 and the municipal elections of 1919, the Democratic leaders chose to avoid a fight. Ritchie was the choice.[1]

---

1. James B. Levin, "Albert C. Ritchie, A Political Biography" (Ph.D. dissertation, City College of New York, 1970), pp. 8-75; J. F. Essary, *Maryland in National Politics from Charles Carroll to Albert C. Ritchie,* 2d ed. (Baltimore: John Murphy Co., 1932), pp. 301-02; William M. Bowen, Jr., "The Period of Ritchie and After," in Morris L. Radoff, ed., *The Old Line State: A History of Maryland* (Annapolis: Hall of Records Commission, 1971), p. 128; Frank F. White, Jr., *The Governors of Maryland, 1777–1970* (Annapolis: Hall of Records Commission, 1970), pp. 256-63. See also "Mrs. Albert Ritchie in the White House," *Woman's Home Companion,* May, 1928, Box 28A, Ritchie Papers, MS 710, M.H.S. See clippings from the *Baltimore American,* May 9,

After a tough campaign against Republican Harry W. Nice, Ritchie became governor by the grace of 165 controversial votes. He did not enter Annapolis under auspicious circumstances. Nationally, the Wilson coalition was disintegrating; the Democrats were wracked by the problem of the League of Nations, the continuing burdens of war taxes, and the high cost of living. In the Old Line State, Ritchie's narrow triumph was won by focusing on local issues of roads, oysters, and education, and by forging a fragile truce in a bitterly divided party. His first and primary task would be to build a viable party to serve as an instrument for administration and policy. It would not be easy.

Maryland's Democrats traditionally existed in an uneasy state-city partnership. As Ritchie began his term, state boss John Walter Smith was beginning his fortieth year of elective office. Born in 1845 in Snow Hill on the Eastern Shore, Smith was successful in banking and lumber enterprises. Elected to the state Senate in 1889, he had subsequently served as president of the Senate, congressman, governor, and United States Senator. The *Sun* described him as a "party man," "who played the game." In 1919 Smith still led the most powerful organization in the state. His defeat for reelection in the Republican avalanche of 1920, his dwindling patronage, and the growing record of Ritchie would seriously erode his dominance. Still, in 1923, Smith's reluctance to support Ritchie's renomination could cause serious concern in the governor's camp. At his death in 1925, Smith left a group of dissident followers, but Ritchie was solidly in control of the Democratic state organization.[2]

In the city, Ritchie's struggle for leadership and unity was more complex. Two warring leaders, John J. "Sonny" Mahon and Frank S. Kelly, had been locked in fierce combat for four years. The aging Mahon represented a typical boss' success story. Leaving school at fourteen, he had worked in a print shop and then entered local politics. At nineteen, he ran the ninth

---

Nov. 9, Nov. 28, 1919, *Sun*, July 14, 1919, *News*, Nov. 5, 1919 in Box 2, Ritchie Papers. Unless otherwise noted all newspapers cited are published in Baltimore.

2. *Biographical Directory of the American Congress, 1774–1961* (Washington: Government Printing Office, 1961), p. 1620; *Sun*, April 20, 1925 in the Democratic Scrapbook, Maryland Room, Enoch Pratt Free Library, Baltimore. Compiled by the Democratic State Central Committee, the Democratic Scrapbook, 1919–1932, provides a rich clipping file.

ward. Advanced in "Boss" Isaac Rasin's organization, Mahon
served fourteen years in the city council. A proud, professional
politician, he asserted: "Politics is my business and I make it
pay. I would be a fool not to." His chief rival and former
lieutenant, Frank S. Kelly, was variously called the "King of the
Underworld," "slot machine Kelly," or simply "The Kelly."
Allegedly, he entered politics by deterring Negro voting in
West Baltimore. He built an organization through his liberal aid
to the poor and his talent at organizing repeaters at the polls.
Together, Kelly and Mahon's men dominated the city council;
as one civic reformer complained, "All that the present council
represents is these two honorable gentlemen."[3]

As the Ritchie campaign began in 1919, Mahon and Kelly had
not spoken for four years. But moved by expediency and in
need of a winner, they grimly and publicly exchanged greetings
and observed a tenuous truce. By 1920 they were again feuding
openly, fielding rival slates for the sensitive Democratic State
Central Committee. Ritchie had to arrange for a neutral emissary to cajole them into supporting the presidential ticket in
1920. Throughout 1921 he worked to prove his evenhanded-
ness in patronage and interest.[4]

Although a field of three Democratic senatorial candidates in
1922 indicated that state factionalism was not yet dead, by the
mayoralty election of 1923 Ritchie could savor Mahon-Kelly
unity in backing Mahon lieutenant, Howard W. Jackson. While
the victory of Jackson would eventually further muddy city
Democratic politics as he built his own faction and alliances, in
1923 Ritchie's mastery at building party solidarity was well recognized in the charges raised against "the machine." In the

---

3. Sonny Mahon, "The Autobiography of a Baltimore Boss," *Sun*, Oct. 1, 8,
15, 22, 1922; Edwin Rothman, "Factional Machine-Politics, William Curran
and the Baltimore City Democratic Organization, 1929–1946" (Ph.D. dissertation, Johns Hopkins University, 1949), pp. 21-27, 230-35. Kelly was more
accessible to constitutents and ward lieutenants; Mahon held court at the
Rennert Hotel. While lieutenants of both of the aging chiefs struggled for
power, Kelly's seemed the younger, more aggressive. Interview with E.
Brooke Lee, March 23, 1972. For 1919 peacemaking see *Evening Sun*, Aug. 7,
1919; *Washington Star*, Aug. 6, 1919; *Baltimore American*, Aug. 7, 1919.

4. Danny Loden, "Inside Stuff," *News*, Aug. 13 and Sept. 1, 1923; Rothman,
p. 61; *Baltimore American*, Sept. 25, 1919, *News*, Dec. 28, 1919; *Sun*, April 13,
1920; *Evening Sun*, March 30, 1921; *Sun*, Aug. 9, 1921; *News*, Aug. 16, 1921;
*Sun*, Aug. 20, 1921.

calm after the Jackson victory, the *Sun* recognized Ritchie as the leader of a new organization "as the old order passeth."[5]

While organizing the Democrats, Ritchie also faced the not inconsiderable opposition of the Maryland Republicans. Newly-elected Senator Ovington Weller, working smoothly with party chairman Galen Tait, and with good contacts in Washington, dominated the GOP in the 1920's. Like Ritchie, he was not without his challengers. Former boss and national committeeman William Jackson bridled in his Eastern Shore semi-retirement when Weller sought to capture his committee seat in 1921. Adding to this friction was the problem of popular maverick and perennial, self-financed, presidential hopeful, Senator Joseph I. France. Finally, the "Maryland Gentleman," former Governor Phillips Lee Goldsborough, western Maryland party leader W. Bladen Lowndes, and Baltimore's Mayor William Broening were intermittently quietly unhappy and openly hostile to the Weller-Tait generalship. Though the factions would agree on a gubernatorial candidate in 1923, their unity, like that of the Democrats, was tenuous. Additionally, the Republicans, divided on the prohibition issue, were pushed by the wet stance of Ritchie into a dry to damp position and party straddle that satisfied neither the wet city forces nor their dry county cousins.[6]

The third political factor that would determine the success of Ritchie was the powerful Baltimore *Sunpapers*. Under publishers Harry and Van Lear Black, the *Sun* fielded an awesome reportorial staff led by columnists Frank Kent and H. L. Mencken. Called the "wet blanket" by one critic and termed the third most significant force in the legislature after Ritchie and the bosses, the *Sun* landed daily on the doorsteps of nine of ten houses in influential Guilford, Homeland, and Roland Park.[7] Fortunately for Ritchie, its policy paralleled his stance on

5. *Sun*, April 17, May 11, Sept. 8, Oct. 7, 1922; *Sun* Jan. 5, 11, April 6, May 6, 9, 10, 1923; Rothman, p. 62; Levin, p. 177. Election statistics for 1922 senatorial race are in *Maryland Manual*, 1923, p. 185.

6. Weller's old business partner was Secretary of War John W. Weeks. *Evening Sun*, Sept. 19, 30, 1921; *News*, Sept. 9, 1922; *Sun*, May 1, Sept. 12, Nov. 8, 9, 1922.

7. Harry J. Green, *A Study of the Legislature of Maryland with Special Reference to the Sessions of 1927 and 1929* (Baltimore: J. H. Press, 1930), p. 103; Gerald W. Johnson, Frank R. Kent, H. L. Mencken and Hamilton Owens, *The Sunpapers of Baltimore* (New York: Knopf, 1951), pp. 364, 383-86, 389.

prohibition, women's suffrage, economy in government, and Old Line State sovereignty. With few exceptions, the *Sun* staunchly supported the governor throughout his fifteen years in office.

The final factor in party building during Ritchie's early years was the policy and program he developed in his first administration. Preeminent was the emergence of his vigorous defense of state's rights in the key issues of women's suffrage, the threatened intervention in the coal strike of 1922, and prohibition.

Ritchie viewed women's suffrage as a problem for the individual states. Joined in his views by Senator Smith, Ritchie had supported an anti-suffrage plank in the Democratic platform of 1919 and had continually rejected suffragists' pleas to support their cause in the legislature. In all of these actions, he was cheered by the *Sun*, which entreated the General Assembly to "Let Maryland remain true to herself. . . . to the knightly creed which recognized in true women the real inspirers of every good work and word." When the legislature, after a day of parades and advocacy, voted down the amendment eighteen to nine in the Senate and sixty-four to thirty-six in the House, the *Sun* cheered "Good Old Maryland."[8]

Yet within seven months, in August 1920, Maryland would bow to the judgment of Tennessee as its ratification of the Susan B. Anthony amendment made women's suffrage the law. Ritchie moved quickly to welcome Maryland's 300,000 new voters; Smith, while stoutly asserting that he was still unconvinced that the majority of women wanted the suffrage, gracefully acceded urging: "Let's do the decent thing and do it in a decent way." A Mahon lieutenant more involved in the immediate scramble for votes urged his precinct captains, "Register everybody you can drag to the polls; there'll be plenty of time to talk politics to them afterward, but they're no good to us unless they're registered."[9]

Both parties hastened to woo the new registrants. In his 1920 campaign Ovington Weller urged a federal department for women and backed legislation limiting women's working hours and establishing old age and mothers' pensions. The Demo-

---

8. *Sun,* Jan. 11, Feb. 18, 1920; *Evening Sun,* Feb. 11, 1920.

9. *Sun,* Aug. 19 and Oct. 1, 1920.

cratic platform pledged efforts to improve working conditions and a state system of child care. Ritchie, concerned by the impact of his wet stance and his prior coolness to voting rights, called a special legislative session to provide for additional registration facilities. He voiced, however, a frequently reiterated southern Democratic concern that "the thoughtful and intelligent white women of Maryland" would not allow "the Negro women and undesirable characters" to form the voting female majority. Subsequently, when Attorney General Armstrong declared that the Nineteenth Amendment applied only to the vote and not to offices where the male pronoun was used, Ritchie successfully urged the legislature in 1922 to pass his bills removing the remaining political disabilities from women by establishing their eligibility for elective and appointive offices and for jury duty.[10]

Ritchie's view of state sovereignty and responsibility emerged more forcefully in the national coal strike of 1922. The struggle of John L. Lewis's United Mine Workers for district agreements dragged on from April through December. Sixty-five mining companies in western Maryland reported their revenue losses at $5,000,000 and wage losses to the strikers of $4,000,000. A concerned President Harding urged the governors of coal producing states to provide national guard protection if and when the mines were reopened and promised federal support if necessary. Ritchie promised cooperation but noted that there had been no request in Maryland for such protection. He added a stinging rebuke: "The traditions of this state are those of a people who have settled such matters as these without the aid of bayonets." If local operators chose to reopen, they could hire their own guards as long as they were Maryland citizens of high character. To Ritchie, the taxpayers should not and would not be burdened.

At Secretary of Commerce Herbert Hoover's request, however, the governor established a coal commission to ensure equitable distribution and announced that he would only move

10. Joseph Chepaitis, "The First Two Administrations of Albert Cabell Ritchie, Governor of Maryland, 1920–1927" (M.A. thesis, Georgetown University, 1965), p. 22; Levin, pp. 162, 191-92, 194; Sharon B. Abell, "The Presidential, Senatorial and Congressional Elections of 1920 in Maryland" (M.A. thesis, Georgetown University, 1970), p. 57; *Sun*, Aug. 20, Sept. 2, 1920; Feb. 19, 1921; *Baltimore American*, Sept. 5, 1920.

further if hospitals and other essential facilities were threatened by shortages. Additionally, he urged operators and miners in the central competitive district to meet and journeyed to New York to confer with John L. Lewis.[11] In Maryland the miners lost the strike, but Ritchie's resistance to police intervention and his efforts to facilitate collective bargaining won him labor's appreciation, while underscoring his position on state and industrial responsibility.

Ritchie's most heated defense of state sovereignty and individual liberty was waged against prohibition. In his campaign in September 1919, he promised opposition against any attack on the liberties of the individual; at the Democratic convention in 1920, he fought for a platform plank repealing the Eighteenth Amendment; in the legislature of 1920, he urged measures to allow Maryland farmers to produce cider and Maryland citizens to have 3½ per cent beer and light wines. When the Supreme Court stated that the states "had no right to be damp," Ritchie's attorney general ruled that local police would not have the power to make arrests under the federal enforcement provision, the Volstead Act. All of this activity earned the enmity of Maryland's superintendent of the Anti-Saloon League, George W. Crabbe, who asserted that Ritchie was "a menace to the good morals of Maryland."[12]

As in the coal strike, Ritchie utilized a federal plea for cooperation by the President in October 1923, to issue a statement opposing the prohibition measure as an invasion of state rights. Trenchantly observing that prohibition cost the nation $38,000,000 in lost taxes and bound all citizens to the decision made by a majority of 2,313 legislators, Ritchie asserted that prohibition was breeding a lawlessness in state and nation that could only be cured by a return to local option—the pre-Eighteenth Amendment arrangement in Maryland.[13]

In other areas, Ritchie consistently opposed child labor amendments as well as federal aid to education and spoke out against the federal encroachments of Coolidge, Hoover, and the burgeoning Washington bureaucracy. Although he would

---

11. Maryland, *Thirty-first Annual Report of the Commissioner of Labor and Statistics of Maryland,* 1922, pp. 141-42, 150-51; Chepaitis, pp. 49-51.

12. Neal Dorsey Thigpen, "The Presidential Aspirations of Albert C. Ritchie" (M.A. thesis, University of Maryland, 1966), p. 19; Levin, p. 106.

13. Levin, p. 106.

cooperate to insure Maryland's fair share of federal largess, he argued earnestly for responsible local government and agreed with Jefferson that citizens closest to problems solved them in the most effective manner.

While opposing federal expansion, Ritchie worked to mold Maryland into a model of state government and to place Maryland's administration "on a strictly business basis." One of Ritchie's first actions was to engage the Griffenhagen firm of Chicago to study Maryland's administrative structure. Rejecting the executive emphasis and sweep of their recommendations, Ritchie appointed a follow-up State Reorganization Committee of 108 Democrats, headed by Judge Charles Burke, to "Marylandize" the Griffenhagen proposals. The Burke Committee's plan, adopted by the legislature in September 1921, overcame the strong opposition of officeholders, particularly old supporters of Smith, who would be replaced by consolidation. It pared down eighty-five executive and administrative agencies to nineteen executive departments. Administrative savings were estimated at $100,000.[14]

In addition to streamlining at the top, Ritchie fulfilled a 1919 campaign promise to work for merit in the civil service ranks. Although the *Sun* was disappointed in his exemptions to the system, Ritchie did eventually include under merit provisions all state employees except those directly appointed by the governor, teachers, and highway patrolmen.[15]

To afford more equitable representation in the legislature, Ritchie redeemed a pledge made to Baltimore's leaders by legislation to increase the city's representation by two additional senators and twelve delegates. Always under-represented, Baltimore's boundaries had been extended again in 1920. This marked increase in population made the disproportionate representation more glaringly evident. Baltimore, with one-half of the state population, had less than one-eighth of the representation in the Senate and less than one-fourth in the House of Delegates. Defeated by rural opposition in his first attempt, Ritchie was faced by Baltimore legislative threats that if he did not wield his strongest influence in the 1921 session, city delegates would fight to defeat his entire program. The

---

14. *Sun,* April 16 and May 31, 1921.
15. *Evening Sun,* Feb. 6, 1920.

difficult and necessary three-fifths vote was finally achieved after a caucus made representation a party measure.[16]

Finally, to put his administrative and political affairs in order, Ritchie promoted the Fewer Elections Act in 1922. Annoyed by annual elections and campaigns, the *Sun* noted "that the Ritchie proposal would be welcomed by sane communities wearied and worn out by perpetual politics." Obviously not moved entirely by pity for the overworked voter, Ritchie was aware of Democratic difficulties in the 1920 Republican landslide and the perennial fuller campaign chests of the GOP. With a continuing emphasis on Maryland primacy, he urged that all state elections, except those for municipal office, be held in non-presidential even years; that delegates, state senators, and county officials be elected every four years; that the terms of comptroller and treasurer be lengthened to coincide with gubernatorial terms. Under the fewer elections measure, the legislature would not assemble after its 1924 session until 1927, and Ritchie anticipated a welcome saving of $350,000. After assuaging the fears of local Democrats at a meeting of forty state leaders, the measure was endorsed by the Senate twenty-two to five and the House seventy-one to thirty-one in the 1922 session.[17]

While efficiency, achieved by government organized on a business basis, was one pillar of Ritchie's administration, economy was the other. Ritchie utilized the budget reforms of the previous administration to tightly monitor state expenses. The executive submitted a two-year budget to the legislature; only reductions could be made. No additional measures could be legislated unless specific funding was provided. To underscore his control and purpose, Ritchie read his first budget message before the legislature. His rigorous scrutiny of new programs and administrative reorganization and reforms, as the institution of a Central Purchasing Bureau, allowed him to achieve one of his proudest boasts in the progressive reduction in state taxes from $36^{31}/_{72}$ cents in 1919 to $25^{74}/_{100}$ cents per $100 assessed evaluation in 1929.[18]

---

16. *Sun*, March 23, 1920; Chepaitis, p. 39; Levin, pp. 28-29.

17. *Sun*, Oct. 13, 14, 1922; Chepaitis, pp. 41-42. Ritchie's programs in conservation, roads, and care for the retarded and insane are concisely noted by White, pp. 260-62.

18. W. L. Fairbanks and W. S. Hamill, *The Manufacturing Industry of*

Administrative efficiency and economy also enabled more responsible and balanced delivery of state services. Ritchie's response to the critical Flexner and Russell Sage reports, which rated Maryland's educational system thirty-seventh among the states, sparked a reorganization plan, higher teachers' salaries, increased emphasis on secondary education, the appointment of a new state superintendent, and, most significantly, an equalization fund to subsidize poorer counties. Additionally, Ritchie sponsored improved facilities for the mentally ill and delinquents, a broadened workmen's compensation measure, and an ambitious road building program.

The first major test of Ritchie's record and organization was his bid for re-election in 1923. No Maryland governor had been returned to Annapolis since the Civil War. Party harmony evident in the "machine" mayoralty victory in April held firm in November. Senator Smith was persuaded by old friend and Democratic angel Frank Furst to withdraw his opposition, while Baltimore's Sonny Mahon issued an endorsement with the acknowledgement that Ritchie had been "regular." The *Sunpapers* and labor, particularly the western Maryland miners, were friendly. The Republican opposition had agreed to back Attorney General Alexander Armstrong. But the coalition of the dry forces and of the Anti-Saloon League and the Ku Klux Klan was the greatest imponderable.[19]

Maryland Klan membership and voter strength was difficult to estimate. One claim of 15,000 members on the Eastern Shore was countered by another of 500. Klan tactics were awkward at best. The Democratic candidate for attorney general, Roman Catholic Thomas H. Robinson, ran better than Ritchie, while the Klan limply explained that it had not been aware of his religion until two days before the election. In addition, Klan influence in the counties was credited with rousing a Roman Catholic and Jewish vote for Ritchie in Baltimore. A *Sun* reporter, interpreting the clashing results, concluded that the Klan "probably is the most overrated organization there ever has been in the state." Most damaging to the Klan-Anti-Saloon League effort to make the 1923 campaign a wet-dry fight was

*Maryland* (Baltimore: Maryland Development Bureau of the Baltimore Association of Commerce, 1932), pp. 180-81; *The Maryland Almanac*, 1929, p. 131; Levin, p. 101; *News*, Feb. 12, 1920.
19. Levin, pp. 188-89; Bowen, p. 130; *Sun*, June 18 and 27, 1923.

the announcement of Alexander Armstrong that personally he was a "wet." On election day many "drys" apparently stayed home.[20]

Triumphing with 175,302 to Armstrong's 136,463, Ritchie led the ticket. But his 38,000 vote bulge was built only through a 41,252 plurality in wet Baltimore City. Armstrong carried fourteen of the twenty-three counties, running particularly well on the lower shore, southern Maryland, and traditionally Republican western Maryland. In the next four years, Ritchie's alliance building and strong record would be needed to keep organizational unity, but in 1925 it could be asserted, "The truth at the present time is that Governor Ritchie is the organization."[21]

In February 1926, Ritchie announced his candidacy for an unprecedented third term. This time his major opposition came within the party from William Milnes Maloy, his rival for the post of attorney general in 1915. Maloy's issues were well chosen. While stressing Ritchie's long incumbency and powerful machine, Maloy vigorously pictured the governor as a friend of the plutocrats and enemy of the people. The focus of his attack was the Conowingo power complex.

Maryland had granted a contract allowing Pennsylvania power interests to build a dam on the Susquehanna at Conowingo to supply Philadelphia's power needs. Baltimore power interests were protected by a fifty-year restriction on the distribution of Conowingo power to the city. While decrying this agreement, Maloy also noted that a loophole allowed the Pennsylvanians to avoid paying Maryland taxes. To Maloy, the political ramifications of the power arrangement seemed particularly damaging. The Arundel Corporation, headed by Board Chairman Frank Furst, had won a $20,000,000 construction contract. *Sunpapers'* support might be traced to Arundel vice-president Lloyd Lowndes, first cousin of publishers Harry and Van Lear Black. Columnist Frank Kent was also a director of the Arundel Corporation.[22]

---

20. John W. Owens series on the Klan is in the *Sun*, Nov. 20 and 21, 1923; Levin, pp. 194, 197.

21. Levin, pp. 98-99; *Sun*, Nov. 5, 1923; *Maryland Manual*, 1924, pp. 188-90; *The Maryland Almanac*, 1924, p. 100; *The Marylander*, May 23, 1925. For continuing factions see *The Observer*, Sept. 18, 1926; *The Marylander*, July 10, 1926; *Sun*, Sept. 9, 1926.

22. *Sun*, March 21, 1926; *The Observer*, May 1, Aug. 28, Oct. 30, 1926; *The Marylander*, June 19, 1926.

In response, Ritchie pointed out that through the contract the state would gain a $1,600,000 bridge at no cost to the taxpayer. Baltimore's development did not need additional power from the Susquehanna resource. Moving from the defensive, he stressed his record safeguarding personal rights and local independence in his opposition to prohibition and federal child labor laws and proudly noted his tax cuts, road and educational development, and conservation efforts. The Conowingo issue proved no match for the Ritchie organization and record. In the primary the governor carried every county over Maloy and won 85 per cent of the Baltimore City vote. The total cost of his effort was $594.10.[23]

The general election pitted Ritchie against Weller's candidate, Addison E. Mullikin. Like Maloy, he stressed long incumbency and Conowingo. However, after a bitter primary and an abortive effort to topple Weller by Broening, William Jackson, Lowndes, and France, the Republican party was described as "a hopeless wreck." Mullikin and Weller, running for reelection to the Senate, were knifed by their Republican rivals and buried under an overwhelming Democratic vote. Ritchie led a strong ticket by 60,000 votes, carried every ward in Baltimore except the Negro fourteenth and seventeenth, and won fourteen of twenty-three counties. In addition to unseating Weller with Democrat Millard Tydings, the Democrats had won all the congressional seats but one. While one caustic critic described the victory as 75 per cent alcoholic and stressed the impact of state employee votes and a divided GOP, clearly Ritchie and his party had won an impressive victory.[24]

Handsome winner in 1926, Ritchie faced a renewed and intensified struggle by Baltimore lieutenants in the 1927 mayoralty race. Incumbent Howard Jackson was under attack for his drinking, absenteeism, the awarding of one-third of the city's $12,000,000 fire insurance to his Riall-Jackson firm,[25] and

---

23. *Sun*, April 4 and Oct. 25, 1926; *Evening Sun*, Sept. 15, 1926.

24. *The Observer*, May 8, 1926; *Sun*, Jan. 27, April 1, June 16, Aug. 13, 14, 21, Oct. 9, 1926; *The Observer*, Oct. 16, 1926; *Sun*, Oct. 20, Nov. 4, 1926; *The Marylander*, Nov. 13, 1926; *The Observer*, Nov. 6, 1926; *Maryland Manual*, 1927, pp. 242-49.

25. *The Observer*, Sept. 6, Oct. 11, 18, 25, 1924; *News*, Feb. 26, 1925; *Evening Sun*, Sept. 21, 1925; *Sun*, Sept. 22, 1925; *News*, March 10, 1926; *Sun*, March 11, 1926; *Evening Sun*, Feb. 17, 1927.

the placing of the bulk of the city bonding through Riall-Jackson with the Fidelity and Deposit Company, where Frank Furst and the *Sunpapers'* Van Lear Black were influential. Although Jackson stressed his record in lowering taxes and improving administration and announced he was ready to run, Ritchie and Kelly turned to East Baltimore lieutenant William Curran as the party choice. A Roman Catholic, Curran faced popular former Mayor William Broening. The *Sunpapers*, stressing the national debate begun in the April *Atlantic Monthly* on Catholicism and the presidential qualifications of Al Smith, viewed the Curran race as an interesting test of the religious impact on the urban voter. But the *Catholic Review*, neutral during the campaign, heatedly rejoined, after Curran was soundly defeated, that the religious issue was a fake. Curran, a divorced man and not a practicing Catholic, would not attract such allegiance.[26] Most significant for Ritchie's harmony hopes was the obvious knifing by Jackson dissidents and jealous rivals. With the death in 1928 of old leaders Sonny Mahon and Frank Kelly, it was clear that Baltimore faced renewed bloodletting. On the eve of Ritchie's 1930 gubernatorial race, city confusion was effectively summarized; "The Democratic situation in Baltimore is now more of a mess than it is anything else."[27]

Ritchie's decision to run once again in 1930 met strong opposition. Insurgent Democrats in the legislative sessions of 1927 and 1929 had increasingly challenged Ritchie and the firm leadership of Speaker E. Brooke Lee. Party leaders William Curran, Howard Jackson, and national committeeman Howard Bruce all advised against the race. Baltimore County's Senator David McIntosh announced his candidacy. The usual dry opposition was augmented by the remnants of the 1928 anti-Smith, anti-wet Independent Citizens, Inc., who claimed 50,000 voters. Additionally, Ritchie had to meet public outcry over his first administrative scandal, the defalcations of two

26. Rothman, pp. 36-42; *The Marylander*, March 19, 1927; *The Catholic Review*, April 1, 8, 22, May 13, 1927; *Sun*, April 7, 1927; Curran "Obituary" *Sun*, Oct. 5, 1951.
27. *The Observer*, April 9, 23, 30, 1927; *Sun*, May 4, 1927; *Baltimore American*, May 4, 1927; *The Observer*, June 9, 1928; *Sun*, June 20, July 13, Dec. 22, 1928; Rothman, pp. 65, 78; *The Observer*, Sept. 30, 1930; *The Marylander*, May 7, 1927; *The Maryland Almanac*, 1928, pp. 108-09.

employees in the State Roads Commission. Yet for all of this initial flurry, by March 1930, McIntosh withdrew; money and Eastern Shore backing had failed to materialize. The anti-Ritchie Baltimore *Post* ruefully observed: "He has been able to build a political organization around himself which is, at least within his own party, impregnable."[28]

In 1930, the Republican opposition was not formidable. A fierce primary fought on the wet-dry issue was won by the wet, William Broening. Pressured by Phillips Lee Goldsborough to assume a drier posture for party unity and preempted from a pure wet stand by the record of Ritchie, Broening finally straddled on this key issue. Trying to capitalize on the roads' scandal, he hit particularly hard on the fourth-term issue and the Republican concern, "Ritchie Forever?" In the final vote, however, Broening's challenge fell short. In a wet-dry contest and against the background of the depression, Ritchie convincingly triumphed 283,639 to 216,864. His 65,861 vote margin in Baltimore represented a sweep of all but the sixteenth and the Negro seventeenth and fourteenth wards. The Democrats won every congressional seat; elected twenty-three of twenty-nine state senators and scored an increase of six in the House of Delegates. The Republican party, the *Sun* crowed, "got exactly what was coming to it." Yet the Democratic triumph was for Ritchie slightly tinged. For the first time incumbent Ritchie lagged behind the state ticket, falling 15,000 votes shy of the 80,000 pluralities of Attorney General William Preston Lane and

28. The Democrats controlled the legislature by large majorities under Ritchie. See Rothman, p. 14. There was a fall from 93–25 to 82–36 in the House of Delegates in the election of 1926. Speaker E. Brooke Lee felt that Ritchie faced his most difficult legislative challenges in the 1927 and 1929 sessions. The administration margin over dissident Democrats and Republicans hovered at a scant four votes. Interview with E. Brooke Lee, March 23, 1972. Also see *The Baltimore Federationist*, May 25, 1928; Sister Rita Marie Helldorfer, S.S.N.D., "The Gubernatorial Career of Albert Cabell Ritchie, Governor of Maryland, 1920–1935" (M.A. thesis, Catholic University of America, 1955), pp. 67-68. Sister Alice Joseph Rohe, O.S.F., "Press Opinion of a Political Leader: Albert Cabell Ritchie and the Democratic Party, 1924–1932" (M.A. thesis, Catholic University of America, 1967), p. 4; *Sun*, Feb. 5, Aug. 25, Nov. 1, 2, 3, 5, 7, 26, 1929; *Evening Sun*, May 10, 1929; *The Observer*, April 28 and May 12, 1928; Levin, p. 325; *Sun*, March 10, May 10, 1929 and March 31, April 4, 6, Oct. 12, 21, 1930. For full clipping file see Box 39, Ritchie Papers; *Maryland Manual*, 1931, pp. 248-59.

Comptroller William S. Gordy.[29] As in 1923, he won only a minority of the counties. Although still the unquestioned leader of his party and the Old Line State, Ritchie might justifiably turn with some concern to meet the increasing crisis of the depression.

While Ritchie dominated the party in Maryland, the presidential and congressional contests from 1920 to 1932 also clearly demonstrated the growing voter strength and effective coalition of the Maryland Democrats.

In the 1920 campaign, Democratic prospects were far from reassuring. The *Sun* consistently and sharply lambasted presidential Republican candidate Warren Harding as "a typical wheelhorse," "a man of negative character," a creature of the Republican senatorial leadership. Though Democratic nominee Cox was also a disappointment to the *Sun*, the editors concluded that "In all of the qualities which qualify a man for the presidency he is immensely superior to his opponent." Both candidates in their Maryland speeches stressed the major issue in the state and in the nation—the League of Nations. In the voting, Harding's 55,491 plurality was the largest ever registered in an Old Line State presidential race. Triumphing in fifteen counties, he carried every ward in Baltimore, except the second and tenth. He ran well in wards with a heavy Irish, Russian, and Polish registration. In the twentieth and twenty-sixth wards with German voting strength, Harding won handily. Mahon's home ninth ward, with many Irish and German voters, returned a Republican majority of 253. The *Sun* estimated that 30 per cent of the registered Democrats either stayed home or voted Republican. While one Baltimore politician blamed the sulking and apathy of warring bosses Mahon and Kelly, the *Sun* perhaps more effectively gauged the results, observing, "Never before were there so many voters with a grouch without knowing how to get rid of it."[30]

---

29. Bel Air *Times*, July 18, 1930, Box 39, Ritchie Papers; *Sun*, April 9 and 16, June 5, Aug. 17, 18, Nov. 2, 1930. *Sun* reporter Franklyn Waltman surveyed the state in the *Sun*, Oct. 26, 27, 29, 30; Levin, p. 333; *Sun*, Nov. 6, 1930; *Evening Sun*, Nov. 6, 1930; *Maryland Manual*, 1931, pp. 250-51.

30. Abel, pp. 13-15, 25-26, 39-42; Levin, pp. 123-24; *Sun*, June 13, July 7, Aug. 8, Sept. 19, 28, Oct. 22, 1920; *Baltimore American*, Oct. 31, 1920; *Evening Sun*, Nov. 1, 1929; *Sun*, Oct. 14, 1920; *The Maryland Almanac*, 1921, pp. 106, 117; *Maryland Manual*, 1921, pp. 133-34.

While the presidential campaign had been described as the quietest in years, the major Maryland confrontation was for the Senate seat held by incumbent John Walter Smith, a dedicated "dry." Facing him was the Republican party boss, Ovington Weller, an advocate of light beer and wines. Both candidates were not classic stump speakers, preferring to work quietly on building party strength with local leaders. Indeed, Weller was described as the "Greatest Living Rival of the Sphinx." Both faced party defections. Democratic bosses Kelly and Mahon in wet Baltimore were not active for Smith. Republican Phillips Lee Goldsborough, resenting upstart Weller, believed that Marylanders would not "reward an ingrate." Additionally, two independent candidates confused the campaign. Baltimore's wet, George D. Iverson, sought backing solely on his anti-prohibition stance. Negro leader Ashbie Hawkins, chafing at miserly Republican patronage for loyal Negro voters, ran in order to chastise the GOP. In the final election results, Weller eked out a victory that lagged 31,080 behind Harding's Baltimore total. Hawkins' 6,538 votes seemed to harm him less than Iverson's 21,345 ballots from the wet ethnic wards in Baltimore damaged Smith.[31]

In the congressional races, prohibition's power as an issue was illustrated in the successful one-issue campaign of Republican John Phillip Hill, the "Babe Ruth of the wets" in Baltimore's third district. Only in the second district was the women's vote credited with unseating an old suffrage antagonist, Carville D. Benson. With the vote totals counted, Maryland's congressional delegation would favor the Republicans four to two. The Democrats had only barely held in the first district on the Eastern Shore with victor T. Alan Goldsborough and in the fourth in Baltimore City with veteran Charles Linthicum.[32]

Four years after the Harding avalanche of 1920, difficulties of the Democrats had only deepened. The cultural issues of prohibition and the re-emergence of the Ku Klux Klan bitterly divided the growing urban, ethnic, "boss" wing and the rural, old stock southern forces. Leading candidate Al Smith, from New

31. Abel, pp. 44-67; *Baltimore American*, April 15, 1920; *News*, May 14, 17, Sept. 29, 1920; *Sun*, Aug. 11, 15, Oct. 28, 1920; *Evening Sun*, Nov. 3, 1920.
32. *Baltimore American*, Sept. 1, 1920; *Sun*, Oct. 28 and Nov. 1, 1920; Abel, pp. 67-73, 76-87; *Maryland Manual*, 1921, pp. 138-41.

York's East Side and Tammany Hall, vied with southern-born, old-stock, William Gibbs McAdoo, chosen candidate of the Klan. Clustered behind these front runners, hopeful of the nomination if an impasse developed, were corporation lawyer John W. Davis, Alabama's Senator Oscar Underwood, and the "wet hope" Albert C. Ritchie.

The Ritchie strategy was to be available and hopefully to be everyone's second choice. In preparation for the New York convention, he built a campaign staff, headed by national committeeman Howard Bruce, that included able E. Brooke Lee, H. L. Mencken and Frank Kent. Having garnered a resolution in the House of Delegates urging his candidacy, he also obtained, after acrimony and heavy persuasion, a delegation named on a state-wide basis that was pledged to the unit rule and to Ritchie for president. As a candidate, he assumed a low profile. Speeches were kept to a minimum. He avoided the Klan issue and de-emphasized prohibition. The primary goal was to avoid alienation of neutral and rival delegations and to demonstrate Ritchie's fitness as a border state, southern, Protestant, wet, unifying candidate.[33]

Although the convention's ovation at Ritchie's nomination reflected some success for this strategy, John W. Davis and his staff were the ultimate beneficiaries on the 104th ballot of the Smith-McAdoo deadlock. Interpretations of Ritchie's defeat varied from Kent's question, "Was he too wet, and Maryland too small?" to the allegation that his "amateur" managers had been bested by the Davis organization. His silence on the Klan issue and his failure to support Smith were cited to explain why Smith's supporters did not turn to Ritchie in the deadlock.[34]

In the presidential campaigning, Ritchie loyally supported Davis. The *Sun* reminded voters that Davis's mother was a Baltimorean, and cited his progressive career, his support of the Clayton anti-trust measure, and his defense of Eugene Debs. In contrast, it caustically criticized Coolidge's acceptance speech for avoiding the Harding scandals and the Klan issue and for an

---

33. Thigpen, pp. 6, 22-23, 30-32, 34; James Levin, "Governor Albert Ritchie and the Democratic National Convention of 1924," *M.H.M.*, XLVI (Summer, 1971), 102-05, 110-11; *The Observer*, May 24, 1924; Frank Kent, "The Great Game of Politics," Jan. 2, 1924, Vol. I, Kent Papers, MS 181, M.H.S.

34. Thigpen, Preface, pp. 44-56; Levin, pp. 18-20, 109; Kent, "The Great Game of Politics," Feb. 19, 1924, Kent Papers; *Sun*, July 10, 1924.

artful "appeal to the materialistic instincts of the voters." Yet in
a campaign that in party unity and funding placed Coolidge as
the undisputed favorite in the Free State and the nation, a questionable factor was the Progressive candidacy of Fighting Bob
LaFollette. If he won six states, Frank Kent argued, Coolidge
could not win.[35]

LaFollette electors, including Dr. Broadus Mitchell, a Johns
Hopkins professor, and Elisabeth Coit Gilman, a daughter of
The Johns Hopkins University's first president, were chosen at
what was claimed to be the first state LaFollette convention.
Three hundred delegates of labor and farm organizations, the
Socialist party, the *Afro-American*, and *American Jewish
Forward* gathered to organize a campaign committee and to
contribute funds. LaFollette's campaign headquarters was established in the Baltimore Federation of Labor offices. LaFollette workers were active in unions and in the counties and
reportedly were making inroads. Late in the campaign LaFollette spoke to 10,000 to 12,000 at the Fifth Regiment Armory in
Baltimore, denouncing tariffs, monopoly, and the sugar trust;
the *Sun* complained that he "assails, indicts and scourges." Noting defensively that the crowd topped Davis's turnout, the *Sun*
reported that there were many non-voters present.[36]

Increasingly, the early predictions that Maryland would fall
into the Coolidge column seemed borne out. In the face of the
LaFollette threat, it was argued, conservative Democrats would
bolt to Coolidge. Yet Coolidge's final Free State margin was a
bare 14,342 votes. LaFollette's 32,947 votes in southern and
eastern wards of the city, where the Baltimore Federation of
Labor was strong, were highly damaging to Davis. The Baltimore *Observer*, estimating an 80 per cent Democratic registration among labor, concluded that in Maryland, LaFollette had
functioned as an assist to the Republican party. The *Sun*, in
assessing the results, argued that with a divided party and no
clear cut vote getting issues, Davis was doomed from the start.

But together the Davis-LaFollette totals in a 65 per cent voter
turnout in Baltimore were 93,180 to Coolidge's 69,588. Combined they would have carried every ward but the Negro four-

35. *Sun*, July 10, 11, Aug. 12, 15, Nov. 1, 4, 1924; *The Observer*, Sept. 13,
1924; Kent column in the *Sun*, July 18, 1924.
36. *Sun*, Aug. 4, 1924; *The Observer*, Sept. 6, 13, 27, 1924; *Sun*, Oct. 28, 1924;
*The Observer*, Nov. 1, 1924.

teenth and seventeenth and the twenty-second and fifth. In the same combination, Davis's eleven-county victory would have been augmented by Frederick, Prince George's, and Washington Counties. LaFollette-Davis statewide totals of 195,229 would have handily defeated Coolidge.[37] For Congress, the Democrats carried the state districts four to two and won the first district seat from the Republicans, who were badly weakened by the death of their leader and incumbent Sidney Mudd.[38]

As early as January 1926, Ritchie was boomed as a possible candidate for the presidency in 1928. The *New York Times* quoted a response to his speech to the "Tammany of the West," Chicago's Iroquois Club, ranking it "in importance with certain epochal pronouncements of James G. Blaine, Stephen A. Douglas and James Monroe." Ritchie, more modestly, agreed that this speech fairly launched him for the 1928 run. Throughout 1926 and 1927, Ritchie maintained a full lecture schedule, addressing, among others, the New York City lawyers, the Virginia Assembly, the Governors' Conference, the National Chamber of Commerce, and the American Historical and American Political Science Associations. Additionally, he contributed articles to the scholarly *Annals of The Academy of Political and Social Science, The Tax Digest, Current History,* and *Plain Talk. Sun* writers profiled him in the *American Mercury, Scribner's,* and *Christian Science Monitor,* and political reporter Charles Merz observed in the *Independent:* "It is not too much to say that in the last three years he had made more speeches in more different parts of the United States than any other man in American life save Lindbergh and Will Rogers."[39]

37. *The Observer,* Aug. 23, 1934; *Sun,* Oct. 23, 31, Nov. 5, 6, 1924; *Baltimore American,* Nov. 19, 1924; *The Observer,* Nov. 1, 8, 1924. Baltimore returns in *The Maryland Almanac,* 1925, p. 19. Campaign efforts are in *The Observer,* Oct. 4, 11, 1924 and *Sun,* Oct. 31, 1924.

38. *Sun,* Oct. 12, 14, 16, 18, 1924; *Maryland Manual,* 1925, pp. 203-11; *Maryland Almanac,* 1925, pp. 15, 18-19. House of Delegates and Senate results in Rothman, p. 14.

39. Clippings on pre-campaign activities in 1926, 1927 and 1928 are collected in Box 28A, Ritchie Papers: *Sun,* Jan. 9, 18, 21, March 6, 1926; *Time,* May 24, 1926; *American Rights,* March 15, 1926; *Sun,* May 5, 18, 19, 20, July 8, 27, Dec. 30, 1927; *Evening Sun,* Aug. 12, 1927; Ritchie articles: "Some Facts Underlying the Relationship Between the United States and Russia," *Annals,* July, 1926; "Reducing Maryland's State Tax Rate," *The Tax Digest,* Oct. 1927; "Is Democracy a Failure," *Current History,* May, 1928; "The Imperialism of

The themes Ritchie reiterated in speeches and articles were articulated most succinctly in his *Plain Talk* article: "the love of liberty, the spirit of toleration, faith in the individual man and in his rights and privileges, freedom, opposition to arbitrary power and excessive Federalism; the pride of self reliance and all the individuality that is humanly possible." In *Scribner's*, he emphasized: "We are developing into the most overgoverned and least self governing of peoples." While inveighing against Coolidge's growing bureaucracy and pleading the case for states' rights and responsibility, Ritchie was also reminding the voters that if prohibition were the major issue in 1928, he was the candidate who had most consistently offered a position. He could be, as the *American Legion Magazine* observed, "a Moses for the Wets."[40]

Yet suddenly, after this full preparation for the Democratic convention, Ritchie announced in June 1928, that he was withdrawing as a candidate in favor of Al Smith. After so much effort, there was wide speculation. The *Sun* reported Ritchie backers to be of the opinion that "this is Smith's year and if he is a candidate and doesn't get it," the nomination would be worthless. Subsequently, theories were hotly disputed by James Farley of a Smith-Ritchie meeting in which Ritchie declared "All right, Al, I'll wait," and agreed to mount his race in 1932. More subtle was the analysis by *Sun* reporter Hamilton Owens, observing in the March 1926 *American Mercury* "that his warmest admirers stand in constant fear that in a rough-and-tumble he may stop to think twice."[41]

At the convention and in the Maryland campaign Ritchie and the *Sunpapers* sounded the theme of Smith—man of the people. Seconding Smith's nomination, Ritchie asserted: "You cannot run human government by dehumanized efficiency experts, who think that charts, blueprints, reports and statistics constitute its whole sum and substance." The *Sun* portrayed the Smith-Hoover match-up as the democrat versus the engineer.

the Dollar," *Atlantic Monthly*, May, 1928; Frank Kent, "Ritchie of Maryland," *Scribner's*, Oct., 1927; Charles Merz, "Preconvention Portraits, VIII: Ritchie of Maryland," *The Independent*, Feb. 25, 1928.

40. Albert C. Ritchie, "Shall We Govern Ourselves," *Scribner's*, April, 1928; "Too Much Government," *Plain Talk*, Feb., 1928, Ritchie Papers, Box 28A. *American Legion* cited Ritchie as "A Moses for the Wets" Jan. 29, 1926, Box 28A.

41. *Sun*, Jan. 3 and June 19, 1928; Thigpen, pp. 65-76; Bowens, pp. 130-31.

Hoover's address on the spiritual ends of national life was assessed as "depressingly uninspired and trite." Additionally, he was actively supported "by the worst elements of his party and is obviously content."[42]

Yet in the Old Line State and the nation, the presidential campaign was to be no people versus the interests fight. From the beginning the 1928 race was characterized by bigotry and whispering. The Anti-Saloon League and the Baltimore Ministerial Association mobilized to fight Smith on the wet issue. The Eastern Shore native son and national champion of the dry cause, Bishop James Cannon, returned home to help to distribute the literature of the prolific and anti-Catholic Fellowship Forum. Senator Bruce estimated that $500,000 worth of these broadsides were distributed in Maryland; typical was a pamphlet asserting: "A Vote for Al Smith is a Vote for the Pope." Ritchie sarcastically countered: "Do you suppose that the Pope has been biding his time for 300 years until Smith was born?" The Democratic National Committee defensively issued fliers on religious toleration.[43]

Race also was utilized as a Maryland issue. Negro Republicans, dismayed at the lily-white southern strategy of the party and the treatment of their suggested planks at the national convention, threatened to continue their slow drift to the Democrats, begun in the 1923 Ku Klux Klan anti-Ritchie campaign. Democrats in Baltimore City had indicated through patronage, particularly in the fourteenth ward, that the latch string was out. So accepted was the probable Negro move to the Republicans, noted Tydings, that the Republicans on the Eastern Shore were using scare tactics by having Negroes ride in cars covered with Smith banners.[44]

The 1928 linkage of alcohol, Romanism, racism, and Tammany Hall made the battleground an Armageddon. A Baltimore Methodist minister asserted that if Smith were elected "homes would become brothels." The *Southern Methodist* declared the victory of "an illiterate, a Roman Catholic, one who indulges

42. *Sun*, June 15, 28, 29, Aug. 12, 15, 23, Sept. 14, 1928.

43. *The Observer*, May 5, 12, 1928; *Sun*, April 7, 8, 11, May 8, 26, Sept. 24, 26, 1928. *Evening Sun*, Aug. 8, 1928; Frank F. White, "The 1928 Presidential Election in Maryland," (M.A. thesis, University of Maryland, 1947), pp. 2-3, 21, 33, 39, 41, 47-48, 58-59; Thigpen, p. 79; *Sun*, July 26, Aug. 9, 19, Sept. 21, 22, Oct. 6, 1928.

44. *The Observer*, Sept. 15, Nov. 3, 1928.

habitually in cocktails, and an inveterate enemy of prohibition would be an insult to the dry protestant democracy of the South."[45] It was obviously a powerful mix. Although united for Smith and outspending the Republicans, the Maryland Democratic leaders were still pleading for funds on the eve of the election. In the voting, Hoover soundly trounced Smith in Maryland 301,479 to 223,626. In the counties only Queen Anne's, home of the Democratic National Committee Chairman, J. J. Raskob, and St. Mary's, with its substantial Roman Catholic population, gave Smith a plurality. In Baltimore City, Hoover swept sixteen of twenty-eight wards, but won only a 9,076 vote edge of 261,282 cast. Reviewing the totals, a *Sun* analyst concluded that in Maryland the religious issue was the most powerful. Farm problems, power questions, and Tammany made little impact. Republicans boasted that prosperity might have led voters to reward the incumbents; yet this too, was not strongly articulated in the Maryland campaign. While the defeat was dramatic, the *Sun* predicted that the Democrats could make important gains for the future; the Negro vote in the seventeenth ward was promising; Roman Catholic identification might remain; wet immigrants seemed firmly in the party ranks. Additionally, the vote of a growing suburban working population on the fringes of Washington in Prince George's and Montgomery Counties, apparently in the LaFollette column in 1924, might land in the Democratic camp.[46]

In the Senate and congressional races, Herbert Hoover's coattails were unimpressive. The Maryland gentleman, Phillips Lee Goldsborough, a former governor and redoubtable votegetter, unseated incumbent William Cabell Bruce. But Bruce was vulnerable for his strong support of the power interests and charges of absenteeism. In the house races, the Democrats managed to win, with some hairbreadth finishes, five of the six seats. Only in traditionally Republican western Maryland, did the GOP triumph.

Four years later, in the depths of the depression, Ritchie made his last run for the presidency. Strengthened by election to an unprecedented fourth term as governor, Ritchie's inau-

---

45. White, "The 1928 Presidential Election in Maryland," p. 17.
46. *Maryland Almanac*, 1929, pp. 76-77, 79-81; White, "The 1928 Presidential Election in Maryland," pp. 66-67; *Sun*, Nov. 8, 1928.

gural speech in January 1931 spurred presidential speculation in the *Chicago Tribune, London Times, Colliers, Saturday Evening Post,* and the *Nation.* The Columbia Broadcasting System broadcast his address over thirty-four New England stations. In April *Cosmopolitan* cited a poll of congressmen that listed fifty-nine for Roosevelt and thirty-seven for Ritchie.[47]

In January 1932, Ritchie officially, if obliquely, announced his candidacy. Asked at a Baltimore Democratic club banquet if he wanted to be president, he responded simply, "Who would not?" As in 1926 and 1927, he undertook extensive speaking engagements to outline the Ritchie platform. Two themes, liberty for the individual and faith in the old ways, were constantly reiterated. In a Menckenesque address at the Governors' Conference he warned: "If you are to be inspected and suspected and never respected by your Government, then the army of experts and near experts who do all these things will be expert enough to see that you pay the piper, even if you cannot always call the tune." His commencement address at Washington College in June clearly developed his faith: "Strange temples are under construction and in them dwell strange gods, who beckon obeisance. But the altar of faith which has brought us safely through all our adventures of peace and war still stands and its fires still burn. I, for one, see no reason for another shrine." More specifically, the *Sun* summarized his program as against paternalism, and for better budgeting procedures, tariff cuts, repeal of the Eighteenth Amendment, and establishment of the thirty-hour week.[48]

Pre-convention and floor strategy echoed 1924. Ritchie did not enter the primaries. With a number of favorite sons, he hoped to be everyone's second choice should front-runner Roosevelt be stopped. The Old Line State gave him a rousing sendoff to Chicago. A crowd of over 30,000 listened to ten brass bands playing, "There's a President in the Heart of Maryland."

---

47. For national press coverage see clippings in Box 38, Ritchie Papers. Also Rohe, p. 55; *Sun,* Jan. 15, 1931.

48. *Sun,* Jan. 8, 1932. Clippings on Ritchie speeches in Box 44, Ritchie Papers. *Sun,* Feb. 18, March 20, April 8, 14, 1932; *Evening Sun,* Feb. 1, March 5, 6, 16, 19, 1932. Washington College address, *Evening Sun,* June 11, 1932; Governor's Conference, Rohe, pp. 68-69; *Sun,* April 27, 1932, *New York Herald-Tribune,* April 28, 1932. Issues surveyed in *Sun,* March 20, April 22, May 20, 26, June 2, 9, 1932.

Planes flew overhead. In Chicago, Ritchie received a tumultuous welcome as over 1,000 traders left the floor of the Chicago Board of Trade to join the 10,000 crowding the streets. At his nomination a boisterous forty-minute demonstration erupted. Yet, as Frank Kent pointed out, Ritchie had more friends and fewer delegates than any other candidate. In the balloting, Ritchie's top vote was 23½ of which 16 were Maryland votes.[49]

As in 1928, Ritchie was eulogized for his gallantry in defeat, and, as in 1924, speculation began on the reasons for his failure. Frank Kent concluded that the villain was Al Smith, leader of the anti-Roosevelt forces, who, seemingly convinced that he could still win the nomination, never worked for an agreement on one "Stop Roosevelt" candidate. Roosevelt manager James Farley and others argued that when the Democrats adopted a plank for prohibition repeal, the major reason for backing Ritchie was removed. "However, Farley actually offered Ritchie the nomination for vice-president after the repeal plank was adopted by the Resolutions Committee." The *Sun* finally concluded that Ritchie was "out of step with too many elements of our national life to have a chance of getting the nomination." A disappointed Mencken described the convention climax as a classic Democratic ending: "The victors are full of uneasiness and the vanquished are full of bile."[50] Yet in the depths of the

---

49. Thigpen, 92-105; clippings on convention in Box 45, Ritchie Papers, *Sun*, June 22, 23, 1932; *News*, June 23, 24, 1932; *Post*, June 29, 1932; *Evening Sun*, June 22, 1932. Farley, concerned at the "Stop Roosevelt" drive asked Ritchie if he would accept the vice-presidency on FDR's ticket. Ritchie declined preferring to be Governor of Maryland. Thigpen, pp. 117-25. E. Brooke Lee was present at the Farley meeting. Interview with E. Brooke Lee, March 23, 1972. Lee felt that Ritchie was closest to the presidential nomination in 1932 than at any other time.

50. Thigpen, pp. 127-40; *Sun*, July 3, 1932; *Jewish Times*, July 8, 1932. *Evening Sun*, July 2, 1932. "Organization of the support for this prohibition repeal plank was put together in Mayor Howard Jackson's room, which was adjacent to Governor Ritchie's. . . . A clear majority of the delegation to the convention had pledged their support of the repeal plank before the Resolutions Committee meeting to act upon the platform.

"Of course I doubt that Jim Farley could have delivered the vice presidential nomination to Governor Ritchie after William Randolph Hearst and the leaders of the California delegation plus the Texas delegation got together for Jack Garner for that nomination. Also, the inclusion of the Volstead Repeal plank in the platform undoubtedly lessened the appeal that a Ritchie candidacy would have added. But a basic fact is that this platform committee fight was organized with Governor Ritchie's full knowledge and approval. . . ." Letter from E. Brooke Lee to the author, June 7, 1972. Ironically, E. Brooke

depression, running against scapegoat Hoover, Roosevelt was assured a handsome victory.

Ritchie and the Old Line State Democrats campaigned loyally and hard for the victors. Maryland resoundingly chose Roosevelt by a margin of 130,000 votes. Winning Baltimore City by an 81,355 plurality, he carried every county but traditionally Republican Allegany, Garrett, and Calvert. Behind Roosevelt on the Democratic ticket, incumbent Senator Millard Tydings trounced Wallace Williams. All six congressional seats fell to the Democrats.[51] Resting on an ethnic and labor vote in Baltimore and industrial county areas, gradually winning a greater share of the Negro urban vote, and relieved of the divisive wet-dry issue with prohibition repeal, the Democrats achieved a stunning reversal of 1920. Functioning effectively in state and national contests, the Democratic coalition and leadership stood triumphant in 1932.

2

ECONOMIC AND SOCIAL ISSUES

As Maryland's political development in the 1920's centered on the leadership of Ritchie, economic growth rested on the dominance of Baltimore. Building from a highly diversified industrial base of textiles, petroleum, smelting and refining, and fertilizers, Baltimore and its booster businessmen successfully attracted 103 new plants during the decade. City salesmanship stressed the solid banking and credit facilities, low power and tax rates, low cost of living, advantageous port position and terminals, relatively tranquil labor conditions, rich consumer market, and Baltimore's primacy as a distribution center for the Southeast. Baltimore became the eastern center of the new glamour aircraft industry as Glenn L. Martin, Berliner-Joyce, Doyle Aero and Curtiss-Caprivi built factories and fields in the area. American Sugar and Western Electric developed major new plants, and Bethlehem Steel invested $100,000,000 to expand its Sparrows Point facility. Bethlehem's president Charles

---

Lee's dogged and successful fight before the platform committee which delayed the convention an entire day and added to Farley's nervousness, might have been a contributing factor to Ritchie's defeat.

51. In the Roosevelt triumph, the Maryland Socialist vote was close to a record, totalling 10,489 for Norman Thomas. *Maryland Manual*, 1933, pp. 283-90.

Schwab congratulated a gratified Baltimore Association of Commerce: "There is no place in the United States so susceptible of successful industrial development. . . ."[52]

Paralleling Baltimore's industrial expansion was the vitality of her import-export trade. The city began the decade ranking seventh in volume of foreign trade; by 1926 it was the third port in export and import cargoes, rated only behind New York and New Orleans. To win this position, the Baltimore Chamber of Commerce (the former Grain and Flour Exchange) worked tirelessly to defend the port's favorable rail differential against the claims of competing Gulf ports, New York, Philadelphia, and Boston. In Congress, the Chamber lobbied with only partial success for federal funds to deepen the channel to forty feet. New grain elevators built by the Western Maryland Railroad at Port Covington, by the Pennsylvania Railroad at Canton, and by the B&O at Locust Point added an 8,000,000 bushel capacity for the port. Ironically, the grain trade, which had prompted the development of these facilities, suffered disastrously throughout the decade. The renewed competition of Russian, Canadian, Argentinian, and Australian wheat at the war's end plummeted exports through Baltimore from 29.7 to 21.7 million bushels in 1921. By 1924 wheat exports dropped to 16,055,643 bushels, with 10 million bushels stored in Baltimore elevators. The Chamber of Commerce recorded the year as one of "disappointments" and "uncertainty." Although Baltimore's volume in other areas allowed it to maintain a healthy tonnage, by 1930 the grain exchange reported exports of all grains had fallen to the lowest total since 1910.[53]

In order to stimulate trade within the state, an ambitious ten-year road-building program was launched by the Ritchie administration by matching federal road appropriations of $850,000 a year to develop trunk lines and post roads. Addition-

---

52. *Baltimore*, XIII (July, 1920), 9; XIII (Aug., 1920), 7; XIX (Dec., 1925), 22; XX (Oct., 1926), 55; XV (May, 1922), 38; XXII (Jan., 1929), 5-6. Schwab is cited in *Baltimore*, XX (Dec., 1926), 5. For a survey of Maryland's industrial growth see Fairbanks and Hamill, *The Manufacturing Industry of Maryland*, pp. 8-45.

53. *Baltimore*, XXI (May, 1928), 62; XIV (Oct., 1920), 7; XXIII (July, 1930), 23. See also *67th Annual Report of the Baltimore Chamber of Commerce for the Year Ending December 31, 1921* (Baltimore: Hess Printing Co., 1922), pp. 10-11; *68th Annual Report, 1922*, pp. 14-15; *70th Annual Report, 1924*, p. 11; *75th Annual Report, 1929*, p. 11.

ally a fund of $750,000 annually was recommended for lateral roads if the counties would pledge to match it. State bond issues and a four-cent gasoline tax supported the completion of Crain Highway and free bridges across the Severn and Susquehanna rivers. By the end of Ritchie's administrations the Old Line State road system of 3,000 miles was adjudged the second best in the nation.[54]

Yet perhaps the most significant transportation development in the decade was the linkage of the Eastern and Western Shores. An abortive effort had been made in the 1916 legislature with the authorization of $50,000 for the State Roads Commission to develop a ferry service between Annapolis and Claiborne. Since the funds would enable purchase of only one ten-car ferry, it was hardly surprising that no action was taken. Three years later, when a group of New York promoters launched the Claiborne-Annapolis Ferry, Inc., and established scheduled runs, six hours were cut from the old mail time. However, this pioneering venture was peculiarly ill-starred. One of the two company vessels, the *General Lincoln*, ran aground in 1920, stranding the cars on board for over a month; the next year a paddle-wheel box broke and lifeboats were needed to rescue the passengers. Discouraged, the original backers withdrew, and the service was taken over by a Maryland group headed by former Governor Emerson C. Harrington. The first round-bottomed double-ended vessel, the *Governor Albert C. Ritchie*, was added in 1926 and soon joined by the *John M. Dennis* and the *Governor Harry W. Nice*. By 1930 a shortened Matapeake route cut the running time from an hour and a half to forty-five minutes. Other lines encouraged by this success joined Bay Shore Park to Rock Hall, Baltimore to Tolchester, and Crisfield to the western shore of Virginia.[55]

Coincident to the launching of the Bay ferry services was the discussion and planning for a bay bridge. In 1927 the Chesapeake Bay Bridge Company was chartered, headed by Baltimoreans, Stuart S. Janney (Ritchie's law partner), W. Roscoe Bonsal, and a group of New York promoters. Senator Tydings gained the approval of the secretary of war and Congress for the

---

54. Chepaitis, pp. 17-18; *The Marylander*, April 2, 1927.
55. Clippings in Vertical File, Enoch Pratt Free Library. Hereafter VFEP. *Sun*, Nov. 22, 1940; *Evening Sun*, Feb. 23, 1924, June 14, 1929, Sept. 26, 1936; *Baltimore American*, July 27, 1952; *Sun*, Aug. 11, 1940.

span, contractors' bids were taken, and hearings were set before the Public Service Commission. However, the combined opposition of anxious Eastern Shore merchants and the Annapolis Ferry Corporation as well as the disastrous impact of the crash of 1929 postponed the project.[56]

Physical expansion in industry, trade, and transportation was paralleled by the organizational development of Baltimore's businessmen. In April 1924 the Baltimore Association of Commerce was formed by the amalgamation of the Merchants and Manufacturers Association, the Export and Import Board of Trade, and the Industrial Bureau of the Board of Trade. In a "spirit of working together," the association labored and lobbied to encourage and protect local interests.

In the state legislature, Baltimore business lobbied against the minimum wage bill, arguing that it should cover all women in agricultural and domestic work, a sure deterrent to rural support. Two workmen's compensation measures were opposed; similarly, in 1924, the Association of Commerce argued against an eight-hour law for women, asserting that it would rob them of their opportunity to work ten hours and force them to work eight hours on Saturday to keep Maryland's textile mills on a competitive level with New York. Consistently and successfully they lobbied against Maryland's adoption of the child labor amendment. Particularly noisome to the association was a state nonpartisan insurance fund proposal, which was denounced as "socialistic and un-American." As a measure of their general lobbying success, the association observed that in the 1922 session, every bill it opposed except a soldiers' bonus was defeated.[57]

While the Association of Commerce did not officially endorse political candidates, its concern in 1924 over a Congress "run wild" did lead it to urge businessmen to work for a victory for "common sense" by striking down LaFollette's "radicalism" with "unrelenting vigor." Relief at Coolidge's "glorious victory" was colorfully expressed in the Association organ,

56. Bridge clippings VFEP. *Sun*, Sept. 5, 1953, *Baltimore*, XLV (July, 1952); *Sun*, Jan. 22, 1927, Jan. 13, 1929, March 15, 1929, July 24, 1952. Clippings also in Box 38, Ritchie Papers. *Maryland Leader*, Nov. 11, 1933; *Sun*, Sept. 30, Nov. 7, 12, 13, 14, 1933. It would be 1952 before the bridge was completed.
57. *Baltimore*, XVII (May, 1924), 7; XIII (April, 1920), 3-7; XVII (Feb., 1924), 7-8; XIII (March, 1920), 26.

*Baltimore*: "The election was a complete routing of ultra radicalism in America. The mere smell of the skunk caused the vast majority of voters to forget other candidates and other issues in a determination to slaughter that malodorous beast."[58]

On the state and local level the association urged business to meet its civic responsibilities in supporting Baltimore school, water and harbor loans, and "proper aid" to the University of Maryland. It backed home rule for Baltimore and campaigned for a one-branch city council. In the area of environment it endorsed efforts to regulate smoke emission in the city and stressed the need of Maryland-Virginia cooperation to protect shad and the blue crab. More tangibly, the Association and Baltimore business met their responsibilities as citizens by successfully organizing and directing the Community Chest Drives.[59]

Throughout the decade, the Association of Commerce in *Baltimore* optimistically prodded the city's conservative and sober businessmen to efficient effort. As the postwar recession of 1921 ebbed, they advised "In closing up your books for 1921, be sure to close out your last remnant of pessimism." By October 1922, *Baltimore* noted that the "general spirit is distinctly optimistic." A year later, business was incited to abandon its caution and ultra conservatism for "the New School of business preaches go-get-it doctrine—whip up the steed and gallop forward." The association applauded 1925 efforts, as business was more active, "evidencing a refreshing smell of confident satisfaction."[60]

Yet within this optimism the association also recognized several "sore spots." Housing remained a troubled industry throughout the decade. Europe's lagging recovery threatened trade. The agricultural depression and the farmers' reduced purchasing power promised serious industrial repercussions.[61] A worrisome industrial sluggishness in 1927 caused Baltimore's

---

58. *Baltimore*, XXVIII (Dec., 1924), 8.

59. *Baltimore*, XIII (Jan., 1920), 40-41; XIII (Sept., 1920), 3; XVII (March, 1924), 7-8; XVII (July, 1924), 21; XVIII (March, 1925), 13-16; XIX (Jan., 1926), 15-16; XXII (Feb., 1929), 45.

60. *Baltimore*, XV (Dec., 1921), 11; XVI (Oct., 1922), 7; XVII (Oct., 1923), 7; XIX (Nov., 1925), 14-15.

61. *Baltimore*, XVI (Nov., 1922), 11; XVII (Nov., 1923), 7-8; XVII (Dec., 1923), 7-8.

unemployment to rise to 25,000. Reflective of a slowdown encompassing the entire east coast, the slump led many businessmen to the unhappy conclusion that the country was "overbuilt."[62]

Though Baltimore business was cushioned by its diversity and its production of necessities rather than luxuries, it continued to be sluggish during 1928. The Baltimore Federation of Labor's claim of 75,000 idle was hotly disputed by the Association of Commerce. However, its own estimate of 30,000 indicated that industrial conditions remained troublesome. It rejoiced that the police census found only 15,473 unemployed. Yet in October 1929, on the brink of the stock market collapse, *Baltimore* reported "satisfactory conditions." Employment was improved; wholesale and retail markets were sound.[63]

While business and political leaders throughout the nation met in troubled conferences to assess the impact of the crash, Baltimore's Mayor William Broening called a meeting of a hundred, "the cream of Baltimore industry." The overwhelming theme was optimism. Retail executives reported plans for expanded business. Daniel Willard of the B&O observed that his road was never in better condition physically; the gas company announced that its 1930 budget was the largest in history. Ralph C. Hudson, president of the Association of Commerce, asserted: "If there is any depression it will be short-lived. Baltimore has little to worry about." Mayor Broening noted that the city would launch a $20,000,000 public improvement program and then summed up the meeting: "Confidence is what is wanted and this extraordinary meeting indicates that we have it." This confidence lasted through 1930. *Baltimore* magazine trumpeted, "Industry is not going to the bow-wows." The newly elected association president, Frank Roberts, reported: "Business and industry have been hit much more lightly in Baltimore during the current economic depression than in other large cities of the United States. Baltimore has fared well in comparison."[64]

While Baltimore business struggled against the impact of the

---

62. *Baltimore*, XX (Aug., 1927), 19; XX (Aug., 1927), 9.

63. *Baltimore*, XXIII (Oct., 1929), 11; XXI (Jan., 1928), 5; XXI (March, 1928), 9; *The Baltimore Federationist*, March 16, 1928.

64. *Baltimore*, XXIII (Dec., 1929), 3; XXIV (Dec., 1930), 5; XXIII (Jan., 1930), 8.

depression of 1929, Maryland's farmers fought the effects of the recession of 1921 throughout the decade. As in industry, Old Line State agricultural diversification helped to soften the blow. Grain, especially wheat, was the major crop, but there was significant acreage in hay, tobacco, vegetables, fruit, and nuts. Forest, dairy, and poultry products added to the diversity. The drop in prices from a 1920 high to 1923, however, graphically indicated the recession's severity in Maryland. Wheat plummeted from $2.80 a bushel to $1.04; corn from $1.85 to $.86; potatoes from $3.52 to $1.12. Tobacco, sharply dropping in 1921, enjoyed a slight upturn in 1923.[65]

Though Marylanders observed that the agricultural recession was not so disastrous as elsewhere, the 1923 "financial stringency" was sufficiently acute for Ritchie to establish a Governor's Committee on Agricultural Program. Charged with recommending solutions for the decline and planning for sound future development, the committee urged further expansion of cooperative organizations of producers, already effectively utilized by the tobacco and dairymen. With the Baltimore Association of Commerce, the committee requested that Congress modify immigration restrictions to help ease the farm labor shortage.[66]

In adversity the farmer strengthened his organizations. The fifty-year-old Maryland Grange was joined in 1923 by the Maryland Farm Bureau Federation and its purchasing adjunct, the Maryland Agricultural Cooperative. The State Extension Service continued its educational work through the county agent system. In the exigencies of the drought of 1930, units of the militant National Farmers Union were established in the Old Line State, particularly in Carroll County.[67]

By the end of the 1920's the number of Maryland farms had declined by 4,704; farm acreage dropped 200,000, half of which

---

65. W. S. Hamill, *The Agricultural Industry of Maryland* (Baltimore: Maryland Development Bureau of the Baltimore Association of Commerce, 1934), pp. 1-2, 120; R. F. Hale, *Prices Paid for Maryland Farm Products, 1851–1927,* (College Park, Maryland: University of Maryland Agricultural Experiment Station, 1930), pp. 55-62.

66. Maryland, *Report of the Committee on an Agricultural Program,* Nov. 20, 1933.

67. Thomas B. Symons, *The Passing of a Decade: A Summary of Extension Activities in Maryland, 1924–1933* (College Park, Maryland: University of Maryland Extension Service, 1934), pp. 28-29.

was on the Eastern Shore. Increased development of hunting and recreational land, the growth of the suburbs in Anne Arundel, Baltimore and Montgomery Counties, and more intensive land use by poultry and dairy interests contributed to the rural population decline. The industrial depression in 1929 only deepened the problems of Maryland agriculture. Estimated gross income from farm production graphically demonstrated the difficulty of Maryland farmers; but again the saving cushion was diversity as the following table shows:

|  | 1929 | 1930 | 1931 | 1932 |
|---|---|---|---|---|
| Corn | $ 2,054,000 | $ 314,000 | $ 1,105,000 | $ 626,000 |
| Wheat | 9,053,000 | 6,884,000 | 3,752,000 | 1,715,000 |
| Tobacco | 3,640,000 | 4,441,000 | 4,981,000 | 6,856,000 |
| Truck crops | 5,486,000 | 6,859,000 | 8,145,000 | 13,485,000 |
| Milk | 25,156,000 | 23,401,000 | 19,945,000 | 16,875,000[68] |

Like the farmer, organized labor faced difficult challenges in the 1920's. Charges of union "radicalism" in the "red scare" of 1919–1920, opposition by vigorous open shop practice of Baltimore management, and an increasing labor surplus placed the American Federation of Labor on the defensive. Problems in union membership were clear. Only 10 per cent of industrial Baltimore was organized, mainly in the textile and building trades. As the Association of Commerce approvingly noted: "The great body of workers in Baltimore are sound in their patriotism, are honest in their motives, and are ready to do the right thing if they are properly led." Most were native born and owned their own homes. In brief, Baltimore's labor force was stable and conservative. If there were difficulties, an "ample supply" of unskilled Negro labor was available.[69]

In attempting to organize this rank and file the AFL leadership was dominated by Baltimore's Henry Broening. Elected in 1920 to head the Baltimore Federation of Labor, Broening's term, rivaling Ritchie's, was only terminated by his death in 1933. Forty years old, a horseshoer by trade, a graduate of Loyola College, who liberally sprinkled his speeches with classical allusions, Broening exemplified the middle-class posture

68. Hamill, pp. 37, 51-52, 81, 107, 110-16, 310.

69. *Baltimore*, XIII (Feb., 1920), 3; XIX (Oct., 1926), 57; Fairbanks and Hamill, *The Manufacturing Industry of Maryland*, pp. 167-99.

and aspirations of the local membership.[70] His programs were in the AFL tradition of bread and butter issues with emphasis on self-help. The Federation of Labor established the Baltimore Labor College; it sponsored radio broadcasts to carry labor's views and programs to the public; it worked for labor representation on the school board and battled against vocational training in the school system. In the legislature, the AFL effectively supported the reorganization of the Bureau of Labor and Statistics, but otherwise made little progress in achieving its major objectives. Attempts to gain Maryland's ratification of the child labor amendment met the adamant opposition of Ritchie in his state rights philosophy. Efforts to reduce the limit of working women's hours from ten to eight were unsuccessful. While amendments to the workmen's compensation law of 1914 were passed in 1920, 1929, and 1931, labor still asserted that disability and death benefits were woefully inadequate.[71]

Child labor was a key issue in Ritchie's stand against federal expansion and for state responsibility. Maryland's child labor legislation restricted employment of children under fourteen in manufacturing, workshops, and canneries, and required work permits for those between fourteen and sixteen to work an eight-hour day. The state screened youthful applicants for health, mental hygiene, and character, insisting on "faithfulness to work, honesty to company, and justice to employers." Throughout the decade a general decline in the issuance of permits perhaps reflected a local labor surplus and emphasis on completion of a high school education. While the number of legal workers dropped, however, an augmented and efficient staff of state inspectors was concerned at the significant numbers still illegally employed in Baltimore City and County.[72] In

---

70. *Twenty-Ninth Annual Report of the Maryland Board of Labor and Statistics, 1920*, pp. 204-05. Broening was the cousin of the incumbent mayor, William Broening.

71. *The Baltimore Federationist*, Sept. 28, 1938, Aug., 28, 1931; *Baltimore*, XXVII (Nov., 1933), 22; *The Baltimore Federationist*, Dec., 14, 1928, May 18, 1928; *Thirty-fourth Annual Report of the Commissioner of Labor and Statistics of Maryland, 1925*, pp. 188-89.

72. Child labor trends are developed in the Twenty-ninth and Thirtieth Annual *Reports* of the Maryland State Board of Labor and Statistics and in the Thirty-first to Thirty-ninth Annual *Reports* of the Commissioner of Labor and Statistics. In Baltimore, most of the permits were issues for work in small retail stores, offices, messenger services and metal and printshops. Child labor applications usually reflected the health of the economy; applications reached

rural areas, the child labor problem was particularly trouble-some. Canneries were not scrupulous in checking proof of age. A survey by the Children's Bureau of Anne Arundel County and Eastern Shore children working in fields and canneries demonstrated that 50 per cent of the white and 71 per cent of the Negro children between eight and sixteen were below average grades for their age.[73]

Moved by these statistics and continued urban violations, the legislature revised the child labor law in 1928. Completion of the elementary grades was required before a work permit would be issued. The State Department of Education provided children with evidence of age before they left school to enable them to work for the canneries; letters were also sent from schools to the row bosses. This improved enforcement procedure and modest educational extension were the only Maryland responses to the child labor problem. The onset of the depression perhaps was more effective in decreasing child labor.[74]

A survey of the hours and working conditions of Maryland women, undertaken at the request of Ritchie, reported conditions "not at all favorable" in the Old Line State. Dangerous defects and fire hazards were cited in 148 of 240 plants inspected. Though concerned about these conditions, the primary stress of the AFL was for legislation lowering the ten-hour law to eight. Enforcement of even the ten-hour provision was difficult. When state investigators acted on complaints, they found that women would not testify for fear of losing their jobs. In 1929, of 61,697 women workers surveyed, only thirty-seven ten-hour violations were discovered. In one case, when two women were found to have been employed over sixty hours a week and ten hours a day, the employer was fined $17.90. Enforcement was not effective; the legal fines were less than a deterrent.[75]

---

17,894 in the postwar boom of 1920 and dropped to 7,684 in the recession of 1921.

73. Alice Channing, *Child Labor on Maryland Truck Farms, 1923*, Children's Bureau, Publication No. 123 (Washington: Government Printing Office, 1923), pp. 23-31, 51-52.

74. *Thirty-eighth Annual Report of the Commissioner of Labor and Statistics of Maryland, 1929*, p. 41; *Thirty-ninth Annual Report, 1930*, pp. 13-14. In 1930, Baltimore city inspectors still found 114 children employed illegally.

75. *Thirtieth Annual Report of the Maryland State Board of Labor and Statistics, 1921*, pp. 81-83; *Thirty-fourth Annual Report, 1925*, p. 45.

Though Maryland had pioneered in workmen's compensation legislation and revised her 1914 law under Ritchie in 1920, 1929, and 1931, organized labor still had serious reservations concerning time limits on reporting injuries and the adequacy of disability and death benefits. The benefits had been appreciably raised, but a 1925 study concluded that in no disability case had the payments been adequate to meet the living expenses of the disabled worker and his family. Similarly, the death benefit, extending over five and a third years, was too brief a time for a widow to become self-supporting.[76] Clearly, in the area of child and women's labor and workmen's compensation, the local labor forces had only modest success in winning legislative support for their objective.

Traditionally, however, the AFL had stressed organization and collective bargaining over politics to achieve labor's goals. In this area, also, labor's failure to achieve union recognition, union shop, and improved wages and hours was painfully obvious. The fight for the union shop met management's dedication to the open shop. A 1920 strike by 6,000 workers at the Maryland Drydock Company, one of the largest city employers, marked the first union shop confrontation. Adamant in its intent to hire without discrimination, the drydock company was backed by the Baltimore Merchants and Manufacturers Association, which stressed the importance to local business of the open shop. As the strike wore on from January through March, violence erupted between pickets, scabs, and police, but by April 1 the workers accepted defeat and the open shop.[77]

In 1922 the troubled railroad industry was the center of labor difficulties. Western Maryland shopmen struck in March, complaining that management was sending its repair work to an outside contracting firm; 1,100 workers walked out in Hagerstown and Cumberland; shopmen in Baltimore cooperated. In a tangled legal wrangle the United States District Court ruled

---

76. Evelyn Ellen Singleton, *Workmen's Compensation in Maryland*, J. H. U. Studies in Historical and Political Sciences, Series LIII, Number 2 (Baltimore: J. H. Press, 1935), pp. 12-19, 52-53, 42-44, 50, 101. A brief experiment in lump sum death payments had also been ineffective since "all the people who established chicken farms failed." Federal vocational rehabilitation funds, available to the states on a matching basis were not utilized in Maryland until 1929.

77. *Twenty-ninth Annual Report of the Maryland State Board of Labor and Statistics, 1920*, pp. 171-83.

that federal railroad legislation which authorized management phase-out of positions had never envisioned dismissal of an entire labor force. The U.S. Railroad Board also decided for the workers, but management ignored the ruling. Four months later, a nationwide shopmen's strike over wage cuts involved Maryland workers in a ten-week walkout. Several workers were found guilty of tar and feathering and assault and battery; and though the AFL decried the verdict as a "frame up for sure," they were sentenced to a minimum five-year prison term.[78]

In 1922 over 5,000 Western Maryland miners struck from April to December for wage increases and the union shop. Four thousand of them proved unsuccessful. The major producer, Consolidated Coal Company, and sixteen of eighteen Garrett County mines remained open-shop. The AFL argued that strikebreakers of "the lowest type" had been imported. Again there was violence; four killings were recorded. As the strike limped to an unsuccessful close, Maryland's Commissioner of Labor and Statistics estimated that 850 miners in the George's Creek area had left the mines to work for Kelly-Springfield Tires in Cumberland; another 650 had been employed by the B&O.[79]

After this initial period of confrontation early in the decade, a period of relative labor quiet followed. The year 1923 showed the smallest loss due to strikes since 1918; in 1924 no major strikes were recorded; similarly in 1926, there seemed remarkable tranquility. The calm perhaps reflected Coolidge prosperity, but more probably, organized labor's acceptance of reality. The sobering defeats in strikes and legislation were accompanied by a distressing rise in unemployment. At the end of the recession of 1921, Baltimore's Merchant and Manufacturers Association still recorded a "distressful total" of idle workers. Throughout the allegedly affluent Coolidge years, a labor surplus was noted by Baltimore business. Additionally, modest as the activities of Baltimore's labor leaders seemed, the local Federation of Labor noted that plants were leaving the city or

78. *Thirty-first Annual Report of the Commissioner of Labor and Statistics of Maryland, 1922*, pp. 174-76. Though they did not achieve a victory, workers did return to the job without discrimination and with no further wage cut.

79. *Thirty-first Annual Report of the Commissioner of Labor and Statistics of Maryland, 1922*, pp. 141-42, 150-51; Chepaitis, pp. 49-51; *Thirty-second Annual Report of the Commissioner of Labor and Statistics, 1923*, pp. 140-42.

contracting jobs out. In April 1930, a Baltimore unemployment survey cited 17,273 men and women "without jobs, able to work and looking for jobs."[80] Although Maryland was "more fortunate" than other states, the hope for relief through local labor organizations seemed slim indeed.

Unsuccessful in lobbying at the legislature and aware of labor's need for a changed political climate, Maryland's organized labor through the AFL State Political League and the Baltimore Federation endorsed sympathetic candidates. The "labor vote" was difficult to estimate, however. An unfriendly *Sun* estimated it to be as high as 100,000 votes; yet the two most identifiable labor candidates, William I. Norris, 1922 Democratic primary candidate for the Senate, and presidential hopeful LaFollette, obviously demonstrated considerably less clout at the polls. In the Smith-Hoover campaign of 1928, the Baltimore Federation favored Smith, but, involved in a running feud with Ritchie, it did not formally endorse his Democratic colleague.[81]

The AFL's relations with Ritchie moved from initially warm support to the calling of a nationwide labor boycott against him. Labor had rated Ritchie over Nice in the 1919 campaign. Ritchie's stand in the coal strike, his "wetness," and the 1923 battle with the Klan had further earned labor's approval. By 1926, however, Ritchie's Conowingo actions and opposition to the child labor amendment led the Baltimore Federation to ask a national AFL boycott. President William Green obliged and announced in 1928 that the AFL would not support Ritchie or Davis for president.[82]

Also supporting labor issues through politics, though not ap-

80. *Baltimore*, XVII (April, 1924), 7-8. There was an unsuccessful textile workers' strike at Baltimore's Mount Vernon-Woodberry Mills, one of several unsuccessful efforts by the Amalgamated Clothing Workers and the ILGWU during the decade. *Thirty-second Annual Report of the Commissioner of Labor and Statistics, 1923*, pp. 124-25; *Thirty-third Annual Report*, pp. 1-3; *Thirty-ninth Annual Report*, pp. 55-66. See also *Baltimore*, XV (March, 1922), 6-8; XVII (June, 1924), 7, 27; *The Baltimore Federationist*, May 11, 1928.

81. *Sun*, Aug. 29, 1920, Aug. 5, 1922, Aug. 24, 1922; *Evening Sun*, Aug. 11, 1924; *The Baltimore Federationist*, Feb. 17, June 2, July 13, Aug. 18, 31, Sept. 21, Oct. 26, 1928.

82. Baltimore *Trade Unionist*, Sept. 1, 1919, and *Washington Star*, Sept. 4, 1919 in Box 2, Ritchie Papers. See also *Sun*, Jan. 28 and June 9, 1928, Oct. 11, 1930. A pamphlet in Ritchie's defense by the Ritchie Citizenship League is in VFEP.

preciably winning a significant labor vote, was Maryland's Socialist party. The articulate Socialist journal, *The Maryland Leader*, advanced a program in its first issue in November 1929: for unemployment insurance, old age pensions, and public ownership of utilities. Like the AFL, the Socialists flayed Ritchie to no avail. An editorial lamented his fourth term announcement in January, 1930, "So Ritchie insists on another term as Governor of Maryland. This will be his fourth term if he gets it. Of course there is Conowingo, the good roads scandal, and ten-cent carfare; but people forget." Socialist candidate for governor in 1930, Elisabeth Gilman, mounted a strenuous campaign and doubled the Socialists' 1926 vote. Her 3,059 total, however, indicated the distance between Socialist rhetoric and influence in the Old Line State.[83]

Economically, in business prosperity and leadership, in the agricultural recession, and in organized labor's distress, Maryland had, with Old Line State variations, reflected a national pattern. Socially, in issues and tensions emerging from social change and mobility, Maryland's development mirrored the nation's experience.

Postwar disillusionment stemmed from various factors: Versailles, a spill over of the hate for the Hun into anti-Bolshevik hysteria, the economic uncertainty and tensions of economic reconversion and inflation, the concern over cars, flappers, movie morals, and the mounting evidence of urban America's increasing dominance led many troubled and insecure citizens to agree with Willa Cather's assessment that "The world broke in two in 1922 or thereabouts." A spate of nostalgic novels, a turning to fundamentalist religion, an emphasis on censorship and blue laws represented rural, old stock Americans' agonized defense of the old ways. The high point of their triumph and the harbinger of their defeat was the prohibition amendment. No issue more significantly divided the nation in the 1920's; in no issue was Maryland's leadership more prominent. Home of the leading national wet politician, Albert C. Ritchie, and the out-

---

83. *Maryland Leader*, Nov. 23, 1929, Jan. 18, Feb. 15, Sept. 20, Oct. 25, Nov. 1, 1930. "Platform and Issues of the Labor Party of Maryland" is in VFEP. The dogged Labor Party faithfully ran presidential, gubernatorial and congressional candidates. They never amassed more than 3,000 votes, mainly from Allegany County and Baltimore's second and third congressional districts.

raged wet H. L.Mencken, Maryland also claimed Bishop James Cannon, a leader of the dry crusade, as a native son.

The official arena was politics; the crux of the post-amendment confrontation was enforcement. As Frank Kent noted in the *Sun*, from 1920 to 1925, prohibition obscured all other issues; Maryland politics were "in a sorry, soggy, sloppy state." In the legislature the dry attempts to pass a state Volstead act were beaten down when a referendum measure was attached and the drys decided not to test their statewide strength. Ritchie's position followed a ruling by Attorney General Armstrong that Maryland's police did not have the power to make arrests under the Volstead Act. As a federal law, it should be federally enforced. With Ritchie's denunciation of Volsteadism in 1922 at Harding's conference of governors and his triumph over dry forces in the 1923 race for reelection, he was encouraged to campaign as a presidential hopeful with a keg of beer and with vine leaves in his hair.[84]

Locally, wet Republican Congressman John Phillip Hill set the conflict sharply between city and rural interests by making cider and wine at "Franklin Farms" in the heart of Baltimore. Hanging apples on a tree and trailing grape vines over his fence, he invited reporters to his harvest. He stoutly insisted that if he were arrested for making 2.75 cider, farmers who were producing it should also be apprehended so that they would feel state oppression. Arrested with his brews by federal officers and tried in federal court, Hill was found not guilty. Although the jury agreed that his product contained more than 12 per cent alcohol, they found it was not "intoxicating."[85]

Hill's flamboyant defiance was matched in a more prosaic manner throughout Baltimore. A west Baltimore restaurateur's radio advertisement promised "good food and everything that goes with it." Natives knew that a red hard crab sign outside a restaurant meant sea food and real beer. The local bootlegging

---

84. A full discussion of the issues in the dry campaign in Baltimore, 1916, is in the clippings of the Association Against the Prohibition Amendment, MS 1544, M.H.S. See also Frank Kent, July 26, 1925, "A Great Game of Politics," Vol. IV, MS 181, M.H.S.; Levin, p. 161, *Sun*, March 4 and Aug. 6, 1920; Hamilton Owens, "Ritchie of the Free State," *American Mercury*, March, 1926, Box 28A, Ritchie Papers.

85. *Sun*, Oct. 22, 1922; *Evening Sun*, Sept. 19, 1924; *Sunpapers of Baltimore*, pp. 396-97.

business was brisk and efficient. Baltimore's harbor proved a good access route for Cuban liquor. Additionally, the U.S. Industrial Alcohol Corporation plant at Curtis Bay was one of the largest in the world. Convictions of local bootleggers were won for the diversion of 110,000 gallons valued at $2,500,000. The new Crain Highway was christened "Bootleg Boulevard." Lincolns drove south to rendezvous with Fords to pick up the country moonshine for sale in thirsty Baltimore. The Bureau of Prohibition summed up the Old Line State enforcement problem: "We have no cooperation in the State of Maryland other than the sheriffs of some of the counties where they have local option laws. We thought we had secured a great deal of cooperation in the Baltimore Police Department when they agreed to protect our men from riot when they were making raids and to preserve public order. That was helpful. Before that we were thrown to the wolves over there."[86]

Federal agents did mount intensive enforcement drives in Baltimore with some success. In 1922 they apprehended 409 Volstead violators; in 1925 they made 1,065 arrests. Meanwhile local Baltimore police arrests for drunkenness soared from a low of 1,785 in 1920 to a 6,029 high in 1924. The WCTU cited figures showing Maryland led in excessive alcohol rates.[87] Wet William Cabell Bruce asserted in the Senate in 1926: "It seems to me that if this state of things continues one-half of the population of the United States will be in jail and the other half will be drunk with nobody to take care of the states at all."

Organizations on both sides mounted campaigns for the cause. An early Association for the Repeal of Prohibition was joined by a Liberty Defense League, and finally by the Maryland division of the National Association Against the Prohibition Amendment. The executive secretary, Robert Ennis, protegé of Democratic leader Frank Furst, well represented the Democratic-wet connection. The Maryland Anti-Saloon

86. John C. Schmidt, "The Wet, Wet Years of Prohibition in the Free State," *Sun*, Jan. 14, 1962; *The Observer*, Aug. 9, and July 5, 1924. There were two lynching threats against agents who killed suspected bootleggers, *Sun*, Aug. 2, Sept. 15, 1925 and April 10, 1926; "Judge Coleman's Charge to the Jury," United States District Court, Feb. 17, 1928, VFEP.
87. Laurence Schmeckebier, *The Bureau of Prohibition: Its History, Activities and Organization* (Washington: The Brookings Institution, 1929), pp. 67-68; *Evening Sun*, Jan. 16, 1933; Address of Senator Bruce in VFEP. See also *Sun*, Feb. 27, 1929.

League, led by Superintendent George Crabbe, the United Law Enforcement Clubs of Maryland, and the Washington County Law and Order League fought back in a losing effort.[88]

With the onset of the depression, Senator Tydings raised the economic benefits that would come to the grain farmer and the taxpayer by repealing prohibition. Hearst and *Literary Digest* polls showed a national and Old Line State sentiment for repeal. When the ratification of a repeal amendment was presented in 1933 to the voters, Maryland voted for wetness five to one; in the city the margin was ten to one. In nine minutes and with a unanimous vote, Maryland's ratifying convention became the twenty-seventh state for repeal. A jubilant Ritchie addressed the delegates: "in this day of Fascism and Sovietism and the subjugation of people to the domination of the state or of a man, this marks a rededication of the people of America to the precepts of Democracy."[89] To rural America, it represented only one more instance of growing immorality and lawlessness in changing America.

The prohibition battle was accompanied by other moral skirmishes throughout the 1920's. The Maryland Board of Censors, created in 1916 to review and license films, screened over 5,000 movies in 1920–1921 and asserted it had "kept the flood of salacious and pernicious films to a great extent out of the state." With the onset of the talkies late in the decade, the censor board complained of "smutty jokes" and reported that "frank discussion of sex is the order of the day." Again, as in the prohibition fight, the *Sun*, led by the ebullient Mencken, raised the standard of personal liberty and decried this rearguard action of the Puritans. But the Board of Censors was applauded by legislative resolution and urged again to prohibit the showing of films calculated to degrade or make light of high ideals.[90]

Gambling, vice, and crime also concerned Marylanders as symptoms of a dangerous moral decline. A 1920 legislative

---

88. *Sun*, May 13, 1922. See also in VFEP, *Sun*, April 8, 26, May 12, 23, 1926; *Evening Sun*, Aug. 8, 1928.

89. *Baltimore American*, March 17, 1923, April 3 and 4, 1926; *Sun*, April 29, April 26, 1932 and Oct. 19, 1933; *Evening Sun*, Aug. 25, 1931, VFEP.

90. *Fifth Annual Report of the Maryland State Board of Motion Picture Censors, 1920–1921*, p. 3; *Fifteenth Annual Report, 1930–31*, pp. 4-5. The *Fifth–Sixteenth Annual Reports* provide a full survey of the decade. See also Frank Porter, "Censored," *Evening Sun*, March 18, 1952 VFEP.

effort to end all race track betting passed the House of Delegates, but was modified by Senate and administrative opposition into a measure for stricter track regulation and control
through the creation of a new Maryland Racing Commission. In
Baltimore, a sensational daylight murder of a local businessman
led to the founding of the citizens' Baltimore Criminal Justice
Commission to monitor city crime-fighting and the courts. Yet,
as with prohibition, the early years of the 1930's found the
moral crusaders on the defensive. A pledge by Baltimore's
Police Chief Charles Gaither to stringently enforce the blue law
code banning Sunday sports, movies, and the sale of commodities led to a vigorous campaign between the Lord's Day
Alliance and the Citizens Liberal Sunday Laws Committee.
Baltimore's liberalizers carried the day in the city and in the
legislature and repealed the old restrictions.[91]

While prohibition was socially the most divisive Free State
issue between the wars, the Ku Klux Klan was the most publi-
cized divisive force. Revitalized in the early years of the 1920's,
the Klan solicited membership in Baltimore in the spring of
1921 through a selective mail campaign. Local King Kleagle,
H. P. Moorehead, explained that the Klan was not "ultra-
exclusive" but was composed of "picked men." The Klan, he
asserted, had the same right to reject Jews as Masons, to reject
Catholics as the Knights of Columbus rejected Protestants, to
reject Negroes because America was a "white man's country."
An exposure series on Klan finances and practices by the *New
York World* in September 1921, and the resulting congressional
investigation, only led in the Old Line State, as in the nation, to
a membership spurt and increased Klan activity.[92] In assessing
which Marylanders joined the Invisible Empire, a *Sun* reporter
concluded: "mainly perfectly good, kindly people, generally
without anything to occupy their minds when they quit work,
looking for novelties, attracted by the idea of something mys-
terious, perhaps a little thrilled at the suggestion that they are
members of a band pledged to support 'Americanism.'" In the
remote districts of the lower shore members were found among

---

91. Baltimore Criminal Justice Commission, Inc., *First Annual Report for the
Year, 1923* (Baltimore: n.p., 1924), p. 3; *The Observer*, May 19, Aug. 23, 1924;
*Sun*, May 3, 1932; Levin, pp. 107-09.
92. Sheldon Smith, "K.K.K. Empire Was Once Strong Here," *Evening Sun*,
Jan. 20, 1966, VFEP. See also *Evening Sun*, April 15, Sept. 9, 13, 19, 1921.

oystermen and farmers. In the towns klansmen were those who liked "controversy." No fostering of the Klan by specific churches was noted and no specific political identification was made. Divided between Democrats and Republicans, most Klansmen seemed to join the organization and, based on its political impact, to "forget it."[93]

Yet, particularly in the early years of the 1920's, the Klan was a highly visible phenomenon in the Free State. The year 1922 was one of demonstrations and parades. Robed Klansmen paraded in Frederick and Baltimore. In October a caravan of Klansmen travelled to Annapolis and held a monster rally of 2,500 at Church Circle. The parade highpoint was achieved in the summer of 1925. In June, 10,000 Klansmen gathered for their first convention held outside Baltimore. Thirteen railroad coaches had journeyed from the city. The Ladies Aluminum Band led the musical festivities, while a plane wrote KKK across the sky. In July 25,000 Klansmen gathered at a Hyattsville rally. The following month Maryland leader Frank Beale announced a Baltimore parade of 12,000 and totaled the state membership as 33,000 in seventy-two dens.[94]

As elsewhere, Maryland Klan activities were a mixture of positive actions and intimidation. Klansmen appeared at church services with charity offerings; 4,000 Klansmen assembled at Havre deGrace to lay a church cornerstone and to honor the pastor, a Klan lecturer; Klansmen arrived in regalia to pay their respects at a funeral. Group baptisms, performed by Protestant clergy at the Hampden Klan No. 57 in Baltimore, underscored the Christian emphasis, while the specific christening of Katerine Karlotta Knickman proved the degree of one family's commitment. Fiery crosses were periodically reported from Salisbury to Elkridge. While there seemed to be little Klan-connected violence, Negro workmen were allegedly intimidated during a Brunswick strike. Night-riders beat and branded a railroad worker who reportedly had beaten his wife. A Smithsburg saw mill was dynamited after repeated Klan threats.[95]

Officially, the Klan found little encouragement in the Old

---

93. John Owens' Klan series in the *Sun*, Nov. 20 and 21, 1923.
94. *Sun*, Sept. 9, Oct. 25 and 29, 1922, June 3, 1925; Smith, *Evening Sun*, Jan. 20, 1966.
95. *Sun*, May 16, 20, 1923, Aug. 19, 1924; *Evening Sun*, June 22, 1923.

Line State. Maryland court action challenged the Klan's tax exempt status. National Guard chief General Reckord forbade the use of the Westminster armory for a Klan rally and Governor Ritchie twice denied the use of the Baltimore armory to the Klan. A Baltimore anti-masking ordinance was directed against Klan parading. Yet it was a combination of external opposition and internal scandals and divisions that would finally lead to the neutralization of the Klan's influence.[96]

As the Klan trumpeted its defense of American ideals, Maryland's excluded minorities asserted their patriotism. Most articulate was the Irish-born successor to Cardinal Gibbons, Archbishop Michael Curley and his diocesan organ, *The Catholic Review*. Catholicism and Americanism were pointedly linked. The first and last American veterans of World War I, the *Review* reported, were Catholics from Baltimore. In September 1921, the *Review* decried a campaign led by a renegade Marist brother, ostensibly aimed at ousting Catholic services from an American Legion hall in Havre de Grace. The *Review* cheered when his assertion that a Catholic could not be a good citizen was met by a barrage of eggs hurled by Aberdeen and Edgewood soldiers. When a group of parents in La Vale, Allegany County, petitioned for the removal of the local principal, the *Review* concluded it was because of his Catholicism. Observing that the principal was a veteran, the editors headlined: "The Blush is on the cheek, Maryland." In February 1927, the *Review* similarly defended the Catholic principal in New Windsor, Carroll County, under fire for not having a flag in front of the school.[97]

Taking a defensive stand against the Klan, *The Catholic Review* applauded the 1921 expose by the New York *World*. Now America could realize "that there were mean fellows, sneaks and cowards who, for the sake of gold, were willing to destroy the very foundation stone of American Liberty." The best answer to the Ku Klux Klan, of course, was "Cardinal Gibbons, Churchman and Citizen." The Klan attempt to oust

---

96. *Evening Sun*, Dec. 30, 1921, July 20, 1922; *Sun*, Dec. 30, 1921, Dec. 15, 27, 1922; Jan. 16, Feb. 17, 1923, May 13, 1925, Sept. 2, 1927; Smith, *Evening Sun*, Jan. 20, 1966.

97. *The Catholic Review*, Nov. 13, 1959, Sept. 24, 1921, Sept. 9, 1922. Bureau of the Census, *Report of Religious Bodies, 1936*, p. 765 lists 272,881 Roman Catholics in Maryland.

Ritchie in 1923 earned the governor firm Catholic support. Archbishop Curley, whose views on child labor and federal aid to education closely matched Ritchie's, announced on the eve of the Democratic national convention in 1924: "I personally know of no one in the country worthier or better qualified to fill the highest executive position or anyone I should prefer to see in the White House. And I feel that I can speak for some 300,000 people."[98]

The response of Maryland's 75,000 member Jewish community was articulated with less heat. The *Jewish Times* also monitored Klan activity, stressed Jewish contributions to the community, and in 1923 solidly endorsed the reelection of Ritchie. The Ritchie record, the *Jewish Times* reminded, included the appointment of Eli Frank to the Supreme Bench of Baltimore; of Philip B. Perlman as Secretary of State; and of prominent Jewish members to the State Board of Welfare, the State Board of Labor and Statistics, and the Governor's Reorganization Committee. In brief, as the understated advertisement in the *Jewish Times* asserted: "Gov. Albert C. Ritchie Has a Splendid Record."[99]

The largest minority in Maryland, excluded by the Klan, was also the most handicapped in achieving full citizenship. The Negro community formed a steady 16.9 per cent of the state's population in the decades between the wars. But within that statistic there was a marked shifting of Maryland Negroes. Seventeen counties, particularly in southern Maryland and the Eastern Shore, registered Negro losses, while Baltimore City, through extension of its boundaries and through migrations claimed 51.4 per cent of the Negro population by 1930 and ranked fourth in the nation in percentage of Negro citizens.[100]

98. *The Catholic Review*, Sept. 24, Dec. 17, 1921; *Sun*, Oct. 14, 1924. Curley is cited in *The Observer*, June 7, 1924.

99. *The Jewish Times*, Sept. 8, 1923.

100. W. L. Fairbanks and W. S. Hamill, *A Statistical Analysis of the Population of Maryland* (Baltimore: Maryland Development Bureau of the Baltimore Association of Commerce, 1937), pp. 56-80, 110-11, 114; Maryland, *Report of the Governor's Commission on Problems Affecting the Negro Population*, Joseph P. Healy, Chairman, March, 1943, pp. 13-16. Hereafter cited as *Healy Report*. Ira DeA. Reid, *The Negro Community of Baltimore* (Baltimore: Baltimore Urban League, 1935), pp. 39-40; *Report of the Survey of the Public School System of Baltimore, Maryland. School Year 1920–1921*, George D. Strayer, Director, I, 192-95. Hereafter cited as *Strayer Report*.

As the Baltimore Negro community expanded, its difficulties seemed only to increase. Negro-owned retail stores ranked lowest in volume of sales of all comparable cities. Negro enterprises were, with few exceptions, small. Negro laborers worked predominantly as common laborers or in areas of personal or domestic service. When they were employed in manufacturing there was little advancement. In the public sector there were no black policemen, firemen, motormen, or librarians. Baltimore's *Afro-American* bitterly concluded: "In most public buildings built and maintained by tax funds, you can't be a scrub woman, run an elevator or fire a boiler. You are a stranger in your own home."[101]

While the employment situation was difficult, the housing conditions were even more discouraging. Baltimore Negroes were crowded along Pennsylvania Avenue and Caroline Street. Only 17 per cent owned their own homes and a third of these took in lodgers. Housing surveys in the early 1930's consistently cited overcrowding, poor sanitation, high disease and crime rates, and social disorganization in the Negro housing areas. Limited in expansion by white neighborhood covenants and by little land area available for development within the city, the Negro density was estimated at 113 dwellings for every thousand Baltimore Negroes.[102]

Separated economically and socially, Negroes developed a sense of community through their churches and over 400 social clubs. The Baltimore Colored Symphony Orchestra, the City-Wide Young People's Forum, and the Colored Division of Recreation brought entertainment to over 85,000. The *Afro-American* reported community events, usually ignored in the white press, and tried to provide leadership for Negro rights and opportunities. Hope for progress in Maryland's racial development came from the Maryland Interracial Commission, the Peoples Unemployment League, the Urban League, National Association for the Advancement of Colored People, YMCA and YWCA. Yet a report in the mid-1930's indicated that the Old Line State's move toward full citizenship was far from aggressive, concluding: "Baltimore offers an excellent example

---

101. Reid, pp. 11-15. Bakeries, gas stations, and lunch rooms were the most numerous Negro businesses.
102. Reid, p. 16; *Healy Report*, pp. 117-18.

of just what takes place and what does not take place at Armageddon; for here, frequently, the groups do not battle, but apparently wait for the Lord."[103]

While Maryland's and Baltimore's Negro communities were seemingly mired in a slow advance toward fuller citizenship, the state witnessed a sudden spate of racial lynchings. In December 1931, a Negro, Mack Williams, accused of murdering his employer, was pulled from a Salisbury hospital and lynched. While decried by Ritchie, the *Worcester Democrat and Ledger-Enterprise* stressed the local "outraged feeling" and "heroic methods of treating such varmient [*sic*]." The Williams' lynching was viewed by the local state's attorney as the culmination of Eastern Shore concern over racial crime.[104] Within two years, there was another lynching; it occurred in Princess Anne. Twenty-eight-year-old George Armwood, accused of attacking an elderly white woman, was dragged by a mob of 5,000 from the jail, hung, mutilated and burned. Mencken and the *Sunpapers* most violently articulated their outrage. Mencken excoriated Wicomico County and complained, "The gallant Wicomicans having butchered a wounded and helpless black man, seem very likely to get away with it."

Local refusal to bring indictments in the Armwood lynching, in spite of a list of accused supplied by the state Attorney General William Preston Lane, caused Ritchie to quietly dispatch 300 National Guardsmen from Baltimore to make the arrests for the state. Arriving in the early morning hours and seizing the local telephone exchange, the troops, led by General Milton Reckord, apprehended four of nine suspects on Lane's list. The subsequent violence, abortive attempts to release the prisoners,

---

103. Reid, pp. 40-44.
104. Lynching statistics in Monroe N. Work, ed., *Negro Year Book* (Tuskegee: Tuskegee Institute, 1923) in VFEP. Mencken-Eastern Shore exchange in VFEP: *Worcester Democrat and Ledger-Enterprise*, Dec. 12, 1931; *Sun*, Dec. 27 and 30, 1931; *Afro-American*, Feb. 23, 1935; *Baltimore Federationist*, Dec. 11, 1931; Levin, p. 351. Two months before, a Negro, Yuel Lee, accused of murdering a family of four, had confessed and then rescinded his admission and secured the counsel of International Labor Defense lawyer, the Communist, Bernard Ades. A Snow Hill mob tried three times to wrest Lee from jail and did succeed in beating the lawyer Ades. Ritchie ordered Lee transferred to Baltimore. The local state's attorney linked the Lee-Williams cases asserting "The International Labor Defense is at the bottom of this trouble. The Negro Williams was a Communist inflamed by their teachings." *Sun*, Dec. 27, 1931.

and threats to lynch Lane were ended when local Judge Robert F. Duer stayed the removal of the prisoners to Baltimore and issued a writ of habeas corpus. After a ten-minute hearing, the prisoners were released due to lack of sufficient evidence. Ritchie heatedly denounced the dismissal, declaring the judges knew "absolutely" that sufficient evidence could have been produced to hold the men. Lane, testifying two months later before a Senate subcommittee hearing on the Costigan-Wagner anti-lynching bill, read into the record the names of those whom he believed had escaped a just conviction, and concluded that "any legislation to stamp out lynching or mob violence is highly commended."[105]

The Maryland Anti-Lynching Federation rallied at a Baltimore meeting. Speakers included liberal editor Oswald Garrison Villard, Walter White of the NAACP, W. W. Alexander and Edward Lewis of the Urban League, and local Socialist leader Dr. S. M. Neistadt. Although backed in its legislative efforts by the Ritchie administration, the anti-lynching movement frustratingly remained unsuccessful in the Old Line State and in Congress throughout the 1930's.[106]

Additionally, the Negro minority found it difficult to achieve self-help at the polls. Less than 17 per cent of the population, they faced the problem of "in the bag" Republican votes. In a Democratic state their Republican backing brought few victories; in the rare instances of Republican victory their constancy brought little reward. The Negro vote was carefully distributed over congressional, Baltimore councilmanic/state assembly lines and ward boundaries. The strongly Negro fifth, fourteenth, seventeenth, and eighteenth wards in Baltimore were divided into the third and fourth congressional districts and into four councilmanic/state legislative districts. Negroes comprising a 55.1 per cent majority in the eighteenth ward were divided into three congressional districts. While Negroes did elect some city councilmen and state senators, their influence was obviously diffuse.

Increasingly, however, in the 1920's the Negro voter drifted to the Democrats. In the 1924 race, *Sun* columnist Frank Kent

105. *Maryland Leader*, Oct. 21, 1933. In VFEP, *Sun*, Oct. 21, Nov. 28, 1933, Feb. 22, 1934; *Evening Sun*, Oct. 23, 1933, Dec. 14, 1931; *New York Times*, Nov. 29, 1933.
106. *Sun*, Oct. 21, 1933; *Maryland Leader*, Nov. 25 and Dec. 2, 1933.

H. L. Mencken (1880-1956),
renowned Baltimore editor, publisher, and author.
*Ray lee Jackson, N.B.C. Studio.*

reported the Negro response to Democrat Davis's strong stand against the Klan. In 1928 and 1932 races, the Negro leadership became increasingly irritated at Republican efforts to crack the solid South. Baltimore's *Afro-American* inveighed against Hoover as the "Grand Kleagle or Dragon of the Lily Whites," and editorially endorsed Franklin D. Roosevelt. But Baltimore's Negro voters changed party affiliation slowly; they would not become "in the bag" Democrats until 1948.[107]

### 3
### CULTURAL AND EDUCATIONAL DEVELOPMENTS

While Ritchie moved Maryland to the national forefront politically, H. L. Mencken led the Free State in the cultural assault of the 1920's on the Babbitts, the booboisie and the puritans. Writing for the *Evening Sun*, while editing the *Smart Set* and then the *American Mercury*, Mencken was judged "the most powerful personal influence on this whole generation of educated people." Cultural hero F. Scott Fitzgerald, another Maryland resident in the 1920's, gratefully dedicated *Tales of the Jazz Age* "To the Notorious H. L. Mencken." A severe literary critic, lexicographer, political reporter, and cultural pundit, Mencken's early column in the *Morning Herald*, "Baltimore & the Rest of the World," typified his Old Line State roots. In the *Nation*, June 13, 1928, he described Maryland as the closest state to utopia:

> Do I limn Utopia? . . .
> When I cross the line I feel safer and happier. The low moan of Methodist divines comes from the swamps of the Chesapeake littoral, but it is only a moan, not a bark of "Attention!" Even coming from New York, that great city, I notice a change of air. The cops grow polite, and hold their cavalry charges for cases of foreign invasion. The Governor writes his own state papers, disdaining the aid of the reverend clergy. When a still blows up, no one is alarmed. The very Babbitts walk lightly with eager eyes upon their betters. It could be better to be sure—but remember what country it is in!

The *New York Times*, caustically noting the Mencken paean,

---

107. Reid, p. 43; *Sun*, Aug. 21 and Sept. 4, 1924; *The Observer*, Sept. 12 and Nov. 3, 1928.

concluded that henceforth after listing Maryland as the home of the Great Crab, the B&O and Barbara Fritchie, a citation should be added: "Site of the Elysian Fields."[108]

Yet culturally the Old Line State and Baltimore lagged considerably behind this Olympian designation. While Maryland writers and artists—Mencken, Fitzgerald, Lizette Woodward Reese, and Rosa Ponselle—were winning recognition, Baltimore's audiences seemed wedded to the tried and familiar. The municipally supported symphony, led by Gustav Strube, primarily featured Richard Wagner, Beethoven, Tchaikovsky, and Brahms. Less than one-sixth of its offerings were modern, leading to one critic's lament: "Musically, the city is conservative to the bone." The annual tours of the Metropolitan Opera added lustre but little innovation. Ford's Theater offered a rich season of try-out plays and those on tour from New York. Not untypical was the 1937 season with presentations including Ina Claire in *End of Summer*, *Stage Door* with Margaret Sullivan, the Lunts in *Idiots' Delight*, Katherine Hepburn in *Jane Eyre*, and the *Ziegfeld Follies*.[109]

By far the most significant cultural achievement of the Free State in the decade between the wars was the transformation of the schools. Maryland had been roundly scored by the 1916 Flexner Report for inefficiency, lack of organization, poorly trained teachers, and obsolete instruction. The state ranked thirty-first in literacy in the 1910 census; 50 per cent of the white children had received no more than a fourth or fifth-grade education. The Flexner recommendations were sweeping: reorganization of the state and county boards of education, an

---

108. Carl Bode, *Mencken* (Carbondale, Ill.: Southern Illinois University Press, 1969), pp. 45-185; Mencken, "Maryland, My Maryland," *The Nation*, May 13, 1928, Box 28A, Ritchie Papers.

109. Weldon Wallace, "Case-History of a Musical City . . . Baltimore," *The Musical Digest*, XXVIII (Dec., 1946) in VFEP. See also Frederick A. Kummer, *The Free State of Maryland, A History of the State and its People, 1634–1941* (Hopkinsville, Kentucky: Historical Records Association, 1941), I, 362-65. John Charles Thomas was another famous native son. For theater see *Baltimore*, XXX (Jan., 1937), 10, (March, 1937), 52, (April, 1937), 16 (May, 1937), 26, XXXI (Nov., 1937), 52. While Marylanders conservatively supported the arts, they relished their sports. *The Maryland Almanac*, 1920–1929 provides a record of major events. See also Frederick G. Lieb, *The Baltimore Orioles* (New York: Putnam, 1952) and VFEP for Preakness accounts and the Pimlico Special in 1938 between War Admiral and Seabiscuit.

end of the "spoils" positions, and increased professionalism throughout the system.[110]

In 1920 newly elected Governor Ritchie acted to reform Maryland education. After consultation with the General Education Board, he chose Baltimore County's superintendent, Albert S. Cook, as his new state superintendent. Later he approvingly observed: "I took great interest in our schools, but all I really did was get a good man, and turn him loose. He found what was needed, and I backed him up." The second key state appointment was Columbia Teachers College graduate, Lida Lee Tall, to head the Maryland State Normal School. Her task was to achieve professionalism and effectiveness in instruction. By 1930, 95 per cent of Maryland's elementary teachers were fully qualified, an increase of 60 per cent in a decade. The legislature in 1922 completed the basis for transformation of the Old Line State schools with the passage of the Equalization Plan. A minimum salary schedule was instituted, with a state subsidy for poor counties from the equalization fund. A subsequent survey concluded that Maryland had perhaps "the most far-reaching and scientific method of equalizing revenues of any state."[111]

While the state moved to upgrade its system, education in Baltimore City faced an equally critical situation. The Strayer Report, completed by a team from Columbia Teachers College in 1920, issued a scathing indictment of the city plant, administration, teaching, educational support, and outcomes. A large number of Baltimore's schools were labeled unsafe, unsanitary, unattractive, inadequately planned, and "almost entirely lacking in the equipment for modern instruction." Over 94 per cent were rated low on fire prevention; 82 per cent on heating and

---

110. Flexner and Bachman, *Public Education in Maryland. A Report to the Maryland Educational Survey Commission.*
111. James Petrie Rouleau, "The Governors of Maryland and Education, 1850–1950" (M.A. thesis, University of Maryland, 1951), pp. 43-46; Maryland, Department of Education, *Fifty-sixth Annual Report of the State Board of Education for the Year Ending, July 31, 1922*, p. 79; *Fifty-seventh Annual Report*, pp. 122-27; Mary C. Cain, *The Historical Development of State Normal Schools for White Teachers in Maryland* (New York: Teachers College, Columbia University, 1941), pp. 603-04. In his message to the General Assembly in 1922, Ritchie stated: "For nothing has the present State Administration been more solicitous than the improvement of the public school facilities of the State," *Message of Governor Albert C. Ritchie to the General Assembly of Maryland, 1922,* (Baltimore: King Bros., n.d.) p. 7.

ventilation. Over a quarter of the schools were placed in the "abandon" category. Not untypical was the report on Leonard Calvert School No. 26: "a totally inadequate site, very dark classrooms, a musty interior, gloomy wall decorations, inadequate stairways and complete lack of fire protection. . . ."[112]

If the plant was inadequate, program, curriculum, and teaching were also found wanting. Baltimore had five high schools and nine preparatory and junior high schools; yet, insisted the Strayer Report, the city had no comprehensive secondary system. Curricula, particularly in the Negro schools, did not meet student needs. Consequently, Baltimore ranked fortieth among forty-one largest cities in the proportion of high school students to total school enrollment. In the elementary schools the major criticism was reserved for teaching methods; the report concluded: "Baltimore teachers must think of school more as a place for instructing pupils and improving their abilities and to consider the school no longer as a place for holding pupils till their work reaches a certain standard." To meet the city's problems, the Strayer Report recommended a ten-year, $23,069,600 program of improvements.

The Baltimore School Board proved as responsive as the state administration. Its 1921 report cited plans for revised curricula, new instructional methods, vocational training improvement, better supervisory personnel, salary increases, and plant upgrading. By 1924 arrangements were made for the merger of the Baltimore Training School with the State Normal School at Towson.[114] One year later, Dr. David Weglein became superintendent, and, like Dr. Cook, became the leader for improved instruction and professionalism.

While state and city schools were upgraded in the 1920's, Negro public schools were by comparison radically upgraded. Baltimore's appropriations to Negro schools quadrupled. In 1922 the first Negro was named Supervisor of Colored Schools; new textbooks, improved instruction, and the celebration of Negro History Week, Negro Health Week, and Negro Week signified a new commitment. The Negro vocational school trip-

---

112. *Strayer Report*, I, 92-3, 100-1.

113. *Ibid.*, I, 153 and 305, *Abstract of the Strayer Report*, pp. 33, 39-44, 46.

114. *Ninety-second Report of the Board of School Commissioners of Baltimore City to the Mayor and City Council for the Scholastic Year Ending, Aug. 31, 1921 and the Fiscal Year Ending Dec. 31, 1921*, pp. 7-10; Cain, p. 112.

led its enrollment, doubled its faculty, and moved to a new facility. Yet a vocational problem remained in the Baltimore Department of Education's policy to train only for a needed trade. For Negroes this resulted in limited offerings. In the early 1920's, over 50 per cent of the students in the Negro vocational school studied carpentry. While the variety of courses improved during the decade to include electricity, auto mechanics, and cosmetology, the offerings clearly lagged behind those of white vocational schools. At the same time a survey of Negro graduates from Douglass High School, 1927–1933, was more encouraging. Over 18 per cent had enrolled in colleges; 14½ per cent in normal schools; 3.1 per cent in professional schools; and 8 per cent were employed. Negro teacher training was also improved through the institution of a four-year program at the Fannie Jackson Coppin Normal School. In the state system, the minimum Negro school term was extended to 160 and then to 180 days. There was also improvement in rural transportation for Negro students.[115]

Several other areas remained separated and unequal throughout the decades between the wars. In the mid-1930's Maryland spent $67.61 on every white student in the system and $48.01 on every Negro student. A fight was mounted by the national NAACP leadership and by Maryland organizations for equal teachers' salaries. Suits brought by individual Negro teachers were settled out of court in Montgomery, Prince George's, and Calvert Counties. Allegany, Baltimore, and Washington Counties equalized their salaries. Finally a Negro principal from Anne Arundel County sought a federal injunction under the Fifteenth Amendment to prevent lower salaries. His victory marked the end of unequal racial salary scales.[116]

In the area of equal educational opportunity the NAACP was active in the Free State, particularly in the City-Wide Youth Forum in Baltimore. The *Afro-American* provided journalistic support; and NAACP attorneys Thurgood Marshall and Charles Houston supplied legal aid in a drive for either separate and

---

115. Reid, pp. 23-27; *Healy Report*, pp. 44-45; Doxey A. Wilkerson, *Special Problems of Negro Education* (Washington: Government Printing Office, 1939), p. 19; Channing, pp. 17-21.

116. Wilkerson, p. 50; *Sun*, March 14, 1935, VFEP; Helen Marie Plater, "A History of the Negro in Maryland, 1865–1940" (M.A. thesis, Howard University, 1942), pp. 146-64.

truly equal Negro education or integration. In the public secondary schools, the target was Baltimore County, which had no Negro high school. Negro county students, after completion of the seventh grade, had to pass a qualifying examination for entry into a Baltimore City high school. In 1936 the NAACP through attorney Thurgood Marshall filed suit for Margaret Williams, who was denied a high school education because she had twice failed the required test. Marshall argued that the Baltimore county Negro elementary schools with "tottering roofs, rotten floors" and impossible access roads led to Negro educational disabilities. Half the students taking the examination failed and were denied secondary education; white students had to meet no such requirement. However, on the grounds that the Williams examinations had been fairly administered, the writ of mandamus asked by the NAACP was denied.[117] Across the Old Line State, Negroes lagged behind in secondary education. The 1940 census indicated that only 3.4 per cent of Negro students completed four years of high school.[118] Equity was still to be achieved.

Finally, the decade of the 1920's saw marked expansion also in the parochial school system of elementary and secondary education. Drs. Cook and Weglein were joined by Archbishop Curley. As the Maryland Equalization Act was passed in 1922, the Baltimore *Catholic Review* headlined that a "Fortune will be Spent on Parochial Schools in this Archdiocese." Some $500,000 was earmarked for education. At his installation in December 1921, the Archbishop declared: "The hope of the harvest is in the seed." If a new parish had to decide between construction of a church building or a school, the diocesan orders were to build the school first. Curley insisted: "Let the church be poor, let it be a mere shack if needs be—God will be content, but God wants the school." In eighteen years, the archbishop raised almost $30 million for parochial schools in Baltimore and the rural parishes. Enrollment increased from 31,802 elementary students in 1921 to 53,912 in 1939; in the

---

117. *Afro-American*, Feb. 15 and 22, 1936; *Sun*, March 15 and 29, 1936.

118. *Healy Report*, p. 101. The 1940 census also demonstrated that of 49,910 illiterates in Maryland 50.2 per cent were Negroes. Over 6 per cent of Maryland's Negroes had completed no years of schooling; 31 per cent had completed up to four years.

secondary schools and colleges the increase was from 4,949 to 20,252.[119]

Higher education in Maryland also witnessed unusual growth and expansion in the decades between the wars. In the first year of Ritchie's administration, the merger between the Baltimore professional schools, comprising the University of Maryland and the small State Agricultural College at College Park, was completed. Long planned and frequently aborted, the merger of the professional schools with an undergraduate affiliate was dictated by a "crunching debt" of $400,000. Rebuffed by St. Johns after a period of voluntary association and refused by Western Maryland College, the university had approached Maryland State College "hat in hand." Introduced by alumnus Millard Tydings, the measure for merger easily passed both legislative houses and was signed with some misgivings by Governor Ritchie.[120]

The new University of Maryland's drive for excellence under President Albert Woods fulfilled Ritchie's apprehensions. Aware of the governor's economy emphasis, Woods submitted his 1922 budget directly to the General Assembly, asking an increase from $540,000 to $1,930,000. Ritchie heatedly noted that Woods was asking as much for 2,000 university students as the state expended on 250,000 in the public schools. He apportioned $793,000 and stressed his responsibility to inform the taxpayers of the costs of the "ambitious plans" of the university. Why, he queried, should funds be markedly increased for the state university when there were several available private alternatives?[121]

In 1924 Ritchie's concerns and Woods' hopes for the university violently collided in what a *Sun* observer called "the most desperate struggle in the legislative history of the present century." Woods asked the legislature for $2,760,000, including a popular appropriation to improve the university hospital in Baltimore. The budget request was supported by Baltimore's Boss Kelly, whose constituents profited from the Baltimore medical services, and was backed by alumni and university lobbying efforts. Ritchie vetoed the appropriation, appearing personally

---

119. *The Catholic Review*, Sept. 2, 1922, Nov. 24, 1939; *Sun*, May 17, 1947.
120. Callcott, *History of the University of Maryland*, pp. 283-89.
121. *Ibid.*, pp. 277-87; *Evening Sun*, Jan. 4, 1922.

before the legislature to explain his actions. He asserted that the merger should be dissolved. College Park should remain under state control. A grant of $500,000 for the hospital, to support needed services and repairs, was offered if the university accepted the separation. Although Ritchie's veto was not overridden, the Senate and House of Delegates upheld the merger and voted the university $927,000. Accepting the inevitable, Ritchie gradually developed a pride in the university, describing it as one of his administration's accomplishments, and "one of the outstanding institutions of learning in the country."[122]

The leadership of the university passed from the academically-oriented Woods in 1926 to the brick and mortar administration of President Raymond A. Pearson. By 1935 the ravages of the depression, the restiveness of the faculty under increasing loads, Pearson's priority on buildings, and the student unrest over faculty resignations led to an overwhelming expression of no-confidence by the tenured faculty and a call by regents for Pearson's resignation. His successor, Vice-President Harry C. Byrd, would prove one of the most remarkable administrators of the university. A gifted leader, administrator, and politician, Byrd not only won for the University of Maryland generous New Deal benefits under WPA, CCC, and PWA, but also succeeded in wresting increases from the state legislature. Yet, for all of Byrd's success and the university's growth, Maryland still lagged behind in support of higher education, assuming only 30 per cent of the total cost of operating the university.[123]

As the state university, the University of Maryland also became a battleground for social and civil rights in the decades between the wars. Feminists skirmished with President Woods. Two Maryland students opposed compulsory ROTC and took their objection to the Supreme Court. The 1934 Murray case, however, was perhaps the most significant confrontation. Supported by the NAACP, Amherst graduate Negro Donald G. Murray applied for admission to the University of Maryland Law School. Arguing that State scholarship aid for Negro students for legal training outside the state had not been funded,

122. Callcott, pp. 284-85; Rouleau, p. 79; Chepaitis, pp. 64-69; *Sun*, March 28, 1924; Thomas O'Neill "Obituary of William Curran," *Sun*, Oct. 5, 1951.
123. Callcott, pp. 308-33; *Maryland Leader*, May 11, 1935.

Murray applied to the university. Refused admission by President Pearson, Murray filed through the NAACP for a writ of mandamus. In hearings before Baltimore's Judge Eugene O'Dunne in June 1935, Murray stressed that all racial groups except Negroes were acceptable at the University of Maryland and that the state scholarship fund was unappropriated. O'Dunne ordered the writ; the order was upheld by the Court of Appeals, and Murray registered in September 1935. By 1937, the legislature amended its oversight and funded the Negro scholarships for out-of-state study. However, by the onset of World War II, all of the professional schools were integrated.[124]

4

THE DEPRESSION AND NEW DEAL

The onslaught of the depression of the 1930's overshadowed Maryland's advances in education and its cultural and moral battles. From October 1929, statistics detailed a growing national misery: forty billion dollars in stock values were lost; bank failures rose to 2,194; unemployment hovered at thirteen million; farm income was reduced by half. But repercussions from the stock crash and national collapse were registered slowly in the Old Line State. Through 1930 Baltimore businessmen insisted the city was "appreciably better off" than its rivals. Five thousand new industrial jobs had held unemployment below the urban average; the slumping building industry improved "in spots"; and port business, in spite of adverse conditions, had "made strides." Early in 1931, when the national indices were at their lowest point since 1914, Baltimore was still "holding up well." Yet by the fall, two-minute radio spots on WBAL and reassuring public messages began to reflect the hollow optimism issued from Washington. Governor Ritchie, in almost an exact echo of Hoover in 1929, asserted: "All the foundations of real and lasting prosperity are still here." The president of the Consolidated Gas, Electric, Light and Power Company agreed that "the basic causes of the depression have com-

---

124. Callcott, pp. 295, 306-07; Rouleau, pp. 80-82; Mencken, "The Murray Case," *Sun*, Sept. 23, 1935. In an attempt to maintain separate but equal undergraduate facilities, the state purchased Princess Anne Academy from Morgan College and in 1939 purchased Morgan College from the Methodist Episcopal Church.

pletely disappeared. What remains is simply fear and lack of confidence." Perceptibly in 1932 Baltimore slid into the recession. By mid-year only 40 per cent of the plants in Maryland were operating full time; the port girded for the impact of the British tariff; wholesale and retail trade were in sharp decline. The Baltimore Association of Commerce, bullish through the first troubled years, finally agreed in December 1932 that although Baltimore had moved in a different manner than the country as a whole, it "finally arrived at about the same place."[125]

The brave statements of Baltimore business in the first two years of the depression were not paralleled by the actions of the unemployed. In March 1930, the Communists mounted a parade of the unemployed. Although only 150 marchers assembled, many hundreds more gathered to hear the speeches at City Hall Plaza. A desperate mother, deserted by her husband, advertised four of her children for placement. Peoples Court Judge T. Bayard Williams, anguished in February 1931, "I've seen hundreds of people come into court, admit they owed back rent and with tears in their eyes plead for a little more time in the hope their luck would turn for the better." By early 1932 hundreds gathered daily in soup and bread lines.[126]

The brunt of relieving this distress fell on the private charity agencies: the Family Welfare Association, the Bureau of Catholic Charities, Associated Jewish Charities, and the Salvation Army. By the end of 1930 they were issuing alarms and appealing to the city for help. In 1931 Hoover's Commission for Unemployment set Baltimore's unemployment rate at 19.2 per cent. While disputing this estimate, the Baltimore Association of Commerce nevertheless spearheaded business and citizen mobilization for relief. The Citizens Emergency Relief Committee of Baltimore was formed to survey relief needs and to secure needed funds. Its March estimate indicated that $300,000 was needed immediately and urgently. Community

125. *Baltimore*, XXIII (May, 1930), 32; XXIV (April, 1931), 25-6; XXV (Nov., 1931), 3-5; XXV (Feb., 1932), 15; XXV (July, 1932), 19; XXVI (Dec., 1932), 5. Albert D. Hutzler still maintained that while 1932 was the "most disappointing" business year of that generation, "the stability of Baltimore was again demonstrated," *Baltimore*, XXVI (Jan., 1933), 3-5.

126. *Maryland Leader*, March 15 and Nov. 29, 1930, Feb. 14, 1931, Jan. 16, 1932; *The Observer*, April 2, 1932.

Fund agencies reported the expenditure of nearly $40,000 a month; Catholic Charities, $17,000; Jewish Charities, $12,000; the Police Department $84,900. By mid-April the CERC had raised $350,000, but Chairman W. Frank Roberts ruefully noted that probably the need was for $600,000. The 1931 Community Fund drive set its goal at $2 million, largest in its history. Additionally, it launched a gift drive for a special emergency unemployment relief fund. Gifts, including $30,000 from the Consolidated Gas, Electric, Light and Power Company and the Savings Bank of Baltimore, totaled $365,000. An additional $125,000 was raised from proceeds set aside by Ritchie from four race track days. However, even this total, added to the $650,000 raised by the CERC and $2 million from the Community Chest, was far from sufficient.[127]

Individual self-help schemes were launched. The *Sunpapers* sponsored a Self-Denial Day in March 1931, urging citizens to drop contributions in 2,400 ballot boxes spread through the city. The national "Give a Job" and "Share the Work" campaigns were enthusiastically supported in the Free State. Some 1,500 B&O workers gave one-half a day's pay for ninety days to help the jobless. The American Legion sponsored "Give-A-Veteran-a-Job Campaign" requesting 30,000 jobs. The Maryland Share-the-Work movement won employer pledges not to lay off any more workers and to take on more men through work sharing. Additionally, the Baltimore Federation of Labor urged all in Maryland with an income over $2,500 to assess themselves 5 per cent and to contribute the funds to relief. All public officials were asked to enforce an eight-hour day and a five-day week as an example to industry.[128]

Baltimore Mayors Broening and Jackson responded in turn to the emergency with direct assistance and expanded public works. A Municipal Free Employment Service was initiated in December 1930. City workers were required to contribute part of their salaries to aid in balancing the city budget and to take one day a month off to help spread the work. City budgets in 1930 and 1931 supported new school construction, the East-

---

127. *Baltimore*, XXIV (March, 1931), 5–6; XXIV (April, 1931), 11-12; XXV (Nov., 1931), 11; XXV (Dec., 1931), 19-20; XXIV (Feb., 1931), 43; XXIV (Aug., 1931), 24-25.

128. *Baltimore*, XXV (Feb., 1932), 12, XXVI (Oct., 1932), 4; *The Baltimore Federationist*, April 10, and Sept. 4, 1931.

Albert C. Ritchie (1876-1936),
Governor of Maryland from 1920 until 1935.
*Harris & Ewing.*

West Viaduct, and extension of Howard Street. Although the Commission on Governmental Efficiency and Economy expressed growing concern at the unbalanced budget, the city council authorized appropriations in 1933 to pay whatever overdraft was created in 1932. If CERC funds were exhausted, the city pledged to meet the needs of the citizen. Jackson's estimate was a city expenditure of over three millions in relief by the end of 1932. These municipal, business, and private citizen efforts, however, were still insufficient. The president of the Community Fund predicted that if the situation in Baltimore continued to worsen, 100,000 people would not have the bare necessities of life by March 1933.[129]

As Baltimore's effort and resources proved inadequate, the city leaders appealed to the state. The Federation of Labor urged Governor Ritchie to expand his public works, build a bay bridge, and call a special session of the legislature to grapple with the severe unemployment problem. During 1931 statistics indicated that Baltimore's distress was reflected throughout the Old Line State. Maryland's unemployment figures worsened throughout the year; coal was depressed in western Maryland; and the major producer, Consolidated Coal Company, was operating at half strength. In Baltimore and Anne Arundel Counties relief funds approached exhaustion.[130]

However, Ritchie was reluctant to use state funds until all other avenues had been explored. He urged business to utilize its statesmanship to attack unemployment; he recommended the thirty-hour week. Government's role was to retrench, to avoid heavy taxes. Following his philosophy of state responsibility, Ritchie organized a Governor's Advisory Committee on Unemployment Relief in mid-1932, one of the first in the country. Sternly opposed to the dole, Ritchie also pledged that his administration would allow no one in the Old Line State to starve. Although Ritchie insisted that local giving should continue to be the major source for aid to the needy, the governor's committee arranged to disburse state funds raised by short term borrowing. By January 1933, the governor asked a 10 per cent salary contribution from state employees, increased Baltimore's

129. *Baltimore*, XXIII (Jan., 1930), 7, XXIV (June, 1931), 43, XXIV (Feb., 1931), 15; *Maryland Leader*, Aug. 22, 1931; *Baltimore*, XXV (April, 1932), 19-20; XXVI (Oct., 1932), 5.

130. *The Baltimore Federationist*, March 6, 1931.

share of the gas tax and motor vehicle funds, and set a bond issue to meet Baltimore's $3,000,000 in relief expenditures. Consistently he worked within the limits of the state economy to increase state jobs and to increase state construction. Reviewing the state efforts, he concluded: "I do not know anything Maryland could do which has not been done in order to accelerate public building and construction work."[131] Yet always this action was well within Ritchie's philosophic and economic parameters. Private property and enterprise guided by responsible business would bring renewed prosperity; the state could prime the pump and issue emergency relief, but its primary contribution would come from solvency and retrenchment.

Ritchie's self-help and state responsibility theory was strongly tested in the severe drought of 1930. When Hoover called a meeting of twelve governors to discuss drought relief, Ritchie, though Old Line State farm losses were estimated at $38,000,000, was not invited. As Ritchie protested this federal oversight, the Republican leader Galen Tait sharply rejoined: "Practically every tenet of Governor Ritchie's theory of Maryland's relation to the nation is opposed to Maryland's true interest." After indicating the Old Line State's interest in sharing in federal drought relief, Ritchie characteristically formed a Maryland committee to coordinate state and federal efforts and to devise a credit program for the distressed farmers. Federal loans would be given with proper security, but, as the Master of the Maryland State Grange angrily observed, 25 per cent of Old Line State farmers were insolvent and could not produce the needed collateral. A Baltimore *Post* editorial pessimistically agreed that since bankers did not lend money without security, "Governor Ritchie's conferences were doomed from the outset." However, the governor's committee, headed by Baltimore banker Waldo Newcomer, did move to establish the Maryland Drought Loan Corporation and a fund to allow loans to farmers without proper collateral. Unfortunately the cumbersome machinery of the new loan corporation and the stipulation that it would not operate until regular banking channels proved unable to provide relief, placed the farmer in "dire straits" until midwinter. Newcomer's committee further urged the governor to move road work ahead of schedule and to utilize as much

131. *Fortieth Annual Report of the Commissioner of Labor and Statistics of Maryland, 1931*, pp. 4-5; *The Maryland Leader*, July 16, 1932.

manual labor as possible for "we can't see people starve and there seems no legal way of getting money to aid the farm laborers and some farmers who have no credit."[132]

Maryland's banking community, pressed into service to organize a rescue for the farmers of the state in 1930, faced grave difficulties of its own in 1931 and 1932. Three national banks and fifteen state banks failed. Generally, Maryland bankers had elected state over national charters; the lower capital requirements and a minimum of red tape were attractive inducements, but significantly, the brunt of the banking collapse was borne by the state institutions. The major failure in 1931 was that of the $8,000,000 Central Trust Company of Frederick and its eleven branches. Its bankruptcy precipitated the demise of fourteen other small banks in western Maryland. The mismanagement and subsequent indictment of President Emory Coblentz and the severe economic blow dealt to an already depressed farming community gave rise to a "dangerous hostility" and the departure of banking officials. In September 1931, Baltimore's $100,000,000 bank, the Baltimore Trust Company, in its new thirty-four story building, weathered numerous withdrawals after the Baltimore Clearing House moved to reassure the public through an advertisement that the local banking situation was sound. But in 1932 the failure of Baltimore's Park Bank and a dangerous run on the Union Trust Company provided additional jolts. Symbolic of the bankers' uneasiness was their request that Ritchie not allow the showing of the film *American Madness* depicting a run on a bank.[133]

The year 1933 opened with the jaunty advertisement of the Union Trust: "Come on America—Let's Go" and with the insistence of President John M. Dennis, "We at Union Trust Company are supremely confident of the return of better business

132. Symons, pp. 16-21; *Sun*, Aug. 15, 16, 17, 22, 23, 26, Sept. 10, 26, 30, 1930; *News*, Aug. 18, 1930; *Post*, Sept. 2, 1930. Clippings in Box 40, Ritchie Papers.
133. Joseph T. Elvove, "State Bank Failures in Maryland" (M.A. thesis, University of Maryland, 1936), pp. 24-36; Charles A. Hales, *The Baltimore Clearing House* (Baltimore: J. H. Press, 1940), pp. 138-41, 156-57, 310-11; *Baltimore*, XXI (Aug., 1928), 31; XXIII (Dec., 1929), 9; Maryland, State Planning Commission, *United States Community Improvement Appraisal, State of Maryland* (n.p.: n.p., March, 1938), "Frederick County Board of Education." This collection of reports examines the CWA, PWA, FERA, WPA and other agencies' impact on the state. It is reproduced through offset process. Hereafter cited as *Community Improvement Appraisal*. Fairbanks and Hamill, *The Manufacturing Industry of Maryland*, pp. 172-76.

and prosperity to Baltimore and the nation." In February it was obvious that the Baltimore banking public was not reassured. The bank holiday in Michigan, the Senate investigation of New York's National City Bank, and the announcement of the closing of Baltimore's $7,000,000 Title Guarantee and Trust Company led to a rush of withdrawals; as a result the State Banking Commissioner estimated that the banks would have to close February 25 if there were no reversal. At a subsequent meeting the banking commissioner, representatives of the clearing house, the Reconstruction Finance Corporation, the Federal Reserve Bank of Richmond, and the states attorney's office agreed to ask that Ritchie institute a banking holiday, pending legislation regulating withdrawals and bank reorganization. Ritchie acted quickly, called the holiday, reassured the public by radio, organized a depositors' committee led by President Joseph S. Ames of Johns Hopkins to consider legislation, prodded the banking commissioner and banking representatives to hammer out a measure, and secured legislative approval by March 4. A Maryland extension of its banking holiday merged into the national holiday called by Franklin D. Roosevelt. When solvent banks in Baltimore and the nation reopened March 14, six local institutions remained closed: the giant Baltimore Trust Company, Union Trust Company, Baltimore Commercial Bank, Commonwealth Bank, Mercantile Bank and Clifton Savings Bank. All restored service by December 1933 except the Baltimore Trust Company, which was finally reorganized by the Reconstruction Finance Corporation as the Baltimore National Bank.[134]

In the aftermath and in the attempt to assess blame, the most frequent conclusion was that the collapse generally came from mismanagement. A legislative resolution demanding publication of all depositors who withdrew over $10,000 in the emergency produced a list of the B&O, $2,557,335.81; Consolidated Gas and Electric Company, $1,915,707.82; Alexander Brown, $708,856.00; A. S. Abell Company (*Sunpapers*), $184,000.00; and the state of Maryland, $861,622.95. The presidents of the Central Trust Company and the Park Bank were indicted for violations of the state banking laws.[135]

---

134. Elvove, pp. 36-54; Hales, pp. 141-67; *Baltimore*, XXVI (Jan., 1933), 23.
135. *Maryland Leader*, March 25, 1933; Levin, p. 397. Archbishop Curley

The jobless-hungry stand in a typical breadline during the depression.
*Library of Congress.*

More positive were the recommendations submitted by the Banking Commission in 1935. Loans to individuals or corporations were limited to 10 per cent; banks and trust companies were required to carry their legal reserves in banking institutions with unimpaired capital and a surplus of not less than $400,000; the amount a state bank or trust company could invest in its bank building was limited, and finally, capital requirements for forming a state bank were changed to conform to the requirements for a national bank.[136]

The failure of national and state recovery and of relief efforts by the end of Hoover's administration was most visibly manifest in the growing organization and action of the unemployed. In the summer of 1932 a contingent of the Bonus Expeditionary Force en route to Washington arrived at Grantsville in western Maryland. The Salvation Army provided food; the workers found shelter; and Ritchie provided trucks to transport the veterans to the capital. Three months later, after the BEF was routed by a regular army force, an angry Ritchie asserted: "It is, to say the least, not edifying to see arms and tanks and sabers and tear bombs used in this way, and men driven out at night at the point of the bayonet." Some 3,000 fugitives streamed into Maryland and again trucks were supplied for those who wanted transport. However, when BEF leader Waters announced the gift of twenty-five acres in Anne Arundel County from a sympathetic Old Line State citizen and his intent to set up a camp, Ritchie, faced with the hard possibility of 7,000 men arriving to swell Maryland's relief rolls, sent sanitation inspectors. Pronouncing the site not fit for habitation, Ritchie negotiated with Waters, and the small outpost disbanded and left the state.[137]

In January 1933, Maryland's own unemployed, led by Socialists Charles W. Whitmore and Elisabeth Gilman, organized the People's Unemployment League. Quickly mushrooming to 2,500 members in fifteen locals, the PUL sent spokesmen to meet with charity and welfare officials to protest the "starva-

---

asserted: "We hear much about the restoration and need of confidence. . . . So long as our wealthy crooks can get away with financial 'murder' there will be no confidence." *Maryland Leader*, April 1, 1933.

136. Maryland, *Report of the Banking Commission of Maryland*, Feb. 20, 1935, pp. 1-8; Elvove, pp. 63-97.

137. *Baltimore American*, May 29, 1932; *Post*, July 30, 1932; *Sun*, July 31, Aug. 2, 3, 1932; *Evening Sun*, Aug. 1, 2, 3, 1932. Clippings in Box 45, Ritchie Papers.

tion" level of a dollar per person per week for food, with no provision for rent. Five months later, representatives of the PUL joined 4,000 delegates to a Washington meeting of the Continental Congress of Economic Reconstruction and joined in their Declaration of Independence. In July a Maryland Congress of Farmers and Workers gathered in Hagerstown. Representatives of eighty state organizations, including the Farmers' Cooperative Milk Corporation, the Maryland and District of Columbia Federation of Labor, the PUL, International Ladies Garment Workers Union, Women's International League for Peace and Freedom, Johns Hopkins University Liberal Club, and the League for Industrial Democracy heard prepared reports on taxation and banking, unemployment relief, civil liberties, and race relations. Charging the Ritchie administration with lack of sympathy for the workers, they urged a special legislative session for relief and social legislation, urged the governor to call for a moratorium on home mortgages, and recommended the socialization of basic industries.[138]

A survey of state needs in the summer of 1933 underscored the urging of the Farmers and Workers Congress for relief. In Garrett County, one in three persons was on relief. Baltimore County's welfare chairman reported that 742 families on relief were receiving 3½¢ per meal. In Anne Arundel County, Dr. J. H. Janney, chairman of the county relief committee, urged the use of land at the county almshouse to build a shelter for those who were on relief and who had been evicted. In eighteen of twenty-three counties relief burdens were high.[139]

In the whirlwind beginning of the New Deal's First Hundred Days, Ritchie, aware of Maryland's relief needs, asserted that the Free State should get her fair share of federal aid. A meeting with the congressional delegation in May underscored the temporary deviation that the emergency had caused in his philosophy of state responsibility. "All hands," the governor announced, "agreed that we ought to get all we can." Ritchie appointed a special liaison man, Frederick P. Lee, to represent state interests in Washington and to monitor federal programs. He appointed a coordinating Committee on Public Works to

---

138. *Maryland Leader*, Jan. 14 and 28, May 13, July 22, 1933; *Sun*, June 22, July 4, 16, 17, 1933.
139. *Maryland Leader*, June 17, July 1, 8, 15, 1933.

prepare a program to submit to the Public Works Administration.[140] His efficiency, organization, and appointment of Lee ruffled congressional feathers anxious for a "fair share" for their own constituents. Complaining that "the Governor didn't consult us about his plans," Congressmen proposed their own plan for $70,000,000 in federal funds for Maryland. Additionally, Baltimore's Mayor Jackson complained that the city was not being fully included in the governor's councils. A beleaguered Ritchie quickly moved to soothe the congressmen and to plan a "peace conference" with Jackson. As finally constituted in June, Ritchie's Committee on Public Works was headed by W. Frank Roberts, former president of the Baltimore Association of Commerce. A special executive committee was comprised of the governor, Mayor Jackson, E. Brooke Lee, and Bernard L. Crozier, Baltimore's engineer. District committees led by the congressmen were established. At-large members, including Attorney General William Preston Lane, Jr., and Henry F. Broening of the Baltimore Federation of Labor, were added. Also created by the General Assembly were the State Planning Commission and Maryland Emergency Housing and Park Commission.[141] The Old Line State, which had tried self-help, stood ready to coordinate relief and recovery efforts with the New Deal.

The New Deal continued, but vastly broadened Hoover's relief and recovery efforts. The Hoover trickle-down approach was accompanied by major efforts to rebuild purchasing power. Emerging from the debates of brain trusters and the programs of Congress, there was indeed federal assistance for every sector.

For the relief of business, the Reconstruction Finance Corporation, initiated by Hoover, broadened its operations. Under the conservative leadership of Texas banker Jesse Jones, the RFC disbursed $124,009,336.47 to Maryland banks and businesses in the first three New Deal years. Ritchie also applied in March 1933, for an RFC loan to provide emergency relief; within six months, twelve Maryland counties had utilized over $176,000. By 1934 the Free State took a more discriminating view of RFC funds; Attorney General Herbert O'Conor ruled that the RFC Mortgage Company operating in the state must, like other

---

140. *Sun*, May 24, 26, June 5, 7, 1933.
141. *Sun*, June 6, 8, 16, Dec. 39, 1933.

Maryland corporations, pay a bonus tax on its stock. In a thin echo of the 1819 M'Culloch v. Maryland confrontation, Maryland won the first court tests until Congress specifically exempted the stock and other RFC holdings.[142]

The beleaguered homeowner was assisted by the Home Owners Loan Corporation. The Maryland director, David Stiefel, estimated that in an eleven-month period some 300 applications a week had been filed, and 6,651 loans, totalling $18,598,009.83, were made in the Old Line State. By June 1936, 15,928 homeowners had mortgages refinanced to the extent of $45,602,271. Although the average Maryland borrower had been two years delinquent in principal and interest, by August 1939 HOLC reported 80 per cent of the borrowers had been able to save their homes, and 11 per cent had a "good chance."[143]

In order to meet the urgent needs of the unemployed, the Federal Emergency Relief Administration was authorized in May 1933. An initial appropriation of $500,000,000 was disbursed to the states and communities on a basis of three dollars from the state or local authorities to one federal dollar for local relief measures. In Maryland a subsidiary of the Board of State Aid and Charities, The Maryland Emergency Relief Administration, (MERA), headed by Harry Greenstein, was created by the legislature to coordinate Free State relief measures. In Baltimore, since the four private agencies were ineligible for FERA funds, the BERC (Baltimore Emergency Relief Commission) was formed as a unit of MERA. Headed by D. Luke Hopkins, it immediately assumed relief obligations for 23,000 families. Ritchie, meanwhile, ordered a survey of state

---

142. *Sun*, May 10, 27, 1933. For a later report see *Reconstruction Finance Corporation Report for the Fourth Quarter of 1938: A Report Covering the Operations of the Reconstruction Finance Corporation for the Fourth Quarter of 1938, and for the Period from the Organization of the Corporation in February 2, 1932, to December 31, 1938, Inclusive.* See also *Evening Sun*, Jan. 30, 1952, VFEP. On taxing RFC operations see *Sun*, April 15, 1935, Feb. 14, 17, 1936, Jan. 12, March 28, 1938, VFEP. The power to exempt from taxation was upheld in March, 1938 in a 4–3 Court of Appeals decision.

143. U.S., National Emergency Council, *Maryland, State and National Reports, 1933–1938* (Washington: National Emergency Council, 1938). This is a collection of eight reports detailing federal expenditures in Maryland. Hereafter cited as *Maryland, State and National Reports, 1933–1938.* See reports 1, 4, 7 for HOLC. See also *Sun*, Jan. 9, June 12, 1934; *Baltimore*, XXVII (May, 1934), 4.

needs by the State Commission on Unemployment Relief and informed FERA head, Harry Hopkins, that Maryland would want funds from the first FERA grants. By September, FERA grants to Maryland totaled $2,500,000.[144]

Still concerned at continued unemployment and at facing the winter of 1933–1934 with lagging recovery efforts, Roosevelt, with the advice of Hopkins, authorized the formation of the Civil Works Administration. A massive emergency program of federal work relief, CWA hoped with an initial $400,000,000 appropriation to make jobs for four million Americans. Maryland's quota was set at 35,000. State Charity Board Chairman Richard Cleveland led the Old Line State effort. Administratively, CWA utilized the same organizations established for FERA, as Harry Hopkins ordered, "the present emergency relief authority in each county is hereby constituted the CWA for that county."[145]

Problems of instituting CWA in Maryland and Baltimore were a microcosm of the national difficulties. As Cleveland explained, with 16,000 men in Baltimore already on work relief projects, it would not be easy to develop quickly effective work for an additional 35,000. The urgency and deadlines of CWA led to an early delay in matching men and supplies. Spades, rakes, and small tools were in short supply. However, in the first five weeks of CWA, 700 state projects were approved, ranging from clearing land in Worcester County, building bulkheads at Cambridge, and rat-catching in Baltimore.[146] The city, concerned at burgeoning budgets and the problems of matching federal dollars, drew up plans through the BCWA for $575,000 in projects, for adult education, street improvement, school repairs, murals for public buildings, and music at ball games. Yet Mayor Jackson's personal penny-watching and delays caused by bad weather led to sharp prodding by the federal Civil Works Administration. Dispelling Baltimore's excuses of weather, red tape, and supply shortages as "bunk, absolute

---

144. *Sun*, May 26, June 14, 1933.

145. Telegram Harry Hopkins to Richard Cleveland, Nov. 10, 1933; telegram Cleveland to Hopkins, Nov. 11, 1933, Box 20, Maryland CWA Correspondence, National Archives; *Sun*, Jan. 14, 1934. Pertinent clippings are in Box 47, Ritchie Papers.

146. *Sun*, Jan. 11, 12, 1934. Listing of approved CWA projects for Baltimore is in the *Sun*, Nov. 23, 1933.

bunk," the CWA threatened to take the money away and advised that "if the rules interfere with the human purposes of CWA set the rules aside." Baltimore's efforts were also plagued by charges of graft and wage disputes. A CWA administrator revealed that Mayor Jackson's insurance firm was insuring 23 per cent of the trucks used in CWA work. In Baltimore organized labor argued for an increased scale for skilled work of $1.10 an hour, while Eastern Shore employers complained that the minimum scale of $13.50 a week was twice the prevailing local wage. The city finally reached its quota January 18, one week before CWA, scheduled for a March expiration, issued its first cutback orders.[147]

The relief confusion created by the end of the CWA and the need to readjust work relief back into the FERA, MERA, and BERC, brought administrative havoc and overwhelming budgetary pressures. The MERA head, Greenstein, observing that one in six Baltimore families was on relief and that the city relief bill had reached a semi-monthly $712,589.29, estimated that city funds would be exhausted by mid-April. The question of how the city needs would be met became increasingly interwoven with the political maneuvering of incumbents Ritchie and Jackson; both candidates for governor in 1934 wanted their administrations to stand as models of fiscal prudence. From Washington, Harry Hopkins insisted that Baltimore and Maryland were "able to spend a lot more money on relief than they have spent." While he trickled some funds into the state to meet the city needs, he pressed for a "showdown" and a precise accounting of how Maryland would meet her relief burdens. The waiting game was described by the *Sun*: "Greenstein is waiting for Ritchie and Jackson to do something: Jackson is waiting for Ritchie to do something. And Ritchie is waiting for Greenstein to do something."[148]

A May meeting between Harry Hopkins and Greenstein finally set Maryland's relief needs at $18,000,000; Hopkins agreed to spend 50 per cent, but insisted that Maryland would

147. *Maryland Leader,* Jan. 27, 1934, reported that the president of the Democratic Club of Maryland was sentenced to 2 years in prison and fined $2,000 for taking fees to obtain jobs in work relief. See also *Sun,* Jan. 17, March 1, 1934; *Evening Sun,* March 4, 1934; *Post,* Jan. 10, 16, 1934.
148. *Sun,* March 15, April 17, May 15, 27, 1934; *Evening Sun,* March 19, 23, 1934; *Baltimore,* XXVIII (July, 1934), 1; XXVIII (Aug., 1934), 2, 25-26.

have to raise $9,000,000. Ritchie's response was to establish a relief advisory committee. Attempting to avoid a legislative session, he urged district officials to examine their needs and exhaust local resources to meet them. Greenstein had been dispatched to urge the counties to assess the eight-cent levy authorized for relief by the legislature. Meanwhile, bad weather conditions on the Bay raised unemployment figures to 46 per cent in Somerset, 35 per cent in Wicomico, 23 per cent in Kent and 16 per cent in Dorchester Counties.[149]

Still, Baltimore remained the hardest hit. Ritchie insisted that the city must assume more local responsibility. The way to break the habit of feeding at the public trough at state expense and to demonstrate the costs, he asserted, was to have individual citizens pay for relief out of their own pockets. Baltimore's method of attack, however, was a concerted scrutiny of relief rolls for "chiselers." Since there was no fat to pare from the quality of relief; the quantity was reduced. Single homeless men without dependents and those who were domestics as well as areas where jobs were plentiful were cut from the rolls. By early May the city caseload was reduced by 450 a week. Greenstein ordered a further cut of 5,910 cases by the end of June. Finally in August the revenue from state bond sales became available, alleviating the worst distress in Baltimore and the state. In a relief denouement in December 1935, the Board of State Aid and Charities ordered BERC and the county boards to stop relief for all employables. In an explanatory statement, Greenstein expressed his hope that the new Works Progress Administration would assume the major work relief burden.[150] The first phase of direct federal relief under Hopkins ended; the earnest private efforts and state attempts to meet relief obligations locally concluded with the acceptance of the longevity and grim reality of the depression and unemployment.

In reviewing the MERA effort, Greenstein summarized the difficulties: "Limitations of funds; payment of wages on a budgetary deficiency basis; uncertainty and lack of continuous employment; impossibility of long range planning." Yet the

149. *Sun,* June 2, 3, 7, 9, March 19, 22, 1934; *Evening Sun,* June 4, 7, 1934.
150. *Sun,* June 3, 5, 9, 15, 1934; *Evening Sun,* March 2, June 5, 1934; *Sun,* Dec. 31, 1935; *Maryland Leader,* Aug. 25, 1934 detailed the reaction of the PUL to the relief cutback.

project results were impressive. The MERA work division constructed seventy-two miles of roads, thirty-three bridges,
twelve schoolhouses, rebuilt Baltimore's Fifth Regiment Armory, landscaped a municipal park at Salisbury, planted 6,232
trees, and improved fish hatcheries and game preserves. In the
area of public health, nurses aided 4,100 persons. The Women's
Division provided sewing rooms to train unskilled workers;
commodities were distributed. If the production record was
good, the report on the workers was equally so. Lowered
efficiency, where it existed, resulted from undernourishment,
loss of work habits from enforced idleness, or inefficient supervision. Most Marylanders who were forced into relief wanted to
work, and worked well.[151]

While highly cost-conscious and conservative in its response
to FERA and CWA, Maryland responded to the Civilian Conservation Corps with enthusiasm. Federally funded, the CCC
proved a highly popular combination of youth rescue, aid to
families on relief, and conservation of the nation's forests and
resources. The Maryland Board of State Aid and Charities
selected youth from eighteen to twenty-five from relief
families; the Department of Labor processed the state selections, and the War Department established camps. By May
1933, Maryland had organized five camps with a complement of
200 in each. Camp Tydings on the Patapsco River near Baltimore was typical. The Maryland Forestry Department directed
efforts of clearing underbrush along the river, building fire
breaks, and laying out paths for hikers. An army captain supervised life in the camp.[152]

As "the sound of axes rang," the CCC accomplishments
mounted with those of CWA and MERA. A preliminary list in
February 1935, revealed 166 miles of telephone lines in forest
areas, 188 miles of forest truck trails, and more than 312 miles of
fire breaks. In the next two years, CCC restored old Fort Frederick, rebuilt the Washington Monument near Boonsboro, and
worked on Eastern Shore drainage projects. Work was provided

---

151. Maryland, *Report of Work Division Activities, Maryland Emergency
Relief Administration*, April, 1934 to July, 1935, pp. v, 11, 31, 74, 96, 102,
112-39, 142-72, 185-88, 197-248, 250-56.
152. Maryland, Board of State Aid and Charities of Maryland, *The Fifth
Civilian Conservation Corps Anniversary in Maryland*, VFEP; *Sun*, May 28,
Dec. 24, 1933, Jan. 15, 1935, July 5, 1936, July 16, 1937, VFEP.

for 21,000 corpsmen at thirty camps; $3,800,000 were sent by the enrollees to dependents, and an estimated 76,000 were taken off the relief rolls. The Maryland contribution in experts, tools, and equipment reaped a rich return. As the state forester observed, CCC efforts had advanced the development of forest lands by twenty-five years. Fish and game resources had more than tripled. More significant, however, was the rehabilitation of youth through "an atmosphere of wholesomeness in the camp. Strapping, clear-eyed, suntanned youths live under strict military discipline, work vigorously, eat enormously and sleep like logs, with supervised recreation and voluntary vocational training in between." As a *Sun* report headlined: "Callow Youths Who Went to Work when Idea Went into Effect Now Hardly Recognizable. Progress Made in Every Direction."[153]

New Deal relief for farmers first responded to the obvious need for credit that was demonstrated in the drought of 1930 and the increasing mortgage foreclosures. In establishing the Farm Credit Administration and to centralize agricultural credit agencies, Roosevelt scored one of his first psychological victories through an invitation to farmers to wire the White House collect should red tape threaten to remain snarled while the sheriff was at the gate with a foreclosure order. In Maryland the need for federal credit was obvious. Thirty per cent of the farm mortgage loans of the Federal Land Bank of Baltimore were delinquent or extended in January 1934. Through February, Prince George's County recorded courthouse sale of nearly 2,000 homesteads in Upper Marlboro and a Montgomery County paper listed forty columns of tax sale notices. With increased federal loan assistance, forced farm sales decreased markedly by 1935.[154]

However, more than stop-gap credit was needed to rehabilitate agriculture. Led by Secretary of Agriculture Henry Wal-

153. *Baltimore,* XXVIII (Feb., 1935), 35; *Community Improvement Appraisal,* pp. 9, 23-24, 28; *Maryland, State and National Reports, 1933–1938,* reports 1, 2, 4, 7; U.S., Office of Government Reports, *Maryland* (Washington: Office of Government Reports, Statistical Section, 1940), II, 50. This is a two volume collection of statistical reports on New Deal agencies' activities in Maryland. Hereafter cited as Office of Government Reports. *Maryland. Sun,* April 22, 1933, April 5, 1936, April 6, 1937, VFEP.
154. *Maryland Leader,* March 17, 1934; Ralph Russell, *Maryland Farm Credit Handbook* (College Park: University of Maryland Agricultural Experiment Station, 1936), pp. 642-43.

lace, the New Deal sought to "rationalize" agriculture. Accepting overproduction and subsequent low commodity prices as central problems, the New Deal Agricultural Adjustment Administration moved to reduce acreage through quota agreements with farmers. Utilizing the county agents of the extension service, AAA subsidized the cooperating farmers through benefit payments raised through a tax on agricultural processors. In Maryland Ritchie appointed a coordinating committee led by Thomas Symons, Director of the Extension Service. A massive wheat adjustment campaign was launched through press, radio, county meetings, letters, and phone calls to wheat growers. Symons described the results as "most gratifying;" 66 per cent of the wheat acreage in Maryland, reflecting the cooperation of 7,739 farmers, was under AAA contract. Wheat benefits of $1,627,000 would be paid in Maryland. In the subsequent 1934 corn-hog campaign, Maryland producers entered contracts, bringing an additional $230,500 in benefits. Tobacco growers reduced acreage and received $77,000. Referendums in 1935 in wheat and corn demonstrated that Maryland farmers were overwhelmingly in favor of continuing the programs.

Maryland's crops fitted very well into the AAA contract programs.[155] The farmers' cash income rose from $41,166,000 in 1932 to $62,820,000 in 1935. Maryland wheat rose from fifty-three cents per bushel to seventy-six cents; corn from forty-four cents to seventy cents; hogs from $4.60 hundredweight to $9.10; tobacco from 16.8¢ to 19.5¢ a pound. Additionally, the cash income from milk production rose 11 per cent, eggs 66 per cent, and truck crops 68 per cent. When the Supreme Court struck down AAA in 1935, the *Sun* estimated that $3,500,000 might be slashed from the state farm income, and a spokesman of the Maryland Farm Bureau Federation asserted: "Organized farmers face the task of drawing up a program for replacing AAA and fighting for its adoption." The substitute measure passed in January 1936 as the Soil Conservation and Domestic Allotment plan and was enthusiastically endorsed.

---

155. Thomas Symons, *Twenty-first Annual Report of the University of Maryland Extension Service for the Year 1935*, p. 5. For further statistics see U.S., Farm Credit Administration, Division of Finance and Statistics, *Monthly Report on Loans and Discounts*, Dec., 1936, p. 8; *Maryland, State and National Reports, 1933–1938*, reports, 1, 2, 4, 7; Office of Government Reports, *Maryland*, II, 15; Russell, p. 641.

Fourteen thousand five hundred farmers signed contracts governing 60 per cent of the crop land in the state. In a year of good weather and good crop yield, the value of Maryland farm products increased $9,000,000 over 1935.[156] Though there was some decline in 1937 and 1938, Maryland agriculture, cooperating under the passage of the second Agricultural Adjustment Act, continued healthy.

The business counterpart of AAA, the National Recovery Administration, was organized in June 1933. Under the leadership of the ebullient General Hugh Johnson and the symbol of the Blue Eagle, the NRA sought federal-business cooperation and planning for recovery. Building on the trade association experience of the 1920's, the NRA monitored business efforts to rationalize production through the establishment of industrial codes and goals. Maryland's business cooperation was enthusiastically promoted by Baltimore's Association of Commerce. A Trade Association Department was established with a branch office in Washington to coordinate efforts and to serve as a clearing house for local trade groups. In August a massive NRA Reemployment Drive was launched in Baltimore, led by Major General Paul B. Malone as "generalissimo," and was supported by 500 business majors, captains and lieutenants as "shock troops." Reportedly, 4,600 workers were added to local payrolls. A parade of 7,000 marchers, twenty bands and a twenty-foot dragon from the Chinese community attacking "Old Man Depression" filed past Governor Ritchie and an estimated 250,000, thus sparking another campaign, "Now is the Time to Start Buying."[157]

Though most Maryland businesses apparently complied with the codes and joined the Blue Eagle campaign, textile companies particularly chafed under the NRA wage and hour provisions. In Baltimore, the J. Schoeneman Company locked out

156. U.S., Department of Agriculture, Agricultural Adjustment Administration, Division of Information, *State Summary Series, Maryland,* revised, pp. 1-6, VFEP; *Sun,* Jan. 7, 1936; Thomas Symons, *Twenty-second Annual Report of the University of Maryland Extension Service for the Year 1936,* pp. 3-5; ibid., 1937, pp. 3-7; U.S., Department of Agriculture, *Agricultural Adjustment, 1937–38,* press release in VFEP. Also in VFEP is *AAA Program Payments, March 25, 1938.*

157. *Baltimore,* XXVI (July, 1933), 1; XXVI (Aug. 1933), 1-2, 5; XXVII (Oct., 1933), 3; XXVII (Jan., 1934), 3. The Baltimore Association of Commerce helped to form seventy trade associations. See also *Sun,* Nov. 20, 1966, VFEP.

900 workers, insisting that a $14.50 weekly wage and a thirty-six hour week were unmanageable. Simultaneously, the firm announced it was leaving the state. L. Greif and Brothers sought an injunction to restrain NRA from interfering with its wage cuts. On the Eastern Shore, cotton garment contractors resisted enforcement; in some cases workers were forced to sign work receipts for twelve dollars when they received only six or eight dollars. Additionally, a Baltimore Fur Workers Union charged that the Baltimore Furriers Association boast of 100 per cent compliance was patently false since furriers were still working forty-eight and forty-four hour weeks. Violations were cited in a special front page box in the Socialist *Maryland Leader* headed "This Week's Chiseler vs. NRA."[158]

The labor provisions of NRA under section 7a, providing for union organization and collective bargaining, and the code provisions against sweatshop and child labor also caused state repercussions. As elsewhere, Maryland industries occasionally translated union organization as "company union"; in Baltimore, a shoe firm locked out 500 members when they elected the AFL over a company union. Teamsters struck the Davidson trucking firm for refusing to honor a union vote. NRA child labor codes, setting a minimum age of sixteen, affected 187 Maryland working children. Additionally, "homework" in the textile industry, a frequent pre-NRA practice in Baltimore, was largely ended by the codes. Labor's support for the NRA was visibly evident in a parade of 10,000 in Baltimore protesting the Supreme Court's 1935 decision of unconstitutionality.[159] Remaining, however, were the long-term benefits of the defunct NRA, the establishment of a minimum wage, maximum hours, the right to collective bargaining, and the end to sweatshops and child labor.

In the last area of recovery undertaken in the first New Deal years, the government moved to prime the pump through direct federal spending. The Public Works Administration, under In-

---

158. *Forty-second Annual Report of the Commissioner of Labor and Statistics of Maryland, 1933*, pp. 6-9; *Maryland Leader*, July 14, 21, 1934, Aug. 12, 19 and Sept. 23, 1933, Nov. 25, 1933; *Baltimore*, XXVII (Sept., 1934), 20; *The Baltimore Federationist*, Dec. 1, 1934.

159. *Maryland Leader*, Aug. 2, 1933. *Forty-third Annual Report of the Commissioner of Labor and Statistics of Maryland, 1934*, pp. 2-3; *Forty-fifty Annual Report, 1935*, p. 2; *Maryland Leader*, July 20, 21, 1934; June 1, 1935.

terior Secretary Harold Ickes, was established as part of NRA in an attempt to parallel business and government recovery efforts. Like FERA, PWA projects called for federal-state funding; early grants generally set the federal contribution at 30 per cent; the state or local contribution at 70 per cent. Again, the budgetary concerns of Ritchie and Mayor Jackson were evident. By February 1934, PWA officials scored the state's delays, which placed Maryland last in spending. Prodded by Free State PWA administrator George L. Radcliffe, the pace increased, and state planning began to show results. The building of the Susquehanna and Potomac River bridges, reconstruction and equipping of the old university hospital as a dispensary, and construction of a dormitory and arts and science building at College Park, building and repair of school buildings throughout the state, and completion of sewage and water systems were only a part of the massive Maryland effort.[160]

Most controversial was the PWA Maryland roads program; the focus of debate was the Philadelphia Road project in 1934. State Roads Commissioner E. Brooke Lee favored widening the old road, while the federal officials and the Maryland Public Works Advisory Board advanced a plan for a new road paralleling the B&O tracks. While protests by merchants along the old route and allegations of political interests delayed choice of route and construction, PWA official W. C. Stettinius warned "if you don't watch out the governor will get a letter from Mr. Ickes taking your money away."[161] An eventual compromise was achieved, yet the incident helped to underscore Maryland's dilemma in the early New Deal. Committed to state responsibility and doggedly attempting to remain master of its own affairs, Ritchie and the state were drawn by relief and recovery needs increasingly into an uneasy partnership with the federal government.

The popularity of the New Deal, the longevity of Ritchie, and the difficulty of maintaining his governmental philosophy ended the Age of Ritchie in the election of 1934. Free State scruples at federal programs were denounced by Republican

---

160. Office of Government Reports, *Maryland*, II, 29-33; *Community Improvement Appraisal*, p. 4. Employment figures are also in *Sun*, July 6, 1934.
161. *Sun*, June 20, 1933, Jan. 27, 29, 30, Feb. 4, 1934; *Evening Sun*, March 2, 21, June 19, 24, 25, 26, 1934. In the midst of the debate E. Brooke Lee resigned from the SRC to return to private business, *Sun*, May 29, 1934.

victor Governor Harry W. Nice, whose platform promised fuller cooperation with the New Deal. Nationwide, the election triumphs of the New Deal, coupled with the increasing fractiousness of business, and pressure from Senator Huey P. Long, Dr. Francis Townsend, Father Charles E. Coughlin, and others led Roosevelt to broaden relief recovery efforts. In the increased stress on federal responsibility and the emergence of the first outlines of the welfare state, the second phase of the New Deal found official Maryland hesitancy radically reduced.

The scope of this post-1934 New Deal phase is clearly seen in the organization of the Works Progress Administration, funded with nearly $5,000,000,000. FERA and CWA paled in comparison. WPA projects in Maryland were highly varied. Construction projects, utilizing 88 per cent unskilled labor, ranged from flood repair at Keedysville, farm-to-market roads in Wicomico, sewers and repairs to the Carroll mansion in Baltimore, and school construction throughout the state. The Department of Health coordinated efforts with the WPA to advance public water and sewage facilities by fifteen years. Recreation projects were administered in twenty-one counties and Baltimore. City school buildings were lighted in the evenings for volleyball, checkers, and music. A household service trained domestics, and women's projects in sewing produced thousands of garments. A nursery school project for low income families was instituted. Maps were drawn, a city atlas prepared, collections at the Baltimore Museum and Enoch Pratt Free Library were catalogued, and customs records since 1790 were listed. A WPA writers' project produced *Maryland, A Guide to the Old Line State*. By June 1939, the WPA had spent $37,738,392 in Maryland and had completed over 167 miles of roads, eighteen bridges, eighty-four playgrounds, seventeen parks, seventy-two miles of water lines, and had constructed or improved 509 buildings.[162]

These Maryland projects produced some of the complaints and problems that were raised nationwide against WPA. Labor asserted that the wage scale was too low in Baltimore, and,

---

162. *Community Improvement Appraisal,* county and municipal reports, Office of Government Reports, *Maryland,* pp. 39-40; *Sun,* June 7, 1936, Jan. 17, 1937, Feb. 14, 1938. For transition problems from CWA-FERA to WPA see *Maryland Leader,* June 7, 23, 1934, Aug. 17, Sept. 21, 28, Oct. 11, 1935 and *Sun,* Dec. 29, 1935 and Jan. 1, 7, 1936.

according to a relief administrator, a Baltimore family of six had an average $6.74 monthly deficit under WPA wages that had to be met by local relief. While urban labor complained of the paucity of WPA wages, rural labor found them highly attractive. Maryland tobacco growers complained that they found it almost impossible to get workers. Local officials in Hancock, Washington County, complained of political influence in the distribution of jobs and a tendency of the WPA workers to congregate in bars on pay day. There was also a fear that receiving federal wages would prove habit forming. As the federal government, still chasing a balanced budget, cut back WPA appropriations in 1937, Maryland was faced with a mounting relief nightmare and asserted it would refuse aid to those dropped from the WPA rolls because they became a federal responsibility. Baltimore also temporarily refused to sign the "sponsors agreement" required for WPA projects, fearing that a federal withdrawal of funds would obligate the city to complete the unfinished work.[163]

While there were objections and concerns, the Maryland reaction to WPA proved generally overwhelmingly favorable. Hagerstown's mayor noted the "salubrious effect on the morale of the community." Williamsport's leaders cited permanent benefits, concluding, "The financial condition of the town has never been better, while the happiness and security of the people, despite the uncertainties of a troubled economic world are well preserved." As a Sharpsburg burgess agreed, "Money spent for work relief is surely a better plan than to spend a great deal more of it in reducing rebellion." Projects had rehabilitated communities, saved morale, and, more importantly, had kept alive "the knowledge that man still has consideration for his fellow man."[164]

Concern for youth was also emphasized in the post-1934 efforts of the New Deal. CCC appropriations were increased. The National Youth Administration was established by execu-

---

163. D. Luke Hopkins, "Relief Supplementation of WPA Wages," *The Councillor,* I (Feb., 1936), 8-9; Robert O. Bonnell, "How Some Families Live on WPA Wages," *The Councillor,* III (Dec., 1938), 27-31; *Community Improvement Appraisal,* municipal report, Hancock; *Sun,* July 24, Aug. 22, 31, 1937; *Evening Sun,* Sept. 7, 1937 in VFEP.

164. *Community Improvement Appraisal,* municipal reports, Hagerstown, Williamsport, Sharpsburg.

tive order to give youth "a definite stake in the life of their time." Maryland's State Youth Administrator, Ryland N. Dempster, worked with five area directors and local advisory committees to coordinate projects that would keep the state's youth in school and to promote training for those out of school and unemployed. NYA tasks varied from guidework at Fort McHenry to maintenance work at Maryland House in Druid Hill Park. Training programs were provided by the Salvation Army in child care; Negroes were trained as orderlies at University Hospital. Projects allowing students to finish their education paid college students up to $20 a month and high school students from three to six dollars monthly. By July 1939, NYA had spent $1,409,451 in Maryland: $570,625 in work projects, and $838,826 for wages to students.[165]

Concern for the elderly, made a national issue by the successful campaigning of Dr. Townsend for his pension scheme, was merged in 1935 with a plan for unemployment compensation; the result was the Social Security Act. Maryland moved immediately to implement Social Security measures for the needy aged, dependent children, and the blind. Not until December 1936, however, did the Free State legislate for unemployment compensation in response to the federal Social Security provisions. Benefits became payable in January 1938; by September 1939, they had totaled $14,463,263.[166]

Other New Deal efforts were directed at rural deprivation. Instituted in 1935, the Rural Electrification Administration filled a major need in Free State rural communities. At its inception, only 15 per cent of Maryland farms were connected to central power station lines. By June 1939, utilizing $629,000 in REA funds, Maryland cooperatives had constructed 400 miles of lines to serve 1,400 members. Increasing farm electrification particularly aided poultrymen and dairymen.[167]

More broadly conceived was the Farm Resettlement Ad-

---

165. Ryland N. Dempster, "For Unemployed Youth," *The Councillor*, II (June, 1937), 18-22; Ryland N. Dempster, "Federal Security Agency, National Youth Administration," *Federal Business in Maryland*, IX (Jan.–March, 1941), 23-25; National Youth Administration of Maryland, *A Special Report to the Advisory Committee of Baltimore City, June 20, 1938*, pp. 4-10; Office of Government Reports, *Maryland*, II, 23.
166. Office of Government Reports, *Maryland*, II, 25.
167. *Ibid.*, p. 19.

ministration under the leadership of the controversial brain-truster Rexford G. Tugwell. Committed to community planning and the wise use of natural resources, Tugwell proposed and initiated a series of "greenbelt" towns. The most fully conceived was Greenbelt, Maryland. Built on cheap acreage by relief labor, located near job opportunities in Washington and the Beltsville agricultural center, providing a ready market for neighboring farmers, and serving as a model for a town rationally planned, Greenbelt richly mixed New Deal relief and recovery measures. Eight hundred and eighty-five families were carefully chosen to pioneer in the new community. However, emphasis on planning, government ownership of the land, the cooperative emphasis of its economic system and government, the cost overruns in construction, and congressional antipathy to the leadership of Tugwell, led to the termination of FRA after only 4,000 families had been relocated.[168]

In the area of urban rehabilitation, the Wagner-Steagall Act created the United States Housing Authority and provided loans for slum clearance and construction of low-rent projects. The Maryland Housing Authority Law of 1937 authorized cities and towns of 1,000 to establish local authorities to plan and construct projects. By October 10, ten were underway, including College Creek Terrace in Annapolis, Edgar Allan Poe Homes in Baltimore, and two in Frederick. Two thousand five hundred and fifty-six families would benefit from the $22,518,000 in USHA loans.[169]

Perhaps the most far-reaching New Deal benefit to any group was the passage of the Wagner National Labor Relations Act in 1935. Labor rights were legislated and guarded by the establishment of the National Labor Relations Board. For the next two years, backed by a sympathetic administration in Washington and led by the drive of the newly formed Committee for Industrial Organization to organize the unorganized, labor

---

168. *Ibid.*, pp. 16-17; *Maryland, State and National Reports, 1933–1938*, report 5; U.S., Department of Agriculture, *Farm Security Administration Announces Greenbelt Rentals*, Sept. 2, 1937, press release in VFEP. See also Leslie G. Hunter, "Greenbelt, Maryland: A City on a Hill," *M.H.M.*, LXIII (June, 1968), 105-36. Rural rehabilitation efforts were continued under FSA and the Bankhead-Jones Tenancy Act.

169. Office of Government Reports, *Maryland*, II, 37-38; *Maryland, State and National Reports, 1933–1938*, report 4. Total of all federal expenses in Maryland with the exception of VA is in *ibid.*, reports 1–8 through June 30, 1938.

tested the implications of the new legislation. The 1936 report of Maryland's commissioner of labor and statistics reported "serious labor unrest" and an unusually large number of strikes. Key Maryland industries of rubber, textiles, maritime, autos, and canning were struck for union recognition and collective bargaining.[170]

Cumberland was the scene of one major confrontation. A CIO United Rubber Workers attempt to organize Cumberland's second largest employer, Kelly-Springfield Tire Company, led to a strike in August 1936, of 1,700 workers over union recognition, wages and hours, and better working conditions. Violence flared briefly as strikers attacked a bus carrying workers into the factory and were repulsed by gas bombs hurled by police from the running boards of escort cars. In September this strike ended unsuccessfully, and the workers returned without discrimination, but in January the United Rubber Workers sat down in the plant for an increase on the piece work base. Kelly-Springfield retaliated by laying off the union leaders and bargaining with the company's Employees Protective Association. In this early test, the NLRB found that the company had not engaged in collective bargaining, ordered it to disband the company union, to reinstate the union employees with back pay, and to post notice that it intended to comply with the Wagner Act.[171]

---

170. The Maryland AFL began the decade of the 1930's with a heated debate over allocation of offices to Baltimore, D.C. and western Maryland. William Green arbitrated the dispute, but the local leadership repudiated his settlement. See *The Baltimore Federationist,* April 17, May 20, 22, 27, July 15, 1932. At Broening's death in 1933, he was succeeded in the Baltimore Federation by Joseph McCurdy. McCurdy had already assumed state leadership. The antipathy of the AFL for the new CIO was obvious in the call for the Cumberland convention in 1938. *The Baltimore Federationist,* April 14, 1938. The CIO formed an executive association of the Baltimore Industrial Council in July 1937. Seventy-seven delegates assembled representing a purported 40,000 workers. Frank Bender was the CIO organizer. In November 1937, the First District Council was organized and chose John Jones of the UMW as president. At this meeting Jones lashed out at McCurdy. *Sun,* July 29, 1937, *Eve. Sun,* Nov. 8, 1937, VFEP. See also *Western Maryland Industrial Voice of Labor,* December issues for 1938 state CIO convention. Also *Forty-fifth Annual Report of the Commissioner of Labor and Statistics of Maryland, 1936,* pp. 6-12.

171. *Ibid.,* pp. 6-12; *Evening Sun,* Aug. 26, 1936; *Sun,* Sept. 2, 1936; *Evening Sun,* Jan. 21, 1937; *Sun,* Nov. 26, 1937. NLRB release, *Consent Decree in Kelly-Springfield Tire Case Announced, May 29, 1938,* VFEP.

In Amcelle, Maryland, close to the Kelly-Springfield plant, the Celanese Corporation's acetate factory was struck by the CIO United Textile Workers of America for collective bargaining, a 15 per cent wage increase, and implementation of grievance procedures. Nine thousand workers walked out in November. Local authorities in the company town called in the state police. In a mutual de-escalation, however, the police agreed to reduce their numbers from fifty to two, if the strikers would reduce their pickets from several hundred to thirty. The detective agencies hired by the Celanese Corporation did not match the low police profile. A clash between detectives and strikers resulted in one stabbing and fifteen other injuries. Tension increased as the B&O, whose tracks ran through the plant, obtained a temporary injunction against interference with its trains. Rumors of scabs arriving on the trains led to stoning incidents at the plant and fifty-four warrants issued for arrests. By December 2, the UTW agreed to end the walkout, and Celanese agreed to deal with the union and to establish grievance procedures and to increase wages. While the UTW saw this as a crack in the textile industry of the solid South, the closed shop was still not achieved.[172]

In Baltimore CIO-United Auto Workers attempted to organize General Motors. The year 1937 opened with an organizing drive and walkout by UAW workers at the Fisher Body plant and Chevrolet. Led by James Blackwell, a UAW organizer fresh from the Celanese strike in Amcelle, the workers confronted the assertion by the local Fisher head that the plant would never close. Non-union workers who wanted to stay on the assembly line presented a scroll bearing 2,400 signatures stating their gratitude for the Christmas bonus and their confidence in General Motors. They denounced outside individuals who were allegedly intimidating "loyal" workers. Although management expressed its surprise at this demonstration, press photographers were there to record the event. Anti-strike workers followed this effort by meeting to plan a march on Washington to petition Roosevelt and Secretary of Labor Frances Perkins to intervene and end the strike. Twenty-two UAW members were forcibly kept out of the meeting in a free-swinging melee. In February the Baltimore strike was settled

---

172. *Evening Sun*, Nov. 15, 17, 1936; *Sun*, Nov. 28, 29, Dec. 2, 3, 1936.

by the Michigan capitulation of General Motors. Within five days of reopening, however, production was again interrupted briefly while some union leaders were ejected from work. Testimony by the plant manager before the LaFollette Civil Liberties Committee shed some light on the Baltimore loyalty movement. Although he insisted that the back-to-work movement in January had originated among the workers, it was acknowledged that the leader was a former Pinkerton employee. Additionally, the loyal leadership had been given the use of the payroll list for mailing purposes. Union men had been threatened and terrorized on the job. By June, the UAW dominated the local and national scene. A sit-down strike of 800 UAW workers at the Baltimore Fisher plant protested the use of non-union men on the trim line. The UAW mounted a 2,000 man picket line. A quick settlement won reemployment of union men, mutual control of assembly line speed, settlement of seniority, and wage increases.[173] However, as in the textile strike, the closed shop was still not achieved.

In June 1937, busy state Labor Commissioner Harry Phoebus had to contend with a walkout of 2,000 workers from the Cambridge canning plants of Phillips Packing Company, Inc. Six plants were closed. There was no organized union, but discontent over wages and a desire to join the AFL were cited as reasons for the strike. Violence flared as a policeman in the Phillips yard allegedly brandished a pistol at the strikers. Enraged, they hurled stones at the plant and police and overturned nineteen Phillips trucks. Phoebus arrived, soothed both sides, extracted a no-violence pledge from the strikers, and arranged for the withdrawal of sheriffs' forces. The workers righted the trucks and began conversations with AFL Baltimore organizer Anna Neary and owner Albanus Phillips.[174] By early July, violence flared again. A strike leader arrested on a drunk and disorderly charge was visited by 200 strikers at the jail and quickly released by the sheriff on collateral of ten dollars. Subsequently a striker, walking past the plant, was shot, allegedly by a guard. Workers began interfering with the Phillips Hardware Com-

173. *Forty-sixth Annual Report of the Commissioner of Labor and Statistics of Maryland, 1937*, pp. 8-16; *Sun*, Jan. 1, 9, 11, 22, 23, 1937; *Evening Sun*, Jan. 29, Feb. 23, 1937; *Sun*, Feb. 19, 24, March 6, June 5, 10, 14, 15, 16, 17, 1937; *Evening Sun*, June 9, 10, 21, 24, 1937, VFEP.
174. *Sun*, June 24, 1937, VFEP.

pany by seizing trucks and threatening employees. In this atmosphere NLRB agents arrived in Cambridge to join Phoebus and Anna Neary. The Cambridge Workers Association, backed by local merchants, as "a home union for home people," was organized and divided the labor forces. AFL's Anna Neary filed a complaint with the NLRB that Phillips Company had "sponsored, dominated, interfered with and controlled the Cambridge Workers Association." Phillips signed a contract with the CWA, however, as the sole bargaining agent. Although the NLRB, finding that the CWA was a company union that had coerced workers, issued an order that Phillips discontinue bargaining with CWA and stop discouraging workers from joining the AFL or CIO, it was two years before compliance was achieved.[175]

The year 1938 was one of relative labor tranquility. Significantly, perhaps, the dominant strike issue was seniority. Labor was further undergirded by the Supreme Court's approval of the NLRB and the passage of the Fair Labor Standards Act. Also, from 1935 Maryland labor was buoyed by the General Assembly's passage of anti-yellow dog and anti-injunction measures, improved workmen's compensation, and old age pensions.[176] Of all of Maryland's citizens, labor through self-help and legislation had advanced most surely in the emergence of federal welfare and concern.

## 5

### THE DEFEAT OF RITCHIE

The impact of the depression and the New Deal and increasing concern over the response of Ritchie and the spectre of his

---

175. *Sun,* June 28, 30, July 2, 3, 9, 24, 1937; *Evening Sun,* Aug. 30, Nov. 13, 1937; *Sun,* Feb. 13, May 7, July 9, 1938. Fears of a farmers' reaction were rising. The tomato crop was still to be harvested and stringbeans especially raised for Phillips were scheduled to arrive at the plant. Strikers drove out to the fields to try to discourage pickers and persuaded 200 Negro migrants to cooperate. Farmers' worries were eased by the assurance that their crop would be marketed by the Queen Anne and Hillsboro cooperatives. See also NLRB release, *Stipulation Effects Compliance with Labor Board Order, Feb. 29, 1940,* VFEP.
176. *Forty-seventh Annual Report of the Commissioner of Labor and Statistics of Maryland, 1938,* pp. 3-8, 12-20; *The Baltimore Federationist,* April 19, 1935, *Baltimore American,* April 14, 1935.

permanent tenure in office produced the highly complex and significant contest at the top of the ticket in 1934. In the summer of 1933, Mencken speculated:

> The weakness of the Ritchie machine lies in the fact that its existence is a standing grief to every member of the Why-Not-Me? Club. . . . I do not predict formally that they will succeed in knocking off the Governor, for he is a more adept politician than any of them and perhaps than all of them taken together; all I venture to say is that many of them are ready to try to knock him off if he ever looks to be wobbly.

By March 1934, the *Sun* listed fifteen possible Democratic and Republican challengers. As late as July 6, Frank Kent still lamented: "the political picture is beginning to resemble the work of a cubist artist."[177]

The major contest loomed in the Democratic party and centered on the fifth-term aspirations of Ritchie and the implications for party control. A three-cornered struggle began to emerge in the spring of 1934 among Ritchie, urged by E. Brooke Lee and other leaders to forego Annapolis and file for the Senate; Mayor Jackson, always anxious to broaden his base and campaigning on Ritchie's accolade that he was the best mayor Baltimore ever had; and Senator Millard Tydings, who had built up a talented political following through New Deal patronage. Below this struggle at the top other Democratic candidates and leaders evinced a growing restlessness with Ritchie's "governeritis contageosus." There was no room at the top, and Ritchie's appointees left little room at the bottom. Baltimore businessman Clarence Miles organized the Maryland Democratic League against long tenure in office. Six alternatives to Ritchie were offered. Frederick's Dr. Charles H. Conley filed for governor, pledged to a constitutional limitation of gubernatorial tenure. In St. Mary's County, state Senator J. Allen Coad threatened to lead an independent Democratic bolt if Ritchie ran. Baltimore leader William Curran summarized: "Our party is in the temper for a good old-fashioned primary fight. . . ."[178]

---

177. H. L. Mencken, "The Governorship," *Evening Sun*, July 3, 1933; *Sun*, March 18, July 6, 1934.

178. *Baltimore American*, Aug. 20, 1933, *Post*, Nov. 3, 1933; *Sun*, Aug. 31, Sept. 26, 27, Nov. 2, 1933; *Post*, Jan. 27, 1934; *Sun*, Feb. 6, 23, June 23, 1934, *Sun*, June 23, 1938. See clippings Box 48, Ritchie Papers. E. Brooke Lee

The New Deal credentials of Ritchie became increasingly central. Observing the federal patronage distributed in Maryland and the accepted adage: "They might as well have hung out a sign No Ritchie or Curran Men Need Apply," the Baltimore County *Jeffersonian* concluded that Ritchie was surely hurting himself by not jumping on the Roosevelt recovery wagon. After a March meeting with Ritchie, old friend Bernard Baruch declared that Roosevelt was urging Ritchie to run for senator rather than governor to retrieve the seat for the party. Not until May 12 did Ritchie, after the usual flurry of petitions urging him to run, announce his candidacy for reelection. Expressing his awareness that his bid for the Senate would be unopposed in the party, he stated his belief that a gubernatorial primary would not imperil the party.[179]

Other Democratic leaders and hopefuls feared that a primary fight would "rock the Democratic party to its foundations" and be "little short of suicidal." An impatient Mayor Jackson, told by Ritchie not to "wait for him," had officially filed his candidacy on April 28. Working anxiously to avoid the bloodbath, Senator Tydings hurriedly sounded out state leaders to build support for a compromise candidate, Roosevelt friend, and state Public Works Administrator, George L. Radcliffe. On May 28 Radcliffe, assured of Tydings' backing, some demonstrated sentiment by local Democrats against a primary, plus a possible quiet Roosevelt encouragement, announced he would run for governor if Jackson and Ritchie withdrew. Neither gentleman would oblige. After a four-hour conference with Tydings, Radcliffe re-announced his candidacy, this time with the hope that Jackson would withdraw and that Ritchie would run for the Senate. The Radcliffe ticket was left hopefully open, but his position was clear and pledged to "upholding the hand" of

---

advised Ritchie to run for the Senate since "such a move would have disengaged most of the ambitious local Democrats who felt that they had no chance against sitting Ritchie appointees as long as he remained in office; and after 15 years of top appointive power Governor Ritchie had actually filled every office in the State.

"Such a move would have also unloaded all of the State issues which were proving troublesome. Nearly all Democrats including most of the more potent leaders of the then Ritchie opposition were expressing themselves as happy to support the Governor for the U.S. Senate." Letter of E. Brooke Lee to author, June 7, 1972.

179. *Evening Sun*, Aug. 3, 1933; *Baltimore American*, March 11, 1934; *Sun*, March 24, May 13, 1934, Box 48, Ritchie Papers.

Franklin D. Roosevelt. An adamant Ritchie, lamenting the injection of the New Deal into the race, indicated he would not be budged. At the formal filing, June 25, he reiterated: "I want to say, and I hope it will be the last time I have to say it, I would rather be Governor of Maryland than Senator from all the United States."[180]

In the impasse all sides vied at applying pressure. Jackson, while asserting his strength, urged an anti-Ritchie candidates' conference to decide on one candidate. Radcliffe's receptivity built speculation that if Ritchie would not withdraw Jackson might run for the Senate on the Radcliffe slate. At the same time, Ritchie asserted that the fifth-term nomination would surely fall to him and talked of Radcliffe on his ticket for senator. Clearly unbudging and rallying his forces effectively, Governor Ritchie could not be balked. After another futile Jackson-Radcliffe conference, Tydings sought a meeting with Ritchie men E. Brooke Lee and William Walsh, admitted defeat, and urged acceptance of Radcliffe on the Ritchie ticket for senator. On July 8 Radcliffe announced his withdrawal, in the interests of harmony, of his candidacy for the Senate. He further explained that state Democratic leaders had urged him to accept the position, pointing out that his New Deal associations would make him an asset as a Maryland senator. Although a disappointed Jackson and Conley vowed to remain in the fight, it was obvious that Ritchie believed the major Democratic battle was won. The day after the Radcliffe settlement, Ritchie announced he would leave for vacation in Europe. As he expected, Jackson's support faltered; on the governor's return he was met by 15,000, and at their head was the mayor.[181]

Left alone to lead the Ritchie dissidents was Dr. Charles H. Conley. Bitterly he inveighed against the rule of "Prince Albert

---

180. *Sun*, April 26, May 1, June 26, 1934; *Baltimore American*, May 6, 1934, Box 48, Ritchie Papers.
181. *Sun*, May 29, June 1, 7, 14, 17, 19, 20, 25, 27, July 1, 2, 8, 9, 29, 1934; *Evening Sun*, May 29, 31, 1934. Rothman, p. 53; Helldorfer, p. 77; Ritchie was so discouraged before his June commencement address at the University of Maryland that he told E. Brooke Lee that he was right in trying to dissuade him from running. He did not believe he could win. When Tydings subsequently capitulated and approached Lee, Ritchie was reluctant to relinquish his backing of Howard Bruce for the Senate. Lee in a marathon telephone session with county leaders achieved backing for the Ritchie-Radcliffe ticket. Interview with E. Brooke Lee, March 23, 1972.

the Fourth." On the Ritchie departure for Europe, he had caustically observed that now the governor could "confer with the British King on the divine right of Kings, with Hitler in Germany on the disposal of political enemies, with King Alphonso on a safe and sane road to abdication." Conley urged Maryland to end the reign and to choose a new dealer and a new deck.[182]

A Ritchie victory in a troubled Democratic vote was predicted, but ironically, a *Washington Post* survey pointed out, the major Conley attack against the rule of Ritchie and his vaunted machine seemed misdirected. In county after county the organization was in difficulties. In Wicomico, ninety-eight Democrats were seeking local offices as the young turks battled for positions; Dorchester was the scene of bob-tailed fighting, every man for himself. Talbot's Democrats were still seeking a leader after the death of a local chieftain. In Cecil, Talbot, Washington, and Baltimore Counties disgruntled factions struggled. In southern Maryland, anti-Ritchie factions had formed, and Ritchie remained unpopular for his wetness and conservation policies.

In spite of a downpour in parts of the state, a heavy primary vote was brought out by the local struggles and the contest at the top of the ticket. Ritchie compiled a three-to-one margin in the city, but Conley registered surprisingly well in the counties; he carried Caroline, Dorchester, Kent, St. Mary's, Talbot, Cecil, Frederick, Queen Anne's, Somerset, Worcester, and Wicomico. A turnover of 2,000 to 2,500 votes distributed among the counties would have given Conley the victory in the state Democratic convention. The *New York Herald Tribune* interpreted the 90,000 Conley votes as representing deep New Deal inroads in Maryland. The following day, Ritchie issued an "unexpected endorsement of President Roosevelt." Subsequently, the first article of the State Democratic Platform adopted at the party convention pledged "one hundred per cent support of the New Deal."[183]

Ritchie's Republican opposition was chosen after a bitterly devisive primary struggle. GOP candidates, agreeing with their Democratic candidates that Ritchie was vulnerable, echoed

---

182. *Washington Herald*, Sept 10, 1934; *Sun*, July 17, 1934, clipping in Box 51, Ritchie Papers.

183. *Sun*, Sept. 14, 21, 1934; *Boston Transcript*, Sept. 29, 1934; Box 51, Ritchie Papers. *The Observer*, Sept. 15, 1934. See also *Sun*, Oct. 28, 1934.

Conley's cry that Maryland wanted not merely a new deal but a brand new deck of cards. GOP factional leaders who had warred intermittently throughout the 1920's, again struggled for dominance: old Eastern Shore chief, William P. Jackson, backed H. Webster Smith, former chairman of the Public Improvement Commission; Ovington Weller and William Broening joined to support Baltimore's Harry W. Nice, the Ritchie foe of 1919; former governor and proven vote getter, Senator Phillips Lee Goldsborough, the Maryland gentleman, urged to make one more run by Eastern Shore and "blue stocking" supporters. Trying to estimate a favorite, the *Washington Post* could only pronounce a mixed bag. With voters marking first and second choices on their ballots, the predictions became even more difficult. Yet issues at the hustings were effectively drawn. Smith's major thrust was for new leadership in the party, since the Weller-Tait-Goldsborough dominance had only resulted in fifteen years of Ritchie. Goldsborough, damaged perhaps by his position as Chairman of the Board of the Baltimore Trust Company, stressed a conservative approach, urging: "Do not ... dull your vision with new-hatched, untried, fledgling doctrines and theories that conflict with the American principles of civil liberty and justice." Nice supported the New Deal. He was a surprisingly early winner in plurality and in the convention vote. Nominated to the tune of "Happy Days Are Here Again," Nice would stand on a platform pledged to secure more New Deal benefits for the Old Line State under his Republican administration.[184]

The Maryland Socialists had no such difficulties in making their 1934 slate: The Johns Hopkins professor, Broadus Mitchell, ran for governor; Elizabeth Gilman for senator. Backed by an endorsement by the *Afro-American*, Mitchell pledged state ownership of transportation, purchase of the coal mines, and racial equality. Lashing out at both capitalists and Ritchie, he asserted: "His philosophy has been preserved like ancient laces in camphor, to let us see what men thought in days forgotten."[185]

184. Helldorfer, p. 74 and 78; *Evening Sun*, April 16, 1934; *Sun*, June 29, 30, Sept. 6, 28, 1934, Box 51, Ritchie Papers. Baltimore City and County favored Nice; Cecil supported Smith; Dorchester backed Goldsborough.
185. *Afro-American*, July 21, 1934, *Sun*, June 19, Sept. 17, 1934, Box 51, Ritchie Papers. Also *Maryland Leader*, May 26, 1934.

The Ritchie-Nice contest, a repetition of the closely fought campaign of 1919 with echoes of "steal," was the scenario for 1934. But while the main combatants were the same, the parties and the issues were significantly altered. The Democratic diplomacy and hard-won harmony of 1919 were lacking in 1934. Defeated Dr. Conley and his supporters, backers of outmaneuvered Howard Jackson and the factions of Mencken's "why not me" persuasion would be less than enthusiastic for the Ritchie-Radcliffe-Tydings accommodation. In the Republican camp the silk-stocking Goldsborough men and anti-New Deal old boss Galen Tait were not adherents of lawyer Harry Nice.[186]

While the Republicans stressed the theme of one-man rule and seemed convinced that if they did not oust Ritchie he would run forever, the other major issue was Ritchie's repugnance to the New Deal. The Republicans continued the Nice primary contention that they could obtain more federal benefits for the Free State. As the *Sun* editorialized, Nice would certainly not shoot Santa Claus. The anti-Ritchie *Baltimore Post* summarized: "To find the Republicans cashing in on the popularity of a Democratic President and to find the Democrats, that is, the Ritchie organization Democrats—weakened by the success of their party nationally, would be a curious paradox. Yet it is one which the Annapolis administration seems to have been at pains to bring about and which the Republicans would be foolish not to formalize."[187]

The impact of the "more New Dealish than the Democrats" issue was seen as Ritchie and Tydings opened the Baltimore campaign and pointed out "a vote for the Republican ticket will be a great slap in the face for the President of the United States." Ritchie made a nationwide broadcast for the NRA, and Ickes praised the Maryland PWA as the most efficient and conscientious in America. James Farley asserted that Ritchie was "one of the most outstanding Democrats and Maryland one of the best governed states." Additionally, Tydings and Radcliffe announced after an October meeting with Roosevelt that PWA funds would be available to modernize the C&O canal. Republican backing of Roosevelt, Tydings insisted, was "political

---

186. *The Observer*, Nov. 10, 1934.

187. *Post*, June 6, 1933, Box 48, Ritchie Papers; *Washington Post*, Sept. 30, 1934; *Sun*, Sept. 28, 1934, clipping in Box 51, Ritchie Papers.

hypocrisy." Radcliffe and attorney general candidate Herbert O'Conor stumped the state, talking of Ritchie's close cooperation with the New Deal. The Democratic slogan was recorded by the Harford County *Aegis*, "Back up the President" with Ritchie.[188]

While the New Deal was the major issue, Republicans also charged Ritchie with bungling the bank crisis of 1933 and favoring the banks headed by political friends, the troubled Baltimore Trust Company, Union Trust Company, and Title Guarantee Company. Nice promised tax relief by lowering the auto tag fee from nine to two dollars. He charged inefficiency in the State Roads Commission. In brief, Nice was preempting Ritchie's old platform of economy and efficiency. Throughout the campaign, Ritchie was on the defensive. He complained of Nice's glittering promises, asserting it was always easier for the "outs" than the "ins." He noted: "We Democrats have no magic and no trick articles to peddle. We are interested only in giving the best government of which we are capable and in recognizing the claim of humanity." In stumping the state, however, Ritchie uncharacteristically tried to match promises with Nice. Pledging roads in Elkton and oyster rehabilitation in Cambridge, he promised a permanent state relief welfare program in Baltimore. When his city lieutenants were accused of links with organized crime, he pointed out Nice's career as a criminal lawyer and his involvement in an alleged movie-house swindle in 1922.[189]

As the campaign, Maryland's "most spirited in a generation," came to a close, the columnists and pundits saw a divided state. Though the Democrats led the Republicans two to one in registration and were conceded Baltimore City, the Democrats acknowledged that the counties might fall to the GOP by 20,000 votes. The continued intransigence of Democrat Conley, and restless county factions, the GOP defection of Galen Tait, and the coolness of Goldsborough and Smith backers were imponderables. The *Sun* supported Ritchie on the basis of his experience and concluded that a vote for Nice could only be a blind

188. Helldorfer, pp. 78-86; *Sun*, Oct. 19, 22, 1934; *Evening Sun*, Oct. 19, 1934, Box 51, Ritchie Papers.

189. Helldorfer, pp. 78-86; *Sun*, Oct. 16, 25, 30, Nov. 1, 2, 3, 1934; *Evening Sun*, Oct. 31, 1934; *Baltimore American*, Sept. 30, 1934, clipping in Box 51, Ritchie Papers; Rothman, p. 99.

gamble: "Mr. Nice is the pleasantest of men and his intentions are good but what more can be said." On the other hand, Nice predicted a victory asserting: "It is Kismet: it is fated to be so."[190]

In the final voting Nice edged Ritchie 253,813 to 247,664. He carried every county but Montgomery, Prince George's, and Baltimore, which he lost by only 487 votes. At the same time Radcliffe was beating Republican opponent Joseph I. France 264,279 to 197,642, and Herbert O'Conor was trouncing his opponent for attorney general 280,957 to 177,689. Radcliffe's Baltimore plurality was 44,000; O'Conor's a stunning 79,000, while Ritchie's hovered at 20,000. A six-man Democratic delegation was returned to Congress. As the *Sun* realistically concluded: "Nice is entitled to say he owes his election to his own enterprise and efforts and found himself on the crest of a wave of revolt vs. Governor Ritchie." The Socialist *Maryland Leader* agreed, as did the *Baltimore American*; it was a protest vote and it was against Ritchie. The *Detroit News* compared it "with the Athenians turning out Aristides through their weariness at hearing him called the Just."[191]

In most precisely pinpointing the reasons for the defeat, the press observed the force of the Conley strength in Frederick county but adjudged Baltimore City "the slaughterhouse." The *New York Times* concluded it was a question of jealous rivals and cutthroat politics. Others cited the racial issue, particularly the impact of Ritchie's calling out of the national guard over the Armwood lynching. Yet in 1930 Ritchie had lost Dorchester and Wicomico Counties and the decline was only slight in 1934. Conversely, the *Afro-American*, angered at Ritchie's refusal to replace the Baltimore Police Chief Charles Gaither, repeal Jim Crow laws, and his failure to appoint Negroes to state offices, claimed that the Negro vote had defeated the governor. In some Negro precincts of Baltimore, Ritchie received as little as 5 per cent of the vote. Labor's vote was counted against Ritchie, as was the oystermen's, angry at a gas tax on work boats and the

---

190. *Sun*, Oct. 12, 18, 1934; *Washington Post*, Nov. 5, 1934, clipping in Box 51, Ritchie Papers.
191. *Sun*, Oct. 11, 15, Nov. 9, 1934; *Detroit News*, Nov. 11, 1934, Box 51, Ritchie Papers; *Maryland Leader*, Nov. 10, 17, 1934; Helldorfer, p. 90. Election returns in *Maryland Manual*, 1935, pp. 266-73. Ritchie's Baltimore total dropped 37,262 votes from 1930.

closing of oyster beds. Anger over the bank failures was an added liability. Finally, the prohibition repeal issue, which had helped Ritchie in the past, was missing. As Tydings summed up: "There were just too many barnacles on the good ship Ritchie for it to have survived the hazards of another battle for the governorship."[192]

Ritchie was eulogized in defeat by the Maryland and national press. His party position was conjectural; Tydings and Jackson, rivals with position and patronage, would surely increase their power. Ritchie observed six weeks of silence after Nice's inauguration and then lashed out: "For the first time in my recollection the State is without a Governor who makes any effort to function."[193]

If his role in the state was contested, Ritchie continued to be a spokesman of states rights and an increasing opponent of the New Deal. Like Al Smith, he wondered aloud what had happened to the party platform of 1932; like Al Smith, he gravitated into the anti-New Deal Liberty League. At his death in February 1936, Old Line State party chieftains were struggling for supremacy; Maryland was fiscally troubled under the administration of Nice, and the New Deal was on the brink of its most stunning victory. In 1936, in spite of the lukewarm straddle of the *Sun* and the lack of ardor of Tydings and Jackson, Franklin Roosevelt in an unprecedented 90 per cent voter turnout achieved an Old Line State and national landslide. The Old Line State "voters," not the leaders, supported Roosevelt in Baltimore City 210,668 to 97,667 and in the state 389,612 to

---

192. *New York Times*, Nov. 9, 1934, Box 51, Ritchie Papers; *Afro-American*, June 2, 1934, clipping in Box 48, Ritchie Papers. E. Brooke Lee believed that Ritchie's length of term in office, his appointments throughout the counties, the restlessness of younger, ambitious leaders all contributed to Ritchie's downfall. Interview with E. Brooke Lee, March 23, 1972. See also Harry W. Kirwin, *The Inevitable Success: Herbert R. O'Conor* (Westminster, Md.: Newman Press 1962), p. 161.

193. *Sun*, Feb. 27, 1935; *Evening Sun*, Feb. 27, 1935; *Washington Post*, Sept. 15, 1934, Box 51, Ritchie Papers. Mencken in "Hail but not Farewell," *Evening Sun*, Jan. 7, 1935, stated: "But if you think he [Nice] will be able to do better for the State on his burning deck than Ritchie would have done in the midst of his well-oiled and efficient (if sometimes rather pungent) machine, then all I can say is that you are almost ripe to believe that the Brain trust really has brains or that Jonah swallowed the whale."

231,435.[194] The Age of Ritchie was over; the Age of Roosevelt was at its height; and Maryland was at the end of one phase of the difficult transition between the wars.

194. Thigpen, p. 144; *The Observer*, Feb., 1936; *Evening Sun*, Nov. 4, 1936. Election returns in *Maryland Manual*, 1937, pp. 305-06. For FDR's abortive "purge" of Tydings in 1938, see Myron I. Scholnick, "The President and the Senator: Franklin Roosevelt's Attempted 'Purge' of Maryland's Millard Tydings in 1938" (M.A. thesis, University of Maryland, 1962). See also Philip A. Grant, Jr., "Maryland Press Reaction to the Roosevelt-Tydings Confrontation," *M.H.M.*, LXVIII (Winter, 1973), 422-37, and for the gubernatorial race of 1938 see Kirwin, pp. 180-216. The candidacies of Jackson, O'Conor, Sasscer, and Gordy aptly indicated the struggle for Democratic leadership after Ritchie.

## BIBLIOGRAPHICAL ESSAY
### CHAPTER IX

As in other periods of the state's history a lamentable dearth of published studies is the case here. The major available sources are government documents, newspapers and clipping files and unpublished dissertations and theses. The richest repository of these is the Maryland Room of the Enoch Pratt Free Library.

To investigate the administrations of Governor Ritchie, the Ritchie papers (MSS. 710, M. H. S.) are invaluable. There is no full length published study of Ritchie, but the unpublished dissertation of James B. Levin, "Albert Ritchie, a Political Biography" (Ph.D., City College of New York, 1970) offers the most complete analysis of his life and career. Unpublished theses by Joseph Chepaitis, "The First Two Administrations of Albert Cabell Ritchie, Governor of Maryland, 1920–27" (M.A. thesis, Georgetown University, 1965) and Sister Rita Marie Helldorfer, "The Gubernatorial Career of Albert Cabell Ritchie, Governor of Maryland, 1920–35" (M.A. thesis, Catholic University of America, 1955) provide helpful administrative studies.

Maryland in national politics is ably examined by Frank F. White, Jr. in "The 1928 Presidential Election in Maryland" (M.A. thesis, University of Maryland, 1947); Neal Thigpen, "The Presidential Aspirations of Albert C. Ritchie" (M.A. thesis, University of Maryland, 1966); Joseph Rohe, O.S.F., "Press Opinion of a Political Leader: Albert Cabell Ritchie and the Democratic Party, 1924–32" (M.A. thesis, Catholic University of America, 1967) and Myron I. Scholnick, "The President and the Senator: Franklin Roosevelt's Attempted 'Purge' of Maryland's Millard Tydings in 1938" (M.A. thesis, University of Maryland, 1962).

For Baltimore's complicated politics, the clipping file of the Democratic State Central Committee, The Democratic Scrapbook, 1919–1932, in the Maryland Room, Enoch Pratt, provides a rich source. The most detailed study of Baltimore bosses in the period is Edwin Rothman's "Factional Machine Politics, William Curran and the Baltimore City Democratic Organization, 1929–46" (Ph.D. dissertation, Johns Hopkins University, 1949).

The history of the interwar period is helped by Frank F. White, Jr., *The Governors of Maryland, 1777–1970* (Annapolis: Hall of Records, 1970) which supersedes the treatment of Ritchie by William M.

Bowen, Jr. in "The Period of Ritchie" in Radoff (ed.) *The Old Line State: A History of Maryland,* 2d. ed. (1971) and the laudatory essay by J. Frederick Essary in *Maryland in National Politics from Charles Carroll to Albert C. Ritchie* (2d ed.; Baltimore: John Murphy Co., 1932). Harry W. Kirwin, *The Inevitable Success: Herbert R. O'Conor* (Westminster, Md.: Neuman Press, 1962) is helpful on law and order issues of the Ritchie period and on the complex elections of 1934 and 1938. Harry J. Green's *A Study of the Legislature of Maryland with Special Reference to the Sessions of 1927 and 1929* (Baltimore: J. H. Press, 1930) is an able institutional study.

Election statistics are available in the *Maryland Manual*; Baltimore ward statistics are found in the *Maryland Almanac*. Evelyn L. Wentworth's *Election Statistics in Maryland, 1934–1958* (College Park: Bureau of Governmental Research, University of Maryland., 1959) surveys the later period.

The politically powerful *Sunpapers* is profiled by staffmen Gerald W. Johnson, Frank Kent, et al, *The Sunpapers of Baltimore* (New York: Alfred Knopf, 1951). The *Sun* columns should be supplemented by the Baltimore *News*, Baltimore *Post*, Baltimore *Afro-American* and Socialist *Maryland Leader*. Two small Baltimore weeklies, the acerbic, anti-Ritchie, *The Observer,* 1924–38, and *The Marylander,* 1925–31, provide controversial but detailed political analysis.

The economic development of Maryland is surveyed by a series of studies sponsored by the Maryland Development Bureau of the Baltimore Association of Commerce. The Maryland Development Bureau published three of the most helpful works for this period: W. L. Fairbanks and W. S. Hamill, *The Manufacturing Industry of Maryland* (Baltimore, 1932); W. S. Hamill, *The Agricultural Industry of Maryland* (1934); W. L. Fairbanks and W. L. Hamill, *A Statistical Analysis of the Population of Maryland* (1931).

The monthly issues of *Baltimore*, the organ of the Baltimore Association of Commerce provide the fullest, albeit optimistic commentary on the industrial and port development. They should be supplemented by the *Annual Report of the Baltimore Chamber of Commerce,* 1921–33, for details of commodity traffic through the port. The issues of the AFL's *The Baltimore Federationist,* 1920–1933 and the *CIO News* (Baltimore, 1939) and *Western Maryland Industrial Voice of Labor* (Cumberland, 1938–39) advance countering opinions to the Association of Commerce and each other.

Useful monographs are Thomas B. Symons, *The Passing of a Decade: A Summary of Extension Activities in Maryland, 1924–1934* (College Park: University Extension Service, 1935); Ralph F. Hale, *Prices Paid for Maryland Farm Products, 1851–1927* (College Park: University of Maryland Agricultural Experimental Station, 1938);

Evelyn E. Singleton, *Workmen's Compensation in Maryland* (Baltimore: J. H. Press, 1937), and Charles A. Hales, *The Baltimore Clearing House* (Baltimore: J. H. Press, 1940). They should be supplemented by the annual reports of the Commissioner of Labor and Statistics and the Banking Commission.

For the depression period, the government reports of the Maryland Emergency Relief Administration, the Reconstruction Finance Corporation and the Departments of Labor and Agriculture are vital. The most helpful compilations of relief activities are in United States Community Improvement Appraisal of the Federal Works Program in Maryland (mimeo.), March, 1938, sponsored by the Maryland Planning Commission and *State Statistics, Maryland*, U.S. Office of Government Reports, Statistical Section, II, 1940. Leslie Gore Hunt, "Greenbelt, Maryland: A City on a Hill," *M.H.M.*, LXIII (June, 1968), 105-36 details one facet of the New Deal in the Free State. Joseph T. Elvove's unpublished thesis, "State Bank Failures in Maryland", (M.A. thesis, University of Maryland, 1936) effectively surveys the development and vulnerability of Maryland's banking system.

In the area of social and cultural development, the concerns of black Marylanders are detailed in Ira DeA. Reid, *The Negro Community of Baltimore* (Baltimore: the Urban League, 1935) and the *Report of the Governor's Commission on Problems Affecting the Negro Population*, 1943. There are no full studies of the other minority targets of the Ku Klux Klan, the Maryland Catholics and Jews, but the *Catholic Review* and the *Jewish Times* provide weekly coverage of their activities and interests. For Klan and prohibition issues, the clipping files in the *Sunpapers'* library and the vertical file of the Maryland Room, Enoch Pratt, are most helpful. *The Annual Reports of the Baltimore Criminal Justice Commission and the Maryland State Board of Motion Picture Censors* are valuable indices of criminal activities and moral sensibilities. Carl Bode's *Mencken* most ably presents the views of the "Sage of Baltimore" on the human foibles of the period.

Education in Maryland is surveyed by Flexner and Bachman, *Public Education in Maryland, A Report to the Maryland Educational Survey Commission*. Baltimore schools are studied in George D. Strayer's *Report of the Survey of the Public School System of Baltimore, Maryland. School Year 1920–1921*. (3 vols. Baltimore: n.p., 1921). George H. Callcott's *A History of the University of Maryland* analyzes not only the development of the university but also the broad social and economic issues confronting higher education between the wars.

# X

## MODERN MARYLAND
## POLITICS AND SOCIAL CHANGE

BY

FRANKLIN L. BURDETTE

UNIVERSITY OF MARYLAND

Maryland in the mid-1930's, somewhat later than much of the nation, encountered political upheaval. Continuing economic dislocations of the depression and a host of varied local dissatisfactions withered support for established leadership. In a long-enduring pattern, new faces and voices rose to compete with the old for the responsibilities and burdens of power.

1

### FROM DEPRESSION TO WAR

Herbert R. O'Conor, for more than a decade the able state's attorney of Baltimore City, led the entire 1934 statewide Democratic ticket in his successful race for attorney general. That leadership gave him a strategic voice in the councils of the Democratic legislature, also elected in that year of Republican Harry W. Nice's narrow victory for the governorship over four-term Albert Cabell Ritchie. Notwithstanding the end of the Ritchie regime, Maryland remained firmly albeit independently Democratic.

Struggle for the ultimate leadership of the Democratic party, particularly after the death of Ritchie early in 1936, overshadowed political activities of the Nice administration. Mayor Howard Jackson of Baltimore, an able administrator, had long wanted to move to the governor's chair, but during Ritchie's tenure it became the better part of valor not to make an overt

773

challenge. He could now point to his withdrawal from consideration for the governorship in 1934 and claim that he had become the logical heir to leadership and service in the state. The Four Horsemen of the Ritchie era, all county leaders who had held high state influence and positions—E. Brooke Lee of Montgomery, David C. Winebrenner III of Frederick (a Ritchie cousin), William Preston Lane, Jr., of Washington, and William C. Walsh of Allegany—soon formed a strong block of support for the mayor. There were others, prominent party figures in the counties and in Baltimore City itself, who had no desire to elevate the mayor from city leader to state leader as well.

The Democratic national convention of 1936, held in Philadelphia, became for Marylanders a conclave to discuss state politics. Mayor Jackson, whose gracious courtesy and phenomenal memory for names were always attractions, gave daily breakfasts so popular that his suite was overrun. Although allied with Jackson, Millard E. Tydings, Maryland's senior United States Senator busily planning to run for reelection two years later, was in no position to engage in factional infighting, whatever his willingness to receive the mantle of party leadership in the state. He loyally seconded the nomination of Franklin D. Roosevelt for reelection to the presidency, causing comment about his unexpected "gyrations around the New Deal." The mayor as well as "stop Jackson" politicians courted Howard Bruce, the national committeeman, a county man with extensive business ties to Baltimore. It was upon these three —Jackson, Tydings, and Bruce—that current Democratic leadership in Maryland was generally expected to rest. For the moment anti-Jackson forces settled on Lansdale G. Sasscer of Prince George's County, president of the state Senate, as a probable candidate for governor. Sasscer, known to his closest friends as Ghiselin, had also had close ties to Ritchie.[1]

Mayor Jackson, in order to forestall others, formally announced his candidacy for governor nearly fifteen months before the 1938 election. Declaring that "Baltimore City is regarded as one of the best managed cities in the United States," he promised a reorganized state government, better budget practices, fully competitive rather than "invited" bids for state highway construction, uniform application of taxes and a pay-

---

1. Baltimore *Evening Sun*, June 29, 1936.

as-you-go policy for capital expenditures, a strengthened merit system, and aid to the oyster industry.[2]

Howard Bruce, not to be outflanked, in a speech at Cambridge denounced the Jackson candidacy and the efforts of Lee and Weinbrenner "to stampede the Democratic Party into dealing out all other contenders but Howard Jackson." He urged a primary contest to test "the real sentiment of the voters," whether the mayor, who "prides himself on being in complete and absolute control of the Democratic organization of Baltimore City," should be given the governorship to "set up in Maryland a political oligarchy which will hold the state in its grasp for years to come."[3]

O'Conor, speaking the same evening at nearby Salisbury, said that the "current flurry of hot-weather politics" by "focusing public attention upon matters of state policy and the proper function of government" would be likely to arouse citizens "to the great need of correction along certain lines." Advocating an administration concerned with roads that will "once again lead the nation" and favoring "returning the county roads to the counties" with provision for maintenance equipment, he called it "no secret" that Maryland had slipped, until today "our roads are rated among the poorest in the nation in proportion to the population and density of traffic."[4]

To counter the momentum of the Jackson boom, Sasscer announced his candidacy in late September. O'Conor formally entered the race in early October with an eleven-point program of social and administrative improvements.[5] Major spokesmen for anti-Jackson Democrats in the state had decided, after discussion about and with candidates, that O'Conor should carry their banner in the primary election. Bruce supported him; and William Curran, one of the most sophisticated and influential Democratic leaders in Baltimore, predicted rightly that O'Conor could carry all six legislative districts in the city.[6] William S. Gordy, Jr., of Salisbury later entered the Democratic

---

2. *Sun*, June 28, 1937.
3. *Ibid.*, Aug. 20, 1937.
4. *Ibid.*
5. *Ibid.*, Sept. 22, Oct. 4, 1937.
6. Harry W. Kirwin, *The Inevitable Success: Herbert R. O'Conor* (Westminster, Md.: Newman Press, 1962), pp. 202-203.

gubernatorial contest. A stalwart supporter of Ritchie on the Eastern Shore, he had served since 1923 as comptroller of the treasury.

National attention first turned to the upcoming Maryland primary when Democratic Congressman David J. Lewis of western Maryland announced on June 1, 1938, that he would run against Senator Tydings. A strong supporter of New Deal policies, Lewis was clearly the candidate in Maryland to carry the torch for President Roosevelt's "purge of 1938." The President was soon specific, praising Lewis as one of four men, "one of the American pioneers," who led the drive in Congress for passing the Social Security Act of 1935. Tydings, who had voted "present" on the measure in the Senate, contended that it should be amended to remove the tax on low-income groups. Indeed, he predicted in a campaign address at Hagerstown, with "fellow candidates" of the Jackson state ticket on the platform, that the new Congress would revise the law. The President almost immediately classed Tydings with "those who have betrayed the New Deal in the past and will again," accusing the senator of wanting "to run with the Roosevelt prestige and the money of his conservative Republican friends both on his side."[7] Roosevelt had felt and remembered the restraining power of Tydings, including the senator's opposition in 1937 to enlarging the Supreme Court.

There was speculation that the national administration, not sure of New Deal fervor among announced candidates for the governorship, might support Dr. H. C. "Curley" Byrd for that office or—until the Lewis announcement—for the Senate.[8] Dr. Byrd, the politically-conservative president of the University of Maryland since 1936, had charmed Washington officialdom in obtaining several millions of dollars in grants for the College Park campus and, in 1937, had published a defense of New Deal spending policies. He came to the attention of Roosevelt himself and was induced to endorse the Lewis candidacy. When the President went to Crisfield in late summer to further his "purge" effort, Byrd (a native of that center of the fishing industry on the Bay) joined him for the occasion.[9] Curley Byrd,

---

7. *Sun,* June 2, Aug. 16, 17, 1938.
8. *Ibid.,* June 2, 1938.
9. Callcott, *A History of the University of Maryland,* pp. 325-26.

affable, hard-driving, and intense, had remarkable success in raising money from Governor Nice, the legislature, and from private donors. His critics called him a political manipulator and his product a machine; his admirers called him a university builder. The foray into big-time politics added, for a time, to the swelling voices of the critics.

Marylanders had little use for the presidential "invasion." The issue, as *The Sun* pointed out, was whether a president was elected to be followed, or whether members of Congress might join in the making of public policy. Millard Tydings was renominated in the September primary by a vote of 189,719 to 124,439. Lewis carried only four counties in western Maryland and two legislative districts in Baltimore City. In the general election, Tydings swamped his Republican opponent, Judge Oscar Leser of Baltimore, by more than two to one.[10]

The gubernatorial primaries were a far more complicated matter. Republican Governor Nice, after vacillation, decided to run for reelection. The vote-gathering strength of his primary opponent, Harry T. Phoebus of Somerset County, proved to be minor. Democrats feared, as Sasscer said candidly, that "ill feeling now raging between the two Baltimore City factions" respectively supporting Jackson and O'Conor might, if either were to be nominated, "be carried into the election with a result that we may have another Republican governor." That fear, Sasscer added, surely with more hope than certainty, "has caused thousands of Democrats who are interested in party success in November to turn their support to my candidacy."[11] To the incumbent governor, Democratic feuding was the most heartening political news that he encountered.

Gerald W. Johnson of the *Sunpapers*, already near the heights he was to scale as a national and Maryland analyst of social movements, assayed the gubernatorial problem. Relationships among the federal government, the states, and the citizens were the central issue. The old landmarks were shifting, and when the new precedents became static those states with "alert and aggressive leadership will be in a position of advantage." The

---

10. For a detailed account of the attempt to defeat Tydings, see Myron I. Scholnick, "The President and the Senator: Franklin Roosevelt's Attempted 'Purge' of Maryland's Millard Tydings in 1938" (M.A. thesis, University of Maryland, 1962).

11. *Sun*, June 6, 1938.

campaign, with all its lackadaisical turmoil, would set the political stage in Maryland for years to come. The greatest of the state's innumerable problems, Johnson wrote, clustered around the Bay, Baltimore City, and western Maryland. The Bay was a great potential supply of seafood and at the same time "a chasm splitting the state, interfering with the free movement of its goods and people." In Baltimore, steadily drained by the counties of its best taxpayers, "expansion of the main business district has been halted for nearly ten years and all around the edge of that district the City has rotted away." In western Maryland, "much of the coal lies too deep to be mined profitably" and the need for new economic development, perhaps as a vacationland, pressed for attention.

Who were the candidates for governor and what could they do? Mayor Jackson, Johnson believed, was undoubtedly a man of unusual ability, with honesty, good sense, and business acumen, "one of the best bookkeepers in the world" who could carry out admirably a "stable setup and a definite program" given to him. O'Conor, a good lawyer and more, could "administer a big office. . . . with high efficiency, and in scrupulous accord with the law." Gordy, "if anything a better bookkeeper than Jackson," could "look after the state's money with the minutest care, and no cracksman, criminal or political, would get away with a cent of it." What would Sasscer, calling himself a New Dealer, mean for Maryland? If the New Deal might be "merely a method of getting money from the Federal Government. . . . we had better elect Curley Byrd who, as a money-getter, can run rings around anybody else in Maryland public life." As for Governor Nice, "it must be plain to the dullest that there isn't a more completely bewildered man in the United States." As a Republican "with a Democratic legislature and a Democratic administration in Washington he has had no chance to be on the inside of any program." Johnson offered "one Democratic opinion that, considering the fix he's in, he has made a surprisingly good governor." But "there is not much point in reelecting a man" who will have no chance "of realigning the position of the state" in its internal affairs or national relations.[12]

Democratic candidates for governor and their campaign

12. *Evening Sun,* June 16, 1938.

strategists, whom Gerald Johnson derided for following at the wrong time an old political rule of saying nothing in sonorous terms, fretted with a logistical problem of another type. Since 1910 Maryland law had provided that a plurality or even a majority of votes would not necessarily determine the winner of a statewide primary race. Instead the nominee would be determined in a state party convention in which each of the twenty-three counties and of the six legislative districts in Baltimore City would have delegates equal in number to its representation in both houses of the legislature, the General Assembly. Each of the separate delegations by law must cast all its votes for the winner in the county or legislative district, and the law also required a majority of the convention for a nomination. This unit-vote system presented another complication: when more than two candidates entered a statewide race, each voter could mark a second choice. On the second ballot at the convention, the lowest-ranking candidate was dropped and his voters' second choices were used to determine, and perhaps change, the unit votes of the county or legislative district in the city. When a delegation's second-ballot choice was eliminated, it was free to vote for any candidate remaining. With four Democratic candidates in the field, the complicated second-choice arrangement might be necessary for a nomination—and was, as the voting turned out. Originally enacted to assure the necessity of substantial county support for a candidate from Baltimore's large voting base, the law had not materially altered the informal practice of geographical ticket building for statewide offices and therefore had not sharply encouraged rural-urban rivalries in elections.[13]

In the primary on September 12, O'Conor gained a plurality of popular votes, leading Jackson by 147,000 to 135,000 and winning in the six legislative districts of Baltimore City. Jackson did surprisingly well in the counties. Gordy and Sasscer stood third and fourth in the ballot count and received a scattering of unit votes. With O'Conor leading in the unit votes but with no candidate having a majority, it was apparent that the convention would go to a third ballot when it convened on September 28. On the night of September 26 Sasscer an-

13. For a more detailed study of the law, see Robert S. Friedman, *The Maryland County Unit System and Urban-Rural Politics* (College Park: Bureau of Governmental Research, University of Maryland, 1958).

nounced that the seven delegates from Prince George's County, bound to him on the first ballot and to Gordy on the second, had agreed at a meeting held secretly in Riverdale to vote for Attorney General O'Conor on the third, assuring him the gubernatorial nomination.[14] The following day the circuit court in Allegany County acted, in effect, to approve a recount giving O'Conor that county's unit votes. Sasscer had expressed his preference; and Jackson acceded to it with grace, knowing that appealing the Allegany litigation could not change the result. Experience with the second-choice ballot provision led to its repeal, but the unit-vote system remained to perplex politicians and the public until it was invalidated in 1963 by a Supreme Court decision involving the state of Georgia.

The November general election was an anticlimax. Governor Nice could have hoped to win only with a more badly divided opposition. A jovial, heavy-set lawyer, he liked people so much that it was easy for him to promise them more than he could deliver. Early in his administration he had leaned toward removing and replacing public employees. In defense of the merit principle Willis Jones and Albert Ward, both influential in the public service, joined others in organizing the Maryland Classified Employees Association with high goals of professionalism. Authorization of voting machines in Baltimore occurred in the Nice administration; and the governor was more willing than his predecessors to break the color line in appointments. Less propitious politically were fiscal difficulties in state matching of federal welfare funds and the application of a state income tax at the opening of 1938. Yet the Republican campaign for the governorship did not encounter the debacle that engulfed Judge Leser, the party's nominee for the Senate. The New Deal was coming to an end. Hitler had been on the move in Europe, seizing Austria in March. At election time many Marylanders, like other Americans, were living in the euphoria of "peace in our time" following the crisis at Munich in September, which resulted in the dismemberment of Czechoslovakia by German annexation of Sudetenland with Hitler's all-too-temporary assurance that Czechs were secure in their republic.

O'Conor was elected governor by 308,372 votes against

14. *Sun*, Sept. 27, 1938.

242,095 for Nice. Democrats carried all the state ticket, enlarged majorities in both houses of the General Assembly, and all representation in Congress. While Tydings was reelected to his Senate seat by 68.3 per cent of the vote, O'Conor won with 54.6 per cent.

Sometimes called "the luckiest man in Maryland politics," O'Conor entered the governorship at the age of forty-two during a time of rising tensions about America's role and security in a world of conflict. Many of the central problems in his years of office were related directly or indirectly to the forerunners, support, and immediate aftermath of World War II. Honest, upright, a devoted Catholic, a hard worker and quick learner, he set for himself and others a high standard of performance.

Knowing the importance of an effective administrative organization in carrying out state programs, the governor-elect created a Committee on the Structure of the Maryland State Government headed by Dr. Isaiah Bowman, president of The Johns Hopkins University. The Bowman report, prepared by a group including such prestigious names as Dean Acheson, Glenn L. Martin, and Lansdale G. Sasscer, was ready before inauguration day. Its recommendations rested on acclaimed administrative practices of consolidation of departments having overlapping functions, clear placement of administrative responsibility in departmental heads by shifting the role of boards to policy making, centralization of authority over accounting functions, regular study of programs by a well-staffed budget bureau, and careful classification of positions under a merit system. The governor-elect called the report "splendid," said that he intended to stand by it, and remarked that he did not wish to talk about "specific items."[15] These words would soon lead him into misunderstanding and controversy.

Headlines about the governor's inaugural address in Annapolis stressed that new, perhaps heavy, taxes could be expected.[16] "We must balance our budget and maintain our credit," he said—and he saw no way out "except through additional taxation." Four social needs "must be driven 'line abreast' under the rein of economy and the spur of efficiency": law and order, public health, roads and other means of transpor-

---

15. *Ibid.*, Jan. 6, 7, 1939.
16. *Ibid.*, Jan. 12, 1939.

tation, and education. He advocated improving administration of justice in the lower courts and abolition of the fee system in them. He proposed a legislative council to study public measures between sessions of the General Assembly. As a Democrat, he pledged to avoid building a personal political organization.[17] O'Conor found the Democratic legislature responsive, as his Republican predecessor had not, and at the end of its biennial session he was able to report in a radio broadcast from Baltimore that most of his program had been adopted. New taxes would bring enough revenue to balance the budget "for the first time in many years," and without an increase in the property tax rate. (The governor did not mention in his broadcast that the new taxes involved a higher income rate plus levies on alcoholic beverages and cigarettes estimated in the aggregate to bring in an additional $17 million.) He had obtained, with most of the recommendations of the Bowman committee, a permanent budget bureau. The Legislative Council had been created. In the lower courts trial magistrates, reduced in number, would be on salary without a fee system. Workmen's compensation would cover occupational diseases. A new law raised standards and salaries for teachers.[18] And the governor's new State Publicity Commission had aptly chosen for Maryland a descriptive slogan, "America in Miniature."

The greatest controversy in the legislative session arose over that portion of the Bowman report proposing consolidation of various conservation agencies into a single Department of Natural Resources. Conservationists believed that the governor had implicitly endorsed the plan in his approval of the Bowman report on governmental organization. Watermen who made their living from the Chesapeake Bay refused to accede to the idea of placing state programs and services for commercial and tidewater fisheries in a single statewide conservation department out of their control. Conservationists contended that the problems of the Bay were virtually statewide, involving upland erosion and industrial deterrents to aquatic life. They pointed out that in the past half century siltation and other problems had reduced the annual harvest of oysters from ten million bushels

---

17. *State Papers and Addresses of Governor Herbert R. O'Conor* (no publisher or date), I, 3-7, 9-10.
18. *Ibid.*, pp. 49-56; *Sun*, April 7, 1939.

to well below two million and that the acreage of oyster beds had decreased from over 200,000 acres to 100,000 in thirty years. Watermen were adamant, however, and conservationists were not well enough organized to counter the political pressures in and out of the legislature for a separate tidewater agency. The governor yielded to the concept of separate agencies and the immediate political aspects of the controversy were postponed.[19] Two years later the issue was compromised by creating a Board of Natural Resources headed by the chairman of the Department of Tidewater Fisheries.

At the end of his first year as governor, O'Conor was happy to report not only that the budget of the state was balanced but that there had been a surplus at the close of the fiscal year of almost $4.5 million. Moreover, $5 million had been budgeted for public assistance and relief; diversion of gasoline tax money had been stopped, and as a consequence $3.8 million had become available for road construction. The governor was also gratified, as many state workers were not, that $371,000 of unexpended departmental appropriations had been returned to the state treasury.[20] Agency heads were learning that by saving money already appropriated they could please the governor, who was at once program conscious and economy-minded.

Mayor Howard Jackson retained his influence in politics by winning reelection in Baltimore in 1939, defeating in the Democratic primary his Curran-backed opponent Charles H. Buck by 36,000 votes in a turnout of 135,000 and going on to win over the Republican nominee, Theodore R. McKeldin, by 24,000. That resurgence of Jackson, after his loss of the city in the gubernatorial primary the year before, and the eclipse of William Curran's Baltimore organization added obstacles to the ambition of Howard Bruce to go to the United States Senate. Not to be deterred, however, Bruce ran in the Democratic primary of 1940 against incumbent Senator George L. Radcliffe, who trounced him by 80,000 votes in the face of strong support of Bruce by Governor O'Conor. In the Republican primary of 1940 former Governor Harry W. Nice of Baltimore defeated a former mayor of the city, William F. Broening, by 17,000 votes for the Senate nomination.

19. Kirwin, *op. cit.*, pp. 236-43.
20. O'Conor, *State Papers and Addresses*, I, 137.

At the 1940 Democratic national convention held in Chicago in July, Senator Tydings received eight and a half of Maryland's sixteen votes for President in protest against the principle of a third term; all of Maryland's votes were later switched to Roosevelt. Leading standpat Roosevelt supporters in the delegation were Governor O'Conor, Mayor Jackson, William Preston Lane, Jr., E. Brooke Lee, James H. Pollack, J. Millard Tawes, and Sumner Welles; they departed company with the favorite-son gesture led by Senators Tydings and Radcliffe, Howard Bruce, and Attorney General William C. Walsh. In the fall election Roosevelt outdistanced Wendell L. Willkie in all parts of the state except five counties and obtained 58.3 per cent of the total vote. Radcliffe was reelected senator with a handsome 64.7 per cent.

## 2

### WORLD WAR II

By mid-1940 America had embarked on major defense efforts. From the preceding September World War II brought catastrophe to western Europe. Hitler had taken Poland, Denmark, Norway, and the low countries; France fell by the middle of June 1940. President Roosevelt declared in a commencement address at the University of Virginia on June 10 that America would aid the opponents of force with the material resources of the nation and prepare for any emergency. In September Congress enacted the first peacetime conscription, providing for registration of men from ages twenty-one to thirty-five and for induction of draftees. Some 200,000 Marylanders registered for the draft in mid-October. The *Sunpapers* reported after a survey that youth viewed the prospect "without too violent complaint," feeling that "the draft is necessary, if not salutary." They were "not thrilled" by the thought of a year's service. They would almost unanimously volunteer to repel an attack but would oppose American entrance into the war for any other reason.[21]

In August Governor O'Conor had met with the new Maryland Council of Defense and Resources, which he appointed to enlist support for preparedness and to study ways that the state

---

21. *Sunday Sun Magazine*, Oct. 13, 1940.

and its people might help in the national effort. His directive covered consideration of policies to eliminate profiteering or unfair practices in defense industries and of lawful efforts to circumvent subversive activities.[22] The majority of agitators and fifth columnists are aliens, he later remarked at ceremonies after a defense parade in Salisbury, and in the light of "admitted dangers" commented that "our government should be much more ready to deport such people."[23]

A year later, by August 1941, defense spending by the national government had stimulated a boom in Maryland industry. Over a billion dollars in direct contracts reached the economic pipelines to Maryland within thirteen months. By adding training and industrial construction costs—plus $500 million of new orders from outside industries for machinery, iron, steel, copper, and raw materials, the total new business amounted to $1.6 billion. Defense plant employment alone had expanded by almost 50,000, and all business employment had risen by nearly 100,000.

Baltimore, with its great industrial complex, was more affected in its way of living than any other single area of the state. Two industries, shipbuilding and aircraft, accounted for a large part of the new workers pouring into the city. Bethlehem-Fairfield Shipping had contracts for sixty-two vessels and the Maryland Drydock Company a vast program of reconversion and repairs. They were seeking 12,000 new employees. The Glenn L. Martin Company had a backlog of $743 million in aircraft orders, $56 million for the British war effort, and the rest from the United States Government. Martin, with 23,000 employees, expected to add over 6,000. Growing industrial output had also moved Baltimore nearer the top of the country's list of smoky cities. The new defense activity taxed the resources of Baltimore in schools, housing, health and sanitation, law enforcement, transportation, and power production. At least 10,000 new housing units were needed. In the state as a whole, communities asked $5 million for schools for the children of defense workers. Harford County expected 1,000 or more at Havre de Grace, Edgewood, and Aberdeen. Prince George's, Anne Arundel, Charles, and Baltimore Counties had

22. O'Conor, *State Papers and Addresses*, I, 215-19.
23. *Ibid.*, p. 233.

problems of space and teachers in schools where new pupils were arriving.[24] As Congressman William D. Byron, from western Maryland, was pointing out, the cities of Baltimore and Washington and the adjacent counties—with their concentration of defense efforts—made virtually one gigantic metropolitan district with administrative problems to be coordinated.[25]

Governor O'Conor was proud of Maryland's defense effort and devoted close attention to it. His Maryland Council of Defense (so named by the 1941 session of the legislature) coordinated policies of civilian defense. In 1941 the legislature authorized a State Guard to replace the National Guard while it was in federal service, and along lines recommended by the national War Department. The Guard's strength of 2,700 was later supplemented by a Special Military Police Force of about 300 to guard bridges, water supplies, and other installations. After the Japanese attack at Pearl Harbor on December 7, 1941, and congressional declaration of war on the Axis powers at the stirring recommendation of President Roosevelt, the governor organized a volunteer reserve militia known as Minute Men. They became available in every section of Maryland, 12,000 strong, for local protection against sabotage or raiding parties. Spotter posts for aircraft warning, over 200 in number by late 1942, were manned at varying times by 15,000 Marylanders.[26] With enemy submarine action reported off the coast and possible aircraft action suspected, Maryland practiced blackouts at night. Rationing of gasoline, rubber, food, and other critical supplies altered the routine of almost every household.

There were tensions for the governor, too, personal and official. He became so engrossed in work that he neglected, even avoided, informal contact with old friends. Always more effective as a public speaker than in social banter, he secluded himself from the casual graces of the politician. Early in 1942 black citizens of Baltimore, protesting ten killings by police, held a mass rally of more than 2,000 with Carl Murphy, editor of the *Afro-American*, presiding to organize a "march" on Annapolis in several hundred cars, twenty chartered buses, and ten special coaches of the Baltimore and Annapolis Railroad.

---

24. *Evening Sun*, Aug. 18, 20, 1941.
25. *Sun*, Feb. 19, 1941.
26. O'Conor, *State Papers and Addresses*, I, 258-59; III, 616-20, 733, 784-90.

"We are in desperation," said Juanita Jackson Mitchell, representative of the National Association for the Advancement of Colored People and a Baltimore leader of the march.[27] They met with the governor, who later appointed a commission headed by Joseph P. Healy to study conditions affecting the Negro population. O'Conor was aware that wartime conditions had given minorities increased prosperity in the midst of discrimination but, clearly on record for even-handed justice, he did not intend to get "too far ahead of the average citizen" on issues of race relations.[28]

In 1942 the governor, regularly active in national meetings on problems of the states, was chosen chairman of the Governors' Conference. The honor fortified his decision to seek a second term. In the Democratic primary he had only token opposition. His opponent in the general election, Theodore R. McKeldin, thirty-nine, virtually drafted for the race, already known for fifteen years in Baltimore as a popular orator, proved to be a shining knight for Republican hopes. O'Conor won the election with an embarrassingly small margin of 19,000 votes in the state, losing three legislative districts in Baltimore and eight counties. His majority in the Democratic city, with the support of both the Jackson and Curran factions, was less than 3,700. He lost thirteen of the twenty-eight wards. His running mate for reelection as attorney general, William C. Walsh of Cumberland, handsomely carried the city and the state; and J. Millard Tawes of Crisfield, running for reelection as comptroller, had no opposition at all.

McKeldin, whom Howard Jackson had defeated for mayor of Baltimore in 1939, promptly capitalized on his political strength and in 1943 retired Jackson by winning the mayoralty with a majority of 20,111 votes. Democratic candidates for all other city offices were successful. In his campaign, directed at Jackson's long continuance in office, McKeldin promised a nonpartisan administration. Both Thomas E. Conlon (speaker of the House of Delegates) and Howard E. Crook, elected respectively president of the city council and comptroller, were political allies of William Curran who were placed on the Democratic city ticket in the new Jackson-Curran political rapproche-

---

27. *Evening Sun*, April 24, 1942.
28. Kirwin, *op. cit.*, p. 300.

ment. Curran had campaigned strenuously for Jackson and had enthusiastically urged support by his own "b'hoys," as the *Sun* called political lieutenants.[29]

In the meantime Governor O'Conor had become a leading champion in the nation of the role of the states. As the president of the Council of State Governments he joined Governor Thomas E. Dewey of New York at a regional conference in that state in pressing for the return of state responsibilities and functions in many areas of local concern. The Maryland governor said that the best way to reverse trends toward centralization of power in Washington was "convincing proof" that the states were capable of meeting "the impact of postwar problems before they get out of hand." He later joined Mayor McKeldin of Baltimore in condemning suggestions that the federal government ignore state boundaries and deal directly with municipalities or other economic areas in handling postwar projects. Dr. Abel Wolman, chairman of the State Planning Commission, said that conditions "call for a stronger form of state review and state planning than previously has been necessary." Roy Barton White, chairman of the Maryland Commission on Postwar Reconstruction and Development and president of the Baltimore and Ohio Railroad, opposed "some federal district subservient only to the federal government in Washington" as a substitute for the states "as they now exist."[30]

Restructuring the Court of Appeals, the highest court in Maryland, and changes in the circuit courts of general jurisdiction became the subject of study by a commission appointed by Governor O'Conor in 1941 at the request of the State Bar Association. Headed by Carroll T. Bond, then Chief Judge of the Court of Appeals, its work remained in controversy until the election of 1944. The General Assembly of 1943 submitted two resulting constitutional amendments which the voters approved. One of them reduced the Court of Appeals from eight judges to five (two from Baltimore City and one from each of three Appellate Judicial Circuits) and provided that its judges serve only on that court instead of acting also as chief judges of trial circuits. This amendment also authorized the governor to appoint judges upon the expiration of terms rather than merely

---

29. *Sun*, May 5, 12, 1943.
30. *Ibid.*, April 10, July 13, 1943.

to fill vacancies, each judge to serve until the next general election occurring after one year. Opponents were skeptical of broadening the appointive power of governors and also argued that the change would deprive judges of the highest court of continuing trial experience and the lower courts of their direct guidance. Endorsed by reform-minded advocates as offering more careful selection and more efficient judicial specialization, while preserving the popular check of election after initial performance, the amendment was overwhelmingly ratified. The second amendment permitted the Court of Appeals, under provisions of general law to be enacted by the General Assembly, to assign judges of the judicial circuits to other circuits for limited periods to relieve accumulated business or because of illness or disqualification of any judge. This arrangement, allowing assignment of trial judges to areas in which they did not live and where they were not subject to election, afforded administrative advantages but aroused more opposition. It was narrowly ratified by 97,995 votes to 94,239; only an affirmative margin of over 11,000 votes in Baltimore City saved the proposal.

Maryland's delegates to the Democratic national convention of 1944 supported Roosevelt for a fourth term in the presidency. They opposed the renomination of Henry Wallace for vice president and, to reserve their votes for the best strategy, ran up the favorite-son flag of O'Conor for the office. The governor and his friends swung the delegation to Harry S. Truman and earned his outspoken gratitude.[31] Republican delegates to their convention, at the urging of Mayor McKeldin, united behind Thomas E. Dewey for president after Paul Robertson, chairman of the party's city committee and often a McKeldin foe, agreed to drop support of Governor John W. Bricker of Ohio.[32] The popular vote separating the Roosevelt-Truman and Dewey-Bricker tickets in Maryland was surprisingly close, 315,000 to 292,000. Dewey carried sixteen counties; only a 40,000 margin in Baltimore City saved the state for Roosevelt. The fourth-term issue, economic dislocations in the lingering war, and concern about national predominance in federal-state relationships contributed to a drop in Democratic enthusiasm and in voter turn-

31. Kirwin, *op. cit.*, pp. 366-67.
32. *Sun*, June 27, 1944.

out at the polls. Millard E. Tydings, still a frequent critic of domestic policies of the administration, had no difficulty in winning reelection as United States Senator, 344,000 to 213,000, over Blanchard Randall, Jr., who had defeated Paul Robertson in the Republican primary.

Although limited in his options by the economic restrictions imposed by the war, the governor made plans for state assumption of its responsibilities in health, education, and welfare. He believed in social progress prudently administered, and he sought also a counterweight to demands for new federal programs. The legislature at his urging tightened the supervisory and coordinating powers of the State Department of Public Welfare; provided medical aid to indigents under the state Department of Health but with administration purposely placed in county health departments under supervision of the medical profession; and advanced educational standards and facilities by making available throughout the state twelve years of public schooling (increasing years from eleven to twelve in twenty counties), by reducing class sizes and raising teachers' salaries, and by affording state aid to county libraries.[33]

3

POSTWAR PROGRESS AND POLITICS

With the successful conclusion of the war in 1945, fear mounted—and continued for some time—that depressed economic conditions would follow even more critically than after World War I. Industrial layoffs of workers in Maryland reached 45,000 by October, all but 6,000 of them in Baltimore. The armed services had released 34,000 Maryland veterans and 170,000 others would soon be faced with seeking employment or remaining in service. The Baltimore *Evening Sun* predicted that 160,000 persons in Maryland might be jobless by spring.[34] The outcome proved to be less fearsome: the war had left a high demand for consumer goods soon to be turned out by industry; aid programs abroad kept the wheels of American enterprise whirring; and substantial federal expenditures at home eased the transition. National laws enacted for the benefit of veterans

---

33. Kirwin, *op. cit.*, pp. 385-92, *passim*.
34. *Evening Sun*, Oct. 2, 1945.

greatly helped their readjustment: payments for service termination, job rights, unemployment compensation, loans for homes, farms, or businesses, health care, and subsidies for education ( the G. I. Bill of Rights). Training schools and colleges in Maryland as elsewhere were soon hard pressed to find classroom space and faculty. An unprecedented expansion of higher education followed, to be continued for more than two decades.

In 1946 it was inflation, spiraling with the relaxation of price controls, that seemed to be most threatening in an uncertain economy. Labor leaders, eager to assure workers wage increases compatible with rising prices, mounted a series of strikes which threatened industrial stoppages. President Truman seized the coal mines in a bitter strike dispute with United Mine Workers' leader John L. Lewis and threatened to use the army to run railroads. As election returns were to demonstrate, public sentiment about labor was more conservative than at the height of the New Deal.

Herbert O'Conor decided to run for the United States Senate, challenging incumbent George L. Radcliffe in the Democratic primary rather than run for a third term in the governorship. O'Conor faced the problem of retaining labor support without alienating his more conservative Democratic friends. He advocated reduction in federal spending, avoidance of compulsory arbitration but insistence that "both labor and industry must be made to realize that the public interest is paramount," more recognition of the debt to veterans, and denial of citizenship "to any person espousing the doctrine of a foreign power in opposition to American principles."[35] His unspectacular victory over Radcliffe by 22,000 was not enough to hide completely difficulties he would encounter in the fall election.

Factional infighting for the Democratic gubernatorial nomination became so intense that for years it affected indirectly the fortunes of the party. At times the popular J. Millard Tawes from the southern Eastern Shore, completing his second term as comptroller of the treasury, seemed to be the leading candidate. He had strong support from Senator Millard E. Tydings and from William Curran, the often dominant but embattled Baltimore City political leader whom O'Conor had appointed attorney general upon the resignation of William C. Walsh in 1945.

---

35. *Sun*, May 2, 1946.

Conservative Baltimore County leader H. Streett Baldwin, in his second term in Congress, entered the contest with the support of Howard Bruce and with charges of bossism against Curran. Baldwin could not fathom, he said, the change in relations between Curran and Tydings. "There are no more bitter political enemies in the state."[36] William Preston Lane, Jr., of Hagerstown, attorney general during Ritchie's fourth term as governor and currently the highly respected Democratic national committeeman, was undeniably a leading candidate. John J. Cornwell tried to persuade Lane to avoid public office and to succeed him as general counsel of the Baltimore and Ohio Railroad. "Pres, I've been governor of West Virginia and I know that it isn't worth it." Lane responded, "John, I've not been governor of Maryland and I want to find out for myself if it's worth it."[37]

Tawes' campaign was soon complicated by the sudden resignation of his manager, Truman B. Cash of Carroll County, coupled with a denunciation of Curran and bossism. Cash, who was both chairman of the Democratic State Central Committee and state Administrator of Loan Laws, declared "I will not bend my knee to a City boss such as Curran" or participate in elevating him "to the virtual governorship of Maryland." Curran replied that Cash was motivated by "malice" springing from failure to get a friend placed on the ticket for attorney general.[38] Senator Tydings, working vigorously for Tawes and saying that he had brought him into the campaign, mystified some observers by his involvement in the State House race. In the hard-fought primary, Lane led Tawes by 104,000 to 86,000, with Baldwin trailing at 49,000. Lane was nominated by capturing a clear majority of unit votes in the state convention. Writing in the *Evening Sun*, Thomas M. O'Neill judged that Tydings, who had sought an ally in the State House for his own race for reelection four years hence, was the greatest loser in political leverage. Curran looked "a little less like the City boss" despite local victories. Another loser was the redoubtable Marie Bauernschmidt, "Mrs. B," a woman of independent means and views who for two decades had titillated Baltimore with caustic radio appraisals of

---

36. *Evening Sun*, March 16, 1946.
37. Author's memorandum (Oct. 1, 1966) of conversation with William Preston Lane, Jr.
38. *Evening Sun*, May 8, 1946.

candidates. She agreed with Curran for a change because she disapproved more of Baldwin and of James H. "Jack" Pollack, leader of Baltimore's fourth district, who, in his usual opposition to Curran, was supporting Lane.[39]

Democrats carried the statewide offices in the fall of 1946, but O'Conor won his Senate seat by a close vote over Republican D. John Markey—so close that recounting and disputing went on for months. Lane secured the governorship in competition with Republican Theodore R. McKeldin by a margin of 46,000, all but 1400 of it in Baltimore City.

Governor Lane came into office five days early in 1947 by election of the Democratic legislature to fill the unexpired term of Governor O'Conor. In his inaugural address for the full term, Lane spoke of the central thrust of his administration: provision of much-needed public services and facilities for modern Maryland. Education should equal in quality that of any other system in the nation. Welfare programs must be improved and new hospital facilities for the needy and greater effort in mental hygiene provided. Maryland must move also to preserve its natural resources. Legislation would be introduced to construct a bridge across Chesapeake Bay to replace the state ferry system. Great, wide, high-speed highways must be built to relieve traffic congestion. "The only practical way to finance such highways . . . is by building toll roads, just as we have built toll bridges across the Susquehanna and the Potomac"—opened in 1940—"and as we propose to do across Chesapeake Bay."[40]

Money would be a problem in an economy of higher costs. The day of state surpluses, to which wartime limitation of supplies and construction had contributed, was over. The proposed budget would be $18 million larger than the current one; Lane and his advisers would have to find money.

The new administration paid careful heed to the report of a commission headed by Judge Joseph Sherbow of Baltimore, appointed by Governor O'Conor, on the Distribution of Tax

---

39. *Ibid.*, June 25, 1946. For a description of persistent factionalism and flexibility of allegiance among Baltimore political leaders, see Edwin Rothman, "Factional Machine-Politics: William Curran and the Baltimore City Democratic Party Organization, 1929–1946" (Ph.D. dissertation, The Johns Hopkins University, 1949), Chs. IV-V.

40. *Ibid.*, Jan. 8, 1947; *Journal of Proceedings of the House of Delegates of Maryland*, January Session, 1947, pp. 98-100.

Revenues. It included such prominent figures as Richard W. Case and Reuben Oppenheimer, Baltimore attorneys, John B. Funk, chairman of the Senate Finance Committee, and former Baltimore Mayor Howard Jackson. The commission borrowed staff from the state and obtained as consultants Professors V. O. Key, Jr., of The Johns Hopkins University and William Paul Walker of the University of Maryland to speed its work. It proposed in great detail readjustment of income taxes and a limited first-call in distribution to local governments to stabilize their income; changes in tax revenues from the four one-mile racetracks (Pimlico, Havre de Grace, Laurel, and Bowie) and the five half-mile tracks (Bel Air, Cumberland, Hagerstown, Marlboro, and Timonium) to increase state receipts from a current $5.1 million to $6.8 million, with percentage distribution to counties and municipalities; alteration of state aid to schools, continuing equalization grants to less affluent counties but adding grants per classroom and pupil and providing matching funds as incentives for increasing teachers' salaries and for school construction; and, recognizing that some counties with rising populations were building roads more rapidly, allocation of portions of the state gasoline taxes to counties on the basis of mileage in their road systems.[41] Around these technical suggestions, planning and political debate about state-local fiscal relationships revolved in determining the shared-revenue policies that were necessary for equitable handling of state services. As the governor pointed out in his inaugural address, they left open the problem of greatly expanding the revenues of the state.

If the state needed money, Lane would approach the problem with his characteristic courage. On February 19 he proposed to the legislature a new 2 per cent sales tax, estimated to yield $18.4 million per year, and increased income taxes, expected to bring additional revenue of $6.8 million.[42] The highly controversial sales tax was explosive in its political consequences, from the time of its enactment marring the Lane administration with open evidences of unpopularity. Crowds tossed pennies at the governor and on occasion at his wife; he felt that disrespect shown to her was the only gesture "out of order" during his

41. *Evening Sun*, Oct. 3–5, Oct. 7–8, 1946.
42. *Ibid.*, Feb. 19, 1947.

term of office. More circumspect opponents of the sales tax, duly enacted by the legislature, pointed out that it was a burden on those least able to pay, whatever its advantages in bringing stable revenue and in openly asking everyone in Maryland to share in the cost of government. The sales tax, however, was fast becoming a fact of American life.

Baltimore returned to a Democratic mayoralty in the spring of 1947 with the election of Thomas D'Alesandro, Jr. Mayor Mc-Keldin, reading the signs aright, did not seek reelection. Tommy D'Alesandro, in his fifth term in Congress and by the quirk of fast turnover the senior member of the Maryland delegation in the house, had long nursed ambition to become mayor of his native city. A protegé of the Curran political organization, he found it firmly committed to City Comptroller Howard E. Crook for the nomination. Emerging as a power in his own right, he swept the primary by 15,000 votes, with the help of a coalition of district leaders who had aided the election of Governor Lane. Among the most prominent of those leaders were Ambrose J. Kennedy, Patrick F. O'Malley, Jack Pollack, and Joseph M. Wyatt. In defeating Crook, who had the support not only of Curran but also of the popular state comptroller and votegetter James J. Lacy, D'Alesandro carried four districts and was narrowly edged in the other two.[43] In a lackluster turnout of less than half the voters, many of them disposed to take the result for granted, D'Alesandro was elected mayor on May 6 by a majority of 15,000 over his Republican opponent, Deeley K. Nice, nephew of the late Governor Harry W. Nice. Destined to serve three consecutive terms as mayor, D'Alesandro was soon a central political figure in the city.

In the meantime, Governor Lane had made a decision, almost routine in itself, that was to involve him and the statewide Democratic party in unanticipated conflict. In the spring of 1947 he announced that he would appoint Stuart Symington Janney, Jr., to the chairmanship of the State Racing Commission at the expiration of the term of George P. Mahoney, who had been appointed by Governor O'Conor. Mahoney, a businessman and paving contractor, had been an owner and lover of horses from his youth. Janney, an attorney in a leading Baltimore law firm, was the owner and rider of the Maryland Stee-

---

43. *Ibid.*, April 2, 1947.

plechase champion, Winton. Supporters of Mahoney praised him for "cleaning up" the Maryland racetracks and for introducing practices copied elsewhere. His detractors, among them horse owners and track officials, claimed that he had painted an unfair picture of racing in Maryland.[44]

The governor's timing of his announcement of replacement of one prominent Baltimore County resident with another was unfortunate. Mahoney, eager for reappointment, had gone that morning to a meeting in Kentucky of the National Association of State Racing Commissioners where he was considered a likely choice for office, probably a vice presidency.[45] "I can't blame Mahoney for being mad," Lane remarked years later, about the timing of the new appointment. The other two racing commissioners complained about Mahoney to the governor, and after he told them that they had the votes to control Mahoney and that they ought to do it he heard no more from them. He concluded that he should replace all three but found that he had no power to do so until their terms expired. He had been delayed in announcing a new chairman because the successor was "slow in making up his mind" to accept.[46] Rumors soon began to fly that Mahoney would run for governor; he became an unannounced candidate and a vocal critic. Was he moved by annoyance and resentment? "I don't know, I never found out" sprang from Lane's judicious reserve, coupled with the caution that "it is often difficult to assess other people's motives from general stories about them or even from what they may say to others."[47]

Maryland Democrats played a role larger than usual in the party's national convention of 1948. Senator Tydings received from the state convention a favorite-son endorsement for vice president and, though claiming after the national conclave that he was "never a serious candidate," figured prominently in national speculation. At the convention a coalition of big-city leaders pushed for Governor Lane as a man acceptable to the South without Tydings' anti-New Deal record in Congress. Lane rejected their overtures, and Tydings seconded the nomi-

44. *Sun*, April 21, 1947.

45. *Ibid.*

46. Author's memorandum of conversation with William Preston Lane, Jr., Oct. 25, 1966.

47. *Ibid.*

nation of Senator Alben W. Barkley of Kentucky, who became President Truman's running mate. Senator O'Conor, as chairman of the convention's rules committee, had a conspicuous part in beating back an attempt by southerners to reinstate the party's abandoned two-thirds majority rule in the convention, a ploy related to their attack against the civil-rights plank in the platform.[48]

In a year in which southern conservatives, under the banner of Strom Thurmond, attacked President Truman from the right for his civil rights advocacy, and from the left liberal Henry Wallace headed a Progressive party with appeals to labor and minorities and opposition to the mounting Cold War crisis with the Soviet Union, discouraged Democrats enjoyed a surprise victory when the President won reelection. In Maryland, however, with no election for statewide offices, Republicans Thomas E. Dewey and Earl Warren carried the state for president and vice president by a plurality of 8,000 votes. They won in fifteen counties with generally slim margins, except for substantial victories in two of the larger, Baltimore and Montgomery; a Democratic plurality of under 24,000 in Baltimore City was not enough to make a difference. The vote of almost 10,000 for Henry Wallace (7,226 of it in Baltimore) if shifted could have changed the result, even without considering 2,941 votes for Socialist Norman Thomas and 2,476 write-in ballots for Thurmond.

Maryland voters adopted in 1948 a constitutional amendment prohibiting a governor who has served two consecutive popularly-elected terms from succeeding to the term immediately following. That measure, a pledge in the Democratic state platform of 1946, met voters' approval everywhere except in Baltimore City and Wicomico County. Another ratified amendment introduced annual sessions of the legislature but stipulated that local laws could not be enacted in short sessions required in even-numbered years.

A more vigorously debated 1948 amendment to the state constitution, overwhelmingly approved by the voters in every county and in Baltimore, made ineligible for public office or employment in the state any person who "advocates the overthrow of the Government of the United States or of the State of

---

48. *Evening Sun*, July 16, 1948.

Maryland through force or violence." The legislative session of 1949, gripped with the alarms of the Cold War and charges of worldwide communist conspiracy, passed almost without dissent the Ober Law (named for Frank B. Ober, chairman of a commission that recommended it) to supplement the new constitutional provision. In a packed joint House of Delegates-Senate hearing in the house chamber, strong statements came from opposing positions. Civic, business, and veterans' organizations approved; labor union spokesmen, representatives of Americans for Democratic Action and other liberal groups, and speakers from the Communist party and Henry Wallace's Progressive party were opponents.[49] Responsible voices differed over the central issue: whether the threat of present danger was sufficient to justify unusual vigilance, or whether the rights of freedom of speech and assembly—as distinct from actual violence—could safely take priority. For all the furor, the statute outlawing subversive organizations and requiring statements of assurance from candidates for office and from public employees[50] never became an effective instrument to find subversives.

The postwar administration over which Lane presided moved apace to construct needed facilities and provide new or expanded services that the war had delayed. Lifted restrictions on supplies and amenities spurred population movements into the suburbs of Baltimore and Washington with a consequent explosion of housing development. The movement outward reinvigorated the era of the automobile, and commuters accepted ever greater distances to acquire the pleasures of green lawns, a few trees, and long curving lines of single-family homes.

Schools in the counties and Baltimore City received priority in the administration's programs, using legislative authorization for $70 million in bonded indebtedness for direct or indirect state aid for constructing hundreds of buildings. In the four-year period public school enrollments increased by some 44,000 to 320,000; annual amounts in state appropriations for school aid moved, including advances in salaries and other expenses, from $9 million to $27 million. Rapid expansion of the

---

49. *Ibid.*, Feb. 8, 10, 1949.
50. *Laws of Maryland, 1949*, Ch. 86.

University of Maryland and the state teachers' colleges also continued. The governor was aware from long experience as newspaper publisher, banker, and public official that, if all else were forgotten, its advancement of every level of education would label the administration a success.[51]

There were other accomplishments indeed. The state constructed new hospitals; under the quietly able direction of Dr. Clifton T. Perkins it improved the antiquated facilities for mental patients and began programs of water pollution control and other health measures. Policies for road improvement accounted for 1,100 miles of new roads; the Bay Bridge construction began and by the end of Lane's administration reached 40 per cent of completion; negotiations advanced for the future Baltimore harbor tunnel.[52] In 1950 President Truman, the governor, and Mayor D'Alesandro dedicated Baltimore's Friendship Airport (in Anne Arundel County), which became a center for international and domestic air traffic.[53] Maryland burgeoned with activity that reshaped its future.

Elections in 1950 shook the Democratic party in Maryland as no others had done since the defeat of Ritchie in 1934 for a fifth term as governor. Senator Tydings had less difficulty winning renomination than did Governor Lane, although the senator's two primary opponents, running without major organization support, amassed more than a third of the votes.

Lane, in his own mind, was reluctant to run again. "I didn't think that I could be elected," but Hooper Miles, the state treasurer, "influenced me very much by saying that I ought not to duck out." The governor consulted his wife, who told him: "'In all the years I have known you, I never knew you to run away.' That settled it."[54]

The gubernatorial primary was both bitter and a mixed blessing to Lane as the nominee. The governor's principal opponent, the ebullient George P. Mahoney, attacked him and the cost of his programs from end to end of the state. He promised to reduce sales and other taxes and to save the state "millions and millions of dollars." Lane pressed him in vain for specific

51. *Evening Sun*, Jan. 6, 1949, June 9, 1950; *House Journal*, 1951, pp. 16-18.
52. *Ibid.*, 1949, pp. 28-29, 95; *ibid.*, 1951, pp. 17-19.
53. *Evening Sun*, June 24, 1950. In 1973 the state changed the name to Baltimore-Washington International Airport.
54. Author's memorandum of conversation with Lane, Oct. 25, 1966.

programs to be curtailed. Mahoney had another theme. "I am fighting against one of the most powerful political machines that has ever ruled this state. . . . but I am going to beat that machine and its powerful bosses and become . . . a free governor of this great Free State."[55] In the outcome Mahoney carried Baltimore by 22,000 votes, narrowly losing only the fourth district—Jack Pollack's domain. Mayor D'Alesandro worked for Lane; "Willie" Curran, for Mahoney. The governor led in the counties (carrying sixteen) by 4,000 votes. Mahoney's popular plurality of 18,000 and his majority of 2,000 over all other candidates in the primary race were brushed aside by the unit system then legally binding the state convention, which voted Lane the nomination.

Senator Tydings' tribulations in the election campaign after the 1950 primaries were bizarre. Regarded as too conservative by strong supporters of the New Deal in its heyday, and having lost enthusiasm among leaders of labor, minorities, and liberals, he now found himself questioned as if he were an apologist for alleged sympathizers with communism. The domestic winds of the Cold War period had turned more turbulent. Senator Joseph R. McCarthy of Wisconsin had charged that communists had infiltrated the Department of State. Alger Hiss had been convicted of perjury in denying that he had given official papers to Whittaker Chambers, his principal accuser, who had hidden a microfilm in a pumpkin at his Pipe Creek Farm in Carroll County. Professor Owen Lattimore, director of the Walter Hines Page School of International Relations at The Johns Hopkins University, whom McCarthy charged with being a "Soviet agent" and the "architect" of American Far East policy, returned from a trip abroad to call the senator from Wisconsin a "base and miserable creature." Lattimore testified before a Senate Foreign Relations subcommittee, headed by Tydings, that he had never been a member of the Communist party and that he did not believe in and had never advocated its principles or cause. Tydings declared that subcomittee members had examined a summary of Lattimore files prepared by J. Edgar Hoover, Director of the Federal Bureau of Investigation, which showed no connection with communism or espionage.[56] Even

55. *Sun*, Sept. 3, 18, 1950.
56. *Evening Sun*, Jan. 21, April 1, 3, 6–7, 1950.

before the Maryland primary election, the Cold War had become heated with invasion of South Korea from the north, followed by President Truman's order directing American aid and the call by the Security Council of the United Nations for assistance to South Korea.

John Marshall Butler, Tydings' Republican opponent in the Senate race, had received like Lane nomination by benefit of unit votes in a state convention. General D. John Markey of Walkersville, whom O'Conor had barely defeated for the Senate in 1946, had led in the 1950 Republican primary by nearly 2,000 votes but had lost in most of the large counties and in all of the districts of Baltimore City. Butler was then little known in the state except, especially among lawyers, as a respected member of the Baltimore bar. His supporters, among them Republican National Committeeman Jacob France, arranged the services of Jon M. Jonkel of Chicago as public relations director and manager of the campaign. The strategy was one of spreading doubt, not accusations, around Senator Tydings, especially doubt of his committee findings about inaccuracies in charges leveled by McCarthy.[57] Tactically, Tydings made a mistake in replying too much, thereby spreading the impact of opposition strategy. On election eve he denounced a four-page tabloid, authorized by Young Democrats for Butler, which used a composite picture—labeled as such—of the senator and Earl Browder, former head of the Communist party of the United States, apparently in conversation. The paper blazed with such headlines as "Senator Tydings Promised Probe, But Gave Whitewash Instead." Tydings accused his opponent of publishing "faked photographs" and "outright falsehoods." Butler, denying that he had seen the tabloid before it was printed, countered that the senator "is now whining because parts of his record have been exposed to the public view." Senator O'Conor supported his Democratic colleague by calling the Butler campaign, which he thought to be directed by "isolationists" from out of the state, "the most deplorable resort to mud slinging and character assassination this state has witnessed in many years."[58]

---

57. See Stanley Kelley, Jr., *Professional Public Relations and Political Power* (Baltimore: J.H. Press, 1956), Ch. IV, "Merchandising Doubt."
58. *Evening Sun*, Nov. 6, 1950.

Lane ran on his substantial record, as in the primary, against Theodore R. McKeldin, who had received the Republican nomination without opposition. Responding to the times, McKeldin strove to show that his views on tax reduction and economy were akin to Mahoney's. While Mahoney asserted his support of the Democratic ticket, many of his lieutenants aided McKeldin. So great were the defections, even among Lane's primary allies, that at the last minute Jack Pollack threw his own precinct to McKeldin.[59] During the fall campaign Lane resigned as national committeeman and Mahoney succeeded him, actions that Lane attributed to the hard-pressed Tydings, whose appeal to the governor was "You are unconsciously helping to assassinate me."[60]

Defeat of Tydings was generally unexpected, for he had been to most Marylanders an admired independent of scintillating mind and rapier tongue and an institution in the Senate for twenty-four years. Even the bookmakers rated him a five to one favorite while calling the governor a seven to five underdog.[61] Butler's lead was 326,291 to 283,180, 53.5 per cent of the two-party vote. McKeldin attained a tremendous victory for a Republican in Maryland, 369,807 to 275,824 for Lane, 57.3 per cent of the total vote, and he carried Baltimore City by 47,000 votes while Butler won it by 17,000. McKeldin was the victor in twenty-six of the twenty-eight city wards, Butler in eighteen of them; in the city Butler led notably in areas where the Negro vote was strongest.[62] Lane won by small leads in only three counties—Dorchester, Kent, and Queen Anne's on the Eastern Shore. Tydings led in ten, doing best in his home county of Harford; he fell behind badly in the suburban counties ringing Washington, in western Maryland, and in Baltimore and Anne Arundel Counties.

Many factors coincided to bring about the Democratic debacle. The sales tax led to Democratic unpopularity and a suicidal gubernatorial primary that hurt the party's morale. The communist issue alienated many conservatives; Tydings himself thought that issue a major one among Catholic voters. Laboring

59. *Ibid.*, Oct. 2, 27, Nov. 4, 8, 1950.

60. Author's memorandum of conversation with Lane, Oct. 25, 1966.

61. *Evening Sun*, Nov. 8, 1950.

62. *Ibid.*

men and the liberals found McKeldin appealing and, in the Senate race, thought Tydings' domestic record conservative. Cries of boss rule in Baltimore and even in the counties were destructive, however unjustly applied to the candidates. Tydings, a critic of national administrations, had become a defender of an increasingly unpopular regime enmeshed in the Korean conflict. Moreover in a rapidly growing population, he and Lane, leaders who deserved well of the people, were distant figures personally unknown to the voters and therefore unprotected from misunderstanding.[63]

### 4

### McKeldin, Beneficiary of Democratic Strife

Theodore Roosevelt McKeldin, the most gregarious of Maryland's modern governors, was in many ways well suited to the role that a Republican chief executive must play with a Democratic legislature and other Democratic colleagues. Genuinely a humanitarian, he was less interested in detail than in the broad outlines of policy. He had a keen sense of political timing, often keeping his own counsel until all about him were left in a quandary about his intentions. Few were really close to him, but everybody knew him. One of the state's most charismatic figures, he was an accomplished and moving orator, sometimes mildly chided for elegance of phrases and repetition of theme. He was interested in the heritage of the state, but most of all in its people. For years he had traveled over the state to meetings large or small, and in office he continued the practice as few governors had done before him. Gracious and cordial, he knew no recreation more absorbing than talking with friends or strangers about the virtues and artifacts of Maryland past or present. He became famous in and out of the state for his gifts of autographed pictures of its governor, of symbols of its tradition, and of tributes he had written to its historic role in America. He was an enthusiast about the ideals of freedom, equality, and progress that Maryland had sought and toward which, as a genuine if groping idealist, he hoped it would continue to strive.

Fractured leadership in the Democratic legislature, resulting

---

63. *Ibid.;* Kirwin, *op. cit.,* pp. 508-11; John H. Fenton, *Politics in the Border States* (New Orleans: Hauser Press, 1957), pp. 182-87.

from searing primaries and disappointing elections for the highest offices in the state, compounded McKeldin's problems as a Republican governor and tested his skills as a negotiator. Like his Democratic predecessor, he saw the continuing need for new road programs and other construction and for a host of public services in an urbanized state. He saw also the pressure for prudent economy without "indiscriminate and arbitrary cuts" arising from "the unchecked inflationary spiral" accompanying the undeclared war in Korea. He would move with caution and with counsel, appointing both a commission to study reorganization of the state government and an advisory council to review highway construction.[64]

Headed by Simon E. Sobeloff, former solicitor of Baltimore City and a political associate of McKeldin, the Commission on the Administrative Organization of the State assembled impressive talent for its work. Carl B. Swisher of The Johns Hopkins University and Elwyn A. Mauck, on loan from the directorship of the state Fiscal Research Bureau, both political scientists, served respectively as directors of research and staff. The revered and influential Horace E. Flack, for a generation director of the Department of Legislative Reference; James V. Bennett of Montgomery County, director of the United States Bureau of Prisons; and civic-minded Malcolm Moos of The Hopkins were among the consultants.

Commission recommendations for a program-oriented budget, municipal home rule, new personnel procedures, and reform of prison and parole administration were soon adopted— the first two requiring constitutional amendments supported by other influential leaders and ratified by the voters in 1952 and 1954. In developing and supporting later implementing legislation for the home rule amendment, the Maryland Municipal League, listening to its knowledgeable executive secretary, Edmund C. Mester, exerted great influence in persuading reluctant members of the Senate—long used to dominance over legislation for municipalities in their counties—that they would escape both criticism and endless detail by effective home rule. The commission, served by Sobeloff as chairman until his appointment by McKeldin as chief judge of the Court of Appeals,

---

64. Inaugural Address, January 10, 1951, pp. 5-7.

did not achieve major goals of thoroughgoing reorganization.[65] Recommendations were nevertheless significant in the administrative and fiscal development of the state, as were those of the Lane-appointed Maryland Tax Survey Commission studying removal of tax inequities, under the chairmanship of Richard W. Case from 1949 to 1951. This commission encountered legislative resistance.

The State Roads Commission and its advisory council, after an eighteen-months' study, proposed in 1952 a twelve-year highway program designed to meet needs for the predictable future. The plan, subsequently approved with minor modifications by the legislature, called for improving 3,450 miles of roads, 300 miles of them to be built in new locations, at an estimated cost of $568 million. Major changes contemplated circumferential highways around Baltimore and Washington, new roads from Annapolis to Baltimore and northward and from Pennsylvania across central Maryland to Virginia, and other improved roads from Glen Burnie to the Potomac River Bridge and on the Eastern Shore. The financing proposals suggested raising the gasoline tax from five to six cents per gallon, increasing automobile license fees, and issuing of new construction bonds.[66] The planning gave Maryland an advance network design for the later federal interstate highway program. Meanwhile the $45 million Chesapeake Bay Bridge from Sandy Point to Kent Island, which Lane had pressed, opened to traffic—4.35 miles from shore to shore with a suspension span of 1,500 feet, allowing 186½ feet above the water in the shipping channel to Baltimore.[67]

National politics, deep rifts in the Democratic party, and the demonstrated Republican leadership of Governor McKeldin intermingled in 1952 Maryland elections. McKeldin left characteristically unclear until the national convention his preference for president; against a chance of being considered for vice president, he was disposed to be a nominal favorite-son candidate for the highest office. He did make clear his support of

65. See Carl T. Richards, "Maryland's Administrative Reorganization: A Study of Decision-Making" (Ph.D. dissertation, University of Maryland, 1972).
66. *Evening Sun*, Nov. 12, 1952.
67. *Ibid.*, July 30, 1952.

Congressman J. Glenn Beall of Frostburg in the primary race for the United States Senate. The governor, identified with the more liberal wing of his party, had no desire to aid H. Grady Gore of Montgomery County, endorsed for the Senate by National Committeeman Jacob France, president of the Midcontinent Petroleum Corporation and Baltimore banker, who had enormous influence in Maryland's Republican politics. He, like Gore, favored the candidacy of Robert A. Taft for President.[68] The primary brought Beall a lead of over 21,000 votes.

At the national convention, McKeldin eagerly accepted an invitation to nominate General Dwight D. Eisenhower and in doing so, as the *Evening Sun* remarked editorially, "pulled out the stops, turned up the volume and poured it on." In organ tones he acknowledged the significance of the opportunity given to "the Governor of a Southern State—indeed the only Republican Governor south of the Mason-Dixon Line." With fourteen of Maryland's twenty-four delegates favoring Robert A. Taft, the governor's persuasiveness brought a vote of sixteen to eight for Eisenhower in the first balloting.[69] General William C. Purnell, counsel of the Western Maryland Railroad, and Senator John Marshall Butler led the Maryland delegates for Taft. McKeldin took France's place as national committeeman; but Miss Bertha Adkins of Salisbury, director of the women's division of the National Committee, remained committeewoman.

Democrats engaged in another party-shattering primary contest for the United States Senate, this time between George P. Mahoney and Congressman Lansdale G. Sasscer. Senator O'Conor, who decided not to seek reelection, broke ranks with the Democratic establishment to endorse his old friend Mahoney, saying that "he possesses not only diligence, integrity and great energy, but also a high degree of ability" and that he was impressed with "his deep concern over un-American activities" and "his intention to adhere to sound fiscal policies."[70] Sasscer made strong bids for Eastern Shore unit votes. J. Millard Tawes, who had regained the state

68. Paul T. David, Malcolm Moos, and Ralph M. Goldman, *Presidential Nominating Politics in 1952* (Baltimore: J.H. Press, 1954), II, "Maryland," 236-45.
69. *Evening Sun*, July 11, 1952.
70. *Ibid.*, April 23, 1952.

comptrollership—first by Lane's appointment and then by election in 1950—often introduced him to town and rural gatherings, where the congressman from southern Maryland emphasized his interest in crops, cattle, and especially watermen's aspirations.[71] Mayor D'Alesandro in Baltimore poked fun at Mahoney and, more seriously, accused him of "wrecking the Democratic Party."[72]

Mahoney won the Democratic primary for the Senate by over 14,000 votes, leading in ten counties and in all of Baltimore City's districts except the fourth, which Jack Pollack saved for Sasscer by 262 votes. Bradford Jacobs wrote in the *Evening Sun* that Mahoney, "self-styled 'one man against the bosses,' blew up the once-potent state Democratic machine to . . . snatch away the senatorial nomination the bosses vowed he should not have."[73] The Democratic state convention, filled with anti-Mahoney delegates legally bound to him under the unit rule, elected E. Brooke Lee of Montgomery County as chairman by 105 votes to 45 for Mahoney's candidate, Joseph George, dominant party leader in Queen Anne's County. It nominated Mahoney and elected him as delegate-at-large to the national convention; but when Jack Pollack's delegates from the fourth district voted for Mahoney's candidate for convention chairman, it pointedly removed Pollack's name from the list of national convention delegates.[74]

In the presidential election of 1952 Eisenhower won Maryland with 55.4 per cent of all the votes, leading Adlai E. Stevenson by 104,000, but losing Baltimore City by 12,000. J. Glenn Beall gained his Senate seat with 52.5 per cent of the votes, leading Mahoney by 43,000 votes, but losing Baltimore by 35,000. In addition to Baltimore City, Mahoney carried four counties, Cecil, Queen Anne's, St. Mary's, and Somerset.

Dissension in the party affected esprit de corps in a Democratic legislature left with factional or sectional allegiance in the absence of a recognized statewide spokesman. So strong were antagonisms in the Senate session of 1953 that Senator George W. Della of Baltimore won reelection as president of

---

71. *Ibid.*, April 17, 1952.

72. *Ibid.*, May 1, 1952.

73. *Ibid.*, May 6, 1952.

74. David *et al.*, *op. cit.*, II, 249-51.

the body on the seventy-eighth ballot by a combination of Republican votes and a minority of Democrats over C. Ferdinand Sybert of Howard County, nominee of the Democratic majority caucus.[75] Baltimore chieftain Jack Pollack openly warred with Dr. H. C. Byrd, president of the University of Maryland and always influential in state politics, for failing to join him in an unsuccessful attempt to defeat reelection of House Speaker John C. Luber, a Pollack antagonist in the city. House Democrats, never free from factionalism, were soon divided into blocs—Baltimore City, Western Shore, and Eastern Shore —with sixteen of the thirty-five from Baltimore often voting with Eastern Shoremen who had provided the key votes for election of Speaker Luber.[76]

Legislatures of the McKeldin years in the governorship engaged in the delicate political task of agreeing with the Republican governor only when necessary, as it frequently was. Many of the most vexatious problems were financial, with both the governor and the General Assembly often preferring to postpone costly expenditure. The governor's first term was far from barren, even if understandably filled with political jockeying. The legislature provided for a $3 million state office building in Annapolis with the hope of bringing from Baltimore to the capital city a larger part of the state's business and workers. Three years later it authorized a $14 million state office building in a redevelopment area north of Baltimore's central business district.

Dr. Byrd, in continuing to obtain construction funds and status for the university, at the same time wielding such political influence in the legislature that some dubbed him a shadow governor, had obviously become a major competitor of the governor for real power, present and future. The legislature at his behest passed over the governor's veto an autonomy bill freeing the university from the supervision of many state agencies, including those setting standards for personnel and purchasing.[77] Within another extended day, the last of the 1952 session, he was back at the State House lobbying on the floor of the house in the hours after midnight for more than $500,000 of additional

75. *Sun,* Jan. 15, 1953.
76. *Ibid.,* Jan. 10, 16, 1953.
77. *Laws of Maryland, 1952,* Ch. 14.

construction money that he had persuaded the Senate to add to a pending bond bill. Prophetically, he was rebuffed. Protest against his amendment and his presence swelled, at first fanned by a few Republicans, but, as taut tempers rose, joined by others in both parties; thirty or forty members leaped to their feet to hoot "get out, get out" as he retreated to watch from the gallery a vote of sixty-seven to thirty-two against him.[78] Stoically he went to his office, as usual at seven o'clock in the morning, for a conference with the president of the student government.

Politicians' minds turned to the setting of the stage for the state elections of 1954. Executive and legislative branches avoided sensitive decisions that might better await the result. The governor was proud of the opening of the final link of the Baltimore-Washington Expressway. The General Assembly passed legislation to require local governing bodies and state boards to take final action in public meetings on all resolutions or rules. It voted a $100 million bond issue for a bonus to veterans, held by the attorney general to have been unconstitutionally enacted; the governor, with the political controversy perhaps softened, vetoed the bill.[79]

Dr. Byrd convinced himself that it was he who must challenge Governor McKeldin's quest for reelection. With some regret and evident nostalgia for his old labors, he asked to be released from the presidency at the beginning of 1954. The regents of the university gave the acting presidency to Dr. Thomas B. Symons, the retired Dean of Agriculture, relaxed, amiable, and respected. In eight months they brought Dr. Wilson H. Elkins to the presidency from a similar position at Texas Western College. A new day of balancing quality with quantity came to the university.[80] Calm, incisive, and informed, Dr. Elkins dealt with the public and its leaders through reasoned statements, sometimes interspersed with wry wit, rather than by casual contact or comment.

Efforts to avert a bitter Democratic primary for the governorship in 1954 proved to be chimerical. Clarence W. Miles, brother of the state treasurer and a power in Democratic coun-

---

78. *Evening Sun*, March 6, 1952.
79. *Laws of Maryland, 1952*, Ch. 13; vetoes, pp. 302-304.
80. Callcott, *op. cit.*, pp. 360-61, 367-70.

sels from the days of O'Conor's governorship, convened a well-attended conclave in Baltimore that brought little more than a resolution, offered by former Senator Millard E. Tydings, that Democrats ought to attack Republicans.[81] H. C. Byrd, candidate of those who considered themselves the regulars of the Old Line State, took a lofty view. "I've got more to offer this job than the job has to offer me," he said to reporters. "I don't believe it is necessary to run around the state importuning every Tom, Dick and Harry."[82] The irrepressible George P. Mahoney, making his third state-wide race in four years, hinted irreverently of Byrd's prospects for the executive mansion: "Government House is not a haven where 'elder statesmen' can spend their days of retirement in peace."[83] Mayor D'Alesandro shelved his own plans to run.

Dr. Byrd broke into the first major headlines of the primary campaign in a television interview in Baltimore. Mahoney had earlier offered to run for comptroller, Byrd said in answer to a reporter's query, adding that he had rejected the idea because he could never desert the incumbent, J. Millard Tawes. Mahoney immediately replied that in a series of meetings with him Byrd had importuned him to run, suggesting that he could handle Tawes and promising to resign the governorship in two years for a Senate race and to throw his support to Mahoney for election as governor by the General Assembly, empowered to fill the vacancy. Charles G. Whiteford, pointing out in the *Sun* that the two agreed only that there had been meetings, wrote that they left no middle ground. "One of the two told less than the truth." He quoted Tawes as having only one thing to say, "Under no circumstances am I going to get into that controversy."[84]

The Democratic candidates facing each other with such belligerence agreed in charging that McKeldin, despite words of economy, had sharply increased the state budget—by 55 per cent Mahoney reiterated. Former Governor Lane campaigned for Byrd to avoid "looking in the direction of bankruptcy" under McKeldin, whose budgets in four years he totaled as half a

---

81. *Sun*, Jan. 5, 1954.
82. *Washington Post*, Jan. 10, 1954.
83. *Baltimore American*, Jan. 24, 1954.
84. *Sun*, Jan. 18–20, 1954.

billion dollars more than those of the preceding quadrennium. Mahoney called Byrd "one of the biggest spendthrifts the State of Maryland has ever had to maintain and support," and pictured himself as the only man "to halt increased spending." Yet he and Byrd agreed that a veterans' bonus bill should be sent to referendum, that better transit facilities should be provided in Baltimore with more money for the Public Service Commission, and that a state port authority should be created for Baltimore to develop its trade in the face of competition from the projected St. Lawrence Seaway. Mahoney supported a $200 million five-year school development plan proposed by the Maryland Congress of Parents and Teachers and the Maryland State Teachers Association. He urged maintenance of expenditure rates for roads to meet construction schedules. At Brunswick he advocated a "dynamic program of industrial development" to reverse trends that were driving young people from small towns; "with the threat of the hydrogen and atomic bombs," he said, decentralizing industries are "looking for sites in smaller towns." Byrd, campaigning by June at stores and gasoline stations, spoke vigorously for a state agency to bring new industry to western Maryland and other sections that needed employment opportunities. Praising organized labor as good for the employer and the employee, he opposed "any Taft-Hartley law and . . . any right-to-work law" regulating union membership.[85]

Late developments in the Democratic primary campaign undoubtedly had more impact on the outcome among voters on the Eastern Shore, with its important county-unit votes, than the statements of the candidates. The Supreme Court of the United States had delivered its decision holding that racially separate public schools are inherently unequal. Some 50,000 cards mailed to the Eastern Shore and southern Maryland quoted Dr. Byrd as saying that he would treat Negroes better than any other governor had ever done. Byrd insisted that what he would do for Negroes would equally benefit whites and accused Mahoney—who denied that he had anything to do with the cards—of fanning racial prejudice. A survey of Democratic

85. *Ibid.*, April 5, May 14, June 3, 26–27, 1954; *Sunday Sun*, April 4, 1954; *Evening Sun*, May 10, June 15, 1954; *Baltimore News-Post*, May 26, 1954; Washington *Evening Star*, June 10, 1954.

leaders on the Eastern Shore reported that injection of the racial issue hurt Byrd among whites in the area. The Monumental Democratic Club in Baltimore distributed folders titled "Why the Negro Should Vote for George P. Mahoney."[86]

Byrd clearly won in the popular balloting on June 28—by a margin of 4,000 votes in the final count—and led in unit votes by eighty to seventy-two. Mahoney won in nine counties and in all of Baltimore's districts except the fourth, getting an especially heavy vote in Negro wards. Byrd carried the counties by 19,000 but lost Baltimore by 15,000. But returns in his favor in Calvert, Queen Anne's, and Talbot Counties and in Baltimore's fourth district were so close that Mahoney obtained recounts and fought unsuccessfully in the courts to overturn confirmation of Byrd's victories. The nominating convention was postponed pending litigation, and it was late August before Byrd's primary victory was finally assured. C. Ferdinand Sybert's nomination for attorney general in a race against Philip H. Dorsey, Jr., a Mahoney supporter from Leonardtown and one of the strongest voices of the party in southern Maryland, made fewer headlines but encountered a similar contest.[87]

Governor McKeldin, renominated in the Republican primary over token opposition that he blithely ignored, toured the state with his customary empathy. Annoyed by statements from Byrd implying financial improprieties in the state government and by criticism of fees to real estate agents for assembling land parcels for approaches to the Baltimore harbor tunnel as examples of "waste and extravagance," the governor moved to a posture of attack. Praising progress of the road program, McKeldin contended that his administration had begun long-range planning to replace "an illogical patchwork of frequently unconnected stretches of macadam."[88]

As rumors began to circulate that there were unfavorable comments in an accreditation report about the university, the governor questioned his opponent's record as its president. Arthur W. Sherwood, Republican nominee for Congress in a Baltimore district, publicly alluded to "a status of probation" given

86. *Sun*, June 27, 30, 1954.
87. *Ibid.*, July 27, Aug. 5, 1954; *Baltimore News-Post*, Aug. 18, 1954; *Washington Post*, Aug. 26, 1954.
88. *Sun*, Oct. 9, 12, 1954.

Thurgood Marshall (1908-    ), Baltimorean who as chief legal counsel
for the NAACP argued the 1954 school desegregation case before the
Supreme Court; appointed an associate justice of that court in
1967 by President Lyndon B. Johnson. *Life Magazine.*

the School of Medicine.[89] So delicate did the issue become that the regents, respecting the confidence of the detailed report, announced that all schools at the university were fully accredited, subject to any necessary review in two years. They confirmed, as Byrd had already stated in the campaign, that there were words of praise for his administration; and they listed five critical areas discussed in the report: administrative centralization, lack of faculty participation in educational policy, the library, status of the School of Medicine, and intercollegiate athletics.[90]

Final weeks of the campaign brought drama both from nature and from candidates for the electorate's favor. Hurricane Hazel wreaked devastation on the boats of watermen of the Eastern Shore and upon the means of livelihood of other workers. They gave much credit to the state administration and to Republican Congressman Edward T. Miller for extensive disaster relief.[91] McKeldin raised the winds of political storm, calling Byrd's continuing charges of financial improprieties in the state administration a "salvo of slander" and charging that his opponent's record was "tyrannical" and "autocratic."[92] The governor announced that he would include in the university budget $2.2 million for a new library that Byrd had not obtained for all his "boasted influence."[93] The issue of race soon became the most exciting one in the contest. Byrd had been on record as favoring local determination of school desegregation but said that he preferred "separate but equal facilities," which "it would not be wise" to end at once. McKeldin, reluctant to speak on the issue during the early phases of the campaign, sensed that the times were ripe for forthright positions. The nation was turning, both on domestic and international fronts, from an era of suspicion and recrimination. He took the leap in St. Mary's County. "Come, come, Dr. Byrd! Come out of the bog of bigotry, out of the puddle of prejudice." McKeldin was not entirely finished with caution; he spoke little of desegregation but insisted that he stood with the law on the question.[94]

---

89. *Ibid.*, Oct. 9, 1954; Washington *Evening Star*, Oct. 11, 1954.
90. Callcott, *op. cit.*, pp. 361-62.
91. *Sun*, Oct. 20, 1954.
92. *Baltimore American*, Oct. 17, 1954; *Evening Sun*, Oct. 18, 1954.
93. *Sun*, Oct. 19, 1954.
94. Washington *Evening Star*, Oct. 21, Nov. 2, 1954.

The election demonstrated again an aphorism in Maryland politics: for a Republican to be elected in a statewide contest he must be more liberal than his Democratic opponent. With the strength of labor growing since the 1930's, both Democratic Baltimore City and Republican western Maryland, the latter with its intermittently employed miners, sympathized more readily with liberal appeals. Even the affluent suburbs often joined them. Only the Eastern Shore and parts of central and southern Maryland responded quickly to a conservative voice. Miscalculating political impacts of rapid population growth in Baltimore and in the widening suburbs northward from Washington, Byrd chose the wrong strategy to build a majority. He lost Baltimore City by 43,000 votes and the counties by over 19,000. McKeldin was elected to a second term by 54.5 per cent of the vote.

A new term did not bring McKeldin at once to pinnacles of leadership in the Democratic legislature. In his inaugural address, he dedicated himself "as the humble and loyal servant of God and the sovereign people of the State of Maryland" to seek anew with others "the further advancement of human values as the greatest contribution we may make to our day and age."[95] But the General Assembly of 1955, as the *Evening Sun* observed, enacted "no major long-range or large-scale program."[96] It battled over taxation, rejecting the governor's proposals for increases in sales and income taxes and substituting a payroll withholding of income taxes to bring a temporary windfall from advance payments. Except for laws giving effect to the new constitutional provision for municipal home rule, beginning the regulation of strip mining of coal, making voting machines mandatory from 1958, and authorizing the future toll highway from Baltimore to the Delaware line, much of the legislative product was routine. Part of the difficulty stemmed from acrimony within and between the legislative chambers.

From the outset of the 1955 session Democratic tempers were ruffled by caucus voting to choose officers of the houses. Speaker John C. Luber of Baltimore, affiliated with a coalition of party leaders who opposed Mayor Thomas D'Alesandro's bid for a third term, secured his own reelection to leadership in the House of Delegates with the support of members from the

95. *House Journal*, 1955, pp. 88-89.
96. *Evening Sun*, April 5, 1955.

Eastern Shore. Angered by the Eastern Shore's rejection of the candidacy of Perry O. Wilkinson of Prince George's County for the speakership, political leaders of southern Maryland retaliated in the Senate. They withdrew expected support from Shoreman Layman J. Redden of Caroline County for the presidency of the Senate and secured the election of Louis L. Goldstein of Calvert County, who would have continued as majority leader in a Redden regime. In the arrangement, ambitious Senator John Grason Turnbull of Baltimore County became majority leader and, in accord with custom, also chairman of the Finance Committee. Senator Frederick C. Malkus, Jr., colorful, shrewd, and independent Democratic Shoreman from Dorchester County, obtained the chairmanship of the Judicial Proceedings Committee. This changing of the guard in the Senate temporarily eclipsed the leadership of Senator George W. Della who, as a coalition opponent of Mayor D'Alesandro in Baltimore, had decided to support Senator Redden rather than fight for a fifth year in the Senate presidency himself.[97]

Opening of the Patuxent Institution in 1955, the outcome of years of effort and planning, brought diagnostic and therapeutic programs—under psychiatric direction—to defective delinquents. Continuing road construction, unexpectedly large use of the Bay Bridge, new investment in manufacturing, a rising labor force, compliance by ten counties with the United States Supreme Court ruling on school integration (without major incidents) all brought the state pride and confidence. In August, however, Hurricane Connie left fourteen dead and $4 million damage in major portions of the state, and five days later the less severe Hurricane Diane whipped coastal areas.

The legislature's short session of 1956 wrestled with financial problems and with developmental issues of great importance to Baltimore City and the state. That session, and a special one called by Governor McKeldin for March 8 to remove all doubts of constitutional procedure, compiled a remarkable legislative record. The General Assembly created the Maryland Port Authority to improve shipping facilities in most of the navigable waters of the state, authorized the city of Baltimore to borrow money for a civic center and for new or improved buildings for the Enoch Pratt Free Library, approved issue of revenue bonds

---

97. *Ibid.*, Jan. 5, 1955; *Sun*, Jan. 6, 1955.

by the University of Maryland for construction of housing, recreational, and service facilities at College Park and Baltimore,
empowered the State Roads Commission to construct a toll expressway to Pennsylvania and Delaware, and extended the borrowing powers of several county governments. The General
Assembly also approved budget requests of more than $300
million, raised salaries and benefits of state employees, and
provided a credit pool of $75 million from which counties could
borrow for school construction.

When the 1956 legislature convened, it was at once faced
with critical problems of a transit strike in Baltimore which
began on January 30 and, when it ended on March 5, had become the longest in the city's history. Some 2,200 members of
the AFL-CIO transit union struck the Baltimore Transit Company, a corporation privately owned by investors chiefly based
in Chicago. Strikers sought wage scales comparable with those
in other eastern cities. At least 150,000 regular passengers
found themselves without bus or streetcar service, and the Retail Merchants Association soon estimated loss of sales by seven
large downtown department stores at $100,000 a day with loss
of 5,500 employee work days in a ten-day span. Smaller stores
averaged 36 per cent reduction in sales.[98]

Governor McKeldin pushed a plan for seizure of the
strikebound transit company; Delegate Marvin Mandel of Baltimore informed Frank P. Baummer, the union president, that
the city delegation of which he was chairman would have to
support a grand inquest by the House of Delegates to investigate the causes of the strike unless workers returned to service.
Mayor D'Alesandro announced his opposition to municipal acquisition and operation of the transit system, at the same time
expressing a preference for local private rather than absentee
ownership.[99] The House of Delegates on February 6 unanimously approved a motion by Delegate Maurice Cardin of Baltimore City for a grand inquest,[100] which began in Annapolis on
February 13. In the outcome the General Assembly, over the
opposition of company and union spokesmen, passed a seizure

98. *Evening Sun*, Jan. 30, Feb. 13, 1956.
99. *Ibid.*, Feb. 2, 13, 1956.
100. *House Journal*, 1956, pp. 117-18.

measure with provisions for compulsory arbitration.[101] On March 5 the governor placed the company under a state administrator and its personnel returned to work the next day as state employees pending the ultimate completion of contract negotiations.[102]

Political ambitions of Governor McKeldin, Republican National Committeeman for Maryland and the dominant party figure in the state, were never far from the surface of public speculation. Early in 1956, with uncertainty about President Eisenhower's health and his intention to seek reelection, there was talk about the governor's willingness to lead the Maryland delegation to the Republican national convention as a favorite-son candidate for president. Later, in the absence of a clear Eisenhower endorsement of Richard M. Nixon's renomination for vice president, speculation turned toward the governor for that office. Malcolm Moos of Baltimore, chairman of the Republican City Committee and rumored to have closer rapport with the White House staff than the ambitious governor, remarked cautiously that "eminently qualified chief executives like Governor McKeldin and Governor Christian A. Herter of Massachusetts have consistently been mentioned as promising running mates."[103] It was hardly a secret that McKeldin, a leading liberal, had sought without success to find a candidate to run in the party primary against the more conservative Senator John Marshall Butler.[104]

The ambition of former Democratic Senator Millard E. Tydings to regain the seat that he had lost to Butler in 1950, and the determination of the perennial George P. Mahoney to run against Tydings in the Democratic primary, soon occupied the center of Maryland's political stage. The contest was a close one. Tydings won the primary on May 7 by less than 8,000 votes. Mahoney had won Baltimore City and ten of the counties, and the prospect for Democratic unity was uncertain. McKeldin promptly spoke out for Butler at the Republican state convention in Baltimore, saying that Tydings had been nominated with the support of a "clique" in the Democratic party

101. *Laws of Maryland, 1956*, Ch. 41; re-enacted with amendments, *Laws of Maryland, Extraordinary Session, 1956*, Ch. 15.

102. *Evening Sun*, March 5–6, 1956.

103. *Ibid.*, March 1, 1956.

104. Washington *Sunday Star*, Sept. 30, 1956.

who had "blacklisted" Mahoney, "the man who has the support of a vast number of his party's members."[105]

Democratic fortunes were further complicated by the illness of Tydings, who resigned the senatorial nomination from a sense of campaign obligation to the party. His supporters suggested to the Democratic State Central Committee, charged by law with making a new nomination, that Mrs. Tydings be named the party candidate. Mahoney, as the close runner-up in the primary, claimed the prize, and the committee in a tense meeting in Baltimore on August 27 chose him over Mrs. Tydings by a vote of ninety-seven to fifty-five.[106]

At Chicago on August 16 Democrats had nominated Adlai E. Stevenson for a second presidential race, and the next day had chosen Senator Estes Kefauver of Tennessee for vice president in a close contest with Senator John F. Kennedy of Massachusetts. Maryland's delegates cast their votes for the nominees. In the following week Republicans at San Francisco unanimously renominated President Eisenhower and Vice President Nixon. Governor McKeldin headed a committee proposing minimal changes in convention rules and served also on the platform subcommittee on civil rights, arguing there for a liberal statement. A moderate one came forth upon insistence of White House aides. The governor was openly disappointed with his role in the convention but announced that without presidential encouragement he would not allow his name to be placed in nomination for vice president. His reward was the last of the seconding speeches for Nixon, in which he praised the party for "reversing the treacherous tides sweeping away the proud sovereignty" of the states.[107]

In the Maryland senatorial campaign Democratic nominee Mahoney focused his efforts with threefold emphasis: attacks on Senator Butler's 1950 campaign tactics against Senator Tydings; criticism of the Butler voting record in the Senate, particularly votes favorable to oil and gas interests; and portrayal of Republicans as the party of the rich and Democrats as defenders of "all the people." Butler on October 15 made a prepared

---

105. *Frederick News*, May 16, 1956.

106. *Evening Sun*, August 28, 1956.

107. Charles A. H. Thomson and Frances M. Shattuck, *The 1956 Presidential Campaign* (Washington: Brookings Institution, 1960), pp. 153, 162, 175, 177-80, 186, 208.

television statement that use in a 1950 tabloid of a composite picture, even if so labeled, showing Tydings with a communist was "in bad taste and a mistake in judgment" of "enthusiastic yet ill-advised friends" for which he would accept responsibility even though he "had nothing to do with its preparation." Thereafter he stressed his record of service to Maryland, one which he thought had seldom been equaled by a first-term senator; and he described himself, despite his more conservative views, as one of the "Eisenhower team." Adlai Stevenson in a Baltimore speech on October 30 declared that Butler in 1950 had conducted "one of the most shameless campaigns of distortion" and for it "deserves to be beaten" even if he "would make us believe that he was just foolish, in order that we do not think him a knave. But neither a knave nor a fool is a fit representative for Maryland in the United States Senate." Both Senators Kefauver and Kennedy spoke in Maryland, the latter expressly to win votes for Mahoney to preserve Democratic control of the Senate. Major labor leaders endorsed Mahoney for the first time in his four campaigns, but some union leaders formed the Baltimore Labor League for Eisenhower and Butler.[108]

The vote-gathering power of Eisenhower was overwhelming in Maryland. He swept every county and the city of Baltimore, the latter by nearly 38,000 votes, winning the state's electoral votes by 559,738 to 372,613, or 60 percent of the popular votes, the largest margin Maryland had ever given a Republican candidate for president. With him he carried Senator Butler to victory, 473,059 to 420,108 (53 per cent). Mahoney won only Calvert, Prince George's, Queen Anne's, and St. Mary's Counties and Baltimore City (the last by 5,137 votes). The senator carried nine of the city wards, four of them with large populations of black voters who had decided to support the Republican ticket. So great was their voting switch that Democratic Congressman George H. Fallon of Baltimore won reelection by a majority of only 6,303. All incumbents in the House of Representatives, four Democrats and three Republicans, held their seats.

Shortly before the 1956 election, the president's brother, Dr. Milton S. Eisenhower, who had served as president of Pennsylvania State University, became president of The Johns Hopkins

---

108. *Evening Sun*, Oct. 16, 29–30, Nov. 2, 1956.

University, where he continued his long career in education, public service, and liberal causes. Governor McKeldin pressed for racial integration in public services, presiding over its application in the National Guard and on the state's beaches. In the election Baltimore County voters followed the earlier example of Montgomery County (1948) by approving a home rule charter but adding the principle of a strong county executive.

McKeldin's last years as governor brought continuing problems of finding revenues to finance expanding programs and services of the state in a period of rising costs. Every issue also felt the effects of rivalry in party politics. Democratic leaders were determined to find a way to reverse a trend toward loss of statewide elections. Many of them, persuaded that divisive primaries were at the root of their problem, were attracted to the idea of negotiating a harmony ticket. Republicans hoped to field a candidate whose voter appeal could retain for their party the governorship that McKeldin could not seek because of a constitutional barrier against more than two consecutive terms. Republican Senator J. Glenn Beall intended to seek reelection in 1958 rather than run for governor, and McKeldin made it clear that he would not challenge him in a primary. The force of these problems entered in one way or another into almost every legislative issue. In dealing with the governor, moreover, the General Assembly, under Democratic control, resisted rising costs, particularly if reflected in rising taxes.

At the beginning of the 1957 General Assembly the governor said to a joint session of the two houses that the "gravest—the most pressing—of all our problems" came from the "constantly mounting conflict" between the necessarily expanding highway system and "the rising rate of death and destruction which accompanies the expansion." He proposed annual inspection of motor vehicles and other traffic safety measures, and it soon became apparent that he favored a tax of five cents on each package of cigarettes to finance them. The governor conceded that his forthcoming budget, the largest in the state's history, was out of balance by $7 million and "will call for some adjustment in our tax structure."[109] The legislature defeated vehicle inspection and almost all other traffic measures, partly because of reluctance of some state department heads to support them.

---

109. *House Journal*, 1957, pp. 34, 37.

The governor called the legislative attitude "cavalier" in its "lack of concern" for public safety. Delegate Lloyd L. Simpkins, chairman of the House Judiciary Committee, said that the remarks were "untrue, unfair, and very unkind."[110]

Pressed by a strong lobby, the legislature approved an increase of $400 per teacher in state aid for salaries, the costs to be covered by a three-cent cigarette tax. The governor vetoed the bill after adjournment of the session with the observation that teachers' salaries should be increased by local governments "primarily responsible" for schools. The legislature in 1958 promptly overrode the veto.[111]

Of the fiscal record of the 1957 session Louis L. Goldstein, president of the Senate, told the Advertising Club of Baltimore that the legislature had cut the governor's budget by $3 million and balanced it at $360 million without new taxes that the governor had proposed. Observing that real property in the state was worth $20 billion, he added prophetically that the state could afford increased spending for needed services. The governor, in a mellow mood, told the same audience that the legislature had done a "marvelous job."[112] That session had also repealed the 1785 compact giving Virginia equal access to the Maryland-owned Potomac River. Great controversy had arisen over violent conflict with Virginia watermen.[113]

A severe drought in the summer of 1957 periled water supplies and reduced agricultural yields. In a happier scene in October, 43,000 football fans cheered Queen Elizabeth II of Britain and her husband Prince Philip at the Maryland-North Carolina game in Byrd Stadium at College Park. Governor McKeldin and Dr. Wilson H. Elkins, president of the University of Maryland, were the principal hosts. In ceremonies heralding alleviation of major traffic bottlenecks in Baltimore, the governor on November 29 opened the Harbor Tunnel, twin tubes of 6,298 feet.

To many of the shrewdest leaders of Maryland's Democratic party it seemed apparent that State Comptroller J. Millard Tawes of Somerset County on the Eastern Shore, by long

110. *Sun*, Feb. 9, April 3, 1957.

111. *House Journal*, 1958, pp. 18-22; *Senate Journal*, 1958, pp. 50-54.

112. *Sun*, April 11, 1957.

113. *Laws of Maryland, 1957*, Ch. 765.

months of quiet negotiation, had become virtually assured of the 1958 nomination for governor. The problem of avoiding a party-splitting primary, potentially devastating to success in the general election, nevertheless loomed before them. The first open step to build a harmony ticket to avert later disaster was the Tawes endorsement of Senate president Louis L. Goldstein, often mentioned for governor himself, for the office of comptroller.[114] Meanwhile Michael J. Birmingham, Democratic National Committeeman and a dominant political figure in Baltimore County, worked diligently with other party leaders to find a way to remove Mayor Thomas D'Alesandro of Baltimore from his already-announced candidacy in the gubernatorial race. Persuading him to run for the United States Senate might provide the solution, but the reluctant mayor demanded strong and even written assurances of support from Tawes-oriented county politicians.

A widely-heralded conclave of more than forty of the state's Democratic leaders of all counties and Baltimore, with Birmingham—sometimes called the White Rabbit in Maryland lore—as chairman, met on the evening of January 8 at Carvel Hall, historic hostelry in Annapolis. Despite their many rivalries, they wrought mightily to bring the Democratic party together as it had not been united in twenty years. Tawes and D'Alesandro, with press releases ready for use if all went well, sat together nervously in a suite in Baltimore's Emerson Hotel. At the meeting in Annapolis J. Newton Brewer of Montgomery County moved endorsement of Tawes and D'Alesandro for governor and senator. Charles County leader Rudolph Carrico asked, "Can we produce?" He wanted to consult his co-workers at home before supporting D'Alesandro; but he signed the resolution with the others after Philip B. Perlman, former solicitor general of the United States, pointed out that the prepared resolution used the words "acting only for ourselves." Voice votes endorsed C. Ferdinand Sybert of Howard County (who had withdrawn from the race for governor two months earlier) for reelection as attorney general and Senator Goldstein for comptroller. Senator Louis N. Phipps, Anne Arundel County leader, lost a motion to include their names in the written document. Mayor D'Alesandro promptly announced his entry in the Sen-

114. *Evening Sun*, Jan. 8, 1958.

ate primary race, contested though it would remain, joining the Tawes harmony ticket in pledges of mutual support. The mayor's switch ended months of resistance to political necessity. Only weeks before he had said airily about overtures from Tawes supporters, "They want a strong Baltimore man on the ticket to help drag an old nag across the finish line."[115]

In truth, J. Millard Tawes had taken over the leadership of the Democratic party in Maryland. In his years as a popular comptroller he had demonstrated that, though never a showman, he was honest, capable, and politically shrewd. His harmony ticket in the 1958 primary, except in the case of D'Alesandro's Senate race, encountered no serious opposition. The Baltimore mayor had entered an already crowded field, and none of the other leading candidates would withdraw from the Senate primary: George P. Mahoney, who in all his campaigns could count a substantial following; James Bruce, wealthy industrialist and once ambassador to Argentina, running with the support of former Governor William Preston Lane, Jr., and of former Senators George L. Radcliffe and Millard E. Tydings; and Dr. Clarence D. Long, professor of economics at The Johns Hopkins University, articulately attractive to many voters. John Grason Turnbull, Baltimore County, majority leader of the Senate, had hoped to be tapped for the national Senate but in the face of the competition accepted his disappointment. All four of the leading Democratic senatorial candidates favored tax cuts to stimulate the developing economic recession, only D'Alesandro giving higher priority to a public works program; all advocated strengthening national defense beyond allocations of the Eisenhower administration; all supported foreign aid programs. Long proposed a minimum national standard for unemployment insurance and denounced American semi-military aid to Arab countries. The Birmingham organization in Baltimore County, in a change of signals, endorsed Mahoney for the Senate.[116]

The Tawes ticket won in the Democratic primary on May 20, Tawes and Goldstein overwhelmingly, Sybert unopposed, and only D'Alesandro eking out a narrow victory. The Baltimore mayor ran less than 6,000 votes ahead of Mahoney, carrying the

---

115. *Sun, Evening Sun*, Jan. 9, 1958.
116. *Evening Sun*, May 5–7, May 12, 14, 1958.

city by 14,000, but losing the popular votes in the counties to
Mahoney by nearly 9,000. Bruce and Long ran third and fourth,
each getting less than half of the votes received by either of the
two leading candidates. D'Alesandro, victor by a plurality of
popular votes although winner of a majority of the unit votes in
the state, was clearly in political trouble.

Republicans had a quiet primary. J. Glenn Beall faced only
token opposition for his Senate seat. Congressman James P. S.
Devereux of Baltimore County, retired brigadier general of
Marines and renowned as the World War II hero of Wake Island, was unopposed for governor. McKeldin had been far from
happy about Devereux's identification with conservatives in
the party; but the general was willing to run, and no liberal
Republican came forth to challenge either his proved voter appeal as a member of Congress or the political anointment given
him by numerous party leaders.

Even before the primary Tawes, as the certain Democratic
nominee for governor, wielded decisive influence in the dead-
locked legislature that was unable to agree on revenue measures to produce the balanced budget required by the constitution. The floor leaders, Senator Turnbull and Delegate A.
Gordon Boone, pressed for Governor McKeldin's proposals to
increase both the sales and income taxes from two to three per
cent but until Tawes' intervention were unable in a series of
votes to get sufficient support from their election-conscious colleagues. Delegate Blair Lee III of Montgomery County, writing
by invitation in the *Evening Sun*, gave thanks to the governor,
the legislative leadership, and "most of all, to Millard Tawes for
acting like a statesman when he might have acted like a
politician."[117] The General Assembly also prohibited pari-
mutuel betting in the state, an issue arising from the controversial introduction of jai alai in Anne Arundel County near Fort
George G. Meade; and it ended operation of slot machines on
piers from the Virginia side of the Potomac River.[118]

Campaigning for the November general elections was extensive but generally dignified. Devereux, without oratorical flair
and almost self-effacing in demeanor, ran for governor with a
candor devoid of political wiles. He told liquor dealers that they

117. *Ibid.*, March 13, 20, 1958.
118. Baltimore *News-Post*, March 6, 1958; *Laws of Maryland, 1958*, Chs. 18,
43.

could expect no special favors and on the traditionally southern-minded Eastern Shore made a strong plea for civil rights. At the convention of the Maryland State Teachers Association Tawes supported further state increases in salaries, but Devereux, supporting Governor McKeldin's pleas for county responsibility, warned the association against "blackjacking of legislators" and "the havoc of a political bulldozer in the marble halls of Annapolis."[119]

In their public appearances both gubernatorial candidates favored stabilizing state tax rates but advocated improved programs in higher education, public health, industrial development, and prison reform. Tawes, with the benefit of long experience in state government, offered a larger variety of proposals, including legislative reapportionment and programs for the aged, highways, utility regulation, and review of administrative organization. Sensitive observers predicted that Tawes would win an easy victory and that the race between Senator Beall and Mayor D'Alesandro would be close. The liberal Jacob Javits, Republican senator from New York, came to Baltimore to speak for Beall, who also received endorsement from the *Sunpapers* and from such influential Baltimore Democrats as Irvin Kovens and Hyman A. Pressman. The *Sunpapers*, moreover, endorsed Republican John A. Derr of Frederick for comptroller.[120]

The Democratic victory in 1958 was tremendous, but Republican J. Glenn Beall was reelected to the Senate by 15,000 votes. Tawes was the hero of his party, regaining Democratic control of the governorship after eight years by carrying every county and every district of Baltimore City with a statewide majority of 207,000 votes (63.6 per cent of the total). D'Alesandro carried only six counties, and his margin of 31,000 votes in Baltimore City contrasted embarrassingly with Tawes' majority of 90,000 there. Goldstein and Sybert easily won the offices of comptroller and attorney general, each receiving in Baltimore a majority greater than that given by the city to the mayor in his Senate race. For the first time since 1940 Democrats won all of the state's seats in the House of Representatives. The Democratic gain of three congressional seats from

---

119. *Baltimore American*, Sept. 28, 1958; *Evening Sun*, Oct. 17, 1958.
120. *Ibid.*, Oct. 30–31, Nov. 1, 3, 1958; *Sun*, Nov. 3, 4, 1958.

Maryland was part of a tide of such victories in the nation. It surged not only from the 1958 economic recession, with rising prices and lingering unemployment, but also from extensive voter dissatisfaction with the rate of progress in education, health, housing, and other social benefits. In the state legislature Democrats increased their strength from twenty-one to twenty-six in the Senate and from ninety-eight to 116 in the House of Delegates, leaving Republicans only three senators and seven delegates—the smallest Republican representation in the General Assembly since 1871.

Although the mayor of Baltimore was chagrined within his own stronghold, his powerful political ally James H. "Jack" Pollack had a different experience. Ethnic change in his fourth district of Baltimore from predominantly Jewish to a majority of black constituents had, after years of ineffectual outcries about bossism and all-Jewish slates, brought about the election of three black legislators in 1954. The winners who opposed the organization machinery were Republican Senator Harry A. Cole and two in the House of Delegates, one a Republican and another an independent Democrat who had been successful in the primary.

At the urging of Dr. Carl Murphy of the *Afro-American*, influential newspaper voice of the black community, Senator Cole in running for reelection in 1958 assembled an all-black coalition of legislative candidates against the Pollack organization. One was Mrs. Verda Welcome, an independent Democrat who had won in the 1958 primary, and another Mrs. Irma Dixon, already nominated for the house with Pollack support. Mrs. Dixon promptly repudiated coalition endorsement. The anti-organization ticket also carried the extra electoral burden of including five Republicans and two Democrats.

In a change of strategy, Pollack had fielded a black nominee, J. Alvin Jones, for the Senate. The battle cries of the endangered organization, often heavy handed in its tactics, were aimed directly against the all-black "segregated" coalition. Established politicians had attained an image of favoring an "integrated" slate assembled under the banner of Pollack's famous political headquarters, the Trenton Club. Churches and civic organizations of the black community—now numbering a majority of the district's registered voters—heavily supported the coalition, despite many protests and misgivings about the im-

plications of "segregation." In fact, the coalition leaders had
been unable to find white candidates who would stand against
the established organization. The election reinvigorated the
Pollack organization. All of its candidates and Mrs. Welcome
—the Democratic primary nominees—were easily elected.[121]

5

TAWES: CONTINUING EXPANSION AND CHANGE

If, as the *Sunpapers* suggested, Governor Tawes "initiated no
big changes of policy" in the early days of his administration, he
himself had given a reason. In his inaugural address on January
14, 1959, he pledged: "I shall offer no program during my administration the end of which cannot be foreseen." He would
never "propose a course of action without a cautious exploration of all its aspects and all its possible consequences."[122]
Moreover, he rightly foresaw expansion not only of population,
industry, and business but of pressures for more and better
highways, schools, and hospitals as well as for improved welfare programs and correctional systems. He was, as it came
about, to do far more in his terms of office.

The legislature met under new leadership with members
ready to respond in most matters to the governor's wishes.
George W. Della of Baltimore City returned by a unanimous
vote to the Senate presidency he had left four years earlier at
the accession of Senator Goldstein, who had now become
comptroller. Other senators at the helm included Edward S.
Northrop, Montgomery County, majority leader and chairman
of the Finance Committee; Frederick C. Malkus, Jr., Dorchester,
continuing as Judicial Proceedings chairman; and Mary L.
Nock, Education chairman. In the House Perry O. Wilkinson,
Prince George's, became speaker, with A. Gordon Boone, Baltimore County, as floor leader and chairman of Ways and
Means; Ridgely P. Melvin, Jr., Anne Arundel, chairman of

121. *Evening Sun*, Oct. 27, 30, 1958; G. James Fleming, *An All-Negro Ticket
in Baltimore* (New Brunswick, N.J.: Eagleton Institute of Politics, Rutgers
—The State University, 1960).

122. *Journal of Proceedings of the Senate of Maryland, January Session,*
1959, p. 38; Conley H. Dillon, ed., *Messages, Addresses, and Public Papers of
J. Millard Tawes, Governor of Maryland* (Annapolis: State of Maryland), I, 3;
*Evening Sun*, April 6, 1959.

Judiciary; and Blair Lee III, Montgomery, chairman of Education.[123]

An outstanding political and legislative accomplishment of the 1959 session was the passage of a proposed constitutional amendment to create a Municipal Court of Baltimore City to replace part-time trial magistrates.[124] Opposed vigorously by the city delegation, the bill to reform the patronage-ridden courts of the city carried only after an unusual call by the governor for support of it as a party measure. The legislative procedure also set a precedent in breaking the custom of honoring the wishes of a delegation in the General Assembly about issues affecting its own area. The amendment to alter the court structure in Baltimore met overwhelming statewide approval in 1960, with Baltimore providing nearly half the opposition. Other legislative achievements in 1959 were the enactment of a point system for traffic violations to be used in suspending or revoking drivers' licenses and approval of the Potomac River Compact of 1958 with Virginia, creating a commission to regulate seafood catches in the river.[125]

Baltimore's primary election on March 3 broke the established patterns of Democratic politics in the city. State's Attorney J. Harold Grady defeated Mayor Thomas D'Alesandro, Jr., by a margin of 33,000 votes, destroying the latter's hope for an unprecedented fourth straight term. Governor Tawes, who endorsed D'Alesandro, his erstwhile senatorial running mate on the harmony ticket of the preceding year, inadvertently became involved in the cries of civic outrage that contributed to the mayor's defeat. The governor's late-winter appointments list —the Green Bag—gave eleven of fourteen positions in Baltimore to adherents of the Pollack-D'Alesandro party organization. Most controversial was the nomination of Paul A. Dorf, Jack Pollack's son-in-law, for chief magistrate of the city Traffic Court. The mayor, actively opposed by George P. Mahoney whom he had defeated in the senatorial primary and by a minority of party professionals, a week before had been favored to win. Yet his policies leading to higher taxes, including a tax on advertising held unconstitutional by the courts, had weakened

123. *Senate Journal*, 1959, pp. 4, 19-20; *House Journal*, 1959, pp. 5-6, 27-29.
124. *Laws of Maryland, 1959*, Ch. 373.
125. *Ibid.*, Chs. 736, 269.

him. He received only 38 per cent of the total vote in a turnout of 54.2 per cent of the city's 332,517 registered Democrats. Nominee Grady's ticket for city-wide offices was also easily successful in the primary: Senator Philip H. Goodman for president of the city council and Dr. R. Walter Graham for renomination as comptroller.[126]

Former Governor Theodore R. McKeldin won the Republican nomination for mayor. He had calculated on running against the weakened D'Alesandro, who might be portrayed as a symbol of outdated boss rule. Against Grady's own image as the reform candidate in a Democratic stronghold, the outlook was different indeed. Yet McKeldin made his appeal, enjoying the campaigning that Grady found tiresome. Minority groups had always supported him, McKeldin said, because he had sympathy for people who are pushed around. "I don't have very much in common with many of the Republicans. I don't have their philosophy." Grady, "proud to be a Democrat," retorted that he was supported by many Republicans because they "prefer a genuine Democrat to a counterfeit Republican."[127]

Pollack told his workers to "vote your conscience" and many of them in the fourth district and in the fifth, to which he had extended his operations, passed out sample ballots for McKeldin. Still, McKeldin had less organized Democratic support in Baltimore than in any other race he had run. D'Alesandro forces worked for Grady, who won the election by better than two to one. Both Goodman and Graham were elected with handsome majorities. McKeldin carried only the fourth district, and that by 4,000 votes.[128]

The Grady regime, soon struggling with fiscal problems of Baltimore, advocated a 1 per cent earnings tax as a source of urgently-needed revenue. As a temporary expedient the city administration sought to eliminate expansion of its budget. At the opening of the year Baltimore had a long-term debt of $309.5 million, an increase of 88 per cent in thirteen years.

In his state-of-the-state message to the General Assembly in 1960 Governor Tawes could report substantial activity. He had obtained legislation for a new Department of Economic De-

126. *Evening Sun*, March 4, 1959.
127. *Ibid.*, April 1–2, 1959.
128. *Ibid.*, May 4–6, 1959.

velopment to encourage expansion of business and industry and for a Commission on Problems of the Aging.[129] He had secured reorganization of various state agencies, notably the State Roads Commission, the newly-named Departments of Tidewater Fisheries and State Planning, and the State Racing Commission.[130] He had leaned to the view that membership of policy boards should be larger in order to represent more sections of the state. "We have completely recovered from the recession"; and services had been expanded with attention to economy and prudent management. "Additional taxation is unthinkable" while revenues "are sufficient."[131] The legislature approved $4.3 million for higher teachers' salaries, resisting teacher requests for $17 million. The governor vetoed a bill, on the ground that it gave no adequate power of enforcement, introduced by Delegate Joseph D. Tydings to regulate savings and loan associations.[132] Criticism of uninsured associations and of savings losses had become a major public issue.

The governor called a conference of nine Appalachian governors at Annapolis in May to lay the groundwork for regional economic development. Although only three of Maryland's westernmost counties are in Appalachia, Governor Tawes' early interest and leadership earned him acclaim for acting to increase the role of the states in intergovernmental cooperation. The Appalachian Regional Commission grew from the conference and was influential in evolving legislation for the broader Area Redevelopment Administration. The city of Cambridge received the second grant given in the country by the administration, $213,000 for sewer facilities to serve new industries.[133]

To the Democratic State Central Committee, meeting in Annapolis in August 1959, Tawes suggested that it "would be wise" for the Maryland party to send an uninstructed delegation—"unfettered" he called it—to the national convention of 1960. He was soon to modify his position, however, for Senator John F. Kennedy in a personal conversation informed him unequivocally that he intended to enter Maryland's presi-

129. *Laws of Maryland, 1959*, Chs. 185, 1.
130. *Ibid.*, Chs. 241, 430, 543, 831.
131. *House Journal*, 1960, pp. 46-54.
132. *Sun*, March 4, 1960; *Laws of Maryland, 1960*, pp. 310-13.
133. Dillon, *op. cit.*, I, 71-75, 187.

dential primary. Within the month the governor issued a statement pointing out the greater "maneuverability" of a free delegation, welcoming the senator in a Maryland primary, and
volunteering that "I have no desire and no intention of entering
such a primary myself." Senator Wayne Morse of Oregon also
entered the contest, and four days before the voting the governor said in Kennedy's presence in Annapolis, "I intend to cast
my ballot next Tuesday for Senator Kennedy" and urged others
"to do the same."[134] He would have preferred such a candidate
as Senator Stuart Symington of Missouri,[135] once a Baltimore
industrialist; but he bowed to reality, for the organized Democratic sentiment for Kennedy was unbeatable in Maryland.
Kennedy outpolled Morse by 201,769 to 49,420 votes; 24,350
Democrats voted for an uninstructed delegation.

Kennedy's nomination on the first ballot at the Los Angeles
Democratic convention in July was quickly followed in
Chicago by the unanimous Republican choice of Richard M.
Nixon, to whom the Maryland party faithful had made an early
commitment. At Chicago Mrs. Alvin L. Aubinoe, a Maryland
delegate from Montgomery County, launched a drive, with the
help of others, to nominate for vice president Miss Bertha S.
Adkins of Salisbury, Undersecretary of Health, Education, and
Welfare.[136] It proved to be a gesture of courtesy. Nixon's choice
of Henry Cabot Lodge was primarily a judgment about ticket
strengthening, as Kennedy's selection of Lyndon B. Johnson
had been.

That the presidential race might be close in Maryland as in
the nation was clear. The somber mood of the country had lifted
since the election of 1958, with more prosperous times and with
American space and earth satellite programs showing promise
of outperforming the earlier successes of the Soviet Union.
Election returns in the state put Kennedy and Johnson in the
lead by a comfortable 76,000 votes. There were warning signals, however, for Democratic strategists. While Kennedy had
been the victor in Baltimore City by 88,000, he had lost the
counties by 12,000. Indeed he had carried only seven of them,

---

134. *Ibid.*, pp. 131, 134-35, 137-38.

135. Albert W. Quinn, "Contemporary Maryland," in Morris L. Radoff, ed.,
*The Old Line State* (Annapolis: Hall of Records Commission, State of Maryland, 1971), p. 454.

136. Baltimore *News-Post*, July 25, 1960.

two on the Eastern Shore, three in southern Maryland, and the populous counties of Montgomery and Prince George's. On the same day Republican Charles McC. Mathias, Jr., member of the House of Delegates from Frederick County, won election to Congress from the western Maryland district, other seats remaining Democratic.

Shortly before the election Mrs. Madalyn E. Murray withdrew her son from junior high school in Baltimore to protest the practice of opening the school day with reading from the Bible. Her case became one in which the Supreme Court of the United States ruled Bible reading in public schools, even when pupils who object are excused, unconstitutional as a religious exercise required by the state in violation of the first amendment.[137]

The census of 1960 verified statistically the tremendous growth of the state's population to a total of 3,100,689. In a decade the increase, much of it in the metropolitan suburbs, was over 750,000—growth by nearly a third above the 1950 population. Baltimore City lost 10,000, but suburban Baltimore County gained 222,000. Montgomery grew by 176,000, Prince George's by 163,000, and Anne Arundel by 89,000. While the state had been predominantly urban since 1910, the urban portion of the state's population had now increased to 72.8 per cent. In the ten-year period the gross state product had increased by 46 per cent in comparison with a growth of 39 per cent in gross national product. Maryland's per capita income now exceeded by 9 per cent that of the nation as a whole. Approximately 70 per cent of the people in Maryland lived in a wide corridor extending from the District of Columbia to the suburbs north of Baltimore.

Governor Tawes saw important implications for public policy in future growth as well as that of the past. He emphasized the need to "reckon . . . with sheer numbers" in the years ahead, in his address to legislators at the opening of the General Assembly's 1961 session. "We must make preparations for the accommodation by 1970 of a total population of nearly 4,000,000, a motor vehicle registration of 1,600,000, a community of more than a quarter of a million people 65 years of age or older." Urbanization must be "uppermost in the minds of those

---

137. *Sun*, Nov. 3, 1960; *Murray* v. *Curlett*, 374 U. S. 203 (1963).

who plan for the State's future." That urbanization would make "the conservation of remaining natural resources and open land an inescapable necessity." In its floodtide it would further complicate relationships of state and local governments, and of local governments with one another.[138]

Legislators assembled with political sensitivity about unemployment in Baltimore, a situation causing the United States Department of Labor to place the city on its critical list, and especially about rifts and rivalries within the governing Democratic party. The session dealt firmly with savings and loan associations, a few of which were still causing scandal and public clamor, by enacting regulatory legislation introduced jointly by Senate President George S. Della and Senators John-Clarence North of Talbot and Edward S. Northrop of Montgomery. It also passed an insurance regulatory bill, introduced by Delegate Joseph D. Tydings of Harford, limiting an insurer's liability for any one loss to 10 per cent of its surplus. It made provisions for the Municipal Court of Baltimore City to carry out the voters' 1960 approval of a constitutional amendment creating the court. The General Assembly enacted legislation, introduced by Speaker Perry O. Wilkinson of Prince George's for the Legislative Council and pressed by liberal Delegate Francis X. Gallagher of Baltimore City, to create a Metropolitan Transit Authority for the Baltimore area. A bill introduced by Senators William S. James of Harford and Mary L. Nock of Wicomico, duly enacted, authorized the board of education in any county or in Baltimore City to maintain community colleges with current expenses financed on the basis of one-third each from the state, the county or Baltimore, and student fees.[139] Upward adjustments in the cigarette and sales taxes, the latter minor, became law. These taxes and other allocations of funds supported increases of $9.5 million in state aid to local governments for welfare and education as proposed by the Legislative Council Committee on Taxation and Fiscal Matters headed by Senator James.[140] The legislature failed to heed the governor's call to act on the explosive issue of reapportioning the House of Delegates.[141]

---

138. *House Journal*, 1961, pp. 27-28.
139. *Laws of Maryland, 1961*, Chs. 205, 482, 616, 670, 134.
140. *Ibid.*, Chs. 321, 655; *Evening Sun*, April 3, 1961.
141. *House Journal*, 1961, p. 34.

Because Jack Pollack and his Baltimore political organization petitioned to put to referendum the savings and loan regulation and the Baltimore Municipal Court arrangements, and could thereby delay them until the election of 1962, Governor Tawes called the General Assembly into special session in June to consider emergency legislation. The laws were reenacted, by the necessary three-fifths majorities of all members elected, to make them effective at once.[142] Both laws were also approved by large majorities, even in Baltimore, in the election of 1962.

In view of mounting tensions in Democratic leadership circles it was apparent by 1961 that the ensuing year's election would be a critical test of the party's ability to continue control of the governorship. Tawes, as a moderate liberal, always ready to move forward after careful appraisal of options, was beset from left and right—called in his own party too slow by eager liberals and too ready for change by the more cautious conservatives. After long deliberation, and to the surprise of many who did not know his courage, the governor announced that he would be a candidate for reelection. George P. Mahoney, in alliance with politician Jack Pollack and vigorously anti-Tawes, was openly running for the governorship. David Hume of Charles County, wealthy newcomer to Maryland politics who had served briefly as treasurer of the state party, planned to run also but at the time seemed to be a distant voice crusading for clean government, particularly the control of slot machines in southern Maryland.[143]

Full slates of candidates for statewide offices in the Democratic primaries of 1962 developed around the Tawes and Mahoney banners. The governor's ticket emphasized both continuity and new recognition of officeholding Democrats. It included for United States Senator Daniel B. Brewster of Baltimore County, two-term member of Congress; attorney general, Thomas B. Finan of Allegany, who had been appointed to that office (after serving as Democratic state chairman) to succeed C. Ferdinand Sybert upon the latter's elevation to the Court of Appeals; Louis L. Goldstein for reelection as comptroller; and House Speaker Perry O. Wilkinson for congressman-at-large. (An eighth congressional seat awarded to Maryland by reapportionment was filled for a time, because of districting controver-

142. *Evening Sun,* June 12, 1961.
143. Washington *Evening Star,* Aug. 26, 1961, Feb. 8, 1962.

sies, by statewide vote.) The Mahoney slate in the Democratic primary offered an unusual assortment of ability and divergent views: for senator, Blair Lee III of Montgomery County, a moderate of balanced judgment awarded much praise for his work in the House of Delegates; attorney general, state Senator Samuel W. Barrick of Frederick; comptroller, Marshall A. Levin, Baltimore; congressman-at-large, Delegate Carlton R. Sickles, Prince George's, widely known as an independent-minded Democrat of liberal leanings; David Hume, running for governor without a slate, endorsed Finan, Goldstein, and Sickles.[144]

Republicans, not at all confident that they could carry the state even with the help of wrangling among Democrats, had difficulty fielding a strong ticket. John Marshall Butler had declared publicly that he would not seek another term in the Senate. Republican leaders hoped that they could build a ticket around former Governor McKeldin, who decided that the year was not an appropriate one. Frank Small, Jr., Prince George's, was eager to run for governor. Despite a term in Congress and various state appointments, he was little known to the public at large. The party leadership endorsed him at a meeting in Baltimore after all hope of McKeldin's candidacy for a third nonconsecutive term had faded. At the same time the leaders endorsed former Congressman Edward T. Miller of the Eastern Shore for the Senate, much to the indignation of his principal opponent, James P. Gleason of Montgomery County.[145] McKeldin had persuaded Miller to enter the Senate race. When the liberal former governor later telephoned to say that he had firmly decided not to run for the governorship after all, Miller knew that he and other statewide Republican candidates had little chance in the fall election.[146] Indeed, the primary itself became a threat to Miller. Gleason ran so vigorous a campaign that the well-known Miller won the primary by less than 9,000 votes. Small, with minor opposition, had an easy primary victory.

Emotion-arousing issues, prominently displayed in the press, deeply affected the Democratic primary of 1962. The first of them, long simmering, was that of equal accommodations for

144. Frederick *News*, May 16, 1962.
145. *Ibid.*, April 12, 1962.
146. Author's memorandum of conversation with Edward T. Miller, Sept. 19, 1966.

Unusual view of Hopkins Plaza, Baltimore.
Photo by Lloyd Pearson, *The Baltimore Sunpapers.*

persons of all races in restaurants and motels. Problems of discrimination had become acute and fanned much protest alongside the roadways leading through the state on the route from Washington to New York. Disappointed with lack of remedial legislation in the regular session of the General Assembly, Governor Tawes, with high hopes, called a special session. There the House of Delegates, after adopting exemption provisions for fifteen counties, still failed to pass an accommodations bill. The vote on the electric board in the house chamber stood sixty to forty-three, two short of the constitutional requirement of a majority of all the members; nineteen were unrecorded, with some members sitting in their seats but refusing to vote. "The saddest day in Maryland's legislative history," said Dr. Furman L. Templeton, executive director of the Urban League in Baltimore, predicting "accelerated demonstrations with all the bitterness that they involve." Some of the recalcitrant legislators, perhaps enough to have saved the bill in the House, had been angered by a telegram to President Kennedy from the Maryland Conference of the National Association for the Advancement of Colored People asking that federal funds be withheld for the relief of storm-devastated Ocean City until "the absolute ending of state-enforced racial discrimination." *The Sun* commented, "Nothing at the moment would ease the tension quite so effectively as a few new examples of voluntary desegregation."[147]

A second politically disconcerting controversy swirled around charges, first given public voice by candidate David Hume, that Jack Pollack had a tape recording of a conversation with Governor Tawes about patronage deals. Pollack later played a tape for newsmen to hear the alleged conversation. Governor Tawes decided to meet the issue in a television address, saying that he had discussed patronage with Pollack in the 1958 campaign but after "about three months" in office had realized that "a workable relationship" with Pollack "would be impossible." The governor said that he had withstood Pollack's patronage demands even "when he threatened to play some kind of tape he said he had." Pollack's endorsement of Mahoney, he added, gave the "best evidence" of failure "to gain a foothold" in state government. In the meantime

147. *Sun*, March 10, 11, 1962.

Mahoney hammered away at Tawes, blaming him especially for failing to prevent citizens' savings and loan losses. The governor struck back in a television appeal, saying that Mahoney had built his campaign "entirely upon dishonest innuendo, character assassination, and unvarnished lies." Hume declared that Mahoney had now joined with Pollack and the lobbyists "who worked longer and harder than anyone else" in trying "to defeat the laws which have regulated" the savings and loan industry.[148]

There were surprises in the Democratic primary returns. While Tawes, with the help of most of the Democratic organizations, received 178,792 votes and the nomination by a plurality, Mahoney obtained 125,966, and Hume an astonishing 118,295. Indeed, Hume outran Mahoney in the counties by over 13,000 votes. The governor led in twenty counties and in two of Baltimore's districts; Mahoney carried four districts in the city; and Hume won in Montgomery, Prince George's, and Washington Counties. Congressman Brewster easily acquired the Senate nomination, joining all other members of the Tawes ticket except Wilkinson in victory. Liberal Carlton R. Sickles easily won the primary over the House speaker for Congressman-at-Large.

Former Mayor D'Alesandro of Baltimore, in a keynote address at the Democratic state convention, warned against the danger of complacency that might give Republicans the election by default. Tawes' peacemaking skills within his party, however, were equal to the need. Small, his Republican opponent, called the governor a "political chameleon" for negotiations that brought endorsements from bitter primary enemies. Not even the organizing capacity of progressive David Scull of Montgomery County, the new Republican state chairman, could lift his party ticket to victory.[149] The success of President Kennedy in standing up to Premier Khrushchev and in securing the Soviet Union's removal of nuclear missiles from Cuba a week before the election undoubtedly aided Democratic candidates in the country and in Maryland.

Tawes won his race for reelection by a majority of 86,800, a

---

148. Dillon, *op. cit.*, I, 144-45; Salisbury *Times*, March 22, 1962; Frederick *News*, April 11, 1962; Hagerstown *Daily Mail*, Dec. 27, 1962.

149. Cumberland *Evening Times*, June 8, 1962; Washington *Sunday Star*, June 17, 1962; Salisbury *Times*, Oct. 22, 1962.

Crowd before the speakers' stand at the opening of the Baltimore Beltway on July 7, 1962. Photograph by Willis Malashuk. *The Baltimore Sunpapers.*

figure that revealed continuing strains in the Democratic party. Although his popularity at the polls had suffered by comparison with the returns four years earlier, he had attained a new distinction. He was the first Democrat to emerge from a primary contest with George P. Mahoney and subsequently win the election. All Democrats on the statewide ticket were readily victorious. It was Goldstein who had the largest majority, 176,834 votes. He and Attorney General Finan became the immediately obvious Democratic candidates for governor in 1966. Carlton R. Sickles was elected to Congress from the state at large by the smallest of the Democratic margins, 79,000 over his Republican opponent Newton I. Steers, Jr., of Montgomery County. Steers was soon to serve as state chairman of his party. Republicans notably increased their representation in the General Assembly. Democrats retained customary control, twenty-two to seven in the Senate and 117 to twenty-five in the house. Because of a state court decision in May holding apportionment of the House of Delegates unconstitutional, Governor Tawes called a second special session of the legislature. It enacted a temporary measure to enlarge the house by nineteen seats apportioned among the largest counties and Baltimore City.[150]

The election victory in 1962 gave to Governor Tawes and his Democratic colleagues a new lease of authority. His second administration brought even greater activity in the shaping of public policy coupled with renewed political controversy and disappointment.

In his first term the governor had worked hard to encourage planned economic growth in the state, to improve both state and local governmental management, and to utilize expanding revenue from existing taxes rather than to raise the rates or impose new levies. Upswing in the economy, a national phenomenon, had brought particular benefits to Maryland. Business spending for new plant and equipment steadily increased. Farmers, declining in numbers, nevertheless worked larger and more profitable enterprises. The fiscal health of the state government was unusual in times of deficit budgets among its counterparts in the nation.[151] Governor Tawes directed the relocation of state agencies in a new state office building, long

---

150. *Evening Sun*, May 24, 1962; *Laws of Maryland, Special Session, May 25, 1962*, Ch. 1.

151. Cambridge *Daily Banner*, April 26, 1963.

projected for a renewal area north of the business center of Baltimore, and in new office facilities in Annapolis. "Lifting the face" of downtown Baltimore, also long in the planning, was announced in 1960 by its civic and political leadership. Charles Center and adjacent structures became a showplace of modern business acumen. The Baltimore-Harrisburg interstate highway was open for traffic in 1959. By 1961 the final leg of the John Hanson Highway, two lanes in each direction, linked Annapolis with Washington; and by 1962 the Baltimore Beltway, thirty-two and four-fifths miles around the city, was also open to motorists and truckers. These and other roadways in the state added immeasurably to its traffic safety and its economic development.

The great problems and controversies of the second Tawes term as governor, inextricably intertwined with changing political power in Maryland, revolved around such disparate issues as civil rights, reapportionment of the General Assembly, educational development, control of slot machines in the southern counties, reorganization of state services and agencies, taxation and the related allocation of state funds, and constitutional revision.

Organization of the General Assembly in 1963 was, in the governor's view, acceptable and workable. William S. James of Harford served as president of the Senate and H. Winship Wheatley, Jr., of Prince George's as majority leader. In the House A. Gordon Boone of Baltimore County was speaker; W. Dale Hess, Harford, majority leader; Thomas Hunter Lowe, Talbot, chairman, Judiciary Committee; Marvin Mandel, Baltimore City, chairman, Ways and Means. Republicans in the Senate chose Edward T. Hall, Calvert, as minority leader to replace the humorously shrewd Harry T. Phoebus of Somerset. In the house they chose as minority leader J. Glenn Beall, Jr., son of the senior United States senator from Maryland.

Control of slot machines in four counties of southern Maryland, where they operated legally as a significant part of the economy, soon became the hottest political issue in the session. To much of the state the gambling devices were politically unacceptable and therefore thorns in the side of the Democratic party. Advocates of local autonomy in matters of regulation bitterly opposed the administration's compromise measure to ban slot machines in the state and to phase them out over a period of five years in counties and municipalities where they had been locally authorized. Once again the Tawes administration moved to override traditional respect for the privilege long accorded members of the General Assembly to exclude their own counties from the application of statewide law. As in the case of reform of the courts of Baltimore, the governor successfully pressed against local opposition for legislative enactment of the regulatory measure.[152] While long in controversy, the law remained in effect.

Democratic intraparty recriminations and voter indifference in the 1963 primary for Baltimore City offices revealed publicly that organizational unity which Tawes and his supporters had arranged for the statewide elections of 1962 remained fragile. In the fall of 1962 the governor appointed Mayor J. Harold Grady to the Supreme Bench of Baltimore. Philip H. Goodman, president of the city council and a former state senator, succeeded to the mayoralty and avidly sought election in his own right. He readily won nomination on March 5, 1963, in alliance with the D'Alesandro organization and with the aid of James H. Pollack and his northwest Baltimore workers. Thomas D'Alesandro III, son of the former mayor, who had replaced Goodman as city council president, was nominated for continuance in office on the ticket built by Mayor Goodman. Many of the Pollack precinct organizers cut D'Alesandro from their sample ballots in favor of Solomon Liss, running on the mayoralty ticket of Dr. R. Walter Graham, Jr., for eight years city comptroller. A third ticket headed by C. Meredith Boyce, businessman and former city treasurer, showed surprising strength without organization support, its citywide candidates running in second place. Hyman A. Pressman, attorney and civic activist, came within 2,000 votes of defeating Henry R. Hergenroeder, the Goodman candidate for comptroller, in a primary that drew only 44 per cent of the registered Democratic voters.[153]

Former Governor Theodore R. McKeldin easily swept the Republican primary for mayor of Baltimore, an office he had held from 1943 to 1947. Hyman A. Pressman accepted the Republican nomination to fill a vacancy on the ticket for comp-

---

152. *Laws of Maryland, 1963*, Ch. 616.
153. *Evening Sun*, March 2, 4–6, 1963.

After a night of rioting: Still smouldering ruins mark the area in Cambridge following a night of violence which left two blocks in flames (July 25, 1967). *The Baltimore Sunpapers.*

troller, joining forces with McKeldin and winning in the Court of Appeals a challenge to the legality of nominally changing parties and running for an office after a primary defeat for it. The campaign was filled with Republican charges of bossism, corruption, and incompetence and Democratic countercharges of opportunism, hypocrisy, and inattention to city needs in the past. The *Sunpapers*, expressing fear of bosses "from Mr. Goodman and Irvin Kovens on down" and balancing individual records, endorsed McKeldin, D'Alesandro, and Pressman. The three were elected in a turnout of 55.7 per cent of the city's 380,000 registered voters, McKeldin by a margin of less than 5,000 votes, Pressman by less than 6,000, but D'Alesandro by two to one over his hapless opponent, Robert J. Gerstung. The city council remained, as it had been for twenty years, unanimously Democratic.[154] The three city-wide winners pledged to work together for the social, economic, and physical improvement of the city. The period of the second McKeldin mayoralty of Baltimore was one of notable progress toward equal opportunity in employment, housing, education, and welfare and in planning development of the Inner Harbor area and other construction.

The General Assembly of 1963 had hesitantly accepted Governor Tawes' recommendation[155] for a law against discrimination in public accommodations. But the statute prohibiting denial of available rooms or food at hotels or restaurants because of race, creed, color, or national origin expressly exempted a dozen counties, most of them on the Eastern Shore.[156]

Racial violence flared in Cambridge on the night of June 11, following weeks of demonstrations by Negroes seeking more rapid school integration, desegregation of eating places, and better employment opportunity. After juvenile court sentencing of two teenage Negroes as delinquents for repeated participation in demonstrations, nearly a hundred Negroes prayed and sang outside the local jail. As they returned to their homes, about the same number of whites followed. Bricks, bottles, and other objects flew between the two groups. During the night three white men received gunshot wounds, fire-bombs caused

154. *Ibid.*, May 2–4, 6–8, 1963.
155. *House Journal*, 1963, I, 30.
156. *Laws of Maryland, 1963*, Ch. 227.

blazes in three white-operated business establishments in the Negro section, and bricks thrown by carloads of white youths injured two Negro teenagers. Negroes pelted firemen and police with bricks as the fires were controlled. The violence preceded by hours the rifle killing of Medgar Evers, civil rights leader, at Jackson, Mississippi; and at Cambridge tension and violence or its threat long distressed the city. "If rational counsel is to prevail among the mass of Negroes," said Representative Charles C. Diggs, Jr., of Michigan to the troubled country, "Congress will have to give the moderates, such as myself, the necessary weapons—and that means the whole civil rights package."[157]

Extending throughout the state the law prohibiting discrimination in places of public accommodation, although excluding bars, was a major legislative accomplishment of 1964. In that year Marvin Mandel became speaker of the House of Delegates and Roy N. Staten of Baltimore County joined him in the legislative leadership as chairman of the House Committee on Ways and Means. The drive for a statewide open accommodations law required a combination of leadership from Governor Tawes, called "remarkable" by the *Sunpapers*, and a growing consensus in the General Assembly that the time had come for action.[158] Promptly petitioned to referendum, the law received approval from the state's voters in the 1964 general election, 342,715 to 301,505. Thirteen counties registered disapproval, including Anne Arundel, Baltimore, three in western Maryland, and six on the Eastern Shore. Baltimore City, in a light vote on the issue, approved by less than 15,000; only Montgomery approached a favorable margin of two to one.

Entry of Governor George C. Wallace of Alabama in the Maryland Democratic presidential primary of 1964 added to the already building tensions of the state's political life. Daniel B. Brewster, who had served over a year in the United States Senate, promptly announced that he would run in that primary to hold Maryland's first-ballot votes in the national convention for President Lyndon B. Johnson. The senator was at first disposed not to "dignify Wallace's campaign with too much attention,"

157. *Evening Sun,* June 12, 13, 1963.
158. *Ibid.,* March 14, 16, 1964; *Laws of Maryland, Special Session, March 11–14, 1964,* Ch. 29.

expressing the belief that "all Maryland Democrats regret" his candidacy.[159] As the governor's appeal and well-financed campaign progressed, Brewster called Wallace "a bigot and an aspiring dictator" who with a push for his opposition to civil rights measures could become "the leader of a modern inquisition in this country." Wallace drew applause from conservative women at a luncheon in Baltimore and was both cheered and heckled by an audience of 7,000 students at the University of Maryland in College Park. Chaplains at the university arranged an anti-Wallace rally where 4,000 students stood in the rain to listen to Brewster and Senator William Proxmire of Wisconsin. Wallace, contending in his campaign that segregationists were not anti-Negro, said that in trips around the nation he had found millions who "don't call themselves segregationists, but they segregate." At Cambridge Wallace's appearance sparked new protests by black and a few white civil rights marchers. Some of them threw bottles, and national guardsmen using tear gas arrested fourteen, including Mrs. Gloria Richardson, Negro civil rights leader. General George M. Gelston of the state's National Guard, with calm words on a second night of confrontation, persuaded the crowds to disperse. Bishop John Wesley Lord of the Washington area of the Methodist Church said that when Wallace's doctrine of states' rights "is used to perpetuate injustice," the moral law supersedes and that "the civil rights issue supported by our President and Senator Brewster represents an awakening of the American conscience." Senator Edward M. Kennedy lent the magic of his presence for parades in South Baltimore to close the Brewster campaign.[160]

Senator Brewster won the presidential primary, but the strength of the opposition and the slimness of his margin over an outside contender were politically embarrassing to him and appalling to many Maryland leaders. The statewide vote stood at 267,106 for Brewster, 214,849 for Wallace, 20,652 split between an "uninstructed delegation" and a minor candidate from Baltimore. Of all the votes cast, Brewster received 53.1 per cent; Wallace, 42.7 per cent. But Wallace carried seventeen of the twenty-three counties. In the total vote of all counties, how-

159. *Sun,* March 16, 1964.

160. *Washington Post,* May 12–13, 15, 1964; Cambridge *Daily Banner,* May 12, 18, 1964; Salisbury *Times,* May 18, 1964.

ever, Brewster had a lead of 49.8 per cent to Wallace's 47 per cent. In Baltimore City, the Maryland senator received the handsome majority of 59.3 per cent of all votes to 34.9 per cent for Wallace. In addition to the city and a bare margin of 324 votes in his home county of Baltimore, the senator carried only Allegany, Garrett, Washington, Frederick, Montgomery, and Prince George's, all but the last with good majorities.

Other developments in the Democratic primary of 1964 foreshadowed serious problems for management of statewide politics under the aegis of the Tawes administration. For several years there had been little secrecy about the governor's preference that his successor, to be elected in 1966, should be Thomas B. Finan of Cumberland, attorney general by the governor's appointment and by subsequent election. Finan had begun his rise in Democratic politics as a younger associate of the highly esteemed William C. Walsh. Known affectionately as the Red Fox of western Maryland, Walsh had been a power in the state from the days of Albert Cabell Ritchie's governorship. The personable and able Finan early became a stalwart supporter and trusted counselor of Tawes. The road to succession, carefully planned as it had been, was not altogether clear even within the administration. An obvious contender for the office was Comptroller Louis L. Goldstein, an indefatigable campaigner with more personal contact in Maryland and a better memory for names than any other official in its modern history. To meet the delicate problem looming for 1966, Goldstein was persuaded to run in 1964 as the administration candidate for the United States Senate.

Joseph D. Tydings, who had been interested in running even in 1962, decided to contest the 1964 Democratic nomination for the senatorial seat. Stepson of Senator Millard E. Tydings, he had been adopted by the elder Tydings during his service in the Senate. Joe Tydings was young, an effective campaigner —and more. A liberal Democrat, he had served in the House of Delegates and had done yeoman work as a manager of the campaign of John F. Kennedy for president. As Kennedy's appointee to the office of United States attorney, he gained new recognition for his prosecutions, particularly those involving the conduct of officers of some Maryland building and loan associations. Tydings' plans for candidacy were almost openly laid with President Kennedy's tacit blessing; and after the

President's assassination the friendly interest of his brothers Robert and Edward, both in high office, remained evident.[161]

The acrimonious and expensive campaign starred the Tydings adaptation of the Kennedy mode of voter appeal. He relied heavily on television exposure and on volunteers for tea-and-coffee receptions and for manning precincts on election day. Tydings, who had the aura of the young knight in shining armor, openly attacked the Tawes administration—sometimes referring to it as "the Hocker-Tawes machine," a whipping-boy reference to the governor's friend George Hocker, prominent spokesman for the brewing industry. At other times Tydings said that he would "knock the tar out of the Hocker-Tawes-Goldstein machine." He endorsed Senator Brewster as a nominal candidate for president despite Brewster's support of Goldstein. Tydings openly stood as the candidate of the Kennedy New Frontier, Goldstein as the faithful servant of Maryland. Both approved civil rights legislation pending in Congress. Tydings persistently criticized Goldstein for a school-revenue increase in the state income tax, passed by the General Assembly at the governor's urging. Goldstein indignantly pointed out that he had opposed the tax increase, which was repealed at the end of the year—too late to undo its political damage.[162] The outcome of the primary in May was a surprisingly large Tydings victory, 279,564 to 155,086.

Emergence of Senator Barry Goldwater of Arizona as a front-running Republican candidate for the presidential nomination aroused controversy among Maryland Republicans that easily matched state Democratic tensions. Goldwater forces at the state party convention in June were able to elect only a minority of delegates to the national convention. Governor William W. Scranton of Pennsylvania, keynote speaker at the Maryland conclave, announced there his candidacy for president in a last-ditch effort to forestall a Goldwater nomination at San Francisco. The outcry among surprised Goldwater backers was publicly derisive as convention chairman Rogers C. B. Morton subtly pled for order and Congressman Charles McC. Mathias,

161. Hagerstown *Daily Mail*, May 4, 1964.

162. *Ibid.; Washington Post*, May 6, 1964; Salisbury *Times*, May 14, 26, 1964; *Laws of Maryland, 1964*, Ch. 17; *Laws of Maryland, Special Session, November 6, 1964*, Ch. 1.

Jr., introduced Governor Scranton.[163] State Chairman Newton I. Steers, Jr., a classmate and longtime friend of Scranton, had invited him to make the keynote speech but had received no firm response until a telephone call at the eve of the convention.[164] The governor, encouraged by former President Eisenhower to make the plunge, was later cautioned by that often nonpolitical eminence that he could make no public endorsement. Scranton ended his torturing vacillation by making a last-minute presidential bid from a sense of civic duty.

At the Democratic state convention a few days later, Governor Tawes and his friends were in control. They elected House Speaker Marvin Mandel convention chairman by a vote of 130 to forty-one over Alfred L. Scanlan, prominent Montgomery County supporter of Joseph D. Tydings for the Senate. The convention gave the Tydings forces three delegates to the national convention, including the senatorial nominee himself, and one alternate. But the state meeting agreed to Tydings-endorsed resolutions for a state constitutional convention and a party constitution. Governor Tawes and Dr. Mildred Otenasek retained membership in the Democratic National Committee.[165]

Maryland Republicans supporting Scranton for president carried their advocacy to the floor of the national convention. Newton I. Steers, Jr., chairman of the Maryland delegation but acting "as a delegate," moved a resolution to ban seating any delegate elected by discriminatory practices. J. Fife Symington, Jr., of Baltimore County, Goldwater leader in the Maryland delegation, complained that the action would "wreck" unity. The motion, Steers said to reporters, had been suggested by former Ambassador Henry Cabot Lodge to turn delegates from Goldwater as Lodge and other Eisenhower strategists had turned the 1952 convention from Robert A. Taft. Delegates shouted down the Steers ploy. Dr. Milton S. Eisenhower, a member of the delegation, nominated Scranton.[166]

---

163. *Washington Post*, June 13, 1964.

164. Author's memorandum of conversation with Newton I. Steers, Jr., Feb. 18, 1973.

165. Washington *Evening Star*, June 16, 1964.

166. *Ibid.*, July 14, 1964; memorandum of conversation with Steers, Feb. 18, 1973; *Official Report of the Proceedings of the Republican National Convention . . . 1964*, pp. 30-34, 333-36.

Goldwater's nomination was far from popular in Maryland, as in much of the country. Charming and reasonable as the senator from Arizona could be in person, he attained the image in the printed and broadcast media as a conservative who might threaten social security and other domestic programs and perhaps involve the nation in hasty international conflict. The country was in no mood to turn from the New Frontier of the stricken Kennedy and the Great Society envisioned by his successor, Lyndon Johnson. Governor Tawes, in welcoming President Johnson to Baltimore near the end of the campaign, praised his successes "in the war on poverty, in the reduction of the federal income tax. . . . in the expansion of human rights . . . in your firm resolve to assist the emerging nations of the world resist the forces of tyranny. . . . in your determination to prevent nuclear holocaust and to end contamination of the air we breathe and the water we drink."[167] Theodore R. McKeldin, Republican mayor of Baltimore who had twelve years before nominated Eisenhower, endorsed Johnson "to join with him" in "the art of uniting rather than dividing, of reconciling differences rather than aggravating them, of reasoning together rather than plotting against one another from strongholds of isolation."[168]

In the atmosphere of consensus which President Johnson confidently sought in 1964, Democratic victories in Maryland were sizable. The president received the voters' approval in the state by a majority of over 345,000; Goldwater won, by small numbers, only in Dorchester and Garrett Counties. Tydings amassed a majority of more than 276,000 to defeat his Republican opponent, the personally popular J. Glenn Beall, who at seventy sought a third consecutive term in the United States Senate. Republicans managed to hold two seats in Congress: Charles McC. Mathias, Jr., won a third term and Rogers C. B. Morton a second; Mathias by a substantial majority and Morton by a comfortable one. Democrat Carlton R. Sickles, running for reelection to Congress from the state at large, obtained the greatest of the statewide majorities—almost 383,000.

Issues of representation in the General Assembly and of electoral districting, there and for congressional seats, propelled

---

167. Dillon, *op. cit.*, II, 143.
168. *Ibid.*, quoted by Tawes, p. 148.

liberal voices into Maryland politics in the 1960's. They pressed vigorously in the courts their demands for more representation of the burgeoning suburbs, and for more equitable distribution of political power on the basis of population. The Maryland Committee for Fair Representation, under such leaders as Royce Hanson and Alfred L. Scanlan—the latter its attorney at every stage of contest—had notable impact in changing the basis of representation in Maryland and the focus of lawmaking power.

Maryland's legislature in both houses had long followed a principle of a fixed membership from each of the counties and from districts within Baltimore City, with some recognition of population in the structure of the House of Delegates. At the opening of the 1960's Baltimore and the four most populous counties, with 75 per cent of the state's population, had ten of twenty-nine senators and sixty of 123 delegates. The Court of Appeals of Maryland, in defending the structure of the Maryland Senate on the ground that it followed the federal plan for the national Senate,[169] opened the way for appeal to the Supreme Court of the United States. No fully population-based reapportionment proved to be acceptable to the General Assembly pending the outcome of that appeal. In the meantime, however, the state's long-standing county unit system of determining the result of statewide primary elections was in effect reversed by the Supreme Court in a Georgia case.[170] The Maryland case defending its Senate, argued for the appellants by Alfred L. Scanlan and for the state by Robert S. Bourbon, attracted the written support of fourteen attorneys general from other states. The Court, seven to two, held the apportionment of the Maryland Senate invalid, in part because of the "overall representation" in the two houses.[171]

Because of failure of the General Assembly to agree upon a reapportionment plan, Governor Tawes called a special session in October 1965. He urged compliance with the mandate of the

---

169. *Maryland Committee for Fair Representation* v. *Tawes*, 229 Md. 406 (1962).

170. *Gray* v. *Sanders*, 372 U. S. 368 (1963); *Evening Sun*, March 18, 1963.

171. *Maryland Committee for Fair Representation* v. *Tawes*, 377 U. S. 656, 673 (1964). See Robert G. Dixon, Jr., *Democratic Representation: Reapportionment in Law and Politics* (New York: Oxford University Press, 1968), pp. 217-26.

Supreme Court to avoid "the far more distasteful alternative of having the courts apportion our legislature for us."[172] The apportionment finally adopted gave the Senate forty-three instead of twenty-nine members with the house remaining at 142. The law provided for senatorial districts, some of them multi-member, which grouped or subdivided counties.[173] While every county received at least one member of the house, population disparities for representation there and in the Senate were far less than in the past. The smallest percentage of the state's population able to achieve a majority in the Senate was 47.8, and in the House of Delegates 49.5; but house districts departed more sharply from equal population than those for the Senate. The General Assembly took the unusual step of enacting also a preferred alternate plan that would have retained a senator for every county.[174] The Court of Appeals, pointing out that 37 per cent of the state's population could elect a majority of the Senate under the preferred alternate, invalidated that plan. It approved as "honest and sincere" the new apportionment left in effect.[175]

Congressional redistricting, mandated by the courts for equity in representation, embroiled the legislature in the issue of preserving three seats for Baltimore City. A deadlock in 1966 between the legislative chambers, the house for retaining three city seats and the Senate opposed, resulted in no legislation at all. A three-judge federal court consisting of District Judges Roszel C. Thomsen and Edward S. Northrop and Circuit Judge Simon E. Sobeloff, all of them Marylanders, promptly divided the state into eight congressional districts of approximately equal population. They followed a compromise plan to give Baltimore City great weight in three districts by adding precincts in adjacent Baltimore and Anne Arundel Counties. The action also parceled Anne Arundel among three districts. Joseph W. Alton, Jr., widely-known Republican county executive in Anne Arundel, appealed to the Supreme Court of the

172. Dillon, *op. cit.*, II, 39-40.

173. *Laws of Maryland, Special Session, Oct. 11, 1965*, Ch. 2.

174. *Ibid.*, Ch. 3.

175. *Hughes* v. *Maryland Committee for Fair Representation*, 241 Md. 471, 487 (1966).

United States, which in a terse order quickly affirmed the districting.[176]

Revenues for expanding and more costly state and local services were crucial in the closing years of the Tawes administration. The governor remarked in 1965 that the major problems he had faced since taking office in 1959 were "related, in one way or another, to finances." One of the most persistently plaguing problems had been "the complicated interrelationship" of "state and local finances." The state had preempted the lucrative sales and income taxes. Local governments, raising about the same amount of money, were largely dependent on property taxes. The burden was especially heavy on property owners in Baltimore City and on those living near it or in the broad Baltimore-Washington corridor.[177]

Two study commissions, one headed by Dr. Paul D. Cooper, director of the State Fiscal Research Bureau, and a legislative group headed by Senate majority leader Harry R. Hughes of Caroline County, had evolved a Cooper-Hughes plan to raise but graduate the state income tax and to reform business taxes. Designed in part to assure state-aided programs in the face of an estimated deficit of $27.7 million, the proposal went to the legislature with administration backing. Shepherded through the Senate by a single vote, the Cooper-Hughes plan was strangled in the house in the final hours of the 1966 session.[178] The governor, conscious of election-year pressures in the General Assembly against new state taxes, supported a temporary measure enacted in special session permitting Baltimore City or any county to levy an income tax of not more than one per cent.[179] The fiscal approach of the Cooper-Hughes proposals later became the policy of the state, in a new political scene, as the 1967 legislature would demonstrate.[180]

Political negotiations for the gubernatorial election of 1966 were also dramatically chaotic. The long-nurtured hope of Governor Tawes that the Democratic party could unite under the

---

176. *Evening Sun*, April 5–6, May 31, 1966; *Maryland Citizens Committee for Fair Congressional Redistricting* v. *Tawes*, 253 F. Supp. 731 (1966); *Alton* v. *Tawes*, 384 U. S. 315 (1966).

177. Dillon, *op. cit.*, II, 547.

178. *Evening Sun*, March 29, 31, 1966.

179. *Laws of Maryland, Special Session, March 30, 1966*, Ch. 2.

180. *Ibid.*, *1967*, Ch. 142.

middle-of-the-road banner of Attorney General Finan was sure to be challenged. Months earlier, Senator Joseph D. Tydings had encouraged his crusading friends by openly doubting that the party "can avoid a factional fight" in the primary. "I'm not interested in any sort of coalition or harmony ticket."[181] The Democratic primary contest for governor emerged as a four-way one. Finan, with support of many of the long-established organizations, ran on his record as attorney general. His platform advocated larger programs in education, economic development, and highways. The *Sunpapers,* in endorsing him, called his record "thoroughly proven" and his program "intelligent, well-rounded and constructive." Carlton R. Sickles, completing two terms as congressman-at-large and supported by Senator Tydings, assumed the reformer's posture to put "integrity back into state government." Mild and contemplative in person, he campaigned with lashing attacks against the administration and its candidate. Never "ashamed of" his "support from labor," he proposed a "new politics" of ideas and programs welling from the people rather than from a system of "politics as usual." George P. Mahoney, for nearly two decades a spectacular but unsuccessful candidate for high office and again lightly dismissed by the politically unwary, based his vigorous campaign largely against enforced open housing, using the slogan "Your Home Is Your Castle—Protect It." A fourth candidate who, like Mahoney, would draw votes from Finan was Clarence W. Miles, a respected Baltimore attorney and banker living across the Bay in Queen Anne's County. He too proposed change, especially in education, police organization, and taxation, accusing his opponents of avoiding the central issues in state government.[182]

Republican leaders early agreed on Spiro T. Agnew as their candidate for governor. His election as county executive by the voters of Baltimore County in 1962 had placed him in the most important administrative office then held by a Republican in the state or its subdivisions. The feat had been facilitated by a factional fight in the Democratic party. Michael J. Birmingham had reasserted dominance of his party in Baltimore County by defeating Democrat Christian H. Kahl for renomination as

181. *Evening Sun,* Aug. 7, 1965.
182. *Ibid.,* Sept. 2, 6–7, 10, 12, 1966.

county executive. Many of Kahl's workers avidly supported Agnew in an election campaign in which the articulate Republican outshone the debate-reluctant Birmingham. In 1966 Agnew, better known at the time in the Baltimore area than to the public elsewhere in the state, directed his active and widely-televised primary campaign for governor toward voter recognition and response. "Ted Agnew's My Kind of Man" was the theme song of his management; summary of the challenges and issues in developing Maryland's progress was the candidate's personal strategy.

As Agnew swept to victory over nominal Republican opposition in the September gubernatorial primary, Democrats were badly divided. With less than a third of the votes cast for a field of six Democratic candidates, Mahoney won the Democratic primary by 148,446 votes to 146,507 for Sickles, 134,216 for Finan, and 42,304 for Miles. Mahoney secured pluralities in twelve counties and Baltimore City. Finan led in eight counties, Sickles only in Montgomery and Prince George's, and Miles only in Queen Anne's. Without Miles in the race, Finan almost certainly would have been nominated.

Although many liberal and moderate Democrats swiftly repudiated Mahoney as the head of the party ticket, Governor Tawes at the state Democratic convention in October endorsed every nominee. "Loyalty to the Democratic Party I conceive to be an obligation." Democratic United States Senators Brewster and Tydings and Congressman Sickles stayed away from the convention. Some Democrats were pleased with the independent race for governor announced by Hyman A. Pressman, comptroller of Baltimore City, a course of action that worried others because of its potential division of the vote. Agnew called his own campaign a "crusade for conscience," stressing before many audiences that "a vote for Pressman is a vote for Mahoney." Mahoney refused to move from his opposition to open housing legislation. He also sternly advocated law enforcement against violent crime. Agnew favored prohibiting racial discrimination in new apartment and other housing developments but exempting existing dwellings. He pressed urgently for educational development, particularly vocational-technical training, and for tax reform to channel funds to such specific needs as education, welfare, and public health. Mass transportation, crime, and both air and water pollution, he declared, were problems that the state must solve. The stirring issue of the campaign remained the underlying issue of racial and economic discrimination. Mahoney denied that race was involved except, he said, "to protect the Negro." Agnew appealed to "decency, integrity, and responsibility"; the voters must choose between the "flame of righteousness" or "the evil of a fiery cross."[183]

Agnew's election pivoted upon substantial leads in Montgomery County (37,000), Baltimore City (almost 24,000), and Prince George's County (14,000). He carried all of western Maryland plus the Eastern Shore counties of Talbot and Wicomico and Harford County, northeast of Baltimore City. Of the total votes, 455,318 were for Agnew, 373,543 for Mahoney, and 90,899 for Pressman. Mahoney led in thirteen of the counties. Estimates of the ethnic vote gave Agnew over four-fifths of the black portion, a lead over Pressman in the Jewish, and Mahoney heavy majorities among Italians and Slavs.

Democrats were entirely successful with their state ticket for other offices: Louis L. Goldstein for reelection as comptroller and Francis B. Burch of Baltimore City for attorney general. Republicans picked up a third member of Congress with the election of Gilbert Gude in a new district based largely upon Montgomery County. Republicans Mathias and Morton were reelected to Congress, the latter defeating the venerable H. C. Byrd, who had returned to the Chesapeake Bay region of his youth for a final fling in politics. Republicans also increased their membership in the state Senate from seven to eight and held their roster of twenty-five in the House of Delegates. Except for the strains of conflict in the party, Maryland was still basically a Democratic state.

In June 1965 Governor Tawes had appointed a Constitutional Convention Commission of twenty-seven members to study the need for revision of the state constitution, including the desirability of a convention and the nature of appropriate change. He appointed as chairman H. Vernon Eney, highly respected Baltimore attorney, whose diligence and mastery of the subject proved to be phenomenal. Former Governor William Preston Lane, Jr., as honorary chairman, participated actively in the commission's work until his death early in 1967. By September

---

183. *Ibid.*, Oct. 13, 18, 25, 27, 29, 1966.

1965 members of the commission recommended a convention. The legislature of 1966 enacted laws submitting a convention call to the voters and providing for convening it in 1967 if approved.[184] In a special election at the time of the 1966 primary, voters in light balloting on the question sanctioned the convention, 160,280 to 31,680. Baltimore City and every county favored it.

Thereafter the Constitutional Convention Commission completed a draft constitution, with detailed studies, destined to be of great influence in the work of the convention. The commission also prepared enabling legislation for the convention, duly enacted with modifications by the legislature in 1967 and approved by Governor Agnew. The commission's draft envisioned a modernized basic law strengthening the Declaration of Rights, liberalizing residence requirements for voters, continuing a bicameral legislature but with automatic reapportionment, increasing the power of the governor as administrator, arranging the courts of the state in a four-tiered system, allowing Baltimore City and the counties all powers not denied by law, and prohibiting public local laws by the General Assembly for particular counties or municipalities.[185]

Another study group, appointed by Governor Tawes in the summer of 1966, also to have impact in subsequent times, was the Commission for the Modernization of the Executive Branch of the Maryland Government. Its chairman, John N. Curlett, president of Baltimore's famous condiment-distributing firm, McCormick and Company, had been active in many civic enterprises, including the chairmanship of the City Board of School Commissioners. Dr. Francis E. Rourke of The Johns Hopkins University served as vice chairman and Dr. Jean E. Spencer of the Bureau of Governmental Research at the University of Maryland as staff director. The commission proposed that the governor be given a much-needed initiative in administrative reorganization of Maryland's state government. His office, it recommended as a first step, should be staffed with program coordinators to "assure effective executive leadership"

184. *Laws of Maryland, 1966*, Chs. 500, 501.

185. *Report of the Constitutional Convention Commission* (Annapolis: State of Maryland, 1967), pp. 19-23, 69-93 *et seq.;* see also *Constitutional Revision Study Documents of the Constitutional Convention Commission of Maryland* (Annapolis: State of Maryland, 1968).

and "full and timely communication" between the governor and the units of the executive branch and also among them.[186]

In the second Tawes administration, higher education in Maryland saw both new directions and great expansion. The University of Maryland became the tenth largest in the nation. Its Catonsville campus, the University of Maryland Baltimore County, opened in 1966. The state made notable investments in construction there, in such examples as the Tawes Fine Arts Center at College Park, the new university law school building and additions to the University Hospital in Baltimore, and in the state college system. In 1963 the legislature, following the advice of a commission on higher education under the chairmanship of John N. Curlett, created a loosely-structured tripartite system. University governance continued under its regents. The five teachers' colleges became state colleges under a separate board, with plans later developed to add liberal arts programs and with provision for Morgan State College to join the system. Community colleges remained under local boards of education. The same statute created an Advisory Council for Higher Education, of which Wesley N. Dorn became director, to study the development and coordination of the state system of public higher education.[187] In the fall of 1965 the state's public institutions of higher learning enrolled 40,786 full-time undergraduates, plus more than 17,000 part-time. The State Department of Education estimated that over 35 per cent of Maryland's high school graduates in 1966 went on to college. During the two terms of Governor Tawes, over $6 million of state aid for laboratories, libraries, and other facilities went to private collegiate institutions: Hood, Johns Hopkins, Loyola, Mount St. Mary's, Notre Dame, St. John's, St. Joseph, Washington, and Western Maryland.[188]

Public school systems also received substantial increases in state aid.[189] By 1965 Maryland ranked ninth in the country in the average of teachers' salaries. The legislature authorized

---

186. *Modernizing the Executive Branch of the Maryland Government* (Baltimore: Report of the Commission for the Modernization of the Executive Branch of the Maryland Government, 1967), pp. 3, 6.

187. *Laws of Maryland, 1963*, Ch. 41. The Advisory Council later became the Maryland Council for Higher Education with powers gradually enlarged.

188. J. Millard Tawes, *Governor's Report to the People, 1959–1966*, pp. 8, 12.

189. *Laws of Maryland, 1964*, Ch. 17.

state bonded indebtedness of $10 million to supplement local financing and equipment for vocational schools.[190] Later it approved educational television for schools, with an initial appropriation of $757,000.[191] By the end of 1965 the state had distributed in seven years $84.8 million for elementary and secondary school construction.[192]

About 1,500 miles of new roads were completed in the Tawes terms in the governorship. In the second term the Northeast Expressway, a toll road dedicated by President Kennedy in 1963 and renamed for him shortly after his death, opened to traffic from the Baltimore Harbor Tunnel to the Delaware line. Governor Tawes opened the Capital Beltway in 1964, a year ahead of schedule. It was destined to become a main street of the Maryland suburbs of Washington, moving light industry and business to Prince George's and Montgomery Counties. Road mileage in the state in 1965 was 23,092 (19,442 paved); railroad track mileage, 2,000.

Traffic congestion at peak hours on the Chesapeake Bay Bridge led Governor Tawes to favor a parallel structure adjacent to the existing bridge from Sandy Point to Kent Island. He believed, despite assurances of "full legal authority" already available, that "an undertaking of such far-reaching importance" should be submitted again to the General Assembly. Influential leaders, in the Baltimore area particularly, with Congressman Clarence D. Long one of the most vocal, contended that a new bridge should be in the northern area of the Bay nearer Baltimore. Some support arose for a southern crossing, probably the most expensive. The General Assembly of 1965 rejected the governor's proposals, but in 1966, with the clear understanding that a parallel bridge would have priority, enacted a measure giving the State Roads Commission authority to construct bridges, tunnels, and motorways, the costs to be repaid from tolls. Tawes remarked that he knew of no other law that had generated so much dissension, misinformation, or conscious distortion.[193] It was petitioned to referendum and rejected at the polls in 1966 by 40,000 votes, Baltimore City and

---

190. *Ibid.*, 1965, Ch. 740.
191. *Ibid.*, 1966, Chs. 202, 138 at p. 276.
192. Tawes, *op. cit.*, pp. 7-8.
193. *Laws of Maryland, 1966*, Ch. 517; Dillon, *op. cit.*, pp. 325-26.

Baltimore County producing enormous majorities against it. The setback was short-lived, for the General Assembly in 1967 enacted a statute approved by Governor Agnew authorizing all three Bay crossings and another Baltimore harbor tunnel. That law, with the requisite three-fifths majorities, passed as an emergency measure to exempt it from referendum. Agnew called it "legislation which will bring order out of chaos" and place authority for planning toll structures "where it rightfully belongs—in our State Roads Commission."[194]

The economy of the state and its people continued to be sound. In 1966 Maryland's unemployment rate dipped to 2.9 per cent in comparison with a national average of 3.8 per cent. There were 55,000 employers in the state and nearly 1.3 million jobholders exclusive of federal workers. Of thirty-seven American corporations netting in 1965 $100 million or more, twenty-two had major facilities in Maryland. Agriculture required larger inputs of capital and less of labor than in the past. Gross cash sales from farms reached $321 million in 1965. Poultry and milk accounted for more than half of the gross sales. In the same year farmers produced, with newer scientific methods, thirty-seven million bushels of corn on 501,000 acres, an average yield per acre of seventy-four bushels. Seven years before, comparable figures for corn were twenty-two and one-half million bushels from 413,000 acres, an average of fifty-four and one-half bushels.[195] Tobacco, livestock, wheat, oats, barley, soybeans, hay, apples, and sweet potatoes were other examples of important agricultural production. Mineral production reached a value of $78 million in 1965, the principal tonnage coming from sand and gravel, stone, coal, clays, and lime. Natural gas extraction was 408 million cubic feet. The commercial catch of fisheries was 86.6 million pounds worth $13.2 million. Leading species were blue crabs, oysters, clams, and menhaden. Oysters were worth almost half of the commercial value.

The greatest economic productivity came from manufacturing, $3.3 billion in added value, much of it centered in the Baltimore area. Principal activity was in primary metals, machinery, transportation equipment, and food products.

---

194. *Laws of Maryland, 1967*, Ch. 387; Governor's Statement on Signing House Bill 348, April 21, 1967.
195. Tawes, *op. cit.*, p. 23; Dillon, *op. cit.*, pp. 74-75, 209.

Waterborne commerce was directly related to the livelihood of half a million Marylanders. The Bethlehem Steel Company at Sparrows Point, one of the largest in the world, employed 30,000 of them in producing annually nine million tons of steel from cargoes of iron ore from Venezuela and in constructing tankers and merchantmen at Bethlehem's nearby shipbuilding yard. The American Sugar Company's plant, another of the world's largest, refined raw sugar imported by ship. Other parts of the state depended also on such commerce: packers near the Bay in Dorchester County upon tuna brought by refrigerated ships; brush and button factories in Frederick and Washington Counties upon bristles from India and the Far East and shell and coral from the Caribbean; coal miners in the western mountains; the Celanese Corporation of America at Cumberland, and the Mack Truck Company at Hagerstown upon overseas markets for part of their products.[196]

For a quarter of a century, Governor Tawes remarked in 1964, three basic problems had confronted the Eastern Shore: "decline of the commercial fishing industry, isolation from the mainland, and a lack of a trained and highly motivated labor force." Isolation had been partly removed. He hoped that the Wye Institute, set up by Arthur Amory Houghton, Jr., and Clarence W. Miles to use private funds for the cultural and economic development of the nine counties of the Eastern Shore, could join in cooperative planning with the state, its citizens, and such organizations as the Delmarva Advisory Council, comprised of members from Maryland, Delaware, and Virginia. The governor was deeply interested in plans for regional development, and by 1965 was proud to list such activity in every section of the state: the interstate Delmarva Advisory Council, the Tri-County Council for Southern Maryland, a western Maryland development organization, and the shift from "development" to "orderly growth" in central Maryland through the work of the Maryland-National Capital Park and Planning Commission and the Baltimore Regional Planning Council.[197]

To Tawes the Chesapeake Bay and its region were always a source of special pride, though never an exclusive interest. The

---

196. Dillon, *op. cit.*, pp. 222-23.
197. *Ibid.*, pp. 189-91, 194-97.

first governor from the Eastern Shore in nearly forty years, he was especially pleased that by 1966 state programs to replenish natural resources of the Bay had restored Maryland to national leadership in oyster production. From 1961 the state had invested more than a million dollars annually in the conservation effort. No less than Baltimore's plans to develop and rebuild its inner harbor, interstate proposals to conserve the Potomac River Basin and the watershed of the Susquehanna held promise for the economic growth of the state. In the same spirit of progress Cambridge developed a new deepwater port.[198]

Preservation of natural resources went hand in hand with measures for public health and recreation. The State Department of Health received authority to help communities plan sewage facilities, with state loans and grants supplementing available federal funds. The Department of Water Resources, evolving from a commission in 1964, assumed control of industrial pollution of streams and also broader responsibility for developing and controlling water resources. The state moved rapidly to abate pollution from detergents, particularly important in view of their greater use by a rapidly expanding population. Water consumption grew in the 1960's from 600 to 800 million gallons per day. In the field of health the state modernized and enlarged public facilities and personnel, including five non-profit nursing homes financed by $5 million in bonds to match federal grants. The number of persons treated annually in the state's mental hospitals rose by a quarter in seven years, but new therapeutic procedures shortened periods of hospitalization and decreased the number of resident patients.[199]

In eight years the number of state parks doubled, from seventeen to thirty-four, with acreage more than doubling to 38,000. Users of the recreational facilities rose from one and three-tenths million to three million. Part of Assateague Island, with two miles of state-owned ocean frontage, linked in 1964 by a 1,640-foot bridge to the mainland of Worcester County, became a state park in 1965, while another portion became a national park. The state acted to replace two miles of barrier dunes and made plans to spend more than $7 million for recreational

198. Tawes, *op. cit.*, pp. 33, 39-40; Dillon, *op. cit.*, pp. 198, 206, 436, 440.
199. Tawes, *op. cit.*, pp. 31-32, 43-48.

facilities in the miles of golden sand and surf.[200] Conservationists hailed the actions as a great victory in saving an ir-
replaceable natural resource from commercial development.

Forests, most of them hardwood, stood on 43 per cent of
Maryland's total land area of 9,891 square miles. Over 90 per
cent of the forest lands were under private ownership. Nearly
200 sawmills in the state cut annually an estimated 188 million
board feet of lumber. Forest fires had mounted in the state, 652
of them in 1965 burning an area of 2,632 acres. Careless smoking accounted for more than a third of the fires, with lightning
the source of only seven.[201]

Maryland's population growth from 1960 to 1965 (13.5 per
cent) ranked fifth among the states. Construction was the hall-
mark of suburbia. New communities such as Joppatowne in
Harford County, the Levitt-built Belair section of Bowie in
Prince George's, Crofton in Anne Arundel, and the Montgomery Village area of Gaithersburg sprang up to meet the needs of
commuters and of others who found local employment. With
the complexities of suburban living came a new upsurge of
civic involvement and organization, particularly in Montgomery County, where it had been an increasingly prominent part
of the local scene from the end of World War II.

Especially notable was the development of Columbia in
Howard County, a planned "new town" thirty miles from
downtown Washington but closer to Baltimore City. Conceived
by James W. Rouse, Baltimore financier and builder born and
reared near Easton, the design for Columbia envisioned a
multi-purpose community with gradual growth to about 100,000
population with 30,000 jobs for some 31,000 houses and apart-
ments. Rouse had built Baltimore's residential and commercial
Cross Keys area, the Mondawmin shopping center, and the enclosed Harundale shopping mall nine miles from the city on the
highway to Annapolis.[202]

Announced as a project in 1963, Columbia moved forward to
an early success. Of its planned 18,000 acres, 3,200 were reserved for parks, playgrounds, golf courses, lakes, and woods.

200. *Ibid.*, pp. 34-36; Dillon, *op. cit.*, pp. 121-24.

201. *Maryland Statistical Abstract* (Annapolis: State Department of Economic Development, 1967), pp. 10, 123-27.

202. Gurney Breckenfeld, *Columbia and the New Cities* (New York: Ives
Washburn, Inc., 1971), pp. 173, 181, 211-14.

From the outset, its population was economically and racially diversified, predominantly middle class with about 15 per cent of its residents black. Opened in 1967 with the first of many concerts by the National Symphony Orchestra in the town's $1 million Merriweather Post Pavilion of Music, Columbia quickly exceeded expectations in sales and rentals. Various businesses and industries also moved to Columbia. Within a few years a new plant of the General Electric Company was employing several thousand workers. Population had grown to about 25,000 early in 1973. The new town by that time enjoyed downtown office buildings, a shopping mall, restaurants, and theaters. One of the seven projected village clusters, Wilde Lake, was complete, and three others were nearly so.[203]

Suburbia felt also the throbbing bustle of the federal government, pushing outward from Washington in company with corporate business—and even to Baltimore—along multi-laned ribbons of highway. Among the nationally famous federal installations in the Washington suburbs were the National Institutes of Health, the Bethesda Naval Medical Center, the Atomic Energy Commission, the Goddard Space Flight Center, and the Agricultural Research Center. The Social Security Administration's great complex was similarly a landmark in Baltimore's environs. Fort George G. Meade, 13,000-acre headquarters of the First Army, had long been important to the defense of Washington, as was the large Andrews Air Force Base. Defense installations in Maryland ranged from the Aberdeen Proving Ground (nearly 75,000 acres) and Edgewood Arsenal in Harford County to the Patuxent Naval Air Test Center in St. Mary's and the Naval Propellant Plant in Charles. The Naval Academy at Annapolis was still one of the first features of Maryland in national symbolism. Historic Fort McHenry, periodically saved from plans to flank it with highways over the harbor of Baltimore, was the chief of the Maryland shrines under the custody of the National Park Service. Federally-owned installations in the state, 304 of them in 1966, included 187,000 acres and 12,000 buildings with a total value of $1.6 billion. While the number of federal holdings had increased by

---

203. *Ibid.,* pp. 172-73, 193, 277; Washington *Sunday Star and Daily News,* April 8, 1973.

forty-four in a decade, federal land had diminished by more than 40,000 acres.[204]

With Baltimore's port ranking third in the country in combined import-export tonnage—outpaced only by New York and Norfolk[205]—the Maryland Port Authority in 1965 laid plans to dredge the shipping channel to forty-five feet and to build a World Trade Center and improved marine facilities at the city's waterfront. For seven weeks in the spring of that year Baltimore's leading newspapers suspended publication because of a strike, led by the American Newspaper Guild, for higher wages and a union shop. News coverage returned to the city upon agreement to arbitrate the issues. In the spring of 1966 the Congress of Racial Equality made Baltimore a "target" for demonstrations against racial discrimination in housing and services. As a result the Downtown Apartment House Association agreed to a policy of open occupancy, a change that the city council had earlier refused to enforce by ordinance. In the fall election Marylanders in Baltimore and in all the counties but Garrett approved a constitutional amendment to reduce the appellate burden of the state's highest court by authorizing intermediate courts of appeal. But no event of the year won more enthusiastic acclaim than the baseball record of the Baltimore Orioles, their first World Series victory—a four-game sweep over the Los Angeles Dodgers.

## 6

### AGNEW: FISCAL REFORM AND SOCIAL TENSION

Spiro T. Agnew, destined to attain more national notice in the course of his subsequent career than any other modern governor before him, came to office at a time of continuing economic growth coupled with great demand for change. "This change, if order is to prevail," he remarked, "cannot go unguided." He hoped to move "the rising and often healthful discontent" from "the morasses of chaos and into the channels of constructive change." He hoped for a "new alliance," without labels, for "people, principle, progress."[206] He had the good sense to rec-

---

204. *Maryland Statistical Abstract, op. cit.*, p. 160.

205. *Ibid.*, p. 104.

206. Inaugural Address, Jan. 25, 1967. Cited addresses and other statements by Governor Agnew are chronologically arranged in the state's forthcoming publication of his gubernatorial papers; quotations are from the galleys.

ognize that to make progress as a Republican governor he must work with colleagues in office, Democrats in control of lawmaking policy and also of administrative decisions by the powerful three-member Board of Public Works that he headed. Weeks before his inauguration he appointed, after agreement with Senate President William S. James and House Speaker Marvin Mandel, a legislative committee on tax reform, "the most critical problem facing the State of Maryland at this moment." Majority Leader Harry R. Hughes of the Senate, experienced drafter of tax legislation, served as chairman with House Minority Leader J. Glenn Beall, Jr. as vice chairman.[207]

Tax reform was the centerpiece of the General Assembly's accomplishment in 1967. Designed to reduce the burden of the local property tax in the counties, the new law graduated the state income tax to 5 per cent and permitted each county and the city of Baltimore to levy, for state collection and rebate, an additional income tax up to half of the taxpayer's payment to the state. Baltimore City's earnings tax, tried for a year, was eliminated. The state would also receive more money for specified grants to local governments, for its own expanded services, and to pay to its employees salaries more nearly competitive with private industry.[208]

There were other notable achievements of the first legislative session after full reapportionment, a record that the *Evening Sun* called "one of the most successful within memory." New faces and voices in the General Assembly added strength to the support for change. New or extended programs were numerous, among them laws on air quality, strip mining control and reforestation, water pollution and sewage treatment, driver education and traffic safety, and cultural-educational television. Enacted also were laws for open-occupancy housing, extension of open public accommodations, a division of consumer protection, revolving credit and second mortgage regulations, and repeal of legal barriers to interracial marriage.[209] Governor Agnew was quick to give credit for constructive cooperation to legislative leaders of both parties. He praised in particular the

207. Statement as Governor-Elect on Appointment of Bipartisan Legislative Committee on Tax Reform, Dec. 7, 1966.
208. *Laws of Maryland, 1967,* Ch. 142; Spiro T. Agnew, "120 Million Dollar Question," A Special Program on Tax Reform, WJZ-TV, Baltimore, March 16, 1967.
209. *Evening Sun,* March 29, 1967.

"firm hand on the tiller" of Speaker Marvin Mandel, who had "squelched" signs of rebellion in the house "between puffs on his meerschaum."[210]

The governor was a lawyer, like Speaker Mandel and Senate President James, but his own experience as a governmental official had been in Baltimore County. Not steeped in the details of state administration but, gifted with insight for summary, he was quick to learn. He early created within his office a Task Force on Modern Management to analyze operations of state programs. He also established, in accord with the Curlett Commission report to Governor Tawes in 1967 and with budgetary approval from the legislature, six program executives in the governor's office to improve administrative communication.

A tugboat strike in Baltimore, continuing for many weeks, engaged the governor's active participation in a settlement for the "economic health" of the port. He called it "one of the longest and most frustrating labor disputes in my memory."[211] Other union pressures in Baltimore less directly involved the state but had far-ranging impact. Noteworthy was the victory of the aggressive Baltimore Teachers Union, in a representation election, over the Baltimore Public School Teachers Association. The latter had persuaded the National Education Association to invoke partial national sanctions against the city schools, warning of deterioration of the system from lack of financial support. The city school budget adopted for the following fiscal year, 1968, showed a record increase of 25.4 per cent.

Escalation in 1967 of America's role in the Vietnam War contributed to the rise of social and political tensions, as it was to do for another half decade. More American servicemen, many of them drafted, died in 1967 than in the preceding six years of the war. National war expenditures ran at the rate of $2 billion a month. The nation, and Maryland too, saw growing division between the "hawks" who supported and the "doves" who opposed the war. Governor Agnew, believing that he had made progress in human relations legislation and in "changing . . . the attitudes of many people who were very much opposed to any

210. Remarks upon B'nai B'rith Man-of-the-Year Award to Marvin Mandel, Pikesville, May 10, 1967.

211. Statement of Agreements, Baltimore Tugboat Strike, April 13, 1967.

sort of step," decried as "grave violence" to the civil rights movement the view of many of its national leaders that the war effort involved racial discrimination at home and in Asia. Holding that only the fullest information, which he did not have, could justify disagreement with the President's war policy, the governor gave his full support "until someone shows me that what he's doing is not the proper solution."[212]

To discuss "progress to afford equal rights for all our citizens" the governor held in July a conference in Annapolis with Roy Wilkins, executive director of the National Association for the Advancement of Colored People, who said that he came as a "supplementary," not "an alternative" voice "of the Negro citizens of Maryland." The governor and his guest talked about needs for education, jobs, housing, and the "entire spectrum" of "civil opportunity" for all citizens. Both leaders pointed out that the meeting had been planned weeks before racial riots in New Jersey. Both praised the work of Mrs. Juanita Jackson Mitchell, head of the NAACP in Maryland, the governor saying "I can't blame her for wanting to see the achievement immediately."[213]

In less than a week rioting exploded in Cambridge after a militant speech by black activist H. Rap Brown, national chairman of the Student Nonviolent Coordinating Committee. Burning and looting destroyed largely Negro-occupied homes, businesses, a school, and a church. The governor at once sent 600 National Guardsmen and stimulated organization of a biracial commission to provide relief for victims and to study long-range causes of trouble in which Negro militants had participated. Agnew denounced Brown in such strong terms that leaders of the Congress of Racial Equality in turn criticized the governor. In a broad policy statement emphasizing the importance of breaking "the senseless and artificial barriers of racial discrimination" and of constructive problem solving, the governor declared that in Maryland "rioting or inciting to riot, no matter what wrong is said to be the cause, will not be tolerated" and that any person "inciting to riot" would be arrested and not allowed "to finish his vicious speech." Soon thereafter the governor, noting "widely misunderstood" meaning, wrote Superin-

---

212. News conferences, April 25, Sept. 14, 1967.
213. Transcript of Joint Press Conference, July 19, 1967.

Maryland Historical Society, showing the older part of the Keyser Building (left) and Thomas and Hugg Memorial Building (with flags over front entrance) which opened in October 1967. *M.H.S.*

tendent Robert J. Lally of the Maryland State Police, "It was never my intention to impose any type of 'prior restraint' on the speech of anyone. . . . It is only in cases where a 'clear and present danger' of violence is present that the speech should be interrupted."[214]

Fears that violence would spread to Baltimore City proved to be unfounded. The state committed $480,000 to a crash summer employment program. Over 2,000 permanent-type jobs became available, more than half of them provided by private industry. In addition, 1,150 youths worked in a temporary cleanup program.[215] The city council approved self-help programs planned by residents in poverty areas to provide landlord-tenant councils, faster refuse collection, community sanitation inspectors, and rental of home-repair tools. Improvements in Charles Center continued with the opening of the seventeen-story Federal Building, the Morris Mechanic Theater for stage productions, a new hotel, and twin-tower high-rise apartments. Work began on the southern end of the north-south Jones Falls Expressway, leading from the beltway to the central city. Development of inner harbor building projects also began. The Maryland Historical Society dedicated in October its expanded headquarters, the new three-story Thomas and Hugg Memorial Building erected from bequests of about $3 million. The second building, adjacent to the now less crowded H. Irving Keyser Building (the older part once the home of Baltimore benefactor Enoch Pratt), was in many respects a monument to the perseverance and sagacity of former Senator George L. Radcliffe in his long service as president of the society, to James W. Foster, long its director, and to Harold R. Manakee, then serving as director.[216]

The Supreme Court of the United States, by a vote of six to three in November, invalidated the state's employee loyalty oath stemming from the Ober Law of 1949, declaring it unconstitutionally vague. Governor Agnew remarked that the law's

---

214. *Evening Sun*, July 25, 1967; Governor's Statement on Destruction in Cambridge, July 25, 1967; News Conference, July 26, 1967; Statement on Civil Rights and Rioting, July 30, 1967; Letter [to Governor Nelson A. Rockefeller of New York] on Civil Rights and Opportunity, Aug. 1, 1967; Letter on Enforcing Laws Against Inciting to Riot, Aug. 21, 1967.

215. Governor's News Conference, Oct. 10, 1967.

216. *New York Times*, Oct. 15, 1967.

purpose is "laudable" but that in practice, with no successful prosecution based on it in eighteen years, "it doesn't seem to do anything but inflame people." The best safeguard, he thought, is investigation of the backgrounds of applicants, because "it's what a person is and not what he claims to be that we're interested in."[217]

Baltimore's voters gave the city an all-Democratic group of elected officials after a campaign marked chiefly by charges, hotly denied, of discrimination against Negroes in building a citywide slate of party candidates. Thomas D'Alesandro III won the mayoralty with a record landslide vote to fill the office which his father had held for three terms, 1947–1959. Mayor McKeldin, undoubtedly sensing the political climate, had prudently decided not to run for reelection. With the new mayor the voters elected his primary running mates: William D. Schaefer for council president and Hyman A. Pressman, safely back in the Democratic fold, reelected comptroller. Loans approved at the polls included funds for urban renewal projects, Friendship Airport improvements, off-street parking, playfields, parks, and (with the largest vote) new school construction.[218]

Governor Agnew gave much thought to problems of poverty in cities and to means of financing and administering remedies. His became a national voice, especially among governors, for action. In Maryland the problem, a multiple rather than a single one, "means first the problem of Baltimore; but it is also the problem of Cambridge, Salisbury and Hagerstown; of Frederick, Annapolis and Cumberland." Like many others in both major political parties, he deplored "the plethora of federal programs sponsored without evaluation or coordination, and without any attempt to assure continuity." Seed money "for a particular anti-poverty program" he called "purposeless" without some program dependability. Agnew suggested the possibility of transferring responsibility for welfare programs to the federal government, with uniform standards and benefits, to reduce dislocations of the financially desperate and to stem "the flow of untrained, unemployed and impoverished to the cities." He had high hopes for "compensatory education for the inner city child," for vocational training as "the key to rehabili-

217. *Evening Sun*, Nov. 6, 1967; Governor's News Conference, Nov. 8, 1967.
218. *Sun*, Sept. 1, 6–8, 1967; *Evening Sun*, Nov. 8, 1967.

tation," for coordinated cooperation among levels of government, and most of all for private investment in social development for the common good.[219]

The long-awaited Constitutional Convention of Maryland began its regular sessions in Annapolis on September 12, 1967. Its 142 members had been elected in nonpartisan balloting on June 13 in the districts for, and in number equal to, members of the House of Delegates. More than half of the convention delegates were lawyers, 65 per cent held professional degrees, a majority of them were Protestants, and more than a third had no previous political experience. Former Governor Tawes had been elected from Somerset County without opposition. Fifteen delegates had served as judges (two of them were sitting circuit judges), eleven were incumbent state legislators (three senators and eight delegates) and twenty-two were former legislators, three had been in Congress (including former Senator J. Glenn Beall), nineteen were women. The newly-elected delegates had met in June for seminars at Goucher College and had convened for a day in July to adopt rules and elect officers: J. Millard Tawes, honorary president; H. Vernon Eney, president; Senator James Clark of Howard County, first vice president; Senator William S. James, Harford, second vice president.[220] Austere only at first impression, Eney was a master of legal detail and scrupulously fair. His hand more than any other was the guiding one in the convention.

Like the proposals of the Constitutional Convention Commission, the product of the convention—although differing in many details—attempted to modernize the basic law of Maryland by increasing citizen control of the state, assuring representativeness and greater effectiveness of the legislature, strengthening the administrative authority of the governor, and creating a four-tiered, unified, professionalized court system. The document submitted to the people proposed lowering the voting age from twenty-one to nineteen and reducing residency requirements; requiring single-member legislative districts,

219. Address to Maryland Manufacturers' Association, Baltimore, Nov. 17, 1967.

220. John P. Wheeler, Jr., and Melissa Kinsey, *Magnificent Failure: The Maryland Constitutional Convention of 1967–1968* (New York: National Municipal League, 1970), pp. 29-40; *Journal of the Constitutional Convention of Maryland of 1967–1968* (Annapolis: Constitutional Convention, 1968), pp. 15-20. The author was a delegate to the Maryland Constitutional Convention. eds.

three of them for elections to the House of Delegates within one for the Senate; lengthening annual legislative sessions and permitting extensions; requiring county home rule and limiting the long-exercised power of the legislature to pass laws of strictly local application; and providing that no person be subject to discrimination by the state because of race, color, religion, or national origin.[221] Politically significant divisions in the convention developed over such issues as proposed retention of the elective office of comptroller with greatly reduced powers, single-member legislative districts, judicial reorganization, local and regional government (including removal of constitutional status for some county offices), and omission by close votes of a guaranty for organizing and collective bargaining rights of labor.[222]

Defeat of the proposed constitution in a special election on May 14, 1968, by 56.4 per cent of the vote in a surprisingly large turnout came as a shock to many of the state's leaders. Ratification of the document had been endorsed by Governor Agnew, former Governors Tawes and McKeldin, the attorney general, both United States senators, seven of the eight Congressmen, a large majority of state legislators, the leadership of the state bar, the metropolitan press, and a host of civic and religious leaders. Only Montgomery and Prince George's Counties returned ratifying majorities. A computer-aided analysis of Baltimore City and six counties (but including 80 per cent of the vote in the referendum) suggested that a combination of rural voters, Baltimore-area suburbanites, and middle class white residents of Baltimore brought about the defeat. Precincts which had supported George Wallace of Alabama for president and George P. Mahoney for governor voted the strongest opposition to constitutional change. Seeing opportunity for political and economic reform, black voters in Baltimore City and voters in the upper levels of education or income, particularly in the Washington suburbs, gave the greatest endorsement.[223]

---

221. *Comparison of Present and Proposed Constitutions* (Annapolis: Constitutional Convention, 1968). Transcripts of Convention debates, over 14,000 pages, are in major libraries of the state.

222. See Marianne Ellis Alexander, "The Issues and Politics of the Maryland Constitutional Convention, 1967–1968" (Ph.D. dissertation, University of Maryland, 1972).

223. Robert D. Loevy, "Vote Analysis Made of Maryland Defeat," *National*

Many Marylanders voted only their fears. Opponents of constitutional change argued that governmental costs and resulting taxes would soar upwards of $150 million, and more sober analysis had little effect. Leaders of Save Our State saw democracy threatened by stronger executive and judicial organization. Dale Anderson and Joseph W. Alton, Jr., respectively the influential Democratic and Republican executives in Baltimore and Anne Arundel Counties, said that regional governments, more restricted in the proposed constitution than in the old, could consolidate their suburban counties with Baltimore City. Race was also an element of attack; charges were leveled that Negro voters in the District of Columbia could enter Maryland elections and that others in Baltimore City could annex all or part of Baltimore County. In Baltimore City before election day sound trucks moved along the streets of low-income white neighborhoods, blaring that the old constitution meant "white power."[224] In reality, political organizations and local officials had no desire to alter their bases of power. The civic-minded framers of a new constitution had failed to sense political reality and to build popular support. Governor Agnew commented to the southern governors that states considering a new constitution should not submit it for ratification as a single document. Moreover, he added, advance samples of public opinion should be used to identify the fears of the people.[225]

Legislative output in 1968, following on the heels of the departing Constitutional Convention, elicited restrained praise. Called productive by the governor and modestly so by the press, the work of the session suffered from plain evidences of a tight budget and the usual distractions of an election year. An outstanding accomplishment was passage of the governor's comprehensive water pollution control program. A new law, one of the more liberal in the country, permitted physicians to

*Civic Review*, LVII (Nov., 1968), 519-522, and his "The Constitutional Referendum in Maryland" in Wheeler and Kinsey, *op. cit.*, pp. 229-39.

224. Howard R. Penniman, "The Constitutional Convention as a Device for Legislative Change," in Donald G. Herzberg and Alan Rosenthal, eds., *Strengthening the States* (Garden City, N. Y.: Doubleday and Co., 1971), pp. 205-14; Wheeler and Kinsey, *op. cit.*, pp. 1-7, 191-212.

225. Summary, The Southern Governors' Conference, Charleston, S. C., June 16–19, 1968 (Chicago: Council of State Governments, mimeo., n. d.), pp. 11-12. For substantive criticism by a convention delegate, see Thomas G. Pullen, Jr., "Why the Proposed Maryland Constitution Was Not Approved," *William and Mary Law Review* X, No. 2, Winter 1968, 378-92.

perform abortions in hospitals to protect the mother's health, to prevent birth of a gravely retarded child, or because of rape. Another statute created a Criminal Injuries Compensation Board to award state payments to victims of crime. Recognizing rapid growth of community colleges throughout the state in number and in enrollments, the legislature established a State Board for Community Colleges and authorized appointment of college boards separate from school boards in the counties or Baltimore City. The administration's highway bills to increase program revenues from higher registration fees for motor vehicles and to create a revolving fund for advance purchase of rights of way, both recommended by a governor's commission headed by Robert Redding of Montgomery County, easily received approval. Lawmakers revised business taxes and lending laws, permitting interest of 8 per cent on mortgage loans. They also tightened regulation of contributions and expenditures in political campaigns; but they lifted a sixty-year ban on campaign gifts by corporations, limiting individual or corporate contributions to $2,500.[226] Legislators buried bills to create a public authority for mass transit in the Baltimore area, to bring liquor and election boards under the merit system, and to increase racetrack payments to the state.[227]

Unrest among students on college campuses, a national collegiate development as the Vietnam war continued to accelerate, reached acute proportions in Maryland at Bowie State College in the spring of 1968. Dr. Samuel L. Myers, president of the predominantly Negro institution, called the situation "intolerable" as students led by "hard core professionals" from off campus blocked faculty and administrators from entry. Governor Agnew, saying that although there were no doubt "legitimate grievances" about college facilities, he would not yield to "demands and threats of those who would take matters in their own hands." He sent state police to control the campus and, as disturbances continued, temporarily closed the college, "a very hard decision" made in dealing with "young people who confused provocation with principle."[228] A student meeting with

226. *Laws of Maryland, 1968*, Chs. 446–48, 452, 454–55, 470, 613.

227. *Evening Sun*, March 27, 1968.

228. *Ibid.*, March 30, 1968; Governor's Statement on Bowie State College, March 30, 1968; news conferences, March 30, April 4, 1968.

the governor alleviated later demonstrations at Maryland State College at Princess Anne.[229]

Rioting, looting, and burning struck Baltimore April 6–9, as in many other American cities, after the assassination of Dr. Martin Luther King, Jr., civil rights leader, in Memphis on April 4. Six persons were killed in Baltimore, and conservative estimates of property damage ran to $14 million. Police, the National Guard, and army troops under the command of Lieutenant General Robert H. York, with a policy of avoiding shooting, prevented serious black-white confrontation. Governor Agnew had requested the aid of federal troops. In the light of the times he had also announced his support of the national open-housing law soon to be enacted by Congress.[230]

Characteristically taking his own counsel and stating his convictions without diplomatic concealment, the governor spoke bluntly after the end of rioting in Baltimore to selected moderates in the leadership of the black community. He told them that several weeks earlier they had courageously condemned remarks of a visiting civil-rights leader who referred to Baltimore police as " 'enemies of the black man,' " only to encounter "a storm of censure from parts of the Negro community" after compliments from white leaders. "And you ran," the governor said. "You met in secret with that demagogue" to agree that "you would not openly criticize any black spokesman." Many in the governor's audience walked out, but he went on at length with his message, calling for work together. "I publicly repudiate, condemn and reject all white racists," asking them to do the same for "all black racists."[231] His statement, widely applauded and criticized, gave him a new and fateful national prominence.

Agnew had already taken an interest in national politics. By early 1967 he had identified himself as a supporter of Governor Nelson A. Rockefeller for the Republican presidential nomination, calling him "a clearly superior choice . . . over everyone

---

229. News conferences, May 21, 23, 1968.

230. Address to Citizens of Maryland on Burning and Looting, April 7, 1968; *Evening Sun*, April 8, 1968; News Release and Letter Supporting Federal Open Housing Legislation, April 6, 1968.

231. Statement at Conference with Civil Rights and Community Leaders, State Office Building, Baltimore, April 11, 1968.

else whom I have heard mentioned."[232] In 1968 Agnew organized draft Rockefeller committees in Maryland and later opened a national office in Annapolis to "give direction," under his temporary chairmanship, to volunteer committees for Rockefeller.[233] Governor Rockefeller's entry into the presidential race was generally expected in a television statement on March 21, but instead he announced that he would not be a candidate. Governor Agnew held a regularly scheduled press conference at the same time, as it happened, but pointed out before the Rockefeller statement that he did not know the decision and that "at the moment" he found it "more comfortable to be in the dark." Later he said, "I confess that I am tremendously surprised. I also frankly add that I am greatly disappointed."[234]

Thereafter Agnew became more restrained about a presidential commitment. He met with Richard Nixon in late March, and after Rockefeller's decision on April 30 to become a candidate Agnew said that he was not less enthusiastic about Rockefeller but more enthusiastic than before about Nixon. In May he thanked Nixon for listing him among several potential vice presidential candidates. To hold open Maryland's options, Agnew accepted an invitation from the Republican State Convention to be a favorite son candidate for president. That nominal posture he held publicly until August, when he endorsed Nixon as the Republican National Convention assembled at Miami Beach. Two days later Agnew made the nominating speech for Nixon, describing him as "the *one* man whom history has so clearly thrust forward." Nixon won nomination on the first ballot early in the morning of August 8 and at noontime announced his recommendation, after consultation with party leaders, that Agnew should be the nominee for vice president.[235] The surprising selection stirred a minor revolt into which Governor George W. Romney of Michigan allowed him-

---

232. News Conference, May 4, 1967.

233. Statement on Formation of Citizen Committees for Rockefeller, Jan. 9, 1968; News Release and Statement on Rockefeller Headquarters in Annapolis, March 14, 1968.

234. News Conference, March 21, 1968.

235. News Conference, May 3, 1968; Comment on Published Reports on Vice Presidency, May 17, 1968; Statement Endorsing Nixon's Candidacy for President, Aug. 5, 1968; Address Nominating Richard M. Nixon for President, Aug. 7, 1968; *Evening Sun*, Aug. 8, 1968.

self to be drawn. The convention nominated Agnew by a vote of 1,128 to 186 for Romney.

Nixon and Agnew were elected, but Maryland did not contribute to the victory. The contest for the electoral votes of the state was close, but the winners were the Democratic nominees, Vice President Hubert H. Humphrey of Minnesota for president and Senator Edmund S. Muskie of Maine for vice president. George C. Wallace's candidacy for president under the banner of the American party was a highly complicating factor, drawing conservative votes that might have gone to Nixon in a two-way race. Humphrey ranked as the most liberal of the three but was handicapped on the one hand by association with the Johnson administration and its war policies and on the other by reaction against demonstrations, dissent, and war resistance. Humphrey carried only Calvert and Montgomery Counties and Baltimore City, but the city margin was nearly 100,000 votes. The popular vote in the state was Humphrey, 538,310; Nixon, 517,995; Wallace, who carried no county but ran second to Nixon in Dorchester, 178,734. Nixon, standing for law and order with economic progress at home and for peace with honor abroad, received in the nation a narrow popular plurality of 510,000 votes but a victory in the electoral college of 301 to Humphrey's 191 and Wallace's forty-six. During the campaign Governor Agnew spoke extensively around the country, returning frequently to his office in Annapolis and, when necessary, keeping in touch by telephone with the state's business through his chief of staff, Secretary of State C. Stanley Blair. Agnew as running mate struck responsive chords as an advocate of tax reform to produce new state and local revenue and, in the South particularly, as an opponent of civil disorder and violence. He was the first Maryland citizen to win office through the electoral college and the first since 1832 to receive a ballot from it.

No little part of the credit for Humphrey's success in carrying Maryland in the 1968 presidential campaign belonged to House Speaker Marvin Mandel of Baltimore, who had been elected Democratic State Chairman early in the year.[236] The state party organization had been virtually stalemated with factional strife after the death of Chairman Harry Troth Gross. Mandel moved

---

236. Baltimore *News-American*, Feb. 19, 1968.

quickly to give it life and to raise funds. Still, the problems were manifold. United States Senator Daniel B. Brewster was in trouble in his campaign for reelection. Many Democrats felt that his independent-minded Republican opponent, Congressman Charles McC. Mathias, Jr., would be able to work harder for their causes. "The accent of Maryland will once again be listened to with attention," the *Evening Sun* phrased it in endorsing him.[237] That race was complicated further by the independent candidacy of George P. Mahoney. Mathias won handily; Brewster carried only Charles and St. Mary's Counties and Baltimore City. Mahoney, whose support[238] and votes closely paralleled those of Wallace for the presidency, ran third everywhere. The eight seats in the national House of Representatives remained equally divided between the parties, J. Glenn Beall, Jr., succeeding Mathias in the western Maryland district. Voters in a statewide referendum overturned the 1967 open housing legislation, only Montgomery County voting to sustain it.

Spiro T. Agnew resigned the governorship on January 7, 1969. He had said to the Republican governors, "I was a controversial Governor. I have been a controversial candidate for Vice President. There is no reason to believe that I will be any less controversial as Vice President." To the General Assembly he noted in farewell that his broad goals had been fiscal reform, administrative reorganization, and constitutional modernization. "The first we have achieved, the second is well under way and the third has failed." Fiscal reform, he said, will stand "as the greatest single accomplishment" of the administration and "quite probably of this Legislature, which has worked so cooperatively with me."

During almost five years in the vice presidency Agnew played roles that made him one of the most conspicuous of all occupants of the office. At first he was nominally in charge, at President Nixon's request, of a great variety of intergovernmental relations. His remarkable and often controversial oratorical talents soon turned, obviously with the president's approval, to

237. *Evening Sun*, Oct. 29, 1968.
238. *Sun*, Nov. 4, 1968.

broader political objectives. Many middle-class Americans and almost all conservatives acclaimed him as a champion of law and order and as a herald of virtue and valor. Many liberals, on the other hand, saw threats to freedom in his colorful language extolling old values and denouncing "disruptive demonstrations" against the Vietnam War. In a 1969 speech at Des Moines, he raised new controversy by charging that "a narrow and distorted picture of America often emerges from the televised news" and by his challenge to the networks to improve "the quality and objectivity of news presentation." During the congressional campaigns of 1970 he was an effective speaker at fund-raising dinners and an acid critic of administration detractors, whether Democratic or Republican.

After his reelection with President Nixon in 1972, there was a "new," more subdued Agnew. His friends were proud that he was untouched by the Watergate crimes and scandals which rocked the national administration, and they broached his name to receptive ears in many states as a presidential candidate in 1976. That dream was shattered by mid-1973 under the blows of an investigation begun by George Beall, United States Attorney for Maryland. Prosecutory inquiries first led to criminal charges against Agnew's Democratic successor as executive in Baltimore County, but they soon gave rise to rumors of charges against Agnew himself.

Agnew made televised statements of innocence and also denounced news leaks that he thought may have come from the Department of Justice. On October 10, 1973, he suddenly resigned the vice presidency and an hour later made in person, in the United States District Court in Baltimore, a plea of no contest to one charge of income tax evasion for the year 1967. Beall as United States Attorney presented a detailed statement of information and the names of witnesses who would testify, in most cases under partial immunity from prosecution, that Agnew had accepted payments from Maryland contractors from the time of his service as county executive. Agnew received a fine of $10,000 and probation for three years. In his statement to the court, he said that his "acceptance of contributions was part of a long-established pattern of political fund-raising in the State," adding that he had at no time enriched himself at the expense of the public trust. Reaction in the state and nation was predominantly one of shock and grief that his service in public office had ended in shambles.[239]

## 7

### Mandel: Accountability and
### Administrative Reorganization

When Agnew resigned the governorship in 1969, the General Assembly in joint session promptly elected Speaker Marvin Mandel for the unexpired term, giving him 126 votes. Republican Congressman Rogers C. B. Morton received twenty-six; Francis X. Gallagher of Baltimore City, long an ally of Senator Joseph D. Tydings, fifteen; and Senate President William S. James, thirteen. The new governor responded, "You know me as a quiet man more inclined to solve problems than talk them to death." He hoped to win "by my actions as Governor" the confidence of voters "who did not have a direct voice in this election." In the spirit that "Maryland cannot mark time" he pledged, "Let there be no mistake in any one's mind, I shall govern."[240]

Mandel, long a major public figure in the state, was the first Maryland governor of Jewish faith. His associates, if not the general public, knew his political perspicacity. He was a good listener, quick to get to the heart of a problem, and astute in working out acceptable solutions. In seventeen years as a member of the House of Delegates, nearly all of them in positions of leadership, he had built confidence among his colleagues that eased the way for him to become, as the new governor, at once the leader of Maryland.

Of enormous long-range significance was Governor Mandel's effective guidance of administrative reorganization and constitutional modernization of the state's government. In his first two years in office he shepherded, with the help of a coopera-

239. Speech at Republican Governors' Conference, Palm Springs, California, Dec. 6, 1968; Farewell Address to Maryland General Assembly, Annapolis, Jan. 7, 1969; see John R. Coyne, Jr., *The Impudent Snobs: Agnew vs. the Intellectual Establishment* (New Rochelle, N.Y.: Arlington House, 1972) for texts of some Agnew addresses from 1968 to 1971; *Sun, Evening Sun, New York Times,* Oct. 11, 1973.

240. *Senate Journal,* Special Session, Jan. 6–7, 1969, pp. 46-48; *House Journal,* same session, pp. 87-89.

tive legislature, organizational changes unprecedented in Maryland experience. As speaker of the house he had served with other legislative leaders as a member of a committee appointed in 1968 by Governor Agnew to study executive reorganization. That committee, another study group under the chairmanship of John N. Curlett, reported in 1969 to Mandel as governor. Its recommendations, modified in some important areas, served as guideposts for streamlining many of the principal state administrative agencies within eleven cabinet-level departments, each headed by a secretary.[241]

Constitutional change was no less the product of executive-legislative cooperation. In 1970 voters of the state approved eight of nine proposals for constitutional revision polished by the General Assembly in two successive years. The adopted amendments borrowed in part from proposals of the rejected document drafted by the Constitutional Convention of 1967–1968 and thereby salvaged significant portions of its work. Approved additions to the constitution lowered the residency requirement for voting to six months and authorized the legislature to provide a shorter period of residence for presidential voting; directed the governor to prepare a plan for redistricting and reapportionment of the legislature after each decennial census, making the governor's plan effective unless the legislature changed it within forty-five days.[242]

Other approved amendments simplified arrangements for choosing boards to draft home-rule charters in counties; created district courts, thereby organizing a four-tiered judicial system; gave the governor initiative in administrative reorganization, subject to legislative disapproval of new programs or changes in existing laws; established the office of lieutenant governor, the person elected running as a designated teammate with the successful candidate for governor; expressly permitted references to God in public places or documents; and lengthened legislative sessions, providing for special ones by request from a majority of each house and requiring a commission to fix every four years the maximum compensation of legislators.[243]

---

241. *Executive Reorganization: A Comprehensive Plan for Maryland* (Baltimore: Report of the Governor's Executive Reorganization Committee, 1969); *Maryland Manual, 1971–1972* (Annapolis: Hall of Records Commission, 1972); Richards, *op. cit.*, Ch. V.

242. *Laws of Maryland, 1969*, Chs. 784-85.

243. *Ibid.*, Chs. 786, 789-90; *ibid.*, 1970, Chs. 532, 558, 576.

The people rejected a proposal to allow the governor to appoint and the Senate to confirm appellate and circuit judges. Only the Washington suburbs reported strong majorities for changing the customary appointment, confirmation, and subsequent election in open contests at the polls.

Governor Mandel's statutory success with the General Assembly was also phenomenal. In 1969 he obtained virtually his entire legislative package, including an increase in the state sales tax from 3 per cent to 4 per cent to finance a budget of nearly $1.3 billion in times of uneasiness about adequate revenues, a bill (much opposed by Baltimore County legislators) for a state authority for low-cost housing, a strengthened Human Relations Commission, a Metropolitan Transit Authority for the Baltimore area, a revised presidential primary, a comprehensive program for treating drug addicts, consumer protection laws, bills to require strip mine operators to reclaim damaged land and oil-pollution offenders to pay for cleaning public waters, a program of purchasing open spaces for parks, and payment of prevailing wages on state contracts.[244]

Previously disappointed conservationists secured in 1970 legislation to control dredging and filling of state or private wetlands affected by tidal waters. Gun control advocates were less successful, obtaining only tighter licensing of explosives necessary for manufacture of ammunition for small arms.[245] The governor vetoed a controversial bill to repeal all abortion laws on the grounds that it contained no residency requirement, no notice to husbands or parents, no limit on extent of pregnancy, and no safeguard for hospital care.[246] The Department of Natural Resources received new powers to control shore erosion and major soil grading and also won broad authority over sewage and garbage disposal in the state. The Department of Health and Mental Hygiene likewise acquired new power to enforce standards of air quality and to regulate distribution of dangerous drugs.[247] The state administration had laid the groundwork for greater activity in new facets of health and the environment.

---

244. *Evening Sun*, March 26, 1969.
245. *Laws of Maryland*, 1970, Chs. 241, 404.
246. *Ibid.*, pp. 2156-60.
247. *Evening Sun*, April 1, 1970.

Much acclaim came to the governor from many citizens for his firm measures to end disruptions at the University of Maryland by a minority of students. Saying that "disorder and dissent are not synonymous," he used the National Guard, commanded by Major General Edwin Warfield III, to quell disturbances and violence on the campus, in some of its buildings, and on adjacent roadways.[248] Causes of student unrest, triggered to violent protest by incidents arousing indignation, were complex and deeply rooted in the Vietnam War, disenchantment with materialistic social values, and the seeming impersonality of both modern technology and big government. In the spring of 1970 the use of American troops in Cambodia stirred violence that increased on many campuses, as in Maryland, after the tragic deaths of four students at Kent State University in Ohio. These causes and episodes came at a time of great changes in style and manners of American youth, evident everywhere in Maryland: long hair for men, informality of language and dress or undress among both sexes, increased use of drugs to the point of national alarm, loosening of family ties linked with permissiveness in youthful living arrangements and sexual practices. Withal, except in the provocative heat of anger, youth of the rising generation displayed generally an amazing politeness and a compassion for the needs and problems of others.

In the meantime Mandel, with all his activity in legislation, negotiation, and travel about the state to meet with officials and the public, had made effective plans for election in 1970 to a full term in the governorship. His friends had raised sizable campaign funds. Sargent Shriver, former ambassador to France and brother-in-law of the late President Kennedy, had assessed the possibility of a campaign of his own but found the prospects preempted. Mandel received the Democratic nomination in the September primary by a ten-to-one vote over four nominal opponents. Republicans chose as their nominee C. Stanley Blair of Harford County, former Maryland secretary of state, who resigned before the primary campaign from his position as chief administrative officer with Vice President Agnew.

The path of liberal Senator Joseph D. Tydings in his campaign for reelection was a troubled one. George P. Mahoney,

---

248. *Sun*, May 6, 1970.

his principal primary opponent, benefited from a crossfire of criticism directed at the senator. Conservatives opposed Tydings' liberal views but attacked him chiefly for his support of gun control legislation and his opposition to the extent of American activity in the Vietnam War. Many liberals objected to his sponsorship of crime control legislation for the District of Columbia because of its provisions for no-knock police entry, mandatory sentences, and preventive detention of some defendants.[249] The senator nevertheless won a majority of the primary votes in a four-way race, but Mahoney carried sixteen of the counties. Voters defeated two of Maryland's senior Democratic congressmen, George H. Fallon and Samuel N. Friedel in safe Democratic districts in Baltimore, giving the respective nominations to Paul S. Sarbanes (an able member of the House of Delegates) and to Parren J. Mitchell. The latter, a member of a family long influential in Baltimore and state politics, became the first black citizen to represent Maryland in Congress.

Running on his record in the fall campaign for governor, Mandel defeated Blair in the election by the historic margin of 325,000 votes. At the same time Republican Congressman J. Glenn Beall, Jr., benefiting from the controversy and from the Nixon administration's strong support, defeated Tydings for the Senate by 24,500. The incumbent senator carried only Baltimore City and Montgomery and Prince George's Counties, but the leads in those populous areas were not enough to turn the tide running against him. Like Mandel, other candidates on the Democratic state ticket scored impressive victories: Blair Lee III for lieutenant governor, and Louis L. Goldstein and Francis B. Burch for reelection respectively as comptroller and attorney general. Democrats retained their usual control of both houses of the General Assembly. Republicans increased their membership in the state Senate from eight to ten but dropped from twenty-five to twenty-one in the House of Delegates. Democrats secured five of the eight seats in Congress, Goodloe E. Byron winning for the party the place left by Republican J. Glenn Beall, Jr., in his successful race for the Senate.

---

249. *Evening Sun*, Sept. 11, 14–15, 1970. See William Lambert, "What the Senator Didn't Disclose," *Life*, LXIX, No. 9, Aug. 28, 1970, 26-29, for an account (rejected by Tydings but important in the campaign) critical of the propriety but not the legality of the senator's investment practices. *The Evening Sun*, Oct. 29, 1970, in endorsing Tydings, called *Life's* story a "low blow."

# 8
## RESOURCES AND CHALLENGES

Maryland's population had increased by 26.5 per cent in the decade of the 1960's, a growth rate twice that of the nation. In thirty years the state's residents had more than doubled in number to 3,922,399, more than three-fourths of them living in urban communities. Forty-second among the fifty states in area, Maryland between 1930 and 1970 moved from the twenty-eighth to the eighteenth rank in population. That transition brought problems of adjustment in land use, employment, public services and finance, and living style.

For the second consecutive census Baltimore City lost population, 3.5 per cent, although the Baltimore urbanized area (including parts of Anne Arundel, Baltimore, and Howard Counties) grew by 160,000. The 1970 census reported the city's total population as 905,759. The Negro portion of its residents increased from 34.7 per cent to 46.4 per cent. In 1970 Baltimore slipped from sixth to seventh in population among America's cities. The Baltimore Standard Metropolitan Statistical Area, including the city and the counties of Anne Arundel, Baltimore, Carroll, Harford, and Howard, grew by 14.8 per cent to a population of 2.1 million, ranking eleventh in the nation. The Maryland portion of the comparable Washington area (2.9 million, seventh in the country) accounted for 1.2 million in Montgomery and Prince George's Counties. Prince George's, with a growth rate of 84.8 per cent from 1960, replaced Baltimore County (26.1 per cent) as the most populous of the state's counties; Montgomery (53.3 per cent growth) ranked third in county population. Among the counties, only Somerset, Dorchester, and Allegany lost population, the first by 3.5 per cent and the last two by less than 1 per cent. Several of the older cities and towns had lost, but unincorporated Dundalk, Towson, Silver Spring, Bethesda, Wheaton, and Catonsville, and the city of Rockville had risen to rank after Baltimore City in population order.[250]

---

250. Bureau of the Census, *Number of Inhabitants: Maryland* (Washington: U. S. Government Printing Office, 1971), pp. 7, 11-12, 15, 21, 23; Bureau of the Census, *Statistical Abstract of the United States, 1971* (Washington: U. S. Government Printing Office, 1971), pp. 14, 21, 164.

Nearly 60 per cent of the people of Maryland lived in Baltimore City and in three metropolitan counties, two of the latter in the suburbs of Washington. All heavily Democratic in voter registration, they were far from operating an effective alliance to determine the policies of the state. The city had retained a twentieth-century tradition of fragmented political organizations with economic and ethnic rivalries, sometimes together and often apart but always important in state affairs. Baltimore County, housing in its upcounty spaciousness many of the most forward-looking businessmen of the city, was in its industrial outskirts the home of thousands of white (and a minimum of black) workers who held at arm's length liberal social movements that might alter their neighborhoods. Prince George's felt the political effects of cleavage between the moderately conservative and equally moderate liberal wings of the majority party, and even more crucially of the widening migration of black citizens seeking suburban relief from the crowded District of Columbia. Montgomery, having attained a reputed affluence with one of the highest median family-income levels in the country and often disdaining overt partisanship, was —despite its tight budgets and the many needs of the less prosperous of its citizens—sometimes humorously and usually politely looked upon by the rest of the state as a political world apart. As a popular place of residence for governmental and business officials temporarily assigned to Washington, Montgomery lived with the consequences of a highly transient portion of its people. "Where else," a leading official of the state asked, "could I go to a meeting without knowing half of the people there?" The Washington suburbs suffered, moreover, from the lack of daily news and contact orienting them toward the state as a whole. Problems of Baltimore and at Annapolis were, for all too many, passing stories from emotionally distant places.

Census data revealed, if statistical demonstration were necessary, unequal burdens in the population. The state's 701,341 Negroes, 17.9 per cent of the population, were often at a disadvantage. Nearly two-thirds of them, in contrast with 54 per cent of whites, were born in the state. The median income for white families was $11,635, for Negroes $7,701; the mean, $13,409 for white but $8,625 for Negro. Of all Negro families, 20.9 per cent had incomes less than the poverty level; of white,

5.3 per cent. Public assistance income went to 14.2 per cent of Negro families; to white, 1.9 per cent. Negro men in the labor force suffered a 4.9 per cent rate of unemployment, white men 2.3 percent; Negro women 6.5 per cent, white women 3.4 per cent. Education was also disparate: more than half of the whites, a third of the Negroes, had completed high school; 15 per cent of whites but 7 per cent of Negroes had finished four years of college.[251]

Maryland's economic life prospered in the 1960's. Non-manufacturing employment led the growth, 50 per cent for that category, with services, government, wholesale and retail trade, finance, insurance, and real estate ranking highest. Services alone attained a 75 per cent gain. Only agriculture, mining, and railroad transportation declined in employment. From 1964 to 1969 farmed land diminished from three and a half million acres to three and three-tenths million, and the number of farms from 23,600 to 18,700. In 1968 farm workers numbered only 33,000, including family and hired workers. Dominated by dairy products and poultry, farm livestock accounted for two-thirds of the value of agricultural commodities in 1967; field crops, led by corn, tobacco, and soy beans, brought 21 per cent of receipts.

Transportation and outlays of the federal government remained major elements of the economy. Baltimore in 1968 ranked as the fourth largest foreign-commerce port in the United States. Large ship-container facilities had become landmarks in Baltimore's port development. In 1967 the Baltimore harbor and channels bore forty-one million tons of commerce; the harbors of Cambridge and Crisfield added 153,000. Waterborne commerce on the principal rivers of the Eastern Shore, the Wicomico, Nanticoke, Choptank, Pocomoke, Tred Avon, and Chester, totaled one and seven-tenths million tons. Average daily vehicle mileage in 1968, on state-maintained roads, was almost thirty million—an increase of 74 per cent in a decade.

In 1968 Maryland ranked ninth among the states in federal funds expended, nearly $6 billion. Outlays in social insurance

---

251. *Ibid.*, p. 27; Bureau of the Census, *General Social and Economic Characteristics: Maryland* (Washington: U. S. Government Printing Office, 1972), pp. 130, 150, 158, 160.

and retirement programs were over $2 billion, and in defense nearly $1.7 billion.

Baltimore's notable *Sunpapers*, published weekdays morning and evening with one edition on Sunday, maintained wide circulation and influence in the state. Other daily newspapers published in Baltimore and Cumberland, and except Sunday in Annapolis, Cambridge, Cumberland, Frederick, Hagerstown, and Salisbury, the semi-weekly Baltimore *Afro-American*, and some seventy weeklies offered a variety of general or local news coverage. By 1970 four commercial television stations operated in Baltimore and other stations in Hagerstown and Salisbury. Radio broadcasting came from fifty-two AM and thirty-one FM stations. Washington daily newspapers and broadcasting facilities, however, dominated the news media in the suburbs of the District of Columbia.[252]

Culturally, Maryland enjoyed and produced art, local groups in many parts of the state studying it, participating in its forms, and exhibiting it. Citizens of Baltimore and elsewhere, at least an artistic-minded minority of them, took pride in the collections of the Peale Museum, the Walters Art Gallery, and the Baltimore Museum of Art. All three were enriched by important gifts, as were the Washington County Museum of Art, the Eastern Shore Galleries in the Tidewater Inn at Easton, and other repositories including the Maryland Historical Society. The State House in Annapolis and the executive mansion across the way displayed traditional portraits and other paintings, many of them significant reminders of the past in Maryland. Expanding upon the work of the public schools, private and public collegiate institutions in the state, from community colleges to the two universities, played a continuing role in art education and exhibition.

Music, like art, invited the active interest of all levels of the educational system. Many churches were also centers of musical talent. In Baltimore the Peabody Conservatory of Music ranked among the most prestigious schools in the East for the professional training of musicians. Around it much of the musical life of Baltimore revolved,[253] supported by an estimated 3

252. *Maryland Statistical Abstract* (Annapolis: State Department of Economic Development, 1970), pp. 88, 165-73, 184-86, 190-95, 199-204, 216-28; *Maryland Manual, 1971–1972, op. cit.*, pp. 833-35.

253. See Lubov Keefer, *Baltimore's Music: The Haven of the American Composer* (Baltimore: Privately published, 1962).

per cent of the metropolitan population. Fund-raising philanthropy financed the symphony orchestra. Facing with other opera companies in the country large expense and a gradually declining attendance, the Baltimore Civic Opera Company offered in a brief season each year several productions with an international repertoire. Among the more popular forms that sprang up in various centers were musical comedy and folk festivals with singing and dancing; moreover, small ensembles, woodwind or strings, moved about the state. The new rock music dominated the night-club life of Baltimore and other places. A vigorous musicians union included in its membership virtually all of the professional workers in music. Staged drama, for which Baltimore had long been known, became popular in other centers of population, often in small theaters with productions requiring limited numbers of actors in resident or traveling companies.[254]

In literature Maryland's name was less clearly identified with the works of her nationally-known authors than in the days of Baltimore's outspoken H. L. Mencken. John Barth, a native of Cambridge but long away from the state, received the votes of other writers as one of the best of America's new novelists in two decades on the basis of his first three books, each of hypnotic complexity with an eastern Maryland scene: *The Floating Opera, The End of the Road*, and *The Sot-Weed Factor*.[255] Rachel Carson, writing in Montgomery County a lyrical exposé of the dangers of pesticides, *The Silent Spring*, aroused environmentalists and influenced national policy.[256] Zenith Jones (Mrs. Ford) Brown, living quietly in Annapolis where her husband taught at St. John's College, produced a shelf of widely-read mysteries written under the pseudonyms Leslie Ford and David Frome.[257] John Dos Passos, a leading liberal novelist after World War I, spent his last winters in Baltimore's Peabody Institute or at the Hopkins library writing conservative historical studies.[258] Bruce Catton completed in Bethesda a Civil War historical trilogy, winning a Pulitzer prize for it.[259] Ogden Nash

254. *Sun*, June 26, 1958; Oct. 26, 1962; La Plata *Maryland Independent*, July 28, 1966; Frederick *News*, June 27, 1967; *Washington Post*, Aug. 13, 1967.
255. Cambridge *Daily Banner*, Aug. 11, 1966; *Sun*, March 31, 1970.
256. *Washington Post*, April 15–16, 19, 1964.
257. *Ibid.*, Potomac Section, May 17, 1970, pp. 33-45.
258. *Sun*, Sept. 29, Oct. 4, 1970.
259. *Ibid.*, March 6, 1955.

wrote in Baltimore for thirty years his droll poems in free verse.[260] William Manchester, to become best known for his account of President Kennedy's assassination, produced a biography of Mencken while writing for the *Sunpapers*;[261] and another adopted Baltimorean, Gary Wills, a former teacher of classics at The Hopkins, attacked in *Nixon Agonistes* an administration and the "main myths" of the old creed of American individualism that he thought "dead or dying."[262] Katherine Anne Porter, novelist and essayist of elegant style, gave manuscripts and memorabilia to the University of Maryland and later moved to College Park.[263] Upton Sinclair, born in Baltimore and living briefly in Rockville late in life, author of eighty-nine books and called the "king of muckrakers," commented that his mother's interest in Baltimore social circles led him to become a socialistic troublemaker.[264]

Among many other modern writers native to Maryland or long associated with it, George Boas and Owen Lattimore of the Hopkins faculty worked respectively in philosophy and Chinese studies; Harry Bard, in Maryland government; George H. Callcott, Margaret Law Callcott, Judge Edward S. Delaplaine, R. Samuel Jett, Harold R. Manakee, Morris L. Radoff, and Charles L. Wagandt, in its history. Commanding a wide national readership were Fulton Oursler, novelist and playwright; Benjamin Quarles, historian on the Morgan State faculty; the Morley brothers, Christopher, Felix, and Frank, writing a great variety of fiction and nonfiction; Walter Lord, raconteur of disaster and high adventure; and James M. Cain of University Park, proving himself master of the vernacular novel in *The Postman Always Rings Twice* and providing sketches redolent of rural Maryland in *Our Government*.

Social change rather than the precedents of past achievement came first to the consciousness of most Marylanders, however difficult the adjustment they found it. Small business had been superseded in the community, not merely by the corporation

---

260. *Ibid.*, May 20, 1971.

261. *Ibid.*, Dec. 7, 1968.

262. *Washington Post*, July 6, 1971; *Nixon Agonistes* (Boston: Houghton Mifflin, 1970), pp. 601-602.

263. Hagerstown *Daily Mail*, Dec. 19, 1966; *New York Times*, April 3, 1970.

264. *Sun*, Dec. 3, 1962; Annapolis *Evening Capital*, Nov. 26, 1968; Frederick *News*, Nov. 26, 1968.

but by the conglomerate. Intricacies of management and of the tax laws had spawned consolidations of diversified businesses in national and international agglomerates. American capital moved abroad, and foreign capital to the United States, for advantages of business investment. Uses of the computer brought countless changes to the practices of big business and big government and to many of their clients a new sense of impersonalization and of distance from management. The average household lived in a day of buy now, pay later, with inviting complexities of credit cards and high interest for delayed payments. Changing technology produced new unemployment, the most skilled often finding it the more difficult to secure new livelihoods. High expenditure, including that of government in war and in domestic programs, added to the pace of mounting inflation. Narcotic addiction and crime incident to its support increased. Baltimore was one of America's cities much affected, but metropolitan suburbs and other areas of the state were by no means immune.

Yet production rose, and basic economic stability seemed secure. There were warning signals, however, that industrial and other technology might seriously drain natural resources and add alarmingly to the pollution of air and water. The action of sunlight on automobile emissions regularly raised air pollution on windless summer days beyond the danger point in the Baltimore and the Washington suburban areas of the state. Official warning alerts and even more drastic plans for traffic curtailment accompanied expanding requirements for motor emission control. Widespread use of air conditioning in offices and homes imperiled the supply of electricity and occasionally resulted in isolated outages and temporary reductions of voltage. Sewer inadequacy and overloading caused public health officials to impose in some areas moratoria on new construction. That precaution, together with rising costs and higher property valuations for taxation, made attainment of private low-income housing more difficult.

Construction of a nuclear power plant, with an investment of some $600 million at Calvert Cliffs on the western shore of Chesapeake Bay, aroused protests from environmentalists. They feared that by raising the temperature of water in the Bay the plant would endanger aquatic life and, along with other industries, permanently impair the natural resources of the state. Dr. Abel Wolman, respected professor emeritus of sanitary engineering at The Johns Hopkins University, praised the service of scientific environmentalists in "raising the horizon" and by "checking on alternatives." Admitting that some of his views were not popular, he opposed the overzealous "doomsday" criers about the threat of pollution (and even, in another field, of overpopulation). He called the Calvert Cliffs site "the best" that could be selected.[265] In 1972 torrential rains in the wake of Hurricane Agnes inflicted damage in the millions of dollars to roads, bridges, and private property in central Maryland. By reducing the salinity of the Bay and introducing bacterial problems, the overflow wreaked havoc affecting for at least several years the harvest of soft-shell clams and other products of the fishing industry.

State assumption of the cost of public school construction, a major decision by Governor Mandel and his administration made in order to relieve and equalize financial burdens of Baltimore City and the counties, received legislative approval in 1971. To the dismay of some school officials, the measure gave final authority over rules and procedures to the state Board of Public Works to assure coordination of standards.[266] Asked when the state could take over from the subdivisions all the funding of public education, the governor estimated "a very long time" because "my first aim is to keep this State fiscally solvent." With the taxable base growing "about $1.7 billion a year . . . we can put more of the money into helping the subdivisions" as the wealth of the state grows. The state's total contributions to its subdivisions projected for fiscal 1972 were $890 million, $200 million of that amount to Baltimore City.[267]

Maryland in 1970 held fifth rank among the states in estimated expenditure, $1,240 that year, per pupil enrolled in the public schools. Students numbered 916,000 in 1,300 schools, 291 of them high schools. In addition Maryland's nonpublic elementary and secondary schools (most of them church-related) enrolled by 1971 a total of 127,000 students, a decrease

265. *Sun*, Feb. 27, 1973.

266. *Laws of Maryland, 1971*, Ch. 624; *Evening Sun*, April 13, 1971. For a view linking the legislation to the sinews of power, see Thomas B. Edsall, "Maryland: The Governor Raiseth," *The Washington Monthly*, III, No. 12, Feb. 1972, 32-33.

267. Press conferences, Jan. 29, July 15, 1971.

of 11,000 in six years.[268] The legislature enacted a need-related scholarship program for students in nonpublic schools, a much-debated bill that attracted the heaviest lobbying pro and con in the 1971 session.[269] Voters in 1972 rejected the statute, 543,241 to 448,702, in a referendum turning on the issue of aid to parochial schools. Only Baltimore City and St. Mary's County gave favorable majorities. Most politicians, whatever their preferences, hoped that the referendum would disentangle the issue from the state elections of 1974.

Governor Mandel said in January 1971 to a joint session of the Senate and House that "it is time for a brief pause" in the pace of new legislative programs.[270] In addition to the major school construction and private-school scholarship measures, the legislature enacted laws to prevent counties from levying local sales taxes, to increase state payments to community colleges, to enable the state to build a bridge over Baltimore's outer harbor, to create a public defender system for criminal trials, to join an interstate compact to protect the Potomac, and to redraw congressional district lines in such a way that the Baltimore urban area would dominate three rather than four districts. The General Assembly ignored efforts of some counties to increase their state-collected surtax on incomes. Legislators accepted a salary increase from $2,400 to $11,000 recommended by a special commission, raised judicial salaries, and tightened their own code of ethics.[271]

Internal politics in the legislative chambers during the 1972 session led to open signs of strain in cooperative relations with the governor, the members overriding a small number of his 1971 vetoes. The administration nevertheless obtained legislative approval of an impressive program. Major laws provided for stricter regulation of handguns; reform of automobile liability insurance including a unique state fund to write high-risk policies; funding for the first phase of Baltimore's rapid mass-transit system (the twenty-eight-mile Owings Mill-Baltimore-Friendship line), similar funding for Washington mass transit in

---

268. Kenneth A. Simon and W. Vance Grant, *Digest of Educational Statistics, 1971 Edition* (Washington: U. S. Government Printing Office, 1972), pp. 24, 31, 33-34, 59.
269. *Laws of Maryland, 1971*, Ch. 7; *Evening Sun*, April 13, 1971.
270. *House Journal*, 1971, p. 142.
271. *Evening Sun*, April 13, 1971.

the Maryland suburbs, and new highway improvements (with an increase in the gasoline tax from seven to nine cents for revenue); a proposed constitutional amendment permitting a state lottery, approved by the voters later in the year, and enabling legislation for it; and lowering the voting age to eighteen in state and local elections. The legislature also authorized state purchase of Friendship Airport and arrangements for a revenue-supported sports complex in downtown Baltimore.[272]

Baltimore City elections in the autumn of 1971 pleased Democrats who were watching for signs that the party might achieve a presidential victory in the fall of 1972. William D. Schaefer, Democratic president of the City Council, won the mayoralty with 88 per cent of the vote in an unusually light turnout. With him, Walter S. Orlinsky secured the council presidency and Hyman A. Pressman a third term as comptroller.[273] The battle had been in the Democratic primary after the decision of Mayor Thomas D'Alesandro III not to seek reelection. George L. Russell, Jr., city solicitor, mounted the first substantial black candidacy for mayor. He and Schaefer each spent more than $250,000 in the primary campaign. The results from a turnout of 45 per cent of the Democrats registered gave Schaefer 56 per cent of the votes, Russell 35 per cent. State Senator Clarence M. Mitchell III, a second black candidate, finished fourth with an unexpectedly low 4 per cent. Friends of the black candidates attributed the poor showing to fear that votes would be split between them and to failure of both to enlist crusading enthusiasm.[274]

Election of Governor Mandel in 1971 as chairman of the Democratic governors and in mid-1972 as chairman of the National Governors' Conference enhanced his nationwide political stature. He was careful not to give public endorsement to any aspirant for the Democratic presidential nomination, although many of his closest political allies worked for Senator Hubert H. Humphrey. The governor was not satisfied with the splintering effect of "this hodgepodge of primaries," often with a multiplicity of names. He suggested that the system be changed to a nationwide primary or a national convention held

272. *Ibid.*, April 11, 1972.
273. *Ibid.*, Nov. 3, 1971.
274. *Ibid.*, Sept. 8, 15, 1971.

without state preferential balloting for candidates. Like others, he regarded the paralyzing gunshot wounds suffered by Governor George C. Wallace of Alabama, while campaigning for president May 15 at Laurel as a "horrible tragedy." Governor Mandel thought that no security arrangements could have prevented it, inasmuch as Wallace was mingling with a shopping-center audience.[275]

Only three of the eleven Democratic candidates in the Maryland presidential primary received a large vote. Wallace led in all but three of the counties, amassing in the state 219,687 votes. Senator Humphrey received 151,982 but led only in Baltimore City and Allegany County; Senator George McGovern of South Dakota, with 126,978, led in Howard and Montgomery. In the Republican primary held at the same time, President Nixon won 99,308 votes to 9,223 for liberal Congressman Paul N. McCloskey, Jr., of California and 6,718 for conservative Congressman John M. Ashbrook of Ohio.

Beset with division even before the July nomination of Senator McGovern for president, the Democratic presidential campaign continued to have insuperable difficulties. The withdrawal of Senator Thomas F. Eagleton of Missouri as the vice presidential nominee and his replacement with R. Sargent Shriver of Maryland, despite the latter's popularity, was a setback that cost a month of distressing publicity and campaign effort. Governor Mandel, working with Democratic State Chairman William S. James and other leaders to offset defections among the party faithful, candidly reflected much opinion by commenting that the "biggest problem" of the McGovern campaign "is to take a firm stand on issues" and "maintain that stand."[276] The Republican ticket of Nixon and Agnew, winning the electoral votes for reelection everywhere in the nation except in Massachusetts and the District of Columbia, carried Maryland by a popular vote of 829,305 to 505,781. McGovern and Shriver ran ahead, by the relatively slim margin of 21,837 votes, only in Baltimore City. Conservative Republican Congressman John G. Schmitz of California, presidential nominee of the American party whose banner Governor Wallace declined to carry in the 1972 race, received 18,726 votes in the

---

275. Press conferences, March 9, May 18, 1972.
276. Press conference, Aug. 24, 1972.

state. Republicans picked up a seat in Congress from Maryland, making the party division four to four with the election of Marjorie S. Holt in the redesigned district comprising Anne Arundel County and southern Prince George's.

High appointive offices in the Nixon administration had already gone to prominent Marylanders. Rogers C. B. Morton, who served from 1969 to 1971 as chairman of the Republican National Committee, resigned that position and the Eastern Shore seat in Congress to become Secretary of the Interior. Among others were Mrs. Helen Delich Bentley of Lutherville, chairman of the Federal Maritime Commission; William O. Doub, member of the Atomic Energy Commission; and former state Senator Louise Gore, ambassador to the United Nations Educational, Scientific and Cultural Organization. David K. E. Bruce, born in Baltimore and the scion of a prominent Maryland family, became in 1973 special envoy to the People's Republic of China.

County home rule made steady progress in Maryland, particularly after the mid-1960's. Approval of a county charter by the voters of Harford in 1972 brought to eight the number of counties with home-rule arrangements, seven of them with formal charters. However, in the 1972 elections Cecil, Dorchester, and St. Mary's Counties rejected charters, largely from local controversy but partly because of much-publicized contention across party lines between elected councils and similarly chosen executives in Montgomery and Prince George's.[277]

The Mandel administration joined many other states in supporting, with high hopes, the principle of federal revenue sharing. States, counties, and cities had seen the program as a means of financing needed services that their own resources could not support, necessarily limited as they were by the already large burden of property taxes and by the high rates of federal income and other taxation. The governor was also familiar with the uncertainties, the frequent change, in federal funding for state and local programs. With the enactment of federal legislation there were unforeseen difficulties with the federal budget, with regulations and payments, with presidential impoundment of funds, and with the fact that congressional authorizations for

---

277. For many earlier actions, see J. Hugh Nichols, "County Home Rule in Maryland" (M.A. thesis, The American University, 1967).

money were often more grandiose than actual appropriations. "Every day," the governor said early in 1973, "we are faced with another crisis or semi-crisis with the Federal government reducing another program or cutting out funds." The problems affected not only the state but also the counties and cities. Moreover, the governor feared that revenue sharing might later be viewed by Congress or the executive branch as "a substitute" for existing categories of federal grants.[278]

Other problems pressed upon the governor and his administration. Public welfare rolls undoubtedly included ineligible recipients, perhaps one in twenty, and in 1971 the program operated at a deficit rate. Administrative difficulties were particularly acute in Baltimore, where welfare workers were under city jurisdiction. The governor and the State Department of Social Services pressed for correction. Asked about an idea that the state take back part of the District of Columbia, the governor gave the answer of most Marylanders, "just leave it alone." Governor Mandel was also aware of an impending national crisis in sources of energy but opposed as premature suggestions for off-shore oil drilling in the Atlantic Ocean.[279] The National Oceanic and Atmospheric Administration appraised the Atlantic as already polluted with oil and plastics.

Ocean City was fast becoming the "boom town" of eastern coastal resorts. On a hot summer weekend the city of less than 2,000 permanent residents welcomed as many as 250,000 visitors to a strip of land ten miles long and about three blocks wide. In the first eight months of 1972, the city issued $62 million in building permits, as high-rise construction moved northward up the beach. Meanwhile the State Department of Natural Resources and its allies opened a battle to protect sand dunes and public use of the beachfront.[280] Howard County in 1972, after vigorous civic protest, rejected a project of the Marriott Corporation to build a giant amusement park intended to attract tourists from around the nation and the world.

Thousands of nonviolent protesters in Prince George's County reacted to the decision, late in 1972, of Federal District

278. Press conferences, July 29, 1971, Jan. 11, 1973; Marvin Mandel, "Revenue Sharing—Supplement or Substitute?" *State Government,* XLVI, No. 1, Winter 1973, 16-18.

279. Press conferences, Aug. 5, Nov. 11, Dec. 9, 1971.

280. Washington *Sunday Star-News,* Sept. 10, 1972; *Star-News,* Jan. 15, 1973.

Aerial view of part of the University of Maryland's College Park Campus.

900

Judge Frank A. Kaufman of Baltimore ordering busing to desegregate schools in the county. Governor Mandel, holding that quality education is the essential question, had said earlier that "busing is not an answer to the problem."[281] Making it clear that he favored desegregation and that he opposed a school boycott, he later advocated school construction to achieve racial balance in compliance with the law and to preserve the principle of a neighborhood school. State Senator Verda Welcome, one of the black leaders of Baltimore, replied in the Senate that "someone is advising him badly" and that he and the county are "headed in the wrong direction."[282] Higher courts allowed Judge Kaufman's decision to stand. Busing became effective early in 1973 without major incident, with plans for additional school construction under study.

New legislation in 1973 lowered the age of majority in Maryland to eighteen except for the purchase and use of alcoholic beverages. Other laws required financial disclosures by elected public officials, eliminated grand juries in some criminal proceedings, enlarged special education for handicapped children, increased state aid to schools, and made assessment of property for taxation entirely a state function. The legislative session was equally notable for what it did not pass. Sidetracked measures would have provided aid for teaching materials in nonpublic schools, made the death penalty mandatory for some capital crimes, and given the state new functions in land use control and more administrative authority over personnel and purchasing at the University of Maryland. The budget enacted for the state approximated $2.5 billion.[283]

The University of Maryland, often a scene of discontent in the war years, had attained its largest enrollments in 1971 and 1972: each year over 70,000 at four state campuses and in far-flung centers at home and overseas. Each of the state campuses operated under the administrative direction of a chancellor, with Dr. Charles E. Bishop serving from 1970 at the flagship campus at College Park. President Wilson H. Elkins reported to the Board of Regents that the university received about half of its requested increases from state support for the

281. Press conference, Oct. 5, 1972; Washington *Star-News*, Dec. 30, 1972.
282. Press conferences, Jan. 4, 11, 1973; Washington *Star-News*, Jan. 16, 1973.
283. *Evening Sun*, April 10, 1973.

year 1973–1974. At The Johns Hopkins University Dr. Steven Muller, in the second year of his presidency, announced a drive to raise $100 million for endowed professorships and other educational support. Community colleges in Maryland, rapidly growing to a total enrollment of 52,000, had increased in number to sixteen. The state college system offered bachelor's and master's degrees in teaching and liberal arts programs with 41,000 enrollments in 1972–1973, over 18,500 of them full-time undergraduates. A board of trustees governed that system, with Edmund C. Mester serving as executive director. Each of the six colleges had its own president and board of visitors. The legislature in 1973 made the University of Baltimore a public institution within the state college system, effective in 1975. St. Mary's College of Maryland remained a separate four-year state college of liberal arts and sciences. Private colleges, especially the smaller ones, felt the threatening pinch of rising costs.

Inauguration of the state lottery and the opening of the second Bay Bridge, both in the first half of 1973, were economically significant symbols of change and venturesomeness among Marylanders. James P. Slicher, long the chief budget officer of the state, directed the lottery, the eighth undertaken among the states in a decade, with George P. Mahoney serving at the governor's request as chairman of a five-member rule-making commission. The bridge brought a new spurt of tourists and vacationers to the Eastern Shore. The lottery, with its many public and private outlets for sale of tickets at fifty cents, each vendor entitled to a commission of 5 per cent, engendered intense interest. That success was followed, however, by an anticipated tapering of purchases. The state, interested in a new source of revenue that it need not depend upon for financing particular programs, hoped for a steady upturn of participation. Both ventures coincided with unusually steep inflation, national price and wage controls, shortages of gasoline, meat and other commodities in the marketplace, and continuing air and water pollution. There were, moreover, warnings of sterner preventive measures to come. By mid-1973 the mood of the nation and of Marylanders, looking to political, business, and civic leadership to provide solutions, was mildly uneasy but confidently optimistic.

Americans could walk on the moon, a triumph to which many Marylanders—at the Goddard Space Flight Center at Greenbelt

Double span Chesapeake Bay Bridge.
Photograph by George H. Cook. *The Baltimore Sunpapers.*

and at other installations—made substantial contributions. Surely, citizens in the state said again and again, the country could arrange against all vicissitudes a stable social order, sensitive to its environment, with justice and even-handed opportunity. For solving problems and building opportunity in Maryland, her best assurance remained her cosmopolitan and culturally diverse population, at base moderate in temper however unpredictable in politics, and her geographical advantages, from the sea and the Bay through the cities and rolling farmlands to the mountains in the west.

## BIBLIOGRAPHICAL ESSAY

### CHAPTER X

Maryland's modern history remains a rich field for exploration. The Maryland Historical Society and the Enoch Pratt Free Library in Baltimore, the Hall of Records in Annapolis, and the McKeldin Library of the University of Maryland, College Park, are among major repositories of printed and manuscript materials. Albert W. Quinn's final chapter in Morris L. Radoff, *The Old Line State* (Annapolis: Hall of Records Commission, 1971), is an outline of major political events; of equal usefulness for the casual reader are the final sections, particularly those on governors from Harry W. Nice to Marvin Mandel, in Frank F. White, Jr., *The Governors of Maryland, 1777–1970* (Annapolis: Hall of Records Commission, 1970).

Two of the modern governors are subjects of full-length biographies. Harry W. Kirwin's *The Inevitable Success: Herbert R. O'Conor* (Westminster, Md.: Newman Press, 1962) is professionally competent. Of various biographies of Spiro T. Agnew, written during his vice presidency, the most detailed about events in Maryland are Joseph Albright, *What Makes Spiro Run* (New York: Dodd, Mead, 1972), Theo Lippman, Jr., *Spiro Agnew's America* (New York: W. W. Norton, 1972), and Jules Witcover, *White Knight* (New York: Random House, 1972).

Detailed summaries of Maryland's wartime roles—military, economic, and home-front—are in *Maryland in World War II*, 4 vols. (Baltimore: Maryland Historical Society, 1950–1958), prepared for the State of Maryland under the supervision of Harold R. Manakee as director of the Society's War Records Division.

Issues of the *Maryland Manual*, now published (usually biennially) by the Hall of Records Commission, are important sources of reference; election returns are most readily found there. *Constitutional Revision Study Documents of the Constitutional Convention Commission of Maryland* (Annapolis, 1968) will remain a storehouse of legal information, much of it historical. Harry Bard's *Maryland Today* (New York: Oxford Book Company, 1961) offers a brief survey of the state and its government; the Tidewater Press, Cambridge, Maryland, is scheduling a new edition. Elizabeth Deussen's *Exploring Baltimore* (Baltimore Public Schools, 1965) deals similarly with the city. Jean E. Spencer, *Contemporary Local Government in Maryland* (College Park: Bureau of Governmental Research, University of Maryland, 1965) is the most thorough general study of its subject. Brief histories of the counties are in *The Counties of Maryland and Baltimore City: Their Origin, Growth and Development, 1634–1967* (Baltimore: State Planning Department, 1968). Monographs published between 1947 and 1961 in *Studies in Business and Economics* (College Park: Bureau of Business and Economic Research, University of Maryland) contain extensive analyses of the state's resources.

# INDEX

## Prepared by Frank F. White, Jr.

## COLOPHON

TYPOGRAPHY: Caledonia, 11 point, 2 point leaded.
V.I.P. photo-composition set by
Monotype Composition Co., Baltimore

PAPER: 60 lb. White Finch Opaque—Smooth.
End leaves: 50 lb. Buff Navajo Cover

CASE-BOUND: Gold and Black Roxite A Vellum Cloth.
over .088 boards, stamped in black foil.

PRODUCTION: Schneidereith & Sons, Baltimore, Maryland

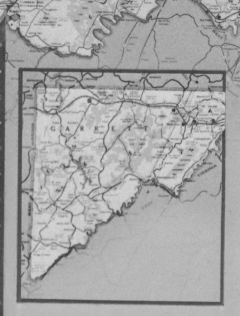

# STATE OF MARYLAND

# STATE HIGHWAY SYSTEM

## AND CONNECTIONS

## 1974

THIS MODERN MAP of Maryland, with its numerous roads, highways, towns and cities, is a dramatic contrast with the earlier map of the state, published in 1795 and found on front end leaf.